D0929930

BOTANICAL LATIN

BOTANICAL LATIN

History, Grammar
Syntax, Terminology and Vocabulary

WILLIAM T. STEARN

DAVID & CHARLES
NEWTON ABBOT   LONDON

ISBN 0 7153 5645 3

Annotated and revised for
second edition 1973
Second impression 1978
Third impression 1980

© 1966, 1973 William T Stearn

All rights reserved. No part of this
publication may be reproduced, stored
in a retrieval system, or transmitted,
in any form or by any means, electronic,
mechanical, photocopying, recording or
otherwise, without the prior permission
of David & Charles (Publishers) Limited

Printed in Great Britain by
Redwood Burn Limited Trowbridge & Esher
for David & Charles (Publishers) Limited
Brunel House   Newton Abbot   Devon

TO
HANNAH THOMPSON CROASDALE
Dartmouth College, Hanover
New Hampshire, U.S.A.
AND
ERIK WIKÉN
Gävle, Sweden
Author of 'Latin för Botanister och Zoologer'

IN APPRECIATION OF THEIR HELP
OVER MANY YEARS TO BOTANISTS PERPLEXED
BY THE LATIN LANGUAGE

ACKNOWLEDGMENTS

Grateful acknowledgment is made to the following for permission to reproduce illustrations: Dr. G. Ainsworth for Fig. 32; the Bentham-Moxon Trustees, Kew, for Figs. 9, 11 and 12; the Commonwealth Mycological Institute, Kew, for Fig. 15; Professor G. H. M. Lawrence and the Macmillan Company, New York, for Figs. 24, 26, 34, 36, 37; the Council of the Marine Biological Association for Fig. 10; Dr. Margaret R. Murley for Fig. 38; Stella Ross-Craig (Mrs. J. R. Sealy) and Messrs. G. Bell & Sons Ltd. for Fig. 8; the Council of the Systematics Association for Fig. 19. Figs. 3, 4, 5, 7, 14 and 30 were specially drawn for this work by Miss Priscilla Fawcett, who has also redrawn Figs. 20, 21, 22, 23, 25, 27, 28, 29 and 35 from the works of Lindley and Josserand. Mr. Maurice Wilson provided Fig. 1, Mrs. T. Threlkeld Fig. 31. To Professor O. E. Nybakken my thanks are due for permission to quote from his *Greek and Latin in scientific Terminology*; to the Royal Horticultural Society of London to reprint part of my article on 'Pronunciation' in the *Dictionary of Gardening, Supplement*. I must also express my gratitude to Miss D. B. Atterton, Mrs. P. Brenan, Miss P. Cazalet, Miss M. Deport, Miss C. J. Hart, Miss C. Roby, Mrs. H. Sabo, Mrs. E. L. Snowdon, Mrs. B. M. Tibbs and Mrs. A. Thompson for the care with which they typed my complicated and much amended manuscript, and to Dr. G. C. Ainsworth, Mrs. F. Balfour-Browne, Mr. J. E. Dandy, Mr. F. C. Deighton, Dr. A. W. Exell, Mr. K. Hulbert, Mr. T. P. R. Layng, Mr. J. H. Price and Mr. P. A. Spalding together with other friends at Kew and the British Museum (Natural History) for the many hours of critical scrutiny they have devoted to reading proofs. Equally appreciated is the care which Messrs. R. & R. Clark of Edinburgh, happily remembered as the printers in 1930 of my first excursion into bibliography, have taken with the printing of this opusculum.

Apologia pro Libro meo

'In all Ages wherein Learning hath Flourished, complaint hath been made of the Itch of Writing, and the multitude of worthless Books, wherein importunate Scriblers have pestered the World . . . I am sensible that this Tractate may likely incur the Censure of a superfluous Piece. . . . *First* therefore, in Excuse of it, I plead, That there are in it some Considerations new and untoucht by others: wherein if I be mistaken, I alledge *Secondly*, that manner of Delivery and Expression may be more suitable to some Mens Apprehension, and facile to their Understandings. If that will not hold, I pretend *Thirdly*, That all the Particulars contained in this Book, cannot be found in any one Piece known to me, but ly scattered and dispersed in many, and so this may serve to relieve those Fastidious Readers, that are not willing to take the Pains to search them out: and possibly, there may be some whose Ability (whatever their Industry might be) will not serve them to purchase, nor their opportunity to borrow, those Books, who yet may spare Money enough to buy so inconsiderable a Trifle.'

Thus begins John Ray's preface to his *The Wisdom of God manifested in the Works of Creation* (1691). These words of a seventeenth-century naturalist and scholar, who wrote extensively in Latin for international convenience but who also compiled a handy *Dictionariolum trilingue* (1675; 8th ed., 1736) of English, Latin and Greek terms for the help of schoolboys, state aptly enough my justification of the present venture, but some account of its intent and origin may nevertheless be added if only to indicate both its sources and shortcomings.

This book aims to provide a working guide to the special kind of Latin internationally used by botanists for the description and naming of plants. Although primarily concerned with grammar, syntax and vocabulary, it attempts also to sketch the historical development of botanical Latin, which is here accepted as a channel of communication now so distinct from classical Latin in spirit and structure as to require independent treatment. Chapter II develops further the theme of the autonomy of botanical Latin. Hence, as Vivian Mercier says of his *The Irish Comic Tradition*, 'this book makes no claim to be the last word on its subject: it is much closer to being the first one'. The realm of literature which a knowledge of botanical Latin opens to botanists is a strange barbarous place for classicists; invited into it

as an interpreter, a good classical scholar may well feel like Alice
meeting Humpty Dumpty through the looking-glass; he must have
local help in order to find his way without misunderstanding of its
long-established rules and customs. Such help the present book tries
to give. The need for it became painfully apparent to me many years
ago.

About 1930, when I was working in a Cambridge bookshop, an
Indian student, now a very distinguished economic botanist, asked
me to translate into Latin some descriptions of new Burmese species
of Charophyta because no scholars in Cambridge would do it for
him. In this, I have subsequently concluded, they wisely recognized
their limitations. But such prudence was of no help at all to my friend,
whose paper had been accepted for publication by a learned society
only on condition that he provided Latin descriptions in accordance
with the *International Rules of botanical Nomenclature*. Hence, reluctantly and laboriously, without having available any descriptions in
Latin of these plants to serve as models and my memories of Virgil's
Aeneid and Caesar's *Gallic War* proving quite useless, I rendered these
imperfectly understood descriptions of plants I had never seen into a
Latin which John Lindley would have justly described as written
'without the incumbrance of previous education' and about which
A. B. Rendle gently wrote that 'the Latin descriptions are merely
literal translations, sometimes faulty, of the English descriptions'.
However, bad though they were, they enabled my friend's otherwise
excellent work to be published; my one regret is that he acknowledged
their origin! It should be noted that, when a botanical author thanks
a professor of classics for providing a Latin description, this is usually
in bad or at any rate unconventional botanical Latin; thus I have
since then found myself erring in very respectable company. This
teenage experience convinced me that someone, but not I, ought to
produce a textbook for the guidance of the likes of me.

During the Second World War, however, when I had to sit for
hour after hour, day after day, staring at the sky from a Royal Air Force
ambulance awaiting planes which, fortunately, rarely crashed, I filled
in time by extracting the descriptive epithets from a series of Floras
lent me by the Lindley Library of the Royal Horticultural Society of
London in the hope of producing some day an etymological dictionary
of botanical names. I did not know that there already existed such
a book, *Verklarend Woordenboek der wetenschappelijke Namen* (1936)
by Cornelis Andries Backer (1874–1963). When, long after the war, I
came across this massive 'boekje', undoubtedly the most comprehensive, reliable and scholarly work of its kind, it seemed foolish to
continue with the preparation of one which would largely duplicate it,

so I decided to expand the grammatical and general chapters of mine, to limit the vocabulary to words used in descriptions and the basic elements of names, and to make it primarily a tool for taxonomists, a 'do-it-yourself' Latin kit. Thus the present work has grown out of war-time notebooks. Its preparation has necessarily been a much interrupted desultory business restricted to occasional evenings, week-ends and days of leave over the last twenty years. My procedure has been to take Latin descriptions by reputable botanical authors, extract the words used, arrange them alphabetically and then correlate them with standard glossaries, notably those by Bischoff, Lindley and Daydon Jackson, and thus to build up a vocabulary based primarily on usage and providing examples more or less ready for use. These examples come from a wide range of botanical literature. As regards the flowering-plants, probably Endlicher's *Genera Plantarum* (1836–50), Bentham and Hooker's *Genera Plantarum* (1863–83) and Urban's *Symbolae Antillanae* (1898–1928) have provided most. Many of those relating to non-vascular cryptogams have come from Montagne's *Sylloge Generum Specierumque Cryptogamarum* (1856), supplemented with a diversity of descriptions by later authors. Dr. G. C. Ainsworth, Mrs. F. L. Balfour-Browne, Mrs. Y. Butler, Mr. E. J. H. Corner, Mr. F. C. Deighton, Mr. A. Eddy, Mr. P. W. James and Mr. R. Ross kindly directed me to good representative descriptions in their respective fields of bryology, lichenology, mycology and phycology.

The name of John Lindley (1799–1865) occurs many times in this book. As a young man I became familiar with the Lindley Herbarium at the Botany School, Cambridge, curiously enough at about the same age as Lindley was when he became assistant librarian to Sir Joseph Banks and acquainted with the Banksian Herbarium. Later, as librarian of the Lindley Library of the Royal Horticultural Society of London, which Lindley also served for many years, I came to know his numerous publications and to admire the industry, tenacity and ability with which he undertook successfully so many different things. In writing this book I have been particularly impressed by the great contribution that Lindley made to exactness and clarity of terminology, notably in his *Introduction to Botany* and *Elements of Botany*, which represent, however, but small parts of his activity, and, like Daydon Jackson and other makers of glossaries, I have taken his work as a foundation. Lindley's books were written vigorously and with good sense, drawing upon extensive reading and experience, and they still repay consulta-tion. In the year of his centenary I am happy indeed to take this opportunity of expressing gratitude both for the example of his life and for his achievements.

The tedious and time-consuming task of sorting thousands of slips into alphabetical sequence, thus bringing together divergent uses of the same word, was greatly lightened by the help of my wife and my son. For much scholarly criticism and advice I am indebted to Mr. J. E. Dandy, the late Mr. N. Y. Sandwith and the late Mr. A. C. Townsend. My greatest debt is, however, to Dr. Hannah Croasdale of Dartmouth College, New Hampshire, U.S.A., who has for many years helped her fellow-workers in phycology to write their Latin descriptions and has made an extensive collection of useful expressions and phrases particularly relating to Algae. These notes, which she generously placed at my disposal, have called my attention to omissions from my vocabulary, suggested additional cross-references, and provided a check on information from other sources.

None of these kind helpers and encouragers is, of course, to be held responsible for the deficiencies of this book, which its unavoidably protracted and intermittent preparation may help to explain though not to excuse. As John Gerard wrote in the preface of his herbal of 1597, 'accept this at my hands (loving countriemen) as a token of my good will, trusting that the best and well minded will not rashly condemne me, although some thing have passed woorthie reprehension.'

W. T. S.

Department of Botany
British Museum (Natural History)

PREFACE TO SECOND EDITION

The writing of his massive *Enthusiasm, a Chapter in the History of Religion* (1950) ended, Monsignor Ronald Knox looked back in 1949 over the thirty years or so of its haphazard preparation amid other tasks, when he must often have feared it would never be completed, and wrote of how 'The Book was what mattered—he had lived with it all these years, fondled it in his waking thoughts, used it as an escape from anxiety, a solace in long journeys, in tedious conversations. . . . The Book haunted his day-dreams like a guilty romance!' Knox, who had indeed written much else, then concluded, 'Do not doubt that one in my position feels, once again, the delicious tremors of first authorship; forgets his bibliography, and ranks in his own mind as *homo unius libri*'. So too it has been with *Botanical Latin*. Off and on, amid other tasks, this occupied the thoughts of its author over some twenty years before it achieved publication in 1966, but the first printing sold out in half as many months.

Since its subject, Botanical Latin, remains and will remain an important international medium for recording and naming plants new to science and since much information is available in no other language, the gratifying world-wide sale of *Botanical Latin* and requests for its re-issue indicate that it has indeed proved as convenient a guide as was hoped. For this new edition, changes have been made throughout with the minimum disturbance of the main text, mostly by the insertion of extra words in Chapters V and XXV and some references in the bibliographies of other chapters. These will help, it is hoped, to maintain the book's usefulness not only to botanists and gardeners but also to historians of science and classical scholars.

W.T.S.

JULY 1972

Contents

List of Illustrations

PART ONE

INTRODUCTORY

CHAPTER I

How to Use this Book

Botanical Latin is an international language used by botanists the world over for the naming and description of plants. Its use is obligatory only in descriptions of plants considered new to science, but little research can be done in systematic botany without recourse to earlier literature written in botanical Latin. Increasing scientific need during the past 250 years for precision and economy in words has made it distinct from classical Latin and it should be treated as such. The present book aims to supply a guide to its grammar, its standard procedures and peculiarities and its basic vocabulary, using examples taken from a wide range of botanical literature, in order that persons ignorant of classical Latin may nevertheless be able to extract the meaning from descriptions in botanical Latin and, if need be, draw up simple, clear and intelligible descriptions of their own. Part I is introductory; Part II deals primarily with grammar; Part III with syntax; Part IV with vocabulary.

The reader having no knowledge of classical Latin must first of all become acquainted with the PARTS OF SPEECH detailed in Chapters V-XII and the concepts of GENDER, NUMBER and CASE (see pp. 59, 60). Examples of these are provided in the sentence *Haec species pulchra crescit maxime in pratis et locis graminosis inter frutices humiles* (This beautiful species grows especially in meadows and grassy places among low shrubs). Here the words *species* (species), *pratis* (meadows), *locis* (places) and *frutices* (shrubs) are NOUNS (see Chapter V), *haec* (this) a PRONOUN (see Chapter IX) adjectivally used, *maxime* (especially) an ADVERB (see Chapter VII), *in* (in, on) and *inter* (among) PREPOSITIONS (see Chapter X), *et* (and) a CONJUNCTION (see Chapter XI), *pulchra* (beautiful), *graminosis* (very grassy) and *humiles* (low) ADJECTIVES (see Chapter VI). The endings of most of these words change according to the meaning intended; such words are said to be *inflected*. The nouns may be masculine, feminine or neuter in *gender* and this, together with their *number* (whether singular or plural) and *case* (whether nominative, accusative, etc.), controls their endings and the endings of their adjectives associated with them. Thus the word *species* used above is of feminine gender, singular number (since only one species is

3

mentioned here) and nominative case ; the adjective *pulchra* associated with it is likewise of feminine gender (hence not masculine *pulcher* or neuter *pulchrum*), singular number and nominative case. The nouns *pratis* and *locis* are of plural number and ablative case, their nominative singular forms being respectively *pratum*, which is neuter, and *locus*, which is masculine. *Frutices* is here the accusative plural form of *frutex*, which is masculine ; the associated adjective *humiles* (of which the masculine nominative singular is *humilis*) agrees with *frutices* in gender, number and case. *Crescit* (it grows) is a VERB (see Chapter XII) agreeing in number with *species*. This example will serve to indicate the complexities of a highly inflected language such as Latin, complexities which, however, lead to clarity.

The VOCABULARY (see Chapter XXV) of botanical Latin is very rich, and a knowledge of it can only be acquired through experience. A useful exercise is to take some descriptions and diagnoses by the botanists mentioned in Chapter II and translate them into English, then later, by use of the Vocabulary, translate them back into Latin. It will be noticed that in a diagnosis such as *pileo 2 cm. lato glabro viridi, stipite 10 cm. longo fistuloso maculis albis consperso, lamellis viridibus liberis, sporis fusiformibus laevibus* (with the pileus 2 cm. broad glabrous green, the stipe 10 cm. long fistular with white spots sprinkled, the lamellae green free, the spores fusiform smooth) many of the words end in *-o*, *-is* and *-ibus* ; these indicate that it is written in the ablative case. Words, however, are listed in dictionaries and glossaries under their nominative form, e.g. under *pileus* (not *pileo*), *latus* (not *lato*), *glaber* (not *glabro*), *viridis* (not *viridi*), *stipes* (not *stipite*), *lamella* (not *lamellis*). The part of the word to which such case-endings are attached is known as its *stem* (see p. 60), e.g. the stem of *pileus* (nominative) and *pileo* (ablative) is *pile-*. Since words with the ablative singular ending, for example, in *-e* and the ablative plural in *-ibus* may have the nominative singular ending in *-en* (e.g. *lichen*), *-er* (e.g. *elater*), *-o* (e.g. *sectio*), *-or* (e.g. *odor*), etc., it is impossible to deduce the nominative singular from the ablative. Hence a given word should be sought in the Vocabulary by its stem rather than by the whole word when not in the nominative case.

Nouns are classified into five main groups or *declensions*, each with a distinctive set of case-endings. The Roman numeral I, II, III, IV or V indicates the declension to which a given noun belongs, the letter *m* (masculine), *f* (feminine) or *n* (neuter) its gender. By reference to Chapter V the correct form to express a particular meaning can easily be found. Adjectives are classified into two main groups indicated by the letters A and B in the Vocabulary. If a particular adjective is to go with, say, a feminine noun of plural number and ablative case, then the feminine plural ablative form of that adjective should be ascertained by reference to Chapter VI. The Vocabulary provides many phrases ready-made which can be adopted or adapted.

A reader intending to describe a plant in Latin should turn to Chapter XIII for examples of DIAGNOSES setting out briefly distinguishing features, to XIV for examples of DESCRIPTIONS stating characters in general, to XV for notes on PUNCTUATION, to XVI for information about HABITATS. In consulting the older literature to check that the plant has not been described and named already, he may find type-localities and distribution there stated in Latin or Latinized GEO-GRAPHICAL NAMES, for which see Chapter XVII.

To provide a new plant with an apt name not already used becomes more and more difficult as more and more names are published. WORDS OF GREEK ORIGIN are just as likely as Latin ones to be pre-occupied. For their formation see Chapters XIX and XX. If these and the Vocabulary do not provide enough material, Roland Wilbur Brown's *Composition of scientific Words* (1956) should be consulted for suggestions, together with Oscar E. Nybakken's *Greek and Latin in scientific Terminology* (1960); in any event, checking with Liddell and Scott's monumental *A Greek-English Lexicon* (new ed. 1940) is advised; for this an acquaintance with the Greek alphabet (see p. 261) is essential. Dictionaries of foreign equivalents should always be used both ways, as a word in one language often has a different range of meaning from a more or less equivalent word in another.

The VOCABULARY (Chapter XXV) of this book is essentially one of botanical Latin and English equivalents and only incidentally explains their meaning and application; this, however, is the function of Chapter XXII, which provides basic Latin-English DESCRIPTIVE TERMINOLOGY taken from Lindley, and of such works as G. W. Bischoff's *Wörterbuch der beschreibenden Botanik* (2nd ed., 1857), J. Lindley's *The Elements of Botany* (1849), A. Gray's *The Botanical Text-Book* (6th ed., Part I, 1879), B. D. Jackson's *A Glossary of botanic Terms* (4th ed., 1928), W. H. Snell and E. A. Dick's *A Glossary of Mycology* (2nd ed., 1971), and the glossaries accompanying many Floras. Moreover it does not set out to state the meanings of specific epithets, although many are incidentally included. For these G. F. Zimmer, *A Popular Dictionary of botanical Names and Terms* (1912), C. A. Backer, *Verklarend Woordenboek van wetenschappelijke Plantennamen* (1936), H. Gilbert-Carter, *Glossary of the British Flora* (3rd ed., 1964) and A. W. Smith and W. T. Stearn, *A Gardener's Dictionary of Plant Names* (1972), may be consulted.

CHAPTER II

Introduction

*Sic enim potius loquamur : melius est reprehendant nos gram-
matici quam non intelligant populi* [Let us rather then declare :
it is better that the grammarians censure us than that the public
does not understand us].

ST. AUGUSTINE OF HIPPO (A.D. 354–430)
Ennar. in Psalm. cxxxviii, 20

'Those who wish to remain ignorant of the Latin language, have no
business with the study of Botany.' So wrote John Berkenhout in
1789. A letter to the *Cambridge Review* of 29 January 1960 by E. J. H.
Corner gives its modern echo : 'We botanists keep Latin alive. We
read it, write it, type it, speak it when mother tongues fail, and succeed
in putting such remarkable things as orchid-flowers and microscopic
fungi into universal understanding through Latin. If we didn't, the
Babel of tongues and scripts would close our accord, and we should
be at the mercy of politics! We have, in fact, our international language ; it is so far evolved that it is almost as different from classical
Latin as modern from Chaucerian English.' Although all too little
appreciated, the international importance of botanical Latin and its
divergence from classical Latin have indeed often been noted. 'Le
latin des botanistes n'est pas cette langue obscure et à réticences de
Tacite, obscure et à périodes pompeuses de Cicéron, obscure et à
graces tortillées d'Horace', wrote Alphonse de Candolle in 1880, 'Ce
n'est pas même la langue plus sobre et plus claire d'un naturaliste, tel
que Pline. C'est le latin arrangé par Linné à l'usage des descriptions et,
j'oserai dire, à l'usage de ceux qui n'aiment ni les complications gram-
maticales, ni les phrases disposées sens dessus dessous.' To learn it,
said this distinguished Swiss botanist, was the work of a month for an
Italian, two months for a Frenchman, three for an Englishman, four
months for a German or Swede not already familiar with a language
of Latin origin. Once acquired it is a valuable working tool, opening
stores of taxonomic information not otherwise available.

Botanical Latin is best described as a modern Romance language
of special technical application, derived from Renaissance Latin with
much plundering of ancient Greek, which has evolved, mainly since

6

1700 and primarily through the work of Carl Linnaeus (1707–78), to serve as an international medium for the scientific naming of plants in all their vast numbers and manifold diversity. These include many thousands of plants unknown to the Greeks and Romans of classical times and for which names have had to be provided as a means of reference. Their description necessitates the recording of structures often much too small for comprehension by the naked eye, hence unknown to the ancients and needing words with precise restricted applications foreign to classical Latin. The use of a modified form of Latin for purposes so remote from classical literature is a consequence of the survival of Latin as a general-purpose language, used in academic, diplomatic, ecclesiastical and legal affairs and even domestic correspondence, long past the crucial period of the sixteenth century when herbalists became aware of the many hitherto unnoticed and unnamed plants around them. They wrote in Latin about these plants because they wrote in Latin about almost everything else. Latin, admittedly derived from the medieval Latin, was then the ordinary generally understood language of educated men. Such indeed it remained all through the eighteenth century. It served not only for international communication, as between Linnaeus and his foreign correspondents, and between Albrecht von Haller (1708–77) and his foreign correspondents, but also for private correspondence between scholars of the same language, possibly because few women then could read Latin. Thus Haller and his friend Johannes Gessner (1709–90), although both German-speaking Swiss, conducted their extensive life-long correspondence in Latin. Study of Latin then began early and led to great fluency in later life. Elias Magnus Fries (1794–1878), the 'founder of modern systematic mycology', tells a little about his own education [1] in his *Historiola Studii mei mycologii* (1857). At the age of twelve when gathering strawberries in a wood he found an unusually large specimen of a fungus (*Hydnum coralloides*), which induced him to begin the study of fungi. He tried to ascertain its name with the aid of Liljeblad's *Utkast til en Svensk Flora* (1792 and 1798), but was soon tripped up by an unknown word *lamella*. 'Shortly afterwards, when out walking with my father, I asked: *Dic, Pater, quid est lamella?* (with my father I was allowed to talk only in Latin, whereby I learned Latin before Swedish). *Lamella*, he replied, *est lamina tenuis*, which explanation given made this term for the fructification of agarics seem particularly apt. . . . Two men especially lit up and fostered my

---

[1] The Latin education of Nils Retzius (1712–57) was rather similar to that of Fries; according to Linnaeus, *Skånska Resa*, 92 (1751), entry of 23 May 1749, when Retzius was about seven or eight years old his tutor spent a year teaching him a Latin vocabulary and then for the next two years allowed him to speak nothing but Latin; thereafter he read Latin authors and conversed in Latin with ease.

studies, the luminaries of Lund botany, one setting (A. J. Retzius), the other rising (C. A. Agardh). . . . From the latter I received Persoon's *Synopsis Fungorum* to make use of, which I soon learned from end to end, from the former Albertini [and Schweinitz's], *Conspectus Fungorum* [*in Lusatiae superioris*] *Agri niskiensis* [*Agro niskiensi crescentium*], which book taught me knowledge of more things than any other' (cf. *Friesia*, 5: 141-143; 1955).

It was natural for men thus reared upon Latin as a living language to use this in their scientific work as well as other matters and to treat it in a free and easy manner, modifying and extending it to meet their needs. From being thus customary and traditional, Latin has now become obligatory for certain botanical purposes. No botanist, however learned, can have a reading knowledge of all the modern languages (said to be about 3,000) from Icelandic and Israeli Hebrew to Burmese, Malay, Chinese and Japanese in which descriptions of new plants might be published. As Linnaeus said as long ago as 1737, when national pride leads individuals to write of their discoveries in their own languages alone, 'the novice may grow old over his literary studies before he is competent to study the sciences' (*Crit. bot.*, no. 229). Moreover, there is no other language in which so much fundamental information of systematic botany, representing an enormous and hard-won grasp upon the facts of the natural world, is recorded. 'Its roots take hold too firmly on the kingdoms of the dead', as Helen Waddell has written of medieval Latin, for it to be discarded. The loss would be too great. Successive international botanical conferences have accordingly decreed its maintenance. A rule (Article 37) of the *International Code of Botanical Nomenclature, 1959* (1961) states that 'in order to be validly published, a name of a new taxon of plants, the bacteria, algae and all fossils excepted, published on or after 1 January 1935 must be accompanied by a Latin diagnosis [i.e. a statement in Latin of characteristics] or by a reference to a previously and effectively published Latin diagnosis' and that 'a name of a new taxon of algae published on or after 1 January 1958 must be accompanied by a Latin diagnosis or by a reference to a previously and effectively published Latin diagnosis'. This rule is scrupulously honoured by most botanists of all nations who thus form an empirical language community, as described by Karl Vossler (*The Spirit of Language in Civilization*, 1932), 'held together by the will to work at a common language material as the special instrument of mutual understanding'. New names published contrary to article 37 are ignored or rejected; they become valid only when provided with a published Latin definition or description of the plant's features. The earlier article 36 of the *Règles internationales pour la Nomenclature botanique, 1905* (1906), namely that 'on or after

1 January 1908, the publication of names of new groups will be valid only when accompanied by a Latin diagnosis', was disregarded by followers of the now obsolete *American Code of Nomenclature* (1907). The probability that new names might be accompanied by descriptions only in Asiatic and African languages was beyond their vision. Experience since 1905 has made the utility of such a rule so evident that the defence of Latin as the one obligatory language for the description of new taxa of plants comes as strongly from Slavonic and Scandinavian botanists as from those of Latin countries. The property of no one nation or linguistic group, Latin has, in consequence of its neutrality, become world-wide. Even if political considerations did not now prevent the adoption of, say, Chinese, English, Russian or Spanish as the *one* international language for the descriptions of new taxa, agreement on one of these would nevertheless not spare research workers in systematic botany the necessity of learning botanical Latin in order to get first-hand information from past work.

The number of original descriptions and diagnoses of plants in Latin certainly exceeds 400,000. Moreover, many standard comprehensive works giving information not elsewhere readily accessible or else important as starting points of nomenclature are in Latin. Among these are J. G. Agardh, *Species, Genera et Ordines Algarum* (1848–98), Bentham & Hooker, *Genera Plantarum* (1862–83), Blume, *Flora Javae* (1828–58), Bornet & Flahault, *Révision des Nostocacées hétérocystées* (1886–88), Brown, *Prodromus Florae Novae Hollandiae* (1810), de Candolle, *Prodromus* (1824–69), De Toni, *Sylloge Algarum* (1889–1907), Endlicher, *Genera Plantarum* (1836–41), Fries, *Systema Mycologicum* (1821–32) and *Lichenographia Europaea* (1831), Gomont, *Monographie des Oscillariées* (1892–93), Halácsy, *Conspectus Florae Graecae* (1900–12), Hayek, *Prodromus Florae Peninsulae Balcanicae* (1924–33), Hedwig, *Species Muscorum* (1801), Hooker, *Flora Boreali-Americana* (1829–40), Kunth, *Nova Genera et Species Plantarum* (1816–25), Ledebour, *Flora Rossica* (1841–53), Linnaeus, *Species Plantarum* (1753) and *Genera Plantarum* (5th ed., 1754), Martius, *Flora Brasiliensis* (1840–1906), Miquel, *Flora Indiae Batavae* (1855–9), Persoon, *Synopsis Plantarum* (1805–7), C. B. Presl, *Tentamen Pteridographiae* (1836), Saccardo, *Sylloge Fungorum* (1882–1931), Spruce, *Hepaticae Amazonicae et Andinae* (1884–85), Urban, *Symbolae Antillanae* (1898–1928), Webb & Berthelot, *Phytographia Canariensis* (1836–50), Willkomm & Lange, *Prodromus Florae Hispanicae* (1861–93), the monographs in de Candolle's *Monographiae Phanerogamarum* (1878–93), and Engler's *Das Pflanzenreich* (1900 onwards), as well as numerous independent monographs. Moreover, certain periodicals, notably Engler's *Botanische Jahrbücher*, Fedde's *Repertorium Specierum Novarum*, Hooker's

Icones Plantarum, Hedwigia and the *Kew Bulletin,* contain many hundreds of descriptions in Latin. There is no shortage of models for those who will take a little trouble to find them.

Botanical Latin could never have been continuously employed for the description of such a diversity of plants but for its progressive development. This has involved the incorporation of a host of terms unknown in classical Latin, e.g. *acarodomatium, achenium, androecium, anthela, ascus, basidium, calyptra, mycelium, ovarium, ovulum, perigonium, sepalum, tepalum* etc., and the use of many classical Latin words with new specialized meanings or with meanings remote from their original usage, e.g. *amentum, bractea, calyx, corolla, pileus, stigma, stipula, velum* (see Chapter III). Side by side with such shifts of application and with enrichment by coinage and taking from other languages, notably Greek, has come a simplification of grammar. In these respects its development has paralleled that of other derivatives from Latin. It illustrates in a small way that relation of science to language picturesquely described by Karl Vossler: 'Science castigates and enriches, conserves and accelerates, prunes and sharpens, obstructs and drives forward linguistic thought in the service of the logos, which it rapes, deprives of its naiveté and enriches instead with innumerable children' (*The Spirit of Language in Civilization,* 1932). No science can advance without forming a specialized vocabulary economical and precise in designating things and concepts; just as the lack of a suitable word hampers discussion, so the provision of one often leads to better understanding of the object or concept concerned; the history of Webber's term 'clone' (*clon*; cf. Stearn, 1949, 1961) [1] provides one example among many. It is to Latin and Greek that those concerned with word-making have mostly turned for material. Although Latin itself has long ceased to be for the botanist 'that universal language which opens to him all the botanical books published in every part of the world', as John Berkenhout described it in 1789, it provides many of the terms used in morphology, anatomy, cytology, physiology, ecology and phytogeography. It no longer serves, however, as the vehicle in which their concepts, ideas, opinions and observations are recorded and discussed. Its function has gradually become almost entirely nomenclatural and descriptive. This limitation of use has made it possible to eliminate from botanical Latin many of the complexities of classical Latin and to impose upon it an easily learned formal style which makes for ease of consultation. It has acquired its own conventions, its own idioms.

The general effect of all this has been to make botanical Latin

[1] W. T. Stearn, 'The use of the term clone', *J. Royal Hort. Soc.,* 74: 41-47 (1949), 'Clone', P. Gray. *Encycl. Biol. Sci.,* 241-243 (1961).

autonomous. It is now as unintelligible to classical scholars as modern English would be to a Frenchman who had learned only Anglo-Saxon. So simple and, to a botanist, self-explanatory a botanical Latin diagnosis as *species scapo conspicue bracteato pubescenti, petalis glandulosis, antheris gynoecio paulo longioribus* treated as classical Latin could be translated as 'kind with the stem conspicuously glistening like gold and reaching the age of puberty with the thin metal plates full of kernels, with the medicines made from flowers a little longer than the woman's apartment', portraying a plant worthy of Edward Lear's *Nonsense Botany*. Botanical Latin is admittedly an artificial language, but then, as stated by L. R. Palmer, 'from its beginning to its end the written Latin language in all its forms is an artificial language'. No more to be regarded as corrupt classical Latin than modern Italian, botanical Latin is an enriched and specialized derivative of the Latin which scholars wrote in the sixteenth century and which in turn was a reformed version of medieval low Latin inspired by the brief Golden Age (81 B.C.–A.D. 14) of classical Latin literature. To discard the medieval legacy and numerous accepted neologisms gathered into botanical Latin during its past three centuries of development would be to destroy those very features from which it derives its utility as an international means of communication. Recognition of its linguistic independence cuts out the need even to consider this.

The relation of botanical Latin to classical Latin is that of a former dependency which by vigorous economic growth over many years has established traditions and divergencies arising out of its special conditions and history that must be accepted, if need be, by proclaiming its status as a language in its own right. From this it follows that there is no good reason to change under pretence of reform the standard spellings and procedures of Latin as used by botanists to make them conform to those of classical Latin. The latter are indeed to be rejected as archaic and incorrect in botanical Latin. Thus *acris* (m.), *palustris* (m.), *laevis, laevigatus, annulus, bacca* and *sylva*, for example, are correct in botanical Latin, *acer* (m.), *paluster* (m.), *levis, levigatus, anulus, baca* and *silva* preferable in classical Latin.

Ben Jonson's posthumous *Timber: or Discoveries made upon Men and Matter* (1641) under the heading 'Consuetudo' sets down neatly the crux of the matter: 'Custome is the most certaine mistresse of language, as the publike stamp makes the current money. . . . The eldest of the present and newest of the past language is the best. For what was the ancient language, which some men so doate upon, but the ancient custome? yet when I name custome, I understand not the vulgar custome . . . but that I call custome of speech, which is the consent of the learned; as custome of life, which is the consent of the good.'

In this book 'the consent of the learned' is taken to be fairly consistent usage by nineteenth-century botanists of acknowledged scholarship. The list of such men to whose works later botanists can well turn for guidance in the skilful handling of Latin is a long one. They include Augustin Pyramus de Candolle (1778–1841), Camille Montagne (1784–1866), Carl Sigismund Kunth (1788–1850), Antoine L. A. Fée (1789–1874), Philip Barker Webb (1793–1854), Karel Boriwog Presl (1794–1852), Carl F. P. von Martius (1794–1868), Elias Magnus Fries (1794–1878), George Bentham (1800–84), Alexander von Bunge (1803–1890), Miles Joseph Berkeley (1803–89) who checked the latinity of Bentham & Hooker's *Genera Plantarum*, Stephan Ladislaus Endlicher (1804–49), Alphonse de Candolle (1806–93), Friedrich Traugott Kützing (1807–93), Edmond Boissier (1810–86), Louis René Tulasne (1815–85) and Charles Tulasne (1816–84), Joseph Dalton Hooker (1817–1911), Richard Spruce (1817–93), Heinrich Moritz Wilkomm (1821–95), Georg Heinrich Mettenius (1823–66), Carl Johann Maximowicz (1827–91), Ludwig A. T. Radlkofer (1829–1927), Franz Stephani (1842–1927), Adolf Engler (1844–1930), Pier Andrea Saccardo (1845–1920), Georg Hieronymus (1846–1921), Giacomo Bresadola (1847–1929), Ignaz Urban (1848–1931), Viktor Ferdinand Brotherus (1849–1929), Edvard August Vainio (1853–1929), Alexander Zahlbruckner (1860–1938), Gustaf O. A. Malme (1864–1937) and others whose output in Latin though of high quality was smaller. Specialists could easily extend such a list. These men not only wrote extensively in Latin; what they recorded in it remains important. A number of them were steeped in the classics. Modern taxonomy being built upon their publications, it obviously makes for consistency and ease of communication to maintain a continuity with their work by using the same expressions and adopting the same style and orthography when relevant and apt.

The care needed to draw up a description in Latin is often in itself an aid to exact description in the writer's mother tongue, wherein an expression may possibly bear several meanings each with a different Latin equivalent; the act of translation reveals ambiguities and forces the writer to become clear in his own mind as to what the original means. Radlkofer in his great work on the *Sapindaceae*, published posthumously 1931–34, described some 140 genera and 2,000 species in Latin. 'I well remember,' wrote Theodor Herzog, 'how Radlkofer, drawing up his Latin diagnoses with a total disregard of the time consumed, would often spend a quarter of an hour in searching for the most apt expression surpassing all others in exactness.' Nevertheless Radlkofer covered over 1,400 pages with them. Those who lack this perfectionist zeal can profit from it by adapting the carefully drafted descriptions of their predecessors to their own use. Unfortunately neglect of such readily available models is all too evident in some modern descriptions.

Reviewing David Don's *Prodromus Florae Nepalensis* (1825), John Lindley said it is 'written in so strange a language, that we can scarcely guess its name, unless, indeed, it be a specimen of some new kind of Latin which may be written "with great facility, after three lessons of an hour each", without the incumbrance of previous education' (*Bot. Reg.*, 11 : sub t. 872 : 1825). Don's work is, however, polished by comparison with some descriptions published in 1962 in which *herbae lignae inferior*; *ramuli annulares*; *ramuli radicantes tangentes terra*; *dens laterales clarissimae*; *radix superioris* is supposed to mean, according to its author, 'herbs woody at soil level; branches annual; branches rooting in contact with the soil; lateral teeth distinctly subtending; radicle superior', and *frutices roundatei, ⅓ lignei ad monei lignei; laminae linearis ad oblanceolate*; *bracteae fructeae pedicelles ad 4 mm., ovoidales, cum 4 pennis* 'rounded shrubs, the lower ⅓ woody to woody throughout; blades linear to oblanceolate; fruiting bracts on pedicels to 4 mm. long, ovoid, bearing 4 wings'!˙ The plants to which these words refer are members of a family which received much attention from Moquin-Tandon, Fenzl and Bunge among others. Study of descriptions by his learned predecessors would have helped the author to make his own descriptions more in keeping with the need of science for intelligibility and accuracy.

CHAPTER III

Development of Botanical
Latin Terminology

ORIGIN OF BOTANICAL LATIN

Botanical Latin derives from the Latin of the Roman writers about plants, notably Pliny the Elder (A.D. 23–79). It accordingly owes its existence to the survival of Latin through the Middle Ages and its retention at the Renaissance and well into the eighteenth century as the one internationally used language of learning among the peoples of Europe, none of which then possessed a vernacular language sufficiently developed and widely enough known to challenge its supremacy in diplomatic, legal and ecclesiastical matters. Had Latin lost this supremacy before the end of the sixteenth century, there would probably be no one international system of botanical nomenclature today, for its use by herbalists and botanists in the sixteenth century established the tradition inherited by the founder of modern botanical nomenclature, Carl Linnaeus (1707–78), that all plants should be given Latin names, or at any rate names of Latin form, independent of local vernacular names, and that works relating to them should also be in Latin. Thus, during the period when scholars interested in plants were few in every country, their use of Latin counteracted their geographical isolation. Written in their own vernaculars, their works would have been largely unread, unknown and ineffective, for the development of any science is necessarily a co-operative effort; in Latin these became direct contributions to a common European pool of learning. Linnaeus owed his scientific career largely to a knowledge of Latin. In turn, botanical Latin owes its present utility, together with its divergence from classical and medieval Latin, largely to Linnaeus. Pliny the Elder, resurrected in the year 1601, would probably have understood without great difficulty the plant descriptions in the just published *Rariorum Plantarum Historia* of Charles de l'Écluse (Carolus Clusius, 1526–1609). Transferred to the nineteenth century, he would have found unintelligible or have grossly misunderstood the detailed and technically excellent descriptions in botanical Latin by such eminent scholars as Antoine L. A. Fée (1789–1874), Philip Barker Webb (1793–1854) and Stephan Ladislaus Endlicher (1804–49), all well versed both in the classics and in botany.

INFLUENCE OF LINNAEUS

This development away from classical Latin in the eighteenth and early nineteenth centuries reflects the progress of formal plant description during that period. As European expansion overseas made known more and more diverse nameless plants, and improved optical aids revealed ever more complex and varied details of structure for which no terms existed in any language, Latin had either to be adapted and extended so that such plants could be given internationally acceptable Latin names and their characters clearly and accurately recorded, or it had to be abandoned for botanical purposes. For Linnaeus indeed there was no choice. Using Latin in works of such importance as his *Genera Plantarum* (1737 ; 5th ed., 1754 ; 6th ed., 1764), *Critica botanica* (1737), *Flora Lapponica* (1737), *Hortus Cliffortianus* (1738), *Philosophia botanica* (1751) and *Species Plantarum* (1753 ; 2nd ed., 1762–63 ; 3rd ed., 1764), which otherwise he could have written only in Swedish, Linnaeus made his principles and methods immediately usable all over Europe. Moreover, by associating them with an acceptable Latin terminology and applying them in encyclopaedic works which botanists had of necessity to consult (for nowhere else was so much information about the kinds of plants to be found so methodically and conveniently assembled) he established a simplified form of Latin as the international language for the formal naming and description of plants. The Romans possessed many words relating to conspicuous plant structures (cf. André, 1956 ; Sprague, 1933 ; Stearn, 1955), notably those of economic use, but lacked precise terms for the parts of the flower, which received little attention before the proof of sexuality in plants at the end of the seventeenth century. It was, however, upon these floral parts that Linnaeus built his 'sexual system' of classification and rather than himself coin entirely new words he had to adapt classical Latin words to his purpose. He took, for example, a word such as *corolla*, meaning in classical Latin 'a little crown or garland', and applied it exclusively to the showy inner envelope of the flower surrounding the sexual organs for which there then existed no convenient unambiguous collective term.   In this way, by stipulative definition,[1] which is an essential process in the development of any science, Linnaeus provided botany with a Latin terminology of great utility, deceptively like classical Latin in appearance, remote indeed from it in spirit and meaning.   He created what was virtually a new Latin botanical language at the very time that the Italian philologists and lexicographers Jacopo Facciolati (1682–1769) and Egidio Forcellini (1688–1768) were purging Latin of its medieval *verba barbara* and ascertaining ancient usage.   Thus has come the great cleavage between Latin as used by botanists and Latin as interpreted by classical scholars.

Following Linnaean precedent, botanical Latin has continued to simplify the grammar of classical Latin and to give to many Latin words restricted and precise meanings often markedly different from those of Roman times; moreover, it has elaborated its vocabulary by adding numerous loan-words and modern compounds.   These innovations are, as John Brand pointed out in 1797, essentially of the same kind as the Romans themselves made when they needed terms to express matters outside their everyday experience.   Thus Cicero himself put into the mouth of Varro, 'the greatest critic and grammarian of the Augustan age', the statement that to unusual subjects one could apply words which had not been in use, and that if Latin could not furnish them recourse could be made to Greek, since to new things new names must be given or those of others transferred to them (*aut enim nova sunt rerum novarum facienda nomina aut ex aliis transferenda*); according to Weise (1893), Varro himself took some 200 words from Greek.   Thanks to such action, botanical Latin has remained an important tool of systematic botany, a language in which even the characteristics of microscopic organisms studied on culture media (see pp. 168, 174) or with the aid of the electron microscope (see pp. 158–161) can be expressed.   This is indeed a remarkable linguistic achievement.   'Call it dog-Latin if you will', R. A. Knox wrote in

---

[1] The essential and constant element of *stipulative definition* is, in the words of Richard Robinson (1950), 'the element of deliberate, arbitrary, self-conscious choice of name for a certain thing or a thing for a certain name. . . . Whether this individual choice agrees with or differs from the common usage of the word defined and whether there is any common usage of it or not is irrevelant to the essence of stipulation. A stipulative definition may vary, in this respect, all the way from stipulating an entirely novel noise as the name of an entirely novel thing to merely confirming and adopting common usage.' It is to be distinguished from *lexical definition*, which states how words have been used and which may supply the material for stipulative definition as it did to Linnaeus. Reference should be made to Robinson's instructive and lucid essay, *Definition* (1950), notably his Chapter 4.

1923 of ecclesiastical Latin, 'there remains a proverb which tells us that a living dog is better than a dead lion, and the difference between the dog-Latin of St. Jerome and the lion-Latin of Cicero is the difference between a living and a dead language.' The same is true of botanical Latin. To assume that a grounding in classical Latin alone will prove adequate for its understanding is to risk much error and misinterpretation.

BEGINNINGS OF PLANT MORPHOLOGY
BY THEOPHRASTUS

The inadequacy of classical Latin by itself as a language for modern botanical use reflects the limited botanical knowledge and needs of the Roman world. The herb-gatherers or rhizotomi of antiquity undoubtedly possessed a wide acquaintance with plants having reputed medicinal value. Thus when we speak in English of anemones, asparagus, crocuses, cyclamens, delphiniums, gentians, lilies, peonies, roses, violets, etc., or of the genera *Achillea*, *Cassia*, *Daphne*, *Narcissus*, *Solanum*, *Viola*, etc., we use names which have come to us with little or no change from the everyday speech and herbalist jargon of ancient Rome and Magna Graecia. Such an extensive vocabulary as is preserved in the works of Pliny the Elder (cf. André, 1956) and Pedianos Dioscorides (cf. André, 1959; Stadler, 1898, 1900; Stromberg, 1940), indicates the ability to distinguish and recognize many plants, but this memorizing of the habit of growth of plants is rarely associated with an interest in their structure deep enough to make the detailed comparisons and the generalizations which bring forth a scientific terminology for their different parts. That is essentially the task of a philosopher rather than a herbalist. It seems to have been first undertaken by Aristotle's disciple and successor Theophrastus of Eresos (370–c. 285 B.C.). He inherited the botanic garden which Aristotle had founded at Athens and here, brooding over the characteristics of some five hundred or so kinds of plants, he arrived at basic concepts of plant morphology which stood essentially unchanged and scarcely enlarged for some nineteen centuries after his death until the development of lenses and the microscope revealed the functions and intimate structure of the flower, using that term in its modern sense as including the calyx and gynoecium as well as the corolla and androecium.

To Theophrastus and his followers for many centuries, indeed up to the seventeenth century A.D., the flower (ἄνθος, *flos*) was the assemblage of organs, essentially leaf-like in almond, apple, pear and plum, but 'hair-like' in grape, mulberry and ivy, which surrounds the organ (the gynoecium of modern botany) that later becomes the fruit or seed. His recognition of these as comparable, despite their great difference in appearance, gave 'to the term ἄνθος, flower, a new definition, a scientific one. The term must (henceforth) embrace whatever is intimately though transiently connected with a fruit-germ, whether laminal and coloured or filamentose and greenish. This, in so far as written records show, is the earliest proposition ever laid down concerning the morphology of the flower; and it was a mighty contribution to scientific botany' (E. L. Greene, 1909). Of Theophrastus's insight and knowledge his two books *De Causis Plantarum* and *De Historia Plantarum* supply many examples, discussed at length by E. L. Greene (1909: 52-142) and by Gustav Senn (1928–43) and summarized by Agnes Arber (1950: 11-23). It may suffice to mention his recognition of the pinnate leaves of ash (*Fraxinus*), mountain ash (*Sorbus*) and elder (*Sambucus*) as leaves comparable with simple leaves and his use of the new word 'pericarp' (περικάρπιον, apparently coined by him or Aristotle) to designate the protective covering around the seeds, whatever its diversity of form and texture. These concepts could not, however, advance satisfactorily beyond the evidence supplied by naked-eye observation. Thus a limit was set to the enrichment of ancient Greek and classical Latin with botanical terms and expressions adequate for modern use.

BEGINNINGS OF PLANT DESCRIPTION
BY THEOPHRASTUS

For those plants which attracted attention by their beauty, economic use or peculiarities, Theophrastus used the current Greek names; the rest he left nameless. He certainly did not set out to describe and name all the plants of his adopted Attica. He nevertheless described a number with remarkable skill. As an example may be quoted his description of the European hop-hornbeam (*Ostrya carpinifolia*: ὄστρυα; Fig. 1): 'It is similar to the beech in *growth* and *bark*; the *leaves* are shaped like a pear's at the base but they are much longer, narrowed to a point, and larger, and have many fibres, which stretch out like ribs from a central straight large fibre and are thick; moreover the leaves are wrinkled along the fibres and have a finely incised edge; the *wood* is hard, colourless and white; the *fruit* is small, oblong and yellow like barley; it has shallow *roots*; it loves water and is found in ravines' (translation by A. Hort, 1916). This description was composed in the infancy of botany, over 2,000 years ago. The description of the same tree appearing in a standard modern work, Alfred Rehder's *Manual of cultivated Trees and Shrubs* (2nd ed.,

1940), is as follows : '*Tree* to 20 metres ; *bark* gray ; young *branchlets* pubescent : *leaves* ovate to ovate-oblong, acuminate, usually rounded at base, sharply and doubly serrate, 4–10 cm. long, dark green and sparingly hairy above, sparingly hairy chiefly on the nerves beneath,

M.Wilson

Fig. 1   *Ostrya carpinifolia* Scopoli ; Hop-hornbeam
(Drawing by Maurice Wilson)

with 12–15 pairs of veins ; *fruiting clusters* 3·5–5 cm. long ; *nutlet* ovoid, 4–5 mm. long, with a tuft of hairs at the apex.' The order of these two descriptions is essentially the same and so is the content. The superiority of the modern description lies chiefly in its use of measurements.

Rehder states that this ostrya is a tree up to 20 metres high with grey bark. Theophrastus states that it is like the beech, which is a tree well known for its grey bark and also 20 metres or more high. Rehder notes that the leaf has 12–15 pairs of side veins; Theophrastus does not mention their number but says that they are many and stout. Rehder mentions hairiness, which is scarcely visible without a lens, but says nothing of the corrugated or wrinkled surface noted by Theophrastus. Rehder describes the leaf-shape in technical terms, 'ovate to ovate-oblong, usually rounded at base'; Theophrastus compares it to that of the pear leaf (noting, however, certain differences), which answers to this description.

In some respects Theophrastus's account is here superior to Rehder's, since it includes facts of economic and ecological interest, namely that the wood is hard and whitish and that the tree loves moisture and grows in ravines. To convey his detail Theophrastus had to make comparisons with better-known plants or objects, i.e. beech, pear and barley, and the ribs of an animal, and this is his general method. Thus in his celebrated description of the sacred lotus (*Nelumbo nucifera*; Fig. 2), to which Cesalpino and more recently

Fig. 2 *Nelumbo nucifera* Gaertner; Sacred Lotus
(Woodcut from Yokusai Iinuma, *Sōmoku Dzusetzu*, 3rd ed.; 1910)

Arber have drawn attention, the thickness of the stalk is compared to that of a man's finger, its air passages to a honeycomb, the size of its leaf-blade to that of a Thessalian hat, the size of its flower to that of a large poppy, its colour to a rose's, its receptacle to a round wasp's nest and its fruits to beans! This a natural and effective method, which has remained in use all through the ages. Even so prominent a systematist as Sir Joseph Dalton Hooker used it late in the nineteenth century. In the technical descriptions of his standard work *The Flora of British India* (1875–97) Hooker did not hesitate to write of a 'stem as thick as the arm or leg', a 'stem as thick as a swan's quill', a 'tuber the size of a walnut', a 'fruit very variable in size, from a hen's egg to a man's fist', a 'drupe the size of a cherry' and so on.

The technical terms used by Rehder in the above description merit attention. 'Tree', 'bark', 'branch', 'leaf', 'cluster', 'tuft' and 'nut' are ordinary English words, either certainly or probably of Teutonic origin; the more technical words such as 'pubescent', 'ovate', 'serrate' and 'ovoid' are of Latin origin, likewise such words as 'base', 'nerve', 'vein', 'apex'. In a longer description the number of Latin-based words would have been much greater. Their use disguises the fact that the same comparative method is being employed. 'Pubescent' comes of a comparison with the hairs which appear on the body at puberty (*pubes*), 'serrate' with a saw (*serra*), 'ovate' and 'ovoid' with an egg (*ovum*). These are well-known concrete things of everyday experience, and, since it is easier to extend the use of words we know than to create new ones, the history of terminology is essentially one of the gradual modification and combination of words linked to such models. Rehder's English description goes readily into botanical Latin.[1] Their degree of resemblance is not accidental. As regards the technical words, it results from the predominant part which Latin has played in the development of the English scientific vocabulary and the deliberate adoption of Linnaeus's Latin terminology by botanists in the late eighteenth century as the basis of the English language of botany (cf. Martyn, 1791; Stearn, 1955).

PLINY THE ELDER AND ISIDORUS

Pliny the Elder undoubtedly incorporated translations into Latin from Theophrastus in his *Historia naturalis* (compiled first century A.D., frequently copied during the Middle Ages, first printed 1469, with 190 editions between 1469 and 1799), which, although 'a great storehouse of misinformation as well as of information, even more valuable as a collection of ancient errors than it is as a repository of ancient science' and, according to Pliny, drawn from works by some 473 authors, 146 Roman and 327 Greek, was of great importance in the medieval and Renaissance period as the major surviving encyclopaedic work

---

[1] *Arbor* ad 20 m. alta; *cortex* griseus; *ramuli* juventute pubescentes; *folia* ovata ad ovato-oblonga, acuminata, basi plerumque rotundata, acute duplicato-serrata, 4–10 cm. longa, supra atro-viridia et sparse hirsuta, venis lateralibus utrinque 12–15; *amenta fructifera* 3·5–5 cm. longa; *nucula* ovoidea, 4–15 mm. longa, apice pilosa.

of Latin antiquity. Many Greek concepts and plant-names came to the notice of the sixteenth-century herbalists through the Latin of Pliny. From Pliny, as Sprague (1933a) has pointed out, Brunfels and Fuchs took much of their terminology. Thus from Pliny's *Historia naturalis* have come many of the terms employed in modern botanical Latin, undergoing much change in meaning on the way. According to Sprague's glossary (1933a), about 187 terms occur in Pliny's *Historia naturalis* which are the same as modern botanical terms or are used in a more or less botanical sense. The resemblance is, however, often deceptive. Thus the word *bractea*, as used by Pliny, means a thin plate of metal or a thin layer of wood, *corona* a garland, *pistillum* a pestle wherewith mustard seed was ground in a mortar, *pollen* a fine flour.

Pliny's vocabulary has indeed a marked economic bias, reflecting a typically Roman preoccupation with matters immediately practical and useful rather than philosophic. The most useful parts of plants are the stems and shoots and their fruits. Of words relating to these parts Pliny had a good store ; *truncus, caudex, caulis, stolo, geniculum, surculus, stipula, vimen, virga, humor, lignum, internodium, liber, ramus, ramulus, medulla, palmes, scopa* and *talea* are among the words he uses for stems and stem-structures. For fruits he had such words as *acinus, baca, balanos, cortex, vasculum, utriculus, glans, granum, lappa, lignum, nucamentum, nux, pappon, pomum, putamen, tegmen, tunica, siliqua, uva.* For leaves and flowers, on the contrary, his vocabulary was very limited. Moreover, the same word could have a variety of meanings. The word *calyx*, according to Sprague, was used by Pliny to designate what we now call an involucre (e.g. in *Tragopogon*), a cupule (e.g. in *Quercus*), a perigon (e.g. in *Lilium*), a calyx (e.g. in *Rosa*), a corona (e.g. in *Narcissus*), a capsule (e.g. in *Papaver*) and a pericarp (e.g. in *Juglans, Punica*) ; he also used it for a covering of wax put around fruit as a preservative, the outer covering of a charcoal heap, the shell of an egg and the shell of a mollusc! Obviously Pliny used any word which seemed apt for the occasion ; it troubled him not at all if the same word was used elsewhere in a different sense. He was, in short, writing as a man of letters, not as a scientist using technical terms with restricted and well-defined meanings. Hence, although Pliny's work [1] is the supreme work in classical Latin about plants, it supplies the raw material for a botanical terminology, and no more.

The same is true of medieval Latin literature about plants. The Spanish encyclopaedist Isidorus Hispalensis (A.D. 560–636) of Seville, whose *Origines sive Etymologiae Libri* is a valuable store of early medieval words relating to all branches of learning, agriculture among

[1] See Gudger (1923), André (1955) and Stahl (1962 : 101-119) for more detailed accounts.

them, has but 74 terms which may be interpreted as botanical (cf. Sprague, 1933c) and most of these are derived from Pliny. He seems, however, to have been the first to list the word *botanicum* (from Greek βοτανη, an herb), a word which did not readily establish itself (cf. Möbius, 1944) before the eighteenth century.

ALBERTUS MAGNUS AND RUFINUS

The next medieval writer of importance upon plants, Albertus Magnus (1193–1280), Bishop of Regensburg, paid considerable attention to plant structure in the midst of his philosophical and theological studies (cf. Balss, 1947 ; Sprague, 1933c, d). His work *De Vegetabilibus Libri VII* contains 142 more or less botanical terms, according to the glossary compiled by Sprague (1933d), who points out that Albertus employed two or three different words in practically the same sense, that many botanical terms still current nowadays were then used in very different senses, and that certain words possessed a more general signification, covering several morphological categories now recognized as distinct. Thus the word *folliculus* was applied by Albertus to a covering of bud-scales, a calyx and a capsule, the word *theca* to an involucre (e.g. of *Castanea* and *Tragopogon*), a calyx, a capsule, a follicle, etc., *siliqua* to a spathe (e.g. of *Phoenix* and *Arum*), glumes, a calyx, a capsule, a legume, the shell of a nut and the core of an apple! Albertus clearly recognized more structures than he had convenient words available. In the flower of borage (*Borago officinalis*; Fig. 3) he distinguished between the different floral whorls and described it as 'arranged like a star composed of five circles consisting of five parts each, namely (1) *theca floris* (calyx), (2) *folia floris* (corolla-lobes), (3) *parvulae eminentiae in flore ipso* (corona-segments), (4) *quinque virgulae* (stamens), and (5) *una virgula* (style), nos. (4) and (5) collectively being termed *spicae floris*' (cf. Sprague, 1933c: 436). The work of Albertus could have provided the foundation for a morphological system had others come forward to extend his observations. As Thorndike (1946) has emphasized, 'in the manuscript age before the development of printing even so celebrated a Schoolman as Albertus Magnus and so important a treatise in the history of botany as *De Vegetabilibus et Plantis* might remain unknown to and unread by other specialists in the same field'. Thus Albertus's work evidently never came into the hands of his lesser-known contemporary, Rufinus of Genoa.

This Rufinus was an Italian monk who compiled a Latin herbal, probably between 1287 and 1300, which was first published in 1946. Its principal interest lies in the observations which Rufinus added to those gathered from his authorities and in his descriptions of plants unknown to them. The descriptive botany of Rufinus, although praised by Thorndike as being for particular plants 'more specific and discriminating than that of any previous author, ancient or medieval', represents no advance on that of Theophrastus. Identification of the plants concerned is almost impossible from the descriptive notes of these authors, unless the plant has very well-marked characters. Such a plant is the one called *centaurea maior* by Rufinus and described

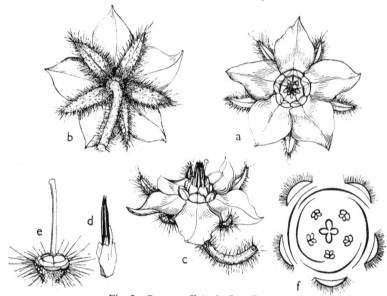

Fig. 3 *Borago officinalis* L.; Borage
a, flos desuper visus; b, flos ab infra visus; c, flos a latere visus; d, stamen; e, pistillum; f, diagramma floris (drawing by Priscilla Fawcett)

as follows: 'Facit gambulam rotundam, lucidam et viridissimam et folia ut matersilve licet parvula, et transit gamba per medium folii, et est spatium inter folium et folium quatuor digitorum et in sumitate gambe facit flores croceos multos. Altitudo gambe est per brachium vel circa, et sapor eius est amarissimus, sed in flore eius sunt octo folia croceissima.' This translates as follows: 'It makes a stem rounded, shining and most green and leaves as those of *mater silva* (*Lonicera periclymenum*) although very small, and the stem passes through the middle of the leaf, and there is a space of four inches between leaf and leaf, and at the top of the stem it makes many yellow flowers. The height of the stem is a cubit or thereabouts, and the taste of it is most bitter, but in the flower of it are eight leaves most yellow.' The plant thus described is undoubtedly *Blackstonia perfoliata* (*Chlora perfoliata*; Fig. 4), easily recognized by its perfoliate leaves and bright yellow flowers.

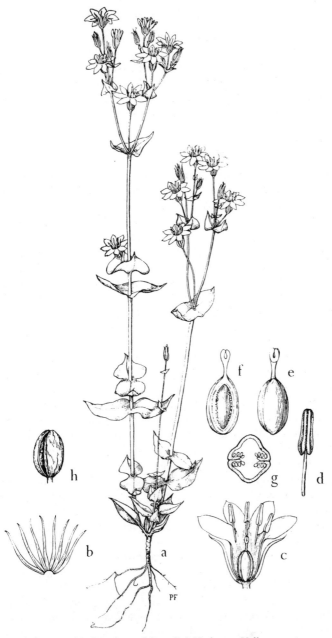

Fig. 4 *Blackstonia perfoliata* (L.) Hudson; Yellow-wort
a, planta integra; b, calyx explanatus; c, flos longitudinaliter sectus
ut stamina et pistillum appareant; d, stamen; e, pistillum; f, pistillum
cum ovario longitudinaliter secto; g, ovarium; h, capsula (drawing
by Priscilla Fawcett)

25

This quotation will suffice to illustrate the rambling style of medieval plant descriptions. Rufinus's use of the words *gamba* and *gambula*, evidently meaning a stem and borrowed from the vulgar Latin *gamba* or *camba* (leg), is of interest, as they do not occur in the glossaries to the works of Pliny, Isidorus and Albertus Magnus. Many long-dead words litter the way to our modern botanical terminology.

VALERIUS CORDUS AND FUCHS

Despite their frequent lack of precision, the Latin words available to a keen and talented observer in the sixteenth century were adequate for giving descriptions of plants that did not require minute detail. Thus Valerius Cordus (1515–44) and Charles de l'Écluse (Carolus Clusius, 1526–1609) in the sixteenth century wrote descriptions so apt and full of significant facts that the plants they had in mind can be confidently identified. Cordus, when he died of a fever at Rome in 1544, aged but twenty-nine years, left a manuscript *Historia Plantarum* containing descriptions of some 500 species, mostly medicinal. According to T. A. Sprague and M. S. Sprague (1939), about 66 were then new. One of these was the flowering rush (*Butomus umbellatus*; Fig. 5) called by Cordus *Gladiolus palustris*. The following extract from his account will serve to illustrate not only his keen observation but the general style of plant description, which prevailed from his time until the early eighteenth century: 'Gladiolus palustris, folia ab una radice erigit multa, iridi similia, angustiora tamen, triquetra & superius in mucronum desinentia, e quorummedio caulis duum triumve cubitorum altitudine erumpit, insigni levore & aequalitate praeditus, in cuius summo flores multi, longis pediculis, ex uno principio nascuntur, in purpura candidi, tribus foliolis constantes, sub quorum intervallis alia tria (sed illis minora) sunt. Stamina in se flores habent numero plerumque novem, croceo in summitate pulvisculo manus attrectantium insicientia. . . . Nascitur autem pinguibus limosis & humentibus locis, quo fluviorum inundationes pervenire possunt'. (Val. Cordus, *De Pl.* Lib. II, Cap. IX, p. 124). This may be translated as follows: 'Gladiolus palustris from one root raises many leaves like those of an iris, yet narrower, three-angled, and ending above in a point, out of the middle of which a stem shoots forth to a height of two or three cubits, provided with notable smoothness and evenness, at the top of which from a main one arise many flowers with long foot-stalks, purple becoming white, consisting of three little leaves, below the intervals of which are another three (but smaller than these). The flowers have stamens within usually to the number of nine, with a yellow powder at the top colouring the hands of those who touch them. . . . It is

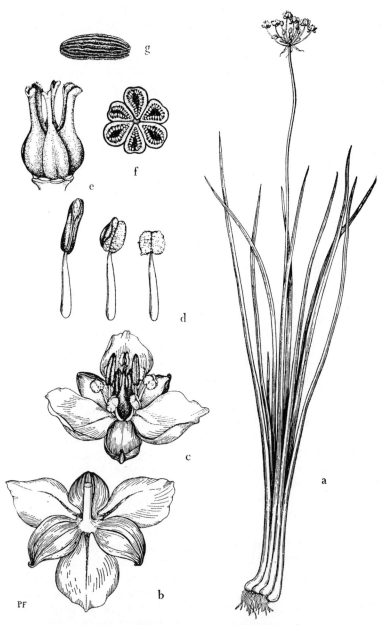

Fig. 5 *Butomus umbellatus* L.; Flowering-rush

a, planta florens; b, flos ab infra visus; c, flos desuper visus; d, stamina; e, gynoecium lateraliter visum; f, gynoecii sectio transversalis; g, semen (drawing by Priscilla Fawcett)

found in lush muddy and wet places, where flooding rivers are able to reach.'

Descriptions of this type, with their active verbs, have a vivid and dynamic quality. Down to the eighteenth century botanists knew their plants mostly in a living state, as organisms shooting up from the root, bursting into leaf and flower, giving birth to the fruit; they wrote in this way of the plant's development because thus it happened under their eyes. Their plants grew in gardens around them or were observed in the wild, which meant that the number available was limited. The elimination of the verb from technical descriptions was symptomatic of a different technique, that of studying by means of herbarium specimens the plants from distant lands, which could not be examined when alive. The herbarium worker usually sees an individual plant only at the stage of development it had reached when gathered and dried for the herbarium. In descriptions of such static material, verbs, of which the essential function is, of course, to express action, are often redundant or indeed misleading.

In Cordus's descriptions there occur a number of words not used today, e.g. *fulcrum* (in classical Latin 'a couch') meaning an adventitious root serving as a prop, *caliculus* (= *cauliculus*) a small stem, *pulvisculus* (in classical Latin 'a fine powder') pollen, *cornicula* (in classical Latin 'little horns') the curved carpels of a peony (*Paeonia*), *apex* the anther; there are also others which are not used today as Cordus used them, e.g. *involucrum* (in classical Latin 'a wrapper') for the spathe of Arum, *apitulum* (in classical Latin 'a small head') and *tuberculum* (in classical Latin 'a small swelling') for the ovary, *caliculus* for the calyx of *Labiatae*: on the other hand most of his words meant the same then as they do now. E. L. Greene (1909) in his enthusiastic appreciation of Cordus as the creator of 'a phytography of a new type' reads rather more into Cordus's use of words than their author intended.

The excellence of the woodcuts with which Cordus's contemporary Leonhart Fuchs (1501–56) illustrated his *De Historia Stirpium* (1542) made detailed descriptions unnecessary but he included an explanation of certain terms, more or less botanical or at least relating to plants, which the inexperienced might find hard to understand. This glossary has been translated into English by Helen A. Choate (1917). Of his botanical terms, 49 remain in use with identical or related meanings, e.g. *aculeus, arista, bacca, bulbus, calyx, culmus, gemma, gluma, spica, unguis*; 18 have changed in meaning, e.g. *capitulum, cyma, conus, lomentum, racemus, stipula*; 43 have become obsolete, e.g. *acinus, acus, alsiosa, apex, asparagus, echinus, iulus, oculus, pampinus, viticula, umbilicus*; 3 terms used in a non-botanical sense by Fuchs have now a botanical application, i.e. *alabastra, amphora* and *ligula*. Fuchs's glossary also includes 15 non-botanical words, e.g. *acetabulum, aluta, amuletum, cyathus, congius, cotyle, cubitus.*

MALPIGHI, CAMERARIUS, JUNG, RAY
AND TOURNEFORT

Understanding of the functions of the floral parts and the provision of terms for them came in the seventeenth and eighteenth centuries. Botanically the seventeenth century began with the publication at Antwerp in 1601 of the *Rariorum Plantarum Historia* by Carolus Clusius (Charles de l'Écluse); towards its end came the publication in London of the two volumes of John Ray's *Historia Plantarum* (1686–88), followed by a supplementary volume in 1704. These two massive works, both written in Latin, are classics of pre-Linnaean literature; sooner or later the student of European plants has to consult one or both. Their descriptions resemble in general style those of Valerius Cordus. The seventeenth century also saw the publication of other works of far-reaching importance for the development of systematic botany although not directly concerned with it, notably Nehemiah Grew's *Anatomy of Vegetables begun* (1672), Marcello Malpighi's *Anatome Plantarum* (1675–79), Joachim Jung's *Isagoge phytoscopica* (1678) and Rudolf Jakob Camerarius's *De Sexu Plantarum Epistola* (1694). They illustrate the first impact of a great technological advance, the development of magnifying glasses, upon plant study. Cordus in the sixteenth century A.D. had been technically no better equipped than Theophrastus in the third century B.C. Even a low magnification reveals structures they could never have seen; moreover, making an object appear big gives it an importance in the mind which provokes enquiry and thought. Thus in the seventeenth century floral structures now received attention in greater detail and botanists fumbled for words to designate them.

Few of the words used by Malpighi have survived into modern botanical terminology. Nevertheless he established the word *calyx* for the outer green covering of the flower, although he applied it to the involucre of *Compositae* as well; sepals and involucral scales he called *foliola calycis*. What we now call the corolla he called the *flos*, using the word *folium* (leaf) when it was of one piece and *folia* (leaves) when divided into petals. The florets of *Compositae* he called *flosculi*. For the filament of the stamen he used the word *petiolus*, for the anther *capitulum* (literally, a little head). The gynoecium as a whole was covered by the word *stylus*, the ovary being distinguished as the *uterus* and the style as the *tubus*; he termed the carpel a *loculus*. He compared

the filamentous corona of *Passiflora* to a crown (*corona*), thus antici-
pating the later technical adoption of the word *corona* for this.

Grew, Sir Thomas Millington and John Ray recognized the sexual
function of the inner parts of the flower; but the honour of proving
this and incidentally of introducing the experimental method into
botany belongs to Rudolf Jakob Camerarius (1665–1721) of Tübingen,
who found that on removing the staminate flowers of the castor oil
plant (*Ricinus*) before the dehiscence of the anthers he never obtained
perfect seeds. He also made observations on mulberry, annual mercury
(*Mercurialis annua*), spinach (*Spinacia oleracea*) and maize (*Zea mays*).
These he recorded in an essay, *De Sexu Plantarum*, printed as an open
letter to Michael Bernhard Valentini (1657–1729) of Giessen. In this
occurs a statement, revolutionary at the time and among the most
important in the whole history of botany, concerning the anthers or
apices as they were then called: 'Aequum ergo omnino videtur, his
ipsis apicibus assignare nobilius nomen, & munus partium genitalium
masculini sexus, ut capsulae eorum sint vascula & conceptacula, in
quibus semen ipsum, pulvis ille, subtilissima plantae portio secernitur,
colligitur, & hinc postmodum dispensatur. . . . Hos uti apices seminis
masculi officinam, ita seminale vasculum cum sua plumula sive stilo
partes genitales, femininio sexui competentes, plantae pariter exhibent.'
(Hence it appears wholly reasonable to assign to the apices themselves
a nobler name and the function of the genital parts of the male sex,
as their capsules are vessels and containers, in which the semen itself,
that powder, the most subtle part of the plant, is produced, collected
and from here afterwards given out. . . . Plants exhibit equally these
apices as the factory of the male semen and the seed-vessel with its
little feather or style as genital parts proper to the feminine sex.)

The effect of this discovery was far-reaching. By concentrating
attention on floral organs, which by means of lenses could now be
examined in detail, as Malpighi and Grew had demonstrated, it stimu-
lated Linnaeus into the production of a system of classification based
solely upon them and made necessary a vast new Latin terminology.
Part of such a terminology was provided by Joachim Jung (1587–
1657) in a little work, *Isagoge phytoscopica* (1678), first published
twenty-one years after his death by his student Johannes Vagetius.
Jung, who was born at Lübeck and studied at Rostock, Giessen and
Padua, taught mathematics at Giessen and Rostock and botany and
zoology at Hamburg. In him the philosophic approach to plant study,
that of Theophrastus, Albertus Magnus and Cesalpino, became once
more alive; he tried to give botanical terminology something of the
precision of mathematics. His work is thus very formal in character,
consisting of aphorisms, of which the following will serve as examples:

'*Folium* est, quod a sede, cui adhaeret, ita in altitudinem, sive longitudinem, & latitudinem extenditur, ut tertiae dimensionis termini inter se differant, h.e.Superficies folii interna ab externa.' (The leaf is that which from its seat of attachment spreads out in height, or length, and breadth in such a manner that the limits of the third dimension differ from one another, i.e. the inner surface of the leaf from the outer.)

'14. *Petiolus*, sive Pediculus folii, est pars in longitudinem extensa, quae folium sustinet, & cauli connectit.' (The petiole, or footstalk of the leaf, is the part stretched in length which supports the leaf and joins it to the stem.)

'15. Petiolus *stricte* dictus a caule usque ad folii initium intelligitur.' (The petiole properly called is understood as being from the stem to the beginning of the leaf.)

'Id., quod inter folia est, *Nervus* saepius, aut *Costa* dicitur.' (The same, which is the middle of the leaves, is called most often the nerve or the rib.)

'16. *Nota*. Folium compositum ab imperitis aut negligenter observantibus pro Ramo aut Surculo habetur, sed discernitur facile, 1. Quod superficiem habet internum & externum, ut & folium simplex. 2. Quia totum autumno decidit, ut & folium simplex.' (The compound leaf is taken by the inexperienced or carelessly observant for a branch or shoot, but is easily to be distinguished (1) in that the surface has an inside and outside, like a simple leaf; (2) because it falls as a whole in autumn, like a simple leaf.)

'*Flos* est pars plantae tenerior, colore, vel figura, vel utroque insignis, rudimento fructus cohaerens.' (The flower is the thinner part of the plant, notable for its colour or shape or both, closely connected with the rudiment of the fruit.)

'*Perianthium* est, quod florem tegit, ideoque crassius est, minus insigne flore ipso. Dicitur enim *calyx*.' (The perianth is that which covers the flower, and therefore it is thicker and less prominent than the flower itself. It is indeed called the calyx.)

'*Flos* vel nudus est, vel perianthio munitus. 2. Flores nudi ut Tulipae, Lilii, Martagi, Colchici, Croci, Polygonati, Sambuci, Fagopyri. 3. Perianthio muniti, ut Borraginis, Buglossae, Papaveris &c.' (The flower is either naked or provided with a perianth. Naked flowers, as those of Tulipa, Lilium, Martagon, Colchicum, Crocus, Polygonatum, Sambucus, Fagopyrum. Provided with a perianth, as those of Borage, Bugloss, Papaver, etc.)

As Arber (1950) has observed, it is remarkable how often the words of Jung's terminology have survived though sometimes changed in meaning, as for example *perianthium* in the above quotation. They owe this largely to their employment by Ray and Linnaeus. Some time before 1660 a manuscript copy of Jung's little treatise, later printed at Hamburg in 1678, came into the hands of John Ray (1628–1705), who gave it a publicity it would never have received in its original state. Ray referred to Jung's work in his *Index Plantarum Agri Cantabrigiensis* (1660) and *Methodus Plantarum nova* (1782) and included Jung's terms and definitions in the glossary to his *Historia Plantarum* (1686). Ray, an internationally minded scholar, naturally wrote in Latin, but he gave English equivalents in his glossary. The first word is *Antherae* of the herbalists, in English 'the Chives', a word which has disappeared from modern English, supplanted by the very word which in 1686 it was used to explain! Earlier writers mostly used the word *apex* (plural *apices*) for the anther. *Capillamenta* (threads) has been displaced by *filamenta*; *julus* and *catulus* (a palm or catkin) by *amentum*; *geniculum* (a joint or knot) by *nodus*; *ossiculum* (the stone of a plum, cherry or the like fruit) by *putamen*. Some words, such as *echinus* (a burr or any prickly fruit), *asparagus* (a tender sprout or shoot of any herb from the ground), *vimen* (a bending twig or wythe) and *vinaceum* (a grape-stone), have been discarded because modern botany does not need special terms for these. Others, such as *corymbus, cyma, folliculus, gluma, perianthium, scapus, siliqua, spatha* and *thyrsus*, survive with slightly or greatly changed meanings.

A number, however, remain essentially the same, e.g. *arista* (the beard or awn), *baccae* (berries), *capitulum, capreolus* (a clasper or tendril), *conus, folium, fructus, gemma* (a bud), *internodium, nervus, panicula, pappus, petalum, pericarpium, petiolus, pomum, spica, stylus, tomentum*, etc. It is worthy of note that the term *flos* (flower) had not yet acquired its comprehensive botanical meaning; it still meant simply the corolla and the androecium and did not include the calyx and gynoecium. Hence the *calyx* is defined by Ray as 'the cup enclosing or containing the flower'. From Fabio Colonna's annotations to F. Hernandez, *Rerum Medicarum Novae Hispanicae* (1649), Ray picked up a valuable suggestion, namely that the floral leaves (*floris foliola*) should be distinguished from the true leaves by a special term, the Greek πεταλον (petalon). Colonna never used this word himself, and to Ray we owe the definite introduction into botanical Latin of *petalum* and thence, with slight modification, into the everyday usage of many modern languages (see below, pp. 40, 46).

A further notable contribution to greater clarity in botanical terminology was made in 1700 by Joseph Pitton de Tournefort (1656–1708) in the introduction to his *Institutiones Rei Herbariae*; here the floral parts and especially the forms of the corolla upon which he largely based his classification are well defined.

SÉBASTIEN VAILLANT

More and more the flower came to be regarded as the most important organ for the classification of plants, and more and more terms came into use to express both its underlying uniformity and its diversity of detail. In 1717 Sébastien Vaillant (1669–1721) published an important address, written in both French and Latin and entitled *Discours sur la Structure des Fleurs, Sermo de Structura Florum*, wherein he wholeheartedly accepted Camerarius's views on the sexuality of flowers and made known a few new words. His introductory remarks touch upon a difficulty which continually faces botanists, the choice between using everyday words with both a common and a specialized meaning or of introducing new words which are unambiguous but may be unpopular. For the male organs Vaillant adopted the word *stamina*, distinguishing the anthers as *capitula* and the filaments as *caudae* or *filamenta*. For the female organ as a whole, the *pistillum* of many authors, he used the word *ovarium*, another innovation, rather than *matrix* proposed by Malpighi. The lower part of this, corresponding to the ovary of later terminology, he called the *corpus* or *venter*, noting that it could be above or below the 'flower', i.e. superior or inferior, and he adopted the word *tubus* for the style. He called attention to the ovules in the ovary. Vaillant's actual words merit quotation: 'Ovaria Malpighio dictae Matrices . . . organa sunt plantarum foeminina', 'Corpus vel venter inferior ovarii pars', 'in ovula Ovarii, . . . in *primula veris*, ubi ovula omnia eidem placentae affixa sitae in ovaria'. Here apparently for the first time in botanical literature are words which have become indispensable: ovary (*ovarium*), ovule (*ovulum*) and placenta adapted in the time-honoured Theophrastan tradition from zoological usage. Vaillant's other new terms have long been forgotten. Such apparent wastage of words occurs throughout the development of a terminology and is by no means regrettable; the greater the production of seed by a plant, the stronger is the chance of a few seedlings reaching maturity. The coining or introduction of new words provides material for the action of linguistic natural selection whereby the most concise, necessary and expressive ones pass into use and the rest perish. No botanist nowadays uses the terms *arinus, aggedula, anabix, besimen, calpa, colesula, elytriculus, erisma, epimenus, gymnocidium, nephrosta, orygoma, perocidium, peridroma, perigynanda, raphida* and *ypomenus* proposed in 1790 by the ingenious and heterodox Noel Joseph de Necker (1729–93), but we owe to him the terms *achena* (achene) and *sepalum* (sepal) put forward in the very same work as these; botanists should hardly need reminding that grain grows on the ear amid chaff.

Classical Greek and Latin are poor in words for parts of the flower, since, as Rickett emphasizes, 'a rational terminology mirrors that upon which it is based, an understanding of the things concerned', and not until the end of the seventeenth century was such an understanding gained.

LINNAEUS'S REFORM OF TERMINOLOGY

The works of Camerarius, Ray and Tournefort which much influenced Linnaeus belong to the latter half of the seventeenth century so immensely important in the development of modern science (cf. Stearn, 1961; Whitehead, 1926). In 1690 their contemporary John Locke (1632–1704) published his *Essay concerning Human Understanding*, the greater part of which he wrote while living in Holland. Locke dealt with 'ideas and words as the great instruments of knowledge' and stated: 'The ends of language in our discourse with others being chiefly these three: first, to make known one man's thoughts or ideas to another. Secondly, to do it with as much ease and quickness as is possible; and, thirdly, thereby to convey the knowledge of things. Language is either abused or deficient when it fails any of these.' To remedy these defects he made various suggestions. He concluded: 'It were therefore to be wished that men, versed in physical inquiries and acquainted with the several sorts of natural bodies, would set down those simple ideas wherein they observe the individuals of each sort constantly to agree. This would remedy a good deal of that confusion which comes from several persons applying the same name to a collection of a smaller or greater number of sensible qualities. . . . methinks it is not unreasonable to propose, that words standing for things that are known and distinguished by their outward shapes should be expressed by little draughts [i.e. outlines] and prints made of them. A vocabulary made after this fashion would perhaps, with more ease, and in less time, teach the signification of many terms than all the large and laborious comments of learned critics.' Locke added: 'In all discourses wherein one man pretends to instruct or convince another, he should use the same word constantly in the same sense.' [1]

Now, this is exactly what Linnaeus set out to do in his *Hortus Cliffortianus* (1738), prepared when he too was a guest of the Dutch. He early grasped the need for precision in terminology and nomenclature, and four pages and two plates of this impressive folio work define the Latin terms used in describing leaves. Most of them remain in use today with essentially the same meanings, but some, e.g. *oblongus* and *lanceolatus*, have diverged; hence it is wise to consult Linnaeus's

---

[1] Locke, like John Stuart Mill later, had botanical interests strong enough to cause him to form a herbarium; cf. J. W. Gough, 'John Locke's herbarium', *Bodleian Library Record*, 7: 42-46 (1962).

illustrations (Figs. 16, 17) when interpreting descriptions from 1753 to about 1800.

In his *Fundamenta botanica* (1736 ; Fig. 6), a little work of 36 pages, Linnaeus had already outlined his procedure in 365 aphorisms reminiscent of Jung's, although not before 1774 did he see a copy of Jung's

CAROLI LINNÆI SVECI

Doctoris Medicinæ

FUNDAMENTA
BOTANICA

quæ

Majorum Operum Prodromi inftar

THEORIAM

SCIENTIÆ BOTANICES

per

breves Aphorifmos

tradunt.

AMSTELODAMI,
Apud SALOMONEM SCHOUTEN.
1736.

Fig. 6   Title-page of Linnaeus's *Fundamenta botanica* (1736)

actual work as distinct from Ray's version of it (cf. Mevius, 1959). He selected from the classical words converted into technical terms by his predecessors those which seemed apt, pleasing and unambiguous, and he added others equally so. His choice largely determined the terms we use now. Thus he adopted the herbalist's *anthera* (in classical Latin a Greek loan-word signifying a 'medicine composed of flowers') instead of *apex* as used by earlier authors and adopted *filamentum* for the support of the anther, reserving *stamen* (in classical Latin 'a thread') for the whole organ as Vaillant had done. He introduced the word *corolla* (in classical Latin 'a little garland'), adopting *petalum* for a flat petal and *nectarium* for a pouched or spurred petal or other nectar-producing structure and distinguishing between the *tubus* and *limbus*. The floral parts he defined concisely by their relative position going from the outside inwards: 'Situs Naturalissimus est, quod *Calyx* involvat Receptaculum, cui *Corolla* alternatim adnascitur; huic autem interius alternatim respondent *Filamenta*, quorum apicibus *Antherae* incumbunt; Centrum Receptaculi occupat *Germen*, cujus apici *Stylus* insidet, summo *Stigma* gerens. Hisce decidentibus Germen in *Pericarpium* crassescit, calyce sustentatum, *Semina* Receptaculo Fructus adnexa includens. *Receptaculum* Floris germini vel subnascitur, vel circumnascitur, vel supernascitur.' This may be translated as follows: 'The most natural arrangement is that the *calyx* envelops the receptacle, to which the *corolla* in alternation is attached; to this moreover on the inside alternately respond the *filaments*, on the tips of which lie the *anthers*; the *germen* occupies the centre of the receptacle and has the *style* seated on top, with the *stigma* borne at the tip. These fallen, the germen fattens into a *pericarp*, supported by the calyx, including within itself the *seeds* joined to the receptacle of the fruit; the *receptacle* of the flower grows below, around or above the germen.'

In 1750, while bed-ridden and so crippled with gout that he had to dictate everything to his student Petrus Loefling, Linnaeus expanded the *Fundamenta botanica* into a book of 364 octavo pages with 11 plates, published in 1751 under the name *Philosophia botanica*. It is the first textbook of descriptive systematic botany and botanical Latin. Linnaeus indicated its history and scope in his first sentence: '*Fundamentis Botanicis* Theoriam atque Institutiones Rei Herbariae sub paucis Aphorismis olim comprehendi, quorum Explicationem per Exempla, Observationes & Demonstrationes, distinctis riteque definitis plantarum Partibus & Terminorum vocibus, *Philosophiam botanicam* dixi, cum in his consistant Praecepta Artis.' This may be translated as follows: 'Some time ago under the name of *Fundamenta botanica*, I expressed in a few concise sentences the theory and elements of botany of which the explanation by examples, observations and demonstrations, with distinct and correctly defined parts of plants and words of definition, I have called *Philosophia botanica*, for in them are the precepts of the art.' Translations and illustrated and expanded versions of the *Philosophia botanica* (see Chapter XXII) soon appeared in England, France and Germany, together with supplementary works, glossaries and dictionaries (for lists, see Rickett, 1944; Systematics Association Committee, 1960), which not only made the new international botanical Latin language easy to learn by anyone possessing the then normal classical education but also added many new terms, some useful, most of them never accepted.

LINNAEUS'S REFORM OF PLANT DESCRIPTION

Linnaeus's most important predecessors in systematic botany were John Ray (1628–1705), who provided him with a comprehensive general survey of the world's flora as known late in the seventeenth century, a concept of species and a basic terminology, Joseph Pitton de Tournefort (1656–1708), who provided him with a methodical illustrated survey of the genera, and Herman Boerhaave (1668–1738), who improved upon Tournefort's method of generic description. Herbalists and botanists long before Tournefort recognized genera (cf. Bartlett, 1940; Stearn, 1960) by grouping under common headings plants with features in common but they did not define genera by providing consistent descriptions of such features. In his *Institutiones Rei herbariae* (1700), which is an improved Latin version of his *Élémens de Botanique* (1694), Tournefort gave definitions of 698 genera and stated the general considerations upon which they were based (for translation into French by G. Becker, cf. Heim, 1957: 239-306). He maintained the old distinction between herbaceous and woody plants, then founded his main classification upon the general form of the flower and recognized two grades of genera, those adequately distinguished by the form of the flower and fruit in combination, e.g. *Campanula*, *Ranunculus*, *Rosa* and *Viola*, and those for which vegetative differences were needed, e.g. *Abies*, *Larix* and *Pinus*.

Linnaeus's debt to Tournefort was indeed great; but he rejected many of Tournefort's names and united many of his genera, holding that vegetative characters should not be used for the definition of genera. He also improved the method of description (cf. Stearn, 1960: x; 1961: lvi), as quickly becomes evident when his and Tournefort's generic descriptions are compared.

The following is a typical description in Tournefort's *Institutiones Rei herbariae* (1700): 'Hyoscyamus est plantae genus, flore A monopetalo, infundibuliformi & multifido: ex cujus calyce C surgit pistillum

D infimae floris parti B adinstar clavi infixum, quod deinde abit in fructum F in ipso calyce reconditum E, ollae similem, operculo HK instructum & in duo loculamenta GG divisum septo intermedio I, cui adhaerescunt plurima semina L.'

The letters A, B, C, etc., refer to the illustration on Tournefort's Plate 41 (Fig. 7). To be noted are the verbs *est*, *surgit*, *abit* and

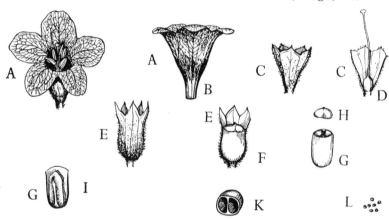

Fig. 7 *Hyoscyamus niger*; Henbane
A, corolla; B, corollae pars inferior; C, calyx; D, pistillum; E, calyx fructifer; E, F, fructus, dimidio calycis demoto; H, fructus operculum a latere visum; G, fructus pars inferior; I, fructus septum; K, fructus operculum ab infra visum; L, semina (drawing by Priscilla Fawcett, based on Tournefort, *Institutiones Rei herbariae*, t. 42; 1700)

adhaerescunt, the whole forming one sentence: 'Hyoscyamus is a genus of plants with a monopetalous funnel-shaped and multifid flower, from the calyx of which arises the pistil', etc.

In 1737 in his *Genera Plantarum* Linnaeus described the same genus as follows:

HYOSCYAMUS * *Tournef.* 42. *Riv.* I. 152, 153.

CAL: *Perianthum* monophyllum, cylindraceum, inferne ventricosum. *ore* quinquefido, acuto, persistens.

COR: *Petalum* infundibuliforme. *Tubus* cylindraceus, brevis. *Limbus* erecto-patens, semiquinquefidus: *laciniis* obtusis, unica reliquis latiore.

STAM: *Filamenta* quinque, subulata, inclinata. *Antherae* subrotundae.

PIST: *Germen* subrotundum. *Stylus* filiformis, longitudine staminum. *Stigma* capitatum.

PER: *Capsula* ovato-obtusa, linea utrinque insculpta, bilocularis, duabus capsulis arcte approximatis, tecta, operculo horizontaliter dehiscente.

SEM: numerosa, inaequalia. *Receptacula* dimidiato-ovata, dissepimento affixa.

The differences between these two descriptions in style and terminology are greater than those between Linnaean descriptions and modern descriptions. Especially to be noted are Linnaeus's elimination of verbs, the use of the nominative case, the separate treatment of each organ, the different terminology, the clear typography. By constructing all his descriptions in the same formal manner Linnaeus facilitated comparison between them and established the concise style which thereafter has been standard in botanical Latin. The development which has taken place in terminology and consequently in botanical Latin since Linnaeus's time reflects above all the innumerable enquiries into the nature of the flower and fruit made in the late eighteenth and early nineteenth centuries. These studies had their origin in the need of systematic botanists to consider as many structures as possible and to describe them accurately; but they were continued for their own interest until plant morphology and anatomy became independent disciplines. The most important investigations of morphology during this period were done by men such as Brongniart, Robert Brown, A. P. de Candolle, J. Gaertner, Lindley, Link, Martius, Mirbel and L. C. Richard, who are today remembered primarily as systematists; and it was they who, following Linnaeus, added most to botanical terminology, since they were compelled to find words for a wealth of hitherto unnoticed or unstudied details.

BOTANICAL LATIN NAMES OF FLORAL PARTS

How comparatively modern (i.e. brought into use between 1736 and 1844) are most of our accepted botanical terms may be illustrated by taking the names of floral parts which can be seen with the naked eye in plants such as *Anemone, Althaea, Narcissus, Nerium, Lilium, Myrtus* and *Vicia* known to Theophrastus, Pliny and many of the early herbalists.

The word *calyx*, as already noted (see p. 22), was used in ancient times for a variety of covering structures, as was the original Greek καλυξ. Early botanical writers fused with this the very similar Latin word *calix*, Greek κυλιξ, meaning a 'cup, goblet, drinking vessel', so that, although separate in classical Latin, *calyx* and *calix* have been used interchangeably in botanical Latin for the outermost covering of the flower or, in *Compositae*, etc., of the flower-head. Malpighi used it in its modern restricted sense in his *Anatome Plantarum* (1751), where he stated 'calyx floris basis est et fulcimentum' and gave numerous illustrations, among them, however, the involucre of *Bellis*. Linnaeus and his contemporaries also included under the term *calyx* various bracteal structures such as the involucre, spathe and glume as well as the calyx proper (their perianthium); to obviate this ambiguous usage, Linnaeus's one-time student Friedrich Ehrhart [1] proposed in 1784 a new term *anthostegium* for this outer structure. *Sepalum* (from σκεπη, covering) was coined by Necker in 1790 (*Coroll. ad Phil. bot.*, 18, 30), undoubtedly in an irregular manner (for *scepalum* would have been a better transliteration) which caused Link to reject it as a barbarous word. Fortunately *sepalum* passed into general use. It satisfies all the requirements specified by Webber (1903) for a new technical word, which should, if possible, be short, euphonious, phonetically spelled, easily pronounced and different from any other word in general use, so that it will not suggest any other meaning than the one desired, and it also possesses 'a derivation which at least suggests its meaning', being linked in form to *petalum*. *Corolla* (in classical Latin, a 'little crown or garland') received its modern application from Linnaeus (*Fundam. bot.*, 10; 1736), who distinguished between the *tubus* and *limbus* of a gamopetalous corolla and the *unguis* (claw) and *lamina* (blade) of a single petal. The word *petalum* (Greek πεταλον, leaf) existed in late Latin with the meaning of 'a metal plate'; in 1649 Fabio Colonna (in Hernandez, *Rerum Med. Novae Hisp. Thesaurus*, 853) suggested its introduction into botany to distinguish the floral leaves from the ordinary leaves, and Ray definitely adopted it in 1682 (*Methodus Pl. nova*: Praef.) and 1686 (*Hist. Pl.*, 1: Term.); thus the word 'petal', which now has such poetic as well as technical associations, was unknown in Shakespeare's time. The companion word *tepalum* originated in 1827 (de Candolle, *Organogr. vég.*, 1: 503), in the French form 'tépale', as an anagram of 'pétale' to designate a division of the perigon. The term *perianthium* as used today is synonymous with *perigonium*. The application of both words has changed somewhat during the past two and a half centuries. *Perianthium* by derivation means something *around* (περι) and hence outside the *flower* proper (ἀνθος), and by 'flower' the earlier writers, from Theophrastus to the botanists of the eighteenth century, as also people in general, meant the coloured delicate part (see p. 18), i.e. the perigon or corolla and sometimes the androecium of modern terminology but

---

[1] Friedrich Ehrhart (1742–95), a Swiss pharmacist who settled in Hanover and who was among the last of Linnaeus's foreign pupils, should not be confused with the pre-Linnaean author and doctor of medicine Balthasar Ehrhart (d. 1756) of Memmingen. F. Ehrhart, who introduced the terms *rhizoma* and *perigonium*, absorbed so thoroughly his master's preoccupation with nomenclature and terminology that he even proposed rules for the naming of German children (cf. *Beitr. Naturk.*, 2: 24: 27; 1788), perhaps because he himself had no children and lacked 'das nöthigste Stück dazu, nemlich eine Frau'!

not the green calyx and the gynoecium. On historical grounds the modern use of the term 'perianth' is absurd and illogical. According to its original use *perianthium* is another name for what we now call the calyx; it originated when the term *calyx* (see above) had a wider and vaguer application; *perianthium*, as used by Jung, by Linnaeus, Patrick Browne, Thomas Martyn and other eighteenth-century botanists, meant parts outside the corolla. This should be kept in mind when consulting their publications. Unfortunately, early in the nineteenth century Mirbel and Robert Brown used *perianthium* as a general word for those floral envelopes outside the androecium which correspond to the calyx and corolla together, especially those of petaloid monocotyledons in which the outer and inner floral envelopes often differ so little in form, colour and texture. Lindley condoned their misuse of the term 'perianth', although de Candolle had already in 1827 protested against such a divergence from traditional and etymologically preferable usage. A collective term for calyx and corolla together being required, de Candolle followed Link (*Phil. bot. novae Prodr.*, 88; 1798) in adopting the word *perigonium* (from περι, around, γονη, offspring, organs of generation) proposed earlier by F. Ehrhart (*Beitr. Naturk.*, 3: 123; 1788) to cover 'mein Calyx und Linnes Corolla'.

The word *stamen* means 'a thread' and it is difficult to establish who first used it in a definite scientific sense for part of the androecium. Adrian van den Spieghel (Spigelius), when he described the flower in 1606 (*Isag. Rem Herb.*, 14) as consisting of three main parts, 'folia, stamina, stylus', certainly used it thus, but was obviously confirming current usage, exemplified by many descriptions in Dodoens, *Stirpium Historiae Pemptades* (1583) and in Clusius, *Rariorum Plantarum Historia* (1601), where descriptive notes such as 'sex alba stamina, flavis apicibus praedita' (six white threads provided with yellow tips) frequently occur. Here the word *stamen* clearly refers to the filament, *apex* to the anther; thus they were used by Tournefort in 1700. No term was then deliberately used for the whole organ. Linnaeus formally adopted *filamentum* for the filament in 1736 (*Fundam. bot.*, 10, 11), thus rejecting the other possible words, *capillamentum, cauda, pediculus* and *stamen*, for this part, and he substituted *anthera* (*Fundam. bot.*, 10, 11) for *apex* (the most commonly used word), *capitulum, capsula, testiculus* and *theca* as the name of the anther (cf. Plantefol & Prévost, 1962). No collective name existed for the whole male part of the flower until in 1826 Roeper (in *Linnaea*, 1: 433; cf. Church, 1919) introduced the term *androeceum* (from ἀνηρ, ἀνδρος, a man, the male sex; οἶκος, house). To correspond with this Roeper (l.c. 438) coined the term *gynoeceum* (from γυνη, woman; οἶκος, house) without reference to the fact that the Romans had latinized as *gynaeceum* and *gynae-cium* the Greek γυναικειον, γυναικων, meaning 'part of the house re-served for women'; in Latin it was applied to the Emperor's seraglio. The term *connectivum* was introduced by L. C. Richard (*Dict. élém. Bot. par Bulliard*) in 1798 (An VII of the First French Republic). The use of the word *pollen* (in Latin 'a fine flour' and thus used by Pliny) as a technical name for the 'prolifick powder analogous to the male sperm in animals' and often called *pulvis* (dust), e.g. by Linnaeus in 1736, we owe to Linnaeus (*Sponsalia Pl.* 31, 53; 1746; reimpr. in *Amoen. Acad.* 1: 85, 103; 1749).

Pistillum (in Latin 'pestle') as a collective name for the female organ occupying the centre of the flower, now usually called the *gynoecium*, was introduced by Tournefort in 1700 (*Inst. Rei Herb.* 1: 70); he had previously adopted 'pistile' in his *Élémens de Botanique* 1: 54 (1694). Vaillant borrowed the term *ovarium* from animal anatomy in 1718; it has displaced Camerarius's *vasculum seminale*, Malpighi's *uterus* and Linnaeus's *germen*; but Vaillant's was probably not the earliest application of it to plants. *Stilus*, although used in Latin for a stake or pointed agricultural implement, usually meant the slender iron writing instrument, pointed at one end but broadened at the other, with which the Romans wrote on wax-covered wooden tablets (cf. Seyffert, *Dict. class. Antiq.*, 700, with fig.; 1891), and the botanical use of the word evidently refers to this. There exists, how-ever, in Greek the word στυλος (stylus) meaning a 'pillar, wooden pole' which the later Greeks at Alexandria used in the sense of the Latin *stilus*. Hence the earlier botanical writers seem to have regarded *stilus* and *stylus* as interchangeable as they did *calyx* and *calix*, probably as a result of the medieval custom of often writing a Latin *i* as *y*. Clusius (*Rar. Plant. Hist.*; 1601) used *stilus*, the preferable spelling, but Spieghel and most writers *stylus*, which through Linnaeus's adop-tion of it has become the standard form in botanical Latin. *Stigma* (στιγμα, tattoo mark, spot) as the name for the pollen-receptive tip of the gynoecium was introduced by Linnaeus in 1736 (*Fundam. bot.*, 10, 12). The term *carpellum* is now applied to a division of the gynoecium at any stage of its development, both before and after pollination. M. F. Dunal, who introduced *carpellum* in 1817 (*Mon. Fam. Anonacées*, 13) as a diminutive of καρπος (fruit), intended it to apply only to a division of the fruit, defining it as 'dans un fruit multiple, le fruit partiel résultant de chaque ovaire fécondé et développé'; for its further history, see Lorch's essay (1963).

Thus a few of these floral terms are Latin words of which the meaning has been restricted to one of its classical uses, e.g. *calyx*; some are words of which the present use diverges little from the classical use, e.g. *filamentum*; most of them, e.g. *corolla, petalum, corona, anthera, pollen, pistillum, stylus, stigma,* are classical words given new specialized meanings; the remainder are either new words coined from classical words in a classical manner, e.g. *perianthium, perigonium, androecium, gynoecium, connectivum, carpellum,* or new words whose connexion with classical words is so slender that they are best regarded as quite new inventions rather than adaptations, e.g. *sepalum* and *tepalum.* Most of them received their present applications between 1736 and 1844. An examination of terms for the types of inflorescence (cf. Rickett, 1944) for fruits and for seeds gives parallel results.

INFLUENCE OF GLOSSARIES

Thus in the course of a century there arose a new Latin language enabling botanists to describe plants with precision. It now seems an exaggeration to call this 'une langue spéciale propre à tout exprimer avec une parfaite exactitude et une extrême brièveté', as Cassini did in 1817 (cf. Cassini, *Opusc. phyt.,* 3 : 212; 1834), when he mentioned Linnaeus's creation of it as 'le titre le plus solide de sa gloire', but without it systematic botany and enquiries in plant geography, ecology, etc., which depend upon identification of plants, could never have made their remarkable progress during the past century. Its success was largely due to the adequate provision of glossaries and good textbooks on plant form. In the second half of the eighteenth century such works were produced by J. Berkenhout in 1764, M. B. Borckhausen in 1797, J. B. F. Bulliard in 1783, P. D. Giseke in 1787, F. G. Hayne from 1799 to 1812, J. Lee in 1765, J. D. Leers in 1775, H. F. Link in 1798, T. Martyn in 1793, C. Milne in 1770, G. C. von Oeder in 1764, L. C. Richard in 1764, H. Rose in 1775, J. Rotheram in 1779, J. A. Scopoli in 1783, R. Weston in 1770, J. J. Plenck in 1798, all of them largely indebted to Linnaeus. In 1800 there appeared the *Versuch einer systematischen vollständigen Terminologie für das Thierreich und Pflanzenreich* by Johann K. W. Illiger (1775–1813), which is especially noteworthy for its logical separation of terms of general application from those limited to particular organs, following the example of Heinrich Friedrich Link (1767–1851) in his *Prodromus Philosophiae botanicae* (1797). Link's work is entirely in Latin, Illiger's in German with Latin equivalents. In 1824 Link published an elaboration of this work entitled *Elementa Philosophiae botanicae,* adding a German version to the second edition of 1837; it is the best exposition in Latin of standard morphological terms. As noted by Lindley, 'little attention, however, was paid to the principles of these authors till the year 1813; when de Candolle adopted them in his *Théorie élémentaire de la Botanique,* with his accustomed skill and sagacity', and Lindley himself developed them still further in his *Introduction to Botany* (1832; 4th ed., 1848). The most elaborate attempt to co-ordinate botanical terms is, however, the *Handbuch der botanischen Terminologie und Systematik* (1830–44) by Gottlieb Wilhelm Bischoff (1797–1854). This so-called handbook consists of three quarto volumes, with 77 plates, the first dealing with terms applicable to flowering plants, the second to cryptogams and the third outlining systems of classification to date; the index alone occupies 338 pages! As a museum of obsolete German and Latin terms it is invaluable; as a textbook it would probably have failed to standardize terminology on account of its unwieldy bulk, had not Bischoff also produced his excellent little *Wörterbuch der beschreibenden Botanik* (1839; 2nd ed., 1857).

A. P. DE CANDOLLE, LINDLEY AND ASA GRAY

Of far greater influence, at any rate outside Germany, have been the works of Augustin Pyramus de Candolle (1778–1841), John Lindley (1799–1865)[1] and Asa Gray (1810–88). All three were busy university teachers and garden directors as well as industrious systematic botanists of great ability. All three were under the necessity of explaining morphological concepts to critical students; all three described and published a great diversity and number of plants new to science; none had time to waste. Their work rests upon a sure understanding of morphology and is illuminated, de Candolle's especially, by an enquiring philosophic attitude leading to a careful choice of words. Consequently their textbooks, despite age, remain instructive and pleasant to read. In de Candolle's *Théorie élémentaire de la Botanique* (1813; 2nd ed., 1819; 3rd ed., 1844) are explained the terms used in

---

[1] John Lindley's work is so often mentioned in this book that it seems fitting to summarize here his industrious career. He was born on 5 February 1799 at Catton near Norwich, Norfolk, England, where his father was a nurseryman seemingly much more skilled in growing and studying plants than in making money and who consequently could afford neither to buy his promising son John a commission in the army nor to send him to a university; indeed, at the age of nineteen John assumed responsibility for the payment of his father's debts. He early acquired a good knowledge of Latin, French and German, and after leaving the Norwich Grammar School at the age of sixteen was sent to Belgium as agent for a London seed merchant. In 1819 he published as *Observations on the Structure of Fruits and Seeds* a translation of L. C. M. Richard's *Démonstrations Botaniques ou Analyse du Fruit* (1808) and in 1820 his *Monographia Rosarum*, the first of his many contributions to systematic botany and horticulture. He became assistant librarian to Sir Joseph Banks in 1819, then in 1822 garden assistant secretary to the Horticultural Society of London; with the management of the Society's affairs he remained busy for the rest of his life, despite being appointed first professor of botany in London University in 1829; he edited the *Botanical Register* from 1836 to 1847 and the *Gardener's Chronicle* from 1841 onwards. He received honorary doctorates from the universities of Munich and Basel. He died at Turnham Green, Middlesex, on 1 November 1865.

his *Systema* (1818–21) and *Prodromus* (Vols. 1–10; 1824–46) and his many *Mémoires* on different families; it remains one of the best and most useful introductions to botanical Latin. The only serious defect of de Candolle's work is its lack of illustrations. However, figures by J. C. Heyland illustrate de Candolle's companion work *Organographie végétale* (1827). The works of John Lindley, who was an excellent draughtsman, abound in illustrations. Of his many publications the most useful today are his *Introduction to Botany* (1832; 4th ed., 1848), and his *Elements of Botany* (3rd ed., 1849; first published in 1830 as *Outline of the First Principles of Botany*).

These works mark the end of the formative period of botanical Latin. Linnaeus about a century earlier had determined its function and nature. His successors in their exploration of plant form had provided more than enough names for most organs of flowering plants and their attributes. The reformation needed was essentially the selection and standardization of the better-known words, i.e. stipulative definition (see p. 16). In this Lindley took an important part. A forceful largely self-taught man, with a good knowledge of Latin, German and French, and also mightily industrious, he surveyed critically the works then available on botanical terminology. The symbol ‡ in his glossary brands the words he considered objectionable, obsolete or rarely used in the sense given. Throughout his textbooks Lindley took care to give brief but exact definitions of the true meanings of words which were then or had been in common use, and in the sense that he defined them they mostly remain in use today. In the United States Asa Gray's *Botanical Text-book, Part 1, Structural Botany* (1842; 6th ed., 1879) performed the same task. Together with Lindley's *Glossary* and J. S. Henslow's *Dictionary of botanical Terms* (1848–56) it forms the basis of B. D. Jackson's *Glossary of botanic Terms* (1900; 4th ed., 1928). Jackson also made much use of E. Germain de St. Pierre's *Guide du Botaniste* (1852) and his *Nouveau Dictionnaire de Botanique* (1870). Thanks to services of the great French botanical draughtsmen A. Faguet, A. Riocreux and L. Steinheil, French botanists also possess excellent illustrated works on terminology in E. Le Maout and J. Decaisne, *Traité général de Botanique* (1868), and H. Baillon, *Dictionnaire de Botanique* (1876–92).

Such works have an important stabilizing influence on terminology and also serve as guides to botanical Latin owing to the close connexion between this and the terms used in English and modern Romance languages. They interact and thus enrich each other. Everyday words such as those for root, leaf and flower differ widely in these languages because they have such a long history behind them, but technical words introduced during the past two and a half centuries remain essentially the same. Thus, for example, 'petal' (*petalum*), 'anther' (*anthera*) 'pollen' (*pollen*), 'carpel' (*carpellum*) and 'stigma' (*stigma*) are 'pétale' 'anthère', 'pollen', 'carpelle' and 'stigmate' in French, 'petalo' 'anthera', 'polline', 'carpello' and 'stimma' in Italian, 'pétala' (Port.) 'pétalo' (Span.), 'antera', 'polen', 'carpelo' and 'estigma' in Portu guese and Spanish, 'petale', 'anterele', 'polenul', 'carpela' and 'stigmatul' in Romanian.

SUMMARY

By the end of the eighteenth century, botanical Latin had thus acquired a vocabulary based indeed on the seventeenth-century legacies of Ray and Tournefort, but enlarged and elaborated by Linnaeus and his successors to meet the needs of most botanists concerned with the flowering-plants in the nineteenth century. Accordingly, when Hum-boldt and Bonpland returned to Europe in 1804, bringing back from tropical America a multitude of plants new to science, botanical Latin provided the ideal medium for their publication, and Kunth's *Nova Genera et Species Plantarum* (1816–25) describing these plants became the forerunner of numerous other elaborate works likewise in botanical Latin which laid the foundations of tropical botany. Study of algae, fungi, lichens and mosses with the aid of the microscope revealed the same need for new terms as had earlier become evident in phanerogamic botany and likewise led to the creation of a new specialized vocabulary, Latin in form but mostly Greek in origin, used in a series of fundamental works by authors of many nationalities. This rich technical vocabu-lary, resting on hard-won knowledge gained largely since 1650 and hence unknown to the ancients, sets botanical Latin apart from classical Latin. It possesses its own standard orthography partly derived from medieval Latin which also diverges from that of classical Latin. The limitation of its subject matter and the adoption of a set formal static method of description for ease of comparison is alien indeed to the spirit of the great Latin literature of the Golden and Silver Ages; it reflects the scientific rationalizing attitude of the first half of the eighteenth century, the period of its birth, and above all the orderly methodical systematizing didactic intellect of Carl Linnaeus, who more than any other man established its present form. As Alphonse de Candolle wrote in 1880: 'C'est le latin arrangé par Linné à l'usage des descriptions. . . . Une langue aussi universelle, aussi précise, aussi bien adaptée par un homme de génie aux besoins de la science ne doit pas être abandonnée' (*La Phytographie*, 35; 1880). Gram-matically, botanical Latin closely follows classical precedent. 'The Latin language', says Michael Grant, with its classical literature in mind, 'is extremely forcible and expressive, very precise when employed,

as it was not always, in its tersest form—and at the same time very
compact; capable of saying much and of saying it well in a brief
space.' In maintaining these virtues so effectively, botanical Latin
joins hands across the centuries with the Latin of ancient Rome.

REFERENCES

ANDRÉ, J. 1955. Pline l'Ancien botaniste. *Revue des Études Latines*, 33 : 297-318.
—— 1956. *Lexique des Termes de Botanique en Latin* (Études et Commentaires, 23). Paris.
—— 1959. *Notes de Lexicographie botanique grecque*. Paris.
ARBER, A. 1938. *Herbals, their Origin and Evolution*. 2nd ed. Cambridge.
[First ed. 1912].
—— 1950. *The Natural Philosophy of Plant Form*. Cambridge.
—— 1953. From medieval herbalism to the birth of modern botany. *Science,
Medicine and History . . . in Honour of Charles Singer*, 2 : 317-336.
BALSS, H. 1947. *Albertus Magnus als Biologe*. Stuttgart.
BARTLETT, H. H. 1940. History of the generic concept in botany. *Bull. Torrey Bot.
Club*, 67 : 349-362.
BISCHOFF, G. W. 1833–49. *Handbuch der botanischen Terminologie und System-
kunde*. 4 vols. Nürnberg.
—— 1833–40. *Lehrbuch der Botanik*. 3 vols. Stuttgart.
—— 1857. *Wörterbuch der beschreibenden Botanik*. 2nd ed. (von J. A. Schmidt).
Stuttgart. [1st. ed., 1839, issued as an appendix to *Lehrbuch der Botanik*.]
BRAND, J. 1797. On Latin terms used in natural history. *Trans. Linnean Soc.
London*, 3 : 70-75.
CAMERARIUS, R. J. 1694. *De Sexu Plantarum Epistola*. Tübingen. (Reprinted
in *Misc. Curiosa Acad. Caesareo-Leop. Nat. Curios*. Dec. iii. 3 App. : 31, 1696,
and J. G. Gmelin, *Sermo academicus*, 83-148, 1749 ; German transl. by M.
Möbius in *Ostwalds Klassiker*, no. 105, 1899).
CANDOLLE, ALPHONSE DE. 1880. *La Phytographie ou l'Art de d'écrire les Végétaux*.
Paris.
CANDOLLE, AUGUSTIN PYRAMUS DE. 1813. *Théorie élémentaire de la Botanique*.
Paris. [2nd ed., 1819 ; 3rd ed., 1844.]
CHOATE, H. A. 1917. The earliest glossary of botanical terms : Fuchs 1542.
Torreya, 17 : 186-201.
CHURCH, A. H. 1919. Androecium and gynoecium. *J. Bot. (London)*, 57 : 220-
223.
FRIZZELL, D. L. 1935. Terminology of types. *Amer. Midland Nat.*, 14 : 637-668.
GEIGER, M. 1945. Prof. Dr. Gustav Senn, 1875-1945. *Verh. Naturf. Ges. Basel*,
56 (ii) : vii-xv. [With a bibliography of Senn's publications.]
GERMAIN DE SAINT PIERRE, E. 1852. *Guide du Botaniste*. Paris.
—— 1870. *Nouveau Dictionnaire de Botanique*. Paris, etc.
GOURLIE, N. 1953. *The Prince of Botanists: Carl Linnaeus*. London.
GRANT, M. 1954. *Roman Literature*. Cambridge. [2nd ed. in Pelican Books,
1958.]
GRAY, A. 1842. *The Botanical Textbook*. New York.
—— 1879. *Structural Botany*. New York & Chicago.
GREENE, E. L. 1909. *Landmarks of botanical History*. Part 1. Washington, D.C.
GUDGER, E. W. 1923. Pliny's Historia naturalis, the most popular natural history
ever published. *Isis*, 6 : 269-281.

48   DEVELOPMENT OF TERMINOLOGY   [CH. II

HELLER, J. L. 1963. The nomenclature of soils, or what's in a name? *Soil Sci. Soc. Amer. Proc.* 27: 216-220.

ILLIGER, J. K. W. 1800. *Versuch einer systematischen völlstandigen Terminologie fur das Thierreich und Pflanzenreich.* Helmstädt.

JACKSON, B. D. 1900. *A Glossary of botanic Terms.* London & Philadelphia [4th ed., 1928.]

JESSEN, K. F. W. 1864. *Botanik der Gegenwart und Vorzeit* in *culturhistorischer Entwickelung.* Leipzig. [Facsimile by Chronica Botanica in 1948.]

JIRÀSEK, V. 1961. Evolution of the proposals of taxonomical categories for the classification of cultivated plants. *Taxon,* 10: 34-45.

JUNG, J. 1747. *Opuscula botanico-physica.* Coburg. [Contains *Doxoscopiae physicae minores,* 1662, and *Isagoge phytoscopia,* 1678.]

KENT, W. 1958. Scientific naming. *Philosophy of Science,* 25: 185-193.

KNOX, R. A. 1923. *See* Lowe, J. E.

LINDLEY, J. 1832. *An Introduction to Botany.* London. [2nd ed., 1835; 3rd ed., 1839; 4th ed., 2 vols., 1848.]

—— 1849. *The Elements of Botany, structural and physiological with . . . Glossary of technical Terms.* London. [5th ed. of *An Outline of the First Principles of Botany,* London, 1830.]

LINK, H. F. 1798. *Philosophiae botanicae novae seu Institutionum phytographicarum Prodromus.* Göttingen.

—— 1824. *Elementa Philosophiae botanicae.* Berlin.

LINNAEUS, C. 1736. *Fundamenta botanica.* Amsterdam. [Facsimile, 1960, Weinheim.]

—— 1737. *Critica botanica.* Leiden. [English translation by A. Hort, publ. by Ray Society, London, 1938.]

—— 1737. *Genera Plantarum.* Leiden. [5th ed., 1754; facsimile, 1960.]

—— 1738. *Hortus Cliffortianus.* Amsterdam.

—— 1751. *Philosophia botanica.* Stockholm.

—— 1753. *Species Plantarum.* 2 vols. Stockholm. [Ray Society facsimile, London, 1957-9.]

—— 1762. *Termini botanici . . . sistit J. Elmgren.* [Reprinted in Linnaeus, *Amoen. Acad.,* 6: 217-246; 1763.]

LOCKE, J. 1690. *An Essay concerning human Understanding.* London. [5th ed., 1706, reprinted in Everyman's Library, 1961.]

LORCH, J. W. 1959. Gleanings on the naked seed controversy. *Centaurus,* 6: 122-128.

—— 1963. The carpel, a case-history of an idea and a term. *Centaurus* 8: 269-291.

LOWE, J. E. 1923. *Church Latin for Beginners.* With a Preface by R. A. Knox. London.

MARTYN, TH. 1791. Observations on the language of Botany. *Trans. Linnean Soc. London,* 1: 147-154.

—— 1793. *The Language of Botany.* London.

MEVIUS, W. 1959. Der Botaniker Joachim Jungius und das Urteil der Nachwelt. *Die Entfaltung der Wissenschaft; zum Gedenken von Joachim Jungius (1587-1657).* Hamburg.

MEYER, E. 1854-7. *Geschichte der Botanik.* Vols. 1-4. Königsberg.

MÖBIUS, M. 1944. Wie sind die Bezeichnungen Zoologie, Botanik und Mineralogie entstanden? *Jenaische Zeitschr. Med. Naturwiss.,* 77: 216-229.

NECKER, N. J. DE. 1790. *Corollarium ad. Phil. botanicam Linnaei spectans.* Neuwied.

PLANTEFOL, L. & PRÉVOST, A. M. 1962. La notion d'étamine à travers ses diverses dénominations. *Revue Philos. France*, 152 : 145-172.

RICKETT, H. W. 1944. The classification of inflorescences. *Bot. Review*, 10 : 187-231.

—— 1954-6. Materials for a dictionary of botanical terms. *Bull. Torrey Bot. Club*, 81 : 1-15, 188-198 (1954); 82 : 419-445 (1956), 342-354 (1956).

ROBINSON, R. 1950. *Definition*. Oxford.

ROSE, H. 1775. *The Elements of Botany*. London. [Mostly translated from Linnaeus, *Philosophia botanica*.]

ROZE, E. 1895. Recherches sur l'origine des noms des organes floraux. *Bull. Soc. Bot. France*, 42 : 213-225.

RUFINUS. 1946. *The Herbal of Rufinus*. Edited from the unique manuscript by L. Thorndike. Chicago.

SALISBURY, R. A. 1800. Remarks on some technical terms used in botany. *Trans. Linnean Soc. London*, 5 : 135-142.

SENN, G. 1928. Theophrasts Differentialdiagnosen für laubwerfende Eichen, Hist. Plant., I₂ 892-7. *Vierteljahrsschr. Naturf. Ges. Zürich*, 73, Beibl. 15 (Festschr. H. Schinz) : 509-541.

—— 1933a. *Die Entwicklung der biologischen Forschungsmethode in der Antike und ihre grundsätzliche Forderung durch Theophrast von Eresos*. (Veroff. Schweiz. Ges. Gesch. Med. Naturw. 8.) Aarau.

—— 1933b. Die Systematik der nordost-mediterranean *Pinus* Arten in Theophrasts Pflanzenkunde III. 9. 1-5. *Verh. Naturf. Ges. Basel.*, 45 : 365-400.

—— 1934. *Die Pflanzenkunde des Theophrast von Eresos*. Basel.

—— 1941. Oak galls in the Historia Plantarum of Theophrastus. *Trans. R. Bot. Soc. Edinburgh,* 60 : 343-354.

—— 1943. Die Beschreibung der Tanne in Theophrasts Pflanzenkunde, Kap., 996-8. *Boissiera*, 7 : 455-484.

—— *See* Geiger, M. 1945.

SPRAGUE, T. A. 1933a. Botanical terms in Pliny's Natural History. *Kew Bull.*, 1933 : 30-40.

—— 1933b. Botanical terms in Isidorus. *Kew Bull.*, 1933 : 401-407.

—— 1933c. Plant morphology in Albertus Magnus. *Kew Bull.*, 1933 : 431-440.

—— 1933d. Botanical terms in Albertus Magnus. *Kew Bull.*, 1933 : 440-459.

—— 1936. Technical terms in Ruellius' Dioscorides. *Kew Bull.*, 1936 : 145-185.

SPRAGUE, T. A. & SPRAGUE, M. S. 1939. The herbal of Valerius Cordus. *J. Linnean Soc. London, Bot.*, 52 : 1-113.

STADLER, H. 1898. Lateinische Pflanzennamen im Dioskorides. *Arch. Latein. Lexikogr.*, 10 : 83-115.

—— 1900. Pflanzennamen im Dioskorides. *Arch. Latein. Lexikogr.*, 11 : 105-114.

STAHL, W. H. 1962. *Roman Science : Origins, Development and Influence*. Madison.

STEARN, W. T. 1955. Linnaeus's 'Species Plantarum' and the language of botany. *Proc. Linnean Soc. London*, 165 : 158-164.

—— 1957. *An Introduction to the 'Species Plantarum' and cognate botanical Works of Carl Linnaeus*. [Prefixed to Ray Society facsimile ˘of Linnaeus, *Species Plantarum*, Vol. i.] London.

—— 1960. *Notes on Linnaeus's Genera Plantarum*. (Prefixed to Historiae Naturalis Classica facsimile of Linnaeus, *Genera Plantarum*, 5th ed., 1754.) Weinheim. [Reprinted 1962 in Stearn, *Three Prefaces on Linnaeus and Robert Brown*.]

—— 1961. Botanical gardens and botanical literature in the eighteenth century. *Cat. Bot. Books, Rachel M. M. Hunt*, 2 : xli-cxl. Pittsburgh.

STRÖMBERG, R. 1937. *Theophrastea. Studien zur botanischen Begriffsbildung*

(Göteborgs Kungl. Vet. Vit.-Samh. Handl. Femte Följden, ser. A. 6 no. 1). Göteborg.

—— 1940. *Griechische Pflanzennamen* (Göteborgs Högsk. Årsskr. 46). Göteborg,

SYSTEMATICS ASSOCIATION FOR DESCRIPTIVE TERMINOLOGY. 1960. Preliminary list of works relevant to descriptive biological terminology. *Taxon*, 9: 245-257.

THEOPHRASTUS. 1916. *Enquiry into Plants*. Transl. by A. Hort. (Loeb Classical Library.) London.

THORNDIKE, L. 1923. *A History of Magic and Experimental Science during the First Thirteen Centuries of our Era*. Vol. 1. London.

TOURNEFORT, J. PITTON DE. 1700. *Institutiones Rei herbariae*. Paris.

VAILLANT, S. 1718. *Discours sur la Structure des Fleurs. Sermo de Structura Florum*. Leiden.

WEBBER, H. J. 1903. New horticultural and agricultural terms. *Science*, new ser., 18: 501-503.

WEIN, K. 1932. Die Wandlung im Sinne des Wortes Flora. *Fedde, Repert. Sp. Nov., Beih.*, 66: 74-87.

WEISE, O. 1893. Zur Lateinisierung griechischer Wörter. *Arch. Latein. Lexikogr.*, 8: 77-114.

WHITEHEAD, A. N. 1925. *Science and the Modern World*. Cambridge.

CHAPTER IV

The Latin Alphabet and Pronunciation

ORIGIN OF THE LATIN ALPHABET

The Latin alphabet by the time of Cicero (106–43 B.C.) consisted of 21 letters derived and modified from the Greek alphabet (see Chapter XIX), possibly through direct contact with the Greek colonists at Cumae in the Bay of Naples, more probably through the intermediary of the widely trading piratical Etruscans of northern Italy, who had contended with the Greeks for maritime supremacy while the Romans were but land-bound farmers in Latium and who had already adopted an alphabet of Greek origin in the seventh century B.C. These letters were the consonants B, C, D, F, G, H, K, L, M, N, P, Q, R, S, T, X, the vowels A, E, O, and the letters I and V which stood for the vowel and consonant sounds now differentiated as I and J, U and W. The Greek alphabet of 24 letters included three, the aspirates θ (theta), φ (phi) and χ (chi), which represented sounds absent from early Latin. Having no phonetic use for them, the Romans converted them into numerals; these ultimately became C (100), M (1,000) and L (50). The Greek κ (kappa) passed out of use: it persisted only in a few words and then only before A. The Roman conquest of Greece in 146 B.C., the bringing of educated Greeks to Rome as slaves, the prestige of Greek culture, the later massive Greek settlements in Rome and the consequent need to transliterate Greek words and names into the inadequate Latin alphabet made the Romans add to it the Greek letters υ (upsilon) and ζ (zeta) as Y and Z and improvise the equivalents TH, PH and CH for the letters θ, φ and χ which they had earlier discarded. E served for both the Greek ε (epsilon) and η (eta); likewise O transliterated both the Greek o (omicron) and ω (omega).

THE LETTERS J, U AND W

The letters J, U (as distinct from V) and W did not exist in the Latin alphabet. The letter J as regards its origin 'is a comparatively late modification of the letter I. In the ancient Roman alphabet, I, besides its vowel value in *ibīdem*, *mīlitis*, had the kindred consonantal value of modern English Y, as in *iactus*, *iam*, *Iouem*, *iustus*, *adiūra*, *maior*, *peior*. . . . The differentiation was made first in Spanish, where from the very introduction of printing (i.e. in books of 1485–7) we see j used for the consonant and i only for the vowel. For the capitals I had at first to stand for both . . . but before 1600 a capital J consonant began to appear in Spanish' (*New Engl. Dict.* under J; 1901). U and V were originally interchangeable forms of the one letter which was employed both for a vowel and the consonant. 'During the sixteenth century, however, continental printers began to distinguish between *u* and *v*, using the former as a vowel and the latter as a consonant. The distinction is found in Italian printing as early as 1524, but its general introduction dates from 1559–60, when it was employed in the *Grammatica* of Ramus. . . . In capitals, however, V for some time continued to serve in the old double function' (*New Engl. Dict.* under U; 1926). The letter W is of medieval origin. 'When in the 7th century, the Latin alphabet was first applied to the writing of English, it became necessary to provide a symbol for the sound (w) which did not exist in contemporary Latin. The sound, a gutturally modified bilabial voiced spirant, is acoustically almost identical with the devocalized (*u*) or (u), which was the sound originally expressed by the Roman U or V as a consonant or symbol, but before the 7th century this Latin sound had developed into (v). The simple *u* or *v* could not be used without ambiguity to represent (w). . . . The ordinary sign for (w) was at first *uu*. . . . The *uu* was carried from England to the continent, being used for the sound (w) in the German dialects and in French proper names and other words of Teutonic and Celtic origin. In the 11th century the ligatured form was introduced into England by Norman scribes' (*New Engl. Dict.* under W; 1928). J, I, U and V with the values thus associated with them are commonly used in botanical Latin. It should be noted, however, that the eighteenth-century printers of Linnaeus's works employed *i* and *j* and *u* and *v* somewhat indiscriminately. At this period *i* often came at the beginning of a word, even though the consonant *j* was intended and *j* often within the word, usually after a vowel but sometimes after a consonant, even though the vowel *i* was intended, as in RHEEDJA and DELPHINJUM. Care should be taken to distinguish between 'f' and 'ſ' in works before 1800. The 'ſ' was used in place of 's' at the beginning of a word and often within it but 's' at the end. Notes on these characters as used in English printing will be found in R. B. McKerrow's *Introduction to Bibliography*, 309–318 (1927).

At first the Latin alphabet existed only in the form of capitals (majuscules), admirable indeed for monumental inscriptions on stone such as the Column of Trajan but much less so for rapid script on papyrus and vellum. By the eighth century A.D. alternative small letters (minuscules, 'lower-case' letters) had developed; those known as Caroline minuscules, which are ancestral to those of modern printing, became firmly and widely established in western Europe during the reign of Charlemagne (c. 742–814). The modern use of capital and lower-case letters together, as in generic names, has no classical precedent. The sloping letters known as *italic*, in which botanical names are usually printed, derive from the hand-writing of fifteenth-century Italian scholars and were made popular by the editions of the classics printed in them by Aldus Manutius (1450–1515) and his sons.

PRONUNCIATION[1]

Botanical Latin is essentially a written language, but the scientific names of plants often occur in speech. How they are pronounced really matters little provided they sound pleasant and are understood by all concerned. This is most likely to be attained by pronouncing them in accordance with the rules of classical Latin pronunciation. There are, however, several systems, since people tend to pronounce Latin words by analogy with words of their own language. Even within the Roman Empire when Latin displaced native languages having different speech rhythms there must have been great regional diversities of pronunciation, as indeed is evident from the different Romance languages, Spanish, Italian, etc., descended from it. Lack of uniformity in pronunciation led Erasmus in 1528 to publish his *De recta Latini Graecique Sermonis Pronunciatione* in which he described how a French ambassador at the court of the Emperor Maximilian made a speech in Latin 'with so Gallic an accent that the Italians present thought he were speaking French'; a German, called upon to reply, sounded as if he was speaking German; 'a Dane who spoke third might have been a Scotchman, so marvellously did he reproduce the pronunciation of Scotland' (cf. Brittain, *Latin in Church*, 26–30). Nevertheless, people were able to make themselves understood despite such differences of pronunciation. In 1608 Thomas Coryat, the author of *Coryat's Crudities*, travelled widely in Europe using Latin as an international language. In 1735–6 Linnaeus visited north Germany, Holland, England and France, likewise using Latin as his major tongue, for he knew little other than his native Swedish.

In English-speaking countries there exist two main systems, the

---

[1] Most of this section is reproduced by permission from the writer's article on the 'Pronunciation of botanical names' in R.H.S., *Dict. Gard. Suppl.*, 301–302 (1956).

traditional English pronunciation generally used by gardeners and botanists and the 'reformed' or 'restored' academic pronunciation adopted by classical scholars as presenting 'a reasonably close approximation to the actual sounds of the language as spoken by educated Romans'. This academic pronunciation comes closer to the usual Latin pronunciation of Continental people than does the conventional English pronunciation.

The pronunciation of a word is determined by the sounds of the individual letters, the length (quantity) of the vowels and the place of stress (accent). Vowels are described as 'long' and often marked with a ⁻ (e.g. *cāke, kīte, ēvil, vōte*) or 'short' and often marked with a ˘ (e.g. *căt, kĭt, ĕgg, pŏt*), according to the relative time spent in saying them.

Words containing more than one vowel or diphthong (i.e. two vowels pronounced as one, e.g. *ae, au, ei, eu, oe, ui*) are divided into *syllables*. Thus *al-bus, ple-nus, mag-nus*, etc., are words of two syllables, and the *stress*, indicated by the sign ' (or by the grave ` to indicate a long vowel in the stressed syllable and the acute ´ to indicate a short vowel), in words of two syllables falls on the first syllable. Most words consist of several syllables, e.g. *al-bi-dus, ple-ni-flo-rus, mag-ni-fo-li-us, ros-ma-ri-ni-for-mis, o-phi-o-glos-so-i-des, Con-stan-ti-no-po-li-ta-nus.*

In Latin every vowel is pronounced, hence *cŏ-tō-nĕ´-ăs-ter* and not *cot-on-easter*. The same applies to the Latinized Greek ending *-ŏ-ī´-dēs* (not *-oi-des*) meaning 'like, having the form of'.

In classical Latin words of several syllables the stress falls on the syllable next to the last one (the penultimate) when this syllable is long (i.e. when it ends in a long vowel or diphthong, e.g. *for-mō´-sus*, or when two consonants separate the two last vowels, e.g. *cru-ĕn´tus*), but falls on the last syllable but two (the antepenultimate) when the last but one is short, e.g. *flō´-ri-dus, la-ti-fŏ´-li-us, sil-vă´-ti-cus*. Diphthongs are treated as long vowels. When, however, two vowels come together in a Latin word without forming a diphthong, the first is short, e.g. *car´-nĕ-us* ; in a word of Greek origin, this does not apply, hence *gi-gan-tē´-us*. The *-inus* ending also varies, being *ī* in some Latin words, e.g. *al-pī´-nus*, but *ĭ* in others, e.g. *se-ro´-tĭ-nus* ; in words of Greek origin, e.g. *bom-by´-cĭ-nus, hy-a-cin´-thĭ-nus*, it is usually *ĭ*.

The above rules of accentuation apply both to the traditional English and the reformed academic pronunciation of Latin. The consonants *b, d, f, h, l, m, n, p, qu, z* are pronounced as in English. The following Table indicates the main differences between the two methods of pronunciation :

REFORMED ACADEMIC	TRADITIONAL ENGLISH
ā as in *father*	*fāte*
ă as in *ăpart*	*făt*

REFORMED ACADEMIC	TRADITIONAL ENGLISH
ae as *ai* in *aisle*	as *ea* in *meat*
au as in *house*	as *aw* in *bawl*
c always as in *cat*	before *a, o, u* as in *cat* before *e, i, y* as in *centre*
ch (of Greek words) as *k* or *k-h* (if possible)	as *k* or *ch*
ē as in *they*	*mē*
ĕ as in *pĕt*	*pĕt*
ei as in *rein*	as in *height*
g always as in *go*	hard before *a, o, u* as in *gap, go* soft before *e, i, y* as in *gem, giro*
ī as in *machīne*	*īce*
ĭ as in *pĭt*	*pĭt*
(consonant i) as *y* in *yellow*	*j* in *jam*
ng as in *finger*	*finger*
ō as in *nōte*	*nōte*
ŏ as in *nŏt*	*nŏt*
oe as *oi* in *toil*	as *ee* in *bee*
ph as *p* or *p-h* if possible	like *f*
r always trilled	
s as in *sit, gas*	*sit, gas*
t as in *table, native*	*table* but *ti* within a word as in *nation*
ū as in *brūte*	*brūte*
ŭ as in *fŭll*	*tŭb*
ui as *oui* (French), *we*	*ruin*
v (consonant *u*) as *w*	as in *van*
ȳ as *u* in French *pur*	as in *cȳpher*
y̆ as in French *du*	as in *cy̆nical*

The pronunciation of Church Latin is based on modern Italian pronunciation, *c* before *i* and *e* being accordingly pronounced as the English *ch* and not as *s* (the conventional English pronunciation) or *k* (the reformed pronunciation).

Whichever system is adopted, the word will sound best and be least objectionable to scholars if a distinction is made between long and short vowels as above and the stress put in the right place according to classical Latin procedure. To do this, reference must be made to a standard dictionary such as C. T. Lewis and C. Short, *Latin Dictionary*, to the works cited below, or to a Flora, such as M. L. Fernald, *Gray's Manual of Botany* (8th ed., 1950), giving careful attention to accentuation.

These rules cannot satisfactorily be applied to all generic names and specific epithets commemorating persons. About 80 per cent of generic names and 30 per cent of specific epithets come from languages other than Latin and Greek. A simple and consistent method of pronouncing them does not exist, because different peoples use the same letters for different sounds and different letters for the same sounds. The *cz* of Polish corresponds to the English *ch* and the Italian *c* before *i* or *e*, but the English *ch* is not the same as the French *ch* or the Italian *ch* before *i* or *e*. The ideal method with most names commemorating persons is to pronounce them as nearly as possible like the original name but with a Latin ending. The uncouth-looking *Warszewiczella* will then be euphoniously pronounced as *var-shĕ-vĭ-chĕl'-la* and not uncouthly as *wars-zew-ic-zell-a*. The main difficulty is that this method involves giving a German pronunciation to *Heuchera*, a French pronunciation to *Choisya*, a Scottish pronunciation to *Menziesia* an Italian pronunciation to *cesatianus*, a Polish pronunciation to *przewalskii*, etc., and to do this is more than most botanists and gardeners can manage.

The ending *-ii* or *iae* of most epithets commemorating persons also creates difficulty if the rules of Latin accentuation are applied strictly, since the accent will then fall on the syllable before the *-ii* or *iae*, which is not its usual place in most personal names, and will thus distort the sound unrecognizably to some ears.

REFERENCES

ALLEN, W. S. *Vox latina: a Guide to the Pronunciation of Classical Latin*. Cambridge.

BLOCH, R. 1952. *L'Épigraphie latine* (Que sais-je? No. 534). Paris.

BRITTAIN, F. 1955. *Latin in Church: the History of its Pronunciation.* 2nd ed. (Alcuin Club Tracts, No. 28). London.

DIRINGER, D. 1962. *Writing* (Ancient Peoples and Places, No. 25). London.

DREWITT, F. G. D. 1927. *Latin Names of common Plants*. London.

ELSE, G. F. 1967. The pronunciation of classical names and words in English. *Classical J.* 62 : 210-214.

GILBERT-CARTER, H. 1964. *Glossary of the British Flora.* 3rd ed. Cambridge.

HIGOUNET, C. 1959. *L'Écriture* (Que sais-je? No. 653). Paris.

KRETSCHMER, P. 1899. *Sprachregeln für die Bildung und Betonung zoologischer Namen.* Berlin.

LOT, F. 1931. À quelle époque a-t-on cessé de parler latin ? *Archivum Latinitatis Medii Aevi,* 6 : 97-159.

McKERROW, R. B. 1927. *Introduction to Bibliography.* London.

MURRAY *et al.* 1901–28. *New English Dictionary on historical Principles.* Vols. 6 (1901), 10 (1926–8). Oxford.

NICHOLSON, G. 1889. *Illustrated Dictionary of Gardening,* 4 : 356-361. London.

PYLES, T. 1939. Tempest in teapot ; the reform in Latin pronunciation. *Journal of English Literary History,* 6 : 138-164.

STEARN, W. T. 1956. Pronunciation of botanical names. Royal Horticultural Society, *Supplement to the Dictionary of Gardening,* 301-302.

STURTEVANT, E. H. 1940. *The Pronunciation of Greek and Latin.* 2nd ed. Philadelphia.

THOMPSON, E. M. 1912. *An Introduction to Greek and Latin Palaeography.* Oxford.

ULLMAN, B. L. 1932. *Ancient Writing and its Influence.* New York & London.

WIKÉN, E. 1951. *Latin för Botanister och Zoologer.* Malmö.

PART TWO

GRAMMAR

CHAPTER V

Nouns

A word which stands for anything that has an existence
is a Noun.

WILLIAM COBBETT, Grammar (1819)

DECLENSION AND AGREEMENT
OF NOUNS AND ADJECTIVES

Latin is a highly inflected language, and its nouns (*substantiva*) have
gender, number and *case*. This means that the ending of a Latin noun
changes not only to indicate that two or more things are being mentioned, as in English 'cow, cows', 'ox, oxen', but also to indicate the
noun's relation to other words in the sentence and to convey meanings
which are expressed in English by its position and by the use of prepositions such as 'of', 'by', 'to', 'with'. It also means that adjectives
associated with a noun must be given corresponding endings so that
the noun and its adjectives agree in gender, number and case. For
example, in the sentences 'the white flower is fragrant' and 'the white
flower has fragrance', the word 'flower' is singular in *number*, because
it refers to only one flower, and is said to be of nominative *case*, because it is the subject of the sentence ; the corresponding Latin word
is *flos*, which is regarded as masculine and hence is said to be of masculine *gender*. The 'white flower' of these sentences would be *flos albus*
in Latin. In such a sentence as 'I pick the white flower', the word 'I'
is the subject and 'flower' the object, although the word 'flower'
itself undergoes no change in English. In Latin 'white flower' as the
direct object of the sentence would be *florem album*, i.e. *flos albus*
changed into the accusative case. 'Of the white flower' in Latin would
be *floris albi*, i.e. in the genitive or possessive case. 'To the white
flower' would be expressed as *flori albo*, i.e. by use of the dative case.
'With the white flower' would be expressed as *flore albo*, i.e. by use of
the ablative case. There are corresponding changes in the form of

Latin words when they refer to more than one thing. Thus referring to 'white flowers' we have *flores albi* (nominative plural), *flores albos* (accusative plural), *florum alborum* (genitive plural), *floribus albis* (dative and ablative plural). From this it will be evident that the use of the correct ending to a word is very important for conveying the intended meaning in Latin.

Gender

Latin words denoting a male, e.g. *vir* (man), *taurus* (bull), are masculine: words denoting a female, e.g. *uxor* (wife), *vacca* (cow), are feminine. In this they correspond to the natural gender or sex of the object concerned. Grammatical gender metaphorically classifies words denoting inanimate objects or qualities which have no natural gender as being nevertheless *masculine* (m.), *feminine* (f.) or *neuter* (n.). The gender assigned to a noun often relates to its ending in the nominative singular or to its meaning, but may be arbitrary. Thus most Latin words ending in -*us* and -*er* are masculine, e.g. *ager* (field), *hortus* (garden), *stylus* (style), *fructus* (fruit); classical names of trees ending in -*us*, such as *juniperus, pinus, prunus, quercus*, are feminine. Most Latin words ending in -*a* and -*es* are feminine, e.g. *corolla* (corolla), *species* (species); most words of Greek origin ending in -*ma*, e.g. *rhizoma* (rhizome), *stigma* (stigma), are neuter. Nouns ending in -*um* and -*u* are neuter, e.g. *herbarium* (herbarium), *petalum* (petal), *sepalum* (sepal), *cornu* (horn). Names of most rivers and mountains (unless they end in -*a* or -*e*) are masculine; those of most countries, islands, cities and trees are feminine, but the numerous exceptions make unreliable most general rules for gender. Schoolboys used to learn rhymes such as the following as aids to memory:

> A woman, island, country, tree
> and city feminine we see:
> Pēnelopē, Cyprus, Germānia, laurus, Athēnae.

Stem and Root

Etymologists call a *stem* that basic part of a Latin word which remains unchanged despite changes in the word as a whole made to express differences of case and number; the endings attached to it to express different meanings—metaphorically like basal leaves, shade leaves, sun leaves, bracts, all of which can be attached to the same stem in a plant—are called *case endings* or *inflexions*. The stem is common to all forms of the same word, or the stem of the nominative singular may be slightly different from the stem of the other cases; thus the stem of *flos* is *flos* in the nominative singular but *flor*- for all the other cases; its case-endings in the singular are -*em* (accusative), -*is* (genitive),

-*i* (dative) and -*e* (ablative) and in the plural are -*es* (nominative and accusative), -*um* (genitive) and -*ibus* (dative and ablative). The term *root* is used by etymologists to denote a part of the stem common to several different words of related meaning; as in plants, several stems may arise from the same root. In a short word the stem and the root may be the same. Thus the stem of *albus* is *alb*-, which is the root not only of *albus* (white) but also of *albor* (whiteness), *albumen* (white of egg), *alburnum* (sap-wood), etc.

In forming compounds the stem of the word as revealed in the genitive case is used. Thus *crux* (cross) has the genitive singular *crucis*, of which *cruc*- is the stem and -*is* is the genitive case-ending; from this are derived *cruciatus* (cross-shaped), *crucifer* (cross-bearing), *cruciformis* (cross-shaped), *crucilabris* (with a cross-shaped lip) and *Crucianella*. The names of families are formed by adding the ending -*aceae* (a nominative plural feminine adjectival ending) to the stem of a legitimate name of an included genus. The stem of *Rosa* (genitive singular *Rosae*) is *Ros*-, hence the family name *Rosaceae*; the stem of *Cannabis* (genitive singular *Cannabis*) is *Cannab*-, hence the family name *Cannabaceae*; the stem of *Salix* (genitive singular *Salicis*) is *Salic*-, hence the family name *Salicaceae*. Words derived from the same Greek element may differ slightly in their stem, according to whether this terminal element was treated by the original author simply as a transliterated Greek word, e.g. *Gyrostemon* (stem *Gyrostemon*-) or was deliberately given a Latin form distinct from that of the corresponding Greek word, e.g. *Podostemum* (stem *Podostem*-), hence the family names *Gyrostemonaceae* and *Podostemaceae*.

Stems of Third Declension nouns

Nouns of the Third Declension (see below) mostly have the stem of the genitive, etc., different from the nominative singular. According to the phonetic nature of the letter ending this stem they are classified (e.g. in Kennedy's *Revised Latin Primer* and in the Vocabulary of the present work) into eleven groups.

(i) Stems ending in **c** or **g** (palatals), e.g. *apex* (tip), stem *apic*-, gen. sing. *apicis*; *calyx* (calyx), stem *calyc*-, gen sing. *calycis*; *Carex* (sedge), stem *Caric*-, gen. sing. *caricis*; *grex* (flock), stem *greg*-, gen. sing. *gregis*; *radix* (root), stem *radic*-, gen. sing. *radicis*; *Panax*, stem *Panac*-, gen. sing. *Panacis*; *spadix* (spadix), stem *spadic*-, gen. sing. *spadicis*. See below, pp. 79, 81.

(ii) Stems ending in **t** or **d** (dentals), e.g. *Abies* (spruce), stem *Abiet*-, gen. sing. *Abietis*; *Cycas* (cycad), stem *Cycad*-, gen. sing. *Cycadis*; -*myces* (-fungus), stem -*mycet*-, gen. sing. -*mycetis*; *pes* (foot), stem *ped*-, gen. sing. *pedis*; *phialis* (phialide), stem *phialid*-, gen.

sing. *phialidis*; *stipes* (stipe), stem *stipit*-, gen. sing. *stipitis*; *varietas* (variety), stem *varietat*-, gen. sing. *varietatis*. See below, pp. 76, 78, 81.

(iii) Stems ending in **b** or **p** (labials), e.g. *ops* (help), stem *op*-, gen. sing. *opis*; *princeps* (the chief), stem *princip*-, gen. sing. *principis*. See below, pp. 85, 86.

(iv) Stems ending in the fricative **s** changing usually to **r**, e.g. *flos* (flower), stem *flor*-, gen. sing. *floris*; *genus* (genus), stem *gener*-, gen. sing. *generis*; *latus* (side), stem *later*-, gen. sing. *lateris*. See below, pp. 85, 87.

(v) Stems ending in **l** or **r** (liquids), e.g. *arbor* (tree), stem *arbor*-, gen. sing. *arboris*; *auctor* (author), stem *auctor*-, gen. sing. *auctoris*; *color* (colour), stem *color*-, gen. sing. *coloris*; *Mucor*, stem *Mucor*-, gen. sing. *Mucoris*; *odor* (smell), stem *odor*-, gen. sing. *odoris*; *sal* (salt), stem *sal*-, gen. sing. *salis*; *ver* (spring), stem *ver*-, gen. sing. *veris*. See below, pp. 75, 77, 84.

(vi) Stems ending in **n** or **m** (nasals), e.g. *aestivatio* (aestivation), stem *aestivation*-, gen. sing. *aestivationis*; *Arundo* (reed), stem *Arundin*-, gen. sing. *Arundinis*; *crassitudo* (thickness), stem *crassitudin*-, gen. sing. *crassitudinis*; *Cyclamen* (sowbread), stem *Cyclamin*-, gen. sing. *Cyclaminis*; *descriptio* (description), stem *description*-, gen. sing. *descriptionis*; *embryo* (embryo), stem *embryon*-, gen. sing. *embryonis*; *hiems* (winter), stem *hiem*-, gen. sing. *hiemis*; *icon* (illustration), stem *icon*-, gen. sing. *iconis*; *longitudo* (length), stem *longitudin*-, gen. sing. *longitudinis*; *margo* (edge), stem *margin*-, gen. sing. *marginis*; *Plantago* (plantain), stem *Plantagin*-, gen. sing. *Plantaginis*; *pollen* (pollen), stem *pollin*-, gen. sing. *pollinis*; *semen* (seed), stem *semin*-, gen. sing. *seminis*; *Senecio* (groundsel), stem *Senecion*-, gen. sing. *Senecionis*; *specimen* (specimen), stem *specimin*-, gen. sing. *speciminis*; *stamen* (stamen), stem *stamin*-, gen. sing. *staminis*. See below, pp. 77, 83.

(vii) Stems of nouns with nominative singular in -**is**, genitive plural in -**ium**, e.g. *clavis* (key), stem *clav*-, gen. sing. *clavis*. See p. 80.

(viii) Stems of nouns with nominative singular in -**es** and genitive plural in -**ium**, e.g. *cautes* (rock), stem *caut*-, gen. sing. *cautis*. See p. 79.

(ix) Stems ending in two consonants and genitive plural ending in -**ium**, e.g. *dens* (tooth), stem *dent*-, gen. sing. *dentis*; *frons* (frond), stem *frond*-, gen. sing. *frondis*; *mons* (mountain), stem *mont*-, gen. sing. *montis*. See below, p. 86.

(x) Stems of nouns with nominative singular in -**e**, -**al** or -**ar** and genitive plural in -**ium**, e.g. *animal* (animal), stem *animal*, gen. sing. *animalis*; *calcar* (spur), stem *calcar*-, gen. sing. *calcaris*; *nectar* (nectar), stem *nectar*-, gen. sing. *nectaris*. See below pp. 75, 76.

Groups vii-x are kept apart principally on historical grounds as nouns with stems in *i*, as distinct from groups i-vi with consonant stems, because they originally differed markedly in declension with -*im* instead of -*em*, -*i* instead of -*e*, -*is* instead of -*es* and -*ium* instead of -*um*, but the *i* of the stem survives only in the genitive plural; e.g. *mons* with stem *monti*- (now reduced to *mont*-) has genitive plural *montium*.

(xi) Stems ending in -**at** of neuter nouns of Greek origin with nominative singular ending in -**ma**, e.g. *Alisma* (water-plantain), stem *Alismat*-, gen. sing. *Alismatis*; *lemma* (lemma), stem *lemmat*-, gen. sing. *lemmatis*; -*nema* (-thread), stem -*nemat*-, gen. sing. -*nematis*; *rhizoma* (rhizome), stem *rhizomat*-, gen. sing. *rhizomatis*; -*sperma* (-seed), stem -*spermat*-, gen. sing. *spermatis*; *stigma* (stigma), stem *stigmat*-, gen. sing. *stigmatis*; *stoma* (stomate), stem *stomat*-, gen. sing. *stomatis*; *systema* (system), stem *systemat*-, gen. sing. *systematis*.

In all the groups above except vii and x the ablative singular is formed by adding -*e* to the stem, e.g. *apex*, stem *apic*-, abl. sing. *apice*; in group vii the ablative singular ends in *e* or *i*, in group x in -*i*, e.g. *calcar*, abl. sing. *calcari*. The dative and ablative plurals in all groups are formed by adding -*ibus* to the stem.

Declension

Many nouns have endings for the different cases the same as those of *flos* given above and are said to be of the same *declension*. Similarly many adjectives follow the same pattern as *albus*. Unfortunately many words follow other patterns. According to their case-endings, nouns may be divided into five main classes known as the First, Second, Third, Fourth and Fifth Declensions and indicated by the Roman numerals I, II, III, IV and V in the Vocabulary. The word *flos* provides an example of a masculine noun of Declension III ending in -*os* in the nominative case; its genitive is *floris*, its stem *flor*-; knowing this we can construct the other cases as needed by adding the appropriate case-endings of Declension III to its stem, e.g. *flor*- + nominative plural ending -*es* gives *flores*, *flor*- + ablative plural ending -*ibus* gives *floribus*. The word *albus* is the masculine nominative singular of an adjective with *alba* as its feminine and *album* as its neuter forms; the masculine and neuter forms are declined like (i.e. follow the same model or *paradigm* as) a noun of Declension II, but the feminine form like a noun of Declension I; such an adjective is indicated by the letter A in the Vocabulary. The word *viridis* (green) represents a second class of adjectives, indicated by the letter B in the Vocabulary, which are declined like Declension III nouns.

Latin dictionaries list nouns in their nominative singular form, then give the genitive case-ending or the whole genitive word when the nominative does not reveal the stem, then the gender and meaning, e.g. **flos**, floris, *m.*, a flower. Facciolati and Forcellini in their great *Totius Latinitatis Lexicon* added a Roman numeral to indicate the declension, a procedure adopted from them in the Vocabulary of this book. The declension can, however, be ascertained directly from the genitive singular case-endings: I, -*ae*; II, -*i*; III, -*is*; IV, -*us*; V, *ei*. Confronted then with a word of which we wish to use the ablative plural, e.g. to translate 'with veins' into Latin, we first ascertain to which declension it belongs. Thus *vena* (vein) has the genitive singular *venae*, i.e. ending in -*ae*, which refers it to Declension I. We next look down the Table of case-endings and find that for Declension I the ablative plural ending is -*is*; we then strip the word to its stem, here *ven-*, and add the appropriate ending to this, *venis* resulting.

An adjective associated with the noun must agree with it in gender, number and case. Thus 'with white veins' would be translated as *venis albis*; 'with green veins' would, however, be *venis viridibus*, because the adjective *viridis* (green), belonging to Group B above, does not follow the same model as *albus*, belonging to Group A above.

Case

Use of cases. In English, as stated above, the relation of a noun to other nouns in a sentence is usually indicated and its meaning accordingly modified by the prepositions 'of', 'by', 'for', etc., whereas in Latin this is done wholly or partly by *case-endings* or *inflexions*, such endings as -*a*, -*am*, -*ae*, -*as*, -*arum*, -*i*, -*o*, -*ibus*, etc., added to the stem of the noun. Particular kinds of endings have particular meanings associated with them. In Latin they belong to six types or *cases*: the *Nominative* (nom.), the *Vocative* (not used in botanical Latin), the *Accusative* (acc.), the *Genitive* (gen.), the *Dative* (dat.) and the *Ablative* (abl.).

The NOMINATIVE is the case of the subject; it is the case under which a word is entered in dictionaries. As Cobbett said: 'A noun is in the *Nominative* case, when it denotes a person, or thing, which *does* something or *is* something; as *Richard strikes*; *Richard is good*.' Or *the plant grows* (in Latin *planta crescit*) or the *plant is tall* (*planta est alta*).

The ACCUSATIVE is usually described as the case of the direct object of a sentence, i.e. 'when the person or thing that it means or denotes is the *object*, or *end*, of some act or of some movement, of some kind or other' (Cobbett). Thus in the description *radix longa caulem singulum edens* (root long a stem single putting forth), the *caulis* (acc. *caulem*) is treated as the object of an act or process (*edens*, present participle of the verb *ēdo*) done by the subject *radix*; hence *radix* is kept in the nominative but instead of *caulis* its accusative *caulem* is used. To quote E. C. Woodcock, here 'the accusative is used as a mere grammatical sign, to indicate the direct object of a verb'.

The accusative also indicates the area over which something is done or occurs or to which it extends or aims. 'The word in the accusative, with or without the aid of a preposition, performs the function of an *adverb*, indicating the goal, direction, or extent of a movement or action, in space or time' (Woodcock). A noun associated in meaning with certain prepositions having this kind of implication, e.g. *ad* (to), *ante* (before), *circa* (about), *inter* (among), *ob* (on account of), *per* (through), *post* (after), *supra* (above), *versus* (towards), is always used in the accusative case. Thus the phrase *apicem versus* (towards the tip), expressing direction, employs the accusative of *apex* (tip); the phrase *per totam longitudinem* (through or over the whole length) employs the accusative of *longitudo* (length). The names of towns and small islands when taken as a point reached are put in the accusative usually without a preposition, e.g. *extensit Delum* (it extends to Delos), but countries, regions and large islands, being regarded as areas on which many points can be reached, require the addition of a preposition such as *in* or *ad*, e.g. *ad Graeciam extensa* (reaching to Greece).

The accusative singular mostly ends in *-am*, *-um*, *-em* or *-im*, less often in *-e*, *-l*, *-r* or *-u*; the accusative plural ends in *-as*, *-os*, *-a*, *-es*, *-ia*, *-us* or *-ua*.

The GENITIVE is the possessive case, with the meaning 'of' or 'belonging to' (genitive of property; possessive genitive). 'A noun is in the Possessive case when it names a person or thing that possesses some other person or thing, or when there is one of the persons or things belonging to the other; as in *Richard's hat*; the *mountain's top*; the *nation's fleet*. Here *Richard*, *mountain* and *nation* are in the Possessive case because they denote persons or things which possess other persons or things, or have other persons or things belonging to them' (Cobbett). Thus the 'tube of the calyx' or 'the tube possessed by the calyx' is translated into botanical Latin as *tubus calycis* or *calycis tubus*, the genitive singular of *calyx* being *calycis*. Its function here is that of an adjective, and the same meaning can often be expressed by the use of a related adjective, e.g. *tubus calycinus* (the calycine tube). As stated by Woodcock, 'the word or words in the genitive define, describe or classify the thing (or person) denoted by noun qualified. The genitive inflexion thus turns a noun or a pronoun into a sort of indeclinable adjective, which is sometimes interchangeable with an adjective.' In such a phrase as *opus magni laboris* (a work of great toil) the genitive is used descriptively, indicating size or quality (genitive of description or quality).

The genitive is much used in specific epithets commemorating persons, e.g. *Euphrasia kerneri* (the eyebright of Kerner; Kerner's eyebright), *Paeonia clusii* (Clusius's peony), *Rosa beatricis* (the rose of Beatrix), *Scabiosa olgae* (Olga's scabious), *Tiarella wherryi* (Wherry's tiarella), *Echeveria baileyorum* (Echeveria of the Baileys). It is less used for geographical epithets, e.g. *Syringa emodi* (the lilac of the Himalaya, the Emodus of classical geographers). In mycology a generic name or hyphened specific name in the genitive[1] is often employed as a specific epithet to indicate the host of a parasitic fungus, e.g. *Phoma betae* (Phoma on Beta), *Fusarium lini* (Fusarium on Linum), *Septoria apii-graveolentis* (Septoria on Apium graveolens), *Phytophthora cactorum* (Phytophthora on cacti), *Urocystis anemones* (Urocystis on Anemone), *Chrysomyza abietis* (Chrysomyza on Abies), *Puccinia iridis* (Puccinia on Iris), *Ophiobolus graminis* (Ophiobolus on grass), *Monoicomyces echidnoglossae* (Monoicomyces on Echidnoglossa), etc.

The genitive singular ends in *-ae*, *-i*, *-is*, *-us* or *-ei* (in *-os* only in a few words transliterated from Greek), the genitive plural in *-arum*, *-orum*, *-um*, *-ium*, *-uum* or *-erum*.

The DATIVE is the case of the indirect object, with the meaning of 'for' or 'to', and denotes that person or thing to or for whom or which something is done. In botanical Latin it is mostly used to indicate affinity, e.g. *Hypno subulato simile* (to Hypnum subulatum similar), *Adonidi vernali affinis* (to Adonis vernalis related). A special use is the 'dative of possession', apparently intended to emphasize the thing possessed and not the possessor, as when the older authors put *mihi* (for me, to me) or *nobis* (for us, to us) immediately after a new botanical name published by them.

The dative is never used with a preposition. The dative singular

---

[1] For some generic names more than one genitive singular form appears in the literature, e.g. *Abutilonis* and *Abutili* for *Abutilon*, *Galeobdoli* and *Galeobdolonis* for *Galeobdolon*. Sometimes the form standard in botanical literature differs from that of antiquity, e.g. *Orchidis* instead of *Orchis* for *Orchis*. In classical Latin, however, a few words had alternative genitive singular forms, e.g. *ficus* (fig), gen. *fici* and *ficus*, *gaster* (belly), gen. *gasteris* and *gastri*, *quercus* (oak), gen. *quercus* and *querci*, *tigris* (tiger), gen. *tigris* and *tigridis*. Hence for some names in use alternative genitive forms can be accepted as permissible; for new names, with epithets in the genitive, convenience will be best served by adopting the most generally used form, e.g. *Phragmitis* rather than *Phragmitidis* for *Phragmites*, *Stachydis* rather than *Stachyos* for *Stachys*, which can often be ascertained from C. A. J. A. Oudemans, *Enumeratio systematica Fungorum* (1919–24). H. K. Airy Shaw and F. C. Deighton have proposed in *Taxon* 12 : 291 (1963) that generic names ending in *-is* or *-ys* should be treated as having the stem *-id* or *-yd* and hence the genitive ending *-idis* or *-ydis*, e.g. *Achlys*, gen. *Achlydis*, *Coris*, gen. *Coridis*, despite a lack of support in classical usage, except that names ending in *-charis* retain the stem *-it*, e.g. *Nomocharis*, gen. *Nomocharitis*, and compounds of *-basis*, *-caulis* and other technical Latin terms retain their customary stem, e.g. *Physocaulis*, gen. *Physocaulis*. Certain names, such as *Azedarach*, *Cacao*, *Gale*, *Kali*, *Manihot*, *Muscari*, *Quamoclit*, are best treated as indeclinable, i.e. as being the same as the nominative in all cases. Statements such as the following in Tournefort's *Institutiones Rei herbariae* (1700) provide a guide to pre-Linnaean usage : 'Abutili species sunt', 'Capparis species sunt', 'Cerinthes species sunt', 'Colocynthidis species sunt', 'Galeopseos species sunt', 'Manihot species sunt', 'Menyanthis species sunt', 'Molles speciem unicam novi', 'Muscari species sunt', 'Nymphoidis species sunt', 'Petasitidis species sunt', 'Stachydis species sunt'.

ends in *-ae*, *-o*, *-i*, *-ui*, *-u* or *-ei*; the dative plural is always the same as the ablative plural and ends in *-is*, *-ibus* or *-ebus*.

The ABLATIVE is the case of the agent, with the meaning usually of 'with' (ablative of accompaniment and of description) but also of 'by' (ablative of instrument or means), 'in' (ablative of respect and of position) or 'from' (ablative of separation and of origin; the true ablative or 'taking away' case). These different functions of the ablative are the result of three originally distinct cases being assimilated into one.

The ablative is much used in diagnoses (see Chapter XIII) stating the essential features *with* which a species is provided, e.g. *Hypericum floribus trigynis, foliis lanceolatis, caule quadrangulo, pericarpiis coloratis* (Hypericum with flowers trigynous, with leaves lanceolate, with stem quadrangular, with pericarps coloured). Linnaean polynomials or phrase-names use the ablative in this manner. Descriptions are written in the nominative, with occasional subordinate clauses in the ablative, e.g. *caulis erectus glaber, inferne radicibus numerosis instructus, superne vaginis imbricatis obtectus* (stem erect glabrous, below with the numerous roots furnished, above with imbricate sheaths covered). Such a contrast between nominative and ablative is particularly useful when distinguishing between an organ and its parts. The ablative is also much used in diagnostic observations, indicating the features *by* which a new taxon differs *from* those already known, e.g. *genus novum floribus pentameris et stipulis connatis a generibus adhuc descriptis recedens* (new genus by pentamerous flowers and by connate stipules from genera up to now described diverging).

The ablative also serves to denote the place *where* or *in which* something happens or is to be found, e.g. *apice* (at the tip), *basi* (at the base), taking over the function of the old locative case.

The ablative singular ends in *-a* (the dative then in *-ae*), *-o*, *-ĕ* or *-i* (the dative then in *-i*), *-u* (the dative then in *-ui* or *-u*), *-ē* (the dative then in *-eī*), the ablative plural (as likewise the dative plural) in *-is*, *-ibus*, *-ebus* or *-ubus*.

The LOCATIVE case, indicating position, was once independent but now resembles in form either the genitive or the ablative. It is thus explained by Woodcock: 'In the first or *-ā* declension *-i* was added to the stem, which produced in Old Latin *Romai*, etc. By a regular phonetic development this had become *Romae* by the beginning of the second century B.C., and was then indistinguishable in form from the genitive. Similarly the locative of the second or *-o* declension was *-oi* (cf. Greek οἶκοι, 'at home'), which became *-i* (e.g. *Arimini*, 'at Ariminum', *domi*, 'at home') and was again indistinguishable from the genitive. . . . Except in singular place-names of the first and second declension and a few other words such as *domi*, etc., the function of the locative was taken over by the ablative.' The locative is used without a preposition when naming a town or small island or other place of limited extent at which something is done, and mainly appears on the title-pages of books to state where they are published, e.g. *Lipsiae* (at Leipzig), *Londini* (at London), *Olisippone* (at Lisbon). See Chapter XVII, p. 208.

TABLE OF CASE ENDINGS

Adapted from Kennedy, *Revised Latin Primer*

Decl.	I	II	III		IV	V	Case
Case	A	O	Consonant	I	U	E	Meaning
				SINGULAR			
	f.	*m. n.*	*m.f. n.*	*f.m. n.*	*m. n.*	*f.*	
Nom.	-a	-us(er) -um	*various*	-is, es -e,l, r	-us -u	-es	Subject
Acc.	-am	-um -um	-em *var.*	-em,im -e,l, r	-um -u	-em	Direct Object
Gen.	-ae	-i	-is	-is	-us	-ei	*of*
Dat.	-ae	-o	-i	-i	-ui (u)	-ei	*to* or *for*
Abl.	-a	-o	-e	-i *or* e	-u	-e	*with, by* or *from*
				PLURAL			
Nom.	-ae	-i -a	-es -a	-es -ia	-us -ua	-es	Subject
Acc.	-as	-os -a	-es -a	-es, is -ia	-us -ua	-es	Direct Object
Gen.	-arum	-orum	-um	-ium	-uum	-erum	*of*
Dat.	-is	-is	-ibus	-ibus	-ibus	-ebus	*to* or *for*
Abl.	-is	-is	-ibus	-ibus	-ibus	-ebus	*with, by* or *from*
				EXAMPLES			
	anthera	folium, *n.*	aestiva-	animal, *n.*	varietas,	facies	
	corolla	herbarium,	tio, *f.*	basis, *f.*	*f.*	fides	
	gluma	*n.*	apex, *m.*	calcar, *n.*	ambitus,	res	
	inflores-	hortus, *m.*	calyx, *m.*	caulis, *m.*	*m.*	series	
	centia	petalum, *n.*	rhizoma,	rhachis, *f.*	fructus,	species	
	lamina	petiolus, *m.*	*n.*		*m.*		
	spatha	pileus, *m.*	stamen,		habitus,		
			n.		*m.*		
			stigma, *n.*		lacus, *m.*		
			stolo, *m.*		sinus, *m.*		
			stoma, *n.*				
			tuber, *n.*				

FIRST DECLENSION

Latin nouns of the First Declension (indicated by I in the Vocabulary) end in *-a* in the nominative singular. They are nearly all feminine. It should be noted that nouns of Greek origin ending in *-ma* are neuter, e.g. *lemma, nema, rhizoma, sperma, systema, trichoma*, and belong to the Third Declension (see p. 82), except when the *-ma* ending is a Latin rendering of the Greek feminine ending *-mē* (*-μη*).

Singular

Nom.	anthera (*f.*)	the anther (as subject)
Acc.	antheram	the anther (as object)
Gen.	antherae	of the anther
Dat.	antherae	to or for the anther
Abl.	anthera	by, with or from the anther

Plural

Nom.	antherae	the anthers (as subject)
Acc.	antheras	the anthers (as object)
Gen.	antherarum	of the anthers
Dat.	antheris	to or for the anthers
Abl.	antheris	by, with or from the anthers

The following feminine nouns are similarly declined : *ala*, wing ; *axilla*, axil ; *ascospora*, ascospore ; *bacca*, berry ; *bractea*, bract ; *bracteola*, bracteole ; *calyptra*, calyptra ; *capsula*, capsule ; *carina*, keel ; *cellula*, cell ; *chalaza*, chalaza ; *coma*, terminal tuft ; *corolla*, corolla ; *costa*, main nerve ; *cyma*, cyme ; *differentia*, distinguishing feature ; *drupa*, drupe ; *familia*, family ; *forma*, form ; *galea*, hood, helm ; *gemma*, bud ; *gluma*, glume ; *herba*, herbaceous plant ; *hypha*, hypha ; *inflorescentia*, inflorescence ; *insula*, island ; *lamina*, blade ; *ligula*, ligule ; *linea*, line, $\frac{1}{12}$ inch ; *macula*, spot, blotch ; *ocrea*, ocrea ; *placenta*, placenta ; *planta*, plant ; *radicula*, radicle ; *rosula*, rosette ; *seta*, bristle ; *siliqua*, siliqua ; *spatha*, spathe ; *spica*, spike ; *spina*, spine ; *spora*, spore ; *squama*, scale ; *stipula*, stipule ; *sylva*, wood ; *umbella*, umbel ; *vagina*, sheath ; *valva*, valve ; *vena*, vein ; *volva*, volva ; *zona*, band.

Generic names ending in -*a*, whether taken direct from Latin, as *Avena, Beta, Castanea, Ferula, Genista, Hedera, Malva, Rosa*, etc., or coined from personal names, as *Abelia, Anaxagorea, Bartsia, Bonnemaisonia, Fuchsia, Jania, Lejeunea, Lobelia, Watsonia*, or non-Latin words, as *Alchemilla, Akebia, Aucuba, Bersama, Dilsea, Kirengeshoma, Madhuca, Nandina, Retama, Rorippa, Vanilla, Yucca, Zebrina*, are likewise treated as belonging to the First Declension, unless derived from neuter Greek names ending in -*ma*, e.g. *Ceratostigma, Ganoderma, Herponema, Monostroma, Tricholoma* (see p. 82).

Here belong geographical names ending in -*a*, e.g. *Anglia* (England), *Asia, China, Gallia* (France), *Helvetia* (Switzerland), *Lapponia* (Lapland), *Marilandia* (Maryland, U.S.A.), *Nigeria, Nova Zelandia* (New Zealand), and in -*ae* (plural form), e.g. *Aquae Gratianae* (Aix-les-Bains), *Athenae* (Athens). The locative case, indicating where something takes place, is the same as the genitive singular, e.g. *Basileae* (at Basel),

Holmiae (at Stockholm), *Romae* (at Rome), or the ablative plural (when the name is of plural form), e.g. *Athenis* (at Athens), and is mainly used on the title-pages of books to record the place of publication.

Feminine personal names, such as *Helena, Lucilia,* together with Latinized surnames of women, e.g. *Sheriffia, Willmottia,* are mostly used as epithets in the genitive, i.e. *helenae, luciliae, sheriffiae, willmottiae.*

The few Latin masculine nouns of the First Declension, e.g. *agricola* (farmer), *incola* (inhabitant), *advena* (newcomer), *poeta* (poet), *scriba* (writer), rarely occur in botanical texts.

To the First Declension also belong a few masculine and feminine nouns of Greek origin. Greek nouns of the First Declension ending in -η (eta) when taken into Latin were given the ending -*a* and declined as *anthera* above during the early period of borrowing from Greek (see p. 51). Later the ending -η was transcribed as -*e*. Modern coinages vary, e.g. *Dimorphotheca, Sarcediotheca, Aphanothece, Cyamathece.* These nouns are mostly generic names, e.g. *Aloe, Alsine, Calocybe, Coniocybe, Psilocybe, Silene,* with the genitive singular formed by adding a terminal -*s*, e.g. *Aloes* (of Aloe), but include a few terms, e.g. *rhaphe* (raphe). The noun *botanica* (in some early authors *botanice*) is peculiar in that, although the nominative ends in -*a*, it has always been declined as if it were *botanice*, with the genitive singular *botanices*, e.g. *professor botanices* (professor of botany); likewise *America* often has the genitive singular *Americes* instead of *Americae.*

Nom.	**Aloe**	**Anemone**	botanica (botanice)
Acc.	**Aloen**	**Anemonen**	botanicen
Gen.	**Aloes**	**Anemones**	botanices
Dat.	**Aloae**	**Anemonae**	botanicae
Abl.	**Aloe**	**Anemone**	botanice
Nom.	**Clitocybe**	**Microchaete**	Microcoryne
Acc.	**Clitocyben**	**Microchaeten**	Microcorynen
Gen.	**Clitocybes**	**Microchaetes**	Microcorynes
Dat.	**Clitocybae**	**Microchaetae**	Microcorynae
Abl.	**Clitocybe**	**Microchaete**	Microcoryne

SECOND DECLENSION

Nouns of the Second Declension (indicated by II in the Vocabulary) end in -*us*, -*er* or -*um* in the nominative singular, in -*i* in the genitive singular, -*orum* in the genitive plural. Those ending in -*us* (often rendering the Greek ending -*os*) are mostly masculine, among the exceptions being feminine *humus* (ground), *fagus* (beech), *pyrus* (pear), *quercus* (oak) and some other names of trees, *methodus* (method) and *hydathodus* (hydathode), neuter *pelagus* (sea) and *virus* (poison); those ending in *-um* or *-on* (transcribed from the Greek ending *-ov*) are neuter.

Nouns ending in *-us* are declined as follows:

Singular

Nom.	**stylus** (*m.*)	the style (as subject)
Acc.	**stylum**	the style (as object)
Gen.	**styli**	of the style
Dat.	**stylo**	to or for the style
Abl.	**stylo**	by, with or from the style

Plural

Nom.	**styli**	the styles (as subject)
Acc.	**stylos**	the styles (as object)
Gen.	**stylorum**	of the styles
Dat.	**stylis**	to or for the styles
Abl.	**stylis**	by, with or from the styles

Similarly declined are the masculine nouns *aculeus*, prickle; *angulus*, angle; *annulus*, annulus; *annus*, year; *apiculus*, small terminal point; *ascus*, ascus; *autumnus*, autumn; *bulbillus*, bulbil; *bulbus*, bulb; *capillus*, hair; *chloroplastus*, chloroplast; *corymbus*, corymb; *culmus*, culm; *discus*, disc; *folliculus*, follicle; *hortulanus*, gardener; *hortus*, garden; *limbus*, limb; *lobus*, lobe; *locus*, place; *nodus*, node; *nervus*, nerve; *nucleus*, nucleus; *numerus*, number; *oculus*, eye; *pappus*, pappus; *pedicellus*, pedicel; *pedunculus*, peduncle; *periplastus*, periplast; *petiolus*, petiole; *pileus*, pileus; *pilus*, hair; *racemus*, raceme; *ramulus*, branchlet; *ramus*, branch; *scapus*, scape; *sorus*, sorus; *strobilus*, cone; *succus*, juice; *sulcus*, furrow; *thallus*, thallus; *thyrsus*, thyrse; *truncus*, trunk; *tubus*, tube; *typus*, type; *utriculus*, utricle; *verticillus*, whorl.

Combinations formed from the above, e.g. *holotypus*, *lectotypus*, are declined in the same way.

Names of genera ending in *-us* are mostly masculine, e.g. *Abelmoschus*, *Acanthus*, *Agaricus*, *Amaranthus*, *Boletus*, *Calochortus*, *Ceanothus*, *Chondrus*, *Cistus*, *Convolvulus*, *Echinocactus*, *Fucus*, *Helianthus*, *Hibiscus*, *Lupinus*, *Paxillus*, *Polyporus*. However, the classical names of trees (and hence of many genera founded on arborescent species) are mostly feminine, e.g. *Alnus*, *Arbutus*, *Buxus*, *Carpinus*, *Cedrus*, *Cissus*, *Cornus*, *Cupressus*, *Crataegus*, *Elaeagnus*, *Fagus*, *Ficus*, *Fraxinus*, *Juniperus*, *Malus*, *Morus*, *Pinus*, *Platanus*, *Prunus*, *Pyrus*, *Ulmus*.

Most masculine personal names are similarly declined, e.g. *Adolphus, Albertus, Ambrosius, Antonius, Bartholomaeus, Bernardus, Carolus, Christianus, Christophorus, Claudius, Edmundus, Franciscus, Georgius, Gottlobius, Gregorius, Gulielmus, Henricus, Hermannus, Hieronymus, Jacobus, Joachimus, Josephus, Laurentius, Ludovicus, Marcus, Martinus, Nicolaus, Paulus, Petrus, Philippus, Ricardus, Robertus, Timothaeus.* Family names when Latinized or of Latin form ending in *-us* are similarly declined when represented by a man (when represented by a woman, see First Declension, above), e.g. *Caesalpinus* (Cesalpino), *Clusius* (de l'Écluse), *Fuchsius* (Fuchs), *Gesnerus* (Gesner), *Hallerus* (Haller), *Linnaeus, Lobelius* (de l'Obel), *Magnus, Mappus, Medicus, Moehringius* (Moehring), *Morisonus* (Morison), *Quercetanus* (Duchesne), *Raius* (Ray), *Renealmus* (Reneaulme), *Rivinus* (Bachmann), *Tragus* (Bock).

Masculine personal names are latinized usually by adding the termination *-ius*, a procedure adopted by the Romans, e.g. when they converted the German 'Hermann' into *Arminius*. The genitive of such names as *Augustus, Cornutus, Franciscus, Linnaeus*, being already of Latin form, takes a single *-i* in the genitive, e.g. *Augusti, Cornuti, Francisci, Linnaei.*

Nom.	**Carolus**	**Linnaeus**	Carl Linnaeus (as subject)
Acc.	**Carolum**	**Linnaeum**	Carl Linnaeus (as object)
Gen.	**Caroli**	**Linnaei**	of Carl Linnaeus
Dat.	**Carolo**	**Linnaeo**	to or for Carl Linnaeus
Abl.	**Carolo**	**Linnaeo**	by, with or from Carl Linnaeus

The locative of geographical names, e.g. *Rhodus* (Rhodes), *Philippi* (Philippi), ends in *-i*, e.g. *Rhodi* (at Rhodes), or in *-is* (when the name is of plural form), e.g. *Philippis* (at Philippi).

Nouns ending in *-er* are declined as follows:

Singular

Nom.	**ager** (*m.*)	the field (as subject)
Acc.	**agrum**	the field (as object)
Gen.	**agri**	of the field
Dat.	**agro**	to or for the field
Abl.	**agro**	by, with or from the field

Plural

Nom.	**agri**	the fields (as subject)
Acc.	**agros**	the fields (as object)
Gen.	**agrorum**	of the fields
Dat.	**agris**	to or for the fields
Abl.	**agris**	by, with or from the fields

Similarly declined are *diameter* (f.), diameter; *liber* (m.), book;

meter (m.), metre ; *vesper* (m.), evening ; *vir* (m.), man ; a few generic names and epithets, e.g. *Cotoneaster, Oleaster, Pinaster*, and some masculine personal names, e.g. *Alexander, Dryander, Sernander, Solander*.

Nouns ending in *-um*, all neuter, are declined as follows :

Singular

Nom.	**folium** (*n.*)	the leaf (as subject)
Acc.	**folium**	the leaf (as object)
Gen.	**folii**	of the leaf
Dat.	**folio**	to or for the leaf
Abl.	**folio**	by, with or from the leaf

Plural

Nom.	**folia**	the leaves (as subject)
Acc.	**folia**	the leaves (as object)
Gen.	**foliorum**	of the leaf
Dat.	**foliis**	to or for the leaves
Abl.	**foliis**	by, with or from the leaves

Similarly declined are the neuter nouns *achenium*, achene ; *amylum*, starch ; *androecium*, androecium ; *apothecium*, apothecium ; *arboretum*, arboretum ; *collum*, neck ; *conidium*, conidium : *dorsum*, back ; *endospermium*, endosperm ; *ericetum*, heath ; *excipulum*, exciple ; *ferrum*, iron, and other names of metals ; *flagellum*, flagellum ; *gonidium*, gonidium ; *gynoecium*, gynoecium ; *herbarium*, herbarium ; *involucellum*, involucel ; *involucrum*, involucre ; *labellum*, labellum ; *labium*, lip ; *lignum*, wood ; *ostium*, entrance, mouth ; *ovarium*, ovary ; *ovulum*, ovule ; *palatum*, palate ; *paramylum*, paramylum ; *perianthium*, perianth ; *perigonium*, perigon ; *petalum*, petal ; *pistillum*, pistil ; *pratum*, meadow ; *regnum*, kingdom ; *rostrum*, beak ; *saxum*, rock ; *scutellum*, scutellum ; *segmentum*, segment ; *sepalum*, sepal ; *sporangium*, sporangium ; *tepalum*, tepal ; *velum*, velum ; *vexillum*, vexillum.

Names of genera ending in *-um* are always neuter, e.g. *Allium, Codium, Crinum, Epimedium, Hypnum, Lilium, Mnium, Olpidium, Stereum*.

Neuter nouns taken from Greek and ending in *-on* (*-ov*) are declined as follows :

Singular

Nom.	**plancton** (*n.*)	the plankton (as subject)
Acc.	**plancton**	the plankton (as object)
Gen.	**plancti**	of the plankton
Dat.	**plancto**	to or for the plankton
Abl.	**plancto**	by, with or from the plankton

Singular

Nom.	Rhododendron	Dinobryon	Trichophyton
Acc.	Rhododendron	Dinobryon	Trichophyton
Gen.	Rhododendri	Dinobryi	Trichophyti
Dat.	Rhododendro	Dinobryo	Trichophyto
Abl.	Rhododendro	Dinobryo	Trichophyto

Here belong such generic names as *Acantholimon, Acroptilon, Antithamnion, Callithamnion, Chrysodendron, Halarachnion, Hydrodictyon, Lithothamnion, Manniophyton, Microdictyon.*

THIRD DECLENSION

Nouns of the Third Declension (indicated by III in the Vocabulary) have their stem ending in a consonant or in the vowels *-i, -o, -u* or *-y*, and form the genitive singular by adding the termination *-is* to this, e.g. *tuber*, gen. sing. *tuberis.* Sometimes the nominative singular and the stem are identical, e.g. *animal*, stem *animal-*, gen. sing. *animalis*, but often the nominative singular has been abbreviated, presenting a 'short stem', and the full stem is used for the other cases, e.g. *varietas*, short stem *variet-*, full stem *varietat-*, gen. sing. *varietatis*, abl. plur. *varietatibus*. The number of nouns belonging to the Third Declension is very large. They are commonly classified by grammarians into groups according to the phonetic nature of the stem as given above (pp. 61-63):

(i) Stems ending in the palatals *c* or *g*. E.g. *radix*, stem *radic-*, gen. sing. *radicis.*

(ii) Stems ending in the dentals *t* or *d*. E.g. *stipes*, stem *stipit-*, gen. sing. *stipitis*; *phialis*, stem *phialid-*, gen. sing. *phialidis.*

(iii) Stems ending in the labials *b* or *p*. E.g. *princeps.*

(iv) Stems ending in the fricative *s* changed usually to *r*. E.g. *flos*, stem *flor-*, gen. sing. *floris.*

(v) Stems ending in the liquids *l* or *r*. E.g. *color*, stem *color-*, gen. sing. *coloris.*

(vi) Stems ending in the nasals *n* or *m*. E.g. *margo*, stem *margin-*, gen. sing. *marginis.*

Five other groups (vii-xi) are also distinguished above. These numbers are used in the Vocabulary.

Erik Wikén's *Latin för Botanister och Zoologer* (1951) classifies nouns of the Third Declension into 19 groups according to the ending of the nominative singular, which is, of course, the form given in dictionaries, and botanists may well prefer such a classification. The

following is a modification of Wikén's system with the endings of the
nominative singular alphabetically arranged:

Those ending in (1) -al; (2) in -ar; (3) in -as; (4) in -ax; (5) in
-e; (6) in -en; (7) in -er; (8) in -es; (9) in -ex; (10) in -i; (11) in -is;
(12) in -ix; (13) in -ma; (14) in -o; (15) in -on; (16) in -or; (17) in
-os; (18) in -s after a consonant (-bs, -ms, -ns, -rs); (19) in -us; (20)
in -ut; (21) in -ys; (22) in -yx.

The locative of geographical names, e.g. *Carthago* (Carthage),
Olisippo (Lisbon), *Neapolis* (Naples), *Gades* (Cadiz), may end in -i or
-e, e.g. *Carthagine*, *Carthagini* (at Carthage), *Olisippone* (at Lisbon),
Neapoli (at Naples), or in -ibus (when the name is of plural form), e.g.
Gadibus (at Cadiz).

1 Ending in -al

Singular

Nom.	**animal** (*n.*)	the animal (as subject)
Acc.	**animal**	the animal (as object)
Gen.	**animalis**	of the animal
Dat.	**animali**	to or for the animal
Abl.	**animali**	by, with or from the animal

Plural

Nom.	**animalia**	the animals (as subject)
Acc.	**animalia**	the animals (as object)
Gen.	**animalium**	of the animals
Dat.	**animalibus**	to or for the animals
Abl.	**animalibus**	by, with or from the animals

2 Ending in -ar

Singular

Nom.	**calcar** (*n.*)	the spur (as subject)
Acc.	**calcar**	the spur (as object)
Gen.	**calcaris**	of the spur
Dat.	**calcari**	to or for the spur
Abl.	**calcari**	by, with or from the spur

Plural

Nom.	**calcaria**	the spurs (as subject)
Acc.	**calcaria**	the spurs (as object)
Gen.	**calcarium**	of the spurs
Dat.	**calcaribus**	to or for the spurs
Abl.	**calcaribus**	by, with or from the spurs

Similarly declined : *nectar* (n.), nectar, *par* (n.), pair, and some
generic names, e.g. *Mikrosyphar*, *Nuphar*.

3 Ending in -as

Singular

Nom.	**varietas** (*f.*)	the variety (as subject)
Acc.	**varietatem**	the variety (as object)
Gen.	**varietatis**	of the variety
Dat.	**varietati**	to or for the variety
Abl.	**varietate**	by, with or from the variety

Plural

Nom.	**varietates**	the varieties (as subject)
Acc.	**varietates**	the varieties (as object)
Gen.	**varietatum**	of the varieties
Dat.	**varietatibus**	to or for the varieties
Abl.	**varietatibus**	by, with or from the varieties

Similarly declined: *Aceras* ; with *d* instead of *t* : *Asclepias* (gen. *Asclepiadis*), *Cycas* (gen. *Cycadis*), *Dryas* (gen. *Dryadis*), *Najas* (gen. *Najadis*), *Serapias* (gen. *Serapiadis*). *Mas* (m.), male, has gen. sing. *maris*.

4 Ending in -ax

Singular

Nom.	**styrax** (*f.*)	styrax (as subject)
Acc.	**styracem**	styrax (as object)
Gen.	**styracis**	of styrax
Dat.	**styraci**	to or for styrax
Abl.	**styrace**	by, with or from styrax

Plural

Nom.	**styraces**	styraces (as subject)
Acc.	**styraces**	styraces (as object)
Gen.	**styracum**	of styraces
Dat.	**styracibus**	to or for styraces
Abl.	**styracibus**	by, with or from styraces

The generic name *Styrax* is treated as feminine, the gum *styrax* (*storax*) as masculine, following Greek usage. Similarly declined: *Donax, Panax, Smilax.*

5 Ending in -e

Singular

Nom.	**vegetabile** (*n.*)	the plant (as subject)
Acc.	**vegetabile**	the plant (as object)
Gen.	**vegetabilis**	of the plant
Dat.	**vegetabili**	to or for the plant
Abl.	**vegetabili**	by, with or from the plant

Plural

Nom.	**vegetabilia**	the plants (as subject)
Acc.	**vegetabilia**	the plants (as object)
Gen.	**vegetabilium**	of the plants
Dat.	**vegetabilibus**	to or for the plants
Abl.	**vegetabilibus**	by, with or from the plants

Similarly declined and likewise neuter : *declive*, slope, *mare*, sea, *Secale*, rye.

6 Ending in -en

Singular

Nom.	**stamen** (*n.*)	the stamen (as subject)
Acc.	**stamen**	the stamen (as object)
Gen.	**staminis**	of the stamen
Dat.	**stamini**	to or for the stamen
Abl.	**stamine**	by, with or from the stamen

Plural

Nom.	**stamina**	the stamens (as subject)
Acc.	**stamina**	the stamens (as object)
Gen.	**staminum**	of the stamens
Dat.	**staminibus**	to or for the stamens
Abl.	**staminibus**	by, with or from the stamens

Similarly declined and likewise neuter : *flumen*, river, *gramen*, grass, *legumen*, legume (pod), *nomen*, name, *pollen*, pollen, *semen*, seed, *specimen*, specimen, *Cyclamen*. Note the change of the *e* of the nominative and accusative singular to *i* in other cases. *Lichen* (m. ; gen. sing. *lichenis*) and *-solen* (m.; gen. *-solenis*), pipe, keep the *e* throughout.

7 Ending in -er

Singular

Nom.	**tuber** (*n.*)	the tuber (as subject)
Acc.	**tuber**	the tuber (as object)
Gen.	**tuberis**	of the tuber
Dat.	**tuberi**	to or for the tuber
Abl.	**tubere**	by, with or from the tuber

Plural

Nom.	**tubera**	the tubers (as subject)
Acc.	**tubera**	the tubers (as object)
Gen.	**tuberum**	of the tubers
Dat.	**tuberibus**	to or for the tubers
Abl.	**tuberibus**	by, with or from the tubers

A number of neuter generic names are similarly declined, e.g. *Acer*, *Papaver*. The masculine noun *aster* (star) and the generic names derived from it, e.g. *Aster*, *Geaster*, *Wardaster*, have the accusative singular *asterem*, the nominative and accusative plural *asteres*. The suffix *-aster*, as in *pinaster*, indicating inferiority or incomplete resemblance (see p. 73), should not be confused with this. *Gaster* (f.; gen. sing *gasteris* or *gastri*) may be declined like *tuber* or like *ager* (p. 72). *Character* (m.) and *elater* (m.) are declined like *aster* above.

8 Ending in **-es**

Those with the genitive singular ending in **-etis** or **-edis** are declined as follows:

Singular

Nom.	**paries** (*m.*)	the wall (as subject)
Acc.	**parietem**	the wall (as object)
Gen.	**parietis**	of the wall
Dat.	**parieti**	to or for the wall
Abl.	**pariete**	by, with or from the wall

Plural

Nom.	**parietes**	the walls (as subject)
Acc.	**parietes**	the walls (as object)
Gen.	**parietum**	of the walls
Dat.	**parietibus**	to or for the walls
Abl.	**parietibus**	by, with or from the walls

Similarly declined: *Abies* (f.), Abies, *myces* (m.), fungus, and compounds of *-myces*, e.g. *Actinomyces*, *Streptomyces*, *Strobilomyces*.

Those with the genitive singular ending in **-itis** are declined as follows:

Singular

Nom.	**caespes** (*m.*)	the tuft (as subject)
Acc.	**caespitem**	the tuft (as object)
Gen.	**caespitis**	of the tuft
Dat.	**caespiti**	to or for the tuft
Abl.	**caespite**	by, with or from the tuft

Plural

Nom.	**caespites**	the tufts (as subject)
Acc.	**caespites**	the tufts (as object)
Gen.	**caespitum**	of the tufts
Dat.	**caespitibus**	to or for the tufts
Abl.	**caespitibus**	by, with or from the tufts

Similarly declined: *Phragmites*.

Those with the genitive singular ending in **-is** without modification of the stem are declined as follows:

Singular

Nom.	pubes (*f.*)	the hair-covering (as subject)
Acc.	pubem	the hair-covering (as object)
Gen.	pubis	of the hair-covering
Dat.	pubi	to or for the hair-covering
Abl.	pube	by, with or from the hair-covering

Plural

Nom.	pubes	the hair-coverings (as subject)
Acc.	pubes	the hair-coverings (as object)
Gen.	pubium	of the hair-coverings
Dat.	pubibus	to or for the hair-coverings
Abl.	pubibus	by, with or from the hair-coverings

Similarly declined are *nubes* (f.), cloud, *rupes* (f.), rock, *sepes* (f.), hedge, *Isoetes* (n.), *Trametes* (f.) and some Greek personal names, e.g. *Orphanides*, gen. sing. *Orphanidis*. Also a number of generic names ending in *-anthes*, *-odes* or *-oides* derived from Greek:

Singular

Nom.	Omphalodes	Nymphoides	Cheilanthes
Acc.	Omphalodem	Nymphoidem	Cheilanthem
Gen.	Omphalodis	Nymphoidis	Cheilanthis
Dat.	Omphalodi	Nymphoidi	Cheilanthi
Abl.	Omphalode	Nymphoide	Cheilanthe

Similarly declined: *Alyssoides, Ammoides, Chrysanthemoides, Dacryodes, Phymatodes, Santaloides*, etc. These are all now treated as feminine (cf. *Taxon*, 3 : 33-34 ; 1954).

Ending in -ex

Singular

Nom.	apex (*m.*)	the tip (as subject)
Acc.	apicem	the tip (as object)
Gen.	apicis	of the tip
Dat.	apici	to or for the tip
Abl.	apice	by, with or from the tip

Plural

Nom.	apices	the tips (as subject)
Acc.	apices	the tips (as object)
Gen.	apicum	of the tips
Dat.	apicibus	to or for the tips
Abl.	apicibus	by, with or from the tips

Similarly declined: *caudex* (m.), stem, rootstock, *cortex* (m.), bark, *frutex* (m.), shrub, *suffrutex* (m.), subshrub ; also such generic

names as *Atriplex* (f.), *Carex* (f.), *Ilex* (f.), *Ulex* (f.), *Vitex* (f.). *Grex*
meaning ' a flock, swarm, troop ', diverges slightly from the above:

Singular

Nom.	**grex** (*f.*)	the flock (as subject)
Acc.	**gregem**	the flock (as object)
Gen.	**gregis**	of the flock
Dat.	**gregi**	to or for the flock
Abl.	**grege**	by, with or from the flock

Plural

Nom.	**greges**	the flocks (as subject)
Acc.	**greges**	the flocks (as object)
Gen.	**gregum**	of the flocks
Dat.	**gregibus**	to or for the flocks
Abl.	**gregibus**	by, with or from the flocks

10 Ending in **-i**

Nouns ending in **-i** are not of Latin origin but taken from Greek
or other languages :

Singular

Nom.	**Thlaspi** (*n.*)
Acc.	**Thlaspem**
Gen.	**Thlaspis (Thlaspeos)**
Dat.	**Thlaspi**
Abl.	**Thlaspe**

Names of non-Greek origin such as *Alhagi, Dipcadi, Kali, Muscari,*
are not declined.

10 bis Ending in **-in**

For compounds of *-glochin*, see p. 90.

11 Ending in **-is**

Those with the genitive singular ending in **-is** (not **-idis**), and thus
the same as the nominative singular, are declined as follows :

Singular

Nom.	**caulis** (*m.*)	the stem (as subject)
Acc.	**caulem**	the stem (as object)
Gen.	**caulis**	of the stem
Dat.	**cauli**	to or for the stem
Abl.	**caule**	by, with or from the stem

Plural

Nom.	**caules**	the stems (as subject)
Acc.	**caules**	the stems (as object)
Gen.	**caulium**	of the stems
Dat.	**caulibus**	to or for the stems
Abl.	**caulibus**	by, with or from the stems

Similarly declined: *axis* (m.), axis, *classis* (f.), class, *clavis* (f.),
ey, *rhachis* (f.), rachis, *unguis* (m.), claw, *vallis* (f.), valley; likewise
many generic names, e.g. *Calotropis, Cannabis, Capparis, Carpopeltis,
Digitalis, Galeopsis, Oxytropis, Sinapis, Vitis* (all feminine).

Generic names compounded from the Greek *cystis* (f.), bladder,
re declined as follows:

Nom.	**Anacystis** (*f.*)
Acc.	**Anacystim**
Gen.	**Anacystis**
Dat.	**Anacysti**
Abl.	**Anacysti**

Similarly declined: *Acrocystis, Ceratocystis, Gloeocystis, Macro-
ystis, Nereocystis.* For declension of *basis* (f.), base, see p. 391.

Those with the genitive singular ending in **-idis** are declined as
follows:

	Singular		Plural	
Nom.	**cuspis** (*f.*)	the cusp (as subject)	**cuspides**	the cusps (as subject)
Acc.	**cuspidem**	the cusp (as object)	**cuspides**	the cusps (as object)
Gen.	**cuspidis**	of the cusp	**cuspidum**	of the cusps
Dat.	**cuspidi**	to or for the cusp	**cuspidibus**	to or for the cusps
Abl.	**cuspide**	by, with or from the cusp	**cuspidibus**	by, with or from the cusps

Similarly declined are *epidermis* (f.), epidermis, *lapis* (m.), stone ;
likewise most generic names ending in *-is*, e.g. *Adonis, Anthemis,
Ascodomis, Bellis, Berberis, Botrytis, Clematis, Crepis, Geopyxis, Orchis,
Oxalis, Phalaris, Pteris, Rhopalostylis.* The genitive of *agrostis* (f.),
couch-grass, is *agrostis* in classical Latin, but for the generic name
Agrostis botanists have preferred the genitive *Agrostidis.*

Those with the genitive ending *-inis* are mostly compounds of
actis (f.), ray, e.g. *Myriactis, Stenactis.*

Those with the genitive ending *-itis* are mostly compounds of
charis, grace, e.g. *Eleocharis, Eucharis, Hydrocharis, Nomocharis.*

12 Ending in -ix

Nouns ending in **-ix** with the genitive singular ending in **-icis** are
declined as follows:

	Singular	
Nom.	**radix** (*f.*)	the root (as subject)
Acc.	**radicem**	the root (as object)
Gen.	**radicis**	of the root
Dat.	**radici**	to or for the root
Abl.	**radice**	by, with or from the root

Plural

Nom.	**radices**	the roots (as subject)
Acc.	**radices**	the roots (as object)
Gen.	**radicum**	of the roots
Dat.	**radicibus**	to or for the roots
Abl.	**radicibus**	by, with or from the roots

Similarly declined : *appendix* (f.), appendix, *cicatrix* (f.), scar, *fili.* (f.), fern, *matrix* (f.), matrix, *spadix* (f.), spadix ; generic names suc as *Larix, Phoenix, Salix, Scandix, Tamarix.*

A few generic names of Greek origin ending in **-ix** have the genitiv singular ending in **-ichis** :

Nom.	**Calothrix** (*f.*)
Acc.	**Calotrichem**
Gen.	**Calotrichis**
Dat.	**Calotrichi**
Abl.	**Calotriche**

Similarly declined : *Acrothrix, Amphithrix, Dichothrix, Schizothrix Ulothrix.* The change from *thrix* in the nominative to *trich-* in othe cases should be noted.

13 Ending in -ma

Nouns ending in **-ma,** with the genitive singular ending in **-atis** are neuter nouns of Greek origin.

Singular

Nom.	**stigma** (*n.*)	the stigma (as subject)
Acc.	**stigma**	the stigma (as object)
Gen.	**stigmatis**	of the stigma
Dat.	**stigmati**	to or for the stigma
Abl.	**stigmate**	by, with or from the stigma

Plural

Nom.	**stigmata**	the stigmas (as subject)
Acc.	**stigmata**	the stigmas (as object)
Gen.	**stigmatum**	of the stigmas
Dat.	**stigmatibus**	to or for the stigmas
Abl.	**stigmatibus**	by, with or from the stigmas

Similarly declined : *-derma,* skin, *lemma,* lemma, *parenchyma* parenchyma, *-plasma,* plasm, *-sperma,* seed, *rhizoma,* rhizome, *synnema* synnema, *systema,* system, *trichoma,* hair ; and numerous generi names, e.g. *Acanthostigma, Aethionema, Aglaeonema, Alisma, Anemo paegma, Arthroderma, Callostemma, Chorizema, Dictyonema Histoplasma, Metastelma, Microloma, Monostroma, Pachyphragma Phyteuma, Saccoloma, Streblonema.*

4 Ending in **-o**

Nouns ending in **-o**, with the genitive singular in **-inis**, are declined as follows :

Singular

Nom.	**margo** (*m.*)	the margin (as subject)
Acc.	**marginem**	the margin (as object)
Gen.	**marginis**	of the margin
Dat.	**margini**	to or for the margin
Abl.	**margine**	by, with or from the margin

Plural

Nom.	**margines**	the margins (as subject)
Acc.	**margines**	the margins (as object)
Gen.	**marginum**	of the margins
Dat.	**marginibus**	to or for the margins
Abl.	**marginibus**	by, with or from the margins

Similarly declined : *altitudo* (f.), altitude, *cotyledo* (f.), cotyledon, *crassitudo* (f.), thickness, *latitudo* (f.), width, *longitudo* (f.), length, *magnitudo* (f.), size, *ordo* (f.), order ; and many generic names, e.g. *Albugo, Arundo, Ferulago, Plantago, Plumbago, Solidago, Tussilago.*

Nouns ending in **-o**, with the genitive singular in **-onis**, are declined as follows :

Singular

Nom.	**sectio** (*f.*)	the section (as subject)
Acc.	**sectionem**	the section (as object)
Gen.	**sectionis**	of the section
Dat.	**sectioni**	to or for the section
Abl.	**sectione**	by, with or from the section

Plural

Nom.	**sectiones**	the sections (as subject)
Acc.	**sectiones**	the sections (as object)
Gen.	**sectionum**	of the sections
Dat.	**sectionibus**	to or for the sections
Abl.	**sectionibus**	by, with or from the sections

Similarly declined are *aestivatio* (f.), aestivation, *descriptio* (f.), description, *editio* (f.), edition, *embryo* (m.), embryo, *mucro* (f.), mucro, *stolo* (f.), stolon, *vernatio* (f.), vernation ; the generic name *Senecio* (m.) and a few personal names, e.g. *Bello*, gen. sing. *Bellonis.*

15 Ending in **-on**

Nouns of Greek origin ending in **-on** (-ων), with the genitive singular ending in **-onis**, are declined as follows :

B.L.—D

Singular

Nom.	**icon** (*f.*)	the illustration (as subject)
Acc.	**iconem**	the illustration (as object)
Gen.	**iconis**	of the illustration
Dat.	**iconi**	to or for the illustration
Abl.	**icone**	by, with or from the illustration

Plural

Nom.	**icones**	the illustrations (as subject)
Acc.	**icones**	the illustrations (as object)
Gen.	**iconum**	of the illustrations
Dat.	**iconibus**	to or for the illustrations
Abl.	**iconibus**	by, with or from the illustrations

Similarly declined: *siphon* (m.), tube; and many generic names, e.g. *Achylogeton, Cotyledon, Endymion, Dendromecon, Dimorphosiphon, Leptochiton, Ophiopogon, Platycodon, Platystemon, Potamogeton, Rhizopogon, Tragopogon.*

A few ending in **-on** have the genitive singular in **-ontis**, e.g. *Didymodon*, gen. sing. *Didymodontis, Erigeron*, gen. sing. *Erigerontis, Leontodon*, gen. sing. *Leontodontis, Sarcodon*, gen. sing. *Sarcodontis.*

16 Ending in **-or**

Singular

Nom.	**arbor** (*f.*)	the tree (as subject)
Acc.	**arborem**	the tree (as object)
Gen.	**arboris**	of the tree
Dat.	**arbori**	to or for the tree
Abl.	**arbore**	by, with or from the tree

Plural

Nom.	**arbores**	the trees (as subject)
Acc.	**arbores**	the trees (as object)
Gen.	**arborum**	of the trees
Dat.	**arboribus**	to or for the trees
Abl.	**arboribus**	by, with or from the trees

Similarly declined are *auctor* (m.), author, *color* (m.), colour, *editor* (m.), editor, *odor* (m.), scent; and a few generic names, e.g *Mucor*, gen. sing. *Mucoris*, and personal names, e.g. *Hector*, gen. sing. *Hectoris*. Some personal names, e.g. *Taylor*, which could have been treated as Third Declension nouns, are commonly latinized as Second Declension nouns, e.g. *Taylorius*, gen. sing. *Taylorii*, instead of *Taylor*, gen. sing. *Tayloris*.

17 Ending in -os

Singular

Nom.	flos (*m.*)	the flower (as subject)
Acc.	florem	the flower (as object)
Gen.	floris	of the flower
Dat.	flori	to or for the flower
Abl.	flore	by, with or from the flower

Plural

Nom.	flores	the flowers (as subject)
Acc.	flores	the flowers (as object)
Gen.	florum	of the flowers
Dat.	floribus	to or for the flowers
Abl.	floribus	by, with or from the flowers

Similarly declined: *ōs* (n.), mouth, gen. sing. *oris*, abl. sing. *ore*, to be distinguished from *ŏs* (n.), bone, gen. sing. *ossis*, abl. sing. *osse*.

There are also generic names of Greek origin ending in -*ōs* (ως) which are commonly declined by analogy with *rhinoceros* (m.), rhinoceros, gen. sing. *rhinocerotis*, abl. sing. *rhinocerote*. Examples are *Anthoceros, Dendroceros, Macroceros* and *Phaeoceros*; although the pre-Linnaean authors Micheli and Dillenius used the genitive singular *Anthoceri*, post-Linnaean authors, among them Richard Spruce, have preferred the genitive singular *Anthocerotis*, hence the family name *Anthocerotaceae*. *Anacampseros* is similarly declined.

18 Ending in -s after a consonant

Nouns ending in -**bs** are declined as follows:

Singular

Nom.	urbs (*f.*)	the city (as subject)
Acc.	urbem	the city (as object)
Gen.	urbis	of the city
Dat.	urbi	to or for the city
Abl.	urbe	by, with or from the city

Plural

Nom.	urbes	the cities (as subject)
Acc.	urbes	the cities (as object)
Gen.	urbium	of the cities
Dat.	urbibus	to or for the cities
Abl.	urbibus	by, with or from the cities

Nouns ending in -**ms** are few, e.g. *hiems* (f.), winter, gen. sing. *hiemis*.

Nouns ending in -ns are declined as follows:

Singular

Nom.	**dens** (*m.*)	the tooth (as subject)
Acc.	**dentem**	the tooth (as object)
Gen.	**dentis**	of the tooth
Dat.	**denti**	to or for the tooth
Abl.	**dente**	by, with or from the tooth

Plural

Nom.	**dentes**	the teeth (as subject)
Acc.	**dentes**	the teeth (as object)
Gen.	**dentium**	of the teeth
Dat.	**dentibus**	to or for the teeth
Abl.	**dentibus**	by, with or from the teeth

Similarly declined are *lens* (f.), lens, *mons* (m.), mountain, *triens* (m.), a third, and a few generic names, e.g. *Fissidens*, *Impatiens*.

Here belong also some nouns with the stem ending in -*d* (not -*t*), e.g. *frons* (f.), frond, gen. sing. *frondis*, *glans* (f.), gland, gen. sing. *glandis*, *Juglans* (f.), walnut, gen. sing. *Juglandis*.

Nouns ending in -ps are declined as follows:

Singular

Nom.	**stirps** (*f.*)	the plant (as subject)
Acc.	**stirpem**	the plant (as object)
Gen.	**stirpis**	of the plant
Dat.	**stirpi**	to or for the plant
Abl.	**stirpe**	by, with or from the plant

Plural

Nom.	**stirpes**	the plants (as subject)
Acc.	**stirpes**	the plants (as object)
Gen.	**stirpium**	of the plants
Dat.	**stirpibus**	to or for the plants
Abl.	**stirpibus**	by, with or from the plants

A few have a change in the stem from the nominative to other cases, e.g. *princeps* (m.) and the generic name *Claviceps* (f.).

Singular

Nom.	**princeps**	the chief (as subject)
Acc.	**principem**	the chief (as object)
Gen.	**principis**	of the chief
Dat.	**principi**	to or for the chief
Abl.	**principe**	by, with or from the chief

Plural

Nom.	principes	the chiefs (as subject)
Acc.	principes	the chiefs (as object)
Gen.	principum	of the chiefs
Dat.	principibus	to or for the chiefs
Abl.	principibus	by, with or from the chiefs

Singular

Nom.	**Claviceps**
Acc.	**Clavicipitem**
Gen.	**Clavicipitis**
Dat.	**Clavicipiti**
Abl.	**Clavicipite**

Nouns ending in -rs are declined as follows:

Singular

Nom.	**pars** (*f.*)	the part (as subject)
Acc.	**partem**	the part (as object)
Gen.	**partis**	of the part
Dat.	**parti**	to or for the part
Abl.	**parte**	by, with or from the part

Plural

Nom.	**partes**	the parts (as subject)
Acc.	**partes**	the parts (as object)
Gen.	**partium**	of the parts
Dat.	**partibus**	to or for the parts
Abl.	**partibus**	by, with or from the parts

19 Ending in **-us**

Nouns ending in **-us** include *corpus* (n.), body, gen. sing. *corporis*, *crus* (n.), leg, gen. sing. *cruris*, *genus* (n.), genus, gen. sing. *generis*, *latus* (side), gen. sing. *lateris*, declined like *tuber* (p. 77), and *palus* (f.), marsh, gen. sing. *paludis*, declined like *cuspis* (p. 81). For compounds of *-pus* (m.), foot, see p. 99.

20 Ending in **-ut**

Nouns ending in **-ut** are declined as follows:

Singular

Nom.	**caput** (*n.*)	the head (as subject)
Acc.	**caput**	the head (as object)
Gen.	**capitis**	of the head
Dat.	**capiti**	to or for the head
Abl.	**capite**	by, with or from the head

Plural

Nom.	**capita**	the heads (as subject)
Acc.	**capita**	the heads (as object)
Gen.	**capitum**	of the heads
Dat.	**capitibus**	to or for the heads
Abl.	**capitibus**	by, with or from the heads

21 Ending in **-ys**

Nouns ending in **-ys** are of Greek origin and are all generic names compounded from such words as *-botrys* (m.), cluster of grapes, *-chlamys* (f.), mantle, *-drys* (f.), oak, *-pitys* (f.), pine, *-stachys* (f.), spike. Those which in Greek have the genitive in -υδος have the Latin genitive *-ydis*; thus *chlamys*, gen. sing. *chlamydis*, has the derivatives *Chlamydocystis*, *Chlamydomonas*, *Chlamydomyces*, *Chlamydopus* and *Chlamydospora*. Those with the Greek genitive -υος should have the Latin genitive *-yos*; but for *Stachys* botanists have preferred *Stachydis* to *Stachyos* (see p. 66). These are declined as follows:

Singular

Nom.	**Leptochlamys**
Acc.	**Leptochlamydem**
Gen.	**Leptochlamydis**
Dat.	**Leptochlamydi**
Abl.	**Leptochlamyde**

Singular

Nom.	**Hypopitys** (*f.*)
Acc.	**Hypopitym**
Gen.	**Hypopityis**
Dat.	**Hypopityi**
Abl.	**Hypopitye**

22 Ending in **-yx**

Nouns ending in **-yx** with the genitive singular ending in **-ycis** are declined as follows:

Singular

Nom.	**calyx** (*m.*)	the calyx (as subject)
Acc.	**calycem**	the calyx (as object)
Gen.	**calycis**	of the calyx
Dat.	**calyci**	to or for the calyx
Abl.	**calyce**	by, with or from the calyx

Plural

Nom.	**calyces**	the calyces (as subject)
Acc.	**calyces**	the calyces (as object)
Gen.	**calycum**	of the calyces
Dat.	**calycibus**	to or for the calyces

Abl.   calycibus   by, with or from the calyces

Those ending in **-yx** with the genitive singular ending in **-ychis** are declined as follows:

Singular

Nom.	**bostryx** (*m.*)	the bostryx (as subject)
Acc.	**bostrychem**	the bostryx (as object)
Gen.	**bostrychis**	of the bostryx
Dat.	**bostrychi**	to or for the bostryx
Abl.	**bostryche**	by, with or from the bostryx

Plural

Nom.	**bostryches**	the bostryces (as subject)
Acc.	**bostryches**	the bostryces (as object)
Gen.	**bostrychum**	of the bostryces
Dat.	**bostrychibus**	to or for the bostryces
Abl.	**bostrychibus**	by, with or from the bostryces

FOURTH DECLENSION

Nouns of the Fourth Declension (indicated by IV in the Vocabulary) have their stem ending in *-u,* the nominative singular in *-us* or *-u,* the genitive singular in *-us*; e.g. *cornu* (n.), horn, stem *cornu-*, gen. sing. *cornus.* Nouns ending in *-us* are mostly masculine, although *quercus* (oak), *manus* (hand) and *tribus* (tribe) are feminine. Nouns ending in *-u* are neuter. Their declension is as follows:

Singular

Nom.	**cornu** (*n.*)	the horn (as subject)
Acc.	**cornu**	the horn (as object)
Gen.	**cornus**	of the horn
Dat.	**cornui**	to or for the horn
Abl.	**cornu**	by, with or from the horn

Plural

Nom.	**cornua**	the horns (as subject)
Acc.	**cornua**	the horns (as object)
Gen.	**cornuum**	of the horns
Dat.	**cornibus**	to or for the horns
Abl.	**cornibus**	by, with or from the horns

Singular

Nom.	**fructus** (*m.*)	the fruit (as subject)
Acc.	**fructum**	the fruit (as object)
Gen.	**fructus**	of the fruit
Dat.	**fructui**	to or for the fruit
Abl.	**fructu**	by, with or from the fruit

Plural

Nom.	**fructus**	the fruits (as subject)
Acc.	**fructus**	the fruits (as object)
Gen.	**fructuum**	of the fruits
Dat.	**fructibus**	to or for the fruits
Abl.	**fructibus**	by, with or from the fruits

Declined like *fructus* are *ambitus* (m.), outline, *conspectus* (m.), survey, *gradus* (m.), grade, *habitus* (m.), habit, *lacus* (m.), lake, *lapsus* (m.), mistake, *sensus* (m.), sense, *sexus* (m.), sex, *situs* (m.), position, *status* (m.), standing, *tribus* (f.), tribe, and *usus* (m.), use. The dative and ablative plural of *lacus* and *tribus* are, however, *lacubus* and *tribubus*

FIFTH DECLENSION

Nouns of the Fifth Declension (indicated by V in the Vocabulary) have their stem ending in -*e*, the nominative singular in -*s* and the genitive singular in -*i*, e.g. *facies*, stem *facie*-, gen sing. *faciei*. They are all feminine except *dies* (m.), day, and *meridies* (m.), midday.

Singular

Nom.	**species** (*f.*)	the species (as subject)
Acc.	**speciem**	the species (as object)
Gen.	**speciei**	of the species
Dat.	**speciei**	to or for the species
Abl.	**specie**	by, with or from the species

Plural

Nom.	**species**	the species (as subject)
Acc.	**species**	the species (as object)
Gen.	**specierum**	of the species
Dat.	**speciebus**	to or for the species
Abl.	**speciebus**	by, with or from the species

Similarly declined: *crassities*, thickness, *facies*, appearance, *fides*, trust, faith, *planities*, plain, *res*, thing, *series*, series, *spes*, hope, *superficies*, surface.

CHAPTER VI

Adjectives and Participles

ADJECTIVES

Adjectives, as Cobbett wrote in his *Grammar* (1819), consist of 'words which are added or put to Nouns, in order to express something relating to the nouns, which something could not be expressed without the help of Adjectives. . . . I want you to go and catch a *turkey*; but I also want you to catch a *white* turkey, and not only a white turkey, but a *large* turkey. Therefore I add, or put, to the noun, the words *white* and *large*, which, therefore, are called Adjectives.' They are dependent words 'added to the name of a thing to describe the thing more fully'. Botanical Latin has a very rich store of such words. Added to generic names they serve as specific epithets, e.g. *Rosa alba*, *R. canina*, *R. carolina*, *R. centifolia*, *R. cinnamomea*. Added to the names of organs they build up the description of the plant, e.g. *flos solitarius nutans ruber* (flower solitary nodding red). In Latin they must agree as to gender, number and case with the nouns they qualify, e.g. *Asparagus albus* (m.), *Betula alba* (f.), *Chenopodium album* (n.). A masculine noun, for example, in the ablative singular must be accompanied by adjectives in the masculine ablative singular, e.g. *flore solitario nutanti rubro*; if they do not thus agree with the noun they qualify, then they may be interpreted as belonging not to it but to something else. Whereas a noun has normally only one gender, adjectives exist in masculine, feminine and neuter states. They have the same five cases as nouns, but for purposes of declension Latin adjectives fall into two main groups distinguished below and in the Vocabulary as A and B; certain adjectives of Greek origin ending in *-es*, etc., are treated as Group C.

PARTICIPLES

Participles are parts of verbs with the functions of adjectives and are used and declined in the same way. Active present participles (treated like Group B adjectives) are exemplified by *attingens* (reaching) *ascendens* (ascending), *emittens* (putting forth), *formans* (forming) *fragrans* (smelling, scented), *nitens* (shining, glossy), *nutans* (nodding hanging), *repens* (creeping), *superans* (overtopping).   Passive pas participles (treated like Group A adjectives) are exemplified by *apertu* (opened), *connatus* (united), *contractus* (drawn together), *dispositu* (arranged), *divisus* (divided), *instructus* (provided with), *lectus* (gathered) *reflexus* (turned back), *visus* (seen).

THE GERUNDIVE

The GERUNDIVE is a kind of participle, passive in meaning, implyin; fitness or potentiality for an act or directing what is to be done, and i used occasionally as a specific epithet, e.g. in *Rhododendron amandum* or in such phrases as *nomen genericum conservandum* (generic name t(be kept), *species excludendae* (species to be excluded), more often t(end a diagnosis, e.g. *species floribus majoribus distinguenda* (species b; its larger flowers to be distinguished).

GROUP A

Adjectives and participles of this group have the nominative singula; endings *-us* (masculine), *-a* (feminine), *-um* (neuter) or *-er* (masculine) *-ra* (feminine), *-rum* (neuter), e.g. *altus, -a, -um* (tall), *ruber, rubra rubrum* (red). Their case-endings are those of nouns of Declension; I and II.

Singular

	M.	F.	N.	
Nom.	longus	longa	longum	the long . . . (as subject)
Acc.	longum	longam	longum	the long . . . (as object)
Gen.	longi	longae	longi	of the long . . .
Dat.	longo	longae	longo	to or for the long . . .
Abl.	longo	longa	longo	by, with or from the long . .

Plural

	M.	F.	N.	
Nom.	longi	longae	longa	the long . . . (as subject)
Acc.	longos	longas	longa	the long . . . (as object)
Gen.	longorum	longarum	longorum	of the long . . .
Dat.	longis	longis	longis	to or for the long . . .
Abl.	longis	longis	longis	by, with or from the long . .

Among the many adjectives and participles declined as above are *acutus* (acute), *albus* (white), *altus* (tall), *crassus* (thick), *cuneatu.* (wedge-shaped), *curvatus* (curved), *ellipticus* (elliptic), *elongatus* (elon-gated), *-fidus* (-split), *hirsutus* (hairy), *lanceolatus* (lanceolate), *latu.*

(broad), *magnus* (big), *nullus* (lacking), *obtusus* (blunt), *ovatus* (ovate), *ovoideus* (ovoid), *parvus* (small), *rotundatus* (rounded), *sparsus* (sparse), *vestitus* (clothed), and geographical adjectives such as *americanus* (American), *anglicus* (English), *hibernicus* (Irish), *lutetianus* (of Paris), *monspeliacus* (of Montpellier).

The gerundives *addendus* (to be added), *conservandus* (to be retained), *distinguendus* (to be distinguished), *excludendus* (to be excluded) are similarly declined.

Singular

	M.	F.	N.
Nom.	florifer	florifera	floriferum
Acc.	floriferum	floriferam	floriferum
Gen.	floriferi	floriferae	floriferi
Dat.	florifero	floriferae	florifero
Abl.	florifero	florifera	florifero

Plural

	M.	F.	N.
Nom.	floriferi	floriferae	florifera
Acc.	floriferos	floriferas	florifera
Gen.	floriferorum	floriferarum	floriferorum
Dat.	floriferis	floriferis	floriferis
Abl.	floriferis	floriferis	floriferis

Like *florifer* (flower-bearing) are declined other compounds of *-fer* and *-ger* as *bulbiger* (bulb-bearing), *fructiger* (fruit-bearing), and adjectives such as *asper* (rough), *lacer* (torn), *liber* (free), *tener* (thin).

Singular

	M.	F.	N.
Nom.	glaber	glabra	glabrum
Acc.	glabrum	glabram	glabrum
Gen.	glabri	glabrae	glabri
Dat.	glabro	glabrae	glabro
Abl.	glabro	glabra	glabro

Plural

	M.	F.	N.
Nom.	glabri	glabrae	glabra
Acc.	glabros	glabras	glabra
Gen.	glabrorum	glabrarum	glabrorum
Dat.	glabris	glabris	glabris
Abl.	glabris	glabris	glabris

Like *glaber* (glabrous) are declined *ater* (black), *integer* (entire), *niger* (black), *pulcher* (beautiful), *ruber* (red), *scaber* (rough).

GROUP B

Adjectives and participles of this group have the nominative singular endings *-is* (masculine and feminine), *-e* (neuter) or *-er* (masculine), *-ris* (feminine), -re (neuter), or -x, -ens, -ans (the same for all genders). Their case-endings are those of Declension III, except that the ablative singular is formed in -i, to avoid confusion with neuter nominative and accusative, whereas ablative singular in -e is markedly more common in Third Declension nouns; the genitive plural ends in -ium.

1 Adjectives with masculine and feminine nominative singular ending in -is, the neuter in -e :

Singular

	M. & F.	N.	
Nom.	brevis	breve	the short . . . (as subject)
Acc.	brevem	breve	the short . . . (as object)
Gen.	brevis	brevis	of the short . . .
Dat.	brevi	brevi	to or for the short . . .
Abl.	brevi	brevi	by, with or from the short . . .

Plural

	M. & F.	N.	
Nom.	breves	brevia	the short . . . (as subject)
Acc.	breves	brevia	the short . . . (as object)
Gen.	brevium	brevium	of the short . . .
Dat.	brevibus	brevibus	to or for the short . . .
Abl.	brevibus	brevibus	by, with or from the short . . .

Singular

	M. & F.	N.
Nom.	lateralis	laterale
Acc.	lateralem	laterale
Gen.	lateralis	lateralis
Dat.	laterali	laterali
Abl.	laterali	laterali

Plural

	M. & F.	N.
Nom.	laterales	lateralia
Acc.	laterales	lateralia
Gen.	lateralium	lateralium
Dat.	lateralibus	lateralibus
Abl.	lateralibus	lateralibus

Like *brevis* (short) and *lateralis* (lateral) are declined *acaulis* (stemless), *affinis* (related), *communis* (common), *edulis* (edible), *fertilis* (fertile), *-formis* (-shaped, as in *cupuliformis, ensiformis, filiformis, fusiformis*, etc.), *-glumis* (-glumed), *gracilis* (slender), *humilis* (low), *laevis* (smooth), *linearis* (linear), *mollis* (soft), *-nervis* (-nerved, as in *paucinervis, multinervis*), *-nodis* (-noded), *omnis* (all), *orbicularis* (orbicular), *originalis* (original), *perennis* (perennial), *sessilis* (sessile), *similis* (like), *tenuis* (thin), *terminalis* (terminal), *viridis* (green), *volubilis* (twining), and other adjectives with the masculine and feminine nominative singular ending in -is, -alis, -aris, -ibilis, -ens, -ilis, among them being compounds of *-caulis* (-stemmed), *-cornis* (-horned) and *-rostris* (-beaked) and most geographical epithets, as *berolinensis* (of Berlin), *cantabrigiensis* (of Cambridge), *lugdunensis* (of Lyons), *monspeliensis* (of Montpellier), *nepalensis* (of Nepal), *oxoniensis* (of Oxford), *parisiensis* (of Paris), *sinensis* (of China), *vindobonensis* (of Vienna).

Here belong in botanical Latin the adjectives *acris* (bitter), *campestris* (relating to plains), *palustris* (marshy), *sylvestris* (woodland, wild) and *terrestris* (earthy), with the nominative masculine singular ending in *-is*, following the usage of Linnaeus, exemplified by *Lathyrus palustris*, *Lathyrus sylvestris*, *Ranunculus acris*, *Scirpus palustris*, *Sonchus palustris*, although in classical Latin these possessed a nominative masculine singular in *-er*, i.e. *acer, campester, paluster, silvester, terrester.*

2 Adjectives and participles with the nominative singular the same in all genders :

Singular

	M. & F.	N.	
Nom.	**simplex**	**simplex**	the simple . . . (as subject)
Acc.	**simplicem**	**simplex**	the simple . . . (as object)
Gen.	**simplicis**	**simplicis**	of the simple . . .
Dat.	**simplici**	**simplici**	to or for the simple . . .
Abl.	**simplici**	**simplici**	by, with or from the simple . . .

Plural

	M. & F.	N.	
Nom.	**simplices**	**simplicia**	the simple . . . (as subject)
Acc.	**simplices**	**simplicia**	the simple . . . (as object)
Gen.	**simplicium**	**simplicium**	of the simple . . .
Dat.	**simplicibus**	**simplicibus**	to or for the simple . . .
Abl.	**simplicibus**	**simplicibus**	by, with or from the simple . . .

Like *simplex* (simple, undivided) are declined *duplex* (twofold), *fallax* (false), *praecox* (early), *tenax* (tough), *triplex* (threefold).

Singular

	M. & F.	N.
Nom.	**repens**	**repens**
Acc.	**repentem**	**repens**
Gen.	**repentis**	**repentis**
Dat.	**repenti**	**repenti**
Abl.	**repenti (-e)**	**repenti (-e)**

Plural

	M. & F.	N.
Nom.	**repentes**	**repentia**
Acc.	**repentes**	**repentia**
Gen.	**repentium**	**repentium**
Dat.	**repentibus**	**repentibus**
Abl.	**repentibus**	**repentibus**

Like *repens* (creeping) are declined other present participles such as *abiens* (departing), *percurrens* (running through), *spectans* (facing, situated towards) (see above, p. 92), adjectives such as *elegans* (elegant), *pubescens* (pubescent) and *recens* (recent), and compounds of *-dens* (toothed), e.g. *brevidens* (short-toothed).

Singular

	M. & F.	N.
Nom.	bicolor	bicolor
Acc.	bicolorem	bicolor
Gen.	bicoloris	bicoloris
Dat.	bicolori	bicolori
Abl.	bicolori	bicolori

Plural

	M. & F.	N.
Nom.	bicolores	bicoloria
Acc.	bicolores	bicoloria
Gen.	bicolorium	bicolorium
Dat.	bicoloribus	bicoloribus
Abl.	bicoloribus	bicoloribus

Like *bicolor* (two-coloured) are declined *multicolor* (many-coloured), *tricolor* (three-coloured), etc.

To Group B also belong various adjectives with unusual nominative endings as *brevipes* (short-footed ; gen. sing. *brevipedis*, abl. sing. *brevipedi*) and other compounds of *-pes*, *longicuspis* (long-cusped ; gen. sing. *longicuspidis*, abl. sing. *longicuspidi*) and other compounds of *-cuspis*, par (equal, paired ; gen. sing. *paris*, abl. sing. *pari*), impar (unequal), *teres* (terete ; gen. sing. *teretis*, abl. sing. *tereti*), *multiceps* (many-headed ; gen. sing. *multicipitis*, abl. sing. *multicipiti*) and other compounds of *-ceps*. Most of such adjectives are really nouns given an adjectival function.

Vetus (old) differs from most other adjectives of Group B in having the ablative singular preferably ending in *-e* not *-i*.

Singular

	M. & F.	N.
Nom.	vetus	vetus
Acc.	veterem	vetus
Gen.	veteris	veteris
Dat.	veteri	veteri
Abl.	vetere	vetere

Plural

	M. & F.	N.
Nom.	veteres	vetera
Acc.	veteres	vetera
Gen.	veterum	veterum
Dat.	veteribus	veteribus
Abl.	veteribus	veteribus

GROUP C

Adjectives of Greek origin, whether directly transliterated from Greek (see Chapter XIX, pp. 260-263) or newly compounded of Greek elements, are mostly used as specific epithets in large genera. When given a Latinized ending in -*us*, as in *arachnoideus* (spidery), *callibotryus* (with beautiful clusters), *leptochilus* (slender-lipped), *macranthus* (large-flowered), *micromerus* (with small parts), *platyphyllus* (broad-leaved), *polychromus* (many-coloured), *rhodorrhizus* (red-rooted), etc., they are treated as ordinary Group A adjectives. Those with Greek endings in -*es*, -*ys*, etc., raise difficulties of declension.

Adjectives ending in -*oides* (resembling) are declined as follows:

Singular

	M. & F.	N.	
Nom.	bryoides	bryoides	the moss-like . . . (as subject)
Acc.	bryoidem	bryoides	the moss-like . . . (as object)
Gen.	bryoidis	bryoidis	of the moss-like . . .
Dat.	bryoidi	bryoidi	to or for the moss-like . . .
Abl.	bryoide	bryoide	by, with or from the moss-like . . .

Plural

Nom.	bryoides	bryoida	the moss-like . . . (as subject)
Acc.	bryoides	bryoida	the moss-like . . . (as object)
Gen.	bryoidum	bryoidum	of the moss-like . . .
Dat.	bryoidibus	bryoidibus	to or for the moss-like . . .
Abl.	bryoidibus	bryoidibus	by, with or from the moss-like . . .

Adjectives ending in -*odes* are similarly declined:

Singular

	M. & F.	N.
Nom.	epiphloeodes	epiphloeodes
Acc.	epiphloeodem	epiphloeodes
Gen.	epiphloeodis	epiphloeodis
Dat.	epiphloeodi	epiphloeodi
Abl.	epiphloeode	epiphloeode

Plural

Nom.	epiphloeodes	epiphloeoda
Acc.	epiphloeodes	epiphloeoda
Gen.	epiphloeodum	epiphloeodum
Dat.	epiphloeodibus	epiphloeodibus
Abl.	epiphloeodibus	epiphloeodibus

Like *epiphloeodes* (epiphloeodal, i.e. growing on the bark) are declined *endophloeodes* (endophloeodal, i.e. growing within the bark), *euodes* (well-scented), *haematodes* (blood-like) and *physodes* (bladder-like).

Such epithets as *aloides*, *alismoides*, *hyacinthoides*, *orchidoides*, *phlomoides*, etc., indicating resemblance to the genera *Aloe*, *Alisma*, *Hyacinthus*, *Orchis*, *Phlomis*, etc., *allantoides* (sausage-like), *deltoides* (triangular), are similarly declined.

NOUNS FUNCTIONING AS ADJECTIVES

An epithet which is really a noun in apposition given an adjectival function should usually be declined like that noun from which it is derived without reference to the gender of the associated generic name.

Singular

Nom.	-botrys	-glochin	-odon
Acc.	-botryn	-glochinem	-dontem
Gen.	-botryis	-glochinis	-odontis
Dat.	-botryi	-glochini	-odonti
Abl.	-botrye	-glochine	-odonte

Plural

Nom.	-botryes	-glochines	-odontes
Acc.	-botryes	-glochines	-odontes
Gen.	-botryum	-glochinum	-odontum
Dat.	-botryibus	-glochinibus	-odontibus
Abl.	-botryibus	-glochinibus	-odontibus

Singular

Nom.	-ops	-pogon	-stachys
Acc.	-opem	-pogonem	-stachydem
Gen.	-opis	-pogonis	-stachydis
Dat.	-opi	-pogoni	-stachydi
Abl.	-ope	-pogone	-stachyde

Plural

Nom.	-opes	-pogones	-stachydes
Acc.	-opes	-pogones	-stachydes
Gen.	-opum	-pogonum	-stachydum
Dat.	-opibus	-pogonibus	-stachydibus
Abl.	-opibus	-pogonibus	-stachydibus

Singular

Nom.	-stemon	-stylis	-thrix
Acc.	-stemonem	-stylidem	-trichem
Gen.	-stemonis	-stylidis	-trichis
Dat.	-stemoni	-stylidi	-trichi
Abl.	-stemone	-stylide	-triche

Plural

Nom.	-stemones	-stylides	-triches
Acc.	-stemones	-stylides	-triches
Gen.	-stemonum	-stylidum	-trichum
Dat.	-stemonibus	-stylidibus	-trichibus
Abl.	-stemonibus	-stylidibus	-trichibus

Some examples of the above are *brachybotrys* (with short raceme), *microglochin* (with small point), *oligodon* (with few teeth), *chrysopogon* (with golden beard), *melanops* (with black eye), *macrostachys* (with large spike), *corynestemon* (with club-shaped stamen), *rhopalostylis* (with club-shaped style), *pyrrhothrix* (with fiery hair).

Compounds of *-pus* (-footed, -based), acc. sing. *-podem*, gen. sing. *-podis*, such as *apus* (footless, sessile), *micropus* (small-footed, with small base or stalk), are similarly declined; there are corresponding compounds of *-podus* (-footed), such as *apodus*, *micropodus*, all derived from Greek.

COMPARISON OF ADJECTIVES

The ordinary state of an adjective, e.g. 'long' (*longus*), is grammatically known as its *positive* degree; its state denoting an increase of the quality concerned, e.g. 'longer', 'rather long' (*longior*), is known as its *comparative* degree, and its state denoting the utmost attainable or an extreme form, e.g. 'longest', 'very long' (*longissimus*), as its *superlative* degree. In Latin the comparative is formed by adding *-ior* (for masculine and feminine) and *-ius* (for neuter) to the stem of the positive, thus *longior*, *longius* (longer) from *longus* (long). The superlative is formed by adding *-issimus* (masculine), *-issima* (feminine) and *-issimum* (neuter) to the stem, thus *longissimus* (most long), except for adjectives ending in *-er* which add *-rimus*, e.g. *tenerrimus* (most thin) from *tener* (thin), and a few ending in *-ilis*, which double the *l* and add *-imus*, e.g. *gracillimus* (most slender) from *gracilis* (slender).

The Comparative is declined as follows:

Singular

	M. & F.	N.	
Nom.	longior	longius	the longer . . . (as subject)
Acc.	longiorem	longius	the longer . . . (as object)
Gen.	longioris	longioris	of the longer . . .
Dat.	longiori	longiori	to or for the longer . . .
Abl.	longiore	longiore	by, with or from the longer . . .

Plural

Nom.	longiores	longiora	the longer . . . (as subject)
Acc.	longiores	longiora	the longer . . . (as object)

Gen.	**longiorum**	**longiorum**	of the longer . . .
Dat.	**longioribus**	**longioribus**	to or for the longer . . .
Abl.	**longioribus**	**longioribus**	by, with or from the longer . . .

Thus 'leaves longer than the spines' would be translated by *folia spinis longiora*, 'leaves shorter than the spines' by *folia spinis breviora* (see Chapter VIII, pp. 115-118).

The Superlative is declined as follows:

Singular

	M.	F.	N.	
Nom.	**longissimus**	**longissima**	**longissimum**	the longest . . . (as subject)
Acc.	**longissimum**	**longissimam**	**longissimum**	the longest . . . (as object)
Gen.	**longissimi**	**longissimae**	**longissimi**	of the longest . . .
Dat.	**longissimo**	**longissimae**	**longissimo**	to or for the longest . .
Abl.	**longissimo**	**longissima**	**longissimo**	by, with or from the longest . . .

Plural

Nom.	**longissimi**	**longissimae**	**longissima**	the longest . . . (as subject)
Acc.	**longissimos**	**longissimas**	**longissima**	the longest . . . (as object)
Gen.	**longissimorum**	**longissimarum**	**longissimorum**	of the longest . . .
Dat.	**longissimis**	**longissimis**	**longissimis**	to or for the longest . . .
Abl.	**longissimis**	**longissimis**	**longissimis**	by, with or from the longest . . .

Unfortunately there are a few adjectives with comparatives and superlatives not formed as above, e.g. *bonus, -a, -um*, good, *melior* (m. & f.), *melius* (n.), better, *optimus, -a, -um*, best; *externus, -a, -um*, outside, *exterior* (m. & f.), *exterius* (n.), outer, *extremus, -a, -um*, outermost; *inferus, -a, -um*, lower, *inferior* (m. & f.), *inferius* (n.), lower, *infimus, -a, -um* or *imus, -a, -um*, lowest; *internus, -a, -um*, inside, *interior* (m. & f.), *interius* (n.), inner, *intimus, -a, -um*, innermost; *magnus, -a, -um*, great, *major* (m. & f.), *majus* (n.), greater, *maximus, -a, -um*, greatest; *multi, -ae, -a* (plural), many, *plures* (m. & f.), *plura* (n.), more, *plurimi, -ae, -a*, most.

Comparison of adjectives ending in *-eus, -ius* and *-uus* is usually made by adding the adverbs *magis* (more), *maxime* (most) to the positive, e.g. *dubius* (doubtful), *magis dubius* (more doubtful), *maxime dubius* (most doubtful).

EXAMPLES OF NOUNS AND ADJECTIVES
DECLINED TOGETHER

1 Masculine noun: *ramulus* (branchlet)

Singular

Nom.	ramulus	glaber	rigidus	gracilis	simplex
	(branchlet)	(glabrous)	(rigid)	(slender)	(unbranched)
Acc.	ramulum	glabrum	rigidum	gracilem	simplicem
Gen.	ramuli	glabri	rigidi	gracilis	simplicis
Dat.	ramulo	glabro	rigido	gracili	simplici
Abl.	ramulo	glabro	rigido	gracili	simplici

Plural

Nom.	ramuli	glabri	rigidi	graciles	simplices
Acc.	ramulos	glabros	rigidos	graciles	simplices
Gen.	ramulorum	glabrorum	rigidorum	gracilium	simplicium
Dat.	ramulis	glabris	rigidis	gracilibus	simplicibus
Abl.	ramulis	glabris	rigidis	gracilibus	simplicibus

2 Feminine noun: *corolla* (corolla)

Singular

Nom.	corolla	glabra	alba	patens	tenuis
	(corolla)	(glabrous)	(white)	(outspread)	(thin)
Acc.	corollam	glabram	albam	patentem	tenuem
Gen.	corollae	glabrae	albae	patentis	tenuis
Dat.	corollae	glabrae	albae	patenti	tenui
Abl.	corolla	glabra	alba	patenti	tenui

Plural

Nom.	corollae	glabrae	albae	patentes	tenues
Acc.	corollas	glabras	albas	patentes	tenues
Gen.	corollarum	glabrarum	albarum	patentium	tenuium
Dat.	corollis	glabris	albis	patentibus	tenuibus
Abl.	corollis	glabris	albis	patentibus	tenuibus

3 Neuter noun: *folium* (leaf)

Singular

Nom.	folium	glabrum	ovatum	ascendens	sessile
	(leaf)	(glabrous)	(ovate)	(ascending)	(sessile)
Acc.	folium	glabrum	ovatum	ascendens	sessile
Gen.	folii	glabri	ovati	ascendentis	sessilis
Dat.	folio	glabro	ovato	ascendenti	sessili
Abl.	folio	glabro	ovato	ascendenti	sessili

Plural

Nom.	folia	glabra	ovata	ascendentia	sessilia
Acc.	folia	glabra	ovata	ascendentia	sessilia
Gen.	foliorum	glabrorum	ovatorum	ascendentium	sessilium
Dat.	foliis	glabris	ovatis	ascendentibus	sessilibus
Abl.	foliis	glabris	ovatis	ascendentibus	sessilibus

POSITION AND CONCORD OF ADJECTIVES

In formal descriptions (see Chapter XIV) an adjective always comes after the noun it qualifies ; in observations and annotations, following classical precedent, it may for emphasis sometimes be placed before the noun.

When two or more nouns of the same gender are qualified by the same adjective, this has the same gender as and takes its number from the noun nearest to it, e.g. *caulis et petiolus glaber* (stem and petiole glabrous), *spatha et corollae glabrae* (spathe and corollas glabrous), *androecium et gynoecium glabrum* (androecium and gynoecium glabrous), or the plural (same gender or neuter) can be used, e.g. *species et forma novae*.

When two nouns are linked by *cum* (with), they are regarded as forming a single unit, and, if the main noun is singular, then the adjective qualifying them will be likewise singular and agree in gender with the main noun, e.g. *lamina cum petiolo 10 cm. longa* (blade together with the petiole 10 cm. long).

When nouns of different gender are qualified by the same adjective, this takes the number and gender of the noun nearest to it, e.g. *calyx et corolla glabra* (calyx and corolla glabrous), *corolla et androecium glabrum* (corolla and androecium glabrous), *androecium et stylus glaber* (androecium and style glabrous), or its neuter plural can be used, e.g. *androecium et stylus glabra*. For emphasis or to avoid ambiguity, the adjective can be repeated after each noun; it then agrees in number and gender with the noun it qualifies, e.g. *caulis glaber, folium glabrum* (stem glabrous, leaf glabrous), *caulis glaber, folia glabra* (stem glabrous, leaves glabrous).

ADJECTIVES AS NAMES OF TAXONOMIC CATEGORIES

The ancients used a number of adjectives as nouns, the qualified word presumably being dropped as redundant. The names of many taxonomic groups in modern systematic botany are similarly of adjectival origin or have been coined by the aid of feminine plural adjectival endings to agree with *plantae*. Under the *International Code of botanical Nomenclature*, particular adjectival plural endings are used to indicate the rank of the group concerned, a method introduced by Lindley in his *Natural System of Botany*, 2nd ed. (1836), where he made all the names of divisions of the same value end in the same way. As he stated, 'the orders [i.e. families] are here distinguished by ending in *aceae*, the suborders [i.e. subfamilies and tribes] in *eae*, the alliances [i.e. orders] in *ales* and the groups [i.e. classes] in *osae*'.

The name of an order (*ordo*) based on the stem of the name of a family has the ending -*ales*, e.g. *Agaricales* from *Agaricaceae*. This is the feminine (and also the masculine) nominative plural ending of group A adjectives such as *muralis* with the suffix -*alis* meaning 'connected with, pertaining to'.

The name of a suborder (*subordo*) based on the name of a family has the ending -*ineae*, e.g. *Solanineae* from *Solanum*. This is the feminine nominative plural ending of group A adjectives such as *cartilagineus* with the suffix -*ineus* indicating resemblance or possession.

The name of a family (*familia*), excluding a few very old names such as *Labiatae*, *Umbelliferae*, *Gramineae*, is formed by adding the ending -*aceae* to the stem of a legitimate name of an included genus, e.g. *Cyatheaceae* from *Cyathea*. This is the feminine nominative plural ending of group A adjectives such as *membranaceus* with the suffix -*aceus* meaning 'made of, resembling'.

The name of a subfamily (*subfamilia*) is similarly formed by adding -*oideae* to the stem of the legitimate name of an included genus, e.g. *Boraginoideae* from *Borago*. This is the feminine nominative plural ending of group A adjectives such as *arachnoideus* with the suffix -*oideus* indicating resemblance. A tribe (*tribus*) is designated likewise but with the ending -*eae* (which is the feminine nominative plural ending of the suffix -*eus*), e.g. *Cyatheeae* from *Cyathea*, and a subtribe (*subtribus*) with the ending -*inae* (from -*inus*).

A generic name formed by treating an adjective as a noun takes its gender from the ending adopted, which is usually feminine, e.g. *Gloriosa* (nominative feminine singular of *gloriosus*).

The name of a subsection or series, i.e. of a group of closely allied species forming a subdivision of a genus below the rank of section, is preferably a plural adjective agreeing in gender with the generic name, e.g. *Cotoneaster* series *Distichi*, series *Microphylli*, etc., *Pedicularis* series *Siphonanthae*, series *Graciles*, series *Myriophyllae*, etc., *Rhododendron* subsect. *Campylogyna*, subsect. *Lepidota*, subsect. *Baileya*, etc. The first authors to employ formally the term *series* were Alexander von Bunge in his revision of *Acantholimon* (1872), wherein he distinguished the series *Microcalycina*, series *Rhodocalycina*, etc., and Carl von Maximowicz in his synopsis of *Lespedeza* (1873), the subgenus *Lespedeza* sect. *Eu-Lespedeza* being here divided into series *Violaceae*, series *Junceae*, etc., and in his publications on *Ribes* (1873), *Cnicus* (1874), *Chrysosplenium* (1876), *Pedicularis* (1877), *Spiraea* (1879), *Viburnum* (1880), etc. (cf. E. G. Bobrov in *Bot. Zhurn.* 44: 1553–1556; 1959). From these Russian publications the term *series* passed into British and German use. Following Maximowicz's example, the name (epithet) of a series is usually the nominative plural of the specific epithet of the best-known or most typical member of the series.

CHAPTER VII

Adverbs

An adverb is a word added to a verb, an adjective or another adverb, but not to a noun or pronoun, to give it greater precision, usually by limiting its meaning. Thus the verb *moveo* refers to any kind of movement; the addition of the adverb *celeriter* (swiftly) would restrict it to rapid movement; the addition of the adverb *tarde* (slowly) would restrict it to slow movement. Just as adverbs are formed from adjectives in English, usually by adding the termination '-ly', as 'rapidly' from 'rapid', in Latin they are formed from adjectives by adding to the stem *-e* (in adjectives of First and Second Declension) or *-ter* or *-iter* (in adjectives of the Third Declension), as *dense* (densely) from *densus* (dense), *frequenter* (frequently) from *frequens* (frequent), *irregulariter* (irregularly) from *irregularis* (irregular). The ablative of some adjectives, pronouns and nouns is also used as an adverb, thus producing adverbs ending in *-o*, as *falso* (falsely), *primo* (firstly), *vulgo* (commonly). The accusative singular neuter of many adjectives and pronouns likewise can serve as an adverb, e.g. *ceterum* (for the rest), *multum* (much), *paulum* (little), *primum* (first). Many adverbs, however, end in *-tim*, e.g. *gradatim* (step by step, gradually) derived through *gradatus* (furnished with steps) from *gradus* (a step), or *-im*, e.g. *sensim* (sensibly, gradually) from *sentio* (be sensible of, perceive). A few adverbs referring to origin end in *-tus*, e.g. *penitus* (deep within, from the innermost part), *intus* (inside, from within). Occasionally two adverbs identical except for the ending have a slight difference in meaning, e.g. *certe* (at least) and *certo* (certainly), *rare* (thinly) and *raro* (seldom), *crebre* (closely, repeatedly) and *crebro* (repeatedly). Adverbs thus display much diversity of ending.

The comparative of an adverb is taken from the accusative singular neuter of the comparative of the corresponding adjective, e.g. *alte* (loftily) has the comparative *altius* (more loftily) from *altus* (lofty, high); likewise *plus* (more) connects with *multum* (much). The superlative of an adverb is formed from the superlative of the corresponding adjective by means of the termination *-e*, e.g. *altissime* (most loftily) from *altissimus* (most lofty), *densissime* (most densely) from *densissimus* (most dense).

The following adverbs occur in botanical Latin:

abrupte: abruptly
acute: acutely
adhuc: until now, as yet
admodum: quite
aegre: unwillingly, hardly, scarcely
aeque: in the manner, equally
aequaliter: uniformly, equally
aliquantum: somewhat
aliter: otherwise
alte: loftily
alternatim: alternately
altius: more loftily
anguste: narrowly
antea: before this, formerly
antice: anteriorly, in the front
arcte (arte): closely, firmly
arcuatim: in the form of a bow, archedly
argute: acutely, sharply
attamen: and that although
bene: well, ably, rightly (opp. to male)
benevole, benigne: kindly
bifariam: on two sides
binatim: in twos
breviter: shortly, briefly
celeriter: quickly
certe: at least
certo: certainly
cetero, ceterum (caeterum): for the rest, besides
cito: quickly
conspicuo: conspicuously
crasse: thickly
crebre: closely, compactly
crebriter, crebro: repeatedly
deinde: thereafter, next
demum: at length
denique: lastly
dense: thickly, closely
deorsum: downwards (opp. to sursum)
dextrorsum: to the right
difficile, difficiliter, difficulter: with difficulty

dilute: slightly, weakly, palely
distincte: distinctly, clearly
diu: a long while, long (in time)
egregie: eminently, excellently
eleganter: gracefully, finely
eodem: to the same place
eximie: excellently
extra, extus: on the outside (opp. to intra, intus)
extrinsecus: from without, outside
facile: easily
falso: falsely, incorrectly
fere: almost, nearly
forsan, forsitan, fortasse: perhaps
fortiter: strongly
frequenter: frequently
gradatim: little by little, gradually
grosse: thickly, coarsely
haud: not at all
hic: here
hinc: hence
hinc inde: on this side and on that side
ibidem: in the same place
identidem: repeatedly
ideo: on that account, for that reason, therefore
inde: from that place, thereafter
infauste: unfortunately, unluckily
inferne: below
initio: at first
inprimis (imprimis): among the first, chiefly, especially
insigniter: remarkably, notably
insuper: moreover
interdum: now and then, sometimes
intra: on the inside
intrinsecus: inwardly, inwards
introrsum: towards the inside
intus: on the inside (opp. to extra, extus)
irregulariter: irregularly
iterum: again, a second time, once more

itidem : in the same way, in like manner
jam (iam) : now, already
late : broadly
lateraliter : laterally
laxe : loosely
leniter : gently, moderately
lente : slowly
leviter : lightly, not heavily
longe : long (opp. to **breviter**)
longitudinaliter : longitudinally
magis : more
magnopere : greatly, very much
male : badly (opp. to **bene**)
manifeste : evidently, manifestly
minime : least of all, very little
minute : minutely
minutissime : most minutely
modice : moderately
molliter : softly
mox : soon
nec, necne, neque : and not
ni : not
nihilominus : notwithstanding, none the less
nimio, nimis : excessively, much, very excessively, overmuch
non : not
nondum : not yet
nonnihil : somewhat
nonnunquam : now and then
nunc : now
nunquam : never
nuper : lately
oblique : obliquely
obscure : darkly, indistinctly
obsolete : obsoletely
olim : formerly, once
omnino : wholly, entirely
paene : almost
pallide : palely (opp. to **saturate**)
parce, parciter : sparingly
pariter : equally, in like manner
parum : too little
passim : in every direction, at random, everywhere
pauce : few

paulatim : little by little
paulum (paullum) : little
paululum : a very little
pauxillum : a little
peltatim : peltately
penitus : inwardly
peranguste : very narrowly
plane : plainly, distinctly
plerumque : mostly, commonly
pluries : often, frequently
post, postea : afterwards
postice : at the back (opp. to **antice**)
postremo : at last, finally
potius : rather
praealte : very deeply
praecipue : chiefly, principally
praesertim : especially
praeterea : moreover, besides
primitus : at first, originally
primo : in the beginning
primum : first
profunde : deeply
prominenter : prominently
promiscue : promiscuously, indiscriminately
prorsus : forwards, straight on
putide : badly, absurdly
quam : as much as, than
quandocumque : whenever, as often as
quaquaversus : to all sides
quodammodo : in a certain manner
rare : thinly   **raro** : seldom
reapse : in fact, actually
remote : remotely
remotiuscule : somewhat remotely
retrorsum : backwards
revera : truly, really
rite : rightly, well
saepe : often, many times
saltem : at least
sat, satis : enough, sufficiently
saturate : fully, richly, intensely (opp. to **dilute, pallide**)
scilicet : that is to say, evidently
secundatim : with parts directed to one side only, all in one direction

sedule : diligently
semel : once
semote : separately
semper : always
seorsim, seorsum : separately
sero : late
sic : so, thus
simul : at the same time, together
similiter : in like manner, similarly
sinistrorsum : towards the left
solemniter : in the usual manner
sordide : dirtily
sparse : sparsely
sparsim : scatteredly, here and there
statim : immediately, at once
subito : suddenly
subtiliter : finely
summe : extremely
superne : from above
sursum : upwards (opp. to deorsum)
tam : so
tamen : notwithstanding, nevertheless
tamquam : as much as, as if
tantum : only, merely

tarde : slowly
tenuiter : thinly
transversa : transversely
tum, tunc : then
ubique : anywhere, everywhere
ultimo : finally
unde : from which place, whence
undecumque : from wherever
undique : from all parts, on all sides, in every part
usque : up to, all the way to (usually with *ad*)
ut : as, in the manner that
utrinque (utrimque) : on both sides, above and below
valde : strongly, very
vehementer : strongly, forcibly
velut : just as, like
vero : certainly, assuredly
verosimiliter (verisimiliter) : most likely
vix : scarcely
vulgo : commonly

A number of phrases are also used adverbially, e.g. *toto caelo* (completely, the width of the sky apart), *in universum* (as a whole), *ut maximum* (at the most), *ut minimum* (at least), *ut videtur* (apparently, as it seems), *ad normam* (customarily), *ad amussin* (exactly).

CHAPTER VIII

Numerals and Measurements

1 Although metric units down to μ have now superseded in botanical
Latin the earlier mensural standards, and although Arabic numerals for
most purposes are preferred to Roman numerals, an acquaintance with
old methods of measurement and dating is essential when consulting
early literature.

KINDS OF NUMERALS

2 Numeral adjectives are of the three kinds, exemplified in English
by *one* (a Cardinal numeral), *first* (an Ordinal numeral) and *one each*
(a Distributive numeral), supplemented by numeral adverbs, exemplified in English by *once*. As stated by Gildersleeve & Lodge, 'the
Cardinal numerals answer the question **quot**, *how many?* and are the
numbers used in counting. The Ordinal numerals are derived from
these and answer the question **quotus**, *which one in the series?'* The
Distributive numerals answer the question **quoteni**, *how many each?* The
numeral adverbs answer the question **quotiens**, *how often? how many
times?*

TABLE OF NUMERALS

3

Arabic Numerals	Roman Numerals	Cardinals		Ordinals	
1	I	unus	*one*	primus	*first*
2	II	duo	*two*	secundus *or* alter	*second*
3	III	tres	*three*	tertius	*third*
4	IIII *or* IV	quatuor	*four*	quartus	*fourth*
5	V	quinque	*five*	quintus	*fifth*
6	VI	sex	*six*	sextus	*sixth*
7	VII	septem	*seven*	septimus	*seventh*
8	VIII	octo	*eight*	octavus	*eighth*
9	VIIII *or* IX	novem	*nine*	nonus	*ninth*
10	X	decem	*ten*	decimus	*tenth*

11	XI	undecim *eleven*	undecimus	*eleventh*
12	XII	duodecim *twelve*	duodecimus	*twelfth*
13	XIII	tredecim	tertius decimus	
14	XIIII *or* XIV	quatuordecim	quartus decimus	
15	XV	quindecim	quintus decimus	
16	XVI	sedecim	sextus decimus	
17	XVII	septendecim	septimus decimus	
18	XVIII *or* XIIX	duodeviginti	duodevicensimus	
19	XVIIII *or* XIX	undeviginti	undevicensimus	
20	XX	viginti	vicensimus (vicesimus)	
21	XXI	unus et viginti	vicensimus primus	
22	XXII	duo et viginti	alter et vicensimus	
23	XXIII	tres et viginti	tertius et vicensimus	
28	XXVIII	duodetriginta	duodetricensimus	
29	XXIX	undetriginta	undetricensimus	
30	XXX	triginta	tricensimus	
31	XXXI	unus et triginta	unus et tricensimus	
40	XXXX *or* XL	quadraginta	quadragensimus	
50	L	quinquaginta	quinquagensimus	
60	LX	sexaginta	sexagensimus	
70	LXX	septuaginta	septuagensimus	
80	LXXX *or* XXC	octoginta	octogensimus	
90	LXXXX *or* XC	nonaginta	nonagensimus	
99	XCIX *or* IC	undecentum	undecentensimus	
100	C	centum	centensimus (centesimus)	
101	CI	centum et unus	centensimus primus	
150	CL	centum quinqua-ginta	centensimus quinquagen-simus	
200	CC	ducenti	ducentensimus	
300	CCC	trecenti	trecentensimus	
400	CCCC	quadringenti	quadringentensimus	
500	IƆ *or* D	quingenti	quingentensimus	
600	IƆC *or* DC	sescenti	sescentensimus	
700	IƆCC *or* DCC	septingenti	septingentensimus	
800	IƆCCC *or* DCCC	octingenti	octingentensimus	
900	IƆCCCC *or* DCCCC	nongenti	nongentensimus	
1000	CIƆ *or* M	mille	millensimus	
1500	CIƆ.IƆ *or* MD	mille quingenti	millensimus quingenten-simus	

1550	CIↃ.IↃL or	mille quingenti	millensimus quingenten-
	MDL	quinquagenta	simus quinquagensimus
1600	CIↃ.IↃC or		
	MDC	mille sescenti	millensimus sescentensimus
1602	CIↃ.IↃCII or	mille sescenti duo	millensimus sescentensimus
	MDCII		alter
1650	CIↃ.IↃ. CL	mille sescenti quin-	millensimus sescentensimus
	or MDCL	quaginta	quinquagensimus
1700	CIↃ.IↃ.CC	mille septingenti	millensimus septingenten-
	or MDCC		simus

An alternative ending for ordinals in *-ensimus*, e.g. *sexagensimus*, is *-esimus*, e.g. *sexagesimus*. *Quatuor* is also spelled *quattuor*.

4 The high numbers in the above table occur only in dates. Thus Clusius's *Rariorum Plantarum Historia* has the date CIↃ.IↃCI (i.e. 1601) on its title-page; in the text (p. 4) he records that fruits of Laurocerasus were sent to him from Constantinople 'anno septuagesimo quarto & octogesimo sexto supra millesimum & quingentesimum', i.e. in the years 1574 and 1586; lower on the same page he refers to 'anno M.D.LXXXI', i.e. 1581. The title-page of Caspar Bauhin's *Pinax* states that it deals with 'plantarum circiter sex millium nomina', i.e. the names of about 6,000 plants; the first edition is dated 'MDCXXIII', i.e. 1623, the second 'CIↃ IↃC. LXXI', i.e. 1671. The use of 'M' for 1,000 comes from its being the first letter of MILLE (thousand); earlier, however, the Romans, according to Mommsen, had assigned the value 1,000 to the Greek letter ϕ (phi), rendered by sixteenth-century printers as CIↃ or C|Ↄ or C|Ↄ, which halved gives IↃ or |Ↄ or |Ↄ or D for 500.

5 Chronograms in works of botanical or horticultural interest are fortunately rare. An example is the apparently undated *Hortus candidus* (cf. Stearn, 1947)[1] with the sentence 'annVite sVperI, fLosCVLVs Vt hIC CanDIDVs VIresCat In saeCLa aVrea' containing letters whose numerical values add up to 1695.

DECLENSION AND USE

6 The CARDINAL NUMERALS *unus* (1), *duo* (2) and *tres* (3) are declined; the others from *quatuor* (4) to *centum* (100) are used unchanged whatever the gender and case of the noun which they qualify, hence *flos unus, flore uno, cellula una, folium unum, folio uno*, but *flores quatuor, floribus quatuor, cellulae quatuor, cellulis quatuor, folia quatuor, foliis quatuor*.

---

[1] W. T. Stearn, 'A curiosity of lily literature, the Ebrach Abbey *Hortus candidus*', Roy. Hort. Soc., *Lily Year Book*, 11 : 97—100 (1947).

	M.	F.	N.	
Nom.	unus	una	unum	one (as subject)
Acc.	unum	unam	unum	one (as object)
Gen.	unius	unius	unius	of one
Dat.	uni	uni	uni	to or for one
Abl.	uno	una	uno	by, with or from one

	M.	F.	N.	
Nom.	duo	duae	duo	two (as subject)
Acc.	duo *or* duos	duas	duo	two (as object)
Gen.	duorum	duarum	duorum	of two
Dat.	duobus	duabus	duobus	to or for two
Abl.	duobus	duabus	duobus	by, with or from two

	M.	F.	N.	
Nom.	tres	tres	tria	three (as subject)
Acc.	tres	tres	tria	three (as object)
Gen.	trium	trium	trium	of three
Dat.	tribus	tribus	tribus	to or for three
Abl.	tribus	tribus	tribus	by, with or from three

7 The ORDINALS *primus* (the first), *secundus* (the second), *tertius* (the third), etc., are declined like *unus* above.

8 The DISTRIBUTIVES denote so many each or at each time:

1	singuli	one each	7	septeni	seven each
2	bini	two each	8	octoni	eight each
3	terni	three each	9	noveni	nine each
4	quaterni	four each	10	deni	ten each
5	quini	five each	11	undeni	eleven each
6	seni	six each	12	duodeni	twelve each

They are declined as plural adjectives of the first and second declension:

	M.	F.	N.	
Nom.	terni	ternae	terna	three each
Acc.	ternos	ternas	terna	three each
Gen.	ternorum	ternarum	ternorum	of three each
Dat.	ternis	ternis	ternis	to or for three each
Abl.	ternis	ternis	ternis	by, with or from three each

They are used when specifying the number of parts at a given position, e.g. the number of leaves in a whorl:

folia verticillata	**quaterna vel sena**
leaves whorled	four or six together
foliis verticillatis	**quaternis vel senis**
with leaves whorled	four or six together

Using ordinals this could be expressed as

folia (foliis) in quoque verticillo quatuor vel sex
leaves (with leaves) in each whorl four or six

In general it is best to avoid both Latin words and Roman numeral
and to use Arabic numerals instead, e.g. to write *folia* 3–14 rather tha
folia tria ad quatuordecim.

9 NUMERICAL ADVERBS denote how many times something happens :

1	**semel**	once	5	**quinquies (quinquiens)**	five times
2	**bis**	twice	6	**sexies (sexiens)**	six times
3	**ter**	thrice	7	**septies (septiens)**	seven times
4	**quater**	four times	8	**octies (octiens)**	eight times

10 Lindley, following A. P. de Candolle, distinguishes the mai
numerical terms as follows :

nullus, absolutely wanting, none
solitarius, unicus, one, growing singly
paucus, few, the number small, not indefinite
numerosus, multus, numerous, so many that they cannot be counted wit
   accuracy ; *or* several, but not of any definite number

MEASUREMENTS

11 Measurements should be expressed in the metric system with th
aid of the adjectives *altus* (high), *longus* (long), *latus* (broad) or *crassu*
(thick), or the nouns *altitudo* (height or depth), *longitudo* (length)
latitudo (breadth), *crassitudo* (thickness), *crassities* (thickness), *profun*
ditas (depth) or *diameter* (diameter) :

valvae 16–30 μ latae, valves 16–30 μ broad
valvis 16–30 μ latis, with valves 16–30 μ broad
latitudo valvarum maxima 28–30 μ minima 16–20 μ,
   width of valves at maximum 28–30 μ at minimum 16–20 μ
arbor 15–50 m. alta, ad 30 cm. diametro, foliis 14–35 cm. longis, 4–10 cm
   latis,
   tree 15–50 m. high, to 30 cm. in diameter, with leaves 14–35 cm. long
   4–10 cm. broad

12 Before the adoption of the metric system, devised in France at th
end of the eighteenth century, authors used the traditional units base
on the human body such as the foot (*pes*), the span (*spithama*), etc
Linnaeus's *Philosophia botanica*, 262, no. 331 (1751) provides a
convenient summary :

Capillus (i.e. a hair's width) = Lineae pars duodecima = $\frac{1}{12}$ Paris line = 0·18 mm.

Linea = Linea una Mensurae parisinae = 2·25 mm.

Unguis (i.e. the length of a finger-nail) = Lineae sex sive uncia dimidia = 6 lines = 1·35 cm. = $\frac{1}{2}$ inch (approx.).

Pollex (i.e. the length of the terminal joint of the thumb) = Uncia una parisina = 1 Paris inch = 12 lines = 2·7 cm. = $1\frac{1}{12}$ inch (approx.).

Digitus (i.e. the length of the index finger) = Unciae duae = 3·4 cm. = $2\frac{1}{8}$ inches (approx.).

Palmus (i.e. the width of the four fingers together) = Unciae tres parisienses = 3 Paris inches = 8 cm. = $3\frac{1}{4}$ inches (approx.).

Dodrans (i.e. the distance between the tips of the thumb and the little finger when extended) = Unciae novem = 9 Paris inches = 24·3 cm. = $9\frac{1}{2}$ inches (approx.).

Spithama (i.e. the distance between the tips of the thumb and the index finger when extended) = Unciae septem = 7 Paris inches = 19 cm. = $7\frac{2}{5}$ inches (approx.).

Pes (i.e. foot) = Unciae duodecim = 12 Paris inches = 32·5 cm. = 13 inches (approx.).

Cubitus (i.e. the distance from the elbow to the tip of the middle finger) = Unciae septendecim = 17 Paris inches = 46 cm. = $1\frac{1}{2}$ feet (approx.).

Brachium (i.e. the distance from the arm-pit to the tip of the middle finger when extended) or Ulna = Unciae viginti quatuor = 24 Paris inches = 65 cm. = 2 feet 1 inch.

Orgya (i.e. the distance between the tips of the middle fingers when the arms are extended) = 6 Paris feet = 1·95 m. = $6\frac{1}{2}$ feet (approx.).

From these are derived the adjectives *uncialis* and *pollicaris* (about 2·7 cm. long), *palmaris* (about 8 cm. long), *spithameus* (about 19 cm. long), *dodrantalis* (about 24·3 cm. long), *pedalis* (about 32·5 cm. long), *cubitalis* (about 46 cm. long), *ulnaris* and *brachialis* (about 65 cm.) and *orgyalis* (about 1·9 m.).

Expressions such as *crassitie pennae cygneae* (with the thickness of a swan's quill) are also used by early authors (see below, p. 118).

NUMERICAL EPITHETS

113 Epithets referring to the number of parts may be formed from Latin or Greek elements or those common to both Greek and Latin or belonging strictly to neither, but as scholars often consider bastard words such as *hexaflorus* to indicate illiteracy, carelessness or bad taste on the part of their coiners it seems proper to avoid unnecessary unions of Greek and Latin; some Greek elements such as *petalum* and *stylus* have become so completely assimilated to Latin that they

now belong equally well to both. The most commonly used of these word-elements in botanical Latin are as follows :

Derived from Latin	Derived from Greek
½—semi- (e.g. semialatus)	hemi- (e.g. hemipterus)
1—uni- (e.g. unifolius)	mono- (e.g. monophyllus)
2—bi- (e.g. biformis)	di- (e.g. dimorphus)
3—tri- (e.g. tripartitus)	tri- (e.g. trimerus)
4—quadri- (e.g. quadricolor)	tetra- (e.g. tetrachromus)
5—quinque- (e.g. quinquenervis)	penta- (e.g. pentaneurus)
6—sex- (e.g. sexangularis)	hexa- (e.g. hexagonus)
7—septem- (e.g. septemcostatus)	hepta- (e.g. heptapleurus)
8—octo- (e.g. octosepalus)	octo- (e.g. octopetalus)
9—novem-	ennea-
10—decem-	deca-
11—undecim-	endeca- or hendeca-
12—duodecim-	dodeca-
20—viginti-	icosa-
few—pauci- (e.g. paucistamineus)	oligo- (e.g. oligostemon)
many—multi- (e.g. multidentatus)	poly- (e.g. polyodontus)

	Derived from Latin	Treated as both Latin and Greek	Derived from Greek
-angled	-angulus		-gonus
	-angulatus		
-anthered		-antherus	
-carpelled	-carpellatus		-gynus
-coloured	-color		-chromus
-flowered	-florus		-anthus
-fruited			-carpus
-leaved	-folius		-phyllus
-lobed		-lobus	
-nerved	-nervis		
	-nervius		-neurus
-petaled		-petalus	
-racemed	-racemosus		-botrys,
			-botryus
-ribbed	-costatus		-pleurus
-seeded	-semineus		-spermus
-sepaled		-sepalus	
-spiked	-spicatus		-stachyus
-spored			-sporus
-stamened	-stamineus		-andrus
			-stemon (us)
-styled		-stylus	
-tepaled		-tepalus	
-toothed	-dentatus		-odon
			-odontus
-veined	-venius		-phlebius
-winged	-alatus		-pterus

4 As regards the origin of those treated above as combining with both Greek and Latin elements, it may be noted that *anthera* (from Greek ἀνθηρα flowering) in classical Latin meant 'a medicine composed of flowers', *stylus* (from Greek στυλος), 'stake', *petalum* (from Greek πεταλον), 'plate'; *lobus* is from Greek λοβος, 'lobe of the ear, pod of leguminous plants', while *sepalum* was coined by Necker in the eighteenth century and *tepalum* by Reichenbach in the nineteenth century. So none is truly classical as now used.

RELATIVE LENGTH

5 The relation in size between parts is often more constant and taxonomically more useful than their actual size. Thus a certain species may be tall or dwarf according to its conditions of growth, but always has the leaves longer than the flower-stem, while another species may always have the leaves shorter than the flower-stem under similar conditions. Examples below indicate how such proportional relations of organs can be expressed using the nominative (nom.) for the subject of the phrase as in a description or the ablative (abl.) as in a diagnosis.

6 When *aequans* (equalling) or *superans* (surpassing, exceeding, overtopping) is used, whether the subject is in the nominative, e.g. *lobi* lobes), *petala* (petals), or in the ablative, e.g. *lobis* (with lobes), *petalis* with petals), the object is put into the accusative, e.g. *tubum* (not *tubus* or *tubo*), *calycem* (not *calyx* or *calyce*):

(a) **lobi tubum aequantes**
   lobes equalling the tube

   lobis tubum aequantibus
   with lobes equalling the tube

(b) **petala calycem superantia**
   petals exceeding the calyx

   petalis calycem superantibus
   with petals exceeding the calyx

Equality of two organs in length is often expressed by *longitudine* (with the length) followed by the genitive, e.g. *tubus longitudine loborum, petala longitudine calycis, filamenta longitudine petalorum.*

7 The insertion of *longitudine* (in length) adds precision:

lobi corollae longitudine tubum paulo superantes
lobes of the corolla in length the tube by a little exceeding

Other useful qualifying words are *haud* (not at all), *fere* (almost), *vix* (hardly), *plus minusve* (more than or less than), *paulo* (by a little), *multo* (by much); more precise are *quarta parte* (by a quarter), etc. (see below); although such expressions as *duabus tertiis partibus* (by two third parts, i.e. $\frac{2}{3}$) or *per duos longitudinis trientes* (for two third of the length) can be used, fractions are best expressed by numerals:

> **prophylla $\frac{2}{3}$ calycis obtegentia**
> prophylls covering $\frac{2}{3}$ of the calyx
>
> **stamina longitudine $\frac{2}{3}$ perigonii partes aequantia**
> stamens in length equalling $\frac{2}{3}$ parts of the perigon

18 When the comparative adjectives *longior* (longer) and *brevio* (shorter) are used to indicate difference, whether agreeing with a wor in the nominative, e.g. *folia* (leaves), *haptonema* (haptonema), *internodi* (internodes), or in the ablative, e.g. *foliis* (with leaves), *haptonemat* (with a haptonema), *internodiis* (with internodes), the name of th thing with which it is compared is put in the ablative, e.g. *scapo* (no *scapus* or *scapum*), *cellula* (not *cellulam*), *ramulis* (not *ramuli* o *ramulos*):

(a) **folia scapo longiora vel paulo breviora**
    leaves longer than or a little shorter than the scape

    foliis scapo longioribus vel paulo brevioribus
    with leaves longer than or a little shorter than the scape

(b) **internodia ramulis 1-5plo longiora**
    internodes 1 to 5 times longer than the branchlets

    internodiis ramulis 1-5plo longioribus
    with internodes 1 to 5 times longer than the branchlets

(c) **perigonium tubulosum diametro suo duplo longius**
    perigon tubular twice as long as its own diameter

    perigonio tubuloso diametro suo duplo longiore
    with perigon tubular twice as long as its own diameter

(d) **filamenta perigonio sesquilongiora, tria interiora tricuspidata cuspid antherifera filamento ipso triplo breviore**
    filaments than the perigon longer by a half, the three inner ones tricusp date with the anther-bearing cusp than its own filament three time shorter (i.e. with the cusp $\frac{1}{3}$ the length of its own filament)

    filamentis perigonio sesquilongioribus, tribus interioribus tricuspidati cuspide antherifero filamento ipso triplo breviore
    with filaments than the perigon longer by a half with the three inner on tricuspidate with the anther-bearing cusp than its own filament thre times shorter

(e) **haptonema cellula 20plo longius**
    haptonema 20 times longer than the cell

    haptonemate cellula 20plo longiore
    with haptonema 20 times longer than the cell

19 Sometimes it is necessary to use both the above modes of expression together, e.g. *superans* (or *aequans*) and *brevior* (or *longior*) in the same phrase :

> **folia internodia aequantia vel eis breviora**
> leaves equalling the internodes or shorter than these

Here *internodia* (abl. plural *internodiis*) is in the accusative plural but *eis* (nom. plural *ea*) is in the ablative plural; since *internodia* is plural, *eis* referring to it is likewise plural.

The order could, however, be reversed :

> **inflorescentia folio caulino brevior vel hoc superans**
> inflorescence than the cauline leaf shorter or this overtopping

Hoc (neuter nom. and acc. singular of *hic*) here takes the place of *folium caulinum.*

20 The adverb *quam* (as, than) exemplified in Caesar's statement, **Hibernia dimidio minor est quam Britannia** (Ireland by half smaller is than Britain), is also used in botanical Latin :

(a) **folia 4-5plo longiora quam latiora**
     leaves 4 to 5 times longer than broad

(b) **foliis 4-5plo longioribus quam latioribus**
     with leaves 4 to 5 times longer than broad

(c) **folia radicalia cauli collateralia breviora quam iste caulis**
     radical leaves collateral to the stem shorter than this stem

When *quam* is used, both nouns compared are both in the same case, e.g. both in the nominative or both in the ablative, as may be necessary.

(d) **internodia quam ramuli multo longiora**
     internodes much longer than the branchlets
     internodiis quam ramulis multo longioribus
     with internodes much longer than the branchlets

21 To indicate the amount of difference in length or width, such expressions as *quarta parte* (by a quarter), *tertia parte* (by a third), *dimidia parte* or *dimidio* (by a half), *sesqui* (one and half; more by a half), *duplo* (twice), *subduplo* (nearly twice), *triplo* (3 times as much), *quadruplo* or *4plo* (4 times as much), *quintuplo* or *5plo* (5 times as much) have often been used. The following are a few examples :

(a) **spatha pedicellis 2-3plo brevior**
     spathe 2-3 times shorter than the pedicels (i.e. spathe $\frac{1}{2}$ to $\frac{1}{3}$ as long as the pedicels)

spatha pedicellis 2-3plo breviore
with the spathe 2-3 times shorter than the pedicels [*breviore* is abl. sing
of *brevior*, and agrees with *spatha*]

(b) **calycis dentes tubo vix longiores**
teeth of the calyx scarcely longer than the tube [*calycis* is gen. sing. of
calyx, *dentes*, the nom. plur. of *dens*; *longiores* agrees with *dentes*]

calycis dentibus tubo vix longioribus
with the teeth of the calyx scarcely longer than the tube

(c) **corolla calyce sesquilongior**
corolla $1\frac{1}{2}$ times longer than the calyx (i.e. proportions of corolla to
calyx = 3 to 2)

corolla calyce sesquilongiore
with the corolla $1\frac{1}{2}$ times longer than the calyx

(d) **filamenta perigonio quarta vel dimidia parte longiora**
filaments longer than the perigon by a quarter or half

filamentis perigonio quarta vel dimidia parte longioribus
with the filaments longer than the perigon by a quarter or half

(e) **staminum filamenta inaequalia, tria exteriora antheras longitudine
aequantia, tria interiora eis dimidio breviora**
filaments of stamens unequal, the outer three equalling the anthers in
length, the inner three half as long [*staminum* is gen. plur. of *stamen*
antheras the accus. plur. of *anthera*, *longitudine* the abl. sing. of
longitudo]

**staminum filamentis inaequalibus, tribus exterioribus antheras longitudine
aequantibus, tribus interioribus eis dimidio brevioribus**
with the filaments of the stamens unequal, the outer three equalling the
anthers in length, the inner three half as long

(f) **stylus perigonium (corollam) longe superans**
style much overtopping the perigon (corolla)

stylo perigonium (corollam) longe superante
with the style much overtopping the perigon (corolla)

(g) **differt floribus dimidio minoribus**
it differs in having flowers half the size

22 Comparison with natural objects taken as standards occurs in many
of the older authors, e.g. :

caulis plus quam humanae altitudinis
stem more than of the height of a human being

verticillastri pisum vix aequantes
verticillasters hardly as big as a pea

verticillastri avellana minores
verticillasters smaller than a hazel-nut

pedunculus crassitudine pennae anserinae
peduncle with the thickness of a goose-quill

Pronouns

A pronoun is a word used in place of a noun to refer to a person or thing already mentioned without naming it, thus avoiding repetition of the noun. Pronouns are little used in botanical Latin.

PERSONAL PRONOUNS

Personal Pronouns refer to the three persons. The Third Person mostly occurs in descriptions, the First Person in comments and annotations, the Second Person in dedications.

	First Person			*Second Person*	
		Singular			
Nom.	ego	I	tu	thou	
Acc.	me	me	te	thee	
Gen.	mei	of me	tui	of thee	
Dat.	mihi	to me	tibi	to thee	
Abl.	me	by, with or from me	te	by, with or from thee	
		Plural			
Nom.	nos	we		you (as subject)	
Acc.	nos	us	vos	you (as object)	
Gen.	nostri	of us, our	vestri	of you, your	
	nostrum		vestrum		
Dat.	nobis	to us	vobis	to you	
Abl.	nobis	by, with or from us	vobis	by, with or from you	

Nomina a me proposita. Names proposed by me.

Haec est facile maxima totius generis species mihi cognita. This is easily the largest species of the whole genus known to me.

Species obscura a nobis non visa. An obscure species not seen by us.

Specimina nobis desunt. Specimens are lacking (not available) to us.

Third Person
Singular

Nom.	is	he	ea	she	id	it (as subject
Acc.	eum	him	eam	her	id	it (as object)
Gen.	ejus	his, of him	ejus	her, hers, of	ejus	its, of it
	(eius)		(eius)	her	(eius)	
Dat.	ei	to him	ei	to her	ei	to it
Abl.	eo	by, with or	ea	by, with or	eo	by, with or
		from him		from her		from it

Plural

Nom.	ei (ii)	they	eae	they	ea	they
Acc.	eos	them	eas	them	ea	them
Gen.	eorum	their, of	earum	their, of	eorum	their, of
		them		them		them
Dat.	eis (iis)	to them	eis (iis)	to them	eis (iis)	to them
Abl.	eis (iis)	by with, or	eis (iis)	by, with or	eis (iis)	by with, or
		from them		from them		from them

With regard to the Third Person, it should be noted that the gender used is that of the noun to which it refers; thus the pronoun for *petiolus* (masculine) would be *is*, for *lamina* (feminine) *ea*, for *folium* (neuter) *id*. Hence in *lamina basi in petiolum angustata eumque marginans* (blade at base narrowed into the petiole and margining it) the pronoun *eum* (masc. acc. sing. of *is*) refers to *petiolum* (acc. sing. of *petiolus*) and agrees with it in gender, case and number.

DEMONSTRATIVE PRONOUNS

Demonstrative Pronouns are *is*, *ea*, *id*, meaning 'that, he, she, it', as above and generally used, and *hic*, *haec*, *hoc*, meaning 'this, he, she, it' with a special sense of nearness, as opposed to *ille*, *illa*, *illud*, 'that he, she, it', with a sense of remoteness, 'yonder'; when a distinction is made between two kinds, *hic* usually indicates the latter one, *ille* the former one.

Singular

	M.	F.	N.	M.	F.	N.
Nom.	hic	haec	hoc	ille	illa	illud
Acc.	hunc	hanc	hoc	illum	illam	illud
Gen.	hujus	hujus	hujus	illius	illius	illius
Dat.	huic	huic	huic	illi	illi	illi
Abl.	hoc	hac	hoc	illo	illa	illo

Plural

	M.	F.	N.	M.	F.	N.
Nom.	hi	hae	haec	illi	illae	illa
Acc.	hos	has	haec	illos	illas	illa
Gen.	horum	harum	horum	illorum	illarum	illorum
Dat.	his	his	his	illis	illis	illis
Abl.	his	his	his	illis	illis	illis

Formas hujus habemus notabiles. We have noteworthy forms of this.

A proxima Poa persica distinguitur radiis patentissimis (in illa erectiusculis). From the very near Poa persica it is distinguished by the very patent rays (in that [i.e. *P. persica*] rather erect).

Spiculae illis C. flavescentis breviores. Spikelets shorter than those of C. flavescens.

Iris notha, I. spuria atque illarum varietates. Iris notha, I. spuria and their varieties.

Folia omnia radicalia, illis S. scopariae similia. Leaves all radical, similar to those of S. scoparia.

Habitu Galio lucido simile, characteribus ad G. palustre magis accedit; ab illo differt foliis floribusque ab hoc habitu. In habit similar to Galium lucidum, by its characters it approaches more to G. palustre; from the former it differs in the leaves and flowers, from the latter in the habit.

His valde affinis est species austro-Africana. To these strongly akin is a South African species.

REFLEXIVE PRONOUNS

Reflexive Pronouns in Latin give the emphasis that the addition of 'self' to a personal pronoun gives in English.

Acc.	se, sese	itself, himself, herself, themselves
Gen.	sui	of itself, etc.
Dat.	sibi	to or for itself, etc.
Abl.	se, sese	by, with or from itself, etc.

Species mexicanae inter sese arcte affines. Mexican species between themselves closely related.

Isandra includit species antheris inter se aequalibus. Isandra includes species with anthers between themselves equal.

POSSESSIVE PRONOUNS

Possessive Pronouns have the function of adjectives.

Singular

	M.	F.	N.	
Nom.	meus	mea	meum	my . . . (as subject)
Acc.	meum	meam	meum	my . . . (as object)
Gen.	mei	meae	mei	of my . . .
Dat.	meo	meae	meo	to or for my . . .
Abl.	meo	mea	meo	by, with or from my . . .

Plural

Nom.	mei	meae	mea	my . . . (as subject)
Acc.	meos	meas	mea	my . . . (as object)
Gen.	meorum	mearum	meorum	of my . . .
Dat.	meis	meis	meis	to or for my . . .
Abl.	meis	meis	meis	by, with or from my . . .

Similarly declined are *tuus, tua, tuum* (thy) and *suus, sua, suum* (his, her, its, their); the plurals *noster, nostra, nostrum* (our) and *vester, vestra, vestrum* (your) are declined like *glaber* (adj. Group A; see p. 93).

> **Specimina pro studiis suis examinata.** Specimens examined for his studies.

> **Linnaeus species suas generis Marrubii in duos ordines instruxit.** Linnaeus arranged his species of the genus Marrubium in two groups.

THE RELATIVE PRONOUN QUI

The Relative Pronoun *qui* (which) is used to add subordinate sentences, usually in diagnoses or titles of books.

Singular

	M.	F.	N.	
Nom.	qui	quae	quod	which (as subject)
Acc.	quem	quam	quod	which (as object)
Gen.	cujus	cujus	cujus	of which
Dat.	cui	cui	cui	to which
Abl.	quo	qua	quo	by, with or from which

Plural

Nom.	qui	quae	quae	which (as subject)
Acc.	quos	quas	quae	which (as object)
Gen.	quorum	quarum	quorum	of which
Dat.	quibus	quibus	quibus	to which
Abl.	quibus	quibus	quibus	by, with or from which

> **Ilex mexicana, quae** [f., nom. sing.] **cum Pileostegia congruit.** Ilex mexicana, which agrees with Pileostegia.

> **Species obscura, cujus** [f., gen. sing.] **folia tantum cognita sunt.** An obscure species, of which only the leaves are known.

> **Species notae 8, quarum** [f., gen. pl.] **1 Novo-Caledonica, 2 Novo Zelandicae, caeterae Australianae.** Known species 8, of which 1 New Caledonian, 2 New Zealand, the rest Australian.

> **Variat magnitudine fructuum qui** [m., nom. pl.] **longitudinem 1–2 cm habent.** It varies in the size of the fruits, which have a length of 1–2 cm.

THE DEFINITE PRONOUN IDEM

The Definite Pronoun *idem* (the same) is declined as follows :

Singular

	M.	F.	N.	
Nom.	idem	eadem	idem	the same (as subject)
Acc.	eundem	eandem	idem	the same (as object)
Gen.	ejusdem	ejusdem	ejusdem	of the same
Dat.	eidem	eidem	eidem	to or for the same
Abl.	eodem	eadem	eodem	by, with or from the same

Plural

	M.	F.	N.	
Nom.	idem, eidem	eaedem	eadem	the same (as subject)
Acc.	eosdem	easdem	eadem	the same (as object)
Gen.	eorundem	earundem	eorundem	of the same
Dat.	isdem	isdem	isdem	to or for the same
Abl.	isdem	isdem	isdem	by, with or from the same

Planta Linnaei eadem ac nostra est. The plant of Linnaeus is the same as ours.

Lilium sinicum idem est ac L. concolor. Lilium sinicum is the same as L. concolor.

In eadem specie variat etiamque in eodem individuo. It varies in the same species and even in the same individual.

Eisdem is sometimes used as the dative or ablative plural instead of *isdem*.

THE INTENSIVE PRONOUN IPSE

The Intensive Pronoun *ipse* (himself), *ipsa* (herself), *ipsum* (itself) is also used for emphasis.

Singular

	M.	F.	N.	
Nom.	ipse	ipsa	ipsum	himself (m.), herself (f.), itself (n.) (as subject)
Acc.	ipsum	ipsam	ipsum	himself (m.), herself (f.), itself (n.) (as object)
Gen.	ipsius	ipsius	ipsius	of himself, etc.
Dat.	ipsi	ipsi	ipsi	to or for himself, etc.
Abl.	ipso	ipsa	ipso	by, with or from himself, etc.

Plural

	M.	F.	N.	
Nom.	ipsi	ipsae	ipsa	themselves (as subject)
Acc.	ipsos	ipsas	ipsa	themselves (as object)
Gen.	ipsorum	ipsarum	ipsorum	of themselves
Dat.	ipsis	ipsis	ipsis	to or for themselves
Abl.	ipsis	ipsis	ipsis	by, with or from themselves

Characteres a me ipso haud observati. Characters by me myself not observed.

B.L.—E 2

THE PRONOUNS ALIUS AND ALTER

Alius (other, another) is declined as follows:

Singular

	M.	F.	N.	
Nom.	alius	alia	aliud	the other (as subject)
Acc.	alium	aliam	aliud	the other (as object)
Gen.	alius	alius	alius	of the other
Dat.	alii	alii	alii	to or for the other
Abl.	alio	alia	alio	by, with or from the other

Plural

	M.	F.	N.	
Nom.	alii	aliae	alia	the others (as subject)
Acc.	alios	alias	alia	the others (as object)
Gen.	aliorum	aliarum	aliorum	of the others
Dat.	aliis	aliis	aliis	to or for the others
Abl.	aliis	aliis	aliis	by, with or from the others

A D. bicolore colore corollae inter alia differt. From D. bicolor it differs among other [characters] by the colour of the corolla.

Adsunt alia specimina in aliis herbariis. There are other specimens in other herbaria.

Species pulchra nulli alii arctius affinis. A beautiful species to no other more closely akin.

Alter (one of two, the other, the second) is declined as follows:

Singular

	M.	F.	N.	
Nom.	alter	altera	alterum	the other, etc. (as subject)
Acc.	alterum	alteram	alterum	the other, etc. (as object)
Gen.	alterius	alterius	alterius	of the other, etc.
Dat.	alteri	alteri	alteri	to or for the other, etc.
Abl.	altero	altera	altero	by, with or from the other, etc.

Plural

	M.	F.	N.	
Nom.	alteri	alterae	altera	the others, etc. (as subject)
Acc.	alteros	alteras	altera	the others, etc. (as object)
Gen.	alterorum	alterarum	alterorum	of the others, etc.
Dat.	alteris	alteris	alteris	to or for the others, etc.
Abl.	alteris	alteris	alteris	by, with or from the others, etc.

Specimen alterum nervos laterales habet. The second specimen of the two has lateral nerves.

Alter is used to indicate one or other of two, *alius* one or other of several.

Prepositions

Prepositions are words inserted to make clear the relation of nouns, adjectives and pronouns to other words in the same phrase or sentence and are used in Latin when this relation is not plainly evident from the case-endings alone. Thus in the phrase *in sylva Amazonica ad fluvium Negro* (in Amazonian forest at the Rio Negro) both *in* (in) and *ad* (at) are prepositions. Likewise in the description *folia infra medium latissima, sed ad basim in petiolum protracta* (leaves below the middle broadest, but at base into the petiole drawn out) the words *infra, ad* and *in* are prepositions.

Most prepositions require that the noun associated with them should be in the accusative case, e.g. *versus basim* (towards the base). Others take the ablative, e.g. *e basi* (from the base). Only a few, e.g. *clam, in, sub, super* and *subter*, can be used with either, according to the context. These take the accusative when they indicate motion towards or into, even if metaphorical, and the ablative when they indicate rest at, i.e. a fixed state. Hence, the organs of plants being usually stationary when described, these prepositions are generally used with the ablative in botanical Latin.

A preposition is usually placed immediately before the noun it governs; but *versus* and *penes* are often placed after it, e.g. *basim versus* (towards the base).

PREPOSITIONS WITH THE ACCUSATIVE

ad: to, towards, at
adversus: opposite to, over against
ante: before
apud: according to, in the writings of
circum: around
circa, circiter: about, around
cis, citra: on this side of

clam: unknown to, without knowledge of
contra: against, contrary to
erga: towards (not used of places)
extra: outside of
in: into
infra: below, beneath
inter: between, among, during

intra : inside, within
juxta : next to, close to, according to, adjoining to
ob : because of
penes : in the power of
per : through, by means of, owing to, during
pone : behind
post : after, behind
praeter : except for
prope : near

propter : on account of
secundum : according to, beside
secus : along
sub : at, to beneath (motion)
subter : to below, beneath
super : over
supra : above
trans : across, on the other side
ultra : beyond
versus : towards, -ward

PREPOSITIONS WITH THE ABLATIVE

a, ab : from, by
absque : without, lacking
clam : unknown to
coram : in the presence of
cum : with
de : concerning, from
e, ex : from, out of
in : in, among

prae : before, in front of
pro : for, on behalf of, as
sine : without, lacking
sub : under (rest)
subter : below, beneath
super : upon
tenus : as far as, reaching to

ENGLISH PREPOSITIONS AND THEIR LATIN EQUIVALENTS

above : supra (acc.) : *supra medium*, above the middle

according to (following) : secundum (acc.), apud (acc.), juxta (acc.) : *juxta opinionem auctoris*, according to the opinion of the author

after : post (acc.) : *post florescentiam*, after flowering

against : contra (acc.)

along : secus (acc.) : *secus venas*, along the veins

amidst : inter (acc.)

among : inter (acc.), in (abl.) : *inter species affines*, among related species

around : circum (acc.)

as : pro (abl.) : *pro specie*, as a species

at : ad (acc.), sub (abl.) : *ad axillas et nodos*, at axils and nodes ; *ad apicem*, at the apex ; *ad angulum 70°*, at an angle of 70° ; *sub angulo 70°*, at an angle of 70° ; *sub anthesi*, at (during) anthesis

before : ante (acc.), prae (abl.) : *ante anthesin*, before anthesis

below : infra (acc.) : *infra medium*, below the middle

beneath : subter (acc. or abl.)

between : inter (acc.) : *diametro inter semi- et sesquimillimetrum*, with diameter between 0·5 and 1·5 mm.

beyond : ultra (acc.) : *ultra petalorum insertionem*, beyond the insertion of the petals

by : a (abl.) *or* ab (abl.) : *a variis auctoribus,* by various authors

concerning : de (abl.) : *de fructibus et seminibus,* concerning fruits and seeds

during : per (acc.)

except for : praeter (acc.) : *praeter aream geographicam,* except for the geographical area

for : pro (abl.) : *pro majore parte,* for the greater part ; *pro mutua commutatione,* for reciprocal exchange

from : e (abl.) *or* ex (abl.), a (abl.) *or* ab (abl.) : *e descriptione,* from (according to) the description ; *ex affinitate,* from (out of) the relationship ; *a praecedenti,* from the preceding ; *a specie altera,* from the other species ; *a speciebus affinibus,* from related species ; *ab illo,* from that

front of, in : prae (abl.)

in : in (acc. or abl.) : *in fructu,* in fruit ; *in sicco,* in a dried state ; *in parte inferiore,* in the lower part ; *in quoque loculo,* in each loculus ; *in specie typica,* in the type species ; *in sylvis,* in woods

in the presence of : coram (abl.), penes (acc.)

into : in (acc.) : *lamina in petiolum angustata,* blade narrowed into the petiole

near : prope (acc.) : *prope apicem,* near the apex

on (above) : supra (acc.)

on (concerning) : de (abl.) : *de plantis labiatis,* on labiate plants

on (in) : in (abl.) : *in pagina inferiore,* on the lower surface

on account of : ob (acc.), propter (acc.) : *ob ovarii formam et structuram,* on account of the shape and structure of the ovary ; *propter habitum, pedunculos erectos et corollas nutantes,* on account of the habit, erect peduncles and nodding corollas

on that (far) side : trans (acc.)

on this (near) side : cis (acc.)

out of : e (abl.) *or* ex (abl.)

outside of : extra (acc.)

presence of, in the : coram (abl.), penes (acc.)

through : per (acc.) : *per regiones temperatas,* through (over) temperate regions

towards : ad (acc.), erga (acc., not used of place), versus (acc.) : *versus folii marginem,* towards the margin of the leaf

under : sub (acc. or abl.) : *sub lente,* under a lens ; *sub microscopio,* under the microscope ; *sub ore,* under (below) the mouth

unknown to : clam (usually acc., sometimes abl.)

up to : ad (acc.) : *a basi ad apicem,* from the base up to the apex

with : cum (abl.) : *cum synonymis,* with synonyms

within : intra (acc.) : *intra corollam,* within the corolla

without (lacking) : sine (abl.) : *sine numero,* without a number

without (outside) : extra (acc.)

CHAPTER XI

Conjunctions

Conjunctions join words, phrases or sentences so as to indicate a connexion between them, which may be additive and positive, e.g. by the use of *et* (and), *-que* etc., or separative and alternative, e.g. by the use of *vel* (or), *-ve* etc., or qualificative and even contrary, e.g. by the use of *sed* (but), but they exercise no direct grammatical control over the words joined comparable to that of a preposition which takes the ablative or accusative. In the above sentence, 'and', 'but', 'or' and 'so as' are conjunctions.

'And' is commonly translated by *et*, which indicates 'an external connexion of different objects with each other', e.g. *in Europa media et australi et in Asia boreali* (in central and southern Europe and in northern Asia), *ex icone et descriptione* (from the illustration and description), *ramulis hornotinis et paniculis* (with branchlets of this year and panicles), *paniculae laterales et terminales* (panicles lateral and terminal), *nomen a Jacquino propositum et a Linnaeo approbatum* (name proposed by Jacquin and accepted by Linnaeus), *habitationes specierum et distributio generis geographica* (habitats of the species and geographical distribution of the genus). 'And also' indicating 'a close internal connexion between single words or whole clauses' is translated by *atque* or *ac* or by the termination *-que* added to the last word of a clause, e.g. *nervis primariis atque rete venularum aequaliter elevatis* (with the primary nerves and the network of veins equally raised), *ovarium dense breviterque hirsutum* (ovary densely and shortly hirsute), *filis intricatissimis moniliformibus geniculatisque* (with filaments most entangled, moniliform and geniculate), *stipulae inferiores multo breviores ac angustiores* (lower stipules by much shorter and narrower).

'Or' is commonly translated by *vel* or by the termination *-ve* added to the last word of a clause, e.g. *folia anguste vel late elliptica apice acuta vel obtusa* (leaves narrowly or broadly elliptic at the apex acute or obtuse), *sporis fuliginosis incoloribusve* (with spores sooty or colourless). A stronger and more positive contrast is expressed by *aut*—'*aut* excludes one term, *vel* makes the two indifferent'—which is occasionally used in botanical Latin. Alphonse de Candolle in his account of *Quercus* in the *Prodromus*, vol. 16 (1864) used *vel* to denote differences in leaf-form apparent on the same branch (represented by a single herbarium specimen) and *aut* to denote those between different branches (represented by different gatherings); thus *foliis basi cordatis vel obtusis vel acutis* (with leaves at base cordate or obtuse or acute) refers to the variation on a single specimen, *foliis basi acutis aut obtusis* (with leaves at base acute or obtuse) to the variation shown by specimens from different branches, probably from different trees.

The conjunction *seu* or *sive* (or if, or else) mostly appears in book titles, e.g. *Nomenclator botanicus seu Synonymia Plantarum universalis, Fuci sive Plantarum Fucorum Icones.*

For emphasis, after the manner of 'both . . . and', 'either . . . or', 'neither . . . nor' in English, pairs of prepositions are sometimes used as correlatives in Latin, e.g. *et . . . et, vel . . . vel, nec . . . nec.*

Other conjunctions sometimes used in botanical Latin include *ut* (so that, in order that), *quod* (because), *si* (if), *etsi* (even if), *licet* (granting that, although).

CHAPTER XII

Verbs

Alice was too puzzled to say anything, so after a minute Humpty
Dumpty began again. 'They've a temper, some of them—particularly verbs, they're the proudest—adjectives you can do anything with,
but not verbs—however *I* can manage the lot.'—LEWIS CARROLL,
Through the Looking-Glass

GENERAL CHARACTERS OF VERBS

Since a major function of verbs is to express action and since botanical
descriptions usually state the characters of plants as observed in the
most inactive of all states, i.e. as dead specimens fastened to sheets
of paper or mounted on microscope slides, verbs have become almost
redundant in modern botanical Latin. Botanists manage verbs best
by avoiding them altogether. Their main use now is in diagnostic
notes. But earlier authors naturally used them freely; and to read a
Latin dissertation or, for example, the extensive phycological discus-
sions in Latin of J. G. Agardh's *Till Algernes Systematik* (1872–90)
requires almost as extensive and sound a knowledge of classical Latin
as a piece of Augustan prose. This is outside the scope of the present
book. For a full treatment of verbs, reference must be made to
standard Latin grammars.

For botanical purposes much of the information given in these is
unnecessary. It is, however, necessary to distinguish Person, Number,
Voice and Tense, which limit the application of the verb, and the parts,
such as Infinitive, Participles and Gerundive, which have no limit of
persons or number. The Third Person, e.g. *est* (it is), *sunt* (they are),
is commonly used, the First Person, e.g. *sum* (I am), *habemus* (we have),
occasionally used, the Second Person, e.g. *es* (thou art), *estis* (you are),
very rarely and then mostly in dedications and prefaces. The First
Person singular in the active voice usually ends in -*m* or -*o*, the
Third Person singular in -*t*, the First Person plural in -*mus*, and the

Third Person plural in *-nt* but in the passive voice the Third Person singular ends in *-tur* and the Third Person plural ends in *-ntur*. The pronouns *ego* (I), *nos* (we), *is* (he), *ea* (she), *id* (it) are rarely used, since the ending of the verb itself indicates both person and number. The Tenses commonly used are the Present and Perfect of the Indicative, e.g. *differt* (it differs), *floret* (it flowers), *video* (I see), *vidi* (I have seen or I saw), *vidit* (he has seen), *vidimus* (we have seen), *viderunt* (they have seen), *distinguitur* (it is distinguished), *coluntur* (they are cultivated). Being essentially adjectival in function, the Present Participle, e.g. *purpurascens* (becoming purple), *radicans* (rooting), *repens* (creeping), the Past Participle Passive (Perfect Participle), e.g. *laevigatus* (made smooth), *lectus* (collected), *missus* (sent), and the Gerundive, e.g. *cognoscendus* (to be known), *distinguendus* (to be distinguished), are much more important; they are treated as adjectives (see p. 91). The Perfect Indicative of the Passive is formed from the Past Participle plus the Present Indicative Active of the verb *sum*, e.g. *visus sum* (I have been seen), *visus est* (he has been seen), *visi sumus* (we have been seen), *visi sunt* (they have been seen).

The Gerund is a verbal substantive ending in *-ndum*, with no plural but declined through the singular like other neuters in *-um*, e.g. *ad regnandum natus* (born to rule), *regnandi studium* (the desire of ruling).

The Gerundive is a verbal adjective in *-ndus* and as such is used in agreement with substantives and pronouns.

Active verbs have *two* participles; e.g. *dicens* (present), *dicturus* (future).

Passive verbs have *one*; e.g. *dictus* (past).

Deponent verbs have *three*; e.g. *sequens* (present), *secutus* (past), *secuturus* (future).

CONJUGATIONS

Verbs are classified into four main groups, called the First, Second, Third and Fourth Conjugations. Those which fit into these are termed 'regular'; there are, however, some 'irregular' verbs which do not. The dictionary entry for a verb states the first person present indicative, e.g. *video* (I see), the first person perfect indicative, e.g. *vidi* (I have seen), the supine (another form of verbal substantive), e.g. *visum* (in order to see) and the number, e.g. 2, of the conjugation to which it belongs, if regular. The conjugation can be recognized by the ending of the infinitive:

1 First Conjugation -*are*, e.g. **emendare** (to correct), **habitare** (to inhabit).
2 Second Conjugation -*ēre*, e.g. **florēre** (to flower), **vidēre** (to see); see p. 133.
3 Third Conjugation -*ĕre*, e.g. **colĕre** (to cultivate); see p. 134.
4 Fourth Conjugation -*ire*, e.g. **invenire** (to find); see p. 136.

It should be noted that the Third Conjugation is not so uniform as the other three, and its perfect participles are formed according to several disconcertingly different patterns.

There are also deponent and irregular verbs; see p. 137.

FIRST CONJUGATION
Active Voice

Present Indicative

habito	I inhabit
habitat	it (he, she) inhabits
habitamus	we inhabit
habitant	they inhabit

Perfect Indicative

habitavi	I have inhabited (I inhabited)
habitavit	it (he, she) has inhabited
habitavimus	we have inhabited
habitaverunt	they have inhabited

Present Infinitive   **habitare**   to inhabit
Present Participle   **habitans**   inhabiting

Passive Voice

Present Indicative

habitor	I am inhabited
habitatur	it (he, she) is inhabited
habitamur	we are inhabited
habitantur	they are inhabited

Perfect Participle   **habitatus** (m.), **habitata** (f.), **habitatum** (n.)
            inhabited

Gerundive   **habitandus** (m.), **habitanda** (f.), **habitandum** (n.)
            to be inhabited

In the following list the first person singular is given first, e.g. *amo* (I love), then the third person singular, e.g. *amat* (it loves), the present participle, e.g. *amans* (loving), and the perfect participle (past participle passive) masculine, e.g. *amatus* (loved).

amo	amat	amans	amatus	*love*
asservo	asservat	asservans	asservatus	*guard carefully*
amplifico	amplificat	amplificans	amplificatus	*enlarge*
angusto	angustat	angustans	angustatus	*make narrow*
cito	citat	citans	citatus	*cite*
comparo	comparat	comparans	comparatus	*compare*
conservo	conservat	conservans	conservatus	*preserve*
determino	determinat	determinans	determinatus	*determine*
discrepo	discrepat	discrepans	——	*differ*
disto	distat	distans	——	*stand apart*
dono	donat	donans	donatus	*give*
emendo	emendat	emendans	emendatus	*amend*

habito	habitat	habitans	habitatus	*inhabit*
illustro	illustrat	illustrans	illustratus	*elucidate*
indico	indicat	indicans	indicatus	*indicate*
observo	observat	observans	observatus	*observe*
plico	plicat	plicans	plicatus	*fold*
quadro	quadrat	quadrans	quadratus	*agree*
revoco	revocat	revocans	revocatus	*recall*
seco	secat	secans	sectus	*cut*
vario	variat	varians	variatus	*vary*

Pulmonaria tuberosa amat loca subumbrosa. Pulmonaria tuberosa loves rather shady places.

Habitat in collibus siccis Galloprovinciae. It dwells on dry hills of Provence.

Ab A. saxatili leguminibus dispermis distat. From A. saxatilis it stands apart by its two-seeded legumes.

Specimen originarium in herbario Linnaei asservatum est. The original [type] specimen is preserved in the herbarium of Linnaeus.

Quoad folia et calycem O. scopariam in memoriam revocat. As regards leaves and calyx it recalls O. scoparia.

SECOND CONJUGATION

Active Voice

Present Indicative

video	I see
videt	he (she) sees
videmus	we see
vident	they see

Perfect Indicative

vidi	I have seen (I saw)
vidit	he (she) has seen
vidimus	we have seen
viderunt	they have seen

Present Infinitive **vidēre** to see

Present Participle **videns** seeing

Passive Voice

Present Indicative

videor	I am seen (I seem)
videtur	he (she, it) is seen, it seems
videmur	we are seen
videntur	they are seen

Perfect Participle Passive **visus** (m.), **visa** (f.), **visum** (n.) seen

Gerundive **videndus** (m.), **videnda** (f.), **videndum** (n.) to be seen

adhaereo	adhaeret	adhaerens	adhaesus	*adhere to*
appareo	apparet	apparens	—	*appear*
augeo	auget	augens	auctus	*increase*
careo	caret	carens	—	*lack*
floreo	floret	florens	—	*flower*
gaudeo	gaudet	gaudens	—	*rejoice in*
habeo	habet	habens	habitus	*have*
misceo	miscet	miscens	mixtus	*mix*
pertineo	pertinet	pertinens	—	*belong*
praebeo	praebet	praebens	praebitus	*exhibit*
teneo	tenet	tenens	—	*hold*
video	videt	videns	visus	*see*

Bazzania brasiliensis habet folia minora flavida. Bazzania brasiliensis has smaller yellowish leaves.

Haec planta medium tenet inter P. montanam et P. tuberosam. This plant holds a position midway between P. montana and P. tuberosa.

Sporas vidi ellipsoideas. I have seen ellipsoid spores.

THIRD CONJUGATION

Active Voice

Present Indicative

    mitto   I send
    mittit   he (she) sends
    mittimus   we send
    mittunt   they send

Perfect Indicative

    misi   I have sent
    misit   he (she) has sent
    misimus   we have sent
    miserunt   they have sent

Present Infinitive   **mittere**   to send

Present Participle   **mittens**   sending

Passive Voice

Present Indicative

    mittor   I am sent
    mittitur   he (she, it) is sent
    mittimur   we are sent
    mittuntur   they are sent

Perfect Participle   **missus** (m.), **missa** (f.), **missum** (n.)
                 sent

Gerundive   **mittendus** (m.), **mittenda** (f.), **mittendum**
              (n.) to be sent

accedo	accedit	accedens	accessus	*approach*
addo	addit	—	additus	*add to*
attingo	attingit	attingens	attactus	*reach*
cingo	cingit	cingens	cinctus	*surround*
cognosco	cognoscit	cognoscens	cognitus	*know*
colligo	colligit	colligens	collectus	*gather*
colo	colit	colens	cultus	*cultivate*
congruo	congruit	congruens	—	*agree*
conjungo	conjungit	conjungens	conjunctus	*unite*
corrigo	corrigit	corrigens	correctus	*correct*
cresco	crescit	crescens	cretus	*grow*
detego	detegit	detegens	detectus	*discover*
dico	dicit	dicens	dictus	*say*
distinguo	distinguit	distinguens	distinctus	*distinguish*
divido	dividit	dividens	divisus	*divide*
ēdo	edit	edens	editus	*publish*
ĕdo	edit	edens	esus	*eat*
emitto	emittit	emittens	emissus	*put forth*
evado	evadit	evadens	evasus	*pass beyond*
facio	facit	faciens	factus	*make*
findo	findit	findens	fissus	*split*
frango	frangit	frangens	fractus	*break*
insero	inserit	inserens	insertus	*insert*
insero	inserit	inserens	insitus	*graft*
instruo	instruit	instruens	instructus	*provide*
jungo	jungit	jungens	junctus	*join*
lego	legit	legens	lectus	*gather*
maturesco	maturescit	maturescens	—	*ripen*
mitto	mittit	mittens	missus	*send*
neglego	neglegit	neglegens	neglectus	*neglect*
occulo	occulit	occulens	occultus	*hide*
occurro	occurrit	occurrens	—	*occur*
percurro	percurrit	percurrens	percursus	*run along*
pingo	pingit	pingens	pictus	*paint*
pono	ponit	ponens	positus	*put*
prodo	prodit	prodens	proditus	*bring forth*
recedo	recedit	recedens	recessus	*recede.*
rejicio	rejicit	rejiciens	rejectus	*cast out*
rumpo	rumpit	rumpens	ruptus	*burst*
scindo	scindit	scindens	scissus	*tear*
scribo	scribit	scribens	scriptus	*write*
sisto	sistit	sistens	—	*stand*
tego	tegit	tegens	tectus	*cover*
vivo	vivit	vivens	—	*live*

Crescit in uliginosis. It grows in marshes.

Linnaeus formam primariam et praeter hanc duas varietates β et γ distinxit. Linnaeus distinguished the primary form (the type) and besides this two varieties β and γ.

FOURTH CONJUGATION

Active Voice

Present Indicative

invenio	I find
invenit	he (she) finds
invenimus	we find
inveniunt	they find

Perfect Indicative

inveni	I have found (I found)
invenit	he (she) has found
invenimus	we have found
invenerunt	they have found

Present Infinitive **invenire**   to find
Present Participle **inveniens**   finding

Passive Voice

Present Indicative

invenior	I am found
invenitur	he (she, it) is found
invenimur	we are found
inveniuntur	they are found

Perfect Participle **inventus** (m.), **inventa** (f.), **inventum** (n.) found

Gerundive **inveniendus** (m.), **invenienda** (f.), **inveniendum** (n.) to be found

aperio	aperit	aperiens	apertus	*open*
convenio	convenit	conveniens	conventus	*agree*
finio	finit	finiens	finitus	*limit*
fulcio	fulcit	fulciens	fultus	*support*
invenio	invenit	inveniens	inventus	*find*
partio	partit	partiens	partitus	*divide*

Species bene notae 2 boreali-Americanae, quarum una etiam in Japonia invenitur. Species properly known 2 north-American, of which one is moreover found in Japan.

Nostra planta cum bahamensi (typo Linnaeano) bene convenit. Our plant agrees well with the Bahaman plant (the Linnaean type).

In itinere quod vere anni 1849 feci duas plantas inveni. On the journey which I made in the spring of the year 1849 I found two plants.

In Cuba insula primus invenit Houstonus. Houstoun first discovered it on the island of Cuba.

DEPONENT AND IRREGULAR VERBS

Deponent and irregular verbs diverge from the patterns of the four conjugations given above.

DEPONENT VERBS have a passive form but an active meaning, except in the gerundive, e.g.:

Present Indicative

utor	I use
utitur	he (she) uses
utimur	we use
utuntur	they use

Perfect Indicative

usus	sum	I have used (I used)
usus	est	he (she) has used
usi	sumus	we have used
usi	sunt	they have used

Infinitive	uti	to use
Present Participle	utens	using
Past Participle	usus	having used
Gerundive	utendus (m.), utenda (f.), utendum (n.)	
	to be used	

IRREGULAR VERBS derived from two roots are exemplified by *sum* (I am) and *fero* (I bear) and their derivatives:

Present Indicative

sum	I am
es	thou art
est	he (she, it) is
sumus	we are
estis	you are
sunt	they are

Future Indicative

ero	I shall be
eris	thou wilt be
erit	he (she, it) will be
erimus	we shall be
eritis	you will be
erunt	they will be

Perfect Indicative

fui	I have been (I was)
fuisti	thou hast been
fuit	he (she, it) has been
fuimus	we have been
fuistis	you have been
fuerunt	they have been

Present Infinitive	esse	to be
Perfect Infinitive	**fuisse**	to have been
Present Participle	none	
Gerundive	none	

Sum is a particularly important verb because it helps to form the passive of other verbs, e.g.:

Divisus est. It has been divided.

Stamina a spiculis examinatis jam delapsa fuerunt. Stamens from the spikelets examined were already fallen.

One of its derivatives is *possum* (I can), used in observations, e.g.

Ad interim juxta J. aculeatum inseri potest. For the present it can be inserted next to J. aculeata.

It is usually associated with the present passive infinitive, e.g. *habitari* (to be inhabited), *videri* (to be seen), *mitti* (to be sent), *inveniri* (to be found).

Present Indicative

possum	I can
potest	he (she, it) can
possumus	we can
possunt	they can

Present Subjunctive

possim	I may be able to (could)
possit	he (she, it) may be able to (could)
possimus	we may be able to (could)
possint	they may be able to (could)

The subjunctive, rare in botanical Latin, is used when one activity is conditional or dependent upon another or to express anticipation.

Subspecies esse possit Lecideae gelatinosae. It could be a subspecies of Lecidea gelatinosa.

Other derivatives of *sum* are:

absum	**abest**	be absent
adsum	**adest**	be present
desum	**deest**	be wanting
prosum	**prodest**	be of use

Genus ex charactere dato videtur Arthropogoni affine sed aristae desunt. The genus from the character given appears akin to Arthropogon but the awns are wanting.

Radix deest et flos unicus adest. The root is lacking and only one flower is present.

Fero (I bear, carry) is mostly used in its present participle *ferens* (bearing, carrying):

Present Indicative

fero	I bear
fert	he (she, it) bears
ferimus	we bear
ferunt	they bear

Infinitive **ferre**   to bear

Present Participle **ferens** bearing

Gerundive **ferendus** (m.), **ferenda** (f.), **ferendum** (n.)
                    to be borne

differo	differt	differens	*differ*
profero	profert	proferens	*bring forth*

Here belongs the verb *refert* (it concerns, it refers to) contracted from *rem fert*, used only in the third person singular.

SYNTAX AND OTHER MATTERS

Diagnoses

The noun *diagnosis* (διαγνωσις) comes from the verb διαγιγνωσκω ('know one from the other, discern, distinguish') and was used by the Greeks in the general sense of 'means of distinguishing, power of discernment, deciding'. Meaning originally a process or the mental instrument of a process, it now designates their result, and has thus several related but divergent applications. A medical diagnosis is an identification of a disease or pathological condition based on observation of the patient's symptoms, etc. A botanical or zoological diagnosis is a brief statement of the distinguishing features of an organism.

TYPES OF DIAGNOSES

Diagnoses were formerly divided into two kinds, one giving *differential* characters, the other *essential* characters. As stated by Lindley, 'differential characters express in the least possible space the distinctions between plants; they should contain nothing superfluous. A differential character moreover conveys no information beyond the differences between one thing and another and can be viewed in no other light than as a convenient method of analysis.' To call a 250-word description of a *Pandanus* holotype a 'diagnosis' is to misuse the term. 'The *essential* character of a plant expresses, as its name implies, those peculiarities known by experience to be most essential to it; but admits nothing unimportant or superfluous or that is common to all the species of the same genus or to all the genera of the same order.' For admirable examples of essential characters Lindley referred to Robert Brown's *Prodromus Florae Novae Hollandiae* (1810).

The drafting of diagnoses accordingly calls for an intimate acquaintance with the members of a group. The features selected must be constant for the taxon and, even if not individually uncommon within the group, those mentioned should together form a unique combination therein. Thus Linnaeus in 1753 distinguished his *Bauhinia aculeata* from all other species of *Bauhinia* by the phrase *caule aculeato* (with prickly stem), this feature being present in none of the others. Usually, however, a diagnosis to be effective must mention a combination of features. Most Linnaean specific names (*nomina specifica legitima* or phrase-names), as distinct from Linnaean binomials, are of this synoptic kind. Thus Linnaeus distinguished his *Bauhinia divaricata* by the phrase *foliis ovatis lobis divaricatis* (with ovate leaves with spreading lobes) from his *B. ungulata* with *foliis ovatis lobis parallelis* (with ovate leaves with parallel lobes) and from his *B. variegata* with *foliis cordatis, lobis coadunatis obtusis* (with cordate leaves, with blunt lobes united at their base). Linnaeus devoted much thought to the drafting of these diagnostic phrases, which were for him the true names of species and hence are very important for the typification of Linnaean binomials (cf. Stearn, 1957: 84–87, 126–132; Stearn, 1961a: 17).

Linnaeus held that these diagnoses should not exceed twelve words in length and he and Jacquin even managed on occasion to reduce them to one word. Thus Jacquin's diagnosis of *Ehretia tinifolia* is simply *Ehretia inermis*, of *E. spinosa* simply *Ehretia spinosa*, here as in his *Rauvolfia hirsuta* and *R. tomentosa* the diagnostic word being the same as the specific epithet. As the number of known species grew, and consequently the number of characters needed to distinguish them, his successors found it impossible thus to limit the number of words in a diagnosis; gradually the diagnostic phrase in the ablative case expanded into a short description likewise in the ablative case, although the nominative case was used for extended descriptions and for mention of non-diagnostic features. Thus Linnaeus in his *Species Plantarum*, 1: 448 (1753) provided *Reseda luteola*, dyer's greenweed (see p. 188), with the diagnostic name *Reseda foliis lanceolatis integris, calycibus quadrifidis* (Reseda with entire lanceolate leaves, with four-cleft calyces), which sufficed to distinguish it from the seven other species of *Reseda* named by him. In 1868 the monographer of the *Resedaceae*, Jean Müller of Aargau, needing to distinguish this from the 52 other species of *Reseda* then known, expanded the diagnosis to *foliis indivisis angustis, calyce 4-partito, lamina petali superioris 3-loba, staminibus circa 25, capsulis depresso-obovoideis undulato-rugosis ore contractis acute et valide 3-cuspidatis, seminibus laevibus parvulis* (with leaves undivided narrow, calyx 4-parted, blade of the upper petal 3-lobed, stamens about 25, capsules depressed-obovoid undulately rugose at the mouth contracted

Fig. 8 *Reseda luteola* L.; Weld, Yellow-weed
A, tota planta; B, folium inferum; C, pars supera ramuli floriferi; D, flos cum bractea; E, sectio longitudinalis floris; F, petalum superum; G, petalum laterale; H, petalum inferum; I, stamen; J, sectio transversa ovarii; K, pars ramuli fructiferi; L, capsula; M, semen (from Stella Ross-Craig, *Drawings of British Plants*; 1950)

E
×6

D
×3

H
×6

G
×6

I
×8

F
×6

J
×12

M
×8

K
R·C
×1

L
×4

C
×1

B
×1

A
×1/6

acutely and strongly 3-cuspidate, seeds smooth rather small). In 1867 Boissier, dealing with 27 oriental species of *Reseda*, gave an even longer diagnosis: *elata glabra parce et stricte ramosa, foliis lanceolato-linearibus elongatis supra basim saepe denticulatis, floribus subsessilibus racemum longissimum strictum formantibus, sepalis persistentibus ovato-oblongis corolla brevioribus, petalorum superiorum laciniis integris vel 2-3-partitis, filamentis persistentibus, capsulis strictis parvis glabris obovato-depressis sub ore contractis acute dentatis profunde 5-sulcatis* (tall glabrous sparingly and erectly branched, with leaves lanceolate-linear elongated above the base often denticulate, flowers almost sessile forming a very long spike-like upright raceme, sepals persistent ovate-oblong shorter than the corolla, laciniae of the upper petals entire or 2-3-parted, filaments persistent, capsules erect small glabrous obovate-depressed below the mouth contracted acutely toothed deeply 5-furrowed). The publication of such comparatively long diagnoses by nineteenth-century authors, who understood very well the distinction between a diagnosis in the ablative dependent upon the generic name and a true description with the organs independently described in the nominative, has misled later authors apparently unaware of this distinction into publishing very long descriptions in the ablative. For this there is no justification in history or convenience.

DIAGNOSTIC OBSERVATIONS

The traditional procedure of authors using diagnoses was to give first the diagnosis usually in the ablative, as exemplified above, then a statement of geographical distribution (see Chapter XVII), then a description in the nominative, often followed by an observation stating how the species differed from its allies, such as *Differt haec species a C. pelviformi caule erecto* etc. (This species differs from *C. pelviformis* by its erect stem, etc.), *Distinctissima foliis maximis racemisque patentissimis* (most distinct by its very large leaves and very outspread racemes) or stating concisely the main characters of other species, e.g. *Optime distinguitur a T. jamaicensi, cujus flores caerulei et capsulae tri-alatae sunt* (It is very well distinguished from *T. jamaicensis*, of which the flowers are blue and the capsules three-winged). Ignatius Urban (1848–1931) in his *Symbolae Antillanae* was probably the last botanist to employ extensively this time-honoured method of presentation. His detailed accounts of new species frequently conclude with a helpful note on related species such as that under *Meliosma recurvata* Urban (1921) of Haiti: *Ob inflorescentias elongatas tenues inter omnes species americanas peculiaris. Aliae species domingenses M. impressa Krug et Urb. cujus fructus ignoti sunt, praeterea foliis apice rotundatis v. truncatis, iargine integris, nervis lateralibus supra sulcato-impressis, M. Herbertii tolfe foliis ad ramos floriferos saltem integris, fructibus pluries majoribus iatim discernendae sunt. M. obtusifolia (Bello) Krug et Urb. (e Portorico), iuae fructibus similibus gaudet, foliis 2-3-plo longius petiolatis, multo iajoribus, margine integris, inflorescentiis crassioribus recedit* (Peculiar ιmong all American species on account of its elongated slender in-ιorescences. The other Dominican species are straightway to be ιistinguished, *M. impressa* Krug & Urban, of which the fruits are ιnknown, moreover by its leaves at the apex rounded or truncate, at ιhe margin entire, with the lateral nerves on the upper side sulcate-ιmpressed, *M. herbertii* Rolfe by its leaves entire only on flowering ιranches, its fruits often larger. *M. obtusifolia* (Bello) Krug & Urban from Puerto Rico), which rejoices in similar fruits, recedes by its ιuch larger leaves entire at the margin with petioles 2 or 3 times ιonger and thicker inflorescences).

Linnaean phrase-names, exemplified by those of *Bauhinia divaricata* ιnd *Reseda luteola*, from which diagnoses, such as those of Mueller, ιoissier and many other authors, notably Robert Brown in his *Prod-ιomus Florae Novae Hollandiae* (1810), were developed, had essentially ιhe same function as the contrasting statements in keys (cf. Stearn 957: 86; 1959: 17, 18; 1961: xxi). The provision of good keys ιakes such diagnoses unnecessary. In their place later authors often ιive diagnostic observations such as *Ab O. calophylla Engler pedicellis ιupra basin articulatis, inflorescentiis longioribus differt* (From *O. ·alophylla* Engler it differs by the pedicels articulate above the base, ιy the longer inflorescences). To these the term 'diagnosis' has now ιeen transferred. Under the International Code of Botanical Nomen-ιlature the publication of such an observation in Latin will suffice ΄or valid publication. Although inadequate as a scientific record, it ιan serve a useful purpose in indicating the affinities of a taxon pro-·ided these are correctly assessed; otherwise it may be virtually useless. Γhus W. Wright Smith mentioned his *Magnolia mollicomata* as 'species ιx affinitate *M. obovatae*, Thunb. (*M. hypoleucae*, Sieb. et Zucc.) et *M. ιfficinalis* Rehder et Wilson'; but this plant has in fact no close ιffinity with either. The following examples illustrate the diversity in ιtyle and content of diagnoses. The English versions follow fairly ιlosely the order of the Latin so as to demonstrate the manner of ιonstruction (see pp. 156, 378), the word order in Latin diverging in ιany respects from that natural in English.

EXAMPLES OF DIAGNOSES

Alsophila ramisora Domin: *A. infestae* Kunze affinis sed textura tenui, ιegmentis sat profunde crenato-dentatis et praesertim venatione et soris ad ·enarum ramos insidentibus notabilis (Domin, 1929).

B.L.—F

Akin to *A. infesta* Kunze but notable for the thin texture, the rather deeply crenate-dentate segments and especially the venation and the so situated on the branches of veins.

Arthothelium adriaticum *A. Zahlbruckner*: *Arthothelium sardoum* Bag. tangit, ob apothecia elongata et ob sporas minores minusque septatas ab e removendum (Zahlbruckner, 1914).

It touches *Arthothelium sardoum* Bagl., by reason of its elongated apotheci and its smaller and less septate spores to be taken away from this.

Brachylophon anastomosans *Craib*; a *B. scortechinii* King foliorur nervis lateralibus paucioribus crassioribus bene intra marginem anasto mosantibus, a *B. curtisii* Oliver foliis tenuioribus, ab ambobus rhach graciliore glabro, pedicellis brevioribus recedit (Craib, 1926).

It separates from *B. scortechinii* King by the fewer thicker lateral nerv of the leaves anastomosing well within the margin, from *B. curtisii* Oliver b the thinner leaves, from both by the more slender glabrous rhachis wit shorter pedicles.

Bryum auratum *Mitten*; *B. filiformi* primo adspectu maxime simile, se foliis fere duplo latioribus cellulis ad eorum apices duplo triplove latioribu et operculo rostrato (Mitten, 1859).

To *B. filiformi* at first sight most similar but with leaves almost twice a broad with the cells at the apices twice or thrice as broad and with the ope culum rostrate.

Corydalis gortschakovii *Schrenk*; species insignis floribus suis aurei majusculis (ad 9 lin. longis), a speciebus nobis notis bene distincta; differt *C. stricta* caule simplicissimo, foliis mollibus, laciniis acutiusculis, bractei herbaceis inferioribus subpinnatifidis, sepalis minutis basi non deorsur auriculatis, calcari elongato; a *C. sibirica* atque *C. impatiente* radice perenn caule simplicissimo, floribus majusculis et praeterea a *priore* lamina peta calcarati obtusissima (in *illa* acuminata) et siliquis ellipticis (in *illa* obovatis, a *posteriore* calcare graciliore limbum aequante (in *C. impatiente* dupl breviore) aliisque notis; a *C. nobili* haud aegre distinguitur caule toto folios (in *illa* a basi ad mediam partem nudo), racemo elongato, bracteis superioribu indivisis longe acutatis (in *illa* obtusis), sepalis parvis, non caudatis nequ peltatis vel deorsum auriculatis, calcari graciliore apice haud incrassat (Schrenk, 1841).

A remarkable species quite distinct from the species known to us by it golden rather large (to 9 lines long) flowers; it differs from *C. stricta* by it completely unbranched stem, soft leaves with acutish laciniae, herbaceou bracts, the lower almost pinnatifid, minute sepals at base not downwardl auriculate, elongated spur; from *C. sibirica* and *C. impatiens* by its perennia root, completely unbranched stem, rather large flowers and moreover fron the *former* by the very obtuse lamina of the spurred petal (in *that* acuminate and elliptic siliquae (in *that* obovate) from the *latter* by the more slender spu equalling the limb (in *C. impatiens* half as long) and other characters; fron

. nobilis it is distinguished without difficulty by its completely leafy stem
(n *that*, naked from the base to the middle part), elongated raceme, the
ndivided long-acute upper bracts (in *that* obtuse), the small sepals neither
audate nor peltate or downwardly auriculate, the more slender spur not
hickened at the tip.

Deutzia staurothrix *Airy-Shaw*; a *D. corymbosa* R. Br. foliorum pilis
tellatis utriusque paginae cruciformibus 4-radiatis, rarius 3- vel 5-radiatis
tatim dignoscenda (Airy-Shaw, 1934).

From *D. corymbosa* R. Br. immediately to be distinguished by the cruci-
orm 4-rayed, rarely 3- or 5-rayed, stellate hairs of each side of the leaves.

Dryopteris crassinervia *C. Christensen* ; habitu et textura *D. unita* e (Blume)
). Kuntze et affinibus similis et nullo dubio his speciebus proxima, praecipue
iffert venis basalibus non vere unitis, glabritie frondis, etc. (Christensen,
934).

In habit and texture like *D. unita* (Blume) O. Kuntze and allies and with-
ut doubt close to those species, it differs especially by the basal veins not
ruly united, by the glabrous state of the fronds, etc.

Galium petiolatum *Geddes*; a *G. rotundifolio* L. foliis petiolatis differt
Geddes, 1928).

From *G. rotundifolium* L. it differs by its petiolate leaves.

Geranium × **magnificum** *Hylander* ; planta inter *G. ibericum* Cav. et *G.*
latypetalum F. & M. quasi intermedia et verisimiliter ex hybridatione harum
pecierum orta, ab ambobus fructibus abortivis differt, quoad formam
oliorum cum *G. iberico* sat congruens sed petalis intensius violaceis, plus
·bcordatis et leviter tantum emarginatis (non ut in *G. platypetalo* margine
itegerrimis et late cuneatis) et indumento pilis eglandulosis longissimis
ilis glandulosis sat brevibus immixtis differt (in *G. iberico* indumentum
antum eglandulosum, in *G. platypetalo* tantum glandulosum) (Hylander,
961).

Plant almost intermediate between *G. ibericum* Cav. and *G. platypetalum*
*. & M. and probably sprung from the hybridization of these species, it
liffers from both by the abortive fruits, agreeing adequately with *G. ibericum*
s regards the shape of the leaves, but it differs in the petals more intensely
iolet, more obcordate and only lightly emarginate (not as in *G. platypetalum*
uite entire and broadly cuneate) and in the indumentum with very long
landless hairs intermixed with moderately short glandular hairs (in *G.*
bericum the indumentum only glandless, in *G. platypetalum* only glandular).

Helotium subconfluens *Bresadola* ; species haec ab *Helotio citrino* (Hedw.)
iffert ascomatibus minoribus minus coloratis, ascis quoque brevioribus, sed
·raesertim sporis fusoideis enucleatis (Bresadola, 1903).

This species differs from *Helotium citrinum* (Hedw.) by the smaller less
oloured ascomata, the asci also shorter, but especially by the enucleate
usoid spores.

Holomitrium muelleri *Hampe*: *Holomitrio crispulo* aemulans, differt foliis integerrimis et perichaetio multo breviore (Hampe, 1870).

To *Holomitrium crispulum* comparable, it differs by its quite entire leaves and much shorter perichaetium.

Kerriochloa *C. E. Hubbard*; genus novum, *Ischaemo* L. affine, a quo racemis solitariis breviter pedunculatis e lateribus spatharum emergentibus, spiculis valde heteromorphis, spiculis sessilibus a latere leviter compressis, gluma inferiore chartacea dorso convexa ecarinata, spiculis pedicellatis dorso compressis ad glumam inferiorem redactis differt (C. E. Hubbard, 1950).

New genus, akin to *Ischaemum* L., from which by the racemes solitary shortly pedunculate out from the sides of the spathes emerging, by the spicules strongly heteromorphic, with the sessile spicules at the side lightly compressed, the lower glume chartaceous on the back convex keelless, with the pedicelled spicules on the back compressed to the lower glume reduced it differs.

Kohautia sennii *Bremekamp*; inter species subgeneris *Pachystigmatis* seriei *Barbatarum* inflorescentia laxa et floribus parvis ad *K. effusam* (Oliver) Brem. accedens sed statura multo minore, pedicellis brevibus, corollae lobis majoribus ab ea recedens (Bremekamp, 1952).

Among species of the subgenus *Pachystigma* series *Barbatae* by its loose inflorescence and small flowers approaching *K. effusa* (Oliver) Brem. but diverging from this by its much lower stature, short pedicels, larger lobes of the corolla.

Lecanora carpathica *A. Zahlbruckner*; quoad habitum et fabricam internam apotheciorum ad *Lecanoram hageni* accedit, sed ab ea differt essentialiter thallo validiore, soralibus obsito, KHO flavescente, praeterea ab ea distat apotheciis minoribus et angustioribus, sporis minoribus e hymenio I persistenter violaceo-coeruleo tincto (Zahlbruckner, 1914).

As to habit and the internal structure of the apothecia it approaches *Lecanora hageni*, but it differs essentially from this by the more robust thallus covered by soralia, turning yellow with KOH, moreover it stands apart from this by its smaller and narrower apothecia, its smaller spores and its hymenium with I persistently violet-blue coloured.

Limonium mouretii (*Pitard*) *Maire*; species maroccana ab aliis speciebus Africae septentrionalis pariter foliis margine sinuatis et caulibus angulatis ve alatis gaudentibus propter folia caulesque glabra, pedunculos spicarum angulatos (nec alatos apicibus alarum in appendices triangulares abeuntibus)

Fig. 9   *Kerriochloa siamensis* C. E. Hubbard

1, planta florens, pars; 2, ligula; 3, rhachidis internodium spiculis sessilibus et pedunculatis; 4, gluma inferior spiculae sessilis; 5, lemma anthoecii inferioris; 6, palea; 7, 8, stamina; 9, lemma anthoecii superioris; 10, palea; 11, lodiculae; 12, 13, 14, caryopsis; 15, spicula pedicellata (by Stella Ross-Craig, from Hooker's *Icones Plantarum*, 35; 1950)

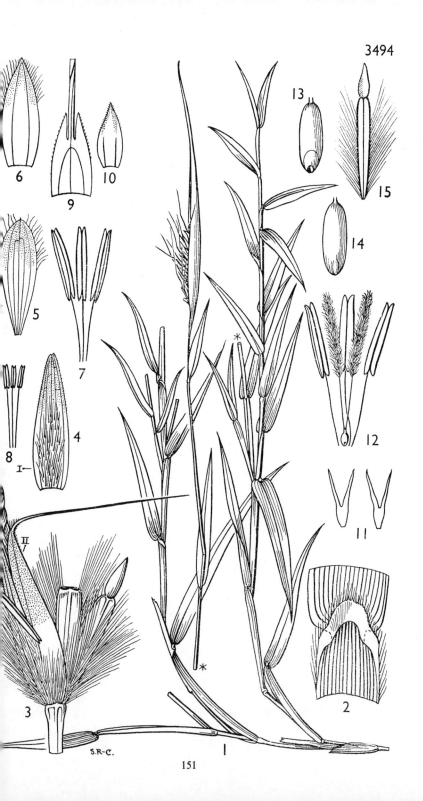

3494

S.R-C.

151

bracteam superiorem apice haud spinosam, calycem anguste infundibuliformem bene distincta (Stearn, 1940).

Moroccan species from other species of north Africa in like manner
furnished with (rejoicing in) leaves sinuate at the margin and angled or
winged stems quite distinct on account of its glabrous leaves and stems,
angled peduncles of the spikes (not winged with the tips of the wings ending
in triangular appendages), upper bract at the tip not spinous, narrowly
funnel-shaped calyx.

Lindsaea coriifolia *Lindman* ; species habitu cum *Lindsaea schomburgkii*
Klotzsch optime congruens, sed differt segmentis crassioribus, coriaceis
longius distantibus, venulis subduplo crebrioribus (Lindman, 1903).

Species in habit with *Lindsaea schomburgkii* Klotzsch best agreeing but it
differs in its thicker coriaceous more widely spaced segments with the venules
nearly twice as crowded.

Malva colmeiroi *Willkomm* ; haec species in Lusitania septentrionali et in
Gallaecia copiosissima ab affinibus *M. moschata* et *M. tournefortiana* carpellis
praeclare distinguitur glabris (aliquando in dorso vix puberulis), maturitate
nigrescentibus, lateribus parum radiato-rugulosis, quae in *M. moschata*
hirsutissima, demum aterrima, lateribus conspicue radiato-rugosis et in *M.
tournefortiana* hirsuta sed etiam maturitate pallida et aliquantulo minora
sunt (Lacaita, 1930).

This species most plentiful in northern Portugal and in Galicia from the
allied *M. moschata* and *M. tournefortiana* is very clearly distinguished by the
glabrous carpels (now and then on the back only just puberulous) at maturity
blackish, with the sides not particularly radiate-rugose, which in *M. moschata*
are most hirsute at length quite black, with the sides conspicuously radiate-
rugose and in *M. tournefortiana* hirsute but even at maturity pale and
somewhat smaller.

Psychotria farameoides *Bremekamp* ; a speciebus quas Mueller Argovensis ad *Eu-psychotriae* species *Bracteosas* ascripsit combinatione florum
subcapitatorum cum foliis basi rotundatis et vix notabile petiolatis distinguenda, a *Ps. bracteata* DC. quam Mueller Argovensis ad *Inundatas* adnumer-
avit forma bractearum lineari-lanceolata et foliis minoribus, pro rata
angustoribus, basi rotundatis et brevius petiolatis diversa (Bremekamp, 1962)

From the species which Müller of Aargau ascribed to *Eu-psychotric*
Bracteosae to be distinguished by the combination of almost capitate flowers
with leaves rounded at base and not notably petiolate, from *Ps. bracteate*
DC. which Müller attributed to the *Inundatae* distinct by the linear-lanceolate
shape of the bracts and the smaller relatively narrower leaves at base rounded
and more shortly petiolate.

Psychotria laurifolia *Swartz* ; differt a *P. glabrata* foliis longioribu
crassiusculis, floribus majoribus, baccis subrotundis (Swartz, 1797).

It differs from *P. glabrata* by its longer somewhat thick leaves, its larger flowers, its almost rotund berries.

Psalliota purpurella *F. H. Möller*; differt a *P. semota* statura minore, lamellis latioribus et colore pilei omnino purpureo (Möller, 1951).

It differs from *P. semota* by its smaller stature, broader gills and the completely purple colour of the pileus.

Reaumuria trigyna *Maximowicz*; quam *R. songarica* m. omnibus partibus multo major et flores non sessiles, ceterum habitu similior quam *R. persicae* Boiss., cui ex characteribus diagnosticis proxima, quae tamen foliis dense fasciculatis ovatis, flore duplo majore filamentisque basi crenatodentatis, praeter alia signa abhorret (Maximowicz, 1881).

Than my *R. songarica* in all parts much bigger and flowers not sessile, otherwise more like [this] in habit than *R. persica* Boiss., to which according to the diagnostic characters [it is] close, [but] which nevertheless differs by having] the leaves densely fasciculate ovate, the flower twice as big and the filaments at base crenate-dentate apart from other features.

Sabal jamaicensis *Beccari*; *S. parviflorae* affinis, a qua imprimis differt ramulis floriferis brevioribus, fructiferis in medio paullo incrassatis et segmentorum laciniis in apicem tenuissimum filiformem productis (Beccari, 1908).

Allied to *S. parviflora*, from which it differs particularly by the shorter flowering branchlets, the fruiting ones at the middle a little thickened and the laciniae of the segments drawn out into a very slender thread-like apex.

Saxifraga geoides *Lacaita*; species nova *S. geo* proxima, cujus flores foliorumque texturam, indumentum et colorem habet. Differt vero statura minore, vix ultra 10 cm., foliorum basi non vel vix cordata, saepe cuneiformi, petiolo breviore (2-3 cm.) latioreque (1·5 mm.), lamina minima, parum longiore (1-1·5 cm.) quam lata, marginis crenaturis paucissimis (6-8) et minus regulariter dispositis (Lacaita, 1930).

New species nearest to *S. geum*, of which it has the flowers and the texture, indumentum and colour of the leaves. It differs in fact by its lower stature, scarcely above 10 cm., by the base of the leaves not or scarcely cordate often cuneiform, by its shorter (2-3 cm.) and broader (1·5 mm.) petiole, very small blade little longer (1-1·5 cm.) than broad, with the crenate teeth of the margin very few (6-8) and less regularly arranged.

Senecio sagitta *Maximowicz*; ex affinitate *S. cacaliaefolii* Schultz Bip. et *S. emodensis* Schultz Bip., ab utroque foliorum forma et venatione distinctus (Maximowicz, 1881).

Of the affinity of *S. cacaliaefolius* Schultz Bip. and *S. emodensis* Schultz Bip., distinct from both by the form and veining of the leaves.

Trichostomum obtusifolium *Brotherus*; species foliis obtusissimis a congeneribus diversa (Brotherus, 1922).

Species by its very blunt leaves different from other members of the genus.

Viburnum × **bodnantense** *Aberconway*; hybrida hortensis e *Viburno fragrante* Bunge et *V. grandifloro* Wallich exorta, magnitudine floris (tubo corollae c. 9 mm. longo) inter parentes media, ad illud habitu et perulis interioribus subglabris, ad hoc foliis plerumque magnis et pedunculo pubescenti accedens (Stearn, 1950).

Garden hybrid originated from *Viburnum fragrans* Bunge and *V. grandiflorum* Wallich, by the size of the flower (with the tube of the corolla about 9 mm. long) midway between the parents, coming near to the former by its habit and almost glabrous inner perules, to the latter by its usually large leaves and pubescent peduncle.

Viburnum × **hillieri** *Stearn*; hybrida hortensis e *Viburno erubescente* DC. et *V. henryi* Hemsley genita, foliis sempervirentibus ad 6 cm. latis, tubo corollae 4-5 mm. longo et aliis characteribus inter parentes media (Stearn, 1956).

Garden hybrid born from *Viburnum erubescens* DC. and *V. henryi* Hemsley, by the evergreen leaves to 6 cm. broad, by the tube of the corolla 4-5 mm. long and by other characteristics midway between the parents.

Viola grandisepala *W. Becker*; ex affinitate *V. smithianae* W. Becker et specierum affinium sepalis late ovatis conspicuis distinguenda (W. Becker, 1928).

From the alliance of *V. smithiana* and related species to be distinguished by its conspicuous broadly ovate sepals.

CHAPTER XIV

Descriptions

Descriptions necessarily vary in length, detail and style according to the purpose for which they are intended and the nature of the organisms concerned; but a complete description, as defined by John Lindley, in which there would be 'a full statement made of all the peculiarities of every part, however obscure or difficult to observe', is rarely needed. A description should, however, state the habit of the plant and the shape and other obvious characters of all its main organs, usually omitting those common to the whole family or genus, when the classification is a well-established one, and give special attention to those characters which separate closely allied species in the group. For many groups there now exists a standard sequence in which organs and their attributes are recorded. With flowering plants it is customary, in accordance with the Linnaean rule 'Descriptio ordinem nascendi sequatur . . . Praestat naturam sequi a Radice ad Caulem, Petiolos, Pedunculos, Flores' (*Philosophia botanica*, no. 328; 1751), to proceed upwards from the root to the flowers and fruit and from the outside inwards.

The order of recording attributes is based on the general principles enunciated by Alphonse de Candolle: 'Pass from the known to the unknown, from definite matters to indefinite ones, from those which are most apparent to those which are less so.' For an individual organ, e.g. a simple leaf, this means stating position and number, general shape or outline, apex, margin, base, length, breadth, pubescence, veining, texture, colour. It is usual to describe the blade of a leaf before the petiole and stipules; the filaments of stamens before the anthers and pollen; the ovary of a pistil before the style and stigma. A set order enables descriptions to be readily compared. When describing a new species, the best policy is to adopt the same sequence and terminology of organs and their attributes as in some standard revision of the group. When preparing a monograph, a good beginning may be made by first describing two of the most diverse species and two of the most closely allied and then, from comparison of these descriptions, drafting a guiding scheme which can serve as a model for all descriptions. All information will then be presented in the same order; a difference in wording should indicate a difference in the plants concerned, similarity in wording a lack of significant difference.

Very long descriptions bury the most commonly needed information in a mass of detail. Hence a description of a new genus or species should be accompanied by a statement supporting its publication by emphasizing the most significant differences from its allies (see Chapter XIII) and placing it systematically. Some authors *italicize* or l e t t e r - s p a c e special features within the description.

Below are descriptions by a diversity of authors referring to diverse groups within the plant kingdom. Some of them may serve as models, others will suggest methods. Preference has been given to modern authors because they often take into consideration various characters ignored by or unknown to earlier authors of repute. The description of new plants in Latin is an act of international co-operation obligatory under the *International Code of botanical Nomenclature*. But it is not easy, and in some groups, notably the Algae (cf. Lund, 1953),[1] may be found very difficult. Hence there is a strong temptation to entrust the translation into Latin of the description of a new taxon to some willing person who may not understand properly the author's intent and may be unfamiliar with the customary terminology of the group (see the Preface to this book!). Professors of the classics are particularly liable to err through ignorance of botanical tradition. No descriptions should be written without study of previous descriptions referring to the same kind of plants. For descriptions in Latin of families and genera Bentham and Hooker's *Genera Plantarum* (1862–83) provides excellent models. For other groups, reference should be made to works by the masters of phytography listed on pp. 9, 12. Whenever possible, therefore, a Latin description should be accompanied by a description in the author's own language and an illustration as a defence against ambiguity and misinterpretation.

The English versions, being intended to illustrate the arrangement and style of the Latin descriptions, follow the latter fairly literally and would sometimes have been differently worded if intended to stand by themselves.

---

[1] J. W. G. Lund, 'Article 44 of the International Code in relation to Algae', *Taxon*, 2: 17-19 (1953).

ALGAE

CYANOPHYTA

Anabaenopsis magna *J. H. Evans* (Nostocaceae)

Trichomata libere natantia, brevia vel longa, circinata anfractibus uno ad octo, constricta ad septa, 10-11 μ lata. *Cellulae* cylindraceae, 8-12 μ ongae, bullis nullis, protoplasmate subtiliter granulari. *Heterocystae* :erminales vel geminatae intercalaresque, fere sphaericae vel ellipsoideae, 16 × 13 μ, poris uno vel duobus parvis munitae. *Sporae* (akinetes) geminatae ntercalares, ab heterocystis remotae, inflato-cylindraceae, 10-11 μ longae, 11 μ latae, protoplasmate fusco denso granulari (Adapted from J. H. Evans in *Hydrobiologia*, 20 : 82; 1962).

Trichomes free-floating, short or long, coiled with 1 to 8 spirals, con-tricted at cross-walls, 10-11 μ broad. *Cells* cylindric, 8-12 μ long, with no oubbles (gas vacuoles), with the protoplasm very finely granular. *Heterocysts* :erminal or paired and intercalary, almost spherical to ellipsoid, 16 × 13 μ, with one or two small pores. *Spores* (akinetes) paired and intercalary, away 'rom the heterocysts, inflated cylindrical, 10-11 μ long, 11 μ broad, with the protoplasm dark dense granular.

Microcoleus vaginatus *Gomont* (Oscillatoriaceae)

Fila sparsim repentia, rarius in stratum nigrum et nitens intricata, tortuosa, haud raro confuse pseudo-ramosa. *Vaginae* cylindraceae, ambitu plus minusve inaequales, agglutinantes, apice acuminatae et clausae, aut apertae et evanescentes, interdum omnino diffluentes, chlorozincico iodurato non caerulescentes. *Trichomata* aeruginosa intra vaginam permulta, arcte con-gesta, plerumque funiformi-contorta, extra vaginam recta, ad genicula haud constricta, apice sublonge attenuata et capitata, 3·5 μ ad 7 μ crassa ; articuli subquadrati, vel diametro trichomatis ad duplo breviores, rarius ad duplo ongiores, 3 μ ad 7 μ longi ; dissepimenta frequenter granulata ; membrana cellulae apicalis superne in calyptram depresso-conicam incrassata (M. Gomont, *Mon. Oscillar.*, 94 ; 1892).

Filaments sparsely creeping, more rarely entangled into a black and glossy layer, tortuous, not rarely confusedly pseudo-branched. *Sheaths* cylindric, in outline more or less unequal, glued together, at the apex acumi-nate and closed, or open and passing away, sometimes entirely dissolving, not turned blue by chlorozinc-iodine. *Trichomes* verdigris, within the sheath very many, tightly congested, commonly twisted like rope, outside the sheath straight, not constricted at the nodes, at the tip somewhat long attenuate and capitate, 3·5 μ to 7 μ thick ; articuli almost quadrate, or up o twice shorter than the diameter of the trichome, more rarely to twice onger, 3 μ to 7 μ long ; end walls frequently granulate ; membrane of the apical cell upwards thickened into a depressed-conical calyptra.

CHRYSOPHYTA

Amphiprora subcostata *Hustedt* (Amphiproraceae)

Membrana frustulorum delicata. *Frustulum* in facie connectivali visun in medio profunde constrictum, 54 μ longum, in medio 8 μ, prope apices 17 ʲ latae; alae ad 7 μ altae. *Linea alarum basalis* convexa non sinuata, irregu laris. *Structura membranae* tenuissima, striis transapicalibus inconspicuis Alae costis transapicalibus circiter 6 in 10 μ, ad marginem versus plerumque furcatis, prope polos saepe anastomosantibus. *Forma valvarum* incognita verisimile lanceolata; superficies valvarum medio valde inflata (F. Husted in *Veröff. Inst. Meeresf. Bremerhaven*, 6 : 77; 1959).

Membrane of frustules delicate. *Frustule* in girdle view at the middle deeply constricted, 54 μ long, in the middle 8 μ broad, near the ends 17 μ broad wings to 7 μ high. *Base line of the wings* convex not sinuate, irregular *Structure of the membrane* extremely thin, with transapical striae incon spicuous. *Wings* with transapical costae about 6 in 10 μ, towards the margin mostly forked, near the poles often anastomatosing. *Shape of the valve.* unknown very probably lanceolate; surface of the valves at the middle strongly inflated.

Asterolampra arrhenii *Kolbe* (Astrolampraceae)

Valvae reniformes planae fragiles, 138-216 μ longae, 84-150 μ latae; aree *centralis* circularis hyalina, radiis 8-14 rectis interdum bifurcatis; *comparti- mentes* circiter ¾ radii occupantes, centrum versus convexi vel truncati areolis distinctis aequalibus 12 in 10 μ; *intervalla* (vectores) 8-14 aequilata (circiter 3 μ) leviter arcuato-curvata vel recta marginem non attingentes (R. W. Kolbe in *Rep. Swed. Deep-Sea Exp.* 6, *Sedim.*, 1 : 47; 1954).

Valves reniform flat fragile, 138-216 μ long, 84-150 μ broad; *central area* circular hyaline, with 8-14 straight sometimes forked rays; *sectors* occupying about ¾ of the radius, towards the centre convex or truncate, with distinct equal areoles 12 in 10 μ; *intervals* (vectors) 8-14 of equal width (about 3 μ gently arcuate-curved or straight not reaching the margin.

Chrysochromulina strobilus *Parke & Manton* (Chrysophyceae)

Cellula in statu erratico satis metabola, depressa, dorso convexo, ventre plano vel cavo; dum quieta lenteve prolabens ephippioides seu a dorso vel

---

Fig. 10 *Chrysochromulina strobilus* Parke & Manton
1, cellula apice tumido tantum haptonematis flexi omnino extensi affixa; 2, cellula ephippioides affixa, flagello more heterodynamico movente, haptonemate per magnam partem longitudinis affixo; 3, cellula ephippioides lente prolabens haptonemate a fronte corporis extendente; 4, cellula in statu primo fissionis lente rotans et movens, haptonemate a fronte corporis omnino extenso; 5, cellula in statu fissionis, flagellis quattuor et haptonematibus duobus ad satis celeriter natandum aptis; 6, individuum natans, flagellis pro specie typicis ad celeriter movendum aptis, haptonemate extenso sed in se circinato et post corpus se trahens; 7, individuum prolabens sine rotatione, flagellis ad motum prolapsionis aptis; 8, cellula deltoides (a ventre visa) lente movens, haptonemate a fronte corporis omnino extenso, flagello altero lente undulanti, altero rigido vel lente vibranti: *c*, chromatophorum globulos saturatos lipidos a 'Sudan Black' tinctos continens, *f*, flagellum, *fb*, globuli

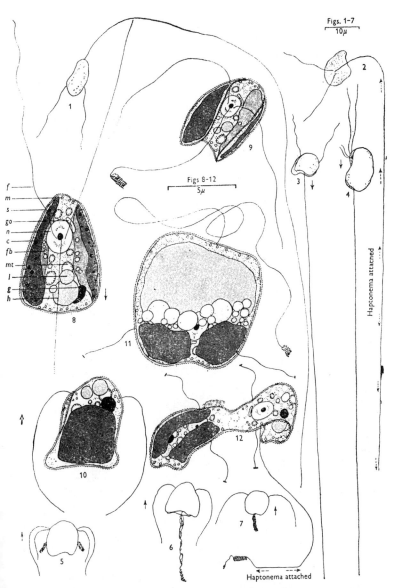

Figs. 1-7
10μ

Figs 8-12
5μ

Haptonema attached

Haptonema attached

lipidi, *g*, graphitum, *gb*, area Golgii, *H*, haptonema, *I*, vesicula leucosinea, *m*, corpus muciferum, *mt*, mitochondrium, *n*, nucleus, *s*, squama cupuliformis; 9, cellula affixa, haptonemate partim circinato et flagello a corpore extenso; 10, individuum natans, flagellis et corpore in statu ad rapide natandum pro specei typico; 11, cellula (e cultura in lumine forti per 10 dies culta) globulos lipidos multos continens, haptonemate paene omnino extenso in se circinato et apice tantum affixo; 12, status fissionis serus; cellula filialis absque chromatophoris (from *J. Marine Biol. Assoc. United Kingdom*, 38; 1959)

ventre visa truncato-ovata ; dum cito natans campanuliformis seu obovata
seu depresse globularis ; 6-10 (raro 5-12) μ longa. *Flagella* duo *haptonemaque*
unicum in facie ventrali sat conferte inserta, plerumque mediana, tertia
cellulae longitudinis parte ab apice rotundato remota ; flagella paene vel
plane aequalia, tenuissima, glabra, ad apices attenuata, nodulo quidque
terminatum (per microscopium electronicum viso), cellula 2-3 plo longiora,
inter motum citum homodynamica, inter lente movendum ut inter quietem
heterodynamica visa ; haptonema flagellis dimidio tenuius, extensum cellula
12-18 (raro -20) plo longius, apice incrassatum, in sectione transversa tres
membranas tubiformes concentricas ostendens fibras 6 in orbem dispositas
induentes, in tota longitudine adhaerendi potens. *Periplastus* pecticus,
squamis dense angulate congestis, 0·15-0·2 μ diametro, marginibus adscen-
dentibus, discis intus mucronato-incrassatis obtectus, alteris illis suppositis
delicatulis, hyalinis, orbicularibus vel ovalibus, 0·3-0·4 μ diametro, costis
radiantibus ornatis.

Nucleus unicus ; stigma nullum. *Chromatophora* 2 vel 4, interdum unum
vel nullum, fulva, in facie externa striatula, inter statum erraticum cellulae
parietalia, catilliformia vel oblonga, pyrenoidibus externis carentia, sed
regione penaria interna manifesta quidque instructum ;. inter statum seden-
tarium pallide aurea, subtilissime lobata. *Synthemata* lipoida et leucosinea.
Corpora mucifera ejectilia parva, in strato externo cytoplasmatis distributa,
in facie dorsali et ventrali posterioris partis ephippii crebriora, inter
metabolam situs mutantia.

Propagatio vegetativa in statu erratico bifissione effecta, cellulis filialibus
plerumque aequalibus ; in statu sedentario fissione iterata cellulae amoe-
boidis, cellulis filialibus 4, ovatis, parietibus subtilibus indutis, quaque earum
cellulam erraticam per porum liberante.

Typus die 9. Maji 1950 in summo mari lat. bor. 49° 21′, long. occ. 04° 54′
lectus, in Plymouth Angliae sub numero 43 cultus, postea in vivario
Cantabrigiensi depositus (M. Parke & I. Manton in *J. Marine Biol. Ass.
U.K.*, 38 : 172 ; 1959).

Cell in a motile state considerably metabolic, depressed, with the dorsal
side convex, with the ventral side flat or concave ; when at rest or slowly
gliding forward saddle-shaped or seen from the dorsal or ventral side trun-
cate-ovate ; when rapidly swimming bell-shaped or obovate or depressed-
globose ; 6-10 (rarely 5-12) μ long. Two *flagella* and one *haptonema* on the
ventral surface fairly closely inserted, usually central, distant one third part
of the length of cell from the rounded apex ; flagella almost or quite equal,
very fine, glabrous, drawn out to the apices, each one terminated by a small
knob (seen by means of the electron microscope), 2-3 times longer than the
cell, during rapid motion appearing homodynamic, during slow movement
as also when at rest heterodynamic ; haptonema half as thin as the flagella,
when extended 12-18 (rarely -20) times longer than the cell, at the apex
thickened, in transverse section displaying three tube-shaped concentric
membranes surrounding 6 fibres arranged in a ring, along its whole length
capable of clinging. *Periplast* pectic, covered with densely angularly crowded
scales 0·15-0·2 μ in diameter with ascending margins and discs on the inside

mucronately thickened, with beneath them placed others [which are] delicate
transparent orbicular or oval 0·3-0·4 μ in diameter ornamented by radiating
ribs.

Nucleus one ; stigma nil. *Chromatophores* 2 or 4, occasionally one or
more, tawny, on the outer face faintly striated, during the motile state of the
cell parietal, saucer-shaped or oblong, lacking external pyrenoids, but each
one provided with an evident internal storage region ; during non-motile
state pale gold, very finely lobed. *Synthemata* with lipids and leucosin.
Ejectile *muciferous bodies* small, distributed in the outer layer of cytoplasm,
on the dorsal and ventral surface of the back of the saddle more numerous,
during metaboly changing position.

Vegetative propagation in the motile state effected by fission into two,
with the daughter cells usually equal ; in the non-motile state by repeated
fission of amoeboid cell, with 4 ovate daughter cells provided with delicate
walls, every one of these liberating the motile cell through a pore.

Type collected on 9 May 1950 at the surface of the sea in lat. 49° 21′ N.,
long. 04° 54′ W., cultured in Plymouth, England under no. 43, later deposited
in the Cambridge living collection.

Chrysosphaerella rodhei *Skuja* (Chrysosphaerellaceae)

Coloniae ± globosae, saepe paululum tetraëdricae vel ellipsoideae,
interdum leviter irregulares, plerumque cellulis 4-32 compositae, 20-45 μ
diametientes, sine tegumento mucoso ; cellulis obovatis vel obovoideo-
piriformibus, 12-19 μ longis, 7-12 μ latis ; flagellis binis valde inaequalibus :
flagello generali cellulae longitudine 1½-2½-plo longiore, flagello altero
brevissimo solum ⅛-1/10 cellulae longitudinis. *Periplastus* sat firmus incoloratus
in parte anteriori squamis silicosis ellipticis, 3·5-3·8 μ × 1·5-2 μ magn., spinisque
1-4-8 vel ultra munitus ; spinis rectis acutis a basi apicem versus gradatim
attenuatis, 6-26 μ longis, inferne ad 0·9 μ crassis, disco duplicato pedali
3-3·5 μ lato, 1·5-3 μ alto praeditis. *Chromatophora* bina, lateralia, brunneo-
luteo-viridia, alveiformia, stigmate uno (raro bina) ovali, fusco-rubro ad
marginem anteriorem. *Vacuola contractilia* binis ad basin flagellorum, gutta
magna leucosini in parte posteriore cellulae ; praeterea granulis minutis
in cytoplasmate hyalino sparsis, nucleo nucleolato centrali. *Cystae* globosae,
13-15 μ diam., membrana hyalina vel pallidissime brunnea, levi, poro 2·5-3 μ
lato praeditae) H. Skuja in *Symb. Bot. Upsal.*, 9, no. 3 : 276 ; 1948).

Colonies more or less globose, often somewhat tetrahedric or ellipsoid,
sometimes slightly irregular, usually composed of 4-32 cells 20-45 μ in diameter without a mucous tegument ; with cells obovate or obovoid-pear-
shaped, 12-19 μ long, 7-12 μ broad ; with two flagella exceedingly
unequal ; with the principal flagellum 1½-2½ times longer than the length of
the cell, the other flagellum very short, only ⅛-1/10 the length of the cell. *Periplast* moderately firm colourless in the anterior part protected by elliptic
siliceous scales 3·5-3·8 μ × 1·5-2 μ in size and 1-4-8 or more spines ; with spines
straight acute from the base to the apex gradually attenuate, 6-26 μ long,
below to 0·9 μ thick, provided with a double foot-like disc 3-3·5 μ broad,

1·5-3 μ high. *Chromatophores* two, lateral, brown-yellow-green, trough-shaped with the eye-spot one (rarely two) oval, brownish red at the anterior margin. *Contractile vacuoles* two at the base of the flagella, with a large drop of leucosin in the posterior part of the cell; moreover with minute granules scattered in the hyaline cytoplasm, with a central nucleolate nucleus. *Cysts* globose, 13-15 μ in diameter, with the membrane hyaline or very pale brown, smooth, provided with a pore 2·5-3 μ broad.

Eunotia taeniata *Hustedt* (Eunotiaceae)

Valvae margine ventrali leniter concava, margine dorsali convexa 4-9-undulata, apicibus obtuse rotundatis, 30-55 μ longae, 6-10 μ latae. *Rhaphai* (rhaphes) breves in limbo valvorum prope polos sitae, apices terminales earum in facie valvarum non surrectae. *Striae transapicales* 12-20 in 10 μ, in apicibus densiores, usque ad circiter 24 in 10 μ. *Costa longitudinalis* fasciam hyalinam modice latam juxta marginem ventralem formans (F. Hustedt in *Bot. Notiser*, 1952: 380; 1952).

Valves with the ventral margin slightly concave, the dorsal margin convex with 4-9 undulations, the ends obtusely rounded, 30-55 μ long, 6-10 μ broad. *Raphes* short situated on the mantle of the valves near the poles, the terminal ends of these not produced on the surface of the valves. *Transapical striae* 12-20 in 10 μ, at the ends denser, up to about 24 in 10 μ. *Longitudinal rib* (pseudoraphe) forming a hyaline fairly broad band close to the ventral margin.

CHLOROPHYTA

Codium duthieae *Silva* (Codiaceae)

Thallus erectus ad 60 cm. alt., dichotome ramosus; rami omnino teretes, solum ad dichotomias aut fere omnino complanati; interdichotomiae 3-14 mm., dichotomiae ad 40 mm. lat. *Utriculi* cylindrici ad clavati, (130-) 175-500 (-720) μ diam. (45-) 670-1800 μ long., apicibus late rotundatis; membrana utricularis 2-6 μ crass., ad apices (ad 42 μ) interdum incrassata. *Pili* (aut pilorum cicatrices) parci, interdum satis multi (ad 12 per utriculum), 185-430 μ infra apicem portati. *Filamenta medullaria* plerumque 43-72 μ diam. *Gametangia* lanceo-ovata, 70-160 μ diam. (235-) 270-430 μ long., aliquot (ad 8) per utriculum, omnia in pediculis c. 15 μ long. in protuberantia 345-675 μ infra apicem portata (P. C. Silva in *Austral. J. Bot.*, 4: 275; 1956).

Thallus erect, to 60 cm. high, dichotomously branched; branches wholly terete, flattened only at the dichotomies, or flattened almost throughout; interdichotomies 3-14 mm. broad, dichotomies to 40 mm. broad. *Utricles* cylindrical to clavate, (130-) 175-500 (-720) μ diam., (45-) 670-1800 μ long, with apices broadly rounded; utricular wall 2-6 μ thick, at apices occasionally thickened (to 42 μ). *Hairs* (or hair scars) occasional, at times fairly numerous (to 12 per utricle), borne 185-430 μ below apex. *Medullary filaments* mostly 43-72 μ diam. *Gametangia* lance-ovoid, 70-160 μ diam., (235)-270-430 μ long, several (to 8) per utricle, all borne on pedicels about 15 μ long on protuberances 345-675 μ below apex.

Cosmarium planogranatum Croasdale (Desmidiaceae)

Cellulae 24-30 μ × 22-26 μ, 8-10 μ latae isthmo, 13-16 μ crassae. *Semicellulae* elliptico-reniformes; sinus inapertus; margines plerumque crenis 14 uniformibus planis praediti; superficies granula 25-35 magna plana, 12 in circulo intramarginali, aliis in tribus ordinibus irregularibus horizontalibus dispositis, praebens; membrana alibi laevis; semicellulae a latere visae circulares, granulis in quattuor ordinibus horizontalibus dispositis, a vertice visae late ovatae sine protuberantia mediana, granulis in duobus ordinibus intramarginalibus dispositis, parte mediana laevi; chloroplastus monocentricus (H. T. Croasdale in *Trans. Amer. Microsc. Soc.*, 81 : 29; 1962).

Cells 24-30 μ × 22-26 μ, 8-10 μ broad at the isthmus, 13-16 μ thick. *Semicells* elliptic-reniform; sinus closed; margins commonly provided with 14 uniform flat crenae; surface with 25-35 large flat granules, with 12 arranged in an intramarginal circle, the others in three irregular horizontal rows; membrane otherwise smooth; semicells in side view circular, with granules arranged in four horizontal rows, in vertical view broadly ovate without a median protuberance, with granules arranged in two intramarginal rows, with the median part smooth; chloroplast monocentric.

Enteromorpha jugoslavica Bliding (Ulvaceae)

Planta fertilis ca. 10-20 cm. alta, diam. 0·1-0·3 cm., inferne ramis paucis simplicibus angustissimis. *Cellulae* series distinctas longitudinales et nonnumquam transversales formantes, a facie visae quadratae, ca. 10 μ × 10 μ, aut rectangulares 11·0-12·7 μ longae, 8·2-9·0 μ latae, in infima parte caulis ca. 16 μ × 12 μ, rotundatae, subordinatae. *Pyrenoides* cellulae 1-3 (-4). *Generationes* alternantes: iso-gameta generationis sexualis minutissima, ca. 4·9 μ longa, 2·6 μ lata; zoosporae generationis asexualis 4-ciliatae, ca. 9·2 μ × 5·1 μ (C. Bliding in *Bot. Notiser*, 113 : 172; 1960).

Fertile plant about 10-20 cm. high, 0·1-0·3 cm. in diameter, below with branches few simple very narrow. *Cells* forming distinct longitudinal and sometimes transverse series, in surface view square, about 10 μ × 10 μ, or rectangular 11·0-12·7 μ long, 8·2-9·0 μ broad, in the lowest part of the stem about 16 μ × 12 μ, rounded, not well ordered. *Pyrenoids* of the cell 1-3 (-4). *Generations* alternating: isogametes of the sexual generation extremely minute, about 4·9 μ long, 2·6 μ broad; zoospores of the asexual generation 4-ciliate, about 9·2 μ × 5·1 μ.

CHAROPHYTA

Nitella moniliformis Zaneveld (Characeae)

Planta monoica, gracilis, humilis, moniliformis, brunneo-viridis, ad 15 cm. alta. *Caulis* tenuis, 150-300 μ in diam. *Internodia* quam ramuli 1-2-plo longiora. *Verticillorum ramuli* steriles fertilibus similes, capita formantes, c. 0·7 cm. diam., plerumque 4-, interdum 3- ad 5-furcati, 0·5 cm. longi; radii primarii 6-7, longitudine ½ totius ramuli; radii secundarii 5-6; radii tertiarii 5-6; radii quaternarii 4-5; radii quintarii (dactyli) 3-5. *Dactyli* plerumque 3-5, plus minusve aequales, bicellulati; cellula inferior 250-530 μ longa, 35-55 μ lata, cylindrica, apice rotundata; cellula superior acuminata, 35-70 μ longa, basi 8-17 μ lata. ♂ et ♀ *gametangia* ad omnes furcationes posita, haud muco circumfusa. *Antheridia* solitaria, terminalia, c. 180 μ diam. *Oogonia* 1-3 aggregata, ad nodos liberos posita, 240-270 μ longa (coronula inclusa), 204-235 μ lata, striis (5-)6; *coronula* persistens, connivens, 50-60 μ alta, basi 65-90 μ lata; *oosporae* aureo-brunneae, 180-225 μ longae, 155-195 μ latae, striis (4-)5; oosporae *membrana* tuberculata (J. S. Zaneveld in *Blumea*, 4 : 79; 1940).

Plant monoecious, slender, low, moniliform, brown-green, up to 15 cm. high. *Stem* slender, 150-300 μ in diam. *Internodes* 1-2 times as long as the branchlets. Sterile *branchlets of the whorls* similar to the fertile ones, forming heads of c. 0·7 cm. diam., frequently 4- sometimes 3- to 5-furcate, 0·5 cm. long; primary rays 6-7, half as long as the entire branchlet; secondary rays 5-6; tertiary rays 5-6; quaternary rays 4-5; quinary rays (dactyls) 3-5. *Dactyls* mostly 3-5, more or less equal, two-celled; basal cell 250-530 μ long, 35-55 μ wide, cylindrical, rounded at the apex; upper cell acuminate, 35-70 μ long, 8-17 μ wide at base. Male and female *gametangia* situate at all forks, not enveloped by mucus. *Antheridia* solitary, terminal, c. 180 μ in diam. *Oogonia* 1-3 together, situate at the free nodes, 240-270 μ long (including coronula), 204-235 μ wide, with (5-)6 striae; *coronula* persistent, connivent, 50-60 μ high, 65-90 μ wide; *oospores* golden-brown, 180-225 μ long, 155-195 μ wide, at base with (4-)5 striae; *membrane* of oospore tuberculate.

PHAEOPHYTA

Lithoderma antarcticum *Skottsberg* (Ectocarpaceae)

Discus minutus suborbicularis obscure fuscus, 180-210 μ crassus, crescentia marginali, substrato firme adhaerens, cellulis quadraticis—hexagonis—rectangularibus 4-10 μ longis et 4-7 μ latis, chromatophoris nonnullis donatis disciformibus. *Fila* verticalia arcte conglutinata, e cellulis cubicis formata. *Sporangia* unilocularia terminalia cylindracea, ad 15-16 longa et 9-10 μ lata. Pili desunt (C. Skottsberg in *Arkiv f. Bot.* II., 2 : 539; 1953).

Disc minute almost orbicular dull dark brown, 180-210 μ thick, with marginal growth, firmly clinging to the substratum, with quadrate to hexagonal to rectangular cells 4-10 μ long and 4-7 μ broad, containing several disc-shaped chromatophores. Erect *filaments* closely stuck together, formed from cubical cells. *Sporangia* unilocular terminal cylindric, to 15-16 μ long and 9-10 μ broad. Hairs lacking.

RHODOPHYTA

Batrachospermum globosporum *Israelson* (Batrachospermaceae)

Frons ad 7 cm. alta, ad 600 μ crassa, nunc laxe nunc abunde ramosa, valde mucosa, saturate viridis, leviter cyanescens. *Verticilli* aut distantes et ellipsoidei, aut contigui et plus minus compressi. *Ramuli secundarii* longi, numerosi, mox totum internodium obtegentes. *Pili* numerosi, plus minus elongati. Monoica. *Ramuli carpogoniferi* e cellulis basalibus ramulorum primariorum orientes, breves, ad 7-cellulares, curvati; carpogonia ad 40 μ longa, trichogyno indistincte pedicellato, elongato-obconico vel raro obovato vel subcylindraceo. *Spermatangia* globosa, 5·5-6 μ longa, 5-6 μ lata, in apicibus ramulorum primariorum et secundariorum evoluta. *Gonimoblasti* singuli vel rarius duo, magni, in centro verticilli inserti, globosi vel semiglobosi, laxi; ramuli gonimoblasti ramulis primariis subsimiles, cellulae basales et subbasales cylindraceae, 2½-5 plo longiores quam latae. *Carpo-sporangia* globosa vel subglobosa, rarius obovata, ad 13 (15) μ longa, ad 11 μ lata (G. Israelson in *Symb. Bot. Upsal.*, 6, no. 1: 44; 1942).

Frond up to 7 cm. high, to 600 μ thick, sometimes sparsely sometimes richly branched, strongly mucilaginous, deep green, lightly blue-tinged. *Whorls* either separated and ellipsoid or touching and more or less compressed. *Secondary branchlets* long, numerous, soon covering the whole internode. *Hairs* numerous, more or less elongated. Monoecious. *Carpogonial branches* arising from the basal cells of the primary branchlets, short, up to 7-celled, curved; carpogonia to 40 μ long, with the trichogyne indistinctly stalked elongated-obconical or rarely obovate or almost cylindrical. *Spermatangia* globular, 5·5-6 μ long, 5-6 μ broad, developed at the apices of the primary and secondary branchlets. *Gonimoblasts* single or more rarely two, large, inserted in the centre of the whorl, globular or semi-globular, loose; gonimoblast branchlets almost the same as the primary branchlets, the basal and almost basal cells cylindrical, 2½-5 times longer than broad. *Carposporangia* globose or almost globose, more rarely obovate, to 13 (15) μ long, to 11 μ broad.

Corallina goughensis *Y. M. Chamberlain* (Corallinaceae)

Planta usque ad 4 cm. alta, frondibus numerosis erectis e crusta basali ortis, per duos longitudinis trientes inferiores simplicibus intergeniculis teretibus, per trientem superiorem dichotome vel corymbose ramosis intergeniculis compressis. *Intergeniculorum cellulae* dispositae in strata horizontalia extremam partem versus deorsum curvata ita corticem formantia; cellulae medianae 35-70 μ longae, 6-8 μ latae, synapsibus lateralibus bene evolutis. *Genicula* unizonalia; cellulae usque ad 250 μ longae. *Conceptacula tetrasporica* terminalia, in sinu inter ramulos duos posita, poris apicalibus. *Tetrasporae* zonatim divisae, c. 160 μ longae, 60 μ latae (Y. M. Chamberlain in *Bull. Brit. Mus.* (*Nat. Hist.*), *Bot.*, 3: 213; 1965).

Plant up to 4 cm. high, with numerous erect fronds springing from a basal crust, for the lower two thirds of [their] length unbranched with terete inter-genicula, for the upper third dichotomously or corymbosely branched with compressed intergenicula. *Cells of intergenicula* arranged in horizontal rows towards the outermost part downwards curved to form a cortex ; central cells 35-70 μ long, 6-8 μ broad, with lateral synapses well developed. *Genicula* unizonal ; cells up to 250 μ long. *Tetrasporic conceptacles* terminal, placed in the angle between two branchlets, with pores apical. *Tetraspores* zonately divided, about 160 μ long, 60 μ broad.

Liagora tetrasporifera *Børgesen* (Helminthocladiaceae)

Frons caespitosa, ca. 7-8 cm. alta, filiformis, teres, 0·5-0·7 mm. crassa, dichotome divisa ; crusta calcarea continua, superficie sublaevi obducta. Color frondis in specimine exsiccato roseo-albidus. *Stratum periphericum* ex filamentis dichotomis plus minus irregulariter evolutis formatum est ; cellulae in parte basali subcylindricae, 5-8 μ latae, in media parte breviores et crassiores, ca. 8-10 μ latae, ad apicem versus breviores et minores ca. 3 μ latae. *Rami carpogonii* fere recti, ex tribus cellulis compositi, ca. 10 μ lati. *Cystocarpia* fere sphaerica ex filis non carposporiferis sed tetrasporangiferis constructa. *Antheridia* ad apices filorum assimilantium nascuntur. Planta monoica est (F. Børgesen in *Danske Vid. Selsk. Biol. Meddel.*, VI, 6 : 39 ; 1927).

Frond caespitose, about 7-8 cm. high, filiform, terete, 0·5-0·7 mm. thick, dichotomously divided ; calcareous crust continuous, covered by an almost smooth surface. Colour of the frond in the dried specimen rosy-white. *Peripheral layer* is formed from dichotomous more or less irregularly developed filaments ; cells in the basal part almost cylindric, 5-8 μ broad, in the middle part shorter and thicker, about 8-10 μ broad, towards the apex shorter and smaller about 3 μ broad. *Carpogonial branches* almost straight, made up of three cells, about 10 μ broad. *Cystocarps* almost spherical formed from filaments not carpospore-bearing but tetraspore-bearing. *Antheridia* are produced at the tips of the assimilating filaments. The plant is monoecious.

Nitophyllum berggrenianum *J. Agardh* (Delesseriaceae)

Fronde subsessili tenue membranacea, venis superficialibus usque ad lacinias superiores continuatis percursa, decomposito-pinnatifida, laciniis supra basem angustiorem mox cuneato-dilatatis, apice obtuso lobatis aut in lacinias angustiores sublineares productis, inferioribus a margine hic illic appendiculatis, soris rotundatis per lacinias medias sparsis.

Caespites minuti 1-2 pollicares rosulati, fronde iterum iterumque decomposita membranaceo-lubrica constituti, sessiles stipite conspicuo nullo. *Rami frondis* singuli supra partem inferiorem angustiorem paulo magis dilatati pinnatifidi, lobis supra sinum rotundatum invicem superpositis, inferioribu margine subinaequalibus sparsim dentatis et hic illic in appendices minuta productis, superioribus cuneatis lobatisque lobis rotundatis. *Sori* pe acinias medias sparsi, majusculi et rotundati. *Venae* evidentes at tenues. *Frondes* nunc appendiculis conglutinantur et praeparatione facilius dilacerantur.

Frondem inferiorem transverse sectam monostromaticam observavi. Caeterum duas formas vidi, quas aetate praecipue diversas judicavi. Una minor, supra praecipue descripta, lubrico-membranacea et chartae arcte adhaerens. Hujus lobi superiores abbreviati, inferioribus evidentius cuneato-dilatatis. Altera major usque 3pollicaris, et quia elongatior laciniis angustioribus, superioribus fere linearibus praedita, magis membranacea et chartae minus adhaerens. Sori melius evoluti lacinias medias occupant, per discum sparsi, nunc in laciniis superioribus secus margines quoque obvenientes, neutiquam vero modo N. lacerati secus margines seriati. Venae superficiales in utraque forma aeque obvenientes. Cellularum superficialium series 2-3, quae margine proximae sunt, ab interioribus parum differunt. Ipsum vero marginem occupant cellulae multo minores, subcubicae, unica serie saepissime dispositae (J. G. Agardh, *Sp. Gen. Ord. Algarum*, 3 : 449 ; 1876).

With the frond subsessile thin membranous, transversed by superficial veins continued up to the upper laciniae, decompound-pinnatifid, with the laciniae soon cuneately expanded above the narrower base, at the apex obtusely lobed or drawn out into narrower almost linear laciniae, the lower ones at the margin here and there appendiculate, with rounded sori scattered over the middle laciniae.

Tufts minute 1-2 inches rosetted, formed by the frond repeatedly decompound membranous-smooth, sessile with no conspicuous stipe. Single *branches of the frond* above the narrower lower part a little more broadened pinnatifid, with the lobes above the rounded sinus mutually overlapping, the lower ones at the margin somewhat unequal sparsely toothed and here and there drawn out into minute appendages, the upper ones cuneate and lobed with the lobes rounded. *Sori* (clusters of tetrasporangia) scattered over the middle laciniae, fairly large and rounded. *Veins* evident yet slender. *Fronds* are now bound together by little appendages and are very easily torn during preparation.

I have observed the lower frond in transverse section to be single-layered. For the rest I have seen two forms which I judge to be different chiefly in age. The smaller one, principally described above, smooth-membranous and firmly adhering to paper. The upper lobes of this abbreviated, with the lower ones more evidently cuneate-broadened. The other one larger up to 3 inches, and because more elongated provided with narrower lacinae having the upper ones almost linear, more membranous and adhering less to the paper. The better developed sori occupy the middle laciniae, scattered over the disc, but often also on the upper laciniae occurring along the margins, not exactly arranged in rows along the margin in the manner of N. laceratum. Superficial veins equally occurring in each form. Series of superficial cells 2-3, which are close to the margin, differ little from the interior ones. In fact much smaller almost cubical cells, most often arranged in a single row, occupy the margin itself.

FUNGI

ASCOMYCETES

Penicillium pusillum G. *Smith* (Aspergillaceae)

Coloniis in agaro Czapekii lentissime crescentibus, restrictis, primo caesiis deinde cum mycelio aerio albo aut vinaceo, paulo funiculosis, rugosis reverso brunneo-purpureo cum agaro paulo concolorato ; guttulis incoloratis ; glomeres mycelii sed nulla sclerotia efficientibus ; *coloniis in musto ex hordeo cum agaro* celerius crescentibus, albis glaucisque, paulo floccosis e funiculosis, rugosis, mox sclerotia brunneola numerosa efficientibus ; *conidiophoris* ex hyphis repentibus vel funiculis hypharum, plerumque non ramosis raro cum uno ramo, glabris, cum apicibus paulo inflatis, 35-55 μ long. et 1·5-2 μ diam. ; *penicillis* monoverticillatis ; *sterigmatibus* paene cylindricis, 10-11 (15) × 1·8-2 μ, aliquando longioribus et septatis ; *conidii* glabris, primo ovatis deinde globosis 2-2·5 μ diam. aut subglobosis 2·3-2·8 × 2-2·2 μ ; *sclerotiis* brunneolis, irregulariter globosis, ferme 300 μ diam. confluentibus (G. Smith in *Trans. Brit. Mycol. Soc.*, 22 : 255 ; 1939).

With *colonies on Czapek agar* very slow-growing, restricted, at first bluish-grey then with a white or vinaceous mycelium, slightly funiculose rugose ; the reverse brownish-purple with the agar almost the same colour droplets colourless ; forming compacted mycelium but no sclerotia ; with *colonies on wort agar* more rapidly growing, white or glaucous, a little floccose and funiculose, rugose, soon forming numerous brownish sclerotia ; *conidiophores* arising from trailing hyphae or ropes of hyphae, mostly unbranched rarely with a single branch, smooth, with the tips a little swollen, 35-55 μ long and 1·5-2 μ diam. ; *penicilli* monoverticillate ; *sterigmata* almost cylindrical, 10-11 (15) × 1·8-2 μ, occasionally longer and septate ; *conidia* smooth, at first ovate then globose 2-2·5 μ in diameter or subglobose 2·3-2·8 × 2-2·2 μ ; *sclerotia* brownish, irregularly globose, for the most part 300 μ in diameter, confluent.

Symphyosirinia E. A. *Ellis* (Helotiales)

Apothecia e synnematibus specierum Symphyosirae exorientia, cupulata stipitata. *Excipulum* prosenchymatosum, totum ex hyphis homomorphis subparallelis constans. *Asci* inoperculati, 8-spori. *Ascosporae* uniseriatae vel in dimidio distali asci biseriatae, demum 1-septatae ; paraphyses cylindricae. Typus [nominis] generis: *S. galii* E. A. Ellis (E. A. Ellis in *Trans. Norfolk & Norwich Nat. Soc.*, 18, no. 3: 5 ; 1956).

Apothecia originating from synnemata of a *Symphyosira*, cupulate, stipitate. *Excipulum* prosenchymatous, composed of uniform subparallel hyphae throughout. *Asci* inoperculate, 8-spored. *Ascospores* uniseriate or becoming biseriate in the distal half of the ascus, ultimately becoming 1-septate; paraphyses cylindrical. Type of [name of] genus: *S. galii* E. A. Ellis.

Symphyosirinia galii E. A. *Ellis*

Synnemata primaria sessilia vel substipitata, alba ; *secundaria* carnosa, clavata, 1-3 mm. alta. *Conidia* cylindrica, obtusa, hyalina usque pallide olivacea, 7-9-septata, 35-60 × 5-7 μ, in cellula distali setas 1-3 usque ad 50 μ longas gerentia. *Apothecia* e synnematibus primariis senescentibus erumpentia, stipitata, cupulata, 1·0-1·5 mm. diametro, ad 3 mm. alta. *Discus* planus, immarginatus, pallide griseo-brunneus. *Asci* cylindrico-clavati, 8-spori, 100-127 × 7-9 μ, poro iodo tincto haud caerulescente. *Ascosporae* uniseriatae, ovoideae, continuae vel 1-septatae, hyalinae, 10-15 × 3·5-4 μ. *Paraphyses* cylindricae, 2 μ latae. *Excipulum* prosenchymatosum (E. A. Ellis in *Trans. Norfolk & Norwich Nat. Soc.* 18, no. 3 : 6 ; 1956).

Primary synnemata sessile or substipitate, white ; *secondary* fleshy, clavate, 1-3 mm. high. *Conidia* cylindrical, obtuse, hyaline to pale olivegreen, 7-9-septate, 35-60 × 5-7 μ, on the distal cell bearing 1-3 setae up to 50 μ long. *Apothecia* erumpent from old primary synnemata, stipitate, cupulate, 1·0-1·5 mm. in diameter, to 3 mm. high. *Disc* flat, immarginate, pale greyishbrown. *Asci* cylindric-clavate, 8-spored, 100-127 × 7-9 μ, with the pore not blued by iodine. *Ascospores* uniseriate, ovoid, continuous or 1-septate, hyaline, 10-15 × 3·5-4 μ. *Paraphyses* cylindric, 2 μ broad. *Excipulum* prosenchymatous.

BASIDIOMYCETES

Aecidium hederae *Wakefield* (Uredinales)

Pycnidia amphigena, praecipue hypophylla, laxe gregaria, primo mellea demum obscurantiora, 80-120 μ diametro. *Aecidia* hypophylla vel petiolicola, conferta, per folii totam superficiem aequaliter distributa, matricem deformantia, cupulata, 0·5-1·5 mm. diametro, margine albido pulchre revoluto 5-7-inciso. *Pseudoperidii cellulae* angulatae, firme conjunctae, 15-20 μ diametro, vel 25 × 20 μ, pariete 2-2·5 μ crasso, verrucoso-striato. *Aecidiosporae* globosae vel subglobosae, leviter angulatae, subhyalinae, laeves, 18-19 × 15 μ, tenuiter tunicatae, poris germinationis 4-5 instructae (E. M. Wakefield in *Kew Bull.*, 1931 : 202; 1931).

Pycnidia amphigenous [i.e. on two sides], chiefly hypophyllous [i.e. on lower side of leaf], loosely clustered, at first honey-coloured later becoming darker, 80-120 μ in diameter. *Aecidia* hypophyllous or on the petiole, crowded, evenly distributed over the whole leaf surface, distorting the host, cupulate, 0·5-1·5 mm. in diameter, with a whitish beautifully revolute 5-7-incised margin. *Cells of the pseudoperidium* angular, firmly united, 15-20 μ in diameter, or 25 × 20 μ, with the wall 2-2·5 μ thick, verrucosely striate. *Aecidiospores* globose or subglobose, slightly angular, almost hyaline, smooth, 18-19 × 15 μ, thin-walled, provided with 4-5 germ pores.

Hygrophorus speciosus *Peck* (Agaricaceae)

Pileo ex ovato vel subconico expanso, margine tenui recurvo, glabro, glutinoso, saepe minute umbonato, nitide rubro vel coccineo, demum lutescente ; *stipite* longo, subaequali, solido, albo vel lutescente, plerumque viscido ; *lamellis* arcuatis, decurrentibus, subdistantibus, candidis, interstitiis venosis ; *sporis* ellipsoideis, 8-9 μ long. Gregarius, 8-13 cm. altus ;

pileus 2½ cm. latus, stipes 6-10 mm. crassus. Pereximia species. Umbo parvus et discus diutius reliquo pileo colorem servant (P. A. Saccardo, *Sylloge Fungorum*, 5 : 415 ; 1887).

With the *cap* at first ovate or subconical, then expanded, the margin thin recurved, glabrous, glutinous, often minutely umbonate, brightly red or crimson, then becoming yellowish ; with the *stem* long, almost equal (i.e. cylindrical), solid, white or yellowish, generally viscid ; with the *gills* arcuate, decurrent, sub-distant, white, with veined interspaces (i.e. anasto- mosing) ; with *spores* ellipsoid, 8-9 μ long. Gregarious, 8-13 cm. high ; cap 2·5 cm. broad, stem 6-10 mm. thick. Very showy species. The small umbo and disc retain colour longer than the rest of the cap. [This description in the ablative should be compared with Bresadola's below in the nominative.]

Hygrophorus speciosus *Peck* (Agaricaceae)

Pileus carnosus, tenuis, e campanulato expansus et umbonatus, laete flavus, umbone aurantio-fulvus, glaber, glutinosus, glutine hyalino, 3-6 cm. latus ; *lamellae* distantes, crassae, albae, ad marginem pilei citrinae, quan- doque totae citrinae, acie alba, in fundo venoso-conjunctae, postice decur- rentes ; *stipes* e farcto subcavus, aequalis, apice albus, infra velum flavus, flocculosus, basi albidus, glutinosus, 3-7 cm. longus, 8-15 mm. crassus ; *velum* inferum, glutinoso-fibrillosum hyalinum, ad stipitem saepe in annulum manifestum ; *caro* alba, sub cuticula citrina, inodora et insapora ; *sporae* obovato-ellipticae, hyalinae, 8-10 ⩽ 5-6 μ ; *basidia* clavata, 50-70 ⩽ 6-8 μ (G. Bresadola, *Iconogr. Mycol.*, 7 : t. 313 ; 1928).

Cap fleshy, thin, at first campanulate then expanded and umbonate, bright yellow, at the umbo orange-tawny, glabrous, glutinous, with hyaline glutin, 3-6 cm. broad ; *gills* distant, thick, white, at the margin of the cap lemon-yellow, sometimes all yellow, with white edge, at the base anastomos- ing, decurrent ; *stem* at first stuffed later somewhat hollow, equal, at the apex white, below the veil yellow, flocculose, at the base white, glutinous, 3-7 cm. long, 8-15 mm. thick ; *veil* inferior, glutinously flocculose hyaline, on the stem often appearing as a ring ; *flesh* white, below the cuticle lemon- yellow, scentless and flavourless ; *spores* obovate-elliptic, hyaline, 8-10 × 5-6 μ ; *basidia* clavate, 50-70 × 6-8 μ.

Puccinia menthae *Persoon* (Uredinales)

Pycnidiis vel in parvos greges dispositis vel sparsis, melleis ; *aecidiis* hypophyllis v. saepe caulicolis, in folio maculis plerumque purpureo-rufis insidentibus et in greges plus minusve regulares dispositis, in caulibus, petiolis et nervis foliorum greges incrassatos saepe valde elongatos formanti- bus, rarius sparsis, irregulariter apertis, margine vix v. irregulariter lacerato, erecto v. parum intus curvato ; *aecidiospuris* subglobosis ellipsoideis v. polygoniis, verruculosis, pallide flavis, 24-40 = 17-28 ; *soris uredosporiferis* hypophyllis, mox maculis flavidis v. brunneolis insidentibus, mox sine maculis, minutis, orbicularibus v. ellipticis, sparsis v. aggregatis, epidermide rupta cinctis, mox nudis, subinde confluentibus, cinnamomeis; *uredosporis* globosis, subglobosis, ellipsoideis v. obovatis, echinulatis, pallide brunneis, 17-28 = 14-19; *soris teleutosporiferis* hypophyllis, rarius caulicolis, sparsis v, aggregatis, minutis, subinde confluentibus, orbicularibus, pulverulentis, atrofuscis; *teleutosporis* ellipsoideis, ovatis v. subglobosis, utrinque rotundatis, apice papilla pallida v. hyalina lata praeditis, medio non v. vix constrictis, verruculosis, obscure brunneis, 26-35 = 19-23; pedicello sporam superante, hyalino, gracili (P. Sydow & H. Sydow, *Monographia Uredinearum*, 1 : 282; 1904).

With *pycnidia* arranged in small groups or scattered, honey-coloured; *aecidia* hypophyllous or often on the stems, situated on the leaves generally as purple-reddish spots and disposed in more or less regular groups, forming on stems, petioles and veins thickened groups often much elongated, rarely scattered, opening irregularly, with the margin scarcely or irregularly torn, erect or slightly incurved; *aecidiospores* subglobose, ellipsoid or polygonal, verruculose, pale yellow, 24-40 by 17-28 μ; *uredosori* hypophyllous, soon in yellowish or brownish spots or lacking spots, minute, roundish or elliptical, scattered or aggregated, surrounded by the torn epidermis, soon naked, sometimes confluent, cinnamon; *uredospores* globose, subglobose, ellipsoid or obovate, echinulate, light brown, 17-28 by 14-19 μ; *teleutosori* hypophyllous, rarely on the stems, scattered or grouped together, minute, sometimes confluent, rounded, powdery, dark brown; *teleutospores* ellipsoid, ovate or subglobose, rounded at both ends, with a broad pale or colourless apical papilla, not or scarcely constricted at the centre, verruculose, dull brown, 26-35 by 19-23 μ; pedicel longer than the spore, colourless, slender.

Puccinia oreogeta *Sydow* (Uredinales)

Uredosori hypophylli, sparsi vel pauci, laxe seriatim dispositi, non confluentes, oblongi, 200-300 μ longi, epidermide tecti, flavidi; *uredosporae* ovato-globosae, ovatae vel late ellipsoideae, subinde etiam irregulares, 22-30 ≈ 17-22 μ, dense verruculoso-echinulatae, membrana hyalina vel subhyalina ca. 1·5 μ crassa, poris germ. indistinctis; *teleutosori* conformes sed obscuriores, brunnei, compacti; *teleutosporae* oblongae usque clavatae, ad apicem plerumque rotundatae, rarius leniter truncatae vel conicoproductae, ad septum plerumque leniter constrictae, postice sensim in pedicellum attenuatae, 35-52 μ longae, cellula superiore 16-21 μ lata, inferiore plerumque paullo longiore et angustiore, episporio ad apicem 8-14 μ crasso et flavo-brunneo; pedicello persistenti, 25-45 μ longo, hyalino vel subhyalino (H. Sydow in *Annales Mycol.*, 35 : 224; 1937).

Uredosori hyphyllous, few or sparse, loosely linearly arranged, not confluent, oblong, 200-300 μ long, covered by the epidermis, yellowish; *uredospores* ovate-globose, ovate or broadly ellipsoid, occasionally also irregular, 22-30 by 17-22 μ, densely verruculose-echinulate [set with small wart-like and spiny projections], with a hyaline or almost hyaline membrane about 1·5 μ thick, with indistinct germ pores; *teleutosori* similar [to the

uredosori] but less conspicuous, brown, compact; *teleutospores* oblong to
club-shaped, at the apex commonly rounded, more rarely somewhat truncate
or conically elongated, often lightly constricted at the septum, postically
tapering into the stalk, 35-52 μ long, with the upper cell 16-21 μ broad, the
lower one commonly a little longer and narrower, with the epispore at the
apex 8-14 μ thick and yellow-brown; with the pedicel persistent 25-45 μ
long, hyaline or almost hyaline.

Ramaria flavoviridis *Corner & Thind* (Clavariaceae)

Ad 17×7 cm., gregaria v. caespitosa, trunco subnullo, e basi multiramosa,
carnosa, laete viridis dein flavoviridis, apicibus concoloribus v. albidulis,
rhizomorphis gracilibus albis copiosis praedita; ramis polychotomis,
superne dichotomis et plus minus compressis; carne alba insipida, Anethi soa
odore.

   Sporae $6-8·3 \times 3-3·7$ μ, brunneolo-ochraceae, ellipsoideae, subverrucu-
losae v. subechinulatae. *Hyphae* in tramis receptaculorum rhizomorphisque
dimiticae; skeletales 3-5 μ latae, tunicis 0·5-1 (-1·5) μ crassis, sparsae sed
conspicuae, vix ramosae, aseptatae, ad 1500 μ longae, apicibus filiformibus
elongatis 1 μ latis vel ut segmenta intercalaria; hyphae tenuitunicatae 2·5-9 μ
latae, hinc inde ad 17 μ, copiosae, fibulatae, cellulis ad 140 μ longis (E. J. H.
Corner & K. S. Thind in *Trans. Brit. Mycol. Soc.*, 44: 236; 1961).

   Up to 17×7 cm., gregarious or clustered, with the main stem almost nil,
from the base much-branched, fleshy, light green then yellow-green, with
the tips concolorous or whitish, provided with slender white abundant
rhizomorphs; with branches polychotomous, above dichotomous and more
or less compressed; with flesh white insipid, having the smell of Anethum
soa.

   Spores $6-8·3 \times 3-3·7$ μ, light brownish-ochraceous, ellipsoid, obscurely
verruculose or almost echinulate. *Hyphae* in the flesh of the receptacles and
in the rhizomorphs dimitic; skeletal hyphae 3-5 μ broad, with 0·5-1 (-1·5)
thick walls, sparse but conspicuous, scarcely branched, without septa, up to
1,500 μ long, with filiform elongated ends 1 μ broad or as intercalary segments;
thin-walled hyphae 2·5-9 μ broad, here and there to 17 μ, plentiful, provided
with clamps, with cells up to 140 μ long.

Sphacelotheca sclerachnes *Wakefield* (Ustilaginales)

   Sori in inflorescentiis evoluti, easque omnino destruentes, primitus a
vagina inclusi circiter 1-2 mm. longi, membrana cellulis subhyalinis 10-12 μ
diametro tecti, columella centrali praediti. *Massa sporarum* atrobrunnea,
mox pulverulenta. *Sporae* maxime variabiles, globosae, subglobosae,
pyriformes vel citriformes, brunneo-violaceae, laeves, 10 μ diametro, vel
$12-15 \times 9-10$ μ (E. M. Wakefield in *Kew Bull.*, 1931: 203; 1931).

   Sori developed in inflorescences and entirely destroying these, at first
enclosed by a sheath about 1-2 mm. long, covered by a membrane with
almost colourless cells 10-12 μ in diameter, provided with a central columella.
Spore mass blackish-brown, soon powdery. *Spores* exceedingly variable,

globose, subglobose, pear-shaped or lemon-shaped, brownish-violet, smooth, 10 μ in diameter, or 12-15 × 9-10 μ.

MYXOMYCETES

Comatricha solitaria *Nannenga-Bremekamp* (Stemonitaceae)

Sporangia solitaria vel subsolitaria, stipitata, erecta, parva, altitudine tota circ. 0·6 mm. *Hypothallus* inconspicuus vel nullus. *Stipes* sporangium altitudine circ. dimidia parte excedens, niger, opacus, basi fibrosus, in sporangium immersum. *Sporangium* globosum, 0·35 mm. diam., saturate brunneum; peridium evanescens; columella usque ad medium sporangium porrecta et ibi in ramulos plures divisa. *Capillitium* sub-nigrum, laxius, e filamentis crassis et rigidis, dichotome ramificatis, vix reticulatim connectis compositum. *Sporae* per saturam saturate brunneae, lucem orientem versus visae griseo-brunneae, globosae, circ. 13 μ diam. in typo, in speciminibus aliis interdum 14-16 (18) μ diam., minute verruculosae. *Plasmodium* hyalinum, incolor (N. E. Nannenga-Bremekamp in *Acta Bot. Neerland.*, 11 : 31 ; 1962).

Sporangia solitary or nearly solitary, stipitate, erect small, with total height about 0·6 mm. *Hypothallus* inconspicuous or lacking. *Stipe* exceeding the sporangium in height by about a half (i.e. about 1½ times the height of the sporangium), black, opaque, fibrous at base, immersed in (i.e. penetrating into) the sporangium. *Sporangium* globose 0·35 mm. in diameter, dark brown; peridium evanescent; columella extended to the middle of the sporangium and then divided into several branchlets. *Capillitium* nearly black, rather lax, formed from filaments thick and rigid, dichotomously branched, scarcely reticulately connected. *Spores* in the mass dark brown, grey-brown seen by transmitted light, globose, about 13 μ in diameter in the type, in other specimens sometimes 14-16 (18) μ in diameter, minutely warty. *Plasmodium* hyaline, colourless.

FUNGI IMPERFECTI

Camarosporium rosae *Grove* (Sphaeropsidales)

Pycnidia dense sparsa, globosa, papillata, parva (ca. 120 μ diam.), atra, velata, dein papillâ per rimam laceratam protrusâ. *Sporulae* oblongae, utrinque obtuse rotundatae, 3-septatae (rarissime 4-5-septatae), septis longitudinalibus uno aut duobus praeditae, aequaliter atro-brunneae, vix constrictae, 16-20 × 5·5-6 μ, sporophoris nullis visis (W. B. Grove, *Brit. Stem- and Leaf-Fungi*, 2 : 362 ; 1937).

Pycnidia densely scattered, globose, papillate, small (about 120 μ in diameter), black, covered, then protruding the papilla through a torn fissure. *Spores* oblong, obtusely rounded at both ends, 3-septate (very rarely 4-5-septate), provided with one or two longitudinal septa, evenly dark-brown, hardly constricted, 16-20 × 5·5-6 μ, with no sporophores seen.

Rhodotorula macerans *Frederiksen* (Cryptococcaceae)

Cultura in extracto malti: Post 3 dies ad 25°C cellulae sunt oblongo-ovales (3·3-5·5 × 7-12 μ), singulae vel binae. Post unum mensem ad 17° C sedimentum atque annulus formati sunt.

Cultura in malto-agar: Post 3 dies ad 25° C cellulae sunt oblongo-ovales (3-5 × 7-12 μ), singulae vel binae. Cultura in striis post unum mensem ad 17° C laevis et nitens est vel ex parte rugosa et opaca, color roseus vel ruber.

Cultura in lamina vitrea: Nullum pseudomycelium.

Fermentatio: Nulla.

Assimilatio sacchari: Glucosis + ; Galactosis + (exigua); Saccharosis + ; Maltosis + ; Lactosis + (saepe exigua).

Assimilatio kaliumnitrati: Adest.

Ethanoleum ut unica origo carbonis: Nullum incrementum.

Decompositio arbutini: Variabilis.

Cultura in pectino: Incrementum observatur.

Productio compositorum amylo similium: Adest.

Culturae huius speciei conservantur in 'Centralbureau voor Schimmelcultures', Delft, Hollandia, item in collectionibus culturarum fungorum, quas Academia regia agriculturae, pars phytopathologica, in Hafnia sustentat (P. S. Frederiksen in *Friesia*, 5: 237; 1956).

Growth on malt extract: After 3 days at 25° C the cells are oblong-oval (3·5-5·5 × 7-12 μ), single or in pairs. After one month at 17° C a sediment and a ring are formed.

Growth on malt-agar: After 3 days at 25° C, the cells are oblong-oval (3-5 × 7-12 μ), single or in pairs. The streak-culture after one month at 17° C is smooth and shiny or in part rugose and dull, the colour rose or red.

Culture on glass slide: No pseudomycelium.

Fermentation: Absent.

Assimilation of sugar: Glucose + ; Galactose + (weak); Saccharose + ; Maltose + ; Lactose + (often weak).

Assimilation of potassium nitrate: Positive.

Ethanoleum as sole source of carbon: No increase.

Decomposition of arbutin: Variable.

Growth on pectin: Increase observed.

Production of compounds like starch: Positive.

Cultures of this species are kept in the Centralbureau voor Schimmel cultures, Delft, Holland, also in the fungus culture collection which the Royal University of Agriculture [i.e. Royal Veterinary and Agricultural College], phytopathological section, in Copenhagen maintains.

[An interesting example of cultural reactions effectively summarized in simple clear Latin. The accepted spellings in pharmaceutical Latin for the sugars are *glucosum, galactosum, saccharosum, maltosum, lactosum*, all neuter and Second Declension like *saccharum* (sugar) and *maltum* (malt).]

Septogloeum punctatum *Wakefield* (Melanconiales)

Maculae aridae, elongatae, angulatae, nervis limitatae, fusco-marginatae circiter 8 mm. latae. *Acervuli* hypophylli, atro-olivacei, punctati, compacti, pulvinati, primo epidermide tecti, demum erumpentes. *Conidiophora* filiformia, densissime aggregata, olivacea. *Conidia* cylindracea, utrinque rotundata, dilute olivacea, 25-32 × 5 (-6) μ, demum 3-septatae (E. M. Wakefield in *Kew Bull.*, 1931 : 204; 1931).

Spots dry, elongated, angular, bounded by the veins, dark-margined, about 8 mm. broad. *Acervuli* hypophyllous [i.e. on lower side of leaf], blackish olive-green, punctate, compact, cushion-shaped, at first covered by the epidermis, at length breaking out. *Conidiophores* filiform, very densely crowded, olive-green. *Conidia* cylindrical, rounded at each end, pale olive-green, 23-32 × 5 (-6) μ, at length 3-septate.

LICHENES

Chiodecton emergens *Vainio* (Chiodectonaceae)

Thallus sat tenuis, verruculoso-inaequalis, cinerascens aut cinereoglaucescens, leviter nitidus, KHO non reagens, creberrime contextus, hypothallo nigricante aut pallido-fuscescente saepe limitatus. *Pseudostromata* leviter aut modice prominentia, rotundata aut raro ellipsoidea, diam. 0·6-0·35 mm., sat crebra, simplicia aut raro 2 confluentia, depressa, sat laevigata, albida aut rarius thallo subconcoloria, leviter nitida, creberrime contexta, KHO non reagentia, basin versus sensim dilatata aut sat praerupta, hymenia solitaria continentia, strato amphitheciali obducta thallino, gonidiis concatenatis, 0·007-0·010 mm. crassis, trentepohlioideis instructo, intus albido. *Disci* rotundati aut raro ellipsoidei, lat. 0·2-0·3 mm., haud aut leviter impressi, plani, livido-rufescentes aut nigricantes, subnudi. *Hypothecium* olivaceofuscescens aut olivaceum, tenue, 0·02-0·03 mm. crassum. *Parathecium* olivaceo-fuscescens, crass. 0·03-0·04 mm. *Hymenium* 0·09-0·12 mm. crassum, jodo fulvo-rubescens aut dilute rufescens (haud caerulescens). *Epithecium* decoloratum. *Paraphyses* ramoso-connexae, gelatinam percurrentes, crass. 0·001 mm., sat crebre septatae. *Asci* clavati, membrana fere tota leviter incrassata. *Sporae* 8 :nae, distichae, decolores, oblongo-fusiformes aut ovoideo-oblongae, rectae, apicibus obtusis, 3-septatae, saepe strato gelatinoso tenui indutae (E. A. Vainio, *Lichenes Ins. Philipp.*, 3 : 283 ; 1920).

Thallus rather thin, verrucosely uneven, greyish or greyish-glaucescent, slightly glossy, KOH –, very densely interwoven, often delimited by a blackish to pale brownish hypothallus. *Pseudostromata* slightly or moderately prominent, rounded or rarely ellipsoid, in diameter 0·6-0·35 mm., rather crowded, simple or rarely 2 confluent, depressed, rather smooth, whitish or more rarely subconcolorous, slightly glossy, very densely interwoven, KOH –, towards the base gradually spreading or somewhat abruptly incised, each containing a solitary hymenium, covered by an amphithecial thallus-like stratum layer, provided with filamentous 7-10 μ thick *Trentepohlia*-like gonidia, within whitish. *Discs* rounded or rarely ellipsoid, 0·2-0·3 mm. broad, not or lightly impressed, plane, becoming livid reddish or blackish, almost naked. *Hypothecium* olive-blackish-brown or olive-green, thin, 20-30

μ mm. thick. *Parathecium* olive-blackish-brown, 30-40 μ thick. *Hymenium* 90-120 μ mm. thick, I+ tawny red or pale reddish (not becoming blue). *Epithecium* colourless. *Paraphyses* anastomosing, within mucilage, 1 μ thick, rather closely septate. *Asci* clavate, with the wall almost uniformly thickened. *Spores* 8, biseriate, colourless, oblong-fusiform or ovoid-oblong, straight, with apices obtuse, 3-septate, often covered with a thin gelatinous layer [i.e. halonate].

Cladonia rotundata *Ahti* (Cladoniaceae)

Podetia albido-cinerascentia et partim rufescentia, acidum fumarpro-tocetraricum et atranorinam continentia, dichotome aequaliter vel sub-aequaliter dense ramosa, axem principalem deficientia vel axes indistinctos formantia, vulgo pulvillos densos rotundatos efficientia, internodiis tenuibus, 0·4-0·8 mm. crassis, in summo ramulis ultimis divaricatis, rufescentibus, medulla exteriore tenui compacta facile disintegrataque. *Pycnidia* globosa vel ovoidea, gelatinam hyalinam continentia (T. Ahti in *Ann. Bot. Soc. Zool.- Bot. Fenn.*, 32, no. 1 : 29 ; 1961).

Podetia whitish-greyish and partly becoming reddish, containing fumar-protocetraric acid and atranorine, equally or almost equally densely dicho-tomously branched, with the principal axis absent or indistinct, commonly making dense rounded cushions, with slender internodes 0·4-0·8 mm. thick, at the apex with divaricate reddish ultimate branches, with thin, compact and easily disintegrating outer medulla. *Pycnidia* globose or ovoid, containing hyaline jelly.

Laurera ambigua *Malme* (Pyrenulaceae)

Crusta tenuissima, olivacea v. sordide cinerea, continua, laevis, subopaca, KOH non reagens. *Apothecia* solitaria vel saepius 2-4 approximata coacerva-tave, hemisphaerica, basi abrupta (haud constricta), denudata (tantum basi thallo obducta), circiter 0·5 mm. lata, atra vel nigricantia, apice nonnihil umbilicata, ostiolo papilla minutissima nigra indicato. *Perithecium* nigricans, integrum, basi tamen paullulo tenuius, KOH haud reagens ; nucleus sub-globosus vel basi nonnihil applanata, pallidus, oleoso-guttulosus, J non reagens (tantum contentu ascorum juniorum sordide rubescente), KOH immutatus. *Asci* inflato-clavati, usque 160 μ longi et 45 μ crassi, mem-brana superne nonnihil incrassata. *Sporae* octonae vel abortu pauciores, irregulariter distichae, incolores, oblongo-ellipsoideae, (40-) 45-55 (-60) μ longae, (14)-15-18 (-21) μ crassae, rectae, utroque apice rotundatae, valde murales, septis transversis circiter 11, halone crassiusculo circumdatae, J haud reagentes. *Paraphyses* ramoso-connexae, vix 1 μ crassae, gelatinam copiosam percurrentes (G. O. A. Malme in *Arkiv f. Bot.*, 19, No. 1 : 24 ; 1924).

Crust very thin, olive-green or sordid grey, continuous, smooth, rather dull, KOH–. *Apothecia* solitary or more often 2-4 confluent, hemispherical, at the base incised (not constricted), naked (only at the base covered by the thallus), about 0·5 mm. broad, black or blackish, at the apex somewhat umbilicate, with the ostiole indicated by a very minute black papilla. *Peri-hecium* becoming black, entire, at base nevertheless a little thinner, KOH – ; nucleus almost globose or with base somewhat flattened, pale, provided with oil droplets, I – (only the content of the younger asci becoming dirty reddish), KOH – . *Asci* swollen-clavate, up to 160 μ long and 45 μ thick, with the membrane towards the apex somewhat thickened. *Spores* eight or by abortion fewer, irregularly biseriate, colourless, oblong-ellipsoid, (40-) 45-55 (-60) μ long, (14)-15-18 (-21) μ thick, straight, at both ends rounded, thickly walled, with about 11 transverse septa, fairly thickly halonate, I – . *Paraphyses* anastomosing, scarcely 1 μ thick, within copious mucilage.

Opegrapha sorediifera P. James (Opegraphaceae)

Thallus epiphloeodes, tenuissimus, plerumque indeterminatus, aliquando hypothallo atro-cinereo limitatus, furfuraceus vel scabridus, impolitus ± rimosus sed non areolatus ; *soralia* numerosa, simplicia, ± punctiformia, parva, ad 1·2 mm. lata, raro 2 vel 3 in areas erosas ad 3 mm. diametro coalescentia, crateriformia, aurea vel ochracea. *Soredia* minute granularia vel farinacea. *Ascocarpi* lirellati, breves, c. 2 mm. longi, 1 mm. lati, simplices, crispi, apice obtusi, margine ± tumidi et nudi; discus non expositus.

Thallus 30-60 μ crassus ; cortex c. 15 μ crassus, strato algaceo medullae indistincte delimitato ; algae ad Trentepohlias pertinentes ; cellulae (4-) 5-7 (-8) μ diametro, flavae ad aurantiaco-brunneae. *Excipulum* nigrum, carbonaceum, ad 60 μ latum; *thecium* 100-120 μ altum; *paraphyses* 1 μ crassae, ramosae, anastomosantes ; *hypothecium* ad 15 μ crassum, incolor ; *asci* 60-80 μ longi, 13-16 μ lati, pariete uniformi 2-3 μ crasso, 8- spori ; *sporae* 30-40 (-45) μ longi, 4-5 μ crassae, primo incolores, raro aetate brunnescentes, 10-14- septatae. *Pycnidosporae* 4-6 μ longae, 0·6-0·8 μ crassae, bacillariformes P. W. James in *The Lichenologist*, 2 : 86 ; 1962).

Thallus epiphloeodal, very thin, mostly indeterminate but occasionally bounded by a grey-black hypothallus, scurfy or scabrid, matt, more or less cracked but not areolate ; *soralia* numerous, simple, more or less punctiform, small, to 1·2 mm. broad, rarely 2 or 3 confluent into erose areas to 3 mm. in diameter, crateriform, golden or buff. *Soredia* minutely granular or farinaceous. *Ascocarps* lirellate, short, about 2 mm. long, 1 mm. broad, unbranched, curled, at the apex obtuse, at the margin more or less tumid and naked ; disc not exposed.

Thallus 30-60 μ thick ; cortex about 15 μ thick, with the algal layer of the medulla indistinctly defined ; algae belonging to *Trentepohlia* ; cells (4-) 5-7 (-8) μ in diameter, yellow to orange-brown. *Exciple* black, carbonaceous, to 60 μ broad ; *thecium* 100-120 μ high ; *paraphyses* 1 μ thick, branched, anastomosing ; *hypothecium* to 15 μ thick, colourless ; *asci* 60-80 μ long, 13-16 μ broad, with the wall uniform 2-3 μ thick, 8-spored ; *spores* 30-40 (-45) μ long, 4-5 μ thick, at first colourless, rarely brownish with age, 10-14-septate. *Pycnidospores* 4-6 μ long, 0·6-0·8 μ thick, bacillariform.

BRYOPHYTA

HEPATICAE

Frullania kehdingiana *Stephani* (Jungermanniaceae)

Dioica magna gracilis olivacea flaccida, effuse caespitans vel pendula. *Caulis* ad 12 cm. longus, regulariter bipinnatus, pinnis ad 15 mm. longis, arcuatim patulis, remotiusculis, sparsim breviterque pinnulatis. *Folia caulina* conferta, recte patula, plano disticha, ovata (1·33 mm. longa, medio 1 mm. lata), apice late rotundata, minute apiculata, dorso truncata, caulem itaque haud superantia, basi antica exappendiculata. *Cellulae superae* 18 × 27 μ, trigonis parvis, basales 18 × 36 μ, trigonis majusculis subnodulosis, parietibus ubique flexuosis. *Lobulus* parvus, a caule remotus, e margine folii oblique patens, cylindricus vel anguste clavatus, conico-papulosus. *Amphigastria caulina* majuscula, caule quintuplo latiora, cordiformia, transverse inserta, ad medium inciso-biloba, sinu angusto, lobis late triangulatis acutis. *Perianthia* obovata, rostro brevissimo, ore truncato anguste recurvo. *Folia floralia* intima caulinis duplo longiora, ligulata, margine (praecipue supero) breviter lacerato ; lobulus ad medium solutus, folio aequilongus basique aequilatus, superne duplo angustior, marginibus praecipue inferis profunde laceratis. *Amphigastria floralia* intima lobulo duplo latiora, ultra medium bifida, marginibus similiter laceratis. *Androecia* in caule ramisque seriata, capitata, sessilia, in pinnulis terminalia (F. Stephani, *Sp. Hepat.*, 4 : 577 ; 1911).

Dioicous large slender dull green (olivaceous) flaccid, effusely tufted or pendulous. *Stem* to 12 cm. long, regularly bipinnate, with the pinnae to 15 mm. long, arcuate-patulous, rather distant from one another, sparsely and shortly pinnulate. *Cauline leaves* crowded, straightly outspread, distichous in one plane, ovate (1·33 mm. long, at the middle 1 mm. broad), at the apex broadly rounded, minutely apiculate, on the back truncate, accordingly not exceeding the stem, at the anticous base not appendiculate. *Upper cells* 18 × 27 μ with small trigones, basal ones 18 × 36 μ, with rather large almost nodulose trigones, with the walls everywhere flexuose. *Lobule* small, remote from the stem, obliquely spreading from the margin of the leaf, cylindric or narrowly clavate, conically papillose. *Cauline amphigastria* rather large five times broader than the stem, heart-shaped, transversely inserted, to the middle incisedly two-lobed, with a narrow sinus, the lobes broadly triangular acute. *Perianths* obovate, with an exceedingly short beak, the mouth truncate narrowly recurved. Innermost *floral leaves* twice as long as the cauline ones ligulate, with the margin (especially the upper) shortly lacerate ; lobule free to the middle, equal in length and at base just equal in breadth to the leaf above half as broad with the margins especially the lower deeply lacerate Innermost *floral amphigastria* twice as broad as the lobule, beyond the middle bifid, with the margins similarly lacerate. *Androecia* arranged in rows on the stem and branches, capitate, sessile, terminal on the pinnules.

Marchantia wilmsii *Stephani* (Marchantiaceae)

Major, dilute viridis vel fuscescens. *Frons* ad 4 cm. longa, 7 mm. lata tenuis ; *costa* haud crassa, sed distincte convexo producta sensim in ala enues excurrens. *Epidermis* tenera. *Stomata* majuscula, parum prominentia, ore interno 4 cellulis plano-conicis circumdato. *Appendicula* squamarum late cordiformia, acuta, margine regulariter breviterque dentata, cellulis majusculis subaequimagnis conflata. *Pedunculus* carpocephali validus ad 3 cm. longus, nudus, apice paleis filiformibus brevibus barbatus; paleae involucrales breves, confertae et numerosissimae, late lanceolatae acuminatae vel longe bi-trifidae. *Capitula* feminea magna 9-lobata, centro magno valde convexo, lobis ex angusta basi optime cuneatim ampliatis, apice rotundatis contiguis, basi sinu rotundato discretis. *Involucra* margine cellulis prominulis longe papulosa. *Perianthia* hyalina, ore contracto integro. *Capsula* fusco-brunnea. *Sporae* sulphureae papillatae 35 μ. *Elateres* flavescentes 600 μ. *Capitula mascula* femineis aequimagna, brevius pedunculata, palmatifida, 8-lobata, lobis vix ad medium solutis, ut in femineis sinu rotundato discretis. *Scyphuli* margine creberrime breviterque ciliati (F. Stephani in *Bull. Herb. Boiss.*, 7 : 398 ; 1899).

Rather large, pale green or becoming blackish brown. *Thallus* (*Frond*) to 4 cm. long, 7 mm. broad, thin ; *midrib* not thick, but distinctly convexly prominent gradually running out into thin wings. *Epidermis* delicate. *Pores* (*Stomata*) rather large, not very conspicuous, with the internal opening surrounded by 4 plano-conical cells. *Ventral scales* (*Appendicula of scales*) broadly heart-shaped, acute, at the margin regularly and shortly dentate, made up of rather large cells equal in size. *Peduncle* of receptacle (carpocephalus) stout to 3 cm. long, naked, at the apex bearded with short filiform scales (pales) ; involucral scales (pales) short, crowded and very numerous, broadly lanceolate acuminate or long bi- or trifid. *Female* receptacles (*capitula*) large 9-lobed, with the centre large strongly convex, the lobes from a narrow base well expanded cuneately, at the apex rounded contiguous, at the base separated by the rounded sinus. *Involucres* at the margin long papillose with rather prominent cells. *Perianths* hyaline, with the mouth contracted entire. *Capsules* dark brown. *Spores* sulphur-coloured papillate 35 μ. *Elaters* yellowish 600 μ. *Male capitula* the same size as the females, shortly pedunculate, palmatifid, 8-lobed, with the lobes hardly free to the middle, as in the females separated by the rounded sinus. *Gemmae cups* (*Scyphules*) at the margin very closely and shortly ciliate.

MUSCI

Pilopogon lorentzii *Fleischer* (Dicranaceae)

Dioecus ; flores feminei terminales et innovando laterales, aggregati ; archegonia elongata. *Plantae* laxe caespitosae, robustae, nitidulae, intense nigrescentes, ad apicem luteo-virides, 3-6 cm. altae. *Caulis* erectus, paulum flexuosus, parce divisus vel dichotome ramosus, inferne ferrugineo-tomentosus, dense foliosus, versus apicem floriferum filiformi-attenuatus, simplex, apice in capitulum incrassatus ; rami steriles robustiores, acuminati. *Folia caulina* sicca erecta vel cauli arcuato-incumbentia, hic illic rugulosa, humida erecto-patentia, concava, marginibus versus apicem convolutis, integris ; *folia ramorum floriferorum* minora, appressa, planiuscula, *omnia* basi in caulem fibroso-decurrentia, oblonga, subulato-acuminata, 4-5 mm. longa et 1-1·3 mm. lata, nervo distincto, in basi tertiam partem folii latitudinis occupante, in sectione transversali e strato medio cellularum magnarum et pluribus stratis stereidarum ventralium et dorsalium composita, dorso levi, haud lamelloso, ad apicem breviter excurrente ; *folia comalia* rosaceo-congesta, latiora, nervo longe excurrente ; cellulis valde incrassatis, lumine angusto, rhombeolinearibus, inferioribus sensim longioribus, ad marginem angustioribus, hyalinis, alaribus distinctis, numerosis, ventricosis, bina strata efficientibus, plerisque quadratis, hyalinis vel fuscescentibus, robustis. *Perichaetia* aggregata ; bracteae externae minores, lanceolato-acuminatae, internae e basi longissime vaginantes subito setaceae, nervo longe excurrente, hyalino, parcissime denticulato. *Seta* in modum colli cygnei curvata, ca. 4 mm. alta, nigrescens, ad apicem tuberculosa ; theca aequalis, ovali-cylindracea, sicca leviter et parce sulcata ; *annulus* latus, duplex ; *operculum* conico-subulatum, parum obliquum. *Calyptra* cuculliformis, basi irregulariter fimbriata. *Peristomii dentes* longiusculi, in conum conniventes, profunde bifidi, inferne indistincte trabeculato-rugosi, cruribus granulosis. *Sporae* globosae, viridulae, leves, 12-15 μ diam., sporodermi distincta (M. Fleischer in *Nova Guinea*, 8, Bot. : 739 ; 1912).

Dioecous ; feminine flowers terminal and by renewed growth lateral, aggregated ; archegonia elongated. *Plants* loosely tufted, robust, somewhat glossy, deeply blackish, at the apices yellow-green, 3-6 cm. high. *Stem* erect, a little flexuose, sparingly divided or dichotomously branched, below rustily tomentose, densely leafy, towards the flowering apex filiform-attenuate undivided, at the apex thickened into a head ; sterile branches more robust, acuminate. *Cauline leaves* when dry erect or curved-incumbent to the stem, here and there slightly rugose, when moist erect-spreading concave, with the margins towards the apex convolute, entire ; *leaves of the flowering branches* smaller, appressed, fairly flat, *all* at base decurrent on the stem oblong subulate-acuminate, 4-5 mm. long and 1-1·3 mm. broad, with the nerve distinct, at base occupying a third of the width of the leaf, in vertical section composed of a middle layer of large cells and several layers of ventral and dorsal stereids, on the back smooth, not lamellate, at the apex shortly excurrent ; *comal leaves* crowded like a rose, broader, with the nerve long-excurrent ; with the cells strongly thickened, with a narrow central cavity rhombic-linear, the lower ones gradually longer, at the margin narrower, hyaline, the alar ones distinct, numerous, swollen, forming two layers, most of them quadrate, hyaline or somewhat dusky, robust. *Perichaetia* crowded ; outer bracts smaller, lanceolate-acuminate, inner ones very long sheathing from the base then suddenly setaceous, with the nerve long excurrent hyaline very sparsely denticulate. *Seta* curved in the manner of a swan's neck, about 4 mm. high blackish, at the apex tuberculose ; *capsule* even, oval-cylindric, in a dried state lightly and sparingly furrowed ; *annulus* broad, double ; *operculum* conic-subulate, slightly oblique ; *Calyptra* hood-shaped, at base irregularly imbriate. *Peristome teeth* rather long, connivent into a cone, deeply bifid, below indistinctly trabeculate-rugose, with the crura granular. *Spores* globose, greenish, smooth, 12-15 μ in diameter, with distinct sporoderm.

Rhynchostegiella opacifolia *Dixon* (Brachytheciaceae)

Caespites densi sed faciliter dilabiles, *fusci*; caules prostrati, dense ramosi, ramis erectis, longis (1 cm. vel ultra), robustiusculis. *Folia* sat conferta, erecto-patentia vel leniter secunda, majuscula, caulina 1-1·25 mm. longa, 0·4 mm. lata, ovato-lanceolata, saepe convoluta, late breviter acuminata, *obtusa*; ramea minora, magis ovalia; omnia sicca plus minusve anguste convoluta; margines plani, a parte inferiore folii ad apicem *arcte ubobtuse pellucide* denticulati. *Costa* validiuscula, superne attenuata, supra medium folium soluta. *Cellulae peropacae, angustissimae, parietibus tenuibus obscuris*; *marginales* saepe *pellucidiores*; versus basim paullo latiores, infimae subrectangulares, *alares paucae vel nullae, omnes obscurae*.

Autoica. *Perichaetium* parvum, bracteis paucis, e basi lata cito in acumen flexuosum subulatum integrum constrictis. *Seta* 1·25 cm. alta vel paullo ultra, *laevis*. *Theca* turgide ovalis, sicca deoperculata angustior, asymmetrica, inclinata, pachydermica, saturate fusca, deoperculata 1·5 mm. longa; operculum curvirostratum (H. N. Dixon in *J. Linn. Soc. London, Bot.*, 50: 111; 1935).

Tufts dense but easily broken asunder, *blackish-brown*; stems prostrate, densely branched, with branches erect, long (1 cm. or more), fairly robust. *Leaves* moderately crowded, erect-spreading or slightly secund, fairly large, the cauline ones 1·25 mm. long, 0·4 mm. broad, ovate-lanceolate, often convolute, broadly shortly acuminate, *obtuse*; those of branches smaller, more oval; all when dry more or less narrowly convolute; margins flat, from the lower part of the leaf up to the apex *closely almost obtusely transparently* denticulate. *Midrib* fairly stout, attenuate upwards, vanishing above the middle of the leaf. *Cells very opaque, extremely narrow, with thin obscure walls; the marginal ones* often *more transparent*; towards the base a little broader, the lowest almost rectangular, *the alar ones few or none, all obscure*.

Autoicous. *Perichaetium* small, with the bracts few, from a broad base suddenly constricted into a flexuose subulate entire acumen. *Seta* 1·25 cm. high or a little more, *smooth*. *Capsule* in a turgid state oval, when dry and deoperculate narrower, asymmetric, inclined, pachydermous, deep blackish-brown, deoperculate 1·5 mm. long; operculum with a curved beak.

Sphagnum thailandense *B. Hansen* (Sphagnaceae)

Planta fusca, habitu Sphagni imbricati similis.

Epidermis caulina stratis 2, efibris, pariete exteriore cellularum superficialium saepe foramine uno instructo. *Cylindrus* lignosus rufofuscus.

Folia caulina ovalia ad lingulato-spathulata, 1·4-2·6 mm. longa, ad mediam partem 0·9-1·6 mm. lata, multifibra, plerumque marginibus lateralibus superne incurva, apice dentata, limbo deorsum angusto. *Cellulae hyalinae* non septatae vel raro uniseptatae, in interiore superficie poris veris, praeter inferiores manifesto anulatis, suborbicularibus, ad commissuras et in cellularum angulis dispositis, in dorso foliorum orbicularibus, sursum manifesto anulatis, deorsum cellulas latitudine aequantibus, vix anulatis, series 2 vel rarius 3 subcontinuas formantibus, duabus ad commissuras dispositis instructae.

Fasciculi ramorum e ramis 2-3 compositi, omnibus plus minus extensis, tertio ceteris multo breviore vel plane deficiente. Parietes radiales cellularum epidermaticarum in quarta parte apicali fibrosi porosi, praeterea porosi solum, tangentiales fibris ut poris destituti.

Folia ramulina imbricata, ovalia, valde cava, 1·0-1·8 mm. lata, 1·5-2·4 mm. longa, multifibra et multipora, sulco resorptorio instructa, in interiore superficie poris veris orbicularibus, anulatis, ad commissuras et in cellularum angulis dispositis et plerumque pseudoporis minutissimis bene anulatis in medio cellularum sitis instructa, in dorso poris similibus sed crebrioribus, in series ad commissuras dispositis. *Cellulae chlorophylliferae* in sectione transversali anguste fusiformes vel orciformes, utrinque liberae. *Cellulae hyalinae* intus in pariete cum chlorophylliferis communi laeves (B. Hansen in *Dansk Bot. Ark.*, 20 : 102 ; 1961).

Plant brownish, in habit similar to Sphagnum imbricatum.

Cauline epidermis with 2 layers not fibrous, with the outer wall of the superficial cells often provided with one foramen (large pore). *Cylinder* woody reddish-brown.

Cauline leaves oval to lingulate-spathulate, 1·4-2·6 mm. long, at the middle part 0·9-1·6 mm. broad, many-fibred, usually at the lateral margins incurved above, at the apex toothed, with the limb narrowed towards the base. *Hyaline cells* not septate or seldom uniseptate, provided on the inner face with almost orbicular true pores manifestly ringed except the lower ones, placed at commissures and in the angles of cells, on the back of the leaves orbicular, above manifestly ringed, downwards equalling the width of the cells, scarcely ringed, forming 2 or rarely 3 almost continuous rows, with two placed at the commissures.

Fascicles of branches formed from 2 or 3 branches, all more or less outspread, with the third one much shorter than the others or completely lacking. Radial walls of the epidermal cells on the apical fourth part fibrous, porose, beyond this only porose, the tangential walls destitute of fibres and pores.

Branch leaves imbricate, oval, markedly hollow, 1·0-1·8 mm. broad 1·5-2·4 mm. long, many-fibred and many-pored, provided with absorption furrow, on the inner face provided with orbicular ringed pores placed at the commissures and in the angles of the cells and often with well ringed very minute pseudopores situate in the middle of the cells, the dorsal pseudopores similar to pores but more crowded together, arranged in rows at the commissures. *Chlorophyll cells* in transverse section spindle-shaped or barrel-shaped, free on both sides. *Hyaline cells* inside on the wall common to them and to the chlorophyll cells smooth.

PTERIDOPHYTA

Cyathea cucullifera *Holttum* (Cyatheaceae)

Frondes 8 vel 10, c. 175 cm. longae, verticillatae, verticillis duobus dispositae. *Stipes* 15 cm. longus, verrucosus, omnino paleis vestitus; paleae maximae 2 cm. longae, ½ mm. latae, atrobrunneae, nitidae, margine pallido setiferae (setae nigrae flexuosae); paleae minores superficiei abaxialis stipitis atrobrunneae, irregulares, interdum apice setiferae. *Rhachis* infra pallida, verruculosa, paleis minimis pallidis ciliatis (non setiferis) conspersis praedita. *Pinnae* infimae 5 cm. longae, superiores sensim longiores, maximae 30 cm. longae. *Pinnulae* sessiles, breve acuminatae, ad 4 cm. longae, steriles 10 mm., fertiles 6-8 mm. latae, fere ad costam lobatae, segmento infimo non libero; costulae inter se 3 mm. (steriles) vel 2-2½ mm. (fertiles) distantes; segmenta laminae contigua, firma, fere integra, apice rotundata; venae 8-9-jugatae (steriles), 6-8-jugatae (fertiles). *Sori* indusiati; indusia hemiteliiformia, cucullata, dorso costulam tangentia, pallide brunnea; paraphyses tenues, breves. *Rhaches pinnarum* infra pallidae, hirsutae, pilis crispatis coarctis, paleis minutis ciliatis et paleis elongatis planis setiferis intermixtis; *costae* infra basin versus paleis angustis setiferis caducis, omnino paleis minutis ciliatis pilisque crispatis, apicem versus paleis pallidis bullatis vestitae; *costulae* infra paleis minutis paleisque parvis bullatis vestitae (R. E. Holttum in *Kew Bull.* 16: 54; 1962).

Fronds 8 or 10, about 175 cm. long, verticillate, disposed in two whorls. *Stipes* 15 cm. long, verrucose, entirely clothed with scales; largest scales 2 cm. long, 0·5 mm. broad, dark brown, glossy, at the pale margin setiferous (the setae black flexuous); smaller scales of the abaxial surface of the stipe dark brown, irregular, sometimes at the apex setiferous. *Rachis* below pale, verruculose, provided with very small pale ciliate (not setiferous) scattered scales. Lower *pinnae* 5 cm. long, upper gradually longer, the largest 30 cm. long. *Pinnules* sessile, shortly acuminate, to 4 cm. long, the sterile ones 10 mm. the fertile ones 6-8 mm. broad, lobed almost to the costa with the lowest segment not free; costules between themselves 3 mm. (sterile) or 2-2·5 mm. (fertile) apart; segments of the blade touching, firm, almost entire, at the apex rounded; veins in 8-9 pairs (sterile), 6-8 pairs (fertile). *Sori* indusiate; indusia like those of Hemitelia, hooded, at their backs touching the costule pale brown; paraphyses thin, short. *Raches* of pinnae pale below, hirsute, with curled hairs pressed together, minute ciliate scales and elongated flat setiferous scales intermixed; *costae* on the lower side towards the base clothed with narrow setiferous soon-falling scales, throughout with minute ciliate scales and curled hairs, towards the apex with pale more or less bullate scales; *costules* on the lower side clothed with minute scales and small bullate scales.

Elaphoglossum urbanii *Brause* (Polypodiaceae)

Rhizoma repens, cr. 2 mm. crassum, paleis clathratis peltatis fuscis brunneo-maculatis e basi rotundata lanceolatis acuminatis ciliatis, 0·5 cm.

longis, 1·5 mm. latis munitum, folia bifaria interstitiis 0·3-1·2 cm. longi
emittens. *Petioli* ochracei basi brunnei paleis iis rhizomatis aequalibus spars
praediti, torti, sterilium foliorum 2-7·5 cm., fertilium 9-23·5 cm. long
Lamina coriacea oblongo-lanceolata margine revoluto, supra glabra, infr
juventute paleis clathratis parvis brunneis laceratis instructa, foliorum
sterilium usque ad 10 cm. longa, 1·5 cm. lata, fertilium 10 cm. longa, 1·
cm. lata ; nervis inconspicuis liberis dichotomis. *Sori* totam laminam occu
pantes, sporis bilateralibus lutescentibus cristis praeditis margine granulos
(G. Brause in Urban, *Symb. Ant.* 7 : 488 ; 1913).

Rhizome creeping, about 2 mm. thick, furnished with clathrate peltat
dark brown-spotted from the rounded base lanceolate acuminate ciliat
pales 0·5 cm. long, 1·5 mm. broad, putting forth two-rowed leaves at interva
0·3-1·2 cm. long. *Petioles* ochraceous at base brown sparsely provided wit
pales equalling those of the rhizome, twisted, of the sterile leaves 2-7·5 cm
of the fertile ones 9-23·5 cm. long. *Blade* coriaceous oblong-lanceolate wit
revolute margin, above glabrous, below in youth provided with clathrat
small brown lacerate pales, of the sterile leaves up to 10 cm. long, 1·5 cn
broad, of the fertile ones 10 cm. long, 1·7 cm. broad ; with the nerves incor
spicuous free dichotomous. *Sori* occupying the whole blade, with spores two
sided yellowish provided with crests and at the margin granular.

Notholaena delicatula *Maxon & Weatherby* (Polypodiaceae)

Plerumque gracilis. *Rhizoma* breve erectum vel obliquum, fronde
plures dense caespitosas emittens, paleis tenuibus brunneis concoloribu
lineari-subulatis longe acuminatis circa 4 mm. longis 0·8 mm. latis integri
cellulis elongatis parietibus tenuibus, onustum. *Stipes* castaneus gracili
teres glaber subnitidus laminam subaequans. *Lamina* plerumque deltoide
fere aequilateralis tripinnata vel inferne subquadripinnata. *Rachis costaequ*
stipiti similes. *Pinnae majores* circa 5-jugae remotae oblongae vel deltoidea
petiolatae. *Pinnulae* structura pinnis similes remotae. *Pinnulae ultima*
in pedicellis brevibus castaneis articulatae, tenuiter herbaceae 4 mm. ve
minus longae, pagina superiore minute glanduliferae, inferiore granis cerace
albidis minutissimis discretis copiose praeditae, subintegrae vel minut
irregulariterque crenatae, margine non revoluto ; *laterales* oblongae ve
ovatae vel inaequilateraliter rhomboideae, apice obtusae, basi subtruncata
vel late cuneatae ; *terminales* vel eorum lobi centrales rhomboideae vel fer
flabelliformes, saepe in basin angustam ex comparatione longam sicu
petiolum abrupte contractae. *Nervillae* evidentes tenues liberae pinnata
1-3-furcatae e costula angulo acuto egredientes, fere per totam longitudiner
sporangiferae. *Sporangia* brevissime stipitata, annulo e cellulis circa 2
composito. *Sporae* brunneae sphaericae jugis tenuibus flexuosis fusci
rugosae, diametro ca. 50 μ (W. R. Maxon & C. A. Weatherby in *Contr. Gra*
Herb. Harvard Univ., 127 : 7 ; 1939).

Commonly slender. *Rhizome* short erect or oblique, putting forth man
densely tufted fronds, laden with thin brown uniformly coloured linear
subulate long-acuminate about 4 mm. long 0·8 mm. broad entire pales, wit

elongated cells with thin walls. *Stipe* chestnut-brown slender terete glabrous almost glossy almost equalling the blade. *Blade* commonly deltate nearly equilateral tripinnate or below almost quadripinnate. *Rachis* and *midrib* similar to the stipe. *Larger pinnae* about 5-paired remote oblong or deltate petioled. *Pinnules* in structure similar to the pinnae remote. *Ultimate pinnules* articulate with short chestnut-coloured pedicels, thinly herbaceous 4 mm. or less long, at the upper surface minutely gland-bearing, at the lower with waxy whitish very minute separate grains copiously furnished, almost entire or minutely and irregularly crenate, with the margin not revolute; the *lateral* ones oblong or ovate or unequal-sidedly rhombic, at the apex obtuse, at the base almost truncate or broadly cuneate; the *terminal* ones or the central lobes of these rhombic or nearly fan-shaped, often into a narrow comparatively long base petiole-like abruptly contracted. *Nervillae* evident thin free pinnate 1-3-forked going out from the costule at an acute angle, for nearly the whole length sporangium-bearing. *Sporangia* very shortly stipitate, with an annulus composed from about 20 cells. *Spores* brown spherical rugose with thin flexuous dark ridges, in diameter about 50 μ.

Polypodium polypodioides (*L.*) *Watt* (Polypodiaceae)

Rhizoma repens, paleis adpressis, lanceolato-subulatis, rigidis, tenuiter ciliatis vel glabris onustum; *folia* subcoriacea; petiolus 1-4″ longus; lamina 2-5″ longa, supra paleis ovatis vel rotundatis denticulatis in setam terminalem productis sparse obsita, denique glabra, infra una cum petiolo paleis membranaceis ad insertionem infuscatis rotundatis vel ovatis obtusis vel acuminatis integris vel denticulatis dense squamosa, ovato-oblonga, profunde pinnatipartita; laciniae ½-1″ longae, 1½-2‴ latae, e basi versus apicem decrescentes vel infimae paullulum abbreviatae, basi superiore latiore, inferiore attenuata et decurrente adnatae et ala angusta confluentes, elongato-oblongae, obtusae vel lanceolato-oblongae, plerumque integerrimae; *sori* impressi, plerumque partem superiorem laciniarum occupantes, utrinque ad costulam 4-6, margini approximati, squamis circumdati (G. H. Mettenius, *Über einige Farngattungen* 1 (*Polypodium*) 69; 1856).

Rhizome creeping, laden with appressed lanceolate-subulate rigid finely ciliate or glabrous pales; *leaves* subcoriaceous; petiole 1-4 inches long; blade 2-5 inches long, on the upper side sparsely covered with ovate or rounded denticulate pales drawn out into a terminal bristle, at length glabrous, on the lower side together with the petiole densely scaly with membranous at insertion darkened rounded or ovate obtuse or acuminate entire or denticulate pales, ovate-oblong, deeply pinnatipartite; segments (laciniae), ½-1 inch long, 1½-2 lines broad, from the base towards the tip diminishing or on the lower ones a little abbreviated, at the base with the upper broader, the lower attenuately and decurrently adnate and by a narrow wing confluent, elongate-oblong, obtuse or lanceolate-oblong, very frequently quite entire; *sori* impressed, mostly occupying the upper part of the segments, on both sides at the costule (costula) 4-6, near to the margin, surrounded by scales.

SPERMATOPHYTA
GYMNOSPERMAE

Abies georgei *Orr* (Pinaceae)

Arbor 40-70-pedalis ; *ramuli* annotini dense ferrugineo-villosi, vetustiores nigrescentes, longe fissi ; *cicatrices* circulares ; *gemmae* ovatae, obtusae, valde resinosae ; *perulae* late ovatae, obtusae, persistentes per annos, ramulorum bases cingentes. *Folia* spiraliter inserta, pectinatim disposita, basi distincte constricta, margine leviter revoluta, apice plerumque emarginata, rare acuta vel obtusa, 15-25 mm. longa et 2 mm. lata, supra distincte canaliculata, subtus carinata et faciebus [*recte* fasciis] latis albis binis stomatiferis praedita ; canales resiniferi marginales ; hypodermis in facie ventrali continua crassa, in facie dorsali tantum sub costa et in marginibus praesens. *Amenta mascula* apicem versus ramulorum aggregata, manifeste stipitata, 30 mm. longa. *Strobili maturi* violaceo-brunnei, ovati, sessiles, circa 9 cm. longi et 4-5 cm. lati, leviter resinosi ; *squamae* late obovato-cuneatae, 2 cm. longae et 2 cm. latae, basi leviter auriculatae, stipitatae, apice rotundatae paulo incurvatae, extus brunneo-tomentosulae ; *bracteae* oblongae et manifeste exsertae, apice triangulari erecto et margine erosa, cuspide 6 mm. longo erecto vel recurvo ; *semina* circa 1 cm. longa et 5 mm. lata, alis squamam aequantibus nitidis brunneis, 5 mm. longis et 1 cm. latis (M. Y. Orr in *Notes R. Bot. Gard. Edinburgh*, 18 : 1 ; 1938).

Tree 40-70 feet ; *branchlets* of current year densely rusty-red-villous, the older ones blackish, long-fissured ; *scars* circular ; *buds* ovate, obtuse, strongly resinous ; *bud-scales* broadly ovate, obtuse, persisting through the years, surrounding the bases of the branchlets. *Leaves* spirally inserted, pectinately arranged, at the base distinctly narrowed, at the margin lightly revolute, at the apex commonly emarginate, rarely acute or obtuse, 15-25 mm. long and 2 mm. broad, above distinctly channelled, below keeled and provided with two white broad stomata-bearing bands ; resin-bearing canals (resin-ducts) marginal ; hypoderm on the ventral surface continuous thick, on the dorsal surface present only under the midrib and at the margins. *Male amenta* crowded towards the apex of the branchlets, manifestly stipitate, 30 mm. long. *Mature cones* violet-brown, ovate, sessile, about 9 cm. long and 4-5 cm. broad, lightly resinous ; *scales* broadly obovate-cuneate, 2 cm. long and 2 cm. broad, at the base slightly auriculate, stipitate, at the apex rounded a little incurved, externally brown-tomentulose ; *bracts* oblong and manifestly exserted, with the apex triangular erect and the margin erose, with the cusp 6 mm. long erect or recurved ; *seeds* about 1 cm. long and 5 mm. broad, with glossy brown wings equalling the scale, 5 mm. long and 1 cm. broad.

ANGIOSPERMAE: DICOTYLEDONES

Eupatorium jenssenii *Urban* (Compositae)

Frutex. *Rami* teretes multistriati pilis brevissimis sursum curvatis nigrescentibus dense obsiti. *Folia* opposita, raro hinc illinc subalterna, 5-10 mm. longe petiolata, triangulari- v. ovato-lanceolata, basi subtruncata, non v.

vix in petiolum protracta, superne sensim et longe acuminata, apice ipso
acuto, 4-8 cm. longa, 1·5-3·5 cm. lata v. in ramulis minora, e basi v. perpaullo
supra basin 3- v. sub-5-nervia, nervis 2 intermediis usque ad v.
supra medium productis, omnibus supra prominulis et ope venarum subhorizontalium grosse
anastomosantibus, margine depresse crenata, crenis minute et obtuse
apiculatis, supra glabra, subtus ad nervos obsolete pilosula, et glandulis
minutissimis pellucidis obsita. *Inflorescentiae* axillares et terminales paniculam amplam formantes, speciales subcorymbosae 4-5 cm. diametro ;
bracteae inferiores euphylloideae lanceolatae parcissime serratae v. integrae
1·5-0·7 cm. longae, caeterae lineares v. sublineares ; pedicelli 0-4 mm. longi.
Involucri squamae biseriatae, cr. 9 valde inaequilongae, pleraeque anguste
lanceolatae 3-nerves 1-2 mm. longae, interiores 1-2 inferne anguste lineares,
supra medium latiores 1-3-nerves usque 3 mm. longae. *Flores* 5-6 in capitulo.
Pappi setae 24-27 sordide albidae 2·5 mm. longae. *Corollae* 3 mm. longae ;
tubus cylindraceus superne sensim usque dimidio ampliatus ; lobi triangulares
tubo 7-8-plo breviores. *Antherae* 1 mm. longae, ligula semiorbiculari loculis
8-plo breviore. *Stylus* 5·5 mm. longus, infra medium bifidus. *Achaenia* (non
plane matura) 2·5 mm. longa, parce brevissimeque pilosa (I. Urban in *Ark*.
f. Bot., 17 no. 7: 64; 1921).

Shrub. *Branches* terete multistriate densely covered with very short
upwards curved blackish hairs. *Leaves* opposite, rarely here and there
almost alternate, with petiole 5-10 mm. long, triangular- or ovate-lanceolate,
at base almost truncate, not or scarcely prolonged into a petiole, above
gradually and long acuminate, at the tip itself acute, 4-8 cm. long, 1·5-3·5
cm. broad or smaller on the branches, from the base or a very little above the
base 3- or almost 5-nerved, with the 2 intermediate nerves prolonged up to or
above the middle, all prominent above and by means of the almost horizontal
veins coarsely anastomosing, at the margin depressed crenate, with the
crenae minutely and bluntly apiculate, glabrous above, below obsoletely
pilosulous at the nerves, and covered with very minute pellucid glands.
Inflorescences axillary and terminal forming an ample panicle, the individual
ones subcorymbose 4-5 cm. in diameter ; lower bracts resembling true leaves
lanceolate most sparingly serrate or entire 1·5-0·7 cm. long, the rest linear or
almost linear ; pedicels 0-4 mm. long. *Scales* of the involucre in two series,
about 9 very unequal, most of them narrowly lanceolate 3-nerved 1-2 mm.
long, the inner ones below narrowly linear, above the middle broader 1-3-
nerved up to 3 mm. long. *Flowers* 5-6 in a capitulum. *Bristles of the pappus*
24-27 dirty white 2·5 mm. long. *Corollas* 3 mm. long ; tube cylindric above
gradually up to halfway enlarged ; lobes triangular 7-8 times shorter than
the tube. *Anthers* 1 mm. long, with the semicircular ligule 8 times shorter
than the locules. *Style* 5·5 mm. long, below the middle bifid. *Achenes* (not
completely mature) 2·5 mm. long, sparingly and very shortly pilose.

Ranunculus longipetalus Handel-Mazzetti (Ranunculaceae)

Perennis, rhizomate brevi tenui descendente, radicibus filiformibus
elongatis, fibris tenuissimis. *Caulis* ½-10 cm. longus, erectus vel ascendens
vel subprocumbens, nudus vel 1-2-folius, glaber vel sparse pilosulus, uniflorus.

Folia basalia ambitu reniformia vel pentagona vel ovata, 3-10 mm. lata et aequilonga vel paulo longiora, basi saepe cordata necnon truncata usque cuneata, tripartita usque trisecta, parte (scil. foliolo) medio obovato integro vel 3-5 lobo, interdum graciliter petiolulato, foliolis lateralibus illi similibus vel 2-4-lobis usque 2-4-partitis, lobis ultimis semiorbicularibus et rotundatis usque lanceolatis et acutis, crassiuscula, glabra ; *petiolus* lamina aequilongus vel usque 4 plo longior, basi in vaginam brunnescentem 1-2 mm. latam sensim dilatatus ; *folium caulinum inferius* foliis basalibus simile, sed brevius petiolatum, *superius* trisectum, segmentis lanceolatis integris. *Pedicellus* 0·8-5 cm. longus. *Flos* luteus, c. 1 cm. diametro. *Sepala* elliptica vel obovata, c. 3 mm. longa, glabra, interdum violaceo-suffusa. *Petala* 5, anguste elliptica, 5 mm. longa et 1½-2 mm. lata, anguste rotundata, basi in ungues fere 1 mm. longos cuneato-angustata, nectario patelliformi minutissimo. *Nucularum capitulum* globosum, c. 2 mm. diametro, receptaculo glabro. *Nuculae* immaturae obovoideae, vix 1 mm. longae, compressae, glabrae, in rostra tenuia iis fere aequilonga leviter curvata subito constrictae (H. Handel Mazzetti in *Acta Horti Gothoburg.*, 13 : 160 ; 1939).

Perennial, with rhizome short thin descending, roots thread-like elongated fibres very thin. *Stem* ½-10 cm. long, erect or ascending or almost procumbent naked or 1-2-leaved, glabrous or sparsely pilosulous, one-flowered. *Basal leaves* in outline reniform or pentagonal or ovate, 3-10 mm. broad and just as long or a little longer, at the base often cordate also truncate to cuneate, tripartite to trisect, with the middle part (that is to say leaflet) obovate entire or 3-5-lobed, sometimes slenderly petiolulate, with the lateral leaflets similar to it or 2-4-lobed to 2-4-parted, with the ultimate lobes semicircular and rounded to lanceolate and acute, somewhat thick, glabrous ; *petiole* as long as the blade or up to 4 times longer, at base gradually expanded into a brownish sheath 1-2 mm. broad ; *lower stem leaf* similar to basal leaves but more shortly petioled, the *upper* one trisect, with entire lanceolate segments. *Pedicel* 0·8-5 cm. long. *Flower* yellow, about 1 cm. in diameter. *Sepal* elliptic or obovate, 3 mm. long, glabrous, sometimes violet-suffused. *Petal* 5, narrowly elliptic, 5 mm. long and 1½-2 mm. broad, narrowly rounded, a base cuneately narrowed into claws almost 1 mm. long, with a most minute patelliform nectary. *Head of nutlets* globose, about 2 mm. in diameter, with the receptacle glabrous. Immature *nutlets* obovoid, scarcely 1 mm. long compressed, glabrous, suddenly constricted into a slender lightly curved beak almost as long as these.

Reseda luteola L. (Resedaceae)

Monotoca, glabra. *Radix* fusiformis flexuosa albens. *Caulis* 6-7½ dcm. elatus saepius solitarius virgato-ramosus vel subsimplex fistulosus striatus stricte erectus foliosus leviter angulatus virens ; rami pauci vel plures erecti. *Folia* 5-7 ctim. × 8-12 mm., lineari- vel spathulato-lanceolata vel lorata integra obtusa plana ; basilaria autem anni primi rosulata oblanceolata margine undulata. *Racemi* elongati densiflori. *Bracteae* 2⅓-3½ mm., demum ad 5 mm., e basi lata triangulari subulatae, praeter nervum viridem pallidae subhyalinae, in apice racemorum comoso-exsertae. *Flores* 4½ mm. diam.

Calycis laciniae persistentes; 2 superiores profundius inter se liberae, oblongo-ovatae obtusae anguste hyalino-marginatae, 2 mm., corollae adpressae. *Corolla* calyce parum longior; petala luteola, superius ex appendice transverse ovali ambitu cuneato-obovatum, fere ad medium 5-7-partitum, lateralia trifida vel interdum bipartita, petalum inferum autem ad lobum intermedium superioris reductum vel utrinque magis minute unilobum (vel interdum 2 infera). *Nectarium* squamiforme crenatum viridulum. *Stamina* circiter 25 (20-25), i.e. 20 vel ultra, petalis longiora; filamenta subulata glabra persistentia; antherae tantum $\frac{1}{2}$-$\frac{3}{4}$ mm. luteae. *Stigmata* virentia. *Ovula* ad quamque placentam circiter 10. *Capsula* 5 mm. longa, 6 mm. lata, breviter stipitata brevis campanulata ambitu subhexagona depresso-obovoidea, ad $\frac{1}{3}$ tricornis, cornubus conniventibus acutis incrassatis, profunde 3-4-sulcata, transverse rugosa, late aperta; placentae superne bilobae. *Semina* 1 mm., rotundo-reniformia fuscato-nigra nitida (F. N. Williams, *Prodr. Fl. Brit.*, 1: 599; 1912). See p. 145, Fig. 8.

Monocarpic, glabrous. *Root* fusiform flexuous white. *Stem* 6-7$\frac{1}{2}$ dm., tall often solitary virgately branched or almost unbranched hollow striate tightly erect leafy lightly angled green; branches few or many erect. *Leaves* 5-7 cm. × 8-12 mm., linear- or spathulate-lanceolate or lorate entire blunt flat: basal ones of the first year on the other hand rosetted oblanceolate at the margin undulate. *Racemes* elongated densely flowered. *Bracts* 2$\frac{1}{2}$-3$\frac{1}{2}$ mm., at length 5 mm., subulate from a broad triangular base, pale almost hyaline except for the green nerve, at the apex of the racemes sticking out as a tuft. *Flowers* 4$\frac{1}{2}$ mm. in diameter. *Segments of the calyx* persistent, the upper 2 more deeply free between themselves, oblong-ovate blunt narrowly hyaline-margined, 2 mm., appressed to the corolla. *Corolla* a little longer than the calyx; petals yellowish, the upper one from a transversely oval appendix in outline cuneate-obovate, almost to the middle 5-7-partite, the lateral ones 3-fid or sometimes 2-partite, the lower petal on the other hand reduced to the middle lobe of the upper or on each side more minutely 1-lobed (or sometimes 2 lower). *Nectary* scale-like crenate greenish. *Stamens* about 25 (20-25), i.e. 20 or more, longer than the petals; filaments subulate glabrous persistent; anthers only $\frac{1}{2}$-$\frac{3}{4}$ mm., yellow. *Stigmas* becoming green. *Ovules* at each placenta about 10. *Capsule* 5 mm. long, 6 mm. broad, shortly stipitate short campanulate in outline almost hexagonous depressed-obovoid, to $\frac{1}{3}$ three-horned, with the horns connivent acute thickened, deeply 3-4-furrowed, transversely rugose, widely open; placentas 2-lobed above. *Seeds* 1 mm., rounded-reniform brownish-black glossy.

Rostellularia linearifolia *Bremekamp* (Acanthaceae)

Herba erecta, circ. 20 cm. alta, sparse ramosa. *Internodia* sexangularia late sed haud profunde bisulcata, 2·5-6 cm. longa et 0·8-1·2 mm. diam., glabra, cystolithis brevibus dense albo-notata. *Folia* subsessilia, anguste linearia, 1·5-2·0 cm. longa et 1·2-1·4 mm. lata, apice basique acuta, margine revoluta, subcoriacea, utrimque glabra et laevia, supra cystolithis transverse lineolata, 1-nervia. *Spicae* pedunculo glabro 3-4 cm. longo elatae, rachide subglabra 2-5 cm. longa, nodo infimo a nodo secundo internodio calyci aequilongo separato, internodiis sequentibus gradatim brevioribus. *Bracteae, bracteolae* et *calycis lobi* 4 majores similiores, subulati, 5-6 mm. longi, acuti, hyalino-marginati, margine et costa ciliati. *Rudimentum lobi calycini quinti* filiforme et hyalinum, 0·5-1·0 mm. longum, difficiliter distinguendum. *Corolla* alba, 6·5 mm. longa, extus labii inferioris apice pubescente excepto glabra, tubo 3·5 mm. longo, labio superiore apice bidentato, labio inferiore lobis rotundatis 0·7 mm. longis instructo. *Stamina* filamentis 3·0 mm. longis, thecis 0·8 mm. longis, superiore 0·5 mm. supra inferiorem inserta, inferiore calcare 0·8 mm. longo instructa; connectivum 0·4 mm. latum. *Granula pollinis* 28 μ longa, 17 μ lata, 15 μ crassa. *Ovarium* 1·3 mm. altum, dimidio superiore pilosulum. *Stylus* 4 mm. longus, dimidio superiore sparse hirtellus. *Capsula* 5·5 mm. longa et 1·7 mm. diam., apicem versus puberula, parte solida 1·2 mm. longa. *Semina* 0·8 mm. alta lataque, carunculata (C. E. B. Bremekamp in *Kon. Nederl. Akad. Wet. Amsterdam, Proc.* C., 60: 5; 1957).

Herb erect, about 20 cm. high, sparsely branched. *Internodes* six-angled broadly but not deeply two-furrowed, 2·5-6 cm. long and 0·8-1·2 mm. in diameter, glabrous, densely white-marked with short cystoliths. *Leaves* almost sessile, narrowly linear, 1·5-2·0 cm. long and 1·2-1·4 mm. broad, at the apex and base acute, at the margin revolute, subcoriaceous, on both sides glabrous and smooth, on the upper side transversely marked with fine lines by the cystoliths, 1-nerved. *Spikes* elevated by a glabrous peduncle 3-4 cm. long, with the almost glabrous rachis 2-5 cm. long, with the lower node separated from the next node by an internode as long as the calyx, with the following internodes little by little shorter. *Bracts, bracteoles* and the 4 larger *lobes of the calyx* similar, subulate, 5-6 mm. long, acute, hyaline-margined, at the margin and midrib ciliate. *Rudiment of the fifth calycine lobe* thread-like and hyaline, 0·5-1·0 mm. long, to be distinguished with difficulty. *Corolla* white, 6·5 mm. long, glabrous outside except for the pubescent apex of the lower lip, with the tube 3·5 mm. long, with the upper lip at the apex bidentate, the lower lip provided with rounded lobes 0·7 mm. long. *Stamens* with filaments 3·0 mm. long, with thecae 0·8 mm. long, the upper one inserted 0·5 mm. above the lower one, the lower one provided with a spur 0·8 mm. long; connective 0·4 mm. broad. *Pollen grains* 28 μ long, 17 μ broad, 15 μ thick. *Ovary* 1·3 mm. high, on the upper half slightly pilose. *Style* 4 mm. long, on the upper half sparsely hirtellous. *Capsule* 5·5 mm. long and 1·7 mm. in diameter, towards the apex puberulous, with the solid part 1·2 mm. long. *Seeds* 0·8 mm. high and broad, carunculate.

Salix dolichostachya *Floderus* (Salicaceae)

Frutex procerus vel arbor ad 6 m. alta. *Ramuli annotini* elongati 2·5-3·5 (-5, surculi -7) mm. crassi recti fusci glaberrimi basi striati, ramulis novellis foliatis, inferioribus 0-2, superioribus 1-2 (-4) et intermediis (amentiferis) c. 3-4 (-8) instructi. *Ramuli novelli* ad 2·5 mm. crassi glabri vel apice sparse brevihirsuti foliis vulgo 13-17 praediti. *Stipulae* parvae (in surculis ad 8 × 5 mm.) semicordatae cuspidatae serratae. *Petioli* c. 10 (7-20) mm. longi supra cano-hirsuti subtus glabri. *Folia* c. 70 × 25 (in surculis ad 160 × 55) mm. magna lanceolato-elliptica vel ovata acuta crenulato-dentata vel integerrima plana, nervis secundariis vulgo 15-25 regulariter arcuatis vix elevatis et reticulo parum distincto instructa, supra viridia (costa puberula excepta) glabra infra pallide glauca glaberrima vel (raro) in costa pilosa. *Amenta* subpraecocia lateralia divaricata demum pendula, e gemmis ad 9 mm. longis ovoideis subacutis badiis glabris erumpentia, pedunculis 8-10 (♂) vel c. 15 (♀) mm. longis crassis cinereo-tomentosis et foliolis vulgo 2-3 suffulta, mascula c. 40 × 8, feminea c. 100 (-222) × 12 mm. magna. *Bracteae* c. 2·5 mm. longae in parte inferiore parce hirsutae, masc. ovatae rufae, femin. ovato-lanceolatae fulvae. *Nectaria* solitaria interna minuta (c. ⅓ mm.). *Stamina* duo libera c. 5 mm. longa flava in dimidia parte inferiore villosa vel glabra ; antherae parvae ovato-rotundatae helvae. *Pedicelli* c. ⅔ mm. longi parce pilosi vel glabri. *Capsulae* c. 6 (-9) mm. longae ovoideo-conicae fulvae glabrae vel basi subpuberulae. *Styli* ⅓-½ mm. longi integri. *Stigmata* c. ⅓ mm. longa integra vel emarginata. *Pappus* albus, pilis subcurvatis ; semina c. 8, 1·5 mm. longa (B. Floderus in *Geografiska Ann.*, 1935 : 311 ; 1935).

Tall shrub or tree to 6 m. high. *Branchlets of last year's growth* elongated 2·5-3·5 (-5, shoots -7) mm. thick straight dark quite glabrous at base striate, furnished with leafy young branchlets, the lower 0-2, the upper 1-2 (-4) and the intermediate (catkin-bearing) about 3-4 (-8). *Young branchlets* to 2·5 mm. thick glabrous or at the apex sparsely short-hirsute commonly provided with 13-17 leaves. *Stipules* small (on shoots to 8 × 5 mm.) semicordate cuspidate serrate. *Petioles* about 10 (7-20) mm. long above canous-hirsute below glabrous. *Leaves* about 70 × 25 (on shoots up to 160 × 55) mm. large lanceolate-elliptic or ovate acute crenulate-dentate or quite entire flat, provided with secondary nerves commonly 15-25 regularly arcuate scarcely raised and with a not particularly distinct network, above green and glabrous (with the puberulous midrib excepted), below pale glaucous quite glabrous or (rarely) pilose on the midrib. *Catkins* almost precocious lateral very divergent at length pendulous, breaking forth from buds up to 9 mm. long ovoid almost acute reddish brown glabrous, supported by peduncles 8-10 (male) or about 15 (female) mm. long thick ash-grey-tomentose and with little leaves commonly 2-3, male catkins about 40 × 8, female about 100 (-222) × 12 mm. large. *Bracts* c. 2·5 mm. long in the lower part sparingly hirsute, male ovate reddish, female ovate-lanceolate tawny. *Nectaries* solitary internal minute (about ⅓ mm.). *Stamens* two free about 5 mm. long yellow in the lower half part villous or glabrous ; anthers small ovate-rounded pale red. *Pedicels* about ⅔ mm. long sparingly pilose or glabrous. *Capsules* about 6 (-9) mm. long ovoid-conical tawny glabrous or at base somewhat puberulous. *Styles* ⅓-½ mm. long entire. *Stigmas* about ⅓ mm. long entire or emarginate. *Pappus* white, with somewhat curved hairs ; seeds about 8, 1·5 mm. long.

Viburnum × hillieri *Stearn* (Caprifoliaceae)

Frutex sempervirens diffusus ad 2 m. altus et latus aestate florens. *Ramuli* hornotini laeves glabri vel pilis stellatis leviter aspersi, vetustiores glabri atrobrunnei ; gemmae hiemales anguste lanceolatae stellato-pilosae. *Folia* petiolata estipulata ; lamina anguste elliptica apice breviter acuminata margine sparsim breviterque serrata basi obtusa 5-15 cm. longa 2-6 cm. lata laevis glabra vel infra pilis stellatis sparsim instructa, venis primariis utroque latere 4-5 supra impressis subter prominentibus pinnatim nervata ; petiolus 7-15 mm. longus plerumque rubicundus. *Inflorescentia* lateralis pedunculata multiflora laxa conica subglabra vel minute pubescens 4·5-6 cm. longa 5-7 cm. lata, ramis horizontaliter patentibus. *Receptaculum* glabrum. *Calyx* glaber c. 1 mm. longus. *Corolla* regularis infundibuliformis alba glabra, tubo 4-5 mm. longo, ore vix 3 mm. diametro, lobis patentibus suborbicularibus c. 3 mm. longis. *Stamina* exserta ad apicem tubi corollae affixa, filamentis albis c. 2 mm. longis, antheris 1-2 mm. longis. *Drupa* late ellipsoidea c. 8 mm. longa 6 mm. diametro primum rubra demum nigra ; putamen compressum 7 mm. longum 4·5 mm. latum 2 mm. crassum a ventre sulco lato profundo in longitudinem exaratum (Stearn in *J. R. Hort. Soc. London*, 81 : 539 ; 1956).

Shrub evergreen diffuse to 2 m. high and broad flowering in summer. *Branchlets* of the current year smooth glabrous or lightly sprinkled with stellate hairs, the older ones glabrous black-brown ; winter buds narrowly lanceolate stellate-pilose. *Leaves* petiolate without stipules ; blade narrowly elliptic at the apex shortly acuminate at the margin sparsely and shortly serrate at the base obtuse 5-15 cm. long. 2-6 cm. broad smooth glabrous or underneath furnished sparsely with stellate hairs, pinnately nerved on both sides with 4-5 veins impressed above raised underneath ; petiole 7-15 mm. long frequently reddish. *Inflorescence* lateral pedunculate many-flowered loose conical almost glabrous or minutely pubescent 4·5-6 cm. long 5-7 cm. broad, with branches horizontally spreading. *Receptacle* glabrous. *Calyx* glabrous about 1 mm. long. *Corolla* regular funnel-shaped white glabrous, with the tube 4-5 mm. long, the mouth scarcely 3 mm. in diameter, the lobes spreading almost orbicular about 3 mm. long. *Stamens* exserted attached to the top of the tube of the corolla, with white filaments about 2 mm. long, anthers 1-2 mm. long. *Drupe* broadly ellipsoid about 8 mm. long 6 mm. in diameter at first red later black ; stone compressed 7 mm. long 4·5 mm. broad 2 mm. thick on the ventral side hollowed out lengthwise by a broad deep furrow.

ANGIOSPERMAE : MONOCOTYLEDONES

Angraecopsis breviloba *Summerhayes* (Orchidaceae)

Herba epiphytica nana ; caulis brevissimus, circiter 1 cm. longus, radices numerosissimas flexuosas simplices applanatas circiter 1·5-3 mm. latas dense

Fig 11 *Angraecopsis breviloba* Summerhayes

1, planta florens ; 2, flos a latere visus ; 3, sepalum intermedium ; 4, sepalum laterale ; 5, petalum ; 6, labellum et columna a latere visa ; 7, labelli lamina antice visa ; 8, sectio transversa lobi intermedii labelli ; 9, columna, anthera secta ; 11, anthera subter visa ; 12-14, pollinarium desuper subter et a latere visum (by Stella Ross-Craig, from Hooker's *Icones Plantarum*, 35 ; 1950)

7

8

11

9

1

12

2

13

14

10

5

4

3

R-C.

emittens. *Folia* pauca, cito decidua, ligulata, usque ad 3 cm. longa et 5 mm. lata, apice obtusa brevissime bilobulata, obscure viridia. *Inflorescentiae* patentes vel adscendentes, usque ad 7 cm. longae, dense multiflorae ; pedunculus 1-2 cm. longus, vaginis paucis instructus ; rhachis flexuosa, angulata ; bracteae 2-4 mm. distantes, arcte vaginantes, obtusae vel acutae, 1-2·5 mm. longae. *Flores* secundi, patentes vel adscendentes, pallide virides ; pedicellus cum ovario circiter 4 mm. longus. *Sepalum intermedium* ± recurvatum, oblongo-lanceolatum, subacutum vel obtusum, 3-4·5 mm. longum, 1-1·5 mm. latum ; *sepala lateralia* parallele porrecta, e basi angustata oblique curvatim lanceolata, acuta, 4-5·5 mm. longa, 1-1·5 mm. lata. *Petala* libera, oblique triangulari-lanceolata, acuta, 2·75-4 mm. longa, prope basin 1-1·5 mm. lata ; omnia tepala trinervia. *Labellum* leviter incurvatum, dimidio inferiore breviter trilobatum, totum 3·75-4·5 mm. longum ; lobus intermedius carnoso-subulatus, 2·5-3 mm. longus ; lobi laterales dentiformes, subacuti, carnosi ; calcar dependens vel leviter incurvatum, e basi angusta valde inflatum, 4·25-4·75 mm. longum, circiter 1 mm. diametro. *Columna* subteres, truncata, 0·65-1 mm. longa, androclinio leviter excavato ; anthera hemisphaerica, antice truncata ; pollinia ovoideo-globosa, 0·5 mm. longa, stipitibus duobus genuflexis apice conniventibus, viscidio communi oblongo postice leviter retuso subtus concavo 0·6 mm. longo ; rostellum leviter productum, porrectum, viscidio amoto bilobum, lobis obtusis. *Capsulae* ellipsoideae vel anguste pyriformi-ellipsoideae, 7-9 mm. longae, 2·5-4 mm. diametro, cum pedicello 2 mm. longo (V. S. Summerhayes in *Hooker's Icones Plantarum*, 35 : t. 3490 ; 1950).

Herb epiphytic dwarf ; stem extremely short, about 1 cm. long, giving out densely very numerous flexuous unbranched flattened roots about 1·5-3 mm. broad. *Leaves* few, quickly falling, lingulate, up to 3 cm. long and 5 mm. broad, at the apex blunt very shortly bilobulate, dull dark green. *Inflorescences* horizontal or ascending, up to 7 cm. long, densely many-flowered ; peduncle 1-2 cm. long, provided with a few sheaths ; rachis flexuous, angled ; bracts 2-4 mm. apart, closely sheathing, blunt or acute, 1-2·5 mm. long. *Flowers* secund, horizontal or ascending, pale green ; pedicel with the ovary about 4 mm. long. *Middle sepal* more or less recurved, oblong-lanceolate, somewhat acute or blunt, 3-4·5 mm. long, 1-1·5 mm. broad ; *lateral sepals* parallelly extended, from the narrowed base obliquely curvedly lanceolate, acute, 4-5·5 mm. long, 1-1·5 mm. broad. *Petals* free, obliquely triangular-lanceolate, acute, 2·75-4·5 mm. long, near the base 1-1·5 mm. broad ; all tepals three-nerved. *Labellum* lightly incurved, the lower half shortly three-lobed, in all 3·75-4·5 mm. long ; middle lobe fleshily subulate, 2·5-3 mm. long ; lateral lobes tooth-shaped, almost acute, fleshy ; spur hanging down or lightly incurved, from the narrow base strongly swollen, 4·25-4·75 mm. long, about 1 mm. in diameter. *Column* almost terete, truncate, 0·65-1 mm. long, with the androclinium lightly hollowed out ; anther hemispherical, at the front truncate ; pollinia ovoid-globose, 0·5 mm. long, with the stalks two genuflexed at the apex connivent, with the common viscidium oblong at the back lightly retuse beneath concave 0·6 mm.

long; rostellum lightly drawn out, extended, bi-lobed with viscidium removed, with the lobes blunt. *Capsules* ellipsoid or narrowly pyriform-ellipsoid, 7-9 mm. long, 2·5-4 mm. in diameter, with the pedicel 2 mm. long.

Juncus grisebachii *Buchenau* (Juncaceae)

Perennis, stolonifer; stolones validi. *Caulis* erectus, 20-50 cm. (raro 60 et ultra) altus, teres (vel superne subcompressus), foliatus, in statu sicco plus minus striatus. *Folia* basilaria 3-4 cataphyllina, sequens et 1-3 caulina frondosa, caulina caulem plerumque superantia. *Vagina* in auriculas duas longas obtusas producta; *lamina* teres, superne canaliculata, intus unitubulosa, septis transversis completis externe plus minus prominentibus intercepta. *Inflorescentia* terminalis, composita, bractea infima foliacea longe superata, caeteris plerumque brevioribus. *Capitula* 3 (raro 2) usque 6, erecto-patentia, magna (diametro ca 15 mm), 7-10 (raro 12) flora. *Bracteae* florum omnes hypsophyllinae, membranaceae, lanceolatae, acutatae, floribus plerumque breviores. *Flores* magni (5-6 mm. longi), in axillis bractearum nudi, breviter pedunculati. *Tepala* membranacea, pallide straminea, trinervia, lanceolata, acuta, aequilonga, vel interna paullo longiora (externa interdum sub apice mucronata). *Stamina* sex, perigonium superantia; *filamenta* filiformia castanea, tepalis aequilonga (vel paullo longiora); *antherae* lineares, flavae, filamentis breviores, deciduae. *Pistillum* perigonium superans; *ovarium* trigonum elongato-ovatum; *stilus* filiformis, ovarium aequans; *stigmata* 3 longa, exserta, dextrorsum torta. *Fructus* perigonio longior, prismatico-ovatus, plus minus rostratus, fere trilocularis; pericarpium firmum nitidum, castaneum (raro pallide castaneum). *Semina* longissima, 2-3 (raro usque 4) mm. longa, scobiformia, alba, nucleo parvo flavo (F. Buchenau in Engler, *Bot. Jahrb.*, 6: 202; 1885).

Perennial, stoloniferous; stolons stout. *Stem* erect, 20-50 cm. (rarely 60 and more) high, terete (or above somewhat compressed), leafy, in a dried state more or less striate. Basal *leaves* 3-4 cataphyllary, the following one and 1-3 cauline ones foliaceous, the cauline ones commonly overtopping the stem. *Sheath* produced into two long obtuse auricles; *blade* terete, caniculate above, inside one-tubed, intercepted by transverse complete externally more or less prominent septa. *Inflorescence* terminal, compound, long overtopped by the lowermost leafy bract, with the others mostly shorter. *Heads* 3 (rarely 2) to 6, erect-spreading, large (in diameter about 15 mm.), 7-10- (rarely 12-) flowered. *Bracts* of flowers all hypsophyllary, membranous, lanceolate, slightly acute, commonly shorter than the flowers. *Flowers* large (5-6 mm. long), naked in the axils of bracts, shortly pedunculate. *Tepals* membranous, palely straw-coloured, three-nerved, lanceolate, acute, equally long or the inner ones a little longer (the outer ones sometimes mucronate below the apex). *Stamens* six, overtopping the perigon; *filaments* filiform chestnut-coloured, equal in length to the tepals (or a little longer); *anthers* linear, yellow, shorter than the filaments, deciduous. *Pistil* overtopping the perigon; *ovary* three-angled elongate-ovate; *style* filiform, equalling the ovary; *stigmas* 3 long, exserted, twisted to the right. *Fruit* longer than the perigon, prismatic-ovate, more or less beaked, almost three-locular; pericarp firm glossy chestnut-coloured (rarely pale chestnut-coloured). *Seeds* extremely long, 2-3 (rarely up to 4) mm. long, sawdust-like in appearance, white, with a small yellow nucleus.

Oryza angustifolia C. E. Hubbard (Gramineae)

Gramen annuum, usque 70 cm. altum. *Culmi* solitarii vel non numquam laxe fasciculati, erecti, vel basi prostrati vel geniculati et e nodis inferioribus radicantes, graciles, siccitate compressi, 3-4-nodes, simplices vel e nodis inferioribus ramosi ramulis erectis, glabri, laeves, internodio supremo filiformi tenuissime striato e vagina suprema demum longe exserto. *Foliorum vaginae* compressae, carinatae, glabrae, laeves, tenues, fere membranaceae, tenuiter nerves, inter nervos transverse nervatae, ore auriculis erectis angustis ligula adnatis praeditae, inferiores laxae, pallidae, internodiis longiores, superiores virides, arcte appressae, internodiis demum breviores; *ligulae* membranaceae, lanceolatae, apice acuto attenuatae et demum fissae, 3-7 mm. longae; *laminae* filiformes, setaceae, apice acutae, 10-30 cm. longae, convolutae, basi carinatae usque 1 mm. latae, superne teretes usque 0·5 mm. diametro, strictae vel leviter flexuosae, virides, glabrae, nervis minutissime granulatae vel apicem versus minutissime scaberulae, inter nervos laterales et costam mediam translucidae et transverse nervatae. *Inflorescentia* angusta, gracilis, secunda, erecta vel leviter curvata, 3-8 cm. longa (aristis exclusis), simplex et racemiformis, vel ramos 1-2 gerens; axis primarius gracillimus, laevis; rami erecti et adpressi vel leviter patentes, 2-4 cm. longi, simplices, secundi, 1-6-spiculati; rhachis laevis; pedicelli apice incrassati et oblique truncati, circiter 1 mm. longi. *Spiculae* anguste oblongae, 5-8 mm. longa, 1-1·3 mm. latae, contiguae vel leviter imbricatae, nervis virides, ceterum albidae vel rubido-suffusae. *Glumae* ad annulum cupulariformem obscurissimum redactae. *Lemmata sterilia* nulla. *Lemma fertile* anguste oblongum, ex apice longe aristatum, coriaceum, lateribus pilis minutissimis adpressis obscure asperulum vel fere laeve, marginibus prope apicem minute scaberulum, carina et marginibus apice pilis setaceis brevibus erectis hispido-ciliatum, 5-nerve; arista longissima, tenuissima, erecta, stricta, 11-18 cm. longa, scaberula, rubida, vel inferne albida et superne viridis. *Palea* lemmate paullo longior, lineari-oblonga, carina prope apicem hispido-ciliata, apice cuspidata, cuspide 1-2 mm. longa. *Antherae* purpureae vel albidae, 3-4 mm. longae· *Caryopsis* anguste oblonga, pallide brunnea, usque 3·5 mm. longa (juvenilis) (C. E. Hubbard in *Hooker's Icones Plantarum*, 35 : t. 3492 ; 1950).

Grass annual, up to 70 cm. high. *Culms* solitary or sometimes loosely bunched, erect, at base prostrate or bent and rooting from the lower nodes,

Fig. 12 *Oryza angustifolia* C. E. Hubbard

1, planta integra ; 2, pars supera caulis floriferi ; 3, ligula ; 4, sectio transversa laminae folii ; 5, pars laminae folii ; 6, pars paginae inferioris laminae folii ; 7, spiculae ; 8, apex pedicelli ; 9, palea explanata ; 10, flos (by Stella Ross-Craig, from Hooker's *Icones Plantarum*, 35 ; 1950)

3492

197

slender, in a dried state compressed, 3-4-noded, simple or branched from the lower nodes with erect branchlets, glabrous, smooth, with the uppermost internode filiform very delicately striate from the uppermost sheath at length long-exserted. *Sheaths of the leaves* compressed, keeled, glabrous, smooth thin, almost membranous, thinly nerved, between the nerves transversely veined, provided at the mouth with erect narrow auricles adnate to the ligula the lower ones loose, pale, longer than the internodes, the upper ones green closely appressed, at length shorter than the internodes; *ligules* membranous, lanceolate, at the acute apex attenuate and at length split, 3-7 mm long; *blades* filiform, setaceous, at the apex acute, 10-30 cm. long, convolute at base keeled up to 1 mm. broad, upwards terete up to 0·5 mm. in diameter straight or lightly flexuous, green, glabrous, at the nerves very minutely granulate or towards the apex very minutely scaberulous, between the lateral nerves and the midrib translucent and transversely nerved. *Inflorescence* narrow, slender, secund, erect or lightly curved, 3-8 cm. (excluding the awns) simple and raceme-like, or bearing 1-2 branches; primary axis very slender smooth; branches erect and appressed or lightly spreading, 2-4 cm. long simple, secund, with 1-6 spikelets; rachis smooth; pedicels thickened at the apex and obliquely truncate, about 1 mm. long. *Spikelets* narrowly oblong, 5-8 mm. long, 1-1·3 mm. broad, touching or lightly overlapping, at the nerves green, for the rest whitish or reddish-tinged. *Glumes* reduced to a cup-shaped very obscure ring. *Sterile lemmas* none. *Fertile lemma* narrowly oblong, from the apex long-awned, coriaceous, at the sides with very minute appressed hairs obscurely asperulous or almost smooth, at the margins near the apex minutely scaberulous, at the keel and margins at the apex with setaceous short erect hairs hispid-ciliate, 5-nerved; awn extremely long, very thin, erect, straight, 11-18 cm. long, scaberulous, reddish or white below and green above. *Pale* a little longer than the lemma, linear-oblong, with the keel near the apex hispid-ciliate, at the apex cuspidate with the cusp 1-2 mm. long. *Anthers* purple or whitish, 3-4 mm. long. *Grain* narrowly oblong, pale brown, up to 3·5 mm. long (juvenile).

CHAPTER XV

Punctuation

Niceties of punctuation did not trouble the Romans. They used the full stop, the *punctum*, but no commas because they had none to use. The unhappy result of pedantically ignoring this invention of medieval scribes and of reverting to ancient practice may be seen in Prain's monumental revision of the Indian species of *Pedicularis* (*Ann. R. Bot. Garden, Calcutta* 3; 1890), where diagnoses in the ablative up to 180 words long dispense entirely with such aids to easy consultation as stops, commas and italics. Fortunately Prain did not repeat this experiment in archaism. Most botanists, however, use more commas than they need. As an American has characteristically observed, 'punctuation is like government, the less you have the better off you are, providing you have enough to maintain order'.

It is traditional to punctuate Latin descriptions which employ the nominative differently from diagnoses which employ the ablative. In a description the account of each organ forms a separate sentence and hence is in the nominative case, as pointed out by Lindley and Asa Gray, the ablative being employed only for subsidiary clauses; except within such clauses, each adjective is usually (though not necessarily) separated by a comma. The whole description is analogous to a paragraph made up of several sentences. Procedure varies, but it seems best to separate the account of one organ from that of another by a full stop and to use semi-colons to mark off the parts of an organ which are separately described. Thus: '*Stamina* 6, fauci perigonii inserta, adscendentia; *filamenta* brevissima; *antherae* oblongae. *Ovarium* cum perigonii tubo adnatum, triloculare, ovulis numerosis; *stylus* filiformis; *stigma* capitatum.'

A description in the ablative is an extended specific character or diagnosis and is essentially a single sentence with all of the ablative clauses hanging, as it were, upon the name of the species at the beginning or on an opening statement in the nominative. It should not be broken into unanchored phrases by capital letters and full stops, this being a procedure both illogical and distasteful, like writing in English: 'Herb perennial. With leaves pinnate. With leaves ovate. With flowers solitary or in pairs. With calyx pilose.' When using the ablative it is best to separate the main clauses (i.e. those relating to different

199

organs) by means of semi-colons and the subsidiary clauses (i.e. those relating to different attributes of the same organ) by means of commas. Putting the names of organs in italic, while unnecessary in a short diagnosis, helps the reader of a long one, thus: 'Frutex erectus 1–2 m. altus; *ramis* hornotinis teretibus pilis albidis vestitis; *foliis* sessilibus obovatis obtusis glabris coriaceis, nervo medio supra impresso, nervis lateralibus e medio sub angulo 60°–80° abeuntibus; *floribus* lateralibus et terminalibus solitariis magnis, pedicellis 1 cm. longis; *calyce* campanulato, lobis rotundatis tubo duplo brevioribus; *corolla* alba, odorem gratum exhalente, tubo 5 cm. longo, lobis orbicularibus 2 cm. longis; *staminibus* exsertis, filamentis pilosis, antheris luteis linearibus.'

Here as a warning to typographical wantons is the same diagnosis entirely free of controlling punctuation, etc.: 'Frutex erectus 1–2 m. altus ramis hornotinis teretibus pilis albidis vestitis foliis sessilibus obovatis obtusis glabris coriaceis nervo medio supra impresso nervis lateralibus e medio sub angulo 60°–80° abeuntibus floribus lateralibus et terminalibus solitariis magnis pedicellis 1 cm. longis calyce campanulato lobis rotundatis tubo duplo brevioribus corolla alba odorem gratum exhalante tubo 5 cm. longo lobis orbicularibus 2 cm. longis staminibus exsertis filamentis pilosis antheris luteis linearibus.' The other objectionable extreme is to retain the ablative case throughout but nevertheless to treat the clauses as separate sentences, thus: 'F r u t e x erectus, 1–2 m. altus. R a m i s hornotinis teretibus, pilis albidis vestitis. F o l i i s sessilibus, obovatis, obtusis, glabris, coriaceis, nervo medio supra impresso, nervis lateralibus e medio sub angulo 60°–80° abeuntibus. F l o r i b u s lateralibus et terminalibus, solitariis, magnis. P e d i c e l l i s 1 cm. longis. C a l y c e campanulato, lobis rotundatis, tubo duplo brevioribus. C o r o l l a alba, odorem gratum exhalante, tubo 5 cm. longo, lobis orbicularibus, 2 cm. longis. S t a m i n i b u s exsertis, filamentis pilosis, antheris luteis linearibus.' This is, of course, much easier to read than the preceding block of uninterrupted type, but betrays an ignorance of the history and function of the ablative case in botanical Latin.

Such a description is better in the nominative. Purged of some superfluous commas, the above would read as follows: 'Frutex erectus 1–2 m. altus. *Rami* hornotini teretes, pilis albidis vestiti. *Folia* sessilia obovata obtusa glabra coriacea, nervo medio supra impresso, nervis lateralibus e medio sub angulo 60°–80° abeuntibus. *Flores* laterales et terminales solitarii magni; pedicelli 1 cm. longi. *Calyx* campanulatus, lobis rotundatis tubo duplo brevioribus. *Corolla* alba, odorem gratum exhalens; tubus 5 cm. longus; lobi orbiculares 2 cm. longi. *Stamina* exserta; filamenta pilosa; antherae luteae lineares.' This clear and simple manner of punctuation, with commas used only to separate major clauses and obviate confusion, is essentially that adopted by J. G. Baker in his revision of *Liliaceae* (*J. Linn. Soc. Bot.*, 13–18: 1872–80).

The colon is now rarely used in botanical Latin, although Linnaeus employed it occasionally, making it function as a point inferior to the comma. As stated by Hugh Rose in 1775 (*Elements of Botany* 341), 'Linnaeus uses the *comma* to distinguish the parts and the *colon* where there is a subdivision of a part, and the *punctum*, or full stop, at the end of the sentence'. Thus: 'LINUM *calycibus acutis alternis, capsulis muticis, panicula filiformi, foliis alternis lanceolatis: radicalibus ovatis*'. Although in this way contrary to modern practice, Linnaeus's use of 'ponctuation, cette grande ressource inconnue aux anciens, est toujours uste', as Alphonse de Candolle remarked. Within limits there are no hard and fast rules about punctuation; its functions are to make for clarity and ease in comparing one description with another and to prevent ambiguity; provided these ends are achieved, a little variation from customary usage does no harm.

CHAPTER XVI

Habitats

The conditions under which plants grow have always interested botan‑ ists. Their technical descriptions usually conclude with an ecologica note summarizing the information given on collectors' labels. The statement traditionally begins with *habitat* (it dwells), which in English has consequently become a noun indicating place of growth, less often with *crescit* (it grows), *occurrit* (it occurs), *amat* (it loves), *incolit* (it inhabits), *viget* (it thrives). As stated by Kerner and Oliver, 'The botanists of former times distinguished such habitats into a large number of different classes, from which we may select the following as the most important: fresh-water springs (*fontes*), salt springs (*salina*), brooks (*amnes*), torrents (*torrentes*), rivers (*fluvii*), pools (*stagna*), lakes (*lacus*), the sea (*mare*), shores of rivers and lakes (*ripae*), sea-coasts (*littora*), marshes (*uliginosa*), swamps which dry up in the summer (*paludes*), peat-bogs (*turfosa*), places that are periodically flooded (*inundata*), pastures (*campi*), steppes (*pascua*), deserts (*deserta*), sunny hills (*colles*), stony places (*lapidosa*), rocky places (*rupestria*), sands (*arena*), argillaceous soil (*argilla*), loam (*lutum*), debris (*ruderata*).' Linnaeus, who was a pioneer ecologist, described plants as growing '*in apricis* (sunny open places), *aquosis* (watery places), *aridis* (dry places), *arvis* (arable fields), *asperis* (rough places), *campis* (plains), *collibus* (hills), *cultis* (cultivated places), *desertis* (deserts), *duris* (hard or rough places), *frigidis* (cold places), *glareosis* (gravelly places), *gramino‑ sis* (grassy places), *hortis* (gardens), *humentibus* (damp places), *inundatis* (flooded places), *litoribus maritimis* (sea shores), *montosis* (mountainous places), *muris* (walls), *nemoribus* (open woodland), *paludibus* (marshes), *pascuis* (pastures), *pratis* (meadows), *ruderatis* (rubbish dumps), *rupibus* (rocks), *sabulosis* (sandy places), *sterilibus* (sterile places), *sylvestribus* (woody or wild places), *sylvis* (woods), *tectis* (roofs), *udis* (damp places), *uliginosis* (marshy places) as well as *ad agros* (fields), *ad agrorum versuras* (edges of fields), *ad fossas* (ditches), *ad ripas fluviorum* (banks of rivers)' (cf. Stearn, 1959 : 89).

The preposition *ad* (at) is used with the accusative, e.g. *ad truncos ramosque*, but *in* (in, on), when denoting rest, with the ablative, e.g. *in truncis ramisque*. To indicate the host-plants of parasites and epiphytes the genitive is also much used, e.g. *ad truncos vetustos arborum Pini, Betulae, Quercus, etc. Sueciae meridionalis* (on the old trunks of trees of Pinus, Betula, Quercus, etc., of southern Sweden). The verbs *amat* (it loves) and *incolit* (it inhabits) are followed by the accusative, e.g. *amat loca humida* (it loves damp places), *incolit rupes* (it inhabits rocks).

PLANTS OF ROCKS, HILLS AND MOUNTAINS

Hab. in montibus altis Jamaicae. It grows in high mountains of Jamaica.

Hab. in locis saxosis montium et etiam collium Delphinatus borealis. It grows in stony places of the mountains and also the hills of northern Dauphiné.

Hab. in collibus petrosis Galloprovinciae. It grows in rocky hills of Provence.

In locis siccis et apertis praesertim ad rupes et muros. In dry and open places especially on rocks and walls.

Communis in muris tectisque. Common on walls and roofs.

Ad rupes calcareas Helvetiae. On calcareous rocks of Switzerland.

Ad saxa et rupes graniticas et micaceas Sveciae totius. On granitic and micaceous stones and rocks of all Sweden.

Ad saxa syenitica, gneissiaca et granitica muscis vestita supra zonam Fagi alpium. On syenite, gneiss and granitic stones clothed with mosses above the beech zone of the alps.

In fissuris rupium siccarum. In fissures of dry rocks.

In cryptis umbrosis inter fragmenta saxorum. In shady pits between broken-off pieces of stone.

In scopulis humidis ad cataractam. On damp rocks at the waterfall.

PLANTS OF WOODS AND THICKETS

Habitat in sylvis montium usque ad 500 m. supra mare. It grows in woods of mountains up to 500 m. above sea-level.

Crescit inter frutices in sylvis frondosis, praesertim prope rivulos in locis lapidosis simulque humidis, radicibus demissis in terram argillaceam, qua fissurae rupium impletae sunt. It grows among shrubs in broad-leaved woods, especially near streams in places rocky and at the same time moist, with the roots planted in clay soil, with which the fissures of the rocks are filled.

In sylvis humidis praecipue quercinis in planitiebus collibus montibusque. In damp woods especially of oak on plains, hills and mountains.

In dumosis collium. In thickets of hills.

In pinetis, betulis, fagetis et etiam castanetis. In woods of pine, birch, beech and also sweet chestnut.

PLANTS OF PASTURES, MEADOWS, FIELDS, ETC.

In pascuis siccis. In dry pastures.
In pratis udis. In moist meadows.
In arvis arenosis. In sandy fields.
In hortis et ad margines agrorum. In gardens and at the margins of fields.

AQUATIC AND COASTAL PLANTS

In terram hyeme inundatam. On land flooded during the winter.
In fossis et stagnis. In ditches and ponds.
In palude alpina et in paludibus regionis inferioris. In the alpine marsh and in marshes of the lower region.
Ad saxa in aquis fluentibus quietisve. On rocks in running or still water.
In aquis dulcibus ad lapides et plantas aquaticas et ad parietes piscinarum e puteorum. In fresh water on stones and aquatic plants and on the wall of cisterns and wells.
Ad·saxa, muros, terram, palos, fucos paulo infra limitem superiorem fluxus in Oceano Atlantico ad oras Galliae et Angliae. On rocks, walls, earth pales, Fuci a little below the upper limit of the tide in the Atlantic Ocean on the coasts of France and England.
Ad oras Atlanticas Europae et Americae borealis. On the Atlantic shores of Europe and North America.

PARASITIC, EPIPHYTIC AND SAPROPHYTIC PLANTS

In foliis caulibusque Labiatarum imprimis Menthae, Thymi, Glechomae, Lamii Hedeomatis. On leaves and stems of Labiatae, particularly of Mentha Thymus, Glechoma, Lamium, Hedeoma.
In plantis Umbelliferarum, e.g. Triniae, Osterici, Anthrisci, Myrrhis, Sileris On plants of Umbelliferae, e.g. of Trinia, Ostericus, Anthriscus, Myrrhis Siler.
In foliis adhuc vivis vel languidis Senecionis jacobaeae. On leaves as ye living or wilted of Senecio jacobaea.
Ad ramos Sarothamni, Calycotomes, Anthyllidis, Genistae. On branches o Sarothamnus, Calycotome, Anthyllis, Genista.
In cortice et ligno Betulae, Alni, Quercus. In the bark and wood of Betula Alnus, Quercus.
In caulibus emortuis Urticae. On dead stems of Urtica.
Ad basim caulium putrescentium Echii vulgaris. At the base of decaying stems of Echium vulgare.
In vaginis Secalis et graminum variorum. On the sheaths of Secale and various grasses.
Ad culmos exsiccatos Phragmitis, Arundinis. On dried culms of Phragmites Arundo.
Ad caules et ramos varios, e.g. Oleae, Arbuti, Quercus, Odontitis. On various stems and branches, e.g. of Olea, Arbutus, Quercus, Odontites.

In pagina superiori vel inferiori vel in utraque pagina foliorum. On the upper or the lower or on each surface of the leaves.

In arborum truncis ramulisque. On the trunks and branchlets of trees.

In sylva Amazonica ubique ad arborum folia viva, interdum ad herbas nobiliores, necnon in filicibus. In the Amazonian forest everywhere on the living leaves of trees, sometimes on the robuster herbs, and also on ferns.

Supra folia coacervata putrida Abietis. Above heaped decayed leaves of Abies.

In ligno carioso. In rotten wood.

Ad truncos prostratos putrescentes saepe cum aliis hepaticis muscisque. On prostrate rotting trunks often with other liverworts and mosses.

Ad fimum vaccinum. On cow dung.

In fimo ovino. On sheep droppings.

Habitat ad epidermidem (in epidermide) capitis humani. It inhabits the skin of the human head.

Ad pedem hominis inter digitos. On the foot of a man between the toes.

In tumore (granulomato) cerebrali feminae. In the cerebral tumour of a woman.

In pure abscessus hominis diabetici. In the pus of an abscess of a diabetic man.

In tumoribus subcutaneis interioribusque in toto corpore disseminatis hominis. In subcutaneous and inner swellings (nodules) scattered over the whole body of a man.

In canibus, equis, bovibus, etc., et in hominibus praecipue infantibus, in quibus eruptionem cutis causat. In dogs, horses, cattle, etc., and in men, especially infants, in whom it causes an eruption of the skin.

In ulceribus canis et muris. In ulcers of a dog and a mouse.

ECOLOGICAL EPITHETS AND TERMS

Epithets relating to habitats (*stationes*) are formed from nouns by using the suffix -*icola* (dweller), e.g. *paludicola* (a marsh-dweller), less often -*gena* (-born), e.g. *paludigena* (marsh-born), or adjectival endings indicating possession or connexion, as -*alis*, -*anus*, -*arius*, -*aticus*, -*inus*, or place of occurrence, as -*ensis*, -*estris*, etc.

In phrases such as *in aridis*, the term *solum natale* (natal soil), abl. pl. *solis natalibus*, used by Linnaeus in the sense of 'habitat', is implied but not expressed; the adjective is treated as a second declension neuter noun, e.g. *aridum* (dry place).

A glossary of Latin ecological words used by Ray, Dillenius and their contemporaries will be found on pp. 75-81 of my introduction to the Ray Society's facsimile (1972) of Ray's *Synopsis methodica Stirpium Britannicarum*, 3rd ed. (1724).

CHAPTER XVII

Geographical Names

KINDS OF GEOGRAPHICAL NAMES

Geographical names used in botanical Latin may be divided historically into three groups corresponding to their period of origin:

(1) Those used by the Romans themselves, such as *Roma, Sicilia,* which have survived through continuous usage or are recorded by the classical geographers.

(2) Those coined during the Middle Ages and the sixteenth century for legal or academic purposes, such as *Oxonia* (Oxford), *Cantabrigia* (now Cambridge), *Lipsia* (by way of Lipzig from Liptziche, now Leipzig).

(3) Those of modern origin, which may be names already of Latin form, as *Argentina, Australia, Czechoslovakia, Indonesia, Liberia, Nigeria,* or native names given a Latin ending, as *Chittagonga,* or Latin equivalent, as *Flumen Januarii* (Rio de Janeiro). Names of Latin form, whatever their origin, are treated grammatically as Latin words. Thus *Africa, Alsatia, Jena, Japonia* and others ending in *-a* are declined as feminine nouns of the First Declension, their genitive singular ending in *-ae*; *Amanus, Emodus,* etc., as masculine nouns, and *Argentoratum, Divionum,* etc., as neuter nouns, both of the Second Declension, with the genitive singular ending in *-i*; *Borysthenes* (m.), *Petropolis* (f.), *Tamesis* (m.), etc., as nouns of the Third Declension, with the genitive singular ending in *-is*. Others are best accepted as indeclinable, i.e. they are cited unchanged, as in the statements: *in itinere per Stiriam superiorem, in valle inter Kapfenberg et Aflenz ab incolis 'Thörlgraben' nominata* (on the journey through upper Steiermark, in the valley between Kapfenberg and Aflenz named 'Thörlgraben' by the inhabitants); *in Scania ad Trollehall, prope Gothoburgum, prope Holmiam, in montibus Sumphallen* (in Skåne at Trollehall, near Gothenburg, near Stockholm, in the Sumphallen mountains); *in montibus Sierra de*

Cazorla, loco dicto 'Cruz del Muchacho' (in the mountains Sierra de Cazorla, at the place called 'Cruz del Muchacho').

GEOGRAPHICAL TERMS

Indeclinable place-names are often qualified by an explanatory geographical term in the appropriate case, e.g.: *in provincia Cajatambo in montibus Cordillera negra ad viam ad oppidum Ocros ad jugum Chonta dictum* (in Cajatambo province in the Cordillera Negra mountains by the way to the town Ocros at the ridge called Chonta); *in sylvis montium Azuay et Guayrapata* (in woods of the mountains Azuay and Guayrapata); *in montibus Chimborazo et Azuay* (on the mountains Chimborazo and Azuay); *in monte Pico de Arvas* (on the mountain Pico de Arvas).

The following are the commonest of such terms:

ager (*m.*): territory, district, domain

comitatus (*m.*): county

convallis (*f.*): valley enclosed on all sides

desertum (*n.*): desert

districtus (*m.*): district, controlled area

ditio (*f.*): dominion, sovereignty

finis (*m.*): boundary, border

flumen (*n.*): river

fluvius (*m.*): river

fretum (*n.*): strait

insula (*f.*): island, isle

isthmus (*m.*): isthmus

jugum (*n.*): mountain ridge, chain of mountains

lacus (*m.*): lake

littus, litus (*n.*): coast, sea-shore

locus (*m*)., **locum** (*n.*): place

mare (*n.*): sea

mons (*m.*): mountain, translating in place-names the German *Berg*, Turkish *daǧ* (*dagh*), Italian *monte*, Chinese *shan*, Turki *tau*, Japanese *yama*, etc.

oppidum (*n.*): town

pagus (*m.*): district, canton; applied to an area with definite boundaries

paroecia (*f.*): parish

peninsula (*f.*): peninsula

planities (*f.*): plain

promontorium (*n.*): promontory, headland, cape

planities (*f.*): plain

provincia (*f.*): province

regio (*f.*): district, territory, region; applied to area of indefinite extent

regnum (*n.*): kingdom, realm

sinus (*m.*): bay, gulf

sylva (*f.*): forest

terra (*f.*): land, territory, region

territorium (*n.*): land around a town, territory, district

vallis (*f.*): valley

Regional names are often formed from these terms by the addition of an adjective, e.g. *ager Lugdunensis* (Lyonnais); *districtus Murmanensis* (Murmansk district); *fretum Magellanicum* (Straits of Magellan); *peninsula Athoa* (Athos peninsula); *regio Danubialis*

(Danube region); *sinus Ligusticus* (Golfo di Genova). This adjective agrees in gender, number and case with the noun, e.g. *in locis sicci, agri Lugdunensis* (in dry places of the Lyon district), *in agro Lugdunensi* (in the Lyon district). It usually follows the noun, but can be placed before it. Further precision may be given by the use of the adjectives :

australis, meridionalis : southern
austro-occidentalis : south-western
austro-orientalis : south-eastern
borealis, septentrionalis : northern
boreo-occidentalis : north-western

boreo-orientalis : north-eastern
centralis, medius : central
occidentalis : western
orientalis : eastern

An example is :

Habitat in parte regionis mediterraneae austro-occidentali, praecipue in Hispania centrali et Lusitania meridionali, ubi occidentem versus abundat. It occurs in the south-western part of the Mediterranean region, especially in central Spain and southern Portugal, where towards the west it abounds.

USE OF LOCATIVE CASE AND PREPOSITIONS

The place at which something happens, e.g. a plant grows or a book is published, may be expressed by means of the locative case (see p. 67) without a preposition. This is commonly used on the title-pages of books. For First Declension nouns the locative singular is the same as the genitive, e.g. *Kilae* (at Kiel), *Lipsiae* (at Leipzig), *Romae* (at Rome), as also for Second Declension nouns, e.g. *Londini* (at London), *Rhodi* (at Rhodes), *Taurini* (at Turin). Names of plural form, though of singular meaning, e.g. *Athenae* (Athens), *Aquae-Carolinae* (Karlsbad), *Delphi* (Delphi), *Parisii* (Paris), have the locative the same as the dative plural, e.g. *Athenis* (at Athens), *Aquis-Carolinis* (at Karlsbad), *Delphis* (at Delphi), *Parisiis* (at Paris). For the Third Declension nouns the locative is sometimes the same as the dative, e.g. *Carthagini* (at Carthage), *Neapoli* (at Naples), *Petropoli* (at St. Petersburg), but usually it is the same as the ablative, e.g. *Hispale* (at Seville), *Olisipone* (at Lisbon), *Oeniponte* (at Innsbruck).

The prepositions *a, ab* (from), *e* or *ex* (from) and *in* are followed by the place-name in the ablative, *ad* (at), *circa* (about), *cis* (on this side of), *per* (through), *prope* (near), *supra* (above) and *trans* (across) by it in the accusative, e.g. *in America a Bolivia per Panamam usque ad Californiam* (in America from Bolivia through Panama up to California).

CLASSICAL NAMES

Names for places in Asia came into classical literature in the first place
largely through the conquests of Alexander the Great (356–323 B.C.).
Under his leadership Greek armies marched across Mesopotamia and
Persia and reached the Oxus (Amu Darya), Iaxartes (Syr Darya) and
Indus rivers. From Asiatic merchants the Greeks learned about the remote eastern islands of Taprobane (Ceylon) and Iabadius (Java). Later
the conquests of Rome created an empire in the west which stretched
from the Atlas mountains of Mauritania (Morocco) to the Vallum
Romanum (Roman Wall) of northern Britain. 'The boundaries of the
empire', as Sir Mortimer Wheeler states in his *Rome beyond the
imperial Frontiers* (1955), 'particularly in the East, were sufficiently fluid
to ensure a constant awareness of more distant horizons, of greater
riches, more marvels, fresh menaces.' Traders from the Roman Empire
penetrated into Germany and Sarmatia (eastern Europe) and foreign-
born slaves, mercenaries and merchants probably brought information
about more distant sparsely populated and inhospitable regions such
as Scandinavia and Scythia. There were, moreover, Roman trading
ports (*emporia*) along both the west and the east coasts of India. Thus
for the Mediterranean region and the adjoining countries which were
or had been under Greek or Roman rule, indeed for the region south
of a line stretching obliquely from Britain and France to the borders
of India and including north Africa, the later geographers of antiquity,
Pliny the Elder, Pomponius Mela and Ptolemy, had much information
available. Hence for many places within this region there exist genuine
classical names. Botanists writing in Latin have made extensive use
of them. Thus Edmond Boissier, lacking convenient modern names
for districts of the nineteenth-century Ottoman Empire, used the old
classical names when recording in his *Flora Orientalis* (1867–84) the
distribution of plants within the Near and Middle East (see Fig. 13).[1]

For such names, reference should be made to standard works on
classical geography, as those of E. H. Bunbury (1879), H. Kiepert
(1818), William Smith (1873), J. O. Thomson (1948), H. F. Tozer
(1939), and atlases, such as those of A. A. M. van der Heyden & H. H.
Scullard (1959), J. B. Grundy (1917), J. O. Thomson (in the Everyman
Library, 1961).

LATER NAMES

During the Middle Ages, when Latin still survived as the official
language for legal, ecclesiastical and other matters, many European

---

[1] The late Professor Ch. Baehni informed me that, judging from Boissier's private
library, he used chiefly A. Brué, *Carte générale de l'Asie Mineure* (1839).

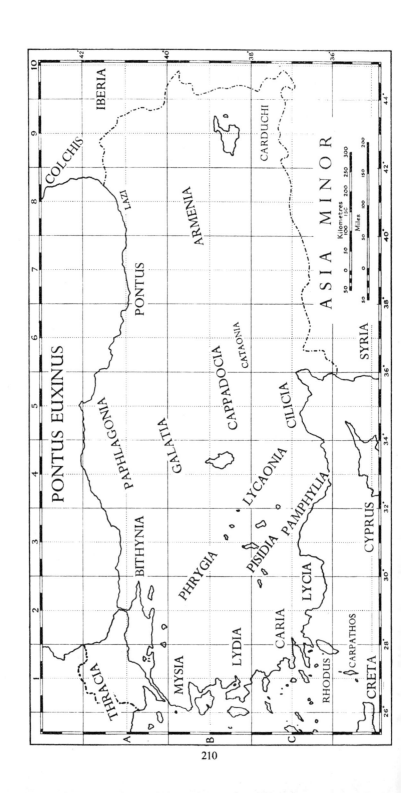

THRACIA

BITHYNIA

MYSIA

LYDIA

PHRYGIA

CARIA

RHODUS

CARPATHOS

CRETA

LYCIA

PISIDIA PAMPHYLIA

LYCAONIA

PAPHLAGONIA

PONTUS EUXINUS

COLCHIS

IBERIA

LAZI

PONTUS

GALATIA

ARMENIA

CAPPADOCIA

CATAONIA

CILICIA

CARDUCHI

ASIA MINOR

SYRIA

CYPRUS

Kilometres
50 0 50 100 150 200 250 300

Miles
50 0 50 100 150 200

210

owns which had not existed in Roman times found it necessary to provide themselves with coined names of Latin form for use in charters and other documents. Usually such names were simply modifications of the original name, e.g. *Cantabrigia* derived by way of Cantebrugge from Grantebrycge (now Cambridge). Sometimes they were translations or equivalents, e.g. *Regiomontum* for Königsberg (now Kaliningrad). Homonyms were usually distinguished by a qualifying word or phrase, e.g. *Francofurtum ad Moenum* (Frankfurt am Main), *Francofurtum ad Oderum* (Frankfurt an der Oder). Such names often occur on the title-pages of books written in Latin.

The store of such Latinized place-names has greatly increased during the last three hundred years. Thus the Cape of Good Hope (not discovered until 1488, then named by the Portuguese King John II *Cabo de Boa Esperança* for the good hope it gave of a sea-route to India) appears in many botanical works as *Caput Bonae Spei* or *Promontorium Bonae Spei*, often abbreviated to *C.B.Spei*, *P.B.Spei* or *C.B.S.*; and the epithet *capensis* forms part of the specific name of many a South African plant. Some of these names were based on local names now obsolete, as *Sebastianopolis* for São Sebastião (now Rio de Janeiro). The works of the Abbé Chevin, P. Deschamps, E. de Toni and J. G. Th. Graesse together include most of them but by no means all. Those which escaped their notice are sometimes very puzzling. Thus *Bisnagaria* is derived from the Portuguese *Bisnaga* which referred to the ancient kingdom of Vijayanagar in southern India east of Malabar and south of the river Kistna. Vellozo's *Pharmacopolis* refers to Parati (formerly Nossa Senhora dos Remedios) in Brazil near Rio de Janeiro. Following Vatican usage (cf. Bacci, 1955), *Neanthopolis* is Addis Ababa, *Antherocrenopolis* Bloemfontein.

LATINIZATION OF PLACE-NAMES

Comparison of classical place-names with their medieval and modern derivatives and of medieval and sixteenth-century place-names with their Latinized versions shows no unvarying pattern of change from one to the other. Thus the ending '-land' may be rendered as *-landia*, e.g. *Gotlandia* (Gotland), *Groenlandia* (Greenland), *Islandia* (Iceland), or translated by *terra*, e.g. *Terra Nova* (Newfoundland), or omitted, e.g. *Gelria* (Gelderland), *Gothia* (Götland), *Jemtia* (Jämtland). Nevertheless certain equivalents, notably of endings, have been widely used, For example, the French 'château' is usually translated by *castrum*.

Fig. 13　Classical Regions of Asia Minor
(Based on A. Brué, *Carte générale de l'Asie Mineure*, 1839, used by Edmond Boissier)

though sometimes by *castellum*, e.g. *Castrum* (or *Castellum*) *Brienti* (Châteaubriand), *Castrum Novum* (Château-Neuf); the German '-burg' is usually rendered by *-burgum*, e.g. *Friburgum* (Freiburg), *Marburgum* (Marburg), the Swedish '-köping' by *-copia*, e.g. *Junecopia* (Jönköping), *Lincopia* (Linköping). The French diphthongs *ai, ei, oi* *ui* become *a, e, o, u*; similarly German *ei, ö,* ü become *i, o, u*. Initial *W* often becomes *V*, occasionally *Gu*.

The following list, based on one compiled by Saalfeld (1885), gives the usual changes of ending made when latinizing medieval and modern place-names:

-ac, -ach, -ack : *-acum, -achium*

-ad : *-adum*

-agne : *-ania*

-ailles : *-alia*

-ain, -aine : *-ania, -anium*

-al : *-alium, -alia*

-am : *-amum*

-an (ain) : *-ānum, -anium* in names of places

-an (ain) : *-ania* in names of regions

-ant, -anz : *-antia*

-ar : *-aria*

-ars : *-acum*

-at : *-atum*

-atsch, -atz : *-atium*

-au : *-avia, -oa, -ovia, -augia* in names of places

-au : *-ovia* in names of regions

-aux : *-atium*

-berg : *-berga, mons*; *-bergia* (region)

-borg : *-burgum*

-born : *-borna*

-burg : *-burgum, -polis* only when first part of name is Greek or Graecized

-c : *-iăcum*

-cester, -chester : *-cestria*

-court : *-curia*

-dorf : *-dorpium*

-e : *-a*

-e, -é : *-as, -aeum*

-eau : *-aldum*

-ec, -eck : *-ecca, -ēca*

-eglia : *-elia*

-ei, -ey : *-eia* in names of places

-ei, -ey : *-ia* in names of regions

-eil, eille : *-elia*

-ein : *-īnum*

-em : *-ēmum*

-en : *-a, -ēna, -um, -ium,* in names of regions also in *-ia*

-ence, -enz : *-entia*

-ent : *-entium*

-er : *-era*

-euil : *-olium*

-ey : see *ei*

-feld : *-felda, -feldia*

-fels : *-felsa*

-ford, -fort : *-fordia*

-furt : *-furtum*

-gard ⎫
-gart ⎪
-garten ⎬ *-gardia*
-gorod ⎪
-grod ⎭

-gen : *-ga* in names of places

-gen : *-gia* in names of regions

-grad : *-polis*

-hafen : *-havia, portus*

-ham : *-hamia, -hamium*

-hausen : *-husa, -husium*

-haven : *-havia, portus*

-heim : *-hemium*

-hof, -hofen : *-hofa, -hovia, -hovium*

-holm : *-holmia*

-holz : *-holtia*

-horst : *-horstium*

-hus, -husen : *-husa, -husium*

-hut : *-hutum*

-ich, -ick ⎫ *-icum*
-ig, -ik ⎭

ie : -ia
igno : -inium
im : -īmum, -īma
in : -īnum, -īnium
ing, ingen : -inga
itsch, -itz : -icium, -itium, -icia
kirchen : -querca, -kerka
köping : -copia
land : -landia, terra
leben : -lēba, -lebia
minster : -monasterium
mold : -moldia
mond, mont : -montium, mons
mouth : -mutha, -muthum, -muthium
münde : -munda
n : -iăcum
o, in Romance names : -um
oglio : -oleum
ogne : -onia
oise : -osia
on : -ona
oping⎫
öping⎭ -opia

-ost : -ostum
-oux : -osum
-ow : -ovia, -ovium
-pol, -poli : -pŏlis
-pré : -pratum
-que : -ca
-r : -iacum
-sand : -sanda
-stadt⎫
-städt⎭ -stadium
-stein : -steinium, -stenium
-stock : -stochium
-t : -iacum
-thal : -thalia, -dalia
-us : -usium
-ville : -villa
-wegen : -vegia
-werth : -verda
-wich, wijk : -vicum
-y : -ium, also -iacum
-zell : -cella
-zza : -ssa

GEOGRAPHICAL EPITHETS

Names of countries and localities used for specific or varietal epithets may be substantives in the genitive, e.g. *saharae* (of the Sahara), *emodi* (of the Emodus, i.e. Himalaya), *sanctae-helenae* (of St. Helena), *maris-nortui* (of the Dead Sea), *novi-belgii* (of the New Netherlands, later New York), *novae-zelandiae* (of New Zealand), *novae-angliae* (of New England), *palinuri* (of Capo Palinuro, Italy), *terrae-novae* (of New-foundland), etc.   The *International Code of botanical Nomenclature*, Rec. 82 E, recommends, however, that epithets taken from geographical names should be adjectives and end in *-ensis* (*-e*), *-anus* (*-a*, *-um*) or *-icus* (*-a*, *-um*), a large number of geographical adjectives having been formed in this way in classical Latin.   Of geographical epithets in *-ensis*, classical examples are provided by *carthaginiensis* (pertaining to Carthage), *castulonensis* (pertaining to Castulo, now Cazorla), *oscensis* (pertaining to Osca, now Huesca), *londinensis* (pertaining to London), etc.   Among epithets in *-anus* are *africanus*, *gaditanus* (pertaining to Gades, now Cadiz), *neapolitanus* (pertaining to Neapolis, now Naples), *romanus* (pertaining to Rome), *pisanus* (pertaining to Pisa), *bactrianus* (pertaining to Bactria, Central Asia).   The terminations *-acus*, *-aeus*, *-enus*, *-inus* and *-us* were also used to form geographical adjectives, e.g. *aetnaeus* (pertaining to Mt. Etna), *alexandrinus* (pertaining to Alexandria), *cyrenaeus* (pertaining to Cyrene, North Africa), *damascenus* (pertaining to Damascus), *etruscus* (pertaining to Etruria now Toscana), *siculus* (pertaining to Sicily), etc.

For botanical purposes *babylonicus* is preferable to *babylonius*, *aegyptiacus* to *aegyptius*, *britannicus* to *britannus*, *hispanicus* to *hispanus*; all were used in classical times.

Some plants have been named after the people whose territory they inhabit. The name of the people is then used in the genitive plural, e.g. *carduchorum* (of the Carduchi, the wild tribesmen of Kurdistan who so severely harried Xenophon and the Ten Thousand).

The termination *-cola* (indicating a dweller or inhabitant) is some times added to a place-name to form a specific epithet, e.g. *morrisoni-cola* (a dweller on Mt. Morrison). Usually, however, *-cola* is used to indicate the habitat rather than the place, e.g. *argillicola* (a dweller on clay), *arenicola* (a dweller on sand), *nubicola* (a dweller among the clouds, i.e. a high-alpine), *linicola* (a dweller among flax, i.e. a weed in flax-fields or a parasite or saprophyte on flax), *rupicola* (a dweller on rocks), *serpentinicola* (a dweller on serpentine rock), *phragmiticola* (a dweller on Phragmites).

Modern adjectives formed by adding *-icus*, *-anus* or *-ensis* to a modern place-name, e.g. *californicus*, *pensylvanicus*, *sibiricus*, *tibeticus*, *japonicus*, *carolinianus*, *americanus*, *mexicanus*, *jamaicensis*, *canadensis*, *nepalensis*, *brasiliensis*, *quebecensis*, *yunnanensis*, *australiensis*, need no explanation. There exist, however, many classical and medieval Latin place-names and adjectives of which the meaning is by no means immediately obvious, e.g. *granatensis*, *lugdunensis*, *lusitanicus*, *moesiacus*, *monspeliensis*, *patavinus*, *rothomagensis*, *salisburgensis*, *suecicus*, *telonensis* (pertaining to Telonis Portus, i.e. Toulon), *vindobonensis* (see below).

SOME GEOGRAPHICAL NAMES USED IN BOTANICAL LATIN

The following list gives modern equivalents for most of the Latin and Latinized place-names used in Linnaeus's *Species Plantarum* (1753) for records of distribution, and on the title-pages of books, to indicate place of publication, together with a number of names used by Boissier and others which may be difficult to interpret. To these have been added specific epithets associated with them. A fairly complete list of Latin and Latinized place-names would probably exceed 15,000 entries. The following list makes no claim to such completeness. For further information, use should be made of the works of Chevin, Deschamps, De Toni, Graesse and Martin.

Names of regions and countries as used by earlier authors, particularly by Linnaeus and his contemporaries, do not necessarily apply to exactly the same regions and countries as possess them today. Sometimes they were vaguely applied ; often boundaries have changed. Many have become obsolete. They have to be interpreted by reference to the extent of botanical exploration at the time (cf. Stearn, 1958). Thus, as stated elsewhere, 'Canada in the Linnaean sense does not correspond to the modern Dominion of Canada but to a region of north-eastern America, partly in Canada, mostly in the United States, where Kalm did much collecting, i.e. roughly from Philadelphia and New York northward, by way of Albany, to Montreal and Quebec and from Albany westward along the Mohawk River to Lake Ontario and Niagara Falls' (Stearn, 1957 : 144).

GEOGRAPHICAL NAMES

Aalandia : Åland Islands (Ahvenanmaa), Finland
Abbatis Cella : Appenzell, N.E. Switzerland (adj. *abbatiscellanus*)
Abellinum : Avellino, S. Italy
Aboa : Åbo (Turku), Finland
Acadia, Accadia : Nova Scotia, Canada (adj. *acadiensis*)
Achaia : Akhaia, Peloponnisos, S. Greece (adj. *achaius*)
Adscensionis Insula: *see* Ascensionis Insula
Aegyptus, Egypt : Egypt, i.e. valley of the Nile between 24° 3′ and 31° 37′ N. (adj. *aegyptiacus*)
Aequatoria : Ecuador (adj. *aequatorialis*)
Aestuarium Reginae Charlottae : Queen Charlotte Sound, New Zealand
Aethiopia : Africa, usually South Africa, in classical use Africa south of Libya and Egypt, hence Abyssinia (adj. *aethiopicus*)
Aetna : Mt. Etna, Sicily, Italy (adj. *aetensis*)
Aetolia : Aitolia, mid Greece (adj. *aetolicus*)
Afghania, Affghania : Afghanistan (adj. *afghanicus*); *see* Bactria
Africa : Africa (adj. *afer, africanus*) ; *see* Aethiopia
Agennum, Aginum, Nitiobrigum : Agen, S. France
Aleppo: Alep (Haleb), N. Syria (adj. *aleppicus, chalepensis, halepensis*)
Alexandria : Alexandria, Egypt (adj. *alexandrinus*)
Algarbia : Algarve, Portugal (adj. *algarvicus*)
Allobrogicae Alpes : Savoy (Savoie), France (adj. *allobrogicus*)
Alpes : European Alps (adj. *alpinus, alpestris* ; often used merely to indicate habitat rather than place)
Alsatia : Alsace (Elsass), France (adj. *alsaticus*)
Altorfia, Altdorffium : Altdorf, W. Germany (adj. *altorfinus, altdorfiensis*)
Alvarnia : Auvergne, France
Amanus : Amanus range, near Iskenderun, Turkey, Asia Minor (adj. *amanus*)
Amboina, Ambona : Ambon, Moluccas, Indonesia (adj. *amboinensis, amboinicus*)
Amicorum Insulae : Tonga Isles (Friendly Isles), Pacific Ocean

Amstelodamum : Amsterdam, Netherlands (adj. *amstelodamensis*)
Anatolia, Natolia : Turkey, Asia Minor (adj. *anatolicus*)
Ancyra : Ankara, Turkey, Asia Minor (adj. *ancyrensis*)
Andegavum : Angers, France (adj. *andegavensis*)
Angelopolis : Puebla (formerly Puebla de los Angeles), Mexico
Angermannia : Ångermanland, mid Sweden
Anglia : England (adj. *anglicus*)
Anneberga : Annaberg, E. Germany
Antillae, India occidentalis : West Indies (adj. *antillanus*)
Antverpia : Antwerp (Anvers), Belgium
Apenninus : the Apennines, Italy (adj. *apenninus*)
Aponus, Balneum Aponense : Abano, N. Italy
Aprutium : Abruzzi, Italy
Aquae Carolinae : *see* Thermae Carolinae
Aquitania : Aquitaine, S.W. France
Arabia : Arabia (adj. *arabicus*)
Arabicus Sinus : *see* Mare Rubrum
Aragonia : Aragon, N. Spain
Arcadia : Arkadhia, Peloponnisos, S. Greece (adj. *arcadiensis*)
Archipelagus : Aegean Islands, E. Mediterranean Sea
Argentoratum : Strasbourg (Strassburg), W. France
Argovia : Aargau (Argovie), Switzerland (adj. *argoviensis*)
Armorica, Aremonica : Brittany (Bretagne), N.W. France
Arvonia : Caernarvonshire, N. Wales, Britain (adj. *arvonicus, arvoniensis*)
Arvonicae Alpes : Snowdon range, N. Wales, Britain
Ascensionis Insula, Adscensionis Insula : Ascension Island, South Atlantic
Atlas : Atlas Mountains, N.W. Africa (adj. *atlanticus* ; gen. *atlantis*)
Atrebatum : Arras, N.E. France (adj. *atrebatensis*)
Atropatene : Azerbaijan, N.W. Iran (adj. *atropatanus*)
Attica : Attiki, S. Greece (adj. *atticus*)
Augusta Allobrogum : *see* Geneva
Augusta Taurinorum : *see* Taurinum
Augusta Vindelicorum : Augsburg, W. Germany
Aurelia, Aurelianum : Orléans, N. France (adj. *aurelianensis*)
Australia, Nova Hollandia : Australia (adj. *australiensis*)
Austria : Austria (Österreich) (adj. *austriacus*)
Avenio : Avignon, S. France
Bactria : N.E. Afghanistan (adj. *bactrianus*)
Baetica : Andalucia, S. Spain (adj. *baeticus*)
Baetis : Guadalquivir R., S. Spain
Bahusia : Bohuslän, S. Sweden (adj. *bahusiensis*)
Balaenae Sinus : Walvis Bay, S.W. Africa
Baleares : Balearic Islands, Spain (adj. *balearicus*)
Balneum Aponense : *see* Aponus
Balticum Fretum, Balticum Mare : The Sound (Öresund), Scandinavia
Banatus : Banat, former Austro-Hungarian crownland, roughly 20°-23° E.,
         45°-46° N., Romania (adj. *banaticus*)

Barbaria : Barbary, i.e. N. Africa W. of Egypt
Barcino : Barcelona, N.E. Spain (adj. *barcinensis*)
Basilea, Basilia : Basel (Bâle), N. Switzerland (adj. *basiliensis*)
Batavia : Dutch Netherlands (adj. *batavus*)
Bathonia : Bath, S.W. England (adj. *bathoniensis*)
Bavaria : Bavaria (Bayern), W. Germany (adj. *bavaricus*)
Belgia : Belgium
Belgium : Netherlands, i.e. the Dutch Netherlands (Belgium Confederatum ; Belgium Foederatum) and modern Belgium (Belgium Austriacum ; Belgia ; Brabantia et Flandria) (adj. *belgicus*)
Bellilua, Balliolum : Bailleul, N. France
Belutchia : Baluchistan, West Pakistan
Benacus Lacus : Lago di Garda, N. Italy
Benghala : Bengal, India and Pakistan (adj. *benghalensis*)
Berna : Bern, Switzerland
Berolinum : Berlin, Germany (adj. *berolinensis*)
Bertiscus : North Albanian Alps, Albania and Yugoslavia
Berytus : Berit Daği (Berytdagh), Central Turkey, Asia Minor (adj. *berytius*)
Berytus : Beirut, Lebanon (adj. *berytensis, berytheus*)
Bipontium : Zweibrücken, W. Germany (adj. *bipontinus*)
Birmania : *see* Burma
Biscaria : Vizcaya, N. Spain
Bisnagaria : S. India, former kingdom of Vijayanagar
Bithynia : N.W. Turkey, Asia Minor (adj. *bithynicus, bithynus*)
Blekingia : Blekinge, S. Sweden
Blesae : Blois, N. France (adj. *blesensis*)
Bodamicus Lacus, Brigantinus Lacus : Lake Constance (Boden See)
Boeotia : Voiotia, mid Greece (adj. *boeoticus*)
Bohemia : Bohemia, W. Czechoslovakia (adj. *bohemicus*)
Bolonia : Boulogne, N.E. France (adj. *boloniensis*)
Bonaria, Bonaeropolis : Buenos Aires, Argentina (adj. *bonariensis*)
Bonna : Bonn, W. Germany (adj. *bonnensis*)
Bononia : Bologna, N. Italy (adj. *bononiensis*)
Borbonia Insula : Réunion, Mascarenes (adj. *borbonicus*)
Borussia : East Prussia, now Poland and U.S.S.R.
Borysthenes : Dnieper R., U.S.S.R. (adj. *borysthenicus*)
Bottnicus Sinus : Gulf of Bothnia, Scandinavia (adj. *bottnicus*)
Brabantia : Brabant, Belgium
Brasilia : Brazil (adj. *brasiliensis*)
Brigantinus Lacus : *see* Bodamicus Lacus
Brigantium : Briançon, S.E. France ; Bregenz, Austria
Britannia : Britain (adj. *britannicus*)
Brugae : Bruges (Brugge), Belgium
Brunna : Brno (Brünn), Czechoslovakia
Brunsviga, Brunswiga : Brunswick (Braunschweig), W. Germany (adj. *brunsvicensis*)
Bruxella : Brussels (Bruxelles, Brussel), Belgium

Buda : Buda, west bank of Danube, Hungary
Budapestinum : Budapest (i.e. Buda and Pest on east bank of Danube), Hungary
Burdigala : Bordeaux, S.W. France (adj. *burdigalensis*)
Burgundia : Burgundy (Bourgogne), E. France
Burma, Birmania : Burma (adj. *burmanicus*)
Byzantium, Constantinopolis : Istanbul, European Turkey (adj. *byzantinus, constantinopolitanus*)
Cadmus : Babadağ, S.W. Turkey, Asia Minor (adj. *cadmicus*)
Cadomum : Caen, N. France
Caesarea Insula : *see* Jersea
Caesarea Mazaca : Kayseri, central Turkey, Asia Minor
Caffraria : S. Africa (adj. *caffer*)
Cairum, Cairus : Cairo, Egypt (adj. *cairicus, kahiricus*)
Calabria : Calabria, S. Italy (adj. *calabricus*)
Caledonia, Scotia : Scotland (adj. *caledonicus, scoticus*)
Calpe : Gibraltar, S. Spain (adj. *calpensis, gibraltaricus*)
Cambria, Cambro-britannia, Wallia : Wales (adj. *cambrensis, cambricus*)
Campechia : Campeche, S.E. Mexico (adj. *campechianus*)
Camschatca : Kamchatka, U.S.S.R. (adj. *camschatcensis*)
Canaria : Gran Canaria or the Canary Islands (Fortunatae Insulae, Insulae Canarienses) as a whole (adj. *canariensis*)
Cantabria : Cantabrica, N. Spain (adj. *cantabricus*)
Cantabrigia : Cambridge, England (adj. *cantabrigiensis*)
Cantabrigia Novae Angliae : Cambridge, Mass., U.S.A.
Cantia, Cantium : Kent, S. England (adj. *cantianus*)
Cappadocia : region of central Turkey, Asia Minor (adj. *cappadocicus*)
Caput Bonae Spei, Cap. B. Spei : Cape of Good Hope, S. Africa (adj. *capensis*)
Caria : A region of S.W. Asia Minor (adj. *caricus*)
Caribaeae, Caribae Insulae : Lesser Antilles, W. Indies (adj. *caribaeus*)
Carinthia : Carinthia (Kärnten), S. Austria (adj. *carinthiacus*)
Carmelus : Mt. Carmel, Israel, Palestine
Carniola : Carniola, former Austrian crownland, N. Yugoslavia (adj. *carniolicus*)
Carolina : Carolina, U.S.A. (adj. *carolinus, carolinensis, carolinianus*)
Carolsruha : Karlsruhe, W. Germany (adj. *carolsruanus, caroliquietanus*)
Carpathus Mons : The Carpathians, E. Europe (adj. *carpathicus, carpaticus*)
Carpetani Montes : Cordillera central of Spain (adj. *carpetanus*)
Carthagena : Cartagena, N. Colombia (adj. *carthaginensis*)
Cashmeria : Kashmir (adj. *cachemirianus, cashmerianus*)
Caspium Mare : *see* Mare Caspium
Cassella, Cassellum : Kassel, W. Germany
Cassubia : region around Danzig (Gdansk), Poland (adj. *cassubicus*)
Castella : Castile (Castilla), Spain (adj. *castellanus*)
Castella Nova : New Castile (Castilla la Nueva), Spain
Castella Vetus : Old Castile (Castilla la Vieja), Spain
Castulo : Cazorla, Andalucia, S. Spain

Castulonensis Saltus : Sierra de Cazorla, Andalucia, S. Spain (adj. *castulonensis, cazorlensis*)

Catalaunia : Catalonia (Cataluña), N.E. Spain (adj. *catalaunicus*)

Cataonia : region of central Turkey, Asia Minor (adj. *cataonicus*)

Caucasia : The Caucasus, U.S.S.R. (adj. *caucasicus*)

Ceylona : *see* Zeylona

Charidemum : Cabo de Gata, near Almeria, S.E. Spain

Charkovia : Kharkov, Ukraine, U.S.S.R.

Chersonesus Taurica : *see* Tauria

Chilonium : *see* Kilia

Christiana : Oslo, S. Norway (adj. *osloensis*)

Cilicia : region of S. Asia Minor (adj. *cilicicus*)

Codanus Sinus : Kattegat, between Denmark and Sweden

Colberga : Kolberg (Kolobrzag), W. Poland

Colonia, Colonia Agrippina : Cologne (Köln), W. Germany

Colonia Allobrogum : *see* Geneva

Conimbrica : Coimbra, Portugal (adj. *conimbricensis*)

Constantinopolis : *see* Byzantium

Cornubia : Cornwall, S.W. England (adj. *cornubiensis*)

Corsica : Corsica (Corse), France (adj. *corsicus*)

Cracovia : Krakow, Poland

Cremsa : Krems, N. Austria

Creta : Crete, Greece (adj. *creticus, cretensis*)

Crocodilorum Insula : one of the Paikuen islands, Fukien, China

Curassao : Curaçao, Caribbean Sea (adj. *curassavicus*)

Curia Rhaetorum : Chur, E. Switzerland

Curonia : Curland (Kurland, Kurzeme), S.E. Latvia, U.S.S.R.

Cyclades : Kikládhes, Greece

Cydonia Cretae : Canea, Crete

Cygnorum Fluvius : Swan River, Western Australia

Cyprus : Cyprus, E. Mediterranean Sea (adj. *cyprius, veneris*)

Cyrenaica, Cyrene : Cyrenaica, N.E. Libya, N. Africa

Dahuria : *see* Dauria

Dalecarlia : Dalarna, mid Sweden (adj. *dalecarlicus*)

Dalia : Dalsland, S. Sweden

Dania : Denmark (adj. *danicus*)

Dantiscum : *see* Gedanum

Danubius : Danube R. (Donau), Europe (adj. *danubialis*)

Dauria, Dahuria, Davuria : a region of S.E. Siberia, U.S.S.R. (adj. *dauricus, dahuricus, davuricus*)

Daventria : Deventer, Netherlands

Delphi Batavorum : Delft, Netherlands

Delphinatus : Dauphiné, E. France (adj. *delphinensis*)

Divionum : Dijon, E. France

Dresda : Dresden, E. Germany

Dyrrachium : Durazzo (Durres), Albania (adj. *dyrrhachinus*)

Eboracum : York, N. England (adj. *eboracensis*)

B.L.—H

Ebrodunum : Yverdon, W. Switzerland
Ebudae Insulae : The Hebrides, W. Scotland (adj. *ebudicus, hebridensis*)
Ecbatana : Hamadan, N.W. Iran
Edessa : Urfa, S.E. Turkey, Asia Minor
Edinum, Edinburgum : Edinburgh, Scotland (adj. *edinensis*)
Egyptus : *see* Aegyptus
Emodus, Emodi Montes : The Himalaya, of which the ancient Greeks knew
   only the western part (gen. *emodi*; adj. *emodensis, himalaicus, himalayensis*
Erfordia, Erfurtum : Erfurt, E. Germany
Erlanga : Erlangen, W. Germany
Erythraeum Mare : *see* Mare Rubrum
Etruria, Hetruria : Tuscany (Toscana), N. Italy (adj. *etruscus*)
Euboea : Evvoi, S.E. Greece
Euganei Montes : Colli Euganei near Padua, N. Italy
Europa : Europe (adj. *europaeus*)
Europa Centralis, Europa Mediterranea : Central Europe
Eustadium : *see* Eystettum
Euxinum Mare, Pontus Euxinus : Black Sea
Exonia : Exeter, S. England (adj. *exoniensis*)
Eystettum, Eustadium : Eichstätt, Bavaria, W. Germany (adj. *eystettensis*)
Fabaria,Thermae Fabriae, Thermae Piperinae : Pfäfers, E. Switzerland
Faeroenses Insulae : The Faeroes (Faeröerne), (adj. *faeroensis*)
Faventia : Faenza, N. Italy
Fennia, Fenningia, Finnia, Finlandia : Finland (Suomi), (adj. *fennicus*)
Flandria : Flanders, Low Countries, i.e. now part of N.E. France, N. Belgium
   and W. Netherlands
Florentia : Florence (Firenze), N. Italy (adj. *florentinus*)
Flumen Januarii, Sebastianopolis : Rio de Janeiro, E. Brazil (adj. *fluminensis*
Formosa : Taiwan, China (adj. *formosanus, taiwanensis*)
Fortunatae Insulae : Canary Islands ; *see* Canaria
Forum Livii, Forolivium : Forlí, N. Italy
Fractus Mons : *see* Pilatus Mons
Francofurtum ad Moenum : Frankfurt am Main, W. Germany
Francofurtum ad Oderum, Francofurtum ad Viadrum, Trajectum ad Viadrum
   Frankfurt an der Oder, E. Germany
Franconia, Francia Teutonica : Franken, central Germany
Friburgum Brisgoviae : Freiburg im Breisgau, W. Germany
Friburgum Helvetiorum : Fribourg, Switzerland
Frisia : Friesland, W. Germany and E. Netherlands
Fuegia, Terra Ignis : Tierra del Fuego, Chile and Argentina (adj. *fuegianus*
Furca Mons : Furka Pass, W. Switzerland
Gades : Cadiz, S. Spain (adj. *gaditanus*)
Gaditanum Fretum, Herculeum Fretum: Strait of Gibraltar
Gaetulia : Sahara, N. Africa (adj. *gaetulicus*)
Galatia : region of central Asia Minor (adj. *galaticus*)
Galitia : Galicia, S. Poland and S.W. Ukraine, U.S.S.R.
Gallecia : Galicia, N.W. Spain

Gallia: France (adj. *gallicus*)
Gallia Monspelii: southern France (Hérault) around Montpellier
Gallia Narbonensis: southern France (Aude) around Narbonne; in Roman times all of southern France
Gallicum Fretum: Strait of Dover (Pas-de-Calais)
Galloprovincia, Provincia: Provence, S. France (adj. *provincialis*)
Gandavum: Gent (Gand), Belgium (adj. *gandavensis*)
Garganus Mons: Monte Gargano, Italy (adj. *garganicus*)
Gedanum, Dantiscum: Danzig (Gdansk), Poland (adj. *gedanensis*); *see* Cassubia
Gelria, Geldria: Gelderland, Netherlands (adj. *gelricus*)
Geneva, Augusta Allobrogum, Colonia Allobrogum: Geneva (Genève), Switzerland (adj. *genevensis, genavensis*)
Genua, Janua Ligurum: Genoa (Genova), N. Italy (adj. *januensis, genuensis*)
Georgia Australis: South Georgia, Antarctica
Germania: Germany (adj. *germanicus*)
Germanicopolis: Čankiri, N. Turkey, Asia Minor
Germanicum Mare: North Sea
Gestricia: Gästrikland, mid Sweden
Gevalia: Gävle, E. Sweden
Gippevicum, Gippeswicum: Ipswich, E. England
Gissa: Giessen, W. Germany (adj. *gissensis*)
Glascovium: Glasgow, S.W. Scotland
Glogovia: Glogow, W. Poland
Glottiana Vallis: Clydesdale, S. Scotland
Gorgades, Insulae Capitis Viridis: Cape Verde Islands, Atlantic Ocean (adj. *gorgoneus*)
Gorlicium: Görlitz, E. Germany
Gotha: Gotha, E. Germany
Gothia: Götland, S. Sweden
Gotlandia: island of Gotland, S. Sweden
Gotoburgum: Gothenburg (Göteborg), S. Sweden (adj. *gotoburgensis, gothoburgensis*)
Gotthardus: St. Gotthard Pass, mid Switzerland
Gottinga, Goettinga: Göttingen, W. Germany (adj. *gottingensis*)
Graecia: Greece (adj. *graecus, hellenicus*)
Granata: Granada, S. Spain (adj. *granatensis*; also used of New Granada, i.e. Colombia)
Granatense Regnum: former kingdom of Granada, S. Spain
Gratianopolis: Grenoble, S.E. France (adj. *gratianopolitanus*)
Groenlandia: Greenland (adj. *groenlandicus*)
Groninga: Groningen, Netherlands (adj. *groningensis*)
Gryphiswaldia, Gryphia: Greifswald, E. Germany (adj. *gryphicus*)
Guadalupa Insula: Guadeloupe, W. Indies (adj. *guadalupensis*)
Guelferbytum, Guelpherpitum: Wolfenbüttel, W. Germany
Guestphalia: Westfalen, W. Germany.
Guinea: W. tropical Africa (adj. *guineensis*)

Haemus Mons: Balkan Mts. (Stara Planina), Bulgaria

Hafnia, Havnia: Copenhagen (København), Denmark (adj. *hafniensis*)

Haga Comitis, Haga Comitum: The Hague (s' Gravenhage), Netherlands

Hala Magdeburgica, Hala Saxonum, Hala ad Salam: Halle an der Saale, E. Germany

Hallandia: Halland, S. Sweden

Hamburgum: Hamburg, W. Germany

Hannovera: Hannover, W. Germany (adj. *hannoveranus*)

Harcynia: *see* Hercynia

Harderovicum: Harderwijk, Netherlands

Harlemum: Haarlem, Netherlands

Hassia: Hessen, W. Germany

Havnia: *see* Hafnia

Helsingforsia: Helsinki (Helsingfors), S. Finland

Helsingia: Hälsingland, S. Sweden

Helvetia: Switzerland (adj. *helveticus*)

Herbipolis: *see* Wirceburgum

Herculeum Fretum: *see* Gaditanum Fretum

Hercynia, Harcynia: Harz region, mid Germany (adj. *hercynicus*)

Hetruria: *see* Etruria

Hibernia, Irlandia: Ireland (adj. *hibernicus, iricus, irensis*)

Hierosolyma: Jerusalem, Palestine (adj. *hierosolymitanus*)

Hippolythum: St. Pölten, N. Austria

Hispahan: Esfahan, Iran

Hispalis: Sevilla, S. Spain (adj. *hispalensis*)

Hispania: Spain (adj. *hispanicus*)

Hispaniola, Sandominicana: Haiti and Dominican Republic, West Indies

Hollandia: Holland, Netherlands (adj. *hollandicus*)

Holmia, Stockholmia: Stockholm, S. Sweden (adj. *holmensis*)

Holsatia: Holstein, W. Germany (adj. *holsaticus*)

Hungaria: *see* Pannonia

Hybla: region of E. Sicily, Italy

Hydaspes: Jhelum R., W. Himalaya (gen. *hydaspidis*)

Hylaea: the wooded plain of the Amazon river, Brazil

Hyrcania: N. Persia bordering the Caspian Sea (adj. *hyrcanus*)

Iabada: *see* Java

Iapygia: Terra d'Otranto (heel of Italy), S. Italy

Iberia: Iberia, Caucasus, corresponding roughly to Georgia, U.S.S.R. (adj. *ibericus*)

Iberia: Iberian Peninsula, i.e. Spain and Portugal

Iberus: Ebro R., N. Spain

Icaria: island of Ikaria, Greece

Iconium: Konya, S. central Turkey, Asia Minor

Illyria, Illyrium: E. coastal region of Adriatic Sea from Trieste S. to N. Albania (adj. *illyricus*)

Ilva: Elba, Italy (adj. *ilvensis*)

India : Indian subcontinent or the Indies (adj. *indicus*)
India occidentalis : *see* Antillae
India orientalis : India and the East Indies
Indiae, India utraque : both East Indies and West Indies
Ingolstadium : Ingolstadt, W. Germany
Ingria : Leningrad region, U.S.S.R. (adj. *ingricus*)
Insubria : region of Lago Maggiore, Lago di Lugano and Lago di Como, N. of Milan, N. Italy and S. Switzerland (adj. *insubricus*)
Interlacum : Interlaken, W. Switzerland
Isauria : region of S. Turkey, Asia Minor (adj. *isauricus*)
Isca : Exe R., S.W. England (adj. *iscanus*)
Islandia : Iceland (adj. *islandicus*)
Jamaica : Jamaica, West Indies (adj. *jamaicensis*)
Japonia : Japan (adj. *japonicus, nipponicus*)
Java, Iabada : Java, Indonesia (adj. *javanicus*)
Jemtia : Jämtland, mid Sweden
Jena : Jena, E. Germany (adj. *jenensis*)
Jersea, Caesarea Insula : Jersey, Channel Islands, Britain
Jura : Jura, S.E. France and N.W. Switzerland (adj. *jurassicus*)
Juressus Mons : Serra do Gerez, Portugal (gen. *juressi*)
Kasanum : Kazan, U.S.S.R.
Kilia, Kilonia, Chilonium : Kiel, W. Germany
Kurdistania : Kurdistan, S.E. Turkey and N. Iraq (adj. *kurdicus*)
Labacum : Ljubljana, N. Yugoslavia
Laconia : Lakonia, Peloponnisos, S. Greece (adj. *laconicus*)
Lapponia : Lapland, N. Scandinavia (adj. *lapponicus*)
Laurentianus Sinus : Gulf of St. Lawrence, Canada (adj. *laurentianus*)
Legio : León, N.W. Spain (adj. *legionensis*)
Lemanus Lacus : Lake of Geneva (Lac Léman), W. Switzerland
Lemgovia : Lemgo, W. Germany
Leodium : Liège, Belgium
Leopolis, Lemberga : Lvov, Ukraine, U.S.S.R. (adj. *leopolitanus*)
Leovardia : Leeuwarden, Netherlands
Libanus Mons : Lebanon range, Lebanon (gen. *libani*; adj. *libanoticus*; *libanensis* refers to Mt. Liban near Santiago de Cuba)
Liburnia : coastal region of Yugoslavia (adj. *liburnicus*)
Libya : Libya, N. Africa (adj. *libycus*); *see also* Cyrenaica, Marmarica, Tripolitania
Liguria : Liguria, N. Italy (adj. *ligusticus*)
Lipsia : Leipzig, E. Germany (adj. *lipsiensis*)
Lisbona : *see* Olisipo
Lombardia, Langobardia : Lombardy, N. Italy
Londinum : London, England (adj. *londinensis*)
Londinum Gothorum : *see* Lunda
Lotharingia : Lorraine, E. France
Lubeca : Lübeck, W. Germany
Luciliburgum : *see* Luxemburgum

Ludovicia : Louisiana or former Louisiana Territory, U.S.A. (adj. *ludovicianus, louisianus*)

Lugdunum : Lyon, S. France (adj. *lugdunensis*)

Lugdunum Batavorum, Leyda : Leiden, Netherlands (adj. *leydensis*)

Lunda, Londinum Gothorum : Lund, S. Sweden (adj. *lundensis*)

Lunella Galliae : Lunel, S. France

Lusatia : Lausitz, region between rivers Oder and Elbe, E. Germany

Lusitania, Portugallia : Portugal (adj. *lusitanicus*)

Lutetia Parisiorum : *see* Parisii

Luxemburgum, Luciliburgum : Luxembourg (Lützelburg) (adj. *luceburgensis*)

Lycaonia : region of central Turkey, Asia Minor (adj. *lycaonicus*)

Lycia : region of S.W. Turkey, Asia Minor (adj. *lycius*)

Lydia : region of W. Asia Minor (adj. *lydius*)

Macedonia : Macedonia, Balkan Peninsula, mostly between 20°-24° E., 40°-42° N. (adj. *macedonicus*)

Machlinium, Mechlinia : Mechelen (Malines), Belgium (adj. *mechlinensis*)

Maclovianae Insulae : Falkland Islands (adj. *maclovianus, falklandicus*)

Maclovium, Aletae : Saint-Malo, N.W. France (adj. *macloviensis*)

Madera : Madeira (adj. *maderensis*)

Maderaspata : Madras region, S. India (adj. *maderaspatanus*)

Madritum : *see* Matritum

Magellanicum Fretum, Magellani Fretum : Strait of Magellan, Chile, S. South America (adj. *magellanicus*)

Malabara : Malabar, S.W. India (adj. *malabaricus*)

Mancunium : Manchester, England (adj. *mancuniensis*)

Manhemium : Mannheim, W. Germany

Maracanda : Samarkand, Uzbekistan, U.S.S.R.

Marburgum, Marpurgum : Marburg, W. Germany

Marchia Brandenburgica, Neomarchia : Brandenburg, E. Germany and W. Poland

Mare Album : White Sea, U.S.S.R.

Mare Caspium : Caspian Sea (adj. *caspicus, caspius*)

Mare Mediterraneum : Mediterranean Sea (adj. *mediterraneus*, midland, remote from the sea, hence also applied to plants of Central Europe)

Mare Mortuum : Dead Sea

Mare Rubrum, Mare Erythraeum, Sinus Arabicus : Red Sea

Margaretha : Isla de Margarita, Venezuela

Mariani Montes : Sierra Morena, S. Spain

Marilandia : Maryland, U.S.A. (adj. *marianus, marilandicus*)

Marmarica : coastal region of Libya and Egypt between Derna and El Alamein (adj. *marmaricus*)

Maroccanum Regnum : Morocco, N. W. Africa (adj. *maroccanus*)

Marpurgum : *see* Marburgum

Martabania : Martaban district, S. Burma (adj. *martabanicus*)

Martinica : Martinique, West Indies (adj. *martinicensis*)

Massilia : Marseille, S. France (adj. *massilianus, massiliensis*)

Matritum, Madritum: Madrid, Spain (adj. *matritensis*)
Mauritania: N.W. Africa (adj. *mauritanicus*)
Mechlinia: *see* Machlinium
Medelpadia: Medelpad, mid Sweden
Media: ill-defined region of W. Asia, with capital first at Rhagae (Tehran), later at Ecbatana (Hamadan), N. Iran
Mediolanum: Milan (Milano), N. Italy
Megalopolis: Mecklenburg, N. Germany (adj. *megalopolitanus*)
Melita: Malta (adj. *melitensis*)
Mervinia: Merioneth, N. Wales, Britain
Mesopotamia: the plain north of Babylon between rivers Euphrates and Tigris, Iraq
Messana: Messina, Sicily, Italy (adj. *messanensis*)
Messenia: Messinia, S. Greece (adj. *messeniensis*)
Michaelopolis: San Miguel de Allende, Mexico; also Archangel, U.S.S.R.
Misnia: Meissen, E. Germany
Moesia: region of mid Balkan Peninsula (adj. *moesiacus*)
Moguntia, Moguntiacum: Mainz, W. Germany
Moldavia: region between 26°-29° E., 46°-48° N., Romania and U.S.S.R. (adj. *moldavicus*)
Moluccae: Moluccas (Amboina, Ceram, etc.), Indonesia (adj. *moluccanus, moluccensis*)
Mona: Anglesey, N. Wales, Britain; Isle of Man, Britain (adj. *monensis*)
Monachum, Monachium: Munich (München), W. Germany (adj. *monacensis*)
Monoecem, Monago, Monoeci Portus: Monaco
Mons Fractus: *see* Pilatus Mons
Monspelgardum, Mons Biligardus: Montbéliard (Mümpelgard), E. France
Monspelium, Monspessulus: Montpellier, S. France (adj. *monspeliensis, monspeliacus, monspessulanus*)
Mosqua: Moscow (Moskva), U.S.S.R. (adj. *mosquensis*)
Murcicum Regnum: Murcia, S. Spain (adj. *murcicus*)
Muschovia: Muscovy, i.e. European Russia, U.S.S.R.
Mysia: region of N.W. Turkey, Asia Minor (adj. *mysicus*)
Nanceium: Nancy, N.E. France
Nannetum: Nantes, N.W. France
Narbona: Narbonne, S. France (adj. *narbonensis*)
Natolia: *see* Anatolia
Nauplia: Návplion, S. Greece
Neapolis: Naples (Napoli), Italy (adj. *neapolitanus*)
Neerlandia: Netherlands (adj. *neerlandicus*)
Nemausus, Nemausium: Nîmes, S. France
Neocomum: Neuchâtel, Switzerland (adj. *neocomensis*)
Neomarchia: *see* Marchia Brandenburgica
Neoweda ad Rhenum: Neuwied, W. Germany
Nepalia: Nepal (adj. *nepalensis, napaulensis*)
Nericia: Närke, S. Sweden
Nicaea: Iznik, Bithynia, N.W. Turkey, Asia Minor

Nicaea Maritima : Nice, S.E. France (adj. *nicaeensis*) : this is the Nicaea of Allioni's *Flora Pedemontana* (1785) ; *Comitatus Nicaeensis*, Comté de Nice

Nidrosia : Trondheim, mid Norway

Nitiobrigum : *see* Agennum

Noricae Alpes : Eastern Alps (Hohe Tauern, etc.), Austria (adj. *noricus*)

Norimberga : Nuremberg (Nürnberg), W. Germany (adj. *norimbergensis*)

Norlandia : Norrland, N. Sweden

Normannia : Normandy, N. France

Norvegia : Norway (adj. *norvegicus*)

Norvicum : Norwich, E. England

Nova Anglia : New England, U.S.A.

Nova Caesarea : New Jersey, U.S.A.

Nova Granata : Colombia ; but more often Gran Colombia (i.e. present Colombia, Ecuador and Venezuela)

Nova Hispania : Mexico (adj. *mexicanus*)

Nova Hollandia : *see* Australia

Nova Wallia Australis : New South Wales, Australia

Noveboracum : New York, U.S.A. (adj. *noveboracensis*)

Novum Castrum : Newcastle upon Tyne, N. England

Nubia : Sudan or N.E. Africa in general (adj. *nubicus*)

Numidia : N.E. Algeria (adj. *numidicus*)

Occitania : Languedoc, S. France (adj. *occitanicus*)

Oceanus Atlanticus : Atlantic Ocean; *cf.* Atlas

Oelandia : island of Öland, S. Sweden (adj. *oelandicus*)

Oenipons : Innsbruck, Austria

Oerebroa : Örebro, S. Sweden

Olbia Galloprovinciae : Hyères, S. France (adj. *olbius*); *see* Stoechades

Olisipo, Olissipo, Ulyssipo, Lisbona : Lisbon (Lisboa), Portugal

Olympus : Olympus, a name applied to many lofty mountains of Greece, Asia Minor and even U.S.A. (adj. *olympicus*)

Olympus Bithynus : Uludağ, near Bursa N.W. Turkey, Asia Minor

Olympus Thessalus : Olimbos, N.E. Greece

Ora Eboris : Ivory Coast, W. tropical Africa

Orcades : Orkney, Scotland (adj. *orcadensis*)

Oruba : island of Aruba, Caribbean Sea (adj. *orubicus*)

Osca : Huesca, N. Spain (adj. *oscensis*)

Ostrobothnia : Österbotten, N.W. Finland

Ostrogothia : Östergötland, S. Sweden

Oxonia : Oxford, England (adj. *oxoniensis*)

Palatinatus : Palatinate (Pfalz), W. Germany (adj. *palatinus*)

Palestina, Palaestina : Palestine (adj. *palestinus, palaestinus*)

Palimbuanum : Palembang, Sumatra, Indonesia

Pamphylia : region of S.W. Asia Minor (adj. *pamphylicus*)

Pannonia, Hungaria, Ungaria : Hungary (adj. *pannonicus, hungaricus*)

Panormus, Panormum : Palermo, Sicily, Italy (adj. *panormitanus*)

Paphlagonia : region of N. Turkey, Asia Minor (adj. *paphlagonicus*)

Papia, Ticinum : Pavia, N. Italy
Parisii, Lutetia Parisiorum : Paris, France (adj. *parisiensis, lutetianus*)
Pascha, Paschatis Insula : Easter Island, Pacific Ocean
Patavium : Padua (Padova), N. Italy (adj. *patavinus*)
Pedemontium : Piedmont, N. Italy (adj. *pedemontanus*)
Peloponnesus : Peloponnisos, S. Greece (adj. *peloponnesiacus*)
Pensylvania : Pennsylvania, U.S.A. (adj. *pensylvanicus*)
Persepolis : Persepolis, S. Iran (adj. *persepolitanus*)
Persia : Iran (adj. *persicus, iranicus*)
Persicus Sinus : Persian Gulf
Peruvia : Peru (adj. *peruvianus*)
Pestinum : Pest, Hungary ; *see* Buda
Petropolis : Leningrad, U.S.S.R. (adj. *petropolitanus*)
Pharmacopolis : Parati, E. Brazil
Philippinae : Philippines (adj. *philippensis, philippinensis*)
Phrygia : region of W. Turkey, Asia Minor (adj. *phrygius*)
Pictavium : Poitiers, N.W. France
Pilatus Mons, Mons Fractus : Pilatusberg, mid Switzerland
Pisidia : region of S.W. Turkey, Asia Minor (adj. *pisidicus*)
Podolia : Podolia, S.W. Ukraine, U.S.S.R. (adj. *podolicus*)
Polonia : Poland (adj. *polonicus*)
Ponteba : Pontebba, N. Italy
Pontus : region of N.E. Asia Minor (adj. *ponticus*)
Pontus Euxinus : *see* Euxinum Mare
Pontus Lazicus : extreme N.E. Turkey, Asia Minor
Portugallia : *see* Lusitania
Portus Lunae : Golfo della Spezia, W. Italy
Portus Lusitaniae, Portus Calensis : Porto, Portugal (adj. *portuensis*)
Posonium : Bratislava, Czechoslovakia
Praetutianus Ager : Abruzzi region, mid Italy (adj. *praetutianus*) ; *see* Aprutium
Praga : Prague (Praha), Czechoslovakia (adj. *pragensis*)
Promontorium Bonae Spei : *see* Caput Bonae Spei
Propontis : Sea of Marmara, Turkey (adj. *proponticus*)
Providentia : New Providence, Bahamas, W. Indies
Provincia : *see* Galloprovincia
Pyrenaei Montes : Pyrenees, France and Spain (adj. *pyrenaicus, pyrenaeus*)
Quatuor Pagorum Lacus : Vierwaldstätter See, near Luzern, Switzerland
Radinga : Reading, S. England
Ratisbona : Regensburg, W. Germany (adj. *ratisbonensis*)
Regiomontum : Kaliningrad, U.S.S.R., formerly Königsberg, E. Prussia (adj. *regiomontanus*)
Rhaeticae Alpes : Alps of E. Switzerland and W. Austria (adj. *rhaeticus*)
Rhenus : Rhine R. (adj. *rhenanus*)
Rhodanus : Rhône R.
Rhodus : Rhodes (Rodhos), Greece (adj. *rhodius*)
Roma : Rome (Roma), Italy (adj. *romanus*)

Romania : Romania (adj. *romanicus*)
Rossia : Russia, U.S.S.R. (adj. *rossicus, russicus*)
Rostochium : Rostock, E. Germany
Roterodamum : Rotterdam, Netherlands
Rothomagus : Rouen, N. France (adj. *rothomagensis*)
Rumelia : Rumili, former division of Ottoman Empire in Europe comprising S. Bulgaria, Greek Thrace and Turkish Thrace, used by Grisebach to cover Bulgaria, S. Yugoslavia, Albania and N. Greece (adj. *rumelicus*)
Ruscino : Perpignan, S.W. France (adj. *ruscinonensis*)
Ruthenia : S. European Russia, U.S.S.R. (adj. *ruthenicus*)
Sabauda : Savoy (Savoie), E. France (adj. *sabaudus*)
Sabbatia : Savona, N. Italy (adj. *sabbatius*)
Salisburgum : Salzburg, Austria (adj. *salisburgensis*)
Salmantica : Salamanca, N. Spain (adj. *salmanticus, salamanticensis*)
Salomonae Insulae : Solomon Islands, Pacific Ocean (adj. *salomonensis*)
Samara : Kuybyshev region, European U.S.S.R.
Sanctae Crucis Insula : St. Croix, West Indies
Sancti Jacobi Insula : St. Jago (S. Iago), Cape Verde Islands, Atlantic Ocean (adj. *jacobaeus*)
Sandominicana : *see* Hispaniola
Sardes : Sart, W. Turkey (adj. *sardensis*)
Sardinia : Sardinia (Sardegna), Italy (adj. *sardous*)
Sarisberia : Salisbury, S. England (adj. *sarisberiensis*, also applied to plants of Salisbury, Rhodesia)
Sarmatia : eastern Europe, mostly European U.S.S.R. (adj. *sarmaticus*)
Sarnia : Guernsey, Channel Islands, Britain (adj. *sarniensis*)
Saxonia : Saxony (Sachsen), E. Germany (adj. *saxonicus*)
Scandia, Scandinavia : Scandinavia (adj. *scandicus, scandinavicus*)
Scania : Skåne, S. Sweden
Scardus : Šar Planina (Shardagh), S. Yugoslavia (adj. *scardicus*)
Scillonia : Isles of Scilly, S.W. England (adj. *scilloniensis*)
Sclavonia : Slavonia, N. Yugoslavia
Scotia : *see* Caledonia
Sebastianopolis : *see* Flumen Januarii
Sedinum : Stettin (Szczecin), W. Poland
Sedunum : Sion, W. Switzerland
Selandia : Zealand (Sjaelland), Denmark
Sena : Siena, N. Italy (adj. *senensis*)
Senegambia : W. tropical Africa (Senegal, Gambia, Portuguese Guinea, Guinea)
Sibiria : Siberia, U.S.S.R. (adj. *sibiricus*)
Sicilia : Sicily, Italy (adj. *siculus*)
Sina : China (adj. *sinensis, chinensis, cathayanus*)
Sinai : Sinai peninsula, Egypt (adj. *sinaiticus, sinaicus*)
Sipylus Mons : Sipuli Dağ, mountain near Manisa and Izmir, W. Turkey, Asia Minor (adj. *sipyleus*)
Sitcha : Sitka, Alaska, U.S.A. (adj. *sitchensis*)

Smolandia : Småland, S. Sweden

Smyrna : Izmir, W. Turkey, Asia Minor (adj. *smyrnaeus*)

Sogdiana : region of Central Asia, between the Amu Darya and Syr Darya rivers, U.S.S.R. (adj. *sogdianus*)

Solodurum : Solothurn, N. Switzerland

Sondershusa : Sondershausen, Switzerland

Songaria, Sungaria, Soongaria : Dzungaria, Sinkiang, Central Asia (adj. *songaricus*, etc.)

Sontius Fluvius : Isonzo R., N. Italy (adj. *sonticus*)

Spetsbergia : Spitsbergen (Svalbard), Arctic Ocean

Sponhemium : Sponheim, near Kreuznach, W. Germany (adj. *sponhemicus*)

Stiria : Steiermark, Austria (adj. *stiriacus*)

Stockholma : *see* Holmia

Stoechades : Îles d'Hyères, S. France; *see* Olbia Galloprovinciae

Stuttgardia : Stuttgart, S.W. Germany

Sudermannia : Södermanland, S. Sweden

Sudeti : Sudeten mountains, N.W. Czechoslovakia and S.W. Poland (adj. *sudeticus*)

Suecia, Svecia : Sweden (adj. *suecicus*)

Suevia : Swabia (Schwaben), S.W. Germany

Sungaria : *see* Songaria

Surinama : Surinam, S. America (adj. *surinamensis*)

Surrejanus Comitatus : Surrey, S. England (adj. *surrejanus*)

Susa : Shush, S.E. Iran (adj. *susianus*)

Syracusae : Syracuse (Siracusa), Sicily, Italy

Syria : Syria (adj. *syriacus*)

Tamesis : Thames R.; S. England (gen. *tamesis*)

Tanais : Don R., U.S.S.R. (adj. *tanaicensis*)

Taprobane : *see* Zeylona

Tataria : Tatary; in Linnaeus's time, Central Asia and European Russia east of the river Don, U.S.S.R.; Little Tatary was the Black Sea region of U.S.S.R. east of the river Dnieper (adj. *tataricus*)

Taurerus Rastadiensis : Radstädter Tauern, W. Austria

Tauria, Chersonesus Taurica : Crimea (Krym), U.S.S.R. (adj. *tauricus*, *chersonensis*)

Taurinum, Augusta Taurinorum : Turin (Torino), N. Italy (adj. *taurinensis*)

Taurus Mons : Taurus (Toros Daglari) mountains, S. Turkey, Asia Minor

Tergeste : Trieste, N. Italy (adj. *tergestinus*)

Terra Ignis : *see* Fuegia

Terra Nova : Newfoundland, Canada

Terulium : *see* Turolum

Thermae Carolinae, Aquae Carolinae : Carlsbad (Karlovy Vary), Czechoslovakia

Thermae Fabriae, Thermae Piperinae : *see* Fabaria

Thessalia : Thessalia, N. Greece (adj. *thessalus*)

Thracia : Thrace, mid Balkan Peninsula (adj. *thracicus*)

Thuringia, Turingia : Thuringia (Thüringen), mid Germany (adj. *thuringiacus*)

Tiberis : Tiber R. (Tevere), Italy

Ticinum : *see* Papia
Tigurum, Turicum Helvetiorum : Zürich, N. Switzerland (adj. *turicensis*)
Tingitana : Tangier, N.W. Africa (adj. *tingitanus*)
Tirolia : Tirol, S. Austria and N. Italy (adj. *tirolensis, tyrolensis*)
Tmolus : Mt. Tmolos near Sardis, W. Turkey, Asia Minor
Toletum : Toledo, mid Spain (adj. *toletanus*)
Tolosa, Tholosa : Toulouse, S. France
Tornacum : Tournai, Belgium (adj. *tornacensis*)
Trajectum ad Mosam, Trajectus Mosae : Maastricht, Netherlands
Trajectum ad Rhenum, Ultrajectum : Utrecht, Netherlands
Trajectum ad Viadrum : Frankfurt an der Oder, E. Germany
Transwallia : Pembroke, Wales, Britain (adj. *transwallianus*)
Trapezus : Trebizond (Trabzon), N.E. Turkey (adj. *trapezuntinus*)
Tridentinae Alpes : Tridentine Alps, N. Italy
Tridentum : Trent (Trento), N. Italy
Trinitatis Insula, Trinitatum : Trinidad, West Indies (adj. *trinitatensis, trinitensis*)
Tripolitania : Tripolitania, N.W. Libya, N. Africa
Troas : Troad region, N.E. Turkey, Asia Minor
Tyrrhenum Mare : Tyrrhenian Sea, W. Mediterranean Sea
Tubinga : Tübingen, W. Germany (adj. *tubingensis*)
Tucumania : Argentina (misrendered as 'Turcomannia' by Linnaeus)
Turcia : Turkey (adj. *turcicus*)
Turicum Helvetiorum : *see* Tigurum
Turingia : *see* Thuringia
Turkestania : Turkistan, Central Asia, U.S.S.R. (adj. *turkestanicus*)
Turolum, Terulium : Teruel, E. Spain (adj. *turolensis*)
Ucrania : Ukraine, U.S.S.R. (adj. *ucranicus*)
Ultrajectum : *see* Trajectum ad Rhenum
Ulyssipo : *see* Olisipo
Ungaria : *see* Pannonia
Uplandia : Uppland, S. Sweden (adj. *uplandicus*)
Upsala : Uppsala, S. Sweden (adj. *upsaliensis*)
Urania : Urnerland, N.E. Switzerland
Valdia, Valdensis Pagus : canton of Vaud, W. Switzerland (adj. *valdensis*)
Valentia : Valencia, E. Spain (adj. *valentinus*)
Valentia Gallorum : Valence, S.E. France
Valentinum Regnum : kingdom of Valencia, E. Spain
Valesia, Valesiensis Ager : Valois, N.E. France
Vallesia : canton of Valais, W. Switzerland
Vallisoletum : Valladolid, N. Spain
Varsavia, Varsovia, Warsavia : Warsaw (Warszawa), Poland (adj. *varsaviensis, warsaviensis*)
Vectis Insula : Isle of Wight, S. England (adj. *vectensis*)
Venetia : Veneto region, N. Italy (adj. *venetus*)
Venetia, Venetiae : Venice (Venezia), N. Italy
Venta Belgarum, Vinconia : Winchester, S. England

Verbanus Lacus: Lago Maggiore, N. Italy and Switzerland (adj. *verbanensis*)
Verona: Verona, N. Italy
Viadrus: Oder R., E. Germany
Vicentia: Vicenza, N. Italy
Vienna Allobrogum: Vienne, S.W. France (adj. *viennensis*)
Vienna Austriae: *see* Vindobona
Vincentii Insula: St. Vincent, West Indies
Vinconia: *see* Venta Belgarum
Vindobona, Vienna Austriae: Vienna (Wien), Austria (adj. *vindobonensis*)
Virtembergia: Württemberg, W. Germany
Visebada: Wiesbaden, W. Germany
Vitemberga: *see* Witeberga
Vratislavia: Wrocław (formerly Breslau), Poland
Wallia: *see* Cambria
Warsavia: *see* Varsavia
Wermelandia: Värmland, S. Sweden
Wessmania: Västmanland, S. Sweden
Westmonasterium: Westminster, London, England
Westrobothnia: N.E. Sweden
Westrogothia: Västergötland, S. Sweden
Wirceburgum, Herbipolis: Würzburg, W. Germany
Witeberga, Vitemberga: Wittenberg, E. Germany
Yermutha: Great Yarmouth, E. England
Zacynthus: island of Zante (Zákinthos), Greece
Zeelandia: Zeeland, Netherlands
Zetlandia: Shetland Isles, Britain (adj. *zetlandicus*)
Zeylona, Ceylona, Taprobane: Ceylon (adj. *zeylanicus, ceylanicus, taprobanicus*)
Zittavia Lusatorum: Zittau, E. Germany

INDEX

Names such as Arabia, Austria, Bohemia, Calabria, Jamaica, of which the native or conventional English form is the same or almost the same as that used in botanical Latin, for the most part are not included in the following index to the above list. Names are arranged alphabetically without regard to diacritical marks.

Argentina, *Tucumania*; Arras, *Atrebatum*; Aruba, *Oruba*; Ascension Island, *Ascensionis Insula*; Atlantic Ocean, *Oceanus Atlanticus*; Atlas Mountains, *Atlas*; Augsburg, *Augusta Vindelicorum*; Auvergne, *Alvarnia*; Avellino, *Abellinum*; Avignon, *Avenio*; Azerbaijan, *Atropatene*.

BAILLEUL, *Bellilua*; Balkan Mountains, *Haemus Mons*; Baltic Sea, *Mare Balti-cum*; Baluchistan, *Belutchia*; Barcelona, *Barcino*; Basel, *Basilea*; Bath, *Bathonia*; Beirut, *Berythus*; Bengal, *Benghala*; Berlin, *Berolinum*; Bern, *Berna*; Beri Daği, *Berytus*; Black Sea, *Euxinum Mare*; Blekinge, *Blekingia*; Blois, *Blesae*; Bodensee, *Bodamicus Lacus*; Bohuslän, *Bahusia*; Bologna, *Bononia*; Bonn, *Bonna*; Bordeaux, *Burdigala*; Bothnia, Gulf of, *Bottnicus Sinus*; Boulogne, *Bolonia*; Bourgogne, *Burgundia*; Brabant, *Brabantia*; Brandenburg, *Marchia Brandenburgica*; Bratislava, *Posonium*; Brazil, *Brasilia*; Bregenz, *Brigantium*; Breslau, *Vratislavia*; Briançon, *Brigantium*; Brittany, *Armorica*; Brno, *Brunna*; Bruges, *Brugae*; Brussels, *Bruxella*; Budapest, *Budapestinum*; Buenos Aires, *Bonaria*.

CABO DE GATA, *Charidemum*; Cadiz, *Gades*; Caen, *Cadomum*; Caernarvon-shire, *Arvonia*; Cairo, *Cairum*; Cambridge, England, *Cantabrigia*; Cambridge, Mass., U.S.A., *Cantabrigia Novae Angliae*; Campeche, *Campechia*; Canary Islands, *Canaria*; Canea, *Cydonia*; Cankri, *Germanicopolis*; Cape of Good Hope, *Caput Bonae Spei*; Cape Verde Islands, *Gotgades*; Carpathians, *Carpathus Mons*; Carthagena, *Cartagena*; Caspian Sea, *Mare Caspium*; Castile, *Castella*; Castile, New, *Castella Nova*; Castile, Old, *Castella Vetus*; Catalonia, *Catalaunia*; Cau-casus, *Caucasia*; Cazorla, *Castulo*; Ceylon, *Zeylona*; China, *Sina*; Chur, *Curia Rhaetorum*; Clydesdale, *Glottiana Vallis*; Coimbra, *Conimbrica*; Colli Eugani, *Enganei Monks;* Cologne, *Colonia;* Columbra, *Nova Granada;* Como, *Novo-Comum* ; Constance, Lake, *Bodamicus Lacus*; Copenhagen, *Hafnia*; Cornwall, *Cornubia*; Crimea, *Tauria*; Curaçao, *Curassao*; Curland, *Curonia*.

DALARNA, *Dalecarlia*; Dalsland, *Dalia*; Danube, *Danubius*; Danzig, *Gedanum*; Dauphiné, *Delphinatus*; Daur, *Dauria*; Dead Sea, *Mare Mortuum*; Delft, *Delphi Batavorum*; Denmark, *Dania*; Deventer, *Daventria*; Dijon, *Divionum*; Dnieper, *Borysthenes*; Don, *Tanais*; Dresden, *Dresda*; Durazzo, *Dyrrhacium*; Dzungaria, *Songaria*.

EASTER ISLAND, *Pascha*; Ebro, *Iberus*; Ecuador, *Aequatoria*; Edinburgh, *Edinum*; Egypt, *Aegyptus*; Eichstätt, *Eystettum*; Elba, *Ilva*; England, *Anglia*; Erfurt, *Erfordia*; Erlangen, *Erlanga*; Etna, *Aetna*; Europe, *Europa*; Europe, Central, *Europa Centralis*; Evvoia, *Euboea*; Exe, *Isca*; Exeter, *Exonia*.

FAENZA, *Faventia*; Falkland Islands, *Maclovianae Insulae*; Finland, *Finlandia*; Florence, *Florentia*; Forli, *Forum Livii*; Franken, *Franconia*; Frankfurt am Main, *Francofurtum ad Moenum*; Frankfurt an der Oder, *Francofurtum ad Oderum*; Freiburg im Breisgau, *Friburgum Brisgoviae*; Fribourg (Freiburg), Switzerland, *Friburgum Helvetiorum*; Friesland, *Frisia*; Furka Pass, *Furca Mons*.

GALICIA (Spain), *Gallecia*; Galicia (E. Europe), *Galitia*; Gargano, Monte, *Garganus Mons*; Gästrikland, *Gestricia*; Gävle, *Gevalia*; Gdansk, *Gedanum*, *Dan-tiscum*; Gdansk region, *Cassubia*; Gelderland, *Gelria*; Geneva, Lake of, *Lemanus Lacus*; Genoa, *Genua*; Gent, *Gandavum*; Gerez, Serra do, *Juressus Mons*; Germany, *Germania*; Gibraltar, *Calpe*; Gibraltar, Strait of, *Gaditanum Fretum*; Giessen, *Gissa*; Glasgow, *Glascovium*; Glogow, *Glogovia*; Görlitz, *Gorlicium*; Gothenburg, *Gotoburgum*; Götland, *Gothia*; Gotland, *Gotlandia*; Göttingen, *Gottinga*; Granada, *Granata*; Greenland, *Groenlandia*; Griefswald, *Gryphis-waldia*; Grenoble, *Gratianopolis*; Groningen, *Groninga*; Guadalquivir, *Baetis*; Guadaloupe, *Guadalupa Insula*; Guernsey, *Sarnia*.

HAARLEM, *Harlemum*; Hague, The, *Haga Comitis*; Halland, *Hallandia*; Halle an der Saale, *Hala Magdeburgica*; Hälsingland, *Helsingia*; Hamadan, *Ecbatana*;

Hamburg, *Hamburgum*; Hanover, *Hannovera*; Harderwijk, *Harderovicum*; Harz, *Hercynia*; Hebrides, *Ebudae Insulae*; Helsinki, *Helsingforsia*; Hessen, *Hassia*; Himalaya, *Emodus*; Holland, *Hollandia*; Holstein, *Holsatia*; Huesca, *Osca*; Hungary, *Pannonia*; Hyères, *Olbia Galloprovinciae*; Hyères, Îles de, *Stoechades*.

ICELAND, *Islandia*; Indies, *Indiae*; Indies, East, *India Orientalis*; Indies, West, *Antillae*; Ingolstadt, *Ingolstadium*; Innsbruck, *Oenipons*; Interlaken, *Interlacum*; Ipswich, *Gippevicum*; Ireland, *Hibernia*; Isfahan, *Hispahan*; Isle of Wight, *Vectis I.*; Isonzo, *Sontius Fluvius*; Istanbul, *Byzantium*; Ivory Coast, *Ora Eboris*; Izmir, *Smyrna*; Iznik, *Nicaea*.

JÄMTLAND, *Jemtia*; Japan, *Japonia*; Jersey, *Jersea*; Jerusalem, *Hierosolyma*; Jhelum, *Hydaspes*.

KALININGRAD, *Regiomontum*; Kamchatka, *Camschatka*; Karlsruhe, *Carolsruha*; Kärnten, *Carinthia*; Kashmir, *Cashmeria*; Kassel, *Cassella*; Kattegat, *Codanus Sinus*; Kayseri, *Caesarea Mazaca*; Kent, *Cantia*; Kharkov, *Charkovia*; Kiel, *Kilia*; Kikladhes, *Cyclades*; Kolberg, *Colberga*; Königsberg, *Regiomontum*; Krakow, *Cracovia*; Krems, *Cremsa*; Kuybyshev, *Samara*.

LAGO DI GARDA, *Benacus*; Lago Maggiore, *Verbanus Lacus*; Lakonia, *Laconia*; Languedoc, *Occitania*; Lapland, *Lapponia*; Lausitz, *Lusatia*; Lebanon Range, *Libanus Mons*; Leeuwarden, *Leovardia*; Leiden, *Lugdunum Batavorum*; Leipzig *Lipsia*; León, *Legio*; Leningrad, *Petropolis*; Leningrad Region, *Ingria*; Leyden, *Lugdunum Batavorum*; Libya, *Cyrenaica, Libya, Marmarica, Tripolitania*; Liège, *Leodium*; Lisbon, *Olisipo*; Ljubljana, *Labacum*; Lombardy, *Lombardia*; London, *Londinum*; Lorraine, *Lotharingia*; Louisiana, *Ludovicia*; Lübeck, *Lubeca*; Lund, *Lunda*; Lunel, *Lunella*; Luxembourg, *Luxemburgum*; Lvov, *Leopolis*; Lyon, *Lugdunum*.

MAASTRICHT, *Trajectum ad Mosam*; Madeira, *Madera*; Madras Region, *Maderaspata*; Madrid, *Matritum*; Mainz, *Moguntia*; Malta, *Melita*; Man, Isle of, *Mona*; Manchester, *Mancunium*; Mannheim, *Manhemium*; Margarita Island, *Margaretha*; Marmara, Sea of, *Propontis*; Marseille, *Massilia*; Martaban Region, *Martabania*; Maryland, *Marilandia*; Mechelen, *Machlinium*; Mecklenburg, *Megalopolis*; Medelpad, *Medelpadia*; Mediterranean Sea, *Mare Mediterraneum*; Meissen, *Misnia*; Merioneth, *Mervinia*; Messina, *Messana*; Mexico, *Nova Hispania*; Milan, *Mediolanum*; Moluccas, *Moluccae*; Monaco, *Monoecum*; Montbéliard, *Monspelgardum*; Montpellier, *Monspelium*; Moscow, *Mosqua*; Munich, *Monachum*; Morocco, *Maroccanum Regnum*; Murcia, *Murcicum Regnum*.

NANCY, *Nanceium*; Nantes, *Nannetum*; Naples, *Neapolis*; Narbonne, *Narbona*; Närke, *Nericia*; Návplion, *Nauplia*; Nepal, *Nepalia*; Netherlands, *Batavia, Belgium, Hollandia, Neerlandia*; Neuwied, *Neoweda ad Rhenum*; New England, *Nova Anglia*; New Jersey, *Nova Caesarea*; New Providence, *Providentia*; New South Wales, *Nova Wallia Australis*; New York, *Noveboracum*; Newcastle upon Tyne, *Novum Castrum*; Newfoundland, *Terra Nova*; Nice, *Nicaea Maritima*; Nikaria, *Icaria*; Nîmes, *Nemausus, Nemausium*; Normandy, *Normannia*; North Sea, *Germanicum Mare*; Norrland, *Norlandia*; Norway, *Norvegia*; Norwich, *Norvicum*; Nova Scotia, *Acadia*; Nuremberg, *Norimberga*.

ODER, *Viadrus*; Oland, *Oelandia*; Olimbos, *Olympus*; Oporto, *Portus Lusitaniae*; Örebro, *Oerebroa*; Oresund, *Balticum Fretum*; Orkneys, *Orcades*; Orléans, *Aurelia*; Oslo, *Christiana*; Ostergötland, *Ostrogothia*; Oxford, *Oxonia*.

PADUA, *Patavium*; Paikuen Islands, *Crocodilorum Insula*; Palatinate, *Palatinatus*; Palembang, *Palimbuanum*; Palermo, *Panormus*; Palestine, *Palestina*; Parati, *Pharmacopolis*; Paris, *Parisii*; Pavia, *Papia*; Pembroke, *Transwallia*; Pennsylvania, *Pensylvania*; Perpignan, *Ruscino*; Peru, *Peruvia*; Pest, *Pestinum*;

Pfäfers, *Fabaria*; Pfalz, *Palatinatus*; Philippines, *Philippinae*; Piedmont, *Pede-montum*; Pilatusberg, *Pilatus Mons*; Poitiers, *Pictavium*; Poland, *Polonia*; Porto, *Portus Lusitaniae*; Portugal, *Lusitania*; Prague, *Praga*; Provence, *Galloprovincia*; Prussia, *Borussia*; Puebla, *Angelopolis*; Pyrenees, *Pyrenaei Montes*.

QUEEN CHARLOTTE'S SOUND, *Aestuarium Reginae Charlottae.*

RADSTÄDTER TAUERN, *Taurerus Rastadiensis*; Reading, *Radinga*; Red Sea, *Mare Rubrum*; Regensburg, *Ratisbona*; Réunion, *Borbonia Insula*; Rhine, *Rhenus*; Rhodes, *Rhodus*; Rhône, *Rhodanus*; Rio de Janeiro, *Flumen Januarii*; Riviera, *Liguria*; Rome, *Roma*; Rostock, *Rostochium*; Rotterdam, *Roterodamum*; Rouen, *Rothomagus*; Roumania, *Romania*; Russia, *Rossia, Ruthenia.*

SAHARA, *Gaetulia*; Saint-Malo, *Maclovium*; Sainte-Croix, *Sanctae Crucis Insula*; St. Jago, *Sancti Jacobi Insula*; St. Pölten, *Hippolythum*; St. Vincent, *Vincentii Insula*; Salamanca, *Salmantica*; Salisbury, *Sarisberia*; Salzburg, *Salisburgum*; Samarkand, *Maracanda*; San Miguel de Allende, *Michaelopolis*; Savona, *Sabbatia*; Savoy, *Allobrogicae Alpes, Sabauda*; Saxony, *Saxonia*; Schwaben, *Suevia*; Scilly Isles, *Scillonia*; Scotland, *Caledonia*; Sevilla, *Hispalis*; Shetland Isles, *Zetlandia*; Shush, *Susa*; Sicily, *Sicilia*; Sienna, *Sena*; Sion, *Sedunum*; Sipuli Dağ, *Sipylus Mons*; Siracusa, *Syracusae*; Sitka, *Sitcha*; Skåne, *Scania*; Slavonia, *Sclavonia*; Småland, *Smolandia*; Snowdon Range, *Arvonicae Alpes*; Södermanland, *Sudermannia*; Solomon Islands, *Salomonae Insulae*; Solothurn, *Solodurum*; Sonderhausen, *Sondershusa*; Sound, The, *Balticum Fretum*; South Africa, *Caffraria*; Spain, *Hispania*; Spitsbergen, *Spetsbergia*; Sponheim, *Sponhemium*; Stara Planina, *Haemus Mons*; Stettin, *Sedinum*; Steiermark, *Stiria*; Stockholm, *Holmia*; Strait of Gibraltar, *Gaditanum Fretum*; Strasbourg, *Argentoratum*; Stuttgart, *Stuttgardia*; Sudan, *Nubia*; Sudeten, *Sudeti*; Surinam, *Surinama*; Surrey, *Surrejanus Comitatus*; Swabia, *Suevia*; Swan River, *Cygnorum Fluvius*; Sweden, *Suecia*; Switzerland, *Helvetia*; Syracuse, *Syracusae*; Szczecin, *Sedinum.*

TANGIER, *Tingitana*; Tatary, *Tataria*; Taurus Mountains, *Taurus Mons*; Terra d'Otranto, *Iapygia*; Tervel, *Torulum*; Thames, *Tamesis*; Thessaly, *Thessalia*; Thrace, *Thracia*; Thüringen, *Thuringia*; Tiber, *Tiberis*; Tierra del Fuego, *Fuegia*; Toledo, *Toletum*; Tonga Isles, *Amicorum Insulae*; Toulouse, *Tolosa*; Tournai, *Tornacum*; Trapzon, Trebizond, *Trapezus*; Trento, *Tridentum*; Tridentine Alps, *Tridentinae Alpes*; Trieste, *Tergeste*; Trinidad, *Trinitatis Insula*; Troad, *Troas*; Trondheim, *Nidrosia*; Tübingen, *Tubinga*; Turin, *Taurinum*; Turkey, *Anatolia, Thracia, Turcia*; Turkistan, *Turkestania*; Turku, *Aboa*; Tuscany, *Etruria*; Tyrol, *Tirolia*; Tyrrhenian Sea, *Tyrrhenum Mare.*

UKRAINE, *Ucrania*; Uludağ, *Olympus Bithynus*; Uppland, *Uplandia*; Uppsala, *Upsala*; Urnerland, *Urania*; Urfa, *Edessa*; Utrecht, *Trajectum ad Rhenum.*

VALAIS, *Vallesia*; Valence, *Valentia Gallorum*; Valencia (town), *Valentia*; Valencia (kingdom), *Valentinum Regnum*; Valladolid, *Vallisoletum*; Valois, *Valesia*; Värmland, *Wermelandia*; Västergötland, *Westrogothia*; Västmanland, *Wessmania*; Vaud, *Valdia*; Venice, *Venetia*; Vicenza, *Vicentia*; Vienna, *Vindobona*; Vienne, *Vienna Allobrogum*; Vierwaldstätter See, *Quatuor Pagorum Lacus*; Vijayanagar, *Bisnagaria*; Vizcaya, *Biscaria.*

WALES, *Cambria*; Walvis Bay, *Balaenae Sinus*; Warsaw, *Varsavia*; West Indies, *Antillae*; Westfalen, *Guestphalia*; Westminster, *Westmonasterium*; White Sea, *Mare Album*; Wiesbaden, *Visebada*; Winchester, *Venta Belgarum*; Wittenberg, *Witeberga*; Wolfenbüttel, *Guelferbytum*; Wrocław, *Vratislavia*; Württemberg, *Virtembergia*; Wurzburg, *Wirceburgum.*

YARMOUTH, *Yermutha*; York, *Eboracum*; Yverdon, *Ebrodunum.*

ZANTE, *Zacynthus*; Zealand (Denmark), *Selandia*; Zeeland (Netherlands), *Zeelandia*; Zittau, *Zittavia Lusatorum*; Zürich, *Tigurum*; Zweibrücken, *Bipontium.*

REFERENCES

BACCI, A. 1955. *Lexicon eorum Vocabulorum quae difficilius Latine redduntur*. 3rd ed. Rome.

BENGTSON, H., & others. 1958. *Grosser historischer Weltatlas*. Teil I: *Vorgeschichte und Altertum*. Munich.

BUNBURY, E. H. 1879. *A History of ancient Geography among the Greeks and Romans*. London.

CARY, M. 1949. *The geographic Background of Greek and Roman History*. Oxford.

CHEVIN, —. 1897. *Dictionnaire latin-français des Noms propres de Lieux ayant une certaine Notoriété principalement au Point de Vue ecclésiastique et monastique*. Bar-le-Duc. (Reprinted London, 1964.)

[DESCHAMPS, P. 1870]. *Dictionnaire de Géographie ancienne et moderne . . . par un Bibliophile*. Paris.

DE TONI, E. 1894. *Repertorium geographico-polyglottum in Usum 'Sylloges Algarum omnium'*. Padua (Patavii).

EGLER, F. E. 1941. The orthography of Pensylvanicus. *Rhodora*, 43 : 220-222.

GRAESSE, J. G. TH. 1971. *Orbis Latinus*. 4th ed., by H. Plechl and G. Spitzbart. Brunswick.

GRUNDY, G. B. *ed.* 1917. *Murray's small classical Atlas*. 2nd ed. [reprinted 1949]. London.

HEYDEN, A. A. M. VAN DER, & SCULLARD, H. H. 1959. *Atlas of the classical World*. Edinburgh.

KIEPERT, H. 1881. *A Manual of ancient Geography*. London.

MARTIN, C. T. 1910. *The Record Interpreter*. 2nd ed. London [see pp. 345-428 for Latin names of places in British Isles].

SAALFELD, G. A. 1885. *Deutsches-lateinisches Handbüchlein der Eigennamen aus der alten, mittleren und neuen Geographie*. Leipzig.

SMITH, WILLIAM, *ed*. 1854-7. *A Dictionary of Greek and Roman Geography*. 2 vols. London.

STEARN, W. T. 1957. *An Introduction to the 'Species Plantarum' and cognate botanical Works of Carl Linnaeus*. London (prefixed to vol. 1 of Ray Society facsimile of Linnaeus, *Species Plantarum*, 1753).

—— 1958. Botanical exploration to the time of Linnaeus. *Proc. Linnean Soc. London*, 169 (1956-7) : 173-196.

STELLFELD, C. 1946. A toponimica latina de Flora Fluminensis. *Tribuna Farmacêutica*, 14 : 246-248.

THOMSON, J. O. 1948. *History of ancient Geography*. Cambridge.

—— *ed.* 1961. *Everyman's classical Atlas*. London.

TOZER, H. F. 1935. *A History of ancient Geography*. 2nd ed., by M. Cary. Cambridge.

WHEELER, M. 1955. *Rome beyond the Imperial Frontiers*. London.

CHAPTER XVIII

Colour Terms

. . . a fisher, on the sand
By Tyre the Old, with ocean-plunder,
A netful, brought to land. . . .

Yet there's the dye, in that rough mesh,
The sea has only just o'er-whispered!
Live whelks, each lip's beard dripping fresh,
As if they still the water's lisp heard
Through foam the rock-weeds thresh. . . .

Mere conchs! not fit for warf or woof!
Till cunning comes to pound and squeeze
And clarify—refine to proof
The liquor filtered by degrees,
While the world stands aloof. . . .

Who fished the murex up?
What porridge had John Keats?

BROWNING, *Popularity* (1842

VAGUENESS OF ANCIENT COLOUR TERMS

Out of the dyestuff and pigment industries of the ancient Mediterranean world have come many colour terms used in botanical Latin, and to this origin is due in part their vagueness of application. As emphasized by Dade (1949), the colours of minerals vary and 'dyes produce different effects according to the mode of their preparation, the materials dyed, and the methods and mordants employed; naturally then the colour conceptions corresponding with the names of these pigments are very broad'. Thus, although the basic colour terms used in botanical Latin were used by the ancients, their application was not necessarily the same then as now. J. König (1927) listed 51 Greek names for colours and 77 Latin ones. Their application has, however, to be guessed from literary references which for the most part are incidental and vague. Homer's certainly odd use of expressions relating to colour led W. E. Gladstone to argue in 1858 that the ancient Greeks were deficient in colour perception. The chemist Sir Humphry Davy had, however, earlier concluded that 'the Greek and Roman painters had almost the same colours as those employed by the great Italian masters at the period of the revival of the arts in Italy. They had indeed the advantage over them in two colours, the Vestorian or Egyptian azure and the Tyrian or marine purple.' The despised dyers, clothiers, artists, decorators and cavalry-men of antiquity, indeed all who in their callings then used colour terms with precision, must have had specialized vocabularies which have left little or no literary record. Colour names as used by poets tend to be metaphorically or indefinitely applied. The lack of colour terms indicates a lack of need, rather than a lack of ability, to perceive and discriminate. The development of a colour vocabulary depends largely upon progress in extracting and manufacturing dyestuffs and paints with consistent results. It is for this reason that modern botanists possess means of precision in colour designation hardly available before the twentieth century.

ANCIENT DYESTUFFS AND COLOUR TERMS

The most celebrated of the ancient dyestuffs was the Tyrian purple, which has given botanical Latin the terms *purpureus, phoeniceus, puniceus, tyrius* and *porphyreus*, the dye of Browning's poem quoted above. Embedded in their soft tissue, certain marine gastropod prosobranch molluscs, notably *Murex brandaris, Murex trunculus* and *Thais haemastoma* (*Purpura haemastoma*), (Fig. 14), have a small oblong hypobranchial gland which secretes a viscid colourless fluid. On exposure to light, however, this molluscan liquid turns yellow and green, then changes to bluish red colours, that of *M. brandaris* becoming deep blue-violet, that of *M. trunculus* and *T. haemastoma* scarlet (cf. Forbes, 1956, also Bouchilloux & Roche, 1955), at the same time giving out a vile penetrating stench. From it the dyers of antiquity made their most costly dye, the purple of Imperial robes and aristocratic togas, known to the Greeks as πορφύρα (porphyra), to the Romans as *purpura*, which apparently was not purple as now understood but crimson. Some 8,000 snails of *Murex brandaris* together yielded 1 gram of dye. Piles of broken shells around Mediterranean coasts

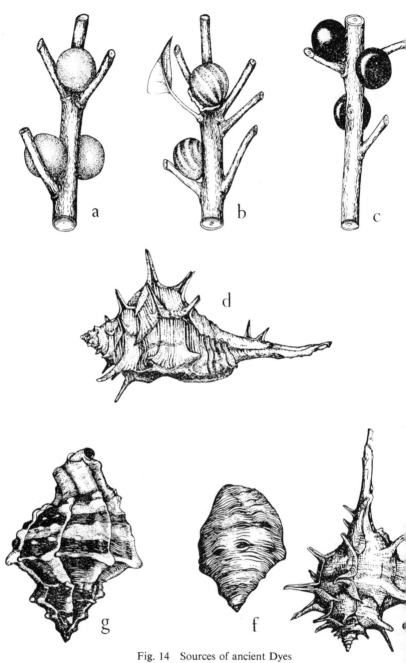

Fig. 14   Sources of ancient Dyes

a, *Kermes vermilio* Planchon f. *typica* ♀;   b, *Kermes vermilio* f.
ballotae ♀; c, *Kermes ilicis* L. ♀ (after A. Balachowsky, 1950); d,
e, *Murex brandaris* L.; f, *Thais haemastoma* (L.); g, *Murex trunculus*
L. (drawing by Priscilla Fawcett)

ndicate where, long ago, Cretans, Phoenicians, Greeks and Romans
ished the murex up and extracted its marine purple (cf. J. W. Jackson,
916). On more than one coast prehistoric fishermen gathering these
hellfish for food must have independently discovered their purple-
roducing secretion, but the Phoenician cities of Tyre and Sidon
Saida) were most responsible for its exploitation on a large scale and
he elaboration of the techniques whereby it yielded a variety of red
nd purple colours (cf. Lacaze-Duthiers, 1859; Forbes, 1956). Their
nanufacturing secrets were lost when the Arabs destroyed the dyeworks
n A.D. 638.

Another source of red dyes in antiquity was provided by the oak-
nfesting coccid insects, *Kermes vermilio* (*Kermococcus vermilio*),
which lives on *Quercus coccifera*, *Q. ilex* and *Q. suber*, and *Kermes
ilicis* (*Kermococcus bauhini*), which lives mostly on *Quercus ilex*, some-
imes on *Q. suber* in the Mediterranean region (cf. Balachowsky, 1950).
The dye was obtained from the female insects swollen with eggs soon
o hatch (Fig. 14). The ancients at one time regarded these globular
gravid females clinging to twigs of oak (Balachowsky, p. 754, figs. 47
nd 48) as a kind of berry (in Greek κοκκος, Latin *coccus*), hence the
djective *coccineus* applied to the scarlet or crimson colour obtained
rom them. It was also recognized that these grains were a kind of
nsect or *vermiculus* (little worm), whence the name 'vermilion'. The
nsect itself later became known by the oriental name *kermes* (derived
rom Sanskrit *krmis*, old Persian *kerema* worm), from which the
djectives *kermesinus*, *chermesinus* and *carmineus* applied to carmine
re derived. There exists a number of other Latin words for red
olours, e.g. *ruber* (red), *sanguineus* (blood red), *roseus* (rose), *miniatus*
scarlet), *cerasinus* (cherry red), there being many substances in nature
rom which these can be produced, and also for yellows, e.g. *croceus*
saffron), *luteus* (yellow), *flavus* (yellow), *aureus* (golden), *cereus* (wax
yellow), *sulphureus* (sulphur), *melleus* (honey yellow). An important
source of yellow dye was the plant *lutum* (weld, *Reseda luteola*), (Fig.
3, p. 145), whence the term *luteus*. There are fewer words for green and
blue. According to Kober (1932), 'it is undoubtedly because it was
so hard for the ancients to produce blue and green that we have so
few words for these colours'. Latin is also deficient in words for grey
nd brown; both *griseus* and *brunneus* used in botanical Latin are
of German origin.

COLOUR NOMENCLATURE AND CHARTS

The application, etymology, etc., of terms for colour used by the
Greeks and Romans are discussed by André (1949), Blumner (1892),

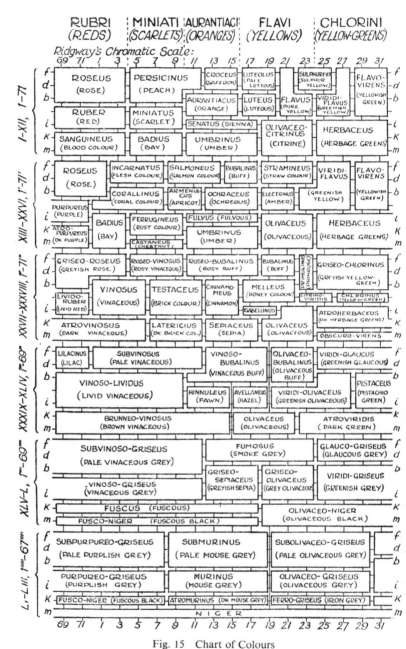

Fig. 15   Chart of Colours

(From H. A. Dade, *Colour Terminology in Biology*, 2nd ed. ; 1949)

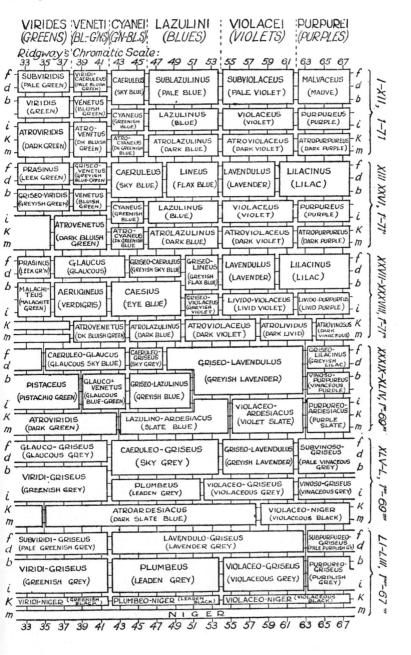

Kober (1932), König (1927), Platnauer (1921), Skard (1946), Vel: Heijn (1958), Wallace (1927) and others. From these surveys it i: evident that the classical use of colour terminology was 'too wide, toc indefinite, too variable' to supply good precedent for modern scientific purposes. Hence authors since the eighteenth century have tendec to restrict classical terms to a part of their original application, tc introduce new terms covering other applications, to make more precisc distinctions, and above all to associate terms with specimens of the colours themselves. A pioneer in this matter was J. A. Scopoli (1723- 1788), who in his *Entomologia Carniolica*, xxxii-xxxiv (1763), gave Latin names which could be used to describe the colours of Lepidoptera During the nineteenth century several botanists, notably A. P. de Candolle in 1813, G. W. Bischoff in 1830 and B. D. Jackson in 1899 produced annotated lists of colour names for botanical use. In 183: John Lindley published a translation into English of Bischoff's list which is reproduced below. The best general survey of English anc Latin equivalents is Dade's *Colour Terminology in Biology* (2nd ed. 1949), which lists the many names now available, selects those bes for use in Latin diagnoses, and defines them by reference to Ridgway': *Color Standards and Nomenclature* (1912), while keeping in mind the desirability of diverging as little as possible from P. A. Saccardo' *Chromotaxia* (1891; 3rd ed., 1912). Dade's chart showing the relation of the names thus selected and defined is reproduced on pp. 240, 241 Wilson's *Horticultural Colour Chart* (1938–41), cited in the vocabular; as *H.C.C.*, has provided a further set of such names. Many name coined in the *H.C.C.* consist of two words, e.g. *ruber monitorius* (signa red), *ruber orientalis* (orient red), etc. Paclt (1958) rejects this binar; nomenclature in favour of having a single Latin term for each of the 93 colours recognized by him. His ten main groups are *ruber* (red) *aurantiacus* (orange), *flavus* (yellow), *chlorinus* (yellow-green), *viridi* (green), *cyaneus* (greenish blue), *violaceus* and *purpureus* (violet) *venetus* (bluish green), *lazulinus* (blue). Whenever possible, livin; material should be matched with the plates in these works or those o Oberthur & Dauthenay (1905), Maerz & Paul (1950), Paclt (1958), o Kornerup & Wanscher (1963) by at least two people—women in genera have a more finely trained colour sense than men—and the use of colou names should be supplemented by precise references to such standards

LIST OF LATIN COLOUR TERMS TAKEN FROM LINDLEY (1832) AND JACKSON (1899)

Entries numbered 1 to 103 below are taken from Lindley's *Introductio* *to Botany*, 402-408 (1832), and based on Bischoff's *Handbuch de*

botanische Terminologie, 1 : 107-115 (1830). The paragraphs of discussion numbered I-XIII are quoted from Jackson's review of the
Latin terms used in botany to denote colour (*J. Bot.* (*London*), 37 :
97-106 : 1899). Together they summarize nineteenth-century usage.

I–II. COLOURLESS AND WHITE

White is usually expressed by *albus*. The following items 1-9
attempt to give more precision.

1 Snow-white (*niveus*) ; as the purest white ; Camellia japonica.
2 Pure white (*candidus*; in Greek composition, *argo-*) ; very pure, but not
so clear as the last ; Lilium candidum.
3 Ivory-white (cream coloured ; *eburneus, eborinus*) ; white verging to yellow,
with a little lustre ; Convallaria majalis.
4 Milk-white (*lacteus*; in words compounded of Greek, *galacto-*) ; dull
white verging to blue.
5 Chalk-white (*cretaceus, calcareus, gypseus*) ; very dull white, with a little
touch of grey.
6 Silvery (*argenteus*) ; a little changing to bluish grey, with something of a
metallic lustre.
7 Whitish (*albidus*) ; any kind of white a little soiled.
8 Turning white (*albescens*) ; changing to a whitish cast from some other
colour.
9 Whitened (*dealbatus*) ; slightly covered with white upon a darker ground.

I Amongst the terms expressive of absence of colour we find *hyalinus,
vitreus, vitricus*, glassy ; *aqueus*, clear as water ; *crystallinus*, clear as ice ;
pellucidus, also implying clearness ; *semi-pellucidus*, some amount of opacity ;
diaphanus, transparent ; *achroos* and *incolor* for scarious. Bischoff also adds
fenestratus, but this use of the word is certainly very unusual.

II WHITE is not a colour, but it produces a feeling of absolute tint, not
the negative considered in the foregoing section. Beginning with the most
general and characteristic of the words expressive of white, we have *albus*, a
dead white ; *niveus*, and occasionally *nivalis*, a brilliantly pure white (as in

Galeandra nivalis Hort.); *virgineus*, unblemished white; *Papyraceus*, paper-white; *candidus* and *candidissimus*, shining white; then the four terms, *cretaceus, calcareus, creteus, gypseus*, seem synonymous, chalk-white; *cerussatus*, plaster-white or white-lead-coloured, must mean the same; *argillaceus*, white clay (but also used for a yellower tint). *Albidus, albidulus, albinus, albineus, albellus, candidulus, exalbidus*, all mean whitish, with probably but little to choose between them; milk-white, that is, having a suffusion of blue, is represented by *lacteus, lacticolor, galactites, galacticolor, galachrous*. Silvery white is *argenteus, argentaceus, argentatus, argyraceus*. Something short of absolute purity is suggested by *albicans, albescens, candicans*, becoming white; ivory-white by *eburneus* and *eborinus*; a yellower tinge by *ermineus, cremeus, cremicolor*, cream-coloured; and an ill-defined 'marble-white' by *alabastrinus* and *marmoratus*, but the latter is used in another sense, and therefore ambiguous.

III. GREY

10 Ash-grey (*cinereus*; in words compounded of Greek, *tephro-* and *spodo-*); a mixture of pure white and pure black, so as to form an intermediate tint.
11 Ash-greyish (*cineraceus*); the same, but whiter.
12 Pearl-grey (*griseus*); pure grey, a little verging to blue.
13 Slate-grey (*schistaceus*); grey, bordering on blue.
14 Lead-coloured (*plumbeus*); the same with a little metallic lustre.
15 Smoky (*fumeus, fumosus*); grey, changing to brown.
16 Mouse-coloured (*murinus*); grey, with a touch of red.
17 Hoary (*canus*, or *incanus*); a greyish whiteness, caused by hairs overlying a green surface.
18 Rather hoary (*canescens*); a variety of the last.

III The lightest tone of GREY is denoted by *canus* and *incanus*; *cinereus* is the grey of wood-ashes, with its allies, *cinerascens* (becoming grey), *cinericius, cineraceus, tephreus, tephrus*; *cretaceo-pallidus* seems to come here; *leucophaeus* must be near this. *Griseus* is darker, but *griseolus* and *grisellus* are perhaps intermediate; *lixivius*, darker than *griseus*, with a suspicion of brown. *Caeius* and *caesiellus* originally represent the blue-grey of the iris of the eye; *liveus, livius, lividus, lividulus*, duller, with less colour. *Spodochrous* is grey in general. *Molybdus, molybdinus, plumbeus* are lead-coloured; about the same intensity with more sheen are *columbianus* and *palumbinus*, which, meaning dove-coloured, seem misappropriated by a grey pigeon. Darker still are *ardesiacus* and *schistaceus*, slate-coloured; while *tylicolor* and *oniscus* are the tints of the wood-louse, and *elephines* and *elephinus* the deep colour of an elephant's hide. *Chalybeus* and *subustulatus* stand for steel-grey; *murinus* and *myochrous* are mouse-coloured (Fries distinguishes between these, the former the lighter); *atroschistaceus*, very dark grey; *fumosus, fumeus, fuligineus, fuliginosus, capnodes, capnoides, subfuscus, subaquilus*, represent smoky or sooty tints; *elbidus*, 'saddest grey'; *nigrescens* and *nigricans* are greys which turn black.

IV. Black

19 Pure black (*ater*; in Greek composition, *mela-* or *melano-*), is black without the mixture of any other colour. *Atratus* and *nigritus*; when a portion only of something is black; as the point of the glumes of Carex.

20 Black (*niger*); a little tinged with grey. A variety is *nigrescens*.

21 Coal-black (*anthracinus*); a little verging upon blue.

22 Raven-black (*coracinus*, *pullus*); black, with a strong lustre.

23 Pitch-black (*piceus*); black, changing to brown. From this can scarcely be distinguished brown-black (*memnonius*).

IV Various qualities of Black have received distinct names; thus *ater* is pure black, without a trace of brown or blue in it; *atricolor* cannot be far off the same; *atramentarius*, inky; *niger*, glistening black, perhaps a trifle rusty; *nigerrimus*, intense black; *anthracinus*, coal-black; *piceus*, pitchy; *piceo-ater* and *furvus* are swarthy and lustreless; *atratus* and *nigritus*, garbed in black; *pullus* and *pullulatus*, about the same tint; *memnonius*, nearly the same as *piceus*, perhaps a little browner; *aethiopicus*, negro-black; *coracinus*, *corvinus*, metallic lustrous black with a tinge of blue; *nigellus*, blackish, and *denigratus*, blackened, are wanting in precision.

V. Brown

24 Chestnut-brown (*badius*); dull brown, a little tinged with red.

25 Brown (*fuscus*; in Greek composition, *phaeo-*); brown, tinged with greyish or blackish.

26 Deep brown (*brunneus*); a pure dull brown. Umber-brown (*umbrinus*) is nearly the same.

27 Bright brown (*spadiceus*); pure and very clear brown.

28 Rusty (*ferrugineus*); light brown, with a little mixture of red.

29 Cinnamon (*cinnamomeus*); bright brown, mixed with yellow and red.

30 Red-brown (*porphyreus*); brown, mixed with red.

31 Rufous (*rufus*, *rufescens*); rather redder than the last.

32 *Glandaceus*; like the last, but yellower.

33 Liver-coloured (*hepaticus*); dull brown, with a little yellow.

34 Sooty (*fuligineus*, or *fuliginosus*); dirty brown, verging upon black.

35 Lurid (*luridus*); dirty brown, a little clouded.

V Brown, a warm tertiary, is treated separately, because of the numerous varieties tending either towards the yellows or reds. *Brunneus* or *bruneus* is a general term for brown, but when restricted, represented by Vandyke brown as a pigment. *Chocolatinus*, *theobrominus*, and *cacainus*, which represent the same thing; *coffeatus*, the colour of roast coffee-beans; *tabacinus*, *nicotianus*, offer a wide range, but are practically restricted to a deep brown. Less precise are *brunnescens* and *bruneolus*, lighter tints. *Umbrinus* would seem to imply the colour of the native earth, but, as we are informed that it is deep brown, it probably is that of burnt umber; *umbricellus* seems ancillary; *boeticus*, 'Spanish brown', must not be confused with the same adjective

when used locally; *castaneus*, chestnut-brown, brings us towards *badiu.*
bay; *russus*, nearly the same; *helvus* and *vaccinus*, 'cow-colour', said to b
near bay; *hepaticus*, liver-coloured, redder; *hiberus*, 'red and black mixec
murrey'; deeper tones being *atro-brunneus*, blackish brown; *ustalis* an
ustulatus, scorched or charred wood. Light browns, akin to yellow, a▪
spadiceus, date-brown; *avellaneus*, *avellinus*, *corylinus*, tint of a new haze
nut, *glandulaceus*, a ripe acorn, come near the tawny shades named unde
orange, as also *ligno-brunneus*, *ligneus*, *lignicolor*, presumably the tint c
recent wood before it becomes grey by exposure, hence yellowish brown.

Bischoff ranks *porphyreus* as amongst the browns; it seems erroneousl▪

VI–VII. Yellow and Orange

36 Lemon-coloured (*citreus*, or *citrinus*); the purest yellow, without a▪
    brightness.
37 Golden yellow (*aureus*, *auratus*; in Greek composition, *chryso-*); pur
    yellow, but duller than the last, and bright.
38 Yellow (*luteus*; in Greek composition, *xantho-*); such yellow as gambog▪
39 Pale yellow (*flavus*, *luteolus*, *lutescens*, *flavidus*, *flavescens*); a pure b▪
    paler yellow than the preceding.
40 Sulphur-coloured (*sulphureus*); a pale lively yellow, with a mixture c
    white.
41 Straw-coloured (*stramineus*); dull yellow, mixed with white.
42 Leather-yellow (*alutaceus*); whitish yellow.
43 Ochre-coloured (*ochraceus*); yellow, imperceptibly changing to brown.
44 *Ochroleucus*; the same, but whiter.
45 Waxy yellow (*cerinus*); dull yellow, with a soft mixture of reddish brow▪
46 Yolk of egg (*vitellinus*); dull yellow, just turning to red.
47 Apricot-coloured (*armeniacus*); yellow, with a perceptible mixture of re▪
48 Orange-coloured (*aurantiacus*, *aurantius*); the same, but redder.
49 Saffron-coloured (*croceus*); the same, but deeper and with a dash c
    brown.
50 *Helvolus*; greyish yellow, with a little brown.
51 Isabella-yellow (*gilvus*); dull yellow, with a mixture of grey and red.
52 Testaceous (*testaceus*); brownish yellow, like that of unglazed earther
    ware.
53 Tawny (*fulvus*); dull yellow, with a mixture of grey and brown.
54 *Cervinus*; the same, darker.
55 Livid (*lividus*); clouded with greyish, brownish and bluish.

VI The type of Yellow is *flavus*, without tending to orange or green o
brown (sometimes indeed used for *ochraceus*); *flavissimus*, an intense shad▪
flavicans, *flavidus*, being tendencies towards *flavus*; *byssinus* is the yellow c
raw silk; *citrinus*, *citreus*, *citrellus*, *citrinellus*, the pure yellow of the rip
lemon-rind; *luteus* is a full strong hue, used by Pliny to denote the yolk c
egg, hence synonymous with *vitellinus*, having a tinge of orange in it. Th▪

Greek forms are *xanthus* and its diminutive *xanthellus; aureus, auricolor, chryseus, chrysellus, chrysitis,* express not only the tint but the lustre of gold ; *auratus,* gilt ; *aureolus,* golden ; *luteolus* and *subflavus,* lighter and less pure but scarcely buff, as given by Ridgway) ; *electricus* and *succineus,* amber ; *sulphureus, sulphurellus, sulphurinus,* sulphur-yellow, pure but light ; *primulinus,* a shade greener than the last ; *stramineus, straminellus, paleus,* straw-colour, like the last, but browner ; *buxeus,* colour of box-wood ; *cerinus,* beeswax when in the comb ; *melleus, mellinus,* honey-colour, the former ambiguous, being also used for smelling of honey ; *ochraceus, ochroleucus, lutosus,* ochre-colour, that is, yellow broken with a tinge of red.

Connected with the foregoing are many mixed tints, tertiaries, such as *fulvus,* buff, with its variants *fulvidus, fulvellus, fulvescens; leochromus, leoninus, cervinus, cervineus, cervicolor, camelinus, mustellinus,* taking their names from the prevalent hue of the lion, stag, camel and weasel, varying buffs and drabs ; *hinnuleus,* fawn-colour, tawny cinnamon. Stronger in tint, but impure, are *galbanus,* the colour of gum galbanum, greenish yellow, and *ictericus, icterinus,* the colour of a person suffering from jaundice. Wharton gives this as 'gall-stone', but in error ; gall-stone is a gorgeous full-toned yellow, while the name implies a muddy hue ; he also cites Fries as using *luridus* for wan yellow, dirtier than *melleus,* and almost 'stone-colour', that is, white broken with ochre, and sometimes umber. *Ravus* and its diminutive *ravidus* seem to be between yellow and grey.

VII ORANGE in its full glow is denoted by *aurantius,* and Fries uses *aurantiacus* as a lighter tint ; *croceus, crocatus, crocinus,* rich orange ; then we have a doubtful set of names, *igneus, ignescens, flammeus, flammeolus,* which have been applied to varied tints of orange, yellow and red ; *auroreus* perhaps should come here, but it is also vague. *Armeniacus,* dull orange, apricot-colour ; *gilvus* by some ranked here, yellower than *cinnamomeus; crustulinus,* the colour of a cracknel biscuit ; *isabellinus,* a dirtier tint ; *rhabarbarinus,* rhubarb colour ; *cupreus* and *cuprescens,* copper-coloured, sometimes with metallic lustre ; *rubiginosus, ferrugineus* and *ferruginosus,* rusty ; *vitelinus,* dormouse-colour, paler and less definite ; *tofaceus* or *tophaceus,* the colour of tufa ; *corneus,* 'horn-colour', whatever that may be ; and *argillaceus,* improperly used for a fawn-coloured clay.

VIII. GREEN

6 Grass-green (*smaragdinus, prasinus*) ; clear lively green, without any mixture.

7 Green (*viridis* ; in Greek composition, *chloro-*) ; clear green, but less bright than the last. *Virens, virescens, viridulus, viridescens,* are shades of this.

8 Verdigris-green (*aeruginosus*) ; deep green, with a mixture of blue.

9 Sea-green (*glaucus, thalassicus, glaucescens*) ; dull green, passing into greyish blue.

0 Deep green (*atrovirens*) ; green, a little verging upon black.

61 Yellowish green (*flavovirens*) ; much stained with yellow.
62 Olive-green (*olivaceus* ; in Greek composition, *elaio-*) ; a mixture of gree and brown.

VIII GREEN is termed *viridis* without more critical definition, its syne nyms, more or less accurate, being *virens, viridans, virescens, viridescen viridulus.* Grass-green is *herbeus, herbaceus, gramineus* (these are practical obsolete) ; *prasinus* is leek-green, practically the same tint as the last *smaragdinus,* emerald-green ; *berylinus,* resembling the last ; *psittaceu* parrot-green, deeper ; *orobitinus,* defined as vetch-green, that is, with a das of black in it ; *atrovirens, atroviridis, melanochlorus, nigro-virens,* very dee green ; and *flavo-virens,* a bright yellowish green. *Chlorascens, chlorinu chloroticus* are greenish.

Aeneus is brassy ; *aereus,* bronze ; *aerugineus, aeruginosus,* verdigri green ; *saligneus,* willow-green, that is, low-toned ; *subviridis* may be th same. *Olivascens, olivaceus, oliveus, olivicolor, olivinus, elaeodes, pausiacu* all express the tint of a ripe olive.

Glaucus, glaucinus, glaucescens, thalassinus, thalassicus, light sea-gree to which may be added *vitreus* of some authors ; *aquamarinus,* a clear se; green verging towards blue ; and *venetus,* a deep sea-green.

IX–X. BLUE, VIOLET AND PURPLE

63 Prussian blue (*cyaneus* ; in Greek composition, *cyano-*) ; a clear brigh blue.
64 Indigo (*indigoticus*) ; the deepest blue.
65 Blue (*caeruleus*) ; something lighter and duller than the last.
66 Sky-blue (*azureus*) ; a light, pure, lively blue.
67 Lavender-coloured (*caesius*) ; pale blue, with a slight mixture of grey.
68 Violet (*violaceus, ianthinus*) ; pure blue stained with red, so as to b intermediate between the two colours.
69 Lilac (*lilacinus*) ; pale dull violet, mixed a little with white.

IX BLUE has a comparatively small list to express its varieties ; *caeruleu caelestis, azureus, caelicolor* are sky-blue ; *cobaltinus* somewhat paler, as *caerulescens; cyanellus,* deeper, and tending towards *cyaneus,* cornflowe blue, *cizatinus* being given as about the same ; *lazulinus* is ultramarine, pigment of various shades, but always a clear bright blue ; *turcoisinus an turcosus* stand for turquoise-blue, that is, with a hint of green in it ; *caesi* and *caesiellus* are the blue-grey of the eye ; *subcaeruleus* and *lividulus,* le; clear, and not very definite ; *scyricum* is given by Charleton as 'Gentianel blew'; *glastinus,* by the same writer as 'woad, watchet and light blew' *indicus,* blue inclining to purple ; *indigoticus,* indigo-blue, having a tinge c black in it ; and dark blue, *cyanater.*

X PURPLE is very variously understood ; practically it is any mixture c blue and red ; Saccardo treats it as synonymous with crimson, but th majority regard it as having more of blue in its composition. *Purpureus, porphyreus*, therefore, are general in their application, followed by *purpurascens, purpurellus, purpurinus* and *porphyreo-leucus; atropurpureus* is familiar to most in the old cultivated 'Sweet Scabious', *Scabiosa atropurpurea*. Royal purple, a warm deep rich tint, is represented by *ostrinus, tyrius, blatteus*. Charleton gives '*dibaphus*, purple-in-grain' as different. The previously mentioned *vinaceus, vinosus* and *vinicolor* come near these hues. Of a lighter tint we find *molochinus* and *malvinus*, both expressing the bluish pink *Malva* flowers; *lilacinus, lilaceus, syringus* recall the tint of *Syringa vulgaris*. Colder in hue we have *violaceus, violascens, violeus, ianthinus, ionides* to recall the violet in all its shades, deeper tones denoted by *amethysteus, amethystinus, hyacinthinus* and *atro-violaceus*.

XI. RED

70 Carmine (*kermesinus, puniceus*) ; the purest red, without any admixture.
71 Red (*ruber* ; in Greek composition, *erythro-*) ; the common term for any pure red. *Rubescens, rubeus, rubellus, rubicundus*, belonging to this.
72 Rosy (*roseus* ; in Greek composition, *rhodo-*) ; pale pure red.
73 Flesh-coloured (*carneus, incarnatus*) ; paler than the last, with a sligh mixture of red.
74 Purple (*purpureus*) ; dull red, with a slight dash of blue [see above].
75 Sanguine (*sanguineus*) ; dull red, passing into brownish black.
76 Phoeniceous (*phoeniceus, puniceus*) ; pure lively red, with a mixture of carmine and scarlet.
77 Scarlet (*coccineus*) ; pure carmine, slightly tinged with yellow.
78 Flame-coloured (*flammeus, igneus*) ; very lively scarlet, fiery red.
79 Bright red (*rutilans, rutilus*) ; reddish, with a metallic lustre.
80 Cinnabar (*cinnabarinus*) ; scarlet, with a slight mixture of orange.
81 Vermilion (*miniatus, vermiculatus*) ; scarlet, with a decided mixture of yellow.
82 Brick-colour (*lateritius*) ; the same, but dull and mixed with grey.
83 Brown-red (*rubiginosus, haematiticus*) ; dull red, with a slight mixture of brown.
84 *Xerampelinus* ; dull red, with a strong mixture of brown.
85 Coppery (*cupreus*) ; brownish red, with a metallic lustre.
86 *Githagineus* ; greenish red.

XI *Ruber* embraces the various forms of RED as a whole: the purest being *carmineus*, cochineal; *coccineus*, perhaps identical; while *kermesinus* and *chermesinus* are the same, and *coccinellus* a lighter tint. *Phoeniceus* is scarlet a little dull, *cinnabarinus* and *scarlatinus* being the fullest in hue; *miniatus, miniaceus*, the more orange tint of red-lead. Verging towards crimson, that is, with blue instead of yellow as the tingeing colour, we have *sanguineus, sanguinolentus, cruentus, cruentatus, haematinus, haematites, haematitius, haematochroos* and *haematicus*, all denoting blood-colour;

puniceus is crimson; *burrhus*, deep crimson, passing into *xerampelinus*, *atro-carmesinus*, *atro-coccineus*, towards *rutilus*, *rutilans*, defined by some as purplish brick-red, but usually brighter in hue; *testaceus*, brick-red, which approaches *gilvus*, *figlinus*, terra cotta; *lateritius*, also brick-red; still deeper in tone, *vinaceus*, and *vinosus*, wine-colour. Rosy reds are *carneus*, *carneolus*, *incarnatus*, flesh-colour; *hysginus*, distinctly redder; *caryophyllaceus*, 'pink'-colour; *erubescens*, blush; *roseus*, *rosaceus*, *rosellus*, *rhodellus*, rose; *corallinus*, coral-red; *salmonaceus*, *salmonicolor*, *salmoneus*, pink with a dash of yellow; *persicus*, *persicinus*, peach-flower colour.

Terms used laxly are *rubescens*, *rufescens*, *rufidulus*, *rufulus*, *rubicundus*, *rufus* or *ruffus*, *sandaricus*, *sandarichinus*, *robeus*, *robus*, *rubens*, *rubellus*, *rubeolus*, *rubidus*, *subrubicundus*, *subrubens*, *sublateritius*, *helvolus*, the last also used for a yellowish drab, but probably pale red, according to the mycological usage of the term; *russus* is also placed amongst the ill-defined reds by some.

Githaginosus (Hayne, Bischoff) and *githagineus* (Lindley) are defined as greenish red, a contradiction; the name is derived from *Githago*, and it refers to red or purple ribs on a green calyx, such as occurs in some species of *Silene*.

XII. VAGUE TERMS

XII Amongst the vague terms must be cited *igneus*, *ignescens*, *flammeus*, *flammeolus*, as they have been used to express different colours; *pallidus* has also been made use of for almost every pale tint of the artist's palette; *luridus* is nearly as indefinite; *tristis* and *sordidus*, any dull uninviting hue, *obscurus* being perhaps a truer term; *coruscans* must mean any strikingly brilliant colour or combination; *metallicus*, any glistening tint suggestive of a metal.

Fulmineus, 'lightning-coloured', according to Wharton, is 'fulvus, fere brunneus' of Fries; it is employed in *Cortinarius fulmineus* Fr.

Other terms which are too vague to be precisely localized are *nebulosus* (Bischoff = *fumosus*); *ferreus*, 'iron-gray' (Charleton).

There yet remain more than a score of terms proposed to express colour, which have not been adopted by others; as they seem to be on record only in the original place of publication (Hayne, *De Coloribus*, 1814), I prefer to give them separately in the order chosen by the author, omitting the zoological and mineralogical terms: *betulinus*, the brownish white of birch-bark; *amiantus*, greenish-white; *cycaceus*, 'sago-grey'; *roborinus*, the grey of last year's oak-twigs; *strychninus*, the colour of the seeds of *Strychnos Nux-vomica; foeninus*, 'hay grey'; *morinus*, mulberry-black; *ureaceus*, charred black; *cascarillus*, the colour of the inner bark of Cascarilla; *guajacinus*, greenish brown; *juniperinus*, bluish brown; *ranunculaceus*, buttercup yellow; *laureolaceus*, the tint of the flowers of *Daphne Laureola*; *pomaceus*, apple green; *pisaceus*, the green of unripe peas; *populeus*, the blackish green of poplar leaves; *capparinus*, brownish green; *endiviaceus*, light blue; *nubilus*, greyish blue; *myrtillinus*, bilberry blue; *pruninus*, plum blue; *parellinus*, litmus violet; *infumatus* is the same as *fumigatus*.

XIII. VARIEGATIONS, MARKINGS AND QUALITY

87 Variegated (*variegatus*); the colour disposed in various irregular, sinuous spaces.

88 Blotched (*maculatus*); the colour disposed in broad, irregular blotches.

89 Spotted (*guttatus*); the colour disposed in small spots.

90 Dotted (*punctatus*); the colour disposed in very small round spots.

91 Clouded (*nebulosus*); when colours are unequally blended together.

92 Marbled (*marmoratus*); when a surface is traversed by irregular veins of colour; as a block of marble often is.

93 Tessellated (*tessellatus*); when the colour is arranged in small squares, so as to have some resemblance to a tessellated pavement.

94 Bordered (*limbatus*); when one colour is surrounded by an edging of another.

95 Edged (*marginatus*); when one colour is surrounded by a very narrow rim of another.

96 Discoidal (*discoidalis*); when there is a single large spot of colour in the centre of some other.

97 Banded (*fasciatus*); when there are transverse stripes of one colour crossing another.

98 Striped (*vittatus*); when there are longitudinal stripes of one colour crossing another.

99 Ocellated (*ocellatus*); when a broad spot of some colour has another spot of a different colour within it.

00 Painted (*pictus*); when colours are disposed in streaks of unequal intensity.

01 Zoned (*zonatus*); the same as ocellated, but the concentric bands more numerous.

02 Blurred (*lituratus*). This, according to De Candolle, is occasionally, but rarely, used to indicate spots or rays which seem formed by the abrasion of the surface; but I know of no instance of such a character.

03 Lettered (*grammicus*); when the spots upon a surface assume the form and appearance of letters; as some Opegraphas.

XIII This subsection consists of terms implying colour, but not mentioning the particular kind, such as *coloratus*, *concolor*, *bicolor*, *mutabilis*, *variegatus*, *pictus*, *guttatus*, *punctulatus* and the like. *Marmoratus* belongs here, although it has been used as synonymous with *alabastrinus*, etc.

INDEX

The numbers below refer to Lindley's numbered entries above.

BADIUS, 24; banded, 97; black, 20; black, pure, 19; blotched, 88; blue, 65; blue, prussian, 63; blurred, 102; bordered, 94; brick-coloured, 82; brown, 25; brown, bright, 27; brown, deep, 26; brown-red, 83; *brunneus*, 26.

CAERULEUS, 65; *caesius*, 67; *calcareus*, 5; *candidus*, 2; *canescens*, 18; *canus,* 17; *carmine*, 70; *carneus*, 73; *cerinus*, 45; *cervinus*, 54; chalk-white, 5; chestnut brown, 24; *chloro-*, 89; *chryso-*, 37; *cineraceus*, 11; *cinereus*, 10; cinnabar, *cinnabarinus*, 80; *cinnamomeus*, cinnamon, 29; *citreus, citrinus*, 36; clouded, 91; coal-black, 21; *coccineus*, 77; coppery, 85; *coracinus*, 22; cream-coloured, 3; *cretaceus*, 5; *croceus*, 49; *cupreus*, 85; *cyaneus, cyano-*, 63.

DEEP BROWN, 26; deep green, 60; *discoideus*, 96; dotted, 90.

EBORINUS, *eburneus*, 3; edged, 95; egg-yolk, 46; *erythro-*, 71.

FASCIATUS, 97; *ferrugineus*, 28; flame-coloured, *flammeus*, 78; *flavescens, flavidus, flavus*, 39; flesh-coloured, 73; *fuligineus, fuliginosus*, 34; *fulvus*, 53; *fumeus, fumosus*, 15; *fuscus*, 25.

GALACTO-, 4; *gilvus*, 51; *githagineus*, 86; *glandaceus*, 32; golden yellow, 37; *grammicus*, 103; grass-green, 56; green, 57; green, deep, 60; green, yellowish, 61; grey, ash, 10; *griseus*, 12; *guttatus*, 89; *gypseus*, 5.

HAEMATITICUS, 83; *helvolus*, 50; *hepaticus*, 33; hoary, 17; hoary, rather, 18.

IANTHINUS, 68; *igneus*, 78; *incanus*, 17; *incarnatus*, 73; indigo, *indigoticus* 64; isabella-yellow, 51; ivory-white, 3.

KERMESINUS, 70.

LACTEUS, 4; *lateritius*, 82; lavender-coloured, 67; lead-coloured, 14; leather yellow, 42; lemon-coloured, 36; lettered, 103; *lilacinus*, lilac, 69; *limbatus*, 94; *lituratus*, 102; liver-coloured, 33; livid, 55; lurid, *luridus*, 35; *luteolus, lutescens,* 39, *luteus*, 38.

MACULATUS, 88; marbled, 92; *marginatus*, 95; *marmoratus*, 92; *mela melano-*, 19; *memnonicus*, 23; milk-white, 4; *miniatus*, 81; mouse-coloured *murinus*, 16.

NEBULOSUS, 91; *niger*, 20; *nigritus*, 19; *niveus*, 1.

OCELLATED, *ocellatus*, 99; *ochraceus*, ochre-coloured, 43; *ochroleucus*, 44; orange-coloured, 48.

PAINTED, 100; pearl-grey, 12; *phaeo-*, 25; *phoeniceous, phoeniceus*, 76; *piceu,* 23; *pictus*, 100; pitch-black, 23; *plumbeus*, 14; *porphyreus*, 30; *prasinus*, 56; prussian blue, 63; *pullus*, 22; *punctatus*, 90; *puniceus*, 70, 76; purple, *purpureu* 74.

RAVEN-BLACK, 22; red, 71; red, bright, 79; red-brown, 30; *rhodo-, roseu* rosy, 72; *rubellus, ruber, rubescens, rubeus, rubicundus*, 71; *rufescens*, rufou *rufus*, 31; rusty, 28; *rutilans, rutilus*, 79.

SAFFRON-COLOURED, 49; sanguine, *sanguineus*, 75; scarlet, 77; *schistaceus*, 13 sea-green, 59; silvery, 6; sky-blue, 66; slate-grey, 13; *smaragdinus*, 56; smok 15; snow-white, 1; sooty, 34; *spadiceus*, 27; *spodo-*, 10; spotted, 89; *stramineu* 41; straw-coloured, 41; striped, 98; sulphur-coloured, 40.

TAWNY, 53; *tephro-*, 10; *tessellatus*, 93; testaceous, *testaceus*, 52; thalassicu 59.

UMBER-BROWN, *umbrinus*, 26.

VARIEGATED, *variegatus*, 87; verdigris-green, 58; *vermiculatus*, vermilion, 81 *violaceus*, violet, 68; *virens, virescens, viridescens, viridis, viridulus*, 57; *vitellinu* 46; *vittatus*, 98.

WAXY YELLOW, 45; white, pure, 2; white, turning, 8; whitened, 9; whitish, ' XANTHO-, 38; *xerampelinus*, 84.

YELLOW, 38; yellow, golden, 37; yellow, pale, 39; yellow, waxy, 45; yolk c egg, 46.

ZONATUS, zoned, 101.

QUALIFYING WORDS

There are also a few useful qualifying adjectives, adverbs and prefixes which can be used together with the colour terms given above:

atro- (prefix): blackish or very dark
dilute (adv.): faintly; **dilutus** (adj.): diluted, faint
floridus (adj.): bright
fuscus (adj.): dark
impolitus (adj.): unpolished, matt
infuscatus (adj.): darkened
intense (adv.): intensely
laete (adv.): brightly; **laetus** (adj.): bright
nitidus (adj.): glossy
obscure (adj.): darkly, dully; **obscurus** (adj.): dark, dull
opacus (adj.): opaque
pallide (adv.): palely; **pallidus** (adj.): pale
pallidulus (adj.): somewhat pale; **perpallidus** (adj.): very pale
purus (adj.): pure
remissus (adj.): faint
saturatus (adj.): full, deep
sordide (adv.): dirtily; **sordidus** (adj.): dull, dirty
suffusus (adj.): tinged
vivide (adv.): brightly; **vividus** (adj.): bright, vivid.

Tingeing, i.e. the addition of a small amount of one colour to another so as to modify slightly the general effect of the latter, is often expressed by means of the preposition *ex* or *e*, indicative of change of state, with the adjective of the modifying colour in the ablative, e.g. *pileus ex olivaceo brunneus* (pileus brown tinged with olive-green), *corolla e roseo alba* (corolla rose-tinged white), *baccae e viridi rubentes* (berries greenish red), *folia ex purpureo vinoso viridia* (leaves green tinged with vinous purple). Similarly, *exalbidus* means 'whitish'.

ELIAS FRIES'S NOMENCLATURE OF COLOURS FOR FUNGI

The *Systema mycologicum* (1821–29), *Elenchus Fungorum* (1828) and other publications by Elias Fries (see p. 7) provide the main taxonomic and nomenclatural foundation of mycology. Fries based them largely on observations he had made from living fungi. In 1884 Henry Thornton Wharton (1846–95) published a study of his use of colour terms. Wharton, a medical man by profession, was a keen amateur mycologist and classical scholar—his publications include a translation of Sappho—and his commentary retains its value. A condensed version is given below:

The subject of colour-names is so vast and intricate that in the following paper I have confined myself to the consideration of those only which occur in Fries' description of the *Agaricini* in his 'Hymenomycetes Europaei'. Even in this restricted field I have found nearly 200 names of colours, although, with one or two exceptions, I have avoided reference to compound names. . . . Perhaps I have omitted some few as it is, for I have had to go over some 20,000 lines of concisely-written Latin to find those that I have gathered together for examination here.

In so long a list of names it is fortunate that not every one requires separate consideration. I have enumerated not only the colour-names used for descriptive purposes by Fries himself, but also most of those used as specific. And in making specific names there is a natural tendency to use a colour-name absolutely synonymous with another, simply from the fact of the most obvious one having been already used. For instance, a describer wishes to name a white species *Agaricus albus*; but when he finds that name is preoccupied, he names his species *Ag. candidus*. Still we need not conclude that he had the strict classical Latin differences of the two words in his mind's eye; he probably never thought that *Ag. albus* was so named because it was of a dead white, nor in speaking of *Ag. candidus* need he have meant to imply that it was of a glistening white, as Cicero might have done. . . .

Another difficulty that constantly presents itself is the indefiniteness with which colour-names were used in classical times. In trying to make out what Fries intended to describe, we are continually hampered by a divergence from the ancient use of the very words he uses. . . . It is my endeavour here to make out the idea in Fries' mind, and only to that end to use the light that can be thrown on the subject from classical sources. Perhaps the best instance of the vague way in which the ancient Romans used the names of colours is to be found in a line by Albinovānus, a Latin poet contemporary with, and a friend of, Ovid's, who flourished about A.D. 28; he describes a woman's arms as whiter than the 'purple' snow:

Brachia purpureâ candidiora nive.

Of course, 'purple' here only means 'glistening' or 'dazzling', but such a use of words does not accord with modern ideas. . . .

In each branch of art or knowledge at the present day different names are used for the same colours. . . . An amusing instance was given me lately by an omnibus-driver. One of his passengers had been much struck by a pair of horses he had been driving, a dun and a strawberry-roan, in the horsey-man's language; the passenger, a tailor, described the one as 'drab', and the other as a 'claret-mixture'.

Consequently mycologists must be a law unto themselves, and if we are willing to hold the illustrious Fries as our law-giver, we must study, not so much what colour-names *should* mean, as in what sense he used them. . . .

We need not be much troubled about classification, for a very simple method is sufficient for our purposes. But it is as well to know how chromatographers ordinarily classify colours; and to this end I copy the following from one of the many editions of Field's book:

Neutral	colours:	white, black
Primary	,,	yellow, red, blue
Secondary	,,	orange, green, purple
Tertiary	,,	citrine, russet, olive
Semi-neutral	,,	brown, maroon, grey

I propose to group the whites and blacks with the greys that come between them; to range the oranges, citrines and browns after the yellows; to include the russets and maroons as subordinate to the reds; to take the purples as variations of the blues; and to comprehend the olives under the greens. Sombre colours dominate so conspicuously among Fungi that we understand their coloration best by regarding their lowly hues as variants from types that owe their names to their very brilliancy. Their complications are so great that it is often difficult, even as it is, to refer them to their proper types; a trouble that was ever present to me when I preliminarily essayed to classify them.

I would begin with the whites and the blacks, and their intermediate greys; I at once discard the trammels that the chromatographers lay down for our deception, when they say that these, in their extremes, are no colours at all.

And first, of the WHITES. My list shows nineteen distinct terms for these. But most of them are made up on the principle that I have already laid down as of constant occurrence, viz., that they owe their appearance to the natural and obvious terms having been already used. The classical distinction of *albus* meaning a dead white, and *candidus* a shining white, has little prominence in Fries' description. To Fries, *albus* is white, and perfect whiteness admits of no qualification. If *albus*, as a specific name, is preoccupied, *albellus*, *albescens*, *albidior*, *albidus* and *albineus* can only express the idea of whiteness, but seem used rather for 'whitish'. *Albicans* and *candicans* should strictly mean 'becoming white'. *Argenteus* and *argyraceus* are a silvery white, silvered. *Dealbatus*, white-washed or plastered, *cerussatus*, coloured with white-lead, and *argillaceus*, like white clay, seem to connote texture or surface along with whiteness. *Eburneus*, ivory-white, *ermineus*, ermine-white, *niveus*, snow-white and *virgineus*, virgin or pure white, have no more distinction than the English terms by which they are naturally translated.

Between the extremes of white and black there can be great varieties of GREYS, and the pure greys run into the blues and browns, so that they are best studied in three groups. Of the pure greys, *canus* and *incanus* are the nearest to white; just as we call white hair or a white horse 'grey'. *Cinereus* is the grey of wood-ashes, *cinerascens* is becoming such a grey; *griseus* seems to be a little darker, and *lixivius* is darker still and inclining to brown. *Cretaceo-pallidus* is a pale chalky grey. *Nigrescens* and *nigricans* do not mean so much dark grey as a grey that turns black with age.

Of greys that incline to blue, *caesius* is the palest; it was the classical term for the blue-grey of the eye. *Glaucus* is a grey that inclines to green, and *glaucescens* denotes a paler shade of the same colour. *Livens* and *lividus* are bluish or leaden-grey, much like *molybdus* and *plumbeus*. *Ardosiacus* is a dull lead-colour. *Ag. (Collybia) tylicolor* and *Ag. (Omphalia) oniscus* seem to owe their specific names to their likeness in colour to a kind of cod-fish known as *oniscus*, and so mean rather a light grey, and not the dark slate-grey of the woodlouse we describe under the name of Oniscus. *Chalybaeus* is a steel or iron-grey; Fries, under *Cortinarius sciophyllus*, explains it as *caeruleo-fuscus*, dusky blue.

Of the brown-greys, *murīnus*, mouse-colour, is the palest (*cf. Paxillus extenuatus*, Fries, p. 402). *Myochrous* should have the same signification, but is used by Fries for a dusky umber. *Argillaceus* is a light brownish ash-colour. *Fuscus*, dusky, is rather a vague term, but it is almost too brown to be classed under the greys at all; *fuscescens* means becoming dusky. *Ravidus* is a dark grey. *Fumosus, fuligineus* and *fuliginosus* are best translated smoky, and not, as the latter might be, sooty black.

Pure BLACKS fortunately do not admit of much variation, although since an absolute black is rarely seen, several terms occur. *Ater* is strictly a lustre-less black, and *niger* is a glistening black; *piceo-ater*, black as pitch, and *furvus*, swarthy, come into the former category; *coracīnus*, raven-black, with a tinge of blue, into the latter. *Atratus* and *pullatus* mean simply 'clothed in black'. *Denigratus*, 'blackened', is used for a dark dusky brown, and not black at all. *Nigerrimus*, 'black as black can be', seems rather pleonastic, but Fries uses it in his descriptions (*Ag. Panaeolus hypomelas*, p. 313).

The next group, the YELLOWS, under which I range the oranges, citrines and browns, presents the greatest difficulties of all, and it is hard to get them into satisfactory order.

The type of pale yellow seems to be *luteus*, like the flowers of the plant woad (*Isatis tinctoria*). Paler than this are *luteolus* and *sulphureus*, sulphur-yellow. *Stramineus*, straw-coloured, denotes a paler and less pure yellow, Naples yellow, of which a deeper, duller shade is *cērĭnus, croceus*, saffron-yellow, being a fuller shade. *Citrīnus* is our lemon-yellow, yellow of wax.

The type of full yellow is *flavus*, gamboge-yellow, which at its fullest brilliancy is *flavissimus*. *Flavidus* is a paler yellow, purer and richer than *luteus*. *Vitellinus*, like the yolk of an egg, is used by Fries, as the Canon reminded us last year, to describe the Chantarelle (*Cantharellus cibarius*). Not far off *flavus* is *aureus*, gold-coloured, which seems to me most like the Cadmium yellow of artists; its diminutive, *aureolus*, does not seem to be a very different shade. *Galbănus*, the colour of the gum galbanum, is a greenish yellow.

The orange-yellows, made up of yellow and red, not brown, are typically two; *aurantius* being a full orange, Cadmium orange, and *aurantiacus* a paler orange, containing less red. *Igneus* and *flammeolus*, denoting the colour of flame, and *fulmineus*, that of lightning, come in this place, but seem to have no very certain application.

Persicinus and *persicolor*, are difficult to describe more intelligibly than by peach colour. *Armeniacus*, apricot-coloured, is explained by Fries as tawny-cinnamon (*fulvo-cinnamomeus*) or yellowish-tan (*helvolo-alutaceus*).

The BROWNS are as extensive as the greys, and comprise every tint between impure yellow and the deepest burnt-umber. Their distinctions are best understood by grouping them into yellow-browns, red-browns and true browns.

Of the yellow-browns *cinnamomeus*, cinnamon, a light yellowish brown, is the palest and most familiar. *Gilvus* is a yellower shade; *Ag.* (*Clitocybe*) *splendens* may be taken in illustrating the type of the colour, a yellowish tan, as it was formerly known as *Ag. gilvus*; classically, *gilvus* was an epithet of a dun or cream-coloured horse. *Alutaceus* has rather a wide signification, but it seems best translated by buff or tan. When it is lighter and yellower it is *helvolus*, the epithet of 'white' wine and 'white' grapes in Pliny: in describing *Cortinarius iliopodius*, Fries explains *helvolus* by *alutaceus*, but there must have been some distinction in his mind between the two terms, for he uses the compound, *helvolo-alutaceus* as 'dusky cinnamon', a fact which appears to show that even Fries himself was not so clear in the application of colour-names as we should like to be. *Crustulinus* seems to be the colour of toast, much darker and warmer than that of a cracknel-biscuit. *Ochraceus* is yellow-ochre, and *melleus*, honey-yellow, is dingier and less yellow; *luridus*, sallow or wan, is still paler and less yellow, almost like that which builders call 'stone-colour'. *Rhabarbarinus* is the light brownish yellow of Turkey rhubarb. *Isabellinus* is a light brownish-yellow or dirty cream-colour.

Fawn-colour does not fall very conspicuously into any of my three divisions of browns, but most of us know the hue so denoted; *cervicolor*, *cervinus* and *hinnuleus* all seem to mean much the same. *Cervinus* is applied to the darkest shade, and Fries explains *hinnuleus* as a tawny-cinnamon (p. 380).

The brownish ochrey yellow colour known to artists as 'gall-stone', only with an inclination to a dirty green, is denoted by *ictericus* or *icterinus*.

The brightest of the red-browns is *lateritius*, the colour of old red tiles; its paler shade, that of *Ag. (Hypholoma) sublateritius*, is familiar to us all. *Testaceus*, brick-coloured, is a reddish brown or rusty bay, almost Venetian red. *Fulvus* is tawny, the colour of a lion, and is also known as *leoninus* or *leochromus*; *fulvellus* seems to be paler and redder, and very like that which gives its name to *Ag. (Collybia) nitellinus*, dormouse-colour. *Helvus* is a light bay or 'cow-colour', like *vaccinus*. *Badius* is a reddish-brown, the colour of a 'bay' horse; *spadiceus*, date-brown, is a duller and darker shade. *Hepaticus*, liver-coloured, is a darker and redder brown than bay. *Ustalis* denotes a warm reddish bay, between red-ochre and brown-madder.

Of the true browns, the type is *brunneus*, Vandyke-brown. *Coffeatus*, like roasted coffee, is very similar. *Ligneo-brunneus* is a lighter or wood-brown. The apparently extinct *Ag. (Lepiota) Paulletii* is described by Fries as *colore* 'de noisette', which must mean a light nut-brown or hazel. *Umbrinus* is a dark brown, brown umber, the colour of a 'brown' horse; indeed, the scale of colours used in describing horses, from dun through chestnut, bay, and brown to black, shows how, in ordinary language, the name of a colour is always taken as of a very extensive connotation, because it is hard to decide where one colour ends and another begins.

We now come to the REDS and their varieties. The palest is *carneus*, with *carneolus* and *incarnatus*, flesh-coloured. *Hysgĭnus* is a more distinctly red flesh-colour. *Roseus* and *rosaceus* imply a rosy pink; *rosellus* seems to mean inclined to pink. There must be some difference between the shades of scarlet or vermilion distinguished as *cinnabarinus* and *miniatus*, because each is compounded with the other as *cinnabarino-miniatus*, but I have not succeeded in finding out what the difference is. *Coccineus*, cochineal red, is a deeper scarlet, carmine. *Sanguineus*, blood-red, is nearly similar. *Rufus*, *ruber* and *russus* are less pure reds. *Rubescens* is merely becoming red. *Rubellus*, *rufidulus* and *rufulus* are reddish. *Rubens* is a brick-red; *rutilus*, *rutilans* a purplish brick-red. *Vinaceus* is reddish rather than claret-coloured, but it does not seem to be ever used in descriptions. Less pure reds are *castaneus*, chestnut; *ferrugineus* and *rubiginosus*, rust-red; and *puniceus*, which is an almost purple red.

BLUES are so rare among Fungi that very few names are required for them. *Caeruleus* is a pale blue, azure; *caerulescens* is becoming blue. *Azureus*, *lazulinus* and *cyaneus* are rather ultramarine. *Cyanellus* is almost sky-blue. *Purpureus* is a bluish purple; *violaceus*, violet, is a reddish purple; *lilacinus* is lilac or mauve. *Ianthinus* and *ionides* alike refer to a violet colour. *Porphyro-leucus* should mean purplish-white, but *Ag.* (*Tricholoma*) *porphyro-leucus*, Bulliard, is described by Fries as 'sooty or dusky, becoming red'.

The type of the GREENS is *viridis*, but it is of no definite hue; *virescens* and *viridans* mean turning green. *Aerugineus* and *aeruginosus* refer to a verdigris or rather bluish-green. *Olivaceus* is olive-green, *olivascens* denoting the preliminary stage of becoming green. *Pausiăcus* describes precisely the same green, from *pausĕa* or *pausia*, a variety of olive; for Fries says of *Ag.* (*Clitocybe*) *pausiacus* that the gills are olivaceous.

REFERENCES

ANDRÉ, J. 1949. *Étude sur les Termes de Couleur dans la Langue latine.* Paris.

BALACHOWSKY, A. 1950. Les Kermes (Hom. Coccoidea) des chênes en Europe et dans le bassin méditerranéen. *Proc. 8th Int. Entomol. Congr.* (*Stockholm*, 1950), 739-754.

BLUMNER, H. 1889. Die rothe Farbe in lateinischen. *Arch. Latein. Lexikogr.*, 6: 399-417.

—— 1892. Die Farbenbezeichnungen bei den romanischen Dichtern. *Berlin. Stud.* 13, no. 3.

BODENHEIMER, F. S. 1928–9. *Materialen zur Geschichte der Entomologie bis Linné.* 2 vols. Berlin.

CARUS, J. V. 1890. *Prodromus Faunae Mediterraneae*, 2: 380-388. Stuttgart.

DADE, H. A. 1949. *Colour Terminology in Biology.* 2nd ed. Kew, Surrey.

DAVY, H. 1815. Some experiments and observations on the colours used in painting by the Ancients. *Phil. Trans. R. Soc.*, 105: 97-124.

FORBES, R. J. 1956. *Studies in ancient Technology*, 4: 98-148. Amsterdam.

JACKSON, B. D. 1899. A review of the Latin terms used in botany to denote colour. *J. Bot.* (*London*), 37: 97-106.

JACKSON, J. W. 1916. The geographical distribution of the shell-purple industry. *Mem. Proc. Manchester Lit. and Phil. Soc.*, 60 n. 7.

KOBER, A. E. 1932. *The Use of Color Terms in the Greek Poets.* New York.

KÖNIG, J. 1927. Die Bezeichnung der Farben: Umfang, Konsequenz und Über-einstimmung der Farbenbenennung. *Archiv. für gesamte Psychologie*, 60: 129-204.

KORNERUP, A. & WANSCHER, J. H. 1963. *Methuen Handbook of Colour.* London (English translation of *Farver i Farver*, Copenhagen, 1961).

LACAZE-DUTHIERS, H. 1859. Mémoire sur la pourpre. *Ann. Sci. Nat., Zool.*, IV. 12: 1-84.

LAUDERMILK, J. 1949. The bug with a crimson past. *Nat. Hist.*, 58: 114-118.
MAERZ, A. & PAUL, M. R. 1950. *A Dictionary of Color*. 2nd ed. New York.
MICHELL, H. 1955. Κοκκος or Kermes. *Classical Rev.*, 69, (N.S. 5): 246.
MÖHRES, F. P. 1962. Purpur. *Die BASF, Arb. Bad. Anil. Soda Fabrik*, 12: 163-167.
OBERTHÜR, R. & DAUTHENAY, H. 1905. *Répertoire de Couleurs*. 2 vols. Paris.
PACLT, J. 1958. *Farbenbestimmung in der Biologie*. Jena [extensive bibliography].
PLATNAUER, M. 1921. Greek colour-perception. *Classical Quarterly*, 15: 153-162.
PLOSS, E. E. 1962. *Ein Buch von alten Farben: Technologie der Textilfarben im Mittelalter*. Heidelberg & Berlin.
—— 1962. Purpurfärben in die Antike. *Die BASF, Arb. Bad. Anil. Soda Fabrik*, 12: 168-171.
RAYNER, R. W. 1970. *A mycological Colour Chart*. Kew, Surrey.
RIDGWAY, R. 1912. *Color Standards and Nomenclature*. Washington, D.C.
SACCARDO, P. A. 1912. *Chromotaxia*. 3rd ed. Padua.
SCHRANK, F. VON P. VON. 1796. Ueber die Linnäischen Farbennamen. Schrank (*Ed.*), *Sammlung naturhistorischer und physikalischer Aufsäze*, 1-96. Nürnberg.
SKARD, S. 1946. The use of color in literature, a survey of research. *Proc. Amer. Phil. Soc.*, 90: 163-249 [extensive bibliography].
VELS HEIJN, N. 1951. *Kleurnamen en Kleurbegrippen bij de Romeinen*. Utrecht.
WALLACE, F. E. 1927. Color in Homer and the Greek poets. *Smith College Classical Studies*, 9.
WANSCHER, J. H. 1953. A simple way of describing flower colours, and a flower colour chart. *R. Vet. Agr. Coll. Copenhagen Yearbook*, 1953: 91-94.
WHARTON, H. T. 1884. On Fries' nomenclature of colours, an examination of the epithets used by him in describing the coloration of the Agaricini. *Grevillea*, 13: 25-31; reprinted in *Trans. Woolhope Nat. Field Club*, 1883–5 (1890): 252-257; for condensed version, see above.
WILSON, R. F. 1938–41. *Horticultural Colour Chart*. 2 vols. London.

CHAPTER XIX

Greek Words in Botanical Latin

INDEBTEDNESS OF BOTANICAL LATIN TO GREEK

Although Latin is the official language for the scientific names of plants, many such names are really of Greek origin. The cause is two-fold. As E. L. Greene noted: 'Pliny, the supreme Latin writer about plants, in translating Theophrastan texts by the hundred into Latin for Roman readers, made use of familiar Latin names in place of the Greek names when there were such, e.g. in place of the Greek *itea* [ἰτεα] [1] he wrote *salix*; in place of *drys* [δρυς], *quercus*; Latin *ulmus*, *sambucus* and *ranunculus* in place of Theophrastan *ptelea* [πτελεα], *acte* [ἀκτη] and *batrachium* [βατραχιον]'. For many plants, however, there were no Latin names available. Pliny overcame this difficulty by transliterating the Greek name into Roman characters, the termination being sometimes changed by him or the not always competent clerks and scribes working hurriedly on his vast compilation, in order to conform to Latin usage. *Aconitum* (ἀκονιτον), *acorus* (ἀκορος), *alsine* (ἀλσινη), *alyssum* (ἀλυσσον), *anchusa* (ἀγχουσα), *anemone* (ἀνεμωνη), *antirrhinum* (ἀντιρρινον) and *aristolochia* (ἀριστολοχια) are but a few of such names taken into Latin from Greek. Linnaeus listed many others in his *Critica botanica*, no. 241 (1737) and *Philosophia botanica*, no. 241 (1751), and himself drew upon ancient names to designate new genera.

There are, however, many botanical names which, although compounded of Greek words, formed no part of ancient Greek. Such names are continually being introduced. This is partly because the apt Latin word has been used already, but chiefly because Greek is a rich flexible language in which pleasing compounds are readily made.

---

[1] In this chapter, as elsewhere in this book, Greek words are given without accents, these being irrelevant to its purpose. As stated by F. K. Smith & T. W. Melluish (*Teach Yourself Greek*; 1947): 'The writing of ac oncents Greek is a conservative tradition from which we might with advantage break away. The ancient Greeks themselves never wrote them. . . . Accents do not appear in manuscripts before the seventh century A.D. The Greek language, however, is quite intelligible without accents. Sappho and Plato did not need them. We may well be rid of an unnecessary burden.'

A pioneer in this modern use of Greek was Pierre Richer de Belleval (c. 1558–1632), founder of the Montpellier botanic garden, who used Latin generic names in Roman characters followed by Greek specific epithets in Greek characters. Thus he proposed the name *Gentianella* ἐαρανθοκυανοχλωρος for the plant later named *Gentiana verna, Fritillaria* πλατυφυλλανθομηλινος for *Fritillaria delphinensis moggridgei*, and so on. Such names he placed on the plates etched and engraved under his direction from 1598 onwards; although known to Linnaeus (cf. *Phil. bot.*, no. 295; 1751), neither they nor any exposition of this system were formally published before 1787. By then the Linnaean system of nomenclature, with Greek words transliterated, had become firmly established.

TRANSLITERATION OF THE GREEK ALPHABET

Under the *International Code of botanical Nomenclature*, principle V (1961), scientific names taken from any language other than Latin or formed in an arbitrary manner are treated as if they were Latin, regardless of their derivation. Latin terminations should be used so far as possible for new names. Greek words must be transliterated into Roman characters when used to form botanical names and epithets, as Linnaeus pointed out in his *Critica botanica*, no. 247 (1737): 'Greek generic names are to be written in Latin characters', since 'in every age it has been the recognized practice among almost all botanists, and even among the most eloquent Romans in ancient times, by Pliny and others, to write Greek names in Roman letters'.

THE GREEK ALPHABET

Numerical Value	Large Character	Small Character	Name	Latin Equivalent	Latinized Transliteration	Examples
1.	'Α	α	alpha	a	a	Ἀκακια, *Acacia*
	'Α	ά		ha	ha	ἀπαλος, *hapalus*
		αι		ai	*usually*	
					ae	Παιονια, *Paeonia*
					less often	
					ai	'Αιρα, *Aira*
		αί			hae	
		αυ		au	au	Δαυκος, *Daucus*
2.	Β	β	bēta	b	b	Βριζα, *Briza*
3.	Γ	γ	gamma	g	g	γιγας, *gigas*
		γγ		gg	ng	Γιγγιδιον, *Gingidium*
		γκ		gk	nc	'Αγκιστρον, *Ancistrum*
		γξ		gx	nx	Σογχος, *Sonchus*
4.	Δ	δ	delta	d	d	Δωδεκαθεον, *Dodecatheon*

Numerical Value	Large Character	Small Character	Name	Latin Equivalent	Latinized Transliteration	Examples
5.	'E	ε	ĕpsilon	ĕ	e	'Εβενος, *E*benus
	'E	ἐ			he	'Ελενιον, *H*elenium
		ει		ei	i *or* e	'Ερεικη, *E*rica.
		ευ				Ποταμαγειτον, Potamogeton
				eu	eu *rarely* ev	Τευκριον, Teu*c*rium
		εὑ		heu	heu	
6.	F *or* Ϝ		digamma	v	v	
7.	Z	ζ	zēta	z	z	Ζεα, *Z*ea
8.	'H	η	ēta	ē	e	'Ηπειρωτης, *E*pirotes
	(final)	η		ē	e *or* a	Αλοη, Aloe, Τυφη, Typh*a*
	'H	ἡ		he	he	'Ηρακλειον, *H*eracleum
9.	Θ	θ	thēta	th	th	Θησειον, *Th*esium
10.	'I	ι	iota	i	i	'Ιρις, *I*ris
					i *or* j	
	'I	ἱ		hi	hi	'Ιππουρις, *H*ippuris
20.	K	κ	kappa	k	c *rarely* k	Κακαλια, *Ca*calia
30.	Λ	λ	lambda	l	l	Μελιλωτος, Me*l*i*l*lotus
40.	M	μ	mu	m	m	Λεμνα, Le*m*na
50.	N	ν	nu	n	n	Νηριον, *N*erium
60.	Ξ	ξ	xi	x	x	Ξανοιον, *X*anthium
70.	'O	ο	omĭcron	o	o	'Ορχις, *O*rchis
	'O	ὁ		ho	ho	'Ολοστεον, *H*olosteum
	(final)	ον		on	um	Μηον, Me*um*
	(final)	ος		os	us *or* os	'Ακανθος, Acanth*us*
						'Ακινος, Acin*os*
		οι		oi	oe	Φοινιξ, Ph*oe*nix
		ου		ou	u	'Αγχουσα, Anch*u*sa
80.	Π	π	pi	P	P	Πεπλις, *P*eplis
	'Ρ	ρ	rho	r	r	Δρυπις, D*r*ypis
100.	'Ρ	ῥ			rh	'Ρηον, *Rh*eum
		ρρ		rr	rrh	Γλυκυρριζα, Glycy*rrh*iza
200.	Σ	σ, ς	sigma	s	s	Σεσελι, *S*eseli.
						στυλος, *s*tylus
300.	T	τ	tau	t	t	Τετραλιξ, *T*etralix
400.	'Υ	υ	upsilon	u	y	θυμος, Th*y*mus
	'Υ	ὑ			hy	'Υσσωπος, *Hy*ssopus
500.	Φ	φ	phi	ph	ph	Φιλαδελφος, *Ph*iladel*ph*us
600.	X	χ	chi	ch	ch	Χελωνη, *Ch*elone
700.	Ψ	ψ	psi	ps	ps	Ψυλλιον, *Ps*yllium
800.	Ω	ὠ	omega	o	o	Ωτιτης, *O*tites, Βρωμος, *B*romus
	'Ω	ὠ			ho	ωρολογιον, *h*orologium

The divisions of Greek texts, e.g. Sprengel's edition (1829–30) of Dioscorides, *Materia medica*, are often numbered with Greek letters having the numerical values given above.

The smooth breathing sign ' (spiritus lenis) associated with an initial letter merely indicates the absence of an aitch (H, h): thus ἀ, ἐ, ἠ, ἰ, ὀ, ῥ, ὐ and ὠ are transliterated as *a*, *ĕ*, *ē*, *i*, *ŏ*, r, y and *ō* respectively.

It should be noted that there is no initial letter corresponding to our H ([h]aitch) in the above Greek alphabet. This sound is one easily lost and also easily but irregularly inserted in many languages. The fate of the letter H (which originally represented an aitch sound) was different in Greek Italy and Greek Asia Minor (Ionia). In Italy the Greeks distinguished between words beginning with an aitch and those not. In Ionia the Greeks dropped their aitches; thus, having no use for this letter in its original sense, they adopted it for the long 'ee' sound. The Ionian alphabet ultimately became the standard Greek alphabet, and to make a distinction between words beginning with an aitch and those not, the Alexandrians split the letter H in two, putting Ⱶ before words beginning with an aitch; this ultimately became ' and is called the rough breathing (spiritus asper); hence ἁ, ἑ, ἡ, ἱ, ὁ, ῥ, ὑ and ὡ are transliterated as *ha*, *hĕ*, *hē*, *hi*, *hŏ*, *rh* and *hō* respectively. Robert Brown overlooked this when he proposed the generic name *Eleocharis*, from ἕλος, ἕλεος 'marshy ground', χαρις 'grace'; he should have written it *Heleocharis*. As regards the transliteration of ῥ, the Romans themselves varied in their practice; thus ῥαφανος (radish), probably an early borrowing, became *raphanus*, but ῥαμνος (buckthorn) *rhamnus*. Hence the original spelling of an author should be accepted.

WORD ENDINGS

The Greek ending -ος (*ŏs*) usually becomes -*us* when transliterated. Thus ὀροβος became *orobus* in Latin, φιλαδελφος *philadelphus*, etc. The Greek ending -ρος (-*ros*), however, often became -*er*, e.g. *Alexander* from 'Αλεξανδρος (cf. Mayer, 1957). The neuter ending -ον (-*ŏn*) often becomes -*um* but sometimes, and then usually in generic names, remains -*on*. Thus ἀνδροσαιμον became *androsaemum* and ὠκιμον (ōkimŏn) *ocimum*, but ῥοδοδενδρον *rhododendron*. The ending -ων (-*ōn*) usually remains -*on*, e.g. *erigeron* (ἠριγερων), *cotyledon* (κοτυλεδων), and compounds of *pogon* (πωγων), *siphon* (σιφων), *stemon* (στημων), etc. Terminal -η sometimes becomes -*a*, e.g. ἐρεικη (ereikē) *erica*; usually, however, it remains -*e*, e.g. *aloe* (ἀλοη), *helxine* (ἑλξινη), *oenanthe* (ὀινανθη), *daphne* (δαφνη), etc. Whereas Latin adjectives in

the nominative end in -*us* (m.), -*a* (f.) or -*um* (n.), -*is* (m., f.) or -*e* (n.)
Greek adjectives display a disconcerting variety of nominative endings,
e.g. -ος (m.), -α (f.), -ον (n.); -ους (m.), -η (f.), -ουν (n.); -ος (m.), -ος
(f.), -ον (n.); -ον (m., f., n.); -ης (m., f.), -ες (n.); -ις (m., f.), -ι (n.),
-ας (m.), -αλη (f.), -α (n.), etc. It is, accordingly, a simplifying procedure when adopting Greek adjectives as botanical epithets to give
them the Latin endings -*us* (m.), -*a* (f.), -*um* (n.). Thus πλατυφυλλος
(m. & f.), -ον (n.) becomes *platyphyllus*, -*a* -*um*. The exceptions are
words ending in -ης, which is better transliterated as -*es*, e.g. γογγυλωδης
(roundish) becomes *gongylodes*, γγ being transliterated as *ng*; -οειδης
becomes -*oides* (see below), but even this can be converted into an
adjective of the First Declension; thus *rhomboides* in botanical Latin
can also be rendered as *rhomboideus* (m.), *rhomboidea* (f.), *rhomboideum*
(n.). For the declension of these, see Chapter V.

However, an adjectival epithet published with a Greek ending
should keep in agreement with the gender of the generic name with
which it is associated, e.g. *acaulos* (m., f.), *acaulon* (n.).

GENDER OF GREEK NOUNS AND ADJECTIVES

Nouns in Greek as in Latin are masculine, feminine or neuter;
qualifying adjectives agree with them in gender, number and case.
A Greek-English lexicon indicates the gender of a noun by adding the
definite article: ὁ (masculine), ἡ (feminine), το (neuter).

Greek nouns taken into Latin retain their original gender, and
compounds derived from two or more Greek words take the gender
of the last unless the ending is altered. Thus *ceras* (κερας, horn) is
neuter, and its compounds, such as *Aceras*, *Aegiceras*, *Xanthoceras*,
are accordingly treated as neuter; their genitive singular ends in
-*ceratis*. Alteration of -*ceras* to -*cera*, as in *Tetracera*, produces, however, a feminine noun, with the genitive singular ending in -*cerae*;
alteration of -*ceras* to -*cerōs* as in *rhinoceros*, *Anthoceros*, *Dendroceros*,
Megaceros, *Phaeoceros*, produces a masculine noun with the genitive
singular ending in -*cerotis*. Similarly *Dipterocarpus*, *Hymenocarpos*,
Stenocarpus and all other modern compounds ending in the Greek
masculine -*carpos* (καρπος, fruit) or -*carpus* are treated as masculine,
but those ending in -*carpa* or -*carpaea*, e.g. *Callicarpa*, *Polycarpaea*,
are treated as feminine, and those in *carpon*, -*carpum* or *carpium*, e.g.
Polycarpon, *Orthocarpum*, *Pisocarpium*, as neuter. These compounds
with Latin endings are to be treated grammatically as Latin words.

Generic names ending in -*codon* (κωδων, bell), -*mecon* (μηκων,
poppy), -*odon* (ὁδων, tooth), -*panax* (παναξ, all-heal), -*stemon* (στημων,
warp, hence stamen), are treated as masculine.

Generic names derived from Greek which end in -*ma* (μα) are neuter, unless this is a rendering of *mē* (μη); hence those ending in *-broma* (βρωμα, food), *-derma* (δερμα, skin), *-loma* (λωμα, hem, fringe), *-nema* (νημα, thread), *-phragma* (φραγμα, fence, hence partition, septum), *-sperma* (σπερμα, seed), *-stemma* (στεμμα, wreath, garland), *-stigma* (στιγμα, spot, hence stigma) and *-stoma* (στομα, mouth), are treated as neuter. Since so many Latin feminine nouns end in *-a*, these neuter nouns of Greek origin ending in *-ma* are somewhat disconcerting. Names derived from the feminine nouns *ŏsmē* (ὀσμη, smell) and *cnēmē* (κνημη, internode, spoke) are likewise feminine even when rendered as osma (e.g. *Meliosma, Xylosma*) and *Knema* (e.g. *Knema, Octoknema*).

Generic names ending in *-anthe* (ἀνθη, flower), *-opsis* (ὀψις, appearance) and *-taxis* (ταξις, order) are treated as feminine.

According to Sprague (1935): 'Modern generic names of plants ending in *-ops* were presumably modelled on the masculine Greek nouns *aigilops* (ἀιγιλωψ), denoting *Quercus Cerris* and also *Aegilops ovatus*, and *cynops* (κυνωψ), a name for *Plantago lanceolata*. They may therefore be regarded as nouns derived from *ōps* (ὠψ), m. f. n., meaning "eye" or "face", hence "facies" or "appearance". The word *cyclōps*, however, is used both as a masculine noun, and as an adjective, meaning "round-eyed", and both *monōps*, "one-eyed", and *chrysōps*, "gold-coloured, shining like gold", are adjectives. As far as their *form* is concerned, modern generic names ending in *ōps* might be either nouns or adjectives . . . since *ōps* itself may be masculine, feminine or neuter, the gender of modern generic names ending in *ōps* may also be masculine, feminine or neuter. Each generic name in *-ōps* will accordingly take the gender originally assigned to it. Thus *Balanops, Dryobalanops, Gyrinops* and *Mimusops* will be treated as feminine, and *Echinops* and *Euryops* as masculine, since these were the genders adopted by the authors of the respective names.'

Botanical generic names ending in *-odes* and *-oides* are now all treated as feminine, in accordance with the *International Code of botanical Nomenclature*, even though a few, e.g. *Santaloides*, have been often treated as neuter. The terminations *-oides* (i.e. -οειδης) and *-odes* (i.e. -ωδης) are adjectival endings indicating resemblance. Consequently generic names such as *Nymphoides* and *Omphalodes* are really adjectives treated as substantives, the word qualified, e.g. βοτανη (f.), *arbor* (f.), *herba* (f.), *planta* (f.), being omitted. Adjectives such as βοτρυοειδης (like a bunch of grapes), δακτυλοειδης (finger-like) and ῥοδοειδης (rose-like) were often used in classical Greek, and an adjective 'was able normally to stand alone without a substantive as subject, object or predicate, or after a preposition, in almost every position indeed in which a substantive might stand' (Atkinson, 1933). Transliterated into Latin, the masculine and feminine ending -οειδης (i.e. *ŏĕĭdēs*) and the neuter -οειδες (i.e. *ŏĕĭdĕs*) become -*oides*. This comprises two parts, i.e. the -*o*- (-*o*-) which belongs to the stem and -ειδης (having the nature of, resembling) from ειδος (shape, kind, nature). The -*oi*- of -*oides* should accordingly be pronounced as *ŏĭ* and not as a diphthong (i.e. not as in English 'adenoid'). In classical Latin such words took the gender of the noun providing the stem— thus *sesamoides* was neuter like *sesamum*—and their gender is not evident from their form. Such names used in zoology are mostly treated as masculine.

Pre-Linnaean authors found the ending -*oides* very handy when naming new genera. To indicate a resemblance to a genus already known, they simply took the stem of its name and added -*oides*. This practice annoyed Linnaeus exceedingly. Denouncing it as the 'common and safe refuge of the idle', he declared in his *Critica botanica* that 'generic names ending in -*oides* are to be banished from the domain of botany', and he himself gave them short shrift. About a hundred generic names in -*oides* coined by Tournefort, Boerhaave, Rivinius, Dillenius, Vaillant, Plukenet, Knaut and others fell before his reforming zeal. Thus *Aloides* became *Stratiotes*, *Plumbaginoides* became *Boerhavia*, *Staphylodendroides* became *Royena*, *Tribuloides* became *Trapa*, and so on. When such pre-Linnaean genera were not sufficiently distinct in his opinion to merit re-naming, he simply treated their offending -*oides* names as synonyms of the genera with which he fused them. *Nymphoides*, for example, became part of *Menyanthes*; *Omphalodes* became part of *Cynoglossum*. When at a later date followers of Tournefort re-established these suppressed genera, they usually restored their pre-Linnaean names. Despite Linnaeus's caustic remarks and his efforts to rid botany of such names for good and all, *Agrimonoides*, *Alyssoides*, *Buglossoides*, *Chrysanthemoides*, *Nymphoides*, etc., still persist as legitimate generic names, and others, such as *Arachnoides*, have been added to them. It is nomenclaturally important to note that when zealous followers of Linnaeus such as Loefling, Jacquin, Rottböll and Solander used such designations as *Celosioides*, *Malpighioides*, *Petesioides*, *Scirpoides*, *Schoenoides*, *Sideroxyloides*, *Staehelinoides*, *Viscoides*, they did not intend these to be permanent generic names but proposed them simply as token names or provisional designations (*nomina fluxa*) indicative of resemblance, to be replaced later by correctly formed names.

FORMATION OF COMPOUNDS

As stated in the *International Code of botanical Nomenclature*, recommendation 73G: '*A compound word or epithet combining elements derived from two or more Greek or Latin words should be formed, as far as practicable, in accordance with classical usage*', i.e. by analogy with words existing in classical Greek or Latin. These are of two main kinds: (1) The co-ordinate compound in which two words of equal importance for the meaning are joined, e.g. *gynandrus* formed from *gyne* (γυνή, woman) and *aner* (ἀνήρ, man) and indicating that the stamens are adnate to the pistil and *hermaphroditus* (ἑρμαφρόδιτος) from *Hermes* ('Ερμῆς, Mercury) and *Aphrodite* (Αφροδίτη, Venus) indicating that both stamens and pistil are present in the same flower. (2) The subordinate compound in which a main element is qualified by a subordinate element joined to it, e.g. *platyphyllus* (πλατύφυλλος, broad-leaved), *macranthus* (μακρανθος, large-flowered); here the element *platy-* (πλατυς, broad) indicates the kind of *phyllon* (φυλλον, leaf), *macro-* (μακρος, large) the kind of *anthos* (ἀνθος, flower). In these the adjectival first components are directly derived from adjectives having an independent existence. The stems of nouns and verbs, followed usually by a connecting vowel, as well as prefixes derived from prepositions and adverbs, can be similarly used. The qualifying subordinate element can, however, be the last component as in *phyllophorus* (φυλλοφορος, leaf-bearing). It then usually refers to some action or process affecting the first component. For the generic name *Cheilolepton* used by Fée instead of *Leptocheilus* (λεπτοχειλος, narrow lip) and adjectives such as *phyllomegus* (with a large leaf) used by Velloso and Steudel, instead of *megalophyllus* (μεγαλοφυλλος, large-leaved), there is some classical precedent in such a noun as *onagros* (ὀναγρος, wild ass, from ὀνας, ass, ἀγριος, wild) with an adjective appended to the stem of a noun.

PREFIXES (see p. 301) include *a-* or *an-* (ἀ- or ἀν-, lacking), *amphi-* (ἀμφι-, in two ways), *di-* (δι-, twice), *ecto-* (ἐκτο-, on the outside), *endo-* (ἐνδο-, on the inside), *epi-* (ἐπι-, upon), *eu-* (εὐ-, good, well), *hemi-* (ἡμι-, half), *para-* (παρα-, near, beside), *peri-* (περι-, around).

SUFFIXES (see p. 305) for forming nouns of Greek origin include those indicative of smallness, e.g. *-ium* or *-ion* (-ιον, n.), *-idium* or *-idion* (-ιδιον, n.) and *-iscus* or *-iscos* (-ισκος, m.) or of relationship, e.g. *-ides* (-ιδης, m.), or the result of a process or action, e.g. *-ma* (-μα, n.), or the agent or doer, e.g. *-tes* (-της, m.). Adjectival suffixes include *-ticus* or *-ticos* (-τικος), attached to the stem of a verb, and *-eus, -eius, -eos* or *-eios* (-εος, -ειος) attached to the stem of a noun, meaning 'pertaining to' or 'noted for'; *-icus* or *-icos* (-ικος) or, after *-i*, *-acus* (-ακος) ' belonging to '; *-inus* or *-inos* (-ινος) 'resembling', often used of colours.

The formation of compounds (both from Latin and Greek) is summarized in the *International Code* as follows:

(a) *In a true compound (as distinct from pseudo-compounds such as* Myos-otis *and* nidus-avis) *a noun or adjective in a non-final position*

appears as a bare stem without case-endings. As examples of accepted
names contrary to this may be cited *Pachysandra* (from παχυς, thick
ἀνηρ, man), instead of *Pachyandra*, and *Peliosanthes* (from πελιος
livid, dark, ἀνθος, flower), instead of *Pelianthes*. When the stem
(see p. 60) of the nominative singular, e.g. *thrix* (θριξ, hair), differ
from that of the genitive singular, e.g. *trichos* (τριχος, of hair), the
latter is normally used as the first component of a compound, although
even here there is classical precedent for the occasional use of both
the short nominative stem and the longer stem as in *Nemastylis* and
Nematostylis; thus *phos* (φως, a contraction of φαος, light) and its
genitive *photos* (φωτος, of light) have yielded *phosphoreo* (φωσφορεω, to
bring light) and *photodotes* (φωτοδοτης, giver of light). The stem of a
word (see p. 61) can be ascertained by removing the case-ending of the
genitive singular; thus the genitive singular of *odous* (ὀδους, tooth)
is *odontos* (ὀδοντος, of the tooth), which yields the stem *odont-* used
in many ancient compounds such as *odontalgia* (ὀδονταλγια, tooth
ache), *odontoides* (ὀδοντοειδης, tooth-shaped), *odontophorus* (ὀδοντοφ
ορος, bearing teeth) and modern compounds such as *Odontadenia, Odon
tochilus, Odontoglossum, Odontopteris, Odontosoria, Odontostigma*
etc. Thus *derma* (δερμα, skin) gives the combining form *dermato-*
gala (γαλα, milk) *galacto-*; *aner* (ἀνηρ, man) *andro-*; and so on.

   (b) *Before a vowel the final vowel of this stem, if any, is normally*
elided (Chrys-anthemum, mult-angulus) *with exception of the Greek y*
and i (Poly-anthus, Meli-osma). Elision is the cutting out of a vowel
or syllable, exemplified in *Hippuris* (ἱππουρις, horsetail, from ἱππος
horse, and ὀυρα, tail). Special cases are provided by *neo-* (νεο-, new
newly) and *pseudo-* (ψευδο-, false) which in classical usage sometimes
occasionally retained their terminal *o* even when followed by a vowel
e.g. *neoades* (νεοαδης, freshly watered), *neoides* (νεοειδης, youthful in
form), *pseudoenedra* (ψευδοενεδρα, feigned ambuscade), *pseudoepec*
(ψευδοεπεο, speak falsely), although in general it was then suppressed
Peri- (περι, around) and *pro-* (προ-, in front of, before) do not change
even before a vowel, e.g. *perianthes* (περιανθης, with flowers all round)
perierctus (περιερκτος, enclosed), *proales* (προαλης, sloping), *proen
gonos* (προεγγονος, great-grandson). Thus the stem and nominative
singular of *limne* (λιμνη, marsh) are identical, but the terminal *-e* (-η)
is normally elided in compounds when it comes before a vowel, e.g
limnasia (λιμνασια, marshy ground), *Limnanthemum, Limnanthes*.

   (c) *Before a consonant the final vowel is normally preserved in Greek*
(mono-carpus, Poly-gonum, Coryne-phorus) *except that* a *is commonly*
replaced by o (Hemerocallis *from* hemera); *in Latin the final vowel is*
reduced to i (multi-color, menthi-folius, salvii-folius). In compounds
of *limne* (see above) the terminal *-e* (-η) is replaced by *-o*, e.g. *limnobio*

(λιμνοβιος, living in a lake), *limnocharis* (λιμνοχαρις, grace of the marsh), *Limnochloa, Limnophila, Limnophyton*. In derivatives of *hals* (ἁλς, salt, sea), *hali-* (ἁλι-) tends to refer to the sea, e.g. *halimus* (ἁλιμος) but *halo-* (ἁλο-) to salt, e.g. *halophilus, Halopegia*, or the sea, e.g. *Halodule, Halophila, Haloragis*.

(d) *If the stem ends in a consonant, a connecting vowel, Greek o, Latin i, is inserted before a following consonant* (Odont-o-glossum, cruc-i-formis). This is a useful general rule to which even in classical times there were exceptions. The connecting vowel makes the word easy to say and pleasant to hear. In late Latin *-o-* sometimes replaced *-i-* as a combining vowel, following the classical precedent of *albogalerus* (i.e. *albus galerus*, white hat) and *albogilvus* (whitish-yellow); its descendant, botanical Latin, thus has *albiflorus* (white-flowered) and *albomarginatus* (white-margined). Similarly the standard combining form of *ater* (black) in botanical Latin is *atro-*, as in *atrocaeruleus* (dark blue), *atrolabius* (black-lipped), *atropurpureus* (black-purple), *atroviolaceus* (black-violet), despite the classical *atricapillus* (black-haired). No connecting vowel follows the prefix *syn-* (συν-, with, united) which becomes *sym-* (συμ-) before *b*, *p* or *ph*, e.g. *symbios* (συμβιος, living together), *symplectus* (συμπλεκτος, twined together), and *sy-* (συ-) before *st-*, e.g. *systylus* (συστυλος, with columns standing close). The stem *melan-* (μελαν-) of the adjective *melas* (μελας, black) is generally followed by the connecting vowel *o*, as in *melanostictus* (μελανοστικτος, black-spotted), but can be used without it, as in *melandryos* (μελανδρυος, dark as an oak).

In classical Greek the rough breathing rendered as *h* was lost when another word was prefixed to it. Thus *haema* (αἱμα, blood) when prefixed by *an-* (ἀν, not, without) became *anaemia*, not *anhaemia*. However, as observed by Nybakken, this elimination of the aspirate has been irregular both in Roman and in modern usage. 'Because of familiarity with the Greek words in their simple form (i.e. not compounded), the aspirate *h* was always felt to be present and therefore an *h* was included in the [transliterated] Greek stem regardless of whether it was used as the first or as a later component term.' Thus the Greek ἀνυδρος became *anhydros* in transliteration. Insertion of the *h* is recommended because it helps to make the meaning and derivation clear. The initial ῥ of a Greek word transliterated as *rh*, e.g. *rhiza* (ῥιζα, root, rhizome), should have an additional *r* added to it when preceded by a vowel, e.g. *Glycyrrhiza* (γλυκυρριζα, liquorice, from γλυκος, sweet, ῥιζα, root), *leptorrhiza* (λεπτορριζα, with a thin root, from λεπτος, small, slender), but as many reputable authors, Linnaeus among them, have omitted this additional *r*, it is best regarded as optional and an author's original spelling, as in *Lemna polyrhiza*, should be accepted.

CONSONANT CHANGES

When joining word elements which begin or end with *mutes*, i.e. the letters

β	(b)	classified as Labial (in Class) and Middle (in Order)
γ	(g)	,,	,, Palatal and Middle
δ	(d)	,,	,, Dental and Middle
π	(p)	,,	,, Labial and Smooth
θ	(th)	,,	,, Dental and Rough
κ	(c, k)	,,	,, Palatal and Smooth
τ	(t)	,,	,, Dental and Smooth
φ	(ph)	,,	,, Labial and Rough
χ	(ch)	,,	,, Palatal and Rough

important changes in consonants take place, of which the following summary is quoted, with accents, from Nybakken (1960):

(*a*) No mute (except κ) can stand before σ because:

π (p), β (b) or φ (ph) before σ (s) = ψ (ps)
$\begin{cases} σῆπ\text{-}σις = σῆψις & \text{(sep-sis} = \text{sepsis)} \\ τρίβ\text{-}σις = τρίψις & \text{(trib-sis} = \text{tripsis)} \\ στρέφ\text{-}σις = στρέψις & \text{(streph-sis} = \text{strepsis)} \end{cases}$

κ (c), γ (g) or χ (ch) before σ (s) = ξ (x)
(except with prefix ἐκ; e.g. ἐκστάς)
$\begin{cases} πρῆκ\text{-}σις = πρῆξις & \text{(prec-sis} = \text{prexis)} \\ λέγ\text{-}σις = λέξις & \text{(leg-sis} = \text{lexis)} \\ θρίχ\text{-}ς = θρίξ & \text{(thrich-s} = \text{thrix)} \end{cases}$

τ (t), δ (d) or θ (th) before σ (s) = σ (s)
(the mute disappears)
$\begin{cases} χάριτ\text{-}ς = χάρις & \text{(charit-s} = \text{charis)} \\ σχίδ\text{-}σις = σχίσις & \text{(schid-sis} = \text{schisis)} \\ ὄρνιθ\text{-}ς = ὄρνις & \text{(ornith-s} = \text{ornis)} \end{cases}$

(*b*) A mute before μ (m) changes as follows:

π (p), β (b) or φ (ph) before μ (m) becomes μ (m): γράφ-μα = γράμμα (graph-ma = gramma)

κ (c), γ (g) or χ (ch) before μ (m) becomes γ (g): πλέκ-μα = πλέγμα (plec-ma = plegma)

τ (t), δ (d) or θ (th) before μ (m) becomes σ (s) or remains unchanged: κλύδ-μα = κλύσμα (clyd-ma = clysma)

(*c*) When a labial or a palatal mute stands before another mute, it must be co-ordinate with the other mute (that is, of the same ORDER; [likewise Smooth, Middle or Rough]). For example:

ἐλλιπ-τικός	(ellip-ticos)	remains	ἐλλιπτικός	(ellipticos)
ἐπιληβ-τικος	(epileb-ticos)	becomes	ἐπιληπτικός	(epilepticos)
τριβ-τικός	(trib-ticos)	becomes	τριπτικός	(tripticos)
στρεφ-τικός	(streph-ticos)	becomes	στρεπτικός	(strepticos)
πραγ-τικός	(prag-ticos)	becomes	πρακτικός	(practicos)
πεγ-τικός	(peg-ticos)	becomes	πεκτικός	(pecticos)

(*d*) When another dental mute (τ, δ, θ) comes before τ, it is changed to σ; for example:

πλατ-τικός   (plat-tikos)   becomes   πλαστικός   (plasticos)
κλυδ-τικός   (clyd-ticos)   becomes   κλυστικός   (clysticos)

(e) Whenever a smooth mute (π, κ, τ) immediately precedes a word beginning with rough breathing, it is changed to the rough mute of the same class; for example:

(1) κατά (cata) plus αἵρεσις (hairesis) = καθαίρεσις (cathairesis). The final -α of κατά elides before the diphthong αι, which brings the smooth mute τ before rough breathing. The mute is then aspirated to θ. The rough breathing mark disappears on the resultant compound term.

(2) ἐπί (epi) plus ἵππιον (hippion) = ἐφίππιον (ephippion). The final -ι of ἐπί elides before the initial vowel of ἵππιον; the smooth mute π becomes aspirated to φ.

(3) ἐκ (ec) plus αἱμάσσω (haimasso) = ἐξαιμάσσω (exaimasso). The smooth mute κ becomes aspirated before the rough breathing of αἱμάσσω.

(f) The consonant ν changes as follows:

(1) Before a labial mute (π, β, or φ) it becomes μ; for example:

ἐν-πάθη   (en-pathe)   becomes   ἐμπάθη   (empathe)
συν-βίος   (syn-bios)   becomes   σύμβιος   (symbios)
συν-φύσις   (syn-physis)   becomes   σύμφυσις   (symphysis)

(2) Before a palatal mute (κ, γ, or χ) it becomes γ (nasal); for example:

συν-κοπή   (syn-cope)   becomes   συγκοπή   (sygcope)
συν-γενής   (syn-genes)   becomes   συγγενής   (syggenes)
συν-χρόνος   (syn-chronos)   becomes   σύγχρονος   (sygchronos)

(3) Before a σ it is dropped; for example:

συν-στολή   (syn-stole)   becomes   συστολή   (systole)
συν-στρεπτός   (syn-streptos)   becomes   συστρεπτός   (systreptos)

(4) Before a λ or a μ it is assimilated; for example:

ἐν-λόβιον   (en-lobion)   becomes   ἐλλόβιον   (ellobion)
συν-μετρία   (syn-metria)   becomes   συμμετρία   (symmetria)

(g) The initial ῥ of a word is doubled whenever another word ending in a vowel is prefixed; but if the prefix ends in a diphthong, the ῥ remains single. For example:

κατα-ῥέω   (cata-rheo)   becomes   καταρρέω   (catarreo)
παρα-ῥυθμός   (para-rhythmos)   becomes   παράρρυθμος   (pararrythmos)
εὐ-ῥυθμός   (eu-rhythmos)   remains   εὔρυθμος   (eurythmos)

GREEK WORD ELEMENTS

The following list gives the more important Greek elements used in
the formation of botanical names. For further suggestions as to
appropriate epithets, reference should be made to the works of R. B.
Brown (1956) and of E. C. Jaeger (1955); epithets chosen should be
checked in Liddell & Scott's *Greek-English Lexicon*. On grammatical
matters, the works of P. Kretschmer (1899), O. E. Nybakken (1960)
and E. Wikén (1951) are particularly helpful. Saint-Lager (1880) and
R. Strömberg (1940) provide lists of Greek plant names with com-
mentaries. André's *Lexique* (1956) lists plant names taken into classical
Latin from Greek.

For Greek prefixes, see p. 304; for Greek adjectival suffixes, see
p. 310; for Greek substantival suffixes, see p. 306.

a- (ἀ): without, not, un-
above: *see* **hyper, epi-**
Acantha (ἀκανθα, *f.*): spine, thorn,
prickle
Achyron (ἀχυρον, *n.*): chaff, husks
acid: *see* **oxys**
Acis, acidos (ἀκις, ἀκιδος, *f.*): pointed
object
Acme (ἀκμη, *f.*): highest point
Acorn: *see* **Balanos**
acros (ἀκρος): at the tip, end, summit
Actis, actinos (ἀκτις, ἀκτινος, *f.*): ray
Aden, adenos (ἀδην, ἀδενος, *f.*): gland
agathos (ἀγαθος): good
Agrostis (ἀγρωστις, *f.*): grass
all-: *see* **pan-**
allo- (ἀλλο-): *prefix*, different, foreign,
strange
alone: *see* **monos**
amblys (ἀμβλυς): blunt, dulled
Ampelos (ἀμπελος, *f.*): climbing plant,
vine
an- (ἀν-): without, not
ancho (ἀγχω): *verb*, strangle; hence
-*anche* as ending of names of
poisonous plants
ancient: *see* **palaeos**
Ancistron (ἀνκιστρον, *n.*): fish-hook
Angion (ἀγγειον, *n.*): vessel, receptacle
Angle: *see* **Gonia**
Anthemon (ἀνθεμον, *n.*): flower
Anthera (ἀνθηρα, *f.*): *in mod. botany*,
anther
antheros (ἀνθηρος): flowering

Anthos (ἀνθος, *n.*): flower; in combinations the Latinized form -*anthus*
is treated as masculine
Apple: *see* **Melon**
arche-, archi- (ἀρχη-, ἀρχι-): first,
chief, arch-
argyros (ἀργυρος): silvery
Aspect: *see* **Opsis**
Ass: *see* **Onos**
Aulos (ἀυλος, *m.*): pipe, flute, tube
Auricle: *see* **Otion**

back, at the: *see* **opisthen**
Back: *see* **Notos**
bad-: *see* **dys-**
Balanos (βαλανος, *f.*): acorn
Ball: *see* **Sphaera**
Band: *see* **Desmos, Taenia,** *also* **Zone,**
Zoster
Bark: *see* **Phloios**
barys (βαρυς): heavy
basis (βασις, *f.*): base, pedestal
bastard: *see* **nothos**
Batos (βατος, *f.*): bramble
Beard: *see* **Pogon**
bearing: *see* **phoros**
Beauty: *see* **Callos**
Bed: *see* **Cline**
Bell: *see* **Codon**
Belly: *see* **Gaster**
Belos (βελος, *n.*): missile, *especially*
dart, arrow
below: *see* **hypo**
Belt: *see* **Zoster, Zone**
bent: *see* **camptos, campylos, cyphos**

Bios (βιος, *m.*) : life

Bird : *see* **Ornis**

Bitter : *see* **picros**

Black : *see* **melas**

Bladder : *see* **Cystis, Physa**

Blastos (βλαστος, *m.*) : shoot

Blepharis (βλεφαρις, *f.*) : eyelash

Blepharon (βλεφαρον, *n.*) : eyelid

Blood : *see* **Haema**

Blood-vessel : *see* **Phleps**

Body : *see* **Soma**

Bone : *see* **Osteon**

Border : *see* **Craspedon, Loma**

botryoides (βοτρυοειδης) : like a bunch of grapes

Botrys (βοτρυς, *m.*) : bunch of grapes

Bowl : *see* **Lecanos**

brachys (βραχυς) : short

Bramble : *see* **Batos**

Branch : *see* **Thallos, Clados**

broad : *see* **platys**

Broma (βρωμα, *n.*) : food

Bryon (βρυον, *n.*) : moss, liverwort

Bundle : *see* **Desme**

Bus (βους, *m., f.*) : cattle

acos (κακος) : bad, ugly

caenos (καινος) : new, fresh ; *to be distinguished from* **cenos** (κενος), empty, **coenos** (κοινος), common

Calamos (καλαμος, *m.*) : reed

calli- (καλλι-) : *in compounds,* beautiful

Callos (καλλος, *n.*) : beauty

calos (καλος) : beautiful

Calymma (καλυμμα, *n.*) : head-covering, hood

Calyptra (καλυπτρα, *f.*) : veil

Calyx (καλυξ, *f.*) : covering of a flower or fruit, *hence* calyx

camptos (καμπτος), **campylos** (καμπυλος) : bent, curved

Cardia (καρδια, *f.*) : heart

Carphos (καρφος, *n.*) : any small dry body, twigs, etc.

Carpos (καρπος, *m.*) : fruit

carrying : *see* **phoros**

Carya (καρυα, *f.*) : nut-bearing tree

Caryon (καρυον, *n.*) : nut

Cattle : *see* **Bus**

Caulos (καυλος, *m.*) : stem

Centron (κεντρον, *n.*) : a sharp point, sting, spur of a cock

Cephale (κεφαλη, *f.*) : head

Ceras (κερας, *n.*) : horn

Chaete (χαιτη, *f.*) : loose flowing hair, mane

Chaff : *see* **Achyron**

chalco- (χαλκο-) : *in compounds,* copper-

chamae- (χαμαι-) : *in compounds,* on the ground, *hence* low-growing

changed : *see* **meta-**

Charis (χαρις, χαριτος, *f.*) : grace

Cheilos, Chilos (χειλος, *n.*) : lip

Chicory : *see* **Seris**

Chion (χιων, *f.*) : snow

Chiton (χιτων, *m.*) : tunic, covering

Chlaena (χλαινα, *f.*) : cloak, covering

Chlamys (χλαμυς, *f.*) : military cloak, mantle

Chloe (χλοη, *f.*) : young green corn or grass

chloros (χλωρος) : greenish-yellow, green

Chroma (χρωμα, *n.*) : colour, complexion

chryso- (χρυσο-) : *in compounds,* gold-

Circle : *see* **Cyclos, Gyros**

Clados (κλαδος, *m.*) : branch, shoot

Class : *see* **Phylon**

Claw : *see* **Onyx**

cleft : *see* **schistos**

cleistos (κλειστος) : closed, shut

Cliff : *see* **Cremnos**

Cline (κλινη, *f.*) : couch

Cloak : *see* **Chlaena, Chlamys**

Club : *see* **Coryne**

Cneme, cnema (κνημη, *f.*) : leg, internode, spoke

Cnemis (κνημις, *f.*) : greave, legging

Coccos (κοκκος, *m.*) : grain, seed, round gall, pill

Codon (κωδων, *m.*) : crier's bell

coelos (κοιλος) : hollow

Colour : *see* **Chroma**

Column : *see* **Stele**

Come (κομη, *f.*) : hair of the head

Cone : *see* **Strobilus**

Conis (κονις, *f.*) : dust

Container : *see* **Thece**

coppery : *see* **chalco-**

Cord : *see* **Sira**

Coryne (κορυνη, *f.*) : club

Cotyle (κοτυλη, *f.*) : small cup, anything hollow

Couch : *see* **Cline**

Course : *see* **Dromos**
Covering : *see* **Calymma, Calyptra, Chiton, Chlaena, Chlamys**
Craspedon (κρασπεδον, *n.*): edge, border
Cremnos (κρημνος, *m.*) : cliff
Crest : *see* **Lophos**
Crinon (κρινον, *n.*) : lily
crooked : *see* **rhaibos**
Crown : *see* **Stelma, Stemma, Stephane, Stephanos**
Ctonos (κτονος, *m.*) : murder
Cup : *see* **Cyathos, Cotyle, Cymbion**
curved : *see* **camptos, campylos, gyros**
Cyanos (κυανος, *m.*) : dark blue colour
Cyathos (κυαθος, *m.*) : ladle, cup
Cybe (κυβη, *f.*) : head
Cyclos (κυκλος, *m.*) : circle
Cymbion (κυμβιον, *n.*) : small cup
cyphos (κυφος) : bent, hunch-backed
Cystis (κυστις, *f.*) : bladder

Dactylos (δακτυλος, *m.*) : finger
Daphne (δαφνη, *f.*) : sweet bay, laurel
dark : *see* **phaeo-**
Dart : *see* **Belos**
dasys (δασυς) : shaggy, hairy, thick-haired
Day : *see* **Hemera**
deca (δεκα) : ten
deltoides (δελτοειδης) : delta-shaped, triangular
Dendron (δενδρον, *n.*) : tree
Derma (δερμα, *n.*) : skin
Desert : *see* **Eremia**
Desme (δεσμη, *f.*) : bundle, handful
Desmos (δεσμος, *m.*) : band, halter, anything used for tying
Dictyon (δικτυον, *n.*) : net
didymos (διδυμος) : double, two-fold, twin
different : *see* **allo-, heteros**
Discos (δισκος, *m.*) : quoit, disc
dolichos (δολιχος) : long
Doron (δωρον, *n.*) : gift, present
Dory (δορυ, *n.*) : shaft, spear
double : *see* **didymos**
Doxa (δοξα, *f.*) : repute, glory
Dromos (δρομος, *m.*) : course, running place
dry : *see* **xeros**
Dung : *see* **Scatos**
Dust : *see* **Conis**
dys- (δυσ-) : bad-, ill-

Ear : *see* **Otion**
earlier : *see* **proteros**
Echidna (ἐχιδνα, *f.*) : viper
Echinos (ἐχινος, *m.*) : hedgehog, sea-urchin
Echis (ἐχις, *m.*) : viper
ectos (ἐκτος) : outside
egg-like : *see* **oodes**
eleo- : *see* **heleo-**
endo- (ἐνδο-) : *prefix*, within, inside
entire : *see* **holos**
entos (ἐντος) : within, inside
epi (ἐπι) : upon
Eremia (ἐρημια, *f.*) : desert, wilderness
Erion (ἐριον, *n.*) : wool
erythros (ἐρυθρος) : red
eu- (ἐυ-) : *prefix*, good, well-developed, normal, true
even : *see* **homalos**
evening : *see* **hesperos**
Eye : *see* **Omma**
Eyelash : *see* **Blepharis**
Eyelid : *see* **Blepharon**

Fan : *see* **Rhipis**
Feather : *see* **pteron**
female : *see* **thelys**, *also* **gyne**
Fern : *see* **Pteris**
few : *see* **oligos**
Fig-tree : *see* **Syce**
Finger : *see* **Dactylos**
Fire : *see* **Pyr**
first : *see* **protos**
Flower : *see* **Anthemon, Anthos**
Folds : *see* **ptyches**
Food : *see* **Broma**
Foot : *see* **Podion**
Forest : *see* **Hyle**
Form : *see* **Morphe**
fragrant : *see* **myristicos**
Fringe : *see* **Loma**
Fruit : *see* **Carpos**
Fungus : *see* **Myces**

Galee (γαλεη, *f.*) : weasel, polecat
Garland : *see* **Stelma, Stemma, Stephane, Stephanos**
Gaster (γαστηρ, *f.*) : belly
Geton (γειτων, *m.*) : neighbour
Gift : *see* **Doron**
Giton (γειτων, *m.*) : neighbour
Gland : *see* **Aden**

Glass : *see* Hyalos

Glochin (γλωχιν, *f.*) : projecting point

Glory : *see* Doxa

Glossa (γλωσσα, *f.*) : tongue

Glottis (γλωττις, *f.*) : mouth of the windpipe

glycys (γλυκυς) : sweet to the taste or smell

Goat, *see* Tragos

gold : *see* chryso-

Gone (γονη, *f.*) : offspring, reproductive organs, womb

gongylodes (γογγυλωδης) : roundish

gongyloides (γογγυλοειδης) : roundish

Gonia (γωνια, *f.*) : angle, corner

Gony (γονυ, *n.*) : knee, node (of grass)

good : *see* agathos

Grace : *see* Charis

Gramma (γραμμα, *n.*) : written character, letter, writing

Gramme (γραμμη, *f.*) : line, stroke of a pen

Grapes, bunch of : *see* Botrys

Graphe (γραφη, *f.*) : drawing, picture, writing

Graphis (γραφις, *f.*) : pencil

Grass : *see* Agrostis, Chloe

Greave : *see* Cneme

green : *see* chloros

gymnos (γυμνος) : naked, unclad, unarmed, stripped

Gyne (γυνη, *f.*) : woman, a female

gyros (γυρος) : rounded, curved

Gyros (γυρος, *m.*) : ring, circle

Haema (αἱμα, *n.*) : blood

Hair : *see* Chaete, Come, Thrix, Trichion

hairy : *see* dasys, lasios

half : *see* hemi-

Hals, halos (ἁλς, ἁλος, *m.*) : salt

Hare : *see* Lagos

Head-band : *see* Mitra

Head-covering : *see* Calymma

Heap : *see* Soros

Heart : *see* Cardia

heavy : *see* barys

Hedgehog : *see* Echinos

hedys (ἡδυς) : pleasant to the taste or smell

helicoides (ἑλικοειδης) : of winding or spiral form

Helios (ἡλιος, *m.*) : sun

B.L.—K

Helix (ἑλιξ, *f.*) : anything of spiral shape

helodes (ἑλωδης) : frequenting marshes

Hem : *see* Loma

Hemera (ἡμερα, *f.*) : day

hemi- (ἡμι-) : *prefix* half-

hesperos (ἑσπερος) : of evening, western

heteros (ἑτερος) : of another kind, different

holos (ὁλος) : whole, entire

homalos (ὁμαλος) : even, level

Honey : *see* Meli

Hood : *see* Calymma

Hook : *see* Ancistron

Horn : *see* Ceras

Husks : *see* Achyron

Hyalos (ὑαλος, *f.*) : glass

Hydor (ὑδωρ, *n.*) : water

hygros (ὑγρος) : wet, moist

Hyle (ὑλη, *f.*) : forest, woodland

Hymen (ὑμην, *m.*) : thin skin, membrane

hyper (ὑπερ) : over, above

hypo (ὑπο) : under, beneath

hypsi- (ὑψι-) : *prefix,* on high, aloft

Hystera (ὑστερα, *f.*) : womb

-idion (-ιδιον, *n.*) : *in compounds, a diminutive suffix,* e.g. oinidion (οἰνιδιον), poor wine

inside : *see* entos

Internode : *see* Cneme

Ion (ιον) : violet

Ios (ιος) : poison, rust

isos (ισος) : equal

K : *see under* C

Keel : *see* Tropis

Kidney : *see* Nephros

Knee : *see* Gony

lagaros (λαγαρος) : thin, narrow, lanky.

Lagos (λαγως, *m.*) : hare

lanky : *see* lagaros

large : *see* macros

lasios (λασιος) : shaggy, woolly

Laurel : *see* Daphne

Leaf : *see* Phyllon

Lecanos, Lecanon (λεκανος, *m.* ; λεκανον, *n.*) : wine-bowl

Lecythos (ληκυθος, *f.*) : oil-flask

Leek : *see* Prason

Legging: *see* **Cnemis**

leios (λειος): smooth to the touch, e.g. **leiophloios** (λειοφλοιος), smooth-barked; **leiophyllos** (λειοφυλλος), smooth-leaved

Leon, leontos (λεων, λεοντος, *m.*): lion

Lepis, lepidos (λεπις, λεπιδος, *f.*): scale (of fish, snake), flake

leptos (λεπτος): fine, thin, slender, weak, e.g. **leptoblastos** (λεπτοβλαστος), with feeble shoots; **leptorrhizos** (λεπτορριζος), with thin delicate root

Leucon (λευκον, *n.*): white colour, e.g. **leucanthemon** (λευκανθεμον, *n.*), white flower; **leucanthes** (λευκανθης), white-flowering; **leucocarpos** (λευκοκαρπος), yielding white fruit

level (even): *see* **homalos**

Lichen (λειχην, *m.*): tree-moss, lichen, liverwort

Life: *see* **Bios**

Lily: *see* **Crinon, Lirion**

Limon (λειμων, *m.*): moist grassy place, meadow

Lion: *see* **Leon**

Lip: *see* **Cheilos**

Lirion (λειριον, *n.*): white lily

Lithos (λιθος, *m.*): stone

Lobos (λοβος, *m.*): lobe of the ear, capsule or pod

Loma (λωμα, *n.*): hem, fringe, border

long: *see* **dolichos**

Lophos (λοφος, *m.*): crest

low-growing: *see* **chamae-**

loving: *see* **phil-**

loxos (λοξος): slanting, oblique, cross-wise

macros (μακρος): large

malacos (μαλακος): soft to the touch

Mallos (μαλλος, *m.*): flock of wool, e.g. **mallotos** (μαλλωτος), fleecy, lined with wool

many: *see* **plei-**

Mark: *see* **Sema**

marshes, of: *see* **helodes, telmatiaeos**

Meadow: *see* **Limon, Nomos**

Mecon (μηκων, *f.*): poppy

megalo- (μεγαλο), **megas** (μεγας): big, large

melas (μελας): black, dark, e.g. **melanostictos** (μελανοστικτος), black-spotted

Meli (μελι, *n.*): honey

Melon (μηλον, *n.*): apple or other tree-fruit

Membrane: *see* **Hymen**

Mene (μηνη, *f.*): moon

Meris (μερις, *f.*): part, portion

mesos (μεσος): middle, in the middle

meta- (μετα): *in compounds*, changed

micro- (μικρος): small, little, e.g. **microcarpos** (μικροκαρπος), bearing small fruit

middle: *see* **mesos**

Milk: *see* **Gala**

Mitra (μιτρα, *f.*): head-band, head-dress

moist: *see* **hygros**

monos (μονος): alone, solitary

Moon: *see* **Mene**

Morphe (μορφη, *f.*): form, shape

Mound: *see* **Soros**

Mountain: *see* **Oreo-, Oros**

Mouse: *see* **Mys**

Mouth: *see* **Stoma**

Murder: *see* **Ctonos, Phonos**

Mushroom: *see* **Myces**

Myces (μυκης, *m.*): mushroom or other fungus

myrios (μυριος): numberless, countless

myristicos (μυριστικος): fragrant

Myron (μυρον, *n.*): sweet oil, perfume

Mys (μυς, *m.*): mouse or rat

naked: *see* **gymnos**

nanos, nannos (νανος, ναννος): dwarf

narrow: *see* **stenos**, *also* **lagaros**

Navel: *see* **Omphalos**

near: *see* **para**

Neighbour: *see* **Geton, Giton**

Nema (νημα, *n.*): thread

neos (νεος): young, new

Nephros (νεφρος, *m.*): kidney

Nesos (νησος, *f.*): island

Net: *see* **Dictyon**

Neuron (νευρον, *n.*): sinew, nerve

Night: *see* **Nyx**

Node: *see* **Gony**

Nomos (νομος, *m.*): pasture

nothos (νοθος): bastard, base-born

Noton (νωτον, *n.*): the back

Notos (νοτος, *m.*): south wind, south or south-west quarter

Notos (νωτος, m.) : the back
numberless : see myrios
Nut : see Caryon
nyctios (νυκτιος) : of the night, nocturnal
Nyx, nyctos (νυξ, νυκτος, f.) : night

oblique : see plagios
ochros (ὠχρος) : pale, wan, sallow, pale yellow, e.g. ochroleucos (ὠχρολευκος), whitish-yellow, yellowish-white
odont- (ὀδοντ-) : relating to teeth
Odour : see Osme
Odus, odontos (ὀδους, ὀδοντος, m.): tooth
Oenos (οἰνος, m.) : wine
Offspring : see Gone
Oil-flask : see Lecythos
oligos (ὀλιγος) : little, small, few, e.g. oligophyllos (ὀλιγοφυλλος), having few leaves
Omma (ὀμμα, n.) : eye
Omphalos (ὀμφαλος, m.) : navel, central part of flower containing seed-vessel
Onos (ὀνος, m., f.) : ass
Onyx (ὀνυξ, m.) : talons, claws, nail, hence clawed base of petal
oodes (ὠωδης) : egg-like
ophio- (ὀφιο-) : in compounds, relating to snakes
Ophis (ὀφις, m.) : snake
opisthen (ὀπισθεν) : behind, at the back
opse (ὀψε) : late
Opsis (ὀψις, f.) : aspect, appearance, hence resemblance
oreo-, ori- (ὀρεο-, ὀρει-) : in compounds, mountain-, e.g. origenes (ὀρειγενης), mountain-born
ores- (ὀρεσ-) : in compounds, mountain-, e.g. oresbios (ὀρεσβιος), living on mountains
Ornis (ὀρνις, m.) : bird
Oros (ὀρος, n.) : mountain, hill
orthos (ὀρθος) : straight, upright
Osme (ὀσμη, f.) : smell, odour, fragrance
Osteon (ὀστεον, n.) : bone
Otion (ὠτιον, n.) : auricle, little ear
outside : see ectos
oxys (ὀξυς) : sharp, keen, shrill, pungent, acid, e.g. oxyodus (ὀξυοδους), with sharp teeth ; oxyphyllos (ὀξυφυλλος), with pointed leaves

pachys (παχυς) : thick, stout, e.g. pachycalamos (παχυκαλαμος), thick-stalked
Paegma (παιγμα, n.) : play, sport
palaeos (παλαιος) : old, ancient
Pale : see ochros
pan- (παν-) : as prefix in compounds, all
para (παρα) : beside, near
Parrot : see Psittacos
Part : see Meris
Partition : see Phragma
Pedestal : see Basis
Pedilon (πεδιλον, n.) : sandal, shoe, boot
penta- (πεντα-) : in compounds, five-
Pera (περα, f.) : leathern pouch, wallet
Perfume : see Myron, Osme
peri (περι) : round about, all round, e.g. pericarpion (περικαρπιον), case of fruit or seed, pod, husk
Petalon (πεταλον, n.) : leaf ; in modern botany, petal
Petra (πετρα, n.) : rock, e.g. petrobaticos (πετροβατικος), given to rock climbing
phaeo- (φαιο-) : dark
phaneros (φανερος) : evident, visible, conspicuous
phil-, philo- (φιλ-, φιλο-) : in compounds, loving, fond of, e.g. philodendros (φιλοδενδρος), fond of trees
philos (φιλος) : beloved, dear
phlebodes (φλεβωδης) : full of veins, with large veins
Phleps (φλεψ, φλεβος, f.) : blood-vessel, vein
Phloios (φλοιος, m.) : bark of trees
phoeniceos (φοινικεος) : purple-red, crimson, red
Pholis, pholidos (φολις, φολιδος, f.) : horny scale, e.g. of reptiles
Phonos (φονος, m.) : murder
Phragma (φραγμα, n.) : fence, screen, partition
phoros (φορος) : bearing, carrying
Phyllon (φυλλον, n.) : leaf
Phylon (φυλον, n.) : race, tribe, class
Physa (φυσα, f.) : bellows, bladder, e.g. physetos (φυσητος), blown, blown out
Phyton (φυτον, n.) : plant
picros (πικρος) : bitter, sharp, pungent in taste

Pilos (πιλος, *m.*): anything made of felt, *especially* a hat

Pine : *see* Pitys

Pipe (tube) : *see* Aulos, Siphon, Solen

Pitys (πιτυς, *f.*) : pine

plagios (πλαγιος) : placed sideways, sloping, oblique

Plant : *see* Phyton

platys (πλατυς) : wide, broad, e.g. platyphyllos (πλατυφυλλος), broad-leaved

pleasant : *see* hedys

plectos (πλεκτος) : plaited, twisted

Plectron (πληκτρον, *n.*) : something to strike with, *hence* a cock's spur

Plegma (πλεγμα, *n.*) : anything twined or twisted

plei- (πλει) : *in compounds*, many-

Pleura (πλευρα, *f.*) : rib

Ploce (πλοκη, *f.*) : anything twisted or woven, web

Podion (ποδιον, *n.*) : foot, e.g. of a vase

poecilos (ποικιλος) : several-coloured, spotted, dappled

Pogon (πωγων, *m.*) : beard

Point : *see* Acis, Glochin

Point, highest : *see* Acme

-pointed : *see* oxys

Poison : *see* Ios

Polecat : *see* Galee

poly- (πολυ-) : *in compounds*, much-, many-

Poppy : *see* Mecon

porphyreos (πορφυρεος) : purple, e.g. porphyranthes (πορφυρανθης), with purple blossom; porphyronotos (πορφυρονωτος), purple-backed

Poros (πορος, *m.*) : ford, strait, passage, pore, opening

Potamos (ποταμος, *m.*) : river

Prason (πρασον, *n.*) : leek

Present (gift) : *see* Doron

Prickle : *see* Acantha

proteros (προτερος) : earlier

protos (πρωτος) : first, foremost

Psammos (ψαμμος, *f.*) : sand

psilos (ψιλος) : bare, stripped of hair, smooth

Psittacos (ψιττακος, *m.*) : parrot

Pteris (πτερις, *f.*) : fern

Pteron (πτερον, *n.*) : feather, wing

Ptyches (πτυχες, *f.*) : folds

purple : *see* phoeniceos, porphyreos

-pus (-πους) : *in compounds*, -footed

Pyr (πυρ, *n.*) : fire

Pyramis (πυραμις, *f.*) : pyramid

Pyren (πυρην, *m.*) : fruit-stone

Pyros (πυρος, *m.*) : wheat

Ragged : *see* rhacois

Rat : *see* Mys

Ray : *see* Actis

red : *see* erythros, phoeniceos

Reed : *see* Calamos

Reproductive organs : *see* Gone

Resemblance : *see* Opsis

Rhabdos (ῥαβδος, *f.*) : rod, wand

rhabdotos (ῥαβδωτος) : striped

Rhachis (ῥαχις, *f.*) : backbone, midrib of a leaf

rhacois, rhacodytos (ῥακοεις, ῥακοδυτος) : ragged, torn, tattered

rhaibos (ῥαιβος) : crooked, bent

Rhipis, rhipidos (ῥιπις, ῥιπιδος, *f.*) : fan

Rhiza (ῥιζα, *f.*) : root

rhodo- (ῥοδο-) : *as prefix in compounds*, rose-, rosy

Rhodon (ῥοδον, *f.*) : rose

Rhynchos (ῥυγχος, *n.*) : snout, muzzle, beak

rhysos (ῥυσος) : shrivelled, wrinkled

Rhytis, rhytidos (ῥυτις, ῥυτιδος, *f.*) : pucker, wrinkled, e.g. rhytidodes (ῥυτιδωδης), wrinkled-looking

Rib : *see* Pleura

River : *see* Potamos

Rock : *see* Petra

Rod : *see* Rhabdos

Root : *see* Rhiza

Rope : *see* Sira

Rose : *see* Rhodon

rosy : *see* rhodo-

rounded : *see* gyros

roundish : *see* gongyloides, gongylodes

Row : *see* Stichos

Rust : *see* Ios

Salt : *see* Hals

Sand : *see* Psammos

Sandal : *see* Pedilon

sapros (σαπρος) : rotten, putrid

Sarx (σαρξ, *f.*) : flesh

Scale : *see* Lepis, Pholis

scato- (σκατο-) : relating to dung

scented : *see* myristicos

schistos (σχιστος): cleft, divided

Scia (σκια, f.): shadow

Sciadion (σκιαδιον, n.): sunshade, parasol, umbel

scleros (σκληρος): hard

Scyphos (σκυφος, m.): cup

Sea: see Thalassa

Seed: see Sperma, also Coccos

Sema (σημα, n.): sign, mark, token

Semia (σημεια, f.): military standard, vexillum

Seris (σερις, f.): endive, chicory

Shaft: see Dory

shaggy: see lasios

Shape: see Morphe

sharp: see oxys

Shoe: see Pedilon

Shoot: see Blastos, Clados

shrivelled: see rhysos

Sideros (σιδηρος, m.): iron

silvery: see argyros

Siphon (σιφων, m.): tube, pipe

Sira (σειρα, n.): cord, rope

Skin: see Derma

slender: see lagaros, leptos

Slice: see Tomos

sloping: see plagios

Smell: see Osme

smooth: see psilos, leios

Snake: see Ophis

Snout: see Rhynchos

Snow: see Chion

soft: see malacos

Solen (σωλην, m.): pipe

solitary: see monos

Soma (σωμα, n.): body

Soros (σωρος, m.): heap, mound

South: see Notos

Spathe (σπαθη, f.): a broad flat blade; in modern botany, spathe

Spear: see Dory

Sperma (σπερμα, n.): seed

Sphaera (σφαιρα, f.): ball, globe, sphere

Spike: see Stachys

Spine (thorn): see Acantha

Spira (σπειρα, f.): anything twisted, wound, coiled

Spiral: see Helix, Spira, also helicoides

Spora (σπορα, f.): seed; in modern botany, spore

spotted: see stictos

Spur: see Centron, Plectron

Stachys (σταχυς, m.): ear of corn; in modern botany, spike

Stalix (σταλιξ, f.): stake

Standard: see Semia

Staphyle (σταφυλη, f.): bunch of grapes

Stege (στεγη, f.), Stegos (στεγος, n.): shelter

Stele (στηλη, f.): monument, column, pillar

Stelma (στελμα, n.): crown, garland, wreath

Stem: see Caulos

Stema (στημα, n.); penis, stamen

Stemma (στεμμα, n.): wreath, garland

Stemon (στημων, m.): thread; in modern botany, stamen

stenos (στενος): narrow, e.g. stenophyllos (στενοφυλλος), narrow-leaved

Stephane (στεφανη, f.), Stephanos (στεφανος, m.): something which surrounds or encircles, hence crown, wreath

Stephos (στεφος, n.): crown, wreath, garland

Stichos (στιχος, m.): row

stictos (στικτος): pricked, tattooed, spotted, dappled

Stigma, stigmatos (στιγμα, στιγματος, n.): tattoo-mark, mark, spot; in modern botany, stigma

Stoma (στομα, n.): mouth, opening

Stone, mineral: see Lithos

Stone of a fruit: see Pyren

stout: see pachys

straight: see orthos

strangle: see ancho, also Ctonos

streptos (στρεπτος): twisted

striped: see rhabdotos

Strobilus (στροβιλος, m.): round ball, spinning top, pine; in modern botany, a cone or cone-like structure

Strophe (στροφη, f.): turning, twist

Stylos (στυλος, m.): pillar, wooden pole, writing implement (through confusion with Latin stilus; see p. 42; hence in modern botany, style)

Sun: see Helios

surrounding: see peri

Swamp: see Telma

sweet: see glycys

Swelling: see Tylos

Sword: see Xiphos

Syce (συκη, f.): fig-tree
Syrinx (συριγξ, f.): pipe

Taenia (ταινια, f.): band, head-band, ribbon
Tail: *see* Ura
Talon: *see* Onyx
tattered: *see* rhacois
Tattoo-mark: *see* Stigma
Taxis (ταξις, f.): arrangement, order, regularity
Teat: *see* Thele
Telma (τελμα, n.): standing water, pond, marsh, swamp; e.g. telmatiaeos (τελματιαιος), of a marsh
ten: *see* deca
Thalassa (θαλασσα, f.): sea
Thallos (θαλλος, m.): branch; *in modern botany*, thallus
Thamnos (θαμνος, m.): bush, shrub
Thece (θηκη, f.): case, chest, container
Thele (θηλη, f.): teat, nipple
thelys (θηλυς): female
thick: *see* pachys
Thorn: *see* Acantha
Thread: *see* Nema
Thrix (θριξ, f.): hair
Tomos (τομος, m.): slice, piece
Tongue: *see* Glossa
Tooth: *see* Odus
trachys (τραχυς): rough, shaggy
Tragos (τραγος, m.): he-goat
Trema (τρημα, n.): aperture, opening
triangular: *see* deltoides
trich- (τριχ-): *in compounds*, hair-
Trichion (τριχιον, n.): small hair
Trochos (τροχος, m.): wheel
Tropis (τροπις, f.): keel of ship
Tube: *see* Aulos, Siphon, Solen
Twist: *see* Plegma, Ploce, Strophe
twisted: *see* plectos
Tylos (τυλος, m.): callus, lump, swelling, knob
Typos (τυπος, m.): blow, impression, print, replica, pattern, model, etc.; *hence in modern botany*, type

Umbel: *see* Sciadion
uneven: *see* anisos
upon: *see* epi

upright: *see* orthos
Ura (ουρα, f.): tail

Veil: *see* Calyptra
Vein: *see* Phleps
Vessel (receptacle): *see* Angion
Violet: *see* Ion
Viper: *see* Echidna

Wallet: *see* Pera
Water: *see* Hydor
Weasel: *see* Galee
Web: *see* Ploce
western: *see* hesperos
Wheat: *see* Pyros
Wheel: *see* Trochos
white: *see* leucos
whole: *see* holos
Wilderness (desert): *see* Eremia
Wine: *see* Oenos
Wing: *see* Pteron
Woman: *see* Gyne
Womb: *see* Gone, Hystera
Wood (forest): *see* Hyle
Wood (timber): *see* Xylon
Wool: *see* Erion, Mallos
woolly: *see* lasios
Wreath: *see* Stelma, Stemma, Stephane, Stephanos
wrinkled: *see* rhysos, Rhytis
Writing: *see* Gramma, Graphe

xanth- (ξανθ-): *in compounds*, yellow-
xanthos (ξανθος): yellow, e.g. xantholeucos (ξανθολευκος), pale yellow
xeros (ξηρος): dry
xiph- (ξιφ-): *in compounds*, sword-
Xiphos (ξιφος, n.): sword
xuthos (ξουθος): *in botany*, golden yellow
Xylon (ξυλον, n.): wood, timber, log

yellow: *see* xanthos
Yoke: *see* Zygon

Zone (ζωνη, f.): belt, girdle, originally a woman's
Zoster (ζωστηρ, m.): belt, girdle, originally a warrior's
Zygon (ζυγον, n.), zygos (ζυγος, m.): yoke

REFERENCES

ANDRÉ, J. 1956. *Lexique des Termes de Botanique en Latin (Études et Commentaires* 23). Paris.
—— 1959. *Notes de Lexicographie botanique grecque.* Paris.
BROWN, R. W. 1956. *Composition of scientific Words: a Manual of Methods and a Lexicon of Materials.* Revised ed. Washington, D.C.
CARNOY, A. 1959. *Dictionnaire étymologique des Noms grecs des Plantes.* Louvain.
DANSER, B. H. 1935. Grammatical objections to the International Rules of Botanical Nomenclature, adopted at Cambridge in 1930. *Blumea*, I: 295-304.
GREENE, E. L. 1909. *Landmarks of botanical History.* Washington, D.C.
INTERNATIONAL COMMISSION ON ZOOLOGICAL NOMENCLATURE. 1961. *International Code of Zoological Nomenclature.* London.
JAEGER, E. C. 1955. *A Source-Book of biological Names and Terms.* 3rd ed. Springfield, Illinois.
KRETSCHMER, P. 1899. *Sprachregeln für die Bildung und Betonung zoologischer und botanischer Namen.* Berlin.
LIDDELL, H. G., & SCOTT, R. 1940. *A Greek-English Lexicon.* New ed., revised by H. S. Jones and R. McKenzie. 2 vols. Oxford.
MAYER, A. 1957. Zur Chronologie der lat. Nomina auf *-er.* *Mnēmēs Charin, Gedenkschrift Paul Kretschmer* (herausg. H. Kronasser), 2: 29-35.
NYBAKKEN, O. E. 1960. *Greek and Latin in scientific Terminology.* Ames, Iowa.
PETZOLD, W. 1886. *Die Bedeutung des Griechischen für das Verständnis der Pflanzennamen.* Brunswick.
ROMAGNESI, H. 1940. Les langues anciennes et la mycologie. *Revue Mycol.* 5: Suppl. 6-10.
SAINT-LAGER, J. B. 1880. Réforme de la nomenclature botanique. *Ann. Soc. Bot. Lyon*, 7: 1-154.
—— 1881. Nouvelles remarques sur la nomenclature botanique. *Ann. Soc. Bot. Lyon*, 8: 149-203.
SAALFELD, G. A. E. A. 1884. *Tensaurus Italograecus.* Vienna.
SAUNIER, J. 1956. *Vocabulaire grec, précédé d'une Introduction sur la Formation des Mots.* 2nd ed. Paris.
SMITH, F. K., & MELLUISH, T. W. 1947. *Teach Yourself Greek.* London.
SPRAGUE, T. A. 1935. The gender of generic names; a vindication of Article 72(2). *Kew Bull.*, 1935: 545-557.
STRÖMBERG, R. 1937. *Theophrastea: Studien zur botanischen Begriffsbildung (Göteborgs Kungl. Vet. Vitt. Handl.*, V Följd., Ser. A, 6, no. 4). Göteborg.
—— 1940. *Griechische Pflanzennamen (Göteborgs Högskolas Årsskr.* 46, no. 1). Göteborg.
WEISE, O. 1893. Zur Latinisierung griechischer Wörter. *Arch. latein. Lexikogr.*, 8: 339-368.
WERNER, C. F. 1956. *Wortelemente lateinisch-griechischer Fachausdrücke in aer Biologie.* Leipzig [2nd ed., 1961].
WIKÉN, E. 1951. *Latin för Botanister och Zoologer.* Malmö.
WOODS, R. S. 1944. *The Naturalist's Lexicon, a List of Classical Greek and Latin Words used or suitable for Use in biological Nomenclature.* Pasadena, California.
ZABINKOVA, N. 1968. Generic names ending in -is and the determination of their stems. *Taxon* 17: 19-33.

CHAPTER XX

Formation of Names and Epithets in Latin

Saepe enim et verba non latina dico ut vos intelligatis. [Often indeed I use non-Latin words in order that you may understand.]
ST. AUGUSTINE OF HIPPO (A.D. 354–430)
Ennar. in Psalm cxxxiii, 8

The discovery of new organisms and the need to provide them and also hitherto misnamed organisms with names, which must not duplicate names already used, together make it necessary for systematists continually to publish new names. Such names are mostly generic or specific. As stated in the *International Code of botanical Nomenclature* (1961): 'The name of a genus is a substantive in the singular number or a word treated as such. It may be taken from any source whatever and may even be composed in an absolutely arbitrary manner.' Likewise 'the epithet of a species may be taken from any source whatever and may even be composed arbitrarily'. Botanical nomenclature has greatly changed since Linnaeus ruled in 1737 (*Critica botanica,* no. 229): 'Generic names which have not a root derived from Greek or Latin are to be rejected'. Nevertheless the *International Code* recommends botanists who are forming names 'to use Latin terminations in so far as possible; to avoid names not readily adaptable to the Latin tongue; not to make names which are very long or difficult to pronounce in Latin'. It is based on the principle that 'scientific names of taxonomic groups are treated as Latin regardless of origin'.

SOURCES OF NAMES

Rabelais (c. 1495–1553) introduced into his account of the herb 'Pantagruelion', i.e. hemp (*Cannabis sativa*), an essay on the origin of plant names (*Pantagruel,* 3 cap. 50; 1546), noting that some plants were named after their first discoverer, cultivator, user, etc., as *Mercurialis* from Mercury, *Gentiana* from Gentius; some from their provenance, as *Ligusticum* from Liguria, *Stoechas* from the Stoechades, etc.; others from their reputed virtues, as *Aristolochia, Malva*, etc.; others by contrast or irony, as *Holosteon* which means 'all bone, because on the contrary there is no herb more fragile and tender'; yet others by allusion to mythological transformations, as *Daphne, Narcissus*, etc.; some from resemblance, as *Hippuris*, like a horse's tail, *Alopecuros*, like a fox's tail, *Delphinium*, like a dolphin, etc. According to their origins the majority of generic names still come within these Rabelaisian groups. Botanists naming a new genus usually try to find a distinctive feature and coin a name by combining Greek or Latin words to express this, or they name it after a person, for preference its discoverer or someone who has studied the group, occasionally a personage of antiquity, as in the names *Caligula, Periclesia, Semiramisia, Proclesia, Sophoclesia, Lysiclesia, Socratesia, Polyboea, Themistoclesia*, etc., given to genera of *Ericaceae*.[1] Less often they adopt or adapt a native name, e.g. *Aucuba, Kokoona, Madhuca, Retama*, or modify the name of a related genus, e.g. by adding prefixes or suffixes such as *Para-, Neo-, -ella, -astrum, -opsis*, etc., to it, or concoct an anagram from such a generic name (see below). The only limitations are those imposed voluntarily by the good taste and common sense of the author (cf. Rowley, 1956). No modern botanist as yet has disregarded the convenience of others by coining generic names quite so long as Dybowski's *Swartschewskiechinogammarus, Toxophthalmoechinogammarus* and *Cornutokytodermogammarus*, although *Pteropentacoilanthus* comes close to them, or has seen fit to suggest a series of amorous incidents with Dolly, Flory, Isa, Mary, Nanny, Peggy, Phyllis and Polly by means of names such as Kirkaldy's *Dolichisme, Florichisme, Isachisme, Marichisme, Nanichisme, Peggichisme, Phyllochisme* and *Polichisme* scarcely relevant to the bugs thus designated.

THE LINNAEAN CANONS

The tendency of early eighteenth-century botanists to use generic names such as *Anapodophyllum, Hydroceratophyllum, Hypophyllocarpodendron*, was effectively checked by Linnaeus from 1737 onwards, partly on aesthetic grounds, mainly, however, because he believed that naturalists should be able to memorize both the names and characters of genera (cf. Cain, 1958; Stearn, 1959) and that awkward, uncouth, very long or meaningless names laid an unnecessary burden on the

---

[1] *Diogenes rotundus*, found in water-tubs, is however, a unicellular green alga.

memory. At the age of twenty-nine he accordingly published in his *Critica botanica* (1737) a series of rules which guided him in his own publications, established standards of procedure for his followers, and led him to discard on a grand scale the names used by his predecessors. As E. L. Greene (1906) observed : 'Such expurgation of generic nomenclature as was then made could never have been effected through the mere will of one individual reformer. Botanists in general as men of culture must have been already more or less disgusted with the abundance of cheap and easily made names that were current.' Linnaeus provided welcome means of reform.

Of those rules which concern the names themselves the following [1] merit attention, not least because the more rigid of Linnaeus's followers, notably Schreber, likewise changed names which did not conform to them.

220 'No sane person introduces "primitives" as generic names. By "primitives", as is well known, are meant words which have no root, no derivation, no significance. What I press is that we should do nothing irrational: wherefore, if we would not be considered utter barbarians, let us not invent names which cannot be derived from some root or other.'

221 'Generic names formed from two complete and distinct words are to be banished from the commonwealth of botany.' Linnaeus therefore replaced the two-word generic name *Caryophyllus aromaticus* by *Caryophyllus*; *Primula veris* by *Primula*, and so on. Later, however, he used many such two-word names as specific epithets (for lists, see Nieuwland, 1911 ; Hylander, 1954).

222 'Generic names compounded of two entire Latin words are scarcely to be tolerated. To make generic names is freely allowed in the Greek language, but not in the Latin. . . . Anyone can readily perceive for himself that Latin words do not combine so easily as Greek.' Linnaeus, nevertheless, accepted such compounds as *Sapindus*, *Passiflora*, *Sanguisorba*, *Saxifraga* and *Sempervivum*.

223 'Hybrid generic names, namely those made from a Greek word compounded with a Latin word, and the like are not to be recognized.'

224 'Generic names compounded of two words, one a piece of a generic term for plants, and an entire word, are unworthy of botanists.' Linnaeus accordingly rejected as generic names *Anemone-Ranunculus*, *Bellis-leucanthemum*, *Chenopodio-morus*, *Lilio-asphodelus* and the like.

225 'A generic name to which one or two syllables are prefixed, to make it denote an entirely different genus from that which it denoted before, is not to be admitted.' Such names rejected by Linnaeus included *Bulbocastanum*, *Chamaebuxus*, *Chamaepericlymenum*, etc.

226 'Generic names ending in *-oides* are to be banished from the domain of botany.' On this matter of *-oides*, see Chapter XIX, p. 266.

---

[1] These are quoted from Sir Arthur Hort's English translation published by the Ray Society in 1938.

227 'Generic names made up of other generic names with a syllable added at the end are not satisfactory.' Names rejected by Linnaeus included those ending in *-ella*, e.g. *Acetosella*, *Cedronella*, in *-astrum*, e.g. *Bellidiastrum*, *Veronicastrum*, in *-aria*, e.g. *Linaria*, *Persicaria*, and in *-ago*, e.g. *Juncago*, *Erucago*.

228 'Generic names with a similar sound give a handle to confusion.' As examples Linnaeus listed, among others, *Alsine*, *Alsinoides*, *Alsinella*, *Alsinastrum*, *Alsinastroides*, *Casia*, *Cassia*, *Cassida*.

229 'Generic names which have not a root derived from Greek or Latin are to be rejected. . . . However, I retain barbarous names when I can obtain a root suggesting a possible derivation from Latin or Greek, in which case such names have the value for me of new coinages, e.g. *Datura*.'

235 'Generic names which are adjectival are less satisfactory than those which are substantives.' Nevertheless Linnaeus used the appropriate name *Gloriosa*.

236 'Generic names should not be misused in order to perpetuate the memory of Saints and men distinguished in some other branch of learning or to secure their favour.'

237 'Generic names taken from poetry or mythology, consecrated names of kings, and names of those who have advanced the study of botany I retain.' Those mentioned include *Andromeda*, *Circaea*, *Daphne*, *Atropa*, *Ixora*, *Nyssa*, *Gentiana*, *Eugenia*, *Asclepias*, *Bignonia* and *Cliffortia*.

238 'Generic names formed to preserve the memory of a botanist who has deserved well of the science I retain as a religious duty.' To this Linnaeus appended an account of links between botanists and the plants named after them, enabling the name to be kept ever in the memory, as *Bauhinia*, which 'has two-lobed leaves or two as it were growing from the same base, being called after the noble pair of brothers Bauhin'. In forming such names, the following points should be observed. 'It must be formed from his surname, not his first name', e.g. *Duranta* (not *Castorea*), *Isnardia* (not *Dantia*). 'One must take care that names do not occur which can be confused with something else.' Thus *Alpina* would be bad, *Alpinia* good. 'The pronunciation of the name should be made as easy as possible.' Hence Linnaeus adopted *Barleria* instead of *Barreliera*. 'Care must be taken that the names are uniform and that they end in *-a*, as though they were feminine substantives.' Thus Linnaeus preferred *Breynia* to *Breyniana*, *Brunia* to *Bruniades*, *Lewisania* to *Lewisanus*. 'Names that are too long must be cut down to avoid getting ell-long names.'

239 'Generic names which have been bestowed without harm to botany should, other things being equal, be allowed to pass.'

247 'Greek generic names are to be written in Latin characters.'

248 'The terminations of generic names and the pronunciation should be made as easy as possible.'

249 'Generic names an ell long, or difficult to pronounce, or unpleasant are to be avoided.' Linnaeus dealt drastically with such caconyms, as Rowley (1956) has termed them. For example, he shortened *Staphylodendron* to *Staphylaea*, *Anapodophyllum* to *Podophyllum*, *Ananthocyclus* to *Anacyclus*,

altered *Leontopetalon* to *Leontice* and substituted *Galanthus* for *Leuco-Narcisso-Lirion*.

Many of these canons have long been disregarded; indeed adherence to Nos. 225, 227 and 229 would deprive botany of the means by which many pleasing and useful names have been coined. Nevertheless, they ensured that modern botanical nomenclature at least began with a series of well-formed, euphonious and convenient names.

FORMATION OF COMPOUNDS IN LATIN

Although Latin does not so abound in compounds as Greek (see Chapter XIX), enough exist in classical Latin to provide models from which procedure can be deduced. The following notes are mostly taken from *Sprachregeln für die Bildung . . . botanischer Namen* 1899) by Paul Wilhelm Kretschmer (1866–1956), a distinguished German classical scholar and philologist, from 1899 to 1937 professor of linguistics at the university of Vienna, for many years editor of the periodical *Glotta*.

1 The first and each non-final component of a Latin compound consists of the stem of a word, to which is usually added the connecting vowel *-i-*. Thus from *flamma* (flame) is derived *flammicomus* (having fiery hair); from *aurum* (gold) *auricomus* (golden-haired); from *anguis* (snake) *anguitenens* (snake-holding); from *flos* (flower; gen. *floris*) *floriger* (flower-bearing); from *odor* (scent) *odorifer* (scented); from *rupes* (rock; gen. *rupis*) *rupicapra* (chamois). A few nouns, namely abstract nouns ending in *-or*, neuter nouns ending in *-us* (gen. *-eris*) and some such as *sanguis*, can form compounds from a shortened stem, e.g. from *vulnus* (wound) *vulnifer* (wound-bringing), *vulnificus* (wound-making); from *sanguis* (blood), *sanguisuga* (blood-sucker) and the alternative forms *sanguilentus* and *sanguinolentus* (bloody).

In classical Latin compounds, when a stem ended in *-i*, as in *gloria*, *medius*, *officium*, etc., this sufficed as a connecting vowel, a single *-i-* being used, instead of the *-ii-* which would result from joining the final *-i* of the stem and a connecting vowel *-i-*, hence *glorificus* (not *gloriificus*), *mediterraneus* (not *mediiterraneus*), *officiperda* (not *officiiperda*). In botanical Latin, however, when the stem of a generic name ends in *-i*, as in *Artemisia* and *Nerium*, this is now retained together with the connecting vowel *-i-*, as in *artemisiifolius* and *neriifolius*. When the stem does not end in *-i*, as in *Anemone*, *Hordeum*, *Halimum*, *Malva*, *Narcissus*, the case-ending is removed and replaced by a single *-i-*, as in *anemonifolius*, *halimifolius*, *malvifolius* and *narcissiflorus*. The stem of many masculine and neuter names plus the connecting vowel *-i* coincides in form with their genitive singular, e.g. *coronop-i-* and *coronopi* (genitive of *coronopus*), *thym-i-* and *thymi* (genitive of *thymus*). Thus, when Linnaeus replaced such pre-Linnaean phrase-names as *Ananthocyclus coronopi folio* (i.e. Ananthocyclus with the leaf of Coronopus) by the binomial *Cotula coronopifolia* and *Genista minima aethiopica foliis thymi confertis* (minute African Genista with crowded leaves of Thymus) by *Aspalathus thymifolia*, the resulting epithets (*coronopifolius, -a, -um, thymifolius, -a, -um,* etc.) were the same as if he had simply appended *-folius, -a, -um,* to the genitive singular. This coincidence obscured the grammatical nature of the connecting *-i-* and misled many later authors into forming epithets in this very manner, e.g. *erucaefolius* (from *Eruca,* gen. *Erucae*) instead of *erucifolius*; *tiliaefolius* (from *Tilia,* gen. *Tiliae*) instead of *tiliifolius,* and so on. This matter is discussed at length by Saint-Lager (1893). Fortunately under the *International Code of botanical Nomenclature* the use of a wrong connecting vowel or vowels in a name or an epithet is to be treated as an orthographic error and corrected.

Adjectives forming the first component are similarly treated, e.g. *alticaulis* (high-stemmed, with tall stems) and *altispex* (looking down from a height) from *altus* (high), *longicaulis* (long-stemmed) and *longipetalus* (long-petalled) from *longus* (long).

In late Latin particularly, but occasionally in classical Latin, owing to the influence of Greek, compounds were sometimes formed with *-o-* instead of *-i-* as a connecting vowel, e.g. *tunicopallium* from *tunica* and *pallium*; such words as *atropurpureus, atrovirens* and *albomarginatus,* are not to be treated as orthographical errors, but accepted as examples of standard procedure in botanical Latin for words beginning with *atro-* and *albo-.*

2 A preposition, an adverbial form or a numeral can serve as the first component of a Latin compound. Thus the preposition *per* (through, all over) when added to an adjective has an intensifying effect, e.g. *amarus* (bitter), *peramarus* (very bitter), *pusillus* (small), *perpusillus* (very small). The preposition *sub* (under, near), on the other hand, has a weakening effect, expressed by 'somewhat' or 'almost' or the termination '-ish', e.g. *subamarus* (somewhat bitter, bitterish), *subsessilis* (almost sessile), or indicates a lower part, e.g. *subcavus* (hollow below), *subscriptus* (written beneath). For other examples, see Chapter X, p. 225. Adverbial forms may be fused with participles, e.g. *suaveolens* (sweet-smelling, fragrant) from *suavis* (sweet) and *olens* (smelling), *altescandens* (high-climbing) from *alte* (highly, on high) and *scandens* (climbing), *longerepens* (long-creeping) from *longe* (long, lengthwise) and *repens* (creeping). Numbers are expressed by *uni-* (1-), e.g. *uniflorus* (one-flowered), *bi-* (2-), e.g. *bifolius* (two-leaved), *tri-* (3-), e.g. *trifoliolatus* (with three leaflets), *quadr-* (4-), *quadri-, quadru-* used before *p* and *m,* e.g. *quadrangulus* (four-angled), *quadridentatus* (four-toothed), *quadrupes* (four-footed), and so on; for further examples, including those of Greek origin, see Chapter VIII, p. 113.

3 The stem of a verb is rarely employed in Latin as the first component of a compound. When so used, it is followed by *-i-,* e.g. *vomificus* (emetic) from *vomo* (vomit).

4 The final vowel of the first component is usually but not invariably cut out when the next component begins with a vowel. Stems of one syllable retain their vowel. Examples are *aequaevus* (of the same age; from *aequus* and *aevus*), *multangulus* and *multiangulus* (many-angled, polygonal; from

multus and *angulus*), *semustus* and *semiustus* (half-burned; from *semi* and *ustus*), *triangulus* (three-angled).

5 In forming adjectives the last component of a compound either stands unaltered or is given a special adjectival ending. Thus the last component is unchanged in the adjective *quadrupes* (four-footed; from *quadrus* and *pes*) and *tricolor* (three-coloured; from *tri-* and *color*). Nouns of the First and Second Declensions (see Chapter V, pp. 68, 70) are converted into adjectives ending in *-us, -a, -um*, e.g. *auricomus* (golden-haired; from *aurum* and *coma*), or in *-is, -e*, e.g. *multiformis* (many-shaped; from *multus* and *forma*), *perennis* (perennial, from *per* and *annus*), *multiramis* (many-branched, from *multus* and *ramus*). Nouns of the Third Declension form adjectives ending in *-us, -a, -um*, e.g. *inodorus* (without smell, from *in-* and *odor*). Nouns of the Fourth Declension form adjectives ending in *-us, -a, -um*, e.g. *multifructus* (many-fruited, from *multus* and *fructus*), or *-is, -e*, e.g. *bicornis* (two-horned, from *bi-* and *cornu*). Compounds formed from *caput* (head) end in *-ceps*, e.g. *multiceps* (many-headed). The terminations *-ius, -ium, -ia* can be used with stems of any group, e.g. *brevinodius* (with a short nodes, from *brevis* and *nodus*).

6 The last component of a compound adjective can also be derived from a verb and usually ends in *-us*, or *-a* when of active meaning, in *-tus* like a participle when of passive meaning. Thus from *vagor* (to wander, range) is derived *montivagus* (mountain-roaming), *nemorivagus* (wandering in woods), etc., from *colo* (cultivate, dwell, inhabit), *undicola* (dwelling in the sea), etc. The verbs *fero* and *gero* (bear, carry) have given numerous compounds in *-fer* and *-ger*, e.g. *florifer* and *floriger* (flower-bearing), *frondifer* (leaf-bearing), *fructifer* (fruit-bearing). Of passive meaning are compounds ending in *-fidus*, e.g. *multifidus* (many-cleft; from *findere*, to split), and *-gena*, e.g. *montigena* (mountain-born; from *gignere*, to bring forth). The perfect passive participle can also be used, e.g. *biformatus* (two-shaped; from *formare*, to shape).

7 The gender, grammatical nature and meaning of a word in Latin can be modified or changed by the use of an appropriate suffix.

A substantival or noun suffix is a component added to the end of the stem or base of a word which converts it into a noun, if a verb, or modifies its meaning, if already a noun. Suffixes (see Chapter XXI) play an important part in the formation of Latin words. Each suffix has characteristics of its own, which concern its general meaning or effect, the kind of word to which it can be attached and the gender which it gives. Thus *-arium* (n.) indicates a place where something is found, usually a receptacle, and hence is attached to the stem of a noun, e.g. *herbarium* (from *herba*, plant), *nectarium* (from *nectar*, nectar); *-orium* (n.) indicates a place or a space of time in which something happens or is done and hence is attached to the stem of the supine of a verb, e.g. *laboratorium* (laboratory, place of work) from *laboratum* (fit to toil), the supine of *laborare* (to toil, take pains). The suffix *-etum* (n.) indicates a habitat dominated by the plant named in the stem, e.g. *quercetum* (an oak-wood) from *quercus* (oak).

The suffixes *-io* (f.) and *-ura* (f.; to be distinguished from the Greek οὐρα or *ura*, tail) designate either an action or the result of an action and hence are attached to the stem of the supine of a verb, e.g. *collectio* (collection ; from *colligere*, to gather), *sectio* (section ; from *secare*, to cut), *fissura* (cleft ; from *findere*, to split). The suffixes *-men* (n.) and *-mentum* (n.), like the Greek *-ma* (n.), likewise designate an action or the result of an action, e.g. *semen* (seed ; from *serere*, to sow), *fragmentum* (a piece broken off ; from *frangere*, to break), *segmentum* (a piece cut off ; from *secare*, to cut). The suffixes *-or* (m.) and *-rix* (f.) indicate the agent of an action and hence are also attached to the stem of the supine of a verb, e.g. *collector* (collector ; from *colligere*, to gather). The suffixes *-bulum* (n.) ; *-brum* (n.) ; *-crum* (n.) and *-trum* (n.) usually indicate the means, the instrument or place of an action, e.g. *infundibulum* (funnel ; from *infundere* to pour into), *involucrum* (involucre ; from *involvere*, to wrap up, cover).

The suffixes above have mostly been used in the formation of technical terms. Suffixes traditionally associated with the stems of nouns and indicating a reduced or smaller state, incomplete resemblance or inferiority take a greater part in the formation of generic and sectional names. Thus, the suffixes *-aster* (m.), *-astra* (f.), *-astrum* (n.), *-ister* (m.), *-istra* (f.), *-istrum* (n.) indicate inferiority or incomplete resemblance and are attached to the stems of generic names, e.g. *oleaster*, *oleastrum* (the wild olive, an inferior kind of *olea*, the olive).

The diminutive suffixes *-lus* (m.), *-la* (f.) and *-lum* (n.) are not used indiscriminately. Their use is normally determined by the gender and declension of the noun providing the stem to which they are attached (cf. Weinhold, 1887). Thus the diminutive of *ramus* (m. ; branch) is formed by adding the suffix *-ulus* (m.) to the stem ram-, this giving *ramulus* (m. ; branchlet). *Capsula* (f. ; capsule, literally 'a small box') is the diminutive of *capsa* (f. ; box). *Vasculum* (n. ; vasculum, literally 'a small vessel') is the diminutive of *vas* (n. ; vessel). The suffixes *-ulus*, *-ula*, *-ulum* or, after *e* or *i*, *-olus*, *-ola*, *-olum*, *-ellus*, *-ella*, *-ellum*, *-illus*, *-illa*, *-illum* form compounds from nouns of the first and second declensions (see Chapter XXI, no. 306). The suffixes *-culus*, *-cula*, *-culum* form compounds from nouns of the Third and Fourth declensions. The suffixes *-cellus*, *-cella*, *-cellum*, *-cillus*, *-cilla*, *-cillum* form compounds from nouns of any declension. In botanical Latin, the suffix *-ella* has now come to be regarded, particularly by mycologists, as being simply a name-forming component to be attached to any personal name or any generic name of either Latin or Greek origin, usually without implication of smallness, e.g. *Englerella*, *Munkiella*, *Microthyriella*, *Phaeodimeriella*. Generic names with diminutive suffixes mostly formed from nouns, a few from adjectives, include *Armillariella*, *Campanula*, *Capsella*, *Fumariola*, *Gentianella*, *Gladiolus*, *Limosella*, *Mitella*, *Pinguicula*, *Pulsatilla*, *Ranunculus*, *Selaginella*.

The feminine suffixes *-ago* and *-ugo* (see p. 305) serve to indicate a resemblance or a property, e.g. *albugo* (a white spot) from *albus* (white), *asperugo* (a rough-leaved plant) from *asper* (rough), *plumbago* (black-lead) from *plumbum* (lead), *tussilago* (the plant coltsfoot) from *tussis* (cough). Their use and history in classical Latin is discussed by Ernout (1941) ; for Kuntze's peculiar use of *-ago*, see p. 293.

NAMES COMMEMORATING PERSONS

When writing in Latin, as they usually did, sixteenth- and seventeenth-century scholars usually gave their names a Latin or Greek form. Thus Charles de l'Écluse (1525–1609), commemorated botanically in the genus *Clusia* and the species *Paeonia clusii, Tulipa clusiana*, etc., latinized his name as *Carolus Clusius*; writing in Italian to Matteo Caccini he signed himself 'Carlo Clusio'. Such scholarly names were formed in various ways, often simply by use of a Latin ending, e.g. Bauhinus from Bauhin, Ferrarius from Ferrari, Fuchsius from Fuchs, or by slight modification, e.g. Bellonius from Belon, Dodonaeus from Dodoens, Lonicerus from Lonitzer, or sometimes by translation, e.g. Camerarius from Kammermeister (the Bamberg family) or Kammerer (the Tübingen family), Melanchthon from Schwarzerd, Tragus from Bock, Tabernaemontanus from Bergzabern. Generic names commemorating them naturally derive from these Latinized forms, e.g. *Bauhinia, Bellonia, Cameraria, Dodonaea, Ferraria, Fuchsia, Lonicera, Tabernaemontana, Tragia*. More modern examples are *Abauria* in honour of G. Doria and *Viridivia* in honour of P. J. Greenway.

As noted by Sarton (*Apprec. of Anc. & Mod. Sci. during the Renaissance*; 1955), 'in the Latin forms, it was often found necessary to duplicate consonants in order to keep preceding vowels short, e.g. Ruellius for Ruel, Bellonius for Belon, Snellius for Snel, Hamellius for Hamel, and then some authors believed wrongly that the original names were Ruelle, Bellon, Snell, Hamelle'.

The changes which Latin words underwent during the evolution of the present Romance languages from vulgar Latin, the standard Latin of the Roman Empire, were not, of course, everywhere the same, but were nevertheless regular enough to permit certain processes to be recognized and to be used in reverse when latinizing present-day names. Thus the Latin *clavis* (key) is the source of the Italian *chiave*, Spanish *clave* and *llave*, French *clef* and *clé*. Hence the Italian N. Chiavena (*d.* 1617) latinized his name as *Clavena* and is commemorated in *Achillea clavenae*. The Latin *columna* (column) remained *columna* in Spanish but became *colonna* in Italian, *colonne* in French. Hence the Italian F. Colonna (1567–1650) latinized his name as *Columna* and is commemorated in the genus *Columnea* and *Romulea columnae*. The Latin *febris* (fever), vulgar Latin *febrem*, has produced Italian *febbre*, Spanish *fiebre*, French *fièvre*; from Latin *peregrinus* (stranger), vulgar Latin *peregrinum* (pilgrim), have come the Italian *pellegrino*, Spanish *peregrino*, French *pèlerin*. The vulgar Latin *calves sorices* (bats) is the source of French *chauves-souris*. In vulgar Latin, words which in classical Latin began with *sc-, sp-, st-* were preceded by an *i*, later changed into *e*-, when spoken in Gaul and the Iberian Peninsula; hence *spatium* (space) by way of *ispatium* has become *espacio* in Spanish, *espace* in French. Knowledge of such changes explains why the Latinized forms made in accordance with them often diverge so much from the originals. Thus Cosson latinized the name of his friend Perraudière as *Perralderius*, commemorated in the genus *Perralderia* and *Epimedium perralderianum*. The course followed in the transformation of a word from French to Latin, and hence to be followed when latinizing a French name, is summarized by Weekley (1899); see also Dauzat (1944), Ewert (1943), Lebel (1959) and Lot (1931). For examples covering the Romance languages in general, see Gröber's elaborate survey (1884–92; A–C, 1884; D–G, 1885; H–M, 1886; M–P, 1887; Q–S, 1888; T–Z, 1889; Summary, 1892).

The final *t* in Latin often became *z* or *zz* in Italian, e.g. *palazzo* (palace) from *palatium* and *Venezia* from *Venetia*. De Notaris and Clementi reversed the process by latinizing Pestalozza as *Pestalotius*; hence the generic name *Pestalotia* commemorating Fortunato Pestalozza.

The invasions of Gaul and Italy by Germanic tribes in the early Middle Ages brought into Latin-speaking areas the German *w* which did not correspond exactly to the Gallo-Latin *v* of the fifth century A.D. and which was rendered sometimes by *v*, more often by *gu*. Thus the German *Waldrik* produced the French *Vaudry* and *Gaudry*; *Wilhelm* became *Villaume*, *Vuillerme*, *Guilhem*, *Guillaume* (cf. Lebel, 1959), whence the Italian *Guglielmo* and the Latinized form *Gulielmus*. When M. Wieland (1515–89) from Königsberg settled in Italy as a young man he italianized his name as 'Guilandini' and latinized it as *Guilandinus*, whence the generic name *Guilandina* commemorating him.

The name Linnaeus, contrary to frequent supposition, is not a Latinized version of Linné, but Linné is a shortened version of Linnaeus, just as Nobel is of Nobelius, Artedi of Arctaedius. Before the eighteenth century many Swedish peasants did not possess family surnames; each added to the baptismal name the genitive of the father's name with the suffix *-son* (son) or *-dotter* (daughter) according to sex. Thus Linnaeus's father was Nils Ingemarsson (1674–1733), the son of Ingemar Bengtsson and Ingrid Ingemarsdotter, and grandson of Bengt Ingemarsson and Ingrid Andersdotter. The family possessed a property in Småland called Linnegård after a big and aged linden tree (*Tilia*), *linn* being a now obsolete Swedish variant of *lind*. On registering at a university, students had to provide themselves with surnames. Ingrid Ingemarsdotter's two brothers Carl and Sven took the name Tiliander from this tree. Her son Nils Ingemarsson coined for himself the name Linnaeus referring to the same family linden, and her grandson

Carl Linnaeus made it famous. In his *Flora Suecica*, 157 (1745) he refers to *Tilia* as being 'vastissima in pago Stegaryd Sunnerboae Smolandiae, unde Tilandri et Linnaei dicti'. The name Linnaeus was thus of Latin form from the start, like many other Swedish family names ending in *-us*.

The *International Code of botanical Nomenclature* recommends that when a new name for a genus, subgenus or section is taken from the name of a person, it should be formed in the following manner:

(*a*) When the name of a person ends in a vowel, the letter *a* is added (thus *Botelua* after Boutelou; *Ottoa* after Otto; *Sloanea* after Sloane), except when the name ends in *a*, when *ea* is added (e.g. *Collaea* after Colla). The purpose of the last provision is to prevent confusion when writing in Latin about the plant and the person commemorated.

(*b*) When the name of a person ends in a consonant, the letters *ia* are added, except when the name ends in *er*, when *a* is added (e.g. *Kernera* after Kerner). In Latinized names ending in *us*, this termination is dropped before adding the suffix *ia* (e.g. *Dillenia* after Dillenius).

(*c*) The syllables not modified by these endings retain their original spelling, unless they contain letters foreign to Latin plant names or diacritic signs.

(*d*) Names may be accompanied by a prefix or a suffix or be modified by anagram or abbreviation. In these cases they count as different words from the original name. Examples are *Durvillea* and *Urvillea*, both after J. S. C. Dumont d'Urville; *Lapeirousia* and *Peyrousea*, both after P. Picot de La Peyrouse; *Englera*, *Englerastrum*, *Englerella*, *Englerina*, *Englerocharis*, *Englerodaphne*, *Englerodendron*, *Englerophoenix*, *Englerophytum*, all after Adolf Engler (1844–1930); *Neourbania*, *Urbania*, *Urbanisol*, *Urbanodendron*, *Urbanodoxa*, *Urbanolophium*, *Urbanosciadium*, after Ignaz Urban (1848–1931); *Bouchea* and *Ubochea*, after C. D. Bouché (1809–81); *Gerardia* and *Graderia*, after John Gerard (1545–1607); *Martia* and *Martiusia*, after K. F. P. von Martius (1794–1868).

'To name one good genus after a man as the ancients did for the Kings Gentius and Eupator, or as later authors have done for Cesalpino, Columna, Ray, Tournefort, Linnaeus, and then stop, *that* is to really *honor* a man, while to use his name as a merely convenient foundation for the making of a dozen different names', wrote E. L. Greene in 1906, 'is not that to openly dishonor him?' Engler certainly did not think so.

INGENIOUS METHODS OF NAME FORMATION

Ingenious ways of making generic names from personal names have been devised by various botanists, notably by Otto Kuntze in 1891.

He used the termination -*ago* from *agere* (to move, perform, achieve, etc.) to commemorate industrious compilers of botanical catalogues, nomenclators, etc., e.g. *Jacksonago, Justago, Koehneago, Pfeifferago, Pritzelago, Richterago, Steudelago*. Botanists who worked on the flora of India and the East Indies received the termination -*inda*, e.g. *Beccarinda, Clarkeinda, Hasskarlinda, Kurzinda, Ridleyinda*; those concerned with the African flora the termination -*afra*, e.g. *Bolusafra, Schinzafra, Schweinfurthafra*; those concerned with the American flora the termination -*amra*, e.g. *Brittonamra, Ernstamra, Kurzamra, Watsonamra*; those concerned with the Asiatic flora the termination -*asia*, e.g. *Itoasia, Maximowasia*. For his services to plant anatomy Radlkofer was awarded the generic name *Radlkoferotoma*! Other nomenclatorial curiosities of Kuntze's making are his *Algogrunowia* and *Algorichtera* commemorating the algologists A. Grunow and P. Richter, *Sirhookera* commemorating Sir Joseph D. Hooker and *Sirmuellera* commemorating Baron Ferdinand von Mueller, *Absolmsia* commemorating Count H. M. C. F. Friedrich zu Solms Laubach and *Aregelia* commemorating E. von Regel, *a* and *ab* being equivalents of the honorific *von* and *zu*, and *Benthamistella* renaming Bentham's *Stellularia*.

Making generic names by compounding a forename (baptismal name) and surname or two parts of a surname is exemplified by Kuntze's *Allenrolfea* commemorating Allen Rolfe, *Albertokuntzea* commemorating Albert Kuntze, *Jamesbrittenia* commemorating James Britten, Beccari's *Petrosavia* commemorating Pietro Savi, O. F. Cook's *Roystonea* commemorating Roy Stone, Dandy's *Elmerrillia* commemorating Elmer D. Merrill and Marquand's *Kingdon-wardia* commemorating F. Kingdon Ward, to whom the genera *Kingdonia* and *Wardaster* are also dedicated. Linnaeus, with his *Rajania* (Plumier's *Jan-Raja*) commemorating John Ray, and the Spanish botanists Ruiz and Pavón, with their *Isidrogalvia* commemorating Isidro Gálvez, *Mecardonia* commemorating Antonio Meca y Cardonia and *Nunnezharia* commemorating Alonso Nuñez de Haro, had given him welcome precedent. Ruiz and Pavón also introduced generic names commemorating two persons simultaneously, as *Juanulloa* in honour of Jorge Juan and Antonio Ulloa, joint authors of *Relación histórica del Viaje a la América meridional* (1748), and *Carludovica* in honour of King Carlos IV of Spain and his queen Maria Luisa. A later example is *Brittonrosea* commemorating the two authors of *The Cactaceae* (1919-23).

For treating initial letters as part of names, as in Kuntze's *Pasaccardoa* after Pier Andrea Saccardo and *Nebrownia* after Nicholas Edward Brown, he had precedent in Fries's *Acurtisia* after A. Curtis and Steudel's *Ifdregea* after I. F. Drege. The generic names *Afgekia* in honour of A. F. G. Kerr and *Resia* in honour of Richard Evan Schultes and the epithet in *Rosa ecae* commemorating E. C. Aitchison are extreme examples of this method used by other authors.

The names *Aschersonia*, *Boecklera*, *Cogniauxia* and *Goeppertia* having been twice (*bis*) used, Kuntze replaced the later homonyms by *Bisaschersonia*, *Bisboeckelera*, *Biscogniauxia* and *Bisgoeppertia*. More often the prefix *neo-* (new) is used, e.g. *Stapfia* and *Neostapfia*, *Marica* and *Neomarica*, to make such a distinction. When a person is particularly associated with one area, geographical prefixes have sometimes been considered appropriate, e.g. *Wilsonia* and *Sinowilsonia*, *Jackia* and *Sinojackia*.

EPITHETS COMMEMORATING PERSONS

Epithets whether specific or infraspecific may be substantival or adjectival. When they are simply nouns in apposition, as in *Rosa rubus*, *Sedum rosea* and *Schinus molle*, they merely follow the generic name, being linked to it not grammatically but by position alone. The name of a person used as an epithet is either put in the genitive case, i.e. given a Latin genitive ending, as in *Rosa farreri*, *R. henryi*, *R. hugonis*, *R. moyesii*, *R. prattii*, *R. murielae*, *R. willmottiae*, or converted into an adjective agreeing in gender with the generic name, as in *Rosa aschersoniana*, *R. forrestiana*, *R. wichuraiana*. Attempts have been made without success to differentiate the application of these adjectival and substantival epithets. Thus John Lindley wrote in 1832: 'If the individual is the discoverer of the plant, or the describer of it, the specific name [i.e. epithet] is then to be in the genitive singular; as *Caprifolium Douglasii*, *Carex Menziesii*; Messrs. Douglas and Menzies having been the discoverers of these species; and *Planera Richardi*, the species so called having been described by Richard: but if the name is merely given in compliment, without reference to either of these circumstances, the name should be rendered in an adjective form, with the termination *anus*, *a*, *um*; as in *Pinus Lambertiana*, in compliment to Mr. Lambert.' Adopted then, this might have made a useful distinction. Apparently, most of those who then and thereafter named new species paid no attention whatever to it; probably they never knew such a distinction had been proposed. However, at the last moment the 1867 Botanical Congress accepted the inclusion in the *Laws of botanical Nomenclature*, drawn up by Alphonse de Candolle, of an article (no. 33) stating that 'names of persons used as specific epithets have a genitive or an adjective form (*Clusii* or *Clusiana*). The first is used when the species has been described or distinguished by the botanist whose name it takes; in other cases the second form is preferred.' Ascherson protested against this rule in 1868. Most botanists continued to disregard it, and in 1883 Alphonse de Candolle declared that 'l'article est tenu pour nul'. Thus, for example, *Rosa willmottiae, Paeonia willmottiae, Corylopsis willmottiae* and *Ceratostigma willmottianum* commemorate Ellen Ann Willmott who collected and described none of them; *Chrysosplenium davidianum, Celtis davidiana, Ampelopsis davidiana, Acer davidii* and *Clematis armandii* commemorate Armand David who collected all of them.

The International Code of botanical Nomenclature recommends that when a new specific or infraspecific epithet is taken from the name of a man it should be formed in the following manner:

(*a*) When the name of the person ends in a vowel, the letter *i* is added (thus *glazioui* from Glaziou, *bureaui* from Bureau), except when the name ends in *a*, when *e* is added (thus *balansae* from Balansa).

(*b*) When the name ends in a consonant, the letters *ii* are added (thus *ramondii* from Ramond), except when the name ends in -*er*, when *i* is added (thus *kerneri* from Kerner).

(*c*) The syllables not modified by these endings retain their original spelling, unless they contain letters foreign to Latin plant names or diacritic signs; these signs must be suppressed and the letters transcribed, e.g. *ä, ö, ü* becoming *ae, oe, ue* respectively, *ø* becoming *oe* and *å* becoming *ao*.

(*d*) When epithets taken from the name of a man have an adjectival form they are formed in a similar way, e.g. *Geranium robertianum, Verbena hasslerana, Asarum hayatanum*.

(*e*) The Scottish and Irish patronymic prefix ' Mac,' ' Mc ' or ' M ', meaning ' son of ', should be spelled ' mac ' and united with the rest of the name, e.g. *macfadyenii* after Macfadyen, *macgillivrayi* after MacGillivray, *macnabii* after McNab, *mackenii* after M'Ken.

(*f*) The Irish patronymic prefix 'O' should be united with the rest of the name or omitted, e.g. *obrienii, brienianus* after O'Brien, *okellyi* after O'Kelly.

(*g*) A prefix consisting of an article, e.g. le, la, l', les, el, il, lo, or containing an article, e.g. du, dela, des, del, della, should be united to the name, e.g. *leclercii* after Le Clerc, *dubuyssonii* after DuBuysson, *lafarinae* after La Farina, *logatoi* after Lo Gato.

(*h*) A prefix to a surname indicating ennoblement or canonization should be omitted, e.g. *candollei* after De Candolle, *jussieui* after de Jussieu, *hilairei* after Sainte-Hilaire, *remyi* after St. Rémy; in geographical epithets, however, 'St.' is rendered as *sanctus* (m.) or *sancta* (f.) e.g. *sancti-johannis*, of St. John, *sanctae-helenae*, of St. Helena.

(*i*) A German or Dutch prefix when it is normally treated as part of the family name, as often happens outside its country of origin, e.g. in the United States, may be included in the epithet, e.g. *vonhausenii* after Vonhausen, *vanderhoekii* after Vanderhoek, *vanbruntiae* after Mrs. Van Brunt, but should otherwise be omitted, e.g. *iheringii* after von Ihering, *martii* after von Martius, *steenisii* after van Steenis, *strassenii* after zu Strassen, *vechtii* after van der Vecht.

If a personal name is already Latin or Greek, the appropriate Latin genitive should be used, e.g. *alexandri* from Alexander, *francisci* from Franciscus, *augusti* from Augustus, *linnaei* from Linnaeus, *hectoris* from Hector.

The same provisions apply to epithets formed from the names of women. When these have a substantival form, they are given a feminine termination, e.g. *Cypripedium hookerae, Rosa beatricis, Scabiosa olgae, Omphalodes luciliae.*

Recommendations *e-i* above were adapted from the *International Code of Zoological Nomenclature* (1961).

ANAGRAMS

When no fitting and meaningful name for a new genus comes to mind, one that is at least euphonious and not over-long can be devised, as a last resort, by rearranging the letters of the name of a closely related genus. Such anagrams are meaningless, but equally so are many plant-names of great antiquity used by the Greeks and Romans. John Lindley accordingly wrote long ago : 'So impossible is it to construct generic names that will express the peculiarities of the species they represent, that I agree with those who think a good, well-sounding, *unmeaning* name as good as any that can be contrived. The great rule to follow is this : In constructing a generic name, take care that it is harmonious, and as unlike all other generic names as it can be' (*Introd. Bot.*, 3rd ed., 531 ; 1839). The first anagrammatic generic name in botanical literature appears to be Linnaeus's *Mahernia* (*Mant. Pl.*, 9 ; 1767) made from *Hermannia* with omission of an *n*. Generic names which are anagrams have been used in most families. Thus *Alchemilla* (Rosaceae) has been transformed into *Lachemilla*; *Allium* (Amaryllidaceae) into *Milula* and *Muilla*; *Arabis* (Cruciferae) into *Sibara*; *Ardisia* (Myrsinaceae) into *Sadiria* ; *Argemone* (Papaveraceae) into

Enomegra; *Aristida* (Gramineae) into *Sartidia*; *Ascyron* (Hyperi-caceae) into *Norysca* and *Roscyna*; *Bouchea* (Verbenaceae) into *Ubochea*; *Cydonia* (Rosaceae) into *Docynia*; *Elvasia* (Ochnaceae) into *Vaselia*; *Elymus* (Gramineae) into *Leymus*; *Filago* (Compositae) into *Gifola, Ifloga, Lifago, Logfia, Oglifa*; *Goldfussia* (Acanthaceae) into *Diflugossia*; *Hariota* (Cactaceae) into *Hatiora*; *Liatris* (Compositae) into *Litrisa* and *Trilisa*; *Mitella* (Saxifragaceae) into *Tellima*; *Monar-della* (Labiatae) into *Madronella*; *Myginda* (Celastraceae) into *Gyminda*; *Pandorea* (Bignoniaceae) into *Podranea*; *Sauvagesia* (Ochnaceae) into *Vausagesia*; *Tacazzea* (Asclepiadaceae) into *Zaca-teza*; *Tephrosia* (Leguminosae) into *Ophrestia*. In the name *Magnolia* sect. *Maingola* the anagrammatic sectional epithet *Maingola* has mean-ing in that *Magnolia maingayi* is the type of the section. The name *Phlebiogonium* retains the meaning of *Goniophlebium*. A few generic names have been formed from anagrams of geographical names, e.g. *Jacaima* (Asclepiadaceae) from Jamaica, *Lobivia* (Cactaceae) from Bolivia. For other examples, see Smith & Stearn (1972: 5)

GEOGRAPHICAL AND ECOLOGICAL EPITHETS

Epithets referring to places of origin and distribution are dealt with in Chapter XVII, those referring to habitats in Chapter XVI.

LATINIZATION OF NATIVE NAMES

Linnaeus, as noted above (p. 255), ruled that generic names not derived from Greek or Latin were to be rejected, which saved botany from being burdened with the uncouth transcriptions of Indian plant-names given in Rheede's *Hortus Indicus Malabaricus* (1678–1703). His real objection was seemingly not to their origin, but to their form; he liked short euphonious names and himself adopted such 'barbarous' names as *Alchemilla, Areca, Berberis, Coffea, Datura, Mammea, Tulipa* and *Yucca*. In fact many plant-names used by the Greeks and the Romans, among them *Anemone, Crocus, Hyssopus* and *Rosa*, were of oriental origin; probably others came from 'a little-known linguistic stratum which, for lack of a more precise name has been called "Mediter-ranean"'. There is no reason whatever against the use of native plant-names as scientific generic names provided that they are fairly short, euphonious and of Latin form or made so. Thus *Aucuba, Kiren-geshoma, Nandina* and *Sasa* are of Japanese origin, *Ailanthus* and *Angraecum* of Malaysian origin, *Madhuca, Manilkara* and *Vanda* of Indian origin, *Nelumbo* and *Wissadula* of Singhalese origin, *Alchemilla, Coffea* and *Taraxacum* of Arabic origin, *Jasminum* of Persian origin,

Poncirus of French origin, *Rorippa* of German origin, *Mammea* and *Zombia* of West Indian origin, *Camassia* of North American Indian origin, and so on.

NAMES OF INTERGENERIC HYBRID GROUPS

The name of a bigeneric hybrid group corresponding to a genus (i.e. a group resulting from hybridization between members of two genera) is formed by combining the names of the two parent genera (i.e. joining the first part or the whole of one name and the last part or the whole of the other) into a single word not exceeding eight syllables, which is regarded as a condensed formula, e.g. × *Adaglossum* (= *Ada* × *Odontoglossum*), × *Dialaelia* (= *Diacrium* × *Laelia*), × *Heucherella* (= *Heuchera* × *Tiarella*), × *Mahoberberis* (= *Berberis* × *Mahonia*).

This method of designating bigeneric hybrid groups by name-blending was introduced by Maxwell T. Masters in 1872 (*Gard. Chron.* 1872 : 358) when he coined the name × *Philageria veitchii* for the hybrid between *Lapageria rosea* and *Philesia magellanica* raised by Messrs. Veitch. Early in the twentieth century orchid-raisers extended its use from bigeneric hybrid groups such as × *Brassocattleya* (= *Brassavola* × *Cattleya*) and trigeneric groups such as × *Brassocatlaelia* (= *Brassavola* × *Cattleya* × *Laelia*) to multigeneric groups such as × *Sophrolaeliacattleya* (= *Cattleya* × *Laelia* × *Sophronitis*). The probability of even more unwieldy designations led E. A. Bowles (cf. Stearn, 1961 : 38) to suggest an alternative method, namely, to abandon all attempts to make combinations of the names of three or more genera and instead to form arbitrary equivalent names by attaching the termination -*ara* to the name of a person. This proposal made at the Brussels Botanical Congress of 1910 was officially accepted at the Stockholm Botanical Congress of 1950.

The name of a multigeneric hybrid group (i.e. one derived from four or more genera) is formed from the name of a person eminent as a collector, grower or student of these plants to which is added the termination -*ara*, e.g. × *Burrageara* (= *Cochlioda* × *Miltonia* × *Odontoglossum* × *Oncidium*) in honour of the Massachusetts horticulturist and geologist Albert C. Burrage (1859–1931). Such a name is regarded as equivalent to a condensed formula.

The name of a trigeneric hybrid group (i.e. one derived from three genera) is formed either like that of a bigeneric hybrid group, by combining the names of the three parent genera into a single word not exceeding eight syllables, or like that of a multigeneric hybrid group, by adding the termination -*ara* to a personal name. Examples are

× *Diacatlaelia* (= *Cattleya* × *Diacrium* × *Laelia*) and × *Rolfeara* (= *Brassavola* × *Cattleya* × *Sophronitis*), commemorating the Kew botanist Robert Allen Rolfe (1855–1921). Names of bigeneric graft-hybrids are similarly formed, e.g. + *Laburnocytisus* (= *Cytisus* + *Laburnum*). Different names must be applied to graft-hybrids and sexual hybrids derived from the same genera, e.g. × *Crataemespilus* (*Crataegus* × *Mespilus*) and + *Crataegomespilus* (*Crataegus* + *Mespilus*)

REFERENCES

CAIN, A. J. 1958. Logic and memory in Linnaeus's system of taxonomy. *Proc. Linnean Soc. London*, 169 : 144-163.

DAUZAT, A. 1944. *Histoire de la Langue française.* (Que sais-je ?, no. 167). Paris.

DYBOWSKI, B. 1926. Synoptisches Verzeichnis mit kurzer Besprechung der Gattungen und Arten dieser Abteilung der Baikalflohkrebs. *Bull. Int. Acad. Polon. Sci. Lett., Cl. Sci. Math. Nat. B.*, 1926 : 1-77.

ELCOCK, W. D. 1960. *The Romance Languages.* London.

ERNOUT, A. 1941. Les noms en -āgŏ, -īgŏ, -ūgŏ du latin. *Revue de Philologie, de Littérature et d'Histoire anciennes*, sér. III. 15 : 85-111.

ERNOUT, A., & MEILLET, A. 1959-60. *Dictionnaire étymologique de la Langue latine.* 4th ed. Paris.

EWERT, A. 1943. *The French Language.* London.

GREENE, E. L. 1906. An unwritten law of nomenclature. *Leafl. Bot. Observ.*, 1 : 201-205.

GRÖBER, G. 1884-92. Vulgärlateinische Substrate romanischer Wörter. *Arch. Latein. Lexikogr.*, 1 : 204-254, 539-556 (1884); 2 : 100-107, 276-288, 424-443 (1885); 3 : 138-143, 264-275, 507-531 (1886); 4 : 116-136, 422-454 (1887); 5 : 12-132, 234-242, 453-486 (1888); 6 : 117-149, 377-397 (1889); 7 : 25-64 (1892).

HYLANDER, N. 1954. Apans stege och Pyrrhas hår . . . reflexions on botanical species names. *Svenska Bot. Tidskr.* 48 : 521-549.

KIRKALDY, G. W. 1904. Bibliographical and nomenclatorial notes on the Hemiptera. *Entomologist*, 37 : 279-283.

KRETSCHMER, P. 1899. *Sprachregeln für die Bildung und Betonung zoologischer und botanischer Namen.* Berlin.

KUNTZE, O. 1891. *Revisio Generum Plantarum.*, 1 : li-lv, cxvi-cxxi. Leipzig, etc.

LEBEL, P. 1959. *Les Noms de Personnes en France.* 4th ed. (Que sais-je ? no. 235). Paris

LINNAEUS, C. 1737. *Critica botanica.* Leyden.

—— 1938. *The 'Critica botanica' of Linnaeus.* Transl. by A. Hort, revised by M. L. Green. London.

LOT, F. 1931. A quelle époque a-t-on cessé de parler latin? *Bull. Du Cange*, 6 : 97-159.

MAYR, E., LINSLEY, E. G., & USINGER, R. L. 1953. *Methods and Principles of systematic Zoology.* New York, etc.

MEYER-LÜBKE, W. 1935. *Romanisches etymologisches Wörterbuch.* 3rd ed. Heidelberg.

NIEUWLAND, J. A. 1911. Some Linnaean trivial names. *Amer. Midl. Nat.*, 2 : 97-112.

NYBAKKEN, O. E. 1959. *Greek and Latin in scientific Terminology.* Ames, Iowa.

ROWLEY, G. 1956.   Caconymy or a few short words against many long ones. *National Cactus & Succ. J.*, 11 : 3-4.

SAINT-LAGER, J. B. 1881.   Nouvelles remarques sur la nomenclature botanique. *Ann. Soc. Bot. Lyon*, 8 : 149-203.

—— 1893.   Un chapitre de grammaire à l'usage des botanistes.   *Ann. Soc. Bot. Lyon*, 18 : 75-95.

SCHULTES, R. E., & PEASE, A.S. 1963.   *Generic Names of Orchids, their Origin and Meaning.*   New York and London.

STEARN, W. T. 1959.   The background of Linnaeus's contributions to the nomenclature and methods of systematic biology.   *Systematic Zoology*, 8 : 4-22.

——1961.   Two thousand years of Orchidology.   *Proc. Third World Orchid Conf.*, 26-42.

SMITH, A. W. & STEARN, W. T. 1972.   *A Gardener's Dictionary of Plant Names.*   London.

WEEKLEY, E. 1899.   *A Primer of historical French Grammar.*   London.

WEINHOLD, A. 1887.   Genuswechsel bei Demunitiva.   *Arch. Latein. Lexikogr.*, 4 : 169-188.

WERNER, C. F. 1956.   *Wortelemente lateinisch-griechischer Fachausdrücke in der Biologie, Zoologie und vergleichenden Anatomie.*   Leipzig.   [2nd ed., 1961.]

WIKÉN, E. 1951.   *Latin för Botanister och Zoologer.*   Malmö.

CHAPTER XXI

Prefixes and Suffixes

An affix is one letter or several letters placed at the beginning of a
word, and then termed a *prefix*, or at the end of a word, and then
termed a *suffix*, to modify its meaning or application or make it distinct
from other words. These elements play an important part in the
formation of words in botanical Latin.

PREFIXES

Prefixes can be attached to both nouns and adjectives. Many Latin
prefixes, e.g. *ad* (to), *circum* (around), *in* (in), *semper* (always), *sub*
(under), are prepositions or adverbs having independent use; these
are called SEPARABLE PREFIXES. Adjectives with a modified ending,
i.e. consisting of the stem and often a connecting vowel, in botanical
Latin may also serve as prefixes, e.g. *hetero-* (different), *neo-* (new),
novi- (new), *pari-* (equal), *pseudo-* (false). Others, e.g. *ambi-* (around),
dis- (apart), *re-* (back, again), *se-* (apart), exist only as part of compounds and are called INSEPARABLE PREFIXES. In general, Latin prefixes should be added only to words of Latin origin and Greek prefixes
to those of Greek origin. Latin *e-*, *ex-* (without) corresponds to Greek
a-, *an-*; Latin *contra-* (against) to Greek *ant-*, *anti-*; Latin *circum-*
(around) to Greek *peri-*; Latin *super-*, *supra-* to Greek *hyper-*; and
so on. Certain words, e.g. *calyx*, *sepalum*, *petalum*, can be treated as
both Latin and Greek, and the Greek *neo-* (new) and *pseudo-* (false)
are commonly prefixed to words which are neither Greek nor Latin
in origin, e.g. *neoguineensis* (pertaining to New Guinea), *Neojunghuhnia*,
pseudomoluccanus (false *moluccanus*), *Pseudopringsheimia*.
    When a prefix ends in a consonant and is placed before a word
beginning with a consonant, e.g. *ad* before *similis*, the final consonant
of the prefix may be changed to that of the word itself, hence *assimilis*,

or to another consonant easier to say in combination; this process is known as ASSIMILATION. Thus *d* usually, but not invariably, becomes *b, f, g, l, n, m, p, r, s* or *t* when placed before a word beginning with these consonants, e.g. *affinis* (bordering, related) from *ad-* and *finis*; thus there may exist alternative forms as *adpressus* and *appressus*, *adligans* and *alligans*. In Greek the final *n* of *syn-* (together) becomes *l* or *r* when placed before these consonants, e.g. *sylloge* from *syn-* and *loge*. The letter *n* before *b* and *p* becomes *m*, e.g. *compositus* from *con-* and *positus*; before *l* the letter *n* usually becomes *l*, e.g. *collimitaneus* (bordering upon) from *con-* and *limitaneus*. The Latin prefixes which usually assimilate to the following word in this manner are *ad-*, *con-, dis-, in-, ob-* and *sub-*. The Latin prefixes ending in a vowel, e.g. *antero-, contra-, de-, extra-, infra-, intra-, intro-, pre-, re-, retro-, semi-, supra-* and *ultra-*, as also the Greek prefixes *amphi-* and *peri-*, retain this vowel even when the following word begins with a vowel, e.g. *extraordinarius, perianthium*. The Greek prefixes ending in *-a*, e.g. *ana-, meta-, para-*, and some ending in *-i* and *-ŏ* (omicron), e.g. *anti-, epi-, apo-, ecto-, endo-*, drop this vowel when they come before a word beginning with a vowel, e.g. *Pararistolochia*.

Many prefixes indicate a relation in space or time or else a degree of development or negation.

LATIN PREFIXES

a-, (before a consonant), **ab-** (before a consonant or vowel), **abs-** (before *c* or *t*): away from, e.g. *abaxialis*, away from the axis; corresponds to Greek *apo-*.

ad-, ac- (before *c*), **af-** (before *f*), **ag-** (before *g*), **al-** (before *l*), **an-** (before *n*), **ap-** (before *p*), **ar-** (before *r*), **as-** (before *s*), **at-** (before *t*): towards, to, near, e.g. *appendix*, something which hangs on.

ai-: *see under* **semper-**.

amb-, ambi-: around, round about.

ana-: *see under* **re-**.

ante-: before, e.g. *antecedens*, going before, preceding.

anti-: *see under* **contra-**.

apo-: *see under* **a-, de-**.

cata-: *see under* **de-**.

circum-: around, e.g. *circumdans*, surrounding, *circumferentia*, circumference; corresponds to Greek *peri-*.

co- (before vowels and *h*), **col-** (before *l*), **com-** (before *b, m* and *p*), **con-** (before *c, d, f, g, j, n, qu, s, t* and *v*), **cor-** (before *r*): with, together with, e.g. *coalitus*, grown together, *collectus*, gathered together, *compositus*, put together, *concordia*, agreeing together, *corrasus*, scraped together; corresponds to Greek *syn-*.

contra-, contro-: against, e.g. *controversus*, turned against; corresponds to Greek *anti-*.

de- : downwards, outwards, from, e.g. *descendens*, sinking down, descending; corresponds to Greek *apo-*, *cata-*.

di- (before some consonants), **dis-** : between, away from, e.g. *dissepimentum*, partition, *dissimilis*, unlike.

dia- : *see under* **pel-**.

e- (before *s* and *d*), **ef-** (before *f*), **ex-** : without, not, lacking, from out, e.g. *edentatus*, toothless, *effusus*, poured out, *exsertus*, thrust out, projecting.

en- : *see under* **il-**.

endo- : *see under* **intra-**.

exo- : *see under* **extra-**.

extra- : on the outside, beyond, over and above, e.g. *extraordinarius*, out of the common order; corresponds to Greek *exo-*.

hemi- : *see under* **semi-**.

hyper- : *see under* **super-**.

hypo- : *see under* **infra-**, **sub-**.

il- (before *l*), **im-** (before *b*, *p*, *m*), **in-** (before vowels and most consonants), **ir-** (before *r*) : in, into, for, contrary, e.g. *illegitimus*, unlawful, *immersus*, plunged into, *ineptus*, unsuitable, *insertus*, put into; corresponds to Greek *en-*.

infra- : below, e.g. *infranodis*, below a node; corresponds to Greek *hypo-*.

inter- : between, e.g. *interjectus*, thrown between, *internodium*, internode, *intervallum*, interval.

intra- : within, e.g. *intra-axillaris*, within the axil; corresponds to Greek *endo-*.

intro- : inside, e.g. *introvenius*, with veins hidden inside the parenchyma.

meta- : *see under* **post-**.

non- : not, e.g. *nonscriptus*, not written upon, without markings.

ob- (before vowels and most consonants), **oc-** (before *c*), **of-** (before *f*), **op-** (before *p*); against, contrary, for, e.g. *obovatus*, obovate.

pel- (before *l*), **per-** : through, extra, very, e.g. *pellucidus*, transparent, *perforatus*, pierced through, *perelegans*, very elegant; partly corresponds to Greek *dia-*.

peri- : *see under* **circum-**.

post- : after, behind, later, e.g. *postmeridianus*, after midday; corresponds to Greek *meta-*.

prae- : before, in front, very, e.g. *praestans*, pre-eminent; partly corresponds to Greek *pro-*.

pro- : for, instead of.

pro- : *see under* **prae-**.

re- : back, against, again, e.g. *resupinatus*, bent back, upside down; corresponds to Greek *ana-*.

retro- : back, behind, e.g. *retrocurvus*, curved back.

se- : out, without, apart, e.g. *segregatus*, kept apart.

semi- : half, e.g. *semicircularis*, semi-circular: corresponds to Greek *hemi-*.

semper- : always, e.g. *sempervirens*, evergreen; corresponds to Greek *ai-*.

sub- (before vowels and most consonants), **suc-** (before *c*), **suf-** (before *f*), **sug-** (before *g*): below, under, almost, approaching, e.g. *subacaulis*, almost stemless, *submersus*, growing under water; corresponds to Greek *hypo-*.

super-: above, e.g. *superpositus*, placed above; corresponds to Greek *hyper-*.

supra-: above, over, e.g. *supracanus*, grey above, *supranodis*, above a node; corresponds to Greek *hyper-*.

syn-: *see under* **co-**.

trans-: beyond, through, across, e.g. *transalpinus*, beyond the Alps, *transportatus*, carried across.

GREEK PREFIXES

a- (before a consonant), **an-** (before a vowel): not, without, less, e.g. *achromus*, without colour, colourless, *anantherus*, without anthers.

ai-: always.

amphi-, ampho-: on both sides, around, both, double, e.g. *amphicarpus*, with two kinds of fruit.

ana-, *ano-*: upon, up, upwards, above.

ant- (before vowels and *h*), **anti-** (before a consonant): against, opposite to, e.g. *antipetalus*, opposite to (not alternate with) petals.

ap- (before a vowel and *h*), **apo-**: from, away, down, downwards.

arche-: original, primitive.

archi-: chief.

cat- (before vowels and *h*), **cata-**: against, along, below.

cato-: down, downwards, below, under.

chori-: separate, apart, e.g. *choripetalus*, with free petals.

dia-: through, across.

dicha-, dicho-: in two, e.g. *dichotomus*, forked, divided in pairs.

dys-: bad, ill, difficult.

ect- (before vowels), **ecto-**: on the outside, outwards.

em- (before *b* and *p*), **en-**: in, within.

endo-, ento-: inside, inwards.

ep- (before vowels and *h*), **epi-**: upon, on, over.

eu-: good, well.

hama-: together with.

hemi-: half.

hyper-: above, over.

hypo-: below, under.

met- (before vowels), **meta-**: next to, among, after.

opistho-: back, behind.

para-: beside, alongside, close by.

peri-: around.

pro-: in front of, before.

pros-: near, in addition.

proso-, prostho-: forward, to the front, before.

sy- (before *s*), **syl-** (before *l*), **sym-** (before *b* and *p*), **syn-**, **syr-** (before *r*), **sys-** (before *s*): together, with, joined.

za-: much.

SUFFIXES

By the use of suffixes a diversity of words may be formed from one word. The suffix determines the meaning, gender and grammatical nature of the compound. Thus the Latin word for 'iron' is *ferrum*, a neuter noun, with the stem *ferr-*. The adjectival ending *-eus* gives the adjective *ferreus* (made of iron). The substantival ending *-ugo*, sometimes indicating a disease, gives the feminine noun *ferrugo* (iron rust); from this, by use of the adjectival ending *-ineus*, is derived the adjective *ferrugineus* (rust-coloured), from which in turn, by use of the participal ending *-escens*, has been coined the adjective *ferruginescens* (becoming rust-coloured, somewhat rust-coloured). Similarly from the masculine noun *flos* (flower), with the stem *flor-*, have come the adjectives *floreus* (made of flowers), *floridus* (flowery) and *floribundus* (full of flowers), the verb *floreo* (flower, flourish) and the masculine diminutive *flosculus* (flowerlet, floret), as well as such compounds as *florifer* and *floriger* (bearing flowers), *florilegium* (a gathering of flowers, hence an illustrated flower book). Latin has numerous suffixes. These are not, however, used indiscriminately. A given suffix usually conveys a limited range of meaning (cf. Leumann, 1944) and is associated with a particular kind of stem to give a word which, according to the suffix, may be an adjective, a verb, an adverb or a noun and then of a particular gender. Latin suffixes should be associated with Latin stems and Greek suffixes with Greek stems, although botanical authors have occasionally done otherwise.

The numerals I–V below indicate the declension of nouns formed by these suffixes.

LATIN SUBSTANTIVAL SUFFIXES

-aculum (n. II): indicates an instrument or means; verb base; e.g. *retinaculum*, hold fast, tether (from *retinere*, to hold back, retain).

-ago (f. III): indicates resemblance or connexion; noun base; e.g. *plumbago*, kind of lead (from *plumbum*, lead). According to Ernout (1941) the ending *-go* originally indicated a force doing something, as in *vertigo*, then a change of state or a state or tendency or malady, e.g. *robigo* (state of being red, tendency to become red, hence iron-rust), *aerugo* (rust of copper), and thus it became a word-forming element to indicate possession of a property, e.g. *lactago* (herb with milky juice), or resemblance, e.g. *ferulago* (inferior or lesser kind of ferula), *cunilago* (a kind of cunila).

-arium (n. II): indicates a place where something is done or a container; e.g. *herbarium*, collection of dried plants (from *herba*, herb), *ovarium*, ovary (from *ovum*, egg).

-aster (m. II), **-astra** (f. I), **-astrum** (n. II); indicates inferiority or incomplete resemblance, hence often applied to the wild equivalent of a cultivated plant; noun base; e.g. *oleaster*, the wild olive (from *olea*, olive); cf. Seck & Schnorr (1884).

-bulum (n. II), **-bula** (f. I); indicates an instrument or means; verb base; e.g. *involucrum*, wrapper, involucre (from *involvere*, wrap up, envelop).

-cellus (m. II), **-cella** (f. I), **-cellum** (n. II); **-cillus** (m. II), **-cilla** (f. I), **-cillum** (n. II); **-culus** (m. II), **-cula** (f. I), **-culum** (n. II); **-ellus** (m. II), **-ella** (f. I), **-ellum** (n. II); **-illus** (m. II), **-illa** (f. I), **-illum** (n. II): diminutive; e.g. *cuticula*, cuticle (from *cutis*, skin), *lamella*, small plate, gill (from *lamina*, plate, blade), *pedicellus*, pedicel (from *pes*, foot). The suffixes *-ulus*, etc., *-ellus*, etc., and *-illus*, etc., form compounds with nouns of the First Declension, *-culus*, etc., with those of the Third and Fourth Declensions, *-cellus*, etc., and *-cillus*, etc., with any declension.

-etum (n. II): indicates collective place of growth, hence plant association; noun base; e.g. *quercetum*, oak-wood (from *quercus*, oak); cf. Mayer (1954).

-ies (f. V): indicates a thing formed; verb base; e.g. *series*, row (from *serere*, to put in a row).

-io (f. III): indicates the abstract or general result of an action; verb base; e.g. *collectio*, a collecting together (from *colligere*, to gather together).

-itas (f. III), **-itia** (f. I), **-ities** (f. III), **-itudo** (f. III): indicates a concept or quality: adjectival or participial base; e.g. *affinitas*, relationship (from *affinis*, bordering), *duritia*, hardness (from *durus*, hard), *longitudo*, length (from *longus*, long), *crassities*, thickness (from *crassus*, thick).

-orium (m. II): indicates place of work or action; verb base; e.g. *laboratorium*, laboratory (from *laborare*, to work, from *labor*, toil).

-ugo (f. III): indicates a substance or property possessed; noun or adjective base; e.g. *asperugo* a prickly plant (from *asper*, rough), *lanugo*, down (from *lana*, wool); cf. *-ago* above, p. 305.

-ullus (m. II), **-ula** (f. I), **-ulum** (n. II): diminutive; noun base of First or Second declension nouns; e.g. *capsula*, a small box, capsule (from *capsa*, box).

-ura (f. I): indicates the result of an action; verb base; e.g. *incisura*, incision (from *incidere*, to cut into).

GREEK SUBSTANTIVAL SUFFIXES

-ias (m. I): indicates a close connexion; noun base; e.g. *Asclepias*.

-cles (m. III): indicates honour or renown, hence abundance of a particular quality, often part of Greek personal names; noun or adjectival base.

-ides (f. III): indicates resemblance; noun base.

-idium (n. II): diminutive; noun base; e.g. *ascidium* (from *ascos*, sack).

-ion (n. II): indicates occurrence; noun base.

-is (f. III): indicates a close connexion; noun base.

-iscus (m. II): diminutive; noun base; e.g. *Asteriscus* (from *aster*, star).

-ites (m. I), **-itis** (m. III): indicates a close connexion; noun base.

-ium (n. II): diminutive; noun base; e.g. *Aspidium*, a little shield (from *aspis*, shield).

-**ma** (n. III): often indicates the result of an action; verb base.

-**mus** (m. II): indicates an action; verb base.

-**osyne** (f. II), **-otes** (f. III): forms abstract nouns indicating a special feature; adjectival base; e.g. *Leptosyne, Leptotes* (from *leptos*, slender, fine).

-**sis** (f. III): indicates an action of a general or abstract nature; verb base; e.g. *diagnosis*, diagnosis (from *diagignoscein*, to know apart).

-**ter** (m. III), **-tes** (m. I), **-tis** (m. III), **-tor** (m. III); **-tria** (f. I): usually indicates the agent or means; verb base.

-**tros** (m. II) or **-trus** (m. II), **-tra** (f. I), **-tron** (n. II) or **-trum** (n. II): indicates a tool or means of doing something: verb or noun base.

LATIN ADVERBIAL SUFFIXES

Latin adverbs possess a variety of endings corresponding to the English '-ly' in meaning. Those formed from adjectives ending in *-er* or *-us* usually end in *-o* or *-e* but may end in *-iter* or *-enter*, e.g. *crebro*, closely, repeatedly, *crebre*, closely, compactly, *crebriter*, repeatedly (all from *creber*, thick, close, repeated). These variants sometimes have different shades of meaning; similarly the adjective *rarus* (far apart, scattered) has given the adverbs *raro, rare, rarenter, rariter*. According to Osthoff (1887), the ending *-iter* originated from the fusion of *iter* (way) with a preceding adjective, e.g. *breviter*, briefly (from *brevis*, short, *iter*, a way). Adjectives ending in *-is* or *-ns* usually have adverbs ending in *-ter* or *-er*, e.g. *fortiter*, strongly (from *fortis*, strong), *frequenter*, frequently (from *frequens*, often, frequent), but may also end in *-e*, e.g. *difficile, difficulter* and *difficiliter* (from *difficilis*, difficult). Adverbs formed from nouns or from past participles of verbs or from adjectives ending in *-atus* frequently end in *-atim*, e.g. *pinnatim*, pinnately (from *pinnatus*, pinnate, from *pinna* or *penna*, feather), *radiatim*, radiately (from *radiatus*, rayed, from *radius*, spoke, ray). A few end in *-am* or *-ies*, e.g. *bifariam*, on two sides, twofold, *bifaries*, twofold.

For further examples see Chapter VII, p. 104.

LATIN ADJECTIVAL SUFFIXES

-**abilis -is -e**: *see below under* **-bilis.**

-**aceus -a -um**: indicates resemblance; noun base; e.g. *coriaceus*, leathery (from *corium*, leather), *rosaceus*, rose-like (from *rosa*, rose).

-**alis -is -e**: belonging or pertaining to; noun base; e.g. *dorsalis*, dorsal (from *dorsum*, back), *autumnalis*, autumnal (from *autumnus*, autumn).

-**aneus -a -um**: indicates resemblance or material out of which something is made; noun base; e.g. *cutaneus*, relating to the skin (from *cutis*, skin).

-**anus -a -um**: indicates position, connexion or possession by; noun base; e.g. *africanus*, African (from *Africa*), *montanus*, relating to mountains (from *mons*, mountain), *clusianus*, belonging to Clusius (from Charles de l'Écluse).

B.L.—L

-aris -is -e: a variant of *-alis* used after stems ending in *l*; e.g. *stellaris*, starry (from *stella*, star), *avicularis*, relating to small birds (from *avicula*, diminutive of *avis*, bird).

-arius -a -um: indicates connexion or possession; noun or numeral base; e.g. *arenarius*, pertaining to sand (from *arena*, sand), *primarius*, chief (from *primus*, the first).

-ascens: indicates process of becoming, hence incomplete manifestation; noun or adjectival base; e.g. *purpurascens*, becoming purple, purplish (from *purpureus*, purple).

-aticus -a -um: indicates place of growth; noun base; e.g. *sylvaticus*, belonging to woods (from *silva*, wood).

-atilis -is -e: indicates place of growth; noun base; e.g. *saxatilis*, dwelling among rocks (from *saxum*, rock).

-atus -a -um: (1) indicates possession or likeness; noun base; e.g. *capitatus*, with a head (from *caput*, head), *ovatus*, egg-shaped (from *ovum*, egg); (2) perfect participial ending of verbs of First Conjugation, indicating an action made or done; e.g. *fucatus*, coloured (from *fucare*, to colour).

-ax: uncommon ending with sense of 'inclining to and apt to'; verb base; e.g. *tenax*, gripping, tenacious (from *tenere*, to hold); *fugax*, apt to flee (from *fugere*, to flee).

-bilis -is -e: indicates capacity or ability; verb base; it becomes *-abilis* with verbs having the infinitive in *-are* and *-ibilis* with those in *-ere* and *-ire*; e.g. *variabilis*, able to change (from *variare*, to change); *flexibilis*, bendable (from *flectere*, to bend).

-bundus -a -um: indicates doing, like a present participle, or action accomplished; verb base; e.g. *floribundus*, flowering, full of flowers (from *florere*, to flower).

-cellus -a -um, -cillus -a -um, -culus -a -um, -ellus -a -um: diminutive; adjectival base; e.g. *pilosiusculus*, slightly pilose (from *pilosus*, pilose, from *pilus*, hair).

-cundus -a -um: indicates an aptitude or constant tendency; e.g. *fecundus* fruitful, *verecundus*, bashful; cf. Beneviste (1933).

-ensis -is -e: indicates country or place of growth or origin or else habitat; noun base; e.g. *bononiensis*, relating to Bononia (now Bologna), *pratensis*, growing in meadows (from *pratum*, meadow).

-escens -is -e: indicates process of becoming, hence not fully achieved resemblance, often expressed in English by the termination '-ish'; verb base, usually itself with a noun or adjectival base; e.g. *senescens*, becoming aged (from *senescere*, to grow old, from *senex*, old), *rubescens*, reddening, reddish (from *rubescere*, to grow red, from *ruber*, red).

-estris (-ester) -is -e: indicates place of growth; noun base; e.g. *rupestris*, dwelling among rocks (from *rupes*, rock). After *u* the *e* is dropped, e.g. *lacustris*, dwelling in lakes (from *lacus*, lake).

-ĕus -a -um: indicates material or colour or resemblance in quality; noun base; e.g. *melleus*, pertaining to honey (from *mel*, honey), *purpureus*, purple (from *purpura*, the mollusc yielding a purple dye; cf. Chapter XVIII). This should not be confused with the Greek *-ēus* meaning 'belonging to' or 'noted for', e.g. *giganteus*, belonging to the giants, hence gigantic.

-ibilis -is -e : *see above under* **-bilis.**

-icans : indicates process of becoming or resemblance sometimes so close as to be almost identical; participal suffix with verb base from noun base; e.g. *nigricans*, blackish (from *nigricare*, to be blackish, from *niger*, black).

-icius -a -um, -itius -a -um : indicates result of an action; verb base; *adventicius*, come from abroad, foreign, out of the ordinary (from *advenire*, to come, arrive); cf. Wölfflin (1888).

-idus -a -um : indicates a state or an action in progress; verb, noun or adjectival base; e.g. *albidus*, whitish (from *albus*, white), *nitidus*, shining, polished (from *nitere*, to shine).

-ilis -is -e : indicates capacity or ability, hence a property or quality; verb base; e.g. *fragilis*, easily broken (ultimately from *frangere*, to break).

-illus -a -um : diminutive, like **-cellus**; *see above.*

-ineus -a -um : indicates material or colour or close resemblance, like **-eus** above; noun base.

-inus -a -um : indicates possession or resemblance; noun base; e.g. *marinus*, belonging to the sea (from *mare*, sea), *ovinus*, belonging to sheep (from *ovis*, sheep), *ursinus*, belonging to a bear, shaggy like a bear (from *ursus*, bear). This comes close to the Greek ινος, Latinized as *inus*, indicating material or colour, hence possession or resemblance, e.g. *hyacinthinus*, of or belonging to the hyacinth (from *hyacinthus*, hyacinth, *Hyacinthos*, pre-Greek name in Greek mythology).

-ius -a -um : means 'characteristic of', hence indicates connexion or resemblance; noun base; e.g. *regius*, royal (from *rex*, king).

-ivus -a -um : indicates capacity, ability, possession by or property of; verb or noun base; e.g. *sensitivus*, capable of feeling (from *sentire*, to feel).

-izans : means 'becoming like, resembling, forming'; noun base; e.g. *graecizans*, imitating the Greeks (from *Graeci*, the Greeks).

-oideus -a -um : indicates resemblance; noun base; *see* **-oides** *below* (p. 310).

-olentus -a -um : *see* **-ulentus** *below.*

-orius -a -um : indicates capability, action, or function; verb base; e.g. *tinctorius*, belonging to dyeing (from *tingere*, to soak in colour).

-osus -a -um : indicates abundance or full or marked development; noun base; e.g. *venosus*, full of veins (from *vena*, vein); cf. Ernout (1949).

-ulentus -a -um, -olentus -a -um : indicates abundance or full or marked development; noun base; e.g. *succulentus*, full of juice, succulent (from *succus* or *sucus*, juice); *vinolentus*, full of wine, drunk (from *vinum*, wine); cf. Ernout (1949) Szemerényi (1954).

-ulus -a -um : (1) diminutive; adjectival base; e.g. *hispidulus*, minutely hispid (from *hispidus*, bristly); (2) indicates a tendency or action; verb base; e.g. *pendulus*, hanging down (from *pendere*, to suspend).

-utus -a -um : indicates possession; noun base; e.g. *cornutus*, horned (from *cornu*, horn).

-uus -a -um : indicates possibility or result of action; verb base, rarely noun base; e.g. *deciduus*, falling off (from *decidere*, to fall down).

GREEK ADJECTIVAL SUFFIXES

-aeus -a -um : indicates 'belonging to'; noun base; e.g. *europaeus*, European (from *Europa*, Europe).

-ĕus -a -um : indicates 'possessed by' or belonging to; noun base, usually the name of a person; e.g. *giganteus*, huge (from *gigas*, giant).

-icus -a -um : indicates 'belonging to'; noun base; e.g. *arcticus*, arctic (from *Arctos*, the Great Bear constellation).

-ineus -a -um : indicates material or colour; e.g. *coccineus*, scarlet (from *coccus*; *see* Chapter XVIII).

-īnus -a -um : indicates material or colour, resemblance or possession; noun base; e.g. *hyalinus*, transparent (from *hyalos*, glass).

-iticus -a -um : indicates fitness or capability for something or possession of.

-ius -a -um : 'characteristic of'; noun base.

-oides (*see* pp. 97, 265), **-oideus -a -um ; -odes :** indicates resemblance; noun base; e.g. *arachnoides*, like a spider's web (from *arachnion*, spider's web), *physodes*, bladder-like (from *physa*, bladder).

-otus -a -um : indicates resemblance or possession; noun base; e.g. *lepidotus*, scaly (from *lepis*, scale).

REFERENCES

BENEVENISTE, E. 1933. Les adjectifs latins en -cundus. *Bull. Soc. Linguist. Paris*, 34 : 186-190.

BUCK, C. D. & PETERSEN, W. 1945. *A reverse Index of Greek Nouns and Adjectives.* Chicago.

ERNOUT, A. 1941. Les noms en -āgō, -īgō, -ūgō du latin. *Revue de Philologie*, III 15 : 85-111.

—— 1949. *Les Adjectifs latins en -ōsus et en -ulentus.* Paris.

FUNCK, A. 1893. Die lateinischen Adverbia auf -im, ihre Bildung und ihre Geschichte. *Arch. Latein. Lexikogr.*, 8 : 77-114.

LEUMANN, M. 1944. Gruppierung und Funktioner der Wortbildungssuffixe des Lateins. *Museum Helveticum*, 1 : 129-151.

MAYER, A. 1954. Die lat. Ortsbezeichnungen auf -etum. *Glotta* 33 : 227-238.

NYBAKKEN, O. E. 1959. *Greek and Latin in scientific Terminology.* Ames, Iowa.

OSTHOFF, H. 1887. Die lateinische Adverbia auf -iter. *Arch. Latein. Lexikogr.* 4 : 455-466.

SCHNORR VON CAROLSFELD, H. 1884. Das lateinische Suffix -anus. *Arch. Latein Lexikogr.*, 1 : 177-194.

SCHÖNWERTH, O., & WEYMER, C. 1888. Über die lateinischen Adjectiva auf -osus *Arch. Latein. Lexikogr.*, 5 : 192-222.

SECK, F., & SCHNORR VON CAROLSFELD, H. 1884. Das lateinische Suffix -aster astra, astrum. *Arch. Latein. Lexikrogr.*, 1 : 390-407.

SWANSON, D. C. 1958. Latin -ensis in verse texts. *Glotta*, 37 : 130-149.

SZEMERÉNYI, O, 1954. The Latin adjectives in -ulentus. *Glotta*, 33 : 266-282.

WERNER, C. F. 1956. *Wortelemente lateinisch-griechischer Fachausdrücke in der Biologie.* Leipzig.

WIKÉN, E. 1951. *Latin för Botanister och Zoologer.* Malmö.

WÖLFFLIN, E. VON. 1888. Die Adjektiva auf -icius. *Arch. Latein. Lexikogr.*, 5 415-437.

—— 1902. Analogiebildungen auf -ellus, -ella-, -ellum. *Arch. Latein. Lexikogr.* 12 : 301-308.

CHAPTER XXII

Descriptive Terminology

LINNAEUS'S PHILOSOPHIA BOTANICA

Modern botanical terminology derives largely from the works of Carl Linnaeus, notably his *Philosophia botanica* (1751 ; cf. Dahlgren, 1951), wherein under each organ, beginning with the root (*radix*) and proceeding upwards by way of the stem (*truncus*), leaf (*folium*), etc., to the seeds (*semina*), he listed the variants of each and thereby provided appropriate words for their recording. Between 1755 and 1824 this book was re-issued or revised eleven times. Every systematic botanist read it ; L. C. Richard said he re-read it every year. Thus it established Linnaean method and terminology. In 1760 James Lee's *An Introduction to Botany* presented it 'cloathed in an English dress', apparently by S. F. Gray the elder ; this was re-issued or revised eight times between 1765 and 1810. Another free translation into English was published in 1775 by Hugh Rose as *The Elements of Botany*.

A more literal French translation, *Philosophie botanique*, appeared in 1788, a Russian one, *Filosofiya botaniki*, in 1800. Thereafter, taking Linnaeus's work as a basis, British, French and German authors produced glossaries and surveys of terminology which added more and more terms and expressions designed to meet the needs of more and more precise observation. As stated by John Lindley, 'the language of Botany was, when Linnaeus left it, admirably suited to the demands then made upon it ; and . . . if the scientific dictatorship which he exercised, had been seized by a successor capable of maintaining his authority, it would, perhaps, have lost none of its excellence. But the wants of science increased with its progress ; as new organs were

CAROLI LINNÆI

ARCHIATR. REG. MEDIC. ET BOTAN. PROFESS. UPSAL.
ACAD. IMPERIAL. MONSPEL. BEROL. TOLOS. UPSAL.
STOCKH. SOC. ET PARIS. CORRESP.

PHILOSOPHIA BOTANICA

IN QVA

EXPLICANTUR

FUNDAMENTA BOTANICA

CUM

DEFINITIONIBUS   PARTIUM,
EXEMPLIS   TERMINORUM,
OBSERVATIONIBUS RARIORUM,

ADJECTIS

FIGURIS ÆNEIS.

CUM PRIVILEGIO.

STOCKHOLMIÆ,
APUD GODOFR. KIESEWETTER
1751.

Fig. 16   Title-page of Carl Linnaeus, *Philosophia botanica* (1751)

distinguished, new substantives were wanted to express them . . . each nation or community studied for itself, thought for itself, and wrote for itself, and hence half a dozen names were proposed in different places to express the same idea.'

GLOSSARIES

This accumulation of words led to the production of yet more glossaries and surveys. They culminated in A. P. de Candolle's *Théorie élémentaire de la Botanique* (1813; 2nd ed., 1819; 3rd ed. 1844), Lindley's *An Introduction to Botany* (1832; 2nd ed., 1835; 3rd ed., 1839; 4th ed., 1848) and *The Elements of Botany* (1847), G. W. Bischoff's *Handbuch der botanischen Terminologie und Systemkunde* (3 vols., 1830–34) and *Wörterbuch der beschreibenden Botanik* (1839; 2nd ed., 1859) and E. Germain de Saint-Pierre's *Guide du Botaniste* (1852) and *Nouveau dictionnaire de Botanique* (1870).

LINDLEY'S SURVEY OF DESCRIPTIVE TERMINOLOGY

Lindley found that 'from one cause or another, whether accident, ignorance, pedantry, over-fastidiousness, vanity or carelessness', the language of botany was 'marvellously in want of reformation'. Following Link (1798), Illiger (1800) and de Candolle (1813), he distinguished the characteristic or common terms of general application from those which applied only to particular organs and he classified these terms into logical groups, as given below. His work, largely owing to the adoption of much of it by George Bentham (1861, etc.) and Asa Gray (1879, etc.), provides the foundation of botanical terminology in English-speaking countries. In his *Introduction* Lindley grouped together words of related meaning and gave Latin and English equivalents associated with definitions in classified order; in his *Elements of Botany* he listed them alphabetically. The abiding international value of these glossaries is indicated by the translation of the first into Spanish at Tucumán in 1951 and its re-issue in California in 1938 and in 1964. Lindley's general survey taken from his *Introduction to Botany*, 3rd ed. (1839) is accordingly reprinted below; most of his examples are either no longer necessary or refer to little-known plants and are omitted, but some additions, placed within square brackets, have been made to indicate divergent later usage. Rickett's four scholarly papers (1954–56), based on the examination of some 25 definitions for each of some important terms, make clear the current lack of consistency and need for standardization. The applications recommended by Rickett are accordingly noted below, together with those for plane shapes provided by the Systematics Association Committee, the chart (1962; Fig. 19) of which is cited below as SADT. Even if standardization becomes general it will nevertheless remain necessary to keep in mind the somewhat different use of some terms in the past when interpreting the descriptions of a given author or period. The most complete glossary in English supplying Latin equivalents for many terms is B. D. Jackson's *Glossary of botanic Terms* (1900; 4th ed. 1928) unfortunately without illustrations. The best illustrated guide is the Russian-Latin *Organographia illustrata Plantarum vascularum* (1956–62) by Theodorov, Kirpicznikov and Artjuschenko.

Lindley's survey of descriptive botanical terminology modified as stated above still provides a basic glossary of botanical Latin even though a few of his English equivalents such as 'leprous' for *lepidotus* (lepidote), 'bossed' for *umbonatus* (umbonate), 'knee pan-shaped' for *patelliformis* (patelliform), 'pointleted' for *apiculatus* (apiculate), are now obsolete. Below its items are numbered continuously instead of section by section.

SYNOPSIS OF TERMINOLOGY

CHARACTERISTIC TERMS are either Individual or Collective.

I CHARACTERISTIC INDIVIDUAL TERMS are either Absolute or Relative.

INDIVIDUAL ABSOLUTE TERMS relate to

    1. *Figure*
        A General or Solid Form (Nos. 1-101)
        B Outlines and Plane Shapes (Nos. 102-138)
        C The Apex (Nos. 139-165)
        D The Base (Nos. 166-178)

Fig. 17   Types of simple Leaves and Indumentum as illustrated in Linnaeus, *Philosophia botanica* (1751)

1, Orbiculatum; 2, Subrotundum; 3, Ovatum; 4, Ovale s. *Ellipticum*; 5, Oblongum; 6, Lanceolatum; 7, Lineare; 8, Subulatum; 9, Reniforme; 10, Cordatum; 11, Lunulatum; 12, Triangulare; 13, Sagittatum; 14, *Cordato-sagitattum*; 15, Hastatum; 16, Fissum; 17, Trilobum; 18, Praemorsum; 19, Lobatum; 20, Quinquangulare; 21, Erosum; 22, Palmatum; 23, Pinnatifidum; 24, Laciniatum; 25, Sinuatum; 26, *Dentato-sinuatum*; 27, *Retrorsum sinuatum*; 28, Partitum; 29, Repandum; 30, Dentatum; 31, Serratum; 32, *Duplicato-serratum*; 33, *Duplicato-crenatum*; 34, Cartilagineum; 35, *Acute crenatum*; 36, *Obtuse crenatum*; 37, Plicatum; 38, Crenatum; 39, Crispum; 40, Obtusum; 41, Acutum; 42, Acuminatum; 43, *Obtusum acumine*; 44, Emarginatum acute; 45, *Cuneiforme emarginatum*; 46, Retusum; 47, Pilosum; 48, Tomentosum; 49, Hispidum; 50, Ciliatum; 51, Rugosum; 52, Venosum; 53, Nervosum; 54, Papillosum; 55, Linguiforme; 56, Acinaciforme; 57, Dolabriforme; 58, Deltoides; 59, Triquetrum; 60, Canaliculatum; 61, Sulcatum; 62, Teres

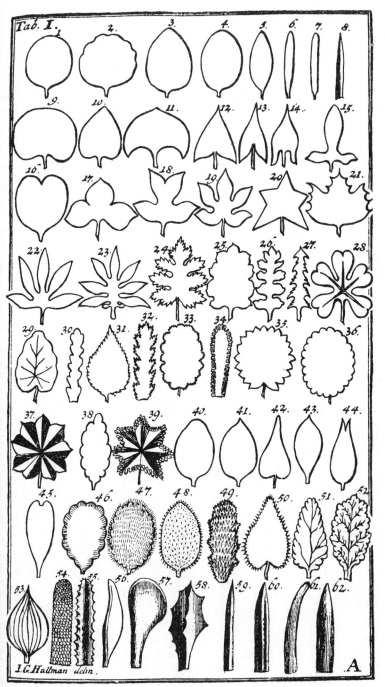

Tab. I.

I.G. Hallman delin.

315

A

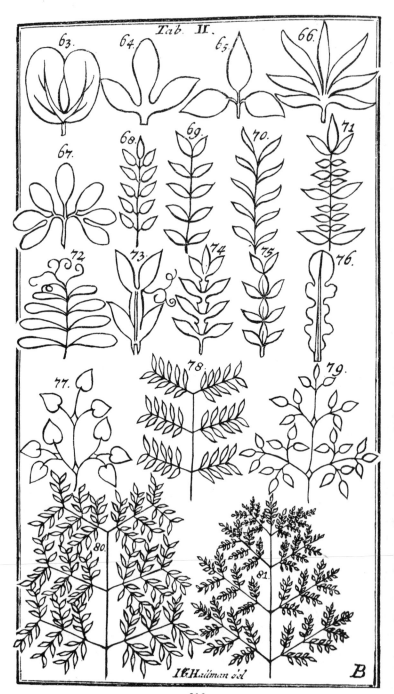

Tab. II.

I.G.Hallman del

B

2. *Division*
    E   The Margin (Nos. 179-188)
    F   Incision (Nos. 189-200)
    G Division or Ramification (Nos. 201-244)
3. *Surface*
    H   Markings or Evenness (Nos. 245-259)
    J   Hair-covering and Superficial Processes (Nos. 260-293)
    K Polish or Texture (Nos. 294-309)
4. *Texture or Substance* (Nos. 310-334)
5. *Size* (Nos. 335-341)
6. *Duration* (No. 342)
7. *Colour* (see Chapter XVIII)
8. *Variegation* (see Chapter XVIII)
9. *Veining* (Nos. 343-364)

INDIVIDUAL RELATIVE TERMS comprehend
  10. *Aestivation and Vernation* (Nos. 365-386)
  11. *Direction* (Nos. 387-436)
  12. *Insertion* (Nos. 437-474)

II CHARACTERISTIC COLLECTIVE TERMS relate to
  13. *Arrangement* (Nos. 475-505)
  14. *Number* (see Chapter VIII)

CLASS I. OF INDIVIDUAL TERMS

The terms which are included in this class are applied to the parts of a plant considered by themselves, and not in masses: they are either *absolute*, being used with reference to their own individual quality; or *relative*, being employed to express the relation which is borne by plants, or their parts, to some other body. Thus, for example, when we say that a plant has a *lateral ovate* spike of flowers, the term *lateral* is relative, being used to express the relation which the spike bears to the stem; and the term *ovate* is absolute, being expressive of the actual form of the spike: and, again, in speaking of a *rugose terminal* capsule, *rugose* is absolute, *terminal* is relative.

Fig. 18 Types of compound Leaves as illustrated in Linnaeus, *Philosophia botanica* (1751)

63, Binatum; 64, Ternatum *foliolis sessilibus*; 65, do. *petiolatis*; 66, Digitatum; 67, Pedatum; 68, Pinnatum *cum impari*; 70, do. *alternatim*; 71, do. *interrupte*; 72, do. *cirrhosum*; 73, do. *conjugatum*; 74, do. *decursive*; 75, do. *articulate*; 76, Lyratum; 77, Biternatum, *Duplicato-ternatum*; 78, Bipinnatum (*Sauvag.*), *Duplicato-pinnatum*; 79, Triternatum, *Triplicato-ternatum*; 80, Tripinnatum (*Sauvag.*), *sine impari*; 81, do. *cum impari*

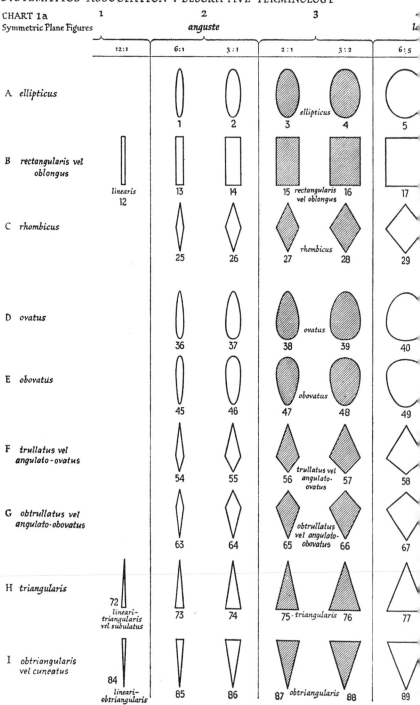

Fig. 19   Chart of simple symmetrical plane Shapes
(From Systematics Association Committee for descriptive Biological
Terminology in *Taxon*, 11 ; 1962)

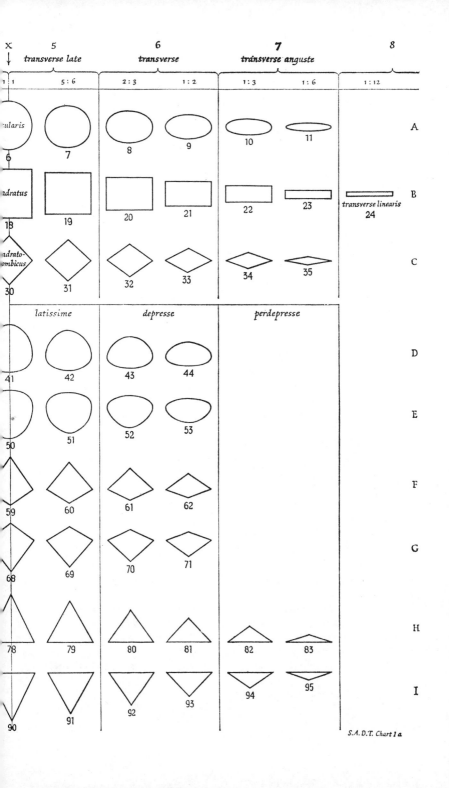

S.A.D.T. Chart 1 a

INDIVIDUAL ABSOLUTE TERMS

These relate to figure, division, surface, texture, size, duration, colour, variegation and veining.

1. *FIGURE*

A. GENERAL OR SOLID FORM

1. **Conicus, pyramidalis** (Conical) : having the figure of a true cone.
2. **Conoideus** (Conoidal) : resembling a conical figure, but not truly one.
3. **Prismaticus** (Prism-shaped) : having several longitudinal angles and intermediate flat faces.
4. **Globosus, sphaericus** (Globose) : forming nearly a true sphere.
5. **Cylindricus** (Cylindrical) : having nearly a true cylindrical figure.
6. **Tubulosus** (Tubular) : approaching a cylindrical figure and hollow.
7. **Fistulosus** (Fistulous) : this is said of a cylindrical or terete body, which is hollow, but closed at each end.
8. **Cubicus** (Cubical) : having or approaching the form of a cube.
9. **Clavatus, claviformis** (Club-shaped) : gradually thickening upwards from a very tapering base.
10. **Turbinatus** (Turbinate or top-shaped) : inversely conical, with a contraction towards the point.
11. **Pyriformis** (Pear-shaped) : differing from turbinate in being more elongated.
12. **Lachrymiformis** (Tear-shaped) : the same as pear-shaped, except that the sides of the inverted cone are not contracted.
13. **Strombuliformis** (Strombus-shaped) : twisted in a long spire, so as to resemble the convolutions of the shell called a Strombus.
14. **Spiralis** (Spiral) : twisted like a corkscrew.
15. **Cochleatus** (Cochleate) : twisted in a short spire, so as to resemble the convolutions of a snail-shell.
16. **Napiformis** (Turnip-shaped) : having the figure of a depressed sphere.
17. **Placentiformis** (Placenta-shaped) : thick, round, and concave, both on the upper and lower surface.
18. **Lenticularis, lentiformis** (Lens-shaped) : resembling a double convex lens.
19. **Scutatus, scutiformis** (Buckler-shaped) : having the figure of a small round buckler ; lens-shaped, with an elevated rim.
20. **Umbonatus** (Bossed) : round, with a projecting point in the centre, like the boss of an ancient shield.
21. **Gibbus, gibbosus** (Gibbous) : very convex or tumid ; as the leaves of many succulent plants : properly speaking, this term should be restricted to solid convexities.
22. **Meloniformis** (Melon-shaped) : irregularly spherical, with projecting ribs : a bad term.

23. **Sphaeroideus** (Spheroidal): a solid with a spherical figure, a little depressed at each end. *De Cand.*

24. **Ellipsoideus** (Ellipsoidal): a solid with an elliptical figure. *De Cand.*

25. **Ovoideus** (Ovoidal): a solid with an ovate figure, or resembling an egg. *De Cand.*

26. **Clypeatus** (Shield-shaped): in the form of an ancient buckler: [almost] the same as scutate, No. 19.

27. **Fusiformis** (Spindle-shaped): thick, tapering to each end.

28. **Teres** (Terete): the opposite of angular: usually employed in contra-distinction to that term, when speaking of long bodies. Many stems are terete.

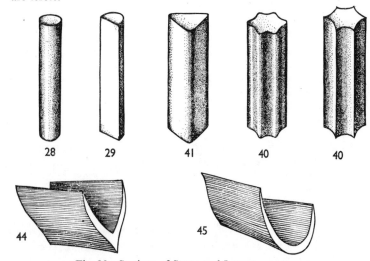

Fig. 20   Sections of Stems and Leaves
27, fusiformis; 28, teres; 29, semiteres; 40, angulosus, 40 sinist., obtusangulus, 40 dext., acutangulus; 41, trigonus; 44, carinatus; 45, canaliculatus (after J. Lindley, *Introduction to Botany*; 1832)

29. **Semiteres** (Half-terete): flat on one side, terete on the other.

30. **Compressus** (Compressed): flattened lengthwise; as the pod of a Pea.

31. **Depressus** (Depressed): flattened vertically.

32. **Planus** (Plane): a perfectly level or flat surface.

33. **Pulvinatus** (Cushioned): convex, or rather flattened.

34. **Discoideus** (Discoidal): orbicular, with some perceptible thickness, parallel faces, and a rounded border.

35. **Arcuatus, curvatus** (Curved): bent, but so as to represent the arc of a circle.

36. **Acinaciformis** (Scimitar-shaped): curved, fleshy, plane on the two sides, the concave border thick, the convex border thin.

37. **Dolabriformis** (Axe-shaped): fleshy, nearly straight, somewhat terete at the base, compressed towards the upper end; one border thick and straight, the other enlarged, convex, and thin.

38. **Falcatus** (Falcate): plane and curved, with parallel edges, like the blade of a reaper's sickle; any degree of curvature, with parallel edges, receives this name.

39. **Linguiformis** (Tongue-shaped): long, fleshy, plano-convex, obtuse.

40. **Angulosus** (Angular): having projecting longitudinal angles. We say *obtuse-angled* [*obtusangulus*] Fig. 40 sinist., when the angles are rounded; and *acute-angled* [*acutangulus*] Fig. 40 dext., when they are sharp. Some call these angles the *acies*.

41. **Trigonus** (Three-cornered): having three longitudinal angles and three plane faces.

42. **Triqueter** (Three-edged): having three acute angles with concave faces; generally used as a synonym of trigonus.

43. **Anceps** (Two-edged): compressed, with two sharp edges.

44. **Carinatus** (Keeled): formed in the manner of the keel of a boat; that is to say, with a sharp projecting ridge, arising from a flat or concave central rib.

45. **Canaliculatus** (Channelled): long and concave, so as to resemble a gutter or channel.

46. **Navicularis, cymbiformis** (Boat-shaped): having the figure of a boat in miniature; that is to say, concave, tapering to each end, with a keel externally.

47. **Flagelliformis** (Whip-shaped): long, tapering and supple, like the thong of a whip. This term is confined to stems and roots.

48. **Funalis** (Rope-shaped): formed of coarse fibres resembling cords. *Mirbel.*

49. **Filiformis** (Thread-shaped): slender like a thread; as the filaments of most plants, and the styles of many.

50. **Capillaris** (Hair-shaped): the same as filiform, but more delicate so as to resemble a hair; it is also applied to the fine ramifications of the inflorescence of some plants.

51. **Moniliformis** (Necklace-shaped): cylindrical or terete and contracted at regular intervals.

52. **Vermicularis** (Worm-shaped): thick and almost cylindrical, but bent in different places. *Willd.*

53. **Torulosus** (Knotted): a cylindrical body, uneven in surface; very nearly the same as moniliform.

54. **Tubiformis, tubatus** (Trumpet-shaped): hollow, and dilated at one extremity, like the end of a trumpet. *De Cand.*

55. **Cornutus, corniculatus** (Horned): terminating in a process resembling a horn. If there are two horns, the word *bicornis* is used; if three, *tricornis*; and so on.

56. **Proboscideus** (Beaked): having a hard terminal horn.

57. **Cristatus** (Crested): having an elevated, irregular, or notched ridge, resembling the crest of a helmet. This term is chiefly applied to seeds and to the appendages of the anthers of some Ericae.

58. **Petaloideus** (Petal-like): having the colour and texture of a petal.

59. **Foliaceus** (Leaf-like): having the texture or form of a leaf.

60. **Alatus** (Winged): having a thin broad margin. In composition *pterus* is used; as *dipterus* for two-winged, *tripterus* for three-winged, *tetrapterus* for four-winged, etc.; *peripterus* when the wing surrounds anything; *epipterus* when it terminates.

61. **Molendinaceus** (Mill-sail-shaped): having many wings projecting from a convex surface.

62. **Gongylodes** (Knob-like): having an irregular roundish figure.

63. **Dimidiatus** (Halved): only half, or partially, formed. A leaf is called dimidiate when one side only is perfect; an anther when one lobe only is perfect; and so on.

64. **Flabelliformis** (Fan-shaped): plaited like the rays of a fan.

65. **Grumosus** (Grumous): in form of little clustered grains.

66. **Testiculatus** (Testicular): having the figure of two oblong bodies.

67. **Ringens, personatus** (Ringent or personate): a term applied to a monopetalous corolla, the limb of which is unequally divided; the upper division, or lip, being arched; the lower prominent, and pressed against it, so that when compressed, the whole resembles the mouth of a gaping animal.

68. **Labiatus** (Labiate): a term applied to a monopetalous calyx or corolla which is separated into two unequal divisions; the one anterior and the other posterior, with respect to the axis; hence bilabiate [*bilabiatus*] is more commonly used than labiate. It is often employed instead of ringent.

69. **Rotatus** (Wheel-shaped): a calyx or corolla, or other organ, of which the tube is very short and the segments spreading.

70. **Hypocrateriformis** (Salver-shaped): a calyx or corolla, or other organ, of which the tube is long and slender, and the limb flat.

71. **Infundibularis, infundibuliformis** (Funnel-shaped): a calyx or corolla, or other organ, in which the tube is obconical, gradually enlarging upwards into the limb, so that the whole resembles a funnel.

72. **Campanulatus, campaniformis** (Bell-shaped): a calyx, corolla or other organ, in which the tube is inflated, and gradually enlarged into a limb, the base not being conical.

73. **Urceolatus** (Pitcher-shaped): the same as campanulate, but more contracted at the orifice, with an erect limb.

74. **Cyathiformis** (Cup-shaped): the same as pitcher-shaped, but not contracted at the margin; the whole resembling a drinking-cup.

75. **Cupuliformis** (Cupola-shaped): slightly concave, with a nearly entire margin.

76. **Patelliformis** (Kneepan-shaped): broad, round, thick; convex on the lower surface, concave on the other: the same as *meniscoideus*, but thicker.

77. **Trochlearis** (Pulley-shaped): circular, compressed, contracted in the middle of the circumference, so as to resemble a pulley.

78. **Scutelliformis** (Scutelliform): the same as patelliform, but oval; not round.

79. **Muscariformis** (Brush-shaped): formed like a brush or broom; that is

to say, furnished with long hairs towards one end of a slender body. [Corresponds to *penicillatus* of later authors].

80. **Acetabuliformis** (Acetabuliform): concave, depressed, round, with a border a little turned inwards.

81. **Crateriformis** (Goblet-shaped): concave, hemispherical, a little contracted at the base.

82. **Cotyliformis** (Cotyloform): resembling rotate [no. 69], but with an erect limb.

83. **Poculiformis** (Poculiform): cup-shaped, with a hemispherical base and an upright limb; nearly the same as campanulate [no. 72].

84. **Scrotiformis** (Pouch-shaped): hollow, and resembling a little double bag.

85. **Digitaliformis** (Foxglove-shaped): like campanulate, but longer, and irregular.

86. **Vascularis** (Vase-shaped): formed like a flower-pot; that is to say, resembling an inverted truncate cone. [*Vascularis* is now rarely if ever used in this sense which corresponds to *olliformis*].

87. **Taenianus** (Tapeworm-shaped): long, cylindrical, contracted in various places, in the manner of the tapeworm.

88. **Botuliformis** (Sausage-shaped): long, cylindrical, curved inwards at each end.

89. **Umbraculiformis** (Umbrella-shaped): resembling an expanded umbrella; that is to say, hemispherical and convex, with rays or plaits, proceeding from a common centre.

90. **Meniscoideus** (Meniscoid): thin, concavo-convex, and hemispherical, resembling a watch-glass.

91. **Fungiformis, fungilliformis** (Mushroom-headed): cylindrical, having a rounded, convex, overhanging extremity.

92. **Modioliformis** (Nave-shaped): hollow, round, depressed, with a very narrow orifice.

93. **Cucullatus** (Hooded): a plane body, the apex or sides of which are curved inwards, so as to resemble the point of a slipper, or a hood.

94. **Selliformis** (Saddle-shaped): oblong, with the sides hanging down, like the laps of a saddle.

95. **Turgidus** (Turgid): slightly swelling.

96. **Inflatus** (Bladdery): thin, membranous, slightly transparent, swelling equally, as if inflated with air.

97. **Ventricosus** (Bellying): swelling unequally on one side.

98. **Regularis** (Regular): in which all the parts are symmetrical. A rotate corolla is regular; the flower of a Cherry is regular.

99. **Irregularis** (Irregular): in which symmetry is destroyed by some inequality of parts. A labiate corolla and the flowers of the Horse-chestnut and the Violet are irregular.

100. **Abnormis** (Abnormal): in which some departure takes place from the ordinary structure of the family or genus to which a given plant belongs. Thus, Nicotiana multivalvis, in which the ovarium has many cells instead of two, is unusual or abnormal.

101. **Normalis** (Normal): in which the ordinary structure peculiar to the family or genus of a given plant is in no wise departed from.

B. OUTLINES AND PLANE SHAPES

[The standardized terms for simple symmetrical plane shapes adopted by the Systematics Association Committee in *Taxon* 11: 145-156, 245-247 (1962) are cited below as SADT; see Fig. 19.]

102. **Ambitus, circumscriptio** (Outline): the figure represented by the margin of a body.

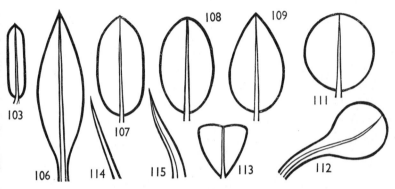

Fig. 21   Outlines of Leaves, etc.
103, linearis, sensu Lindleyi (=anguste oblongus);   106, lanceolatus, sensu Lindleyi (=anguste ellipticus);   107, oblongus;   108, ellipticus; 109, ovatus;   111, rotundus;   112, spatulatus;   113, cuneiformis;   114, subulatus;   115, acerosus (after J. Lindley, *Introduction to Botany*; 1832)

103. **Linearis** (Linear): narrow, short, with the two opposite margins parallel: [*= anguste oblongus* SADT nos. 13-14; length: breadth = 6: 1 to 3: 1].

104. **Fasciarius** (Band-shaped): narrow, very long, with the two opposite margins parallel: [*= linearis* SADT no. 12; length: breadth = 12 or more: 1].

105. **Ligulatus, loratus** (Strap-shaped): narrow, moderately long, with the two opposite margins parallel: [*= anguste oblongus* SADT nos. 13-14].

106. **Lanceolatus** (Lanceolate): narrowly elliptical, tapering [equally] to each end; as the leaf of Plantago lanceolata, Daphne Mezereum, etc.: [*= anguste ellipticus* SADT nos. 1-2; length: breadth = 6: 1 to 3: 1; the discordant use of *lanceolatus* by Lindley and Asa Gray is discussed by Alph. de Candolle, 1880: 198-200].

107. **Oblongus** (Oblong): elliptical, obtuse at each end: [*= oblongus* SADT nos. 15-16; length: breadth = 2: 1 to 3: 2, the sides almost parallel; discussed by Rickett, 1954a: 14].

108. **Ellipticus, ovalis** (Oval): elliptical, acute at each end: [*= ellipticus*

SADT nos. 3-4; length: breadth 2:1 to 3:2 with sides curved equally from middle].

109. **Ovatus** (Ovate): oblong or elliptical, broadest at the lower end, so as to resemble the longitudinal section of an egg: [SADT nos. 38-39; length: breadth = 2:1 to 3:2, broadest below the middle].

110. **Orbicularis** (Orbicular): perfectly circular: [= *circularis* SADT no. 6].

111. **Rotundus, subrotundus, rotundatus** (Roundish): orbicular, a little inclining to be oblong [= *late ellipticus* SADT no. 5; length: breadth = 6:5, broadest at middle].

112. **Spatulatus** (Spatulate): oblong, with the lower end very much attenuated, so that the whole resembles a chemist's spatula.

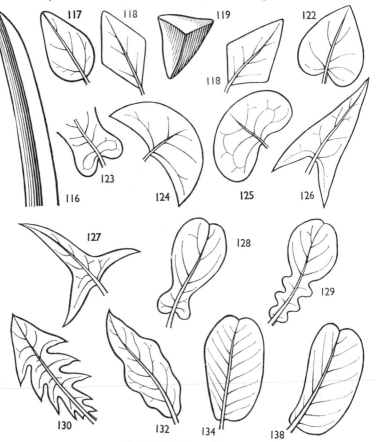

Fig. 22 Outlines of Leaves

116, ensiformis; 117, parabolicus; 118, rhombeus; 119, deltoides; 122 cordiformis; 123, auriculatus; 124, lunatus; 125, reniformis; 126, sagittatus; 127, hastatus; 128, panduratus; 129, lyratus; 130, runcinatus; 132, undulatus; 134, inaequalis; 138, dimidiatus (after J. Lindley, *Introduction to Botany*; 1832)

113. **Cuneiformis** (Wedge-shaped): inversely triangular, with rounded angles: [=*obtriangularis* SADT no. 90].

114. **Subulatus** (Awl-shaped): linear, very narrow, tapering to a very fine point from a broadish base.

115. **Acerosus** (Needle-shaped): linear, rigid, tapering to a fine point from a narrow base.

116. **Ensiformis, gladiatus** (Sword-shaped): lorate, quite straight, with the point acute.

117. **Parabolicus** (Parabolical): between ovate and elliptical, the apex being obtuse.

118. **Rhombeus, rhomboideus** (Rhomboid): oval, a little angular in the middle: [=*rhombicus* SADT nos. 27, 28].

119. **Deltoides** (Deltoid): a solid, the transverse section of which has a triangular outline, like the Greek Δ.

120. **Triangularis** (Triangular): having the figure of a triangle of any kind: [SADT nos. 73-85].

121. **Trapeziformis** (Trapeziform): having four edges, those which are opposite not being parallel.

122. **Cordatus, cordiformis** (Heart-shaped): having two round lobes at the base [*cordatus*], the whole resembling the heart in a pack of cards [*cordiformis*].

123. **Auriculatus** (Eared): having two small rounded lobes at the base.

124. **Lunatus, lunulatus, semilunatus** (Crescent-shaped): resembling the figure of the crescent.

125. **Reniformis** (Kidney-shaped): resembling the figure of a kidney, that is to say crescent-shaped, with the ends rounded.

126. **Sagittatus** (Arrow-headed): gradually enlarged at the base into two straight lobes, like the head of an arrow.

127. **Hastatus** (Halbert-headed): abruptly enlarged at the base into two acute diverging lobes, like the head of a halbert.

128. **Panduratus, panduriformis** (Fiddle-shaped): obovate, with a deep recess or sinus on each side.

129. **Lyratus** (Lyre-shaped): the same as panduriform, but with several sinuses on each side, which gradually diminish in size to the base.

130. **Runcinatus** (Runcinate or hook-backed): curved in a direction from the apex to the base [i.e. with prominent teeth pointing towards the base].

131. **Attenuatus** (Tapering): gradually diminishing in breadth.

132. **Undulatus** (Wavy): having an uneven, alternately convex and concave margin.

133. **Aequalis** (Equal): when both sides of a figure are symmetrical.

134. **Inaequalis** (Unequal): when the two sides of a figure are not symmetrical.

135. **Aequilaterus** (Equal-sided): the same as equal.

136. **Inaequilaterus** (Unequal-sided): the same as unequal.

137. **Obliquus** (Oblique): when the degree of inequality in the two sides is slight.

138. **Dimidiatus** (Halved): when the degree of inequality is so great that one half of the figure is either wholly or nearly wanting [see no. 63].

C. THE APEX

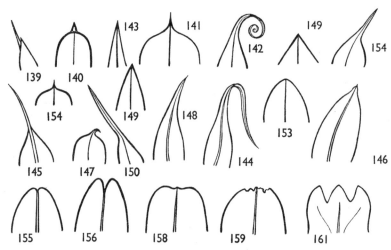

Fig. 23 Apices of Leaves, etc.

139, aristatus; 140, mucronatus; 141, cuspidatus; 142, cirrhosus; 143, pungens; 144, setosus; 145, piliferus; 146, apiculatus; 147, uncinatus; 148, rostratus; 149, acutus; 150, acuminatus; 153, obtusus; 154, obtusus cum acumine; 155, retusus; 156, emarginatus; 158, truncatus; 159, praemorsus; 161, tridentatus (after J. Lindley, *Introduction to Botany*; 1832)

[The divergent use of terms to describe apices is discussed by Rickett in *Bull. Torrey Bot. Club*, 83: 342-354 (1956).]

139. **Aristatus** (Awned): abruptly terminated in a hard, straight, subulate point of various lengths: [provided with a bristle-like appendage, cf. Rickett, p. 349]. The arista is always a continuation of the costa, and sometimes separates from the lamina below the apex.

140. **Mucronatus** (Mucronate): abruptly terminated by a hard short point: [cf. Rickett, p. 348].

141. **Cuspidatus** (Cuspidate): tapering gradually into a rigid point. It is also used sometimes to express abruptly acuminate [cf. Rickett, p. 348].

142. **Cirrhosus** (Cirrhous): terminated by a spiral, or flexuose, filiform appendage. This is due to an elongation of a costa.

143. **Pungens** (Pungent): terminating gradually in a hard sharp point.

144. **Setosus** (Bristle-pointed): terminating gradually in a very fine sharp point. [*Setosus* usually means 'beset with bristles', as in *hispidus*, no 227, *echinatus*, no. 263].

145. **Piliferus** (Hair-pointed): terminating in a very fine weak point.

146. **Apiculatus** (Pointleted): terminating abruptly in a little point; differing from mucronate in the point being part of the limb, and not arising wholly from a costa.

147. **Uncinatus, uncatus** (Hooked) : curved suddenly back at the point.
148. **Rostratus, rostellatus** (Beaked) : terminating gradually in a hard, long, straight point.
149. **Acutus** (Acute, or sharp-pointed) : terminating at once in a point, not abruptly, but without tapering in any degree [i.e. with two almost straight lines converging at an angle of less than 90° ; cf. Rickett, p. 343].
150. **Acuminatus** (Taper-pointed) : terminating very gradually in a point [now 'applied to an apex bounded by lines or surfaces which change from straight or convex to concave and converge gradually to a point' ; cf. Rickett, p. 346].
151. **Acuminose** (Acuminose) : terminating gradually in a flat narrow end.
152. **Caudatus** (Tail-pointed) : excessively acuminated, so that the point is long and weak, like the tail of some animal [cf. Rickett, p. 350].
153. **Obtusus** (Blunt) : terminating gradually in a rounded end [i.e. rounded enough for an angle of 90° to be placed inside it ; *rotundatus*, like an arc of a circle ; cf. Rickett, p. 343].
154. **Obtusus cum acumine** (Blunt with a point) : terminating abruptly in a round end, the middle of which is suddenly lengthened into a point.
155. **Retusus** (Retuse) : terminating in a round end, the centre of which is depressed [with a rounded sinus at the apex ; cf. Rickett, p. 350].
156. **Emarginatus** (Emarginate) : having a notch at the end, as if a piece had been taken out [indented with acute sinus ; cf. Rickett, p. 350].
157. **Accisus** : when the end has an acute sinus between two rounded angles. *Link*. [Essentially as emarginate.]
158. **Truncatus** (Truncate) : terminating very abruptly, as if a piece had been cut off.
159. **Praemorsus** (Bitten) : the same as truncate, except that the termination is ragged and irregular, as if bitten off.
160. **Daedaleus** (Daedaleous) : when the point has a large circuit, but is truncated and rugged. *W*.
161. **Tridentatus** (Trident-pointed) : when the point is truncated, and has three indentations *W*.
162. **Capitatus** (Headed) : suddenly much thicker at the point than in any other part ; a term confined to cylindrical or terete bodies ; glandular hairs, etc.
163. **Lamellatus, lamellosus** (Lamellar) : having two little plates at the point.
164. **Hebetatus** (Blunted) : having a soft obtuse termination.
165. **Muticus** (Pointless). This term is employed only in contradistinction to some other that indicates being pointed ; thus, if, in contrasting two things, one were said to be mucronate, the other, if it had not a mucro, would be called pointless ; and the same term would be equally employed in contrast with cuspidate or aristate, or any such. It is also used absolutely.

D. THE BASE

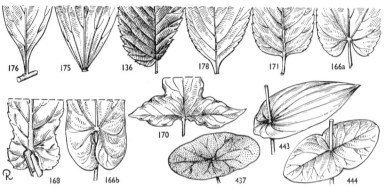

Fig. 24   Bases of Leaves

136, inaequilaterus; 166a, cordatus; 166b, profunde cordatus lobis basalibus imbricatis; 170 (127), hastatus; 171 (158), truncatus; 168 (123), auriculatus; 175, cuneatus; 176, angustatus; 178, breve angustatus; 437, peltatus; 443, perfoliatus; 444, connatus (by Marion E. Ruff, from G. H. M. Lawrence, *Introduction to Plant Taxonomy*; 1955)

[Lindley did not deal specifically with terms relating to the base but included those relevant under B. nos. 122 (*cordatus*), 123 (*auriculatus*), 126 (*sagittatus*), 127 (*hastatus*); C. nos. 154 (*obtusus*), 158 (*truncatus*) above; and under nos. 437 (*peltatus*), 443 (*perfoliatus*) and 444 (*connatus*) below. G. M. Schulze (1953) has provided a useful summary of other terms (Nos. 172-178 below)].

166. **Cordatus** (Cordate): having two equal more or less rounded lobes forming a deep sinus at base.
167. **Subcordatus** (Subcordate): having two slight lobes and a shallow sinus.
168. **Auriculatus** (Auriculate): having two rounded lobes at base which stand out from the rest of the leaf-blade like little ears.
169. **Sagittatus** (Sagittate): having two equal pointed more or less triangular lobes at base directed downward.
170. **Hastatus** (Hastate): having two equal pointed more or less triangular lobes at base directed outwards.
171. **Truncatus** (Truncatus): as if cut straight across.
172. **Rotundatus** (Rounded): rounded like an arc of a circle.
173. **Obtusus** (Blunt): rounded enough for an angle of 90° to be placed inside.
174. **Acutus** (Acute): with sides equally curved convexly to the base, the whole base going within an angle of 90°.
175. **Cuneatus** (Wedge-shaped): with straight sides converging at the base which is described as *late cuneatus* when they make an angle of 90° or more, *anguste cuneatus* when they make an angle of less than 90°.

176. **Angustatus** (Attenuate): with convex curved sides narrowed gradually and concavely to the base.
177. **Cuneato-angustatus** (Cuneate-attenuate): with convex curved sides narrowed abruptly into a straight-sided triangular base.
178. **Breve angustatus** (Shortly attenuate), **Brevissime angustatus** (Very shortly attenuate): with a more or less rounded base abruptly extended downward as a very short triangle.

2. *DIVISION*

E. THE MARGIN

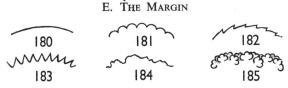

Fig. 25   Types of Margin
180, integerrimus; 181, crenatus; 182, serratus; 183, dentatus; 184, erosus; 185, crispus

179. **Integer** (Entire): Properly speaking, this means having no kind of marginal division; but sometimes it has been used to indicate not pinnatifid, and also nearly destitute of marginal division.
180. **Integerrimus** (Quite entire): perfectly free from division of the margin.
181. **Crenatus** (Crenated) [the diminutive is *crenulatus*, minutely crenate]; having convex teeth. When these teeth are themselves crenated, we say *bicrenate* [*bicrenatus*].
182. **Serratus** (Sawed): having sharp [more or less] straight-edged teeth pointing to the apex. [When the teeth are very small, we say *serrulate* or *serrulatus*.] When these teeth are themselves serrate, we say *biserrate*, or *duplicato-serrate* [or *biserratus*, *duplicato-serratus*].
183. **Dentatus** (Toothed): having sharp teeth with concave [or straight] edges [usually pointing directly outwards]. When these teeth are themselves toothed, we say *duplicato-dentate*, or doubly toothed [*duplicato-dentatus*], but not *bidentate*, which means two-toothed. [The diminutive is *denticulatus*, minutely dentate.]
184. **Erosus** (Gnawed): having the margin irregularly toothed, as if bitten by some animal.
185. **Crispus** (Curled): having the margin excessively irregularly divided and twisted.
186. **Repandus** (Repand): having an uneven slightly sinuous margin.
187. **Angulatus, angulosus** (Angular): having several salient angles on the margin [see no. 40].
188. **Sinuatus** (Sinuate): having the margin uneven, alternately with deep concavities and convexities.

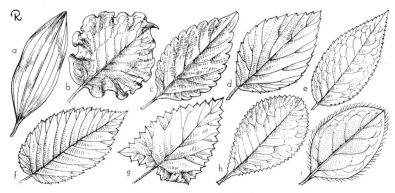

Fig. 26   Types of Margin
a, integer;   b, undulatus;   c, crenatus;   d, serratus;   e, serrulatus;
f, duplicato-serratus;   g, dentatus;   h, denticulatus;   i, ciliatus (by
Marion E. Ruff, from G. H. M. Lawrence, *Introduction to Plant
Taxonomy*; 1955)

F. INCISION

189. **Lacerus** (Torn): irregularly divided by deep incisions.

190. **Incisus** (Cut): regularly divided by deep incisions.

191. **Laciniatus** (Slashed): divided by deep, taper-pointed, cut incisions.

192. **Squarroso-laciniatus** (Squarrose-slashed): slashed with minor divisions at right angles with the others.

193. **Lobatus** (Lobed): partly divided into a determinate number of segments. We say *bilobus*, two-lobed; *trilobus*, three-lobed; and so on.

194. **Fissus** (Split): divided nearly to the base, into a determinate number of segments. We say *bifidus*, split in two; *trifidus*, in three; and so on. When the segments are very numerous, *multifidus* is used.

195. **Partitus** (Parted): divided into a determinate number of segments, which extend nearly to the base of the part to which they belong. We say *bipartitus*, parted in two; *tripartitus*, in three; and so on.

196. **Palmatus** (Palmate): having five lobes, the midribs of which meet in a common point, so that the whole bears some resemblance to a human hand.

197. **Pedatus** (Pedate): the same as palmate, except that the two lateral lobes are themselves divided into smaller segments, the midribs of which do not directly run into the same point as the rest.

198. **Digitatus** (Fingered): the same as palmate, but the segments less spreading, and narrower [this distinction between *palmatus* and *digitatus* is obsolete].

199. **Pinnatifidus, pinnatipartitus, pinnatiscissus** (Pinnatifid): divided almost to the axis into lateral segments, something in the way of the side divisions of a feather. De Candolle distinguishes several modifications of pinnatifidus: 1. *Pinnatifidus*, when the lobes are divided

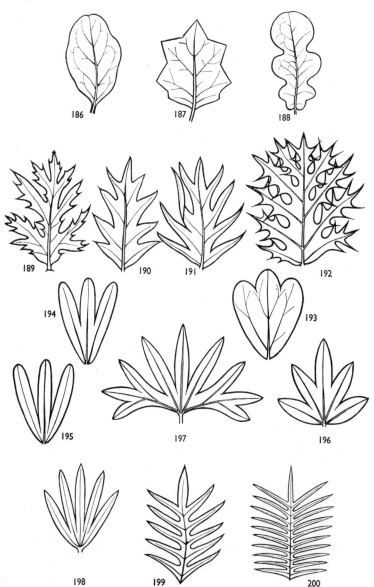

Fig. 27 Shapes of Leaves, etc.

186, repandus; 187, angulatus; 188, sinuatus; 189, lacerus; 190, incisus; 191, laciniatus; 192, squarroso-laciniatus; 193, lobatus; 194, fissus; 195, partitus; 196, palmatus; 197, pedatus; 198, digitatus; 199, pinnatifidus; 200, pectinatus (after J. Lindley, *Introduction to Botany*; 1832)

down to half the breadth of the leaf [mostly within the outer $\frac{1}{4}$]; 2. *pinnatipartitus*, when the lobes pass beyond the middle [or within the middle $\frac{1}{3}$], and the parenchyma is not interrupted; 3. *pinnatisectus*, when the lobes are divided down to the midrib, and the parenchyma is interrupted; 4. *pinnatilobatus*, when the lobes are divided to an uncertain depth; *lyrate* and the like belong to this modification. He has similar variations of palmatus and pedatus; viz. *palmatifidus*, *palmatipartitus*, *palmatisectus*, *palmatilobatus*; and *pedatifidus*, *pedatipartitus*, *pedatisectus* and *pedatilobatus*.

200. **Pectinatus** (Comb-shaped): the same as pinnatifid; but the segments very numerous, close and narrow, like the teeth of a comb.

G. Division or Ramification

201. **Simplex** (Simple): scarcely divided or branched at all.

202. **Simplicissimus** (Quite simple): not divided or branched at all.

203. **Compositus** (Compound): having various divisions or ramifications. As compared with the two following, it applies to cases of leaves in which the petiole is not divided.

204. **Decompositus** (Decompound): having various compound divisions or ramifications. In leaves it is applied to those the petiole of which bears secondary petioles.

205. **Supradecompositus** (Supradecompound): having various decompound divisions or ramifications. In leaves it is applied to such as have the primary petiole divided into secondary ones, and the secondary into a third set.

206. **Bifoliolatus, binatus** (Bifoliolate): when in leaves the common petiole is terminated by two leaflets growing from the same point. This term has the same application as *unijugus* and *conjugatus*. We say *trifoliolate*, or *ternate*, when the petiole bears three leaflets from the same point; *quadrifoliolate*, if there are four from the same point; and *quinquefoliolate*, or *quinate*, if there are five from the same point; and so on.

207. **Vertebratus** (Vertebrate): when the leaf is contracted at intervals, there being an articulation at each contraction. *Mirb.*

208. **Pinnatus** (Pinnate): when simple leaflets are arranged on each side of a common petiole.

209. **Imparipinnatus** (Pinnate with an odd one): when the petiole is terminated by a single leaflet or tendril. If there is a tendril, as in the Pea, it is called *cirrhosus*.

210. **Paripinnatus, abrupte pinnatus** (Equally pinnate): when the petiole is terminated by neither leaflet nor tendril.

211. **Alternatim pinnatus** (Alternately pinnate): when the leaflets are alternate upon a common petiole. *Mirb.*

212. **Interrupte pinnatus** (Interruptedly pinnate): when the leaflets are alternately small and large.

213. **Decrescente pinnatus** (Decreasingly pinnate): when the leaflets diminish insensibly in size, from the base of the leaf to its apex. *Mirb.*

214. **Decursive pinnatus** (Decursively pinnate): when the petiole is winged by the elongation of the base of the leaflets. *Mirb.* This is hardly different from pinnatifid.

215. **Digitato-pinnatus** (Digitato-pinnate): when the secondary petioles, on the sides of which the leaflets are attached, part from the summit of a common petiole. *Mirb.*

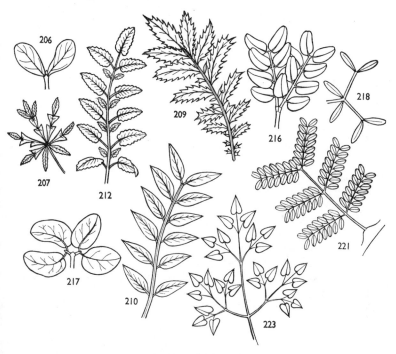

Fig. 28   Division of Leaves
206, bifoliolatus ;   207, vertebratus ;   209, imparipinnatus ;   210, paripinnatus ; 212, interrupte pinnatus ; 216, bidigito-pinnatus ; 217, bigeminatus ; 218, tergeminus ; 221, bipinnatus ; 223, triternatus (after J. Lindley, *Introduction to Botany* ; 1832)

216. **Bidigitato-pinnatus, biconjugato-pinnatus** (Twin digitato-pinnate): the secondary petioles, on the sides of which the leaflets are arranged, proceed in twos from the summit of a common petiole. *Mirb.*

217. **Bigeminatus, biconjugatus** (Bigeminate): when each of two secondary petioles bears a pair of leaflets. *Mirb.*

218. **Tergeminus, tergeminatus** (Tergeminate): when each of two secondary petioles bears towards its summit one pair of leaflets, and the common petiole bears a third pair at the origin of the two secondary petioles. *Mirb.*

219. **Tridigitato-pinnatus, ternato-pinnatus** (Thrice digitato-pinnate) : when the secondary petioles, on the sides of which the leaflets are attached, proceed in threes from the summit of a common petiole. *Mirb.*

220. **Quadridigitato-pinnatus** and **multidigitato-pinnatus** are rarely used, but are obvious modifications of the last.

221. **Bipinnatus, duplicato-pinnatus** (Bipinnate) : when the leaflets of a pinnate leaf become themselves pinnate.

222. **Biternatus, duplicato-ternatus** (Biternate) : when three secondary petioles proceed from the common petiole, and each bears three leaflets. *Mirb.*

223. **Triternatus** (Triternate) : when the common petiole divides into three secondary petioles, which are each subdivided into three tertiary petioles, each of which bears three leaflets.

224. **Tripinnatus** (Tripinnate) : when the leaflets of a bipinnate leaf become themselves pinnate.

225. **Conjugatus, unijugus, unijugatus** (Paired) : when the petiole of a pinnated leaf bears one pair of leaflets. *Bijugus* is when it bears two pairs ; *trijugus, quadrijugus, quinquejugus,* etc., are also employed when required. *Multijugus* is used when the number of pairs becomes very considerable.

226. **Ramosus** (Branched) : divided into many branches ; if the divisions are small, we say *ramulosus*.

227. **Subramosus** (Somewhat branched) : having a slight tendency to branch.

228. **Excurrens** (Excurrent) : in which the axis remains always in the centre, all the other parts being regularly disposed round it.

229. **Ramosissimus** (Much-branched) : branched in a great degree.

230. **Deliquescens** (Disappearing) : branched, but so divided that the principal axis is lost trace of in the ramifications ; as the head of an oak tree.

231. **Dichotomus** (Dichotomous) : having the divisions always in pairs : if they are in threes, we say *trichotomus*.

232. **Didymus** (Twin) : growing in pairs, or divided into two equal parts.

233. **Furcatus** (Forked) : having long terminal lobes, like the prongs of a fork.

234. **Stellatus** (Stellate) : divided into segments, radiating from a common centre ; as the hairs of most malvaceous plants.

235. **Articulatus** (Jointed) : falling in pieces at the joints, or separating readily at the joints : it is also applied to bodies having the appearance of being jointed.

236. **Granulatus** (Granular) : divided into little knobs or knots.

237. **Byssaceus** (Byssaceous) : divided into very fine pieces, like wool.

238. **Dendroideus** (Tree-like) : divided at the top into a number of fine ramifications so as to resemble the head of a tree.

239. **Aspergilliformis** (Brush-shaped) : divided into several fine ramifications, so as to resemble the brush (*aspergillus*) used for sprinkling holy water in the ceremonies of the Catholic Church.

240. **Loculosus, septatus** (Partitioned) : divided by internal partitions into cells.

241. **Anastomozans** (Anastomosing): the ramifications of any thing which are united at the points where they come in contact are said to anastomose. The term is confined to veins.

242. **Ruminatus** (Ruminate): when a hard body is pierced in various directions by narrow cavities filled with dry cellular matter.

243. **Cancellatus** (Cancellate): when the parenchyma is wholly absent, and the veins alone remain, anastomosing and forming a kind of network.

244. **Pertusus** (Perforated): when irregular spaces are left open in the surface of any thing, so that it is pierced with holes.

3. *SURFACE*

H. MARKINGS OR EVENNESS

[A glossary of terms for the surfaces of fungi in particular is provided by Murrill (1905), for the surface of seeds in particular by Murley (1951); see p. 507.]

245. **Rugosus** (Rugose): covered with reticulated lines, the spaces between which are convex; [wrinkled, the elevations irregular].

246. **Reticulatus** (Netted): covered with reticulated lines which project a little.

247. **Semireticulatus** (Half-netted): when, of several layers of any thing, the outer one only is reticulated.

248. **Scrobiculatus** (Pitted): having numerous small shallow depressions or excavations.

249. **Lacunosus** (Lacunose): having numerous large deep depressions or excavations.

250. **Favosus, alveolatus** (Honeycombed): excavated in the manner of a section of honeycomb.

251. **Areolatus** (Areolate): divided into a number of irregular squares or angular spaces.

252. **Cicatricatus** (Scarred): marked by the scars left by bodies that have fallen off; the stem, for instance, is scarred by the leaves that have fallen.

253. **Annulatus** (Ringed): surrounded by elevated or depressed bands.

254. **Striatus** (Striated): marked by longitudinal lines.

255. **Lineatus** (Lined): the same as striatus.

256. **Sulcatus** (Furrowed): marked by longitudinal channels.

257. **Aciculatus** (Aciculated): marked with very fine irregular streaks, as if produced by the point of a needle.

258. **Punctatus** (Dotted): covered by minute impressions, as if made by the point of a pin.

259. **Aequatus** (Even): the reverse of any thing expressive of inequality of surface.

J. HAIR-COVERING AND SUPERFICIAL PROCESSES

[The nature of hair-covering is determined by the length, direction, form and quantity of the hairs together, and for precision these characters should be stated individually, as plants possess more types of hair-covering than there exist special terms to designate them, hence the uncertain and overlapping use of many terms, even though their main meanings are clear (cf. Forbes, 1884 ; Lawrence, 1955 ; Roe, 1971).]

260. **Inermis** (Unarmed) : destitute of any kind of spines or prickles.

261. **Spinosus** (Spiny) : furnished with spines.

262. **Aculeatus** (Prickly) : furnished with prickles.

263. **Echinatus** (Bristly) : furnished with numerous rigid hairs, or straight prickles.

264. **Muricatus** (Muricated) : furnished with numerous short hard excrescences.

265. **Spiculatus** (Spiculate) : covered with fine, fleshy, erect points.

266. **Scaber, asper, exasperatus** (Rough) : covered with hard short, rigid points.

267. **Scabridus** (Roughish) : slightly covered with short hardish points.

268. **Tuberculatus, verrucosus** (Tubercled) : covered with little excrescences or warts.

269. **Papillosus, papulosus** (Pimpled) : covered with minute tubercles or excrescences, of uneven size, and rather soft.

270. **Pilosus** (Hairy) : covered with short, weak, thin hairs ; as the leaf of Prunella vulgaris, Daucus Carota.

271. **Pubens, pubescens** (Downy) : covered with very short, weak, dense hairs ; as the leaves of Cynoglossum officinale, Lonicera Xylosteum, etc. Pubescens is most commonly employed in Botany, but pubens is more classical.

272. **Incanus** (Hoary) : covered with very short dense hairs, placed so closely as to give an appearance of whiteness to the surface from which they grow ; as the leaf of Mathiola incana.

273. **Hirtus, villosus** (Shaggy) : covered with long weak hairs ; as Epilobium hirsutum.

274. **Tomentosus** (Tomentose) : covered with dense, rather rigid, short hairs, so as to be sensibly perceptible to the touch ; as Onopordum Acanthium, Lavatera arborea, etc.

275. **Velutinus** (Velvety) : the same as the last, but more dense so that the surface resembles that of velvet ; as Cotyledon coccineus.

276. **Lanatus** (Woolly) : covered with long, dense, curled, and matted hairs, resembling wool ; as Verbascum Thapsus, Stachys germanica.

277. **Hispidus** (Hispid) : covered with long rigid hairs ; as the stem of Echium vulgare.

278. **Floccosus** (Floccose) : covered with dense hairs, which fall away in little tufts ; as Verbascum floccosum, and pulverulentum.

279. **Glandulosus** (Glandular) : covered with hairs bearing glands upon their tips ; as the fruit of Roses, the pods of Adenocarpus.

280. **Barbatus, crinitus** (Bearded): having tufts of long weak hairs growing from different parts of the surface. It is also applied to bodies bearing very long weak hairs in solitary tufts or parcels.

281. **Strigosus** (Strigose): covered with sharp, appressed, rigid hairs. *W.* Linnaeus considers this word synonymous with hispid.

282. **Sericeus** (Silky): covered with very fine close-pressed hairs, silky to the touch; as the leaves of Protea argentea, Alchemilla alpina, etc.

283. **Peronatus** (Peronate): laid thickly over with a woolly substance, ending in a sort of meal. *W.* This term is only applied to the stipes of Fungi.

284. **Arachnoideus** (Cobwebbed): covered with loose, white, entangled, thin hairs, resembling the web of a spider; as Calceolaria arachnoidea.

285. **Ciliatus** (Ciliated): having fine hairs, resembling the eyelash, at the margin; as the leaves of Luzula pilosa, Erica Tetralix, etc.

286. **Fimbriatus** (Fringed): having the margin bordered by long filiform processes thicker than hairs; as the petals of Cucubalus fimbriatus.

287. **Plumosus** (Feathery): consisting of long hairs, which are themselves hairy; as the pappus of Leontodon Taraxacum [Taraxacum officinale], the beard of Stipa pennata.

288. **Urens** (Stinging): covered with rigid, sharp-pointed, bristly hairs, which emit an irritating fluid when touched; as the leaves of the Urtica urens.

289. **Farinosus** (Mealy): covered with a sort of white scurfy substance.

290. **Lepidotus, leprosus** (Leprous): covered with minute peltate scales.

291. **Ramentaceus** (Ramentaceous): covered with weak, shrivelled, brown, scale-like processes.

292. **Squamosus** (Scaly): covered with minute scales, fixed by one end.

293. **Paleaceus** (Chaffy): covered with small, weak, erect, membranous scales, resembling the paleae of Grasses.

K. POLISH OR TEXTURE

294. **Nitidus** (Shining): having a smooth, even, polished surface; as many leaves.

295. **Laevis, glaber** (Smooth): being free from asperities [*laevis*] or hairs [*glaber*], or any sort of unevenness [*glabratus*, become glabrous having been otherwise, *glabrescens*, becoming glabrous].

296. **Laevigatus, politus** (Polished): having the appearance of a polished substance.

297. **Splendens** (Glittering): the same as polished, but when the lustre is a little broken, from slight irregularity of surface.

298. **Nudus, denudatus** (Naked): the reverse of hairy, downy, or any similar term; it is not materially different from *glaber*.

299. **Opacus, impolitus** (Opaque): the reverse of shining, dull.

300. **Viscidus, glutinosus** (Viscid): covered with a glutinous exudation.

301. **Mucosus** (Mucous or slimy): covered with a slimy secretion; or with a coat that is readily soluble in water, and becomes slimy.

302. **Unctuosus** (Greasy): having a surface which, though not actually greasy, feels so.

B.L.—M

303. **Roridus** (Dewy): covered with little transparent elevations of the parenchyma which have the appearance of fine drops of dew.

304. **Lentiginosus** (Dusty): covered with minute dots, as if dusted.

305. **Pruinosus** (Frosted): nearly the same as *roridus*, but applied to surfaces in which the dewy appearance is more opaque, as if the drops were congealed.

306. **Pulverulentus** (Powdery): covered with a fine bloom or powdery matter.

307. **Glaucus** (Glaucous): covered with a fine bloom of the colour of a Cabbage leaf.

308. **Caesius** (Caesious): like glaucous, but greener.

309. **Dealbatus** (Whitened): covered with a very opaque white powder.

4. *TEXTURE OR SUBSTANCE*

310. **Membranaceus** (Membranaceous): thin and semitransparent, like a fine membrane; as the leaves of Mosses.

311. **Papyraceus, chartaceus** (Papery): having the consistence of writing-paper, and quite opaque; as most leaves.

312. **Coriaceus** (Leathery): having the consistence of leather; as the leaves of Prunus Laurocerasus, and others.

313. **Crustaceus** (Crustaceous): hard, thin and brittle.

314. **Cartilagineus** (Cartilaginous): hard and tough.

315. **Laxus** (Loose): of a soft cellular texture, as the pith of most plants. The name is derived from the parts of the substance appearing as if not in a state of cohesion.

316. **Scariosus** (Scarious): having a thin, dry, shrivelled appearance.

317. **Suberosus** (Corky): having the texture of the substance called cork.

318. **Corticatus** (Coated): harder externally than internally.

319. **Spongiosus** (Spongy): having the texture of a sponge; that is to say, very cellular, with the cellules filled with air.

320. **Corneus** (Horny): hard, and very close in texture, but capable of being cut without difficulty, the parts cut off not being brittle.

321. **Oleaginosus** (Oleaginous): fleshy in substance, but filled with oil.

322. **Osseus** (Bony): hard, and very close in texture, not cut without difficulty, the parts cut off being brittle.

323. **Carnosus** (Fleshy): firm, juicy, easily cut.

324. **Ceraceus, cereus** (Waxy): having the texture and colour of new wax.

325. **Lignosus, ligneus** (Woody): having the texture of wood.

326. **Crassus** (Thick): something more thick than usual. Leaves, for instance, are generally papery in texture; the leaves of cotyledons, which are much more fleshy, are called *thick*.

327. **Succulentus** (Succulent): very cellular and juicy.

328. **Gelatinosus** (Gelatinous): having the texture and appearance of jelly.

329. **Fibrosus** (Fibrous): containing a great proportion of loose woody fibre.

330. **Medullosus** (Medullary or pithy): filled with spongy pith.
331. **Farinaceus** (Mealy): having the texture of flour in a mass.
332. **Tartareus** (Tartareous): having a rough crumbling surface.
333. **Baccatus** (Berried): having a juicy succulent texture.
334. **Herbaceus** (Herbaceous): thin, green and cellular; as the tissue of membranous leaves.

5. *SIZE*

Most of the terms which relate to this quality are the same as those in common use; and, being employed in precisely the same sense, do not need explanation. But there are a few which have a particular meaning attached to them, and are not much known in common language. These are:

335. **Nanus, pumilus, pygmaeus** (Dwarf): small, short, dense, as compared with other species of the same genus, or family. Thus, Myosotis nana is not more than half an inch high; while the other species are much taller.
336. **Pusillus, perpusillus** (Very small): the same as the last, except that a general reduction of size is understood, as well as dwarfishness.
337. **Humilis** (Low): when the stature of a plant is not particularly small, but much smaller than of other kindred species. Thus, a tree twenty feet high may be *low*, if the other species of its genus are forty or fifty feet high.
338. **Depressus** (Depressed): broad and dwarf, as if, instead of growing perpendicularly, the growth had taken place horizontally.
339. **Exiguus** (Little): this is generally used in opposition to large, and means small in all parts, but well proportioned.
340a. **Elatus, procerus** (Tall): this is said of plants which are taller than their parts would have led one to expect.
340b. **Exaltatus** (Lofty): the same as the last, but in a greater degree.
341. **Giganteus** (Gigantic): tall, but stout and well proportioned.

6. *DURATION*

342. [Terms expressive of life-span include *monocarpus* or *hapaxanthus* (bearing fruit but once and then dying after fructification) of which there are three forms: *annuus* (annual, living but one year), *biennis* (biennial, living two years, or within two calendar years), *plietesialis* (requiring several or many years to reach the flowering state, then dying immediately after fruiting), these being distinguished from *polycarpicus* (having the power of bearing fruit many times without perishing) or *perennis* (perennial, lasting for several or many years). The terms expressive of the duration of parts include *caducus* (falling

off very early), *deciduus* (deciduous, finally falling off), *persistens* (persistent, neither falling off nor withering until the part which bears it is perfected), *marcescens* (withering or fading, not falling until the part which bears it is perfected but withering long before that time), *fugax* (fugacious, falling off or perishing very rapidly).]

7 & 8. *COLOUR AND VARIEGATION*

[For colour terms adopted by Lindley, see Chapter XVIII.]

9. *VEINING*

[Arising out of the need to describe fossil leaves and leaf-impressions, C. von Ettingshausen introduced in 1861 a more precise terminology, which is outlined in the vocabulary Chapter XXV under Veining.]

In terms expressive of this quality the word nerves is generally used, but very incorrectly.

343. **Nervosus, nervatus** (Ribbed): having several ribs.

344. **Uninervis, costatus** (One-ribbed): when there is only one rib as in most leaves.

345. **Trinervis** (Three-ribbed): when there are three ribs all proceeding from the base; *Quinquenervis*, when there are five; *Septemnervis*, when there are seven; and so on.

346. **Triplinervis** (Triple-ribbed): when of three ribs the two lateral ones emerge from the middle one a little above its base; *Quintuplinervis* [five-ribbed], etc., are used to express the obvious modifications of this.

347. **Indirecte venosus**: when the lateral veins are combined within the margin and emit other little veins. *Link*.

348. **Evanescenti-venosus**: when the lateral veins disappear within the margin. *Id*.

349. **Combinate venosus**: when the lateral veins unite before they reach the margin. *Id*.

350. **Rectinervis, parallelinervis** (Straight-ribbed): when the lateral ribs are straight. *Mirb*. When the ribs are straight and almost parallel, but united at the summit. *De Cand*.

351. **Curvinervis, converginervis** (Curve-ribbed): when the ribs describe a curve, and meet at the point.

352. **Ruptinervis**: when a straight-ribbed leaf has its ribs interrupted at intervals. *De Cand*.

353. **Penniformis**: when the ribs are disposed as in a pinnated leaf, but confluent at the point. *Id*.

354. **Palmiformis**: when the ribs are arranged as in palmate leaves. *Id*.

355. **Penninervis**: when the ribs are pinnated. *Id*.

356. **Pedatinervis**: when the ribs are pedate. *Id*.

357. **Palminervis**: when they are palmated. *Id.*

358. **Peltinervis**: when they are peltate. *Id.*

359. **Vaginervis**: when the veins are arranged without any order; as in Ficoideae. *Id.*

360. **Retinervis**: when the veins are reticulated, or like lace. *Id.*

361. **Nullinervis, enervis**: when there are no ribs or veins whatever. *Id.*

362. **Falsinervis**: when the veins have no vascular tissue, but are formed of simple, elongated, cellular tissue; as in Mosses, Fuci, etc.

363. **Hinoideus**: when all the veins proceed from the midrib, and are parallel and undivided. *Link.* When they are connected by little cross veins, the term is *venuloso-hinoideus. Id.*

364. **Venosus**: when the lateral veins are variously divided. *Id.* [When the veins are prominent on the leaf surface.]

[For angles of divergence of veins, see p. 540. Otto Berg in *Flora Brasiliensis* 14.i : 3 (1857), describing leaves of *Myrtaceae*, used *arrectus* for veins diverging at 5-30°, *subpatens* for about 40°, *patens* for 45°, *suberecto-patulus* for 50°, *subpatulus* for 70°, *patulus* for 75°, *subdivaricatus* for 80°, *divaricatus* for 90°.]

OF INDIVIDUAL RELATIVE TERMS

These are arranged under the heads of *Aestivation*, or the relation which organs bear to each other in the bud state; *Direction*, or the relation which organs bear to the surface of the earth, or to the stem of the plant which forms the axis, either real or imaginary, round which they are disposed; and *Insertion*, or the manner in which one part is inserted into, or adheres to, another.

10. *AESTIVATION AND VERNATION*

The term *aestivation*, or *praefloration*, is applied to the parts of the flower when unexpanded; and *vernation* is expressive of the foliage in the same state. The ideas of their modifications are, however, essentially the same.

365. **Involutiva, involuta** (Involute): when the edges are rolled inwards spirally on each side (*Link*); as the leaf of the Apple.

366. **Revolutiva, revoluta** (Revolute): when the edges are rolled backwards spirally on each side (*Link*); as in the leaf of the Rosemary.

367. **Obvolutiva, obvoluta**, *Link*; **semi-amplexa**, *De Cand.* (Obvolute): when the margins of one alternately overlap those of that which is opposite to it.

368. **Convolutiva, convoluta** (Convolute): when one is wholly rolled up in another, as in the petals of the Wallflower.

369. **Supervolutiva** (Supervolute): when one edge is rolled inwards, and is enveloped by the opposite edge rolled in an opposite direction; as the leaves of the Apricot.

370. **Induplicativa** (Induplicate): having the margins bent abruptly inwards, and the external face of these edges applied to each other without any twisting; as in the flowers of some species of Clematis.

371. **Conduplicativa, conduplicata** (Conduplicate): when the sides are applied parallelly to the faces of each other.

372. **Plicativa, plicata** (Plaited): folded lengthwise, like the plaits of a closed fan; as the Vine and many Palms.

373. **Replicativa** (Replicate): when the upper part is curved back and applied to the lower; as in the Aconite.

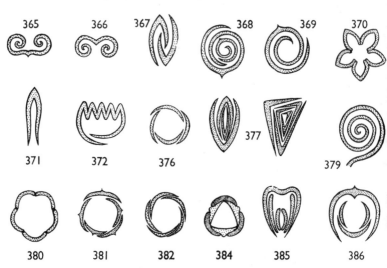

Fig. 29   Types of Aestivation and Vernation
365, involuta; 366, revoluta; 367, obvoluta; 368, convoluta; 369, supervolutiva; 370, induplicativa; 371, conduplicata; 372, plicata; 376, imbricata; 377, equitativa; 379, circinata; 380, valvata; 381, quincuncialis; 382, torsiva; 384, alternativa; 385, vexillaris; 386, cochlearis (after J. Lindley, *Introduction to Botany*; 1832)

374. **Curvativa** (Curvative): when the margins are slightly curved, either backwards or forwards, without any sensible twisting. *De Cand.*

375. **Corrugata, corrugativa** (Wrinkled): when the parts are folded up irregularly in every direction; as the petals of the Poppy.

376. **Imbricativa, imbricata** (Imbricated): when they overlap each other parallelly at the margins, without any involution. This is the true meaning of the term. De Candolle applies it in a different sense (*Théorie*, ed. 1, p. 399).

377. **Equitativa, equitans**, *Link*; **amplexa**, *De Cand.* (Equitant): when they overlap each other parallelly and entirely, without any involution.

378. **Reclinata** (Reclinate): when they are bent down upon their stalk.

379. **Circinata** (Circinate): when they are rolled spirally downwards.

380. **Valvata, valvaris** (Valvate): applied to each other by the margins only.

381. **Quincuncialis** (Quincunx): when the pieces are five in number, of which two are exterior, two interior and the fifth covers the interior with one margin, and has its other margin covered by the exterior.

382. **Torsiva, spiraliter contorta** (Twisted): the same as contorted, except that there is no obliquity in the form or insertion of the pieces. [For the direction of overlap expressed by the terms *dextrorsum* (to the right) and *sinistrorsum* (to the left) see below under no. 418 (*Volubilis*).]

383. **Contorta** (Contorted): each piece being oblique in figure, and over-lapping its neighbour by one margin, its other margin being, in like manner, overlapped by that which stands next it.

384. **Alternativa** (Alternative): when, the pieces being in two rows, the inner is covered by the outer in such a way that each of the exterior rows overlap half of two of the interior.

385. **Vexillaris** (Vexillary): when one piece is much larger than the others, and is folded over them, they being arranged face to face.

386. **Cochlearis** (Cochlear): when one piece, being larger than the others, and hollowed like a helmet or bowl, covers all the others.

11. *DIRECTION*

387. **Erectus, arrectus** (Erect): pointing towards the zenith.

388. **Rectus** (Straight): not wavy or curved, or deviating from a straight direction in any way.

389. **Strictus** (Very straight): the same as the last, but in excess.

390. **Natans** (Swimming): floating under water.

391. **Fluitans** (Floating): floating upon the surface of water.

392. **Submersus, demersus** (Submersed): buried beneath water.

393. **Descendens** (Descending): having a direction gradually downwards.

394. **Dependens** (Hanging down): having a downward direction, caused by its weight.

395. **Ascendens, assurgens** (Ascending): having a direction upwards, with an oblique base.

396. **Verticalis, perpendicularis** (Perpendicular): being at right angles with some other body.

397. **Obliquus** (Oblique): when the margin points to the heavens, the apex to the horizon.

398. **Horizontalis** (Horizontal): when the plane points to the heavens, the apex to the horizon.

399. **Inversus** (Inverted): having the apex of one thing in an opposite direction to that of another.

400. **Revolutus** (Revolute): rolled backwards from the direction ordinarily assumed by similar other bodies; as certain tendrils, and the ends of some leaves.

401. **Involutus** (Involute): rolled inwards.

402. **Convolutus** (Convolute): rolled up.
403. **Reclinatus** (Reclining): falling gradually back from the perpendicular.
404. **Resupinatus** (Resupinate): inverted in position by a twisting of the stalk.
405. **Inclinatus, declinatus** (Inclining): the same as reclining, but in a greater degree.
406. **Pendulus** (Pendulous): hanging downwards, in consequence of the weakness of its support.
407. **Cernuus** (Drooping): inclining a little from the perpendicular, so that the apex is directed towards the horizon.
408. **Nutans** (Nodding): inclining very much from the perpendicular, so that the apex is directed downwards.
409. **Secundus** (One-sided): having all the parts by twists in their stalks turned one way.
410. **Inflexus, curvus, introflexus, introcurvus, infractus** (Inflexed): suddenly bent inwards.
411. **Reflexus, recurvus, retroflexus, retrocurvus, refractus** (Reflexed): suddenly bent backwards.
412. **Deflexus, declinatus** (Deflexed): bent downwards.
413. **Flexuosus** (Flexuose): having a gently bending direction, alternately inwards and outwards.
414. **Tortuosus** (Tortuous): having an irregular, bending and turning direction.
415. **Geniculatus** (Knee-jointed): bent abruptly like a knee.
416. **Spiralis, anfractuosus** (Spiral): resembling in direction the spires of a corkscrew, or other twisted thing.
417. **Circinatus, gyratus, circinalis** (Circinate): bent like the head of a crosier.
418. **Volubilis** (Twining): having the property of twisting round some other body:
    a. To the right hand (*dextrorsum* [*e centro vis.*, *intus vis.*]): when the twisting is from left to right, or in the direction of the sun's course; as the Hop [Humulus].
    b. To the left hand (*sinistrorsum* [*e centro vis.*, *intus vis.*]): when the twisting is from right to left, or opposite to the sun's course; as Convolvulus sepium.
    [These terms as given above are used by the de Candolles, Bischoff, Hiern, etc. They are reversed by those, e.g. Eichler, Duchartre, A. Gray, etc., who regard the observer not as placed within the spiral but looking at it from outside; *a* is then *sinistrorsum externe vis.*, *b* is *dextrorsum externe vis.*; cf. B. D. Jackson, *Glossary*, 4th ed., p. 477.]
419. **Retrorsus** (Turned backwards): turned in a direction opposite to that of the apex of the body to which the part turned appertains.
420. **Introrsus, anticus** (Turned inwards): turned towards the axis to which it appertains.
421. **Extrorsus, posticus** (Turned outwards): turned away from the axis to which it appertains.

422. **Procumbens, humifusus** (Procumbent): spread over the surface of the ground.

423. **Prostratus, pronus** (Prostrate): lying flat upon the earth, or any other thing.

424. **Decumbens** (Decumbent): reclining upon the earth, and rising again from it at the apex.

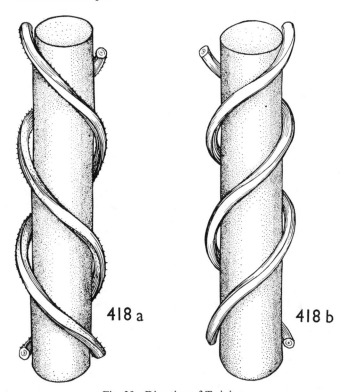

Fig. 30   Direction of Twining
418a, dextrorsum volubilis e centro visus (sinistrorsum externe visus);
418b, sinistrorsum volubilis e centro visus (dextrorsum externe visus)
(drawing by Priscilla Fawcett)

425. **Diffusus** (Diffuse): spreading widely.

426. **Divaricatus** (Straggling): turning off from any thing irregularly, but at almost a right angle; as the branches of many things.

427. **Brachiatus** (Brachiate): when ramifications proceed from a common axis nearly at regular right angles, alternately in opposite directions.

428. **Patens** (Spreading): having a gradually outward direction; as petals from the ovarium.

429. **Connivens** (Converging): having a gradually inward direction; as many petals.

B.L.—M 2

430. **Adversus** (Opposite): pointing directly to a particular place; as the radicle to the hilum.
431. **Vagus** (Uncertain): having no particular direction.
432. **Peritropus** (Peritropal): directed from the axis to the horizon. This and the four following are only applied to the embryo of the seed.
433. **Orthotropus** (Orthotropal): straight, and having the same direction as the body to which it belongs.
434. **Antitropus** (Antitropal): straight, and having a direction contrary to that of the body to which it belongs.
435. **Amphitropus** (Amphitropal): curved round the body to which it belongs.
436. **Homotropus** (Homotropal): having the same direction as the body to which it belongs, but not being straight.

12. *INSERTION*

A. With Respect to the Mode of Attachment or Adhesion

437. **Peltatus, umbilicatus** (Peltate): fixed to the stalk by the centre, or by some point distinctly within the margin. [Cf. Fig. 24, no. 437.]
438. **Sessilis** (Sessile): sitting close upon the body that supports it, without any sensible stalk. [Cf. Fig. 24, no. 175.]
439. **Decurrens, decursivus** (Decurrent): prolonged below the point of insertion, as if running downwards.
440. **Amplectens** (Embracing): clasping with the base.
441. **Amplexicaulis** (Stem-clasping): the same as the last, but applied only to stems.
442. **Semi-amplexicaulis** (Half-stem-clasping): the same as the last, but in a smaller degree.
443. **Perfoliatus** (Perfoliate): when the two basal lobes of an amplexicaul leaf are united together, so that the stem appears to pass through the substance of the leaf. [Cf. Fig. 24, no. 443.]
444. **Connatus** (Connate): when the bases of two opposite leaves are united together. [Cf. Fig. 24, no. 444.]
445. **Vaginans** (Sheathing): surrounding a stem or other body by the convolute base; this chiefly occurs in the petioles of Grasses.
446. **Adnatus, annexus** (Adnate): adhering to the face of a thing.
447. **Innatus** (Innate): adhering to the apex of a thing.
448. **Versatilis, oscillatorius** (Versatile): adhering slightly by the middle, so that the two halves are nearly equally balanced, and swing backwards and forwards.
449. **Stipitatus** (Stipitate): elevated on a stalk which is neither a petiole nor a peduncle.
450. **Palaceus** (Palaceous): when the foot-stalk adheres to the margin. *Willd.* [Used in contrast to *peltatus*, no. 437; cf. Fig. 24, no. 171, etc.]
451. **Liber, solutus, distinctus** (Separate): when there is no cohesion between parts.

452. **Accretus** (Accrete): fastened to another body, and growing with it. *De Cand.*

453. **Adhaerens** (Adhering): united laterally by the whole surface with another organ. *De Cand.*

454. **Cohaerens, coadnatus, coadunatus, coalitus, connatus, confluens** (Cohering): this term is used to express, in general, the fastening together of homogeneous parts. *De Cand.* Such are De Candolle's definitions of these three terms [nos. 452-454]; but in practice there is no difference between them.

455. **Articulatus** (Articulated): when one body is united with another by a manifest articulation.

B. WITH RESPECT TO SITUATION

456. **Dorsalis** (Dorsal): fixed upon the back of any thing.

457. **Lateralis** (Lateral): fixed near [or upon] the side of any thing.

458. **Marginalis** (Marginal): fixed upon the edge of any thing.

459. **Basilaris** (Basal): fixed at the base of any thing.

460. **Radicalis** (Radical): arising from the root.

461. **Caulinus** (Cauline): arising from the stem.

462. **Rameus, ramealis** (Rameous): of or belonging to the branches.

463. **Axillaris, alaris** (Axillary): arising out of the axilla.

464. **Floralis** (Floral): of or belonging to the flower.

465. **Foliaris, epiphyllus** (Epiphyllous): inserted upon the leaf.

466. **Terminalis** (Terminal): proceeding from the end.

467. **Petiolaris** (Of the leaf-stalk): inserted upon the petiole.

468. **Coronans** (Crowning): situated on the top of any thing. Thus, the limbs of the calyx may crown the ovary; a gland at the apex of the filament may crown the stamen; and so on.

469. **Epigaeus** (Epigeous): growing close upon the earth.

470. **Hypogaeus, subterraneus** (Subterranean): growing under the earth.

471. **Amphigenus** (Amphigenous): growing all round an object.

472. **Epigynus** (Epigynous): growing upon the summit of the ovarium.

473. **Hypogynus** (Hypogynous): growing from below the base of the ovarium.

474. **Perigynus** (Perigynous): growing upon some body that surrounds the ovarium.

CLASS II. COLLECTIVE TERMS

It has been already explained, that collective terms are those which apply to plants, or their parts, considered in masses; by which is meant that they cannot be applied to any one single part or thing, without a reference to a larger number being either expressed or understood. Thus, when leaves are said to be *opposite*, that term is used with respect to several, and not to one; and when a panicle is said to be lax, or loose, it means that the flowers of a panicle are loosely arranged; and so on.

13. *ARRANGEMENT*

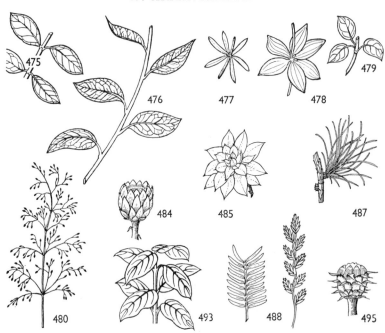

Fig. 31   Arrangement of Leaves, etc.

475, oppositus; 476, alternus; 477, stellatus (verticillatus foliis angustis); 478, verticillatus; 479, ternatus; 480, laxus; 484, imbricatus; 485, rosulatus; 487, fasciculatus; 488, distichus; 493, decussatus; 495, squarrosus (drawing by Gisena B. Threlkeld)

475. **Oppositus** (Opposite): placed on opposite sides of some other body or thing on the same plane. Thus, when leaves are opposite, they are on opposite sides of the stem; when petals are opposite, they are on opposite sides of the ovary; and so on.

476. **Alternus** (Alternate): placed alternately one above the other on some common body, as leaves upon the stem.

477. **Stellatus, stelliformis, stellulatus** (Stellate): the same as verticillate, except that the parts are narrow and acute.

478. **Verticillatus** (Whorled): when several things are in opposition round

a common axis, as some leaves round their stem; sepals, petals and stamens round the ovarium, etc.

479. **Ternus** (Ternate): when three things are in opposition round a common axis.

480. **Laxus** (Loose): when the parts are distant from each other, with an open light kind of arrangement; as the panicle among the other kinds of inflorescence.

481. **Sparsus** (Scattered): used in opposition to whorled, or opposite, or ternate, or other such terms.

482. **Compositus** (Compound): when formed of several parts united in one common whole; as pinnated leaves, all kinds of inflorescence beyond that of the solitary flower.

483. **Confertus** (Crowded): when the parts are pressed closely round about each other.

484. **Imbricatus** (Imbricated): when parts lie over each other in regular order, like tiles upon the roof of a house.

485. **Rosulatus, rosularis** (Rosulate): when parts which are not opposite, nevertheless become apparently so by the contraction of the joints of the stem, and lie packed closely over each other, like the petals in a double rose; as in the offsets of Houseleek.

486. **Caespitosus** (Caespitose): forming dense patches, or turfs; as the young stems of many plants.

487. **Fasciculatus** (Fascicled): when several similar things proceed from a common point.

488. **Distichus, bifarius** (Distichous): when things are arranged in two rows, the one opposite to the other.

489. **Serialis** (In rows): arranged in rows which are not necessarily opposite each other: *biserialis*, in two rows; *triserialis*, in three rows: but these are seldom used. In their stead, we generally add *fariam* to the end of a Latin numeral: thus, *bifariam* means in two rows; *trifariam*, in three rows; and so on.

490. **Unilateralis, secundus** (One-sided): arranged on, or turned towards, one side only.

491. **Aggregatus, coacervatus, conglomeratus** (Clustered): collected in parcels, each of which has a roundish figure.

492. **Spiralis** (Spiral): arranged in a spiral manner round some common axis.

493. **Decussatus** (Decussate): arranged in pairs that alternately cross each other; as the leaves of many plants.

494. **Fastigiatus** (Fastigiate): when all the parts are nearly parallel, with each pointing upwards to the sky.

495. **Squarrosus** (Squarrose): when the parts spread out at right angles, or thereabouts, from a common axis.

496. **Fasciatus** (Fasciated): when several contiguous parts grow unnaturally together into one.

497. **Squamosus** (Scaly): covered with small scales, like leaves.

498. **Depauperatus** (Starved): when some part is less perfectly developed

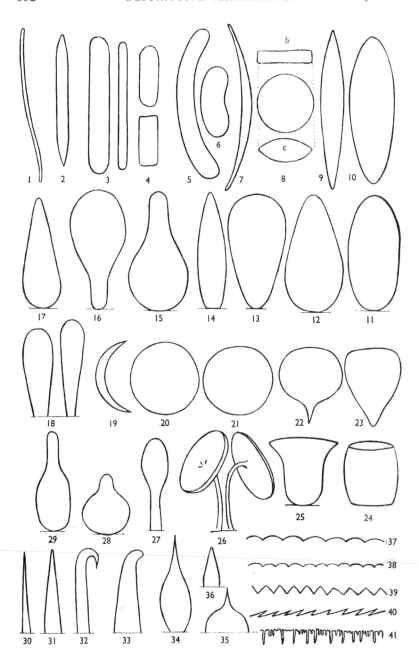

than is usual with plants of the same family. Thus, when the lower scales of a head of a Cyperaceous plant produce no flowers, such scales are said to be starved.

499. **Distans, remotus, rarus** (Distant): in contradiction to imbricated, or dense, or approximated, or any such words.

500. **Interruptus** (Interrupted): when any symmetrical arrangement is destroyed by local causes, as, for example, a spike is said to be interrupted when here and there the axis is unusually elongated, and not covered with flowers; a leaf is interruptedly pinnated when some of the pinnae are much smaller than the others, or wholly wanting; and so on.

501. **Continuus** (Continuous or uninterrupted): the reverse of the last.

502. **Intricatus** (Entangled): when things are intermixed in such an irregular manner that they cannot be readily disentangled; as the hairs, roots, and branches of many plants.

503. **Duplicatus, geminatus** (Double or twin): growing in pairs.

504. **Rosaceus** (Rosaceous): having the same arrangement as the petals of a single rose.

505. **Radiatus** (Radiant): diverging from a common centre, like rays; as the ligulate florets of any compound flower.

INDEX

When a Latin term and its English equivalent are almost identical, as *cylindricus* and 'cylindrical', *ovoideus* and 'ovoid', usually the Latin term alone is indexed below, but when they are markedly different, as *fusiformis* and 'spindle-shaped', both are indexed.

Fig. 32   Shapes of Spores, etc., illustrating some Terms as used
in Mycology

1, filiformis; 2, acerosus; 3, cylindricus; 4, oblongus apicibus obtusis (figura superior) et apicibus truncatis (figura inferior); 5, allantoideus, botuliformis; 6, reniformis; 7, falcatus; 8, discoideus vel lenticularis; *b*, discoideus et *c*, lenticularis; 9, fusiformis; 10, 11, ellipticus (ellipsoideus); 11, ovalis; 12, ovatus (ovoideus); 13, obovatus (obovoideus); 14, navicularis; 15, obpyriformis; 16, pyriformis; 17, obclavatus; 18, clavatus; 19, lunatus; 20, sphaericus, globosus; 21, subglobosus; 22, napiformis; 23, turbinatus; 24, doliformis; 25, campanulatus; 26, peltatus; 27, spathulatus; 28, ampulliformis; 29, lageniformis (sensu Josserandi); 30, acicularis; 31, subulatus; 32, hamatus, uncinatus; 33, cornuiformis; 34, ventricosus; 35, apex mucronatus; 36, apex acutus; 37, crenatus; 38, crenulatus; 39, dentatus; 40, serratus; 41, laciniatus (from G. C. Ainsworth & G. R. Bisby, *Dictionary of the Fungi*, 5th ed.; 1961)

alaris, 463; alatus, 60; alternatim pinnatus, 211; alternativus, 384; alternus, 476; alveolatus, 250; ambitus, 102; amphigenus, 471; amphitropus, 435; amplectans, 440; amplexicaulis, 441; amplexus, 377; anastomozans, 241; anceps, 43; anfractuosus, 416; angulatus, 187; angulosus, 40, 187; angustatus, 176; angustatus, breve, brevissime, 178; annexus, 446; annulatus, 253; annuus, 342; anticus, 420; antitropus, 434; apiculatus, 146; arcuatus, 35; areolatus, 251; aristatus, 139; arrectus, 387; arrow-headed, 126; articulatus, 235, 455; ascendens, 395; asper, 266; aspergilliformis, 239; assurgens, 395; attenuate, 176; attenuatus, 131; auriculatus, 123, 168; awl-shaped, 114; awned, 139; axe-shaped, 37; axillaris, 463.

BACCATUS, 333; band-shaped, 104; basilaris, 459; beaked, 56, 148; bell-shaped, 72; bellying, 97; berried, 333; biconjugato-pinnatus, 216; biconjugatus, 217; biennis, 342; bifariam, 489; bifarius, 488; bifoliolatus, 206; bigeminatus, 217; binatus, 206; bipinnatus, 221; biternatus, 222; bitten, 159; bladdery, 96; blunt, 153, 173; blunt with a point, 154; blunted, 164; boat-shaped, 46; bony, 322; bossed, 20; botuliformis, 88; brachiatus, 427; branched, 226; branched, much, 229; branched, somewhat, 227; breve, brevissime angustatus, 178; bristle-pointed, 144; bristly, 263; brush-shaped, 79, 239; buckler-shaped, 19; byssaceus, 237.

CADUCUS, 342; caesius, 308; caespitosus, 486; campaniformis, campanulatus, 72; canaliculatus, 45; cancellatus, 243; capillaris, 50; capitatus, 162; carinatus, 44; carnosus, 323; cartilagineus, 314; caudatus, 152; ceraceus, cereus, 324; cernuus, 407; channelled, 45; chartaceus, 311; cicatricatus, 252; ciliatus, 285; circinalis, 417; circinatus, 379, 417; cirrhosus, 142, 209; clavatus, claviformis, club-shaped, 9; clustered, 491; clypeatus, 26; coacervatus, 491; coadnatus, coadunatus, coalitus, 454; coated, 318; cochlearis, 386; cochleatus, 15; co-haerens, 454; combinate venosus, 349; comb-shaped, 200; compositus, compound, 203, 482; compressus, 30; conduplicativus, conduplicatus, 371; confertus, 483; confluens, 454; conglomeratus, 491; conicus, 1; conjugatus, 225; connatus, 444, 454; connivens, 429; conoideus, 2; continuus, 501; contortus, 383; converginervis, 351; converging, 429; convolutivus, 368; convolutus, 368, 402; cordatus, 122, 166; cordiformis, 122; coriaceus, 312; corky, 317; corneus, 320; corniculatus, cornutus, 55; coronans, 468; corrugatus, 375; corticatus, 318; costatus, 344; cotyliformis, 82; crassus, 326; crateriformis, 81; crenatus, 181; crescent-shaped, 124; crested, 57; crispus, 185; cristatus, 57; crowded, 483; crowning, 468; crustaceus, 313; cubicus, 8; cucullatus, 93; cuneato-angustatus, 177; cuneatus, 175; cuneiformis, 113; cup-shaped, 74; cupola-shaped, cupuliformis, 75; curled, 185; curvativus, 374; curvatus, curved, 35; curve-ribbed, curvinervis, 351; cushioned, 33; cut, 190; cuspidatus, 141; cyathiformis, 74; cylindricus, 5; cymbiformis, 46.

DAEDALEUS, 160; dealbatus, 309; deciduus, 342; declinatus, 405, 412; decompositus, 204; decreasingly pinnate, 213; decrescente pinnatus, 213; decumbens, 424; decurrens, 439; decursive pinnatus, 214; decursivus, 439; decussatus, 493; deflexus, 412; deliquescens, 230; deltoideus, 119; demersus, 392; dendroideus, 238; dentatus, 183; denudatus 298; depauperatus, 498; dependens, 394; depressus, 31, 338; descendens, 393; dewy, 303; dextrorsum, 418; dichotomus, 231; didigitato-pinnatus, 216; didymus, 232; diffusus, 425; digitaliformis, 85; digitato-pinnatus, 215; digitatus, 198; dimidiatus, 63, 138; disappearing, 230; discoideus, 34; distans, distant, 499; distichus, 488; distinctus, 451; divaricatus, 426; dolabriformis, 37; dorsalis, 456; dotted, 258; double, 503; downy, 271; drooping, 407; duplicato-pinnatus, 221; duplicato-ternatus, 222; duplicatus, 503; dusty, 304; dwarf, 335.

ECHINATUS, 263; elatus, 340; ellipsoideus, 24; ellipticus, 108; emarginatus, 156; embracing, 440; enervis, 361; ensiformis, 116; entangled, 502; entire, 179; epigaeus, 469; epigynus, 472; epiphyllus, 465; equal, 133; equal-sided, 135; equally pinnate, 210; equitans, equitativus, 377; erectus, 387; erosus, 184; evanescenti-venosus, 384; even, 259; exaltatus, 340; exasperatus, 266; exiguus, 339; extrorsus, 421.

FALCATUS, 38; falsinervis, 362; fan-shaped, 64; fariam, 489; farinaceus, 331; fascarius, 104; fasciatus, 496; fascicled, fasciculatus, 487; fastigiatus, 494; favosus, 250; fibrosus, fibrous, 329; fiddle-shaped, 128; filiformis, 49; fingered, 198; fissus, 194; fistulosus, 7; five-ribbed, 346; flabelliformis, 64; flagelliformis, 47; fleshy, 323; flexuosus, 413; floating, 391; floralis, 464; fluitans, 391; foliaceus, 59; foliaris, 465; forked, 233; foxglove-shaped, 85; frosted, 305; fugacious, 342; fugax, 342; funalis, 48; fungiformis, fungilliformis, 91; funnel-shaped, 71; furcatus, 233; furrowed, 256; fusiformis, 27.

GELATINOSUS, 328; geminatus, 503; geniculatus, 415; gibbosus, gibbus, 21; giganteus, 341; glaber, glabrous, 295; gladiatus, 116; glaucus, 307; glittering, 297; globosus, 4; glutinosus, 300; gnawed, 184; goblet-shaped, 81; gongylodes, 62; granulatus, 236; greasy, 302; grumosus, 65; gyratus, 417.

HAIR-POINTED, 145; hair-shaped, 50; hairy, 270; halbert-headed, 127; half-netted, 247; half-stemclasping, 442; half-terete, 29; halved, 63, 138; hanging down, 394; hapaxanthus, 342; hastatus, 127, 170; headed, 162; heart-shaped, 122; hebetatus, 164; herbaceus, 334; hinoideus, 363; hirtus, 273; hispidus, 277, hoary, 272; homotropus, 436; honey-combed, 250; hooded, 93; hook-backed, 130; hooked, 147; horizontalis, 398; horned, 55; horny, 320; humifusus, 422; humilis, 337; hypocrateriformis, 70; hypogaeus, 470; hypogynus, 473.

IMBRICATIVUS, 376; imbricatus, 376, 484; imparipinnatus, 209; impolitus, 299; inaequalis, 134; inaequilaterus, 136; incanus, 272; incisus, 190; inclinatus, inclining, 405; incurvus, 410; indirecte venosus, 347; induplicativus, 370; inermis, 260; inflatus, 96; inflexus, infractus, 410; infundibularis, infundibuliformis, 71; innatus, 447; integer, 179; integerrimus, 180; interrupte pinnatus, 212; interruptus, 500; intricatus, 502; introcurvus, introflexus, 410; introrsus, 420; inversus, inverted, 399; involutivus, 365; involutus, 365, 401; irregularis, 99.

JOINTED, 235.

KEELED, 44; kidney-shaped, 125; knee-jointed, 415; kneepan-shaped, 76; knob-like, 62; knotted, 53.

LABIATUS, 68; lacerus, 189; lachrymiformis, 12; laciniatus, 191; lacunosus, 249; laevigatus, 296; laevis, 295; lamellatus, lamellosus, 163; lanatus, 276; lanceolatus, 106; lateralis, 457; laxus, 315, 480; leaf-like, 59; leathery, 312; lens-shaped, lenticularis, 18; lentiginosus, 304; liber, 451; ligneus, lignosus, 325; ligulatus, 105; linearis, 103; lineatus, lined, 255; linguiformis, 39; little, 339; lobatus, 193; loculosus, 240; lofty, 340; loose, 315, 480; loratus, 105; low, 337; lunatus, lunulatus, 124; lyratus, lyre-shaped, 129.

MARCESCENS, 342; marginalis, 458; matt, 299; mealy, 331; medullary, medullosus, 330; meloniformis, 22; membranaceus, 310; meniscoideus, 90; millsail-shaped, 61; modioliformis, 92; molendinaceus, 61; moniliformis, 51; monocarpus, 342; much-branched, 229; mucosus, mucous, 301; mucronatus, 140; multidigitato-pinnatus, 220; multifugus, 225; muricatus, 264; mushroom-shaped, 91; muticus, 165.

NAKED, 298; nanus, 335; napiformis, 16; natans, 390; nave-shaped, 92; navicularis, 46; necklace-shaped, 51; needle-shaped, 115; nervatus, nerved, nervosus, 343; netted, 246; nitidus, 294; nodding, 408; normalis, 101; nudus, 298; nullinervis, 361; nutans, 408.

OBLIQUUS, 137, 397; oblongus, 107; obtusus, 153, 173; obtusus cum acumine, 154; obvolutivus, obvolutus, 367; oleaginosus, 321; one-sided, 409, 490; opacus, opaque, 299; opposite, 430; oppositus, 475; orbicularis, 110; orthotropus, 433; oscillatorius, 448; osseus, 322; outline, 102; ovalis, 108; ovatus, 109; ovoideus, 25.

PALACEUS, 450; paleaceus, 293; palmatus, 196; palmiformis, 353; palminervis, 357; panduratus, panduriformis, 128; papery, 311; papillosus, papulosus, 269; papyraceus, 311; parabolicus, 117; parallelinervis, 350; paripinnatus, 210; parted, 195; partitioned, 240; partitus, 195; patelliformis, 76; patens, 428; pear-shaped, 11; pectinatus, 200; pedatus, 197; pedatinervis, 356; peltatus, 437; peltinervis, 358; pendulus, 406; penicillatus, 79; penniformis, 353; penninervis, 355; perfoliatus, 443; perforated, 244; perigynus, 474; peritropus, 432; peronatus, 283; perpendicular, 396; perpusillus, 336; persistent, 342; personatus, 67; pertusus, 244; petaloideus, 58; petiolaris, 467; piliferus, 145; pilosus, 270; pimpled, 269; pinnate, 208; pinnatifidus, 199; pinnatipartitus, pinnatiscissus, 199; pinnatus, 208; pinnatus, abrupte, 210; pinnatus, alternatim, 211; pinnatus, decrescente, 213; pinnatus, interrupte, 212; pitcher-shaped, 73; pitted, 248; placentiformis, 17; plaited, 372; plane, planus, 32; plicativus, plicatus, 372; plietesialis, 342; poculiformis, 83; pointless, 165; pointleted, 146; polished, politus, 296; polycarpicus, 342; posticus, 421; pouch-shaped, 84; powdery, 306; praemorsus, 159; prickly, 262; prism-shaped, prismaticus, 3; proboscideus, 56; procerus, 340; procumbens, 422; pronus, prostratus, 423; pruinosus, 305; pubens, pubescens, 271; pulley-shaped, 77; pulverulentus, 306; pulvinatus, 33; pumilus, 335; punctatus, 258; pungens, 143; pusillus, 336; pygmaeus, 335; pyramidalis, 1; pyriformis, 11.

QUADRIDIGITATO-PINNATUS, 220; quincuncialis, 381; quintuplinervis, 346.

RADIANT, radiatus, 505; radicalis, 460; ramealis, rameus, 462; ramosissimus, 229; ramosus, 226; rarus, 499; reclinatus, 378, 403; reclining, 403; rectinervis, 350; rectus, 388; recurvus, reflexus, refractus, 411; regularis, 98; remotus, 499; reniformis, 125; repandus, 186; replicativus, 373; resupinatus, 404; reticulatus, 246; retinervis, 360; retrocurvus, retroflexus, 411; retrorsus, 419; retusus, 155; revolutivus, 366; revolutus, 400; rhombeus, rhomboideus, 118; ribbed, 343; ringed, 253; ringens, 67; rope-shaped, 48; roridus, 303; rosaceus, 504; rosetted, 485; rostellatus, rostratus, 148; rosularis, rosulatus, 485; rotatus, 69; rotundatus, 172; rotundus, 111; rough, 266, roughish, 267; rounded, 172; rows, in, 489; rugosus, 245; ruminatus, 242; runcinatus, 130; ruptinervis, 352.

SADDLE-SHAPED, 94; sagittatus, 126, 169; salver-shaped, 70; sausage-shaped, 88; sawed, 182; scaber, 266; scabridus, 267; scaly, 497; scariosus, 316; scarred, 252; scattered, 481; scrobiculatus, 248; scrotiformis, 84; scutatus, 19; scutelliformis, 78; scutiformis, 19; secundus, 409, 490; selliformis, 94; semi-amplexus. 367; semilunatus, 124; semireticulatus, 247; semiteres, 29; separate, 451; septatus, 240; serialis, 489; serratus, 182; sessilis, 438; setosus, 144; shaggy, 273; sharp-pointed, 149; sheathing, 445; shield-shaped, 26; 'shining, 294; simple, simplex, 201; simplicissimus, 202; sinistrorsum, 418; sinuatus, 188; slashed, 191; slimy, 301; smooth, 295; solutus, 451; sparsus, 481; spatulatus, 112; sphaericus, 4; sphaeroideus, spheroidal, 23; spiculatus, 265; spindle-shaped, 27; spinosus, spiny, 261; spiralis, 14, 416, 492; spiraliter contortus, 382; splendens, 297; split, 194; spongiosus, spongy, 319; spreading, 428; squamosus, 292, 497; squarrose-slashed, squarroso-laciniatus, 192; squarrosus, 495; starved, 498; stellatus, 234, 477; stelliformis, stellulatus, 477; stem-clasping, 441; stipitatus, 449; straggling, 426; straight, 388, 389; straight-ribbed, 350; strap-shaped, 105; striatus, 254; strictus, 389; strombuliformis, 13; subcordatus, 167; suberosus, 317; submersus,

392; subramosus, 227; subrotundus, 111; subterraneus, 470; subulatus, 114; succulentus, 327; sulcatus, 256; supervolutivus, 369; supradecompositus, 205; swimming, 390; sword-shaped, 116.

TAENIANUS, 87; tail-pointed, 152; tall, 340; taper-pointed, 150, tapering, 131; tapeworm-shaped, 87; tartareus, 332; tear-shaped, 12; teres, terete, 28; tergeminatus, tergeminus, 218; terminalis, 466; ternate, 479; ternato-pinnatus, 219; ternus, 479; testiculatus, 66; thick, 326; thread-shaped, 49; three-cornered, 41; three-edged, 42; three-ribbed, 345; thrice digitato-pinnate, 219; tomentosus, 274; tongue-shaped, 39; toothed, 183; top-shaped, 10; torn, 189; tortuosus, 414; torsivus, 382; torulosus, 53; trapeziformis, 121; tree-like, 238; triangularis, 120; trident-pointed, tridentatus, 161; tridigitato-pinnatus, 219; trigonus, 41; trinervis, 345; tripinnatus, 224; triple-ribbed, triplinervis, 346; triqueter, 42; triternatus, 223; trochlearis, 77; trumpet-shaped, 54; truncatus, 158, 171; tuberculatus, 268; tubatus, tubiformis, 54; tubulosus, 6; turbinatus, 10; turgidus, 95; turned backwards, 419; turned inwards, 420; turned outwards, 421; turnip-shaped, 16; twin, 232, 503; twin digitato-pinnate, 216; twining, 418; twisted, 382; two-edged, 43.

UMBILICATUS, 437; umbonatus, 20; umbraculiformis, umbrella-shaped, 89; unarmed, 260; uncatus, uncinatus, 147; unctuosus, 302; undulatus, 132; unequal, 134; unequal-sided, 136; unijugatus, unijugus, 225; unilateralis, 490; uninervis, 344; uninterrupted, 501; urceolatus, 73.

VAGINANS, 445; vaginervis, 359; vagus, 431; valvaris, valvatus, 380; vascularis, vase-shaped, 86; velutinus, velvety, 275; venosus, 364; venosus, combinate, 349; ventricosus, 97; vermicularis, 52; verrucosus, 268; versatilis, 448; vertebratus, 207; verticalis, 396; verticillatus, 478; vexillaris, 385; villosus, 273; viscidus, 300; volubilis, 418.

WAVY, 132; waxy, 324; wedge-shaped, 113, 175; wheel-shaped, 69; whip-shaped, 47; whitened, 309; whorled, 478; winged, 60; woody, 325; woolly, 276; worm-shaped, 52; wrinkled, 375.

REFERENCES

References relevant to this chapter are given in the General Bibliography (Chapter XXVI).

CHAPTER XXIII

Chemical Reactions and Tests

CHEMICAL REACTIONS OF LICHENS

The ancient and widespread use in dyeing of different species of lichens to produce different colours indicates an awareness of easily detected correlated morphological and chemical characters among these plants which was empirically recognized in the far distant past but which the Scandinavian lichenologist William Nylander (1822–99) was the first to employ scientifically as an aid to their identification. In a paper of 1866 on chemical criteria for the study of lichens, Nylander pointed out that certain species of *Parmelia*, for example, turned red when treated with a solution of bleaching powder (*solutio hypochloritis calcici*, $CaCl_2O$) while others showed no reaction, and that caustic potash (*kali causticum*, KOH) turned some species red, others yellow. He noted such reactions in his subsequent descriptions, and the recording of these is now standard procedure in lichenology, even though their taxonomic value has been very diversely assessed (cf. Almborn, 1952; Hale, 1961). Further investigations, notably by Asahini (1954; cf. also Hale, 1961), have revealed an extraordinary variety of organic compounds in lichens, among the most widespread of these being usneic acid (*acidum usneicum*, $C_{18}H_{16}O_7$), lecanoric acid (*acidum lecanoricum*, $C_{16}H_{14}O_7$), gyrophoric acid (*acidum gyrophoricum*, $C_{24}H_{20}O_{10}$) and atranorine (*atranorinum*, $C_{19}H_{18}O_8$).

The presence of such substances is easily recorded in Latin descriptions, e.g. *podetia acidum fumarprotocetraricum et atranorinum continentia* (podetia containing fumarprotocetraric acid and atranorine). When stating the results of colour tests, lichenologists use the abbreviation C or Cl for a saturated aqueous solution of calcium hypochlorite ($CaCl_2O$), J or I for iodine solution (I), K or KOH or KHO for an aqueous solution of potassium hydroxide (KOH), P or PD for *p*-phenylenediamine ($C_6H_4(NH_2)_2$). When two reagents are applied one after

358

the other, the appropriate abbreviations follow the same order, e.g. KC, i.e. K then C. The minus sign (−) or a phrase, e.g. *non reagens* (not reacting), *non tinctus* (not coloured), *immutatus* or *non mutatus* (not changed), indicates no colour reaction. The plus sign (+) indicates a positive colour reaction. These signs may be placed one above the other to indicate different reactions in the upper cortex and the medulla ; thus K± indicates a positive reaction to K by the upper cortex, a negative reaction by the medulla. With a positive reaction, the colour is then stated. Thus with K + the lichen studied may become yellow-ish (*flavescens, sublutescens, lutescens, subluteus*) or yellow (*flavus, luteus*), tawny (*fulvescens, fulvus*), rust-coloured (*ferrugineus*), orange-tawny (*aurantiaco-fulvus*), rose-tinged (*roseo-tinctus*) or blood-red (*sanguineo-rubens, kermesinus*). With J + it may become yellowish (*flavescens*, etc.) or bluish (*coerulescens*), blue (*coeruleus*) or violet-blue (*violaceo-coeruleus*). In Latin descriptions these descriptive adjectives agree grammatically with the name of the organ qualified, e.g. *thallus K luteus* (thallus turned yellow by K), *thecium J violaceo-coeruleum, K non reagens* (thecium turned violet-blue by J, not reacting to K), *hyphae J non reagentes* (hyphae not reacting to J), *hymenio J non tincto, sporis J lutescentibus* (with the hymenium not coloured by J, the spores turned yellowish by J). For further words relating to colours, see Chapter XVIII.

CHEMICAL REACTIONS OF ALGAE AND FUNGI

Chemical tests have also proved helpful in identifying other groups of cryptogams. Thus the phrase *chlorozincico iodurato* is used in descriptions of Algae to state their reaction to Schulze's solution (chlor-zinc-iodine). In the fungus genus *Russula*, for example, *R. xerampelina* turns green (*viridescens*) when treated with iron sulphate (*ferri sulphas*) whereas most species turn pink (*roseus*). Yeasts (cf. Frederiksen, 1956 ; Pedersen, 1958) are necessarily distinguished by their growth (*crescentia*) on culture media (*substrata nutricia*), e.g. malt extract (*extractum malti*) or malt agar (*agar maltatus*), their assimilation (*assimilatio*) of sugars, e.g. glucose (*glucosum*), galactose (*galactosum*), lactose (*lactosum*), maltose (*maltosum*) or saccharose (*saccharosum*), and of potassium nitrate (*kalii nitras*), and other reactions. Frederiksen (1956) provides a good example of a description (see p. 174) in modern Latin simply and ingeniously overcoming the difficulty of dealing with matters so remote from the themes of classical Latin literature. Behaviour on different culture media also needs study, for example, in *Aspergillus* and *Penicillium*.

CHEMICAL NAMES

In introducing chemical data into Latin descriptions, chemical formulae should be given whenever possible and the Latin names of substances should be those traditionally used in pharmaceutical Latin (cf. Cooper & McLaren, 1950) or constructed in the same manner. Thus an 'acid' is *acidum* (n.), 'acetic acid' *acidum aceticum*, hence 'usneic acid' is *acidum usneicum*. The names of acid radicles ending in English as '-ate' end in pharmaceutical Latin in *-as* (m.), e.g. *chloras* (chlorate), *nitras* (nitrate), *sulphas* (sulphate); those in '-ite' end in *-is*, e.g. *nitris* (nitrite), *sulphis* (sulphite). Salts ending in English as '-ide' end in Latin as *-idum*, e.g. *chloridum* (chloride). The name of the element is given in the genitive, e.g. *zinci chloridum* (chloride of zinc). Names of oxides end in *oxidum* (n.), e.g. *dioxidum* (dioxide), *hydroxidum* (hydroxide), *peroxidum* (peroxide). Those of sugars end in *-osum*, e.g. *glucosum* (glucose). Since the Latin names of most of the chemical elements (cf. Flood, 1963) end in *-um*, as also those of many compounds, it is simplest when in doubt to form other names by analogy with these and treat them as neuter.

The following is a list of the more important words relating to chemical matters which can be used in Latin descriptions: s. = noun; m. = masculine; f. = feminine; n. = neuter; adj. = adjective; part = participle; gen. sing. = genitive singular; the numerals I, II, III, IV and the letters A, B, indicate declensions (see pp. 63, 68, 92, 93).

Acetate : acetas (s.m. III), *gen. sing.* acetatis.
acetic : aceticus (adj. A).
Acid : acidum (s.n. II), *gen. sing.* acidi.
acidic : acidus (adj. A).
aethylicus : *see* ethyl.
Agar : agar (s.m. II), *gen. sing.* agari; *agar Czapekii*, Czapek's solution agar (cf. Thom & Raper, *Man. Aspergilli* 32; 1945); *agar ex infusione foeni*, hay infusion agar (cf. Thom & Raper, l.c. 35); *malto-agar, agar maltatus*, malt agar. *See* Must.
Alcohol : alcohol (s.n. III), *gen. sing.* alcoholis; *ethanoleum, alcohol ethylicum*, ethyl alcohol; *alcohol methylicum*, methyl alcohol.
Aluminium (Al) : aluminium (s.n. II), *gen. sing.* aluminii.
Ammonia : ammonia (s.f. I), *gen. sing.* ammoniae.
Amylum : *see* Starch.
Arbutin : arbutinum (s.n. II), *gen. sing.* arbutini.
Arsenic (As) : arsenicum (s.n. II), *gen. sing.* arsenici.
arsenical : arsenicalis (adj. B).
Atranorine : atranorinum (s.n. II), *gen. sing.* atranorini.
Aurum : *see* Gold.
Butter : butyrum (s.n. II), *gen. sing.* butyri.
Calcium (Ca) : calcium (s.n. II), *gen. sing.* calcii.

Carbon (C): carbo (s.m. III), *gen. sing.* carbonis.
Carbonate: carbonas (s.m. III), *gen. sing.* carbonatis.
caustic: causticus (adj. A).
Chlorate: chloras (s.m. III), *gen. sing.* chloratis.
Chloride: chloridum (s.n. II), *gen. sing.* chloridi.
Chlorine: chlorinum (s.n. II), *gen. sing.* chlorini.
Copper (Cu): cuprum (s.n. II), *gen. sing.* cupri.
Dextrose: *see* Glucose.
distilled: destillatus (part A); *aqua destillata*, distilled water.
Ethanol: ethanoleum (s.n. II), *gen. sing.* ethanolei; *see* Alcohol.
ethyl: ethylicus (adj. A), aethylicus (adj. A).
Extract: extractum (s.n. II), *gen. sing.* extracti; *cultura in extracto malti*, culture on malt extract.
Ferrum: *see* Iron.
Fructose: fructosum (s.n. II), *gen. sing.* fructosi.
fumarprotocetraric: fumarprotocetraricus (adj. A).
Gelatin: gelatinum (s.n. II), *gen. sing.* gelatini.
Gelatina: *see* Jelly.
Glucose: glucosum (s.n. II), *gen. sing.* glucosi.
Gold (Au): aurum (s.n. II), *gen. sing.* auri.
gyrophoric: gyrophoricus (adj. A).
Hydrargyrum: *see* Mercury.
hydrochloric: hydrochloricus (adj. A), muriaticus (adj. A).
Hydroxide: hydroxidum (s.n. II), *gen. sing.* hydroxidi.
Hypochlorite: hypochloris (s.m. III), *gen. sing.* hypochloritis.
Infusion: infusum (s.n. II), *gen. sing.* infusi.
Iodine (I): iodum (s.n. II), *gen. sing.* iodi; jodum (s.n. II), *gen. sing.* jodi.
Iron (Fe): ferrum (s.n. II), *gen. sing.* ferri.
Jelly: gelatina (s.f. I), *gen. sing.* gelatinae.
Jodum: *see* Iodine.
Kalium: *see* Potassium.
Lactose: lactosum (s.n. II), *gen. sing.* lactosi.
Laevulose: *see* Fructose.
Lead (Pb): plumbum (s.n. II), *gen. sing.* plumbi.
lecanoric: lecanoricus (adj. A).
Malt: maltum (s.n. II), *gen. sing.* malti.
Malt-agar: malto-agar (s.m. II), *gen. sing.* malto-agari; agar (s.m. II) maltatus (adj. A).
malted: maltatus (adj. A).
Maltose: maltosum (s.n. II), *gen. sing.* maltosi.
Mercury (Hg): hydrargyrum (s.n. II), *gen. sing.* hydrargyri.
methyl: methylicus (adj. A).
Mixture: mistura (s.f. I), *gen. sing.* misturae.
moistened: madefactus (part. A).
muriaticus: *see* hydrochloricus.
Must: mustum (s.n. II), *gen. sing.* musti; *in musto ex hordeo cum agaro*, on wort agar.

Nitrate : nitras (s.m. III), *gen. sing.* nitratis.

nitric : nitricus (adj. A).

Nitrite : nitris (s.m. III), *gen. sing.* nitritis.

Oil : oleum (s.n. II), *gen. sing.* olei ; *guttula oleosa*, oil droplet.

oily : oleosus (adj. A).

oxalic : oxalicus (adj. A).

Oxide : oxidum (s.n. II), *gen. sing.* oxidi.

Pectin : pectinum (s.n. II), *gen. sing.* pectini.

Peroxide : peroxidum (s.n. II), *gen. sing.* peroxidi.

Phosphate : phosphas (s.m. III), *gen. sing.* phosphatis.

Plumbum : *see* Lead.

Potassium (K) : kalium (s.n. II), *gen. sing.* kalii ; potassium (s.n. II), *gen. sing.* potassii.

Propionate : propionas (s.m. III), *gen. sing.* propionatis.

protocetraric : protocetraricus (adj. A).

Saccharose : saccharosum (s.n. III), *gen. sing.* saccharosi.

Salt : sal (s.m. and n. III), *gen. sing.* salis.

Silver (Ag) : argentum (s.n. II), *gen. sing.* argenti.

Sodium (Na) : natrium (s.n. II), *gen. sing.* natrii ; sodium (s.n. II), *gen. sing.* sodii.

Solution : solutio (s.f. III), *gen. sing.* solutionis.

Stannum : *see* Tin.

Starch : amylum (s.n. II), *gen. sing.* amyli.

starchy : amylaceus (adj. A).

sterilized : sterilisatus (adj. A), sterilifactus (adj. A).

Sucrose : sucrosum (s.n. II), *gen. sing.* sucrosi.

Sugar (in general) : saccharum (s.m. II), *gen. sing.* sacchari.

Sulphate : sulphas (s.m. III), *gen. sing.* sulphatis.

Sulphide : sulphidum (s.n. II), *gen. sing.* sulphidi.

Sulphite : sulphis (s.n. III), *gen. sing.* sulphitis.

Sulphur (S) : sulphur (s.n. III), *gen. sing.* sulphuris; sulfur (s.n. III), *gen. sing.* sulfuris.

sulphuric : sulphuricus (adj. A).

sulphurous : sulphurosus (adj. A).

Temperature : temperatura (s.f. I), *gen. sing.* temperaturae.

Tin (Sn) : stannum (s.n. II), *gen. sing.* stanni.

usneic : usneicus (adj. A).

Zinc (Zn) : zincum (s.n. II), *gen. sing.* zinci.

REFERENCES

ALMBORN, O. 1952. A key to the sterile corticolous crustaceous lichens occurring in South Sweden. *Bot. Notiser*, 1952 : 239-263.

ASAHINA, Y. 1954. *Chemistry of Lichen Substances*. Tokyo.

COOPER, J. W., & McLAREN, A. C. 1950. *Latin for pharmaceutical Students*. 5th ed. London.

FLOOD, W. E. 1963. *The Origins of chemical Names.* London.

FREDERIKSEN, P. S. 1956. A new Rhodotorula species, *Rhodotorula macerans* sp.n., isolated from field-retted flax straw. *Friesia,* 5 : 234-239.

HALE, M. E. 1961. *Lichen Handbook. A Guide to the Lichens of Eastern North America.* Washington, D.C.

KOVATS, M. 1822. *Lexicon mineralogicum enneaglottum.* Pest.

NYLANDER, W. 1866. Circa novum in studio Lichenum criterium chemicum. *Flora (Regensburg),* 49 : 198-201.

PEDERSEN, T. A. 1958. *Cryptococcus terricolus* nov. spec., a new yeast isolated from Norwegian soils. *Comptes rendus Trav. Lab. Carlsberg,* 31, no. 7 : 93-103.

CHAPTER XXIV

Symbols and Abbreviations

To save both space and time, botanical Latin employs a number of symbols and abbreviations which by frequent and consistent association with certain meanings have become so familiar that they 'avoide the tediouse repetition of these words' (Robert Recorde's justification in 1557 for introducing the = sign for equality; cf. Cajori, 1923; Tanner, 1963); in certain contexts they express facts more simply than would a full verbal explanation. The + (more, plus) and − (less, minus) signs came into commercial use at the end of the fifteenth century and were given mathematical application by Recorde in 1540. Thomas Harriot posthumously introduced the > (greater than) and < (less than) signs in 1631 (cf. Tanner, 1963). Much earlier the medieval alchemists had used the planetary symbols to signify metals, e.g. ♄ (Saturn) for lead, ♃ (Jupiter) for tin, ♂ (Mars) for iron, ♀ (Venus) for copper (cf. Partington, 1937). The first use of symbols in biology dates from the mid-eighteenth century and stands to the credit of Linnaeus. Mathematics and chemistry gave him good precedent for the introduction of symbols into botanical Latin. In 1751 in the dissertation *Plantae hybridae* he used the sign ♀ for female and the sign ♂ for male (cf. Stearn, 1962). In 1753 in the *Species Plantarum* he added yet others (cf. Stearn, 1957); see below. The great convenience of these symbols led later authors, notably Willdenow, A. P. de Candolle, Trattinick, Loudon and Kuntze, to introduce many others, of which only a few were sufficiently needed as 'stand-in for words' to pass into general use; Kuntze (1893) and Renkema (1942) have dealt with their history.

LINNAEAN SIGNS

The following is Linnaeus's usage in the *Species Plantarum* (1753), prior astrological and alchemical usage and his usage in the *Genera Plantarum* (1737 et seq.) being given between square brackets.

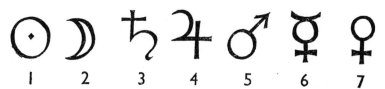

Fig. 33 Medieval planetary Symbols used in Alchemy and Botany
1, the Sun (gold; annual); 2, the Moon (silver); 3, Saturn (lead;
woody); 4, Jupiter (tin; perennial); 5, Mars (iron; male); 6,
Mercury (mercury; hermaphrodite); 7, Venus (copper; female)
(woodcuts by Fritz Kredel, from R. Koch, *Das Zeichenbuch*, 3rd ed.;
1940)

In citations of literature
* indicates a good description to be found at the place cited, e.g. *Hort.
cliff.* 13 * (cf. Sprague & Exell, 1937; Svenson, 1939) [in the
Genera Plantarum, however, * indicates a genus of which Linnaeus
had studied living material].

† indicates an imperfectly known species or some doubt or obscurity
[in the *Genera Plantarum* † indicates that Linnaeus knew the
genus only from herbarium material; absence of * and † indicates
here that he knew it only from the literature].

♂   [Mars; iron] male   Used under *Arctopus, Can-
♀   [Venus; copper] female   nabis,   Carica,   Clutia,
☿   [Mercury; mercury] hermaphrodite   *Ficus, Humulus, Hydro-
                                           charis, Mercurialis, Nyssa*
                                           and *Spinacia*.

In statements of life-span and habit (after 'Habitat')
♄   [Saturn; lead] woody, i.e. tree or shrub.
♃   [Jupiter; tin] perennial.
♂   [Mars; iron] biennial.
○   [Sun; gold] annual.

In the margin and annotations
α (alpha), β (beta), γ (gamma), δ (delta), ε (epsilon) and other Greek
letters indicate varieties; cf. Chapters X, XVII of Stearn, 1957.

In the margin as part of an epithet (nomen triviale)
▽   [water] aquaticus -a -um, e.g. *Plantago* ▽ = *Plantago-aquatica,
Anagall.* ▽ = *Anagallis-aquatica, Nasturtium* ▽ : m = *Nasturtium-
aquaticum.*
♀   [Venus; copper] *Veneris*, e.g. *umbilicus* ♀ = *umbilicus-veneris,
Pecten* ♀ = *pecten-veneris, speculum* ♀ = *speculum-veneris.*

'Symbols forming part of a specific epithet proposed by Linnaeus must be transcribed' (*Int. Code bot. Nom.* 1961, Art. 23). He used them under *Alisma, Campanula, Cotyledon, Scandix, Sisymbrium* and *Veronica*.

OTHER SIGNS

In 1839 Lindley gave an extensive survey of signs proposed up to then, most of which never gained currency. Survivors are given below. It should be noted that certain books have their own special signs and abbreviations; the preface or introduction may provide explanations. Thus in Swartz's *Nova Genera et Species Plantarum seu Prodromus* (1788) an asterisk (*) at the end of a diagnosis indicates that this is based not on a specimen collected by Swartz but on material from other collectors sent to Sir Joseph Banks from the West Indies and hence now in the British Museum (Natural History), London. In Stapf's *Index Londinensis* (1929–31) and its *Supplement* (1941), and also in Stearn's monograph of *Epimedium* and *Vancouveria* (*J. Linnean Soc. London, Bot.*, 51: 409-535; 1938), an asterisk against a citation denotes a coloured illustration; in supplements to the *Index Kewensis* from no. 10 (1947) onwards it simply denotes an illustration. In Kunth's *Nova Genera et Species Plantarum* (1816–25) the names of species and genera new to science collected by Humboldt and Bonpland are marked with †. In his *Prodromus Florae Novae Hollandiae* (1810), however, Robert Brown used the sign † to indicate species known to him only from the account in Labillardière's *Novae Hollandiae Plantarum Specimen* (1804–07). In Acharius, *Lichenographiae Suecicae Prodromus* (1798), the Swedish species are numbered, non-Swedish species unnumbered but marked with an asterisk denoting that Acharius had carefully studied material or the sign † denoting otherwise, i.e. that he knew the species only from literature.

The following have been extensively used:

!	seen by the Author. After a citation of a specimen it means that this has been examined by the author citing it; after a citation of literature, notably by de Candolle, it means that he has examined an authentic specimen from the author whose work is cited.
§	section or other divisions of a genus.
*	in Nyman's *Conspectus Florae Europaeae* (1878–82) before a binomial indicates the rank of subspecies; in other works * between a specific name and an added epithet or name indicates the rank of subspecies.
°	degree of longitude, latitude or temperature.
′	foot, e.g. 2′ = 2 feet (61 cm.); minute of longitude or latitude.
″	inch, e.g. 3″ = 3 inches (7·5 cm.); second of longitude or latitude.
‴	line, e.g. 4‴ = 4 lines ($\frac{4}{12}$ inch = 0·8 cm.).

∝   very numerous ; a large indefinite number.
+   in Nyman's *Conspectus* indicates a doubtful plant ; before or in a
              name indicates a graft hybrid, e.g. + *Laburnocytisus*.
+   more, present.
○   lacking, absent.
⊙   monocarpic (hapaxanthus, monocarpicus).
⊙ or ①   annual (annuus).
⊙ or ①   biennial (biennis).
♃   perennial (perennis).
ђ   shrub or woody plant (frutex vel suffrutex).
ђ   tree (arbor).
×   hybrid (hybrida).
× or ≈   degree of magnification, e.g. × 10 = enlarged by 10 times ; by, e.g.
              20 × 10 cm. = measuring 20 cm. in one direction by 10 cm. in
              another.
≡   identical ; based on the same type ; nomenclatural synonym.
±   plus minusve, more or less.
†   before a personal name indicates deceased ; referring to a specimen
              indicates destroyed.
‡   poisonous.
⧻   very poisonous.
⊕   actinomorphic, regular.
·|·   zygomorphic, irregular.
μ   micron, one thousandth of a millimetre, 0·0001 cm., approx.
              $\frac{1}{25,000}$ inch ; symbol introduced by W. F. R. Suringar in 1857
              (*Diss. Obs. Phyc.*, xiii) and 1870 (*Algae Jap.*, 3).
>   greater than.
<   smaller than.

STANDARD ABBREVIATIONS

a.   *anno* : in the year.
ad int.   *ad interim* : for the present, meanwhile, provisionally.
adv.   *advena* : alien, *hence* introduced from another country.
aet.   *aetatis* : of his age ; *aet. 60*, aged 60 years.
aff.   *affinis* : akin to, bordering.
al.   *alii* : others ; *aliorum*, of others.
alt.   *alter* : second of two ; *ed. alt., editio altera*, second edition.
              altus : high or deep.
alt. s.m.   *altitudine supra mare* : at a height above sea-level.
ampl.   *ampliatus, amplificatus* : enlarged, extended.
ap.   *apud* : with, at the house of, *hence* in the publication of.
auct.   *auctorum* : of authors ; *auct. div., auctorum diversorum*,
                 of various authors ; *auct. mult., auctorum multorum*, of
                 many authors ; *auct. nonn., auctorum nonnullorum*, of
                 some authors ; *auct. omn., auctorum omnium*, of all

authors; *auct. pl., auctorum plurimorum*, of most authors; *sec. auctt., secundum auctores, ex auctt., ex auctoribus*, according to authors.

austr.	*australis*: southern.
b.	*beatus*: blessed, deceased.
bor.	*borealis*: northern.
c., ca.	*circa, circiter*: about.
c. descr.	*cum descriptione*: with description.
c. fr.	*cum fructibus*: with fruits.
c. ic.	*cum icone*: with illustration.
c. s.	*cum suis*: with collaborators.
cap.	*caput*: chapter.
cel.	*celeberrimus*: most celebrated.
centr.	*centralis*: central.
cet.	*cetera*: the rest, the remainder.
cf., cfr.	*confer*: compare.
char.	*character*: character, characteristics.
cit.	*citatus*: cited.
cl.	*clarissimus*: most renowned, celebrated.
cm.	*centimetrum*: centimetre.
coll.	*collegit*: he gathered.
comb.	*combinatio*: combination; *comb. nov., combinatio nova*, new combination of name and epithet.
comm.	*communicavit*: he communicated.
cons.	*conservandus*: to be kept; *nom. cons., nomen conservandum*, conserved name.
corr.	*correxit*: he corrected.
cult.	*cultus*: cultivated.
cv.	*cultivarietas*: cultivar.
d.d.d.	*dono dedit dedicavit*: as a gift he gave and dedicated; *dat donat dedicat*: he gives, presents and dedicates.
dat.	*datus*: given.
ded.	*dedit*: he gave.
del.	*delineavit*: he drew, he portrayed.
descr.	*descriptio*: description.
det.	*determinavit*: he determined, he identified.
diam.	*diametro*: in diameter.
distr.	*districtus*: district.
distrib.	*distributio*: distribution, range.
div.	*diversus*: various.
dom.	*dominus*: master (Mr., Herr, Monsieur, etc.).
	domina: mistress (Mrs., Frau, Madame, etc.).
don.	*donavit*: he gave.
e descr.	*e* (or *ex*) *descriptione*: from the description, according to the description.
e num.	*e numero*: from the number.
e.g.	*exempli gratia*: by way of example, for example.

ᴇ.p.	*ex parte*: in part, partly; *e.p., quoad spec. Jamaic. cit.*, in part, as to Jamaican specimen (species) cited.
ᴇj.	*ejus*: of it.
ᴇjusd.	*ejusdem*: of the same author.
ᴇl.	*elaboravit*: he revised.
ᴇm.	*emendatus*: emended.
	emendavit: he emended.
ᴇrr. typogr.	*errore typographico*: by a printing mistake.
ᴇxc.	*exceptus*: excepted.
ᴇxcl.	*exclusus*: excluded; *typo excluso*, with the type excluded.
ᴇxs.	*exsiccatus*: dried.
., fig.	*figura*: Figure, illustration: *t.* 6 *f.* 2, Plate 6, Figure 2.
.	(before a personal noun) *fide*: according to.
	(after a personal noun) *filius*: son; *Hook. f.*, Hooker filius, J. D. Hooker, son of W. J. Hooker.
	(before an epithet) *forma*: form; *f. sp., forma specialis*, special form.
ᴇm.	*femineus*: female.
il.	*filius*: son.
ꜰl.	*floret*: it flowers; *fl. aest., floret aestate*, it flowers in summer.
	floruit: (of a person) he flourished, he lived at this period.
	flore: with flower, in flower.
ꜰl. pl.	*flore pleno*: with a double flower.
ꜰol.	*folio, foliis*: with leaf, in leaf, with leaves; *fol. var., foliis variegatis*, with variegated leaves.
ꜰr.	*fructus*: fruit, in fruit.
ꜰ., gen.	*genus*: genus.
ɢ.M.	*pro gradu doctoris medici*: for the degree of doctor of medicine, used of certain Linnaean dissertations.
ʜ.	*hortus*: garden.
ʜab.	*habitat*: it inhabits, *hence* place of growth; *hab. c.b.s., habitat ad Caput bonae spei*, it grows at the Cape of Good Hope.
ʜb., herb.	*herbarium*: herbarium.
ʜexap.	*hexapodium*: fathom, 6 feet (1·8 m.).
ʜort.	*hortorum*: of gardens; *hortulanorum*: of gardeners.
ɪ.e.	*id est*: that is.
ɪb.	*ibidem*: the same, in the same place.
ɪc.	*icon*: illustration.
ɪd.	*idem*: the same.
ɪgn.	*ignotus*: unknown.
ɪl.	*illustris*: celebrated.
ɪn adnot.	*in adnotatione*: in annotation, in a note.
ɪn litt.	*in litteris*: in correspondence.
ɪn loc. cit.	*in loco citato*: in the place cited.
ɪn obs.	*in observatione*: in observation.

in sched.	*in schedula*: on a herbarium sheet or label.
in syn.	*in synonymia, in synonymis*: in synonymy.
inc. sed.	*incertae sedis*: of uncertain position.
incl.	*inclusus*: included; *typo incl., typo incluso*, with the type included.
ined.	*ineditus*: unpublished.
infl.	*inflorescentia*: inflorescence.
inq., inquil.	*inquilinus*: naturalized.
ins.	*insula*: island, isle.
i.q.	*idem quod*: the same as.
l.	*vel*; or (*l* for *vel*, like *h* for *nihil*, derives from the procedure of medieval scribes who did not necessarily use an initial letter when abbreviating).
l.c., loc. cit.	*loco citato*: at the place cited.
lat.	*latus*: broad, wide.
leg.	*legit*: he gathered.
lg.	*longus*: long.
lin.	*linea*: linea (c. 2 mm.); cf. p. 113.
lith.	*lithographit*: he lithographed.
m.	*mihi*: to me, of me (dative of possession).
	metrum, meter: metre.
	manu: by the hand; *m.L.f., manu Linnaei filii*, in the handwriting of the younger Linnaeus.
m., mt.	*mons, montes*: mountain, mountains.
m.s.m.	*metra supra mare*: metres above sea-level.
magn.	*magnitudo*: size; *magn. nat., magnitudine naturali*, at natural size.
masc.	*masculus*: male.
mer.	*meridionalis*: southern.
mm.	*millimetrum*: millimetre.
MS., MSS.	*manuscriptum, manuscripta*: manuscript, manuscripts.
min. parte	*pro minore parte*, for the smaller part.
mult.	*multa, multis*: many.
mus.	*museum*: museum; *Herb. Mus. Brit., Herbarium Musei Britannici*, Herbarium of the British Museum.
mut. char.	*mutatis characteribus*: with the characters changed.
n.	*nobis*: to us, of us (dative of possession).
	nomen: name.
	novus: new.
n.v.	*non visus*: not seen.
	non vidi: I have not seen.
nm.	*nothomorpha*: nothomorph.
no.	*numero*: number.
nom.	*nomen*: name; *nom alt., nomen alternativum*, alternative name; *nom. ambig., nomen ambiguum*, ambiguous name; *nom. confus., nomen confusum*, confused name; *nom. cons., nomen conservandum*, name conserved in

International Code of botanical Nomenclature; *nom. illeg., nomen illegitimum*, illegitimate name, *nom. legit., nomen legitimum*, legitimate name; *nom. nud., nomen nudum, nom. sol., nomen solum*, name unaccompanied by a description or reference to a published description; *nom. obsc., nomen obscurum*, obscure name; *nom. tant., nomen tantum*, name only; *nom. superfl., nomen superfluum*, name superfluous when published.

non al.	*non aliorum*: not of other authors.
nov.	*novus*: new.
obs.	*observatio*: observation.
occ., occid.	*occidentalis*: western.
omn.	*omnis*: all.
op. cit.	*opere citato*: in the work cited.
orb.	*orbis*: the world; *orb. nov., orbis novus*, the New World; *orb. vet., orbis vetus*, the Old World.
or.	*orientalis*: eastern.
p.	*pagina*: page.
p.d.	*proprie dicta*: properly speaking.
p.m.	*plus minusve*: more or less.
p.p.	*pro parte*: partly, in part; *p.mag.p., pro magna parte, p.p.maj., pro parte majore*, for the greater part; *p.p.max., pro parte maxima*, for the greatest part, almost entirely; *p.p.min., pro parte minore*, for a small part.
ped.	*pedalis*: a foot (30 cm.) long; cf. p. 113.
pinx.	*pinxit*: he painted.
pl.	*planta*: plant; *p.p. quoad pl. brit., pro parte quoad plantam britannicam*, in part as regards the British plant.
plur.	*plurimus*, most.
poll.	*pollicaris*: an inch (2·5 cm.) long; cf. p. 113.
praec.	*praecipue*: especially.
	praecedens: preceding.
prop.	*propositus*: proposed.
prov.	*provincia*: province.
	provisorius: provisional.
q.e.	*quod est*: which is.
q.v.	*quod vide*: which see.
quor., quorumd.	*quorumdam*: of some authors.
r., rr.	*rarus, rarissimus*: rare, very rare.
recent.	*recentiorum*: of recent authors.
reg.	*regio*: district, region, territory.
s.	*seu, sive*; or.
s. ampl.	*sensu amplificato*: in an enlarged sense.
s.l.	*sensu lato*: in a broad sense.
s.n.	*sine numero*: without a number, unnumbered.
s. str.	*sensu stricto*: in a narrow sense.
sched.	*scheda*: label; *in sched.*, on a herbarium label.

scrips.	*scripsit* : he has written.
sec.	*secus, secundum* : following, according to.
sect.	*sectio* : section.
sens.	*sensu* : in the sense of.
sept.	*septentrionalis* : northern.
seq.	*sequens* : following ; *et seqq., et sequentes,* and the following.
	sequitur : it follows.
ser.	*series* : series.
sp.	*species* : species ; *pro sp., pro specie,* as a species.
	specificus : specific.
spec.	*specimen* : specimen.
sphalm.	*sphalmate* : by mistake, mistakenly.
ssp.	*subspecies* : subspecies.
st., stat.	*status* : rank ; *stat. nov., status novus,* new rank.
syn.	*synonymon, synonymia* : synonym, synonymy.
t., tab.	*tabula* : Plate.
t.	*teste* : on the evidence of.
t., tom.	*tomus* : volume ; *t.c., tomus citatus,* volume cited.
trans. nov.	*translatio nova* : new transfer ; used of epithets transferred without change of rank of the taxon ; cf. *comb. nov., st. nov.* above.
typ.	*typus* : type.
u.s.	*ut supra* : as above.
v., var.	*varietas* : variety ; *pro var., pro varietate,* as a variety.
v.	*vel* : or.
	vide : see
	visum : seen.
	vidi : I have seen ; *v.c., vidi cultam,* I have seen it cultivated ; *v. in hb., vidi in herbario,* I have seen it in the herbarium ; *v.s., vidi siccam,* I have it in a dried state ; *v. spont., vidi spontaneum,* I have seen native or wild material ; *v.v., vidi vivam,* I have seen it in a living state.[1]
v., vol.	*volumen* : volume.
verisim.	*verisimiliter* : probably.
vet.	*veteres* : the ancients.
viz.	*videlicet* : namely.

REFERENCES

CAJORI, F. 1923. Mathematical signs of equality. *Isis,* 5 : 116-125.

CAPELLI, A. 1954. *Lexicon Abbreviaturarum; Dizionario di Abbreviature latine ed italiane.* 5th ed. Milan.

CROSSLAND, M. P. 1962. *Historical Studies in the Language of Chemistry.* London Melbourne and Toronto.

---

[1] *plantam,* plant, is here understood.

FEDOROV, A., & KIRPICZNIKOV, M. 1954. *Abbreviationes, Designationes Institutae Nomina geographica.* Moscow and Leningrad.

FURTADO, C. X. 1937. Asterisks in Linnaeus's *Species Plantarum. Gard. Bull. Straits Settlements,* 9 : 310-317.

KOCH, R. 1940. *Das Zeichenbuch welches alle Arten von Zeichen enthält.* 3rd ed. Leipzig. (English translation by V. Holland, *The Book of Signs,* London, 1930, reprinted New York, 1964.)

KUNTZE, O. 1893. *Revisio Generum Plantarum,* 3 : ccclxxvii-ccclxxxvi. Leipzig, etc.

LINDLEY, J. 1839. *An Introduction to Botany,* 3rd ed. (pp.496–505). London.

PARTINGTON, J. R. 1937. The origins of the planetary symbols for metals. *Ambix,* 1 : 75-77.

RENKEMA, H. W. 1942. Oorspong, beteekenis en toepassing van de in de botanie gebruikelije teekens ter aanduiting van het geslacht en den levensduur. Nederlandsche Dendrologische Vereeniging, *Gedenkb. J. Valckenier-Suringar,* 96-108.

SPRAGUE, T. A., & Exell, A. W. 1937. Citations marked with an asterisk in Linnaeus's *Species Plantarum. J. Bot. (London),* 75 : 78.

STEARN, W. T. 1957. An Introduction to the *Species Plantarum* and cognate botanical Works of Carl Linnaeus, 162-163 (prefixed to Ray Society facsimile of Linnaeus, *Species Plantarum,* vol. 1).

—— 1962. The origin of the male and female symbols of biology. *Taxon,* 11 : 109-113.

SVENSON, H. K. 1939. The asterisk in Linnaeus's *Species Plantarum. Rhodora,* 41 : 139-140.

TANNER, R. C. H. 1963. On the role of equality and inequality in the history of mathematics. *Brit. J. Hist. Sci.,* 1 : 159-169.

PART FOUR

VOCABULARY AND BIBLIOGRAPHY

CHAPTER XXV

Vocabulary

This vocabulary attempts to provide Latin-English and English-Latin equivalents for most of the terms and expressions used in describing plants, together with a number of Latin and Greek word elements often used in forming their names. It does not claim to list every word which has ever been used in descriptive botany, or to provide meanings and explanations as distinct from equivalents for more than a limited number: for those not included the meaning should either be evident from that of a related word or, if not, should be found in a dictionary of classical Latin, if of a general nature, or in a glossary of technical terms relating to a particular field, when of more restricted use. Attention is directed to the lists of names and terms in

Not all of these are included below.

A. P. de Candolle included Latin and French terms in one alphabetical sequence, treating as one entry those which differed only in termination and were evidently the same, e.g. *androgynus* and *androgyne*. In like manner English and Latin terms are here listed together, without cross-references when they would come more or less side by side, e.g. *ovate* and *ovatus*. Sometimes the Latin form has been used for the heading of the entry, sometimes the English. Latin words are followed by an indication of their grammatical nature, e.g. *ad* (prep. with acc.), *Annus* (s.m. II), *annuus* (adj. A), *asymmetrice* (adv.), *at* (conj.), *attingens* (part. B). Nouns are listed in the entry headings with capital letters, other parts of speech with lower-case letters. Since Latin and English words may be only partly equivalent in their range of meaning, the user of this vocabulary, as indeed of any bilingual vocabulary, is recommended to refer backwards and forwards from one language to the other, particularly as owing to the unfortunately but unavoidably desultory method of compilation (see Preface) of this vocabulary the

information needed may be given under either. If, alas, it occurs under
neither, study of analogous words may yield it. Scattered through the
vocabulary are many examples taken from a wide range of botanical
literature. Some of these with but slight modification can be transferred ready-made into descriptions of new taxa ; others may be useful
as models. Hence the English versions follow the Latin more or less
literally. Thus the literal English version of *caules plures sinistrorsum
volubiles glabri aculeis armati virides vel rubri* as given here is 'stems
several to the left twining slender glabrous with prickles armed green
or red' but a translation would read 'stems several, twining to the
left, glabrous, armed with prickles, green or red'.

Some important or frequently used or anomalous terms have been
declined in full. For many others only the cases most used in botanical
Latin, e.g. the ablative, have been given. For yet others it has seemed
adequate to mention simply their grammatical classification in brackets
following the word, e.g. the entry *Hibernaculum* (s.n. II) indicates that
this is a noun (s.) of neuter gender (n.) belonging to the Second Declension (II), and hence will be declined like other neuter Second Declension
nouns in accordance with the model on p. 73.

The numbers at the end of paragraphs, e.g. **365, 386,** refer to the
numbered definitions and figures of Lindley's glossary (Chapter XXII).

ABBREVIATIONS—*abl.* : ablative case (see p. 67) ; *acc.* : accusative case
(see p. 64) ; *adj.* : adjective (for Declension A, see p. 92 ; for Declension B,
see p. 93) ; *adv.* : adverb (see p. 104) ; *c.* : common gender ; *cf.* : confer,
consult ; *class.* : classical ; *comp.* : compound words ; *compar.* : comparative ; *conj.* : conjunction (see p. 128) ; *dat.* : dative case (see p. 66) ; *dem.* :
demonstrative ; *e.g.* : for example ; *f.* : feminine gender ; *fr.* : from ;
gen. : genitive case (see p. 65) ; *Gk.* : Greek ; *H.C.C.* : Horticultural
Colour Chart (1938–41) ; *i.e.* : that is ; *L.* : Latin ; *lit.* : literally ; *m.* :
masculine gender ; *n.* : neuter gender ; *nom.* : nominative case ; *opp.* :
opposite ; *part.* : participle (see p. 91 ; for Declension A, see p. 92 ; for
Declension B, see p. 95) ; *pl.* : plural ; *prep.* : preposition (see p. 125) ;
pron. : pronoun ; *q.v.* : which see ; *s.* : noun, substantive (see p. 59 ; for
Declension I, see p. 68 ; II, p. 70 ; III, p. 74 ; IV, p. 89 ; V, p. 90) ; *sing.* :
singular ; *usu.* : usually.

A

a- (Gk. prefix): *in Gk. comp.*, without,
destitute of, lacking, un-, -less ; see E-,
EX- ; *achlamydeus*, without perianth, *lit.*
'without a cloak' ; *apetalus*, without
petals ; before a vowel *a-* becomes *an-*.

a, ab (prep. with abl.): away from, out of,
from, by, at, in ; *a priore differt indumento*, from the first it differs in indumentum ; *ab affinibus distincta*, from its
relatives distinct ; cf. SEEN.

abaxialis (adj. B): abaxial, away from the
axis or central line, turned towards the
base, ventral ; cf. ADAXIALIS.

abbreviatus (part. A): shortened.

aberrans (part. B): aberrant, departing
from the usual ; cf. ABNORMAL, ANO-
MALUS, ATYPICUS. **100**

abeuntes (nom. pl., part. B): *see* ABIENS.

abhorrens (part. B): differing from, not
agreeing with.

abhymenialis (adj. B): abhymenial, opposite the hymenium.

abiens (part. B): departing, changing suddenly into (with *in* and acc.), passing
away, leaving off ; cf. ANGLE.

able: aptus (part. A).

abnormal: abnormalis (adj. B), abnormis
(adj. B) ; cf. ABERRANS, ANOMALUS,
ATYPICUS.

Abode: sedes (s.f. III), *gen. sing.* sedis; habitatio (s.f. III), *gen. sing.* habitationis.
Abortion: abortio (s.f. III. vi), abortus (s.m. IV): *fructus bilocularis sed saepius ut videtur abortu monospermum*, fruit two-chambered but most often apparently through abortion one-seeded. **abortive**: abortivus (adj. A).
abounding with: scatens (part. B).
about: circa (adv.), circum (adv.), circiter (adv.), fere (adv.), quasi (adv.).
above: super (prep. with acc., rarely abl.), supra (prep. with acc.), insuper (prep. with abl., rarely acc.).
 above all: imprimis (adv.).
 from above: desuper (adv.), insuper (adv.), superne (adv.).
above-ground: supraterraneus (adj. A).
Abridgment: breviarium (s.n. II).
abrumpens (part. B): breaking off.
abrupt: abruptus (adj. A). **abruptly**: abrupte (adv.). **abruptly pinnate**: paripinnatus (adj. A).
abscissus (part. A): cut off, steep, precipitous.
absconditus (part. A): hidden, concealed.
Absence: absentia (s.f. I). **absent**: absens (part. B), carens (part. B); cf. LACKING.
absque (prep. with abl.): without; *absque descriptione*, without a description.
abundant: abundans (part. B), abundus (adj. A), largus (adj. A).
abundantly: abundanter (adv.), copiose (adv.), abunde (adv.).
ac (conj.): and, q.v.
acanth-, acantho-: *in Gk. comp.*, spiny, thorny.
Acarodomatium: acarodomatium (s.n. II); *acarodomatia nulla*, acarodomatia nil; *nervi in axillis acarodomatiis dense pilosis instructi*, nerves at the axils with densely pilose acarodomatia furnished.
acaulescens (adj. B), **acaulis** (adj. B): stemless, or apparently so.
accedens (part. B): approaching, coming near to, resembling (with dat. or *ad* and acc.).
accessorius (adj. A): accessory, additional.
accidental: fortuitus (adj. A). **accidentally**: fortuito (adv.).
acclivis (adj. B): uphill, sloping upwards; cf. DECLIVIS.
accompanied: concomitatus (part. A), comitatus (part. A); *asci clavati paraphysibus filiformibus fine incrassatis concomitati*, asci club-shaped accompanied by paraphyses thread-like at the end thickened.
according to: teste, q.v., fide, q.v., secundum (prep. with acc.).
accordingly: ergo (adv.), igitur (conj.), itaque (conj.).
accrescent: accrescens (part. B), auctus (part. A), increscens (part. B); *calyx*

fructifer saepe plus minus auctus, fruiting calyx more or less enlarged; *calyx demum increscens saepe inflatus*, calyx at length increased, often inflated.
accretus (part. A): grown together. **452**
accumbens (part. B): accumbent, lying along or against another body, e.g. the cotyledons having their edges against the radicle; *cotyledones accumbentes*, cotyledons accumbent.
accurate (adv.), **accuratim** (adv.): carefully, exactly. **accuratus** (adj. A): prepared with care, studied, exact (*not used of persons*); cf. DILIGENS, EXACT.
-aceae (adj. A): nom. f. pl. suffix added to stem of name or synonym of type genus to form name of family, e.g. *Cyperaceae* from *Cyperus*, *Rosaceae* from *Rosa*, *Orchidaceae* from *Orchis*, *Asclepiadaceae* from *Asclepias*, *Boraginaceae* from *Borago*.
acer (adj. B), **acerbus** (adj. A): bitter.
acerosus (adj. A): needle-shaped, like leaves of *Pinus*. **115**
acervatus (part. A): heaped. **acervulatus** (adj. A): in little heaps. **Acervulus**: acervulus (s.m. II), *abl. sing.* acervulo, *nom. pl.* acervuli, *abl. pl.* acervulis; *acervuli sparsi convexi velati, dein epidermiden stellate rumpentes, extus atri intus albi*, pustules (cushion-like masses of hyphae) scattered convex covered, then bursting the epidermis in a stellate fashion, outside black inside white; *acervuli minutissimi immersi dein poro lato emergentes*, pustules very minute immersed, then emerging by a wide opening.
acetabuliformis (adj. B): saucer-shaped, q.v. **80**
-aceus (adj. A): suffix with sense of 'resembling, having the nature of, belonging to', used to form adj. from nouns, e.g. *foliaceus* from *folium*, *orchidaceus* from *Orchis*, *rosaceus* from *Rosa*.
Achene: achenium (s.n. II), *abl. sing.* achenio, *nom. pl.* achenia, *abl. pl.* acheniis. Introduced in 1790 by Necker as *achena* (s.f. I) and used by him for indehiscent one-seeded coriaceous fruits in Ranunculaceae, Cyperaceae, etc., but not for the cypselae (formed from inferior ovary) of Compositae; see Chapter III. Also spelled *achaenium* (s.n. II) and *achaena* (s.f. I); *achenia parva 4-5 mm. longa griseo-brunnea, in parte superiore tuberculis mediocris longitudinis dense obsita et saepe tota rugulosa, in rostrum attenuata*, achenes small 4-5 mm. long grey-brown in upper part with tubercles of medium length densely covered and often completely rugulose,

into a beak drawn out; *achenia in eodem capitulo heteromorpha*, achenes in the same head of differing shape; *achenia subglobosa vel oblique ovoidea transverse costata pilosa apice rostrata*, achenes subglobose or obliquely ovoid transversely ribbed pilose at the tip beaked; *achenium tenue longitudinaliter sulcatum*, achene thin longitudinally furrowed; *achenia tenuia longitudinaliter sulcata*, achenes thin longitudinally furrowed. cf. CYPSELA.

achromaticus (adj. A), **achromus** (adj. A): colourless.

acicularis (adj. B): acicular, i.e. narrow, stiff, pointed, like a needle.

aciculatus (adj. A): marked with very fine irregular streaks. 257

Acid: acidum (s.n. II); *fructus succosi acidis malico, citrico necnon tannico instructi*, fruit juicy, provided with malic, citric and also tannic acid; see Chapter XXIII. **acid**: acidus (adj. A); cf. BITTER.

Acies (s.f. V): sharp edge, angle; *lamellae acie denticulatae*, gills at the edge denticulate.

aciformis (adj. B): needle-like.

Acorn: glans (s.f. III. ix), *abl. sing.* glande, *nom. pl.* glandes, *abl. pl.* glandibus. **Acorn-cup**: cupula (s.f. I), *abl. sing.* cupula, *nom. pl.* cupulae, *abl. pl.* cupulis; *cupula turbinata, basi in stipitem squamosum conicum angustata, squamis laxe adpressis ovatis obtusis velutinis, glande ellipsoidea dimidio exserta*, cup topshaped, at base narrowed into a stalk scaly conical, with scales loosely appressed ovate blunt velvety, with acorn ellipsoid by half exserted; *cupulae hemisphaericae pubescentes, squamis lanceolatis acutis, glande ovoidea cupulam dimidio superante*, cups hemispherical pubescent, with scales lanceolate acute, with acorn ovoid overtopping the cup by half.

acranthus (adj. A): with flowers at apices of shoots. **acrocarpus** (adj. A): with terminal fruit. **acrodromus** (adj. A): acrodromous; see VEINING. **acrogenus** (adj. A): borne at apices. **acropetus** (adj. A): acropetal; *see* BASIFUGIENS. **acroscopicus** (adj. A): facing or directed towards the apex.

Acta (s.n. II. pl.): record of events, reports, proceedings, transactions; *Acta Anglica*, Philosophical Transactions of the Royal Society of London.

actino-: *in Gk. comp.*, rayed, star-like, radiating from a centre. **actinodromus** (adj. A): with veins radiating from a centre.

actinomorphus (adj. A): actinomorphic, regular.

active: agilis (adj. B), mobilis (adj. B). **actively**: impigre (adv.).

aculeatus (adj. A): prickly, spine-like. **Aculeus** (s.m. II): prickle. 262

Acumen: acumen (s.n. III. vi), *abl. sing.* acumine.

acuminatus (part. A): acuminate, i.e. tapering gradually or abruptly from inwardly curved sides into a narrow point. 150

acutangularis (adj. B), **acutangulatus** (adj. A), **acutangulus** (adj. A): sharp-angled.

acutatus (adj. A): sharpened, making an acute angle. **acut-**: *in L. comp.*, pointed; *in Gk. comp.*, oxy-; *acutiflorus, oxyanthus*, with pointed flowers; *acutifolius, oxyphyllus*, with pointed leaves. **acutiusculus** (adj. A): slightly acute. **acutus** (adj. A): acute, pointed, i.e. narrowed gradually and making an angle of less than 90°. 149, 174

ad (prep. with acc.): to, near to, at; *certe ad speciem descriptam pertinet*, certainly to the species described it belongs; *quoad folia ad Lyoniam costatam, quoad fructus ad L. haitiensem accedit*, as to leaves to Lyonia costata, as to fruit to L. haitiensis it comes near; *caules ad nodos radicantes*, stems at the nodes rooting; *folia ad nervos pilosa*, leaves at the nerves pilose; *inflorescentiae ad ramos ramulosque terminales*, inflorescences terminal on branches and branchlets; *tubus a basi ad medium ampliatus, a medio ad apicem contractus*, tube from the base to the middle broadened, from the middle to the tip contracted.

adamantinus (adj. A): very hard.

adaxialis (adj. B): adaxial, i.e. towards the axis or centre, turned towards the apex.

added: adjectus (part. A).

ademptus (part. A): taken away, deprived of.

aden-: *in Gk. comp.*, gland-; *adenospermus*, with glandular seeds.

adest: it is present; cf. ADSUNT, PRESENT.

adhering: adhaerens (part. B), haerens (part. B); *thallus substrato adhaerens*, thallus to the substratum clinging. 453

adhibitus (part. A): used, employed, put to use.

adhuc (adv.): to this place, hitherto, thus far, until now; *alliorum adhuc cognitorum monographia*, of the alliums up to the present known a monograph.

adjectus (part. A): added.

adjoining: contiguus (adj. A), confinis (adj. B; usu. followed by dat.).

adligans (part. B), **alligans** (part. B): clasping, adhering to; *radices adligantes*, clasping roots.

admodum (adv.) : fully, wholly, much.
admonens (part. B) : bringing to mind, suggesting; cf. REVOCANS.
adnascens (part. B) : growing to or upon.
adnatus (part. A) : adnate, attached the whole length or by the whole length or broadly attached. **446**
adnexus (part. A), **annexus** (part. A) : adnexed (used of gills which just reach the stem).
adpressus (part. A), **appressus** (part. A) : appressed, lying flat against.
adscendens (part. A) : ascending. **395**
adspersus (part. A), **aspersus** (part. A) : scattered.
adsunt : they are present; cf. ADEST, DEEST, DESUNT, PRESENT.
adulescens (part. B) : not yet mature.
adult : adultus (part. A), maturus (adj. A).
Adumbratio (s.f. III) : sketch, outline.
aduncatus (adj. A), **aduncus** (adj. A) : hooked.
adustus (part. A) : blackened, scorched.
advanced : provectus (part. A).
advectus (part. A) : carried, brought; ex Asia advectus, introduced from Asia.
adventitious : adventitius (adj. A); gemmae adventitiae, adventitious buds.
adversum (adv. with acc., prep.) : opposite to, against, before. **adversus** (part. A) : turned towards, opposite. **430**
Aecidium : aecidium (s.n. II).
aeger (adj. A) : diseased, sick.
aegerrime (adv.) : with very great difficulty. **aegre** (adv.) : with difficulty, scarcely; capsula valvis carnosis aegre dehiscentibus, capsule with valves fleshy hardly dehiscing.
aegrotus (adj. A) : diseased, sick; cf. LANGUESCENS, MORBIDUS.
aemulans (part. B), **aemulus** (adj. A) : rivalling, more or less equalling.
aeneus (adj. A) : bronze, brazen.
aequabilis (adj. B) : uniform, consistent.
aequabiliter (adv.), **aequaliter** (adv.) : evenly.
aequalis (adj. B) : equal. **aequans** (part. B) : equalling. **aeque** (adv.) : in like manner, equally, uniformly. **aequicrassus** (adj. A) : of even thickness. **aequidistans** (adj. B) : equidistant, the same length apart. **aequilaterus** (adj. A) : equal-sided. **aequilongus** (adj. A) : of the same length. **133, 135**
aequatorius (adj. A) : equatorial.
aequatus (part. A) : even, levelled. **259**
Aerenchyma : aerenchyma (s.n. III).
aerial : aerius (adj. A); radices aeriae, aerial roots.
aerobic : aerobius (adj. A).
Aerophore : aerophorum (s.n. II).
aerugineus, aeruginosus (adj. A) : verdigris (H.C.C. 6.55).

Aes (s.n. III. iv) : copper; see ILLUSTRATION.
Aestas (s.f. III. ii) : summer; aestate ineunte, at beginning of summer; aestate, in summer. **aestivalis** (adj. B), **aestivus** (adj. A) : pertaining to summer.
Aestivation : aestivatio (s.f. III. vi), abl. sing. aestivatione; praefloratio (s.f. III. vi), abl. sing. praefloratione. The term aestivatio for the arrangement of the parts of calyx or corolla in the flower-bud was introduced by Linnaeus in 1762 (cf. VERNATION). It is said to be open (aestivatio aperta) when the parts do not touch one another, valvate (valvata, valvaris) when the parts touch along their margins without overlapping, induplicate (induplicativa) when the margins are bent abruptly inwards and their outer faces touch without overlapping, reduplicate (reduplicativa) when the margins are bent abruptly outwards and their inner faces touch without overlapping. When the parts overlap, the aestivation may be simply imbricate (aestivatio imbricata), the parts overlapping parallelly at the margins; quincuncial (quincuncialis; quincunciali-ter imbricata) when of five parts two have their margins both inside, two with margins both outside, one with one margin inside and the other outside; cochlear (cochlearis; cochleari-imbricata) when one part being larger than the rest and hollowed like a spoon covers all the rest, of which one will be totally inside and the other three with one margin inside and one outside; vexillary (vexillaris) when one part, the vexillum or standard, is much larger than the others and is folded over them, they being face to face, so that the posterior part overlaps the lateral parts and the lateral parts overlap the anterior parts; ascendent (ascendens; ascendenti-imbri-cata), like vexillary aestivation but with anterior parts overlapping the posterior ones; alternative (alternativa) when the parts are in two whorls, the outer parts cover and alternate with the inner parts; contorted or twisted (contorta, torsiva, convoluta) when each part successively overlaps the one in front and is over-lapped by the one behind so that each part has an inner covered margin and an outer exposed margin, the direction being to the right (dextrorsum) or to the left (sinistrorsum) as viewed from the outside (cf. CLOCKWISE, TWINING); corru-gated or crumpled (corrugata) when the parts are folded irregularly together in every direction. In plicate aestivation

(aestivatio plicata) the whole organ (calyx or corolla) is not divided into parts but folded and sometimes also twisted lengthwise; *sepala 5 libera in aestivatione quincuncialiter imbricata*, sepals 5 free in aestivation quincuncially imbricate; *calyx 5-lobus, lobis in aestivatione valvatis*, calyx 5-lobed, with lobes in aestivation valvate; *petala in aestivatione cochleari-imbricata*, petals in aestivation cochlear; *corolla infundibuliformis limbo quinquepartito laciniis per aestivationem contortis vel valvatis*, corolla funnel-shaped with the limb 5-parted with the segments during aestivation contorted or valvate; *corolla lobis aestivatione varie imbricatis nec plicatis nec valvatis nec regulariter contortis*, corolla with lobes at aestivation variously imbricate not plicate not valvate not regularly contorted; *corolla limbo patente, lobis saepius contorto-imbricatis, sese invicem nunc dextrorsum nunc sinistrorsum (ab exteriore spectanti) obtegentibus, in directione contraria vel rarius in eadem directione curvis et in alabastro tortis vel fere rectis, rarissime valvatis*, corolla with limb spreading, with lobes very often contorted-imbricate, by one another in turn at one time to the right at another time to the left (from the outside viewed) overlapping, in direction opposite or very rarely in the same direction curved and in bud twisted or almost straight, most rarely valvate; *corollae lobi in aestivatione valvati*, the lobes of the corolla in aestivation valvate; *corollae loborum aestivatio helicte (sinistrorsum sensu Eichleri) contorta, si imbricata lobo mediano externo*, aestivation of the lobes of the corolla helictically (sinistrorsely in the sense of Eichler) contorted, if imbricate then the middle lobe outside. **365-386**

aestuans (part. B): moving to and fro; cf. ERRATICUS, OSCILLANS.

Aestuarium (s.n. II): estuary, q.v.

Aestus (s.m. IV): tide, q.v.

Aetas (s.f. III. ii): age, q.v.

affectus (part. A): affected; *morbo affectus*, attacked by disease.

affinis (adj. B): neighbouring, allied to, akin to (*with gen. or dat.*). **Affinitas** (s.f. III. ii): affinity, relationship.

affixus (part. A): attached, fastened to.

after: post (adv. & prep.), postea (adv.).

again: denuo (adv.); *radii in radiis minoribus denuo furcati*, rays into lesser rays again forked. **again and again**: etiam atque etiam, iterum atque iterum.

agamicus (adj. A), **agamus** (adj. A): asexual.

Agar: agar (s.m. II), *gen. sing.* agari, *abl. sing.* agaro.

Age (time of life): aetas (s.f. III. ii), *gen. sing.* aetatis, *abl. sing.* aetate; *aetate provecta*, in advanced age. **Youth**: juventus (s.f. III. ii), *gen. sing.* juventutis, *abl. sing.* juventute. **young**: juvenilis (adj. B) 'youthful', novellus (adj. A) 'new', hornus (adj. A) *and* hornotinus (adj. A) *both* 'of the present year's growth, less than 12 months old'. **Maturity, Ripeness**: maturitas (s.f. III. ii), *gen. sing.* maturitatis, *abl. sing.* maturitate. **mature**: maturus (adj. A). **Old age**: vetustas (s.f. III. ii), *gen. sing.* vetustatis, *abl. sing.* vetustate, senectus (s.f. III. ii), *gen. sing.* senectutis, *abl. sing.* senectute. **aged**: vetus (adj. B) 'old', vetustus (adj. A) 'that has existed a long time', senectus (adj. A) 'very old', annotinus (adj. A) 'a year old, of last year's growth'. **Adverbs, etc., of age**: (first) primum (adv.), primo (adv.), initio (abl. of *initium*) 'at the beginning', ab ineunte (abl. part. B) 'from the beginning'; 'then, thereupon', tum (adv.) deinde (adv.); 'afterwards', postea (adv.); 'at last', demum.

Ager (s.m. II): field, territory, district.

agglomeratus (part. A): collected into a head.

agglutinatus (part. A): glued to, adhering as if glued together.

aggregatus (part. A): clustered, collected together; cf. COACERVATUS. **491**

agilis (adj. B): active, swift-moving.

agreeable: gratus (adj. A).

agreeing: congruens (part. B), consentaneus (adj. A), conveniens (part. B.); all with dat. or *cum* with abl.

agrestis (adj. B): pertaining to fields or cultivated land.

Air-chamber: cavernula (s.f. I) aëria (adj. A); *strato cavernularum aëriarum*, with layer of air-chambers; see AERIAL, PNEUMATICUS.

Akinetum (s.n. II): akinete, non-motile spore.

Ala (s.f. I): wing, flange.

Alabastrum (s.n. II): flower bud.

Alar cell: cellula (s.f. I) alaris (adj. B); *cellulae alares multae magnae hyalinae auriculis instructae*, cells at basal angle of leaf many large hyaline with auricles provided; *cellulis alaribus 7-9-seriatis hexagonis*, with cells at basal angle of leaf 7-9 rowed hexagonal.

alaris (adj. B): axillary. **463**

alatus (adj. A): winged. **60**

albens (part. B): whitened. **albescens** (part. B): becoming white, whitish. **albidus** (adj. A): somewhat white, whitish. **albus** (adj. A): white, particularly a dull rather than a glossy white; *see* CANDIDUS.

Albumen: albumen (s.n. III. vi), *acc. sing.* albumen, *gen. sing.* albuminis, *dat. sing.* albumini, *abl. sing.* albumine, *lit.* 'the white of an egg'; endospermium (s.n. II) *acc. sing.* endospermium, *gen. sing.* endospermi, *dat. and abl. sing.* endospermo. This store of starchy or oily food-material accompanying the embryo, by which it is absorbed during germination, instead of during seed-formation as in exalbuminous seeds (*semina exalbuminata*) which lack such a separate store at maturity, may be abundant (*albumen copiosum*), or scanty (*parcum*), its substance mealy (*farinaceum*), oily (*oleosum*), fleshy, i.e. firm but easily cut (*carnosum*), mucilaginous (*mucilaginosum*) or even fluid (*liquidum*), cartilaginous (*cartilagineum*), horny (*corneum*), bony (*osseum*), hard (*durum*) or almost woody (*subligneum*), stony (*scleroideum*), solid (*solidum*), and uniform (*aequabile*), or hollow (*cavum*), with a central or ventral cavity (*cavitate centrali vel ventrali exsculptum*), or ruminate (*ruminatum*) by intrusions of the seed-coat (*plicis irregularibus testae*); *albumen copiosum carnosum nec farinaceum*, albumen abundant fleshy not floury; *embryo intra albumen parcissimum mucilaginosum homotrope arcuatus*, embryo within the very scanty mucilaginous albumen in the same direction as the seed curved.

albuminatus (adj. A): albuminate, provided with albumen (endosperm). **albuminosus** (adj. A): albuminate, provided with abundant albumen.

alcalinus (adj. A): alkaline.

Alcohol: alcohol (s.n. III), *gen. sing.* alcoholis. **alcoholic**: alcoholicus (adj. A).

-ales (adj. B): nom. f. pl. suffix added to stem of name of type family to form name of order, e.g. *Leguminales* from *Leguminosae*, *Iridales* from *Iridaceae*.

Alga: alga (s.f. I), *gen. sing.* algae, *abl. sing.* alga, *nom. pl.* algae, *gen. pl.* algarum, *abl. pl.* algis, *lit.* 'seaweed, a 'thing of little value'. **algaceus** (adj. A), **algensis** (adj. B): pertaining to seaweed.

algidus (adj. A): cold.

alibi (adv.): elsewhere.

alibilis (adj. B): nutritious.

alicubi (adv.): anywhere.

alienus (adj. A): foreign, alien, belonging to another, not related, incongruous, different from; *genus quodammodo Asperugini affine etsi habitu calycibus et nuculis alienum*, genus in a certain manner to Asperugo akin, although by habit, calyces and nutlets different.

aliformis (adj. B): wing-shaped.

alike: conformis (adj. B), similaris (adj. B).

Alimentum (s.n. II): nourishment.

aliquam (adv.): somehow, to some extent. **aliquamdiu** (adv.), **aliquantisper** (adv.): for a while, for some time. **aliquando** (adv.): sometimes, at some time, any time. **aliquanto** (adv.) somewhat, rather. **aliquantum** (adv.), **aliquantus** (adv.): somewhat, (with reference to quantity) in some quantity either great or small.

aliqui, aliqua, aliquod (adj.): some. **aliquot** (adv.) somewhat (with reference to number). **aliquot** (num. indecl.): some, a few, several.

aliquoties (adv.): several times.

aliquoversum (adv.): one way or another.

-alis (adj. B): suffix with sense of 'belonging to, resembling, provided with, pertaining to', used to form adj. from nouns, e.g. *dorsalis* from *dorsum* 'back', *pedalis* from *pes* 'foot', *viminalis* from *vimen* 'pliant twig'.

aliter (adv.): otherwise, in another manner; *non aliter, haud aliter*, just as if, not otherwise.

alius, alia, aliud (adj. A): another, other (of several); *alius . . . alius*, the one . . . the other; *verticilli alii post alios*, whorls one after another, i.e. successively; *formae alia in aliam transeuntes*, forms passing one into another; *alius ex alio*, one after another.

alive: vivens (part. B), vivus (adj. A).

alkaline: alcalinus (adj. A).

all: omnis (adj. B), totus (adj. A). **in all**: omnino (adv.), in summa.

allantoideus (adj. A): sausage-shaped.

allatus (part. A): brought.

alligans: *see* ADLIGANS.

allo-: *in Gk. comp.*, other, another.

allochrous (adj. A): changing from one colour to another; cf. MUTABILIS.

almost: fere (adv.), paene (adv.), propemodo (adv.), quasi (adv.), sub- (prefix).

along: secus (prep. with acc.). **along with**: cum (prep. with abl.).

alpinus (adj. A): alpine, growing in the Alps or in the alpine zone of other mountains.

alte (adv.): on high, high up, deeply.

alter (adj. A): other (of two), second.

altered: mutatus (part. A).

alternate: alternus (adj. A). **alternately**: alternatim (adv.), alterne (adv.). **alternating**: alternans (part. B): *zonis latis et angustis alternantibus*, with broad and narrow zones alternating. **Alternation**: alternatio (s.f. III). **alternative**: alternativus (adj. A). **384, 476**

although: etsi (conj.), quamquam (conj.).

Altitudo (s.f. III): altitude, depth.

altogether: omnino (adv.).

Altum (s.n. II): a height, a depth. **altus** (adj. A): high, elevated, tall.

alutaceus (adj. A): leather-coloured, pale brown.

alveiformis (adj. B): trough-shaped.

Alveola (s.f. I): cavity, pore, alveole. **alveolaris** (adj. B), **alveolatus** (adj. A): pitted, honeycombed, alveolate. **Alveolus** (s.m. II): a small cavity. **250**

always: semper. **nearly always**: persaepe (adv.), saepissime (adv.).

amans (part. B): loving; cf. -PHILUS. **amat** (3rd person sing. pres. indic. of *amo*): 'it loves'.

amarus (adj. A): bitter.

amber-coloured: sucinacius (adj. A), succineus (adj. A), sucineus (adj. A).

ambiens (part. B): going around, surrounding.

ambiguus (adj. A): doubtful, uncertain.

Ambitus (s.m. IV): circumference, outline.

ambly-: *in Gk. comp.*, blunt, obtuse; *amblyantherus*, blunt-anthered; *amblyanthus*, blunt-flowered; *amblyphyllus*, blunt-leaved.

ambo (num. adj.): both together, the two; *ambae species distinctae sunt*, the two species are distinct.

Ambulacrum (s.n. II): avenue of trees.

ambustus (part. A): burned.

amentaceus (adj. A): in the form of a catkin. **Amentum** (s.n. II): catkin.

amethysteus (adj. A), **amethystinus** (adj. A): amethyst, violet (H.C.C. 35); also applied to colour-range between purple and violet.

ammo-: *in Gk. comp.*, sand-; *ammobius*, dwelling on sand; *ammophilus*, sand-loving.

Amnis (s.m. III): torrent, rapidly flowing river; cf. RIVER.

amoeboid: amoeboideus (adj. A).

amoene (adv.): beautifully. **amoenus** (adj. A): beautiful, pleasing.

among: inter (prep. with acc.); *inter species antillanas valde peculiaris*, among West Indian species very extraordinary: *inter omnia Vitacearum genera partitione foliorum atque forma segmentorum insignis*, among all genera of Vitaceae by the division of the leaves and the shape of the segments remarkable; cf. IN.

amorphus (adj. A): shapeless, of indefinite shape.

amotus (part. A): removed, withdrawn.

amphi-: *in Gk. comp.*, around, double, on both sides, of two kinds; *amphibius*, living in water and on land; *amphicarpus*, producing two kinds of fruit,

e.g. aerial and subterranean; *amphigenus*, growing all round an object.

Amphigastrium: amphigastrium (s.n. II), *nom. pl.* amphigastria, *abl. pl.* amphigastriis; *amphigastria foliis aequilonga, ex angusta basi ovata, ad ⅓ profunde lunatim excisa, laciniis lanceolatis porrectis*, amphigastria as long as the leaves, from a narrow base ovate, to ⅓ deeply lunately cut, with segments lanceolate directed outwards and forwards.

Amphithecium: amphithecium (s.n. II), *abl. sing.* amphithecio.

amphitropus (adj. A): amphitropous, i.e. with the ovule bent so that both ends are near each other. **435**

amplectens (part. B): clasping. **440**

amplexicaulis (adj. B): stem-clasping, amplexicaul.

ampliatus (part. A): enlarged, increased.

Amplificatio (s.f. III): enlargement.

amplus (adj. A): ample, abundant, large, great.

Ampulla (s.f. I): flask-like bladder. **ampullaceus** (adj. A), **ampullaris** (adj. B), **ampulliformis** (adj. B): flask-shaped, swollen below like a short flask.

amussim, ad: according to rule, exactly.

amylaceus (adj. A): starchy.

amyloideus (adj. A): resembling starch, i.e. giving a blue reaction to iodine.

Amylum (s.n. II): starch.

an (conj.): or rather, or, or perhaps, perhaps, probably (*implies doubt*).

an-: *in Gk. comp. before a vowel*, without, destitute of, lacking, un-, -less (*see* A-); *anandrus*, without stamens; *anantherus*, without anthers; *ananthus*, flowerless; *anaerobius*, able to live without free oxygen.

ana-: *in Gk. comp.*, upwards, back, again, *with general sense of* increasing, strengthening, repeating; *anabaptistus*, renamed.

Analysis: analysis (s.f. III).

anarthrodactylus (adj. A): same meaning as MONARTHRODACTYLUS, q.v.

anastomosans (part. B): united by running together irregularly to form a network. **Anastomosis** (s.f. III. vi): joining of veins or hyphae into a network; *see* VEINING. **241**

Anatomia (s.f. I): anatomy.

anatropous: anatropus (adj. A).

anceps (adj. B), **ancipitius** (adj. A): two-edged.

ancient: antiquus (adj. A).

and: et (conj.), atque (conj.), ac (conj.), -que (conj. suffix), necnon (conj.), neque non (conj.); *et* joins both words and sentences and is repeated between each thing connected, as *radix et folia et flores*, or left out entirely, as *radix folia* *flores*, hence best used to connect two things, as *radix et folia*; *atque* and *ac*, which is used only before consonants, indicate a close connexion between the ideas, etc., joined, as in the celebrated *ave atque vale*, 'hail and farewell'. *-que* is added to the second of two words closely connected, as *foliis margine carinaque laevibus* 'with leaves at margin and keel smooth', or to the last of several, as *epicalyx calyx corollaque*; *necnon* 'and also' is used for emphasis.

andro-, -andrus: *in Gk. comp.*, male.

Androecium: androecium (s.n. II).

androgynus (adj. A): androgynous, having male and female flowers in the same inflorescence.

Androphorum (s.n. II): androphore, e.g. the basal tube formed by united filaments of stamens in Malvaceae.

Androsporangium: androsporangium (s.n. II).

Androspore: androspora (s.f. I).

anemo-: *in Gk. comp.*, pertaining to the wind; *anemophilus*, wind-loving; *anemon-* refers, however, to the genus Anemone; *anemonoides*, anemone-like.

anfractuosus (adj. A): sinuous, spirally twisted (this meaning rare); cf. ZIGZAG. **416**

anfractus (part. A): winding, bending, crooked.

angiospermus (adj. A): having enclosed seeds; by Linnaeus used to distinguish plants such as Scrophulariaceae which have seeds in capsules from those such as Labiatae and Boraginaceae which have exposed nutlets.

Angle: angulus (s.m. II), *abl. sing.* angulo; *spinae ad angulum 45° patentes*, spines spreading out at an angle of 45°; *nervis sub angulo 45° abeuntibus*, with nerves going forth at an angle of 45°. **angled**: angulatus (part. A), angularis (adj. B); **-angled**: *in L. comp.*, -angulus, *in Gk. comp.*, -gonus; cf. VEINING. **40, 187**

anguilliformis (adj. B): eel-like, worm-like, i.e. long, slender, curved.

angularis (adj. B), **angulatus** (part. A): angled. **angulosus** (adj. A): strongly angled, with prominent angles.

Angulus (s.n. II): angle, corner.

angustatus (part. A): narrowed. **anguste** (adv.): narrowly. **angusti-**: *in L. comp.*, narrow; *angustifolius*, narrow-leaved. **angustus** (adj. A): narrow. **178**

Animal: animal (s.n. III), *gen. sing.* animalis. **Animalcule**: animalculum (s.n. II), *gen. sing.* animalculi.

anisatus (adj. A): flavoured or smelling of aniseed. **anisodorus** (adj. A): aniseed-smelling.

aniso-: *in Gk. comp.*, unequal, uneven; *anisodontus*, unevenly toothed; *anisomeres, anisomerus, anisomericus*, with uneven parts; *anisomorphus*, dissimilar in shape; *anisopetalus*, having unequal petals; *anisophyllus*, with leaves of a pair markedly unequal in size or shape; *anisosepalus*, having unequal sepals; *anisostemonus*, having unequal stamens; *anisostichus*, having unequal rows.

annexus (part. A): *see* ADNEXUS.

anniculus (adj. A): a year old.

Annotatio (s.f. III): remark, annotation.

annotinus (adj. A): a year old, belonging to last year; cf. AGE, ANNICULUS, HORNOTINUS, PRAETERITUS.

annual: annuus (adj. A). **342**

annually: quotannis (adv.).

annularis (adj. B): ring-shaped, arranged in a circle; **annulatim** (adv.): in the form of a ring, ring-wise; **annulatus** (adj. A): marked with rings, surrounded by raised rings or bands, having a ring; **annuliformis** (adj. B): ring-shaped; **Annulus** (s.m. II): annulus, ring. **253**

Annus (s.m. II): year.

annuus (adj. A): annual. **342**

anomalus (adj. A): diverging from the usual, abnormal; cf. ABERRANS, ABNORMAL, ATYPICUS.

anonymos (adj. A): nameless. Used as a token word in Walter's *Flora Caroliniana* (1788) in place of a generic name for unnamed genera; cf. T. A. Sprague in *Kew Bull.*, 1939: 331–334 (1939), D. B. Ward in *Rhodora*, 64: 87–92 (1962), R. L. Wilbur in *J. Elisha Mitch. Sci. Soc.*, 72: 125–132 (1962).

anserinus (adj. A): pertaining to geese.

answering: respondens (part. B).

Ant: formica (s.f. I), *nom. pl.* formicae, *gen. pl.* formicarum, *abl. pl.* formicis. **Ant-**: *in L. comp.*, formic-, *in Gk. comp.*, myrmec-. **full of ants**: formicosus (adj. A). **pertaining to ants**: formicarius (adj. A).

ante (prep. with acc.): before, in front of.

antea (adv.): before, formerly, in time past.

antecedens (part. B): preceding, going before.

Anterides (s.f. III. pl.): buttresses, q.v.

anterior: anticus (adj. A).

Anthela: anthela (s.f. I), *abl. sing.* anthela; *anthela simplex patens erecta*, anthela simple spreading erect; *anthela irregulariter paniculata, ramis suberectis*, anthela irregularly paniculate, with branches almost erect.

Anther: anthera (s.f. I), *gen. sing.* antherae, *abl. sing.* anthera, *nom. pl.* antherae, *acc. pl.* antheras, *gen. pl.* antherarum, *abl. pl.* antheris, *lit.* 'a medicine composed of flowers'; *antherae biloculares ovatae basifixae sacculis usque ad apicem connectivo conjunctis utrinque longitrorsum dehiscentes*, anthers twolocular ovate basifixed with sacs (thecae) up to the tip to the connective joined on each side longitudinally dehiscent; *antherarum thecae glabrae divaricatae*, of the anthers the thecae glabrous spreading abruptly at an obtuse angle; *antherarum loculi per anthesin paralleli seu divergentes usque ad basin dehiscentes, apice plus minus coadunati*, of the anthers the loculi (thecae) through anthesis parallel or divergent down to the base dehiscent at the tip more or less united; *antherae glabrae vel lanatae sagittatae vel hippocrepiformes loculis distinctis vel apice confluentibus, denique rima unica deorsum usque ad medium dehiscentes, basibus saccatis*, anthers glabrous or woolly, sagittate or horseshoe-shaped with the loculi (thecae) distinct or at the tip merged together, and then by a single slit downwards to the middle dehiscent, with the bases saccate; *stamina didynama, antheris apiculatis, thecis basi in calcar longum curvatum productis, ad fissuram ciliatis*, stamens didynamous, with anthers apiculate with thecae at base drawn out into a spur long curved, at the fissure ciliate; *antherae membrana inflexa terminatae*, anthers by membrane inflexed terminated; *antherae 2-loculares, loculis connectivo lato oblongo apice cornuto disjunctis aequalibus parallelis*, anthers 2-locular, with the loculi (thecae) by a broad oblong connective separated equal parallel; *antherae apicibus in orbem cohaerentes loculis subparallelis distinctis contiguis a basi ad apicem late apertis*, anthers by the tips into an orb cohering with the loculi (thecae) almost parallel distinct close together from base to tip wide open; *tubus stamineus cylindratus apice antheras permultas monothecas globum formantes gerens*, staminal tube cylindric, bearing at the tip the anthers many one-celled forming a glove; *antherae lineares connectivo in laminam triangularem obtusam supra loculos producto*, anthers linear with the connective prolonged into a blade triangular blunt above the loculi (thecae).

Antheridiophore: antheridiophorum (s.n. II), *abl. sing.* antheridiophoro.

Antheridium: antheridium (s.n. II), *abl. sing.* antheridio, *nom. pl.* antheridia, *abl. pl.* antheridiis; *antheridia solitaria, ad furcas secundas et tertias* (*rarius primas*) *ramulorum primariorum nonnunquam ad ramulos secundarios posita, diametro 0·2 mm.*, antheridia solitary, at second and third (rarely first) forks of the primary branchlets sometimes on secondary branchlets placed, 0·2 mm. in diameter.

antherless: anantherus (adj. A), anantheratus (adj. A); *stamina ananthera* (*staminodia*) *iis fertilibus alterna*, stamens without anthers (staminodes) with fertile ones alternate.

Anthesis (s.f. III): anthesis, period during which flower is open; *ante anthesin*, before flowering; *sub anthesi*, at flowering; *per anthesin*, during flowering; *post anthesin*, after flowering; *anthesis peractione, sub finem anthesis*, at end of flowering; *anthesis initio*, at beginning of flowering; cf. EFFLORESCENTIA, FLORESCENTIA.

Anthodium (s.n. II): capitulum of Compositae.

Anthoecium: anthoecium (s.n. II); *anthoecium unum hermaphroditum*, anthoecium (spikelet) one hermaphrodite; *anthoecium inferius glumis paullo brevius vel glumas aequans vel superans*, lower anthoecium than the glumes by a little shorter or the glumes equalling or overtopping.

anti-: *in Gk. comp.*, against; *antidysentericus*, against dysentery; *antisyphiliticus*, against syphilis.

antice (adv.): in front. **anticus** (adj. A): anterior, at the front, remote from *or* turned away from the axis; (of anthers) introrse; (of Hepaticae leaves) on upper or dorsal side; *lobi 3, postico obtuso, anticis acutis*, lobes 3, with the posterior one blunt, the anterior ones acute; *sepalum posticum cymbiforme, sepala antica plana*, posterior sepal boat-shaped, anterior sepals flat; *sepala 2 antica ceteris paulo minora*, 2 anterior sepals than the rest a little smaller; cf. POSTICUS. **420**

antihelicte (adv.): anti-clockwise, in a direction passing from left to right, dextrorse (in the sense of Eichler, A. Gray, etc.), sinistrorse (in the sense of de Candolle, etc.); cf. HELICTE, TWINING.

antipetalus (adj. A): antipetalous i.e. opposite a petal or placed upon one, not alternating with petals.

antiquus (adj. A): ancient, old, former.

antrorsus (adj. A): antrorse (directed upwards); cf. RETRORSUS.

anularis: *see* ANNULARIS. **Anulus**: *see* ANNULUS.

-anus (adj. A): suffix with sense of belonging to, connected with, pertaining to, used to form adj. from nouns, particularly from geographical and personal names, e.g. *africanus* from *Africa, romanus* from *Roma, Lamarckianus* after Lamarck, *Hassleranus* after Hassler, *montanus* from *mons* 'mountain'.

anvil-shaped: incudiformis (adj. B).

any: ullus (adj. A). **anywhere**: alicubi (adv.). **at any time**: aliquando (adv.).

apart: seorsum (adv. followed by abl.); distans (part. B); *see* DISTANT, SEPARATE.

aperiens (part. B): opening. **Aperture**: apertura (s.f. I); *cf.* CHINK, FISSURE, OPENING. **apertus** (adj. A): open.

Apertio (s.f. III): opening, unfolding; *ante· apertionem floris*, before the opening of the flower.

Apertura (s.f. I): aperture, hole, opening; *cf.* CHINK, FISSURE, FORAMEN, RIMA.

apertus (adj. A): open.

apetalus (adj. A): without petals.

Apex: apex (s.m. III. i); *see* TIP.

aphyllus (adj.): without leaves; *cf.* NUDUS.

apical: apicalis (adj. B): *cellula apicalis*, apical cell; *crescentia apicali*, by apical growth; *cf.* ACRANTHUS.

apicifixus (adj. A): attached by the apex. **apiculatus** (adj. A): ending abruptly in a short point or apiculum. **Apiculum**: apiculum (s.n. II), *abl. sing.* apiculo. **146**

Aplanospore: aplanospora (s.f. I).

apo-: *in Gk. comp.*, from, away from, out of, asunder, free; *apocarpus*, with carpels free from one another; *apopetalus*, with free petals.

Apoblastus (s.m. II): apoblast, i.e. vigorous barren shoot resulting from cutting back.

apodus (adj. A): sessile, without a stipe.

apomicticus (adj. A): apomictic.

Apophysis: apophysis (s.f. III. vii); *see* PARAPHYSIS.

Apothecium: apothecium (s.n. II), *abl. sing.* apothecio, *nom. pl.* apothecia, *abl. pl.* apotheciis; *apothecia lecideina sessilia rotundata ad basin leviter constricta parva 0·4 mm. crassa*, apothecia lecideine sessile rounded at base lightly constricted small 0·4 mm. thick.

apotropus (adj. A): apotropous.

Apparatus: apparatus (s.m. IV).

apparently: ut videtur, apparenter (adv.).

Appearance, general: facies (s.f. V), *abl. sing.* facie; aspectus (s.m. IV), *abl. sing.* aspectu; habitus (s.m. IV), *abl. sing.* habitu; *herba aspectu Saxifragae*, herb with appearance of a Saxifrage; *habitu similis Solano havanensi*, in appearance similar to Solanum havanense.

appearing: precise meaning should be sought, e.g. first seen (primum visum), first growing (primum crescens).

appendiculatus (adj. A): appendiculate, with small appendages, hanging in small fragments.

Appendix: appendix (s.f. III. i), *abl. sing.* appendice, *nom. pl.* appendices, *abl. pl.* appendicibus.

applanatus (adj. A): flattened or horizontally expanded.

apple-green: pomaceo-viridis (adj. B).

applicitus (part. A): lying upon, lying close to.

appositus (part. A): placed against, side by side with.

appreciably: evidenter (adv.), manifeste (adv.).

appressed: adpressus (part. A), appressus (part. A).

apprime (adv.): first of all, especially.

approaching: accedens (part. B).

approbavit: he has confirmed, approved, accepted as good; used of names already on herbarium sheets.

approximately: circa (adv.), circum (adv.), quasi (adv.).

approximatus (part. A): near each other, close together.

apricot-coloured: armeniacus (adj. A).

Apricum (s.n. II): an open sunny place; *buxus amat aprica*, the box loves sunny places; *habitat in apricis*, it grows in sunny places. **apricus** (adj. A): uncovered, exposed to the sun, sunny, growing in the sunshine.

aptus (part. A): suitable, fit for, appropriate, able.

apud (prep. with acc.): with, near, in the writings of.

Aqua (s.f. I): water, q.v. **Aquae** (s.f. I. pl.): medicinal springs; *Aquae Aureliae*, Baden-Baden; *Aquae Calidae*, Vichy. **aquaticus** (adj. A), **aquatilis** (adj. B): growing in water. **aqueus** (adj. A): clear as water. **Aquosum** (s.n. II): watery place. **aquosus** (adj. A): watery, full of water.

arachnoideus (adj. A), **araneosus** (adj. A): cobwebby.

Arbor (s.f. III. v): tree. **arborescens** (part. B): becoming tree-like. **Arboretum** (s.n. II): living collection of trees. **arboreus** (adj. A): tree-like. **arboricola** (adj. A): dwelling in a tree. **Arbuscula** (s.f. I): a small tree.

Arc: arcus (s.m. IV), *gen. sing.* arcus, *abl. sing.* arcu.

Arch: fornix (s.m. III), *gen. sing.* fornicis; arcus (s.m. IV), *gen. sing.* arcus.

arched: arcuatus (adj. A) 'curved like an arch', fornicatus (adj. A) 'provided with an arch-like structure'. **arched inward**: recavus (adj. A).

Archegoniophore: archegoniophorum (s.n. II), *abl. sing.* archegoniophoro.

Archegonium: archegonium (s.n. II), *abl. sing.* archegonio.

Archipelago: archipelagus (s.n. II).

arcte (adv.), **arte** (adv.): closely, firmly, tightly.

arctic: arcticus (adj. A).

arctus (adj. A), **artus** (adj. A): close, confined, tight.

arcuatus (part. A): curved like a bow. **Arcus** (s.m. IV): curve, arc. **35**

Ardella: ardella (s.f. I), *abl. sing.* ardella.

ardesiacus (adj. A): slate-coloured.

Area: area (s.f. I), *abl. sing.* area; *area hyalina circa rhaphem*, area hyaline around raphe.

arefactus (part. A): made dry, dried: *folia in statu naturali vivo patentia, in statu arefacto ad caulem appressa*, leaves in a natural living state spreading, in a dried state appressed to the stem.

Arena (s.f. I): sand, sandy place, sandy desert. **arenaceus** (adj. A): sandy; *saxum arenaceum*, sandstone. **arenarius** (adj. A): growing on sand, sandy. **Arenosum** (s.n. II): sandy place. **arenosus** (adj. A): full of sand.

Areola (s.f. I): areole, a space marked out on a surface by cracks or ridges. **areolatus** (adj. A): areolate, marked out into small usually angular spaces. **Areolation**: areolatio (s.f. III. vi), *abl. sing.* areolatione. **251**

arescens (part. B): becoming dry.

argenteus (adj. A): silvery. **Argentum** (s.n. II): silver.

Argilla (s.f. I): clay. **argillaceus** (adj. A): clayey, growing on clay, clay-coloured, yellowish-brown. **argillosus** (adj. A): full of clay, clayey.

argute (adv.): sharply. **argutus** (adj. A): sharp, sharp-toothed.

argyr-: *in Gk. comp.*, silver-; *argyrocalyx*, with silvery calyx; *argyrophyllus*, with silvery leaves.

aridus (adj. A): dry, withered.

Aril: arillus (s.m. II), *abl. sing.* arillo, **arillatus** (adj. A): provided with an aril.

Arillode: arillodium (s.n. II), *abl. sing.* arillodio.

-aris (adj. B): suffix with sense of 'belonging to, resembling, provided with', used to form adj. from nouns, especially with stems ending in *l* or *r*, e.g. *acicularis* from *acicula* 'small needle', *orbicularis* from *orbiculus* 'small disc'.

arisen from: ortus (part. A), exortus (part. A). **arising**: oriens (part. B). exoriens (part. B). **arising from**: exoriens (part. B), enascens (part. B); *organa sporangifera sub apice frondis*

exorientia, sporangium-bearing organs arising below the apex of the frond.

Arista: arista (s.f. I), *abl. sing.* arista, *nom. pl.* aristae, *abl. pl.* aristis; *see* AWN. **aristate**: aristatus (adj. A). **139**

Arm: brachium (s.n. II).

armatus (part. A): equipped, armed; *oculo armato*, with the eye equipped, i.e. seen under a lens.

armeniacus (adj. A): apricot-coloured (H.C.C. *60*.9); also used as geographical epithet, pertaining to Armenia.

aromatic: aromaticus (adj. A).

around: circa, circum (adv. and prep. with acc.).

arranged: dispositus (part. A), ordinatus (part. A), digestus (part. A).

Arrangement: collocatio (s.f. III. vi), dispositio (s.f. III. vi). **Arrangement of Leaves**: phyllotaxis (s.f. III. vii); dispositio (s.f. III. vi) foliorum; situs (s.m. IV) foliorum. Leaves may be *basal* (folia basalia; folia caulina), and possibly then *in a rosette* (folia rosulata; *see* ROSETTE), or *cauline*, i.e. carried on an evident stem (folia caulina), being then *spirally arranged* (spiraliter disposita), *alternate* (alterna), possibly *two-rowed* (biseriata, disticha), *scattered* (sparsa, dissita, dispersa), or *crowded* (aggregata, conferta), *decussate* with each node bearing two leaves at right angles to the pair below (decussata) or *whorled* (verticillata) with leaves *three* together (terna), *four* (quaterna), *five* (quina), *six* (sena) *or more* (vel ultra) at each node. *caulis infra nudus vel dimidio inferiore et paullo ultra foliis paucis sparsis praeditus, tunc verticillo foliorum manifesto usque 16-folio et supra verticillum foliis parvis paucis sparsis vel raro verticillo altero paucifolio instructus*, stem naked below or for the lower half and a little more with a few sparse leaves, then furnished with a well-marked whorl of leaves up to 16-leaved and above the whorl with a few small sparse leaves or rarely another whorl of few leaves furnished; *folia dispersa vel inferne aggregata*, leaves scattered or below crowded; *folia verticillata usque 12 folia per verticillum*, leaves whorled up to 12 leaves a whorl; *folia 5-6 in verticillo disposita*, leaves 5-6 in a whorl arranged; *caulis e basi per 4-20 cm. nudus, deinde cataphyllis 1-2, tum foliis 2-4 brevibus remotis, postremo parte media et supera verticillis foliorum usque 8-foliatis 2-4 inter se 2 cm. distantibus vestitus*, stem from the base for 4-20 cm. naked, then clothed with 1-2 cataphylls, then 2-4 short well-spaced leaves, finally in the middle and upper part with 2-4 whorls of leaves up to 8-leaved between themselves 2 cm. apart.

arrectus (adj. A): set upright, pointing upwards, diverging from axis at angle of less than 30°. **387**

arrhizus (adj. A): rootless.

arrow-headed: sagittatus (adj. A). **126**

arte (adv.): *see* ARCTE.

arthro-: *in Gk. comp.*, jointed. **arthrodactylus** (adj. A): *in Charophyta*, having the ultimate rays or dactyls each composed of more than one cell.

articulatus (part. A): articulate, jointed. **Articulus** (s.m. II), joint, part between nodes, segment. **235, 455**

artifactus (adj. A): artificial, man-made.

artificial: artificialis (adj. B), artificiosus (adj. A), factitius (adj. A).

-arum: gen. pl. ending of s. I and adj. A f., meaning 'of'; *descriptiones plantarum novarum*, descriptions of new plants; *palmarum familia*, family of palms; *algae insularum britannicarum*, algae of the British Isles; *monographia Lobeliacearum*, monograph of the Lobeliaceae; *simiarum*, of the monkeys.

arvalis (adj. B), **arvensis** (adj. B): pertaining to fields or cultivated land. **Arvum** (s.n. II): arable field, cultivated land.

as (in the same manner): atque (conj.). **as being, namely**: ut pote (adv.). **as being such**: pro (prep. with abl.). **as far as, reaching to**: tenus (prep. with abl. or gen. placed after noun). **as if, as it were**: velut (adv.). **as (in comparison of size)**: quam (adv.); *cellulae duplo longiores quam latae*, cells twice as long as wide. **as in**: ut (adv.); *ut in typo*, as in the type. **as yet**: adhuc (adv.).

ascending: ascendens (part. B), assurgens (part. B); *cf.* DIRECTION. **395**

-ascens (part. B): present part. ending used in forming adj. to indicate a process of becoming but also a lack of full attainment, e.g. *purpurascens*, becoming purple, purplish.

Ascidium (s.n. II): pitcher, as in *Nepenthes*.

Ascoma: ascoma (s.n. III), *gen. sing.* ascomatis.

Ascospore: ascospora (s.f. I); *see* SPORE.

Ascus: ascus (s.m. II), *abl. sing.* asco, *nom. pl.* asci, *abl. pl.* ascis; *asci usque ad 10 in successione maturescentes, sessiles globosi vel ovati, 30 μ diam., octospori aparaphysati*, asci up to 10, in succession maturing, sessile globose or ovate, 30 μ in diameter, 8-spored without paraphyses; *ascis clavatis paraphysatis octosporis*, with asci club-shaped accompanied by paraphyses 8-spored; *asci clavati vel fusiformes magni 1·5 mm.*

longi octospori paraphysibus immixti, asci club-shaped or fusiform large 1·5 mm. long 8-spored with paraphyses intermingled.

aseptatus (adj. A): without septa.

asexual: agamicus (adj. A), agamus (adj. A), asexualis (adj. B), vegetativus (adj. A).

aspectabilis (adj. B): visible, worthy of being seen.

Aspectus (s.m. IV): appearance, aspect, view; *see* APPEARANCE.

asper (adj. A): rough, uneven, harsh, rugged. **266**

asperatus (adj. A): rough with points or short stiff hairs. **Asperitas** (s.f. III): roughness. **Asperum** (s.n. II): uneven, rough place.

aspergilliformis (adj. B): brush-shaped. **239**

Aspergo (s.f. III): spray (of water), sprinkling.

aspersus (part. A): *see* ADSPERSUS.

aspiciens (part. B): looking forward, facing.

asservatus (part. A): kept, preserved.

assimilating: assumens (part. B), assimilativus (adj. A), assimilans (part. B); *phaeophora in cellulis assimilantibus numerosa*, phaeophores (chromatophores) in assimilating cells numerous.

associated: consociatus (part. A), una cum.

Association (s.n. II): consortio (s.f. III. vi), consortium (s.n. II).

assumens (part. B): taking up, receiving, assimilating.

assurgens (part. B): rising upwards. **395**

Aster (s.m. III): star, starwort.

-aster (m.), **-astrum** (n.): *in L. comp.*, suffix to nouns indicating incomplete likeness or inferiority, often used to distinguish a wild from a cultivated kind, e.g. *oleaster*, *oleastrum*, wild olive, from *olea*, cultivated olive, *pinaster*, wild pine, from *pinus*, pine, particularly the stone-pine with edible seeds, *mentastrum*, wild mint, from *menta*, *mentha*, mint, and definitely derogatory in such words as *formaster*, dandy, *philosophaster*, bad philosopher; also suffix to adjectives in diminutive sense, e.g. *surdaster*, somewhat deaf, compared with *surdus*, deaf; see p. 305.

asterinus (adj. A): aster-violet (H.C.C. 38).

astero-, **astro-**; *in Gk. comp.*, starry, stellate; *asterocalyx*, with star-like calyx; *asterotrichus*, *astrotrichus*, with stellate hairs, stellately hairy.

astictus (adj. A): unspotted, spotless.

astrictus (part. A): drawn together, tight, narrow.

astylus (adj. A): without a style.

asymmetrice (adv.): asymmetrically. **a-symmetricus** (adj. A): asymmetric, irregular.

at (conj.): but, yet, but then.

at: in the sense of 'at which', 'place where' is expressed by *ad* (prep. with acc.), e.g. *ad basim* 'at the base', *ad extremum* 'at the end'; *in* (prep. with abl.), e.g. *in angulis* 'at the angles', or simply with the abl., e.g. *basi* 'at base'; but for places such as towns and small islands by the old locative case (the same as gen. sing. in s. I and s. II, as abl. sing. in s. III, s. IV, s. V), e.g. *Gedani*, at Danzig, *Gottingae*, at Göttingen, *Holmiae*, at Stockholm, *Lipsiae*, at Leipzig, *Lugduni*, at Lyon, *Lugduni Batavorum*, at Leiden, *Lutetiae*, at Paris, *Patavii*, at Padua, *Tiguri*, at Zurich, *Ultrajecti*, at Utrecht.

at least: saltem (adv.), quidem (adv.).

at present: nunc (adv.).

ater (adj. A): black, *esp.* dull black.

atomatus (adj. A): sprinkled with minute particles.

atque (conj.): and, q.v.

atrans (adj. B): darkening. **atri-, atro-**: *in L. comp.*, black, dark, q.v.; *atrolabius*, black-lipped; *atropurpureus*, dark purple; *atrovirens*, dark green; *atri*- is preferable in classical L., but *atro*- in bot. L.

atratus (part. A): blackened, dark.

attached: affixus (part. A), with dat. or with *ad* and acc. or *in* and abl. to indicate place of attachment, *per* and acc. to indicate means by which attached.

attaining: attingens (part. B); *cellulae usque ad 12 μ diametro attingentes*, cells up to 12 μ in diameter attaining.

attamen (adv.): nevertheless.

Attempt: tentamen (s.n. III. vi).

attenuate: attenuatus (part. A). **131, 176**

attingens (part. B): reaching to, attaining; *antherae labium inferius attingentes*, anthers reaching the lower lip.

-atus (part. A): ending of perfect part. passive of verbs with *a*- stems, the infinitive in *-are*, indicating action completed, hence 'provided with, pertaining to' and used also to form adj. from nouns. *attenuatus* 'drawn out' from *attenuo* 'make thin'; *maculatus* 'spotted' from *maculo* 'make spotted' from *macula* 'a spot'; *orbiculatus* 'circular' from *orbiculus* 'small disc'.

atypicus (adj. A): not typical, abnormal; cf. ABERRANS, ABNORMAL, ANOMALUS.

Auctor (s.c. III. v): author, writer, defender of a thesis (not necessarily its actual author) in a public disputation; cf. C. Häberlin in *Zentralbl. Biblioth.*, 43 : 174 (1926).

auctus (part. A): enlarged, increased, added to.

Augmen (s.n. III), **Augmentum** (s.n. II): increase, growth.

aulac-: *in Gk. comp.*, furrow; *aulacospermus*, with furrowed seeds; *aulacanthus*, having spines in furrows, the secondary rows being more prominent than the primary rows bearing the spine-cells.

aurantiacus (adj. A): orange (H.C.C. 12), between yellow and scarlet.

auratus (adj. A): flecked with gold.

aureolinus (adj. A): aureolin yellow (H.C.C. 3). **aureus** (adj. A): golden yellow.

Auricle: auricula (s.f. I), *abl. sing.* auricula, *nom. pl.* auriculae, *abl. pl.* auriculis.

auriculatus (adj. A): auriculate, i.e. furnished with ear-like appendage. **123, 168**

auriformis (adj. A): ear-shaped.

auritus (adj. A): eared, auriculate.

Aurum (s.n. II): gold.

australis (adj. B): south, southern.

aut (conj.): or, q.v.

aut-, auto-: *in Gk. comp.*, self.

autem (conj.): on the other hand, but, nevertheless.

authentic: authenticus (adj. A), genuinus (adj. A), verus (adj. A).

autoicus (adj. A): autoicous, i.e. having male and female organs in separate inflorescences on the same plant.

Autopsia (s.f. I): personal examination.

Autumn: autumnus (s.m. II); *autumno florens*, flowering in autumn; *in serum autumnum*, in late autumn. autumnal: autumnalis (adj. B).

auxiliary: auxiliaris (adj. B).

available: suppetens (part. B), in promptu.

avellaneus (adj. A): hazel, nut-brown.

avenis (adj. B), **avenius** (adj. A): veinless, without perceptible lateral nerves and veins; opposite of VENOSUS.

Avenue: ambulacrum (s.n. II).

aversus (part. A): turned backwards, behind, on the back; *pagina aversa*, lower side of leaf.

avulsus (part. A): pulled off, plucked.

awl-shaped: subulatus (adj. A), lesiniformis (adj. B). **114**

Awn: arista (s.f. I), *abl. sing.* arista, *nom. pl.* aristae, *abl. pl.* aristis; *arista inferne tortilis*, awn twisted below; *valvula aristam terminalem simplicem emittens*, valvule putting forth an awn terminal simple; *aristae nudae scabrae*, awns naked scabrid; *gluma e sinu aristata, arista tenui inferne parum torta, infracta et quidpiam flexuosa 2-pollicari*, glume from the notch awned, with the awn thin below a little twisted bent and somewhat flexuous 2 inches long. **awned**: aristatus (adj. A). **awnless**: muticus (adj. A). **139, 165**

axe-shaped: dolabriformis (adj. B). **37**

axialis (adj. B): axial, relating to the axis, located along the axis.

Axil: axilla (s.f. I), *abl. sing.* axilla, *nom. pl.* axillae, *abl. pl.* axillis, *lit.* 'armpit'. *paniculae e foliorum summorum axillis ortae*, panicles from the axils of the upper leaves arising. **axillary**: axillaris (adj. B), *less often* alaris (adj. B); *inflorescentia axillaris*, inflorescence axillary; *spicae terminales vel ad apicem ramorum axillares*, spikes terminal or at tip of branches axillary; *floribus axillaribus solitariis*, with flowers axillary solitary. **463**

Axis: axis (s.m. III. vi), *acc. sing.* axem *or* axin, *abl. sing.* axe, *nom. pl.* axes, *abl. pl.* axibus; *axis mas femineus vel asexualis*, axis male female or asexual; *axis transapicalis*, transverse axis; *secus axem, secus axin*, along the axis; *axes mares feminei et asexuales simplices vel ramosi*, axes male female and asexual simple or branched; *frustula circum axem apicalem torta*, frustules twisted around the apical axis.

azonatus (adj. A), **azonus** (adj. A): azonate, without zones.

azureus (adj. A): azure, pure deep blue.

Azygospore: azygospora (s.f. I).

B

Bacca (s.f. I): berry, q.v. **baccans** (adj. B): becoming juicy and berry-like, as calyx of Coccoloba. **baccatus** (adj. A): berry-like, pulpy. **baccifer** (adj. A): berry-bearing. **bacciformis** (adj. B): shaped like a berry. **333**

bacillaris (adj. B), **bacilliformis** (adj. B), **baculiformis** (adj. B): rod-shaped, rod-like.

Back: dorsum (s.n. II), *less often* tergum (s.n. II); *pars a tergo visa*, part seen from the back. **on the back**: dorsalis (adj. B). **at the back**: postice (adv.).

back, backwards: recessim (adv.); *in L. comp.*, retro-; *retrocurvatus*, curved back; *retroflexus*, bent back; *retrofractus*, refracted, bent sharply backward from the base; cf. RETRORSUS.

Bacterium (s.n. II): bacterium.

bad: malus (adj. A). **very bad**: pessimus (adj. A). **badly**: male (adv.).

badius (adj. A): bay, reddish-brown, dull brown, chocolate-brown.

bald: calvus (adj. A).

balteiformis (adj. B): belt-shaped.

band-shaped: vittiformis (adj. B), taeniatus (adj. A), fasciarius (adj. A): cf. STRAP-SHAPED.

banded: fasciatus (adj. A) 'with transverse stripes of one colour crossing another', vittatus (adj. A) 'with longitudinal stripes'. **104**

Bank (of river): ripa (s.f. I), *acc. sing.* ripam, *gen. sing.* ripae, *abl. sing.* ripa, *nom. pl.* ripae, *acc. pl.* ripas, *gen. pl.* riparum, *abl. pl.* ripis. **pertaining to banks**: riparius (adj. A).

Banner-petal: vexillum (s.n. II); *see* STANDARD PETAL.

Bar (cross-beam): transtrum (s.n. II).

Barb: hamus (s.m. II), uncus (s.m. II), hamulus (s.m. II).

Barba (s.f. I): beard. **barbatus** (adj. A): bearded, provided with tufts of long weak hairs. **barbellatus** (adj. A): with short stiff hairs as in pappus of some Compositae.

barbed: hamatus (adj. A), uncinatus (adj. A), glochideus (adj. A).

bare: nudus (adj. A); cf. DENUDATUS.

barely: vix (adv.); cf. TANTUM.

Bark: cortex (s.f. III), *acc. sing.* corticem, *gen. sing.* corticis, *abl. sing.* cortice; *ad corticem arborum inter muscos*, on the bark of trees among mosses; cf. CORTICATUS, DECORTICATUS.

Barrel: dolium (s.n. II); the Roman dolium was, however, a large wide-mouthed globular jar. **barrel-shaped**: cupiformis (adj. B), doliiformis (adj. B), orculiformis (adj. B.).

barren: sterilis (adj. B).

basal: basalis (adj. B), basilaris (adj. B). **459**

basally: basaliter (adv.).

Base: basis (s.f. III), fundus (s.m. II), imum (s.n. II), infimum (s.n. II); *basis*, a loan-word from Greek, can be variously declined, e.g. *acc. sing.* basim, basin *or* basem, *gen. sing.* basis *or* baseos, *dat. sing.* basi, *abl. sing.* basi *or* base, *nom.* and *acc. pl.* bases, *gen. pl.* basium, *dat.* and *abl. pl.* basibus; *e basi*, from the base; *basi*, at the base; *prope basin*, near the base; *basin versus*, towards base; *supra basin*, above the base; *ab imo ad summum*, from bottom to top; *stamina imo corollae tubo inserta*, stamens at bottom of corolla-tube inserted; *petala fundo calycis inserta*, petals at bottom of calyx inserted; *see* BOTTOM.

basic: basicus (adj. A): *numerus basicus chromosomatum*, basic chromosome number.

Basidiospore: basidiospora (s.f. I); cf. SPORE.

Basidium: basidium (s.n. II), *abl. sing.* basidio, *nom. pl.* basidia, *abl. pl.* basidiis; *basidia tetraspora clavata*, basidia

4-spored club-shaped; *basidiis bisporis hyalinis*, with basidia 2-spored hyaline.

basifixus (adj. A): attached by the base.

basifugus (adj. B): developing from below upwards, i.e. away from the base (basifugal) and towards the apex (acropetal).

basilaris (adj. B): basal.

basin-shaped: crateriformis (adj. B), lebetiformis (adj. B), pelviformis (adj. B).

basiramifer (adj. A): bearing branches from the base, branched from the base.

Basis (s.f. III): base, q.v.

basiscopicus (adj. A): facing or directed towards the base; cf. ACROSCOPICUS.

Beak: rostrum (s.n. II), *abl. sing.* rostro. **beaked**: rostratus (adj. A), *in L. comp.* rostris (adj. A), -rostrus (adj. A). **slightly beaked**: rostellatus (adj. A). **148**

bean-shaped: fabiformis (adj. B).

Beard: barba (s.f. I). **bearded**: barbatus (adj. A). **beardless**: imberbis (adj. B).

bearing: ferens (part. B), gerens (part. B), both with acc.; praeditus (part. A), instructus (part. A), both with abl. **-bearing**: *in L. comp.*, -fer, -ger, *in Gk. comp.*, -phorus.

beatus (part. A): prosperous, blessed (used only of deceased botanists).

beautiful: pulcher (adj. A), formosus (adj. A), concinnus (adj. A). **beautifully**: pulchre (adv.).

because of: ob (prep. with acc.), propter (prep. with acc.).

becoming: usually expressed by participle ending -ESCENS or -ASCENS.

Bed: lectus (s.m. II).

Beer: cerevisia (s.f. I).

before: ante (prep. with acc.), antea (adv.), antequam (conj.).

Beginning: initium (s.n. II), *acc. sing.* initium, *abl. sing.* initio; *ad initium florendi*, at beginning of flowering; cf. ANTHESIS.

begoniinus: begonia (H.C.C. 6.19), a colour near coral pink.

beheld: spectatus (part. A).

behind: post (prep. with acc.).

bell-: *in L. comp.*, campani-, *in Gk. comp.*, codon-; *campaniflorus, codonanthus*, bell-flowered.

bell-shaped: campanulatus (adj. A), campaniformis (adj. B). *Campaniformis* means 'bell-shaped' whereas *campanulatus* means 'pertaining to a Campanula', the name *Campanula* being coined by Fuchs in 1742 for the species now called *Campanula trachelium*. But both are used for shapes agreeing with the type of corolla usual in *Campanula*, i.e. with a broad rounded base, a gradually expanded tube not more than twice as long as broad and the upper

part (corresponding to the sound bow of a church bell) diverging outwards often above a slight incurve (corresponding to the waist of a bell). For the pileus of an agaric without the campanulaceous incurve, the term *parabolicus* may be used, following Josserand. **72**

belonging: pertinens (part. B); *algae Trentepohlias pertinentes*, algae belonging to Trentepohlia.

below: infra (adv. and prep. with acc.), sub (prep. with abl.), subter (prep. with abl.); *infra medium*, below the middle. **below-ground**: subterraneus (adj. A), hypogaeus (adj. A).

belt-shaped: balteiformis (adj. B).

Bend: flexus (s.m. IV). **bent**: flexus (part. A); cf. OBSTIPUS.

bene (adv.): well, rightly, excellently.

benevole (adv.): kindly.

berried: baccatus (adj. A) 'juicy and succulent', baccifer (adj. A) 'berry-bearing'. **333**

Berry: bacca (s.f. I), *nom. pl.* baccae, *abl. pl.* baccis; *in class. L. usu.* baca, 'any small round fruit' *bacca*; *globosa 1 cm. lata polysperma pulposa acris inedulis rubra nitida fragrans calyce persistente coronata*, berry globose 1 cm. broad many-seeded pulpy acid uneatable red glossy fragrant by the persistent calyx crowned. **berry-bearing**: baccifer (adj. A). **berry-like**: baccatus (adj. A). **becoming berry-like**: baccans (adj. B).

beset: *see* PROVIDED WITH.

betinus (adj. A): beetroot purple.

better: melior (adj. comp.), melius (adv.).

between: inter (prep. with acc.).

beyond: ultra (adv.), ulterius (adv.); *see* TRANS-.

bi-: *in L. comp.*, two-; *biaristatus*, two-awned; *biauritus*, with two auricles; *bibracteatus*, two-bracted; *bicalcaratus*, two-spurred; *bicapsularis*, with two capsules *or* a two-chambered capsule; *bicarinatus*, two-keeled; *bicontortus*, twice twisted; *bicolor*, two-coloured; *biconvexus*, convex on two sides; *bicornis*, two-horned; *bicostatus*, two-ribbed; *bicruris*, two-legged; *bicuspidatus*, with two sharp points; *bidentatus*, two-toothed; *bifacialis*, bifacial; *bifarius*, two-rowed; *bifidus*, two-cleft to about halfway; *biflorus*, two-flowered; *bifoliolatus*, with two leaflets; *bifrons*, two-faced, growing on both sides; *bifurcus, bifurcatus*, twice forked; *biglumis*, two-glumed; *bijugus*, with two pairs of leaflets; *bilabiatus*, two-lipped; *bilamellatus*, with two lamellae; *bilobus, bilobatus*, two-lobed; *bilocularis*, two-chambered; *bimaculatus*, two-spotted; *binervis*, *binervius*, two-nerved; *binotatus*, two-marked; *biovulatus*, two-ovuled; *bipartitus*, divided almost to the base into two parts; *bipinnatus*, twice pinnate, each division of a pinnate leaf being itself pinnate; *biporosus*, two-pored; *bipunctatus*, two-spotted; *birimosus*, opening by two slits; *biseptatus*, with two septa; *biserratus*, doubly serrate, the teeth being themselves toothed; *bisetus*, with two bristles; *bisexualis*, with both sexes together; *bisulcatus*, two-furrowed; *biternatus*, twice ternate, each of the three main divisions being itself divided into three parts; *biuncialis*, two inches (about 5 cm.) long; *bivalvis*, two-valved. Many analogous L. compounds are formed with the L. numerical prefixes *uni-* 'one-', *tri-* 'three-', *quadr-* 'four-', *quinqu-* 'five-', *sex-* 'six-', *septem-* 'seven-', *pauci-* 'few-', *multi-* 'many-', etc.; *see* TWO, DI-.

biatorinus (adj. A): biatorine, i.e. resembling lichen genus *Biatora* in having apothecium without thalline margin and with soft almost colourless excipulum.

bibulus (adj. A): absorbing moisture, drinking readily, *hence applicable to certain fungi*; *charta bibula*, blotting paper.

biconjugatus (adj. A): twice-conjugate. **217**

biennial: biennis (adj. B): symbol ⊙ or ②; *herba biennis*, herb biennial. **342**

bifariam (adv.), **bifarius** (adj. A): in two rows; cf. DISTICHUS. **488, 489**

bigeminatus (adj. A): twice-conjugate. **217**

big: grandis (adj. B), magnus (adj. A).

binary: binarius (adj. A): *per fissionem binariam*, by binary fission.

binatim (adv.): in pairs, by twos.

binatus (adj. A): with a pair, as a leaf divided into two leaflets. **206**

binding together: colligans (part. B).

bini (adj. num. distr. pl.): two each, paired; *cystocarpis singulis aut binis*, with cystocarps single or paired.

Bipartitio (s.f. III): division into two; *multiplicatio cellularum bipartitione vegetativa*, multiplication of cells by vegetative division into two.

bis (adv.): twice; used as a prefix by Otto Kuntze and others in coining new generic names to replace or avoid later homonyms, e.g. *Bisgoeppertia*.

biscoctiformis (adj. B): biscuit-shaped (from med. L. *biscoctus* (s.m. II) 'biscuit', the biscuit envisaged by nineteenth-cent. German botanists being apparently the finger biscuit or the Katzenzünglein kind, i.e. oblong with

the ends rounded and the middle slightly constricted).

bistratose: bistratus (adj. A), distromaticus (adj. A).

bistre (warm brown colour): sepiaceus (adj. A).

Bit: frustum (s.n. II).

bitter: amarus (adj. A), acidus (adj. A), acer (adj. B), acerbus (adj. A).

-bius (adj. A): *in Gk. comp.*, -living; *amphibius*, double-living, i.e. in water or on land.

black: ater (adj. A) 'dull black', niger (adj. A) 'glossy black', anthracinus (adj. A) 'coal black'; *in L. comp.*, atri-, atro-, *in Gk. comp.*, melan-, melano-. **blackened**: denigratus (part. A). **blackening**: denigricans (part. B).

Bladder: vesica (s.f. I), *in Utricularia* ampulla (s.f. I). **bladdery**: vesicarius (adj. A); *in Gk. comp.*, physo-. **96**

Blade: lamina (s.f. I), *abl. sing.* lamina, *nom. pl.* laminae, *abl. pl.* laminis.

blast-, blasto-: *in Gk. comp.*, shoot-.

blephari-, blepharid-, blepharo-: *in Gk. comp.*, relating to eye-lashes or eye-lids, i.e. marginally fringed with hairs, ciliated; *blepharicarpus*, with ciliated fruit, as in Lathyrus species; *blepharidanthus*, with ciliated flower; *blephariglossus*, *blepharoglossus*, with ciliated tongue; *blepharopetalus*, with ciliated petals; *blepharophorus*, bearing cilia; *blepharophyllus*, with ciliated leaves; *blepharosepalus*, with ciliated sepals; *dolichoblepharus*, with long cilia.

Blepharoplast: blepharoplastus (s.m. II).

blister-shaped: pustuliformis (adj. B).

blood-red: sanguineus (adj. A), sanguinolentus (adj. A), haematicus (adj. A), haematinus (adj. A), haematochrous (adj. A), haematodes (adj. B); *in L. comp.*, sanguineo-, *in Gk. comp.*, haem-, haemat-; *sanguineomaculatus*, *haematostictus*, with blood-red spots; cf. HAEM-.

Blotch: macula (s.f. I), *abl. sing.* macula, *nom. pl.* maculae, *abl. pl.* maculis; *macula basilaris atra flavo-cincta late elliptica rotundata vel acuta 2-3 cm. longa*, basal blotch black yellow-margined broadly elliptic rounded or pointed 2-3 cm. long; *perigonium segmentis basi macula oblonga nigrescente flavo-cincta notatis*, perigon with segments marked at base with a blotch oblong blackish yellow-margined; *folia radicalia maculis albidis majoribus confluentibus et minoribus irregulariter sparsis variegata*, leaves radical variegated with whitish blotches the larger merging together and the smaller irregularly sprinkled; *maculae*

foliicolae rotundatae brunneo-olivaceae,
spots growing on leaves rounded olive-
brown ; *maculae albae farinosae parum
densae aut confertae irregulares in pagina
inferiori foliorum,* spots white floury
not very dense or crowded irregular on
lower surface of leaves ; *thallus epilithicus maculas irregulares et bene limitatas
albidas vel flavas haud virides formans,*
thallus growing on stone forming spots
irregular and well-defined whitish or
yellow never green ; *plagas sive maculas
latas in ambitu vagas et attenuatas
efficit,* it produces tracts or broad spots
in outline indefinite and drawn out.
  blotched : maculatus (part. A).
blown out : inflatus (part. A), sufflatus
  (part. A).
blue : azureus (adj. A), caeruleus (adj. A),
  caesius (adj. A), cyaneus (adj. A),
  cobaltinus (adj. A), lazulinus (adj. A),
  venetus (adj. A) ; *in L. comp.,* caesio-,
  in Gk. comp., cyaneo-.
blunt : obtusus (adj. A) ; *in L. comp.,*
  obtusi- *in Gk. comp.,* ambly-. **blunted** :
  obtusatus (adj. A). **153, 173**
Boat :   navicula   (s.f. I).   **boat-shaped** :
  navicularis   (adj.   B),   naviculiformis
  (adj. B), cymbiformis (adj. B). **46**
Body : corpus (s.n. III).   Special terms
  are also used : *granum paramylaceum,*
  paramylon body ; *gutta olei,* drop of
  oil, oil-body.
Bog : palus (s.f. III) 'marsh' ; turbarium
  (s.n.II) 'peat-bog'. **boggy** : uliginosus (adj.A).
bombycinus (adj. A) : silky.
bonus (adj. A) : good.
bony : osseus (adj. A). **322**
Book : liber (s.m. II).
Border : margo (s.f. and m. III. vi) ; *see*
  MARGIN. **bordered** : marginatus (part.
  A), limbatus (part. A), limbatus (adj.
  A). **bordering** : affinis (adj. B).
borealis (adj. B) : north, northern.
born : natus (part. A), genitus (part. A).
  born within : innatus (part. A), *with dat.
  or with* in *and abl.*
borne : portatus (part. A).
Boss : umbo (s.m. III. vi), *abl. sing.*
  umbone. **bossed** : umbonatus (adj. A).
  20
Bostryx : bostryx (s.m. III).
botanic, botanical : botanicus (adj. A).
  Botanist : botanicus (s.m. II). **Botany** :
  botanice (s.f. I), *gen. sing.* botanices ;
  phytologia (s.f. I), *gen. sing.* phyto-
  logiae ; *Botanice est Scientia Naturalis,
  quae Vegetabilium cognitionem tradit*
  (Linnaeus, *Phil. Bot.,* 1 ; 1750), botany
  is the natural science which transmits
  knowledge of plants ; *botanices professor,* professor of botany.

both : ambo (num. adj.), duo (num.),
  uterque (pron.) ; *ambo* refers to two
  objects, considered as a pair, their
  association being assumed as known ;
  duo when their association not already
  known, *uterque* when considered sever-
  ally ; *in superficiebus ambabus folii,* on
  both surfaces of the leaf. **both . . .
  and . . . :** et . . . et. **on both sides** :
  utrinque (adv.), utrinsecus (adv.).
bothr- :   *in Gk. comp.,*   pit ;   *bothryo-
  spermus,* with pitted seeds.
botry-, -botrys :   *in Gk. comp.,*   bunch,
  raceme ; *botryoides, botryoideus,* like a
  bunch of grapes.
Bottom : fundus (s.m. II), *abl. sing.* fundo ;
  imum (s.n. II), *abl. sing.* imo ; infimum
  (s.n. II), *abl. sing.* infimo ; solum (s.n.
  II), *abl. sing.* solo ; *ab infimo,* from
  below ; *infime, ad infimum,* at the
  bottom ; *in solum maris arenosum,* on
  the sandy bottom of the sea ; cf. BASE,
  FUNDUS.
Boundary : finis (s.f. III), *gen. sing.* finis ;
  limes (s.m. III), *gen. sing.* limitis.
  bounded : definitus (part. A), limitatus
  (part. A).
bow-curved : arcuatus (adj. A). **35**
bowl-shaped : crateriformis (adj. B). **81**
brachialis (adj. B) : arm-long, i.e. 2 ft.
  (65 cm.) long. **brachiatus** (adj. A) :
  having decussate branches provided
  with arms. **Brachium** (s.n. II) : arm,
  distance from arm-pit to tip of middle
  finger, hence 2 ft. (65 cm.). **427**
brachy- : *in Gk. comp.,* short ; *brachy-
  andrus,* with short stamens ; *brachy-
  anthus,* with short flowers ; *brachy-
  carpus,* with short fruit ; *brachycalyx,*
  with short calyx ; *brachyceras,* with
  short spur ; *brachypodus,* short-stalked.
Brachyblastus (s.m. II) : short-shoot, spur ;
  brachyblasti floriferi, flower-bearing
  short-shoots ; *inflorescentiae a brachy-
  blastis productae,* inflorescences produced from short-shoots.
brackish : salsugineus (adj. A), salsuginosus
  (adj. A).
Bract : bractea (s.f. I), *abl. sing.* bractea,
  nom. pl. bracteae, *abl. pl.* bracteis, *lit.*
  'a thin plate of metal'. *bracteae concavae obtusae virides in apice juvenili
  inflorescentiae diu imbricatae,* bracts
  concave blunt green at the young apex of
  the inflorescence for a long time imbricate. **bracteate** : bracteatus (adj. A).
bracteolate : bracteolatus (adj. A). **Bracteole** :   bracteola   (s.f. I),   *abl. sing.*
  bracteola, *nom. pl.* bracteolae, *abl. pl.*
  bracteolis.
bran-like : furfuraceus (adj. A).

Branch: ramus (s.m. II), *abl. sing.* ramo, *nom. pl.* rami, *gen. pl.* ramorum, *abl. pl.* ramis; *rami floriferi teretes tenuiter striati, in sicco nigrescentes, pube brevi adpressa vestiti*, flowering branches terete thinly striate, in a dried state blackish, with a short adpressed pubescence clothed; *ramis hornotinis teretibus striatis, pilos parcos breves gerentibus, mox glabrescentibus*, with branches of this year's growth terete striate, carrying sparse short hairs, soon becoming glabrous. **branch-bearing:** ramifer (adj. A); cf. BASIRAMIFER, INFERIORAMIFER, MEDIORAMIFER. **branched:** ramosus (adj. A). **very much branched:** ramosissimus (adj. A). **Branching:** ramificatio (s.f. III. vi). **branching:** ramificans (part. B). **226, 227, 229**

Branchlet: ramulus (s.m. II), *abl. sing.* ramulo, *nom. pl.* ramuli, *abl. pl.* ramulis; *ramuli primarii duplo vel triplo furcati, radiis primariis totam longitudinem ramulorum* $\frac{1}{3}$-$\frac{3}{5}$ *aequantibus*, primary branchlets 2 or 3 times furcate with primary rays the total length of the branchlets $\frac{1}{3}$-$\frac{3}{5}$ equalling; cf. WHORL.

Breadth: latitudo (s.f. III. vi), *abl. sing.* latitudine; *in processus duplo longiores latitudine corporis*, into processes twice as long as breadth of the body.

breaking: frangens (part. B); *see* BROKEN. **breaking apart:** rumpens (part. B). **breaking forth:** erumpens (part. B). **breaking off:** disrumpens (part. B). **breaking open:** refringens (part. B).

brevi-: *in L. comp.*, short; *brevispinus*, short-spined; *brevicollis*, short-necked.

Breviarium (s.n. II): summary, abridgment.

brevis (adj. B): short, of small extent. **brevissimus** (adj. A): extremely short. **breviter** (adv.): shortly, briefly.

Brevitas (s.f. III): shortness.

brick-red: latericius (adj. A), lateritius (adj. A), testaceus (adj. A).

Bridge: *in Silicoflagellates* ponticulus (s.m. II).

bright: clarus (adj. A), vividus (adj. A). **brightly:** clare (adv.), laete (adv.), vivide (adv.), splendide (adv.).

bringing forth: edens (part. B), efferens (part. B), pariens (part. B), gignens (part. B); cf. PRODUCING.

Bristle: seta (s.f. I), *abl. sing.* seta, *nom. pl.* setae, *abl. pl.* setis. **bristle-bearing:** setifer (adj. A). **bristle-like:** setaceus (adj. A). **bristle-shaped:** setiformis (adj. A). **bristly:** setosus (adj. A), echinatus (adj. A), hispidus (adj. A). **144, 227, 263**

brittle: fragilis (adj. B), friabilis (adj. B).

brittleness: fragilitas (s.f. III).

broad: latus (adj. A); *latus factus*, made broad, broadened. **broadly:** late (adv.).

brochidodromus (adj. A): brochidodrome; *see* VEINING.

broken: fractus (part. A), ruptus (part. A). **broken off:** effractus (part. A).

bronze: aeneus (adj. A).

Brook: rivus (s.m. II), *acc. sing.* rivum, **pertaining to brooks:** rivalis (adj. B). **Brooklet:** rivulus (s.m. II).

broom-like: scoparie (adv.), scopiformis (adj. B), scopulatus (adj. A).

brought: advectus (part. A), allatus (part. A).

brown: brunneus (adj. A), fuscus (adj. A), castaneus (adj. A), badius (adj. A), spadiceus (adj. A). **brownish:** brunneolus (adj. A); infuscatus (adj. A).

Bruise: contusum (s.n. II). **bruised:** contusus (part. A).

brumalis (adj. B): wintry.

brunneolus (adj. A): brownish. **brunneus** (adj. A): brown.

brush-like: aspergilliformis (adj. B), penicillatus (adj. A), q.v. **79, 239**

bryo-: *in Gk. comp.*, relating to mosses. **Bryologia** (s.f. I): the study of mosses.

bubalinus (adj. A): buff.

Bubble: bulla (s.f. I). **bubble-like:** bulliformis (adj. B).

Bud: gemma (s.f. I), *nom. pl.* gemmae, *abl. pl.* gemmis; *unopened flower*, alabastrum (s.n. II): *perigonium in alabastro globosum*, perigon in bud globose; *lobi calycis in aestivatione imbricati alabastrum ovatum obtusum formantes*, lobes of calyx in aestivation imbricate an ovate obtuse bud forming.

bud-bearing: gemmatus (adj. A), gemmifer (adj. A), gemmiparus (adj. A). **Budding:** gemmatio (s.f. III). **budding off:** pullulans (part. B). **bud-like:** gemmiformis (adj. B).

buff: bubalinus (adj. A).

Bulb: bulbus (s.m. II), *gen. sing.* bulbi, *abl. sing.* bulbo, *nom. pl.* bulbi, *gen. pl.* bulborum, *abl. pl.* bulbis. The diminutives *bulbilus* and *bulbulus* are similarly declined; *bulbus ovoideus 12-15 lineae crassus prolifer, bulbilis copiosis sub tunicis inclusis et bulbulis foliiferis liberis circumdatus*, bulb globose 12-15 lines (3·4 cm.) thick proliferous, with bulbils abounding under the tunics enclosed and by bulblets leaf-bearing free surrounded; *bulbus globosus 1-3 uncias diametro, tunicis papyraceis vestitus, sapore acerrimo, bulbillis inter tunicas exteriores plurimis parvis brunneis ovoideis sessilibus vel filo brevi fragili stipitatis*, bulb globose 1-3 inches (2·7-8 cm.) in diameter, with tunics papery clothed, with flavour most pungent, with bulbils between outer tunics many small brown ovoid sessile or by a short fragile thread stalked ; *bulbus parvus simplex conicus, tunicis interioribus reticulatim nervatis, exterioribus castaneis reticulato-fibrosis superne in collum longum productis, bulbillo extra tunicas hornas solitario anguste conico sessili vel longe stipitato stipite usque ad unciam unam longo,* bulb small simple conical with inner tunics reticulately nerved, outer chestnut-coloured reticulate-fibrous, above into a long neck lengthened out, with bulbil outside this year's tunics solitary narrowly conical sessile or long stalked with the stalk up to one inch (2·7 cm.) long ; *herba bulbis magnis venenatis tunicis membranaceis,* herb with bulbs large poisonous with tunics membranous ; *bulbus squamosus (tunicis nullis) juvenile albus deinde roseus vel luci expositus purpureus, primo globosus deinde oblatus, usque ad 6 cm. altus 9 cm. latus, squamis paucis vel multis acutis in bulbo juvenili fere orbicularibus in maturo late ovatis,* bulb scaly (with no tunics) youthfully white afterwards rose or when to light exposed becoming purple, at first globose later oblate, up to 6 cm. high 9 cm. broad, with scales few or many acute in the young bulb almost orbicular in the mature one broadly ovate. **Bulb-plate**: lectus (s.m. II). **bulb-shaped**: bulbiformis (adj. B).

Bulbil, Bulblet: bulbilus *or* bulbillus (s.m. II), *abl. pl.* bulbillis; bulbulus (s.m. II), *abl. pl.* bulbulis; *caulis in axillis foliorum superiorum bulbillis magnis viridibus vel brunneis praeditus,* stem in axils of upper leaves with bulbils large green or brown provided ; *caulis bulbilifer,* stem bulbil-bearing.

Bulbotuber (s.n. III) : corm.

bulbous: bulbosus (adj. A).

Bulge: protuberatio (s.f. III). **bulging**: protuberans (part. B), tumescens (part. B).

Bulla (s.f. I): bubble.

bullatus (adj. A): bullate, blistered or puckered.

bulliformis (adj. B): bubble-like.

Bundle: fascis (s.m. III), fasciculus (s.m. II).

Bung: obturamentum (s.n. II).

buried: infossus (part. A), obrutus (part. A), defossus (part. A).

burned: ambustus (part. A), ustulatus (part. A).

Bursicule: bursicula (s.f. I), *abl. sing.* bursicula.

Bush: frutex (s.f. III. i). **bushy**: fruticosus (adj. A), dumalis (adj. B).

but: sed (conj.), autem (conj.); *testa distincte sed subtiliter granulata,* testa distinctly but subtly granulate; *testa haud granulata autem striata,* testa not granulate but striate; *sed* usu. restricts meaning, *autem* emphatically introduces something different or contrary. **but for** (except for): praeter (prep. with acc.). **but indeed**: vero (adv.).

buttery: butyraceus (adj. A).

button-like: globuliformis (adj. B).

Buttresses: anterides (s.f. III pl.), *gen. pl.* anteridum; *anterides gralliformes,* stilt buttresses.

butyraceus (adj. A): buttery, butter-like.

by: 'near' ad (prep. with acc.), 'along' secundum (prep. with acc.), 'by whom *or* which done' a *or* ab (prep. with abl.), per (prep. with acc.); often expressed by abl. alone; *specimina a Linnaeo descripta,* specimens described by Linnaeus ; *lamina per tuberculationes asperata,* blade by tuberculations roughened ; *dimidio minor est,* it is less by half.

byssaceus (adj. A), **byssinus** (adj. A.), **byssoideus** (adj. A): byssoid, filamentous, cobwebby, made of fine threads, cottony. **237**

C

Cacumen (s.n. III. vi): peak, extreme top.

caducus (adj. A): falling, dropping off early. **cadens** (part B): falling. **342**

caelestis (adj. B): heavenly blue.

Caelum (s.n. II): the sky, the heavens; *toto caelo,* by the whole of heaven, exceedingly.

Caeoma (s.n. III): caeoma.

caeruleus (adj. A): blue, *esp.* the deep blue of the Mediterranean sky at midday. **caeruleo-griseus** (adj. A): sky grey. **caerulescens** (adj. B): becoming sky blue.

caesariatus (adj. A): covered with hair, long-haired.

caesius (adj. A): lavender blue (often applied by Romans to blue eyes).

Caespes (s.m. III. ii): tuft, sod of turf. **Caespitulus** (s.m. II), a little tuft. **caespiticius** (adj. A): made of turf, turf-like. **caespitosus** (adj. A), **cespitosus** (adj. A): growing in tufts or patches, caespitose. **486**

caeterum, etc. : *see* CETERUM.

Calathidium (s.n. II), **Calathium** (s.n. II): capitulum of Compositae.

calathiformis (adj. B), **calathinus** (adj. A): cup-shaped.

Calcar (s.n. III. x): spur, hollow nectar-producing appendage of calyx or corolla. **calcaratus** (adj. A): spurred. **calcariformis** (adj. B): spur-like.

calcareus (adj. A): chalky, limy; cf. CALX; *saxum calcareum*, limestone.

calceiformis (adj. B), **calceolatus** (adj. A): slipper-shaped.

Calcium: calcium (s.n. II).

calculated: computatus (part. A).

Caldarium (s.n. II): heated greenhouse, stove house, hot-house.

calendulinus (adj. A): marigold orange (H.C.C. 11).

calidus (adj. A): warm, hot.

calli-: *in Gk. comp.*, beautiful; *callianthus*, with beautiful flowers; *callicarpus*, with beautiful fruits; *callichromus*, beautifully coloured; cf. CALO-.

callifer (adj. A), **callosus** (adj. A): callose, bearing a callus or hardened thickening. **Callus**: callus (s.m. II), *abl. sing.* callo; callum (s.n. II), *abl. sing.* callo.

calm: tranquillus (adj. A); cf. QUIETUS.

calo-: *in Gk. comp.*, beautiful; *calochromus*, beautifully coloured; *caloneurus*, beautifully nerved; *calophlebius*, beautifully veined; *calophyllus*, with beautiful leaves; cf. CALLI-.

calvatus (adj. A), **calvifactus** (adj. A): made bald. **calvescens** (part. B): becoming bald. **calvus** (adj. A): bald, hairless, glabrous.

Calx (s.f. III): lime; *folia calce incrustata*, leaves encrusted with lime.

calyciformis (adj. B): calyx-like. **calycinus** (adj. A): belonging to the calyx, with a well-developed calyx.

calyculatus (adj. A): provided with a calyculus. **Calyculus** (s.m. II): epicalyx, whorls of bracts below the calyx, cup-like structure at the base of the sporangium.

-calymma (s.n. III. ix): *in Gk. comp.*, covering, veil.

Calyptra: calyptra (s.f. I), *gen. sing.* calyptrae, *abl. sing.* calyptra, *nom. pl.* calyptrae, *abl. pl.* calyptris; *calyptra longissima conica, latere fissa, basin versus pilis onusta*, calyptra very long conical, at the side split, towards the base with hairs burdened. **calyptratus** (adj. A): bearing a calyptra or cap-like covering. **calyptriformis** (adj. B): shaped like a conical cap.

Calyx: calyx (s.m. III. i), *gen. sing.* calycis, *abl. sing.* calyce, *nom. and acc. pl.* calyces, *dat. and abl. pl.* calycibus; *calyx cupuliformis truncatus irregulariter fissus c. 20 mm. longus intus glaber extus parce pilosus ruber vel viridis vel flavus, venulis multis percursus, costis haud*

prominentibus, calyx cupola-shaped truncate irregularly cleft about 20 mm. long inside glabrous outside sparingly pilose red or green or yellow, traversed by many veinlets, with ribs not prominent; *calyx cylindraceus 5-nervis, ore obliquo bilabiato, labio postico integro, labio antico 4-dentato dentibus aequalibus acutis*, calyx cylindric 5-nerved, with the mouth oblique two-lipped, with the posticous lip entire, with the anticous lip 4-toothed with equal acute teeth; *calyx deciduus campanulatus, vertice truncato, sed in lobos quinque breves imbricatos semicirculares rotundatos ciliatos ad 2 mm. longos ad 3 mm. latos divisus*, calyx deciduous campanulate, with the top truncate, but divided into five short imbricate semicircular rounded ciliate lobes to 2 mm. long 3 mm. broad; *calyx brevis inaequaliter et obtuse 5-fidus, laciniis in aestivatione valvatis sub bacca patens*, calyx short unequally and bluntly 5-cleft, with the segments valvate in aestivation, outspread beneath the berry; *bracteae amplae calycem includentes*, bracts large enclosing the calyx; *calycis tubus cylindricus extra (basi excepta) tomentosus intus glaber*, tube of the calyx cylindric outside (except at base) tomentose inside glabrous; *calycis segmenta rotundata*, segments of the calyx rounded; *calyce colorato vel viridi hirsuto vel glabro 2 cm. longo, basi attenuato, tubo corollae multo breviore, fructifero clavato, dentibus omnibus acutis*, with the calyx coloured or green hairy or glabrous 2 cm. long, with the base attenuate, much shorter than the tube of the corolla, in a fruiting state club-shaped, with the teeth all enlarged.

Cambium: cambium (s.n. II).

campaniformis (adj. B), **campanulatus** (adj. A): campanulate; *see* BELL-SHAPED. **campanulinus** (adj. A): campanula violet (H.C.C. 37). **campanuloides** (adj. B): resembling a campanula. **72**

campester (adj. B), **campestris** (adj. B): pertaining to plains or flat areas as opposed to hills and mountains; cf. COLLINUS, MONTANUS.

campo-, campso-, campto-, campylo-: *in Gk. comp.*, bent.

camptodromus (adj. A): camptodrome; *see* VEINING.

campylotropus (adj. A): campylotropous, i.e. with ovule curved on to its side so that the micropyle comes near the funicle.

canaliculatus (adj. A): canaliculate, i.e. with a longitudinal groove or channel. **45**

Canalis (s.m. III): groove, channel, canal.
canarinus (adj. A): canary yellow (H.C.C. 2).
cancellatus (adj. A): latticed; cf. CLATH-RATUS, CRIBRATUS. **243**
candicans (part. A): becoming pure white.
candidus (adj. A): pure glossy white; cf. WHITE.
canescens (part. B): becoming grey, greyish; cf. CANUS.
canino-: in L. comp., pertaining to dogs.
canus (adj. A): greyish white, usu. applied to hair-covering.
Cap: see OPERCULUM, PILEUS, PYXIDATUS.
cap-shaped: pileatus (adj. A).
capable: usu. expressed by verbal adj. ending in -ans or -ens when active, -bilis or -ilis when passive; cellulae divisibiles, cells capable of division.
caperatus (part. A): wrinkled.
capiens (part. B): containing.
capillaceus (adj. A), **capillaris** (adj. B), **capilliformis** (adj. B): capillary, hairlike, thread-like; see CAPILLUS. **50**
Capillitium: capillitium (s.n. II), abl. sing. capillitio.
Capillus (s.m. II): hair, hair's width, $\frac{1}{12}$ Paris line, 0·18 mm.
capitatus (adj. A): capitate, with a knoblike head or tip. **162**
Capitulum (s.m. II): head, q.v.
Capreolus (s.m. II): tendril.
capsicinus (adj. A): capsicum red (H.C.C. 1.15).
capsularis (adj. B): capsular, capsule-like.
Capsule: capsula (s.f. I), gen. sing. capsulae, nom. pl. capsulae, abl. pl. capsulis, lit. 'a small box or chest'; capsula calyce persistente paulo longior vel paulo brevior vel calycem aequans cylindracea membranacea apice in dentes 6 breves et stellatim patentes mox reflexos et revolutos dehiscens, capsule by a little longer or by a little shorter than the persistent calyx or equalling the calyx cylindric membranous dehiscing at the tip into 6 short and stellately spreading teeth soon reflexed and revolute; capsulae glabrae pars seminifera globosa 1 cm. alta, rostrum 2 cm. longum, of the glabrous capsule the seed-bearing part globose 1 cm. high, the beak 2 cm. long; capsula fusiformis 4-seminalis, retinaculis parvis acutis, capsule fusiform 4-seeded with retinacula small acute; capsula ima basi circumcirca rumpens, capsule at the very base all around breaking, i.e. circumscissile; capsula clavata fere ad medium solida, capsule club-shaped solid almost to the middle; capsula 3-5-locularis, valvis obtusis aut ad basin aut prope apicem sitis dehiscens, capsule 3-5-locular, dehiscing by blunt valves placed either at base or near the tip; capsulae torulosae (id est circum semina dilatatae inter semina constrictae) uniloculares bivalves, valvis oblongis a basi ad apicem dehiscentes, capsules torulose (i.e. around the seeds swollen, between the seeds constricted) one-chambered two-valved, with valves oblong from base to tip dehiscing; capsula nutans, ab apice ad basin dehiscens, capsule nodding, from tip to base dehiscing; capsula erecta ovato-cylindrica, vaginula vix longior, sub ore tantillum constricta, foliis perichaetii immersa absconditaque, capsule erect ovate-cylindric scarcely longer than the vaginule, below the mouth just a little constricted, by the leaves of the perichaetium covered and concealed.
capucinus (adj. A): nasturtium red (H.C.C. 14); cf. TROPAEOLINUS.
Caput (s.n. III. ii): head, in geographical names cape.
Carbo (s.m. III. vi): carbon, charcoal. **carbonaceus** (adj. A): black (and brittle) like charcoal. **carbonarius** (adj. A): pertaining to charcoal. **Carbonas** (s.m. III. ii): carbonate.
cardia-, cardio-: in Gk. comp., heart-.
cardinalis (adj. B): cardinal red (H.C.C. 8.22), lit. 'pertaining to a door-hinge'.
carefully: diligenter (adv.).
carelessly: neglectim (adv.), negligenter (adv.).
carens (part. B with abl.): lacking; cf. ABSENT.
Caries (s.f. III): decay.
Carina (s.f. I): keel, q.v. carinalis (adj. B): belonging to the keel; puncta carinalia, keel puncta. **carinatus** (adj. A); keeled. **44**
cariosus (adj. A): rotten, decayed.
carmesinus (adj. A): crimson, q.v.
carmine: carminus (adj. A), carmineus (adj. A), (H.C.C. 21); also coccineus (adj. A), carmesinus (adj. A).
carneus (adj. A): flesh-coloured.
carnosulus (adj. A): slightly fleshy. **carnosus** (adj. A): fleshy, succulent, soft but firm. **323**
Caro (s.f. III. vi): flesh; fructus carne alba aromatica dulci, fruit with flesh white aromatic sweet; caro pilei pallida, odore nauseoso, sapore amaro, fracta et exsiccata flavida, flesh of pileus pale with a sickening smell, with bitter taste, when broken and dried yellowish.
carp-, carpo-: in Gk. comp., relating to the fruit; see -CARPUS.
Carpel: carpellum (s.n. II), carpidium (s.n. II).
carpicus (adj. A): relating to the fruit.
Carpidium (s.n. II): carpel.

Carpocephalum: carpocephalum (s.n. II), *abl. sing.* carpocephalo.

carpogonial: carpogonialis (adj. B.). **Carpogonium**: carpogonium (s.n. II). **carpogonium-bearing**: carpogonifer.

Carpophorum (s.n. II): carpophore.

-carpus (s.m. II; adj. A), **-carpa** (s.f. I), **-carpium** (s.n. II): *in Gk. comp.*, -fruit, -fruited.

carried: portatus (part. A), vectus (part. A).

carrot-red: daucinus (adj. A). **carrot-shaped**: dauciformis (adj. B).

carrying: ferens (part. B), gerens (part. B); *in L. comp.*, -fer (adj. A), -ger (adj. A); *in Gk. comp.*, -phorus (adj. A).

cartilaginous: cartilagineus (adj. A). Usu. means 'flexible but firm and tough', but was used by E. Fries to indicate a polished cartilage-like aspect, hence 'ce mot est un des plus beaux traîtres du vocabulaire mycologique'. **314**

Caruncle: caruncula (s.f. I).

caryo-: *in Gk. comp.*, nut-, nucleus-.

Caryopsis: caryopsis (s.f. III. ii), *abl. sing.* caryopside, *nom. pl.* caryopsides, *abl. pl.* caryopsidibus; *caryopsis oblonga teres brunnea, glumis membranaceis involuta, libera, scutello tertiam partem caryopsis aequante, hilo basali anguste elliptico,* caryopsis (grain) oblong terete brown, by glumes membranous enclosed, free, with scutellum a third part of the caryopsis equalling, with hilum basal narrowly elliptic.

cask-shaped: cupiformis (adj. B), doliiformis (adj. B), orculiformis (adj. B).

cassideus (adj. A): helmet-shaped. **Cassis** (s.f. III): helmet, q.v.

cassus (adj. A): empty, devoid of (with gen. or abl.).

cast off: exutus (part A), rejectus (part A).

castaneus (adj. A): chestnut-coloured, from *Castanea*, the sweet chestnut.

castratus (part. A): castrated; applied to staminodes or filaments of stamens without anthers.

Catalogue: catalogus (s.m. II).

Cataphyll: cataphyllum (s.n. II), kataphyllum (s.n. II), *contrasting with* euphyllum 'true leaf'; *innovatio e duobus internodiis constans, quarum alterum breve duo cataphylla* (Niederblätter *Germanorum*) *opposita cito decidua, alterum longum duo euphylla* (Laubblätter *Germanorum*) *fert,* new shoot from two internodes consistently made, of which the short one bears two opposite quickly falling cataphylls (Niederblätter of the Germans), the other two true leaves (Laubblätter of the Germans).

Cataract: cataracta (s.f. I), *gen. sing.* cataractae, *nom. pl.* cataractae, *acc. pl.* cataractas; *in scopulis humidis ad cataractam Agoyan,* on wet rocks at the cataract Agoyan; *ad cataractas fluvii Negro,* at cataracts of the Rio Negro.

Catena (s.f. I): chain; *plantae in catenam cellularum sphaericarum dividentes,* plants into a chain of spherical cells dividing. **catenatus** (part. A): chained, chain-like. **cateniformis** (adj. B): chain-like. **catenulatus** (adj. A): resembling a little chain.

Caterva (s.f. I): crowd, company, group. **catervatim** (adv.): crowdedly, in groups.

catilliformis (adj. B): saucer-shaped, q.v.

Catkin: amentum (s.n. II), *abl. sing.* amento, *nom. pl.* amenta, *abl. pl.* amentis, *lit.* 'strap, thong'; julus (s.m. II); *flores dioici in amenta dispositi,* flowers dioecious in catkins arranged; *amentum masculum parvum gracile 2 cm. longum,* male catkin small slender 2 cm. long; *amenta villosa erecta densa ante foliorum evolutionem prodeuntia,* catkins villous erect dense before unfolding of leaves produced; *arbores vel frutices amentis sessilibus vel pedunculatis coaetaneis aut praecocibus,* trees or shrubs with catkins sessile or peduncled at the same time as the leaves or before them.

caudatus (adj. A): caudate, i.e. ending with a tail-like appendage. **152**

Caudex (s.m. III. i): rootstock, *lit.* 'trunk of tree'; cf. CAULORHIZA.

Caudicle: caudicula (s.f. I), *abl. sing.* caudicula, *nom. pl.* caudiculae, *abl. pl.* caudiculis; *caudiculae horizontales geniculatae 0·1 mm. longae apicem versus dilatatae,* caudicles horizontal abruptly bent 0·1 mm. long towards the tip broadened.

cauliflorus (adj. A): cauliflorous, bearing flowers or inflorescences direct from the main stem or older branches of a tree. **caulinus** (adj. A): cauline, pertaining to the stem, placed on the stem. **Caulis** (s.m. III. vii): stem, q.v.

Caulorhiza (s.f. I): rootstock.

Causa (s.f. I): cause, reason; *honoris causa,* for the sake of honour; *alimenti causa cultus,* for food cultivated.

causing: efficiens (part. B).

Cautes (s.f. III. vi): rough pointed rock.

Cave: caverna (s.f. I), spelunca (s.f. I).

cavernosus (adj. A): full of hollows *or* cavities. **cavernula**: *see* AIR-CHAMBER.

Cavitas (s.f. III. ii): cavity, hollow interior; *cavitatem versus,* towards the cavity.

Cavum (s.n. II): a hole, cavity. **cavus** (adj. A): hollow.

cecidiophorus (adj. A): gall-bearing.
celans (part. B): hiding.
celatus (part. A): hidden, concealed, q.v.
celeriter (adv.): quickly, with speed.
Cell: cellula (s.f. I), *abl. sing.* cellula, *nom. pl.* cellulae, *gen. pl.* cellularum, *abl. pl.* cellulis, *lit.* 'a small store-room or apartment'; *cellula apicalis aut supeme rotundata aut elongata conoidea acutaque,* apical cell either rounded above or elongated cone-shaped and acute; *cellulis magnis olivaceis in filis minoribus unicis, in majoribus divisione peripherica cellulae primariae pluribus zonas transversales distinctas formantes,* with cells large olive-green, in smaller filaments single, in larger ones by peripheral division of the primary cell several, forming transverse distinct zones; *folia rete pellucido, cellulis basilaribus rectangularibus ceteris hexagonis vel rhombeis 25-30 μ longis 8 μ latis, parietibus tenuibus flexuosis,* leaves with a pellucid network, with basal cells rectangular the others hexagonal or rhombic 25-30 μ long 8 μ broad, with the walls thin waved; *cellulis alaribus hexagonis, suprabasilaribus linearibus, ceteris quadratis, omnibus valde chlorophyllosis,* with alar cells hexagonal, those above the base linear, the rest quadrate, all containing much chlorophyll; *cellulis inter alias algas libere natantibus rectis solitariis 2-3 μ crassis,* with cells among other algae freely swimming straight solitary 2-3 μ thick; *fila e cellulis 10-20 elongatis composita,* filaments from cells 10-20 elongated made up; *dentes peristomii ad basin 3 cellulas lati,* teeth of peristome 3 cells wide at base.
-celled: -cellularis; *unicellularis,* one-celled; *bicellularis,* two-celled; *multicellularis,* many-celled; cf. LOCULUS.
cellular: cellulosus (adj. A).
Cellulose: cellulosa (s.f. I).
celsus (adj. A): high, lofty.
centensimus (adj. A): hundredth.
centi-: *in L. comp.,* hundred-; *centifolius,* with a hundred leaves, 'actually more than can be readily counted'. **centiens** (adv.), **centies** (adv.): hundred times, hundredfold.
Centimetre: centimetrum (s.n. II); cm.
central: centralis (adj. B), medius (adj. A); *ad centrum,* at the centre; *area centralis,* central area.
Centralium: centralium (s.n. II).
Centre: centrum (s.n. II) *dat. and abl. sing.* centro; *in centro laminae,* at the centre of the blade; *macula centrum occupans,* blotch occupying the centre; *a centro,* away from the centre.

centrifugus (adj. A): centrifugal, developing from the centre outwards.
centripetus (adj. A): centripetal, developing from outside towards the centre.
centum (num. adj. indecl.): hundred.
Cephalodium: cephalodium (s.n. II), *abl. sing.* cephalodio, *nom. pl.* cephalodia, *abl. pl.* cephalodiis.
-cephalus: *in Gk. comp.,* -headed; *monocephalus,* with a single head; *oligocephalus,* with few heads.
Cera (s.f. I): wax. **ceraceus** (adj. A): waxy, like bees-wax, wax-gold. **324**
-ceras (s.n. III): *in Gk. comp.,* -horn, horn-like projection.
cerasinus (adj. A): cherry red (H.C.C. *1.*22).
cerato-: *in Gk. comp.,* horned; *ceratothecus,* with horned thecae.
cerebriformis (adj. B): having an irregular brain-like appearance.
cereus (adj. A): waxen, waxy. **cerinus** (adj. A): waxy yellow, 'dull yellow with a soft mixture of reddish brown' (Lindley), wax-gold. **324**
cernuus (adj. A): slightly drooping. **407**
certainly: certe (adv.), nimirum (adv.).
certus (adj. A): definite, settled, specified.
cerussatus (adj. A): coloured with *or* as white lead.
cespitosus (adj. A): *see* CAESPITOSUS.
cetero (adv.), **ceteroquin** (adv.), **ceterum** (adv.): for the rest, otherwise. **ceterus** (adj. A): the other.
-chacta, -chaete (s.f. I): *in Gk. comp.,* bristle, long hair.
chaffy: paleaceus (adj. A).
Chain: catena (s.f. I). **chained, chain-like**: catenatus (part. A). **chain-like**: cateniformis (adj. B); cf. MONILIFORMIS.
Chalaza: chalaza (s.f. I), *abl. sing.* chalaza.
chalky: calcareus (adj. A), cretaceus (adj. A).
chalybeus (adj. A): steel-grey.
chamae-: *in Gk. comp.,* on the ground, lowly, creeping.
chambered: locellatus (adj. A).
chance, by: fortuito (adv.).
changed: mutatus (part. A), transmutatus (part. A), transformatus (part. A).
Channel: canalis (s.m. III).
channelled: canaliculatus (adj. A).
Character: character (s.m. III. v), *gen. sing.* characteris, *nom. pl.* characteres, *abl. pl.* characteribus; signum (s.n. II), *gen. sing.* signi, *nom. pl.* signa, *abl. pl.* signis; nota (s.f. I) characteristica (adj. A. f.); *scias characterem non constituere genus, sed genus characterem, characterem fluere e genere, non genus e charactere* (Linnaeus, *Phil. Bot.* no. 169), know that the character does not make the genus but the genus the

character, that the character derives from the genus not the genus from the character; *characteres e distributione venarum desumpti*, characters from the distribution of the veins taken. **characteristic**: proprius (adj. A), characteristicus (adj. A). **characteristically**: proprie (adv.).

chartaceus (adj. A): papery. **311**

checkered, chequered: tessellatus (adj. A).

cheil-, cheilo-: *in Gk. comp.*, lip-.

Cheilocystidium: cheilocystidium (s.n. II), *nom. pl.* cheilocystidia, *abl. pl.* cheilocystidiis.

cherry-red: cerasinus (adj. A).

chestnut-coloured: castaneus (adj. A).

chief: primarius (adj. A). **chiefly**: imprimis (adv.) 'in the first place', praesertim (adv.) 'put foremost, especially', praecipue (adv.) 'especially, particularly, taken first', maxime (adv.) 'in the highest degree', maxima pro parte (adv. phrase) 'for a very large part', apprime (adv.) 'at the very first'.

-chilus (adj. A): *in Gk. comp.*, -lipped.

Chink: rima (s.f. I), fissura (s.f. I); *see* CRACK.

chion-: *in Gk. comp.*, snow-.

-chiton (s.m. III): *in Gk. comp.*, covering, coat, tunic.

chlamyd-: *in Gk. comp.*, wearing a cloak *or* mantle.

Chlamydospore: chlamydospora (s.f. I), *abl. sing.* chlamydospora, *nom. pl.* chlamydosporae, *abl. pl.* chlamydosporis.

Chlamys (s.f. III): *in Gk. comp.*, cloak, mantle, covering.

chlor-, chloro-: *in Gk. comp.*, green-; *chloranthus*, green-flowered; *chlorocarpus*, green-fruited; *chloroleucus*, greenish-white; *chlorophyllus*, green-leaved; *chlorospathus*, with a green spathe; *chlorostictus*, green-spotted; *chloroxanthus*, greenish-yellow. These and similar Latinized Gk. comp. are used only as epithets.

Chlor-zinc-iodine: chlorozincus (s.m. II) ioduratus.

Chloride: chloridum (s.n. II). **Chlorine**: chlorinum (s.n. II).

chlorinus (adj. A): yellow-green.

Chlorophyll: chlorophyllum (s.n. II), *abl. sing.* chlorophyllo; *cellulae chlorophyllo impletae*, cells with chlorophyll filled. **chlorophyllose**: chlorophyllosus (adj. A); *cellulis chlorophyllosis*, with cells containing much chlorophyll.

Chloroplast: chloroplastus (s.m. II), *abl. sing.* chloroplasto, *nom. pl.* chloroplasti, *abl. pl.* chloroplastis.

Chlorozincus (s.m. II) ioduratus: chlor-zinc-iodine (Schulze's Solution of 30

gr. zinc chloride, 5 gr. potassium iodide, 1 gr. iodine, in 14 cc. distilled water); *vaginae chlorozinco iodurato caerulescentes*, sheaths treated with chlor-zinc-iodine becoming blue.

chocolate-brown: badius (adj. A).

chondroideus (adj. A): chondroid, hard and tough like cartilage, the hyphae of the thallus forming a solid mass.

chori-: *in Gk. comp.*, separate, free. *choripetalus*, having separate petals.

chosen: lectus (part. A), excerptus (part. A).

chrom-, chromat-, -chromus: *in Gk. comp.*, pertaining to colour, coloured.

Chromatophore: chromatophorum (s.n. II).

Chromosome: chromosoma (s.n. III), *nom. pl.* chromosomata, *gen. pl.* chromosomatum, *abl. pl.* chromosomatibus. **Chromosome-number**: chromosomatum numerus; *cf.* -PLOIDEUS.

-chromus: *in Gk. comp.*, -coloured; *heterochromus*, with diverse colours.

chroolepoideus (adj. A): resembling the lichen genus *Chroolepis*.

-chrous: *in Gk. comp.*, -coloured; *cf.* -CHROMUS.

chrys-, chryso-: *in Gk. comp.*, golden-; *chrysanthus*, golden-flowered; *chrysocarpus*, golden-fruited; *chrysocephalus*, with golden head; *chrysocladus*, with golden twigs; *chrysographes*, with golden markings; *chrysospermus*, with golden seeds. These and similar Latinized Gk. comp. are used only as epithets.

cibarius (adj. A): relating to food; *cf.* EDULIS. **Cibus** (s.m. II): food.

cicatricatus (adj. A): scarred. **252**

cicatricosus (adj. A): covered with scars. **Cicatrix** (s.f. III. i): scar. **285**

ciliate: ciliatus (adj. A). **Cilium**: cilium (s.n. II), *abl. sing.* cilio, *nom. pl.* cilia, *gen. pl.* ciliorum, *abl. pl.* ciliis.

Cincinnus: cincinnus (s.m. II), *acc. sing.* cincinnum, *abl. sing.* cincinno.

cinctus (part. A): encircled, girdled, enclosed.

cinerascens (part. B): greyish, becoming ash grey. **cinereus** (adj. A): ash grey.

cingens (part. B), **circumdatus** (part. A): surrounding, encircling, girdling. **Cingulum**: cingulum (s.n. II).

cinnabarinus (adj. A): vermilion (H.C.C. 18).

cinnameus (adj. A): smelling of cinnamon. **cinnamomeus** (adj. A): cinnamon-coloured, 'light brown mixed with yellow and red' (Lindley). **cinnamominus** (adj. A): of cinnamon.

circa (adv.), **circiter** (adv.), **circum** (adv.): around, in the neighbourhood, near, about, approximately. **circa, circiter, circum** (all three prep. with acc.) : near to, around. **circumcirca** (adv.): all around.

circinalis (adj. B), **circinatus** (part. A) : coiled inwards from the tip. **circinatim** (adv.) : in a coiled manner. **379, 417**

circularis (adj. B) : circular. **circulatim** (adv.) circulary. **Circulus** (s.m. II): circle; cf. ORBIS. **110**

circum, circumcirca : *see* CIRCA.

circumdatus : *see* CINGENS.

Circumference : ambitus (s.m. IV), circumferentia (s.f. I), circumscriptio (s.f. III. vi), peripheria (s.f. I).

circumnexus (part. A) : wrapped around, surrounding.

circumscissilis (adj. B), **circumscissus** (part. A) : circumscissile, opening by a complete transverse split cutting off the top like a cap or lid ; *capsula supra medium circumscissa, operculo deciduo,* capsule above the middle circumscissile, with the lid deciduous.

Circumscriptio (s.f. III. vi) : boundary, outline, circumference.

circumtextus (part. A) : woven all round.

cirratus (adj. A), **cirrhatus** (adj. A), **cirrosus** (adj. A), **cirrhosus** (adj. A) : tendrilled, ending in a narrow curled or wavy appendage. **cirriformis** (adj. B) : tendril-like. **Cirrus** (s.m. II), **Cirrhus** (s.m. II) : tendril, *lit.* 'curl of hair'. **142**

cis (prep. with acc.) : on this side. **cis-** : *in geographical comp.,* on this side of, i.e. nearest the writer ; *in regionibus cis- et transbaicalensibus,* in regions this side (west) and the other side (east) of Lake Baikal ; *cisalpinus,* this side (south) of the Alps.

Cisterna (s.f. I): cistern, reservoir.

cito (adv.) : quickly, speedily, soon.

citriformis (adj. B) : lemon-shaped.

citrinus (adj. A) : lemon yellow (H.C.C. 4). **viridis citrinus**: citron green (H.C.C. *1*.63).

City : urbs (s.f. III), *gen. sing.* urbis ; cf. TOWN.

clad-, -cladus (s.m. II) : *in Gk. comp.,* branch, shoot.

cladocarpus (adj. A) : cladocarpous, with fruit terminating a short special branch.

Cladode : cladodium (s.n. II) ; *see* PHYLLO-CLADE.

Cladophyll : cladophyllum (s.n. II) ; *see* PHYLLOCLADE.

Clamp-connexion : fibula (s.f. I), *abl. sing.* fibula, *nom. pl.* fibulae, *abl. pl.* fibulis ; *hyphae fibulis nullis,* hyphae with no clamps ; *hyphis fibulatis, hyphis fibuligeris,* with hyphae possessing clamps. The term *colligatio* (s.f. III) *unciformis* (adj. B), nom. pl. *colligationes unciformes,* has also been used.

clare (adv.) : clearly.

clasping : amplectens (part. B), adligans (part. B). **440**

Class : classis (s.f. III. vii), *abl. sing.* classi *or* classe, *nom. pl.* classes, *abl. pl.* classibus.

clathratus (adj. A) : latticed or pierced with openings like a grating or trellis ; cf. LATTICED.

clausus (part. A) : closed, q.v.

clavate : clavatus (adj. A). **9**

clavi- : *in L. comp.,* club-, cudgel-; *claviflorus,* with club-shaped flowers ; *claviformis,* club-shaped ; *clavipes,* with club-shaped pedicel. **9**

Clavis (s.f. III. vii) : key, series of statements of contrasting characters arranged to facilitate identification. For kinds, see *R.H.S. Dict. Gard. Suppl.,* 251-3 (1956); *in clavi*: in the key.

Clavula (s.f. I) : a little club, club-like receptacle of Clavaria ; *clavula filiformis tenax 10 mm. longa fistulosa ochroleuca,* club thread-like tough 10 mm. long fistular yellowish.

Claw : unguis (s.m. III. xii), *abl. sing.* ungue, *nom. pl.* ungues, *abl. pl.* unguibus. **clawed** : unguiculatus (adj. A).

Clay : argilla (s.f. I). **clay-coloured** : argillaceus (adj. A). **clayey** : argillaceus (adj. A), argillosus (adj. A).

clean : mundus (adj. A). **cleansed** : repurgatus (part. A).

clear : liquidus (adj. A), pellucidus (adj. A), hyalinus (adj. A). **clearly** : clare (adv.), perspicue (adv.), manifeste (adv.).

Cleft : fissura (s.f. I) ; *see* CRACK. **cleft** : fissus (part. A).

cleistocarpus (adj. A) : cleistocarpous, i.e. with fruit breaking open irregularly, not by a lid or valves.

cleistogamus (adj. A) : cleistogamous, i.e. fertilized within the unopened flower.

-clema (s.n. III), **-clemus** (adj. A) : *in Gk. comp.,* twig, branch, shoot. This has been used to form a number of adjectival terms for description of Charophyta; *gymnoclemus,* with ecortiate branchlets ; *heteroclemus,* having more than one form of branchlet in the same whorl ; *homoeoclemus,* having all branchlets in the same whorl alike ; *leptoclemus,* with slender branchlets ; *macroclemus,* with large branchlets ; *microclemus,* with small branchlets ; *orthoclemus,* with straight branchlets, *pachyclemus,* with thick branchlets ; *phloeoclemus,* with corticate branchlets ; *spanioclemus,* with few branchlets ; *streptoclemus,* with twisted branchlets.

-cles : *in Gk. comp.,* famous for, noted for, endowed with.

Cliff: scopulus (s.m. II), praeruptum (s.n. II).

climaticus (adj. A): climatic.

climbing: scandens (part. B); *see* TWINING.

Clinandrium: clinandrium (s.n. II), *abl. sing.* clinandrio.

clinging closely: adhaerens (part. B), haerens (part. B), cohaerens (part. B).

Clivus (s.m. II): slope of a hill; *clivorum*, of the slopes, growing on slopes.

Clock: horologium (s.n. II), *lit.* 'a water-clock *or* sun-dial'. clockwise: secundum horologii motum, helicte, sinistrorsum extus vis. anti-clockwise, counter-clockwise: contra horologii motum, anti-helicte, dextrorsum extus vis.; *see* TWINING.

Clone: clon (s.m. III), *acc. sing.* clonem, *gen. sing.* clonis, *nom. pl.* clones.

close together: approximatus (part. A), confertus (part. A), creber (adj. A); *see* COMPACTLY, CONTRACTUS.

closed: clausus (part. A), inapertus (adj. A), impervius (adj. A), reconditus (part. A), praeclusus (part. A).

closely: arte (adv.), arcte (adv.).

clothed: vestitus (part. A). clothing: investiens (part. B), vestiens (part. B).

Clothing: vestimentum (s.n. II), indumentum (s.n. II).

Cloud: nubes (s.f. III). clouded: nebulosus (adj. A). cloudy: nubilus (adj. A).

Club (cudgel): clava (s.f. I). club-shaped: clavatus (adj. A), claviformis (adj. B).

club-: *in L. comp.*, clavi-, *in Gk. comp.*, coryne-, coryno-; *clavigerus, corynephorus*, club-bearing; *clavistamineus, corynestemon*, with club-shaped stamen.

Clump: caespes (s.m. III) 'turf sod', fasciculus (s.m. II) 'little bundle'.

Cluster: fasciculus (s.m. II). clustered: fasciculatus (adj. A); cf. CROWDED. 487, 491

clypeatus (adj. A): shaped like the circular Roman shield (*clipeus*), as distinct from the oblong or oval shield (*scutum*); *see* SHIELD-SHAPED. 26

coacervatus (part. A): heaped together; cf. CUMULATUS. 491

coactus (part. A): felted.

coadunatus (part. A): united, fused together; *see* JOINED. 454

coaetaneus (adj. A): of the same age, i.e. appearing or maturing at the same time as leaves and flowers; *folia radicalia coaetanea linearia*, leaves radical appearing with the flowers linear; cf. HYSTERANTHUS, PRAECOX, PROTERANTHUS, SYNANTHUS.

coalescens (part. B): uniting together by growth.

coalitus (part. A): united by growth. 454

B.L.—O

coarctatus (part. A): pressed together, close-set, narrowed.

coarse: grossus (adj. A). coarsely: grosse (adv.); *folia grosse serrata*, leaves coarsely serrate.

Coast: ora (s.f. I), *acc. sing.* oram, *nom. pl.* orae, *acc. pl.* oras; cf. SEA-SHORE.

Coat: *see* TUNIC.

cobaltinus (adj. A): cobalt blue (H.C.C. 44).

cobwebby: arachnoideus (adj. A), araneosus (adj. A), byssaceus (adj. A).

coccineus: deep red, from scarlet to carmine (H.C.C. 21) and crimson (H.C.C. 22); cf. CRIMSON.

Coccolith: coccolithus (s.m. II).

Coccus: coccus (s.m. II), *abl. sing.* cocco, *nom. pl.* cocci, *abl. pl.* coccis.

cochlariformis (adj. B), cochlearis (adj. B): concave like a spoon, spoon-like, cochlear in aestivation. 386

cochleatus (adj. A): coiled like a snail's shell. 15

-codon (s.m. III): *in Gk. comp.*, bell, e.g. Codonopsis, Platycodon; *Platycodonis*, of Platycodon.

coelospermus (adj. A): hollow-seeded, i.e. having a seed or seed-like fruit hollowed out on one side.

Coenobium (s.n. II): colony, *lit.* 'cloister, convent'; cf. COLONY.

coenocyticus (adj. A): possessing a cell with many nuclei or a filament without septa between nuclei. Coenocytum (s.n. II): coenocyte.

coeruleus: *see* CAERULEUS.

coetaneus: *see* COAETANEUS.

coffeatus (adj. A): coffee-coloured, i.e. the brown of roasted coffee beans.

cognatus (adj. A): related.

cognitus (part. A): known, investigated, understood; *novarum et minus cognitarum stirpium descriptiones*, of new and little-known plants the descriptions; *species minus cognita*, a species little known; *species minus cognitae*, some species little known; *monographia tabulis omnium specierum hactenus cognitarum illustrata*, monograph illustrated with plates of all species up to this time known.

cohaerens (part. B): clinging together, cohering. Cohaerentia (s.f. I): coherence. 454

Cohort: cohors (s.f. III).

Coil: spira (s.f. I); cf. SPIRAL, TURN.

coiled inwards: circinatus (adj. A). 417

-cola (s.f. I; adj. A. f.): -dweller; exists only in L. comp. such as *agricola* (countryman), *monticola* (mountaineer); used adjectivally in such comp. as *ruricola* (dwelling in the country) but then treated as a noun in apposition the same for all genders even though the generic name is m. or n. despite the use by some authors of *-colus, -cola, -colum* as adjectival endings; cf. INCOLA.

cold: frigidus (adj. A), gelidus (adj. A), algidus (adj. A).

collapsing: collabens (part. B). **collapsed**: collapsus (part. A).

Collar: collum (s.n. II), q.v.

collateralis (adj. B): standing side by side.

collected: lectus (part. A). **Collection**: collectio (s.f. III. vi). **collective**: collectivus (adj. A). **Collector**: collector (s.m. III).

collenchymatosus (adj. A): collenchymatous, i.e. elongated and having the walls thickened at the angles; cf.· TRIGONES.

colliculosus (adj. A): covered with little rounded *or* hillock-like elevations.

colligans (part. B): binding together.

Colligatio (s.f. III): ligature, fastening, clamp. **colligatus** (part. A): joined together.

collinus (adj. A): pertaining to hills. **Collis** (s.m. III. vii): a hill.

Collocatio (s.f. III): arrangement, a putting together. **collocatus** (part. A): placed (*used in relation to other objects*).

Collum (s.n. II): neck, neck-like prolongation of organ, collar; *collum-cygni*, neck of a swan, an epithet applied to Aerangis and Psittacanthus species; *tunica in collum elongatum producta*, tunic into a long neck drawn out.

colonial: colonialis (adj. B). **Colony**: colonia (s.f. I), *acc. sing.* coloniam, *abl. sing.* colonia, *nom. pl.* coloniae, *abl. pl.* coloniis; *coloniae atrae hypophyllae effusae*, colonies black on the lower side of leaves outspread; *see* PLAGULA, COENOBIUM.

Colour: color (s.m. III. v), *gen. sing.* coloris, *abl. sing.* colore, *nom. pl.* colores, *abl. pl.* coloribus; see Chapter XVIII); *petala paene vel omnino ejusdem coloris quam sepala*, petals almost or quite the same colour as the sepals; *sine colore*, without colour. **changing colour**: allochrous (adj. A), mutabilis (adj. B), versicolor (adj. B). **coloured**: coloratus (part. A), fucatus (part. A), pictus (part. A). **-coloured**: *in L. comp.*, -color (adj. B), *in Gk. comp.*, -chrous, -chromus; *unicolor*, one-coloured; *bicolor, dichrous*, two-coloured; *concolor*, of the same colour; *discolor, heterochromus*, of different colours; *multicolor, polychromus*, many-coloured; *see* VARIEGATED *and under individual colours.*

colourless: incolor (adj. B), incoloratus (adj. A), achromaticus (adj. A), achromus (adj. A), sine colore; cf. TRANSPARENT.

Colpus (s.m. II): colpus.

Columella: columella (s.f. I), *gen. sing.* columellae, *abl. sing.* columella.

Column: columna (s.f. I), *gen. sing.* columnae, *abl. sing.* columna; *in Gk. comp.*, -stele; *columna-Trajana*, Trajan's Column, an epithet applied to a Pachycereus. **columnar**: columnaris (adj. B).

Coma (s.f. I): coma, i.e. hair-tuft on some seeds, tuft of leaves at top of an inflorescence, leafy crown of a palm tree; *semen fusiforme 3 mm. longum coma alba vel flava*, seed fusiform 3 mm. long with hair-tuft white or yellow. **comalis** (adj. A): comal, relating to a coma.

Comb: pecten (s.m. III. vi); *pectensimiarum*, monkey's comb; *see* PECTEN. **comb-**: *in L. comp.*, pectini-, *in Gk. comp.*, cten-, cteno-; *pectinifer*, combbearing; *ctenopetalus*, with petals cut like a comb. **comb-like**: pectinatus (adj. A). **200**

Combinatio (s.f. III): a joining two by two; *combinatio nova*, abbrev. **comb. nov.** or *n.c.*, nomenclatural new combination usually made by transferring an epithet from one generic name to another, often to displace one in common use.

combinatus (part. A): combined, united.

comesus (part. A): devoured, eaten up.

coming forth: oriens (part. B), prodiens (part. B), proveniens (part. B).

Comitatus (s.f. IV): county.

comitatus (part. A): accompanied, attended.

Commentarium (s.n. II), **Commentarius** (s.m. II): commentary, exposition, annotation.

commiscens (part. B): intermingling.

commissural: commissuralis (adj. B). **Commissure**: commissura (s.f. I), *abl. sing.* commissura, *nom. pl.* commissurae, *abl. pl.* commissuris.

common: communis (adj. B) 'possessed by several' as of an organ covering others, vulgaris (adj. B) 'occurring in plenty, ordinary', pervulgatus (part. A) 'very common'. **commonly**: plerumque (adv.), vulgo (adv.). **in common**: communiter (adv.), conjunctim (adv.).

comosus (adj. A): bearing a tuft of hairs or leaves, *lit.* 'with much *or* long hair', in Pliny, 'with many leaves'.

compact: compactus (part. A); cf. CLOSE TOGETHER, CONDENSATUS, CONTRACTUS, SPISSUS. **compactly**: confertim (adv.), spisse (adv.).

Compages (s.f. III): structure, a joining together; cf. FABRICA, STRUCTURA.

compaginatus (part. A): packed closely one over the other.

comparable: comparandus (adj. A).

comparate (adv.): relatively, comparatively.

Comparison: comparatio (s.f. III): *ex comparatione*, from a comparison.

complanatus (part. A): flattened out (usu. in one plane). complanus (adj. A): on the same plane, flush with.

complens (part. B): filling.

complete: completus (part. A) *lit.* 'filled full', totus (adj. A) 'all'. completed: effectus (part. A). completely: omnino (adv.), penitus (adv.), perfecte (adv.).

complex: complexus (part. A), tortuosus (adj. A).

complicatus (part. A): folded upon itself.

compluriens (adv.), compluries (adv.): several times.

compositus (part. A): put together, made up, united, compound. 203, 482

compressus (part. A): flattened, usually laterally; cf. COMPLANATUS. 30

con-: *see under* CUM.

concatenatus (part. A): linked, connected, joined.

concavus (adj. A): concave, curved inwards, hollowed out; cf. RECAVUS.

concealed: absconditus (part. A), tectus (part. A), occultus (part. A), celatus (part. A), reconditus (part. A).

concentric: concentricus (adj. A).

Conceptacle: conceptaculum (s.n. II) *lit.* 'a receptacle'; *conceptacula lateralia sphaerica sporas globosas purpureas foventia*, conceptacles lateral spherical the spores globose purple cherishing (enfolding); *conceptaculis sphaericis secus ramulos vel ad eorum basim sessilibus*, with conceptacles sphaerical along the branchlets or at the base of these sessile.

concerning: de (prep. with abl.).

Concha (s.f. I): shell of a mollusc. conchatus (adj. A), conchiformis (adj. B): shell-shaped, like the half-shell of a bivalve mollusc.

concinnus (adj. A): neat, pretty, elegant.

concolor (adj. B), concolorans (adj. B), concolorus (adj. A): of the same colour (as the subject of comparison), uniform in colour, of one colour throughout.

concomitatus (adj. A): attended, accompanied, associated.

concretus (part. A): grown together, hence 'with the prevailing idea of uniting, and generally of soft or liquid substances which thicken', compound, condensed, hardened, thickened; *fila intricata inter sese varie concreta*, filaments entangled between themselves variously grown together.

Conculta (s.f. I): convariety, group of cultivars.

condensatus (part. A): condensed (used of inflorescences with numerous flowers on short pedicels, hence very close to the axis).

Condition: status (s.m. IV); cf. STATE.

conditus (part. A): stored.

conduplicatus (part. A): conduplicate, i.e. folded together lengthwise. 371

Condylus (s.m. II): condyle, in drupes of Menispermaceae a projection of the endocarp into the seed-cavity, around which projection the seed is moulded.

Cone (fruit of Coniferae): strobilus (s.m. II); *see* STROBILE. Cone (solid figure): conus (s.m. II). cone-bearing: conifer (adj. A). cone-shaped: conicus (adj. A), conoideus (adj. A). cone-like: strobilaceous (adj. A), strobiliformis (adj. B), strobilinus (adj. A); cf. OB-.

confectus (part. A): made complete by.

conferruminatus (part. A): fused, joined together; cf. JOINED.

confertim (adv.): compactly, close together, densely. confertus (part. A): pressed close together, crowded, densely. 483

confervaceus (adj. A), confervoideus (adj. A): composed of loose filaments resembling genus Conferva.

confestim (adv.): immediately, speedily.

confictus (part. A): formed by, fabricated.

confined to: limitatus (part. A, with *ad* and acc.).

confinis (adj. B): bordering on, adjoining.

conflatus (part. A): produced, melted together, united; *frondes cellulis paucipluristratis conflatae*, fronds with cells in few to many layers united.

confluens (part. B): confluent, running together, blended into one; *folia maculis plusminusve confluentibus conspersa*, leaves with spots more or less confluent sprinkled. 454

Conformatio (s.f. III); shape, form; *ex conformatione disci*, according to the shape of the disc; cf. STRUCTURE.

conformis (adj. B): agreeing closely, of the same shape as.

confused: confusus (part. A).

Congener (s.m. II): member of the same genus.

congestus (part. A): crowded together.

conglomeratus (part. A): clustered, often spherically. 491

conglutinatus (part. A): glued together, united firmly together.

congruens (part. B): agreeing with, corresponding to (used with dat. or *cum* with abl.).

conical: conicus (adj. A); *see* CONE-SHAPED. **conically**: conice (adv.).

Conidiophore: conidiophorum (s.n. II), *nom. pl.* conidiophora, *abl. pl.* conidiophoris; *conidiophora simplicia recta*, conidiophores simple straight.

conidial: conidicus (adj. A).

Conidium: conidium (s.n. II), *abl. sing.* conidio, *nom. pl.* conidia, *abl. pl.* conidiis; *conidium hyalinum vel brunneum septatum*, conidium hyaline or brown septate; *conidia ovata vel obovata, in floccis peculiaribus erectis acrogena, nuncque in monilia contigue catenata, nunc et multo rarius solitaria, parce aut copiosius genita, semper autem candida et levissima*, conidia ovate or obovate, on special erect flocci acrogenous, and sometimes in necklaces closely linked, sometimes and much less often solitary, sparsely or more copiously produced, always white and quite smooth.

conifer (adj. A): cone-bearing, coniferous; *ad lignum arborum coniferarum*, on wood of coniferous trees.

Coniocyst: coniocysta (s.f. I), *abl. sing.* coniocysta; *see* CYST.

Conjugation: conjugatio (s.f. III), *gen. sing.* conjugationis; copulatio (s.f. III), *gen. sing.* copulationis; *cellulae post conjugationem*, cells after conjugation.

conjugatus (part. A), **conjunctus** (part. A): joined, connected, (*in Charophyta*) with antheridia and oogonia (sporophydia) at the same nodes, coupled. **225**

conjunctivus (adj. A): connecting, serving to unite.

conjungens (part. B): conjugating, fusing; *tubus conjungens*, conjugating tube.

connatus (part. A): connate, fused so as not to be separated without injury. **444**

connected: connexus (part. A), consociatus (part. A); cf. JOINED.

Connective: connectivum (s.n. II), *abl. sing.* connectivo; *antherarum connectivum crassum glabrum vel dorso barbatum*, of the anthers the connective thick glabrous or on the back bearded; *antherae connectivo crasso glabro vel dorso barbato*, anthers with the connective thick glabrous or on the back bearded; *antherae introrsae, loculis longitudinaliter dehiscentibus intus contiguis dorso connectivo lato sejunctis*, anthers introrse, with the loculi (anthercells) longitudinally dehiscing on the inside touching on the back by a broad connective separated; *connectivum lineari-filiforme postice ascendens loculum perfectum* (i.e. *fertilem*) *ferens, antice dejectum vel porrectum loculum cassum* (i.e. *sterilem*) *rarius perfectum ferens vel nudum acutum*, connective linear-filiform, at the front ascending a perfect (i.e. fertile) loculus carrying, at the back descending or straight a loculus empty (i.e. sterile) more rarely perfect carrying or naked acute; *connectivum supra antheram dilatatum*, connective above anther enlarged; *connectivum ultra loculos productum*, connective beyond the loculi continued.

connexus (part. A): connected.

connivens (part. B): connivent, coming in contact, converging. **429**

conoideus (adj. A): almost conical. **2**

consentaneus (adj. A): agreeing with, suited to.

conservatus (part. A): preserved, kept safe; cf. ASSERVATUS.

consequently: itaque (adv.).

considerably: aliquantum (adv.); cf. MUCH.

consimilis (adj. B): similar in all respects.

Consistentia (s.f. I): texture, consistence.

consisting of: constans (part. B) ex (with abl.).

consociatus (part. A): united, closely associated, connected.

Consocies (s.f. III): cluster; *consocies glandularum*, gland-field.

Consortio (s.f. III. vi), **Consortium** (s.n. II): community, company, fellowship, association: *in consortio algarum*, in company of algae, i.e. associated with algae.

Conspectus (s.m. IV): survey, short general view.

conspersus (part. A): sprinkled.

conspicue (adv.): remarkably, conspicuously. **conspicuus** (adj. A): striking, remarkable, conspicuous.

constans (part. B): constant, uniform, consistent, consisting of (with *ex* and abl.).

constantly: constanter(adv.), perpetuo(adv.).

constatus (part. A): composed of.

constipatus (part. A): crowded closely together.

constitutus (part. A): constituted, arranged, fixed; cf. COMPOSITUS.

constricted: constrictus (part. A), contractus (part. A). **Constriction**: constrictio (s.f. III), *abl. sing.* constrictione; strictura (s.f. I), *abl. sing.* strictura.

constructed: constructus (part. A) contextus (part. A), exstructus (part. A), fabricatus (part. A).

consumens (part. B): consuming, devouring, destroying.

consutus (part. A): joined together.

contained: contentus (part. A); *materia contenta*, contents.

containing: capiens (part. B); continens (part. B); *fructus oleum essentiale continens*, fruit containing essential oil.

contaminatus (part. A): polluted, contaminated, impure.
Contents: contentum (s.n. II), *abl. sing.* contento, *nom. pl.* contenta; contentus (s.m. IV), *abl. sing.* contentu, *nom. pl.* contentus; cf. CONTAINED.
contentus (part. A): contained, held together.
contextus (part. A): woven together, put together, constructed. Contextus (s.m. IV): hyphal mass between upper surface and subhymenium or trama of pileus, flesh, *lit.* connexion; cf. SUBSTANCE.
contiguus (adj. A), contingens (part. B): touching, adjoining, neighbouring.
continens (part. B): containing, holding together.
continentalis (adj. B): continental, relating to mainland as distinct from islands.
continuus (adj. A): continuous, uninterrupted, non-septate. **501**
contorted: contortus (part. A), *lit.* 'powerful, vehement, involved'. **383**
contortuplicatus (adj. A): entangled, intricate.
contra (adv. & prep. with acc.): against, opposite to, facing.
contractile: contractilis (adj. B); *vacuola contractilis*, contractile vacuole; cf. PULSANS.
contractus (part. A): drawn together into a narrow space, compressed, narrowed, contracted.
contrarius (adj. A): in an opposite direction, opposite, contrary; cf. CONVERSUS.
contributing: donans (part. B), contribuens (part. B).
controlled: gubernatus (part. A), q.v.
Contusum (s.n. II): bruise. contusus (part. A): bruised.
Conus (s.m. II): cone, q.v.
Convariety: convarietas (s.f. III), *nom. pl.* convarietates; conculta (s.f. I), *nom. pl.* concultae.
conveniens (part. B): agreeing.
converging: convergens (part. B), *to* ad (with acc.), *from* ab (with abl.), connivens (part. B); cf. CONNIVENT.
conversus (part. A): changed round, reversed; cf. OB-.
convexus (adj. A): convex, curved outwards. In class L. both *convexus* and *concavus* were used in the sense of 'vaulted, arched, curved'.
convolutus (part. A): convolute, rolled up longitudinally; cf. VERNATION. **368, 402**
copiose (adv.): plentifully, abundantly.
copiosus (adj. A): well-supplied, abounding, plentiful.
Copper-engraving: icon (s.f. III) in aes incisa; *see* ILLUSTRATION.

coppery: cupreus (adj. A), cuprinus (adj. A).
copro-: *in* Gk. *comp.*, relating to dung, excrement; *coprobius*, living on dung; *see* DUNG.
Copula (s.f. I): intercalary band of diatom.
Copulatio (s.f. III): conjugation, q.v.
coralliformis (adj. B): coral-like in form. corallinus (adj. A): coral red. coralloides (adj. B): of coral, coral-like.
Corculum (s.n. II): plumule.
cordatus (adj. A): cordate, i.e. with two equal rounded lobes at base, *lit.* 'of good heart, wise, prudent'. cordiformis (adj. B): heart-shaped. **122, 166**
coriaceus (adj. A): coriaceous, leathery.
Corium (s.n. II): skin, rind, covering. **312**
Cork: suber (s.n. III. v), *gen. sing.* suberis, *abl. sing.* subere. corky: suberosus (adj. A) (not to be confused with *suberosus*, slightly erose). **317**
Corm: cormus (s.m. III), *abl. sing.* cormo, *nom. pl.* cormi, *abl. pl.* cormis, *lit.* 'a trunk'; for the solid bulb-like stem-base of monocotyledons, the older authors, e.g. Ker-Gawler, used *bulbo-tuber*; *cormus magnus sub-globosus 5 cm. crassus, tunicis brunneis membranaceis*, corm large almost globose 5 cm. thick, with tunics brown membranous.
Corner: angulus (s.m. II).
corneus (adj. A): horny, hard and close-textured but not brittle. **320**
Cornfield: seges (s.f. III. ii). pertaining to cornfields: segetalis (adj. B).
cornflower blue: cyaninus (adj. A), *also* cyaneus (adj. A).
corniculatus (adj. A): with a small horn-like appendage, curved in the form of a horn. Corniculum (s.n. II): small horn-like appendage. **55**
-cornis (adj. B), -cornutus (adj. A): *in* L. *comp.*, -horned; *bicornis*, two-horned; *tricornis*, *tricornutus*, three-horned. Cornu (s.n. IV): horn, horn-like process, spur; *cornu bovis*, horn of an ox; *cornu caprae*, horn of a she-goat; *cornu cervi*, horn of a deer; *cornu damae*, horn of a fallow deer. cornutus (adj. A); horn-shaped. **55**
Corolla: corolla (s.f. I), *acc. sing.* corollam, *gen. sing.* corollae, *dat. sing.* corollae, *abl. sing.* corolla, *nom. pl.* corollae, *acc. pl.* corollas, *gen. pl.* corollarum, *abl. pl.* corollis; *corolla rotata tubulosa infundibuliformis vel campanulata, intus glabra pilosa vel villosa*, corolla rotate tubular funnel-shaped or campanulate, on the inside glabrous pilose or villous; *corolla (tubo subnullo) explanata quadrifida bilabiata*, corolla (with an almost non-existent tube) outspread four-cleft two-lipped; *corolla flava, medio 6 mm.*

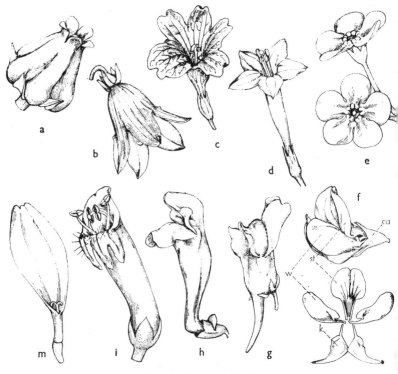

Fig. 34   Types of Corolla

a, urceolatus; b, campanulatus; c, infundibularis; d, hypocrateriformis; e, rotatus; f, papilionaceus (ca, calyx; st, vexillum; w,
alae; k, carina); g, personatus basi calcaratus; h, bilabiatus tubo
basi geniculato superne dilatato; i, bilabiatus tubo fere cylindrico;
m, ligulatus (drawing by Marion E. Ruff, from G. H. M. Lawrence,
Taxonomy of vascular Plants; 1951)

crassa, ad faucem ampliata, corolla
yellow, at the middle 6 mm. thick,
widened at the throat; *stamina tot quot
corollae lobi iisque alterna, fauci vel
tubo corollae affixa,* stamens as many as
the lobes of the corolla and alternate
with these, attached to the throat or
tube of the corolla; *filamenta corollae
adnata,* filaments adnate to the corolla.

corollaceus (adj. A): corolla-like, petaloid, coloured and shaped like a corolla.
corollatus (adj. A): provided with a
corolla. **corolliflorus** (adj. A): having
the calyx, corolla and ovary inserted on
the disc and the stamens inserted on the
corolla. **corollinus** (adj. A): corolla-
like, belonging to the corolla, inserted
on the corolla.

Corona: corona (s.f. I), *acc. sing.* coronam,
gen. sing. coronae, *abl. sing.* corona;
*corona magna infundibuliformis alba vel
flavescens margine sexloba,* corona
large funnel-shaped white or yellowish
at the margin six-lobed; *coronae
rudimentum 3 mm. longum,* of the
corona the rudiment 3 mm. long; cf.
PARASTAS.

coronans (part. B): crowning. **coronatus**
(part. A): crowned. **coronarius** (adj.
A): coronary, of a wreath, suitable for
garlands. **468**

coroniformis (adj. B): having the form of
a corona or coronula.

Coronule: coronula (s.f. I), *gen. sing.*
coronulae, *abl. sing.* coronula; *coronula
persistens 0·7 mm. lata, 0·4 mm. alta,*

coronule persistent 0·7 mm. broad, 0·4 mm. high.

Corpus (s.n. III): body.

Corpuscle: corpusculum (s.n. II).

corrected: emendatus (part. A).

correctly: rite (adv.).

corresponding to: congruens (part. B), consentaneus (adj. A).

corrugatus (part. A): corrugated, crumpled irregularly, furrowed or in folds. **375**

Cortex (s.m. III. i): bark, cortex or substantial outer layer. **corticalis** (adj. B), **corticeus** (adj. A): cortical. **corticatus** (adj. A): covered with bark, a cortex or (in Lichens) a continuous layer of hyphal tissue, corticate, coated. **318**

Cortina: cortina (s.f. I).

Corymb: corymbus (s.m. II), *abl. sing.* corymbo, *gen. sing.* and *nom. pl.* corymbi, *abl. pl.* corymbis, *lit.* a cluster of flowers or of fruits, particularly ivy-berries; *corymbus terminalis 10 cm. latus*, corymb terminal 10 cm. broad; *corymbi flores omnes fertiles conformes*, of the corymb the flowers all fertile alike; *capitula in corymbum disposita*, heads in a corymb arranged. **corymbose**: corymbosus (adj. A). **corymbosely**: corymbose (adv.).

cosmopolitus (adj. A): world-wide.

Cost: impensa (s.f. I), sumptus (s.m. IV).

Costa (s.f. I): midrib. **costalis** (adj. A): relating to the midrib. **costatus** (adj. A): ribbed, having one or more primary veins or ridges; *see* VEINING. **344**

cottony: gossypinus (adj. A), byssaceus (adj. A), q.v.

Cotyledon: cotyledon (s.f. III. vi), *abl. sing.* cotyledone, *nom. pl.* cotyledones, *abl. pl.* cotyledonibus; *cotyledones magnae crassae aequales (vel una majore) carnosae liberae sed arcte contiguae radicula brevis vel brevissima longiores*, cotyledons large thick equal (or with one larger) fleshy free but tightly touching than the short or most short radicle longer; *embryo rectus, cotyledonibus angustis liberis radicula brevi vel brevissima longioribus*, embryo straight, with cotyledons narrow free than the short or most short radicle longer; *cotyledones breves obtusae non raro cum radicula in massam homogeneam carnosam coalitae*, cotyledons short blunt not rarely with the radicle into a fleshy homogeneous mass fused; *embryo cotyledonibus conferruminatis*, embryo with cotyledons fused together.

counterfeiting: mentiens (part. B).

countless: innumerus (adj. A), innumerabilis (adj. B); *in Gk. comp.*, myri-, myrio-.

County: comitatus (s.f. IV); *in comitatu Nicaeensi*, in Comté de Nice.

covered: tectus (part. A), obtectus (part. A), obductus (part. A), velatus (part. A); cf. EXPOSED. **covering**: tegens (part. B), obtegens (part. B), obducens (part. B).

Crack: rima (s.f. I), *abl. sing.* rima, *nom. pl.* rimae, *abl. pl.* rimis, fissura (s.f. I), *abl. sing.* fissura, *nom. pl.* fissurae, *abl. pl.* fissuris.

cracked: rimosus (adj. A). **minutely cracked**: rimulosus (adj. A).

craspedromus (adj. A): *see* VEINING.

crassiusculus (adj. A): moderately thick. **crassus** (adj. A): thick. **326**

Crater (s.m. III): bowl.

crateriformis (adj. A): bowl-shaped, i.e. hemispherical and concave. **81**

cream-coloured: cremeus (adj. A) 'a very pale greyed yellow' (H. A. Dade), cremicolor (adj. B), eburneus (adj. A) 'ivory'.

creber (adj. A): close, pressed together, frequent, numerous. **crebro** (adv.): in close succession, often, repeatedly.

creeping: repens (part. B), reptans (part. B), serpens (part. B).

cremeus (adj. A): cream-coloured, q.v.

Cremocarp: cremocarpium (s.n. II), *abl. sing.* cremocarpio.

Crena (s.f. I): rounded tooth on leaf-margin, etc. **crenatus** (adj. A): crenate, having rounded teeth, scalloped. **crenulatus** (adj. A): crenulate, having small rounded teeth. **181**

crescens (part. B): growing.

crescent-shaped: lunaris (adj. B), lunatus (adj. A). **124**

Crest: crista (s.f. I); *in Gk. comp.*, loph-, lophio-, lopho-. **crested**: cristatus (adj. A) **57**

cretaceus (adj. A): chalky, chalk-white.

cretus (part. A): increased, enlarged.

Crevice: rima (s.f. I), fissura (s.f. I).

cribratus (adj. A), **cribrosus** (adj. A): sieve-like, profusely perforated, with numerous small holes; cf. LATTICED.

crimson: carmesinus (adj. A), kermesinus (adj. A), *also* coccineus (adj. A). These words together with 'carmine' all derive ultimately from the names of the oak-dwelling cochineal insects, in L. *coccum*, from Gk. *kokkos* 'berry', and Persian *qirmiz*, cognate with Sanskrit *krmis* 'worm' and L. *vermis* 'worm', whence French 'vermillon', English 'vermilion'; *See* Chapter XVIII.

Crinis (s.m. III): the hair. **crinitus** (adj. A): having tufts of long weak hairs.

crispatus (part. A), **crispus** (adj. A): crisped, irregularly waved and twisted, kinky, curled. **185**

Crista (s.f. I): crest, terminal tuft; *crista galli*, cock's comb, an epithet applied to species of Corydalis, Erythrina,

Polygala, Rhinanthus, etc. **cristatus** (adj. A): crested. **57**

croceus (adj. A): saffron yellow (H.C.C. 7), cadmium yellow, from the stigmas of *Crocus sativus*.

Cross: crux (s.f. III. i), *gen. sing.* crucis, *abl. sing.* cruce. **cross-shaped**: cruciatus (adj. A), cruciformis (adj. B). **crosswise**: cruciatim (adv.).

Cross-beam: transtrum (s.n. II).

Cross-wall: septum (s.n. II), *abl. sing.* septo, *nom. pl.* septa, *abl. pl.* septis.

Crowd: turba (s.f. I). **crowded together**: aggregatus (part. A), coarctatus (part. A), coacervatus (part. A), confertus (part. A), congestus (part. A), constipatus (part. A), creber (adj. A), conglomeratus (part. A), catervatim (adv.). **483**

crowned: coronatus (part. A). **crowning**: coronans (part. B). **468**

cruciatim (adv.): cross-wise. **cruciatus** (adj. A), **cruciformis** (adj. B): cross-shaped.

crudus (adj. A): raw, uncooked, immature.

cruentus (adj. A): blood-stained.

crumbling: fatiscens (part. B).

crumpled: corrugatus (part. A).

Crus (s.n. III. iv): leg.

crushed: obtritus (part. A).

Crusta (s.f. I): crust, upper surface of pileus of an agaric or thallus of a lichen; *pileus crusta resinosa laccata nitenti tectus*, pileus with a crust resinous varnished shining covered. **crustaceus** (adj. A): hard, thin and brittle, as the thin closely adhering thallus of a lichen, crust-like forming a crust. **313**

Crux (s.f. III. i): cross; *crux maltae*, *crux melitensis*, Maltese cross.

crypt-, crypto-: *in Gk. comp.*, covered, hidden, concealed.

cryptogamicus (adj. A), **cryptogamus** (adj. A): cryptogamic, relating to cryptogams.

Cryptosome: cryptosoma (s.n. III. ix), *nom. pl.* cryptosomata, *abl. pl.* cryptosomatibus.

Crystal: crystallum (s.n. II); *thallus crystallis minutis quarciticis obtectus*, thallus with crystals minute quartz-like covered. **crystalline**: crystallinus (adj. A).

cten-, cteno-, -ctenium (s.n. II): *in Gk. comp.*, comb, e.g. *Ctenolophon* 'comb-crest', *Pithecoctenium* 'monkey's comb'.

cubical: cubicus (adj. A), cubiformis (adj. B). **8**

Cubitus (s.m. II): elbow, cubit, ell, the distance from the elbow to the tip of middle finger, 1½ feet, approx. 46 cm. **cubitalis** (adj. B): 1½ feet long.

cucullatus (adj. A): hooded. **Cucullus** (s.m. II): hood.

cujus (gen. sing. of *qui*): of which, whose.

cujusvis (m.), **cujavis** (f.), **cujumvis** (n.): of any one; *folia cujusvis rami variabilia*, leaves of any one branch variable.

Culm: culmus (s.m. II), *abl. sing.* culmo, *nom. pl.* culmi, *abl. pl.* culmis; *culmus cum panicula 2-3 pedalis erectus*, culm including panicle 2-3 feet high erect; *culmi erecti vel basi leviter geniculati robusti glabri teretes simplices vel ramosi glauci multinodes, internodiis 20 cm. vel ultra longis*, culms erect or at base somewhat abruptly bent robust glabrous terete simple or branched glaucous many-noded, with internodes 20 cm. or more long; *gramina culmis erectis simplicibus vel ramosis, ad genicula sericeo-barbatis, cetero glabris*, grasses with culms erect simple or branched, at nodes silkily bearded, for the rest glabrous.

Culmen (s.n. III. vi), **Culmen superius**: crownshaft, trunk-like extension of top of palm trunk formed by erect petiole-bases enclosing terminal bud; cf. *Gentes Herb.*, 7: 178 (1946).

Cultigen: cultigenum (s.n. II), *nom. pl.* cultigena. **Cultiplex**: cultiplex (s.m. II), *nom. pl.* cultiplices. **Cultivar**: cultivarietas (s.f. III), *nom. pl.* cultivarietes; cultivar (s.n. III), *nom. pl.* cultivaria. **cultivated**: cultus (part. A); cf. SATIVUS. **Cultivation**: cultura (s.f. I); cf. FIELD, GARDEN, NURSERY, SEED-LIST. **Culture**: cultura (s.f. I); *in culturis vetustioribus*, in older cultures; *in cultura pura in agaro Bristolii*, in pure culture on Bristol's agar.

cultratus (adj. B): cultrate, i.e. shaped like a knife-blade, the sides parallel with length to breadth about 6 to 1; essentially the same as *loratus*. **cultriformis** (adj. B): 'curved like a short wide scimitar' (H. N. Dixon).

cum (conj.), **quum** (conj.): when, while, whereas, although, then; cf. TUM.

cum (prep. with abl.): with, together with, along with. In compounds before *b, m, p* the earlier form *com-* is preserved, as in *combinatio, commissura, compositus*, but it becomes *cor-* before *r*, as in *corrugatus, corruptus*, and often *col-* before *l*, as in *collectio, collegium*, and *con-* before most consonants, as in *concolor, condensatus, confertus, congestus, conspicuus*, and is contracted to *co-* before *h* and vowels, as in *coarctatus, cohaerens*. Its effect is to indicate bringing together or intensification or completion; *stamina cum antheribus 5 mm. longa*, stamens together with (including) anthers 5 mm. long; *stylus* *cum stigmate 4 mm. longus*, style together with the stigma 4 mm. long; *calyx in parte inferiore cum ovario connatus*, calyx in lower part with (to) the ovary connate; *ovarium cum disco confluens*, ovary with (into) disc confluent; *cum descriptione latina*, with (having) Latin description; *specimen jamaicense cum typo e Cuba bene congruens*, Jamaican specimen with type from Cuba well agreeing; *speciminibus omnino cum descriptione Kunthii convenientibus*, with specimens entirely with (to) the description of Kunth conforming.

cumulatus (part. A): heaped; cf. COACERVATUS. **Cumulus** (s.m. II): heap, pile.

cunctanter (adv.): slowly, with delay.

cuneate: cuneatus (adj. A), cuneiformis (adj. B). **broadly cuneate**: late cuneatus (adj. A). **narrowly cuneate**: anguste cuneatus (adj. A); *foliis basi late vel anguste cuneatis*, with leaves at base broadly or narrowly cuneate. **113, 175**

Cup: cupula (s.f. I), *abl. sing.* cupula, *nom. pl.* cupulae, *abl. pl.* cupulis; *cupulae minutissimae 0·5-1 mm. in vivo at exsiccatae vix 0·3 mm. crassae hemisphaericae vel obconicae viridi-caerulescentes gelatinosae glaberrimae*, cups very minute 0·5-1 mm. thick in a living state but scarcely 0·3 mm. when dried hemispherical or obconical of greenbluish colour gelatinous quite glabrous; *see* ACORN-CUP. **cup-**: *in L. and Gk. comp.*, calath-, cotyl-, cyath-, cymbio-, scyph- (all of Gk. origin but adopted and latinized by Romans); *in L. comp. only* acetabul-, pocul-, *in Gk. comp. only* peli-. L. *calix* on account of its resemblance to the loan-word *calyx* (Gk. καλυζ) should not be used.

cup-shaped: cupulatus (adj. A), calathinus (adj. A), cyathiformis (adj. B), poculiformis (adj. B); cf. OLLIFORMIS. **74, 83**

cupelliformis (adj. B): like a little cask.

cupiformis (adj. B): cask-shaped, tub-shaped; cf. BARREL-SHAPED, DOLIIFORMIS.

cupola-shaped: cupuliformis (adj. A). **75**

cupreus (adj. A), **cuprinus** (adj. A): coppery.

Cupule: cupula (s.f. I): *see* ACORN-CUP, CUP.

Curator: custos (s.c. III).

curiosus (adj. A): careful, diligent, inquisitive, curious (in the seventeenth- and eighteenth-century sense, not of modern booksellers' catalogues); *rhabarbarologia seu curiosa rhabarbari disquisitio, illius etymologiam differentiam locum natalem formam temperamentum vires detegens*, 'rhubarbology' or an assiduous

B.L.—O 2

investigation of rhubarb, its etymology, distinguishing feature, place of origin, form, constitution and virtues revealing (title of a work, 782 pages long, of 1679, by a German professor of medicine, Mathias Tiling).

curled: crispus (adj. A), crispatus (part. A). **185**

curtus (adj. A): shortened, short.

Curvature: curvatura (s.f. I). **Curve**: curvamen (s.f. III), *abl. sing.* curvamine; arcus (s.m. IV), *abl. sing.* arcu. **curve-**: *in Gk. comp.*, cyrto-, *in L. comp.*, curvi-; *curvisepalus, cyrtosepalus*, with curved or bent sepals; *curvicaudatus*, with a curved tail; *curvinervis, curvinervius*, with more or less parallel curved nerves; *curvirostratus*, with a curved beak; *curviserratus*, with curved teeth pointing forwards; *curvispinus*, with curved spines. **curved**: curvus (adj. A), curvatus (part. A), arcuatus (part. A); cf. BENT. **curvedly**: curvatim (adv.). **35, 351**

Cushion: pulvinus (s.m. II), *abl. sing.* pulvino, *nom. pl.* pulvini, *abl. pl.* pulvinis; used both for plants of cushion-like growth and for the cushion-like swollen base of a petiole; *herba caespitosa pulvinos hemisphaericos formans*, herb tufted forming hemispherical cushions. **cushion-shaped**: pulvinatus (adj. A), pulviniformis (adj. B). **33**

Cusp: cuspis (s.f. III), *abl. sing.* cuspide. **cuspidate**: cuspidatus (adj. A). **141**

Custom: consuetudo (s.f. III), *abl. sing.* consuetudine; mos (s.f. III), *abl. sing.* more; *more*, according to custom; *contra morem consuetudinemque*, contrary to custom. **customarily**: consuete (adv.), ad normam (adv. phrase).

Custos (s.c. III): keeper, curator; *custos sylvarum*, forest-officer.

Cut (s.): incisura (s.f. I). **Cut** (adj.): scissus (part. A), sectus (part. A) 'cut to reach midrib', incisus (part. A) 'cut deeply', partitus (part. A) 'reaching more than half-way to midrib', fissus (part. A) 'reaching half-way or less to midrib'. **cut into, engraved**: incisus (part. A), insculptus (part. A). **cut off**: abscissus (part. A). **cut out**: exsectus (part. A). **189-195**

Cuticle: cuticula (s.f. I), *abl. sing.* cuticula; cutis (s.f. III), *abl. sing.* cute (used mostly in mycology). **cuticular**: cuticularis (adj. B).

Cutting: talea (s.f. I).

cyan-, cyano-: *in Gk. comp.*, blue; *cyananthus*, blue-flowered; *cyanospermus*, blue-seeded. **cyanescens** (adj. B): becoming blue. **cyaneus** (adj. A): dark blue. **cyaninus** (adj. A): cornflower blue (H.C.C. *1*.42).

cyath-: *in Gk. and L. comp.*, cup-; *cyathifer, cyathophorus*, cup-bearing; *cyathiflorus*, with cup-shaped flowers. **cyathiformis** (adj. B): cup-shaped, a little wider at the top than the bottom. **74**

Cyathium: cyathium (s.n. II), *gen. sing.* cyathii, *abl. sing.* cyathio, *nom. pl.* cyathia, *abl. pl.* cyathiis, *gen. pl.* cyathiorum; *cyathium primarium masculum, cyathia secundaria bisexalia,* cyathium primary male, cyathia secondary bisexual; *herba cyathiis in cymam unitis vel in cymas usque 8 apice caulis dispositis,* cyathia in one cyme or in up to 8 cymes at tip of stem arranged.

cyclicus (adj. A): coiled into a circle, relating to a circle. **cyclicalis** (adj. B): rolled up circularly. **cyclo-**: *in Gk. comp.*, circular. **-cyclus**: *in Gk. and L. comp.*, whorled.

cygneus (adj. A): relating to swans, curved suddenly downwards like a swan's neck. **Cygnus** (s.m. II): swan; *collum cygni,* swan's neck; *fluvius cygnorum,* river of swans, i.e. Swan River Colony, Western Australia.

Cylinder: cylindrus (s.m. II). **cylindric**: cylindraceus (adj. A), cylindricus (adj. A), cylindratus (adj. A). **cylindrically**: cylindrice (adv.).

Cymba (s.f. I): woody durable persistent boat-like spathe *or* spathe-valve of palm, *lit.* 'a boat'.

cymbiformis (adj. B): boat-shaped. **46**

Cyme: cyma (s.f. I), *gen. sing.* cymae, *abl. pl.* cyma, *nom. pl.* cymae, *abl. pl.* cymis, *lit.* 'young sprout of cabbage'.

Cypsela: cypsela (s.f. I).

Cyst: *as technical term*, cysta (s.f. I), *gen. sing.* cystae, *abl. sing.* cysta, *nom. pl.* cystae, *gen. pl.* cystarum, *abl. pl.* cystis; *in Gk. comp.*, cysto- *as prefix*, e.g. Cystopteris, *but* -cystis (s.f. III), *gen. sing.* -cystis, *abl. sing.* -cysti, *nom. pl.* cystes, *abl. pl.* cystibus *as final element,* e.g. Macrocystis. This unexpected divergence probably arose through confusion or association of L. *cista* (Gk. κιστη) 'box, chest' and Gk. κυστις 'bladder'.

Cystidium: cystidium (s.n. II), *nom. pl.* cystidia, *abl. pl.* cystidiis; *cystidia numerosa, praesertim prope aciem lamellarum, 40-80 × 5-10 μ fusiformia projicientia, ad apicem incrustatione succinea ornata,* cystidia numerous, especially at edge of gills, 40-80 μ long by 5-10 μ wide fusiform projecting, at the tip with amber-coloured incrustation ornamented; *cystidiis numerosis projicientibus fusiformibus, haud clavatis, tenuiter tunicatis laevibus hyalinis,* with cystidia fusiform, not clavate, thinly tunicate smooth hyaline. Buller, *Researches on Fungi,* 3 (1924), distinguished *caulocystidia* on the stipe, *cheilocystidia* at the edge of a gill, *pilocystidia* (for which Fayod's term *dermatocystidia* is preferable) on the surface or pellicle of the pileus and *pleurocystidia* on the side of a gill; see also Josserand, *Descr. Champign.*, 195 (1952).

Cystocarp: cystocarpium (s.n. II).

Cystolith: cystolithus (s.m. II), *abl. pl.* cystolithis; *folia cystolithis supra minutis punctiformibus subtus creberrimis breviter linearibus quaquaversus directis crassiusculis albidis,* leaves with cystoliths on upper side minute punctiform on lower side very numerous shortly linear to all directions set rather thick whitish.

cyto- *in Gk. comp.*, relating to the cell (*from* κυτος, 'receptacle'): **Cytologia** (s.f. I): cytology. **Cytoplasma** (s.n. III. xi): cytoplasm; cf. PROTOPLASM.

D

dacryoideus (adj. A): dacryoid, tear- or pear-shaped, from a broad rounded end tapering to a pointed end.

Dactyl: dactylus (s.m. II), *nom. pl.* dactyli, *abl. pl.* dactylis; *dactyli plerumque inaequales interdum omnes abbreviati 2- (vel interdum 3-) cellulares,* dactyls (ultimate rays of branchlets in Charophyta) commonly unequal sometimes all abbreviated; *dactyli 2-cellulati quam radii penultimati paulum longiores,* dactyls 2-celled than the penultimate rays a little longer.

dactyl-: *in Gk. and L. comp.*, finger-; *dactylifer,* finger-bearing; *dactylocarpus,* with fruit like a finger; *dactyloides,* finger-like. **dactylinus** (adj. A), **dactyloideus** (adj. A): divided into finger-like structures.

daedaleus (adj. A): marked with sinuous intricate lines, *or* irregularly plaited, *or* with the mouth or apex irregularly jagged or ragged. **160**

Damage: laesio (s.f. III); cf. INJURY.

damaged: laesus (part. A).

damp: udus (adj. A); cf. MOIST.

dark: deep shades of colour are usually indicated by adding the prefix *atro-* to the colour-name; *atroardesiacus,* dark slate-blue; *atrocyaneus,* dark greenish-blue; *atropurpureus,* dark purple; *atrosanguineus,* dark blood-red; *atrovenetus,* dark bluish-green; *atrovinosus,* dark wine-colour, i.e. 'deep shades of the moderately greyed series of purpureus and of ruber' (H. A. Dade); *atroviolaceus*, dark violet; *atrovirens*, *atroviridis*, dark green; *fuscus*, strictly a sombre brown and often applied to a dark-skinned or sun-tanned person, is sometimes used to indicate darkness of other colours. The prefix *per*- indicates intensity of colour; *perviridis*, deep green. **darkened**: fuscatus (part. A). **darkening**: atrans (adj. B), fuscans (part. B).

dasy-: *in Gk. comp.*, shaggy, thickly or markedly hairy; *dasyanthus*, with thickly hairy flowers; *dasychlamys*, with a shaggy covering; *dasycarpus*, with shaggy fruits; *dasyphyllus*, with markedly hairy leaves; *dasystemon*, with shaggy stamens; *dasystylus*, with shaggy styles; cf. PSIL-.

date-coloured: spadiceus (adj. A).

datus (part. A): given.

dauciformis (adj. A): carrot-shaped. **daucinus** (adj. A): carrot-red (H.C.C. 6.12).

Daughter: filia (s.f. I). **Daughter-cell**: cellula filialis, *abl. pl.* cellulis filialibus.

Day: dies (s.m. V), *abl. sing.* die, *nom. pl.* dies, *abl. pl.* diebus; *in diem*, in the space of a day: *die et nocte*, by day and night. **belonging to day-time**: diurnus (adj. A).

de (prep. with abl.): concerning, with respect to, out of, from.

dead: mortuus (part. A), emortuus (part. A) *used of organs*; *in Gk. comp.*, necro-. *See* DECEASED.

deadly: funestus (adj. A); lethalis (adj. B).

dealbatus (part. A): covered with a white powder, *lit.* 'whitewashed'.

debilis (adj. B): weak.

deca-: *in Gk. comp.*, ten-; *decandrus*, 10-stamened, *decapetalus*, 10-petalled; *decaphyllus*, 10-leaved; *see* DECEM-, TEN-.

decalvatus (part. A): made *or* become glabrous.

Decas (s.f. III. ii): decade, set of 10; cf. DECURIA.

Decay: caries (s.f. III).

decayed: cariosus (adj. A), putrefactus (part. A); cf. ROTTEN. **decaying**: putrescens (part. B).

deceased: mortuus (part. A), defunctus (part. A) (used of organisms), beatus (part. A), q.v. (used of a person named).

decem (num. adj. indecl.): ten. **decem-**: *in L. comp.*, ten-; *decemfidus*, 10-cleft; *decemjugus*, with 10 pairs of leaflets; *see* DECA-, TEN-.

decidedly: perspicue (adv.), valde (adv.).

deciduous: deciduus (adj. A), caducus (adj. A). **342**

deciens (adv.), **decies** (adv.): ten times, tenfold.

Decimetrum (s.n. II): decimetre.

decimus (adj. A): tenth.

decipiens (part. B): deceiving (used of a species closely resembling another); cf. FALLAX.

declinatus (part. A): bent *or* curved downwards *or* forwards. **405, 412**

declivis (adj. B): sloping downwards, steep; cf. DEVEXUS.

Decoction: decoctum (s.n. II).

decolor (adj. B), **decoloratus** (part. A): deprived of its natural colour, discoloured, faded. **decolorans** (part. B): losing colour.

decomposed: *see* ROTTEN.

decompound: decompositus (adj. A). **204**

decorated: ornatus (part. A).

decorticans (part. B): with bark peeling off. **decorticatus** (part. A): stripped of bark, with bark peeled off.

decrescens (part. B): growing less, diminishing, narrowing. **decrescente** (adv.): decreasingly.

decumbens (part. B): decumbent, prostrate with tip rising upwards. **424**

Decuria (s.f. I): decade, set of ten; cf. DECAS.

decurrent: decurrens (part. B), decursivus (adj. A); *pileus lamellis longe decurrentibus*, pileus with gills running down the stipe. **439**

decurved: decurvus (adj. A), decurvatus (adj. A).

Decus (s.n. III. iv): ornament, grace, splendour; *decus montium*, ornament of the mountains.

decussatus (adj. A): decussate, i.e. in pairs that alternately cross each other at right angles, thus making four rows; marked with lines intersecting cross-wise; derived from *decussis*, 'the number ten', *hence* 'the crosswise intersection of two lines like the Roman numeral X'. **493**

deep: profundus (adj. A). **deeply**: penitus (adv.), profunde (adv.).

deest (3rd person sing. indic. pres. of *desum*): 'it is wanting'; cf. ABSENCE, ADEST, DESUNT, E-, EX-, EXPERS, LACKING, PRESENT, WANTING, WITHOUT.

defective: defectivus (adv. A), imperfectus (adj. A), mancus (adj. A).

Defectus (s.m. IV): failure, lack.

deficiens (part. B): wanting, lacking.

definite (adv.): precisely, definitely.

Definition: definitio (s.f. III. vi).

definitus (part. A): definite, of a fixed number less than 20; terminating in a flower; cf. CERTUS.

deflexus (part. A): deflected, bent or turned abruptly downwards; *per angulum 50° deflexus*, deflexed through an angle of 50°. **412**

defloratus (part. A): with flowers withered or fallen.

Defoliatio (s.f. III. vi): leaf-fall.

deformans (part. B): deforming, disfiguring.

deformis (adj. B): misshapen.

defossus (part. A): buried in the earth.

Dehiscence: dehiscentia (s.f. I). dehiscing: dehiscens (part. B); cf. RUPTILIS, SEPTICIDALIS.

dein (adv.), deinde (adv.): thereafter, thereupon, then.

dejectus (part. A): low, fallen; *in ramis dejectis lectum*, on fallen branches collected; *ad ramos dejectos cortice denudatos*, on fallen branches stripped of bark.

delapsus (part. A): fallen away.

Delectus (s.m. IV); selection; *delectus seminum*, seed-list (*usu. of botanic garden*).

delicate: subtilis (adj. B), tenuis (adj. B), tenellus (adj. A); delicatus (adj. A), rarely used, means 'addicted to pleasure, dainty, fastidious'.

Deliciae (s.f. pl. I): pleasure, delight, pastime.

Delineatio (s.f. III. vi): sketch, drawing. delineatus (part. A): drawn (*commonly abbreviated to* del.).

deliquescens (part. B): deliquescent, becoming fluid when mature; repeatedly branching, *and thus metaphorically* melting away. **230**

deltate, deltoid: deltatus (adj. A), deltoideus (adj. A), triangularis (adj. B). **119, 130**

demersus (part. A): submerged, sunk in water. **392**

deminuens (part. B): diminishing. deminutus (part. A): diminished, small, diminutive, reduced.

demissus (part. A): low, lowly, humble, drooping.

demonstrable: demonstrabilis (adj. B).

demotus (part. A): put aside, removed.

demptus (part. A): taken away, subtracted.

demum (adv.): at length, at last; *nunc demum*, now; *post demum*, afterwards, not until after.

dendr-, dendro-, -dendron (s.n. II): *in Gk. comp.*, tree; *dendriticus, dendroideus, dendromorphus*, tree-like, resembling a tree in shape; *dendrophilus*, tree-loving. **238**

Dendrologia (s.f. I): study of trees. dendrologicus (adj. A): relating to the study of trees.

deni (num.): ten each, ten at a time.

denigricans (part. B): blackening, becoming black. denigratus (part. A): blackened.

denique (adv.): at last, at length, finally.

Dens (s.m. III. ix): tooth, prong; *dens canis*, tooth of a dog; *dens leonis*, tooth of a lion.

dense: densus (adj. A), confertus (part. A). densely: dense (adv.), confertim (adv.), spisse (adv.).

dentatus (adj. A): toothed, usu. with sharp teeth pointing outwards. denticulatus (adj. A): denticulate, i.e. with very small teeth. denti-: *in L. comp.*, tooth-; *dentiformis*, tooth-like. **183**

denudatus (part. A): denuded, stripped, having the leaves or hairs worn off. **298**

denuo (adv.): again, anew, once more.

deorsum (adv.): downward, below (*opposite of* SURSUM).

depauperatus (adj. A): undeveloped, reduced, depauperate, starved. **498**

dependens (part. B): suspended, hanging down. **394**

depending: secundum (prep. with acc.); *secundum aetatem*, depending on age, according to age.

depictus (part. A): portrayed in colour.

deplanatus (part. A): levelled off, made level.

Depressio (s.f. III): a depression.

depressus (part. A): flattened from above, somewhat sunken at the centre. **31, 338**

Depth: altitudo (s.f. III), profunditas (s.f. III); *in profunditate 1-2 orgyarum*, at a depth of 1-2 fathoms.

depulsus (part. A): driven away, expelled, dislodged.

derasus (part. A): smoothed off, shaved off; *area derasa*, scar area on seed of Sapotaceae.

derelictus (part. A): abandoned, neglected.

derived from: oriundus (adj. A).

Derma (s.n. III. ix), dermato-: *in Gk. comp.*, skin, e.g. *Argyroderma* 'silver skin', *Scleroderma* 'tough skin'.

Dermatocystidium: dermatocystidium (s.n. II), *nom. pl.* dermatocystidia, *abl. pl.* dermatocystidiis; cf. CYSTIDIUM.

descending: descendens (part. B); *also* cernuus (adj. A), declinatus (part. A), deflexus (part. A), nutans (part. B); cf. DIRECTION. **393**

described: descriptus (part. A). Description: descriptio (s.f. III. vi), *abl. sing.* descriptione, *nom. pl.* descriptiones, *abl. pl.* descriptionibus: *descriptiones et icones plantarum rariorum*, descriptions and illustrations of rare plants; *nomen absque descriptione*, name without a description.

Desert: desertum (s.n. II), *gen. sing.* deserti, *abl. sing.* deserto, *nom. pl.* deserta, *gen. pl.* desertorum, *abl. pl.* desertis. desert-: *in L. comp.*, deserti-, *in Gk. comp.*, erem-; *deserticola*, dweller in deserts; *eremophilus*, desert-loving; *eremicus*, pertaining to deserts; cf. TESCA.

desiccatus (part. A): dried up.

designated: designatus (part. A).

desinens (part. B): ending, stopping, ceasing.

-desma (s.n. III. ix): *in Gk. comp.*, band.

-desma (s.f. I): *in Gk. comp.*, bundle.

desquamatus (part. A): scaled off, peeled, rubbed bare.

destitutus (part. A): forsaken by, lacking, used with *abl.*; *thallus sorediis et isidiis destitutus*, thallus lacking soredia and isidia.

destroying: destruens (part. B), consumens (part. B).

destructus (part. A): destroyed. **destruens** (part. B); destroying, ruining.

desumptus (part. A): chosen, selected, picked out of a multitude.

desunt (3rd person pl. indic. pres. of *desum*): 'they are wanting'; cf. DEEST.

desuper (adv.): from above, from overhead.

det.: *see* DETERMINAVIT.

detached: separatus (part. A).

detectus (part. A): revealed, discovered.

detergendus (gerund. adj. A), **detergibilis** (adj. B): easily wiped off *or* removed (as glaucous 'bloom' of fruits).

determinatus (part. A): definite in outline, limited in number or extent.

determinavit (3rd person sing. active perfect of *determino*): 'he has enclosed within boundaries', i.e. he has identified it, ascertained the systematic position and the name. This word, or its abbreviation *det.*, is commonly used in annotating herbarium specimens; *det. A. Gray*, identified by A. Gray.

detersus (part. A): wiped clean, removed.

detrusus (part. A): pushed down or into.

deustus (part. A): burned up.

deuter- *in Gk. comp.*, second; *deuteronymus*, named a second time, an epithet (comparable with *anabaptistus*) applied to a species for which the first name given cannot be used.

developed: evolutus (part. A), effectus (part. A).

devexus (adj. A): sloping, steep; cf. DECLIVIS.

devoid of: carens (part. B with acc.); *see* DEEST, EXPERS, LACKING.

devoured: comesus (part. A).

dexter (adj. A): to the right, on the right-hand side; cf. SINISTER. **dextrorsum** (adv.): towards the right; cf. TWINING.

Dextrose: dextrosum (s.n. II), *gen. sing.* dextrosi.

di-: *in Gk. comp.*, two-; *diadelphus*, with stamens in two sets; *diandrus*, two-

stamened; *dichroanthus*, with two-coloured flowers; *diclinus*, with unisexual flowers, *lit.* 'in two beds'; *digynus*, with two styles or carpels; *dimerus*, with parts in twos; *dimorphophyllus*, with two kinds of leaves; *dimorphotrichus*, with two kinds of hairs; *dipetalus*, two-petalled; *dipterocarpus*, with two-winged fruits; *dipyrenus*, with two pyrenes; *dispermus*, two-seeded; *see* BI-, TWO.

Diagnosis: diagnosis (s.f. III); *diagnoses plantarum novarum Asiaticarum*, diagnoses of new Asiatic plants. **diagnostic**: diagnosticus (adj. A).

diagonally: diagonaliter (adv.).

Diagram: diagramma (s.n. III); *diagramma floris*, floral diagram.

dialy-: *in Gk. comp.*, separated, disbanded; *dialypetalus*, with separate petals.

Diameter: diameter (s.m. II), *acc. sing.* diametrum, *gen. sing.* diametri, *abl. sing.* diametro; diametrum (s.n. II), *acc. sing.* diametrum, *gen. sing.* diametri, *abl. sing.* diametro; *4 cm. diametro*, 4 cm. in diameter; *segmenta aeque longa ac diametrum vel breviora*, segments as long as the diameter or shorter; *pilis longis diametrum caulis aequantibus*, with long hairs equalling the diameter of the stem; abbrev. *diam.*

diaphanus (adj. A): colourless and nearly or quite transparent, diaphanous; cf. HYALINUS, PELLUCIDUS, TRANSPARENS, VITREUS.

Diaphragm: diaphragma (s.n. III).

Diarium (s.n. II): journal; cf. ACTA.

diarthrodactylus (adj. A): (in *Charophyta*) having each ultimate ray two-celled.

dibrachiatus (adj. A): two-branched (used of hairs); cf. MALPIGHIACEUS.

Dichasium: dichasium (s.n. II), *acc. sing.* dichasium, *abl. sing.* dichasio.

dichotome (adv.): dichotomously, **dichotomus** (adj. A): dichotomous, having divisions always in pairs. **231**

dictus (part. A): stated, declared, called; *loco dicto 'Kadamak'*, at the place called 'Kadamak'.

didymus (adj. A): didymous, in pairs, divided into two lobes, *in mycology* two-celled. **232**

didynamus (adj. A): didynamous, i.e. with two stamens long, two stamens short.

Dies (s.m. V): day.

different: dissimilis (adj. B), diversus (part. A); cf. ALIUS, ALTER.

Differentia (s.f. I): distinguishing feature; cf. CHARACTER.

differently: aliter (adv.), alio modo (adv. phrase).

differing: abhorrens (part. B), differens

(part. B), discrepans (part. B), divergens (part. B).

differt (3rd person sing. pres. indic. active of *differo*, 'carry asunder, differ, be distinguished from'): 'it differs'; cf. Chapter XIII.

difficile (adv.), **difficiliter** (adv.), **difficulter** (adv.) : with difficulty.

difficilis (adj. B) : difficult.

diffluens (part. B) : flowing in different directions, dissolving.

difformis (adj. B) : irregularly *or* unevenly *or* differently formed, unlike what is usual.

diffractus (part. A) : broken in pieces, shattered.

diffusus (part. A) : diffuse, loosely, irregularly *or* widely spreading, with branches diverging from axis at an angle of 45°-90°. **425**

digestus (part. A) : set in order, arranged.

digitatus (adj. A) : digitate, e.g. with leaflets radiating from tip of leaf-stalk. **198**

digitiformis (adj. B) : finger-like.

dilabens (part. B) : falling asunder, melting away, disappearing ; *sepala post anthesin dilabentia*, sepals after anthesis falling away.

Dilatatio (s.f. III) : swelling, expansion, widened part. **dilatatus** (part. A) : broadened, expanded, widened.

diligens (part. B) : careful, attentive, accurate. **diligenter** (adv.) : carefully.

dilute (adv.) : slightly, weakly. **dilutus** (part. A) : diluted, thin, weak (*mostly used of faint colours*).

Dimension : dimensio (s.f. III. vi).

dimidiatus (part. A) : dimidiate, with one part of an organ so much smaller than the other that only half of the whole organ seems present ; divided through the middle ; actually halved, with the outer wall of perithecium covering only the upper half. **Dimidium** (s.n. II) : the half. **dimidio** (adv.) : by half. **dimidius** (adj. A) : half. **63, 138**

diminishing : deminuens (part. B), minuens (part. B), imminuens (part. B), decrescens (part. B).

diminutus (part. A) : made small, diminished.

dimissus (part. A) : discharged, sent forth, let go.

dimorphus (adj. A) : having two forms, e.g. short- or long-styled.

dingy : sordidus (adj. A).

Dio : *see* DIVUM.

dioecious, dioicous : dioecius (adj. A) ; *in bryology usu.* dioicus (adj. A).

diplecolobeus (adj. A) : with incurved cotyledons twice folded transversely, as in Heliophila.

diplo- : *in Gk. comp.*, double ; *diploceras*, with two horns ; *diplocyclus*, with two whorls ; *diploscyphus*, with a double cup ; *diplostemonus*, diplostemonous, i.e. having stamens twice as many as the petals, the stamens of the outer whorl opposite the sepals, the stamens of inner whorl opposite the petals ; *diplostephanus*, having a double circle of stipulodes at the base of each whorl of branchlets ; *diplostichus*, in two rows, *in Charophyta* having two rows of cells to each branchlet.

diploid : diploideus (adj. A) ; cf. CHROMOSOME, -PLOIDEUS.

Direction : cursus (s.m. IV), *abl. sing.* cursu 'line of motion, course' ; directio (s.f. III), *abl. sing.* directione 'a making straight, aiming'. The poise of an organ when directed upwards may be indicated by *erectus*, *arrectus* (erect), *ascendens*, *assurgens* (ascending), when directed outwards by *horizontalis*, *patens* (spreading), when directed downwards by *descendens*, *nutans* (nodding), *cernuus* (nodding), *deflexus*, *declinatus*, *reclinatus* (bent downwards), when hanging down by *dependens*, *pendulus*, when having a gradually inward direction by *connivens*, when flat on the ground by *humifusus*, *procumbens*, *pronus*, *prostratus*, *decumbens*. The part. *spectans* (looking at, facing, situated towards), is sometimes used with adverbs *deorsum* (downwards), *sursum*, *sursus* (upwards), *extrorsus* (outwards) ; the adv. *versus* or *versum* (turned in the direction of) usu. follows the name of part (in acc.) to which direction is indicated ; *apicem versus*, towards the tip, *deorsum versus*, downwards ; *quoquoversus*, in every direction ; *spinae a se ex adverso flexae*, spines turned in opposite directions from each other. Cf. OVULE, VEINING.

directus (part. A) : straight, going direct (*whether horizontally or vertically*).

disagreeing : discrepans (with *in*, abl. or dat.)

disappearing : evanescens (part. B) ; cf. DELIQUESCENS, DILABENS, FATISCENS.

Disc : discus (s.m. II), *gen. sing.* disci, *abl. sing.* disco (*generally used*), torus (s.m. II), *gen. sing.* tori, *abl. sing.* toro (*used only of receptacle*) ; *thallus e disco basali et filis erectis constructus*, thallus from a basal disc and erect filaments constructed ; *discus basalis paucistratus e filamentis repentibus cohaerentibus compositus*, basal disc several-layered from creeping cohering filaments composed ; *capituia heterogama, floribus radii uniseriatis fertilibus, disci sterilibus*, heads heterogamous with flowers of the circumference in one series fertile, of the disc sterile; *achenia disci bialata*, achenes of the disc two-winged. **disc-like**: disciformis (adj. B), discoideus (adj. A), discoidalis (adj. B).

discedens (part. B): separating, dividing, contrasting.

discernible: distinguibilis (adj. B).

discharged: dimissus (part. A), emissus (part. A). **discharging**: emittens (part. B.).

disciformis (adj. B): disc-like. Used also of Compositae when in a capitulum having central and marginal florets distinct the outer female florets do not rise above the disc. **discoideus** (adj. A): discoid, with a rounded blade and thickened margin. Used also of Compositae with all the florets regular and alike. **discoidalis** (adj. B): orbicular. **34**

discolor (adj. B): of another colour, not of the same colour (*as when two faces of a leaf are unlike in colour*), variegated.

discovered: inventus (part. A).

discrepans (part. B): differing.

discretus (part. A): separated, set apart, loose.

Discrimen (s.n. III. vi): that which separates two things from each other, distinction, difference.

Disease: morbus (s.m. II); cf. -OSIS.

diseased: aeger (adj. A), aegrotus (adj. A), morbidus (adj. A), morbosus (adj. A); cf. INFECTUS, LANGUESCENS, TABESCENS.

dish-shaped: patelliformis (adj. B).

disintegrating: fatiscens (part. B).

disjuncte, disjunctim (adv.): separately. **disjunctus** (part. A): separate, distinct.

Disk: *see* DISC.

dislodged: depulsus (part. A).

disorderly: inordinate (adv.), inordinatim (adv.).

dispansus (adj. A): opened out widely, with gaping cracks.

dispar (adj. B): unlike, unequal.

disparatus (part. A): separated.

disperse (adv.), **dispersim** (adv.): dispersedly, here and there. **Dispersio** (s.f. III): dispersion, scattering. **dispersus** (part. A): scattered.

dispersing: spargens (part. B).

displaying: ostendens (part. B), praebens (part. B).

displicatus (part. A): scattered.

Dispositio (s.f. III. vi): regular arrangement. **dispositus** (part. A): arranged, disposed, placed here and there, spaced.

disrumpens (part. B): breaking off, bursting asunder. **disruptus** (part. A): broken off.

dissectus (part. A): dissected, deeply divided or cut into numerous segments.

Dissepimentum (s.n. II): dissepiment, partition, dividing wall.

Dissertatio (s.f. III. vi): discourse, dissertation (*originally a spoken one*), thesis.

dissiliens (part. B): bursting elastically, springing apart.

dissimilis (adj. B): unlike, dissimilar (*generally referring to variation in the form of a given organ on the same plant*).

dissiti-: *in L. comp.*, remote, apart; *dissitiflorus*, with well-spaced flowers. **dissitus** (adj. A): lying apart, remote, well-spaced.

dissocians (part. B): dissociating; cf. DISCEDENS.

dissolutus (part. A): dissolved.

dissolving: diffluens (part. B), dissolvens (part. B).

distalis (adj. B): distal, remote from place of attachment.

Distance: distantia (s.f. I), *abl.* distantia, spatium (s.n. II), *abl.* spatio.

distant: distans (part. B), 'standing apart', semotus (part. A) 'far removed'; cf. DISSITUS, REMOTUS. **499**

distentus (part. A): distended; cf. TURGIDUS.

distichus (adj. A): distichous, arranged in two opposite rows. **488**

distinct: distinctus (part. A) 'separated', proprius (adj. A) 'on its own'; *species propria*, a distinct species. **451**

distinguibilis (adj. B): discernible, distinguishable; cf. EVIDENT.

Ditch: fossa (s.f. I), *gen. sing.* fossae; scrobis (s.m. III), *gen. sing.* scrobis.

Ditio (s.f. III. vi): authority, administrative district.

distributed: distributus (part. A). **Distribution**: distributio (s.f. III); *distributio geographica*, geographical distribution.

District: regio (s.f. III); ager (s.m. II).

disturbed: turbatus (part. A).

diu (adv.): a long time, long (*in sense of time*). **diuscule** (adv.): a little while. **diutinus** (adj. A). **diuturnus** (adj. A): long-lasting, of long duration. **diutius** (adv.): very long, longer (*both in sense of time*). **diutule** (adv.): a little while.

diurnus (adj. A): belonging to the day; cf. DAY, NOCTURNUS, VESPERTINUS.

divaricatus (part. A): divaricate, spreading asunder at a wide angle; *see* VEINING. **426**

divergens (part. B): diverging, going different ways.

diverse (adv.); in different directions, differently, diversely; cf. VARIE. **diversi-**: *in L. comp.*, diverse, various; *diversicolor, diversicolorus*, of various colours; *diversiflorus*, with flowers of different kinds; *diversifolius*, with leaves of different shapes on the same individual; *diversiformis*, of varying form.

diversus (part. A): turned different ways, diverse, contrary, opposite, different, distinct.

dives (adj. B): rich, plentiful; *arbor succo viscido lacteo dives*, tree rich in viscid milky juice.

divided: divisus (part. A). **dividing**: dividens (part. B), discedens (part. B).

Division: divisio (s.f. III. vi) 'act of dividing, part divided off', divisura (s.f. I) 'place of division, fork, incision', pars (s.f. III. ix) (part), caput (s.n. III. ii) (heading, chapter); *cellulae ante divisionem, divisione, post divisionem ovoideae*, cells before division, at division, after division ovoid.

divulgatus (part. A): widespread, q.v.

divulsus (part. A): torn asunder, separated, removed.

Divum (s.n. II): the sky; *sub divo, sub dio*, in the open air.

Docks: navalia (s.n. II, pl.).

doctus (part. A): learned, skilled.

dodeca-: *in Gk. comp.*, twelve-; *dodecandrus*, 12-stamened.

Dodrans (s.m. III. ix): three-quarters, distance between tips of thumb and little finger when extended, 9 inches, approx. 24 cm. **dodrantalis** (adj. B): 9 inches long.

dolabriformis (adj. B): dolabriform, i.e. in shape somewhat resembling an axe. **37**

dolich-, dolicho-: *in Gk. comp.*, long-; *dolichanthus*, long-flowered; *dolichobotrys*, with a long raceme; *dolichocalyx*, with a long calyx; *dolichocentrus*, *dolichoceras*, long-spurred; *dolichopetalus*, long-petalled; *dolichophyllus*, long-leaved; *dolichopodus*, long-stalked; *see* BRACHY-, LONG-.

doliiformis (adj. B): barrel-shaped; cf. CUPIFORMIS.

Domatium; domatium (s.n. II), *nom. pl.* domatia, *abl. pl.* domatiis; *see* ACARODOMATIUM.

Dome: tholus (s.m. II). **dome-shaped**: tholiformis (adj. B).

Domina (s.f. I): mistress, Mrs. **Dominilla** (s.f. I): Miss. **Dominus** (s.m. II): master, Mr.

dominans (part. B): dominating, dominant.

donans (part. B): giving. **donatus** (part. A): given.

donec (conj.): while, until.

dormiens (part. B): sleeping, resting; *gemmae dormientes*, resting buds.

dorsal: dorsalis (adj. B), dorsualis (adj. B). **dorsally**: dorsaliter (adv.). **dorsifixed**: dorsifixus (adj. A). **456**

Dorsum (s.n. II): back, lower *or* outer side of an organ.

Dot: punctum (s.n. II), *abl. pl.* punctis; *petala flava punctis nigris basim versus notata*, petals yellow with black dots towards the base marked. **dot-like**: punctiformis (adj. B). **dotted**: punctatus (adj. A). **258**

Dotting: punctatio (s.f. III. vi), *abl. sing.* punctatione; *valvae sine punctatione distincta*, valves without distinct dotting.

double: duplex (adj. A). In florist's sense of having much more than the usual number of petals, *duplex, flore pleno, pleniflorus, plenus* (full), *trigintipetalus* (thirty-petalled), *centifolius* (hundred-leaved) have been used. **doubly**: duplo (adv.). **doubly-**: *in L. comp.*, duplicato-, *in Gk. comp.*, diplo-; *folia duplicato-serrata*, leaves doubly serrate.

doubled: geminatus (part. A), duplicatus (part. A). **503**

Doubt: dubitatio (s.f. III. vi). **doubtful**: dubius (adj. A). **doubtfully**: dubie (adv.). **without doubt**: sine dubio, sine ulla dubitatione.

downward: deorsum (adv.); *folia pilis deorsum curvatis*, leaves with hairs downwards curved.

downy: pubescens (part. B), pubens (adj. B). **271**

-doxa (s.f. I), **-doxus** (adj. A): *in Gk. comp.*, glory, splendour, good repute, e.g. *adoxus* 'without glory', *eudoxus* 'of good repute', *chionodoxa* 'glory of the snow', *helodoxa* 'glory of the marsh'.

dragging: trahens (part. B).

Drawing: delineatio (s.f. III. vi). **drawn**: delineatus (part. A).

drawn out: extensus (part. A), extractus (part. A), productus (part. A).

dredged: subductus (part. A), prolatus (part. A).

drepan-: *in Gk. comp.*, curved like a sickle, sickle-; *drepanophyllus*, with sickle-shaped leaves; *see* FALCATE.

Drepanium: drepanium (s.n. II), *acc. sing.* drepanium, *abl. sing.* drepanio.

dried: exsiccatus (part. A), siccatus (part. A); desiccatus (part. A), arefactus (part. A); *exsiccatum, specimen exsiccatum*, dried specimen; *exsiccata, flora exsiccata*, set of dried specimens.

drooping: cernuus (adj. A), demissus (part. A). **407**

Drop: gutta (s.f. I). **Droplet**: guttula (s.f. I).

drum-shaped: tympaniformis (adj. B).

drupaceus (adj. A): drupe-like. **Drupe**: drupa (s.f. I), *abl. sing.* drupa, *nom. pl.* drupae, *abl. pl.* drupis, *lit.* 'an over-ripe wrinkled olive'. **Drupelet**: drupeola (s.f. I); cf. FRUCTICULUS.

dry: siccus (adj. A), aridus (adj. A); *hortus siccus*, herbarium; *caules in sicco nigrescentes*, stems in a dried state blackish; *folia siccitate membranacea*, leaves by drying membranous; *habitat in aridis*, it dwells in dry places.

Dubitatio (s.f. III. vi): doubt; *sine ulla dubitatione*, without any doubt; *sine dubio*, without doubt, indisputably. **dubie** (adv.): doubtfully. **dubius** (adv. A): doubtful.

Ducatus (s.m. IV): duchy.

dulcis (adj. B): sweet, pleasant; cf. AMARUS.

dull: hebes (adj. B), *acc. sing.* hebetem, *gen. sing.* hebetis, *abl. sing.* hebeti; cf. MATT. **dull**: obscure (adv.).

dull-coloured: tristis (adj. B) 'sad', obscurus (adj. A) 'dusky', sordidus (adj. A) 'dingy'.

dum (conj.): while, whilst, now.

Dumetum (s.n. II): thorn-scrub, thicket. **Dumicola** (s.m. I): dweller in thickets. **dumosus** (adj. A): full of thorn-bushes, of bushy habit *or* aspect. **Dumus** (s.m. II): thorn-bush.

dumtaxat (adv.),: exactly, only, not more, not less.

Dune: thinium (s.n. II), *abl. pl.* thiniis.

Dung: stercus (s.n. III), *acc. sing.* stercorem, *gen. sing.* stercoris, *abl. sing.* stercore; fimus (s.m. II), *acc. sing.* fimum, *gen. sing.* fimi, *abl. sing.* fimo; *ad fimum equinum*, on horse-droppings; *in stercore vaccino*, in cow-dung. **dung-loving** (growing on dung): coprophilus (adj. A), fimicola (s.f. I). **pertaining to dung**: stercorarius (adj. A); *in Gk. comp.*, apopato-, copro-, ontho-, scato-, scybalo-, *in L. comp.*, fimi-, sterc-, sterco-. **stinking like dung**: stercoreus (adj. A).

duo (adj. num.): two, q.v.

duodeciens (adv.), **duodecies** (adv.): twelve times. **duodecim** (num. adj. indecl.): twelve. **duodecimus** (num. adj. A): twelfth.

duplex (adj. B): double, q.v.

duplicato (adv.): twice as much. **duplicato-crenatus** (adj. A): doubly crenate, each tooth itself toothed. **duplicato-pinnatus** (adj. A): bipinnate. **duplicato-serratus** (adj. A): doubly serrate.

duplicatus (part. A): doubled, paired. **221, 503**

duplo (adv.): doubly.

Duration: duratio (s.f. III. vi), *abl. sing.* duratione. **during**: per (prep. with acc.), tempore (*abl. sing.*, s.n. III), (with gen.) (at the time of); *tempore conjunctionis sexualis*, during sexual union.

Duritia (s.f. I): hardness.

duriusculus (adj. A): somewhat hard. **durus** (adj. A): hard.

dusky: furvus (adj. A).

dwarf: nanus (adj. A), pumilus (adj. A). **335**

Dyer: tinctor (s.m. III), q.v.

dying off: emoriens (part. B).

dysentericus (adj. A): reputed to cause dysentery.

E

e (prep. with abl.): from, out of; *see* EX.

e- (L. prefix): *in L. comp.*, without, lacking, destitute of, un-, -less; *see* EX, A-; *ebracteatus*, without bracts; *ecalcaratus*, spurless; *ecallosus*, lacking callosities; *ecarinatus*, not keeled; *eciliatus*, without cilia; *ecorticatus*, without bark or bark-like covering; *ecristatus*, not crested; *efoliatus*, without leaf-like scales; *eglandulosus*, eglandular, destitute of glands, glandless; *enervis*, *enervius*, with no ribs or veins apparent; *enotatus*, without markings; *epapillosus*, not papillose; *epetiolaris*, *epetiolatus*, without petiole; *epunctatus*, without dots; *erostris*, beakless; *estipitatus*, not stalked; *estipulatus*, without stipules; *e-* is never used before a vowel, *h*, *t* and *q*, rarely before *p* and *s*.

each: can be expressed in several ways according to meaning; *inter se*, between each other, to each other; *in quoque segmento*, on each segment; *venae sibi parallelae*, veins parallel to each other. **each** (of two): uterque (pron. m.), utraque (f.), utrumque (n.). **each single one** (of a number of objects): unusquisque (compar. pron. m.), unaquaeque (f.), unumquidque (n.). **each and every**: omnis (adj. B).

-eae (adj.): nom. f. pl. suffix added to stem of name or synonym of type genus to form name of tribe, e.g. *Datureae*

Ear: (*of cereal*) spica (s.f. I), (*of leaf-base*) auricula (s.f. I). **eared**: spicatus (adj. A), q.v.; auriculatus (adj. A), q.v.

early: mature (adv.), praecox (adj. B).

Earth: *see* SOIL.

easily: facile (adv.). **easy**: facilis (adj. B).

East: oriens (s.m. III. ix), *gen. sing.* orientis; *ad orientem*, to the east. **east, eastern**: orientalis (adj. B).

eaten up: exesus (part. A).

Ebb: recessus (s.m. IV), refluxus (s.m. IV); cf. TIDE.

ebbing: minuens (part. B); *minuente aestu*, at the ebbing of the tide.

ebeneus (adj. A): ebony black.

eburneus (adj. A): ivory white, i.e. white with yellow tinge.

-ebus: abl. and dat. pl. ending of s. V., meaning mostly 'with' but also 'from, by, in' (when abl.) and 'to, for' (when dat.

ecarinatus (adj. A) : without keel, keelless.

eccentricus (adj. A) : *see* EXCENTRICUS.

echinatus (adj. A) : echinate, armed with numerous rigid hairs or straight prickles or spines, from *echinus* (s.m. II), 'hedge-hog, sea-urchin', *hence* 'prickly husk of sweet chestnut'. **echinulatus** (adj. A) : with very small prickles, echinulate. **263**

ecorticatus (adj. A) : without bark.

edens (part. B) : giving out, putting forth ; *radix caules edens*, root putting forth stems.

edentatus (adj. A) : untoothed, toothless.

Edge : *see* MARGIN.

edible : edibilis (adj. B), edulis (adj. B), esculentus (adj. A).

Editio (s.f. III. vi) : edition ; *editio altera*, second edition. **editus** (part. A) : (*relating to books, etc.*) published, (*relating to places*) high, lofty.

edulis (adj. B) : eatable ; *see* EDIBLE.

eel-like : anguilliformis (adj. B), q.v.

Eelworm : vermiculus (s.m. II) nematoideus (adj. A), nematodum (s.n. II).

effaced : obliteratus (part. A).

effectus (part. A) : completed, accomplished, developed.

efferens (part. B) : bringing forth, producing.

efficiens (part. B) : effecting, presenting, making, causing.

effiguratus (adj. A) : effigurate, having a definite form or figure.

Efflorescentia (s.f. I) : the period of opening of the flower ; cf. ANTHESIS.

effoetus (adj. A) : worn out by bringing forth young, exhausted.

effractus (part. A) : broken off.

effusus (part. A) : spread out, indeterminate, straggling, wide (*referring to habit of growth*), *lit.* 'poured out'.

egg-yolk yellow : vitellinus (adj. A).

eglandulatus (adj. A) : **eglandulosus** (adj. A) : eglandular, non-glandular, glandless.

egrediens (part. B) : coming forth, passing out of.

egregie (adv.) : excellently. **egregius** (adj. A) : excellent.

eight : octo (num. adj. indecl.) 'eight', octavus (adj. A) 'eighth', octies (adv.), octiens (adv.) 'eight times', octanus (adj. A) 'eight at a time'.

eight- : *in L. and Gk. comp.*, octo- ; *octopetalus*, 8-petalled ; *see* OCTO-.

either : alteruter (adj. A) ; cf. BOTH, EACH, UTERQUE.

ejected : ejectus (part. A), expulsus (part. A).

ejusdem : of the same ; *see* IDEM.

elabens (part. B) : escaping, slipping away.

elasticus (adj. A) : elastic, returning to its original position when pressed or bent.

Elater : elater (s.m. III. v), *gen. sing.* elateris, *abl. sing.* elatere, *nom. pl.* elateres, *gen. pl.* elaterum, *abl. pl.* elateribus ; *elateres in omnibus fere dispiri rare monospiri vel 3-4-spiri decidui, perpauci heteromorphi interdum in capsulae fundo apiceve diutius persistentes, demum idem ac normales decidui*, elaters in nearly all with two spiral fibres rarely with a single spiral or with 3 or 4 spirals deciduous, a few abnormal heteromorphic ones sometimes persisting longer at the base or the apex of capsule, at last deciduous the same as the normal ones ; *elateres valde numerosi, tota facie capsulae interna primum insidentes, capsula dehiscente omnes decidui, angusti utroque fine tenuiores tortiles*, elaters very numerous, the whole inner surface of the capsule at first occupying, with the capsule bursting all falling out, slender at each end narrower twisted ; *elateres nulli*, elaters none ; *elateres vel monospiri vel fibram solam flexuosam (nec spiralem) continentes*, elaters either with one spiral or containing a single flexuous (not spiral) fibre ; *elaterum fibra perfecte spiralis*, of the elaters the fibre perfectly spiral.

elatus (part. A) : tall, q.v. **340**

electron : electronicus (adj. A) ; *flagellum per microscopum electronicum visum*, flagellum seen by means of the electron microscope.

elegans (adj. B) : elegant. **eleganter** (adv.) : elegantly.

elevated : elevatus (part. A).

eleven : undecim (num. adj. indecl.) 'eleven', undecimus (adj. A) 'eleventh', undecies (adv.) undeciens (adv.) 'eleven times'. **eleven-** : *in Gk. comp.*, hendeca-, *less correctly* endeca- ; *endecaphyllus, hendecaphyllus*, with 11 leaves or leaflets.

Ell : cubitus (s.m. II), *nom. pl.* cubiti.

ellipsoid : ellipsoideus (adj. A), ellipsoidalis (adj. B). **24**

elliptic, elliptical : ellipticus (adj. A). **very narrowly elliptic** : peranguste ellipticus. **narrowly elliptic** : anguste ellipticus. **broadly elliptic** : late ellipticus. **108**

-ellus (adj. A, suffix) : used to form diminutives ; in colour-names indicates a pale tint.

elongated : elongatus (adj. A), productus (part. A), prolatus (part. A).

elsewhere : alibi (adv.).

emarcidus (adj. A) : withered.

emarginatus (part. A) : emarginate, shallowly notched (*usu. at tip*), (in Fungi) with a sudden curve or notch at point of attachment to stipe. **156**

embedded : *see* IMBEDDED.

embracing: amplectens (part. B). **440**

Embryo: embryo (s.m. III. vi), *gen. sing.*
embryonis, *abl. sing.* embryone. The
form *embryum*, to be expected from Gk.
ἔμβρυον (s.n.), has been rarely if ever used;
*embryo magnus arcuatus, cotyledonibus
planis, plumula inconspicua, radicula
brevi*, embryo large curved like a bow,
with cotyledons flat, plumule inconspicuous, radicle short; *embryo in albumine carnoso periphericus linearis curvus
vel spiraliter tortus (haud rectus) indivisus, cotyledonibus inconspicuis*, embryo
within fleshy endosperm peripheral
linear curved or spirally twisted (not
straight), with cotyledons inconspicuous;
*embryo nunc rectus, cotyledonibus latis
foliaceis conduplicatis albumen longitudinaliter involvens radicula brevi infera,
nunc incurvus, cotyledonibus incumbenti-
bus convolutis albumen involventibus, vel
cotyledonibus angustis albumini appli-
citis, radicula elongata extraria infera*,
embryo straight, with the cotyledons
broad leafy conduplicate the albumen
lengthwise enveloping (i.e. the embryo
covering the albumen with its cotyledons), or with the cotyledons narrow
applied to the albumen, with the radicle
elongated external lower; *embryonis
exalbuminosi cotyledones circinatim convolutae*, of the exalbuminous embryo the
cotyledons coiled from the tip; *species
structura embryonis plane diversa*, species
by the structure of the embryo clearly
different; *species habitu praecedentis sed
embryone diversa*, species with the habit
of the preceding but by the embryo
different. **embryonalis** (adj. B): pertaining to the embryo. **embryonatus**
(adj. A): provided with an embryo.

Embryotega: embryotega (s.f. I), *abl. sing.*
embryotega.

Emendatio (s.f. III. vi): correction, amend-
ment. **emendatus** (part. A): freed of
faults, corrected.

emerald-green: smaragdinus (adj. A).

emergens (part. B); emerging, half-
uncovered.

emeritus (part. A): 'that has become unfit
for service, worn out, burned out, ex-
tinguished' (Lewis & Short); applied by
Ovid to horses, by modern universities
to retired professors.

emersus (part. A): raised up, brought
forth, standing above.

eminens (part. B): standing out, projecting.

Eminentia (s.f. I): projection, protuberance.

emissus (part. A): sent forth, released,
discharged.

emittens (part. B): emitting, giving forth,

releasing; *zoosporangia 4 zoosporas
emittantia*, zoosporangia emitting 4
zoospores.

emoriens (part. B): dying off.

emortuus (part. A): dead, perished.

empty: cassus (adj. A), inanis (adj. B),
vacuus (adj. A), *in some contexts*,
nudus (adj. A), 'naked'). cavus (adj. A)
'hollow', evacuatus (part. A) 'emptied
out'.

emulsivus (adj. A): milk-like in texture.

enantio-: *in Gk. comp.*, opposite.

enatus (part. A): issuing from, arising from.

encircled: cinctus (part. A), circumdatus
(part. A). **encircling**: cingens (part. B),
circumdans (part. B).

enclosed: inclusus (part. A). **enclosing**:
includens (part. B).

encrusted: incrustatus (part. A).

encysted: incystatus (adj. A).

End: extremum (s.n. II), *abl. sing.* ex-
tremo, *nom. pl.* extrema, *abl. pl.* ex-
tremis; extremitas (s.f. III. ii), *abl. sing.*
extremitate, *abl. pl.* extremitatibus;
finis (s.f. III), *abl. sing.* fine, *abl. pl.*
finibus; *folia in extremitatibus ramulorum tantum*, leaves at the ends of the
branches only.

end-, endo-: *in Gk. comp.*, within, inside.

endeca-: *in Gk. comp.*, eleven-.

ended: terminatus'(part. A, used with abl.).

endemic: endemicus (adj. A).

Endexine: endexinium (s.n. II).

ending in: desinens (part. B, used with *in*
and acc.), terminans (part. B, used with
in and acc.).

endo-: *in Gk. comp.*, within, inside.

endogenus (adj. A): endogenous, arising
from deep-seated tissue, growing immersed for the most part in the substratum (*as certain lichens*), produced
within another body.

endolithicus (adj. A): endolithic, growing
immersed in stone.

Endoperidium: endoperidium (s.n. II).

endophloeodes (adj. Gk.), **endophloeodicus**
(adj. A): endophloeodal, i.e. inhabiting
the cork layer of tree bark and immersed
in it: *thallus endophloeodes*, thallus
endophloeodal.

endophyticus (adj. A): endophytic, growing within plant tissue.

Endosperm: endospermium (s.n. II), *abl.
sing.* endospermio.

Endospore: endosporium (s.n. II), *abl.
sing.* endosporio.

Endothecium: endothecium (s.n. II), *abl.
sing.* endothecio.

endozoicus (adj. A): living inside an
animal. **endozoophyticus** (adj. A):
growing in *or* among zoophytes.

enecans (part. B): killing completely.

enervis (adj. B), enervius (adj. A): without nerves; cf. NERVOSUS. **361**

engraved: sculptus (part. A), insculptus (part. A), sculpturatus (adj. A).

enim (conj.): truly, certainly, for.

enlarged: amplificatus (part. A) 'made wider', auctus (part. A) 'increased by growth', dilatatus (part. A) 'spread out', accrescens (part. B) 'enlarging by growth with age'; cf. ACCRESCENT.

Enlargement: amplificatio (s.f. III).

ennea-: *in Gk. comp.*, nine-; *enneandrus*, 9-stamened; *enneaphyllus*, with 9 leaves or leaflets; *enneaspermus*, 9-seeded; *see* NINE-.

enodis (adj. B): without nodes; cf. NODOSUS.

ensatus (adj. A), ensiformis (adj. B): sword-like, 'shaped like a two-edged sword, gradually tapering to the point' (Berkenhout); cf. GLADIATUS. **ensifer** (adj. A): sword-bearing. **ensifolius** (adj. A): sword-leaved. **116**

-ensis (adj. B): adjectival suffix indicating origin or place, e.g. *hortensis* relating to gardens, *kewensis*, relating to Kew.

ensnaring: illaquens (part. B).

entangled: intricatus (part. A), implicatus (part. A), contortuplicatus (adj. A). **502**

entering: ingrediens (part. B), iniens (part. B).

entire: integer (adj. A): *labello integro*, with labellum entire; *folia integra viridia*, leaves entire green; *foliis integris viridibus*, with leaves entire green; *bractea integra*, bract entire; *scapus bractea integra*, scape with bract entire; *bracteae integrae virides*, bracts entire green; *pedicelli bracteas membranaceas virides integras duplo superantes*, pedicels twice as long as the membranous green entire bracts; *bracteis integris*, with entire bracts: **entirely**: omnino (adv.); sometimes expressed by the use of adj. in the superlative. **179**

enumerated: enumeratus (part. A), noncupatus (part. A). **Enumeration**: enumeratio (s.f. III. vi), recensio (s.f. III. vi).

Envelope: involucrum (s.n. II). **enveloped**: involutus (part. A). **enveloping**: involvens (part. B); *see* EMBRYO.

ephemeral: ephemerus (adj. A), fugax (adj. B).

ephippioideus (adj. A), ephippiomorphus (adj. A): saddle-shaped.

epi-: *in Gk. comp.*, upon, over, on top of, added to; *epidendrus*, on trees; *epigeios*, on the earth; *epihydrus*, on the water, i.e. floating; *epipsilus*, bare above; *epitrichus*, hairy above.

Epicalyx: epicalyx (s.m. III. i), *gen. sing.* epicalycis, *abl. sing.* epicalyce; *see* CALYX.

Epicarp: epicarpium (s.n. II).

epicorollinus (adj. A): inserted on the corolla.

Epicotyl: internodium (s.n. II) epicotylum (adj. A), epicotylus (s.m. II).

Epicutis: epicutis (s.f. III. vii), *gen. sing.* epicutis, *abl. sing.* epicute.

epidermal: epidermalis (adj. B), epidermicus (adj. A).

Epidermis: epidermis (s.f. III. ii), *gen. sing.* epidermidis, *abl. sing.* epidermide.

epidermoideus (adj. A): epidermis-like.

epigaeus (adj. A): epigeal, growing upon the ground or rising a little above it. **469**

epigenus (adj. A): epigenous, growing on the surface.

epigynicus (adj. A), epigynus (adj. A): epigynous, situated on the upper part of the ovary or above the oogonium. **472**

epilithicus (adj. A): epilithic, growing on the surface of stone, roof-tiles, etc.

epiphloeodes (adj. Gk.), epiphloeodicus (adj. A): growing on the surface of bark or wood; cf. ENDOPHLOEODES.

Epiphragm: epiphragma (s.n. III. xi), *abl. sing.* epiphragmate; tympanum (s.n. II), *abl. sing.* tympano.

epiphyllus (adj. A): epiphyllous, growing on leaves or leaf-like organs on, *in mycology*, the upper surface of leaves; *in epiphyllo*, on the upper leaf-surface.

epiphyticus (adj. A): epiphytic, growing on other plants but not parasitic.

Epispore: episporium (s.n. II), *abl. sing.* episporio; *episporio laevi vel granuloso asperoque, hyalino vel fuscescente*, with epispore smooth or granular and rough, hyaline or becoming brownish. **episporiatus** (adj. A): provided with an epispore.

Epithallus: epithallus (s.m. II), *abl. sing.* epithallo.

Epitheca: epitheca (s.f. I), *abl. sing.* epitheca; epivalva (s.f. I), *abl. sing.* epivalva. **Epithecium**: epithecium (s.n. II), *abl. sing.* epithecio.

Epivalve: *see* EPITHECA.

epizoophyticus (adj. A): growing on zoophytes but not parasitic.

equal: aequalis (adj. B), aequus (adj. A), parilis (adj. B), consimilis (adj. B), 'very like'. **equalling**: aequans (part. B, with acc.). **equally**: pariter (adv.), aeque (adv.).

equal-sided: aequilaterus (adj. A). **135**

Equator: aequator (s.m. III).

equatorial: aequatorius (adj. A).

equidistant: aequidistans (adj. B).

equinus (adj. A): pertaining to horses: *stercus equinus*, horse manure, horse droppings. **equorum**: of horses, *gen. pl. of* equus (s.m. II).

equitans (part. B): equitant, conduplicate and overlapping in two ranks, the base of the folded outer leaf clasping the base of the one opposite and this in turn clasping the base of the leaf opposite it; *lit.* 'riding', the lower leaf when turned horizontally seeming to ride upon the one above it. **377**

erasus (part. A): scraped off, e.g. when the outer layer has been lost or shed.

erect: erectus (part. A), arrectus (part. A). **erectiusculus** (adj. A): somewhat or almost erect. **erecto-patens** (adj. B): spreading at an angle of about 45°. **387**

erem-: *in Gk. comp.*, desert-.

erga (prep. with acc.): over against, opposite to.

ergo (adv.): because of (with gen.), accordingly, therefore.

erigens (part. B): rising, raising itself.

erio-: *in Gk. comp.*, woolly-, wool-*eriocalyx*, with woolly calyx; *eriogynus*, with woolly ovary; *eriophorus*, wool-bearing; *eriophyllus*, woolly-leaved; *eriorrhachis*, with woolly rachis; *eriospermus*, with woolly seeds. These and similar Latinized Gk. compounds are used only as epithets.

erosus (part. A): erose, having an irregularly toothed or apparently gnawed margin. **184**

erraticus (adj. A): wandering to and fro.

Error: erratum (s.n. II), *abl. sing.* errato, *nom. pl.* errata; error (s.m. III. v.), *abl. sing.* errore, *nom. pl.* errores.

erubescens (part. B): reddening, blushing, rose.

eruditus (part. A): learned, cultured.

erumpens (part. B): breaking through; *acervuli erumpentes*, acervuli bursting the surface.

Eruptio (s.f. III): a bursting forth, eruption, explosion.

erythrinus (adj. A): red. **erythro-**: *in Gk. comp.*, red-; *erythrocalyx*, with red calyx; *erythrocarpus*, red-fruited; *erythrochilus*, red-lipped; *erythrogrammus*, with red lines; *erythromelanus*, blackish red; *erythropoecilus*, red-spotted; *erythrorhachis*, with red rachis; *erythrosepalus*, red-sepalled; *erythrostachys*, with red spike; *erythrostictus*, red-spotted; *erythrotrichus*, red-haired. These and similar Latinized Gk. compounds are used only as epithets.

escaping: evadens (part. B), elabiens (part. B).

-escens (part. B): present part. ending used in forming adjective to indicate a process of becoming without full attainment reached.

esculentus (adj. A): edible, q.v.

eseptatus (adj. A): not partitioned, lacking septa.

especially: apprime (adv.), praecipue (adv.), praesertim (adv.).

essential: essentialis (adj. A): *character essentialis*, diagnosis, brief statement of most important characters. **essentially**: admodum (adv.) 'fully', quasi (adv.) 'almost', revera (adv. phrase) 'in fact'.

estriatus (adj. A): not striate.

Estuary: aestuarium (s.n. II), *acc. sing.* aestuarium, *abl. sing.* aestuario, *nom. acc. pl.* aestuaria, *abl. pl.* aestuariis; *species intertropicae littora limosa ad aestuaria fluviorum vegetatione arborea insalubri dense obumbrant*, the inter-tropical species the muddy shores at the estuaries of rivers with unhealthy woody vegetation densely cover over.

et (conj.): and, q.v.

etiam (conj.): and also, furthermore, even; *etiam atque etiam*, constantly, again and again.

etsi (conj.): although.

-etum (s.n. II): *in L. comp.*, place dominated by a given plant; *castanetum*, a wood of chestnut; *ericetum*, heath.

eu-: *in Gk. comp.*, well, good, thoroughly, completely, truly, as in the generic names *Eucalyptus*, 'well-covered'; *Eucharis*, 'charming'; *Euclidium*, 'well-shut'; *Eulophia*, 'with a good crest'; *Euonymus*, 'of good name, fortunate', ironically referring to its poisonous properties (recorded in Theophrastus, *Enqu.* III. xviii. v. 37); *Euptelea*, 'good elm'; *Euscaphis*, 'good vessel'; *Eusideroxylon*, 'true ironwood'. Also formerly much used in sense of 'true, original, primitive' in subgeneric and sectional names and infraspecific epithets for the subdivision containing the type of the name thus prefixed without reference to its linguistic origin, as in *Rhododendron* subg. *Eurhododendron*, *Prunus* sect. *Euprunus*, *Bowlesia* sect. *Eubowlesia*, *Saxifraga pedemontana* subsp. *eupedemontana*, *S. tridactylites* subsp. *eutridactylites*. Some generic names beginning with *Eu-* commemorate persons, e.g. *Eugenia* after Prince Eugen of Savoy, *Eulalia* after the botanical artist Eulalie Delile, *Eupatorium* after King Mithridates VI Eupator of Pontus and *Euphorbia* after the Numidian physician Euphorbus; *euanthus*, with beautiful flowers; *eubotryus*, with well-developed clusters; *eucallus*, beautiful; *euchaites*, with long hair; *euchromus*, *euchrous*, well-coloured; *eudoxus*, of good report; *eumorphus*, well-formed; *euprepes*, comely.

eucarpic: eucarpicus (adj. A).

Euphyllum (s.n. II): true leaf, foliage leaf as opposed to cataphyll (bract, reduced or rudimentary form of leaf); *see* CATAPHYLL. **euphylloideus** (adj. A): resembling foliage leaves; *bracteae primariae euphylloideae*, primary bracts like foliage leaves.

eutopicus (adj. A): twining with the sun, twisted from left to right; *see* TWINING.

evacuatus (part. A): left empty; cf. EMPTY.

evadens (part. B): escaping, going out.

evanescens (part. B), **evanidus** (adj. A): vanishing, passing away, quickly disappearing or fading, lasting only a short time. **evanidinervius** (adj. A): with nerves becoming faint and disappearing before reaching the margin.

even (adv.): etiam (adv.).

even (adj.): planus (adj. A) 'flat', aequus (adj. A) 'uniform', aequatus (part. A), 'made even, levelled'. **259**

Evening: vesper (s.m. II or III), *gen. sing.* vesperi *or* vesperis, *abl. sing.* vespero *or* vespere. **belonging to evening**: vespertinus (adj. A).

evenly: aequaliter (adv.), aequabiliter (adv.).

eventually: demum (adv.), denique (adv.).

ever: aliquando (adv.) 'at any time', semper (adv.) 'always, at all times'.

evergreen: sempervirens (adj. B); cf. PERHIEMANS.

eversus (part. A): everted, abruptly turned outwards, turned inside o ıt.

every: omnis (adj. B); *in fere omni segmento*, in almost every segment; *e fere omni cellula*, from nearly every cell; cf. QUISQUE.

everyway: quoquoversus (adv.), omnino (adv.).

everywhere: ubique (adv.), passim (adv.).

evident: evidens (adj. B), manifestus (adj. A), perspicuus (adj. A), visibilis (adj. B). **evidently**: evidenter (adv.), manifeste (adv.), perspicue (adv).

evolutus (part. A): unfolded, unrolled, developed.

evulgatus (part. A): published.

ex, e (prep. with abl.): from, out of, away from, after, through, by reason of; *ex* is always used before vowels, and even before consonants is used quite as commonly as *e*; *lamina e basi ad apicem 4 cm. longa*, blade from the base to the tip 4 cm. long; *ex affinitate Epidendri ramosi*, of the affinity of Epidendrum ramosum; *inflorescentiae ex axillis foliorum summorum 1-3 prodeuntes*, inflorescences from axils of upper leaves 1-3 produced; *ex comparatione speciminum siccorum cum planta viva in horto*, from comparison of dried specimens with a living plant in the garden; *e descriptione*, according to the description, judging from the description alone; *flores caerulei* (*e collectore*), flowers blue (according to the collector); *pulvini e ramis numerosis aggregatis compositi*, cushions out of numerous crowded together branches made up; *ovarium constat ex duobus carpellis*, ovary consists of two carpels; *ex Rossia specimina plura vidi*, from Russia many specimens I have seen; *ex speciminibus siccis originariis et ex litteris auctoris*, from original dried specimens and from letters of the author; *hybrida ex Pulmonaria mollissima et P. officinali*, hybrid from Pulmonaria mollissima and P. officinalis; *folia nervis lateralibus e nervo medio sub angulo 70°-80° abeuntibus*, leaves with lateral nerves from mid nerve at angle of 70°-80° departing; *semina ex horto botanico*, seeds from botanic garden; *baccae e viridi rubentes*, berries from green becoming red, berries greenish-red; *baccis e nigro rufis*, with berries red inclining to black; *magna ex parte*, in a great degree; *ex more*, according to custom; *ex contrario*, on the other hand, on the contrary; *nomen derivatum ex rhachi foliorum alata*, name derived from winged rachis of leaves; *nomen e lingua graeca sumptum est*, name from the Greek language taken is; *ex sententia cl. monographi generis, qui plantam nostram vidit, species nova ex Antillis minoribus est*, according to the distinguished monographer of the genus, who our plant saw, a new species from the Lesser Antilles it is.

ex- (prefix): *in L. comp.*, without, lacking, destitute of, un-, -less; *see* E-, AN- *exalatus*, wingless; *exalbuminatus, exalbuminosus*, without endosperm, the embryo occupying the whole space within the seedcoat; *exannulatus*, without an annulus; *exaristatus*, awnless; *exindusiatus*, without an indusium; *exscapus*, stalkless; *exstipulatus*, without stipules; *exsuccus*, without juice, dry.

exact: accuratus (part. A) (used only of statements and things), diligens (part. B) (used of persons), exactus (part. A) (measured; used only of numbers). **exactly**: accurate (adv.), diligenter (adv.), ad amussim (adv. phrase).

exalbescens (part. B): becoming white. **exalbidus** (adj. A): whitish.

exaltatus (part. A): raised high, lofty. **340**

exaratus (part. A) : furrowed (*usu. with more or less parallel grooves*, *lit.* 'ploughed').

exasperatus (part. A) : covered with short hard points, *lit.* 'roughened'. **266**

excavatus (part. A) : hollowed out in a curve, e.g. at insertion of leaf, or as a deep pit.

excedens (part. B) : rising above, overtopping, exceeding.

exceedingly : admodum (adv.), magnopere (adv.), summopere (adv.), valde (adv.).

excellent : optimus (adj. A), egregius (adj. A).

excellently : optime (adv.), egregie (adv.), eximie (adv.)

excelsus (part. A) : lofty, high.

excentricus (adj. A) : eccentric, one-sided, placed out of the centre ; *stipes excentricus*, stipe attached between centre and edge of pileus ; *oosporis gutta excentrica*, with oospores having an oil-drop to one side.

except for : praeter (adv. and prep. with acc.) ; *herba praeter inflorescentiam hirsutam glabra*, herb except for the hairy inflorescence glabrous ; *praeter titulum mutatum nulla nota differt*, except for the changed title by no matter it differs ; cf. NISI. **excepting, excepted** : exceptus (part. A) ; *herba (scapo glabro excepto) hirsuta*, herb (with the glabrous scape excepted) hairy.

excerptus (part. A) : taken from, selected, chosen.

excessively : nimis (adv.)

Excipule : excipulum (s.n. II), *abl. sing.* excipulo, *nom. pl.* excipula, *abl. pl.* excipulis ; *excipulum integrum fuligineum ad basim planatum, labiis erectis superne conniventibus*, excipule entire dark brown at base flattened, with lips erect above coming together.

excisus (part. A) : cut out (*often referring to sinuses*).

exclusively : solum (adv.), nonnisi (adv.), omnino (adv.).

exclusus (part. A) : excluded ; *descriptione exclusa*, with the description excluded.

excrescens (part. B) : growing out, enlarging, usually abnormally.

excretus (part. A) : full grown.

excurrens (part. B) : excurrent, running out beyond, e.g. mainstem of a conifer, veins of a leaf ; *folia costa percurrente vel breviter excurrente*, leaves with midrib percurrent or shortly excurrent.

excussus (part. A) : shaken off, removed, plucked out.

Exemplum (s.n. II) : example, specimen.

exesus (part. A) : eaten up, irregularly eroded on the surface.

exhauriens (part. B) : making empty, taking out, exhausting.

exhausted : effoetus (adj. A).

exhibiting : exhibens (part. B), ostendens (part. B), praebens (part. B).

exiens (part. B) : going forth, springing forth, coming up ; *inflorescentiae ex axillis exeuntes*, inflorescences arising from the axis ; cf. INIENS.

exiguus (adj. A) : weak, feeble, little. **339**

exiliens (part. B) : springing out.

exilis (adj. B) : small, meagre, weak, thin, slender.

eximie (adv.) : exceedingly, excellently.

Exit : exitus (s.m. IV).

exo- : *in Gk. comp.*, outward, outside ; *opposite of* ENDO- ; *exostylis*, with projecting style.

Exocarp : exocarpium (s.n. II), *abl. sing.* exocarpio.

exogenus (adj. A) : exogenous, produced from outer tissue or on the outside of another body.

Exoperidium : exoperidium (s.n. II), *abl. sing.* exoperidio.

exoriens (part. B) : coming out, arising. **exortus** (part. A) : sprung from, arisen out of.

Exospore : exosporium (s.n. II), *abl. sing.* exosporio.

Exothecium : exothecium (s.n. II), *abl. sing.* exothecio.

exotic : exoticus (adj. A) ; cf. ALIENUS, FOREIGN.

Expansio (s.f. III) : expansion ; *ante expansionem*, before expansion.

expansus (part. A) : expanded, spread out.

expelled : depulsus (part. A).

expers (adj. B) : devoid of, without ; used with gen. and abl. ; *sepala glandum expertia*, sepals devoid of glands.

explanatus (part. A) : flattened, outspread, explained : *in statu explanato*, in a flattened-out state.

Explicatio (s.f. III) : explanation, exposition, analysis.

exploding : explodens (part. B).

explosively : eruptione (*abl. sing. of* eruptio, q.v.).

exposed : expositus (part. A), apertus 'open', nudus (adj. A) 'naked'.

expressus (part. A) : prominent, clearly exhibited ; *costa supra anguste impressa infra late expressa*, midrib narrowly impressed above broadly prominent below.

expulsus (part. A) : ejected, expelled.

exsculptus (part. A) : chiselled out, pitted with small depressions.

exsertus (part. A) : exserted, thrust forth, protruding from *or* extending beyond surrounding organs.

Exsiccata (s.f. I): an exsiccata, a set of dried specimens usually provided with printed labels.

Exsiccatum (s.n. II): dried specimen; cf. DRIED.

exsiccatus (part. A): dried; *plantae exsiccatae*, herbarium specimens; *fungi exsiccati*, dried fungi.

exstans (part. B): projecting.

exstipulate: exstipulatus (adj. A), estipulatus (adj. A).

exstructus (part. A): put together, constructed.

exsuccus (adj. A): juiceless.

exsudans (part. B): exuding. **Exsudatum** (s.n. II): exudate.

exsulcus (adj. A): not furrowed.

exsurgens (part. B): rising out of.

extended: extensus (part. A), productus (part. A), prolongatus (part. A), provectus (part. A). **extending**: extensus (part. A). **Extension**: extensio (s.f. III).

extense (adv.): at length, extensively (part. A). **extensus** (part. A): stretched out, extended.

exter (adj. A): on the outside, from *or* of another country, foreign. **exterior** (adj. comp., m. and f.), **exterius** (n.): outward, outer, exterior. **externus** (adj. A): outward, external.

external: *see* EXTER, OUTER. **externally**: *see* EXTRA, OUTSIDE.

extimus (adj.): outermost, farthest, most remote.

Extine: extina (s.f. I).

extra (prep. with acc.): outside of, beyond, apart from, besides, in addition to. **extra** (adv.): on the outside, externally. **extra-axillaris** (adj. B): extra-axillary, i.e. arising on internode beyond or outside an axil, not direct from an axil. **extraneus** (adj. A): extraneous, strange, foreign, not related.

extractus (part. A): drawn forth, dragged out.

extrarius (adj. A): outward, external, placed on the outside.

extremely: maxime (adv.), magnopere (adv.). **Extremum** (s.n. II): an end, the end, the last; *ad extremum*, at the end.

Extremitas (s.f. III): extremity; *folia ad extremitates ramorum*, leaves at tips of branches.

extremum (adv.): at last, finally. **extremus** (adj. A): outermost, extreme, last. **extrinsecus** (adv.): from outside, on the outside.

extrorsus (adv.): extrorsely, towards the outside, opening on the outside. **421**

extrusus (part. A): pushed out.

extus (adv.): outside, on the outside.

Exudate: exsudatum (s.n. II). **exuding**: exsudans (part. B).

Exul, Exsul (s.f. III. x): exile, banished person; *Plantagineae ex nullo climate exules*, the Plantagineae from no climate exiles.

exutus (part. A): stripped off, cast off, shed.

Eye: ocellus (s.m. II), oculus (s.m. II), *in Gk. comp.*, omma- (s.n. III.), -ophthalmus (adj. A); *melanophthalmus*, black-eyed. **marked with eye-like spots**: ocellatus (adj. A). **Eye-spot**: stigma (s.n. III). **with naked eye**: oculo nudo (adv. phrase).

F

fabiformis (adj. B): bean-shaped.

Fabrica (s.f. I): structure; *genus fabrica antherarum distincta*, genus distinct by the structure of the anthers; cf. COMPAGES, STRUCTURE. **fabricatus** (part. A): constructed, fashioned.

Face: superficies (s.f. V). **facial**: facialis (adj. B).

faciens (part. B): making, producing, creating.

Facies (s.f. V): shape, general appearance, external form; *see* APPEARANCE, VIEW.

facile (adv.): easily. **facilis** (adj. B): easy.

facing: aspiciens (part. B), spectans (part. B).

factitius (adj. A): artificial, made by art.

factus (part. A): made, done.

facultative: facultativus (adj. A).

faded: decolor (adj. B).

faecal: faecalis (adj. B). **Faeces**: faeces (*nom. pl. of* faex, s.f. III), *gen.* faecum *or* faecium, *abl.* faecibus.

faint: dilutus (part. A), tenuis (adj. B), inconspicuus (adj. A). **faintly**: dilute (adv.) (*used only of colours*), leviter (adv.).

fairly: satis (adv.).

falcatus (adj. A): falcate, curved like a sickle. **falcato-secundus** (adj. A): falcate and turned to one side of the stem. **falciformis** (adj. B): shaped like a scythe or sickle. **38**

Fall: lapsus (s.m. IV), q.v.

fallax (adj. B): deceptive, fallacious; cf. DECIPIENS.

fallen: caducus (adj. A), delapsus (part. A). **falling**: cadens (part. B).

false: falsus (adj. A), *in comp.* pseudo-. **falsely**: false (adv.), spurie (adv.), perperam (adv.).

falsinervis (adj. B): with nerves formed of cellular (not fibrovascular) tissue. **362**

Family: familia (s.f. I), *acc. sing.* familiam, *nom. pl.* familiae, *acc. pl.* familias.

fan-shaped: flabellatus (adj. A), flabelliformis (adj. B).

far off; procul (adv.), longe (adv.).

farciminiformis (adj. B): sausage-shaped.

farctus (part. A): stuffed, filled, or solid with tissue softer than the outside; cf. HOLLOW.

-fariam (adv.): *in L. comp.*, -ranked, in a row or line; *unifariam*, in one row; *bifariam*, in two rows. **489**

Farina (s.f. I): flour-like powdery covering. **farinaceus** (adj. A): starchy. **farinosus** (adj. A): mealy, covered with farina. **331**

-farius (adj. A): *in L. comp.*, -ranked; *folia quadrifaria*, leaves four-ranked.

farthest: ultimus (adj. A), extremus (adj. A).

fartilis (adj. B): stuffed; cf. FARCTUS.

fasciarius (adj. A): band-shaped. **fasciatus** (adj. A): fasciate, teratologically grown together, as of several stems into one; marked transversely with broad parallel stripes of colour. **104, 496**

Fascicle: fasciculus (s.m. II), *acc. sing.* fasciculum, *abl. sing.* fasciculo, *nom. pl.* fasciculi, *acc. pl.* fasciculos, *abl. pl.* fasciculis; *inflorescentia ad fasciculum simplicem reducta*, inflorescence to a simple cluster reduced; *fasciculi brevissimi vix ad 1 millimetrum longi, in vivo purpureo-sanguinei* (*fide Ehrenb.*), *in speciminibus siccis griseo-virides*, fascicles very short scarcely 1 mm. long, in a living state purple-blood-red (according to Ehrenberg), in dried specimens greygreen; *trichomata in fasciculos squamuliformes discretos libere natantes aggregata*, trichomes in fascicles scale-like separate freely swimming clustered together.

fasciculatus (adj. A): clustered, growing in bundles. **Fasciculus** (s.m. II): fascicle, bundle, cluster of pedicels, etc., part ('livraison', 'Heft') of volume. **487**

fastened to: affixus (part. A).

fastigiatus (adj. A): fastigiate, with branches clustered, parallel and erect, giving a narrow elongated habit, (*in bryology*) with branches reaching to the same height. Not to be confused with *fastigatus* (part. A), high, exalted. **494**

fastuosus (adj. A): proud, haughty.

Fat: sebum (s.n. II), *gen. sing.* sebi; pingue (s.n. III), *gen. sing.* pinguis. **fat**: pinguis (adj. B), obesus (adj. A).

Fathom: orgya (s.f. I), hexapodium (s.n. II).

fatiscens (part. B): disintegrating, crumbling, disappearing.

Fauces (s.f. III. i. pl.): throat, defile, gorge. In class. L. used only in pl., in bot. L. mostly in singular. **Faux** (s.f.

III. i): upper part of throat, orifice of calyx or corolla, mouth, entrance, narrow way, defile, gorge, pass.

faveolatus (adj. A): finely honeycombed.

favosus (adj. A): honeycombed, i.e. covered with regular angled depressions. **250**

fawn: hinnuleus (adj. A); *in Gk. comp.*, elapho-.

Feature: proprietas (s.f. III).

Fecundatio (s.f. III): fertilization; *varietates e fecundatione artificiali ortae*, varieties derived from artificial fertilization. **fecundus** (adj. A): fruitful, fertile; cf. STERILE.

felted: coactus (part. A).

female: femineus (adj. A), foemineus (adj. A); *flores feminei*, female flowers; *in Gk. comp.*, gyn-, thely-.

Fenestra (s.f. I): window. **fenestratus** (adj. A), **fenestralis** (adj. B): windowed, provided with openings. **fenestrellatus** (adj. A): with little windows or openings.

-fer (adj. A, suffix): *in L. comp.*, -carrying. *caulis florifer*, flower-bearing stem; *panicula fructifera*, fruit-bearing panicle.

ferax (adj. B): fruitful, fertile. Not to be confused with *ferox*.

fere (adv.): nearly, almost, for the most part, about.

ferens (part. B): carrying, bearing.

ferment-producing: zymogenus (adj. A).

Fermentation: fermentatio (s.f. III).

Fermentum (s.n. II): yeast.

Fern: filix (s.f. III. i), *gen. sing.* filicis, *nom. pl.* filices. **fern-like**: filicinus (adj. A); cf. FILIC-.

ferox (adj. B): fierce. Generally used of very spiny plants.

ferreus (adj. A): iron, relating to iron; *via ferrea*, railway.

ferruginescens (adj. B): becoming rustyred. **ferrugineus** (adj. A): rusty, light brown with a little mixture of red. **Ferrum** (s.n. II): iron.

fertile: fertilis (adj. B), fecundus (adj. A).

Fertilization: fecundatio (s.f. III).

ferus (adj. A): wild; cf. SYLVESTRIS.

few, a: aliquot (num. indecl.), q.v. **few**: paucus (adj. A). **few-**: *in L. comp.*, pauci-, *in Gk. comp.*, oligo-, spano-.

Fibre: fibra (s.f. I), *nom. pl.* fibrae, *acc. pl.* fibras, *abl. pl.* fibris; *bulborum tunicae tandem in fibras paralleas apicem versus vel in totum solutae*, of the bulbs the tunics at length into fibres parallel towards the tip or entirely breaking up; *vitta fibrarum seriebus 2-3 formata*, band formed from 2-3 series of fibres.

Fibril: fibrilla (s.f. I).

fibrillosus (adj. A): fibrillose, covered with firm thin threadlike fibres. **fibrosus** (adj. A): composed of separable threads or fibres, fibrous. **329**

Fibula (s.f. I): clamp connexion of fungal hypha, *lit.* 'clasp, buckle, pin, brace'. **fibulatus** (adj. A): provided with clamps. **fibuliger** (adj. A): clamp-bearing.

fici- : *in L. comp.*, relating to figs; *see* FIG-.

ficulneus (adj. A): of the fig-tree.

fide (abl. sing. of *fides*): according to, *lit.* by the faith, by the assurance (of); *fide Smith in litt.*, according to Smith in a letter; *fide collectoris*, according to the collector; cf. TESTE.

-fidus (adj. A): *in L. comp.*, divided (*usually within outer third*). **199**

Field : ager (s.m. II), *abl. pl.* agris, 'cultivated land, whether arable or pasture, as opposed to the wild', arvum (s.n. II), *abl. pl.* arvis, 'arable land as opposed to pasture'. **pertaining to fields** : agrestis (adj. B), arvalis (adj. B), arvensis (adj. B).

fierce : ferox (adj. B), q.v.

Fig : ficus (s.f.), *gen. sing.* fici *or* ficus, *abl. sing.* fico *or* ficu, *nom. pl.* fici, *gen. pl.* ficorum, *abl. pl.* ficis.

fig- : *in L. comp.*, fici-, *in Gk. comp.*, syco-; *ficifolius*, fig-leaved, i.e. with deeply 3-7-lobed digitate leaves suggesting those of Ficus carica; *sycocarpus*, with fig-like fruit.

Figura (s.f. I): shape, figure. **figuratus** (part. A): of definite shape.

Filament : filum (s.n. II), *abl. sing.* filo, *nom. pl.* fila, *abl. pl.* filis, filamentum (s.n. II), *abl. sing.* filamento, *nom. pl.* filamenta, *abl. pl.* filamentis ; *fila laxe intricata vel valde contorta vix flexilia haud sine ruptura extricanda*, filaments loosely entangled or strongly intwisted together scarcely pliant not without breaking to be unravelled ; *fila repentia irregulariter ramosa e cellulis oblongis composita*, filaments creeping irregularly branched from cells oblong made up ; *thallus e disco basali et filis erectis constructus*, thallus from a basal disc and erect filaments built up ; *discus basalis e filis repentibus coherentibus subdichotome divisis compositus*, basal disc from filaments creeping cohering almost dichotomously divided made up ; *filamenta simplicia fere per longitudinem aequabiliter 4 μ crassa*, filaments simple almost throughout their length evenly 4 μ thick ; *alga filamentis erectis parallelis vel intricatis fragilibus a basi ad apicem gradatim angustatis*, alga with

filaments erect parallel or entangled fragile from base to tip gradually narrowed; *filamentum* is used both for the filaments of stamens and the vegetative filaments of Algae, *filum* only for the latter ; cf. STAMEN.

filamentous : filamentosus (adj. A).

fili- : *in L. comp.*, thread-; *filicaulis*, with thread-like stem ; *filifer*, thread-bearing ; *filifolius*, thread-leaved ; *filipendulus*, hanging by a thread, e.g. the swollen parts of tuberous roots connected by narrow thread-like parts.

Filia (s.f. I): daughter.

filic- : *in L. comp.*, relating to ferns; *filicifolius*, with fern-like leaves ; *filiciformis, filicinus*, fern-like.

filiformis (adj. B): thread-like. **49**

Filius (s.m. II): son ; *Hooker filius*, *Hook. fil., Hook. f.*, the younger Hooker, i.e. Joseph Dalton Hooker (1817–1911), son of William Jackson Hooker (1785–1865).

Filix (s.f. III. i): fern.

filled : impletus (part. A), refertus (part. A), repletus (part. A), completus (part. A), plenus (adj. A); *semen dorso late concavum, sulco arillo spongioso repleto*, seed on the back broadly concave, with the furrow by a spongy aril filled ; *protoplastus olei plenus*, protoplast full of oil. **filling** : complens (part. B). implens (part. B) ; *chlorophyllum cellulam complens*, chlorophyll filling the cell.

Filum (s.n. II): thread, filament of alga ; *see* FILAMENT.

fimbri- : *in L. comp.*, fimbriate; *fimbricalyx*, with fimbriate calyx.

Fimbria : fimbria (s.f. I): *nom. pl.* fimbriae, *abl. pl.* fimbriis. **fimbriate** : fimbriatus (adj. A).

fimecarius (adj. A): growing on dung. **Fimus** (s.m. II): dung, q.v.

final : ultimus (adj. A). **finally** : postremo (adv.), extremum (adv.), ad extremum, denique (adv.), tandem (adv.).

findens (part. B): tearing, splitting.

fine : tenuis (adj. B). **finely** : subtiliter (adv.).

fingens (part. B) : representing.

Finger : *see* DACTYL.

finger-like : digitiformis (adj. B).

Finis (s.f. III) : boundary, limit, border, end.

finished : terminatus (part. A).

firm : firmus (adj. A) 'stable, steady', solidus (adj. A) 'dense, not hollow'. **firmly** : firme (adv.), solide (adv.).

first : primus (adj. A). **firstly** : primitus (adv.), primo (adv.), primum (adv.), initio (abl. of *initium*) 'in the beginning'.

Fish : piscis (s.m. III), *gen. sing.* piscis. **Fish-pond** : piscina (s.f. I).

fissi- : *in L. comp.*, split-; *fissidens*, with split teeth ; *see* SPLIT. **fissilis** (adj. B) : easily split. **Fissio** (s.f. III) : fission.

Fissure : fissura (s.f. I), rima (s.f. I) : *areolae fissuris tenuibus separatae*, areoles by narrow fissures separated. **fissured** : fissuratus (adj. A).

fissus (part. A) : cleft, i.e. cut to about midway or more. **194**

fistulosus (adj. A) : fistular, i.e. hollow throughout, like a pipe, but closed at ends ; cf. PERFOSSUS. **7**

fit : aptus (part. A), aptatus (part. A) ; *ad vescendum aptum*, fit to eat.

fitted together : interordinatus (adj. A).

five : quinque (num. adj. indecl.) 'five', quintus (adj. A) 'fifth', quini (num. adj. distr. pl.), 'five each', quinquiens (adv.) 'five times' ; *petala quinque rubra*, petals 5 red ; *petalis quinque rubris*, with petals 5 red. **five** : *in L. comp.*, quinqu-, quinque-, quinqui-, *in Gk. comp.*, penta- ; *pentagonus, quinquangularis, quinquangulatus*, 5-angled ; *pentachaetus, quinquesetus*, 5-bristled ; *pentanthus, quinqueflorus*, 5-flowered ; *pentaphyllus, quinquefolius*, with 5-leaves or leaflets ; *pentaneurus, quinquenervus, quinquenervis*, 5-nerved ; *pentagynus, quinquestylus*, 5-styled ; *pentaphlebius, quinqevenosus*, 5-veined ; *see* PENTA-, QUINQUE-.

fixed : certus (adj. A) 'certain', fixus (part. A) 'immovable'. **fixed to** : affixus (part. A), with dat. or *ad* and acc.

flabellatus (adj. A), **flabelliformis** (adj. B) : flabellate, fan-shaped. **64**

flaccidus (adj. A) : flaccid, not able to hold up its own weight.

flagellar : flagellaris (adj. B).

flagelliform : flagelliformis (adj. B), flagellaris (adj. B). **47**

Flagellum : flagellum (s.n. II), *nom. pl.* flagella, *abl. pl.* flagellis.

flammeus (adj. A) : flame-coloured, fiery red, scarlet.

flask-shaped : ampulliformis (adj. B).

flat : planus (adj. A). **flattened** : complanatus (part. A). **flattened horizontally** : applanatus (adj. A).

flavescens (adj. B), **flavidus** (adj. A) : yellowish, pale yellow. **flavovirens** (adj. B) : green stained with yellow, yellowish-green. **flavus** (adj. A) : yellow, paler than *luteus* ; *flavus dresdanus*, dresden yellow (H.C.C. 64) ; *flavus imperialis*, empire yellow (H.C.C. 60.3) ; *flavus neapolitanus*, naples yellow (H.C.C. 40. 3).

Flesh : caro (s.f. III. vi), *abl. sing.* carne. **flesh-coloured** : carneus (adj. A). **fleshy** : carnosus (adj. A), succulentus (adj. A).

flexibilis (adj. B), **flexilis** (adj. B) : flexible. **flexuosus** (adj. A) : flexuosus, zigzag, bent alternately in opposite directions. **flexus** (part. A) : bent. **413**

floating : natans (part. B), fluitans (part. B) ; *folia natantia*, floating leaves. **391**

floccosus (adj. A) : floccose, with tufts of soft hairs, (in Algae) having appearance of matted woolly hairs.

flooded : inundatus (part. A), q.v.

Flora : flora (s.f. I).

floralis (adj. B) : floral, relaᵤᵢₙₒ to the flower.

Florescentia (s.f. I) : period of flowering.

Floret : flosculus (s.m. II), *abl. sing.* flosculo, *nom. pl.* flosculi, *abl. pl.* flosculis.

floribundus (adj. A) : profusely flowering.

floribus (dat. and abl. pl. of flos) : with flowers ; *see* FLOWER.

Floricane : floricanna (s.f. I) ; *primocannae erectae, floricannae procumbentes, foliis floricannarum trifoliolatis*, primocanes (biennial shoots in first year) erect, floricanes (biennial shoots in second year, i.e. flowering state) procumbent, with leaves of floricanes 3-foliolate.

floridus (adj. A) : abounding in flowers, profusely flowering. **florifer** (adj. A), **floriger** (adj. A) : bearing flowers, flowering. **Florilegium** (s.n. II) : a collection of paintings of flowers ; cf. Blunt & Stearn, *Art. Bot. Illustr.* 123-131 (1950). **florosus** (adj. A), **florulentus** (adj. A) : abounding in flowers, (profusely flowering.

Florula (s.f. I) : a small flora.

Flos (s.m. III. iv) : flower, q.v. **Flosculus** (s.m. II) : floret, q.v.

Flour : farina (s.f. I), *abl. sing.* farina. **floury** : farinosus (adj. A) 'covered with meal', farinaceus (adj. A) 'of mealy composition', aleurodes (adj. Gk.), (*used only as specific epithet*).

flourishing : vigens (part. B).

Flow : fluxus (s.m. IV).

Flower : flos (s.m. III. iv), *acc. sing.* florem, *gen. sing.* floris, *dat. sing.* flori, *abl. sing.* flore, *nom. and acc. pl.* flores, *gen. pl.* florum, *dat. and abl. pl.* floribus ; *flos solitarius sessilis magnus fragrans*, flower solitary sessile large fragrant ; *flore solitario sessili fragranti*, with flower solitary sessile fragrant ; *pedicelli florem superantes*, pedicels exceeding the flower ; *pedicelli longitudine florum*, pedicels the length of the flower ; *color florum variabilis*, colour of flowers variable ; *flores parvi lutescentes*, flowers small yellowish ; *floribus erectis parvis*, with flowers erect small ; *spatha arte floribus accumbente, flore duplo majore*, with spathe lying closely upon the flowers, twice as big as the flower.

flowering: florens (part. B).

Flowering, Period of: florescentia (s.f. I); *see* ANTHESIS; flowering before the leaves, *see* PROTERANTHUS, PRAECOX; flowering with the leaves, *see* COAETANEUS, SYNANTHUS; flowering after the leaves, *see* HYSTERANTHUS.

flowing: profluens (part. B).

fluitans (part. B): floating, swimming. **391**

Flumen (s.n. III. vi): river, stream; *see* RIVER. **fluminalis** (adj. B), **flumineus** (adj. A): pertaining to rivers. **fluminensis** (adj. B): pertaining to Rio de Janeiro, Brazil.

flush with: complanus (adj. A), with *dat.*

fluted: striatus (adj. A).

fluviaticus (adj. A), **fluviatilis** (adj. B): pertaining to rivers. **Fluvius** (s.m. II): river (*not so frequently used as* flumen); *see* RIVER.

Flexus (s.m. IV): flow, flux.

foaming: spumeus (adj. A), spumosus (adj. A).

Fodder: pabulum (s.n. II).

foecundus (adj. A): fruitful, fertile; cf. STERILE.

foemineus (adj. A): female.

foetens (part. B), **foetidus** (adj. A), **foetulentus** (adj. A): stinking, evil-smelling.

Fold: plica (s.f. I), *abl. sing.* plica, *nom. pl.* plicae, *abl. pl.* plicis. **folded**: plicatus (adj. A).

foliaceus (adj. A): foliaceous, leafy, leaf-like in texture or shape. **folianeus** (adj. A): taking the place of a leaf. **foliaris** (adj. B): relating to the leaf. **foliatus** (adj. A): provided with leaves, leaf-bearing. -**foliatus** (adj. A), -**folius** (adj. A): *in L. comp.*, -leaved; *unifoliatus*, *unifolius*, with one leaf, one-leaved; *bifoliatus*, *bifolius*, two-leaved. **foliifer** (adj. A): leaf-bearing. **foliiformis** (adj. B): leaf-like. **foliosus** (adj. A): leafy, full of leaves, many-leaved. **Folium** (s.n. II): leaf, q.v. -**foliolatus**: leaf-letted. **Foliolum** (s.n. II): leaflet. **59, 465**

Follicle: folliculus (s.m. II), *abl. sing.* folliculo, *nom. pl.* folliculi, *abl. pl.* folliculis; *folliculi erecti pubescentes, reticulato-venosi vel etiam corrugati, stylis persistentibus 5 mm. longis inclusis 20 mm. longi*, follicles erect pubescent, reticulately veined or even corrugated, with the persistent 5 mm. long styles included 20 mm. long. **follicle-like**: follicularis (adj. B).

following: sequens (part. B), secundus (adj. A); secundum (prep. with acc.), post (prep. with acc.).

Fons (s.m. III. ix): spring of water, fountain-head. **fontanus** (adj. A), **fontinalis** (adj. B): growing in or by springs.

Food: cibus (s.m. II), pabulum (s.n. II), nutrimentum (s.n. II), alimentum (s.n. II). **pertaining to food**: cibarius (adj. A).

Foot: pes (s.m. III. ii), *acc. sing.* pedem, *gen. sing.* pedis, *abl. sing.* pede, *nom. and acc. pl.* pedes, *gen. pl.* pedum, *abl. pl.* pedibus; *ad altitudinem 4,000 pedum super oceanum*, at 4,000 ft. (1220 m.) altitude above the ocean; *see* -PODUS.

Footpath: semita (s.f. I).

for: enim (conj.); per (prep. with acc.); *sinus per quasi dimidium longitudinis clausus*, sinus for almost half of its length closed; cf. PRO, PROPTER.

Foramen (s.n. III); opening, aperture; cf. APERTURA, RIMA.

foratus (part. A): pierced with holes.

foreign: exoticus (adj. A), peregrinus (adj. A), alienus (adj. A); INQUILINUS.

Forest: sylva (s.f. I). **Forester**: sylvarius (s.m. II), saltuarius (s.m. II), custos (s.m. III) sylvarum.

Fork: furca (s.f. I), *acc. sing.* furcam, *abl. sing.* furca, *nom. pl.* furcae, *acc. pl.* furcas, *abl. pl.* furcis; *see* ANTHERIDIUM, RAY. **forked**: furcatus (adj. A). **233**

Forma (s.f. I): form, figure, shape (*referring to general build, etc.*), form (*as taxonomic unit inferior to variety*); *planta sub variis formis invenitur, quarum primariae sunt sequentes*, the plant is found under various forms, of which the chief are the following; *forma specialis*, special form, one distinguished by physiological rather than morphological characters.

formed: factus (part. A), formatus (part. A), instar (s. indecl. with gen.) 'with form of'. -**formed**: *in L. comp.*, -formis, *in Gk. comp.*, -morphus. **forming**: faciens (part. B), formans (part. B).

formerly: antea (adv.), olim (adv.), pridem (adv.), quondam (adv.).

Formica (s.f. I): ant; *formicarum*, of ants. **Formicarium** (s.n. II): swelling at base of leaf or top of petiole or at node inhabited by ants. **formicarius** (adj. A): pertaining to ants. **formicosus** (adj. A): full of ants.

formosus (adj. A): finely formed, handsome, beautiful. Not to be confused with *formosanus*, 'relating to Formosa (Taiwan)'.

fornicalis (adj. B): with arches, relating to arches. **fornicatus** (adj. A): arched, provided with small arched scale-like appendages in corolla-tube, *lit.* 'vaulted'. **Fornix** (s.m. III. i): small scale, *lit.* 'arch, vault, brothel'; *corolla fauce* *fornicibus lanceolatis integris vel bilobis in conum conniventibus clausa*, corolla at the throat by lanceolate entire or 2-lobed scales coming together as a cone closed ; *fornices corollae prominuli vel exserti papillosi*, scales of the corolla prominent or exserted papillose.

fors (adv.), **forsan** (adv.) : perhaps, perchance. **fortasse** (adv.) : perhaps, possibly, probably. **forte** (adv.) : by chance, by accident, perhaps.

fortis (adj. B) : strong, powerful, vigorous. **fortiter** (adv.) : strongly, vigorously.

fortuito (adv.) : at random, by chance, fortuitously, accidentally. **fortuitus** (adj. A) : accidental.

forwards : prorsum (adv.), prorsus (adv.).

Fossa (s.f. I) : ditch, trench ; *in fossis*, in ditches. **Fossula** (s.f. I) : a little furrow.

foul : foedus (adj. A). **fouled** : foedatus (part. A), inquinatus (part. A).

found : inventus (part. A).

Fountain-head : fons (s.m. III. ix), *nom. pl.* fontes.

four : quattuor, quatuor (num. adj. indecl.) 'four', quaterni (num. adj. dist. pl.) 'four each, four together', quartus (adj. A) 'fourth', quater (adv.) 'four times' ; *sepala quatuor viridia*, sepals 4 green ; *sepalis quatuor viridibus*, with sepals 4 green. **four-** : *in L. comp.*, quadr-, quadri, *in Gk. comp.*, tetra-; *quadrangularis, tetragonus*, 4-angled ; *quadricolor, tetrachromus*, 4-coloured ; *quadricornis, quadricornutus, tetraceras*, 4-horned ; *quadrifolius, tetraphyllus*, 4-leaved ; *quadrifarius, tetrastichus*, 4-rowed ; *quadrialatus, tetrapterus*, 4-winged ; *see* QUADR-, TETRA-.

Fovea (s.f. I) : a small pit. **foveatus** (adj. A) : pitted. **foveolatus** (adj. A) : minutely pitted.

fovens (part. B) : embracing, enfolding, cherishing : *rhachis scrobiculis calyces fructigeros foventibus insculpta*, rachis sculptured with pits holding tightly the fruiting calyces.

fractiflexus (adj. A) : zigzag. **fractus** (part. A) : broken.

fragile : fragilis (adj. B), friabilis (adj. B).

Fragmentum (s.n. II) : piece broken off, fragment ; *see* FRUSTILLUM.

fragrant : fragrans (part. B) ; *see* SMELL.

fraternus (adj. A) : brotherly, closely allied.

freckled : lentiginosus (adj. A).

free : liber (adj. A), discretus (part. A). **freely** : libere (adv.) 'unrestrictedly', copiose (adv.) 'abundantly'.

frequent : frequens (adj. B). **frequently** : saepe (adv.), plerumque (adv.), increbre (adv.).

fresh : dulcis (adj. B) (*used of water*) ; novus (adj. A) 'new', vivus (adj. A) 'living'.

Fretum (s.n. II), **Fretus** (s.m. IV) : strait, sound, channel ; *in freto Magellanico*, in Straits of Magellan ; *fretum Herculeum*, the Strait of Gibraltar.

friabilis (adj. B) : fragile.

Frigidarium (s.n. II) : cool greenhouse, orangery. **frigidus** (adj. A) : cold.

Fringe : fimbria (s.f. I). **fringed** : fimbriatus (adj. A), *in Gk. comp.*, thysano-.

from : a or ab (prep. with abl.) 'distant from', e or ex (prep. with abl.) 'going away from' ; unde (adv.) 'from which' ; *plantae e basi ramosae*, plants branched from the base ; *species nova a speciebus aliis floribus pedicellatis distinguenda*, new species from other species by its pedicellate flowers to be distinguished ; *varietas a typo divergens*, variety diverging from the type ; *planta ex Algeria introducta*, plant introduced from Algeria. **from above** : desuper (adv.).

Frond : frons (s.f. III. ix), *gen. sing.* frondis, *abl. sing.* fronde, *nom. pl.* frondes, *gen. pl.* frondium, *abl. pl.* frondibus ; *frons bipinnata ambitu ovata 25 cm. longa*, frond bipinnate in outline ovate 25 cm. long ; *fronde late triangulari bipinnata, pinnis ad angulum 70°-80° patentibus*, with frond broadly triangular bipinnate, with pinnae at an angle of 70°-80° spreading ; *frondes lineares iteratim dichotomae angulo acuto (40°-60°), rarissime pinnatim divisae 2-3 pollicares, furcis mediis 8 mm. longis*, fronds linear repeatedly dichotomous at an acute angle (40°-60°) very rarely pinnately divided 2-3 inches long, with middle forks 8 mm. long.

Frondescentia (s.f. I) : leafing, the unfolding of leaves.

frondosus (adj. A) : leafy, leaf-like, leaf-bearing, with well-developed leaves, full of leaves.

Frondula (s.f. I) : division of a pinnate frond.

Front : frons (s.f. III) ; *a fronte visus*, seen from the front. **front** : anticus (adj. A). **frontal** : frontalis (adj. B). **in front** : antice (adv.).

frothy : spumeus (adj. A).

frozen : gelatus (part. A).

Fructiculus (s.m. II) : a single fruiting carpel of an apocarpous fruit ; cf. DRUPELET. **fructifer** (adj. A) : fruit-bearing. **fructificans** (part. B) : fruiting. **Fructificatio** (s.f. III. vi) : fruit-body, fructification (as used by Linnaeus, the flowering and fruiting organs ending one period of generation and beginning the next one, i.e. calyx, corolla, androecium, gynoecium, fruit and seed). **fructuosus** (adj. A): fruitful, abounding in fruit.

frugifer (adj. A): fruit-bearing.

Fruit: fructus (s.m. IV), *gen. sing.* fructus, *abl. sing.* fructu, *nom. pl.* fructus, *gen. pl.* fructuum, *abl. pl.* fructibus; frux (s.f. III), *nom. pl.* fruges, is rarely used in bot. L., although in class. L. *fructus* seems to have referred chiefly to tree-fruits, as *frux* to those growing on the ground, as peas and beans, and *frumentum* to cereals, as wheat and barley, all basically meaning 'produce for enjoyment' from *fruor* 'enjoy'; *fructus nunc baccatus indehiscensque, nunc capsularis, supra medium circumscisse dehiscens pericarpii parte superiore decidua, vel septicide bivalvis, valvis integris bifidisve*, fruit sometimes baccate and indehiscent, sometimes capsular, above the middle transversely dehiscent with the upper part of the pericarp deciduous, or septicidally 2-valved, with the valves entire or 2-fid; *fructus varius, superus vel plus minus inferus, nudus vel calycis tubo persistente inclusus, drupaceus pomaceus follicularis vel ex achaeniis drupisve indefinitis toro sicco vel carnoso impositis compositus*, fruit varied, superior or more or less inferior, naked or by the persistent tube of the calyx covered, drupaceous pomaceous follicular or from achenes or drupes of indefinite number on a dry or fleshy torus placed made up.

Fruit-body: fructificatio (s.f. III. vi), *abl. sing.* fructificatione; receptaculum (s.n. II), *abl. sing.* receptaculo. *fructificatio resupinata, juvenilis tenuis citrino-viridis, maturitate subgelatinosa lutea*, fructification resupinate, when young thin citron-green, at maturity almost gelatinous.

fruitful: fecundus (adj. A), fertilis (adj. B), fructuosus (adj. A).

fruiting: fructifer (adj. A), frugifer (adj. A), fructificans (part. B).

Frustillum (s.n. II): a small piece, a scrap; *see* FRAGMENTUM. **Frustrum** (s.n. II): bit, piece.

Frustule: frustulum (s.n. II), *nom. pl.* frustula, *abl. pl.* frustulis; *frustula oblonga vel rectangularia in fascias conjuncta mox soluta et per isthmum angulis concatenata*, frustules oblong or rectangular in bands joined together soon free and linked through an isthmus by the angles.

frutescens (part. B): becoming shrubby. **Frutex** (s.m. III. i): shrub, bush. **fruticans** (part. B): becoming shrubby. **fruticosus** (adj. A): shrubby, bushy.

fucatus (part. A): painted, coloured, stained.

fuchsinus (adj. A): fuchsine pink (H.C.C. 6.27).

fugax (adj. B): fleeting, transitory, ephemeral; *floribus fugacibus*, with flowers quickly withering. **342**

fulciens (part. B), **fulcrans** (part. B): supporting. **fulcratus** (part. A): supported. **Fulcrum** (s.n. II): prop, support (used by Linnaeus for subsidiary organs such as petioles, stipules, tendrils, prickles, bracts, pedicels).

fulgens (part. B), **fulgidus** (adj. A): shining, bright-coloured.

fuligineus (adj. A): dirty-brown, almost black, sooty. **fuliginosus** (adj. A): full of soot, sooty. **Fuligo** (s.f. III. vi): soot.

full: plenus (adj. A), repletus (part. A), (*in some contexts*) farctus (part. A). fartilis (adj. B), onustus (adj. A), solidus (adj. A). **full-grown**: adultus (part. A). **fully**: plene (adv.), perfecte (adv.), admodum (adv.).

fultus (part. A): supported.

fulvescens (adj. B): becoming tawny, somewhat tawny. **fulvi-, fulvo-**: *in L. comp.*, tawny, yellowish-brown; *fulvicaulis*, with tawny stem; *fulvinervis*, with tawny nerves; *fulvisericeus*, silky with tawny hairs; *fulvispinus*, with tawny spines. **fulvidus** (adj. A): somewhat tawny. **fulvus** (adj. A): tawny, 'dull yellow with a mixture of grey and brown' (Lindley), yellowish-brown.

fumeus (adj. A), **fumidus** (adj. A), **fumosus** (adj. A): smoky.

funalis (adj. B): rope-like. **48**

functioning: fungens (part. B); *zoosporis velut isogametae fungentibus*, with zoospores functioning as if isogametes.

Fundamentum (s.n. II): groundwork, basis.

Fundus (s.m. II): the bottom of anything, base; *corolla fundo violaceo excepto lutea*, corolla yellow except for the violet base.

funestus (adj. A): causing death, deadly, fatal, killing.

fungal: fungalis (adj. B). **Fungus**: fungus (s.m. II), *gen. sing.* fungi, *abl. sing.* fungo, *nom. pl.* fungi, *gen. pl.* fungorum, *abl. pl.* fungis; *sylloge fungorum omnium hucusque cognitorum*, summary of the fungi all thus far known, i.e. of all known fungi.

fungens (part. B): functioning.

fungiformis (adj. B), **fungilliformis** (adj. B): mushroom-shaped. **91**

fungosus (adj. A): spongy. The word *fungus*, orig. *sfungus*, is cognate with *spongia*, Gk. σπογγια, sponge.

Funicle: funiculus (s.m. II), *abl. sing.* funiculo.

funicularis (adj. B), **funiformis** (adj. B): rope-like. **funiculosus** (adj. A): occurring in ropes *or* bundles, rope-like. **Funiculus** (s.m. II): funicle, cord, slender rope. **Funis** (s.m. III): rope.

funnel-shaped: infundibuliformis (adj. B), infundibularis (adj. B).

Furca (s.f. I): fork, q.v. **furcatus** (adj. A): forked, having two long terminal lobes. **233**

furfuraceus (adj. A): scurfy, covered with bran-like scales or powder, *lit.* 'like bran'.

furnished: *see* PROVIDED WITH.

Furrow: sulcus (s.m. II), *abl. sing.* sulco, *nom. pl.* sulci, *abl. pl.* sulcis; *sulci ampli, magnam valvae partem occupantes,* furrows big, a large part of the valve occupying. **furrowed**: exaratus (part. A), sulcatus (adj. A), valleculatus (adj. A); cf. ALVEIFORMIS, CHANNELLED.

furvus (adj. A): dark, dusky, almost black.

fuscans (part. B): darkening. **fuscatus** (part. A): darkened.

fusci-, fusco-: *in L. comp.*, dark or dark brown; *fusciflorus,* with dark brownish flowers.

fuscus (adj. A): a sombre brown, 'brown tinged with greyish or blackish' (Lindley), 'very dark blackish brown' (Dade), but often used to indicate darkness of colour.

fused: connatus (part. A), coalitus (part. A), conferruminatus (part. A), conjunctus (part. A).

fusiformis (adj. B): fusiform, swollen at middle and tapering to each end like a spindle, narrowly ellipsoid. **27**

fusing: conjungens (part. B), coalescens (part. B). **Fusion**: conjunctio (s.f. III); *in locus conjunctionis,* at point of fusion.

future: futurus (part. A).

G

gal-, gala-, galacto-: *in Gk. comp.*, milk, milky (*referring either to milky colour or production of latex*); *galactanthus, galanthus,* with milk-white flowers; *galachrous,* milk-coloured; *see* LACTI-, MILK-.

Galactose: galactosum (s.n. II), *gen. sing.* galactosi.

Galbulus: galbulus (s.m. II), *abl. sing.* galbulo, *nom. pl.* galbuli, *abl. pl.* galbulis.

galbus (adj. A): yellow (*in this sense probably a loan-word from German*), smooth.

Galea (s.f. I): helmet, q.v. **galeatus** (adj. A): provided with a helmet. **galeiformis** (adj. B): helmet-shaped. **galericulatus** (adj. A): provided with a little helmet-like skull-cap or *galerum* (s.n. II).

Gall: galla (s.f. I), *lit.* 'oak-apple'. **gall-bearing**: cecidiophorus (adj. A).

Galla (s.f. I): gall, oak-apple.

Gametangium: gametangium (s.n. II), *abl. sing.* gametangio, *nom. pl.* gametangia, *abl. pl.* gametangiis; *gametangia ad nodos primarios et ad basim verticillorum posita,* gametangia at primary nodes and at base of whorls situated.

Gamete: gameta (s.f. I), *abl. sing.* gameta, *nom. pl.*, gametae, *abl. pl.* gametis.

gamo-: *in Gk. comp.*, united; *gamopetalus,* with petals united from base upwards; *gamophyllus,* with perigon segments likewise united; *gamosepalus,* with sepals likewise united.

gangliiformis (adj. B): knot-like. **Ganglion** (s.n. II): knot, swelling along stem. **ganglioneus** (adj. A): with knot-like swellings.

gaping: hians (part. B), ringens (part. B).

Garden: hortus (s.m. II), *gen. sing.* horti; cf. VIRIDARIUM.

gas-, gaseous: gaseosus (adj. A); *vacuola gaseosa,* gas vacuole.

gaudens (part. B): rejoicing in, *hence* happily possessing.

Gelatina (s.f. I): jelly.

Gelatinum (s.n. II): gelatin.

gelatinous: gelatinosus (adj. A). **328**

gelatinus (adj. A): jelly-like, jelly-.

gelatus (part. A): frozen.

gelineus (adj. A): jelly-like, jelly-.

gemellus (adj. A), **geminus** (adj. A): twin-born, paired. **geminatus** (part. A): made double, doubled, paired. **503**

Gemma (s.f. I): bud, bud-like organ capable of reproducing the plant. **Gemma-cup**: scyphulus (s.m. II). **Gemmatio** (s.f. III): budding. **gemmatus** (adj. A): provided with buds, budded. **gemmifer** (adj. A), **gemmiparus** (adj. A): bearing buds. **gemmiformis** (adj. B): bud-like. **-gemmis** (adj. B), **-gemmius** (adj. A): *in L. comp.*, -budded; *multigemmius,* many-budded.

Gemmula (s.f. I): ovule; *gemmulae in loculis solitariae,* ovules in the loculi solitary. **gemmulifer** (adj. A): ovuliferous, ovule-bearing; *amenta gemmulifera,* female catkins.

general: generalis (adj. B); *index abecedarius generalis,* general alphabetical index. **generally, in general**: generatim (adv.), generaliter (adv.), plerumque (adv.), universe (adv.), in universum.

Generation: generatio (s.f. III); cf. MULTIPLICATION, PROPAGATION.

generic: genericus (adj. A); *nomen genericum*, generic name; *nomina generica conservanda*, generic names to be kept; *propter semina deficientia positio generica incerta*, on account of seeds wanting generic position uncertain; see GENUS.

Generitypus (s.m. II): generitype, type-species of the genus.

genetic: geneticus (adj. A). **genetically:** genetice (adv.).

-geneus (adj. A): *in Gk. comp.*, of a particular kind; *homogeneus*, all of the same kind; cf. -GENUS.

geniculatus (adj. A): geniculate, bent abruptly like a knee, *lit.* 'with bended knee'. **Geniculum** (s.n. II): node, joint.

Genitalia (s.n. pl. II): stamens and pistil, androecium and gynoecium, sexual organs; cf. ORGAN.

genitus (part. A): produced, born of, arising from; *hybrida a Viburno erubescente et V. henryi genita*, hybrid from Viburnum erubescens and V. henryi brought forth.

Gens (s.f. III. ix): race, clan, swarm; *gentes herbarum*, the kinds of herbs (or plants generally).

gentianinus (adj. A): gentian-blue (H.C.C. 42).

gently: leniter (adv.).

genuflexus (adj. A): bent like a knee; cf. GENICULATUS.

genuinus (adj. A): genuine, authentic, *hence* applied to type element of a species.

Genus: genus (s.n. III. iv), *gen. sing.* generis, *abl. sing.* genere, *nom. and acc. pl.* genera, *abl. pl.* generibus; *genus novum*, new genus; *pro genere*, as a genus; *genera autem tot sunt, quot attributa communia proxima distinctarum specierum secundum quae in primordio creata fuere: confirmant haec revelata inventa observata*; *hinc omnia genera naturalia sunt* (Linnaeus), there are as many genera as the common approximating attributes of distinct species according to which they were created in the beginning: revelation, discovery, observation confirm this; hence all genera are natural (Linnaeus); *punctis more generis*, with dots after the manner of the genus; *foliis pro genere parvis*, with leaves for the genus small; *revisio generis Achilleae*, revision of the genus Achillea; *generitypus est*, it is the type of the generic name.

-genus (adj. A): *in comp.*, born or produced in a certain place or condition;

alpigenus, alp-born, native of the Alps; *primigenus*, first produced.

geographical: geographicus (adj. A); *distributio geographica*, geographical distribution.

geotropus (adj. A): turning towards the ground.

-ger (adj. A): *in L. comp.*, carrying, bearing; *ramus floriger*, flowering branch.

geraniius (adj. A): geranium lake (H.C.C. 20).

gerens (part. B): carrying.

Germen (s.n. III. vi): ovary.

germinalis (adj. B): germ-; *filum germinale*, germ-thread.

germinating: germinans (part. B); *arbores littorales tropicae seminibus intra pericarpium cum stirpe matre cohaerens germinantibus et radices in terram agentibus singulares*, trees coastal tropical remarkable by the seeds within the pericarp attached to the mother plant germinating and roots into the earth driving. **Germination:** germinatio (s.f. III. vi), *gen. sing.* germinationis.

gerontogeus (adj. A), **gerontogaeus** (adj. A): pertaining to the Old World; *species gerontogea*, a species of the Old World; *species omnes gerontogeae*, species all belonging to the Old World; cf. NEO-.

-geton (s.m. III): *in Gk. comp.*, neighbour, a dweller; *potamogeton*, river-neighbour; *aponogeton*, neighbour of Aponos (from Gk. *a* 'without', *ponos* 'trouble'), the healing springs of Bagni d'Abano.

gibbosus (adj. A), **gibbus** (adj. A): gibbous, more swollen in one place than another, with a pouch-like swelling, with hump-like swellings, *lit.* 'hunch-backed'. **21**

giga-, gigant-: *in Gk. comp.*, giant, very large; *gigalobius*, with very large pods; *gigantostachys*, with very large spikes. **giganteus** (adj. A): giant, gigantic, very large. **Gigas** (s.m. III): a giant. **341**

Gibba (s.f. I): hump, swelling.

gignens (part. B): begetting, bringing forth.

Gill: lamella (s.f. I), *nom. pl.* lamellae, *abl. pl.* lamellis. As regards their attachment, following Josserand, *Descript. Champ. Supér.* 237 (1952) especially, several types may be distinguished; *lamellae omnino liberae, basi stipitem non attingentes* (or *basi intervallo a stipite separatae*), gills entirely free, at base the stipe not reaching (or at base by a gap from the stipe separated), Fig. A; *lamellae liberae, basi attenuatae stipitem vix attingentes*, gills free, at base narrow the stipe just reaching, Fig. B; *lamellae subliberae*, gills almost free, i.e. attached at base by only part

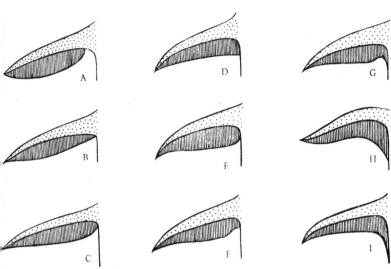

Fig. 35   Types of Attachment of Gill
(After M. Josserand, *Description des Champignons supérieurs*; 1952)

of their width, Fig. C; *lamellae simpliciter adnatae*, gills simply adnate, i.e. attached at base to the stipe by their whole width, Fig. D; *lamellae basi adnatae rotundatae* (or *basi rotundato-adnatae*), gills at base rounded adnate, i.e. rounded and diminished in width before joining stipe, Fig. E; *lamellae basi adnatae emarginatae* (or *basi emarginato-adnatae*), gills at base adnate emarginate, i.e. diminished in width by a hollow curve before joining stipe, Fig. F; *lamellae uncinatae*, gills uncinate, i.e. with a notch before joining stem, Fig. G; *lamellae decurrentes*, gills decurrent, i.e. carried downwards on stipe, Fig. H, I; *lamellae angustissimae 3 mm. latae, basi rotundatae stipitique contiguae sed haud vero adnatae, ambitum versus attenuatae, albae, pileo candidiores, acie acutae at non denticulatae, confertissimae*, gills very narrow 3 mm. broad, at base rounded and touching the stipe but not truly adnate, towards the circumference attenuate, white, than the pileus a more brilliant white, at the edge acute yet not denticulate, very close together; *lamellis subdistantibus tetradymis acute decurrentibus medio ventricosis antice attenuatorotundatis albis angustissimis*, with gills somewhat distant tetradymous sharply decurrent at the middle swollen in the front (i.e. outside) attenuate-rounded white very narrow.

gilvus (adj. A): dull yellow, yellowish tan, but also applied to reddish or greyish colours found on horses.

Girdle: cingulum (s.n. II), *abl. sing.* cingulo; zona (s.f. I), *abl. sing.* zona; *aspectu cingulari*, in girdle view.

given: datus (part. A), donatus (part. A). **giving forth**: edens (part. B), emittens (part. B).

glabrate, glabrescent: glabratus (adj. A) 'made nearly glabrous', glabrescens (part. B), 'becoming glabrous or nearly so', glabriusculus (adj. A), 'almost glabrous', decalvatus (part. A), 'become glabrous'. **glabrous**: glaber (adj. A), glabellus (adj. A); *herba omnino glabra*, herb entirely glabrous; *folium glabrum*, leaf glabrous; *herba monophylla folio glabro*, herb one-leaved with the leaf glabrous; *folia glabra*, leaves glabrous; *ramuli glabri tenues foliis glabris*, branchlets glabrous thin with leaves glabrous; *calyx glaber*, calyx glabrous. **glabrous-**: *in L. comp.*, glabri-, *in Gk. comp.*, psilo-; *psilandrus*, with glabrous stamens; *glabriflorus*, *psilanthus*, with glabrous flowers; *glabripetalus*, with glabrous petals; *glabrispiculus*, with glabrous spikelets; **Glabrous state:** glabritia (s.f. I). **295.**

glacialis (adj. B): frozen, glacial.

Gland: glans (s.f. III. ii), *abl. sing.* glande, *nom. pl.* glandes, *abl. pl.* glandibus, *lit.* 'acorn'; glandula (s.f. I), *abl. sing.* glandula, *nom. pl.* glandulae, *abl. pl.*

glandulis. Despite past inconsistency and also the use, which is historically correct, of the term *glans* for an acorn or similar fruit and of *glandula* for the rostellar gland of Orchidaceae, it would seem best to apply *glans* to a secretory area or mass and the diminutive *glandula* to a single secretory cell or a few-celled isolated very small secretory organ; the use of the term *glans* for swellings without secretory functions should now be avoided; *glans hemisphaerica viscida viridis vel lutea*, gland hemispherical sticky green or yellow; *glande viridi vel lutea*, with gland green or yellow; *glandibus geminatis viridibus vel luteis*, with glands paired green or yellow; *glandula sessilis sphaerica unicellularis minuta impleta succo viscido ochroleuco vel incolorato*, gland sessile spherical one-celled minute filled with juice sticky yellowish white or colourless; *colleterae constant ex singulis glandulis terminantibus cellulas uniseriales cylindraceas*, colleters (mucilaginous hairs) are made up from solitary glands terminating cylindric cells in one series; *bracteae ut et rhachis inflorescentiae pedicellique glandulis longiuscule stipitatis dense obsitae*, bracts as also the rachis of the inflorescence and the pedicels with glands rather long stalked densely covered. **gland-bearing, glandular:** glandifer (adj. A), glandulifer (adj. A), glandulosus (adj. A); *colleterae a phytographis 'pili glanduliferi' nominatae sunt*, colleters by plant-describers 'hairs glandule-bearing' are named; *calyx extus glandulosus*, calyx on the outside glandular; *folia utrinque glandulosa*, leaves on both sides glandular. **glandless:** eglandulatus (adj. A), eglandulosus (adj. A), glandibus destitutus (adj. A), sine glandibus.

Glandule: glandula (s.f. I); *see* GLAND.

Glans (s.f. III. ii): gland (secretory organ), swelling or appendage resembling a gland in appearance, nut (one-seeded dry indehiscent fruit with hard pericarp) borne in a cupule as an acorn, beech-mast, sweet chestnut, etc.

Glara (s.f. I): scree, q.v.

Glarea (s.f. I): gravel, shingle.

glareosus (adj. A): pertaining to gravel.

Glass: vitrum (s.n. II). **glassy:** vitreus (adj. A).

Glasshouse: *see* GREENHOUSE.

Glaucescence: glaucedo (s.f. III); *species foliorum glaucedine insignis*, species notable for the glaucous condition of the leaves. **glaucescent:** glaucescens (adj. B). **glaucous:** glaucus (adj. A).

glaucous-: *in L. comp. usu.* glauci-, *in Gk. comp.* glauco-; *glaucifolius*, *glaucophyllus*, glaucous-leaved; *glauciifolius*, with leaves of sea poppy (Glaucium); *glaucocarpus*, glaucous-fruited. **307**

gleaming: fulgens (part. B), fulgidus (adj. A), micans (part. B), nitens (part. B), nitidus (adj. A), lucidus (adj. A).

Gleba: gleba (s.f. I), *abl. sing.* gleba; *gleba pluricellulosa a peridio non separabilis candida immutabilis lactiflua demum farinacea*, gleba (sporing tissue) many-celled from the peridium not separable pure white unchanging milky at length floury.

glebosus (adj. A): full of clods, lumpy.

Glebula: glebula (s.f. I), *abl. sing.* glebula.

glebulosus (adj. A): glebulose, with rounded elevations.

Gleocystidium: gloeocystidium (s.n. II).

glistening: lucens (part. B); *see* GLOSSY.

glob-, globi-: *in L. comp.*, ball-like, globose; *globifer, globiger*, globe-carrying, i.e. with a spherical organ. **globosus** (adj. A): round like a ball, globose, spherical. **globularis** (adj. B), **globulifer** (adj. A), **globulosus** (adj. A): globule-bearing, globular. **globuliformis** (adj. B): button-like. **Globulus** (s.m. II): a little ball, globule. **Globus** (s.m. II): a round body, ball, globe, sphere. **4**

Glochid: glochin (s.f. III. ii), *abl. sing.* glochide, *nom. pl.* glochides, *abl. pl.* glochidibus, *lit.* 'projecting part, barb of arrow'; glochidium (s.n. II), *abl. sing.* glochidio, *nom. pl.* glochidia, *abl. pl.* glochidiis. **glochideus** (adj. A), **glochidiatus** (adj. A): glochidate, provided with barbs.

gloeo-: *in Gk. comp.*, glue-, sticky; *gloeocalyx*, with a viscous calyx. **gloeocarpus** (adj. A): having the reproductive organs enveloped in mucus. **Gloeocystidium** (s.n. II): gleocystidium.

Glome: glomus (s.n. III. iv), *abl. sing.* glomere, *nom. pl.* glomera, *abl. pl.* glomeribus, *lit.* 'ball of yarn', etc.

glomeratus (part. A): collected closely together into a head. **glomerulatus** (adj. A): provided with glomerules.

Glomerule: glomerulus (s.m. II), *abl. sing.* glomerulo, *nom. pl.* glomeruli, *abl. pl.* glomerulis; *glomeruli florum inferiores remoti, superiores approximati, omnes folio suffulti*, glomerules (clusters of capitula with an involucre) of flowers lower remote, upper close together, all by a leaf subtended.

Glossiness: nitor (s.m. III).

glosso-: *in Gk. comp.*, tongue-; *glossophyllus*, with tongue-shaped leaves. **Glossologia** (s.f. I): terminology.

glossy: nitidus (adj. A), politus (part. A), inunctus (part. A); *see* GLEAMING, GLISTENING, POLISHED.

Glucose: glucosum (s.n. II), *gen. sing.* glucosi.

Glue: glutinium (s.m. II), ichthyocolla (s.f. I). **glued to**: agglutinatus (part. A), adglutinatus (part. A). **glued together**: conglutinatus (part. A).

glumaceus (adj. A): glumaceous, like the glumes of grasses. **Glume**: gluma (s.f. I), *abl. sing.* gluma, *nom. pl.* glumae, *abl. pl.* glumis; *glumae aequales similes concavae uninerves dorso rotundatae vel carinatae, primo erectae tandem divergentes*, glumes equal alike concave onenerved on the back rounded or keeled, at first erect at length divergent.

glutinous: glutinosus (adj. A), viscidus (adj. A); *cf.* GLOEO-. **300**

glyco-: *in Gk. comp.*, sweet of taste or smell; *glycosmus*, sweet-smelling.

glypto-: *in Gk. comp.*, cut into.

going forth: exiens (part. B).

golden-yellow: aureus (adj. A), auratus (adj. A) 'ornamented with gold'; *in L. comp.*, aurei-, aureo-, auri-, *in Gk. comp.*, chrys-, chryso-; *aureiflorus, chrysanthus*, golden-flowered; *auricolor, chrysochromus*, gold-coloured; *aureilabris, chrysochilus*, with golden lip.

-gŏne (s.f. I), **-gonium** (s.n. II): *in Gk. comp.*, reproductive organs.

gongylodes (adj. A): knob-like. **62**

goni-, gonia-: *in Gk. comp.*, angled, angular; *goniocalyx*, with angled calyx; *goniocarpus*, with angled fruits; *goniospermus*, with angled seeds.

Gonidium: gonidium (s.n. II).

Gonimoblast: gonimoblastus (s.m. II).

Gorge: fauces (s.f. III. i, pl.), *abl. pl.* faucibus; *in faucibus crescens*, in the gorge(s) growing.

gossypinus (adj. A): cottony, q.v.

governed: gubernatus (part. A).

gracilis (adj. B): thin, slender.

gradatim (adv.): little by little, gradually.

gradually: gradatim (adv.), paulatim (adv.), sensim (adv.), leniter (adv.).

Graft (scion): insitum (s.n. II). **grafted**: insiticius (adj. A), insititius (adj. A).

Grain: granum (s.n. II); *granum paramylaceum*, paramylon grain; *cf.* POLLEN.

gralliformis (adj. B): stilt-like; *radices gralliformes*, stilt-roots.

Gramen (s.n. III. vi): grass, q.v. **gramineus** (adj. A): grassy, grass-like. **graminifolius** (adj. A): grass-leaved.

grammatus (adj. A): striped with raised lines.

grandi-: *in L. comp.*, large, big; *grandiflorus*, large-flowered. **grandis** (adj. B): large, great, big, tall, lofty.

granular, granulate, granulose: granularis (adj. B), granulatus (adj. A), granulosus (adj. A). Indiscriminate use has made these terms virtually interchangeable; to the earlier authors *granulatus* meant 'consisting of many little knobs attached by small strings, as in the *Saxifraga granulata*' (Berkenhout, 1799). **Granule**: granulum (s.n. II), *abl. sing.* granulo, *nom. pl.* granula, *abl. pl.* granulis; *granulis distinctissimis aequidistantibus et aequimagnis polygoniis vel quadraticis papillosis*, with granules most distinct (all) at the same distance apart and of the same size many-angled or quadrate papillose; *granulis margaritaceis usque ad semi-radium subaequalibus dein majoribus demumque ad marginem decrescentibus*, with granules pearly to half-radius almost equal thereafter bigger and finally at the margin diminishing. **236**

Granum (s.n. II): grain; *see* POLLEN.

Grape (fruit): uva (s.f. I). **grape-bearing**: uvifer (adj. A). **like a cluster of grapes**: botryoideus (adj. A), uvarius (adj. A).

grasping: prehendens (part. B), prehensilis (adj. B).

Grass: gramen (s.n. III. vi), *gen. sing.* graminis, *abl. sing.* gramine, *nom. pl.* gramina, *gen. pl.* graminum, *abl. pl.* graminibus; *gramen perenne multicaule caespitosum gracile, inflorescentia inclusa 10-20 cm. altum*, grass manystemmed tufted slender, with inflorescence included 10-20 cm. high; *gramina perennia vel annua, nunc elata ramosa nunc humilia caespitosa, basi saepe decumbentia interdum bulboso-incrassata, foliis planis mollibus vel setaceis rigidis*, grasses perennial or annual, now tall branched now dwarf tufted, at base often decumbent sometimes bulbously thickened, with leaves flat soft or setaceous rigid; *descriptiones et icones graminum*, descriptions and illustrations of grasses; *de graminibus*, concerning grasses. **grass-**: *in L. comp.*, gramini-, *in Gk. comp.*, agrosto-; *agrostologia*, agrostology, the study of grasses; *graminifolius, agrostophyllus*, grass-leaved; *graminiformis*, grass-like. **grassy**: gramineus (adj. A).

gratus (adj. A): pleasing, agreeable.

Gravel: glarea (s.f. I). **gravelly**: glareosus (adj. A).

graveolens (adj. B): strong-smelling.

gravis (adj. B): heavy, weighty.

gray: *see* GREY.

greasy: sebosus (adj. A), unctus (part. A).

great: magnus (adj. A), amplus (adj. A). **great as**: tantus quantus (adj. A). **greatly**: magnopere (adv.), multum (adv.).

green: viridis (adj. B); *folia atro-viridia vittis pallide viridibus vel etiam albidis secus venas currentibus notata*, leaves dark green marked with bands pale green or even whitish along the veins running; *ovarium viride*, ovary green. **green-**: *in L. comp.*, viridi-, *in Gk. comp.*, chlor-, chloro-; *viridi-albus, chloroleucus*, greenish-white; *viridiflorus, chloranthus*, green-flowered; *viridipes, chloropodus*, with a green stalk. **bluish-green**: venetus (adj. A). **deep-green**: atrovirens (adj. B), perviridis (adj. B). **emerald-green**: smaragdinus (adj. A). **greenish**: virellus (adj. A), viridulus (adj. A), *prefix* viridi-, e.g. *viridi-flavus*, greenish-yellow. **leek-green**: porraceus (adj. A), prasinus (adj. A). **malachite-green**: malachiteus (adj. A). **olive-green**: olivaceus (adj. A). **pea-green**: pisinus (adj. A). **sea-green**: glaucus (adj. A). **yellowish-green**: flavo-virens (adj. B), chlorinus (adj. A). **uranium-green**: luteoviridis (adj. B); *see* VIRIDIS.

Greenhouse: caldarium (s.n. II) 'hothouse', tepidarium (s.n. II) 'warm house', frigidarium (s.n. II) 'cool house', hibernaculum (s.n. II).

gregarius (adj. A): gregarious, growing in company but not united or matted together. **gregatim** (adv.): in clusters.

Grex (s.m. or f. III. i): flock, herd, drove, swarm, *hence* a group of species or hybrids; *grex hybrida polymorpha hortensis*, hybrid-swarm polymorphic belonging to gardens.

grey: canus (adj. A), cinereus (adj. A), cineraceus (adj. A), griseus (adj. A), schistaceus (adj. A). **grey-**: *in Gk. comp.*, polio-, spod-, spodo-, tephro-, *in L. comp.*, cano-, cinereo-. **greyish**: cinerascens (part. B), ravidus (adj. A).

griseus (adj. A): grey, pearl-grey, pure grey a little verging to blue.

Groove: sulcus (s.m. II), *abl. sing.* sulco; *putamen a ventre sulvo lato profundo in longitudinem exaratum*, stone on the ventral side by a furrow broad deep lengthwise ploughed out.

grooved: sulcatus (adj. A), canaliculatus (adj. A); cf. CHANNELLED, ENGRAVED, FURROWED.

grosse (adv.): coarsely, larger than usual. **grossus** (adj. A): thick, coarse.

Ground: terra (s.f. I); cf. SOIL.

Group: turma (s.f. I), grex (s.m. or f. III. i), caterva (s.f. I). **grouped**: aggregatus (part. A), dispositus (part. A); *cellulae*

binae quaternaeque aggregatae, cells in groups of two and four.

growing: crescens (part. B).

grumosus (adj. A): broken into grains *or* small tubercles.

gubernatus (part. A): governed, controlled, managed.

Gum: gummi (s.f. indecl.). **gummy**: gummosus (adj. A).

Gustus (s.m. IV): taste, flavour.

Gutta (s.f. I): a drop of fluid, oil-droplet in spores or hyphae of fungi. **guttatus** (adj. A): spotted. **Guttula** (s.f. I): oil-droplet in fungus. **guttulatus** (adj. A): guttulate, provided *or* apparently sprinkled with dots of oil or resin.

gymno-: *in Gk. comp.*, naked. **gymnocarpus** (adj. A): with the fruit naked, i.e. without perianth, hairs, mucus (e.g. in Charophytes) or some other covering. **gymnostomaticus** (adj. A): gymnostomous.

gyn-, gyno-: *in Gk. comp.*, female or pertaining to female organs.

Gynandrium: gynandrium (s.n. II), *abl. sing.* gynandrio. **Gynobase**: gynobasis (s.f. III); *see* BASIS. **gynobasic**: gynobasicus (adj. A). **gynodynamous**: gynodynamicus (adj. A), gynodynamus (adj. A).

Gynoecium: gynoecium (s.n. II), *abl. sing.* gynoecio; pistillum (s.n. II), *abl. sing.* pistillo. **Gynophore**: gynophorum (s.n. II), *abl. sing.* gynophoro. **Gynostegium**: gynostegium (s.n. II), *abl. sing.* gynostegio; *gynostegium sessile 2 mm. altum*, gynostegium sessile 2 mm. high; *caput gynostegii convexum semiglobosum rostro brevi vix 1 mm. longo alte bifido ornatum*, head of the gynostegium convex hemispherical ornamented with a beak short scarcely 1 mm. long deeply bifid.

gypseus (adj. A): gypsum-like. **Gypsum** (s.n. II): gypsum.

Gyroma (s.n. III): annulus of ferns.

gyrosus (adj. A): curved backwards and forwards in turn, spiral.

Gyrus (s.m. II): circle, ring, annulus.

H

habitat: 'it grows'. **Habitatio** (s.f. III. vi): place of growth; usually the place of growth is associated with the verb *cresco* 'grow' or *habito* 'have possession of, inhabit, dwell' in the 3rd pers. sing. pres. active (*crescit, habitat*); *regiones temperatas, rarius calidas, totius orbis terrarum habitat*, regions temperate, more rarely hot, of the whole world it inhabits; cf. SOLUM.

labitus (s.m. IV) : condition, appearance, posture, nature, habit, manner of growth ; *see* APPEARANCE. **habitus** (part. A) : well-conditioned, fleshy, corpulent.

actenus (adv.) : thus far, until now.

aec (dem. pron.) : this, she, these.

aem-, haem- : *in Gk. comp.*, blood-red; *haemanthus*, with blood-red flower; *haematocarpus*, with blood-red fruit; *haematocephalus*, with blood-red head; *haematochrous*, blood-coloured ; *haematolasius*, woolly with blood-red hairs; *haematophyllus*, with blood-red leaves; *haematospermus*, with blood-red seeds; *haematostachys*, with blood-red spike.

laematochrome : haematochroma (s.n. III).

aerens (part. B) : adhering, clinging, remaining, attached.

lair : pilus (s.m. II), *nom. pl.* pili, *abl pl.* pilis ; trichoma (s.n. III); *nom. pl.* trichomata, *abl. pl.* trichomatibus. As to direction, a hair (pilus) may be *erect* (erectus, part. A) or *spreading* (patulus, adj. A), *leaning* (inclinatus, part. A), *bent forwards* (pronus, adj. A), *bent back* (resupinus, adj. A), *appressed* (appressus, part. A); as to texture, *soft* (mollis, adj. B), *stiff* (rigidus, adj. A), *harsh* (asper, adj. A); as to form, *simple* (simplex; adj. B), *straight* (rectus, adj. A), *twisted* (tortus, part. A), *curled* (crispus, crispatus, adj. A), *curved* (curvus, curvatus, part. A), *flexuose* (flexuosus, adj. A), *unicellular* (unicellularis, adj. B), *multicellular* (multicellularis. adj B), *moniliform*, like a string of beads (moniliformis, adj. B), *club-shaped* (clavatus, adj. A), *hooked* (uncatus, uncinatus, adj. A), *barbed* (glochideus, glochidiatus, adj. A), *branched* (ramosus, adj. A), *forked* (furcatus, adj. A), *feathery* (plumosus, adj. A), *stellate* (stellatus, adj. A), *sessile* (sessilis, adj. B), *stalked* (stipitatus, adj. A), *glandular* (glandulifer, adj. A), etc. They may be *sparse* (pili sparsi), *bunched together* (fasciculati), *dense* (densi), etc.; *folia pilis mollibus sparsis vestita*, leaves with soft sparse hairs clothed ; *corollae tubus introrsum medio circulo pilorum ornatus, supra et infra hunc circulum saepissime pilis minutis conspersus*, tube of the corolla on the inside at the middle with a circle of hairs adorned, above and below this circle most often with minute hairs sprinkled ; *trichomata, quae caulem et folia vestiunt*, hairs, which clothe stem and leaves ; *folia margine pilis albis longiusculis multicellularibus induta*, leaves at the margin with white rather long multicellular hairs furnished ; *utrinque pilis adpressis malpighiaceis hic illic nonnunquam satis regulariter conspersa*, on both surfaces with hairs appressed malpighiaceous here and there sometimes fairly regularly sprinkled ; *calyx pilis longis teneris rectis pellucidis apice glandulosis quibus nonnullae setae rigidae intermixtae sunt*, calyx with hairs long thin straight transparent at the tip glandular, with which some bristles rigid intermixed are ; *planta pilis eglanduligeris omnino destituta, pilis glanduligeris tantum obsita*, plant entirely lacking eglandular hairs, with gland-bearing hairs alone covered.

Hair-covering : indumentum (s.n. II), *gen. sing.* indumenti, *abl. sing.* indumento ; hirsuties (s.f. V), *gen. sing.* hirsutiei, *abl. sing.* hirsutie ; crinis (s.m. III), *gen. sing.* crinis, *abl. sing.* crine, *rarely used.* **hair-like** : capillaceus (adj. A), capillaris (adj. B), capilliformis (adj. B), trichoideus (adj. A); cf. THREADLIKE.

hairy : *see* CILIATUS, HIRSUTUS, HIRTUS, HISPIDUS, INCANUS, LANATUS, PILIFER, PILOSUS, PUBENS, PUBESCENS, STRIGOSUS, TOMENTOSUS, TRICH-, VELUTINUS, VILLOSUS. **270-287**

Half (s.) : dimidium (s.n. II), *abl. sing.* dimidio ; *fissura ad dimidium radii attingens*, fissure reaching down to half of the radius; *in dimidio inferiore*, on the lower half ; *sori dimidium distale obducentes*, sori covering the distal half. **half** (adj.) : dimidius (adj. A). **half-** : *in L. comp.*, semi-, *in Gk. comp.*, hemi-; *hemisphaericus, semiorbicularis*, hemispherical ; *hemipterus, semialatus*, half-winged ; *hemicryptus, semioccultus*, half-hidden.

Halipedum (s.n. II) : a plain by the sea.

halo- : *in Gk. comp.*, salt ; *halophilus*, salt-loving.

halonatus (adj. A) : surrounded by an outer circle, from *halos* (s.f.) 'halo, circle around the sun or moon'.

halved : dimidiatus (part. A); *cellulae magnitudine dimidiata*, cells half the size. **16, 138**

hamatus (adj. A) : barbed, hooked at the tip. **hamosus** (adj. A) : hooked. **hamulatus** (adj. A), **hamulosus** (adj. A) : armed with small hooks. **Hamulus** (s.m. II) : small hook, barb. **Hamus** (s.m. II) : hook, barb.

hanging down : dependens (part. B), pendens (part. B), pendulus (adj. A), pendulinus (adj. A), dependulus (adj. A). **394**

hapalo-: *in Gk. comp.*, soft-; *hapalophyllus*, soft-leaved.

hapaxanthus (adj. A): having a single flowering period, then dying; cf. MONOCARPUS. **342**

haplo-: *in Gk. comp.*, single-; *haplocaulis*, single-stemmed. **haplostephanus** (adj. A): (in *Charophyta*) having a single circle of stipulodes at the base of each whorl of branchlets. **haplostichus** (adj. A): with a single row.

Hapteron: hapteron (s.n. II).

Haptonema: haptonema (s.n. III. xi); cf. p. 161.

hard: durus (adj. A). **hardened**: induratus (part. A). **hardening**: indurescens (part. B).

hardly: vix (adv.), aegre (adv.).

Hardness: duritia (s.f. I).

harmful: noxius (adj. A).

hastatus (adj. A): hastate, i.e. with equal more or less triangular basal lobes directed outwards. **hasti-**: *in L. comp.*, spear-; *hastifer, hastiger*, spear-bearing; *hastifolius*, spear-leaved; *hastilabius*, with spear-like lip; *hastipetalus*, with spear-like petals. **hastilis** (adj. B): spear-shaped. **127, 170**

Hastula (s.f. I): terminal part of petiole of palms, also called a ligule, *lit.* 'a little spear'; cf. *Gentes Herb.*, 7: 179 (1946).

haud (adv.): not at all, by no means; used with adv., verbs and adj. **haudquaquam** (adv.): by no means whatever.

Haustorium: haustorium (s.n. II); *fruticulus parasiticus caulibus volubilibus haustoriis affixis*, shrublet parasitic with stems twining by haustoria attached.

hazel-coloured: avellaneus (adj. A).

Head: capitulum (s.n. II), *acc. sing.* capitulum, *abl. sing.* capitulo, *nom. and acc. pl.* capitula, *abl. pl.* capitulis; *flores in capitulum globosum aggregati*, flowers in head globose crowded together; *capitulum magnum terminale 3 cm. latum*, head large terminal 3 cm. broad; *capitula homogama discoidea terminalia*, capitula homogamous with disc-florets terminal; *capitula heterogama radiata nutantia parva mediocriave magna ad apices ramorum solitariave in axillis superioribus pedunculata*, capitula heterogamous rayed nodding small medium-sized or large at tips of branches solitary or in upper axils peduncled.

head-: *in L. comp.*, capit-, capiti-, *in Gk. comp.*, cephal-, cephalo-. **-headed**: *in L. comp.*, -ceps, *in Gk. comp.*, -cephalus.

heaped: acervatus (part. A).

Heart: cor (s.n. III. ii); *folia obtusata forma fere cordis humani*, leaves blunt with the shape almost of the human heart.

heart-shaped: (at base with two rounded lobes) cordatus (adj. A), (in general form) cordiformis (adj. B); *in L. comp.* cordi-, *in Gk. comp.*, cardio-; *cordifer, cardiophorus*, heart-carrying, i.e. with a heart-shaped structure of some kind **122**

heavy: gravis (adj. B), 'weighty', densus (adj. A), 'thick', ponderosus (adj. A), 'heavy'.

hebdomalis (adj. B): weekly. **Hebdomas** (s.f. III): week.

hebetatus (part. A): dimmed, with the brightness taken off, matt, blunted.

hecat-, hecto-: *in Gk. comp.*, hundred-.

Hedge: sepes (s.f. III. viii), *gen. sing* sepis, *nom. pl.* sepes, *gen. pl.* sepium. In class. L. also *saepes*.

hedy-: *in Gk. comp.*, sweet; *hedyosmus*, sweet scented.

Height: altitudo (s.f. III): *ad altitudinem mediam*, at mid height.

heleo-, helo-: *in Gk. comp.*, marsh; *helodes* (*often wrongly transcribed as* elodes), growing in marshy places; *helodoxa*, glory of the marsh.

helic-: *in Gk. and L. comp.*, coiled, spirally twisted; *helicantherus*, with twisted anthers. *Heliconia* and derivatives, such as *heliconiifolius, heliconioides, heliconiopsis*, refer however to Mt Helikon in Greece.

helicte (adv.): clockwise, in a direction passing from right to left when seen from the outside, sinistrorse (in the sense of Eichler, A. Gray, etc.), dextrorse (in the sense of de Candolle, etc.); cf. ANTIHELICTE, TWINING.

heliotrope-coloured: heliotropinus (adj. A) (H.C.C. 6.36).

Helmet: cassis (s.f. ii), *gen. sing.* cassidis, *abl. sing.* casside (used for the upper hooded sepal of Aconitum); galea (s.f. I), *gen. sing.* galeae, *abl. sing.* galea (used for hooded upper lip of corolla of Pedicularis, etc.). In class. L. *cassis* denoted usually a metal helmet, *galea* a leather one; *cassis ascendens* (*haud horizontalis*) *valde incurva longirostris 3 cm. lata, apice inflata*, ascending (never horizontal) strongly incurved long-beaked 3 cm. broad, at the tip inflated; *cassidis symmetricae margo inferior horizontalis recta*, of the symmetrical helmet the lower margin horizontal straight; *galea purpurea in rostrum praelongum angustum primo contortum apice truncatum attenuata*, helmet purple into a beak very long narrow at first twisted at the tip truncate drawn out; *corolla galeae rostro* *lineari proboscideo contorto apice truncato*, corolla with the beak of the helmet linear proboscis-like twisted at the tip truncate; *galeae pars verticalis c. 6 mm. longa leviter reflexa margine breviter bidentata, pars antherigera 10 mm. longa apice sensim in rostrum breve conicum attenuata*, of the helmet the vertical part about 6 mm. long lightly reflexed at the margin shortly two-toothed, the anther-bearing part 10 mm. long at the tip gradually into a beak short conical drawn out. **helmet-shaped**: galeiformis (adj. B), cassideus (adj. A).

helvus (adj. A): light bay, pale red, 'the dingy colour of oxen' (H. A. Dade).

hemi-: *in Gk. comp.*, half-; *hemicryptus*, half-hidden; *hemipterus*, half-winged; *hemisphaericus*, hemispherical.

Hemisphere: hemisphaerium (s.n. II): *in regionibus intertropicis utriusque hemisphaerii*, in intertropical regions of each hemisphere.

hence: hinc (adv.), igitur (adv.), quamobrem (adv.).

hendeca-: *in Gk. comp.*, eleven-; *see* ELEVEN-.

hepaticus (adj. A): liver-coloured, dark reddish-brown.

hepta-: *in Gk. comp.*, seven-; *heptadactylus*, with 7 digitately arranged finger-like lobes; *heptagynus*, with 7 styles or carpels; *heptamerus*, with parts in sevens; *heptanthus*, 7-flowered; *heptapetalus*, 7-petalled; *heptaphyllus*, with 7 leaves or leaflets; *see* SEPTEM-, SEVEN-.

Herb: herba (s.f. I); *herbae annuae vel perennes erectae vel repentes, glabrae*, herbs annual or perennial, erect or creeping, glabrous.

herbaceus (adj. A): herbaceous, i.e. grass-green *or* yellow-green in colour, *or* green and slightly fleshy, as opposed to faded, colourless and dry, particularly with reference to bracts, or with annual usually juicy stems as opposed to perennial woody stems. **334**

Herbarium: herbarium (s.n. II), *gen. sing.* herbarii, *abl. sing.* herbario; *herbarium normale*, standard herbarium; *ex Herbario Musei Britannici*, from the Herbarium of the British Museum; *revisio lichenum in herbario Linnaei asservatorum*, revision of lichens in herbarium of Linnaeus preserved; *synonymia muscorum Herbarii Linnaeani*, synonymy of mosses of Linnaean Herbarium; cf. DRIED, EXSICCATA, EXSICCATUM, HORTUS.

herbidus (adj. A): rich in herbs, grass-green.

Herbula (s.f. I): a little herb.

here: hic (adv.). **here and there**: disperse

(adv.), dispersim (adv.), hic illic (adv.), passim (adv.). **hereafter**: posthac (adv.).

hermaphrodite: hermaphroditus (adj. A), bisexualis (adj. B); *flores hermaphroditi unisexuales vel polygami*, flowers hermaphrodite unisexual or polygamous.

Hesitatio (s.f. III): hesitation; *haud sine hesitatione a sequente separavi*, not without hesitation have I separated it from the following.

hetero-: *in Gk. comp.*, different, other, uneven; *heterocarpus*, producing different colours; *heterogamus*, bearing two or more kinds of flowers (e.g. neuter, or unisexual, and bisexual) in one cluster; *heteromerus, heteromericus*, not corresponding in number; *heteromorphus*, diverging from usual structure, having organs of varying form *or* length; *heterophyllus*, having leaves of more than one form; *heterosporus*, having two kinds or sizes of spores; *heterotrichus*, having hairs of more than one kind or length. Similar Gk. comp. but of contrary meaning are formed with *homo-*, alike, similar, agreeing.

Heterocyst: heterocysta (s.f. I), *gen. sing.* heterocystae, *abl. sing.* heterocysta, *nom. pl.* heterocystae, *gen. pl.* heterocystarum, *abl. pl.* heterocystis; *heterocystae ad basim pseudo-ramorum nullae*. heterocysts at base of pseudo-branches none; *heterocystae basilares, in unica specie intercalares*, heterocysts basal, in one species between the apex and the base; *heterocystis intercalaribus vel basalibus sphaericis vel ovalibus 6 μ longis 8 μ crassis*, with heterocysts intercalary or basal spherical or oval 6 μ long 8 μ thick; *sporae ab heterocystis remotae*, spores distant from heterocysts; *sporae heterocystis contiguae*, spores adjacent to heterocysts.

heterogeneus (adj. A): heterogeneous, not uniform in structure. **heteroicus** (adj. A): heteroecious, with stages of development on different hosts, with more than one form of inflorescence in the same species. **heteromorphus** (adj. A): heteromorphic, having organs of varying form or length, (in *Charophyta*) with sterile and fertile whorls dissimilar. **heterostylus** (adj. A): heterostylous, i.e. with styles of different length in individuals of the same species and the stamens correlatedly varying in length or position; *planta heterostyla, androdynamica a gynodynamica nisi stylo abbreviato et filamentis exsertis vix diversa*, plant heterostylous, the androdynamous one from the gynodynamous except for the abbreviated style and exserted filaments scarcely different;

flores heterostyli, stylo in flore dolicho-stylo 4 mm. longo, in flore brachystylo 1 mm. longo, flowers heterostylous, with the style in a long-styled flower 4 mm. long, in a short-styled flower 1 mm. long.

hexa- : *in Gk. comp.*, six; *hexandrus, hexastemonus*, 6-stamened; *hexagynus* with 6 styles *or* carpels; *hexamerus*, with parts in sixes; *hexapetalus*, 6-petalled; *hexapyrenus*, with 6 pyrenes; *hexasepalus*, 6-sepalled; *hexaspermus*, 6-seeded; *hexastachys, hexastachyus*, 6-spiked; *see* SEX-, SIX-.

hexagonal : hexagonus (adj. A), sexangularis (adj. B).

Hexapodium (s.n. II): fathom, toise.

hians (part. B) : gaping, open-mouthed.

Hibernaculum (s.n. II) : winter-bud, glass-house. **hibernus** (adj. A) : belonging to winter, wintry; cf. HIEMALIS.

Hibrida : *see* HYBRID.

hic (adv.) : in this place, here; *hic illic*, here and there, sporadically; *hic inde*, locally.

hic (dem. pron. m.), **haec** (dem. pron. f.), **hoc** (dem. pron. n.) : this, he, she, it.

hidden : occultus (part. A), celatus (part. A); *see* CONCEALED. **hiding** : occultans (part. B).

hiemalis (adj. B), **hyemalis** (adj. B) : belonging to winter, wintry; cf. HIBERNUS. **Hiems** (s.f. III. vi) : winter.

high : altus (adj. A), celsus (adj. A), elatus (part. A), excelsus (part. A), procerus (adj. A). **highly** : maxime (adv.), alte (adv.) (used of height).

hilaris (adj. B) : relating to the hilum.

Hill : collis (s.m. III. vii), *abl. pl.* collibus. **pertaining to hills** : collinus (adj. A).

Hilum : hilum (s.n. II), *abl. sing.* hilo, *lit.* ' a trifle '; *hilum rotundatum basale 4 mm. diametro*, hilum rounded basal 4 mm. in diameter; *semina globosa hilo rotundato*, seeds globose with hilum rounded.

himanto- : *in Gk. comp.*, strap-shaped; *himantoglossus*, with a strap-shaped tongue.

hinc (adv.) : from this place, from this side, from this time, after this; *hinc atque illinc*, on both sides; *hinc et inde*, from different directions; *hinc . . . hinc . . .*, on this side . . . on that side . . ., here . . . there. . . .

hinnuleus (adj. A) : fawn-coloured.

hippocrepicus (adj. A), **hippocrepiformis** (adj. B) : shaped like a horseshoe, i.e. bent almost into a circle, but with a distinct opening.

hircinus (adj. A) : smelling like a goat.

Hirsuties (s.f. III) : rough hair-covering. **hirsutus** (adj. A) : hirsute, covered with fairly coarse and stiff long erect *or* ascending straight hairs.

hirti- : *in L. comp.*, hairy, particularly with long distinct hairs; *hirticalyx*, with hairy calyx; *hirticaulis*, with hairy stem; *hirtiflorus*, with hairy flowers; *hirtistylus*, with hairy style. **hirtus** (adj. A) : hairy : *see* HIRSUTUS. **273**

hispidus (adj. A) : hispid, covered with coarse rigid erect hairs or bristles harsh to the touch. **277**

Historia (s.f. I) : history, systematic account of natural phenomena.

hoary : incanus (adj. A). **272**

hodiernus (adj. A) : relating to the present time.

Holdfast : hapteron (s.n. II). **Holdfast-cell** : cellula (s.f. I) hapteroidea, tenaculum (s.n. II).

holding : tenens (part. B), retinens (part. B) 'keeping hold of', continens (part. B) 'containing', haerens (part. B) 'clinging'.

Hole : foramen (s.n. III) 'a round hole made by boring', cavum (s.n. II) 'hollow, cavity'. **holed** : foratus (part. A), porosus (adj. A), perforatus (part. A) ; cf. LATTICED.

hollow : cavus (adj. A). **hollowed out** : excavatus (part. A), exaratus (part. A) 'ploughed out'; *semina obovata ventre excavata*, seeds obovate in the lower side hollowed out; *putamen compressum a ventre sulco lato profundo in longitudinem exaratum*, stone compressed at the lower side by a wide deep furrow lengthwise ploughed out.

holo- : *in Gk. comp.*, entire, complete, whole, undivided; *holocarpus*, with undivided fruits; *holodontus*, with entire teeth; *hologynus*, with entire ovary.

holodactylus (adj. A) : has same meaning as *monarthrodactylus*.

Holotype : holotypus (s.m. II).

homo-, homoeo-, homoio- : *in Gk. comp.*, like, of the same kind, agreeing; *homocarpus*, with one kind of fruit only; *homogamus*, with only one kind of flower in the cluster; *homosporus*, with spores of the same kind and size; cf. HETER-, SAME.

homoeomorphus (adj. A) : (in *Charophyta*) with sterile and fertile whorls similar.

homogeneus (adj. A) : homogeneous, uniform in structure.

Homogonium : homogonium (s.n. II).

homoimerous, isomerous : homoimerus (adj. A), isomerus (adj. A).

homomallus (adj. A) : homomallous, i.e. all turned in the same direction.

Homonymum (s.n. II): homonym.

homotropus (adj. A) : turned or curved in one direction. **436**

Honey : mel (s.n. III. v), *gen. sing.* mellis. **honey-coloured** : melleus (adj. A).

Honey-comb: favus (s.m. II). **honey-combed**: favosus (adj. A). **250**
Hood: cucullus (s.m. II). **hooded**: cucullatus (adj. A). **93**
Hook: uncus (s.m. II): **hook-shaped**: unciformis (adj. B). **hooked**: uncatus (adj. A), uncinatus (adj. A), hamatus (adj. A), aduncus (adj. A). **147**
horizontal: horizontalis (adj. B). **horizontally**: horizontaliter (adv.). **398**
Hormogon: hormogonium (s.n. II), *nom. pl.* hormogonia, *abl. pl.* hormogoniis; *hormogonia lateralia verticillata 45 µ lata e cellulis 10-12 composita*, hormogons lateral verticilate 45 µ broad from 10-12 cells made up; *hormogoniis terminalibus vel lateralibus oppositisque 45 µ longis*, with hormogons terminal or lateral and opposite 45 µ long.
Horn: cornu (s.n. IV), *gen. sing.* cornus, *abl. sing.* cornu, *nom. pl.* cornua, *abl. pl.* cornibus; *in L. comp.*, -cornu, -cornis, corni-, *in Gk. comp.*, -ceras, -ceros, cerato-; *bicornis, diceras*, two-horned; *brevicornu, brachyceras*, with short horn; *corniger, ceratophorus*, horn-bearing. **horned**; cornutus (adj. A). **horn-shaped**: cornuatus (adj. A). **horny**: corneus (adj. A). **55, 320**
hornotinus (adj. A): belonging to the present year, not a year old; *ramuli hornotini pilosi, annotini glabri, vetustiores crassi cortice griseo fisso*, branchlets of this year's growth pilose, of last year's growth glabrous, the older ones thick with the bark grey fissured.
Horologium (s.n. II): clock; *horologium florae*, floral clock.
Horreolum (s.n. II): an organ or area on which pollen collects, *lit.* 'a little granary'.
horricomis (adj. B): bristly, shaggy. **horridus** (adj. A): sticking out, prickly, rough, bristly.
Horse: equus (s.m. II), *gen. pl.* equorum *or* equum. **pertaining to horses**: equinus (adj. A); *in Gk. comp.*, hippo-.
horseshoe-shaped: hippocrepicus (adj. A), hippocrepiformis (adj. B).
hortensis (adj. B): pertaining to gardens, raised in a garden. **Hortulanus** (s.m. II): gardener; *hortulanorum*, of gardeners. **Hortus** (s.m. II): garden; *hortorum*, of gardens; *hortus siccus*, herbarium; *Hortus Medicus*, Physic Garden; cf. OLERARIUM, SEMINARIUM.
Host (*of parasite*): hospes (s.m. II. ii), *gen. sing.* hospitis, *abl. sing.* hospite; *see* NOURISHING, NUTRIX.
hot: calidus (adj. A); cf. TEMPERATE. **Hot Springs**: thermae (s.f. II. pl.); *in thermis euganeis*, in hot springs of the Colli Euganei near Padua.

B.L.—P 2

Hot-bed: pulvillum (s.n. II).
Hot-house: calidarium (s.n. II).
huc (adv.): to this point, in this direction.
humectatus (part. A), **humefactus** (part. A): moistened. **humectus** (adj. A): moist, damp; cf. HYGRO-.
Humerus (s.m. II): shoulder.
humi (adverbial form of *humus*): on the ground. **humifusus** (adj. A): spread out over the ground, procumbent. **422**
humidus (adj. A): moist, damp.
humilis (adj. B): low, low-growing. **337**
Humus (s.m. II): the earth, the soil.
hundred: centum (num. adj. indecl.) 'hundred', centensimus (adj. A) 'hundredth', centies (adv.), centiens (adv.) 'hundred times'. **hundred-**: *in L. comp.*, centi-, *in Gk. comp.*, hecat-, hecto-; *centifolius*, 100-leaved, in *Rosa centifolia* referring to large number of petals, in *Lilium centifolium*, to large number of leaves.
hyacinthinus (adj. A): hyacinth-blue (H.C.C. 40), violet, (*rarely*) like a hyacinth in habit. **hyacinthoides** (adj. B): hyacinth-like.
hyalinus (adj. A): hyaline, colourless and transparent, *lit.* 'of glass or crystal'.
hybospermus (adj.A): with tuberculate seeds.
Hybrid (s.): hybrida (s.c. I), *abl. sing.* hybrida, *nom. pl.* hybridae, *abl. pl.* hybridis. **hybrid** (adj.): hybridus (adj. A), hybridogenus (adj. A). As epithets to designate hybrids *adulterinus, digeneus, hybridus, miscellus, misturatus, mistus, nothus* and *spurius* are used, but not *bastardi*; *taxa hybridae originis, taxa hybridogena*, taxa of hybrid origin.
Hydathode: hydathodus (s.f. II), *abl. sing.* hydathodo, *nom. pl.* hydathodi, *abl. pl.* hydathodis.
hydro-: *in Gk. comp.*, water; *hydrophilus*, water-loving.
hydrochloric: hydrochloricus (adj. A), muriaticus (adj. A). **Hydrochloride**: hydrochloridum (s.n. II).
hyemalis (adj. B), **hiemalis** (adj. B): pertaining to winter, wintry.
hygro-: *in Gk. comp.*, damp, moist, moisture; *hygrophilus*, moisture-loving. **hygrometricus** (adj. A), **hygroscopicus** (adj. A): hygroscopic, i.e. readily absorbing moisture and then changing form or poise by expansion. **hygrophanus** (adj. A): hygrophanous, translucent when wet, opaque when dry.
hymen-: *in Gk. comp.*, membrane, membranous, skinny; *hymenocarpus*, with membranous fruits; *hymenosepalus*, with membranous sepals.
Hymenium: hymenium (s.n. II), *gen. sing.* hymenii, *abl. sing.* hymenio.

hyp-, hypo- : *in Gk. comp.*, below, under, beneath, lower; *hypargyreus*, silvery beneath; *hypochryseus*, golden beneath; *hypogaeus*, below the ground; *hypoglaucus*, glaucous beneath; *hypolasius*, woolly beneath; *hypolepidotus*, scaly beneath; *hypoleucus*, white beneath; *hypophaeus*, dark beneath; *hypophyllus*, beneath the leaf; *hypostictus*, spotted beneath.

Hypanthium : hypanthium (s.n. II), *abl. sing.* hypanthio.

hyper- : *in Gk. comp.*, beyond, over, above.

hyperboreus (adj. A): belonging to the extreme north, northern; cf. BOREALIS.

Hypha : hypha (s.f. I), *nom. pl.* hyphae, *gen. pl.* hypharum, *abl. pl.* hyphis; *hyphae hyalinae haud inflatae 2-3 μ latae plus minusve crasse tunicatae septatae, fibulis carentes vel eis solum ad basim basidiorum praeditae*, hyphae hyaline never inflated 2-3 μ broad more or less thickly tunicated septate, lacking fibulae or provided with these only at the base of the basidia; *hyphis albidis rectis vel leniter undulatis 6-8 μ crassis septatis (articulis 20 μ longis) unilateraliter ramosis fibulatis*, with hyphae whitish straight or gently undulate 6-8 μ thick with joints 20 μ long on one side branched possessing clamp-connexions; cf. TEXTURA.

Hyphopodium : hyphopodium (s.n. II), *nom. pl.* hyphopodia, *abl. pl.* hyphopodiis : *hyphopodia capitata alternata suberecta plerumque recta 20-30 μ longa, cellula basali cylindracea 3-6 μ longa, cellula apicali irregulariter stellato-lobata*, capitate hyphopodia alternate almost erect commonly straight 20-30 μ long with basal cell cylindric 3-6 μ long with apical cell irregularly stellate-lobed; *hyphopodia mucronata nulla*, mucronate hyphopodia nil.

hyphosus (adj. A): full of hyphae.

Hypnospore : hypnospora (s.f. I): *see* SPORE.

hypo- : *see* HYP-.

Hypocotyl : hypocotylus (s.m. II), internodium (s.n. II), hypocotylum. **hypocotylary** : hypocotylus (adj. A).

hypocraterimorphus (adj. A), **hypocrateriformis** (adj. B): hypocrateriform, salver-shaped, i.e. with a long narrow tube abruptly expanded into a shorter flat or spreading limb. **70**

Hypoderm : hypoderma (s.n. III), *abl. sing.* hypodermate.

hypodermicus (adj. A): under the epidermis.

hypogaeus (adj. A): hypogeal, growing or remaining below ground. **470**

Hypogynium : hypogynium (s.n. II), *abl. sing.* hypogynio.

hypogynus (adj. A): hypogynous, i.e. situated below base of ovary or oogonium. **473**

hypophyllus (adj. A): hypophyllous, i.e. growing on the underside of leaves; *in hypophyllo*, on the lower leaf-surface.

Hypothallus : hypothallus (s.m. II), *abl. sing.* hypothallo. **hypothallinus** (adj. A): relating to the hypothallus.

Hypotheca, Hypovalve : hypotheca (s.f. I), *abl. sing.* hypotheca; hypovalva (s.f. I), *abl. sing.* hypovalva.

hypsophyllinus (adj. A): hypsophyllary, bracteal. **Hypsophyllum** (s.n. II): hypsophyll, i.e. bract of the inflorescence.

hysteranthus (adj. A): following the flowers; used of leaves produced later than the flowers, as in the almond, many species of Colchicum, etc.; cf. PRAECOX, SYNANTHUS, *also* COAETANUS, PROTERANTHUS.

hysterinus (adj. A), **hysteriformis** (adj. B), **hysterioideus** (adj. A): hysterine i.e. long and cleft like the sporocarp (hysterothecium, fruit-body) of Hysterium.

hysterogenus (adj. A): late-produced, e.g. leaves produced after flowering; cf. PRIMIGENUS.

I

iadinus (adj. A): jade-green (H.C.C. 54).

iam : *see* JAM.

ibi (adv.): there, on the spot, then, thereupon.

-ibus : abl. and dat. pl. ending of s. III, s. IV and adj. B, meaning mostly 'with' but also 'from, by, in' (when abl.) and 'to, for' (when dat.); *planta floribus patentibus, staminibus viridibus*, plant with spreading flowers, with green stamens.

Ice : glacies (s.f. V).

Icon (s.f. III): illustration, plate; *icones plantarum novarum, rariorum vel minus cognitarum*, illustrations of new, rare or little known plants; *nova genera plantarum descripta et iconibus illustrata*, new genera of plants described and with plates illustrated; *ex icone*, from (according to) the illustration; *see* ILLUSTRATION.

icosandrus (adj. A): with twenty stamens.

icterinus (adj. A): jaundice-yellow.

Ictus (s.m. IV): stab, bite, sting; *nomen Pruni cornutae datum ob ovaria insectorum ictu in cornu excrescentia*, name of Prunus cornuta given on account of the ovaries by the sting of insects growing out into a horn.

idem, eadem, idem (pron.): the same; *color pilei idem ac Polypori adusti*, colour of pileus the same as that of Polyporus adustus.

identical with: idem atque, idem ac, simillimus (adj. A); *see* SAME.

ideo (adv.): for that reason, therefore.

idonee (adv.): suitably, fitly. **idoneus** (adj. A): suitable, convenient, sufficient.

if: si (conj.); *caulis solidus aut si cavus nunc firmus*, stem solid or if hollow then firm; *vix aut haud*, scarcely if at all.

igitur (adv.): then, therefore, accordingly.

ignescens (part. B): glowing, burning, i.e. bright-red. **igneus** (adj. A): fire-red (H.C.C. 15), flame-colour. **ignivomus** (adj. A): fire-vomiting, volcanic.

ignotus (adj. A): unknown; *see* INCOGNITUS.

illa (adv.): in that direction.

illaqueans (part. B): ensnaring, entrapping.

ille (dem. pron. m.), **illa** (dem. pron. f.), **illud** (dem. pron. n.): that, he, she, it; sometimes used to indicate celebrity or emphasis, e.g. *Winnie ille Pu*, Winnie-the-Pooh; in contrasts *hic* indicates the nearer, *ille* the more remote; *hic ... ille ...*, this ... that ..., the one ... the other.

illecebrosus (adj. A): alluring, attractive.

illegitimus (adj. A): unlawful; *nomen illegitimum*, name contrary to the rules of nomenclature, illegitimate name.

illic (adv.): in that place, there; cf. HIC.

illinc (adv.): from that place, thence.

illinitus (part. A): smeared, daubed over, overspread.

illustrated: illustratus (part. A). **Illustration**: icon (s.f. III), *gen. sing.* iconis, *abl. sing.* icone, *nom. pl.* icones, *gen. pl.* iconum, *abl. pl.* iconibus; imago (s.f. III), *gen. sing.* imaginis, *abl. sing.* imagine, *nom. pl.* imagines, *gen. pl.* imaginum, *abl. pl.* imaginibus; figura (s.f. I), *nom. pl.* figurae, *abl. pl.* figuris; illustratio (s.f. III), *nom. pl.* illustrationes, *abl. pl.* illustrationibus; tabula (s.f. I), *nom. pl.* tabulae, *abl. pl.* tabulis. *icones sunt ligneae, aeneae, fundamentales absque umbra, fucatae vivis coloribus, originales ex foliis ipsis loco typi, pretiosae, malae*, illustrations are wooden (i.e. woodcuts), copper (i.e. copper engravings), plain without shading, painted in natural colours, original from the leaves themselves (i.e. nature prints), of great value, bad; *icones selectae ex vivo delineatae*, selected illustrations drawn from living material; *iconum botanicarum index locupletissimus*, of illustrations botanical an index most rich; *explicatio iconis*, explanation of the illustration; *species graminum iconibus illustratae*, species of grasses with plates illustrated; *icones aeri sculptae*, illustrations on copper engraved; *tabulae coloratae et tabulae nigrae analyticae aeri incisae*, plates coloured and plates black (i.e. black-and-white) analytical on copper engraved; *tabulae pictae*, plates painted; *plantarum imagines in aes incisae et vivis coloribus pictae*, of plants the likenesses in copper engraved and with living (i.e. natural) colours painted; *xylographia exhibit stirpem foliis lanceolatis eximie maculatis*, the woodcut shows a plant with leaves lanceolate exceedingly spotted; *cum figuris xylographice expressis*, with woodcut figures; *figurae plantarum maxima pro parte ex Passaeo petitae*, figures of plants for the most part from Passeus (i.e. Crispin de Passe) taken; *ut in illustratione originali*, as in the original illustration. *See* W. Blunt & W. T. Stearn, *The Art of Botanical Illustration* (1950), C. Nissen, *Die botanische Buchillustration* (1951-52), S. Sitwell & others, *Great Flower Books* (1956).

Imago (s.f. III. vi): likeness, figure; *see* ILLUSTRATION.

imbecillis (adj. B), **imbecillus** (adj. A): weak, feeble.

imbedded: inclusus (part. A) in (prep. with abl.); *in gelatina inclusus*, imbedded in gelatine.

imberbis (adj. B): beardless.

imbricate: imbricatus (part. A), imbricans (part. B); *imbricativus* (adj. A) is used only of aestivation. **376, 484**

imitating: mentiens (part. B), simulans (part. B); *involucrum calycem mentiens*, involucre imitating a calyx.

immaculatus (adj. A): unspotted, unstained.

immarginatus (adj. A): without a distinct margin, border or rim.

immature: immaturus (adjA), crudus (adjA)

immediately: statim (adv.) 'at once, forthwith', confestim (adv.) 'speedily, forthwith', proxime (adv.) 'nearest, next'; *proxime super nodum*, immediately above the node; *cellula quasi confestim mobili facta*, cell almost immediately made motile.

immensus (adj. A): immense, vast, boundless.

Immersio (s.f. III): immersion.

immersus (part. A): submerged, imbedded, covered up, immersed.

imminens (part. B): overhanging; cf. IMPENDENS.

imminuens (part. B): diminishing. **imminutus** (part. A): diminished, reduced in size.

immixtus (part. A): intermixed, mingled with.

immo (adv.): on the contrary, by no means.

immobile: immobilis (adj. B), fixus (part. A), immotus (adj. A).

immutabilis (adj. B), **immutatus** (adj. A): unchangeable, unchanged.

impar (adj. B): uneven, unequal, dissimilar. **impariter** (adv.): unequally.

imparipinnate: imparipinnatus (adj. A). 209

impassable: impervius (adj. A).

impeditus (part. A): hindered, obstructed, *hence* not completely formed.

impellucidus (adj. A): opaque, not pellucid.

impendens (part. B): overhanging; cf. IMMINENS.

impenetrable: impenetrabilis (adj. B).

Impensa (s.f. I): outlay, cost, expense; *impensis Salvii*, at the cost of Salvius.

imperfect: imperfectus (adj. A), inchoatus (part. A), mancus (adj. A), mendosus (adj. A).

imperforatus (adj. A): not perforated.

impervius (adj. A): impassable.

impigre (adv.): actively, energetically.

implens (part. B): filling.

impletus (part. A): filled, q.v.

implexus (part. A), **implicatus** (part. A), **implicitus** (part. A): entangled, entwined, interwoven, interlaced.

impolitus (adj. A): unpolished, matt. 299

impositus (part. A): laid upon, placed upon, i.e. of an organ or part not gradually passing into another.

impressi-: *in L. comp.*, sunken, impressed; *impressinervis*, with sunken nerves; *impressivenius*, with sunken veins. **impressus** (part. A): impressed, sunk below the surface as if pressed in; *nervo medio supra bene impresso*, with middle nerve above well impressed.

imprimis (adv.): in the first place, chiefly.

impudicus (adj. A): immodest, shameless.

impure: impurus(adjA),contaminatus(adjA)

impunctatus (adj. A): not punctate; cf. PUNCTATUS.

Imum (s.n. II): lowest part, bottom. **imus** (adj. A): lowest, lowermost.

in (prep. with abl. and acc.): in, within, among, at, into, on to, towards, during, on. Used with *acc.* when motion or growth or action of some kind towards or into something may be envisaged by an ingenious effort of the imagination, with *abl.* when rest is indicated, a more usual botanical condition. *ex* and *in* are associated in phrases indicating progression, just as are *ab* and *ad*. 'in' is sometimes best translated by *per* or *velut*, q.v.; *in sylva Amazonica, in foliis vivis, raro in cortice crescens*, in Amazonian forest, on living leaves, rarely on bark growing; *in corticibus arborum tropicarum*, on barks of tropical trees; *in arboribus et rupibus inter muscos in America tropica*, on trees and rocks among mosses in tropical America; *species 8 in aquis dulcibus Americae temperatae vel tropicae dispersae, una in variis locis Europae inquilina*, species 8 in fresh waters of temperate or tropical America dispersed, one in various places of Europe naturalized; *herba in siccis frequens*, herb in dry places frequent; *species in silvis Italiae indigena et hinc in hortos Europae mediae translata, hodie quoque in hortis botanicis culta et passim in nemoribus subspontanea facta*, species in woods (*abl.*) of Italy indigenous and from here into gardens (*acc.*) of central Europe transported, today also in botanic gardens (*abl.*) cultivated and here and there in groves (*abl.*) subspontaneous made, i.e. naturalized; *folia in rhizomate conferta*, leaves on the rhizome crowded together; *planta in statu florendi*, plant in flowering state; *indumentum canum in inflorescentiis floribus petiolis foliorumque nervis mox deciduum, jam tempore florendi in nodis ramulorum et in extremitatibus inflorescentiarum tantum persistens*, hair-covering grey on the inflorescences, flowers, petioles and nerves of the leaves soon falling, already at the time of flowering on nodes of branchlets and tips of inflorescences alone persisting; *dentibus in quoque latere 5-10*, with teeth on each side 5-10; *folia in paribus aequimagna*, leaves of the same pair equal in size; *petala in aestivatione valvata*, petals in aestivation valvate; *folia basi in petiolum cuneatum angustata*, leaves at base into a cuneate petiole narrowed; *pedicelli in calycem sensim ampliati*, pedicels into the calyx gradually expanded; *corona in denticulos lineares lacerata*, corona into little linear teeth lacerated; *ovarium viride in stylos purpureos transiens*, ovary green into styles purple passing gradually; *filamenta in foveolam dorsalem antherarum intrusa*, filaments into a little dorsal pit of anthers thrust (inserted); *in hoc libro*, in this book; *semen a latere visum*, seed in side view, seed seen from the side; *costa in sectione transversali e 3 stratis cellularum formata, ventrali e cellulis amplis inanibus, interno e cellulis incrassatis, dorsali e cellulis parvis*, midrib in transverse section from 3 layers of cells formed, with the ventral from large empty cells, the inner from thickened cells, the dorsal from small cells.

inactive: iners (adj. B); cf. AGILIS, MOBILIS.

-inae: adj. nom. f. pl. ending added to stem of name of synonym of type genus to form name of subtribe, e.g. *Rutinae* from Ruta.

inaequabilis (adj. B), inaequalis (adj. B): unequal. inaequi-: *in L. comp.*, unequal, uneven; *inaequilateralis*, *inaequilaterus*, with unequal sides; *inaequimagnus*, not of the same size. inaequaliter (adv.): unequally. **134, 136**

inamyloideus (adj. A): not amyloid; *hyphis omnibus inamyloideis*, with all hyphae not giving a blue reaction to iodine.

inanis (adj. B): empty.

inapertus (adj. A): not open, closed, although normally open.

inarticulatus (adj. A): without divisions.

incanus (adj. A): hoary, white. **272**

incarnatus (part. A): flesh-coloured.

incertus (adj. A): uncertain, doubtful.

Inch: pollex (s.m. III. i), *nom. pl.* pollices 'thumb'; uncia (s.f. I), *nom. pl.* unciae 'twelfth part'; approx. 2·5 cm. inchlong: pollicaris (adj. B), uncialis (adj. B).

inchoatus (part. A): incomplete, unfinished, imperfect, rudimentary.

incidens (part. B): meeting.

incisifolius (adj. A): with deeply cut leaves.

Incision: incisura (s.f. I).

incisus (part. A): cut deeply and sharply. **190**

inclinatus (part. A): bent down, diverging downwards from the horizontal. **405**

includens (part. B): including.

inclusus (part. A): included, enclosed, not projecting, comprised within; *stamina inclusa*, stamens not projecting; *folium* (*petiolo 3 cm. longo incluso*) *10 cm. longum*, leaf (with petiole 3 cm. long included) 10 cm. long. *cum* can also be used, e.g. *cellula* (*cum tuberculo*) *1 mm. longa*, cell (including tubercle) 1 mm. long.

incoctus (adj. A): uncooked, raw.

incognitus (adj. A): unknown; cf. IGNOTUS.

Incola (s.c. I): dweller, inhabitant, resident; *species montium Africae tropicae imprimis orientalis incola*, the species of the mountains of tropical Africa particularly eastern an inhabitant. incolens (part. B): inhabiting, q.v.; cf. -COLA, INHABITANT.

incolor (adj. B), incoloratus (adj. A): colourless.

incomparabilis (adj. A): beyond compare, unequalled.

incomplete: incompletus (adj. A), inchoatus (part. A), imperfectus (adj. A).

inconspicuous: inconspicuus (adj. A).

inconstans (adj. B): changeable, not constant (opp. of IMMUTABILIS).

incorrect: mendosus (adj. A). incorrectly: perperam (adv.), errore, mendose (adv.): cf. ERROR, FALSELY.

incrassatus (part. A): thickened.

Increase: augmen (s.n. III), *gen. sing.* augminis; augmentum (s.n. II), *gen. sing.* augmenti.

increased: auctus (part. A). increasing: crescens (part. B). increasing in thickness: spissescens (part. B).

increbre (adv.): frequently.

Incrementum (s.n. II): increase, increment.

incrusted: incrustatus (part. A). incrusting: incrustans (part. B).

incubaceus (adj. A): lying on the ground.

incubus (adj. A): incubous, obliquely inserted on the stem so that the leaf edge nearest the shoot-tip overlaps and thus covers the lower edge of the leaf above.

incudiformis (adj. B): anvil-shaped.

incultus (adj. A): untilled, not cultivated, used of habitats. Incultum (s.n. II): wasteland, uncultivated ground.

incumbens (part. B): incumbent, folded inwards and lying upon, used of cotyledons having the radicle resting on one side of a cotyledon instead of along the edge; *cotyledones incumbentes*, cotyledons incumbent.

incurrens (part. B): over-running; *see* INCUBUS.

incurvatus (adj. A), incurvus (adj. A): curved inwards. **410**

incystatus (adj. A): encysted.

inde (adv.): from that place, thence, from that time, thenceforward, after that, then.

indefessus (adj. A): unwearied, indefatigable; an epithet often and rightly applied to the great eighteenth- and nineteenth-century systematists.

indefinite: indefinitus (adj. A).

indehiscens (adj. B): indehiscent, not opening at all or not splitting in a regular manner, e.g. by valves or along a definite line, when ripe; cf. SEPTICIDALIS, SYNCLISTUS.

indented: indentatus (adj. A).

indescriptus (adj. A): undescribed.

indeterminate: indeterminatus (adj. A).

Index (s.m. III. i): catalogue, list, index.

Indicatio (s.f. III): indication. indicatus (part. A): pointed out, showed, revealed.

indigenous: indigenus (adj. A).

Indigo: indicum (s.n. II), *abl. sing.* indico; *fructibus contusis indici colorem conspicuum exhibentibus*, with bruised fruits the conspicuous colour of indigo exhibiting; *filamentis indico coloratis*, with filaments coloured with indigo; *flores colore indici tincti*, flowers with the colour of indigo tinged. **indigo-coloured**: indigoticus (adj. A).

indirectly: indirecte (adv.).

indiscriminately: promiscue (adv.) 'in common, promiscuously', passim (adv.) 'hither and thither, at random'.

indistinctus (adj. A): not distinct, unclear, ill-defined.

indistinguishable: haud distinctus (part. A), simillimus (adj. A).

Individual (s.): individuum (s.n. II), *abl. sing.* individuo, *abl. pl.* individua, *abl. pl.* individuis; *individua libera solitaria vel binatim cohaerentia vel seriata vel varie consociata*, individuals free solitary or by pairs cohering or in series or variously united; *individua in muco nidulantia radiatim in circulum plus minus completum planum coadjuncta*, individuals in slime nestling, radiately into a circle or less complete flat joined together. **individual** (adj.): singulus (adj. A) (*generally used in pl.*); *singulae cellulae*, individual cells. **individually**: singulatim (adv.), singulariter (adv.).

indivisus (adj. A): undivided.

Indoles (s.f. III): inborn quality, nature.

Indumentum (s.n. II): hair-covering, q.v.

induplicatus (adj. A): induplicate, i.e. having the margins bent abruptly inwards and the outer face of these folds applied to each other without any twisting. **370**

induratus (part. A): hardened. **indurescens** (part. B): becoming hard.

indusiatus (adj. A): indusiate, possessing an indusium. **Indusium**: indusium (s.n. II), *gen. sing.* indusii, *abl. sing.* indusio, *nom. pl.* indusia, *gen. pl.* indusiorum, *abl. pl.* indusiis, *lit.* 'a woman's under-garment'.

indutus (part. A, with abl.) clothed with.

Induviae (s.f. I. pl.): persistent parts, e.g. withered leaves nevertheless persisting on the shoot or accrescent or withered calyx, corolla or perigon clothing the fruit. **induviatus** (adj. A): clothed with withered parts, as a stem with persistent dead leaves; cf. MARCESCENS, REMANENS.

-ineae (adj. A): nom. f. pl. ending added to stem of name of type of family to form name of suborder, e.g. *Malvineae* from *Malvaceae*.

inermis (adj. B): unarmed, without spines, prickles or stings. **260**

iners (adj. B): inactive, sluggish, inert, stagnant.

inexspectatus (adj. A): unexpected, q.v.

infectus (part. A): spoiled, infected.

inferior (adj. comp.): lower. **inferne** (adv.): below, beneath, in lower part.

inferioramifer (adj. A): branched in the lower part.

infernus (adj. A), **inferus** (adj. A): lower, that which is beneath; *ovarium inferum*, ovary inferior, i.e. bearing at its top the perigon, etc.

infestans (part. B): infesting, attacking.

infestus (adj. A): troublesome, becoming a weed.

inficiens (part. B): tainting, infecting, spoiling.

infime (adv.): at the bottom. **Infimum** (s.n. II): lowest part, bottom. **infimus** (adj. A): lowest, lowermost.

inflatus (part. A): bladdery, i.e. thin, membranous and swollen; cf. VESICARIUS. **96**

inflexus (adj. A): bent inwards; cf. INTROFLEXUS. **418**

Inflorescence: inflorescentia (s.f. I), *abl. sing.* inflorescentia, *nom. pl.* inflorescentiae, *abl. pl.* inflorescentiis, 'flowering', adopted by Linnaeus for the manner in which flowers are arranged on the plant and hence for the flowers themselves considered collectively with their supports, this constituting a flower-bearing branch or system of branches with no ordinary foliage leaves between the flowers. Types of inflorescence are the *anthela* (anthela, s.f. I), *bostryx* (bostryx, s.m. III. i), *catkin* (amentum, s.n. II), *cincinnus* (cincinnus, s.m. II), *corymb* (corymbus, s.m. II), *cyathium* (cyathium, s.n. II), *cyme* (cyma, s.f. I), *dichasium* (dichassium, s.n. II), *drepanium* (drepanium, s.n. II), *head* (capitulum, s.n. II), *panicle* (panicula, s.f. I), *raceme* (racemus, s.m. II), *rhipidium* (rhipidium, s.n. II), *spadix* (spadix, s.m. or f. III. i), *spike* (spica, s.f. I), *spikelet* (spicula, s.f. I), *thyrse* (thyrsus, s.m. II), *umbel* (umbella, s.f. I), *verticillaster* (verticillaster, s.m. II). These nouns may be used, or else the term *inflorescentia* may be qualified by an adjectival form as *corymbosa, cymosa, dichasialis, capitato-paniculata, racemosa, spicata, thyrsigera, umbellata*; see H. W. Rickett, 'The classification of inflorescences', *Bot. Review*, 10 : 187-231 (1944); *flores in axillis foliorum 2-4 umbelliformi-dispositi e rhachi subnulla prodeuntes*, flowers 2-4 in axils of leaves umbellately arranged, from an almost non-existent rachis produced; *inflorescentia simplex vel ramosa e rhipidiis multis ad 10-floris composita*, inflorescence simple or branched from many rhipidia up to 10-flowered put together; *inflorescentia varia floribus in corymbos umbelliformes vel thyrsos densifloros vel paniculas axillares vel terminales dispositis,* inflorescence varied, with the flowers in corymbs umbel-like or thyrses dense-flowered or panicles axillary or terminal arranged; *inflorescentia normaliter 2-3-chotome cymosa, cymis terminalibus paniculatis vel axillaribus,* inflorescence normally di- or trichotomously cymose, with the cymes terminal paniculate or axillary; *inflorescentia racemosa simplex erecta glabra pauciflora (floribus 4-5), folio caulino brevior, 5-10 cm. longa,* inflorescence racemose simple erect glabrous few-flowered (with flowers 4-5), shorter than the stem leaf, 5-10 cm. long; *inflorescentiae masculae ad apices ramorum parcae breviter pedunculatae, femineae ad axillas foliorum sessiles numerosae, omnes glomeratae multiflorae,* male inflorescences at tips of branches few shortly pedunculate, female at axils of leaves sessile numerous, all compactly clustered many-flowered.

infossus (part. A): buried, sunken.
infra (adv.): on the underside, beneath, below. **infra** (prep. with acc.): below, under, later than, less than. **infra-apicalis** (adj. B): placed below the apex. **infra-axillaris** (adj. B): placed below the axil. **infracentralis** (adj. B): placed below the centre.
infractus (part. A): sharply bent, incurved. **410**
inframedianus (adj. A): slightly or somewhat below the middle.
infraterminalis (adj. B): below the apex.
infrequent: infrequens (adj. B). **infrequently**: infrequenter (adv.), rarius (adv.), interdum (adv.), sparse (adv.).
infundibularis (adj. B), **infundibuliformis** (adj. B): funnel-shaped. **71**
infuscatus (adj. A): brownish.
Infusion: infusum (s.n.II), decoctum (s.n.II)
ingens (adj. B): exceeding the size usual for the group, huge.
ingratus (adj. A): unpleasant, disagreeable.
ingrediens (part. B): entering, going in.
Inhabitant: incola (s.f. I); *species hemisphaerii borealis incolae,* species inhabitants of the northern hemisphere.
inhabiting: incolens (part. B), habitans (part. B), crescens (part. B), indigenus (adj. A), próveniens (part. B), vigens (part. B); *arbor parva Malabariae littora incolens,* tree small of Malabar the coasts inhabiting; *arbores Asiae littora tropica incolentes,* trees of Asia

the tropical coasts inhabiting; *frutex in India boreali crescens,* shrub in north India growing; *frutices in America et Africa tropica crescentes,* shrubs in America and tropical Africa growing; *herba in Capite Bonae Spei indigena,* herb at the Cape of Good Hope indigenous; *herbae in Europa australi indigenae,* herbs in southern Europe indigenous; *species in aridis Europae orientalis et Asiae mediae provenientes,* species in dry places of eastern Europe and central Asia occurring; *species littora lacuum habitantes,* species inhabiting the shores of lakes; *frutices in insula Madagascar crescentes,* shrubs in the island Madagascar growing.
iniens (part B): entering, going in; cf. INGREDIENS.
Initial (s.): initium (s.n. II). **initial** (adj.): primus (adj. A).
Initium (s.n. II): beginning.
injurious: noxius (adj. A). **Injury**: noxa (s.f. I); cf. ICTUS, LAESIO, VULNUS.
innatus (part. A): innate, borne on apex of supporting part, adhering by growing into. **447**
inner: interior (adj. comp.); *segmenta interiora,* inner segments; *intra margines interiores,* within the inner margins. **innermost**: intimus (adj. A).
innocuus (adj. A), **innoxius** (adj. A): harmless, i.e. lacking poisonous properties, spines, bristles, etc.
innominatus (adj. A): unnamed, nameless.
innovans (part. B): renewing.
Innovation: innovatio (s.f. III. vi), *abl. sing.* innovatione, *nom. pl.* innovationes, *gen. pl.* innovationum, *abl. pl.* innovationibus; *gramen perenne, innovationibus intravaginalibus,* grass perennial, with new basal vegetative shoots growing up within the sheath; *innovationes extravaginales,* new shoots outside the sheath.
innoxius (adj. A): *see* INNOCUUS.
innumerabilis (adj. B), **innumerus** (adj. A): countless, innumerable.
inodorus (adj. A): without smell, scentless.
inoperculatus (adj. A): without a lid or operculum.
inopinatus (adj. A): unexpected, q.v.
inordinate (adv.), **inordinatim** (adv.), **inordinaliter** (adv.): irregularly, disorderly. **inordinatus** (adj. A): irregular, disordered.
inquilinus (adj. A): naturalized, introduced.; cf. FOREIGN.
inquinatus (part. A): fouled, stained, polluted, dirty, blackish.
insculptus (part. A): engraved, cut into, with sunken markings, embedded in.

Insect: insectum (s.n. II), *gen. sing.* insecti, *abl. sing.* insecto, *nom. pl.* insecta, *gen. pl.* insectorum, *abl. pl.* insectis. **insect-**: *in L. comp.*, insecti-, *in Gk. comp.*, entomo-; *insectifer,* bearing an insect, i.e. with flower shaped like an insect; *insectifugus,* driving away insects; *insectivorus,* insect-eating.

inserted: insertus (part. A), affixus (adj. A); *stamina tubo corollae supra basin sed infra medium inserta,* stamens to tube of corolla above base but below middle inserted; *stamina 4 exserta, corolla ad aut sub sinubus affixa,* stamens 4 exserted, to the corolla at or below the sinuses attached. **Insertion**: insertio (s.f. III. vi).

insertus (part. A): affixed to, placed on, originating from.

Inside (s): pars (s.f. III) interior. **inside** (adj.): internus (adj. A), penitus (adj. A). **on the inside**: intra (adv.), intus (adv.), intrinsecus (adv.), interius (adv.), introrsum (adv.), penitus (adv.); *see* OUTSIDE. **towards the inside**: introrsum (adv.).

insidens (part. B, with dat.): sitting upon, situated upon; *bulbus cylindricus rhizomati tenero insidens,* bulb cylindric on a slender rhizome mounted; *perianthium germini insidens,* perianth (i.e. calyx) on the ovary situate (i.e. with a superior calyx).

insignis (adj. B): distinguished by, remarkable for, outstanding, noted. **insignite** (adv.): remarkably, notably.

insimul (adv.): at the same time.

insipidus (adj. A): tasteless, insipid.

insiticius (adj. A), **insititius** (adj. A): grafted.

Insitum (s.n. II): a graft, scion.

inspersus (part. A): interpenetrated with granules, sprinkled upon.

inspissatus (adj. A): thickened.

Instar (s. indecl.): manner, likeness, form; *ad instar* (with gen.), like, in the form of.

instead of: vice (with gen.), ad invicem; *ordines dentium duos vice unius,* two rows of teeth, instead of one.

Institutio (s.f. III. vi): arrangement, custom, principle, element of instruction; *institutiones rei herbariae,* elements of botany.

Institutum (s.n. II): institute, organization set up to promote a particular study; *institutum botanicum academiae,* botanical institute of the academy.

instructus (part. A): provided with.

insuetus (adj. A): unusual.

Insula (s.f. I): island, q.v. **insularis** (adj. B): pertaining to islands, insular.

insuper (adv.): above, on top, from above, moreover, besides. **insuper** (prep. with acc. and abl.): over, above.

intactus (adj. A): untouched, intact, entire.

integer (adj. A): entire, undivided, simple, without teeth or lobes or notches. **integerrimus** (adj. A): absolutely entire. **179, 180**

integri-: *in L. comp.*, entire; *integrifolius,* with entire leaves; *integrilabris,* with entire lip.

Integument: integumentum (s.n. II).

intense (adv.): intensely.

inter (prep. with acc.): between, among, in the midst of, surrounded by, during. **inter** (adv. rarely used): in between, in the midst. **interaneus** (adj. A): inward, interior, internal.

intercalaris (adj. B): intercalary, arising between base and apex; *heterocystae intercalares,* heterocysts intercalary; *heterocystis intercalaribus,* with heterocysts intercalary; cf. COPULA.

interceptus (part. A): interrupted, intercepted.

intercurrens (part. B): running between.

interdum (adv.): sometimes, now and then, occasionally.

interea (adv.): meanwhile, in the interim.

interfoliaceus (adj. A): interfoliaceous, i.e. placed between two opposite leaves.

interim (adv.): meanwhile, for a time, in the meantime.

interior (adj. comp.): inner, interior. **interius** (adv.): in the inner part, on the inside, within.

interjacens (part. B): intervening, coming between.

interjectus (part. A): cast between, placed between, intermediate between.

intermediate: intermedius (adj. A); but interjectus (part. A), interpositus (part. A), medius (adj. A) may also be applicable.

interne (adv.): inwardly, internally. **internus** (adj. A): inward, internal.

Internode: internodium (s.n. II), *abl. sing.* internodio, *nom. and acc. pl.* internodia, *abl. pl.* internodiis; *internodia ramulis 2-5 plo longiora,* internodes than the branchlets 2-5 times longer; *caulis internodiis elongatis,* stem with elongated internodes; *caules ad internodia radicantes,* stems at internodes rooting.

interordinatus (adj. A): fitted together, fitted into one another.

interpetiolar: interpetiolaris (adj. B).

interpositus (part. A): placed between *or* among, interposed.

interruptedly: interrupte (adv.); *interrupte pinnatus,* interruptedly pinnate. **212**

interruptus (part. A): interrupted, not continued. **500**

interspersus (adj. A): strewn, interspersed.

Interstitium (s.n. II): space between, interstice.

Interval: intervallum(s.n.II),spatium(s.n.II)

intervening: interjacens (part. B).

interwoven: intertextus (part. A), implexus (part. A).

intestinalis (adj. B): relating to or found in the intestines. **intestiniformis** (adj. B): intestine-like (*applied to lax hairs bent irregularly backwards and forwards and slightly constricted at intervals*).

intestinus (adj. A): internal.

intime (adv.): in the inmost part, inwardly, internally. **intimus** (adj. A): inmost, innermost.

into: in (prep. with acc.); cf. IN.

intonsus (adj. A): unshaven, *hence* bristly, shaggy.

intortus (part. A): twisted or bent upon itself.

intoxicated: temulentus (adj. A).

intra (adv.): on the inside, inwardly. **intra** (prep. with acc.): within, into, during.

intracalycinus (adj. A): intracalycine, within the calyx.

intracellularis (adj. B): within a cell.

intramarginalis (adj. B): intramarginal, within and near the margin.

intrarius (adj. A): lying on the inside, turned inward to the axis.

intrastaminalis (adj. B): intrastaminal, within the stamens.

intricatus (part. A): entangled; cf. TEXTURA. **intricate** (adv.): intricately. **502**

intrinsecus (adv.): on the inside, inwardly, towards the inside, inwards.

intro (adv.): inwardly, internally, to the inside (indicating motion).

introduced: introductus (part. A); cf. INQUILINUS.

introflexus (adj. A): bent inwards; cf. INFLEXUS. **410**

intromissus (part. A with *in* and acc.): sent in, introduced into.

introrsum (adv.): towards the inside, inwardly, on the inside.

introrsus (adj. A): introrse, turned towards the axis. **420**

intrusus (part. A): thrust in, inserted.

Intuitus (s.m. IV): look, view; *primo intuitu*, at first glance.

intumescens (part. B): swelling up.

intus (adv.): on the inside, within; *see* INSIDE, OUTSIDE.

inunctus (part. A): anointed, i.e. glossy as if oiled.

inundatus (part. A): flooded, usu. applied to places covered with water during part of the year, more or less dry the rest of the year.

invadens (part. B): attacking, invading. **invasus** (part. A): attacked, invaded.

inventus (part. A): found.

inverse (adv.), **inversum** (adv.): upside down. **inversus** (part. A): turned upside down or turned about. **399**

investiens (part. B): clothing.

Investigatio (s.f. III. vi): investigation, research, enquiry.

invicem (adv.): in turn, one after another, alternately; *ad invicem*, instead of.

invisible: invisibilis (adj. B).

Involucel: involucellum (s.n. II), *abl. sing.* involucello, *nom. pl.* involucella, *abl. pl.* involucellis. **involucralis** (adj. B): involucral, of the involucre. **involucratus** (adj. A): involucrate, having an involucre or ring or rings of bracts around the base of an inflorescence. **Involucre**: involucrum (s.n. II), *gen. sing.* involucri, *abl. sing.* involucro, *nom. pl.* involucra, *gen. pl.* involucrorum, *abl. pl.* involucris. *flores (flosculi auct. plur.) plures in receptaculo communi (clinanthio auct. pl.) sessiles involucro communi (periclinio auct. pl.) e bracteis (squamis, phyllis vel phyllariis auct. plur.) 1-∞-seriatis liberis concretisve cincti, capitulum (anthodium vel calathidium auct. plur.) florem singulum simulans formantes*, flowers (florets of many authors) many on a common receptacle (clinanthium of many authors) sessile, by a common involucre (periclinium of many authors) out of bracts (scales, phylla or phyllaries of many authors) in one to an indefinite number of series free or joined together surrounded, forming a head (anthodium or calathidium of many authors) resembling a single flower; *involucrum cylindraceum angustum post anthesin basi aequale vel parum ampliatum, bracteis pauciseriatis scarioso-marginatis fructiferis immutatis, intimis elongatis subaequalibus, exterioribus gradatim brevioribus vel paucis brevissimisque*, involucre cylindric narrow after anthesis at the base even or little increased, with bracts in few series scariose-margined in the fruiting state unchanged, with the innermost ones elongated almost equal, with the outer ones gradually shorter or few and very short; *involucri cylindrici viridis bracteae pauciseriatae scarioso-marginatae acuminatae*, of the cylindric green involucre the bracts in few series scariose-margined acuminate; *involucra e basi late rotundata fere semiglobosa dense nigro-glandulosa, squamis lanceolatis acutis usque ad 1 cm. longis*, involucre from the base broadly rounded almost half-globose densely black-glandular, with the scales lanceolate acute up to 1 cm. long; *involucris hemisphaericis vel campanulatis viridibus glandulosis*, with involucres hemispherical or campanulate green glandular; *involucri campanulati phylla imbricata nigra, praeter marginem interdum ciliatum glabra, quoad formam et magnitudinem valde variabilia, exteriora ovata, interiora oblonga*, of the campanulate involucre the phylla overlapping black, except for the sometimes ciliate margin glabrous, as to shape and size very variable, the outer ovate the inner oblong. The divisions of the involucre have been variously termed, e.g. *bractea, phyllum, phyllarium, squama, tegula*.

involutus (part. A): involute, rolled inwards. **involvens** (part. B): enveloping. **365, 401**

inwardly: intrinsecus (adv.), intro (adv.), intime (adv.), introrsum (adv.).

io-: *see* ION-.

Iodate: iodas (s.m. III. ii), *gen. sing.* iodatis. **Iodide**: iodidum (s.n. II), *gen. sing.* iodidi. **Iodine**: iodum (s.n. II), *gen. sing.* iodi, *abl. sing.* iodo; *granulae iodo soluto madefactae vulgo colorem caeruleum ducentes*, granules with dissolved iodine moistened commonly a blue colour producing. **iodized**: iodisatus (adj. A), iodatus (adj. A).

ion-, io-: *in Gk. comp.*, violet-coloured; *ionandrus*, with violet stamens; *ionanthus*, with violet flowers; *ionoglossus*, with violet tongue; *ionophyllus*, with violet leaves; *see* VIOLET.

ipse (demonst. pron.): self, himself, herself, itself.

Iron: ferrum (s.n. II). **iron**: ferreus (adj. A), q.v.

irpicinus (adj. A): like a rake or harrow.

irregular: irregularis (adj. B), asymmetricus (adj. A) 'asymmetric', zygomorphicus (adj. A) 'divisible into equal halves along one plane only', inordinatus (adj. A) 'disordered, haphazard', insolitus (adj. A) 'unusual', abnormis (adj. B) 'without rule, abnormal'. **irregularly**: irregulariter (adv.), irregulatim (adv.), asymmetrice (adv.). **99**

irriguus (adj. A): well-watered, wet, soaked.

irritabilis (adj. B): sensitive, responding to stimuli.

isabellinus (adj. A): isabella, soiled tawny yellow. The tale that it depicts the colour of the Archduchess Isabella's under-garments after three years of continuous wear without changing and washing is unfounded but suggests the colour.

ischno-: *in Gk. comp.*, thin, slender; *ischnopetalus*, narrow-petalled.

Isidium: isidium (s.n. II), *abl. sing.* isidio, *nom. pl.* isidia, *abl. pl.* isidiis; *isidia claviformia coralliformia cylindrica, soredialia squamiformia vel verruciformia*, isidia club-shaped coral-like cylindric, soredial scaly or warty; cf. Geesteranus in *Blumea*, 6: 47 (1947).

Island: insula (s.f. I), *gen. sing.* insulae, *abl. pl.* insula, *nom. pl.* insulae, *gen. pl.* insularum, *abl. pl.* insulis; *arbor Insulae Norfolk*, tree of Norfolk Island; *herbae in insula Madagascar crescentes*, herbs on island Madagascar growing; *Insulae Britannicae*, British Isles; *Americae tropicae et insularum Indiae occidentalis incolae*, of tropical America and of the islands of the West Indies dwellers; *species insularum Oceani pacifici*, species of islands of the Pacific Ocean; *frutices in insulis Canariis indigeni*, shrubs in the Canary Islands indigenous; *ex eadem insula*, from the same island; *in Bodotriae insulis*, on islets of the Firth of Forth, Scotland; *species pro insula diu cognita*, species for the island a long while known. **pertaining to islands**: insularis (adj. B); *in Gk. comp.*, neso-; *nesophilus*, island-loving.

iso-: *in Gk. comp.*, equal, like; *isochilus*, with lip equal to other parts, equal-lipped; *isolepis*, with equal scales; *isomerus*, with equal parts, i.e. with the number of parts in one floral whorl the same as in another whorl; *isophyllus*, with equal leaves.

isodiametrus (adj. A): isodiametrical, with vertical and horizontal diameters equal.

Isogamete: isogameta (s.f. I).

isolated: sejunctus (part. A), segregatus (part. A).

isolateral: aequilateralis (adj. B).

isostichus (adj. A): having equal rows.

Isthmus: isthmus (s.m. II).

it: usually implied and not expressed, particularly when 3rd person sing. verb is used; cf. p. 120.

ita (adv.): in this manner, thus.

itaque (conj.): and so, accordingly, for that reason, consequently.

itch-causing: pruriens (part. B).

Iter (s.n. III): journey, q.v.

iterum (adv.): again, a second time, once more; *iterum atque iterum*, again and again.

itidem (adv.): likewise.

itinerarius (adj. A): relating to journeys or travelling; *unio itineraria*, society or club to promote exploration and travel.

Iulus: *see* JULUS.

ivory-white: eburneus (adj. A).

J

jam (adv.), **iam** (adv.): now, at present, already, till now.

jamdudum (adv.): long before, a long time ago.

Jelly: gelatina (s.f. I), substantia (s.f. I) gelinea.

jelly-like: gelineus (adj. A), gelatinus (adj. A), tremelloideus (adj. A).

Jodum (s.n. II): iodine, q.v.

Join (union): junctura (s.f. I) ; *stamina ad corollae tubi cum ovario juncturam inserta*, stamens at junction of tube of corolla with ovary inserted ; **joined**: junctus (part. A), colligatus (part. A), conferruminatus (part. A), conjunctus (part. A), conflatus (part. A), consociatus (part. A).

Joint: articulus (s.m. II). **jointed**: articulatus (part A) ; cf. ARTHRO-, GENICULATUS. **235, 455**

Journal: diarium (s.n. II) ; cf. ACTA.

Journey: iter (s.n. III), *gen. sing.* itineris, *abl. sing.* itinere ; *hepaticae amazonicae et andinae quas in itinere suo per tractus montium et fluviorum Americae aequinoctialis decerpsit R. Spruce*, liverworts Amazonian and Andean which R. Spruce in his journey through the region of mountains and rivers of Equatorial America gathered ; cf. ITINERARIUS.

Juba (s.f. I): panicle of grasses, *lit.* 'mane' ; *juba 2-pedalis stricta sicca grisea*, panicle 2-feet long narrow when dried grey. **jubatus** (adj. A): maned (*i.e. with mane-like appearance*).

Judex (s.c. III): judge ; *me judice*, in my judgment, with me as judge.

Judicium (s.n. II): judgment, decision, opinion ; cf. OPINION.

jugatus (adj. A): yoked together, in pairs ; *trijugatus*, with three pairs. **Jugum** (s.n. II): pair, ridge, chain of mountains. -jugus (adj.A): *in L. comp.*, -paired

Juice: succus (s.m. II), *abl. sing.* succo ; *herbae succo croceo praeditae*, herbs with juice saffron-coloured provided. **juicy**: succidus (adj. A), succosus (adj. A).

juiceless: exsuccus (adj. A).

julaceus (adj. A) ; julaceous, smoothly cylindrical, catkin-like, bearing catkins. **Julus** (s.m. II): catkin.

Juncetum (s.n. II): rushy place. **junceus** (adj. A): rush-like, made of rushes. **juncifolius** (adj. A): rush-leaved. **juncosus** (adj. A): full of rushes.

Junctura (s.f. I): join, joint, uniting. **junctus** (part. A): joined, united, connected together.

just: admodum (adv.), modo (adv.). **just as**: sicut (adv.).

juste (adv.): rightly, duly, justly. **justus** (adj. A): rightful, true, just.

jutting out: procurrens (part. B), projectus (part. A), exstans (part. B).

juvenalis (adj. B): youthful, juvenile, pertaining to Port Juvenal near Montpellier, e.g. Godron's *Florula Juvenalis* (1854). **juvenilis** (adj. B), **juvenis** (adj. B): young, youthful. **Juventus** (s.f. III. ii): season of youth, youth, youthful state.

juxta (adv. and prep. with acc.): near, nearby, by the side of, next to, very near, approaching.

K

Kalium (s.n. II): potassium.

Keel: carina (s.f. I), *acc. sing.* carinam, *gen. sing.* carinae, *abl. sing.* carina ; *carina rectiuscula vel incurva, apice obtusa vel acuta*, keel almost straight or incurved, at the tip blunt or acute ; *carinae obtusae petala dorso apice connata*, of the blunt keel the petals on the back of the tip joined ; *corolla alba carina alas longitudine aequante extus pilosa*, corolla white with the keel equalling the wings in length outside pilose ; *corolla bicolor, ad vexilli basim et ad carinae apicem violacea*, corolla two-coloured, at the base of the standard and at the tip of the keel violet ; *carinae lamina purpurea unguem suum albidum longitudine aequans*, of the keel the purple lamina its whitish claw in length equalling. **keeled**: carinatus (adj. A) 'provided with a keel', carinalis (adj. B) 'relating to the keel'. **keelless**: ecarinatus (adj. A).

Keeper: custos (s.c. III).

keeping back: retinens (part. B). **keeping together**: continens (part. B).

kept: conservatus (part. A), asservatus (part. A).

kermesinus (adj. A): crimson.

Key (statement of contrasting characters): clavis (s.f. III. vii), *abl. sing.* clave. **Key** (indehiscent winged fruit): samara (s.f. I), *abl. sing.* samara.

kidney-shaped: reniformis (adj. B) (*used of outlines and flat objects*), nephroideus (adj. A.) (*used of solid objects*).

killing: enecans (part. B), funestus (adj. A); *in L. comp.*, -cidus, *in Gk. comp.*, -ctonus.

kindly: benevole (adv.).

Kingdom: regnum (s.n. II).

kinky: crispus (adj. A).

knee-jointed, kneed: geniculatus (adj. A).

knobbed: torulosus (adj. A). **knobby**: nodosus (adj. A). **knob-like**: gongylodes (adj. B) ; cf. UMBONATUS. **62**

knot-like: gangliiformis (adj. B).
known: cognitus (part. A).

L

Labellum: labellum (s.n. II), *abl. sing.*
labello, *nom. pl.* labella, *abl. pl.* labellis;
labellum orbiculare flabellatum vel ellip-
ticum apice excisum 2-3 mm. latum
multinervosum basi ante ostium callo in-
structum, labellum orbicular fan-shaped
or elliptic at the tip cut out (notched)
2-3 mm. broad many-nerved at base in
front of the opening with a thickening
provided; *labellum ex ungue brevissimo*
ambitu ovatum obscure quadrilobatum,
lobulis lateralibus quam intermediis
majoribus, omnibus rotundatis, labellum
from a very short claw in outline ovate
obscurely four-lobed, with the lateral
lobules than the middle ones larger, all
of them rounded.
labiatus (adj. A): lipped, used of corolla
tubular at base but expanded above into
one or two lips. **68**
labilis (adj. B): slippery, perishable.
labiosus (adj. A): large-lipped, with well
developed labium. **Labium** (s.n. II):
labium, lower lip of corolla.
labyrinthine: labyrinthinus (adj. A),
daedaleus (adj. A) (*from Daedalus,*
mythical builder of the Cretan labyrinth)
'marked with sinuous intricate lines',
labyrinthiformis (adj. B) 'irregularly
bent and crumpled'.
Lac (s.n. III. ii): milky juice; *see* LATEX.
laccatus (adj. A): looking as if varnished.
lacerate: lacerus (adj. A), laceratus
(part. A). **189**
lachno-: *in Gk. comp.,* woolly; *lachno-*
spermus, with woolly seeds.
Lacinia: lacinia (s.f. I), *abl. sing.* lacinia,
nom. pl. laciniae, *abl. pl.* laciniis, *lit.*
'flap of garment'. **laciniatus** (adj. A):
slashed into narrow divisions with taper-
pointed incisions. **laciniifolius** (adj. A):
laciniate-leaved. **191**
laciniosus (adj. A): very laciniate. **Laci-**
nula (s.f. I): lacinule, a small *or* fine
lacinia.
lacking: destitutus (part. A), carens (part.
B), nullus (adj. A), demptus (part. A),
deficiens (part. B); cf. ABSENCE, DEEST.
Lacrima (s.f. I), **Lacryma** (s.f. I): tear-
drop; *lacryma Jobi,* tear of Job. **lacri-**
miformis (adj. B): tear-shaped, obovoid,
i.e. solid and more or less obovate in
outline. **12**
lactaneus (adj. A), **lacteus** (adj. A), **lac-**
tineus (adj. A): milky, milk-white, white
with a blue tinge. **lactarius** (adj. A):
milky, made of milk. **lacti-:** *in L.*

comp., milk, milky, referring either to
milky colour or production of latex.
lactifer (adj. A): milk-producing; *see*
GAL-, MILK-.
Lactose: lactosum (s.n. II), *gen. sing.*
lactosi.
Lacuna (s.f. I): lacuna, air-space in tissue,
depression in lichen-thallus, pool, pond.
lacunosus (adj. A): covered with depressions, pitted with shallow holes
larger than those described as alveolate.
249
Lacus (s.m. IV): lake; *habitat in fundo*
lacuum, it inhabits the bottom of lakes;
in lacubus Sueciae, Borussiae, in lakes of
Sweden and Prussia. **lacuster, lacustris**
(adj. B): inhabiting lakes.
ladder-like: scalariformis (adj. B), scalaris
(adj. B).
laden: onustus (adj. A).
Laesio (s.f. III): damage, injury, wound,
lesion. **laesus** (part. A): damaged.
laetus (adj. A): cheerful, pleasant, bright.
laete (adv.): lightly, not severely, brightly.
laevigatus, levigatus (adj. A): smooth and
polished. **296**
laevis, levis (adj. B): smooth, free from
unevenness, hairs or roughness. **295**
Laevulose: laevulosum (s.n. II), *gen. sing.*
laevulosi.
lageniformis (adj. B): flask-shaped; cf.
RETORT-CELL.
lago-: *in Gk. comp.,* hare-, mostly with
reference to rough furriness like a hare's
foot; *lagopus, lagopodus,* hare-footed.
Lake: lacus (s.m. IV), q.v.
Lamella (s.f. I): thin plate of tissue, gill,
q.v. **lamellaris** (adj. B), **lamellatus** (adj.
A), **lamellosus** (adj. A): lamellate, composed of or arranged in layers or thin
plates. **Lamellula** (s.f. I): !amellule,
a short gill not reaching the stipe.
Lamina (s.f. I): blade; *lamina vitrea,* glass
slide. **laminiformis** (adj. B), **laminaris**
(adj. B): blade-like.
lampro-: *in Gk. comp.,* bright, lustrous,
shining.
Lana (s.f. I): wool. **lanatus** (adj. A):
woolly. **276**
lanceatus (adj. A): lanceolate (in sense of
A. P. de Candolle and Lindley).
lanceolate: lanceolatus (adj. A); a term
of varied application; *lanceolatus,*
'armed with a little lance or point', as
used by all authors represents a comparatively narrow shape with curved
sides tapering to a pointed end; in
Linnaeus's sense, a shape broadest at
the middle and tapering to each end,
typified by *Plantago lanceolata* (with
length to breadth roughly 6 to 1) i.e.
very narrowly elliptic; in the sense of

A. P. de Candolle, Lindley and many German authors, a shape broadest at the middle, tapering to each end with length to breadth about 3 to 1, i.e. narrowly elliptic; in the sense of Bentham, A. Gray and most English-speaking authors from 1865 onwards, a shape broadest below the middle with length to breadth about 3 to 1. For discussion, see Alphonse de Candolle, *Phytographie*, 198-200 (1880). **106**

lanci- : *in L. comp.*, lanceolate; *lancifolius*, with lanceolate leaves; *lancilabris*, with lanceolate lip; *lancipetalus*, with lanceolate petals.

Land : terra (s.f. I). **land** : terrestris (adj. B), *in Gk. comp.*, geo-.

laneus (adj. A) : woolly, wool-like.

Language : lingua (s.f. I).

languescens (part. B) : wilting, withering.

lani- : *in L. comp.*, woolly; *lanicaulis*, with woolly stems; *laniger*, woolbearing. **lanosus** (adj. A) : woolly.

lanuginosus (adj. A) : woolly, downy.

lapidescens (part. B) : becoming stonehard, petrifying. **lapideus** (adj. A) : stone-hard, made of stone. **lapidosus** (adj. A) : full of stones, stony. **Lapis** (s.m. III. ii) : stone.

Lappa (s.f. I) : bur. **lappaceus** (adj. A) : bur-like.

Lapsus (s.m. IV) : fall, shedding; *calyx post lapsum fructus persistens*, calyx persisting after fall of the fruit.

Laqueus (s.m. II) : noose, snare; *laquei hyphales*, hyphal snares.

large : grandis (adj. B), magnus (adj. A), amplus (adj. A). **large-** : *in L. comp.*, grandi-, magni-, *in Gk. comp.*, macro-, mega-, megalo-. **largely** : magnopere (adv.).

largus (adj. A) : abundant, plentiful, abounding.

lasi-, lasio- : *in Gk. comp.*, hairy, woolly; *lasiandrus*, with woolly stamens; *lasiantherus*, with woolly anthers; *lasianthus*, with woolly flowers; *lasiobotrys*, with woolly racemes; *lasiocalyx*, with woolly calyx; *lasiocarpus*, with woolly fruit; *lasiocladus*, with woolly twigs or shoots; *lasiogynus*, with woolly pistil; *lasioneurus*, with woolly nerves; *lasiophlebus*, with woolly veins; *lasiophyllus*, with woolly leaves; *lasiorhynchus*, with woolly snout or beak; *lasiosiphon*, with woolly tube; *lasiostemon*, with woolly stamens; *lasiostylus*, with woolly style.

last : extremus (adj. A), postremus (adj. A), ultimus (adj. A). **at last** : demum (adv.), ad postremum (adv.). **lastly** : denique (adv.), postremo (adv.).

late : serotinus (adj. A) : *see* SLOW.

late (adv.) : broadly, widely.

later : postea (adv.), demum (adv.) 'at last', tandem (adv.) 'at last'.

lateral : lateralis (adj. B). **457**

lateri- : *in L. comp.*, at the side, lateral to; *laterifolius*, on the side of a leaf at the base.

lateritius, latericius (adj. A) : dark brick red, like old red tiles.

Latex : latex (s.m. III. i), *abl. sing.* latice; lac (s.n. III. ii), *abl. sing.* lacte; *herba latice flavo*, herb with yellow latex; *latex copiosus albus immutabilis*, latex abundant white not changing.

lati- : *in L. comp.*, broad, wide; *latibasis*, with broad base; *latibracteatus*, with broad bracts; *latifolius*, broad-leaved; *latilabris*, broad-lipped; *latilobus*, with broad lobes; *latipes*, with broad foot *or* stalk; *latisectus*, cut into broad divisions; *latisepalus*, broad-sepalled; *latistipulatus*, with broad stipules.

latinus (adj. A) : Latin; *lingua latina*, the Latin language; *latine*, in Latin.

Latitude : latitudo (s.f. III).

latrorsus (adj. A) : directed towards the sides, along the sides.

latticed : cancellatus (adj. A), clathratus (adj. A). **243**

latus (adj. A) : broad, wide.

Latus (s.n. III. iv) : side, flank : *ligula apice et lateribus ciliata*, ligule at the tip and the sides ciliate.

lavandulaceus, lavandulus (adj. A) : lavender-violet.

laxe (adv.) : loosely. **laxi-** : *in L. comp.*, loose. **laxus** (adj. A) : flaccid, loose, i.e. with parts distinct and apart from one another or in an open or loose arrangement. **315, 480**

Layer : stratum (s.n. II), *abl. sing.* strato, *nom. pl.* strata, *abl. pl.* stratis; *testa e stratis tribus formata stratum exterius tenuissimum, medium fibrosum, interius spongiosum*, testa from layers three formed, the outer one very thin, the middle one fibrous, the inner one spongy; *stratum filamentorum laxe intricatorum tenue viride vel rubescens mucosum*, layer of loosely entangled filaments thin green or reddish slimy. **Layer** (used in vegetative propagation) : propago (s.f. III), *gen. sing.* propaginis. **-layered** : *in L. comp.*, -stratus (adj. A), *in Gk. comp.*, -stromaticus; *unistratus, monostromaticus*, one-layered; *bistratus, distromaticus*, two-layered; *tristratus, tristromaticus*, three-layered; *paucistratus, oligostromaticus*, few-layered; *multistratus*, many-layered.

Lead : plumbum (s.m. II). **leaden** : plumbeus (adj. A). **leaden-grey** : molybdeus (adj. A).

Leaf: folium (s.n. II), *abl. sing.* folio, *nom. pl.* folia, *gen. pl.* foliorum, *abl. pl.* foliis; *folium basale solitarium lineare vel lanceolatum planum acutum 6-9 poll. longum 3-4 lin. latum*, leaf basal solitary linear or lanceolate flat acute 6-9 inches (15-23 cm.) long 3-4 lines (7-9 mm.) broad; *folia caulina opposita, suprema 4-6 saepe valde conferta, in eodem pari subaequimagna usque valde inaequimagna et inaequilonge petiolata, plus minus orbicularia, basi rotundata vel cordata margine integro dense ciliata, apice obtusissima, e basi 3-nervia, supra in facie subtus ad nervos pilosa*, leaves cauline opposite, the upper 4-6 often very much crowded together, in the same pair almost equal in size to very unequal in size and unequally stalked, more or less circular, at base rounded or cordate, at the entire margin densely ciliate, at the tip extremely blunt, from the base 3-nerved, above on the face below at the nerves pilose; *folia basi ad ⅓ latitudinis imbricata, angulo fere recto divergentia, subduplo longiora quam lata, in dimidio supero lingulata*, leaves at base for ⅓ of width imbricate, almost at a right angle diverging, almost twice as long as broad, in the upper half lingulate; *folia alterna, ambitu ovata, usque ad 9 cm. diametro, ad basin trisecta*, leaves alternate, in outline ovate, up to 9 cm. in diameter, to the base three-cut; *foliorum basalium atque caulinorum infimorum petioli laminam circiter aequantes*, of basal and lower cauline leaves the petioles about equalling the blade; *caulis e basi per 20 cm. nudus, cum foliis 4 brevibus remotis, postremo verticillis foliorum usque 8-foliatis vestitus*, stem from base upwards for 20 cm. naked, then with leaves 4 short remote, finally with whorls of leaves up to 8-leaved clothed; *foliis parvis ovatis hirsutis atroviridibus*, with leaves small ovate hairy dark green; **leaf-bearing**: foliifer (adj. A), foliatus (adj. A). **leaf-like**: foliiformis (adj. B).

Leafing: frondescentia (s.f. I), *acc. sing.* frondescentiam; *folia saepius vere ante frondescentiam novam cadunt*, the leaves most often in spring drop off before the production of new foliage.

leafless: aphyllus (adj. A), foliis carens (part. B with abl.).

Leaflet: foliolum (s.n. II), *abl. sing.* foliolo, *nom. pl.* foliola, *gen. pl.* foliolorum, *abl. pl.* foliolis.

leafy: frondosus (adj. A), foliaceus (adj. A), foliosus (adj. A). **59**

leaning: inclinatus (part. A).

learned: doctus (part. A), eruditus (part. A), peritus (adj. A).

least: minimus (adj. A). **at least**: minimum (adv.); saltem (adv.), quidem (adv.), ut minimum (adv. phrase).

leather - coloured: alutaceus (adj. A). **leathery**: coriaceus (adj. A). **312**

-leaved: *in L. comp.*, -folius, -foliatus, *in Gk. comp.*, -phyllus.

lebetiformis (adj. B): basin-shaped, bowl-shaped.

lecanorinus (adj. A): having light-coloured margin of apothecium formed by thallus, as in the lichen genus Lecanora.

lecideinus (adj. A): having apothecia, as in the lichen genus Lecidea, with dark-coloured excipulum proprium.

Lectotype: lectotypus (s.m. II).

lectus (part. A): collected, picked, selected.

Lectus (s.m. II): bed, couch, bulb-plate.

leek-green: porraceus (adj. A), prasinus (adj. A).

left behind: relictus (part. A).

legitimus (adj. A): allowed by the law, proper, genuine, legitimate.

Legume: legumen (s.n. III. vi), *abl. sing.* legumine, *nom. pl.* legumina, *abl. pl.* leguminibus; *legumen rectum lineare sesquipollicare calyce persistente cinctum 6-8-spermum dorso carinatum*, legume straight linear 1½ inches long by the persistent calyx surrounded 6-8-seeded on the back keeled; *legumen oblongum obliquum, rarius falcatum, membranaceum coriaceum carnosum vel durum, indehiscens vel bivalve, intus continuum vel inter semina farctum vel septatum*, legume oblong oblique, rarely falcate, membranous leathery fleshy or hard, indehiscent or two-valved, inside continuous or between the seeds filled or septate; *legumen incurvum crassum exalatum subcompressum, epicarpio fragili, mesocarpio pulposo, endocarpio coriaceo*, legume incurved thick wingless somewhat compressed, with the epicarp brittle, the mesocarp pulpy, the endocarp leathery; *legumen sessile vel stipitatum, teres vel turgidum vel inflatum, ad suturam superiorem incrassatum*, legume sessile or stipitate, terete or swollen or inflated, at the upper suture thickened; *legumine subgloboso vel ovoideo glabro vel piloso (pilis albis copiose tecto) inermi vel spinoso indehiscenti vel tardius bivalvi*, with the legume almost globose or else ovoid glabrous pilose (with white hairs plentifully covered) unarmed or spiny indehiscent or at length two-valved; *leguminibus horizontaliter patentibus linearibus imperfecte bilocularibus, calyce membranaceo persistente quinquies longi-*

oribus in dorso carinatis, in ventre convexis, c. 5 cm. longis 5 mm. latis, with legumes horizontally spreading linear incompletely bilocular, than the membranous persistent calyx five times longer, on the back keeled, on the lower side convex, about 5 cm. long 5 mm. broad. **leguminaceus** (adj. A): having the character of a legume. **leguminosus** (adj. A): legume-bearing.

lei-, leio-: *in Gk. comp.,* smooth; *leianthus,* smooth-flowered.

Lemma: lemma (s.n. III), valva (s.f. I) gluma (s.f. I) florens; *lemma spiculam aequans, erectum, 3-nerve,* lemma equalling spikelet, erect, ovate, 3-nerved; *lemmata erecta oblonga, ciliata,* lemmas erect oblong ciliate.

lemon-coloured: citrinus (adj. A). **lemon-scented**: citriodorus (adj. A).

Length: longitudo (s.f. III. vi), *abl. sing.* longitudine; *pro longitudine,* for the length; *per totam longitudinem rhachidis,* over the whole length of the rachis.

lengthened: protentus (part. A), elongatus (adj. A). **lengthwise**: longistrorsum (adv.), in longitudinem, longitudinaliter (adv.); *rami longistrorsum sulcati,* branches lengthwise furrowed.

leniter (adv.): gently, mildly, gradually.

Lens: lens (s.f. III) *gen. sing.* lentis, *abl. sing.* lenti *or* lente; *sub lente,* under a lens (the usual expression of eighteenth-century authors is, however, *oculo armato*); *perithecia aculeis (vix oculo armato manifestis at ope microscopii compositi perspicuis) obruta,* perithecia with prickles (hardly evident under a lens but with the help of the compound microscope quite clear) covered. **lens-shaped**: lenticularis (adj. B), lentiformis (adj. B).

lente (adv.): slowly, leisurely.

Lenticel: lenticella (s.f. I), *abl. pl.* lenticellis.

lenticularis (adj. B), **lentiformis** (adj. B): lens-shaped, i.e. resembling a double convex lens. **18**

lentiginosus (adj. A): freckled. **304**

lentus (adj. A): pliant, flexible, sluggish, thick-flowing, viscous.

lepido-: *in Gk. comp.,* scale-, scaly. **lepidotus** (adj. A): covered with small scales.

leprosus (adj. A): having a scurfy appearance, 'spotted like a leper' (Berkenhout), *lit.* 'leprous'.

lept-, lepto-: *in Gk. comp.,* slender, thin, narrow; *leptanthus,* slender-flowered; *leptocarpus,* slender-fruited; *leptochilus,* narrow-lipped; *leptocladus,* with slender shoots; *leptodermaticus, leptodermicus,*

leptodermus, thin-skinned, the wall of the cell thinner than the cavity; *leptodictyus,* with a fine network; *leptogrammus,* with fine or narrow markings; *leptolobus,* with slender pods; *leptomerus,* with slender, small or delicate parts; *leptoneurus,* fine-nerved; *leptopetalus,* slender-petalled; *leptophyllus,* slender-leaved; *leptopterus,* narrow-winged; *leptopodus,* with slender petiole; *leptorrhizus,* with slender rhizome.

lesiniformis (adj. B): awl-shaped.

Lesion: laesio (s.f. III).

less: minor (adj. B; comp. of *parvus*): *ramuli minores,* lesser branches; *strato minus quam 10 μ crasso,* with layer less than 10 μ thick; **less**: minus (adv.); **-less**: expressed sometimes by addition of prefix *ex-* or *e-* to adj. or prep. *sine* with abl. of noun.

lethalis (adj. B): lethal, deadly.

Letter (of alphabet): littera (s.f. I). **Letter** (epistle): litterae (s.f. I pl.), epistola (s.f. I).

leuc-, leuco-: *in Gk. comp.,* white-. Associated with colour terms it indicates paleness; *leucacanthus,* with white spines or prickles; *leucanthus,* white-flowered; *leucocarpus,* white-fruited; *leucocladus,* with white shoots; *leuconeurus,* white-nerved; *leuconotus,* white-backed; *leucopetalus,* white-petalled; *leucophaeus,* pale grey; *leucophlebius,* white-veined; *leucophyllus,* white-leaved; *leucospermus,* white-seeded; *leucotaenius,* white-banded.

level: planus (adj. A); cf. PLAIN. **levelled**: deplanatus (part. A), aequatus (part. A). **259**

leviter (adv.): lightly, mildly.

Liane: liana (s.f. I).

Libellus (s.m. II): booklet, pamphlet; *in hoc libello,* in this pamphlet.

Liber (s.m. II): inner bark of a tree, book.

liber (adj. A): free, not joined together; *styli liberi vel connati,* styles free or united. **liberatus** (part. A): set free, released. **libere** (adv.): freely, without restraint. **451**

liberated: liberatus (part. A).

Lichen: lichen (s.m. III), *gen. sing.* lichenis, *nom. pl.* lichenes, *gen. pl.* lichenum, *abl. pl.* lichenibus.

Lid: operculum (s.n. II), *abl. sing.* operculo; *ascidii operculum ascendens ovatum, facie inferiore prope apicem appendice instructum, basim versus carinatum,* of the pitcher the lid ascending ovate, on the lower surface near the tip with an appendage provided, towards the base keeled. **lidded**: operculatus (adj. A).

Life: vita (s.f. I).

Light: lux (s.f. III), *gen. sing.* lucis, *abl. sing.* luce; cf. TRANSMITTED.

light: dilutus (part. A), pallidus (adj. A). **lightly**: laete (adv.), modice (adv.), leviter (adv.).

lignatilis (adj. B) : growing on wood.

lignescens (adj. B) : becoming woody.

ligneus (adj. A), **lignosus** (adj. A) : woody, wooden, ligneous, made of wood. **Lignum** (s.n. II) : wood; *arbor ligno duro albo*, tree with wood hard white. **325**

ligulate: ligulatus (adj. A). **105**

Ligule: ligula (s.f. I), *lit.* 'a little tongue', *nom. pl.* ligulae, *abl. pl.* ligulis; *ligula linea brevior truncata ciliata*, ligule than a line ($\frac{1}{12}$ inch) shorter truncate ciliate ; *ligulae ad marginem ciliolatum redactae*, ligules to a ciliolate margin reduced ; *ligulae anguste oblongae truncatae scariosae*, ligules narrowly oblong truncate scarious ; *corollae radii ligulatae, ligula brevi obovata* corollas of the radius (i.e. ray-florets) ligulate, with ligula short obovate.

liguliforus (adj. A) : having a capitulum of only ligulate florets.

like: similis (adj. B, followed by dat. or gen.), ad instar (with gen.).

Likeness: similitudo (s.f. III. vi).

likewise: item (adv.), itidem (adv.), similiter (adv.), similimodo ac.

lilacinus (adj. A) : lilac, i.e. 'pale dull violet mixed a little with white' (Lindley) but with more red in it and nearer purple than *lavandulaceus*, which has more blue and is nearer violet, both being greyed and light.

liliaceus (adj. A) : lily-like; *flos liliaceus*, flower bell-shaped or funnel-shaped with six perigon segments.

lilliputanus, lilliputianus (adj. A) : small enough to inhabit the land of Lilliput in Swift's *Gulliver's Travels* (*applied to species of Lejeunea, Harposporium, Veronica, etc.*).

Limb: limbus (s.m. II); *limbus corollae pelviformis, mutabilis, in aestivatione ruber, sub anthesi violaceus et priusquam corolla decidit caeruleus, 15 mm. latus*, limb of corolla saucer-shaped, changeable, in bud red, at anthesis violet and before the corolla falls blue, 15 mm. broad.

limbalis (adj. B) : applied to connecting marginal nerve of anastomosing nerves of leaves.

limbatus (adj. A) : bordered, i.e. with one colour edged by another more broadly than in *marginatus*.

Limbidium: limbidium (s.n. II), *abl. sing.* limbidio.

Lime: calx (s.f. III), *gen. sing.* calcis, *abl. sing.* calce; *fila pulvinos calce induratos*

foriantia, filaments forming cushions hardened by lime ; *stratum calce incrustatum*, layer by lime encrusted ; *ad terram calcariam*, on calcareous ground ; *planta calcaria carbonica zonatim incrustata*, plant by calcium carbonate in bands encrusted ; *filis carbonate calcario saepe incrustatis*, with filaments by calcium carbonate often encrusted.

Limes (s.m. III) : boundary, limit.

Limestone: saxum (s.n. II) calcareum ; calcarius (s.m. II) densus.

limi-: *in L. comp.*, pertaining to mud, mud-; *limicola*, a dweller on mud.

limitatus (part. A) : bounded, limited, bordered, enclosed within limit.

limn-: *in Gk. comp.*, pertaining to standing water, pools, lakes; *limnophilus*, pondloving.

limosus (adj. A) : muddy, growing in muddy places. **Limus** (s.m. II) : mud, slime.

limpidus (adj. A) : clear, transparent.

Linea (s.f. I) : line, $\frac{1}{12}$ inch ; English line, 2·1 mm., French line 2·3 mm.

linear: linearis (adj. B). **103**

linearifolius (adj. A) : linear-leaved.

lineatus (adj. A), **lineolatus** (adj. A) : marked by fine parallel lines. **255**

Lingua (s.f. I) : tongue, language.

linguiformis (adj. B), **lingulatus** (adj. A) : tongue-shaped. **39**

linifolius (adj. A) : flax-leaved.

linked: concatenatus (part. A); cf. JOINED.

linquens (part. B) : leaving, departing from.

Lip: labium (s.n. II), *abl. sing.* labio.

lipped: labiatus, *in Gk. comp.*, -chilus, -cheilus.

liquescens (part. B) : becoming liquid.

Liquidum (s.n. II) : liquid.

liquidus (adj. A) : clear.

Lirella: lirella (s.f. I), *abl. sing.* lirella.

lirellatus (adj. A) : provided with lirellae. **lirellinus** (adj. A) ; long and narrowly furrowed.

lith-, litho-: *in Gk. comp.*, stone- ; *lithophilus*, loving stones ; *lithospermus*, with seeds hard as stone.

litoralis (adj. B) : *see* LITTORALIS.

Littera (s.f. I) : letter of alphabet. **Litterae** (s.f. I pl.) : letter, epistle, letters of alphabet ; *in litteris*, in a letter.

little ; parvus (adj. A), minutus (adj. A). **very little**: minimus (adj. A) ; **extremely little**: minutissimus (adj. A).

littoralis (adj. B), **litoralis** (adj. B), **littoreus** (adj. A) : pertaining to the sea-shore.

Littus (s.n. III), **Litus** (s.n. III) : sea-shore, beach, bank.

Litura (s.f. I) : irregular blurred fleck or marking.

lividus (adj. A) : livid, a vague term which 'may be defined as the peculiar livery effect of adding grey and black to the range of hues between blue and red' (H. A. Dade), originally a blue or leaden colour.

living : vivens (part. B), vivus (adj. A) : *in statu vivo*, in a living state : cf. INHABITING.

lobatus (adj. A) : lobed. **193**

Lobe : lobus (s.m. II), *abl. sing.* lobo, *nom. pl.* lobi, *abl. pl.* lobis ; *folia lobis lateralibus distantibus triangularibus acutis integris, lobo terminali hastato parvo acuto*, leaves with lateral lobes well apart triangular acute entire, terminal lobe hastate small acute. **lobed** : lobatus (adj. A) ; *in L. comp.*, -lobus ; *parvilobus*, with small lobes ; *trilobus*, three-lobed.

Lobule : lobulus (s.m. II) : *abl. sing.* lobulo, *nom. pl.* lobuli, *abl. pl.* lobulis ; *folia imbricata, supra lobulum semierectum divergentia*, leaves imbricate, above the half-erect lobule diverging ; *lobulo ovoideo turgido*, with lobule ovoid swollen.

localis (adj. B) : local, belonging to a given place ; *varietates locales speciei*, local varieties of the species.

Locality : locus (s.m. II), *nom. pl.* loci, 'single places', *or* loca, 'connected places, regions'.

located : locatus (part. A).

locellatus (adj. A) : locellate, divided into small secondary compartments. **Locellus** : locellus (s.m. II), *nom. pl.* locelli, *abl. pl.* locellis ; *loculi antherarum in locellis 2 divisi*, loculi of anthers in 2 locelli divided.

locularis (adj. B), **loculatus** (adj. A) : having cavities or loculi ; *plurilocularis*, with many loculi. **loculicide** (adv.) : loculicidally. **loculicidus** (adj. A) : splitting down the back of loculus or chamber, not at the septa ; *see* SEPTICIDALIS. **loculosus** (adj. A) : divided internally into cells or by partitions.

Loculus : loculus (s.m. II), *abl. sing.* loculo, *nom. pl.* loculi, *abl. pl.* loculis ; *loculi biovulati, ovulis collateralibus*, chambers [of ovary] two-ovuled, with the ovules side by side ; *pori nectariferi cum loculis alternantes*, nectar-pores with loculi alternating ; *ovarium 3-loculare, ovulis in quoque loculo solitariis vel paucis*, ovary trilocular, with ovules in each loculus solitary or few ; *semina in loculis contigua, loculum arcte implentia*, seed in the loculi touching, the loculus tightly filling ; *antherarum loculi paralleli contigui, poro terminali dehiscentes*,

of the anthers the loculi parallel touching, by a terminal pore dehiscing. **240**

Locus (s.m. II) : place, locality.

Locusta (s.f. I) : spikelet of a grass.

Lodicule : lodicula (s.f. I), *abl. pl.* lodiculis, *lit.* 'a small blanket, coverlet' ; glumella (s.f. I), *abl. pl.* glumellis ; *lodiculae duae hyalinae truncatae vel bilobatae glabrae, 1·3 mm. longae*, lodicules 2 hyaline truncate or 2-lobed glabrous 1·3 mm. long.

lofty : celsus (adj. A), excelsus (adj. A), exaltatus (part. B). **340**

-logia (s.f. I) : *in Gk. comp.*, study of (*from* λογος, *discourse*) ; *agrostologia*, study of grasses ; *botanologia*, botany, study of plants ; *bryologia*, study of mosses ; *crocologia*, study of crocuses (*used by Hertodt for a treatise on saffron*) ; *mycologia*, study of fungi ; *see* CURIOUS.

lomato- : *in Gk. comp.*, fringed, bordered.

Loment : lomentum (s.n. II). **lomentaceus** (adj. A) : bearing *or* resembling a loment.

long : longus (adj. A) : *folium 3 pollices longum*, leaf 3 inches long ; *folio longo*, with the leaf long ; *foliis longis*, with leaves long ; *folia ramulorum longorum ovata 3 cm. longa*, leaves of the long branchlets ovate 3 cm. long ; *petiolus longus*, petiole long ; *caules ad 30 cm. longi, ramis 10-20 cm. longis*, stems to 30 cm. long, with branches 10-20 cm. long. **long-** : *in Gk. comp.*, dolicho-, *in L. comp.*, longi-. **longer** : longior, longior, longius (adj. compar.). **moderately long** : longiusculus (adj. A). **very long** : longissimus (adj. A).

longaevus (adj. A) : of great age, long-lived. **longe** (adv.) : lengthwise, long, for a long time, at a distance ; *longe lateque*, in length and breadth. **longi-** : *in L. comp.*, long- ; *longialatus*, long-winged ; *longibarbatus*, long-bearded ; *longicalcaratus*, long-spurred ; *longicalyx*, with long calyx ; *longicaudus*, long-tailed ; *longicaulis*, long-stemmed ; *longicuspis*, with a long point *or* cusp ; *longiflorus*, long-flowered ; *longipetalus*, long-petalled ; *longiracemosus*, with long racemes ; *longisepalus*, long-sepalled ; *longistylus*, long-styled. **longissimus** (adj. A) ; extremely long. **longistrorsum** (adv.) : lengthwise, longitudinally. **Longitudo** (s.f. III. vi) : length, q.v.

longinquus (adv.) : far off, a long way off.

longitudinal : longitudinalis (adj. B). **longitudinally** : *see* LENGTHWISE.

Longiturnitas (s.f. III. ii) : duration.

longiusculus (adj. A) : moderately long, fairly long.

loose: laxus (adj. A) 'not crowded', liber (adj. A) 'free', incohaerens (part. B) 'not clinging together'. **loosely**: laxe (adv.). **315, 480**

loph-, lopho-: *in Gk. comp.*, crest-, crested; *lophophorus*, crest-bearing, crested; *lophospermus*, with crested seeds.

loratus (adj. A), **loriformis** (adj. B): ligulate, strap-shaped, i.e. moderately long with the two margins parallel. **105**

Lorica (s.f. I): lorica, entire siliceous covering of diatom cell, *lit.* 'leather cuirass'; *lorica simplex bivalvis silicea compressa, valvibus inaequalibus*, lorica simple 2-valved siliceous compressed, with valves unequal. **loricatus** (part. A): loricate, armoured with a hard scaly exterior.

loriformis (adj. B): *see* LORATUS.

love: amo (verb, conj. I): *amat umbras*, it loves shady places. **loving**: amans (part. B); *in Gk. comp.*, -philus.

low: humilis (adj. B), demissus (part. A); *aestus recessu*, at low tide. **337**

lower: infernus (adj. A), inferus (adj. A), inferior (adj. compar.); *folia in eodem ramo quoad dispositionem variabilia, infima rosulata, inferiora remota, superiora c. 2 cm. distantia, summa conferta*, leaves on the same branch as regards arrangement variable, the lowermost in a rosette, the lower ones well apart, the upper 2 cm. apart from each other, the uppermost crowded together. **lowermost**: infimus (adj. A), imus (adj. A).

lubricus (adj. A): smooth and slippery.

lucens (part. B): shining, polished, glistening.

lucidus (adj. A): shining, clear, transparent.

Lucus (s.m. II): sacred thicket, wood.

lukewarm: tepidus (adj. A).

lumbricalis (adj. III. vi): cavity or space **lumbriciformis** (adj. B): worm-shaped.

Lumen (s.n. III. vi): cavity or space within a cell, *lit.* 'light, opening'.

lumpy: glebosus (adj. A).

lunaris (adj. B), **lunatus** (adj. A): crescent-shaped. **lunulatus** (adj. A): ornamented with little crescents, crescent-shaped. **124**

luridus (adj. A): dirty brown, smoky yellow, drab yellow; sometimes confused in application with *lividus*.

Lusus (s.m. IV): a sport or variant, *lit.* 'a game, something done as an amusement or joke'.

lutarius (adj. A), **lutensis** (adj. B): living in *or* on mud.

luteolus (adj. A): pale yellow, yellowish. **lutescens** (adj. B): becoming yellow, yellowish. **luteus** (adj. A): deep yellow,

golden-yellow, buttercup-yellow (H.C.C. 5). In general deeper than *flavus* and not verging to red as *croceus*; the name from *lūtum*, weld, dyer's rocket (*Reseda luteola*); *luteus chromaticus*, chrome yellow (H.C.C. *60.5*); *luteus ranunculinus*, buttercup-yellow (H.C.C. 5).

Lŭtum (s.n. II): mud.

Lux (s.f. III): light; cf. TRANSMITTED.

luxuriant: luxurians (part. B).

lying above; superjectus (part. A). **lying beneath**: subjectus (part. A). **lying between**: interjectus (part. A).

lyrate: lyratus (adj. A). **129**

M

macer (adj. A): thin, meagre.

maceratus (part. A): macerated, i.e. softened by soaking.

macilentus (adj. A): thin, meagre.

macr-, macro-: *in Gk. comp.*, long, large, great; *macrandrus*, with large anthers; *macranthus*, large-flowered; *macroblastus*, with large embryo; *macrocalyx*, with large calyx; *macroglossus*, long-tongued; *macrophyllus*, large-leaved; *macropodus*, with large foot or support; *macrorrhizus*, with large root *or* rhizome; *macrostomus*, wide-mouthed; *macrotrichus*, with long bristles.

Macrocyst; macrocysta (s.f. I).

Macrospora (s.f. I): macrospore, megaspore.

Macrosporangium (s.n. II): macrosporangium, megasporangium.

Macula (s.f. I): spot, blotch, mesh of network. **maculatus** (part. A); spotted, blotched. **maculiformis** (adj. B): spot-shaped. **maculosus** (adj. A): full of spots, mottled.

made: factus (part. A). **made up of**: constatus (part. A) (*followed by* e *or* ex *and* abl.), compositus (part. A).

madefactus (part. A): made wet, moistened, soaked; cf. MOISTENED. **madidus** (adj. A): moist, wet, soaked; cf. MOIST.

Mador (s.m. III): moisture, wetness.

maeandriformis (adj. B): meandriform, having an irregularly winding *or* meandering direction.

magenteus (adj. A): magenta (H.C.C. 27), red-purple.

magis (adv.): more, more completely; *non magis quam*, not more than.

magni-: *in L. comp.*, large; *magnistipulus*, with large stipules; *magniguttatus*, having large oil globules.

Magnification: magnificatio (s.f. III); *magnificatione*, at a magnification. **magnified**: amplificatus (part. A), auctus (part. A); *folia oculo nudo vel negligentius perscrutanti glaberrima sed revera pilis minutis oculo armato aspectabilibus conspersa,* leaves to the naked eye or by careless examination quite glabrous but in fact sprinkled with minute hairs visible under the lens ; *figurae octies auctae,* figures 8 times magnified ; *semina sub lente reticulata,* seeds seen under the lens reticulate ; *see* LENS.

Magnitudo (s.f. III. vi) : size ; *magnitudine naturali,* at natural size.

magnopere (adv.) : greatly, strongly, extremely.

magnus (adj. A) : big, great, large (*compar.* major ; *superl.* maximus).

main : principalis (adj. B). **mainly** : praecipue.

major (adj. compar. of *magnus*) : greater.

making : efficiens (part. B), faciens (part. B), formans (part. B).

malachiteus (adj. A) : malachite-green.

male : mas (adj. B), *gen. sing.* maris, *abl. sing.* mare, *gen. pl.* marium, *abl. pl.* maribus ; masculus (adj. A) ; masculinus (adj. A) ; symbol ♂ ; *planta mascula tantum descripta,* male plant only described ; *flores masculini,* flowers male ; *flores hermaphroditi masculos aequantes,* flowers hermaphrodite the male ones equalling.

male (adv.) : badly, ill ; *planta male descripta,* plant badly described.

malpighiaceus (adj. A) : relating to or resembling *Malpighia* ; *pili malpighiacei,* hairs attached at the middle with two stiff pointed radiating branches ; *cf.* DIBRACHIATUS.

Malt : maltum (s.n. II), *gen. sing.* malti ; *cultura in extracto malti,* culture on malt-extract.

Maltose : maltosum (s.n. II), *gen. sing.* maltosi.

malus (adj. A) : bad.

malvaceus (adj. A) : pertaining to mallow (Malva) ; *flos malvaceus,* flower with 5 clawed petals fused with staminal tube.

malvettinus (adj. A) : mauvette (H.C.C. 5.37).

malvicolor (adj. B), **malvinus** (adj. A) : mauve (H.C.C. 6.33).

Mamilla (s.f. I) : nipple, teat, small projection. **mamillatus** (adj. A) : mamillate, having small nipple-like projections. **mamilliformis** (adj. B) : nipple-shaped. **mammiformis** (adj. B) : nipple-shaped. **mammosus** (adj. A) : having large breasts, resembling a large nipple, as fruit of *Solanum mammosum.*

mancus (adj. A) : defective, imperfect, as Hector Léveillé's descriptions of new species.

mandarinus (adj. A) : mandarin-red (H.C.C. 17).

manifeste (adv.), **manifesto** (adv.) : evidently, manifestly. **manifestus** (adj. A) : evident, clear, apparent, manifest ; *see* EVIDENT, PERCEPTIBLE, PHANER-.

Manipulus (s.m. II) : handful, bundle.

Manner : modus (s.m. II) (*with gen.*). Can also be expressed by *instar* (s. indecl.) ; *modus vitae,* manner of life ; *in modum, ad modum, ad instar, more* (*with gen.*), after the manner.

Mantissa (s.f. I) : make-weight, worthless addition, *hence* supplement.

Manubrium (s.n. II) : a projecting cell in Characeae ; the long more or less cylindrical base of a woody spathe (cymba) in palms, *lit.* 'a handle' ; *cf. Gentes Herb.,* 7 : 179 (1946).

Manure : *see* DUNG.

many : multus (adj. A), numerosus (adj. A) ; *flores multi,* flowers many ; *stolonibus numerosis,* with numerous stolons. **as many as** : tot quot (adj. indecl.) ; *corolla lobis tot quot sepalis,* corolla with lobes as many as the sepals ; *stamina tot quot corollae lobi iisque opposita,* stamens as many as lobes of the corolla and opposite to these. **just as many as** : totidem quot (adj. indecl.) ; *laminis totidem quot undulationibus,* with just as many laminae as undulations.

many- : *in L. comp.,* mult-, multi-, *in Gk. comp.,* poly- ; *multicolor, polychromus,* many-coloured ; *multiflorus, polyanthus,* many-flowered ; *multifolius, polyphyllus,* many-leaved ; *multiformis, polymorphus,* many-shaped, very variable ; *multifructus, polycarpus,* many-fruited ; *multinodus,* with many nodes or knots ; *multiceps,* many-headed ; *multicellularis, pluricellularis,* many-celled.

marbled : marmoratus (adj. A), q.v.

marcescens (part. B) : withering but not falling off, *hence* dry and persistent. **marcidus** (adj. A) : withered.

Mare (s.n. III. x) : the sea ; *cf.* MALE.

margaritaceus (adj. A), **margaritatus** (adj. A) : pearly, pearl-like.

Margin : margo (s.m. and f. III. vi), *acc. sing.* marginem, *abl. sing.* margine ; *folia margine incrassata,* leaves at the margin thickened ; *folia margine incrassato,* leaves with the margin thickened ; *folia ad marginem incrassata,* leaves at the margin thickened. **marginal** : marginalis (adj. B). **margined** : marginatus (adj. A), limitatus (part. A), praetextus (part. A) ; *cf.* LIMBATUS. **-margined** : *in L. comp.,* -marginatus, *in Gk. comp.,* -craspedus ; *aureomarginatus, chrysocraspedus,* golden-margined, **342**

yellow-edged. **margining**: marginans (part. B). **458**

marginicidalis (adj. B): marginicidal, i.e. in septifragal dehiscence of a capsule when the margins of the valves are opposite and not between the dissepiments; *see* SEPTICIDALIS.

marinus (adj. A): growing in the sea.

maritimus (adj. A): growing by the sea.

Mark: nota (s.f. I), signum (s.n. II); cf. MACULA. **marked**: notatus (part. A), signatus (part. A). **markedly**: valde (adv.), sigillatim (adv.).

marmoratus (adv. A): marbled, irregularly striped *or* veined, the veins *or* the area along them irregularly coloured differently from rest of surface.

marroninus (adj. A): maroon (H.C.C. 10.30).

Marsh: palus (s.f. III. ii), *abl. sing.* palude. **marshy**: palustris (adj. B), *in Gk. comp.*, helo-.

marsupiatus (adj. A): pouched. **marsupiformis** (adj. B): pouch-shaped, pocketlike. **Marsupium** (s.n. II): pouch, pocket, marsupium, fruiting receptacle of *Hepaticae*.

mas (adj. B), **masculus** (adj. A), **masculinus** (adj. A): male.

Massa (s.f. I): dough-like mass, lump; *massa pollinis, massula*, pollen mass.

mastoideus (adj. A): nipple-like.

Mat: teges (s.f. III): *filamenta tegetes formantes*, filaments forming mats.

Material: materia (s.f. I).

maternal: maternus(adjA),matricalis (adjB)

matricalis (adj. B): maternal, uterine, within the ovary; *cellulae matricales*, mother cells.

Matrix: matrix (s.f. III), *gen. sing.* matricis.

matt: hebetatus (part. A) 'made dull', impolitus (adj. A) 'unpolished', opacus (adj. A) 'shaded, darkened'. **299**

matted: implicitus (part. A), implexus (part. A).

Maturatio (s.f. III): ripening. **maturescens** (part. B): ripening.

mature: maturus (adj. A), adultus (part. A); cf. EXCRETUS. **mature** (adv.): early.

Maturitas (s.f. III): ripeness, maturity; *usque ad fructus maturitatem persistens*, remaining up to the maturity of the fruit.

mauve: malvinus (adj. A), malvicolor (adj. B).

maxime (adv.): in the highest degree, extremely. **maximus** (adj. A, superl. of *magnus*): greatest; *maximam partem, pro maxima parte*, for the most part.

maybe: fortasse (adv.).

Mazedium: mazaedium (s.n. II).

Meadow: pratum (s.n. II), *abl. pl.* pratis. **pertaining to meadows**: pratensis (adj. B).

meagre: macilentus (adj. A), macer (adj. A), exilis (adj. B).

mealy: farinosus (adj. A). **331**

Means: ops (s.f. III), q.v.

meanwhile: interea (adv.).

measured: mensus (part. A). **measuring**: metiens (part. B); *pori 1 ad 2 mm. diametro metientes*, pores measuring 1-2 mm. in diameter; cf. MENSURA.

mechanicus (adj. A): mechanical.

Medianum (s.n. II): the middle. **medianus** (adj. A): middle.

medicinal: medicinalis (adj. B), medicus (adj. A), officinalis (adj. B).

Medietas (s.f. III): the middle.

medifixus (adj. A): attached by *or* at middle.

mediocris (adj. B): middling, not remarkable, between large and small.

medioramifer (adj. A): branched at the middle.

Mediostratum: mediostratum (s.n. II).

mediterraneus (adj. A): inland, in the middle of the land, remote from the sea. In this sense, opposed to *maritimus*, used by classical authors and older botanical authors, e.g. Sloane, but often used by others as referring to coasts, etc., of Mediterranean Sea; *in sylvis mediterraneis Jamaicae*, in inland woods of Jamaica; *in mediterraneis Hispaniae*, in the inland parts of Spain; *in mare atlantico et mediterraneo*, in Atlantic Ocean and Mediterranean Sea; *in regione mediterranea*, in the Mediterranean region; *algae maris mediterranei*, algae of the Mediterranean Sea.

Medium (s.n. II): the middle; *in medio*, in the middle. **medius** (adj. A): middle, that is midway between; *species inter praecedentem et sequentem media, a quibus foliis hirsutis dignoscitur*, species between the preceding and the following midway, from which by hairy leaves it is distinguished.

medivalvis (adj. B): attached to the middle of a valve.

Medulla: medulla (s.f. I). **medullary**: medullosus (adj. A). **330**

meeting: conveniens (part. B), incidens (part. B) (with acc.).

mega-, megalo-: *in Gk. comp.*, big, great, large, very; *megacalyx, megalocalyx*, with large calyx; *megacanthus*, with large thorns; *megalanthus*, large-flowered; *megalobotrys*, with large racemes; *megacarpus, megalocarpus*, large-fruited; *megacephalus, megalocephalus*, with large head; *megacheilus, megalochilus*, with large lip; *megaphyllus, megalo-*

phyllus, large-leaved ; *megapotamicus*, pertaining to a big river, i.e. the Rio Grande of Brazil ; *megaspermus, megalospermus*, large-seeded ; *megalosorus*, with large sori ; *megastigma*, with large stigma. Vellozo unorthodoxly made the compounds *perianthomegus*, 'with large perianth' and *phyllomegus*, 'with large leaves'.

Megasporangium : megasporangium (s.n. II), macrosporangium (s.n. II).

Megaspore : megaspora (s.f. I), macrospora (s.f. I).

megisto- : *in Gk. comp.*, very big, very large; *megistophyllus*, with very large leaves.

mei-, meio- : *in Gk. comp.*, less, smaller, fewer ; *meiogyrus*, rolled slightly inward.

Mel (s.n. III. v) : honey.

mel-, melan-, melano- : *in Gk. comp.*, black, very dark; *melanacanthus*, with black thorns or prickles ; *melanantherus, melantherus*, black-anthered ; *melancholicus*, melancholy, i.e. with downcast inflorescences or dingy flowers ; *melanocarpus*, black-fruited : *melanocaulis*, black-stemmed ; *melanophloeus*, with black bark ; *melanophthalmus*, black-eyed ; *melanorrhizus*, with black roots ; *melanospermus*, black-seeded ; *melanosporus*, black-spored ; *melanostictus*, black-spotted ; *melanotrichus*, black-haired.

melius (adv.) : better (compar. of *bene*).

melleus (adj. A) : honey-coloured, honey-like. **mellitus** (adj. A) : pertaining to honey, honey-sweet.

melting : deliquescens (part. B) : *ad nives deliquescentes*, at the melting snows.

Membrane : membrana (s.f. I), *abl. sing.* membrana ; *membrana connectivali longitudinaliter plicata*, with connecting membrane longitudinally folded. **membrane-bearing** : membranifer (adj. A).

membranous : membranaceus (adj. A). **membranous-leaved** : membranifolius (adj. A). **310**

mendosus (adj. A) : incorrect, full of faults.

meniscatus (adj. A) : shaped like a half-moon *or* crescent. **meniscoideus** (adj. A) : thin and concavo-convex, like a watch-glass. **90**

Mens (s.f. III) : power of recollection, mind, intellect.

Mensis (s.m. III. vii) : month. **menstruus** (adj. A) : monthly, lasting for a month.

Mensura (s.f. I) : a measure. **mensus** (part. A) : measured.

mentiens (part. B) : counterfeiting, imitating.

Mentum (s.n. II) : chin, projection, mentum.

meo : *see* MEUS.

mere : merus (adj. A). **merely** : tantum (adv.), tantummodo (adv.), solummodo (adv.).

merging : transiens (part. B), commiscens (part. B).

Mericarp : mericarpium (s.n. II).

meridionalis (adj. B) : south, southern ; *see* AUSTRALIS.

Meristem : meristema (s.n. III).

-merus : *in Gk. comp.*, referring to parts or their number, from *meros*, share; *dimerus*, with two parts *or* two members of a given part *or* whorl ; *trimerus*, with three parts *or* three members of a given part *or* whorl ; *isomerus*, having members of successive whorls the same in number ; *leptomerus*, with slender parts.

Mesh : macula (s.f. I), q.v. Can sometimes be rendered by *interstitium*.

meso- : *in Gk. comp.*, middle-; *mesochorus*, midland ; *mesostylus*, intermediate between long-styled and short-styled.

Mesocarp : mesocarpium (s.n. II).

mesodermaticus (adj. A) : with wall and cavity of cell equally thick.

Mesonervus (s.m. II) : main vein of frond.

Mesophyll : mesophyllum (s.n. II).

meta- : *in Gk. comp.*, associated with, changed, substituted for.

metallic : metallicus (adj. A).

Method (*system of teaching*) methodus (s.f. II), (*manner*) modus (s.m. II).

metiens (part. B) : measuring.

Metre : metrum (s.n. II), meter (s.m. II). **metre-long** : metralis (adj. B).

Metuloid : metuloida (s.f. I), *nom. plur.* metuloidae, *abl. pl.* metuloidis; *metuloidis hymenii 30-70 μ longis 10-20 μ latis crasse tunicatis crystallo-coronatis ventricosis*, metuloids (encrusted cystidia) of the hymenium 30-70 μ long 10-20 μ broad thick-walled crystal-crowned (i.e. with crystalline incrustation at tip) ventricose.

meus (pron. adj.) : my, mine, belonging to me ; *sensu meo, me judice*, in my opinion; *exemplaria mea in herbario meo asservata*, my specimens in my herbarium preserved.

micaceus (adj. A) : covered with glistening particles, growing on mica.

micans (part. B) : gleaming, with a slight metallic lustre.

micro- : *in Gk. comp.*, little, small; *micranthus*, small-flowered ; *microcarpus*, small-fruited; *microdontus*, with small teeth ; *microglossus*, with small tongues or rays ; *microphyllinus*, with minute leaflets *or* leafy scales ; *microstegius*, with small bracts ; *microstomus*, small-mouthed ; *microthyrsus*, with small thyrse; *microtrichus*, short-haired; *microtus*, small-eared.

Micropyle: micropyle (s.f. I, Gk.), *acc. sing.* micropylen, *gen. sing.* micropyles, *abl. sing.* micropyle.

Microscope: microscopium (s.n. II); *per microscopium electronicum*, by means of the electron microscope. **microscopic**: microscopicus (adj. A).

Microspore: microspora (s.f. I).

mid : medius (adj. A), q.v.

Middle : medium (s.n. II), medianum (s.n. II); *caule ad medium usque foliato*, with stem up to the middle leaf-bearing. **middle** : medius (adj. A), medianus (adj. A). **middle-, mid-** : *in L. comp.*, medi-, *in Gk. comp.*, meso-. ; *cf.* INFRAMEDIANUS.

midland : mediterraneus (adj. A), mesochorus (adj. A) ; *see* MEDITERRANEUS.

Midrib : costa (s.f. I) ; *cf.* VEINING.

mihi (pron. dat.) : to me ; often abbreviated to *m*. and used after a name to indicate the author's responsibility for it (dative of the possessor ; *est mihi*), as *Onosma hispanica* mihi.

mild : mitis (adj. B). **mildly** : leniter (adv.).

Milk : lac (s.n. III. ii), *abl. sing.* lacte ; latex (s.m. III, i), *abl. sing.* latice. **milk-** : *in L. comp.*, lacti-, *in Gk. comp.*, gal-, gala-, galacto- ; *lacticolor, galachrous*, milk-coloured ; *lactiflorus, galactanthus, galanthus*, with milk-white flowers ; *see* GAL-, LACTI-. **milk-white** : lactaneus (adj. A), lacteus (adj. A), lacticolor (adj. B), lactineus (adj. A). **milky** : lacteus (adj. A), lactarius (adj. A).

mille (num. adj. indecl.) : thousand.

mimosinus (adj. A) : mimosa - yellow (H.C.C. 60.2).

mingled : mixtus (part. A), mistus (part. A), immixtus (part. A), miscellus (adj. A), misturatus (adj. A).

miniatus (adj. A) : saturn-red (H.C.C. 13), flame-scarlet, *lit.* 'painted with red lead'.

minime (adv.) : least, very little, extremely seldom. **minimopere** (adv.) : not at all. **minimum** (adv.): at least. **minimus** (adj. A ; superl. of *parvus*) : very little, very least.

minor (adj. B ; compar. of *parvus*) : smaller, inferior, lesser.

minuens (part. B) : lessening, ebbing, waning.

minus (adv.) : less ; *haud minus quam*. not less than ; *nihil minus*, by no means ; *si minus*, if not, otherwise.

minute (adv.) : finely, minutely. **minutus** (part. A) : very small, minute.

mire (adv.) : wonderfully. **mirimodis** (adv.) : in an astonishing manner. **mirus** (adj. A) : wonderful, extraordinary, remarkable.

miscellus (adj. A) : mixed.

misshapen : deformis (adj. B).

missus (part. A) : sent ; *secundum exemplar unicum herbarii Linnaeani, ab Alstroemerio missum*, according to the one specimen of the Linnaean herbarium, by Alströmer sent.

Mistake : erratum (s.n. II), *abl. sing.* errato, *nom. pl.* errata; error (s.m. III. v), *abl. sing.* errore, *abl. pl.* errores.

misturatus (adj. A), **mistus** (part. A) : mixed, mingled.

mitis (adj. B) : mild, mellow, innoxious, soft.

mitre-shaped : mitriformis (adj. B).

mixed : *see* MINGLED.

Mixomorph : mixomorpha (s.f. I), *nom. pl.* mixomorphae.

mixtus (adj. A) : mixed.

mobile : mobilis (adj. B) ; *cf.* AGILIS.

moderately : moderate (adv.), modice (adv.), bono modo (adv.), parce (adv.).

modice (adv.) : moderately, not very, not much, lightly.

Modification : modificatio (s.f. III. vi).

modioliformis (adj. B) : nave-shaped. **92**

modo (adv.) : only, merely ; *bono modo*, moderately ; *non modo*, not only ; *nullo modo*, in no way ; *modo . . . tum . . .* at first . . . then. . . .

Modus (s.m. II) : standard, measure, manner, way of conduct *or* happening.

moist : humidus (adj. A) ; madidus (adj. A), udus (adj. A). **moistened** : humectatus (part. A), humefactus (part. A), madefactus (part. A) ; *in statu sicco vel humectato*, in dry or moistened state; *thallus in sicco cinereus, madefactus rosaceo-cinerascens*, thallus in a dry state grey, when moistened rosy-greyish ; *foliis siccitate appressis, humiditate recurvatis*, with leaves by drying appressed, by moistening recurved. **Moistness, Moisture** : mador (s.m. III), *abl. sing.* madore ; *cf.* HYGRO-.

molendinaceus (adj. A) : furnished with large wing-like expansions. **61**

mollis (adj. B) : soft, pliant. **molliusculus** (adj. A) : somewhat soft.

molybdeus (adj. A) : leaden grey.

Momentum (s.n. II) : circumstance, influence, weight, importance ; *notae haud sunt magni momenti*, the characters are not of great importance.

mon-, mono- : *in Gk. comp.*, one- ; *monadelphus*, with filaments or stamens united in one ; *monandrus*, with one stamen ; *monantherus*, with one anther ; *monanthus*, one-flowered ; *monaxialis* having a single axial filament ; *monocephalus*, with one head ; *monochlamydeus*, with one kind of perigon ;

monochrous, of a single colour; *mono-gynus*, with one style *or* carpel; *mono-petalus*, having petals joined in one, gamopetalous; *monophyllus*, one-leaved; *monospermus*, one-seeded; *monostachyus*, with a single spike; *monosiphonus*, consisting of one continuous tube; *monostichus*, in one row; *monotypicus*, with only one member.

Monas (s.f. III): unit.

moniliformis (adj. B): moniliform, i.e. cylindrical but contracted at regular intervals like a string of beads. **51**

monocarpic: monocarpus (adj. A), monocarpicus (adj. A), monocarpaeus (adj. A), hapaxanthus (adj. A), monotocus (adj. A). Such plants, which flower and fruit but once and then die, may be annual or monocyclic (annuus), biennial or dicyclic (biennis), lasting for several years or polycyclic (plietesialis). **342**

monochasial: monochasialis (adj. B). **Monochasium**: monochasium (s.n. II).

Monocotyledon: monocotyledon (s.m. III), *nom. pl.* monocotyledones.

monoecious: monoecius (adj. A), monoicus (adj. A).

Monopodium: monopodium (s.n. II). **monopodial**: monopodialis (adj. B).

monotocus (adj. A): producing offspring but once: cf. MONOCARPIC.

Mons (s.m. III. ix): mountain.

monstruosus (adj. A), **monstrosus** (adj. A): monstrous, abnormal, teratological.

montanus (adj. A): pertaining to *or* growing on mountains, montane.

Month: mensis (s.m. III. vii), *gen. sing.* mensis; *per duos vel tres menses*, for two or three months; *primo mense*, at the beginning of the month. **monthly**: menstruus (adj. A), q.v.

morbidus (adj. A): diseased, causing disease.

morbosus (adj. A): sickly, diseased.

Morbus (s.m. II): disease.

morchelliformis (adj. B): morel-shaped, i.e. ovoid with a honeycomb-like pitted surface, resembling the fruit-body of *Morchella esculenta*.

more: plus (adj.), *gen. sing.* pluris, *nom. pl.* plures, plura, *gen. pl.* plurium. **more**: (in quantity) plus (adv.), (in degree) magis (adv.); *plus minusve*, more or less. **little more than**, quasi (adv.). **more than**: ultra (adv.), plus quam.

More (abl. sing. of *Mos*, s.m. III. iv): according to custom, in the manner of, like; *more Phomatis*, in the manner of Phoma; *pro more*, customarily; *more suo*, in his own way, after his fashion.

Morphology: morphologia (s.f. I).

-morphus: *in Gk. comp.*, -shaped; *dimorphus*, existing in two forms; *dimorpho-phyllus*, with leaves of two shapes.

mosaic: mosaicus (adj. A).

moschatus (adj. A): musky, musk-scented.

Moss: muscus (s.m. II): *in Gk. comp.*, bryo-, -bryon, -bryum.

mostly: maximam partem, pro parte maxima 'for the most part', plerumque (adv.) 'generally', vulgo (adv.) 'commonly', ut maximum (adv. phrase) 'at most'.

Mother: mater (s.f. III), *gen. sing.* matris. **mother**: maternus (adj. A), matricalis (adj. B).

motile: mobilis (adj. B), movens (part. B); *cellulae formam mutantes dum movent*, cells changing shape when they move.

motionless: immobilis (adj. B).

Motus (s.m. IV): movement.

mouldy: mucidus (adj. A), mucedinosus (adj. A).

Mound: tumulus (s.m. II); **mounded**: acervatus (part. A), cumulatus (part. A).

Mountain: mons (s.m. III. ix), *gen. sing.* montis, *abl. sing.* monte, *nom. pl.* montes, *gen. pl.* montium, *abl. pl.* montibus; *area geographica speciei extenditur per montes Carpatorum*, geographical area of the species extends through the mountains of the Carpathians; *in silvis montium Jamaicae*, in woods of the mountains of Jamaica; *in montibus excelsis*, in high mountains. **mountain**, **montane**, **pertaining to mountains**: montanus (adj. A); *in locis udis regionis montanae et subalpinae*, in damp places of the montane and subalpine region; *prope rivulos in convallibus montanis*, near streams in mountain valleys. **mountain-**: *in L. comp.*, monti-, *in Gk. comp.*, oreo-; *monticola*, a dweller on mountains; *montigenus*, *oreogenus*, mountain-born; *montivagus*, wandering over mountains; *oreophilus*, mountain-loving.

Mouth: os (s.n. III. iv), *acc. sing.* orem, *abl. sing.* ore; orificium (s.n. II), *acc. sing.* orificium, *abl. sing.* orificio; ostium (s.n. II), *acc. sing.* ostium, *abl. sing.* ostio; *corolla sub ore constricta*, corolla below the mouth constricted; *theca infra orificium constricta*, theca below the mouth (opening) constricted; *tubus calycinus capsulae ostium superans*, calyx tube the mouth of the capsule overtopping; cf. RICTUS.

Movement: motus (s.m. IV).

movens (part. B): moving, motile; *cellulae leniter moventes*, cells gently moving.

mox (adv.): soon, presently.

mucedinosus (adj. A), **mucidus** (adj. A): mouldy.

much: multus (adj. A). **much**: multum (adv.), multo (adv.) (in comparisons); **much as**: tanquam (adv.); **much more** . . . **than**: multo magis (adv.) . . . quam. **not much**: vix (adv.), non nihil (adv.), paulo (adv.). **too much**: nimis (adv.)

muciger (adj. A): mucus-bearing, mucus-producing.

Mucilage: mucus (s.m. II), *acc. sing.* mucum, *abl. sing.* muco; *vaginae in mucum amorphum gelatinosum diffluentes*, sheaths into amorphous gelatinous mucilage dissolving; *planta gloeocarpa dicta, i.e. verticillis fertilibus in muco involutis*, plant termed 'gloeocarpous' i.e. with fertile whorls in mucilage enveloped; cf. GLOEO-. **mucilaginous**: mucilaginus (adj. A), mucosus (adj. A).

mucosus (adj. A): slimy, mucous, mucilaginous. **301**

Mucro: mucro (s.m. III. vi), *abl. sing.* mucrone. **mucronate**: mucronatus (adj. A). **140**

Mud: limus (s.m. II), lutum (s.n. II); *in L. comp.*, limi-. **mud-dwelling**: lutarius (adj. A), lutensis (adj. B); cf. LIMOSUS.

mult-, multi-: *in L. comp.*, many-; on the analogy of *multicaulis*, many-stemmed, *multifidus*, cleft into many parts, *multiflorus*, abounding in flowers, *multiformis*, many-shaped, manifold, *multijugus*, with many yoked together, *multinodus, multinodis*, having many knots, *multipartitus*, much divided, *multiplex*, many-folded, etc., which exist in classical L., botanists have coined some 50 epithets or terms, the meanings of which are, however, usually self-evident; *multangulus*, many-angled; *multiaxialis*, having a core of axial filaments; *multiceps*, many-headed, i.e. with many shoots from a single crown; *multinervis, multinervius*, many-nerved; *multiseptatus*, with many partitions; *multiserialis*, many-ranked; *multivalvis*, many-valved. **225**

multifariam (adv.); in many rows. **multifarius** (adj. A): many-rowed.

multiplex (adj. A): with many parts of the same kind together, as in a double flower.

Multiplication: multiplicatio (s.f. III. vi); *multiplicatio vegetativa divisione cellularum, propagatio agamica zoosporarum ope, generatio sexualis zoogametarum ope*, vegetative multiplication by division of the cells, agamic propagation by means of zoospores, sexual generation by means of zoogametes. **multiplied**: multiplicatus (part. A), auctus (part. A).

multo (adv.): by much, much. **multoties** (adv.): many times. **multum** (adv.):

much, often, frequently, greatly. **multus** (adj. A): many, much, great.

munitus (part. A): provided with, *lit.* 'fortified, protected'; *folia spinis recurvis nigris munita*, leaves by recurved black spines defended.

muralis (adj. B): belonging to *or* growing on walls.

muriaticus (adj. A): hydrochloric.

muricatus (adj. A): muricate, i.e. rough with short hard points like the shell of Murex (see Chapter XVIII). **264**

muriformis (adj. B): muriform, having the appearance of bricks in a wall.

murinus (adj. A): mouse-grey, pale brownish-grey.

Murus (s.m. II): wall.

muscosus (adj. A): mossy, moss-like. **Muscus** (s.m. II): moss.

Museum: museum (s.n. II), *gen. sing.* musei; *ex Herbario Musei Britannici*, from the Herbarium of the British Museum.

mushroom-shaped: fungiformis (adj. B), fungilliformis (adj. B). **91**

musky: moschatus (adj. A).

mutabilis (adj. B): changeable.

Mutation: mutatio (s.f. III), *gen. sing.* mutationis.

mutatus (part. A): changed.

muticus (adj. A): without a point, awnless, blunt. **165**

mutilatus (part. A): mutilated, cut short.

mutue (adv.): mutually, in relation to each other, reciprocally.

myc-, mycel-, myceto-, myco-, -myces: *in Gk. comp.*, fungal, fungus-, -fungus.

mycelial: mycelialis (adj. B); *setae myceliales numerosae erectae rectae simplices acutae atrae 180-200 μ longae basi 7-9 μ crassae*, mycelial setae numerous erect straight unbranched acute black 180-200 μ long at base 7-9 μ thick; *setae myceliales nullae*, mycelial setae none; *setis mycelialibus numerosis erectis simplicibus vel apice irregulariter furcatis*, with mycelial setae numerous erect simple or at the tip irregularly forked. **Mycelium**: mycelium (s.n. II), *gen. sing.* mycelii, *abl. sing.* mycelio; *mycelium epiphyllum ex hyphis brunneis undulatis septatis 10 μ crassis (cellulis plerumque 30 μ longis) opposite vel irregulariter ramosis laxe reticulatis compositum*, mycelium growing on upper side of leaves from hyphae brown undulate septate 10 μ thick (with cells usually 30 μ long) opposite or irregularly branched loosely reticulate composed. **Mycology**: mycologia (s.f. I)

myri-, myrio-: *in Gk. comp.*, countless, very many; *myrianthus*, with numerous

flowers; *myrioneurus,* with numerous
nerves; *myriophyllus,* with numerous
leaves or leaf-divisions; *myriostictus,*
with numerous spots or dots.

myrme-, myrmec-, myrmeco-: *in Gk.
comp.,* pertaining to ants; *myrmeco-
calyx,* with calyx inhabited by ants;
myrmecophilus, ant-loving, i.e. providing
structures liked by ants.

myx-, myxo-: *in Gk. comp.,* slimy, slime-,
mucus-.

N

naked: nudus (adj. A); (without leaves)
aphyllus (adj. A); cf. GYMNO-. **somewhat
naked:** nudiusculus (adj. A). **298**

nam (conj.): thus, for example. **namque**
(conj.): for indeed.

Name (s.n. III. vi): nomen (s.n. III. vi),
gen. sing. nominis, *abl. sing.* nomine,
nom. pl. nomina, *abl. pl.* nominibus;
see NOMEN. **named:** nominatus (part.
A).

namely: id est, scilicet (adv.).

nan-, nann-, nano-, nanno-: *in Gk. comp.,*
dwarf. **nanandrus:** nanandrous.

nanus (adj. A): dwarf. **335**

napiformis (adj. B): turnip-shaped.

narcotic: narcoticus (adj. A).

narrow: angustus (adj. A). **narrowed:**
angustatus (part. A), attenuatus (part.
A), contractus (part. A); *lamina in
petiolum alatum angustata,* blade into
a winged petiole narrowed; *lamina basi
sensim in petiolum attenuata vel subito
contracta,* blade at base gradually into
the petiole drawn out or abruptly contracted. **narrowing:** decrescens (part.
B); *lamina in petiolum canaliculatum
gradatim decrescens,* blade into a
channelled petiole gradually narrowing.
narrowly: anguste (adv.); *anguste
ovatus,* narrowly ovate. **most narrow:**
angustissimus (adj. A). **very narrow:**
perangustus (adj. A). **very narrowly:**
peranguste (adv.).

nascens (part. B): arising, beginning.

natalis (adj. B): pertaining to birth;
locus natalis, place of birth, locality for a
plant, station; cf. SOLUM.

natans (part. B): swimming, floating on
or under the surface of water. **390**

native: indigenus (adj. A), (inborn)
nativus (adj. A).

natural: naturalis (adj. B).

naturalized: inquilinus (adj. A).

Nature: natura (s.f. I).

natus (part. A): born.

nauseosus (adj. A): producing sickness,
nauseous.

Navalia (s.n. II. pl.): docks.

Navel: umbilicus (s.m. II). **navel-shaped:**
umbilicatus (adj. A), umbiliciformis (adj.
B); *in Gk. comp.,* omphalo-.

Navicula (s.f. I): a boat. **navicularis** (adj.
B), **naviculiformis** (adj. B): boat-shaped.
46 Navis (s.f. III): ship.

ne (adv. & conj.): no, not.

near: prope (prep. with acc.). **near:**
propinquus (adj. A), proximus (adj. A).
nearly: fere (adv.), paene (adv.), prope
(adv.), quasi (adv.), propemodum (adv.).

nebulosus (adj. A): clouded, cloudy, with
unevenly blended colours.

nec (adv. and conj.), **neque** (adv. and conj.):
not, and not, also not; *nec . . . nec,
neque . . . neque,* neither . . . nor; *nec
. . . . et, neque . . . et,* not only . . .
but also. **necnon** (conj.), **neque non**
(conj.): and also, and yet, likewise.

Neck: collum (s.n. II), *acc. sing.* collum,
gen. sing. colli, *abl. sing.* collo.

-necked: *in L. comp.* -collis (adj. B).

necklace-like: moniliformis (adj. B). **51**

necnon, neque: *see* NEC.

necro-: *in Gk. comp.,* dead.

Nectar: nectar (s.n. III. x), *abl. sing.* nectare.
nectar-bearing, nectarial: nectarifer (adj.
A), nectarifluus (adj. A), nectareus (adj.
A): *sulco nectarifero glabro viridi,*
with nectarial furrow glabrous green.

Nectary: nectarium (s.n. II), *abl. sing.*
nectario, *nom. pl.* nectaria, *abl. pl.*
nectariis.

needle-like: acicularis (adj. B), aciformis
(adj. B), acerosus (adj. A). **115**

neglected: neglectus (part. A), praetermissus (part. A), omissus (part. A).

negligently: neglecte (adv.), neglectim
(adv.), negligenter (adv.).

neighbouring: vicinus (adj. A), propinquus
(adj. A).

neither . . . nor: *see* NEC.

-nema (s.n. III. xi): *in Gk. comp.,* thread.
nemato-: *in Gk. comp.,* thread-like;
nematospadix, with thread-like spadix.

Nematode: nematodum (s.n. II); vermiculus (s.m. II) nematoideus (adj. A).

nemoralis (adj. B), **nemorosus** (adj. A):
pertaining to woods and groves.

nempe (conj.): certainly, namely.

Nemus (s.n. III. iv): grove, open woodland.

neo-: *in comp.,* new-. Mostly used as
prefix to avoid or remedy the creation
of generic homonyms or to connect a
new group with a closely related one,
e.g. *Neocolletia* and *Colletia, Neolitsea*
and *Litsea, Neomarica* and *Marica;
neogaeus,* pertaining to the New World;
neoguineensis, pertaining to New
Guinea; *neotropicus,* pertaining to the
American tropics.

nephro-: *in Gk. comp.*, kidney-; *nephrolepis*, with kidney-shaped scales; *nephrophyllus*, with kidney-shaped leaves. **nephroideus** (adj. A): kidney-shaped (*used of solid objects such as seeds*).

nervalis (adj. B): situated on a nerve.

Nervation: nervatio (s.f. III). **Nerve**: nervus (s.m. II), *abl. sing.* nervo, *nom. pl.* nervi, *abl. pl.* nervis; cf. VEINING. **nerved**: nervatus (adj. A), nervosus (adj. A). **nerve-**: *in L. comp.*, nervi-, *in Gk. comp.*, neuro-; *nervifolius*, *neurophyllus*, with strongly nerved leaves; *neurocarpus*, with strongly nerved *or* ribbed fruit. **-nerved**: *in L. comp.*, -nervis (adj. B), -nervius (adj. A), *in Gk. comp.*, -neurus (adj. A); *triplinervis*, three-nerved; *quintuplinervis*, five-nerved, *multinervis*, many-nerved; *parallelinervius*, *paralleloneurus*, parallel-nerved; *dictyoneurus*, with netted nerves. **nerveless**: enervis (adj. B), enervius (adj. A), nullinervius (adj. A). **343, 361**

nervisequens (adj. B): following the nerves, along the nerves.

Nervule: nervillus (s.m. II), nervulus (s.m. II).

neso-: *in Gk. comp.*, pertaining to islands.

Nest: nidus (s.m. II). **nestling**: nidulans (part. B), q.v.

Net: rete (s.n. III. x), *abl. sing.* reti *or* rete. **net-**: *in L. comp.*, reti-, *in Gk. comp.*, dictyo-; *dictyophlebius*, net-veined. **net-like, netted**: reticulatus (adj. A). **Network**: reticulum (s.n. II). **246**

neuter: neuter (adj. A), *lit.* 'neither the one nor the other'.

neutriquam (adv.): by no means.

never: nunquam (adv.), haud (adv.), nullo modo (adv.), nec unquam (adv.).

nevertheless: attamen (adv.), tamen (conj.).

new: novus (adj. A); *nomen novum*, new name substituted for a name not available; *in comps.*, neo-, novo-, novi-, with novae (genitive sing. f. of *novus*) mostly in geographical names; *novae-hollandiae*, of New Holland, i.e. Australia; *novi-belgii*, of New Netherlands, i.e. Manhattan, N.Y., U.S.A.; *novo-granatensis*, pertaining to New Granada.

next: proximus (adj. A with dat.).

next to: juxta (prep. with acc.)

nexus (part. A): tied together, interlaced, entwined.

nidulans (part. B): nestling, nesting, partially encased or lying in a cavity, embedded in pulp; *apothecia in tomento folii nidulantia*, apothecia partially encased in the tomentum of the leaf.

Nidus (s.m. II): nest.

niger (adj. B): black, *esp.* glossy black. **nigrifactus** (part. A): blackened.

nigrescens (part. B): becoming black.

nigricans (part. B): blackish, swarthy.

Night: nox (s.f. III), *gen. sing.* noctis, *abl. sing.* nocte, *nom. pl.* noctes, *abl. pl.* noctibus. **at night**: nocte (adv.), noctu (adv.). **belonging to night**: nocturnus (adj. A).

Nihil (s.n. indecl.), **nihilum** (s.n. II), **nil** (s.n. indecl.): nothing. **nihil** (adv.): by no means. **nihilominus** (adv.): nevertheless, notwithstanding.

nimirum (adv.): without doubt, certainly, surely.

nimis (adv.): too much, excessively, very much; *non nimis*, not too much, not very.

nine: novem (num. adj. indecl.) 'nine', novenus (adj. A) 'nine each, nine, ninth', novies (adv.), noviens (adv.) 'nine times'. **nine-**: *in L. comp.*, noven-, novem-, *in Gk. comp.*, ennea-; *enneaphyllus*, with nine leaves or leaflets; *novemnervius*, nine-nerved.

Nipple: mamilla (s.f. I), papilla (s.f. I). **nipple-shaped**: mammiformis (adj. B), mastoideus (adj. A).

nisi (conj.): if not, unless; *nisi si*, except if; *nisi ut*, except that.

nitens (part. B), **nitidus** (adj. A): shining, polished. **Nitor** (s.m. III): brightness, sheen, glossiness, shine. **294**

Nitrate: nitras (s.m. III. ii), *gen. sing.* nitratis. **nitric**: nitricus (adj. A). **Nitrogen**: nitrogenium (s.n. II), *gen. sing.* nitrogenii.

nivalis (adj. B): pertaining to snow, snowy, snow-like. **nivescens** (part. B): becoming snow-white. **niveus** (adj. A): snowy, snow-white. **nivosus** (adj. A): full of snow.

Nix (s.f. III): snow.

Nobis (pron. dat.): to us; *see* MIHI.

noctiflorus (adj. A): night-flowering. **nocturnus** (adj. A): belonging to the night; *cf.* DIURNUS, VESPERTINUS.

nodding: nutans (part. B). **408**

Node: nodus (s.m. II), *abl. sing.* nodo, *nom. pl.* nodi, *acc. pl.* nodos, *abl. pl.* nodis; geniculum (s.n. II) is little used; *rami ad nodos incrassati*, branches at nodes thickened; *culmi nodis incrassatis pilosis*, culms with nodes thickened pilose. **-noded**: *in L. comp.*, -nodus (adj. A), -nodis (adj. B); *multinodus, multinodis*, many-noded.

Nodifrons (s.f. III. ix): nodifrond, leafy nodal bract subtending inflorescence in palms.

nodosus (adj. A): knotted, knobby.

Nodule: nodulus (s.m. II), *abl. sing.* nodulo, *nom. pl.* noduli, *acc. pl.* nodulos, *abl. pl.* nodulis; *valvae typice nodulo* *centrali singulo rotundato magno nodulisque terminalibus 2 donatae*, valves typically with a central solitary rounded large nodule and 2 terminal nodules presented; *circa nodulum centralem*, around the central nodule. **nodulebearing**: nodulifer (adj. A). **nodulelike**: noduliformis (adj. B).

Nodus (s.m. II): node, q.v.

Nomen (s.n. III): name; *nomen illegitimum*, illegitimate name, i.e. one not in accordance with the rules of nomenclature; *nomen a Linnaeo adhibitum*, name by Linnaeus employed; *nomen usitatum*, usual name; *specimen sphalmate sub nomine 'tricerospermo' emissum*, specimen by error under the name 'tricerospermum' sent out; *Benthamius hoc nomen citavit*, Bentham this name cited; *nomina nova in opere meo inclusa*, new names in my work included.

Nomenclature: nomenclatura (s.f. I), *gen. sing.* nomenclaturae; *secundum leges nomenclaturae internationales*, following the international laws of nomenclature; *contra regulam codicis nomenclaturae*, against a rule of the code of nomenclature.

nominatus (part. A): named.

non (adv.): not; *nonnihil*, not much; *non vero*, truly not; *nonnisi, non nisi*, only: *non fere*, scarcely, hardly; *see* NOT.

nondum (adv.): not yet.

none: nullus (adj. A).

nonnullus (adj. A): some, several.

nonnunquam (adv.): sometimes.

nonus (adj. A): ninth.

nor : necque (conj.) ; see NEC.

normal : normalis (adj. B). Used as epithet to distinguish completely green from variegated forms and single- from double-flowered forms. **101**

North: septentrio (s.m. III), *gen. sing.* septentrionis; *ad septentriones*, to the north, *lit.* 'to the seven stars of the Great Bear'. **north, northern**: septentrionalis (adj. B), borealis (adj. B).

noster (pron. adj. A): our, ours.

not : non (adv.), nihil (adv.), nullo modo. *non* is generally used and comes immediately before the word or words negatived. *nihil*, 'not at all', is used only with verbs. *nequaquam, nullimodo, nullo modo*, 'by no means, in no way', *numquam*, 'at no time, never', *haud*, 'not at all, by no means', are more emphatic. In phrases *nec . . . nec*, 'neither . . . nor', *neque . . . neque*, 'neither . . . nor', *nec . . . et*, 'not only . . . . but also', may be employed; *seminum testa non crustacea*, of the seeds the testa not crustaceous; *ramis*

teretibus neque triquetris neque alatis, with branches terete neither triquetrous nor winged; *fructus nondum descriptus verisimiliter non dehiscens*, fruit not yet described very likely not dehiscent; *labellum medio non sulcatum*, labellum at the middle not grooved; *flores non visi*, flowers not seen; *discus nec albus nec ater*, disc neither white nor black.

Nota (s.f. I): that by which a thing is known, distinguishing mark, feature.

notabilis (adj. B): noteworthy, remarkable; cf. WONDERFUL.

notable: insignis (adj. B), notabilis (adj. B). **notably**: insigniter (adv.).

notatus (part. A): marked.

Notch: incisura (s.f. I).

noth-, notho- : *in Gk. comp.*, false-. Used in coining generic names indicating close but incomplete agreement, e.g. *Nothofagus*. **nothus** (adj. A): false, not genuine, mongrel, hybrid.

nōto- : *in Gk. comp.*, southern, south-; *Notelaea*, southern olive.

nōto- : *in Gk. comp.*, dorsal, back-, on the back; *Notoceras*, dorsal spur ; *Notylia*, dorsal hump.

Notula (s.f. I): a little mark, a small note *or* article.

nourishing: nutricius (adj. A), nutritorius (adj. A), alibilis (adj. B) ; *planta nutricia*, host-plant. **Nourishment**: alimentum (s.n. II), nutrimentum (s.n. II) ; *see* FOOD.

novellus (adj. A): young.

novem (num. adj. indecl.): nine. **novem-, noven-** : *in L. comp.*, nine-. **novenus** (adj. A): nine each, nine. **noviens** (adv.), **novies** (adv.): nine times, ninefold.

Novitates (s.f. III. ii. pl.): new things, novelties.

now: nunc (adv.), jam (adv.).

nowhere: nullibi (adv.), nusquam (adv.).

Noxa (s.f. I): injury, hurt. **noxius** (adj. A): harmful, injurious.

nubilis (adj. B): ready for pollination.

nubilus (adj. A): cloudy, dark, greyish-blue.

nucamentaceus (adj. A): in the form of a nutlet. **nucatus** (adj. A): nut-brown. **nucifer** (adj. A): nut-bearing. **nuciformis** (adj. B): nut-shaped.

nucleatus (adj. A): with a kernel or stone, with a nucleus.

Nucleus : nucleus (s.m. II), *abl. sing*, nucleo.

Nucula (s.f. I): nutlet.

nudiusculus (adj. A): somewhat naked. **nudus** (adj. A): naked, i.e. devoid of leaves or some other clothing, lacking usual covering, bare. **298**

nullibi (adv.): nowhere.

nullimodo (adv.): by no means, in no way.

nullinervius (adj. A): nerveless, q.v. **361**

nullus (adj. A): not any, none, lacking, absent.

Number: numerus (s.m. II), *acc. sing.* numerum, *abl. sing.* numero; *inflorescentia quoad florum numerum variabilis*, inflorescence with respect to number of flowers variable; *numero 1-6 varians*, with number from 1 to 6 varying; *stamina numero perigonii phyllis aequalia*, stamens to the number of leaves of perigon equal; *auctor numerum specierum generis valde reduxit*, the author greatly reduced the number of species of the genus.

Numerals: these are listed in Chapter VIII (pp. 108-110). In descriptions Arabic figures are generally preferable to Latin words, e.g. *calyx 10-nervis 5-dentatus* rather than *calyx decemnervis quinquedentatus*. In forming names and epithets, Gk. numerical prefixes should be united to words of Gk. origin, L. prefixes to L. words, avoiding such hybrids as *quadragonus, sexandrus*. When a word though of Gk. origin has become completely latinized, as *calyx, lobus, petalum*, or is neither Gk. nor L. but accords with both, as *tepalum*, it can take either a Gk. or a L. prefix, Gk. being usually preferred: 1-, *L.* uni-, *Gk.* mono-; 2-, *L.* bi-, *Gk.* di-; 3-, *L. Gk.* tri-; 4-, *L.* quadri-, *Gk.* tetra-; 5-, *L.* quinque-, *Gk.* penta-; 6-, *L.* sex-, *Gk.* hex-; 7-, *L.* septem-, *Gk.* hepta-; 8-, *L., Gk.* octo-; 9-, *L.* noven-, novem-, *Gk.* ennea-; 10-, *L.* decem-, *Gk.* deca-; 11-, *L.* undecim-, *Gk.* hendeca-; 12-, *L.* duodecim-, *Gk.* dodeca-; 20-, *L.* viginti-, *Gk.* icos-; few-, *L.* pauci-, *Gk.* oligo-; several- to many-, *L.* pluri-; many-, *L.* multi-, *Gk.* poly-; hundred-, *L.* centi-, *Gk.* hecto-, hecato-; very many, *Gk.* myri-; see ONE-, TWO-, THREE-.

numerous: numerosus (adj. A), multus (adj. A), plurimus (adj. A).

numquam: *see* NUNQUAM.

nunc (adv.): now, at present; *nunc . . . olim . . .*, now . . . formerly.

nuncupatus (part. A): enumerated, named.

nunquam (adv.): at no time, never, by no means.

nuper (adv.): recently, not long ago.

nusquam (adv.): nowhere.

Nut: nux (s.f. III. i), *gen. sing.* nucis, *abl. sing.* nuce, *nom. pl.* nuces, *gen. pl.* nucum *or* nucerum; *nux initio conica vel rotundata denique oviformis vel subglobosa obtusa glabra vel pilis stellatis vestitata*, nut at first conical or rounded at length egg-shaped or subglobose blunt glabrous or with stellate hairs clothed.

nutans (part. B): nodding. **408**

Nutlet: nucula (s.f. I).

nutricius (adj. A): nourishing, that nourishes or nurses. **nutriens** (part. B): nourishing, feeding, sustaining with food. **Nutrimentum** (s.n. II): nourishment. **nutritorius** (adj. B): nourishing, nutritious. **Nutrix** (s.f. III. i): host-plant, *lit.* 'wet-nurse, nurse'.

Nux (s.f. III): nut, q.v.

nyct-: *in Gk. comp.*, pertaining to night.

O

ob (prep.): *when used with verbs of motion* towards, *with verbs of rest usually* on account of, by reason of. In Class. L. *ob* was used with acc., in late L. also with abl.; *species nova ob bulbum parvum, folia laevia, calycem glandulosum, petala alba inter species sectionis Leiophylli ponenda*, new species on account of the bulb small, leaves smooth, calyx glandular, petals white among species of section Leiophyllum to be placed.

ob- (prefix): inversed-, reversed-, the other way round; *obclavatus*, club-shaped but attached by thicker end; *obcompressus*, flattened above and below instead of from side to side, so that two sutures of fruit, for example, are brought close together; *obconicus*, conical but with apex downward; *obcordatus*, reversed cordate with deep sinus remote from attachment; *obdiplostemonus*, with twice as many stamens as petals to which the outer series are opposite; *oblanceolatus*, oblanceolate, i.e. reversed lanceolate, the broadest part above the middle, length to breadth about 3 to 7; *obovatus*, obovate, i.e. reversed ovate, the broadest part above the middle, length to breadth about 3 to 2; *obpyramidatus*, reversed pyramidal; *obtriangularis*, obtriangular; *obtrullatus*, obtrullate, angular-obovate.

obducens (part. B): covering, spreading over. **obductus** (part. A): covered over, overspread.

obesus (part. A): fat, stout, plump.

oblatus (adj. A): oblate, i.e. almost circular but flattened above and below so that length to breadth is about 3 to 4.

obligatus (part. A): bound, obligatory.

oblique: obliquus (adj. A). **obliquely**: oblique (adv.). **137, 397**

obliteratus (part. A): effaced, i.e. so weakly developed as to be hardly perceptible.

oblitus (part. A): smeared, filled to excess; cf. TEXTURA.

oblong: oblongus (adj. A). broadly oblong: late oblongus. narrowly oblong: anguste oblongus. very broadly oblong: perlate oblongus, latissime oblongus. 107

obrutus (part. A): buried, covered.

obscure (adv.): indistinctly, obscurely. obscurus (adj. A): dark, shady, indistinct.

observed: observatus (part. A). Observation: observatio (s.f. III), nom. pl. observationes.

obsessus (part. A): occupied.

obsitus (part. A): covered over with, beset.

obsolescens (part. B): becoming obsolete, disappearing. obsoletus (adj. A): rudimentary, suppressed, scarcely apparent. obsolete (adv.), obsoletely.

obstipus (adj. A): bent forward, bent to one side.

obstructus (part. A): blocked up, obstructed.

obtectus (part. A): covered over, concealed, protected. obtegens (part. B): covering over.

obtextus (part. A): woven over, overspread.

obtritus (part. A): crushed, broken.

obturamentum (s.n. II): stopper, bung. obturatus (part. A): stopped up.

obtusangulus (adj. A): obtuse-angled. obtusatus (adj. A): blunted, obtuse. obtuse (adv.): obtusely. obtusiuscule (adv.): somewhat obtusely. obtusus (part. A): blunt, obtuse. 153, 173

obtutus (s.m. IV): observation, looking upon, seeing.

obvallatus (part. A): surrounded with a wall or rampart.

obverse-lunatus (adj. A): inversely crescent-shaped, the horns projecting away from the axis.

obverse-ovatus (adj. A): obovate.

obversus (part. A): turned towards, directed towards opposite, broader at or towards the top or apex than towards the base or in the lower part.

obvious: manifestus (adj. A). obviously: manifeste (adv.), manifesto (adv.).

obvius (adj. A): at hand, in the way, obvious, exposed.

obvolutus (part. A): wrapped around, e.g. when margins of one organ alternately overlap those of an opposite organ. 367

occasionally: subinde (adv.) 'repeatedly', aliquando (adv.) 'now and then', interdum (adv.) 'sometimes'.

occidentalis (adj. B): west, western.

occlusus (part. A): closed up.

occultans (part. B): hiding. occultus (part. A): hidden.

occupied: occupatus (part. A), obsessus (part. A); caulis erectus tertio vel quarto supero inflorescentia occupatus, stem erect with the upper third or quarter by the inflorescence occupied. occupying: occupans (part. B); discus fundum tubi calycis occupans, disc the bottom of tube of calyx occupying.

occurring: praesens (adj. B) 'present', dispositus (part. A) 'placed here and there', repertus (part. A) 'found, discovered'.

oceanicus (adj. A): pertaining to the ocean. Oceanus (s.m. II): the ocean; in oceano atlantico, pacifico et indico, in the Atlantic Ocean, Pacific Ocean and Indian Ocean.

ocellatus (adj. A): marked with two-coloured spots, having a centre of one colour surrounded by a broad ring of another. Ocellus (s.m. II): eye, distinctly coloured or otherwise noticeable zone in mouth of corolla, small thickening in valve-wall of certain diatoms.

ochraceus (adj. A): ochre-yellow, yellowish-brown.

Ocrea: ocrea (s.f. I), ochrea (s.f. I), lit. 'greave'; ocreae in apice ramorum tantum visae, adpressae, membranaceae, 6 mm. longae, cito deciduae, ocreae at tip of branches only seen, appressed, membranous, 6 mm. long, quickly falling.

octavus (adj. A): eighth. octiens (adv.), octies (adv.): eight times, eightfold. octo (num. adj. indecl.): eight. octo-. in both L. and Gk. comp., eight-; octandrus, with 8 stamens; octofarius, arranged in 8 rows; octoflorus, 8-flowered; octogonus, 8-angled; octonervis, octonervius, 8-nerved; octopetalus, 8-petalled; octorrhabdos, 8-striped; octovulatus, 8-ovuled. octoni (num. adj.): eight together, eight each; folia octona, leaves eight together.

Oculus (s.m. II): eye; oculo armato, with the aid of a lens; oculo nudo, with the naked eye; specimina ante oculos, specimens seen, i.e. before or under the eyes.

odd-pinnate: imparipinnatus (adj. A). 209 -odes: see -OIDES.

odon-, odont-, odonto-: in Gk. comp., toothed, tooth-; odontochilus, with toothed lip; odontoglossus, with toothed tongue; odontopetalus, with toothed petals; odontorrhizus, with root or rhizome tooth-bearing. -odon, -odontus: in Gk. comp., -tooth, -toothed; oligodon, with few teeth; macrodon, with large tooth or teeth; *macrodontus*, large-toothed; *octodontus*, eight-toothed.

Odor (s.m. III. v): smell of any kind, odour, perfume, stench, fragrance. **odoratus** (part. A), **odorifer** (adj. A), **odorus** (adj. A): having a smell, usually sweet-smelling; *convallariodorus*, fragrant like lily of the valley (Convallaria); cf. OLENS, OLIDUS, OSM-, REDOLENS.

-oecium (s.n. II): in Gk. *comp.*, -house, -room, e.g. συνοικιον latinized as *synoecium* (s.n. II) 'a room where several people dwell together', whence the 'homologized expressions' *androecium* and *gynoecium* (not *gynaeceum*) for the male and female systems of the flower; cf. A. H. Church in *J. Bot.* (*London*), 57 : 220-223 (1919).

Oecologia (s.f. I): ecology.

Oecotypus (s.m. II): ecotype.

oedo-: in Gk. *comp.*, swollen; *oedocarpus*, with swollen fruit.

of: usually expressed by use of genitive case; when 'from' or 'by' can be used instead of 'of', use *e* or *ex* (prep. with abl.).

officinalis (adj. B): used in medicine. This epithet more often refers to the past than the present; it is derived from *opificina*, shortened to *officina*, originally a workshop or shop, later a monastic storeroom, then a herb-store, pharmacy or drug-shop.

Offset: propagulum (s.n. II), *abl. sing.* propagulo; cf. PROLIFER.

Offspring: progenies (s.f. V); cf. PROLES.

often: saepe (adv.) 'many times', crebro (adv.) 'in close succession', compluriens (adv.), compluries (adv.) 'several times'. **very often**: persaepe (adv.), plerumque (adv.), saepissime (adv.).

-oideae: ending, derived from nom. pl. f. ending of adj. A, added to the stem of the name, or of a synonym, of the type genus of a subfamily to form name of this subfamily, e.g. *Boraginoideae* from *Borago*, *Heliotropioideae* from *Heliotropium*.

-oides, -odes, -oideus: in Gk. *comp.*, like, resembling, having the form *or* nature of. Generic names ending in *-oides* or *-odes*, e.g. *Nymphoides*, *Omphalodes*, are treated as feminine.

Oidium: oidium (s.n. II), *abl. sing.* oidio, *nom. pl.* oidia, *abl. pl.* oidiis.

Oil: oleum (s.n. II), *gen. sing.* olei; *guttae olei*, oil-bodies, drops of oil. **oily**: oleosus (adj. A), oleaceus (adj. A.); *corpora oleosa*, oil-bodies.

old: vetus (adj. B), *gen. sing.* veteris, *abl. sing.* vetere, *nom. pl.* veteres, *gen. pl.* veterum, *abl. pl.* veteribus; cf. AGED.

oleaceus (adj. A): relating to the olive tree, hence oily. **oleagineus** (adj. A), **oleaginosus** (adj. A): fleshy and oily, as pulp of the olive (*Olea*). **321**

olens (part. B): smelling, odorous, pleasant or unpleasant; *graveolens* strong-smelling, ill-smelling; *suaveolens*, sweet-smelling; cf. ODORATUS, OLIDUS, REDOLENS.

oleosus (adj. A): oily, full of oil.

oleraceus (adj. A): pertaining to kitchen gardens, either as a pot-herb or vegetable or as a weed. **Olerarium** (s.n. II), **Holerarium** (s.n. II): vegetable garden, kitchen garden.

Oleum (s.n. II): oil.

olidus (adj. A): emitting a smell.

olig-, oligo-: in Gk. *comp.*, few-; *oliganthus*, few-flowered; *oligoblepharus*, with few cilia; *oligocarpus*, with few fruits; *oligodon, oligodontus*, with few teeth; *oligomerus*, with few parts; *oligophlebius*, with few veins; *oligophyllus*, sparse-leaved; *oligosorus*, with few sori; *oligostachys*, with few spikes.

olim (adv.): formerly, in time past.

olivaceus (adj. A): olive-green. **oliviformis** (adj. B): olive-shaped.

Olla (s.f. I): pot, jar. **olliformis** (adj. B) pot-shaped; cf. BARREL-SHAPED, CUP-SHAPED.

omissus (part. A): neglected, left out, disregarded.

omnifariam (adv.), **omnilateraliter** (adv.) on all sides. **omnino** (adv.): altogether entirely. **omnis** (adj. B): all, every, the whole: *planta omnis glabra*, the whole plant glabrous; *in omnibus quae vidi exemplaribus*, in all specimens which I have seen.

on: in (prep. with abl.), used to indicate position generally; super (prep. with abl.), used to indicate position directly above or over; *insidens* 'sitting on' takes dat.

once: semel (adv.). **once more**: iterum (adv.).

onco-: in Gk. *comp.*, swollen, puffed out, bulky; *oncocarpus*, with swollen fruit cf. OEDO-.

one: unus (adj. A) 'one', unicus (adj. A 'one and no more, unique', singulari (adj. B) 'alone, single, one at a time' solitarius (adj. B) 'alone, by itself solitary', primus (adj. A) 'first', singul (num. distr. adj.) 'one each', semel (adv.) 'once'; *folium solitarium*, lea solitary; *caulis folio unico ovato*, stem with one ovate leaf; *ad unum*, all together; *in unum*, into one; *flores unu ad sex*, flowers one to six; *flore numero inter unum et sex*, flowers i number between one and six; *unus tantum*, one only.

one-: *in L. comp.*, uni-, *in Gk. comp.*, mon-, mono-; *unicolor, monochrous*, of one colour; *uniflorus, monanthus*, one-flowered; *unifolius, monophyllus*, one-leaved; *unistratus, monostromaticus*, one-layered, *unispicatus, monostachyus*, with a single spike; *unialatus, monopterus*, one-winged; *see* MON-, UNI-.

one-sided: secundus (adj. A); used of inflorescence with flowers directed to one side only and of other organs with parts so placed, often by twisting. **409, 490**

only (adj.): unicus (adj. A), unus (adj. A), solus (adj. A), singularis (adj. B). **only** (adv.): tantum (adv.), solum (adv.), non nisi (adv.) modo (adv.); *nervis laevibus non nisi sub apice scabris*, with nerves smooth only under the tip scabrid.

onustus (adj. A): laden, overloaded, full.

Oogonium: oogonium (s.n. II).

Oosporangium: oosporangium (s.n. II), *abl. sing.* oosporangio, *nom. pl.* oosporangia, *abl. pl.* oosporangiis; *oosporangium brunneum manifeste complanatum, 0·2-0·4 mm. longum, 0·2-0·3 mm. latum, 8-9 liras evidentes sed apice excepto non prominentes exhibens, membrana leviter granulata*, oosporangium brown decidedly flattened, 0·2-0·4 mm. long, 0·2-0·3 mm. broad, showing 8-9 ridges evident but except at the tip not prominent, with membrane lightly granulate.

Oospore: oospora (s.f. I), *abl. sing.* oospora, *nom. pl.* oosporae, *abl. pl.* oosporis; *oospora aureo-fusca ellipsoidea vel globosa jugis 6 leviter alata*, oospore golden-brown ellipsoid or globose lightly flanged with 6 ridges; *oospora brunnea vel nigra paulo complanata, 0·5-0·6 mm. longa 0·5 mm. lata, 6-8 liras tenues et prominentes exhibens, membrana crassa irregulariter granulata*, oospore brown or black a little flattened, 0·5-0·6 mm. long, 0·5 mm. broad, showing 6-8 ridges thin and standing out, with membrane thick irregularly granulate. According to Horn af Rantzien in *Bot. Notiser*, 109: 218 (1956), the term *oospora* as used by most writers on the fructifications of *Charophyta* should be replaced by *oosporangium*.

opacus (adj. A): darkened, dull, not shining, opaque. **299**

opaque: opacus (adj. A), impellucidus (adj. A), non translucidus (adj. A).

Ope: *see* OPS.

open: apertus (part. A), reclusus (part. A). **opening**: aperiens (part. B), dehiscens (part. B). **Opening**: orificium (s.n. II), *acc. sing.* orificium, *abl. sing.* orificio; apertura (s.f. I), *acc. sing.* aperturam, *abl. sing.* apertura; foramen (s.n. II), *acc. sing.* foramen, *abl. sing*, foramine. These are used for actual openings, but *apertio* (s.f. III) for the process of opening; cf. CRACK, OS.

operculate: operculatus (adj. A). **Operculum**: operculum (s.n. II), *abl. sing.* operculo, *nom. pl.* opercula, *abl. pl.* operculis, *lit.* 'a cover'; *operculum conicum oblique rostratum capsulam longitudine fere aequans*, operculum conical obliquely beaked the capsule in length almost equalling; *ascidia peristomio applanato operculum versus expanso, operculo ovato*, pitchers with the peristome flattened towards the lid expanded, with the lid ovate.

opertus (part. A): hidden, concealed.

ophio-: *in Gk. comp.*, pertaining to snakes, snake-like; *ophiocarpus*, with a slender twisted fruit; *ophiolithicus*, growing on serpentine (ophiolite) rock; *ophiophyllus*, with twisted *or* coiled leaves.

Opinion: judicium (s.n. II), sententia (s.f. I), opinio (s.f. III. vi); *auctor hanc sententiam comprobavit*, the author this opinion wholly approved; *mea quidem sententia*, in my opinion (way of thinking) at least; *meo judicio*, in my opinion (judgment); *ut opinio mea est*, as my opinion (supposition) is; cf. JUDEX, SENTENTIA.

Oppidum (s.n. II): town.

opposite: oppositus (adj. A); *stamina petalis opposita*, stamens opposite to the petals. **opposite-leaved**: oppositifolius (adj. A). **475**

Ops (s.f. III): ability, means, help, support, aid; *frutex ope cirrhorum scandens*, shrub with the aid of tendrils climbing; *motus ciliarum ope*, movement by means of cilia.

optime (adv.): well, exceedingly; *cum typo optime congruit*, with the type it agrees well. **optimus** (s. adj. A): best; superl. of *bonus*.

Opus (s.n. III): work, labour. **Opusculum** (s.n. II): a little work, pamphlet.

or: vel (conj.), -ve (conj. suffix), aut (conj.), seu (conj.), sive (conj.). *vel*, abbreviated as *v.* or *l.*, is commonly used. Most botanists apparently regard all the above as interchangeable. Following classical usage *aut* generally indicates a more important or real difference, 'an absolute or essential opposition', 'an alternative inconsistent with another alternative', *vel* or the termination *-ve* a less important difference, often one that 'concerns the expression more than the substance'; they have the sense of 'either . . . or', whereas *seu* and *sive*, abbreviated as *s.*, are essentially conditional with the sense of 'whether or', 'or else', and are less frequent except in book titles; in DC., *Prodromus* 16. i (1864) Alphonse de Candolle used *vel* (or *nunc* . . . *nunc*) when describing differences in form seen by him on the same specimen or the same branch and *aut* to contrast those of specimens coming from different branches and possibly or certainly from different trees; *pedicelli glabri aut ovarium glandulosum*, pedicels glabrous or ovary glandular; *calcar aut nullum aut saccatum album vel luteum*, spur either lacking or saccate white or yellow; *foliis nunc cordatis nunc obtusis*, with leaves sometimes cordate sometimes blunt; *foliis oblongis ellipticisve basi cordatis vel obtusis aut rarius cuneatis*, leaves oblong or elliptic at base cordate or obtuse or rarely [on specimens from a different tree] cuneate; *hortus bogoriensis descriptus seu Retziae editio nova*, Bogor garden described or of Retzia a new edition; *flora seu descriptio plantarum*, flora or description of plants; *Fuci, sive plantarum Fucorum generi a botanicis adscriptarum icones*, Fuci, or illustrations of plants to the genus of Fucus by botanists referred.

Ora (s.f. I): coast; *in Mari Pacifico (in Oceano Pacifico) ad oras Peruviae*, in Pacific Ocean on the coasts of Peru; *ad oras Peruanas Oceani Pacifici*, on the Peruvian coasts of the Pacific Ocean.

orange: aurantiacus (adj. A), croceus (adj. A), calendulinus (adj. A), armeniacus (adj. A), tangerinus (adj. A).

orbatus (part. A): stripped of, deprived of, *lit.* 'bereaved'; *arbores foliis pro empore orbatae haud sempervirentes*, trees for a time stripped of leaves not evergreen.

orbicular: orbicularis (adj. B), orbiculatus (adj. A); *see* CIRCULAR. **110**

Orbis (s.m. III. vii): ring, circle, orb, the world.

orchideus (adj. A): orchid-like.

orculiformis (adj. B): cask-shaped, q.v.

Order: ordo (s.m. III. vi), *nom. pl.* ordines; *folia ⅜ ordine disposita*, leaves in ⅜ order (phyllotaxis) arranged.

ordinary: usitatus (part. A); *cf.* CUSTOM.

ordinate (adv.), **ordinatim** (adv.): in order or succession, in good order, regularly.

Ordinatio (s.f. III): arrangement, pattern. **ordinatus** (part. A): arranged.

oreo-, ores-: *in Gk. comp.*, pertaining to mountains; *oreophilus*, mountain-loving; *oresbius*, mountain-dwelling.

Organ: organum (s.n. II), *nom. pl.* organa; *organa affixionis*, organs of attachment; *organa reproductionis*, organs of reproduction.

Orgya (s.f. I): fathom (1·83 m.), toise (6 feet, 1·95 m.), the distance between tips of middle fingers when arms are extended. **orgyalis** (adj. B): fathomlong, 6 feet long or high.

Oriens (s.m. III. x): the east. **oriens** (part. B): coming forth, arising, originating.

orientalis (adj. B): eastern.

Orifice: orificium (s.n. II), *acc. sing.* orificium, *abl. sing.* orificio; *cf.* OPENING.

Origin: origo (s.f. III. vi), *acc. sing.* originem, *abl. sing.* origine. **original**: originalis (adj. B), originarius (adj. A).

oriundus (adj. A): descended from, originating in, derived from; usually with *ab* or *ex*; *cf.* ORTUS, OFFSPRING.

Ornament: decus (s.n. III. iv), ornamentum (s.n. II).

ornatus (part. A): furnished, equipped, adorned, embellished.

ornith-: *in Gk. comp.*, pertaining to birds, bird-like; *ornithopodus*, bird-footed.

orth-, ortho-: *in Gk. comp.*, straight, erect; *orthacanthus*, with straight spines; *orthocarpus*, with straight fruits; *orthoneurus*, with straight nerves; *orthotropus*, orthotropous, i.e. when the ovule has a straight axis. **433**

ortus (part. A): descended from, arisen out of; *cf.* ORIUNDUS.

-orum: gen. pl. ending of s. II and adj. A. m. n., meaning 'of'; *amicorum*, of the friends, sometimes referring to the Friendly Islands; *anthropophagorum*, of the cannibals; *Baileyorum*, of the Baileys (Liberty Hyde B. and Ethel Zoe B.); *icones fungorum*, illustrations of fungi; *anglorum*, of the English; *germanorum*, of the Germans.

oryziformis (adj. B): like a grain of rice.

Os (s.n. III. iv), *gen. sing.* oris: mouth.

Os (s.n. III. iv), *gen. sing.* ossis: bone.

oscillans (part. B): swinging, oscillating; *cf.* AESTUANS. **oscillatorius** (adj. A): capable of swinging movement. **448**

-osis (s.f. III): suffix used in mycology to coin names of diseases; *Aspergillosis*, disease caused by Aspergillus.

osm-: *in Gk. comp.*, scented. **-osma** (s.f. I): *in Gk. comp.*, -scent.

osseus (adj. A): bony, of bone-like hardness. **ossiformis** (adj. B): bone-shaped, having a terminal knob.

ostendens (part. B) : displaying, exposing to view.

Ostiole : ostiolum (s.n. II), *abl. sing.* ostiolo, *nom. pl.* ostiola, *abl. pl.* ostiolis, *lit.* 'a little door' ; *ostiolum centrale cylindricum apice in fibrillas decolores hyalinasve solutum*, ostiole central cylindric at the tip into fibrils faded or hyaline breaking up ; *ostiolo longissimo concolori apice fibroso*, with ostiole very long of one colour at the tip fibrous.

Ostium (s.n. II) : door, entrance or exit, mouth (of a river) ; *in ostio fluminis*, in the mouth of the river.

-osus (adj. A) : suffix indicating abundance *or* marked development.

other : alius (adj. A) 'another among several or many', alter (adj. A) 'the other of two', diversus (adj. A) 'different', ceterus (adj. A) 'the other, the rest'.

otherwise : aliter (adv.) 'differently', alio modo, alia ratione 'by another method', cetera (adv.) 'for the rest' ; *aliter quam*, otherwise than ; *aliter velut in specie*, otherwise just as in the species.

outer : exterior (adj. comp.), externus (adj. A). **outermost** : extimus (adj. A).

Outline : ambitus (s.m. IV), circumscriptio (s.f. III. vi), circumferentia (s.f. I). **102**

Outside : pars (s.f. III) exterior. **outside** : externus (adj. A). **on the outside** : extra (adv., class. L.), extus (adv., mod. L.), extrinsecus (adv.) ; *calycis tubus extra intraque glaber*, tube of the calyx on the outside and on the inside glabrous ; *corolla supra basin extrinsecus glabra*, corolla above the base on the outside glabrous ; *perigonium extus pilosum intus glabrum*, perigon pilose outside glabrous inside ; *segmenta extus flava lineis purpureis ornata intus omnino purpurea*, segments outside yellow with purple lines ornamented inside entirely purple.

outwardly : extrinsecus (adv.).

ovalis (adj. B) : oval, elliptic, i.e. broadest at the middle, the sides curved and length : breadth usually 2 : 1. **108**

Ovary : ovarium (s.n. II), *abl. sing.* ovario, *nom. pl.* ovaria, *abl. pl.* ovariis ; *ovarium sessile dimidio superiore pubescens biloculare utroque loculo ovulis 3-8*, ovary sessile in the upper half pubescent 2-chambered, with each cell (loculus) with 3-8 ovules ; *ovarium primis vitae stadiis quadriloculare ab apice usque ad imum, mox uniloculare*, ovary in its first stages of life 4-chambered from tip to base, soon one-chambered ; *ovarium subglobosum triloculare in stylum longum productum*, ovary sub-

globose 3-chambered into a long style drawn out ; *ovarium stipitatum in medio dilatatum apice basique distincte attenuatum hexagono-sulcatum, poris nectariferis ad basem imam tribus*, ovary stalked, in the middle broadened, at tip and base distinctly attenuate, hexagonous-sulcate, with pores nectar-bearing at the very base three ; *ovarium inferum vel semisuperum vel superum*, ovary inferior or half-superior or superior ; *see* PLACENTA. **ovary-bearing** : ovariifer (adj. A).

ovate : ovatus (adj. A). **broadly ovate** : late ovatus. **narrowly ovate** : anguste ovatus. **very broadly ovate** : perlate ovatus, latissime ovatus. **109**

over : super (adv., prep. with acc.) 'extending over' ; plus quam (adv.) 'more than'.

overall : ubique (adv.).

overhanging : imminens (part. B), impendens (part B), superpendens (part. B).

overlapping : imbricatus (part. A), superpositus (part. A) ; cf. INCUBUS, SUCCUBUS.

overlooked : praetermissus (part. A).

overmuch : nimis (adv.).

overspread : obductus (part. A), obtectus (part. A).

overtopped : superatus (part. A), q.v.

overtopping : superans (part. B), excedens (part. B) ; *styli antheras longe superantes*, style the anthers long overtopping.

ovi- : *in L. comp.*, egg- ; *oviformis*, egg-shaped ; *oviflorus*, with egg-shaped flowers.

ovinus (adj. A) : pertaining to sheep.

ovoid : ovoideus (adj. A). **25**

ovulate : ovulatus (adj. A) ; *ovarium pauciovulatum, ovulis pendulis*, ovary few-ovuled, with the ovules pendulous.

Ovule : ovulum (s.n. II), *abl. sing.* ovulo, *nom. pl.* ovula, *abl. sing.* ovulis ; *ovula in quoque loculo duo collateralia vel plurima biseriatim superposita, rarius in loculis solitaria vel numerosissima irregulariter conferta, anatropa vel in paucis generibus orthotropa, basi medio vel apice lateraliter affixa vel rarius horizontalia*, ovules in each loculus two side by side or many in two series with one ovule above the other, rarely in the loculi solitary or most numerous irregularly crowded together, anatropous or in a few genera orthotropous, at base in the middle or at the top laterally fastened or rarely horizontal; cf. OVARY, PLACENTA.

own, its : suus (adj. A), proprius (adj. A).

Ozonium : ozonium (s.n. II).

P

pabularis (adj. B): fit for fodder. **Pabulum** (s.n. II): food, nourishment, fodder.

pachy-: *in Gk. comp.*, thick-, stout-; *pachydermus, pachydermicus*, thick-skinned, with wall of cell thicker than cavity; *pachycarpus*, with thick pericarp, thick-fruited; *pachycladus*, with thick branches; *pachyphyllus*, thick-leaved; *pachypodus*, with a thick support (petiole, peduncle, pedicel); *pachypterus*, with stout wings; *pachyrrhizus*, with thick root or rhizome; *pachystachys, pachystachyus*, with thick spike; *pachystylus*, with thick style.

packed: contiguus (adj. A) 'touching', farctus (part. A) 'stuffed', impletus (part. A) 'filled full'; *cellulae arcte contiguae*, cells closely packed; *cellulae guttis olei impletae*, cells packed with oil-bodies.

-paegma (s.n. III. ix): *in Gk. comp.*, play (although *paegmium* (s.n.) 'plaything, toy', may be intended).

paene (adv.): nearly, almost.

Page: pagina (s.f. I), *gen. sing.* paginae, *abl. sing.* pagina. pagina, *nom. pl.* paginae, *abl. pl.* paginis.

Pagina (s.f. I): page, surface.

Paint: pigmentum (s.n. II). **painted**: fucatus (part. A), pictus (part. A).

Pair: par (s.n. III); *paribus oppositis*, in opposite pairs; 'in pairs' can be expressed by *binatim* (adv.). **paired**: binatus (adj. A), bini (adj. A. pl.), gemellus (adj. A), geminus (adj. A), geminatus (adj. A), -jugus (adj. A).

palaceus (adj. A): margin-attached; attached by the edge to its support, as the blade of a non-peltate leaf to its petiole or of a spade (*pala*) to its sleeve and handle. **450**

palaemoneus (adj. A): shrimp-red (H.C.C. 6.16).

palaeo-: *in Gk. comp.*, ancient, old; *palaeobotanicus*, relating to fossil plants; *palaeotropicus*, relating to the Old World tropics; cf. NEO-.

palaris: relating to stakes, stake-like; *radix palaris*, tap-root.

Palate: palatum (s.n. II), *abl. sing.* palato.

palatus (adj. A): variant of PALACEUS used by Diels.

pale: dilutus (part. A), pallens (part. B), pallidus (adj. A). **becoming pale**: pallescens (part. B).

Pale, Palea: palea (s.f. I), *abl. sing.* palea, *nom. pl.* paleae, *abl. pl.* paleis.

paleaceus (adj. A): chaffy, of chaff-like texture. **293**

palely: pallide (adv.), dilute (adv.).

paliformis (adj. B): stake-like; *cellulae paliformes*, palisade cells.

Palisade: vallum (s.n. II).

pallens (part. B), pale. **pallescens** (part. B): becoming pale. **pallide** (adv.): palely. **pallidus** (adj. A): pale.

Palma (s.f. I): palm of the hand (*hence* width of 3 in.), a palm-tree; *palma scandens gracilis sparse armata glabra ad 2 m. alta*, palm climbing slender scantily armed glabrous to 2 m. high; *palma elata erecta valida, trunco annulato spinis nigris horrido*, palm tall erect strong-growing, with trunk annulate bristling with black spines. **palmaris** (adj. B): equalling the width of the palm of the hand, about 3 in. (8 cm.).

palmatim (adv.): palmately. **palmatus** (adj. A): palmate, i.e. lobed or divided in the manner of an outspread hand with the sinuses between the lobes pointing to the place of attachment. **196, 354**

palud-: *in L. comp.*, pertaining to marshes; *paludicola*, a dweller in marshes; *paludigena*, marsh-born, growing in marshes; *paludosus*, marshy, swampy, boggy. **Palus** (s.f. III. ii): marsh, swamp, bog, fen, pool. **palustris** (adj. B): swampy, marshy; *palustria*, swampy places.

Palynologia (s.f. I): the study of pollen and spores.

Pamphlet: libellus (s.m. II).

pan-: *in Gk. comp.*, all; *pantropicus*, throughout the tropics.

panduratus (adj. A), **panduriformis** (adj. B): fiddle-shaped, i.e. broadest near the top, curving inwards in the lower part, then curving outwards again above the base. **128**

Panicle: panicula (s.f. I), *acc. sing.* paniculam, *gen. sing.* paniculae, *abl. sing.* panicula; *panicula ramosissima, erecta vel demum nutans, folia superans*, panicle most branched erect or at length nodding, overtopping the leaves; *capitula in paniculam terminalem amplam disposita*, heads in a panicle terminal ample arranged. **panicle-like**: paniculiformis (adj. B). **paniculate**: paniculatus (adj. A). **paniculately**: paniculatim (adv.).

panniformis (adj. B), **pannosus** (adj. A): felted, with appearance *or* texture of felt.

papaverinus (adj. A): poppy red (H.C.C. 16).

papery: papyraceus (adj. A), chartaceus (adj. A). **311**

papilionaceus (adj. A): butterfly-like, papilionaceous, with corolla like that of pea, bean, etc.; *see* Fig. 34 f (p. 408).

Papilla: papilla (s.f. I), *nom. pl.* papillae, *abl. pl.* papillis.
papillatus (adj. A): papillate, having papillae. **papilliformis** (adj. B): nipple-like. **papillosus** (adj. A): papillose, covered with papillae. **269**
Pappus (apical tuft of hair or bristles or homologous appendages on fruits of Compositae and Valerianaceae): pappus (s.m. II), *gen. sing.* pappi. On a seed, such a tuft is termed COMA, q.v.; *pappus uniserialis albus setaceo-paleaceus breviter plumosus*, pappus in one series white bristle-like and chaffy shortly plumed; *pappus biserialis*, pappus in two series; *pappus duplex*, pappus double; *pappus multiserialis*, pappus in many series; *pappi series exterior cupulam 1 mm. altam fimbriatam formans, interior e paleis multis basi cohaerentibus longis superne plumosis constans*, of the pappus the outer series forming a cup 1 mm. high fimbriate, the inner composed from pales many at base cohering long in the upper part plumed; *pappus multiserialis basi in annulum conferruminatus*, pappus many-seried at base into a ring cemented together; *pappi paleae 2-seriales, exteriores ellipticae tenerae persistentes, interiores ovatae caducae*, of the pappus the pales in 2 series, the outer elliptic thin persistent, the inner ovate deciduous; *pappi duplicis setae exteriores 1 mm. longae scabridae, interiores 1 cm. longae plumosae, omnes nigrae*, of the double pappus the outer bristles 1 mm. long scabrid, the inner 1 cm. long plumose, all black.
Papula (s.f. I): pustule, a relatively large papilla or nipple-like projection. **papulosus** (adj. A): pustular.
papyraceus (adj. A): papery, as most leaves are when dried. **311**
Par (s.n. III): pair; *internodio inter par infimum et infimum proximum 1 cm. longo*, with internode between the lowest pair of leaflets and the next lowest 1 cm. long; *tria paria pinnarum*, three pairs of pinnae; *paribus infimis deflexis*, with the lowest pairs deflexed.
para-: *in Gk. comp.*, by the side of, near, compared with (*sometimes implying superiority*), similar to, as in generic names *Pararistolochia* (near *Aristolochia*), *Paranephelium* (near *Nephelium*), etc.
parabolicus (adj. A): used of more or less ovate leaves abruptly contracted below the rounded apex; cf. BELL-SHAPED. **117**
parallel: parallelus (adj. A); *parallelus ad axem*, parallel with axis. **parallel-**

nerved, -veined: parallelinervius (adj. A), paralleloneurus (adj. A), parallelivenius (adj. A). **in a parallel manner**: parallele (adv.). **350**
Paramylon: paramylon (s.n. II); *granum paramyli*, paramylon body.
Paranema: paranema (s.n. III. xi), *nom. pl.* paranemata, *abl. pl.* paranematibus; *paranemata (seu paraphyses) praesentia*, paranemata (or paraphyses) present.
Paraphyllium: paraphyllium (s.n. II), *nom. pl.* paraphyllia, *abl. pl.* paraphylliis.
Paraphysis: paraphysis (s.f. III. vii), *abl. sing.* paraphyse, *nom. pl.* paraphyses, *abl. pl.* paraphysibus; *paraphyses simplices septatae 100 μ longae, basim versus 6 μ latae, apicem versus 4 μ latae*, paraphyses simple septate 100 μ long, towards the base 6 μ broad, towards the tip 4 μ broad: *paraphysibus brevibus articulatis copiosis*, with paraphyses short articulated abundant.
Parasite: parasitus (s.m. II), parasita (s.f. I). **parasitic**: parasiticus (adj. A). In referring to hosts of fungi the adj. *parasiticus* is usually omitted, being understood, *in* with abl. being used alone; *parasitatur in arboribus variis at praesertim in Corylo, Fraxino et Betula*, it plays the parasite on various trees but especially Corylus, Fraxinus and Betulus; *frequens in pagina aversa foliorum Aceris*, frequent on lower surface of leaves of Acer; *in foliis vivis*, in (on) living leaves; cf. HOST.
Parastas (s.f. III): coronal ray of Passiflora, *lit.* 'doorpost'; *parastades filiformes albae*, coronal rays thread-like white.
paratus (part. A): prepared, provided with, equipped with.
parce (adv.): sparingly, moderately. **parcus** (adj. A): sparing, moderate, frugal.
parchment-like: pergamaceus (adj. A), pergamenus (adj. A).
Parenchyma: parenchyma (s.n. III), *abl. sing.* parenchymate; *cellulae pigmentosae in parenchymate numerosae*, pigmented cells in the parenchyma numerous. **parenchymatous**: parenchymatus (adj. A), parenchymaticus (adj. A).
Parent: parens (s.m.f. III. ix), *gen. sing.* parentis, *abl. sing.* parente, *nom. pl.* parentes, *abl. pl.* parentibus; *hybrida inter parentes crescens ac optime intermedia*, hybrid among the parents growing and beautifully intermediate.
parental: parentalis (adj. B).
pariens (part. B): bringing forth, producing.

Paries (s.m. III): wall. **parietalis** (adj. B): parietal, borne on the wall; *chromatophoro parietali*, with parietal chromatophore.

parilis (adj. B): equal, like.

paripinnatus (adj. A): paripinnate, i.e. pinnate and ending with a pair of leaflets (not a single terminal leaflet). **210**

Parish: parochia (s.f. I).

pariter (adv.): equally, in like manner.

paroecius (adj. A), **paroicus** (adj. A): paroecious, i.e. having male and female organs in the same inflorescence but separate, the male ones in the axils of lower bracts.

Part: pars (s.f. III), *abl. sing.* parte, *nom. pl.* partes, *abl. pl.* partibus; *ex parte*, in part, partly; *pro parte majore*, for the greater part; *pro parte minore*, for the smaller part; *in omnes partes*, *omnibus partibus*, in all respects, altogether; *nulla parte*, not at all.

parted: partitus (part. A), q.v. **195**

partial: partialis (adj. B).

partibilis (adj. B): divisible, ultimately separating *or* easily separated.

Particle: particula (s.f. I).

particular: peculiaris (adj. B). **particularly**: praesertim (adv.), praecipue (adv.), imprimis (adv.).

partim (adv.): partly, in part.

Partitio (s.f. III): a division.

Partition: dissepimentum (s.n. II), disseptum (s.n. II), septum (s.n. II).

partitus (part. A): partite, divided into parts, the division reaching almost to the base or into the inner ⅓; *multipartitus*, divided into many parts: *palmatipartitus*, palmately partite; *pinnatipartitus*, pinnately partite. **195, 199**

partly: partim (adv.), ex parte, in parte.

parum (adv.): too little, not enough, not very.

parumper (adv.): for a short time.

Parvitas (s.f. III): smallness.

parvus (adj. A): little, small, puny.

Pascuum (s.n. II): pasture. **pascuus** (adj. A): pastural, relating to pastures.

passim (adv.): at random, here and there, far and wide, everywhere.

passing into: transiens (part. B), confluens (part. B), decrescens (part. B); *ovarium cum disco confluens*, ovary into the disc flowing; *ovarium sensim in stylos ovario fere aequilongos transiens*, ovary gradually into styles almost as long as the ovary passing; *lamina basi in petiolum gradatim decrescens*, blade at base into the petiole gradually diminishing.

past: praeteritus (part. A).

pastural: pascuus (adj. A). **Pasture**: pascuum (s.n. II), *abl. pl.* pascuis.

Patella: patella (s.f. I), *lit.* 'small dish, plate'.

patelliformis (adj. B): dish-shaped, saucer-shaped; cf. PELVIFORMIS. **76**

patens (part. B): spreading, outspread, diverging from the axis at almost 90°. **patenter** (adv.): patently. **patentissimus** (adj. A): very widely spreading. **428**

pateriformis (adj. A): saucer-shaped.

patho-: *in Gk. comp.*, relating to suffering and to diseases.

Patria (s.f. I): native land.

Pattern: ordinatio (s.f. III): *ordinatione spinarum diversa*, with a different pattern of spines.

patulus (adj. A): spread, outspread.

pauci-: *in L. comp.*, few-; *paucidentatus*, few-toothed; *pauciflorus*, few-flowered; *paucifolius*, few-leaved; *paucijugus*, with few pairs of leaflets; *paucinervis*, *paucinervius*, few-nerved; *paucipunctatus*, with a few spots; *pauculus* (adj.), very few.

paucus (adj. A): few.

paulatim (adv.): little by little, gradually; *see* SENSIM.

paulisper (adv.): for a short time.

paulo (adv.), **paullo** (adv.): by a little, somewhat, a little.

pausiacus (adj. A): olive-green.

pavoninus (adj. A): peacock-eyed.

Pea: pisum (s.n. II); *magnitudine pisi*, the size of a pea. **pea-green**: pisinus (adj. A), pisaceus (adj. A). **pea-shaped**: pisiformis (adj. A).

peach-coloured: persicinus (adj. A).

pear-shaped: pyriformis (adj. B). **11**

pearly: margaritaceus (adj. A), perlarius (adj. A).

Peat-bog: turbarium (s.n. II).

peaty: turfosus (adj. A). **Peaty Moor**: turfosum (s.n. II).

pectic: pecticus (adj. A).

pectinatim (adv.): in the form of a comb. **pectinatus** (adj. A): pectinate, i.e. with narrow close-set divisions like a comb. **200**

peculiaris (adj. B): special, particular, not held in common with others.

pedalis (adj. B): a foot long (about 30 cm.).

pedatus (adj. A): pedate, i.e. palmate, q.v., but with the lateral lobes or divisions themselves divided. **pedati-**: *in L. comp.*, pedately; *pedatinervis*, pedately nerved. **197**

Pedicel: pedicellus (s.m. II), *abl. sing.* pedicello, *nom. pl.* pedicelli, *acc. pl.* pedicellos, *abl. pl.* pedicellis; *pedicelli 5 cm. longi filiformes glabri*, pedicels 5 cm. long thread-like glabrous; *pedicellis glabris perigonium aequantibus vel* *eo brevioribus*, with pedicels glabrous equalling the perigon or shorter than this ; *spatha pedicellos initio aequans, demum iis duplo brevior*, spathe at first equalling the pedicels, ultimately twice shorter than these (i.e. ½ their length).

pedicellaris (adj. B), **pedicellatus** (adj. A) ; provided with a pedicel, pedicelled.

Peduncle : pedunculus (s.m. II), *abl. sing.* pedunculo, *nom. pl.* pedunculi, *abl. pl.* pedunculis ; *pedunculus elongatus terminalis glaber*, peduncle elongated terminal glabrous ; *pedunculi terminales et axillares nudi glabri uniflori*, peduncles terminal and axillary naked (i.e. without bracts) glabrous one-flowered ; *pedunculis patentibus, inferioribus silicula duplo saltem longioribus*, with peduncles spreading, the lower at least twice longer than the silicle ; cf. SCAPE.

peduncularis (adj. B), **pedunculatus** (adj. A) : provided with a peduncle, pedunculate.

pelagicus (adj. A) : pertaining to the sea.

Pellicle : pellicula (s.f. I), *abl. sing.* pellicula ; *pileus pellicula viscida absitus*, pileus with a viscid pellicle covered ; *caro sub pellicula flava*, flesh under the pellicle yellow.

Pellis (s.f. III) : skin.

pellucidus (adj. A) : translucent but not hyaline.

peltate : peltatus (adj. A), peltiformis adj. B) ; cf. PALACEUS, SHIELD-SHAPED. **437**

pelviformis (adj. B) : basin-shaped ; cf. PATELLIFORMIS.

penarius (adj. A) : relating to provisions ; *regione penaria manifesta*, with well-marked storage region.

pencilled : lineolatus (adj. A), q.v.

pendulous : pendens (part. B), pendulus (adj. A), cernuus (adj. A) 'with face towards the ground', nutans (part. B) 'nodding'. **406-408**

penetrans (part. B) : penetrating.

penicillatus (adj. A), **penicilliformis** (adj. B) : shaped like a pencil *or* an artist's camel-hair brush. **Penicillum** (s.n. II) : brush-like tuft of hairs.

Peninsula : peninsula (s.f. I), paeninsula (s.f. I) ; *flora Peninsulae Balcanicae*, flora of the Balkan Peninsula.

penitus (adj. A) : inward, inner, interior. **penitus** (adv.) : inwardly, in the inside, deeply, completely.

pennatus (adj. A) : pinnate, q.v.; *pennatus* is preferred in class. L., *pinnatus* in bot. L.; *penna* (s.f. I) and *pinna* (s.f. I) 'feather, wing, pen', were often used indiscriminately.

penninervis (adj. B) : pinnately nerved. **pennivenius** (adj. A) : pinnately veined.

penta- : *in Gk. comp.*, five- ; *pentacarpus*, 5-fruited ; *pentacyclus*, with 5 twists ; *pentadactylus*, digitately divided into 5 finger-like lobes ; *pentagynus*, with 5 styles or carpels ; *pentamerus*, with parts in fives ; *pentandrus*, 5-stamened ; *pentapetalus*, 5-petalled ; *pentapterus*, 5-winged ; *pentasepalus*, 5-sepalled ; *pentaspermus*, 5-seeded ; *pentastachys*, with 5 spikes ; *pentastichus*, in 5 series *or* lines ; *pentastictus*, 5-spotted ; *see* FIVE-, QUINQU-.

Pepo (s.m. III) : pumpkin, fruit of Cucurbitaceae.

per (prep. with acc.) : through, throughout, all over, all along, during, by means of, by, on account of ; *flores per ramos in ramulis abbreviatis congesti*, flowers crowded all along the branches on branchlets abbreviated ; *species per regiones temperatas calidioresque dispersae*, species through regions temperate and warmer dispersed. **per-** : *in L. comp.*, through, very, completely, exceedingly ; *peraeque*, quite equally, uniformly ; *peralbus*, pure white ; *peranguste*, very narrowly ; *peraridus*, very dry ; *perasper*, very rough ; *percoloratus*, deeply coloured ; *percrudus*, quite immature ; *perdifficiliter*, with great difficulty ; *perdulcis*, very sweet ; *perdurus*, very hard ; *perelegans*, very elegant ; *perexigue*, very sparingly ; *pergrandis*, very large ; *peridoneus*, very suitable, well adapted ; *permale*, very badly ; *permultum*, very much ; *perpallidus*, very pale ; *perparvus*, very small ; *perutilis*, very useful.

peragratus (part. A) : traversed.

perceptible : perceptibilis (adj. B) ; *nervis exilibus vel exilissimis vix perceptibilibus*, with nerves feeble or very feeble scarcely perceptible ; cf. INVISIBLE, MANIFESTUS.

percurrens (part. A) : percurrent, i.e. extending the whole length of an organ but not continued beyond it ; *folia costa percurrente*, leaves with a percurrent midrib ; *costa percurrens haud excurrens*, midrib percurrent never excurrent.

perducens (part. B) : leading through, traversing. **perductus** (part. A) : traversed, conducted.

perdurans (part. B) : persistent, enduring.

peregrinus (adj. A) : foreign.

perennating : perennans (part. B). **perennial** : perennis (adj. B).

perfecte (adv.) : fully, completely. **perfectus** (adj. A) : complete, hermaphrodite, perfect.

perfoliate : perfoliatus (adj. A). **443**

perforatus (adj. A): pierced with holes *or* pores *or* sprinkled with translucent dots; cf. PERTUSUS.

perfossus (part. A): pierced through, hollow; cf. FISTULOSUS.

pergamaceus (adj. A), **pergamenus** (adj. A), **pergamentaceus** (adj. A): parchment-like; cf. PAPYRACEUS.

perhaps: fors (adv.), forsan (adv.), fortasse (adv.), forte (adv.), forsitan (adv.).

perhiemans (part. B): persisting through the winter, remaining all winter.

peri-: *in Gk. comp.*, about, around, surrounding.

Perianth: perianthium (s.n. II), *gen. sing.* perianthii, *abl. sing.* perianthio, *nom. pl.* perianthia, *abl. pl.* perianthiis. Applied by Linnaeus and his contemporaries to the calyx exclusive of the corolla, but by Mirbel, Robert Brown and later authors to the perigon, i.e. the floral envelope outside the stamens when not differentiated into calyx and corolla, and applied in Hepaticae to the colesule, i.e. the inflated envelope around the archegonium; *perianthium quadripartitum, persistens,* perianth (calyx) 4-parted, persistent; *perianthium infundibulare sex-partitum corollinum viridulum extus pilosum,* perianth (perigon) funnel-shaped 6-parted corolla-like greenish on the outside pilose; *perianthia basi nuda* (*i.e. a bractea remota*) *foliis caulinis subaequilonga pyriformia, tota longitudine acute 5-carinata, laevissima, apice rotundato obsolete rostellata,* perianths (colesules) naked at base (i.e. at a distance from the bract) about as long as the stem-leaves, for the whole length acutely 5-keeled, quite smooth, at the rounded apex obsoletely beaked; *see* PERIGON.

Pericarp: pericarpium (s.n. II), *gen. sing.* pericarpii, *abl. sing.* pericarpio.

perichaetial: perichaetialis (adj. B); *bracteae perichaetiales, perichaetii bracteae,* perichaetial bracts. **Perichaetium**: perichaetium (s.n. II), *abl. sing.* perichaetio.

Peridiolum: peridiolum (s.n. II), *abl. sing.* peridiolo.

Peridium: peridium (s.n. II), *abl. sing.* peridio.

Perigon: perigonium (s.n. II), *gen. sing.* perigonii, *abl. sing.* perigonio; *perigonium deciduum vel persistens hexaphyllum,* perigon deciduous or persistent six-leaved; *perigonii phylla* (*segmenta*) *oblonga,* leaves (segments) of the perigon oblong; *stamina longitudine ⅔ perigonii partes aequantia,* stamens in length

equalling ⅔ of the perigon; *stamina perigonio duplo breviora,* stamens twice shorter than (i.e. half the length of) the perigon; *filamentis perigonium duplo superantibus, ima basi inter se et cum perigonio coalitis,* with filaments twice exceeding the perigon, at the very base between themselves and with the perigon united; *see* PERIANTH. **perigonial**: perigonialis (adj. B); *bracteae perigoniales,* perigonial bracts.

Perigynium: perigynium (s.n. II), *gen. sing.* perigynii, *abl. sing.* perigynio.

perigynous: perigynus (adj. A). **474**

Period: periodus (s.f. II).

Peripheria (s.f. I): circumference; *chloroplastus plus quam dimidium peripheriae cellulae circumiens,* chloroplast more than half of the circumference of the cell encircling; *peripheriam versus,* towards the circumference. **periphericus** (adj. A), **peripheralis** (adj. B): pertaining to the boundary *or* outer surface, peripheral.

Periphysis: periphysis (s.f. III), *nom. acc. pl.* periphyses, *abl. pl.* periphysibus.

Periplast: periplastus (s.m. II); cf. PROTOPLAST.

peristomate: peristomatus (adj. A).

Peristome: peristomium (s.n. II), *gen. sing.* peristomii, *abl. sing.* peristomio; peristoma (s.n. III), *gen. sing.* peristomatis, *abl. sing.* peristomate; *peristomium duplex, exterius e dentibus crassis trabeculatis constans, interius obsoletum,* peristome two-fold, the outer from teeth thick cross-barred made, the inner obsolete; *see* PITCHER.

Perithecium: perithecium (s.n. II), *abl. sing.* perithecio, *nom. pl.* perithecia, *abl. pl.* peritheciis; *perithecia globosa folii parenchymati omnino immersa,* perithecia globose completely sunk in the parenchyma of the leaf; *perithecia numerosa in hyphis mycelii lateralia subglobosa hyalina levia,* perithecia many lateral in hyphae of the mycelium almost globose hyaline smooth.

peritropus (adj. A): directed horizontally. **432**

peritus (adj. A): skilful, learned, experienced.

perlarius (adj. A): pearly.

permanens (part. B): persistent, lasting.

perniciosus (adj. A): destructive, ruinous; cf. NOXIUS.

peronatus (adj. A): thickly overlaid with a woolly substance that becomes mealy. **283**

perpaucus (adj. A): very few, very little.

perpaulum (adv.): a very little indeed. **Perpaulum** (s.n. II): a very little; *perpaulo,* by a very little.

perpendicularis (adj. B): perpendicular, used of organs which go downwards; for stems, etc., *erectus, strictus,* etc., are used. **396**

perperam (adv.): incorrectly, falsely.

perpetuo (adv.): constantly, uninterruptedly, always.

perplexus (adj. A): confused, intricate, obscure.

perplurimus (adj. A): very many.

perquam (adv.): as much as possible, extremely.

perruptus (part. A): broken through.

persaepe (adv.): very often.

persicinus (adj. A): peach-coloured.

persistent, persisting: persistens (part. B), perdurans (part. B), permanens (part. B), remanens (part. B); *calyx ad maturitatem fructus persistens,* calyx to the ripening of the fruit remaining; *folia persistentia,* leaves evergreen. **342**

personatus (adj. A): wearing a mask, i.e. with a 2-lipped corolla having a prominent palate, 'so that when compressed the whole resembles the mouth of a gaping animal' (Lindley), as in many members of the *Scrophulariaceae,* the *Personatae* of Linnaeus or with spore-bearing pustules bursting through the epidermis like little open mouths. **67**

perspicue (adv.): evidently, manifestly, decidedly. **perspicuus** (adj. A): transparent, clear, evident.

pertinens (part. B): belonging to. **pertinet** (3rd person sing. indic. pres. of *pertineo*): it belongs to.

pertusus (part. A): having holes or slits, perforated. **244**

perulatus (adj. A): having buds covered with scales (perules).

Perule: perula (s.f. I), *nom. pl.* perulae, *abl. pl.* perulis; *rami hornotini basi perulis scariosis triangularibus vel lanceolatis 1-2 cm. longis cincti,* branches of current year girdled at base with perules (scales of leaf bud) scarious triangular or lanceolate 1-2 cm. long.

pervagatus (part. A): spread out, widespread, common.

pervalvaris (adj. B): pervalvar, transapical.

pervius (adj. A): perforate, having a passage-way through.

pervulgatus (part. A): very common.

Pes (s.m. III. ii): foot; English foot, 30·5 cm.; Paris foot, 32·5 cm.; *caulis duo pedales vel ultra altus,* stem 2 feet or more high; *pes caprae,* foot of a goat; *pes tigridis,* foot of a tiger; *ad pedes montis,* at the foot of the mountain.

pessimus (adj. A): very bad, utterly bad; superl. of MALUS.

Pest: pestis (s.f. III).

Petal: petalum (s.n. II), *gen. sing.* petali, *abl. sing.* petalo, *nom. pl.* petala, *gen. pl.* petalorum, *abl. pl.* petalis; *petalum latum obovatum,* petal broad obovate; *petala cum sepalis alterna iisque breviora, ad basin disci inserta, in aestivatione aperta, sub anthesi erecta,* petals alternating with the sepals and shorter than these, at the base of the disc inserted, in aestivation open, at anthesis erect; *petala lutea sepalis longiora, 1 cm. longa, patentia, obovata, apice rotundata, nectario squama oblonga obtecto,* petals yellow longer than the sepals, 1 cm. long, outspread, obovate, at the tip rounded, with the nectary covered by an oblong scale; *petalorum laminis obovatis ungue suo paulo brevioribus,* with the blades of the petals obovate shorter a little than the claw; *petalis numerosis cuneatis apice rotundatis aureis glabris calyce patente villoso longioribus,* with petals numerous cuneate at the tip rounded golden glabrous longer than the outspread villous calyx.

petalinus (adj. A), **petaloideus** (adj. A): petal-like. **58**

petiolaneus (adj. A): consisting of a petiole only. **petiolaris** (adj. B): borne on a petiole *or* relating to a petiole, petiolar. **petiolatus** (adj. A): provided with a petiole, petiolate. **467**

Petiole: petiolus (s.m. II), *gen. sing.* petioli, *abl. sing.* petiolo, *nom. pl.* petioli, *acc. pl.* petiolos, *gen. pl.* petiolorum, *abl. pl.* petiolis; *petiolus gracilis ad 5 cm. longus, quam lamina multo brevior, supra planus subtus carinatus, glaber, viridis,* petiole slender to 5 cm. long, than the blade much shorter, above flat beneath keeled, glabrous, green; *petiolus valde sulcatus, in foliis exterioribus et mediis distincte alatus,* petiole strongly grooved, in outer and middle leaves distinctly winged; *petiolus basi teres paulum incrassatus, laminam versus supra applanatus,* petiole at base terete little thickened, towards the blade flattened out; *lamina basi sensim in petiolum attenuata,* blade at base gradually attenuate into the petiole; *petiolus difficillime a lamina distinguendus,* petiole with extreme difficulty from blade to be distinguished; *petioli foliorum basalium lamina quarta vel tertia parte breviores,* petioles of basal leaves shorter than the blade by a quarter or third part; *petioli brevissimi,* petioles extremely short; *folia basi in petiolum superne alatum inferne sensim angustatum contracta,* leaves at base contracted into a petiole winged in the upper part gradually narrowed in the lower part; *petiolis glabris alatis 10 cm. longis*, with petioles glabrous winged 10 cm. long.

petiolulate: petiolulatus (adj. A). **Petiolule**: petiolulus (s.m. II); declined like *petiolus*.

Petra (s.f. I): rock, stone. **petraeus** (adj. A): growing among rocks. **petrensis** (adj. B); found among rocks. **Petrosa** (s.n. II. pl.): rocky places. **petrosus** (adj. A): full of rocks, rocky.

phae-, phaeo-: *in Gk. comp.*, dark-; *phaeadenius*, with dark-coloured glands; *phaeanthus*, dark-flowered; *phaeocephalus*, with dark heads; *phaeoglossus*, dark-tongued; *phaeoneurus*, with dark-coloured nerves; *phaeus*, dark-coloured, dark grey.

Phaeophorum (s.n. II): chromatophore.

phaner-: *in Gk. comp.*, manifest, visible, easily seen; *phanerantherus*, with protruding anthers; *phanerophlebius*, conspicuously veined; *phanerosorus*, with conspicuous sori.

Phialide: phialis (s.f. III. ii), *gen. sing.* phialidis, *abl. sing.* phialide.

-philus: *in Gk. comp.*, -loving; *dendrophilus*, tree-loving, epiphytic; *xerophilus*, loving dry places.

-phlebius: *in Gk. comp.*, -veined; *dictyophlebius*, net-veined. **phlebo-**: *in Gk. comp.*, vein-; *phlebocarpus*, vein-fruited, with veined fruits; *phlebophyllus*, vein-leaved, with conspicuously veined leaves.

phloginus (adj. A): phlox-pink (H.C.C. 6. 25).

phoeniceus (adj. A): bright red, scarlet.

-phorum (s.n. II): *in Gk. comp.*, -carrier, signifying a part which bears some other parts, a stalk or support; *gynophorum*, gynophore, the support of the gynoecium. **-phorus** (adj. A): *in Gk. comp.*, -bearing, -carrying; *lophophorus*, crest-bearing.

photographic: photographicus (adj. A).

-phragma (s.n. III. ix): *in Gk. comp.*, -screen, -partition.

phyco-: *in Gk. comp.*, relating to Algae, algal.

Phycologia (s.f. I): phycology, algology, the study of Algae.

Phycoma (s.n. III): the whole plant-body of an alga; thallus; *phycoma sphaericum duriusculum lubricum intus non distincte zonatum, ex trichomatibus flagelliformibus turgidis simplicibus centro concretis compositum*, plant-body (thallus) spherical somewhat hard slippery (slimy) inside not distinctly zoned, made up from filaments whip-

like turgid simple at the centre thickened together; *phycomatibus numerosis dense intricatis*, with thalli numerous densely entangled; *phycomate lineari complanato*, with thallus linear flattened.

phyll-: *in Gk. comp.*, relating to leaves; *phyllocephalus*, with leafy heads.

Phyllary: phyllarium (s.n. II); cf. TEGULUM.

Phylloclade: phyllocladium (s.n. II), *abl. sing.* phyllocladio, *nom. pl.* phyllocladia, *abl. pl.* phyllocladiis; cladodium (s.n. II), *abl. sing.* cladodio, *nom. pl.* cladodia, *abl. pl.* cladodiis. These terms are preferable to *cladophyllum*.

Phyllode: phyllodium (s.n. II).

Phyllopodium: phyllopodium (s.n. II).

Phyllum (s.n. II): leaf. To be distinguished from *phylum* (s.n. II), tribe; *involucri phylla*, involucral bracts.

-phyllus: *in Gk. comp.*, -leaved; *macrophyllus*, large-leaved; *microphyllus*, small-leaved; *monophyllus*, one-leaved; *diphyllus*, two-leaved.

phymatodeus (adj. A): warty, verrucose.

physo-: *in Gk. comp.*, bladdery; *physocarpus*, with bladder-like fruits.

phyt-: *in Gk. comp.*, relating to plants; *phytographia*, description *or* portrayal of plants; *phytologia*, study of plants, botany; *phytopathologia*, study of plant diseases.

-phyton, -phytum (s.n. II): *in Gk. comp.*, -plant.

piceus (adj. A): black as pitch.

picro-: *in Gk. comp.*, bitter; *picrorrhizus*, with bitter roots.

pictus (part. A): coloured, painted; *see* FUCATUS.

Piece: frustrum (s.n. II), pars (s.f. III).

Pigment-spot: stigma (s.n. III. xi).

pigmentifer (adj. A): pigmented. **pigmentivorus** (adj. A): paint-eating, paint-destroying. **pigmentosus** (adj. A): full of pigment, well coloured.

Pigmentum (s.n. II): colouring matter, pigment.

Pile: cumulus (s.m. II), *abl. sing.* cumulo; *sporis in cumulo*, with spores in a heap.

pileatus (adj. A): cap-shaped.

Pileus (s.m. II), *abl. sing.* pileo, *lit.* 'a felt cap'; mitra (s.f. I), *abl. sing.* mitra, *lit.* 'turban', is used only for the more or less globose or conical cap of Morchella and related Discomycetes; *pileus membranaceus profunde umbilicatus flocculosus 2-3 cm. latus, udus striis seu lituris croceis et alternatim flavis ad marginem radiantibus virgatus, siccus unicolor ferrugineus*, pileus (cap) membranous deeply depressed in the middle (umbilicate) finely woolly 2-3 cm. broad, when moist banded with orange yellow and alternate lemon yellow stripes or smears to the margin radiating, when dry uniformly rust-coloured; *pileus horizontalis suborbicularis laccatus, primitus e strato poroso albo tenuissimo constans, sensim dilatatus, primum planus cut modice convexus, fuligineus, opacus, zonis concentricis paucis obscurioribus notatus, margine patente tandem deflexo*, pileus horizontal almost circular apparently varnished, at the very first from a layer porous white very thin composed, gradually enlarged, at first flat or moderately convex, sooty, dull, with zones concentric few rather obscure marked, with margin spreading finally deflexed; *pileo horizontali suborbiculari laccato 3 cm. lato fuligineo zonis concentricis notato*, with pileus horizontal suborbicular apparently varnished 3 cm. broad sooty with concentric zones marked; *pileo albido vel eburneo, dein alutaceo, hygrophano, in statu sicco albo, levi glabro convexo umbonato*, with pileus whitish or ivory, afterwards leather-coloured, hygrophanous (watery-looking when wet, opaque when dry), in a dry state white, smooth glabrous convex but umbonate (i.e. with a rounded elevation in the centre).

pilifer (adj. A): bearing hairs. **piliformis** (adj. B): hair-like. **Pilositas** (s.f. III): pilosity, hair-covering. **pilosus** (adj. A): pilose, hairy with distinct long ascending hairs. **Pilus** (s.m. II): hair. **145, 270**

Pinax (s.m. III): a picture, *hence* a general survey *or* representation.

Pingue (s.n. III): fat, grease. **pinguis** (adj. B): fat, fatty.

pink: roseus (adj. A), erubescens (part. B), persicinus (adj. A), phloginus (adj. A), pudorinus (adj. A), rubellus (adj. A), carneus (adj. A). **pinkish**: subroseus (adj. A).

Pinna (s.f. I): primary division of a compound leaf.

pinnate: pinnatus (adj. A), *less often* pennatus (adj. A). **pinnately**: pinnatim (adv.). **pinnately cleft**: pinnatifidus (adj. A). **pinnately nerved**: pinnatinervis (adj. B), pinnatinervius (adj. A). **pinnatisect**: pinnatisectus (adj. A). **199, 208**

Pinnule: pinnula (s.f. I), *nom. pl.* pinnulae; pinnella (s.f. I), *nom. pl.* pinnellae.

piriformis: *see* PYRIFORMIS.

Piscina (s.f. I): fish-pond. **Piscis** (s.m. III): fish.

pisiformis (adj. B): pea-shaped. **pisinus** (adj. A): pea-green (H.C.C. 61). **Pisum** (s.n. II): pea.

Pistil: pistillum (s.n. II), *abl. sing.* pistillo; gynoecium (s.n. II), *abl. sing.* gynoecio. **pistillate**: pistillatus (adj. A), femineus (adj. A).

Pit: fovea (s.f. I), *abl. sing.* fovea; lacuna (s.f. I), *abl. sing.* lacuna; *folia 3-7 fovearum remotarum calcem secernentium serie notata*, leaves marked with a series of 3-7 remote pits secreting lime.

Pitcher: ascidium (s.n. II), *abl. sing.* ascidio, *nom. pl.* ascidia, *abl. pl.* ascidiis; *ascidia inferiora magna vel parva, parte ⅖ inferiore subglobosa, abrupte in partem superiorem anguste infundibuliformem transiente alis fimbriatis, persistomio in collum 2-3 cm. longum prolongato, sub operculo spinas 2 ferente, applanato ad 10 cm. lato, costis 2 mm. distantibus, operculo reniformi*, lower pitchers large or small, with the lower ⅖ part subglobose abruptly passing into the narrowly funnel-shaped upper part, with the wings fimbriate, with the peristome extended into a neck 2-3 cm. long, under the lid bearing 2 spines, flattened, to 10 cm. broad, with ribs 2 mm. apart, with the lid kidney-shaped.

pitcher-shaped: urceolatus (adj. A). **73**

Pith: medulla (s.f. I). **pithy**: medullosus (adj. A). **330**

pitted: foveatus (adj. A), lacunosus (adj. A). **minutely pitted**: foveolatus (adj. A), scrobiculatus (adj. A). **248, 249**

Place: locus (s.m. II), *nom. pl.* loci 'single places', loca 'places connected with one another'; *hoc loco*, at this place; *loco citato*, at the place cited. **placed**: positus (part. A), dispositus (part. A), locatus (part. A), collocatus (part. A). **placed among**: interpositus (part. A). **placed upon**: superpositus (part. A).

Placenta: placenta (s.f. I), *gen. sing.* placentae, *abl. sing.* placenta, *nom. pl.* placentae, *gen. pl.* placentarum, *abl. pl.* placentis; *ovula 2 ab apice vel sub apice placentae centralis pendula*, ovules 2 from the apex or below the apex of the central placenta pendulous; *ovula in placentis numerosissima*, ovules on the placentas most numerous; *ovula plura placentae centrali liberae sessili vel stipitatae inserta*, ovules many inserted onto the central free sessile or stipitate placenta; *ovarium nunc uniloculare placentis 2 parietalibus, nunc biloculare placentis septo adnatis*, ovary now one-chambered with 2 parietal placentas, now two-chambered with placentas joined to the partition; *ovarium placentis valde prominulis in laminas 2 latas revolutas in medio loculo approximatas vel contiguas divisis, ovarium in loculos 2 vel 4*

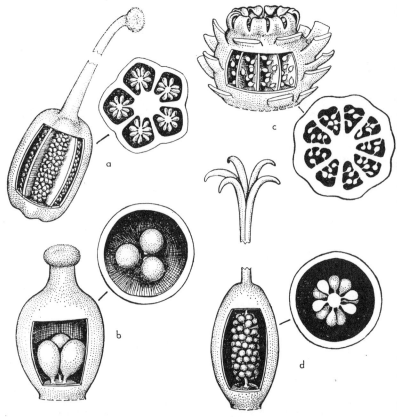

Fig. 36 Types of Placentation
a, ovarium quinqueloculare, placentatione axiali; b, ovarium uniloculare, placentatione basilari; c, ovarium pluriloculare, placentatione laminali, ovulis disseptimentorum parietibus undique insertis;
d, ovarium uniloculare, placentatione centrali libera (drawing by
Marion E. Ruff, from G. H. M. Lawrence, *Introduction to Plant
Taxonomy*; 1955)

imperfecte dividentibus, ovary with
strongly prominent placentas divided
into 2 broad revolute blades in the middle
of the chamber coming together or
touching, the ovary into 2 or 4 chambers
imperfectly dividing; *styli placentarum
numero*, styles with the number of the
placentas, i.e. the styles the same in
number as the placentas; *stigmata tot
quot placentae*, stigmas as many as the
placentas. **placenta-bearing**: placentifer
(adj. A).

Placentation: placentatio (s.f. III. vi),
abl. sing. placentatione; *placentatio
parietalis*, parietal placentation; *pla-*
centatio axilis, axile placentation; *placentatio centralis libera*, free central
placentation; *placentatio basalis*, basal
placentation; *placentatio laminalis*, lamellate placentation.

placentiformis (adj. B); circular and flat,
like a flat cake.

placodioidus (adj. A), **placodiomorphus**
(adj. A): placodioid, with the thallus
as in Placodium.

Plaga (s.f. I): flat surface, region.

plagio-: *in Gk. comp.*, oblique; *plagio-
neurus*, obliquely nerved.

Plagula (s.f. I): fungal colony; *plagulae
epiphyllae rarius hypophyllae et caulicolae*

orbiculares velutinae tenues atrae 1-4 mm. diametro saepe confluentes, colonies growing on upper side of leaves, rarely on the lower side, and on stems orbicular often confluent velvety thin black 1-4 mm. in diameter.

Plain: campus (s.m. II), planum (s.n. II), planities (s.f. V). **pertaining to plains**: campester, campestris (adj. B).

plane (adv.): clearly, distinctly, quite.

Planities (s.f. V): flat surface, plain.

planiusculus (adj. A): fairly flat.

Plankton: plancton (s.n. II), *gen. sing.* plancti. **planktonic**: planctonicus (adj. A).

plano-compressus (adj. A): compressed so as to have two opposite flat sides.

Plant: planta (s.f. I), *gen. sing.* plantae, *abl. sing.* planta, *nom. pl.* plantae, *acc. pl.* plantas, *gen. pl.* plantarum, *abl. pl.* plantis; *plantae annuae vel perennes, terrestres limnobiae vel aquaticae,* plants annual or perennial, terrestrial growing on mud or aquatic.

Plantula (s.f. I): seedling.

Planum (s.n. II): level ground, plain, plane. **planus** (adj. A): even, flat. **32**

Plasmodium: plasmodium (s.n. II), *abl. sing.* plasmodio.

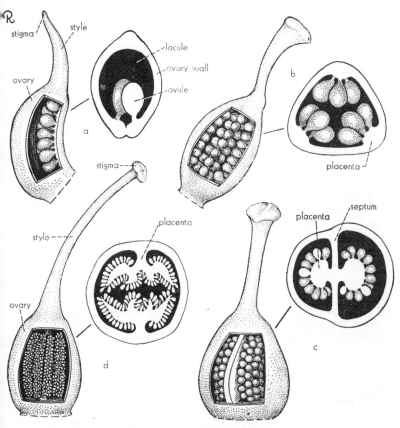

Fig. 37 Types of Placentation
a, ovarium simplex uniloculare, placentatione marginali, ovulis biseriatis; b, ovarium compositum, placentatione parietali; c, ovarium compositum biloculare, placentatione axiali; d, ovarium compositum uniloculare, placentatione parietali, placentis valde intrusis (drawing by Marion E. Ruff, from G. H. M. Lawrence, *Introduction to Plant Taxonomy*; 1955)

platy-: *in Gk. comp.*, broad; *platycaulis*, with broad stems; *platylobus*, with broad lobes; *platypetalus*, broad-petalled; *platyphyllus*, broad-leaved.

pleated: plicatus (adj. A). **372**

pleio-: *in Gk. comp.*, more than usual; *pleiopetalus*, with more petals, as in a 'double' flower.

pleisto-: *in Gk. comp.*, most.

pleniflorus (adj. A): with 'double' flowers, the centre of the flower being filled with petals.

plentiful: *see* ABUNDANT.

plenus (adj. A): full; *flore pleno*, with a 'double' flower.

pleraque (adv.), **plerumque** (adv.): for the most part, very frequently.

Pleuridium: pleuridium (s.n. II).

pleur-, pleuro-: *in Gk. comp.*, lateral, in a sideways position, ribbed; *pleurocarpus*, with the fruit lateral; *pleurogenus*, borne laterally. pleurogenous; *pleuranthus*, with ribbed flowers.

Plexus (s.m. IV): network.

pliant: flexibilis (adj. B), lentus (adj. A).

Plica (s.f. I): fold. **plicatus** (adj. A): folded into pleats *or* furrows, usually lengthwise. **372**

plietesialis (adj. B): plietesial, i.e. monocarpic but living for several years. **342**

-ploideus (adj. A): ending of cytological terms relating to number of sets of chromosomes, derived from Gk. *idios* (private, peculiar, individual), not *eidos* (form), by way of Weismann's term *Id*, introduced in German in 1893 to designate the hereditary germplasm, and Strasburger's terms *Haploid* (single id; gametophyte) and *Diploid* (double id; sporophyte), introduced in German in 1905; cf. *Brittonia*, 4: 338 (1943); *diploideus*, diploid; *hexaploideus*, hexaploid; *tetraploideus*, tetraploid.

plucked: avulsus (part A).

Plug: obturamentum (s.n. II).

plum-coloured: prunicolor (adj. B), pruninus (adj. A).

plumbeus (adj. A): leaden grey.

plumosus (adj. A): feathery.

Plumule: plumula (s.f. I).

pluri-: *in L. comp.*, several-, many-; *pluricostatus*, several-ribbed; *pluriflorus*, several-flowered; *plurifolius*, several-leaved; *plurijugus*, with several pairs of leaflets; *plurilocularis*, several-chambered; *plurinervis, plurinervius*, several-nerved.

pluries (adv.): often, frequently.

plurimum (adv.): very much.

plurimus (adj. A): most.

plus (adv. comp.): more. *plus minusve*, more or less.

Pluvia (s.f. I): rain; *tempore pluviarum*, at the time of the rains. **pluvialis** (adj. B), **pluviatilis** (adj. B): relating to rain.

pneumaticus (adj. A): relating to air, air-.

Pocket: marsupium (s.n. II). **pocket-like**: marsupiiformis (adj. B).

poculiformis (adj. B): cup-shaped. **83**

pod-, podo-: *in Gk. comp.*, foot-; *podophyllus*, with a foot-like leaf. The generic name *Podophyllum* is a contraction of *Anapodophyllum*.

Pod: (*in Leguminosae*) legumen (s.n. III. vi), *abl. sing.* legumine, *nom. pl.* legumina, *abl. pl.* leguminibus; (*in Cruciferae*) siliqua (s.f. I), *abl. sing.* siliqua, *nom. pl.* siliquae, *abl. pl.* siliquis.

Podetium: podetium (s.n. II). **-podus** (adj. A): *in Gk. comp.*, -footed, -based.

poecil-, poecilo-: *in Gk. comp.*, many-coloured, spotted, variegated, dappled, of various colours. Sometimes uncommendably transliterated as *poikil-*; *poecilanthus*, with speckled or variegated flowers; *poecilodermus*, with mottled skin.

Pogon (s.m. III): *in Gk. comp.*, beard; *pogonanthus*, with bearded flowers; *pogonocheilus, pogonochilus*, with bearded lip; *pogonoptilus*, with bearded plume; *pogonostemon*, with bearded stamen.

Point: punctum (s.n. II) 'dot', acumen (s.n. III) 'sharp end'. **pointed**: acutus (adj. A). **pointless**: muticus (adj. A).

poisonous: venenatus (part. A), venenosus (adj. A), toxicarius (adj. A), virosus (adj. A).

polar: polaris (adj. B).

polarilocular: polarilocularis (adj. B).

Pole: polus (s.m. II); *cellulae polis rotundatis*, cells with rounded poles; *ad polos*, at the poles.

polished: politus (part. A), nitidus (adj. A), laevigatus (adj. A), levigatus (adj. A), rasilis (adj. B). **296**

politus (part. A): polished.

Pollen: pollen (s.n. III. v), *gen. sing.* pollinis, *abl. sing.* polline; *antherae violaceae pollen dilute luteum valde irregulare continentes*, anthers violet containing light yellow very irregular pollen; *antherae polline omnino fertili*, anthers with pollen completely fertile; *polline pro parte majore sterili*, with pollen for the greater part sterile. **Pollen-grain**: pollinis granum (s.n. II); pollinis granulum (s.n. II). For terminology see Wodehouse, *Pollen Grains* (1935), Faegri & Iversen, *Textbook of Pollen Analysis* (1964), Erdtman, *Pollen Morphology* (1952), and Kremp, *Morphologic Encyclopedia of Palynology* (1965). Among the many terms are *annulus* (s.m. II), *aperture* (apertura; s.f. I), *colpus* (s.m. II), *dyad* (dyas; s.n. III), *equator* (aequator; s.m. III. v), *exine* (exinium; s.n. II), *exitus* (s.m. IV), *face* (facies; s.f. V), *foramen* (s.n. III. vi), *lumen* (s.n. III. vi), *mesocolpium* (s.n. II), *murus* (s.m. II), *polar area* (area polaris; s.f. I, adj. B), *pole* (polus; s.m. II), *pore* (porus; s.m. II), *reticulum* (s.n. II), *ruga* (s.f. I), *spine* (spina; s.f. I), *stria* (s.f. I), *sulcus* (s.m. II), *tetrad* (tetradium; s.n. II), *ulcus* (s.m. II), *valla* (s.f. I), *verruca* (s.f. I). In taxonomic descriptions of Acanthaceae authors sometimes use the German terms 'Faltenpollen', 'Rippenpollen', etc., proposed by Radlkofer and Lindau, notably in Engler, *Bot. Jahrb.*, 18 : 36 (1893), Engler & Prantl, *Pflanzenfam.* IV., 3b : 280 (1895), Urban, *Symb. Antill.*, 2 : 173 (1900); *pollinis grana parva (25-35 μ) tripora utroque latere pororum serie singula scutellorum magnorum ornata*, pollen grains small (25-35 μ) 3-pored on each side of the pores with a single row of large shields ornamented; *grana virgata, virgis septatis tortis*, grains banded, with bands septate twisted; *grana globosa leviter reticulata echinulata, spinulis intra reticuli spatia in circulos dispositis*, grains globose lightly reticulate somewhat spiny, the little spines inside the spaces of the network in circles arranged; *pollinis granula e typo 'Stachelpollen'*, pollen grain from the type 'Stachelpollen' (spine-pollen); *pollinis granula c. 60 μ diametro sphaeroidea ad typum 'Wabenpollen' nominatum pertinentia*, pollen grains about 60 μ in diameter to the type named 'Wabenpollen' (honeycomb-pollen) belonging; *grana poris 3 aequatorialibus exinio punctato*, grains with 3 equatorial pores, the exine punctuate; cf. HORREOLUM.

Pollex (s.m. III. i): thumb, length of first joint of thumb, 1 inch, approx. 2·5 cm.; same as UNCIA, q.v. **pollicaris** (adj. B): 1 inch long.

pollinaris (adj. B), **pollinicus** (adj. A): pertaining to pollen. **pollinifer** (adj. A): pollen-bearing.

Pollinium: pollinium (s.n. II), *abl. sing.* pollinio, *nom. pl.* pollinia, *abl. pl.* polliniis; *pollen in massas 'pollinia' dictas in quoque loculo solitarias conglutinatum*, pollen in masses called 'pollinia' in each loculus solitary joined together; *pollinia globosa oblonga vel pyriformia vel apice basive in acumen breve vel caudiculam longam producta*, pollinia globose oblong or pear-shaped

or at apex or base into a short point or long caudicle drawn out.

polluted: contaminatus (part. A), pollutus (part. A); *see* INQUINATUS.

poly-: *in Gk. comp.*, many, numerous; *polyanthus*, many-flowered; *polyarthrus*, many-jointed; *polybotrys*, with many racemes; *polycarpus*, with many fruits; *polycladus*, with many shoots; *polychromus*, many-coloured; *polyedricus*, with many flat sides; *polyembryonalis*, with many embryos; *polyneurus*, many-nerved; *polyphlebius*, many-veined; *polyphyllus*, many-leaved; *polypleurus*, many-ribbed; *polypterus*, many-winged; *polyrrhizus*, with many roots; *polyschistus*, split into many parts; *polyspermus*, with many seeds.

polyadelphus (adj. A): having stamens in several groups, each group formed by the union of filaments.

polyarthrodactylus (adj. A): having the ultimate rays *or* dactyls of Charophyta each composed of more than two cells.

polycarpicus (adj. A): polycarpic, i.e. having the power to bear fruit many times, not dying after fruiting but once. **342**

polygamus (adj. A): polygamous, i.e. having both unisexual and bisexual flowers on the same individual or on different individuals of the same species.

polygynus (adj. A): with many pistils or styles.

polymorphus (adj. A): very variable in form.

polypetalus (adj. A): having petals all distinct and free from one another.

polyphagus (adj. A): occurring on a diversity of host plants.

polystichus (adj. A): in many ranks, rows *or* series.

pomaceo-viridis (adj. B): apple-green.

Pome: pomum (s.n. II), *abl. sing.* pomo.

pomeridianus (adj. A): opening in the afternoon.

Pond, Pool: stagnum (s.n. II), lacuna (s.f. I); cf. PISCINA.

ponderosus (adj. A): weighty, heavy.

Ponticulus (s.m. II): a small bridge.

poorly: infirmus (adj.), debiliter (adv.).

porandrus (adj. A): with anthers opening by pores.

poratim (adv.): by pores.

porcatus (adj. A): ridged.

Pore: porus (s.m. II), *abl. sing.* poro, *nom. pl.* pori, *abl. pl.* poris; spiramentum (s.n. II), *abl. sing.* spiramento, *nom. pl.* spiramenta, *abl. pl.* spiramentis; *pori inaequales ampli citrini angulati cum tubulis concolores*, pores uneven large lemon-yellow angled the same colour as the tubules; *pori simplices minuti subrotundi*, pores simple minute almost round; *poris albis magnis concentrice dispositis*, with pores white large concentrically arranged; *poris primo pallidis demum cum pileo concoloribus minimis angulatis (penta-hexagonis) intus nudis*, with pores at first pale at length the same colour as the pileus most small angled (5-6 angled) naked inside; *antherae poris terminalibus rotundatis vel elongatis dehiscentes*, anthers dehiscing by pores terminal rounded or elongated.

porosus (adj. A): pierced with small holes.

porphyr-, porphyro-: *in Gk. comp.*, purple; *porphyrandrus, porphyrantherus*, purple-anthered; *porphyranthus*, purple-flowered; *porphyrocalyx*, with purple calyx; *porphyroneurus*, purple-nerved; *porphyrophyllus*, purple-leaved; *porphyrotaenius*, purple-banded. **porphyreus** (adj. A): purple.

porraceus (adj. A): leek-green; *see* PRASINUS.

porrectus (part. A): stretched outwards and forward; cf. TEXTURA.

portatus (part. A): carried.

Porus (s.m. II): pore, *q.v.*

Positio (s.f. III. vi): position, situation.

positus (part. A): placed.

possibly: forte (adv.) 'by chance', fortasse (adv.) 'perhaps'.

post (adv.): (*of place*) behind, back; (*of time*) after, afterwards. **post** (prep. with acc.): (*of place*) behind; (*of time*) after, since; *post anthesin*, after anthesis.

postea (adv.): after that, thereafter, afterwards, later.

posterior (adj. compar.): following after, later.

posterior: posticus (adj. A). **posteriorly**: postice (adv.).

posterius (adv.): later, afterwards.

posthaec (adv.): afterwards, after this.

postice (adv.): at the back, rearwards. **posticus** (adj. A): that which is behind, at the back, posterior; (*of anthers*) extrorse, facing outward and away from the axis of the flower; (*of corolla*) nearest the axis; (*of Hepaticae*) on the lower or ventral (rooting) side; *calycis lobus posticus acutus*, of the calyx the posterior lobe acute; *limbus bilabiatus, lobo postico brevi emarginato vel bifido, lobis lateralibus brevibus, antico ceteris longiore*, limb 2-lipped, with the posterior lobe short emarginate or bifid, the lateral lobes short, the anterior one longer than the others. **421**

postremo (adv.); at last, finally; *calyx sub anthesi 5 mm. postremo 8 mm. longus*, calyx at flowering time 5 mm. ultimately

8 mm. long, cf. DEMUM. **postremus** (adj. A): hindmost, last.

potamophilus (adj. A): river-loving.

Potassium: kalium (s.n. II), *gen. sing.* kalii; potassium (s.n. II), *gen. sing.* potassii.

potest (3rd sing. pres. indic. of verb *possum*): 'it is possible'.

potius (adv.): rather, preferably.

pot-shaped: olliformis (adj. B).

Pouch: saccus (s.m. II), *abl. sing.* sacco; sacculus (s.m. II), *abl. sing.* sacculo; marsupium (s.n. II), *abl. sing.* marsupio. **pouched**: saccatus (adj. A); marsupiatus (adj. A). **pouch-shaped**: marsupiiformis (adj. B), scrotiformis (adj. B). **84**

Powder: pulvis (s.m. III. v), *abl. sing.* pulvere; farina (s.f. I), *abl. sing.* farina. **powdered**: pulveratus (part. A), pulverulentus (adj. A), farinosus (adj. A). **powdery**: pulveraceus (adj. A), pulvereus (adj. A). **306**

praebens (part. B): holding forth, offering, making, exhibiting (*used with acc.*).

praecedens (part. B): preceding.

praecipitatus (part. A): cast down, precipitated.

praecipue (adv.): chiefly, especially, mainly.

praeclare (adv.): very clearly, admirably, very well.

praeclusus (part. A); closed, shut.

praecox (adj. B): precocious, developing early, over-hasty, bearing flowers before the leaves; cf. HYSTERANTHUS, PRIMIGENUS.

praeditus (part. A): provided with, possessed of.

Praefloratio (s.f. III. vi): aestivation, q.v.

Praefoliatio (s.f. III. vi): vernation.

praegnans (adj. B): pregnant, swollen, swollen with, full of (with abl.); *herba succo praegnans*, herb full of juice.

praemorsus (adj. A): premorse, as if bitten off. **159**

Praerupta (s.n.pl. II): steep *or* rugged places, cliffs.

Praesentia (s.f. I): presence.

praesertim (adv.): chiefly, especially.

praeter (adv. and prep. with acc.): beyond, besides, except for.

praeteritus (part. A): past and gone, past; *rosulae anni praeteriti*, rosettes of the past year; cf. ANNOTINUS.

praetermissus (part. A): left out, omitted, overlooked, neglected.

praetextus (part. A): bordered, fringed.

prasinus (adj. A): leek-green; *see* PORRACEUS.

pratensis (adj. B): growing in meadows. **Pratum** (s.n. II): meadow; *in pratis*, in meadows.

preceding: praecedens (part. B), antecedens (part. B).
precipitated: praecipitatus (part. A).
precisely: adamussim (adv.), accurate (adv.), definite (adv.); cf. EXACTLY.
pregnant: praegnans (adj. B).
prehendens (part. B), prehensilis (adj. B): grasping, taking hold of.
premens (part. B): pressing.
premorse: praemorsus (adj. A).
Presence: praesentia (s.f. I); cf. ABSENCE.
present (adj.): praesens (adj. B) 'at hand, in sight', suppetens (part. B) 'at hand, in store'; *folia praesentia*, leaves present; *semina in speciminibus suppetentibus immatura*, seeds in available specimens immature.
present time, at (adv.): nunc (adv.) 'now', hodie (adv.) 'today', praesenti tempore 'at the present time', jam (adv.) 'at this time'.
present, to be (verb): adsum; *summitas caulis tantum adest*, the top of the stem only is present; *caules (qui adsunt) 5 mm. crassi*, the stems (which are present) 5 mm. thick; *plantae unisexuales frequenter adsunt*, unisexual plants frequently present; cf. DEEST, SUPPETO.
presenting: efficiens (part. B), praebens (part. B), ostendens (part. B).
preserved: conservatus (part. A), asservatus (part. A), servatus (part. A).
pressing upon: premens (part. B).
Pressio (s.f. III. vi): pressure, a pressing down.
previously: *see* FORMERLY.
Prickle: aculeus (s.m. II), *nom. pl.* aculei, *abl. pl.* aculeis; *aculei inaequales sparsi validi*, prickles unequal sparse stout; *caulis aculeis multis inaequalibus rectis vel curvatis*, stem with prickles many unequal straight or curved. **prickly**: aculeatus (adj. A). **261**
pridem (adv.): long ago, formerly.
primaevus (adj. A): in the first period of life, youthful.
primarius (adj. A): of the first rank, chief.
primigenus (adj. A): first produced.
Primitiae (s.f. I, pl.): first things, first fruits, beginnings; *primitiae florae amurensis*, beginnings of an Amur flora.
primitivus (adj. A): primitive, the first *or* earliest of its kind; cf. PRISTINUS.
primitus (adv.): at first, for the first time.
primo (adv.): at first, at the beginning.
Primocane: primocanna (s.f. I), *abl. sing.* primocanna, *nom. pl.* primocannae, *abl. pl.* primocannis; *primocannae aestate arcuatae autumno apice decumbentes ad 2 m. longae 1-5 cm. crassae teretes aculeis multis curvatis armatae*,

primocanes (biennial shoots in the first year) in summer arching in autumn at the tip decumbent to 2 m. long 1·5 cm. thick terete armed with prickles many curved; *folia primocannarum magna 5-foliolata*, leaves of primocanes large with 5 leaflets; *primocanna* is adopted here as being etymologically preferable to *primocanus* (s.m. II), nom. pl. *primocani* (which could mean 'the first grey hairs'), used by L. H. Bailey in *Gentes Herb.* 2: 279 (1932).
primordialis (adj. B): primordial, first-formed.
Primordium (s.n. II): beginning, commencement.
primotinus (adj. A): growing first (*opp. of* SEROTINUS).
primum (adv.): first, firstly, primarily; *primum ... deinde ... tum ... postremo*, first ... next (then) ... then ... lastly.
primus (adj. A): first.
principalis (adj. B): chief, principal, main.
principally: praecipue (adv.).
Principia (s.n. II. pl.): foundations, principles, elements.
prion-: *in Gk. comp.*, saw-; *prionodes, prionoides, prionotus*, like a saw, serrated; *prionochilus*, with a serrated lip; *prionophyllus*, with serrated leaves.
prior, prius (adj. compar.): previous, first, fore; *nomen prius*, first name.
Priority: prioritas (s.f. III).
prismaticus (adj. A): having several longitudinal angles and intermediate flat surfaces. **3**
pristinus (adj. A): early, original.
prius (adv.): before, sooner.
priusquam (adv.): before that.
pro (prep. with abl.): before, in face of, on, in place of, just as, as; *pro genere*, as a genus; *pro synonymo*, as a synonym; *pro rata*, in proportion; *pro parte*, in part; *pro parte majore*, for the greater part.
probable: probabilis (adj. B). **probably**: probabiliter (adv.), verosimiliter (adv.).
proboscideus (adj. A): having a terminal snout-like *or* elongated projection or horn. **Proboscis** (s.f. III. ii): proboscis, terminal projection. **56**
Procarp: procarpium (s.n. II).
procerus (adj. A): very tall, high. **340**
Process: processus (s.m. IV), *abl. sing.* processu, *nom. pl.* processus, *abl. pl.* processibus, *lit.* 'a going forward'; *valvis fere in latere apicum in processus adparenter cavos magnos et in directiones oppositas inclinatos terminantibus*, with valves almost at the side of the tips in processes (projections) apparently hollow large and turned in opposite

directions terminating; *valvae ellipticae processibus conspicuis basi inflatis opposite inclinatis truncatis vel rotundatis, spatio inter bases processuum convexo,* valves elliptic with processes conspicuous at base inflated oppositely inclined truncate or rounded, with the space between bases of processes convex; *peristomium internum e processibus subulatis superne papillosis irregularibus compositum,* inner peristome made from processes subulate above papillose irregular.

procreans (part. B): bringing forth, producing.

procul (adv.): at a distance, far, far from, unconnected with.

procumbent: procumbens (part. B), humifusus (adj. A), prostratus (part. A). **422**

procurrens (part. B): extending, jutting out, projecting.

prodiens (part. B): coming forth, springing from, appearing, produced; *fructus solitarius e folii axilla prodiens,* fruit solitary from the axil of leaf coming forth.

Prodromus (s.m. II): forerunner, preliminary work which should be followed by a more complete one.

producing: efferens (part. B), procreans (part. B), producens (part. B), faciens (part. B), pariens (part. B).

productus (part. A): extended, elongated, stretched, brought forward; *see* PROLONGATUS.

Professor (s.m. III. v): 'one who makes instruction in any branch a business (post-Aug.)' (Lewis & Short); *botanices professor,* professor of botany.

profluens (part. B): flowing; *aqua profluens,* running water.

profunde (adv.): deeply. **Profunditas** (s.f. III): great depth. **profundus** (adj. A): deep.

profuse (adv.): lavishly, profusely. **profusus** (part. A): spread out, extended, profuse.

Progeny: progenies (s.f. V), proles (s.f. III).

progrediens (part. B): advancing by growth and dying off behind.

projecting: procurrens (part. B), projectus (part. A), exstans (part. B), eminens (part. B). **Projection**: projectura (s.f. I), prominentia (s.f. I).

prolabens (part. B): gliding *or* slipping forward.

prolatus (part. A): lengthened, extended, enlarged, drawn out towards the poles, prolate (describing pollen).

Proles (s.f. III. ii): progeny, race, group of closely related taxa.

prolifer (adj. A), **prolificans** (adj. B), **pro-**

lificus (adj. A): producing offsets, bearing progeny as offshoots.

Prolificatio (s.f. III. vi): prolification.

prolongatus (part. A): lengthened, extended; *see* PRODUCTUS, PROTENTUS.

Prolusio (s.f. III. vi): prelude, preliminary way; cf. PRODROMUS.

prominens (part. B): prominent, standing *or* jutting out. **Prominentia** (s.f. I): projection.

prominently: manifeste (adv.).

prominulus (adj. A): slightly raised, standing out a little.

promiscue (adv.): promiscuously, indiscriminately. **promiscuus** (adj. A): mixed, indiscriminate, promiscuous.

Promontorium (s.n. II): promontory, headland; *Promontorium Bonae Spei,* Cape of Good Hope.

promptus (part. A): apparent, manifest, at hand, ready.

Prong: dens (s.m. III. x); cf. TRIBULIFORMIS, TRINACRIFORMIS.

pronus (adj. A): leaning forward, inclined downward, prostrate. **423**

Propagatio (s.f. III. vi): propagation (*usually asexual*); *propagatio vegetativa in statu erratico, haud in statu sedentario* vegetative propagation in the mobile state, not in the stationary state; *propagatione asexuali per divisionem cellularum in membrana maternali,* with asexual propagation by means of division of cells within the maternal membrane.

Propago (s.f. III): layer; cf. CUTTING.

Propagulum (s.n. II): offset.

Propatulum (s.n. II): an open or uncovered place, stomatal aperture.

prope (adv. and prep. with acc.): near.

propemodo (adv.): nearly, almost.

Property: proprietas (s.f. III), q.v.

Prophyll: prophyllum (s.n. II).

propinquus (adj. A): near, neighbouring.

Proportion: proportio (s.f. III. vi), *abl. sing.* proportione; *differt staminum cum perigonio proportione diversa,* it differs by the different comparative relation of the stamens to the perigon. **proportionally**: proportione (adv.).

propositus (part. A): proposed, displayed.

proprie (adv.): specially, for oneself, properly, characteristically. **proprius** (adv. A): one's own, special, particular, characteristic; *sectio flore saepius 4-mero pro genere proprio saepe sumitur,* the section with flower most often tetramerous as a genus on its own is often taken; *genus ovario uniloculari seminibus multis insigniter proprium,* genus by the unilocular ovary with many seeds specially characterized.

Proprietas (s.f. III): special property, feature, peculiarity; cf. CHARACTER, QUALITAS.

propter (adv. and prep. with acc.): near, on account of, because of.

propullulans (adj. B): putting out, budding, shooting forth.

propulsus (part. A): driven forward.

prorsum (adv.): forwards, directly. **prorsus** (adv.): certainly, exactly, precisely.

prorsus (adj. A): straightforward, direct.

prorumpens (part. B): breaking forth, bursting through.

Prosenchyma (s.n. III. xi): prosenchyma (tissue of lengthened cells with tapering ends which overlap and fit together). **prosenchymatus** (adj. A): prosenchymatous.

prostrate: prostratus (part. A), pronus (adj. A); cf. PROCUMBENT. **423**

protentus (part. A): stretched out, lengthened.

proter-: *in Gk. comp.*, first in time. **proterandrus** (adj. A): protandrous, i.e. with anthers shedding pollen before the stigma of the same flower is mature. **proteranthus** (adj. A): before the flowers (*used of leaves produced before the flowers*); cf. HYSTERANTHUS, SYNANTHUS). **proterogynus** (adj. A): protogynous, i.e. with the stigma pollen-receptive before the anthers of the same flower are mature.

Prothallus: prothallus (s.m. II), *abl. sing.* prothallo.

protinus (adv.): (*of position*) forwards, (*of time*) forthwith, from the very first.

proto-: *in Gk. comp.*, first, original, chief.

Protonema: protonema (s.n. III. xi), *abl. sing.* protonemate.

Protoplasm: protoplasma (s.n. III. xi), *abl. sing.* proplasmate: *protoplasma uniformiter granulosum*, protoplasm uniformly granular. **protoplasmic**: protoplasmicus (adj. A).

Protoplast: protoplastus (s.m. II), *abl. sing.* protoplasto, *nom. pl.* protoplasti, *abl. pl.* protoplastis.

protractus (part. A): drawn out, lengthened.

protrudens (part. B), **protrusus** (part. A): pushed out, exserted.

protuberans (part. B): bulging, swollen. **Protuberatio** (s.f. III): bulge, swelling.

provectus (part. A): advanced, carried forward, extended.

proveniens (part. B): coming forth, coming from.

provided with: instructus (part. A) 'furnished', munitus (part. A) 'fortified', indutus (part. A) 'clothed', vestitus (part. A) 'clothed', refertus (part. A) 'well-supplied', paratus (part. A) 'prepared', praeditus (part. A) 'endowed', obsitus (part. A) 'sowed with, covered over', onustus (adj. A) 'laden, burdened, full', gaudens (part. B) 'rejoicing in', armatus (part. A), 'armed', ornatus (part. A) 'splendidly furnished'.

Province: provincia (s.f. I): *provincialis*, pertaining to Provence, southern France.

provisional: provisorius (adj. A): *nomen provisorium*, provisional name.

proximalis (adj. B): proximal, nearest to the axis.

proxime (adv.): very near, nearest, next, very closely. **proximus** (adj. A): nearest, next.

Pruina (s.f. I): waxy whitish powdery 'bloom' or secretion on surface of some plants. **pruinatus** (adj. A), **pruinosus** (adj. A): pruinose, covered with a pruina. **305**

prunicolor (adj. B), **pruninus** (adj. A): plum-coloured, purple.

pruriens (part. B): causing itching, stinging.

psammo-: *in Gk. comp.*, sand-; *psammophilus*, sand-loving.

pseud-, pseudo-: *in Gk. comp.*, false-, i.e. resembling but not equalling. Frequently and sometimes ridiculously used as a prefix in epithets to indicate a close resemblance leading to confusion; among the worst of such compounds are *pseudonebrownii*, not, however, intended as an insult to N. E. Brown, and *pseudoanacamptophyllus*.

Pseudobulb: pseudobulbus (s.m. II); cf. BULB.

Pseudocilium: pseudocilium (s.n. II).

Pseudocyphylla: pseudocyphylla (s.f. I).

Pseudoelater: pseudoelater (s.m. III. v).

pseudolateralis (adj. B): morphologically terminal but appearing lateral.

Pseudoperianth: pseudoperianthium (s.n. II).

Pseudopodium: pseudopodium (s.n. II); *pseudopodia simplicia e variis locis corporis sed praecipue postice extendentia*, pseudopodia simple from various places of the body but especially at the rear stretching out.

Pseudoraphe: pseudorhaphe (s.f. III), pseudoraphe (s.f. III), costa (s.f. I) longitudinalis; cf. RAPHE.

Pseudoseptum: pseudoseptum (s.n. II).

psil-, psilo-: *in Gk. comp.*, bare, bald, smooth; *psilanthus*, with glabrous flowers; *psilocarpus*, with smooth *or* glabrous fruits; *psilocladus*, with smooth *or* glabrous shoots.

psittacinus (adj. A): parrot-like, i.e. with green *or* contrasting colours.

pter-, pterygo- : *in Gk. comp.*, wing-, winged; *pterospermus, pterygospermus,* with winged seeds. **-pterus** (adj. A): *in Gk. comp.*, winged; *tetropterus,* four-winged. **60**

ptycho- : *in Gk. comp.*, referring to folds, pleats, clefts or deep grooves; *ptychocalyx,* with pleated calyx.

pubens (adj. B): downy. **puberulus** (adj. A): minutely pubescent, downy with very short soft hairs. **Pubes** (s.f. III. viii): pubescence, hairiness. **pubescens** (part. B): hairy as opposed to glabrous, downy with short soft hairs. **Pubescentia** (s.f. I): pubescence, hairiness. **pubi-** : *in L. comp.*, softly *or* weakly hairy; *pubinervis, pubinervius,* with pubescent nerves. **271**

Publication : liber (s.m. II) 'book, treatise', libellus (s.m. II) 'pamphlet'. Statement of the issue of a publication is illustrated by the following: *fasciculus primus hujus voluminis publici juris factus est mense Octobri 1811, secundus mense Decembri ejusdem anni, tertius et quartus Martio 1812, quintus et sextus Novembri 1813, septimus et octavus Februario 1815; nonus et decimus tandem nunc prodeunt* (J. F. Jacquin, *Ecl. Pl.*), the first fascicle of this volume was made available for public judgment in the month of October 1811, the second in December of the same year, the third and fourth in March 1812, the fifth and sixth in November 1813, the seventh and eighth in February 1815; the ninth and tenth at last now come forth; *in lucem prodiere Fasc. 1 die 15 m. Septembris 1903, Fasc. II die 18 m. Februarii 1904,* into the public view were brought forth Fasc. 1 on the 15th day of the month September 1903, Fasc. 2 on the 18th day of February 1904; *opus rarissimum nunquam in bibliopoliis venale, quidem sexaginta exemplaribus divulgatum est,* a most rare work, at no time in bookshops for sale, however in sixty copies it was published; *pars prima sistens p. 1 ad 434 edita fuit mense Julio 1862,* the first part presenting p. 1 to p. 434 has been published in the month of July 1862; *pars secunda editur mense Aprili 1883,* the second part is being published in the month of April 1883.

published : divulgatus (part. A), evulgatus (part. A).

Pugillus (s.m. II): a handful; *novarum stirpium pugillus,* of new plants a handful; cf. SERTUM.

pugioniformis (adj. B): dagger-shaped.

pulchellus (adj. A): beautiful and little.

pulcher (adj. A): beautiful. **pulchre** (adv.): beautifully, excellently.

pullatus (adj. A): clothed in black, i.e. dark brown.

pulled off: avulsus (part. A).

pullulans (part. B): budding off, sprouting.

pullus (adj. A): very dark, blackish.

Pulpa (s.f. I): pulp, flesh of fruit; cf. CARO. **pulposus** (adj. A): fleshy, pulpy.

pulveraceus (adj. A), **pulvereus** (adj. A): powdery, powder- *or* dust-like.

pulveratus (part. A), **pulverulentus** (adj. A): powdered, dusty, covered with powder; cf. FARINOSUS, PULVIS. **306**

Pulvillum (s.n. II): hot-bed.

pulvinatus (adj. A): cushion-shaped, strongly convex. **pulviniformis** (adj. B): cushion-shaped.

Pulvinulus (s.m. II): excrescence on lichen-thallus.

Pulvinus (s.m. II): swollen base of petiole, cushion; *thallus pulvinum formans,* thallus forming a cushion.

Pulvis (s.m. III. v): powder; *folium pulvere flavo conspersum,* leaves with yellow powder sprinkled.

Pumilio (s.m. and f. III. vi): a dwarf, pygmy. **pumilus** (adj. A): dwarf, close-growing, short. **335**

punctatus (adj. A): dotted, marked with dots, spots, minute glands, etc. **puncticulatus** (adj. A), **puncticulosus** (adj. A): minutely or finely dotted. **punctiformis** (adj. B): dot-like, reduced to a mere point. **Punctuatio** (s.f. III. vi): dotting. **punctulatus** (adj. A): minutely dotted. **Punctulum** (s.n. II): a minute dot. **Punctum** (s.n. II): point, position, dot, small spot. **258**

pungens (part. B): piercing, pungent, terminating in a hard sharp point. **143**

puniceus (adj. A): phoenician purple, crimson.

pure: purus (adj. A); (*as colour term, also*) vividus (adj. A), laetus (adj. A).

purple- : *in L. comp.*, purpureo-, *in Gk. comp.*, porphyr-, porphyro-.

purpuratus (adj. A): dressed in purple, empurpled. **purpurascens** (part. B): purplish, becoming purple. **purpureus** (adj. A): purple, 'dull red with a slight dash of blue' (Lindley). *Purpura* (s.f. I), Gk. πορφύρα (s.f.), was originally the name for the shell-fish of the eastern Mediterranean Sea yielding to the Phoenicians, particularly the Tyrians, a liquid for the manufacture of the celebrated purple dye of classical antiquity, later the name of the dye itself. This varied according to the shellfish used and the processing applied, and the epithet *purpureus* came to cover various red colours; now it embraces colours between red and violet (H.C.C. 27-34).

purus (adj. A): clean, pure, unstained.

-pus (adj. Gk.): *in Gk. comp.*, -footed; *apus*, gen. sing. *apodis*, footless, sessile.

pushed down: detrusus (part. A).

pusillus (adj. A): very small. **336**

Pustula (s.f. I): pustule, low projection like a blister or pimple, but larger than a papilla.

pustulatus (adj. A): having pustules. **pustuliformis** (adj. B): blister-shaped.

put: *see* PLACED.

Putamen (s.n. III. vi): stone or woody endocarp of a drupe; *putamen compressum 1 cm. longum 5 mm. latum 2 mm. crassum laeve*, stone compressed 1 cm. long 5 mm. broad, 2 mm. thick smooth; *putamine subgloboso foveato 1 cm. diametro*, with the stone almost globose pitted 1 cm. in diameter.

putide (adv.): disgustingly, badly.

putrescens (part. B): rotting. **putridus** (adj. A): rotten.

putting forth: edens (partB), emittens (partB)

pycn-, pycno-: *in Gk. comp.*, close, dense, compact; *pycnanthus*, with flowers crowded together; *pycnostachyus*, with dense spike.

Pycnidiospore: pycnidiospora (s.f. I).

Pycnidium: pycnidium (s.n. II).

Pycniospore: pycniospora (s.f. I).

Pycnium: pycnium (s.n. II).

pygmaeus (adj. A): pygmy, dwarf. **335**

-pyle (s.f. I): *in Gk. comp.*, -opening.

pyr-, pyro-: *in Gk. comp.*, fire-, fiery, hence red or yellow.

pyramidalis (adj. B): pyramid-shaped.

Pyrene: pyrena (s.f. I), *abl. sing.* pyrena, *nom. pl.* pyrenae, *abl. pl.* pyrenis; *less used is* pyren (s.f. III), *abl. sing.* pyrene, *nom. pl.* pyrenes, *abl. pl.* pyrenibus.

Pyrenoid: pyrenoides (s.f. III), *abl. sing.* pyrenoide, *nom. pl.* pyrenoides, *abl. pl.* pyrenoidibus.

pyriformis (adj. B): pear-shaped, i.e. obovoid or narrowly obovoid with a tapering base. **11**

pyrrh-, pyrrho-: *in Gk. comp.*, fire-red, ruddy, flame-coloured.

Pythmen (s.m. III. vi): pythmen. **pythmenophorus** (adj. A): pythmen-bearing.

pyxidatus (adj. A): furnished with a lid, having a pyxidium; *see* OPERCULATUS.

Pyxidium: pyxidium (s.n. II), *abl. sing.* pyxidio.

Pyxis: pyxis (s.f. III. ii), *abl. sing.* pyxide, *nom. pl.* pyxides, *abl. pl.* pyxidibus.

Q

qua (abl. sing. f. of pron. *qui*): from which; *see* QUI.

quaqua (adv.): wheresoever.

quaquaversum (adv.): to all sides, in all directions.

quaque (abl. sing. f. of pron. quisque): each; *foliola 12-24 in quaque pinna*, leaflets 12-24 in each pinna.

quadr-, quadri-: *in L. comp.*, four-; *quadrangularis, quadrangulatus, quadrangulus*, 4-angled; *quadrialatus*, 4-winged; *quadribracteatus*, 4-bracted; *quadridens, quadridentatus*, 4-toothed; *quadrifarius*, in 4 ranks; *quadrifidus*, 4-cleft, deeply divided into 4 parts; *quadriflorus*, 4-flowered; *quadrifolius*, 4-leaved; *quadrilateurus*, 4-sided; *quadrilobatus, quadrilobus*, 4-lobed; *quadrilocularis*, 4-chambered, 4-locular; *quadrinervis, quadrinervius*, 4-nerved; *quadriradiatus*, 4-rayed; *quadrivalvis*, 4-valved; *quadrivulnerus*, with 4 red or purple spots like wounds; *see* FOUR, QUATER, TETRA-.

Quadrans (s.m. III): quarter, one fourth.

quadrans (part. B): agreeing. **quadrat**: it agrees.

quadratim (adv.): four-fold.

quadrato-rhombicus (adj. A): quadrate-rhombic, i.e. square but with a corner at apex and base.

quadratus (part. A): squared, square.

quadri-: *see* QUADR-. **quadruplo** (adv.): four-fold. **quadruplus** (adj. A): four-fold.

quae (pron. f.): which; *see* QUI.

qualis (pron. adj.): what kind of?; of what kind, such as, as for instance.

Qualitas (s.f. III, ii): property, condition.

quam (adv.): than, by how much the more, as much as, in what way; *folia 9plo longiora quam latiora*, leaves 9 times longer than broad (the use of two comparatives, e.g. *longiora* and *latiora* connected by *quam*, is generally considered preferable to a comparative followed by a positive, e.g. *folia 9plo longiora quam lata*); *lamina foliorum aestivalium magis dilatata quam foliorum autumnalium*, blade of summer leaves more broadened than [the blade] of autumn leaves; *labello latiore quam longiore*, with labellum longer than broad; *costa magis prominente quam nervis*, with midrib more prominent than the nerves; *foliis plus quam duplo majoribus*, with leaves more than twice as big.

quamobrem (prep.): on which account, hence.

quamquam (conj.): though, although.

quamvis: (adv.) very much; (conj.) although.

quandoque (adv.): now and then, sometimes.

Quantitas (s.f. III. ii): quantity, extent.

quantus (adj. A): how great, as.

quarciticus (adj. A): quartz, quartz-like.

quare (adv.) : on what account, for which reason.

Quarter : quadrans (s.m. III), *abl. sing.* quadrante; quarta (s.f. I), *abl. sing.* quarta ; *in tribus circuli quadrantibus,* on three-quarters of a circle ; *in quarta parte inferiore,* on the lower quarter.

quartus (adj. A) : fourth.

quasi (adv.) : as if, as it were, about, nearly.

quater (adv.) : four times. **quaternarius** (adj. A) : consisting of four each, containing four. **quaternatim** (adv.) : in fours. **quaterni** (num. adj. distr. pl.) ; four each, four ; *sepala quaterna,* sepals four.

quattuor, quatuor (num. adj. indecl.) : four.

-que (conj. suffix) : and, q.v.

qui (rel. pron.), **quae, quod** : who, which ; commonly used in *abl. sing. f.* qua, *gen. sing.* cuius *or* cujus, *abl. pl.* quibus; *species affinis H. indicae a qua floribus minoribus differt,* species akin to H. indica from which by its smaller flowers it differs.

quickly : celeriter (adv.), cito (adv.), prompte (adv.), *spatha cito caduca,* spathe quickly falling off.

quidam (pron. indef.), **quaedam, quoddam** : a certain (sing.), some (pl.) ; *quodam tempore,* once (indefinite), *quaedam quaestiones,* some inquiries, some disputed matters.

quidem (adv.) : indeed, however, but, at least.

quidpiam (adv.) : in any respect, somewhat.

quiescens (part. B) : resting.

quiet : quietus (adj. A), tranquillus (adj. A) : *in aquis quietis,* in still waters.

quin (conj.) : or even, truly, indeed ; *pedalis quin bipedalis,* a foot or even two feet long.

quinarius (adj. A), **quinatus** : containing five, consisting of five ; *folium quinatum,* leaf with 5 leaflets ; *see* FIVE-, PENTA-.

quincuncialis (adj. B) : quincuncial, containing five-twelfths ; *aestivatio quincuncialis,* having five parts, of which two have their margins completely outside, two have their margins completely inside and the fifth one has one margin outside and the other inside, as in the calyx of Rosa, whence the medieval Latin riddle of the five brothers : *Quinque sunt fratres, Duo sunt barbati, Sine barba sunt duo nati, Unus ex his quinque Non habet barbam utrinque,* of which there are several renderings, e.g. *Quinque sumus fratres, unus barbatus et alter, Imberbesque duo, sum semiberbis ego,* rendered in English by E. B. Cowell as 'Five brethren of one birth are we, All in a

little family, Two have beards and two have none, And only half a beard has one'. 381

quini (num. adj. distr. pl.) : five each, five ; *folia quaterna vel sena* (*raro terna vel quina*), leaves 4 or 6 together (rarely 3 or 5).

quinqu-, quinque-, quinqui- ; *in L. comp.,* five- ; *quinquecostatus,* 5-ribbed ; *quinquedentatus,* 5-toothed ; *quinquefarius,* 5-rowed ; *quinquifidus,* 5-cleft ; *quinquefoliolatus,* with 5 leaflets ; *quinquelobus,* 5-lobed ; *quinquelocularis,* 5-chambered ; *quinquepartitus,* 5-parted ; *quinquevalvis,* 5-valved ; *quinquevulnerus,* with 5 red or purple spots or blotches like wounds ; *see* FIVE-, PENTA-. **quinque** (num. adj. indecl.) : five. **quinquiens** (adv.) : five times. **quintuplex** (adj. B) : five-fold. **quintuplinervis** (adj. B) : five-nerved, i.e. with four strong lateral nerves arising from the midrib above its base and running forward towards the tip, as distinct from *quinquenervis,* with all five parting from the same point at the base. **quintus** (adj. A) : fifth. 346

quisque (pron.), **quaeque, quodque** : each, everyone ; cf. QUAQUE, QUOQUE.

quite : admodum (adv.), omnino (adv.), plane (adv.), sat (adv.), satis (adv.).

quoad (adv.) : as to, with respect to ; *pro parte quoad plantam typicam,* in part as regards the type plant : *perigonii quoad formam compagem et colorem diversitas,* diversity of the perigon as to shape, structure and colour.

quoque (abl. sing. m. and n. of pron. quisque) : each ; *ovula in quoque loculo duo vel plurima,* ovules in each loculus two or many.

quoquoversus (adv.) : everyway, in every direction.

quot (adj. indecl.) : as many as, all, every, how many ; *quot annis,* every year.

quotidianus (adj. A) : every day, daily, common, usual.

quum (conj.) : *see* CUM (conj.).

R

Race : proles (s.f. III).

Raceme : racemus (s.m. II), *acc. sing.* racemum, *abl. sing.* racemo, *nom. pl.* racemi, *acc. pl.* racemos, *abl. pl.* racemis ; *racemus elongatus axillaris vel terminalis multiflorus,* raceme elongated axillary or terminal many-flowered. **racemi-** : *in L. comp.,* in *or* with a raceme or racemelike bunch ; *racemifer, racemiger,* bearing a raceme ; *racemiflorus,* with flowers in a raceme. **racemose** : racemosus (adj. A).

rach-, rhach- : *in Gk. comp.,* pertaining to the main axis, spine or backbone. The

Greek ῥάχις ('spine, backbone, ridge', used by Theophrastus for the midrib of an oak leaf) should properly be transliterated as *rhachis*, but has so commonly been rendered as *rachis* (cf. 'rachitis' and 'rachianaesthesia' in medicine), just as ῥαφή ('seam') has produced 'raphe' and ῥαφίς ('needle') 'raphid', that retention or omission of the *h* is optional in all these, despite its unvarying retention in 'rhizome', 'rheumatism' and 'rhythm'; for this inconsistency there is classical precedent, ῥάφανος being latinized as *raphanus* but ῥοδόδενδρον as *rhododendron*.

Rachilla: rhachilla (s.f. I), *abl. sing.* rhachilla; rhacheola (s.f. I), *abl. sing.* rhacheola; both also spelled *rachilla* and *racheola*; *rhachilla tenuis, supra glumas disarticulans*, rachilla thin, above the glumes breaking up; *spiculae rhachilla tenui supra glumas disarticulantes*, spikelets with rhachilla thin above the glumes breaking up; *spicularum rhachilla brevissima ultra florem non producta*, of the spikelets the rachilla most short above the flower not extended; *rhachilla inter flores vel sub floribus articulata*, rachilla between the flowers or under the flowers articulated.

Rachis: rhachis (s.f. III. ii), *acc. sing.* rhachim *or* rhachin, *gen. sing.* rhachidis, *dat. and abl. sing.* rhachidi, *nom. and acc. pl.* rhachides, *gen. pl.* rhachidum, *dat. and abl. pl.* rhachidibus. This form with a consonant stem in *-d* makes a clear distinction between *nom. sing.* rhachis and *gen. sing.* rhachidis. *Alternatively* rhachis (s.f. III. vii), *acc. sing.* rhachim, *gen. sing.* rhachis, *dat. and abl. sing.* rhachi, *nom. and acc. pl.* rhaches, *gen. pl.* rhachium, *dat. and abl. pl.* rhachibus. In this classically preferable form with an *-i* stem, *nom. sing.* and *gen. sing.* are both rhachis. The latter is closer to the transliterated Gk. *nom. sing.* rhachis, *acc. sing.* rhachin, *gen. sing.* rhacheos, *dat. sing.* rhachei. 'rachis' is now mostly used in English, *rhachis* and *rachis* are both well supported in bot. Latin. The term refers to the axis of a leaf above the petiole, i.e. the part bearing leaflets, or to the axis of an inflorescence above the peduncle, i.e. the part bearing flowers or fruits, not to the whole axis, but it has been used for the petiole of a fern frond; *folia paripinnata, rhachidi (rhachi) breviter pubescente vel subglabra*, leaves paripinnate, with the rachis shortly pubescent or almost glabrous; *rhachis straminea, pilis brevibus sed patentibus pubescens, apicem versus bisulcata*, rachis straw-coloured, with short but spreading hairs pubescent, towards the apex two-grooved; *pili rhachidis (rhachis) glandulosi*, hairs of the rachis glandular; *rhachidibus (rhachibus) sparsim paleaceis purpureis supra sulcatis*, with rachides (rachises) sparsely paleaceous purple furrowed above; *foliola opposita ad rhachin usque ad par proximum (inferius) late cuneatim decurrentia, quam ob rem bina cum dilatatione rhacheos limbum obtriangularem formant*, leaflets opposite to the rachis down to the next pair (lower) broadly cuneately decurrent, on which account together with the broadening of the rachis an inverted triangular limb they form.

radial: radialis (adj. B).

radians (part. B): radiating, spreading straight outwards from a common centre.

radiatiformis (adj. B): having outer florets of the capitulum larger than those of the disc but not ligulate.

radiatim (adv.): in a radiating manner.

radiatus (part. A): radiate, bearing rays or ray-florets, having corollas of outer florets ligulate; *multiradiatus*, many-rayed; *pauciradiatus*, few-rayed. **505**

radicalis (adj. B): radical, basal, arising from root or root-stock. **460**

radicans (part. B): rooting, putting forth aerial roots. **radicatus** (part. A): having roots.

Radicella (s.f. I): rootlet, q.v. **radicellosus** (adj. A): covered with rootlets.

Radicle: radicula (s.f. I).

radicosus (adj. A): with many roots, full of roots, with a large root.

Radicula (s.f. I): radicle, the rudimentary root of the embryo.

radiosus: *see* RADIATUS.

Radius (s.m. II): ray; in Compositae, the outer ligulate florets as distinct from the tubular florets of the disc; in Umbelliferae, the partial umbel; *capitula heterogama radiata, floribus radii uniseriatis neutris, disci hermaphroditis fertilibus*, capitula heterogamous radiate, with flowers of the ray uniserate neuter, of the disc hermaphrodite fertile; *corollae radii ligulatae, disci tubulosae*, corollas of the ray ligulate, of the disc tubular; *see* RAY.

Radix (s.f. III. i): root, q.v.; *ad radices montium* at the foot of mountains; *in radicibus montium Caucasi*, in the lower part of the mountains of the Caucasus.

Radula: radula (s.f. I).

radulans (adj. B): rasping, rough as a rasp, scabrous. **radulifer** (adj. A): rasp-bearing.

ragged: laceratus (part. A).

Railway: via (s.f. I) ferrea; *secus viam ferream*, along the railway.

Rain: pluvia (s.f. I). **rainy**: pluvialis (adj. B).

raised: elevatus (part. A), prominens (part. B).

ramealis (adj. B), **rameus** (adj. A): belonging to a branch. **rameanus** (adj. A): taking the place of a branch, e.g. a thorn *or* tendril. **462**

ramentaceus (adj. A): covered with ramenta. **Ramentum** (s.n. II): a thin membranous *or* chaffy flattened scale.

rameus (adj. A): *see* RAMEALIS.

rami-: *in L. comp.*, pertaining to branches, branched-; *ramicola*, growing on branches; *ramifer*, branch-bearing; *ramiflorus*, flowering on older branches; *ramiformis*, shaped like a branch; *ramigenus*, producing branches; *ramisparsus*, spread along the branches; *ramispinus*, with branched spines. **ramificans** (adj. B): branching. **Ramificatio** (s.f. III. vi): the branching, branch-system, place where a branch arises. **ramosissimus** (adj. A): very much branched. **ramosus** (adj. A): branched, bearing branches (usually many), much-branched. **226, 229**

ramulinus (adj. A): belonging to branchlets. **ramulosus** (adj. A): bearing branchlets, usually many. **Ramulus** (s.m. II): branchlet, q.v.

Ramunculus (s.m. II): twig, the ultimate division of a branch.

Ramus (s.m. II): branch; *rami hornotini ascendentes 3-6 cm. longi glabri*, branches of the present year's growth ascending 3-6 cm. long glabrous; *ramis floriferis ad nodos ramorum validiorum fasciculatis*, with flowering branches at the nodes of the stronger branches clustered; *rami ramuliquе graciles, inferne cinerascentes, ad apicem in parte hornotini brunei*, branches and branchlets slender, below becoming grey, at the tip in the part of current growth brown; *see* BRANCH.

random (adj.): fortuitus (adj. A). **at random**: fortuito (adv.), temere (adv.).

Range: jugum (s.n. II) 'mountain range', area (s.f. I) geographica 'geographical area', magnitudo (s.f. III) variationis 'size of variation'. **ranging**: extensus (part. A) 'spread over', varians (part. B) 'varying'.

-ranked: *in L. comp.*, -farius (adj. A), -seriatus (adj. A), -ordinatus (adj. A), *in Gk. comp.*, -stichus (adj. A); *folia bifaria, folia disticha*, leaves in two ranks

ranunculinus (adj. A): resembling a buttercup (Ranunculus), buttercup-yellow (H.C.C. 5).

Raphe: raphe (s.f. III), *abl. sing.* raphe, *nom. pl.* raphes, *abl. pl.* raphibus, *rarely but more correctly* rhaphe (cf. RACH-): *ovulum raphe ventrali*, ovule with raphe ventral; *testa raphe longitudinali filiformi*, seedcoat with raphe longitudinal thread-like; *valvae planae raphe recta vel incurva*, valves flat with raphe straight or incurved; *secus raphem*, along the raphe. **Raphe-valve**: raphovalva (s.f. I).

Raphid: rhaphis (s.f. III. ii), *abl. sing.* rhaphide, *nom. pl.* rhaphides, *abl. pl.* rhaphidibus. Commonly used in pl. either as *rhaphides* or *raphides*.

rapidly: celeriter (adv.) 'quickly', abrupte (adv) 'abruptly', prompte (adv) 'promptly'

rapiformis (adj. B): turnip-shaped, with a swollen turnip-like root.

rare (adv.): far apart, sparsely. **rarenter** (adv.), **raro** (adv.): seldom, rarely. **rariflorus** (adj. A): with flowers sparse *or* well separated. **rarior** (adj. compar.): rather rare, more rare, rarer; *plantae novae vel rariores*, plants new or rather rare; *rariorum plantarum historia*, a history of rarer plants.

rarissimus (adj. A): very rare. **rarus** (adj. A): far apart, scattered, rare. **499**

rasilis (adj. B): scraped, shaved, smoothed, polished.

rasp-like: radulans (adj. B), radulifer (adj. A).

rather: potius (adv.) 'preferable', citius (adv.) 'sooner', paulo (adv.) 'a little', aliquantum (adv.) 'considerably'; cf. SOMEWHAT, SUB-.

Ratio (s.f. III. vi): reckoning, calculation, relation, condition; *semina pro ratione magna*, seeds relatively large, i.e. by comparison with those of related plants; *quoad rationes longitudinis petalorum*, as to the relations in length of petals.

ravidus (adj. A): greyish.

ravus (adj. A); greyish-yellow, yellowish-grey, tawny.

raw (uncooked): crudus (adj. A), incoctus (adj. A); *fungus crudus venenatus, coctus esculentus*, fungus when raw poisonous, when cooked edible.

Ray: radius (s.m. II), *gen. sing.* radii, *abl. sing.* radio, *nom. pl.* radii, *acc. pl.* radios, *gen. pl.* radiorum, *abl. pl.* radiis; *radii ad furcam primam 7-10, quorum 1-3 plerumque simplices, ad furcam secundam 4-7, quorum 0-2 in radiis 4-5 denuo furcati, radiis ultimis bicellularibus, cellula inferiore versus basin cellulae ultimae sensim angustata, cellula ultima parva angusta acuta*, rays at the first fork 7-10, of which 1-3 commonly simple at the second fork 4-7, of which 0-2 into rays 4-5 once more forked, with ultimate rays 2-celled, with the lower cell towards the base of the end (apical) cell gradually narrowed, the end cell small acute; *radii primarii 7-10, secundarii 4-7, tertiarii 2-3*, primary rays 7-10, secondary 4-7, tertiary 2-3 ; *see* RADIUS.

reaching : attingens (part. B).

ready : promptus (part. A).

really : revera (adv.), vero (adv.).

rear : posterior (adj. comp.), posticus (adj. A).

recalling : admonens (part. B), revocans (part. B), referens (part. B).

recavus (adj. A) : arched inward, concave.

receding : recedens (part. B).

recens (adj. B) : fresh, young, recent ; *in statu recenti*, in a fresh state (*opp. to* in sicco, *dried*).

Recensio (s.f. III. vi) : enumeration, review.

recently : nuper (adv.).

Receptacle : receptaculum (s.n. II), *abl. sing.* receptaculo : *receptaculum longitudine calycis, hemisphaericum vel globosum, 8-10 mm. longum latumque, basi villosum*, receptacle the length of the calyx, hemispherical or globose, 8-10 mm. long and wide, villous at base.

recessim (adv.) : backwards.

Recessus (s.m. IV) : ebb, retreat, departure ; cf. TIDE. **recessus** (part. A) : receding.

reciprocally : mutuo (adv.), mutue (adv.).

reckoned : computatus (part. A).

reclinatus (part. A) : turned or bent downward upon some other part ; cf. REPLICATUS. **378, 403**

reclusus (part. A) : opened, laid open, unclosed ; cf. APERTUS.

recognitus (part. A) : recognized, authenticated. **recognoscendus** (gerund. A) : to be investigated.

reconditus (part. A) : closed, hidden, shut up, not easily seen ; cf. OCCULTUS.

Rectangle : rectangulum (s.n. II), figura (s.f. I) quadrilatera rectangula. **rectangular** : rectangularis (adj. B), oblongus (adj. A).

rectangulatus (adj. A), **rectangulus** (adj. A) : right-angled.

recte (adv.) : rightly, correctly.

recti- : *in L. comp.*, straight, upright ; *rectifolius*, with straight (*not curved*) leaves ; *rectinervis*, with straight nerves. **rectiusculus** (adj. A) : fairly straight. **rectus** (part. A) straight, upright, **350,388**

recurvatus (part. A), **recurvus** (adj. A) : recurved, curved backwards.

recutitus (adj. A) : apparently bare of epidermis, skinned.

red : ruber (adj. A). This term covers *cinnabarinus*, vermilion (H.C.C. 18),

scarlatinus, scarlet (H.C.C. 19), *sanguineus*, blood-red (H.C.C. 8.20), *ruber ribis*, currant-red (H.C.C. 8.21), *carmesinus*, crimson (H.C.C. 22), *cerasinus*, cherry-red (H.C.C. 7.22), *cardinalis*, cardinal-red (H.C.C. 8.22), and *ruber rosae*, rose-red (H.C.C. 7.24). The lighter tones of these are often described as ROSEUS. Through addition of blue they pass into *purpureus*, of yellow into *aurantiacus*; *caulis ruber*, stem red ; *corolla rubra*, corolla red ; *folia subtus rubra*, leaves red beneath ; *baccis rubris*, with red berries ; *see* RUBER, RUBINEUS, etc. **red-** : *in L. comp.*, rubri-, rubro-, *in Gk. comp.*, erythro-, rhodo- ; *rubrocinctus, rubrolimbatus, rubromarginatus*, red-margined ; *erythrorrhizus*, with red roots ; *erythrophyllus, rubrifolius*, red-leaved ; *erythrostictus, rubropunctatus*, red-dotted ; *erythroneurus, rubronervis*, red-nerved ; *rhodo-* used strictly indicates rose-red, *erythro-* any red.

redactus (part. A) : reduced, diminished ; *folia anisophylla, normalia petiolata valde obliqua, redacta inferiora normalibus similia, superiora sessilia basi cordata*, leaves anisophyllous, the normal ones stalked very oblique, the lower reduced ones similar to the normal ones, the upper reduced ones sessile cordate at base.

reddening : rubescens (part. B).

reddish : rubellus (adj. A), rubens (part. B), rufus (adj. A).

redivivus (adj. A) : reviving from a dry state, living again.

redolens (part. A) : diffusing an odour, scented ; *see* ODORATUS.

reduced : deminutus (part. A), redactus (part. A), reductus (part. A) ; *figurae dimidia parte magnitudinis naturalis deminutae sunt*, the figures are reduced to half natural size.

reduncus (adj. A) : curved *or* bent backwards.

referens (part. B) : representing, referring to, calling to mind.

refertus (part. A) : crammed, filled full ; *see* FARCTUS.

reflexus (part. A) : reflexed, bent abruptly backwards at more than 90°.

Refluxus (s.m. IV) : ebb, back flow ; cf. TIDE.

reformandus (gerundive of *reformo*) : to be reformed ; needing revision.

refractive : refractivus (adj. A).

refractus (part. A) : bent *or* curved back abruptly and strongly.

refringens (part. B) : breaking up, breaking open.

Refugium (s.n. II) : refuge.

Regio (s.f. III. vi) : region, usu. of indefinite extent, tract, province.

Region : regio (s.f. III. vi). In morphology it is often best translated by *pars* (s.f. III), 'part'.

Regma (s.n. III. xi) : regma, a fruit with elastically dehiscing segments or cocci as in Euphorbia.

Regnum (s.n. II) : kingdom.

regularis (adj. B) : regular, actinomorphic, having all the parts of each series uniform ; *flores regulares et symmetrici*, flowers regular and symmetrical. **98**

regularly : ordinate (adv.), ordinatim (adv.), regulatim (adv.).

rejectus (part. A) : rejected, cast off.

rejiciendus (gerundive of *rejicio*) : fit to be cast out, to be rejected ; *nomina generica rejicienda*, generic names to be rejected.

related : affinis (adj. B), cognatus (part. A).

relatively : relative (adv.), comparate (adv.), pro ratione.

released : liberatus (part. A).

relictus (part. A) : left behind.

Reliquiae (s.f. I. pl.) : remains, relics, remnants. **reliquus** (adj. A) : remaining.

remanens (part. B) : remaining behind, staying, abiding, persisting.

remarkable : *see* NOTABLE.

Remnant : vestigium (s.n. II), reliquiae (s.f. I pl.).

remotiusculus (adj. A) : somewhat scattered. **remotus** (adj. A) : scattered, remote, not close together ; used of gills that do not reach the stem but leave a free space around it ; cf. DISTANT, PARUS, SEPARATE. **499**

removed : amotus (part. A), demotus (part. A), divulsus (part. A), excussus (part. A), repurgatus (part. A).

reniformis (adj. B) : kidney-shaped. **125**

Renovatio (s.f. III. vi) : renewal shoot.

repandus (adj. A) : repand, having a slightly uneven and waved margin. **186**

repeatedly : iterum atque iterum (adv.), repetite (adv.), identidem (adv.).

repens (part. B) : creeping, prostrate and rooting ; *see* REPTANS.

Repertorium (s.n. II) : repertory. **repertus** (part. A) : found, discovered.

repletus (part. A) : filled full ; cf. FARCTUS, IMPLETUS, REFERTUS.

replicatus (adj. A) : turned or folded back upon itself so that the upper and lower parts come together ; (in Algae) with annular ingrowth of transverse walls of filaments. **373**

Replum : replum (s.n. II), *abl. sing.* replo.

representing : fingens (part. B), referens (part. B).

Reproduction : reproductio (s.f. III. vi), *gen. sing.* reproductionis, *abl. sing.*

reproductione. **reproductive** : reproductivus (adj. A) ; cf. MULTIPLICATION.

reptans (part. B) : creeping, prostrate and rooting (*see* REPENS) ; arching and then rooting (*see* SARMENTOSUS).

repullulans (part. B) : sprouting again, renewing growth.

repurgatus (part. A) : cleaned, cleansed, removed.

Res herbaria : botany ; *institutiones rei herbariae*, elements of botany.

Research : investigatio (s.f. III. vi).

Resemblance : similitudo (s.f. III. vi). **resembling** : similis (adj. B), simulans (part. B), ad instar (n. indecl. with gen.) ; *fructus forma atque magnitudine fructum Citri aurantifoliae simulans*, fruit by its shape and size the fruit of Citrus aurantifolia imitating.

Residue : reliquiae (s.f. I. pl.), residuum (s.n. II) ; *collo in speciminibus vetustioribus residuis vaginarum subfibrosis comato*, with the collar (neck) in the older specimens by the almost fibrous remains of the sheath clothed as if with hair ; *caudex apice reliquiis foliorum emortuorum marcidis laceratis brunneis involucratus*, root-stock at the tip with the withered tattered brown remains of dead leaves wrapped.

resiliens (part. B) : springing back.

Resine : resina (s.f. I). **resine-producing** : resinifer (adj. A) ; *canales resiniferi*, resin ducts. **resinous** : resinaceus (adj. A), resinosus (adj. A).

resorptus (part. A) : absorbing again ; *sulco resorpto marginali laterali*, with absorption channel on the side of the margin.

Respectus (s.m. IV) : regard, respect, consideration ; *respectu*, with regard to.

respondens (part. B) : answering, answering to, corresponding with.

rest, for the : cetero (adv.).

resting : quiescens (part. B), quietus (adj. A), dormiens (part. B) ; *sporae quiescentes*, resting spores ; *cellula in statu quieto*, cell in the resting state.

restricted : restrictus (part. A).

restrictus (part. A) : tight, close, restricted.

resupinatus (part. A) : resupinate, reversed, inverted by twisting of stalk, turned upside down or apparently so. **resupinus** (adj. A) ; bent back *or* backwards. **404**

retaining : retinens (part. B). **retained** : retentus (part. A).

Rete (s.n. III. x) : network ; *rete venularum*, network of veinlets ; cf. RETICULUM.

retentus (part. A) : retained.

reticulate (adv.), **reticulatim** (adv.) : reticulately, like a network. **reticulato-venosus** (adj. A) : net-veined. **reticu-**

latus (adj. A) reticulate, netted, marked with a network; *cormus tunicis demum in fibras reticulatas brunneas solutis*, corm with tunics as length into brown reticulate fibres breaking up ; *folia utrinque et praesertim subtus manifeste reticulata*, leaves on both sides and especially below obviously reticulate. **Reticulum** (s.n. II): network; cf. RETE. **retiformis** (adj. B): net-like. **246**

Retinaculum: retinaculum (s.n. II), *abl. sing.* retinaculo ; *retinaculum crassum, parte majore superiore a dorso visa late triangulari acuta, parte inferiore cuneata*, retinaculum thick, with the larger upper part seen from the back broadly triangular acute, with the lower part cuneate.

retinens (part. B) : keeping back, retaining.

retinervis (adj. B), **retinervius** (adj. A) : reticulately nerved. **360**

Retort-cell: cellula (s.f. I) lageniformis (adj. B) poro apicali.

retortus (part. A) : twisted *or* bent back.

retractus (part. A) : drawn back (*as of an embryo hidden between the cotyledons*).

retro (adv.) : backwards.

retrocurvatus (adj. A), **retrocurvus** (adj. A) : curved back. **retroflexus** (part. A) : bent back, reflexed ; cf. REFLEXUS. **retrorsum** (adv.), **retrorsus** (adv.) : backwards. **retrorsus** (adj. A) : retrorse, turned backwards. **retroserratus** (adj. A) : saw-edged with teeth pointing towards base ; cf. RUNCINATUS. **411, 419**

retusus (part. A) : retuse, i.e. with rounded shallowly notched end. **155**

revealed: detectus (part. A), manifestus (adj. A), indicatus (part. A).

revera (abl. sing. of *res vera*) : in fact, truly, actually.

reversus (part. A) : turned about, reversed.

Revisio (s.f. III. vi) : revision ; *revisio critica generis Epimedii*, critical revision of the genus Epimedium.

revocans (part. B) : recalling : *in mentem revocans*, recalling to mind ; *in memoriam revocans*, recalling to mind.

revolubilis (adj. B) : capable of being rolled back, of becoming revolute. **revolutivus** (adj. A) : (*in aestivation*) when the two edges of facing leaves are rolled back.

revolutus (part. A) : revolute, rolled back from edge (i.e. towards the lower side) *or* tip ; cf. INVOLUTUS. **366, 400**

Rhacheola (s.f. I), **Rhachilla** (s.f. I) : *see* RACHILLA.

Rhachis (s.f. III. ii): *see* RACHIS.

Rhaphe (s.f. III) : *see* RAPHE.

Rhaphid : *see* RAPHID.

rheo- : *in Gk. comp.*, pertaining to flowing water; *rheophilus*, loving rivers, etc.

Rhipidium : rhipidium (s.n. II), *acc. sing.* rhipidium, *abl. sing.* rhipidio.

rhiz-, rhizi- : *in Gk. comp.*, pertaining to roots or root-like organs; *rhizanthus*, flowering on the root or seeming to do so ; *rhizocarpus*, fruiting on the roots or seeming to do so ; *rhizomorphus*, root-like, root-shaped ; *rhizophilus*, root-loving, living on roots ; *rhizophorus*, root-bearing ; *rhizophyllus*, producing roots from the leaves.

Rhizina (s.f. I) : rhizine, fastening organ on lower side of lichen thallus, root-hair of moss, root-like hair of fungi ; *rhizinis numerosis*, with rhizines numerous.

Rhizoid : rhizoideum (s.n. II), *gen. sing.* rhizoidei, *abl. sing.* rhizoideo, *nom. pl.* rhizoidea, *gen. pl.* rhizoideorum, *abl. pl.* rhizoideis.

Rhizoma (s.n. III. xi) : *see* RHIZOME.

rhizomatosus (adj. A) : provided with a well-developed rhizome.

Rhizome: rhizoma (s.n. III), *gen. sing.* rhizomatis, *abl. sing,* rhizomate, *abl. pl.* rhizomatibus ; *rhizoma elongatum tenuissimum 3 mm. crassum flavidum*, rhizome elongated very slender 3 mm. thick yellowish ; *rhizoma adscendens, crassitudine valde inaequali, partes juniores plerumque 5 mm. adultae ad 18 mm. incrassatae, qua ex causa rhizoma stirpium veterum saepissime nodosum vel gangliosum*, rhizome ascending, with the thickness very uneven, the younger parts commonly 5 mm. the mature to 18 mm. thickened, from which reason the rhizome of old plants most often nodose or full of swellings ; *herba perennis rhizomate brevi crasso*, herb perennial with rhizome short thick ; *innovationes rhizomatis elongatae graciles*, new growths of rhizome elongated slender ; *bulbus cylindricus rhizomati brevi descendenti insidens*, bulb cylindric upon a short descending rhizome seated.

Rhizomorph: rhizomorpha (s.f. I), *abl. sing.* rhizomorpha, *nom. pl.* rhizomorphae, *abl. pl.* rhizomorphis.

Rhizophore: rhizophorum (s.n. II), *abl. sing.* rhizophoro, *nom. pl.* rhizophora, *abl. pl.* rhizophoris.

rhodo- : *in Gk. comp.*, rose-, rosy-red; *rhodanthus*, rosy-flowered ; *rhodocarpus*, rosy-fruited ; *rhodochilus*, rosy-lipped ; *rhodochrous*, rosy-coloured ; *rhodopetalus*, rosy-petalled ; *rhodospathus*, rosy-spathed ; *rhodospermus*, rosy-seeded ; cf. ERYTHRO-, RED-.

Rhodologia (s.f. I) : the study of roses (Rosa).

rhombic: rhombeus (adj. A), rhombicus (adj. A), rhombiformis (adj. B). The

B.L.—R

forms *rhomboideus* (adj. A) and *rhomboidalis* (adj. B) are to be avoided; cf. -OIDES. **118**

rhopalo- : *in Gk. comp.*, club-, cudgel- ; cf. CLAVATUS, CLUB-, CORYNE-.

rhyac- : *in Gk. comp.*, pertaining to rushing streams, torrents; *rhyacophilus*, torrent-loving.

rhynch-, rhyncho- : *in Gk. comp.*, provided with a snout or beak, i.e. a projecting appendage; *rhynchantherus*, with beaked anthers ; *rhynchocarpus*, with beaked fruits.

rhyti-, rhytido- : *in Gk. comp.*, wrinkled, rumpled ; *rhytidophyllus*, with wrinkled leaves ; *rhytidospermus*, *rhytispermus*, with wrinkled seeds; cf. RUGOSUS.

Rib : costa (s.f. I) (*usually applied to midrib of leaf*), stria (s.f. I) (*used of cryptogams*) ; cf. VEINING. **ribbed** : costatus (adj. A), nervatus (adj. A). **343, 344**

Ribbon : taenia (s.f. I).

rice-like : oryziformis (adj. B).

rich : dives (adj. B).

Rictus (s.m. IV) : an opened mouth.

Ridge : crista (s.f. I) *lit.* 'crest' ; dorsum (s.n. II) *lit.* 'back' ; jugum (s.n. II), *lit.* 'yoke' ; porca (s.f. I), *lit.* 'ridge between two furrows made in plowing'. **ridged** : porcatus (adj. A).

rigens (part. B) : stiff, rigid, unbendable. **rigescens** (part. B) : rigescent, rather stiff, becoming stiff.

right (adj.) : rectus (part. A) 'straight, correct' ; dexter (adj. A) 'opposite to left'. **right, to the** : dextrorsum (adv.). **rightly** : recte (adv.), rite (adv.).

rigid : rigidus (adj. A), rigens (part. B). **rigidly** : rigide (adv.). **rigidiusculus** (adj. A), **rigidulus** (adj. A) : somewhat rigid.

Rima (s.f. I) : cleft, fissure, chink, crack. **rimiformis** (adj. B) : shaped like a cleft. **rimosus** (adj. A) : full of cracks, marked with numerous cracks.

Ring : annulus (s.m. II). **ring-shaped** : annularis (adj. B), annuliformis (adj. B). **ringed** : annulatus (adj. A). **253**

ringens (part. B) : gaping. **67**

Ripa (s.f. I) : bank of stream or river. **riparius** (adj. A) : frequenting banks of streams *or* rivers, riverside.

ripe : maturus (adj. A). **Ripeness** : maturitas (s.f. III). **Ripening** : maturatio (s.f. III). **ripening** : maturescens (part. B).

rising : errigens (part. B).

rite (adv.) : properly, rightly, duly, correctly.

rivalis (adj. B) : pertaining to brooks.

rivalling : aemulans (part. B), aemulus (adj. A).

River : flumen (s.n. III. vi), *acc. sing.* flumen, *abl. sing.* flumine ; fluvius (s.m. II), *gen. sing.* fluvii ; *abl. sing.* fluvio ;

less often amnis (s.m. III. vii), *acc. sing.* amnem, *abl. sing.* amne. **pertaining to rivers** : fluvialis (adj. B), fluviaticus (adj. A), fluviatilis (adj. B), flumineus (adj. A), amnicus (adj. A); *in Gk. compounds*, potamo- ; *planta ad fluvii Negro cataractas lecta*, plant at cataracts of Rio Negro collected ; *in planitie ad fluvium Danuvium*, in level place at (by) the river Danube; *in sylvis ripariis humidis juxta flumen Amazonum, praecipue secus fluvios Pastasa Bombonasa etc.*, in damp riverside woods near the river Amazon, especially along the rivers Pastasa, Bombonasa, etc.; *ad fluminis Amazonum affluentes inferiores*, at lower tributaries of the river Amazon.

river-loving : potamophilus (adj. A).

rivularis (adj. B) : pertaining to brooklets.

rivulosus (adj. A) : having fine wavy grooves.

Rivulus (s.m. II) : brooklet, rivulet.

Rivus (s.m. II) : brook, small stream.

Road : via (s.f. I).

roaming : erraticus (adj. A), vagus (adj. A).

robust : robustus (adj. A), validus (adj. A).

Rock : petra (s.f. I), *abl. sing.* petra, *abl. pl.* petris 'rock, crag' ; rupes (s.f. III. viii), *abl. sing.* rupe, *abl. pl.* rupibus 'steep rock, cliff' ; scopulus (s.m. II), *abl. sing.* scopulo, *abl. pl.* scopulis 'pointed *or* projecting rock, cliff, crag' ; saxum (s.n. II), *abl. sing.* saxo, *abl. pl.* saxis 'large stone, detached rock'. *inter saxa rupesque*, among stones and rocks ; *habitat in rupibus calcareis*, it lives on limestone rocks ; cf. CAUTES.

rock- : *in L. comp.*, rupi-, saxi-, *in Gk. comp.*, litho-, petro- ; *petrophyes, rupicola*, growing on rocks. **rock-dwelling** : petraeus (adj. A), petrensis (adj. B), rupestris (adj. B), saxatilis (adj. B). **rocky** : petrosus (adj. A), rupestris (adj. B), saxeus (adj. B), saxosus (adj. A), scopulosus (adj. A).

Rod : virga (s.f. I). **rod-shaped** : bacilliformis (adj. B), bacillaris (adj. B).

rolled back : revolutus (part. A). **rolled inward** : involutus (part. A).

Roof : tectum (s.n. II), *gen. pl.* tectorum.

Root : radix (s.f. III. i), *acc. sing.* radicem, *gen. sing.* radicis, *abl. sing.* radice, *nom.* and *acc. pl.* radices, *gen. pl.* radicum, *dat* and *abl. pl.* radicibus ; *radix longa crassiuscula caulem singulum edens*, root long moderately thick putting forth a single stem ; *herba biennis radice dauciformi*, herb biennial with root carrot-like ; *radice crassa descendente, fibris numerosis tenuibus*, with (main) root thick descending, with fibrous roots numerous slender ; *radices pigmentiferae, calyptris* *acutis, seriatim fasciculatae, usque ad 17, quarum primae 3-5 folium rudimentale perforantes, ceterae liberae,* roots pigmented, the root-caps acute, clustered in rows, up to 17, of which the first 3-5 pierce through the rudimentary leaf, the rest free; *habitat ad radices arborum,* it lives at *or* on the roots of trees; *caulis elongatus radices numerosas flexuosas ramosas laeves 3-4 mm. diametro emittens,* stem elongated sending forth roots numerous somewhat zigzag branched smooth 3-4 mm. in diameter; *radicibus paucis fusiformibus ad 1 cm. crassis albis,* with roots few fusiform to 1 cm. thick white; *fasciculus fibrovasalis totam radicis longitudinem percurrens,* fibrovascular bundle running down the whole length of the root.

rooted, provided with roots: radicatus (part. A). **rooting, putting forth roots:** radicans (part. B); *caules subterranei repentes ad nodos radicantes,* stems subterranean creeping rooting at the nodes.

Rootlet: radicella (s.f. I), *nom. pl.* radicellae, *acc. pl.* radicellas, *abl. pl.* radicellis; *radicellae solitariae vel marginales 4-5nae,* rootlets solitary or marginal 4-5 together; *caulis basi radicellas multas emittens,* stem at the base many rootlets putting forth; *radices paucae attenuatae, radicellis nullis vel sparsis,* roots few attenuate, with rootlets none or sparse.

Rootstock: caudex (s.m. III), *gen. sing.* caudicis; caulorhiza (s.f. I), *gen. sing.* caulorhizae; *caudex multiceps lignosus, caudiculis brevibus,* rootstock manyheaded woody, with short divisions.

Rope: funis (s.m. III), funiculus (s.m. II). **rope-like:** funicularis (adj. B), funiformis (adj. B), funiculosus (adj. A), funalis (adj. B). **48**

roridus (adj. A): bedewed, dewy, appearing as if covered with fine dewdrops. **303**

rosaceus (adj. A): like the flower of a single rose (Rosa), i.e. with 5 outspread petals and many stamens. **504**

rose: roseus (adj. A); erubescens (part. B) 'reddening' has the same meaning. **rose-, rosy-:** *in L. comp.,* rosei-, roseo-, *in Gk. comp.,* rhod-, rhodo-; *roseocinctus, rhodocraspedus,* rosy-edged; *roseiflorus, rhodanthus,* rosy-flowered; *roseiflorus* should not be confused with *rosiflorus* or, less correctly, *rosaeflorus,* 'having flowers like a rose'. **roseolus** (adj. A): pink, pale rose.

Rosette: rosula (s.f. I), *abl. sing.* rosula, *nom. pl.* rosulae, *abl. pl.* rosulis. The alternative form *rosella* (s.f. I) is rarely used; *foliorum rosula sempervirens c. 10 cm. diametro;* rosette of leaves ever-

green c. 10 cm. across; *caulis infra rosulam terminalem foliorum vivorum foliis mortuis vestitus,* stem below terminal rosette of living leaves with dead leaves clothed. **rosetted:** rosularis (adj. B), rosulatus (adj. A), rosulans (adj. B); *folia ad apicem caulis rosulata,* leaves at tip of stem in a rosette; *caulis folia rosularia superans,* stem overtopping the rosette-leaves; *folium caulinum foliis rosularibus simile,* stem-leaf similar to the rosette-leaves; *lamina foliorum rosularium glauca,* blade of rosette-leaves glaucous. **485**

rostellatus (adj. A): somewhat beaked, provided with a short beak. **Rostellum:** rostellum (s.n. II), *abl. sing.* rostello. **rostratus** (adj. A): beaked, provided with a long beak. **rostriformis** (adj. B): beak-like. **Rostrum** (s.n. II): beak. **-rostris** (adj. B), **-rostrus** (adj. A). *in L. comp.,* -beaked; *brevirostris,* short-beaked; *longirostris,* long-beaked; *tenuirostris,* slender-beaked. **148**

Rosula (s.f. I): rosette, q.v. **rosulans** (adj. B), **rosulatim** (adv.): in the form of a rosette. **rosulatus** (adj. A): rosetted, rosulate, provided with *or* in the form of a rosette. **485**

rotatus (adj. A): wheel-shaped. Used of a gamopetalous corolla with a spreading almost flat and circular limb and a very short tube. **69**

rotten, rotting: putrefactus (part. A), putridus (adj. A), putrescens (part. B), cariosus (adj. A); *ad lignum cariosum,* on rotten wood; *in ligno putrescente,* in rotting wood; *in ramis siccis vel putridis,* on dry or rotting branches; *ad caules plantarum putridos,* on rotten stems of plants.

rotundatus (part. A): rounded. **153, 172**

rotundus (adj. A): almost circular, with length to breadth about 6 to 5. **111**

rough: asper (adj. A), exasperatus (part. A), scaber (adj. A). **roughly (approximately):** plusminusve (adv.). **Roughness:** asperitas (s.f. III. ii). **266**

round in outline: rotundus (adj. A), q.v., circularis (adj. B), orbiculatus (adj. A). **round and solid:** globosus (adj. A), sphaericus (adj. A). **4, 110, 111**

rounded: rotundatus (part. A).

Row: series (s.f. V), q.v. **in rows:** serialis (adj. B), seriatus (adj. A), seriatim (adv.); cf. -FARIUS, -STICHUS. **489**

rubbed: tritus (part. A).

Rubbish dump: ruderatum (s.n. II), *abl. pl.* ruderatis; *species in ruderatis et hominum domiciliorum vicinis inveniuntur,* the species on rubbish dumps and in vicinity of the dwellings of men are found ; *circa ruderata et hominum domilicia sedem figunt,* around rubbish dumps and dwellings of men they fix their abode.

rubellus (adj. A) : reddish.

rubens (part. B) : reddish.

ruber (adj. A) : red ; *calyx ruber,* calyx red ; *corolla rubra,* corolla red ; *corollae limbus in aestivatione rubescens, sub anthesi ruber, postremo rubro-violaceus,* limb of corolla in aestivation reddening, at anthesis red, finally red-violet ; *folium subtus rubrum,* leaf red beneath ; *floribus rubris,* with red flowers. **rubescens** (part. B) : turning red, reddening. **rubicundus** (adj. A) : red, ruddy. **rubidus** (adj. A) : red. **rubiginosus** (adj. A) : rusty-red ; *see* FERRUGINEUS. **rubineus** (adj. A) : ruby-red (H.C.C. 8. 27). **rubr-, rubro-** : *in* L. *comp.,* red- ; *see* RED-.

ruby-red : rubineus (adj. A).

ruddy : rubicundus (adj. A).

ruderalis (adj. B) : growing among rubbish. **Ruderatum** (s.n. II) : rubble, rubbish dump, q.v.

Rudiment : rudimentum (s.n. II), *abl. sing.* rudimento. **rudimentary** : rudimentalis (adj. B), rudimentarius (adj. A).

rufus (adj. A) : reddish.

Ruga (s.f. I) : wrinkle or fold. **rugiformis** (adj. B) : wrinkle-like. **rugulosus** (adj. A) : somewhat wrinkled. **rugosus** (adj. A), **rugatus** (part. A) : wrinkled, rugose. **245**

ruined : destructus (part. A). **ruining** : destruens (part. B). **ruinous** ; ruinosus (adj. A)

ruminatus (adj. A) : ruminate, i.e. very uneven and looking as if chewed ; *albumen durum copiose plicato-ruminatum,* albumen hard copiously folded and ruminate. **242**

rumpens (part. B) : bursting, tearing, breaking open *or* through irregularly.

runcinatus (adj. A) : runcinate, i.e. pinnatifid *or* coarsely serrate with teeth pointing towards the base ; cf. RETROSERRATUS. **130**

Runner : sarmentum (s.n. II), *abl. sing.* sarmento, *nom. pl.* sarmenta, *abl. pl.* sarmentis ; stolo (s.m. III. vi), *abl. sing.* stolone, *nom. pl.* stolones, *abl. pl.* stolonibus ; flagellum (s.n. II), *abl. sing.* flagello, *nom. pl.* flagella, *abl. pl.* flagellis. These are used for long slender aboveground lateral rooting shoots, the term *flagellum* or *sarmentum* being applied to a naked whip-like runner rooting and producing leaves at its tip, as in Fragaria, and *stolo* to a runner leafy its whole length, as in Ajuga, Gslechoma and Hieracium. The term *soboles* is used for

an underground runner, as in Aegopodium.

running : profluens (part. B) (*used only of water*), currens (part. B).

Rupes (s.f. III. viii) : rock, cliff ; cf. ROCK. **rupestris** (adj. B) : rocky, rock-dwelling. **ruptilis** (adj. B) : dehiscing irregularly. **rupturing** : rumpens (part. B). **ruptus** (part. A) : broken, burst asunder. **ruralis** (adj. B) : belonging to the country, rural ; cf. URBANUS.

rush-like : junceus (adj. A), junciformis (adj. B).

russet : russus (adj. A).

rusticanus (adj. A) : belonging to the country, rural.

rusty-red : ferrugineus (adj. A), rubiginosus (adj. A).

rutilans (part. B), **rutilus** (adj. A) : red with yellow admixture, reddish-orange.

S

Sabuleta (s.n. pl. II) : sandy places. **Sabulo** (s.m. III. vi) : coarse sand, gravel. **Sabulosum** (s.n. II) : sandy place. **sabulosus** (adj. A) : sandy, growing in sandy places.

saccatus (adj. A) : pouched, bag-shaped, saccate.

saccharatus (adj. A) : sugary, sugared, looking as if sprinkled with sugar. **saccharifer** (adj. A) : sugar-bearing. **saccharinus** (adj. A) : sugary. **Saccharosum** (s.n. II) : saccharose. **Saccharum** (s.n. II) : sugar.

sacciformis (adj. B) : bag-shaped, sac-shaped.

Sacculus (s.m. II) : a little sac, loculus of anther.

sad : tristis (adj. B). Applied to dull colours.

Saddle : ephippium (s.n. II), sella (s.f. I) ; *ephippii instar, similis ephippio,* resembling a saddle. **saddle-shaped** : ephippioideus (adj. A), ephippiomorphus (adj. A), selliformis (adj. B) ; *sella* (s.f. I) denotes many kinds of seat, *ephippium* a horse-saddle exclusively. **94**

saepe (adv.) : often. **saepenumero** (adv.) : again and again. **saepissime** (adv.) : very often, nearly always. **saepiuscule** (adv.) : fairly frequently.

Saepes (s.f. III.) : *see* SEPES.

saffron-yellow : croceus (adj. A).

sagittatus (adj. A), **sagittiformis** (adj. B) : sagittate, i.e. shaped like an arrow-head with two equal sharp basal lobes directed downwards. **126, 169**

Sal (s.m. III. v) : salt. **saline** : salsus (part. A), salinus (adj. A).

salient : prominens (part. B).

salignus (adj. A): willowy, willow-like.
saline: salinus (adj. A), salsus (part A).
Salinity: salsitudo (s.f. III).
salmoneus (adj. A): salmon-pink (H.C.C. 4.12).
Salsitudo (s.f. III): salinity.
salsuginosus (adj. A): growing in brackish places, i.e. within the reach of salt water.
salsus (part. A): salted, saline.
Salt: sal (s.m. III. v), gen. sing. salis, abl. sing. sale. salt-: in Gk. comp., hal-, hali-, halo-; halophilus, salt-loving. salted, salty: salinus (adj. A), salsus (part. A); salsugineus (adj. A) and salsuginosus (adj. A) refer to brackish places; species in littoribus et in desertis salsis obviae, species on shores and in salt deserts present; species littora lacuum salsorum habitantes, species the shores of salt lakes inhabiting; palus salsa, salt marsh.
saltem (adv.): at least, at all events; frutex saltem partibus vegetativis glaber, shrub at least as to vegetative parts glabrous.
Saltuarius (s.m. II): forester, forest officer.
saltuensis (adj. B): of or belonging to a forest.
Saltus (s.m. IV): forest pasture, woodland, valley, ravine, pass.
salver-shaped: hypocrateriformis (adj. B), hypocraterimorphus (adj. A).
Samara: samara (s.f. I), abl. sing. samara.
same, the: nom. sing. m. idem, f. eadem, n. idem (pron.): planta Jamaicensis eadem est ac planta Cubensis, the Jamaican plant is the same as the Cuban plant; color seminum in eadem planta variabilis, colour of seeds on the same plant variable; ex eadem insula, from the same island; in eodem rhizomate, on the same rhizome; longitudo quasi eadem atque in specie, the length almost the same as in the species; eodem modo ac in, the same as in; cf. TOT, TOTIDEM.
same time, at the: simul (adv.).
Sand: arena (s.f. I), sabulo (s.m. III. vi). sandy: arenarius (adj. A), arenosus (adj. A), sabulosus (adj. A). Sandy place: arenosum (s.n. II), sabulosum (s.n. II), sabuleta (s.n. II. pl.). sand: in Gk. comp., ammo-, psammo-, in L. comp., areni-; ammobius, arenicola, dwelling on sand; ammophilus, psammophilus, sand-loving. Sandstone: lapis (s.m. III) arenarius, saxum (s.n. II), arenaceum. sandy: arenaceus (adj. A).
sandal-shaped: soleiformis (adj. B).
sanguineus: (adj. A): blood-red.
Sap: succus (s.m. II). sappy: succosus (adj. A).
sapidus (adj. A): savoury, well-flavoured; cf. INSIPIDUS.

saponaceus (adj. A), saponarius (adj. A): soapy.
Sapor (s.m. III. v): taste, q.v.
saprophytic: saprophyticus (adj. A).
sarc-, sarco-: in Gk. comp., flesh-, fleshy; sarcanthus, with fleshy flowers; sarcophagus, devouring flesh.
Sarcocarp: sarcocarpium (s.n. II).
sarmentosus (adj. A): producing long runners. Sarmentum (s.n. II): long slender runner: see RUNNER, STOLON.
sat (adv.), satis (adv.): enough, sufficiently, moderately.
sativus (adj. A): sown, planted, cultivated; opp. of FERUS, SYLVESTRIS.
saturate (adv.): deeply, richly, fully. Applied to colours; opp. of DILUTE and PALLIDE.
saucer-shaped: acetabuliformis (adj. B), catilliformis (adj. B), patelliformis (adj. B), pateriformis (adj. B).
sausage-shaped: allantoideus (adj. A), botuliformis (adj. B), farciminiformis (adj. B). 88
Savanna: savanna (s.f. I).
saw-edged: serratus (adj. A). 182
saxatilis (adj. B): dwelling or found among rocks. Saxosa (s.n. pl. II): rocky or stony places. Saxum (s.n. II): large stone, detached rock; in saxis graniticis, on granitic rocks; cf. ROCK.
scaber (adj. A): scabrous, i.e. rough or gritty to the touch on account of numerous minute projections. scaberulus (adj. A), scabrellus (adj. A): minutely scabrous, slightly rough to the touch. scabri-: in L. comp., rough, scabrous; scabriflorus with scabrous flowers. scabridus (adj. A): somewhat scabrous. scabridiusculus (adj. A): minutely scabrous, slightly rough to the touch. scabrosus (adj. A): distinctly scabrous; cf. RADULANS. 266, 267
scalariformis (adj. B): having ladder-like markings or appearance. scalaris (adj. B): ladder-like.
Scale: squama (s.f. I), abl. sing. squama, nom. pl. squamae, abl. pl. squamis. scaled off: desquamatus (part. A). scaly: squamatus (adj. A), squamosus (adj. A), lepidotus (adj. A). 497
scalpelliformis (adj. B): shaped like a scalpel or lancet.
scalpratus (adj. A): having a sharp or cutting edge.
scalpturatus (adj. A): engraved, scratched.
scaly: see under Scale.
scandens (part. B): climbing; cf. TWINING.
scap-, scapi-: in L. comp., relating to a scape, i.e. a leafless or almost leafless peduncle or floral axis arising directly from the rootstock; scapiflorus, having

flowers on a scape; *scapifer, scapiger,* bearing a scape; *scapiformis,* resembling a scape; *scaposus,* having well-developed scapes.

Scape: scapus (s.m. II), *dat. and abl. sing.* scapo; *scapus robustus viridis glaber sursum angulatus, racemo laxo multifloro terminatus,* scape stout green glabrous angled above, by a loose many-flowered raceme terminated.

Scaphidium: scaphidium (s.n. II).

Scar: cicatrix (s.f. III. i), *abl. sing.* cicatrice, *nom. pl.* cicatrices, *abl. pl.* cicatricibus; *vibex* (s.f. IV) is rarely used; *rami cicatricibus foliorum delapsorum semiorbicularibus notati,* branches with semiorbicular scars of fallen leaves marked; cf. HILUM.

scarcely: vix (adv.), aegre (adv.); *vix* is generally used; *aegre* means 'reluctantly, with difficulty'.

scariosus (adj. A): scarious, i.e. of thin dry membranous texture and not green (*opp. of* HERBACEUS). **316**

scarlet: scarlatinus (adj. A), H.C.C. 19. More or less synonymous, as used by some authors, are *cinnabarinus, coccineus, miniatus.*

scarred: cicatricatus (adj. A), cicatricosus (adj. A). **252**

scatens (part. A with abl.): abounding with, gushing forth with.

scattered: dispersus (part. A), sparsus (part. A), displicatus (part. A), dissitus (adj. A), distans (part. B), remotus (part. A) 'being apart, well separated'. Opposite of *aggregatus, approximatus, confertus, creber, spissus,* and of special terms such as *oppositus, ternatus, verticillatus.* **Scattering**: dispersio (s.f. III).

scattering: spargens (part. B). **481**

scaturiginus (adj. A): relating to springs of water. **Scaturigo** (s.f. III. vi): gushing *or* bubbling water, a spring.

sceleratus (part. A): wicked, hurtful, poisonous; cf. NOXIUS.

Sceletus (s.m. II): skeleton; *nervi sceletum folii constituunt,* the nerves constitute the skeleton of the leaf.

Scheda (s.f. I), **Schedula** (s.f. I): sheet of paper, *hence* label; *in scheda,* on an herbarium label; *schedae ad floram exsiccatam Austro-Hungaricam,* labels to the dried Austro-Hungarian flora, i.e. to dried specimens of the Austro-Hungarian flora.

schist-, schisto-: *in Gk. comp.,* split, cleft, deeply divided; *schistoglossus,* with a split tongue, i.e. labellum; *polyschistus,* much divided; cf. SCHIZ-.

schistaceus (adj. A): relating to schistaceous rocks, slaty, slate-grey.

schiz-, schizo-: *in Gk. comp.,* split, cleft, deeply divided; *schizochilus,* with a split lip; *schizopetalus,* with deeply cut petals; cf. SCHIST-.

Schizocarp: schizocarpium (s.n. II).

Schola (s.f. I): lecture, debate, disputation.

scilicet (adv.): evidently, certainly, of course, that is to say.

scissus (part. A): torn. **Scissura** (s.f. I): split, cleft, longitudinal narrow opening; cf. FISSURE.

scitulus (adj. A): pretty, neat, trim; cf. CONCINNUS.

scler-, sclero-: *in Gk. comp.,* hard-.

Scleranthium: scleranthium (s.n. II).

Sclerenchyma: sclerenchyma (s.n. III), *abl. sing.* sclerenchymate.

scleroideus (adj. A), **scleroticus** (adj. A): sclerotic, hardened, of stony texture.

Sclerotium: sclerotium (s.n. II), *abl. sing.* sclerotio, *nom. pl.* sclerotia, *abl. pl.* sclerotiis.

scobiculatus (adj. A), **scobiformis** (adj. B): in fine grains like sawdust, having the appearance of sawdust.

scoparie (adv.): in the form of a broom, i.e. fastigiately.

scopatus (adj. A): densely covered with bristly hairs. **scopiformis** (adj. B), **scopulatus** (adj. A): like a broom or brush.

Scopulus (s.m. II): pointed rock, cliff, crag; cf. ROCK.

scorpioid: scorpioideus (adj. A), scorpioides (adj. B); *inflorescentia dichotome cymosa, cymae ramis scorpioideis, vel cymae ad racemum simplicem scorpioideum reductae,* inflorescence dichotomously cymose, with branches of the cymes scorpioid, or cymes to a simple scorpioid raceme reduced.

Scrap: frustillum (s.n. II), fragmentum (s.n. II) mancum.

scraped: rasilis (adj. B).

scratched: sculpturatus (adj. A).

Scree: glara (s.f. I) adapted from Spanish, scritha (s.f. I) adapted from Old Norse; *glara vel scritha est clivus alpestris saxis deorsum conjectis coopertus,* a scree is an alpine slope wholly covered by rocks thrown downwards.

Scriptum (s.n. II): written matter. **scriptus** (part. A): written. **scripsit** (3rd pers. perf. indic. of *scribo*): 'he has written it'.

Scritha (s.f. I): scree, q.v.

scrobicularis (adj. B), **scrobiculatus** (adj. A): marked by numerous small pits or depressions, minutely pitted; distinct from LACUNOSUS, with large pits: cf. FOVEOLATUS, PUNCTATUS. **Scrobiculus** (s.m. II): pit, depression. **Scrobis** (s.m. III): ditch, trench. **248**

scrotiformis (adj. B): pouch-shaped. **84**
Sculptura (s.f. I): sculpturing relief, carving out of surface.
sculptus (part. A): engraved, carved out.
scurfy: furfuraceus (adj. A).
scutatus (adj. A), scutiformis (adj. B): shield-shaped, q.v. **19**
Scutellum: scutellum (s.m. II), *abl. sing.* scutello; *scutellum dimidiam partem caryopsis aequans,* scutellum a half part of the caryopsis equalling; *see* CARYOPSIS.
Scutula (s.f. I): scutula.
scyph-, scyphi-, scypho-: *in Gk. and L. comp.,* cup-; *scyphifer, scyphiger,* cup-bearing; *scyphocalyx* with a cup-like calyx; *scyphiformis, scyphoides,* cup-like.
Scyphulus: scyphulus (s.m. II).
Scyphus: scyphus (s.m. II), scypha (s.f. I).
Sea: mare (s.n. III. x), *gen. sing.* maris, *abl. sing.* mari (*rarely* mare); *in Mari Antillarum,* in the Caribbean Sea: *in Mare Septentrionali et Baltico,* in the North Sea and the Baltic Sea; *solum maris,* bottom of the sea; cf. MARITIMUS, PELAGICUS.
sea-green: glaucus (adj. A), thalassicus (adj. A).
Sea-shore: littus (s.n. III), *nom. pl.* littora. **pertaining to the sea-shore:** littoralis (adj. B).
Season: tempus (s.n. IV) anni; *ver, aestas, autumnus, hiems sunt tempora anni,* spring, summer, autumn, winter are the seasons of the year.
seated upon: insidens (part. B) (*usu. with dat., rarely with acc.*); *bulbis rhizomati horizontali repenti ramoso insidentibus,* with bulbs on a horizontal creeping rhizome seated ; cf. SESSILIS.
sebaceus (adj. A): tallowy, with appearance and consistency of tallow. **sebifer** (adj. A): wax-bearing. **sebosus** (adj. A): greasy.
sec.: *see* SECUNDUM.
secedens (part. B): splitting apart, at first attached but later separating.
secernens: (part. B): secreting, separating off.
secessus: (part. A): put aside, removed.
second: secundus (adj. A), alter (adj. A).
secondary: secundarius (adj. A), partialis (adj. B); *radii primarii 2-5, secundarii etiam ad 8,* primary rays 2-5, secondary ones furthermore up to 8.
secreting: secernens (part. B); *cellulae mucilaginem secernentes,* cells secreting mucilage. **Secretion:** secretio (s.f. III. vi). **secretory:** secretorius (adj. A).
sectilis (adj. B): cut into small pieces.
Section: sectio (s.f. III. vi), *gen. sing.*

sectionis, *abl. sing.* sectione, *nom. and acc. pl.* sectiones, *dat. and abl. pl.* sectionibus; *revisio specierum sectionis Brachyspathae,* revision of species of section Brachyspatha; *cellulae in sectione transversali ellipticae,* cells in transverse section elliptic.
sectus (part. A): cut; *in L. comp.,* divided to the base; *pinnatisectus,* pinnately divided; *trisectus,* divided into three segments.
secundum (prep. with acc.): according to, following, depending on; *sec. auct. plur., secundum auctores plures,* according to many (more) authors; *secundum iconem Plumieranam,* according to Plumier's illustration.
secundus (adj. A): next, following, second; secund, i.e. having organs (leaves, flowers, etc.) turned towards the same side. **409, 490**
secus (prep. with acc.): along, on; *secus rhachim,* along the rachis; *secus nervos et venas,* along the nerves and the veins. **-secus:** *in L. comp.,* -side; *altrinsecus,* on the other side; *circumsecus,* on all sides; *utrinsecus* on both sides.
sed (conj.): but, yet.
sedecim (num. adj.): sixteen.
sedentarius (adj. A): sedentary, stationary.
Sedes (s.f. III): seat, abode, place, position; *species sedis dubiae (incertae sedis),* species of uncertain position.
Sediment: sedimentum (s.n. II).
Seed: semen (s.n. III), *gen. sing.* seminis, *abl. sing.* semine, *nom. pl.* semina, *gen. pl.* seminum, *abl. pl.,* seminibus; *semen globosum, testa nigra fragili, cotyledonibus margine tantum coalitis, embryone minuto,* seed globose, with seed-coat black fragile, with cotyledons at the margin alone joined together, with embryo minute; *semina tota pilis longis hygrometricis vestita,* seeds entirely in long water-absorbing hairs clothed; *semina compressa dorso convexa, tuberculis seriatis scabra, facie concava laevia,* seeds compressed on the back convex, rough with tubercules in rows, on the front concave smooth; *semina brunnea fere tota pilis madefactis elastice erigentibus vestita,* seeds brown almost entirely with hairs when made wet elastically raising themselves clothed; *semina parva uniserialia aut biserialia globosa aut pyriformia exalata, funiculo circa hilum in arillum album cristatum expanso,* seeds small in 1 series or in 2 series globose or pear-shaped wingless, with the funicle around the hilum into a white crested aril expanded; *semina oblique ovata, pleraque latere altero*

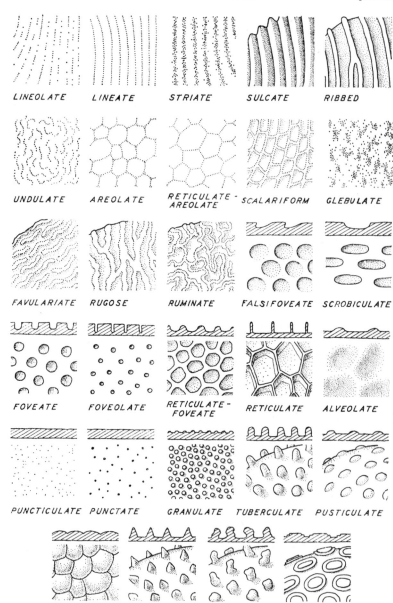

Fig. 38   Types of Surfaces of Seeds
(Drawing by Margaret R. Murley, from *American Midland Naturalist*,
46; 1951)

convexa, altero acutata, sed saepius mutua pressione multiangulata, seeds obliquely ovate, for the most part with one side convex, the other acutate, but very often on account of mutual pressure, many-angled. seeded- : in L. comp., -seminalis, in Gk. comp., -spermus; capsula quadriseminalis, capsula tetrasperma, capsule four-seeded. Usually it is best simply to use numerals, e.g. capsula 2-4-seminalis, capsula seminibus 2-4, capsula semina 2-4 habens. See -SPERMUS. seed-bearing : seminiger (adj. A), seminifer (adj. A).

Seed-bed : seminarium (s.n. II).

Seed-coat, outer : testa (s.f. I), abl. sing. testa. In texture it may be cartilaginea (adj. A), i.e. hard and tough, crustacea (adj. A), i.e. thin, hard and brittle, mucilaginosa or mucosa (adj. A), i.e. mucilaginous, when moist (madida) or made wet (madefacta). For description of surface the following glossary has been compiled from M. R. Murley, 'Seeds of the Cruciferae', Amer. Midl. Nat. 46: 1-81 (1951): aculeate (aculeata, adj. A), i.e. bristly with small pointed projections; alveolate (alveolata, adj. A), i.e. honey-combed, the elevation not rounded off, the depression or area outlined by the elevation being called an insterstice (interstitium, s.n. II); areolate (areolata, adj. A), marked off into little rounded areas by fine lines; colliculate (colliculata, adj. A), i.e. with rounded broad elevations closely spaced covering the seed-coat; falsifoveate (falsifoveata, adj. A), i.e. with pits that do not have the same depth throughout, as a little depression made laterally; favulariate (favulariata ; adj. A), i.e. with the surface finely ribbed, the ribs separated by zigzag furrows; foveate (foveata, adj. A), i.e. pitted; foveolate (foveolata, adj. A), i.e. marked with little pits; furrowed (sulcata, adj. A); glebulate (glebulata, adj. A), i.e. with small clumps of irregularly placed granules; lineate (lineata, adj. A), i.e. marked with fine lines; lineolate (lineolata, adj. A), marked with fine broken lines; punctate (punctata, adj. A), i.e. marked with dots looking like pencil marks variously scattered; puncticulate (puncticulata, adj. A), i.e. minutely punctate, the surface being almost smooth; ocellate (ocellata, adj. A), i.e. having eye-like depressions, each with a raised circular border; pusticulate (pusticulata, adj. A), i.e. with small broad slight elevations not so high or abundant as on a colliculate surface and

not having as abrupt elevations as a minutely tuberculate surface; reticulate (reticulata, adj. A), i.e. with a raised network of narrow and sharply angled lines frequently presenting a geometric appearance, each area or depression outlined by the reticulum being an interspace (interstitium, s.n. II, interspatium, s.n. II); reticulate-foveate (retifoveata, adj. A), i.e. intermediate between reticulate and foveate; rugose (rugosa, adj. A), i.e. wrinkled, the irregular elevation making up the wrinkles and running mostly in one direction; rugulose (rugulosa, adj. A), i.e. with very small wrinkles; ruminate (ruminata, adj. A), i.e. penetrated by irregular channels giving an eroded appearance and running in different directions; scalariform (scalariformis, adj. B), i.e. with small fairly regular cross-band markings suggesting the steps of a ladder; scrobiculate (scrobiculata, adj. A), i.e. with elongated shallow depressions or pits; smooth (laevis, adj. B) and glossy (nitida, adj. A) if polished (polita, adj. A); striate (striata, adj. A), i.e. marked with a series of fine narrow parallel bands (striae, s.f. I pl.) wider than the lines of a lineate surface; sulcate (sulcata, adj. A), i.e. grooved or furrowed with long V-formed depressions; tuberculate (tuberculata, adj. A), i.e. with small smooth rounded projections or knobs; verrucate or warty (verrucata, adj. A), i.e. with irregular projections or knobs; verruculate (verruculata, adj. A), i.e. covered with closely spaced tiny irregular projections; testa laevis madida intumescens, demum mucilaginosa, seed-coat smooth when moistened swelling up, at length mucilaginous.

Seed-list : delectus (s.m. IV) seminum, index (s.c. III. i) seminum, enumeratio (s.f. III. vi) seminum, catalogus (s.m. II) seminum; Delectus Seminum ex Horto Cantabrigiensis Academiae, Selection of Seeds from the Garden of the Cambridge Academy, i.e. the Cambridge University Botanic Garden ; Index Seminum quae Hortus Botanicus Imperialis Petropolitanus pro mutua commutatione offert, Index of Seeds which the Petrograd Imperial Botanic Garden for reciprocal exchange offers.

Seedling : plantula (s.f. I).

seemingly : ut videtur (adv. phrase).

seen : visus (part. A), spectatus (part. A); externe visus, seen from outside ; a latere visus, seen from the side ; a vertice visus, in vertical view ; see VIEW, VISUS.

Seges (s.f. III. ii): cornfield. **segetalis** (adj. B): belonging to *or* growing among standing corn.

Segment: segmentum (s.n. II), *abl. sing.* segmento, *nom. pl.* segmenta, *abl. pl.* segmentis. **segmented**: segmentatus (adj. A) *in class. L.* 'ornamented with tinsel'.

segregatus (part. A): set apart, separated. **sejunctim** (adv.): separately. **sejunctus** (part. A): disunited, separated, isolated.

seldom: raro (adv.).

selected: lectus (part. A), selectus (part. A), desumptus (part. A)

sellaeformis (adj. B), **selliformis** (adj. B): saddle-shaped, q.v. **Sella** (s.f. I), saddle, q.v. **94**

semel (adv.): once, a single time; *semel atque iterum*, once and again; *semel aut iterum*, only once or twice; *plus semel*, more than once; *ramis semel aut bis dichotomis*, with branches once or twice dichotomous.

Semen (s.n. III. vi): seed, q.v.

semi-: *in L. comp.*, half-; *semiadhaerens*, *semiadnatus*, adhering in lower part; *semiamplexicaulis*, with leaf-base half-embracing the stem; *semicordatus*, with one lobe cordate; *semiduplex*, semi-double, with the outer stamens petaloid, the inner stamens normal; *semicircularis, semiorbiculatus*, semicircular; *semiseptatus*, half-partitioned; *see* HEMI-

Semifacies (s.f. V): half of leaf in Selaginella; *folia lateralia semifacie superiore basi cordata, semifacie inferiore basi truncata*, lateral leaves with upper half cordate at base, with lower half truncate at base; *sporophylla dorsalia semifaciem in lumen inclinatam latiorem et semifaciem alteram dimidio angustiorem gerentia*, dorsal sporophylls bearing the half inclined in the light broader and the other half narrower by half; *semifacie luci inclinata laete viridi et semifacie altera pallescente*, with the half inclined to the light bright green and the other half paler.

seminalis (adj. B): relating to the seed.

Seminarium (s.n. II): nursery, seed-plot.

seminifer (adj. A), **seminiger** (adj. A): seed-bearing.

seminiger (adj. A): seed-bearing.

Semita (s.f. I): footpath.

semotus (part. A): distant, far removed.

semper (adv.): always, at all times.

sempervirens (adj. B): evergreen.

senatus (adj. A): sienna.

Senectus (s.f. III): old age; *in senectute*, in old age. **senescens** (part. B): growing old, becoming aged.

seni (num. adj. distr. pl.): six each, six together; *see* SIX.

sensim (adv.): gently, gradually; cf. GRADATIM, PAULATIM.

sensitive: sensitivus (adj. A) 'responsive to stimulus', sensibilis (adj. B) 'manifesting irritability'.

Sensus (s.m. IV): perception, opinion, thought, sense, view, signification, meaning; *sensu stricto*, in a narrow sense; *sensu lato*, in a broad sense, with a wide *or* general interpretation; *sensu Engleri*, in the opinion of Engler, as interpreted by Engler.

Sententia (s.f. I): way of thinking, judgment, opinion; *ex mea sententia*, in my opinion; *juxta meam sententiam*, according to my opinion; cf. JUDEX, OPINION.

senticosus (adj. A): full of thorns or prickles.

seorsim (adv.), **seorsum** (adv.): separately; *seorsim impr. ex Actis Societatis*, separately printed, i.e. issued as a separate from, the Transactions (Abhandlungen, etc.) of the Society (Gesellschaft, etc.). **seorsus** (adj. A): sundered, separate.

Sepal: sepalum (s.n. II), *acc. sing.* sepalum, *gen. sing.* sepali, *dat. and abl. sing.* sepalo, *nom. and acc. pl.* sepala, *gen. pl.* sepalorum, *dat. and abl. pl.* sepalis; *sepalum summum ovatum*, uppermost sepal ovate; *calcar sepalo suo aequilongum vel paulo longius*, spur its own sepal equalling or a little longer than; *sepala lateralia ovata, inferiora et supera lanceolata*, lateral sepals ovate, lower sepals and upper sepals lanceolate; *sepala patentia 2 exteriora trinervia, 2 interiora tantum nervo centrali prominente*, sepals spreading, 2 outer three-nerved, 2 interior with only the central nerve prominent; *sepala dextrorsum tegentia (i.e. sinistrorsum convoluta), libera vel ad ⅓ longitudinis coalita*, sepals overlapping to the right (i.e. twisted to the left), free or to ⅓ of the length joined; *sepalis a bracteolis omnino obtectis*, with sepals by the bracteoles wholly covered; *sepalis ovatis rotundatis viridibus*, with sepals ovate rounded green; cf. CALYX.

sepalinus (adj. A): relating to sepals. **sepaloideus** (adj. A): sepal-like. **-sepalus** (adj. A): *in Gk. and L. comp.*, -sepalled; *erythrosepalus*, red-sepalled.

separabilis (adj. B): separable, not adnate.

separate, separated: separatus (part. A), discretus (part. A), disjunctus (part. A), disparatus (part. A), divulsus (part. A), segregatus (part. A), sejunctus (part. A), seorsus (adj. A); *areolae rimis profundis separatae*, areoles by deep cracks separated, cf. DISTANT, SCATTERED. **separately**: discretim (adv.), disjuncte (adv.), disjunctim (adv.), seorsim (adv.), seorsum (adv.). **separating**: secedens (part. B), discedens (part. B). **Separation**: separatio (s.f. III). **451**

Sepes (s.f. III. viii): hedge; *sepium*, of hedges. **sepiarius** (adj. A): growing in hedges, used for hedging.

sepiaceus (adj. A): sepia.

Sepimentum (s.n. II): partition.

sept-, septem-, septen-: *ir L. comp.*, seven; *septangularis*, 7-angled, *septemfidus*, 7-cleft; *septifarius*, arranged in sevens; *septifolius*, 7-leaved; *see* HEPTA-, SEVEN.

septalis (adj. B): belonging to a septum. **septatus** (adj. A): septate, i.e. divided by partitions. **240**

septem (num. adj.): seven. **septenarius** (adj. A), **septenatus** (adj. A): consisting of seven. **septeni** (num. adj. distr.): seven each; *see* SEVEN.

serpentinus (adj. A): snake-like, i.e. bent backwards and forwards into a wavy line (cf. FLEXUOSUS, MEANDRINUS); growing on serpentine rock (cf. OPHIOLITHICUS).

Serratura (s.f. I): serration, toothing. **serratus** (adj. A): serrate, i.e. saw-edged with sharp teeth pointing forwards, as opposed to RETROSERRATUS, q.v., with teeth pointing backward; cf. CRENATUS, DENTATUS. **serrulatus** (adj. A): finely serrate. **182**

Sertum (s.n. II): wreath *or* garland of flowers. Used figuratively in book-titles to indicate a selection of plants.

serus (adj. A): late.

servatus (part. A): preserved, protected, kept unharmed; *typus in Herb. Mus. Brit. servatus*, type in Herbarium of the British Museum preserved.

a   b   c   d   e

Fig. 39   Dehiscence of Fruits

a, indehiscens; b, septicidalis; c, loculicidalis; d, septifragus marginicidalis; e, septifragus loculicidalis

septentrionalis (adj. B): north, northern; cf. BOREALIS, AUSTRALIS, MERIDIONALIS.

septicidalis (adj. B), **septicidus** (adj. A): septicidal, i.e. when a capsule splits into its component carpels along the lines of junction or the dissepiments (inward-running partitions), as opposed to LOCULICIDALIS, q.v., when the carpels split down the back half-way between (and not along) the lines of junction or the dissepiments. **septifragus** (adj. A): septifragal, i.e. when the valves or backs of carpels break away from the dissepiments. **Septum** (s.n. II): partition, cross-wall, dissepiment.

septiens (adv.), **septies** (adv.): seven times. **septimus** (adj. A): seventh.

sequens (part. B): next, next following; *in specie sequenti*, in the species following.

serialis (adj. B), **seriatus** (adj. A): arranged in rows; cf. -FARIUS. **seriatim** (adv.): in rows, serially. **489**

sericeus (adj. A): sericeous, i.e. silky with long straight close-pressed glossy hairs.

Series: series (s.f. V), *gen. sing.* seriei, *abl. sing.* serie, *nom. pl.* series, *gen. pl.* serierum, *abl. pl.* seriebus.

sero (adv.): late, at a late hour. **serotinus** (adj. A): late-coming, late to leaf *or* flower *or* to appear (*opp. of* PRAECOX, q.v.).

serpens (part. B): creeping; *see* REPENS.

sesqui-: *in L. comp.*, one and a half; *sesquipedalis*, one and a half feet (about 45 cm.) long; *sesquifolius*, anisophyllous, one leaf of a pair being much smaller than the other.

sessil-, sessili- *in L. comp.*, sessile-; *sessilantherus*, with sessile anthers; *sessiliflorus*, with sessile flowers; *sessilifolius*, with sessile leaves. **sessilis** (adj. B): sessile, stalkless, or apparently so, sitting close upon the body that supports it. **438**

Seta (s.f. I): bristle, bristle-like organ, as the fruit-stalk (sporophore) of a moss. **setaceus** (adj. A), **setiformis** (adj. B): setaceous, bristle-like. **setifer** (adj. A): bristle-bearing. **setosus** (adj. A): setose, bristly, i.e. beset with scattered ascending stiff hairs. **Setula** (s.f. I): a kind of cystidium. **setulosus** (adj. A): minutely setose.

seu (conj.): or, q.v.

seven: septem (num. adj. indecl.) 'seven', septimus (adj. A) 'seventh', septies (adv.), septiens (adv.), 'seven times'. **seven-**: *in L. comp.*, septem-, *in Gk. comp.*, hepta-; *septemlobus, heptalobus*, 7-lobed; *see* HEPTA-, SEPTEM-.

several: aliquot (adj. indecl.), plures (adj. pl. B); *aliquot per utriculum*, several to an utricle. **several times**: compluriens (adv.), compluries (adv.), aliquoties (adv.).

Sex: sexus (s.m. IV), *nom. pl.* sexus; *sexus masculinus*, male sex, symbol ♂; *sexus femineus*, female sex, symbol ♀.

sex (num. adj. indecl.): six, 6. **sex-**: *in L. comp.*, six-; *sexdentatus*, 6-toothed *sexfidus*, 6-cleft; *sexlocularis*, 6-chambered; *sexpartitus*, 6-parted; *sexvalvis*, 6-valved; *see* HEXA-, SIX-. **sexiens** (adv.), **sexies** (adv.): six times. **sextus** (adj. A): sixth.

sexualis (adj. B): sexual; *Ego sexuale systema secundum numerum proportionem situm staminum cum pistillis elaboravi* (Linnaeus, *Phil. bot.* No. 68; 1751), I have worked out the sexual system according to the number, relation and position of the stamens with the pistils. **sexualiter** (adv.): sexually.

Shade: umbra (s.f. I), *acc. sing.* umbram. **shady**: umbrosus (adj. A).

Shaft: scapus (s.m. II), q.v.

shaggy: hirtus (adj. A), villosus (adj. A). **273**

Shallow: vadum (s.n. II). **shallow**: vadosus, non altus (adj. A), non profundus (adj. A).

Shape: forma (s.f. I); cf. FORMED.

sharp: acutus (part. A.) 'pointed', acer (adj. B) 'pungent, bitter', amarus (adj. A) 'bitter, sour', argutus (adj. A) 'distinct, clear'. **sharply**: acute, *less often* argute (adv.). **149**

shattered: diffractus (part. A).

Sheath: vagina (s.f. I), *abl. sing.* vagina, *nom. pl.* vaginae, *gen. pl.* vaginarum, *abl. pl.* vaginis; *folia basi vaginis foliorum deciduorum persistentibus inter se obvoluti obtecta, vaginarum tandem deciduarum basibus cupelliformibus*, leaves at base covered with the sheaths of deciduous leaves persistent between themselves wrapped around with the bases of the at length deciduous sheaths shaped like small casks; *vaginae mucosae aetate provecta interdum diffluentes semper hyalinae*, sheaths mucous with advanced age sometimes disappearing (wasting away) always hyaline; *trichomata intra vaginam plura*, trichomes within the sheath several; *trichomata evaginata aut vaginis pertenuibus fragilibus mucosis inclusa*, trichomes sheathless or by sheaths very thin fragile mucous enclosed. **sheathed**: vaginatus (adj. A). **sheathing**: vaginans (adj. B). **445**

shed: exutus (part. A).

Sheen: nitor (s.m. III): *plantae nitore fere destitutae*, plants almost lacking sheen.

Shell of mollusc: concha (s.f. I): *in saxis conchisque*, on rocks and shells. **shell-shaped**: conchatus (adj. A), conchiformis (adj. B).

shield-shaped: clypeatus (adj. A), scutatus (adj. A), scutiformis (adj. B). The Roman *clipeus* was a small round shield, the *scutum* a large oblong shield. **19, 26**

Shingle: glarea (s.f. I): *glarea maritima*, seaside shingle; *glarea fluviatilis*, river shingle.

shiny: nitens (part. B), nitidus (adj. A); cf. LAMPRO-, LUCENS, POLISHED. **294**

Ship: navis (s.f. III).

Shoot: surculus (s.m. II). **Short-shoot**: brachyblastus (s.m. II).

shooting forth: propullans (part. B).

Shore: litus, littus (s.n. III); *plantae in litus ejectae*, plants cast on to the shore. **pertaining to the shore**: litoralis, littoralis (adj. B).

short: brevis (adj. B), curtus (adj. A). **short-**: *in Gk. comp.*, brachy-, *in L. comp.*, brevi-. **very short**: brevissimus (adj. A). **shortened**: abbreviatus (part. A).

shortly: (*in length*) breviter (adv.); (*in time*) mox. **Shortness**: brevitas (s.f. III), *gen. sing.* brevitatis.

Shoulder: humerus (s.m. II). **shouldered**: humeratus (adj. A).

showing: praebens (part. B); *marginibus duas series praebentibus*, with margins showing two series.

shrimp-red: palaemoneus (adj. A).

Shrub, Bush: frutex (s.m. III. i), *nom. pl.* frutices; *frutex omnino glaber ramosissimus sempervirens ad 1 m. altus, ramulis hornotinis ancipitibus*, shrub entirely glabrous much branched evergreen to 1 m. high, with this year's branchlets two-edged. **shrubby**: fruticosus (adj. A).

Shrublet: fruticulus (s.m. II), *nom. pl.* fruticuli; *fruticuli ericoidei capenses madagascarienses et mauritiani sed non mauritanici*, shrublets heath-like of the Cape, Madagascar and Mauritius but not Morocco.

sic (adv.): in this manner, thus.

siccatus (part. A): dried. **Siccitas** (s.f. III. ii): dryness, dried state; *in siccitate*, in a dried state. **siccus** (adj. A): dry; *in sicco*, in a dry state.

sick: *see* DISEASED.

sickle-shaped: falcatus (adj. A).

sicut (adv.): so as, just as.

sicyoideus (adj. A): gourd-shaped, i.e. swollen below with a long neck above; cf. LAGENIFORMIS.

Side: latus (s.n. III. iv), *gen. sing.* lateris, *abl. sing.* latere, *nom. pl.* latera, *gen. pl.* laterum, *abl. pl.* lateribus, in sense of 'flank, right or left side'; pagina (s.f. I), *gen. sing.* paginae, *abl. sing.* pagina, *nom. pl.* paginae, *gen. pl.* paginarum, *abl. pl.* paginis, in sense of 'page, upper

or lower surface, back or front side';
facies (s.f. V), *gen. sing.* faciei, *abl. sing.*
facie, *nom. pl.* facies, *gen. pl.* facierum,
abl. pl. faciebus, *in sense of* 'aspect, face';
*folia basi inaequilatera, latere altero
quam altero 2-3 mm. longius descendente,* leaves at base unequal-sided, with
one side than the other 2-3 mm. lower
descending; *folia nervis utroque costae
latere 8,* leaves with nerves to both sides
of the mid-rib 8; *gluma a latere compressa, lateribus ciliatis,* glume from the
side compressed, with the sides ciliate;
latus valvare asymmetricum, valvar side
asymmetrical; *frustula e latere visa,*
frustules from the side observed; *flagellum unicum e latere vel apice oriens,*
flagellum one from the side or apex
arising; *folia pagina superiore viridi
glabra inferiore rubra hirsuta,* leaves with
the upper surface green glabrous the
lower red hirsute; *folia in pagina
superiore setis aequalibus vestita,* leaves
on the upper surface with bristles of
equal length clothed; *lamina pubescens
deinde facie inferiore glabrescens,* blade
pubescent afterwards at the lower face
becoming glabrous; *hinc . . . illinc . . .,*
on this side . . ., on that side . . .;
utrinque, on both sides; *undique,* on all
sides. **side-** : *in L. comp.,* lateri-, *in Gk.
comp.,* pleur-, pleuro-.
sieve-like : cribratus (adj. A), cribrosus
(adj. A); cf. LATTICED.
sigillatim (adv.) : markedly. **sigillatus**
(adj. A) : sigillate, i.e. as if marked with
impressions of a seal.
sigmoideus (adj. A) : sigmoid, i.e. curved
like the letter S (Gk. *s,* sigma); *valvae
plus minus sigmoideae,* valves more or
less sigmoid.
Signum (s.n. II) : mark, sign.
siliceus (adj. A) : siliceous, flinty.
Silicule : silicula (s.f. I), *abl. sing.* silicula,
nom. pl. siliculae, *abl. pl.* siliculis.
Siliqua : siliqua (s.f. I), *abl. sing.* siliqua,
nom. pl. siliquae, *abl. pl.* siliquis. In
Roman times *siliqua* was mostly used for
the pod of Leguminosae, but also applied
to capsules and follicles; *siliqua elliptica
compressa polysperma, rarius oligo-
sperma, valvis planiusculis, septo membranaceo, stylo elongato,* siliqua elliptic
compressed many-seeded, rarely few-
seeded, with valves rather flat, with septum membranous, with style elongated;
*siliqua elongata teres, continua vel moni-
liformis, laevis vel costata, coriacea
suberosa vel fungosa, intus continua vel
isthmis transversis multilocellaris, locellis
seminiferis interdum locellis vacuis alternantibus,* siliqua elongated terete continuous (uninterrupted) or moniliform
(like a string of beads), smooth or ribbed,
leathery corky or spongy, inside continuous or by transverse contractions
many-chambered, with chambers (locelli) seed-bearing sometimes with chambers empty alternating; *siliqua a latere
compressa, valvis carinatis,* siliqua from
the side compressed, with valves keeled;
*siliqua globosa vel inflata, hispida vel
subechinata,* siliqua globose or inflated,
hispid or almost spiny. **siliquose** : sili-
quosus (adj. A).
silky : sericeus (adj. A), bombycinus
(adj. A); cf. COTTONY.
Silva : *see* SYLVA. **silvaticus** : *see* SYLVATI-
CUS. **silvestris** : *see* SYLVESTRIS.
silvery : argenteus (adj. A); *in Gk. comp.,*
argyro-.
similaris (adj. B) : similar. **similis** (adj. B) :
like, resembling, similar (*used with gen.
or dat.*). **similiter** (adv.) : in like
manner. **Similitudo** (s.f. III. vi) : likeness, resemblance, similarity.
simplex (adj. B) : simple, undivided, unbranched, of one piece or series, not
consisting of several distinct parts (*opp.
of* COMPOSITUS, DUPLEX, RAMOSUS, etc.);
caulis simplex uniflorus, stem unbranched
one-flowered; *caule simplici unifloro,*
with stem unbranched one-flowered;
pili longi simplices nec ramosi, hairs long
simple not branched; *folia simplicia pilis
longis simplicibus vestita,* leaves undivided with long simple hairs clothed.
simplici- : *in L. comp.,* simple-, undivided; *simplicicaulis,* with unbranched
stem; *simplicifolius,* with simple leaves;
simplicifrons, with undivided frond;
simplicivenius, with unbranched veins.
simplicissimus (adj. A) : completely unbranched, quite entire. **simpliciter**
(adv.) : simply, only, plainly. **Simplum**
(s.n. II) : medicinal herb, simple. **201,
202**
simul (adv.) : at the same time.
simulans (part. B) : imitating, resembling;
cf. MENTIENS.
simultaneus (adj. A) : at the same time,
simultaneous : *folia et flores simultanei,*
leaves and flowers together; cf. COAE-
TANEUS.
sine (prep. with abl.) : without, lacking
(*opp. of* CUM); *nomen sine descriptione,*
name without description, nomen nudum; *sine floribus,* without flowers;
sine numero, without a number.
singularis (adj. B) : alone, solitary, alone
of its kind, unique. **singulariter** (adv.),
singulatim (adv.) : singly, separately, one
by one, individually. **singulus** (adj. A) :
one to each, cf. SOLITARIUS, UNICUS.

sinister (adj. A): on the left, left. **sinistorsum** (adv.): towards the left; cf. TWINING. **418**

sino-corallinus (adj. A): chinese-coral (H.C.C. 6.14).

sinuato-dentatus (adj. A): sinuate and dentate at the same time. **sinuatus** (part. A): sinuate, i.e. strongly waved, the margin alternately uneven with concavities and convexities. **sinuolatus** (adj. A): faintly sinuate; cf. REPANDUS. **sinuosus** (adj. A): sinuate, very sinuate. **188**

Sinus (s.m. IV): recess, rounded inward curve between two projecting lobes, bay; *folia profunde cordata sinu basali ob margines contiguos vel imbricatos valde angusto vel clauso*, leaves deeply cordate with the basal sinus very narrow or closed on account of the touching or overlapping margins; *in Sinu Neapolitano*, in the Bay of Naples; *in sinubus Europaeis et Africanis Oceani Atlantici*, in European and African bays of the Atlantic Ocean; *staminodia sub sinubus corollae affixa*, staminodes below the sinuses of the corolla inserted.

Sipho (s.m. III. vi): siphon, i.e. elongated tube in frond of alga; *siphonibus distinctis linearibus non utriculatis*, with tubes separate, linear not bladder-like. **siphon-, siphono-,-siphonius**: *in Gk. comp.*, relating to a tube *or* pipe; *monosiphonius*, with a single tube; *polysiphonius*, with many tubes; *siphonanthus*, with a tubular flower; *siphonocalyx*, with a tubular calyx. **siphonaceus** (adj. A): with elongated tubes or non-septate filaments.

sistens (part. B): standing, appearing, supporting, placing.

Situs (s.m. IV): position occupied by an organ; *situs foliorum*, arrangement of leaves, phyllotaxis.

situs (part. A): set down, placed, left, permitted; cf. PLACE.

sive: or, q.v.

six: sex (num. adj. indecl.) 'six', seni (num. adj. distr. pl.) 'six each, six together', sextus (adj. A) 'sixth', sexies (adv.), sexiens (adv.) 'six times'; *segmenta in quaque serie quatuor ad sex*, segments in each series four to six; *stamina sex vel duodecim rarius indefinita*, stamens 6 or 12 more rarely indefinite; *folia semper sena*, leaves always six. **six-**: *in L. comp.*, sex-, *in Gk. comp.*, hexa-; *sexangularis, sexangulus, hexagonus*, 6-angled; *sexflorus, hexanthus*, 6-flowered; *sexfarius, hexastichus*, 6-rowed; *sexstylosus, hexastylis, hexastylus*, 6-styled; *sexalatus, hexapterus*, 6-winged; *see* HEXA-, SEX-.

Size: amplitudo (s.f. III. vi), *abl. sing.* amplitudine; magnitudo (s.f. III. vi), *abl. sing.* magnitudine; statura (s.f. I), *abl. sing.* statura; *statura variabilis, pro genere minima, perpusilla, pusilla, parva, minor, mediocris, magna, major, vel maxima*, size variable, for the genus very small indeed (the smallest), very small, very small (bigger than *perpusilla*), small, smaller, medium-sized, large, larger, or very large (the greatest); *folia caulina amplitudine admodum variabilia*, cauline leaves as to size very variable.

Skeleton: sceletus (s.m. II).

Sketch: delineatio (s.f. III. vi).

Skin: pellis (s.f. III), *gen. sing.* pellis.

skinned: recutitus (adj. A).

Sky: caelum (s.n. II). **sky-blue**: caelestis (adj. B).

slanting: obliquus (adj. A); *in Gk. comp.*, plagio-. **slantingly**: oblique (adv.).

slate-coloured: ardesiacus (adj. A). **slate-blue**: lazulino-ardesiacus (adj. A). **dark slate-blue**: atro-ardesiacus (adj. A). **slate-purple**: purpureo-ardesiacus (adj. A). **slate-violet**: violaceo-ardesiacus (adj. A). **slaty**: schistaceus (adj. A).

Sleep: somnus (s.m. II).

slender: gracilis (adj. B), exilis (adj. B), tenuis (adj. B).

Slide, glass: lamina (s.f. I) vitrea.

slight: exiguus (adj. A). **slightly**: leviter (adv.) 'lightly', parum (adv.) 'a little', plus minusve (adv.) 'more or less', leniter (adv.) 'mildly'; cf. SOMEWHAT.

Slime: mucus (s.m. II); *in Gk. comp.*, myx-, myxo-. **slimy**: mucosus (adj. A). **301**

slipper-shaped: calceiformis (adj. B), calceolatus (adj. A).

slippery: lubricus (adj. A).

slipping away: elabens (part. B).

Slit: rima (s.f. I).

Slope: clivus (s.m. II), declivitas (s.f. III. ii). **sloping**: devexus (adj. A). **sloping downwards**: declivis (adj. B), devexus (adj. A). **sloping upwards**: acclivis (adj. B), subvexus (adj. A).

slow: tardus (adj. A); *motus tardus*, movement slow. **slowly**: tarde (adv.), lente (adv.), cunctanter (adv.); *cellula dum quieta, lenteve prolabens*, cell when resting or slowly gliding.

small: parvus (adj. A), pusillus (adj. A). **very small**: parvulus (adj. A), perparvus (adj. A). **extremely small**: minimus (adj. A).

Smallness: parvitas (s.f. III).

smaragdinus (adj. A): emerald-green, dark bluish-green.

smeared: illinitus (part. A).

Smell, Scent, Odour: odor (s.m. III. v), olor (s.m. III. v), fetor (s.m. III. v);

frutex odorem gratum exhalens, shrub a pleasing odour giving out. **smelling** (*of anything*) : olens (part. B), olidus (adj. A). **scented pleasantly, fragrant** : suaveolens (adj. B), odorus (adj. A), odoratus (adj. A), fragrans (part. B), aromaticus (adj. A); *flores die inodori noctu fragrantes*, flowers by day scentless, at night fragrant. **smelling unpleasantly, stinking** : graveolens (adj. B), foetidus (adj. A), foetulentus (adj. A), putidus (adj. A), stercoreus (adj. A).

smoke-grey : fumosus (adj. A), fumeus (adj. A).

smooth : laevis (adj. B), levis (adj. B), laevigatus (part. A), levigatus (part. A), rasilis (adj. B) 'not rough', glaber (adj. A) 'without hairs'. **295, 296**

snail-shaped : cochleatus (adj. A).

snake- : *in Gk. comp.*, ophio-; *ophioglossus*, snake-tongued, i.e. with a forked tongue ; *ophiophyllus*, snake-leaved, i.e. with twisted or flexuose leaves. **snaky** : serpentinus (adj. A) q.v.; cf. FLEXUOSUS.

Snout : rostrum (s.n. II).

Snow : nix (s.f. III), *gen. sing.* nivis, *abl. sing.* nive. **Snow-patch** : locus ubi nix longe perdurat. **snow-white** : nivalis (adj. B), niveus (adj. A), candidus (adj. A). **snowy, consisting of snow** : nivalis (adj. B), niveus (adj. A), nivosus (adj. A); *in Gk. comp.*, chion-, chiono-.

so : sic (adv.) 'thus' *with verbs*, ita (adv.) 'thus' *with adj.*, ergo (adv.) 'therefore, hence'. **so that** : ut (conj. *with subjunctive*).

soaked : madefactus (part. A), madidus (adj. A), irriguus (adj. A); cf. HUMECTATUS.

Sobol : soboles (s.f. III. vi), *acc. sing.* sobolem, *gen. sing.* sobolis, *abl. sing.* sobole, *nom. and acc. pl.*, soboles, *abl. pl.* sobolibus. The term *soboles*, referring to the underground creeping base of a stem, is synonymous with *caulis basi stoloniformis* of some authors. **sobolifer** (adj. A) : sobol-bearing ; cf. RUNNER.

Society : societas (s.f. III. ii), *gen. sing.* societatis.

Sodium : sodium (s.n. II), *gen. sing.* sodii.

soft : (*to the touch*) mollis (adj. B), mitis (adj. B), lenis (adj. B); (*to the taste*) mitis (adj. B) ; (*in colour*) lenis (adj. B) ; *aqua pluvialis*, rain (soft) water. **softly** : molliter (adv.), leniter (adv.).

Soil : solum (s.n. II), *acc. sing.* solum, *gen. sing.* soli ; cf. HUMUS, TERRA.

soiled : sordidus (adj. A) ; cf. STAINED.

solaeformis (adj. B), **soleiformis** (adj. B) : sandal-shaped, sole-shaped.

solely : solum (adv.), tantum (adv.).

solemniter (adv.) : customarily.

solferinus (adj. A) : solferino-purple (H.C.C. 26).

solid : solidus (adj. A) ; cf. FARCTUS.

solidinervis (adj. B), **solidinervius** (adj. A) : with undivided nerves running from base to apex.

solitarius (adj. A) : alone, by itself, solitary; *see* ONE, SINGULARIS, UNICUS.

solitus (part. A) : usual, customary.

solstitialis (adj. B) : pertaining to summer.

solubilis (adj. B) : which may be taken apart, coming apart, separating into pieces.

Solum (s.n. II) : lowest part, bottom, floor, soil, earth ; *solum natale*, habitat.

solummodo (adv.) : merely.

solus (adj. A) : alone, single, sole.

Solution : solutio (s.f. III. vi).

solutus (part. A) : set free, not adherent, completely separate from adjacent parts, breaking up, disappearing (*opp. of* ADNATUS, *etc.*). **451**

Soma (s.n. III. ix) : *in Gk. comp.*, body ; cf. CHROMOSOMA.

somatic ; somaticus (adj. A) : *cellulae somaticae*, somatic cells.

some : aliquot (num. indecl.); aliqui, aliqua, aliquod (adj.), *nom. pl.* aliqui, aliquae, aliqua ; nonnullus (adj. A). **somehow** : aliquam (adv.). **sometimes** : interdum (adv.), aliquando (adv.), nonnunquam (adv.). **somewhat** : aliquantum (adv.) 'in some quantity', aliquot (adv.) 'in some numbers', nonnihil (adv.) 'not much' ; cf. SLIGHTLY.

Somnus (s.m. II) : sleep.

soon : mox (adv.), jam (adv.), cito (adv.).

Soot : fuligo (s.f. III. vi). **sooty** : fuligineus (adj. A), fuliginosus (adj. A).

Soralium : soralium (s.n. II).

sordidus (adj. A) : dirty-looking, dingy, soiled.

Sorede : soredium (s.n. II), *nom. pl.* soredia ; *thallus sorediis minutis crebris convexis rarius confluentibus*, thallus with soredia minute crowded convex rarely confluent.

sorifer (adj. A) : sorus-bearing.

Sorocarp : sorocarpium (s.n. II), *abl. sing.* sorocarpio.

Sorophore : sorophorum (s.n. II), *abl. sing.* sorophoro.

Sorus : sorus (s.m. II), *nom. pl.* sori, *gen. pl.* sororum, *abl. pl.* soris; synonymous with *sporothecium*; *sori nudi, apice venarum simplicium*; sori naked, at the apex of simple veins ; *sori numero et loco irregulares plerumque conferti seriemque nervo intermedio approximatam irregularem formantes*, sori in numbers and position irregular, most of them crowded together and forming an irregular series close to the intermediate nerve ; *sori uniseriati exacte inter marginem et costulam* *intermedii*, sori in a single series exactly halfway between the margin and costula; *sori varii, nempe globosi, lineares, oblongive, indusiati aut nudi, saepissime dorso venarum, interdum parenchymati insidentes*, sori various, namely globose, linear, or oblong, with an indusium or naked, most often at the back of the veins, sometimes situated on the parenchyma; *sori simplices pauci obliqui vel fere recti, in venulis superioribus insidentes et hanc ob causam a costa valde remoti et margini approximati*, sori simple few oblique or almost straight, on the upper veinlets situated and hence from the costa very remote and the margin approaching; *sori inter costam et marginem uniseriati denique confluentes et excepto angusto margine totam paginam inferiorem obtegentes*, sori between costa and margin in a single series at length confluent and except for a narrow margin the whole lower surface covering; *sori inframarginales, in dorso dentium vel in sinu dentium (aut dentis dorsum vel illius sinum occupantes)*, sori inframarginal, on the back of teeth or in the recess of teeth (the back of a tooth or its recess occupying); *sororum series segmentorum apicem haud attingentes*, series of sori the apex of the segments not reaching; *soris marginalibus linearibus*, with sori marginal linear.

-sorus: *in Gk. and L. comp.*, pertaining to the sori.

sour: *see* BITTER.

Source: origo (s.f. III. vi).

South: meridies (s.m. V), *gen. sing.* meridiei; *ad meridiem*, to the south; *versus meridiem et orientem a loco dicto*, south-east of the place named. **south, southern**: meridionalis (adj. B), australis (adj. B); *in Gk. comp.*, noto-, *in L. comp.*, austro-.

Space of limited extent: spatium (s.n. II), *abl. sing.* spatio, *nom. and acc. pl.* spatia; *spatio centrali nullo*, with central space nil; *cf.* DISTANCE, INTERSTITIUM, INTERVAL. **spaced**: dispositus (part. A) 'distributed, arranged', dispersus (part. A) 'scattered'.

spadiceus (adj. A): date-coloured, a deep reddish-brown.

Spadix: spadix (s.m. or f. III. i), *gen. sing.* spadicis, *abl. sing.* spadice, *nom. pl.* spadices; *lit.* branch, esp. infructescence of palm; *spadix spatha brevior, totus inclusus, sessilis, basi femineus, superne hermaphroditus, appendice erecta clavata*, spadix than the spathe shorter, all included, sessile, at the base female, above hermaphrodite, with appendage erect

club-shaped; *palma spadicibus inter frondes erumpentibus*, palm with spadices between the fronds breaking out, i.e. with interfoliar spadices; *flores monoici in distinctis spadicibus*, flowers monoecious on different spadices; *spadices sessiles vel pedunculati pluripedales, basi et ad ramos compressos spathis incompletis vaginati, interdum vaginas foliorum perforantes*, spadices sessile or pedunculate several feet long, at base and at the compressed branches by incomplete spathes sheathed, sometimes the sheaths of leaves perforating.

Span: spithama (s.f. I), *nom. pl.* spithamae. **span-long**: spithameus (adj. A).

span-, spano-: *in Gk. comp.*, few, scanty, scarce; *spanospermus*, few-seeded; *spananthus*, few-flowered; *cf.* OLIG-.

spargens (part. B): scattering, dispersing, spreading abroad; *fructibus odorem spargentibus*, with fruits giving out a scent.

sparingly: parce (adv.).

sparsim: (adv.): scatteredly, sparsely. **sparsus** (part. A): sparse, scattered. **481**

spathaceus (adj. A): spathe-like, provided with a spathe.

Spathe: spatha (s.f. I), *abl. sing.* spatha, *nom. pl.* spathae, *lit.* 'a broad flat wooden or metal blade'. Applied to spathe of palms by Theophrastus and Pliny; *spatha erecta ovata viridis longitudinaliter albo-vittata marcescens, inferne convoluta, superne aperta*, spathe erect ovate green longitudinally white-banded withering without falling, below with margins overlapping, above open; *spathae duae, inferiore membranacea decidua inermi, superiore lignosa persistenti aculeata*, spathes 2, with the lower one membranous deciduous unarmed, the upper one woody persistent prickly.

spathiformis (adj. B): spathe-like.

Spathilla: spathilla (s.f. I).

spathulatus (adj. A): spathulate, spatula-shaped, i.e. from a broad rounded upper part tapering gradually downwards into a stalk. **spathuli-**: *in L. comp.*, spathulate; *spathulifolius* with spathulate leaves. **112**

spatiosus (adj. A): of great extent, ample. **Spatium** (s.n. II): space, distance, interval, extent; *axis inferne per spatia pollicaria radios emittens*, axis in lower part at inch-long intervals giving out rays.

spatulatus: *see* SPATHULATUS.

special: peculiaris (adj. B), proprius (adj. A), specialis (adj. B).

specialis (adj. B): particular, special, not general; *formae speciales*, special forms, i.e. parasitic forms restricted to certain hosts despite lack of morphological differentiation.

Species: species (s.f. V), *acc. sing.* speciem, *gen. sing.* speciei, *abl. sing.* specie, *nom. and acc. pl.* species, *gen. pl.* specierum, *dat. and abl. pl.* speciebus; *species nova a specie praecedente bene distincta*, new species from the preceding species well distinct; *ex Haiti hanc speciem non vidi*, from Haiti this species I have not seen; *descriptio speciei novae*, description of a new species; *species omnes tropicae*, species all tropical; *icones specierum novarum vel minus cognitarum*, illustrations of new or little-known species; *species haec et sequentes inter sese valde affines sunt*, this species and the following ones between themselves are very closely akin. **specific**: specificus (adj. A); *differentia specifica continet notas, quibus a speciebus congeneribus differt* (Linnaeus, *Phil. bot.*, No. 256), the specific differential contains the distinctive features by which it differs from species of the same genus. **specifically**: specifice (adv.); *planta certe specifice non distincta*, plant certainly not specifically distinct.

Specimen: specimen (s.n. III. vi), *abl. sing.* specimine, *nom. pl.* specimina, *abl. pl.* speciminibus; exemplum (s.n. II), *abl. sing.* exemplo, *nom. pl.* exempla, *abl. pl.* exemplis; *specimen originarium in herbario auctoris prope . . . collectum*, original specimen in the herbarium of the author near . . . collected; *specimina in herbariis asservata non raro aliis speciebus commixta sunt*, specimens in herbaria preserved not rarely with other species are mixed; *in speciminibus cultis*, in cultivated specimens; *cum exemplaribus Europaeis ad amussim convenit*, with European specimens it agrees precisely; cf. EXSICCATA, HERBARIUM.

speciosus (adj. A): showy, splendid.

Speck: gutta (s.f. I).

spectans (part. B): looking towards, situated towards, lying towards; *flagellum anticum protinus, posticum retro spectans*, front flagellum forwards, back one backwards lying.

spectatus (part. A): beheld, seen, esteemed.

speedily: cito (adv.) 'quickly', confestim (adv.) 'forthwith'.

Spelunca (s.f. I): cave.

-sperma (s.n. III. ix): *in Gk. comp.*, -seed; *see* -SPERMUS.

Spermagonium: *see* SPERMOGONIUM.

Spermatange: spermatangium (s.n. II), *abl. sing.* spermatangio, *nom. pl.* spermatangia, *abl. pl.* spermatangiis.

Spermatiophore: spermatiophorum (s.n. II).

Spermatium: spermatium (s.n. II).

Spermatocystidium: spermatocystidium (s.n. II).

Spermidium: spermidium (s.n. II).

Spermodermium: spermodermium (s.n. II).

Spermodochidium: spermodochidium (s.n. II).

Spermodochium: spermodochium (s.n. II).

Spermogonium: spermogonium (s.n. II).

Spermospore: spermospora (s.f. I).

-spermus (adj. A): *in Gk. comp.*, -seeded; *aulacospermus*, with furrowed seeds; *argyrospermus*, with silvery seeds; *baliospermus*, with spotted seeds; *chrysospermus*, with golden seeds; *dictyospermus*, with seeds having a raised network on the surface; *erythrospermus*, with red seeds; *leucospermus*, with white seeds; *melanospermus*, with black seeds; *monospermus*, one-seeded; *oligospermus*, few-seeded; *pleiospermus*, polyspermus, many-seeded; *leiospermus*, smooth-seeded; *rhytidospermus*, with wrinkled seeds; *trachyspermus*, rough-seeded; *macrospermus*, large-seeded; *microspermus*, small-seeded; *pterospermus*, with winged seeds; *sphaerospermus*, with globose seeds.

sphacelatus (adj. A): with brown *or* blackish speckling.

sphaericus (adj. A): globose, spherical. **sphaero-**: *in Gk. comp.*, globose, spherical; *sphaerocarpus*, with globose fruit; *sphaerocephalus*, with globose heads. **4**

sphaeroideus (adj. A): globose with somewhat compressed *or* flattened poles. **23**

Sphalma (s.n. III. ix): stumble, error, mistake; *sphalmate*, by mistake.

sphen-, spheno-: *in Gk. comp.*, wedge-; *sphenobasis*, with wedge-shaped base; *sphenochilus*, with wedge-shaped lip; *sphenophyllus*, with wedge-shaped leaves; cf. CUNEATUS.

Spica (s.f. I): spike, q.v. **spicatus** (adj. A): spicate, bearing a spike, **spicifer** (adj. A): bearing a spike. **spiciformis** (adj. B): resembling a spike.

Spicilegium (s.n. II): a gleaning.

Spicula (s.f. I): spikelet, q.v.

spiculatus (adj. A): covered with fine points. **265**

Spiculum (s.n. II): spicule.

Spike: spica (s.f. I), *acc. sing.* spicam, *abl. sing.* spica, *nom. pl.* spicae, *acc. pl.* spicas, *abl. pl.* spicis; *spica erecta densiflora cylindrica*, spike erect densely flowered cylindric; *spicae erectae, superiores approximatae, inferiores distantes, omnes densiflorae*, spikes erect, the upper close together, the lower remote, all many-flowered; *verticillastri in spicas axillares vel terminales conferti*, verticillasters in spikes axillary or terminal crowded.

Spikelet: spicula (s.f. I), 'secondary spike, unit of the inflorescence in grasses', *to be distinguished from* spiculum (s.n. II) 'a little sharp point'; *spicula biflora*, spikelet 2-flowered; *spiculae biflorae, flore inferiore masculo vel neutro, superiore hermaphrodito, nunc solitariae, nunc geminae vel plures congestae*, spikelets 2-flowered with lower flower male or neuter, upper one hermaphrodite, now solitary, now paired or several crowded together; *spiculae in quoque pari altera sessilis altera pedicellata*, spikelets in each pair one sessile the other pedicelled; *spiculae homogamae masculae vel steriles lanceolatae 3 cm. longae acutae, spiculae fertiles oblongae fere teretes*, spikelets with one kind of flower (i.e. one-sexed) male or sterile lanceolate 3 cm. long acute, spikelets fertile oblong almost terete.

spindle-shaped: fusiformis (adj. B). **27**

Spine: spina (s.f. I), *abl. sing.* spina, *nom. pl.* spinae, *abl. pl.* spinis; *spinae validae pubescentes ad 2 cm. longae*, spines stout pubescent to 2 cm. long; *fruticuli spinis axillaribus vel nullis vel teneris brevibus vel validis lignosis ad 1 cm. longis, rectis vel recurvatis, saepe horizontaliter patentibus, initio puberulis mox glabris armati*, shrublets armed with axillary spines none or slender short or stout woody to 1 cm. long, straight or recurved, often horizontally spreading at first puberulous soon glabrous; cf. ACULEUS. **spine-bearing**: spinifer (adj. A). **Spine-cell**: spinula (s.f. I). **spine-like**: spiniformis (adj. B). **spinescent**: spinescens (part. B). **Spinule**: spinula (s.f. I). **spinulose**: spinulosus (adj. A). **spiny**: spineus (adj. A), spinosus (adj. A). **261**

Spira (s.f. I): coil, spiral.

spiral: spiralis (adj. B); cf. CIRCINATUS, GYRATUS, HELIC-, STROMBULIFORMIS. **Spiral-cells**: cellulae (s.f. pl. I) spirales (adj. B. pl.). **spirally**: spiratim (adv.), spiraliter (adv.), in cochleam, in spiram; *trichomata in cochleam torta*, trichomes into a spiral twisted; *trichomata in spiram laxam contorta*, trichomes into a loose spiral twisted. **spirally twisted**: torsivus (adj. A), etc.; cf. SPIRALLY. **14, 382, 416, 492**

Spirit: spiritus (s.m. IV).

spirostylis (adj. B), **spirostylus** (adj. A): with spirally twisted style.

spisse (adv.): densely, compactly, closely. **spissescens** (part. B): becoming thick,

thickening. **spissus** (adj. A): dense, compact, close together.

Spithama (s.f. I): span, distance between tips of thumb and first finger when outstretched, 7 inches, approx. 19 cm. **spithameus** (adj. A): a span long *or* high.

splendens (part. B): shining, gleaming, brilliant. **297**

Split: fissura (s.f. I); cf. RIMA, SCISSURA. **split**: fissus (part. A), fissilis (adj. B); *in Gk. comp.*, schizo-, *in L. comp.*, fissi-; *schizophyllus, fissifolius*, with deeply divided leaves. **splitting**: findens (part. B), secedens (part. B). **194**

spod-, spodo-: *in Gk. comp.*, ash-grey-; *spodochrous*, grey-coloured, ash-grey.

Spongiola (s.f. I): a little sponge. Formerly used of the root-tip, the stigma and the caruncle when spongy.

spongiosus (adj. A): spongy, porous, soft and water-soaked, like a wet sponge; cf. FUNGOSUS. **319**

spontaneus (adj. A): naturally growing wild (*opp. of* CULTUS, SATIVUS).

spoon-shaped: cochleariformis (adj. B), cochlearis (adj. B).

sporadic: sporadicus (adj. A): *see* HERE AND THERE.

Sporangium: sporangium (s.n. II), *abl. sing.* sporangio, *nom. pl.* sporangia, *abl. pl.* sporangiis. **sporangium-bearing**: sporangifer (adj. A).

Spore: spora (s.f. I), *acc. sing.* sporam, *gen. sing.* sporae, *abl. sing.* spora, *nom. pl.* sporae, *acc. pl.* sporas, *gen. pl.* sporarum, *abl. pl.* sporis. The terms applied to leaf-shapes and to ornamentation of pollen (cf. POLLEN) are suitable for description of spores, with addition of *allantoideus* (sausage-shaped), *doliiformis* (barrel-shaped), *lageniformis* (gourd-shaped, swollen at base narrowed rather abruptly into a long neck); *sporae oblongae utrinque obtusatae continuae dein 1-septatae tandem 3-septatae brunneae leviter fuligineae at non opacae raro constrictae 12-20μ longae 5-6μ latae*, spores oblong at both ends blunt continuous then 1-septate at length 3-septate brown lightly fuliginous but not opaque rarely constricted 12-20μ long 5-6μ broad; *sporae 30μ in diametro triletae haud monoletae laeves*, spores 30μ in diameter trilete never monolete; *sporae subglobosae leviter sex-angulatae nitentes carneae in cumulo*, spores subglobose lightly 6-angled shining flesh-colour in a heap; *sporae conglobatae brunneae oblongae utrinque rotundatae uniseptatae constrictae 25 × 14μ, cellulis subaequalibus, episporio dense subtiliter verrucoso-punctato*, spores collected into a ball brown oblong at both ends (on both sides) rounded 1-septate constricted 25 by 14μ, with cells almost equal, with the epispore densely finely verrucose-dotted ; *sporis ovatis oblongis vel subglobosis apice non incrassatis medio leviter constrictis brunneis verruculosis 16-20× 20-30μ*, with spores ovate oblong or almost globose at the tip not thickened at the middle lightly constricted brown verruculose 16-20 × 20-30μ ; *sporis albis levibus vel valde aculeatis botuliformibus vel anguste oblongis vel ovoideis 1-guttatis haud amyloideis*, with spores white smooth or strongly spiny sausage-shaped or narrowly oblong or ovoid with 1 oil-drop not amyloid (i.e. not giving a blue reaction to iodine) ; see p. 352, Fig. 32.

spore-bearing : sporifer (adj. A), sporophorus (adj. A). **-spored** : *in comp.* -sporus (adj. A).

Sporidiole : sporidiolum (s.n. II).

Sporidium : sporidium (s.n. II).

Sporocarp : sporocarpium (s.n. II).

Sporoclade : sporocladium (s.n. II).

Sporocyst : sporocysta (s.f. I), sporocystis (s.f. III. vi).

Sporodochidium : sporodochidium (s.n. II).

Sporodochium : sporodochium (s.n. II).

sporogenus (adj. A) : producing spores.

Sporophore : sporophorum (s.n. II).

Sporophydium : sporophydium (s.n. II), *abl. sing.* sporophydio, *nom. pl.* sporophydia, *abl. pl.* sporophydiis ; *sporophydia solitaria vel aggregata*, sporophydia solitary or clustered. Concerning this term, the OOGONIUM, q.v., of most writers on Charophyta, *see* H. Horn af Rantzien in *Bot. Notiser* 109 : 215 (1956).

Sporophyll : sporophyllum (s.n. II).

Sporostegium : sporostegium (s.n. II), *abl. sing.* sporostegio, *nom. pl.* sporostegia, *abl. pl.* sporostegiis.

Sporothecium : sporothecium (s.n. II) ; *see* SORUS.

Spot : macula (s.f. I) 'blotch', q.v., punctum (s.n. II) 'dot, point, prick', gutta (s.f. I) 'drop, speck'. **spotless** : immaculatus (adj. A), purus (adj. A). **spotted** : maculatus (adj. A), punctatus (adj. A), guttatus (adj. A) ; *in Gk. comp.*, balio-, sticto-.

Spray : aspergo (s.f. III), *abl. sing.* aspergine.

spreading : (outstretched) effusus (part. A), expansus (part. A), patens (part. B), patulus (adj. A) ; (extending) extendens (part. B). **428**

Spring (season) : ver (s.n. III. v), *gen. sing.* veris. **belonging to spring** : vernalis (adj. B), vernus (adj. A).

Spring (water) : scaturigo (s.f. III. vi), fons (s.m. III. ix). **belonging to springs** : fontanus (adj. A), fontinalis (adj. B), scaturiginus (adj. A).

springing back : resiliens (part. B). **springing out** : exiliens (part B).

sprinkled : conspersus (part. A), adspersus (part. A).

sprouting again : repullulans (part. B).

spumeus (adj. A) : frothy, foaming. **spumosus** (adj. A) : full of foam, frothy, frothlike.

Spur : calcar (s.n. III. x), *gen. sing.* calcaris, *abl. sing.* calcari, *nom. pl.* calcaria, *abl. pl.* calcaribus ; *calcar leviter incurvatum cylindricum viride apice leviter angustatum 5 mm. longum 1 mm. diametro*, spur slightly incurved cylindric green at the tip slightly narrowed 5 mm. long 1 mm. in diameter ; *labellum ante orificium calcaris callosum*, lip in front of opening of spur callose ; *labellum calcari ellipsoideo viridi apice rotundato intus prope ostium pilis patentibus instructo 3 mm. long*, lip with spur ellipsoid green at the tip rounded on the inside near the mouth with spreading hairs furnished 3 mm. long. **spur-like** : calcariformis (adj. B). **spurred** : calcaratus (adj. A); cf. -CERAS.

spurious : fictus (part. A), spurius (adj. A) ; cf. FALSE. **spuriously** : spurie (adv.).

squalidus (adj. A) : dirty, neglected, squalid.

Squama (s.f. I) : scale. **squamatus** (adj. A) : furnished with scales. **Squamella** (s.f. I), **squamellula** (s.f. I) : a little scale, lodicule (*in Gramineae*), subdivision of papus (*in Compositae*). **squamiformis** (adj. B) : shaped like a scale. **squamosus** (adj. A) : scaly, covered with coarse scales. **Squamula** (s.f. I) : lodicule in grasses, small lobe of thallus in lichens. **squamulosus** (adj. A) : minutely scaly, covered with small scales. **497**

square : quadratus (adj. A).

squarrosus (adj. A) : squarrose, i.e. rough with scales, tips of bracts, etc., projecting outwards usually at about 90°. **495**

stabilis (adj. B) : firm, steadfast, stable.

stachy-, stachyo-, -stachys, -stachyus : *in Gk. comp.*, relating to a spike ; *nom. sing.* stachys, *acc. sing.* stachyn, *gen. sing.* stachyis, *abl. sing.* stachye, *nom. and acc. pl.* stachyes, *gen. pl.* stachyum, *dat. and abl. pl.* stachyibus ; gen. sing. of generic name *Stachys* (s.f.) is *Stachydis*, hence the epithet *stachydifolius*, woundwort-leaved ; *barystachys*, with a heavy spike ; *leptostachys, leptostachyus*, with a slender spike ; *macrostachys, macrostachyus*, with a large spike ;

polystachyus, with many spikes; *stachyurus*, with a tail-like pendulous spike.

stagnalis (adj. B), **stagnatilis** (adj. B): growing in standing water, belonging to ponds *or* pools.

stagnant: stagnans (part. B), iners (adj. B).

Stagnum (s.n. II): a piece of standing water, a pool, pond *or* swamp.

Stain: labes (s.f. III), *abl. sing.* labe.

stained: (*by dyeing*) coloratus (part. A), fucatus (part. A), tinctus (part. A); (*by soiling*) foedatus (part. A), inquinatus (part. A).

Stalk: (*of leaf*) petiolus (s.m. II); (*of frond*) stipes (s.m. III. ii); (*of inflorescence*) pedunculus (s.m. II); (*of flower or fruit*) pedicellus (s.m. II); (*of moss capsule*) seta (s.f. I); (*of agarics, etc.*) stipes (s.m. III. ii).

stalkless: apodus (adj.A), sessilis (adj.B).

Stamen: stamen (s.n. III. vi), *acc. sing.* stamen, *gen. sing.* staminis, *dat. sing.* stamini, *abl. sing.* stamine, *nom. and acc. pl.* stamina, *gen. pl.* staminum, *dat. and abl. pl.* staminibus; *stamen unicum*, stamen one; *stamina tot quot lobi corollae et iis alterna, apicem versus tubi inserta e fauce emergentia*, stamens as many as the lobes of the corolla and alternate with these, towards the apex of the tube inserted from the throat emerging; *stamina libera vel basi tantum vel in tubum alte connata*, stamens free or at base alone or into a tube high united; *stamina exserta, basi corollae affixa, filamentis elongatis*, stamens exserted, to the base of the corolla attached, with filaments elongated; *stamina inclusa, medio vel supra medium corollae inserta*, stamens included, at the middle or above the middle of the corolla inserted; *petalis oblongis stamina duplo superantibus*, with petals oblong twice as long as the stamens; *corolla intus ad basin staminum partium liberarum barbata*, corolla inside at the base of the free parts of the stamens bearded; *staminibus perigonium paulo usque plus sesqui superantibus*, with stamens the perigon by a little up to by 1½ times overtopping; *staminibus inclusis, quam petala brevioribus*, with stamens included, shorter than the petals. **-stamened**: *in Gk. comp.*, -andrus, -stemon, *in L. comp.*, -stamineus.

staminalis (adj. B), **staminaris** (adj. B), **staminealis** (adj. B), **stamineus** (adj. A): relating to stamens, staminal. **staminatus** (adj. A): provided with stamens (*used of wholly male flowers on monoecious or dioecious plants*). **staminifer** (adj. A): stamen-bearing.

Staminode: staminodium (s.n. II), *abl. sing.* staminodio, *nom. pl.* staminodia, *abl. pl.* staminodiis; *stamina 4, quinto postico ad staminodium anantherum reducto, rarius 5 perfecta*, stamens 4, with the fifth posticous one to an antherless staminode reduced, more rarely 5 perfect; *staminodium ad apicem tubi squamiforme suborbiculare vel latius quam longum integrum vel retusum glabrum*, staminode at the top of the tube scale-like almost orbicular or broader than long entire or retuse glabrous; *staminodia tot quot stamina et iis eadem serie alterna petaloidea dentata vel lacera*, staminodes as many as stamens and with those in the same series alternate petaloid dentate or lacerate; *staminodia acuminata staminibus alterna et cum iis tubum connata*, staminodes acuminate alternate with the stamens and with these at base into a tube united.

staminosus (adj. A): with very prominent stamens.

Standard petal: vexillum (s.n. II), petalum (s.n. II) posterius magnum; *vexillum late obovatum vel fere orbiculare c. 3 cm. longum 2·5 cm. latum, marginem versus pallide purpureum, medium versus violaceum, in medio ipso lacteum maculis purpureis notatum*, standard broadly obovate or almost orbicular about 3 cm. long 2·5 cm. broad, towards the margin pale purple, towards the middle violet, in the middle itself milkwhite with purple spots marked; *corolla flava vexillo orbiculari vel oblongo, sursum curvato, basim versus cuneato vel in unguem angustum diminuato*, corolla yellow with standard orbicular or oblong, above curved, towards the base cuneate or into a narrow claw diminished.

standing out: exstans (part. B), prominens (part. B); *folio ad angulum 50° a caule exstante*, with leaf at an angle of 50° from the stem standing out.

stans (part. B): standing upright.

Star: stella (s.f. I); *ad instar stellae*, in the form of a star, like a star; cf. STELLATIM.

Starch: amylum (s.n. II), *gen. sing.* amyli; *cellulae amylo impletae*, cells filled with starch. **starch-like**: amyloideus (adj. A). **starchy**: amylaceus (adj. A).

starry: stellatus (adj. A), q.v.

State: status (s.m. IV), *abl. sing.* statu; *in statu erratico*, in the mobile state; *in statu juvenili*, in the young state; *in statu vivo*, in the living state; *in statu sicco*, in the dried state; *in statu maturo*, in the mature state.

stated: dictus (part. A).

statim (adv.): at once, immediately.

stationary: sedentarius (adj. A), immobilis (adj. B) ; cf. QUIETUS, STILL.

Statura (s.f. I) : size, stature.

Stauros: stauros (s.m. II), *abl. sing.* stauro ; *valvae stauro praeditae*, valves with a stauros provided.

steel-grey: chalybeus (adj. A).

-stela (s.f. I), **-stele** (s.f. I) : *in Gk. comp.*, column ; *gen. sing.* steles ; used in names of *Orchidaceae*, e.g. *Platystele, Rhyncostele, Thecostele*.

Stella (s.f. I) : star, q.v. **stellaris** : *see* STELLATUS. **stellatim** (adv.) **ad instar stellae** : star-wise. **stellato-pilosus** (adj. A) :· having stellate hairs. **stellatus** (adj. A), **stellaris** (adj. B) : stellate, starry, i.e. with narrow divisions radiating from a centre like the rays of a star ; *folia pilis stellatis adspersus*, leaves with stellate hairs sprinkled ; cf. ASTEROTRICHUS. **stellinervis** (adj. B) : stellately nerved. **234, 477**

Stellula : stellula (s.f. I).

Stem: caulis (s.m. III. vii), *abl. sing.* caule, *nom. and acc. pl.* caules, *abl. pl.* caulibus ; *caulis florifer singulus 10 cm. altus erectus vel ascendens viridis vel ruber monophyllus*, flowering stem single 10 cm. high erect or ascending green or red oneleaved ; *herba caule 10 cm. alto erecto vel ascendenti viridi vel rubro inferne foliato superne nudo*, herb with stem 10 cm. high erect or ascending green or red below leafy above naked ; *caules plures sinistrorsum volubiles graciles glabri aculeis armati virides vel rubri*, stems several to the left twining slender glabrous with prickles armed green or red ; *frutex alte scandens caulibus gracilibus glabris aculeis armatis viridibus vel rubris*, shrub high climbing with stems slender glabrous with prickles armed green or red. Cf. CULM. **stem, pertaining to the** : caulinus (adj. A). **stem-clasping** : amplexicaulis (adj. A). **stemless** : acaulis (adj. B). **-stemmed** : *in Gk. and L. comp.*, -caulis (adj. B); *erythrocaulis, rubricaulis*, red-stemmed. **441**

-stemma (s.n. III. ix) : *in Gk. comp.*, garland, wreath. Not to be confused with *stema* (s.n. III. ix) penis, stamen.

-stemon (s.m. III) : *in Gk. comp.*, -stamen ; *callistemon*, with beautiful stamens ; *platystemon*, with broad stamens ; cf. STAMENED.

Steppe: steppa (s.f. I).

stercorarius (adj. A) : pertaining to *or* growing on dung. **stercoreus** (adj. A) : dungy, stinking. **Stercus** (s.n. III) : dung ; *see* DUNG, FAECES.

Stereid: stereida (s.f. I), *nom. pl.* stereidae, *gen. pl.* stereidarum, *abl. pl.* stereidis ; *stratis pluribus stereidarum ventralium et dorsalium*, with several layers of ventral and dorsal stereids.

Sterigma: sterigma (s.n. III. xi), *abl. sing.* sterigmate, *nom. pl.* sterigmata, *abl. pl.* sterigmatibus.

sterile: sterilis (adj. B). **Sterility** : sterilitas (s.f. III. ii). **sterilized** : sterilifactus (adj. A), sterilisatus (adj. A).

Stichid: stichidium (s.n. II).

-stichus: *in Gk. comp.*, in a row or line ; *distichus*, in two rows ; *hexastichus*, in six rows, *polystichus*, in many rows ; *see* -FARIUS, ROW.

sticky: glutinosus (adj. A), viscidus (adj. A), viscosus (adj. A).

stict-, sticto- : *in Gk. comp.*, spotted, dotted ; *stictocarpus*, with spotted fruit. **stictus** (adj. A) : dotted.

stiff: rigidus (adj. A), rigens (part. B). **becoming stiff** : rigescens (part. B).

Stigma: stigma (s.n. III. xi), *gen. sing.* stigmatis, *abl. sing.* stigmate, *nom. pl.* stigmata, *gen. pl.* stigmatum, *abl. pl.* stigmatibus. The forms assumed by this organ are described as follows : *stigma indivisum parvum punctiforme*, stigma undivided small reduced to a mere point ; *stigma dilatatum et obsolete trilobum interdum excavatum viride vel album*, stigma broadened and faintly three-lobed sometimes hollowed out green or white ; *stigma simplex sed variis formis ludens, discoideum maximum radiatim quadrilobatum, perigonii faucem claudens, vel hemisphaericum vel conicum vel globosum*, stigma simple but making play with various forms, disc-like most large radiatingly four-lobed, the mouth of the perigon closing, or hemispherical or conical or globose ; *stigma terminale brevissime bilobum*, stigma terminal very shortly two-lobed ; *stigma lineare decurrens 2 mm. longum*, stigma linear decurrent 2 mm. long ; *stigma infra apicem styli laterale excavatum ciliatum*, stigma below apex of style lateral hollowed out ciliated ; *stigma aequaliter bilamellatum, lamellis (vel styli lobis) ovatis vel oblongis 2-4 mm. longis intus stigmatosis*, stigma evenly two-lamellate, with the lamellae (or lobes of the style) ovate or oblong 2-4 mm. long on the inside stigmatic ; *stigma capitatum rubrum vel purpureum c. 1 mm. diametro*, stigma capitate red or purple about 1 mm. in diameter ; *stigma penicillato-multifidum*, stigma divided into many parts in the form of a brush ; *stylus clavatus, stigmate terminali vel sublaterali vel prope apicem laterali*, style club-shaped with stigma terminal or almost lateral or near the apex lateral; *stylus filiformis, stigmate subgloboso integro 3 mm. lato vel didymo vel bigloboso*, style thread-like, with stigma almost spherical entire 3 mm. broad or deeply two-lobed or forming two spheres; *stylus glaber in stigmata duo linearia 2 mm. longa exiens*, style glabrous into stigmas two linear 2 mm. long running out; *stylus nunc indivisus, stigmate rotundato in discum expanso, nunc apice in lobos 2 vel 3 brevissimos intus stigmatosos divisus*, style sometimes undivided, with stigma rounded into a disc expanded, sometimes at the tip into lobes 2 or 3 very short on the inside stigmatic divided; *styli apex supra annulum stigmatosum productus*, apex of style above the stigmatic ring drawn out; *stylus apice indusio cupulato stigma includenti instructus*, style at the tip with cup-like indusium enclosing the stigma provided; *stylus elongatus bifidus, ramis breviter vel profunde bifidis, stigmatibus capitatis vel clavatis*, style elongated bifid, with branches shortly or deeply bifid, with the stigmas capitate or clavate; *stigmata terminalia parva punctiformia vel per styli lobos decurrentia*, stigmas terminal small point-like or along the lobes of style running downwards; *stigmata basin antherarum haud attingentia*, stigmas the base of the anthers not reaching; *stigmata aurantiaca integra antheros multo superantia*, stigmas orange entire the anthers by much overtopping; *stigmata placentarum numero in capitulum connata*, stigmas the same number as the placentas into a small head united; *stigmata unum ad tria indivisa purpurea plumosa pilis simplicibus vel ramosis*, stigmas one to three undivided purple plumose with hairs simple or branched; *stigmata radii e corolla exserta, disci inclusa*, stigmas of the ray-area from the corolla exserted, of the disc included; *stigmata ramosa ramis capillaceis*, stigmas branched with branches hair-like; Gk. neuter words ending in *-ma*, such as *lemma, parenchyma, protonema, rhizoma, stoma, systema* and *trichoma*, together with generic names of Gk. origin formed from *-calymma, -derma, -desma, -nema, -paegma, -phragma, -soma, -sperma, -stelma, -stemma, -stigma* and *-stoma*, are treated like *stigma* above. The term *stigma* is also used for 'eye-spot'.

stigmaticus (adj. A): stigmatic, i.e. provided with a papillose or sticky pollen-receptive surface, relating to a stigma. **stigmatifer** (adj. A): stigma-bearing. **stigmatiformis** (adj. B), stig-

matoideus (adj. A): shaped like *or* having the appearance of a stigma. **stigmatosus** (adj. A): having especially well-developed or conspicuous stigmas.

Stigmatocyst: stigmatocysta (s.f. I).

Stigmatopod: stigmatopodium (s.n. II).

stilbeus (adj. A), **stilbiformis** (adj. A), **stilboideus** (adj. A): having a long stalk of hyphae and a head of spores, as in *Stilbaceae*.

still: quietus (adj. A), tranquillus (adj. A); *in aquis tranquillis*, in still waters.

stilt-like: gralliformis (adj. B), q.v.; BUTTRESS.

stimulans (part. B): stinging. **stimulosus** (adj. A): well provided with stings; cf. URENS.

Stimulus (s.m. II): sting.

Sting: (*organ*) stimulus (s.m. II), (*wound*) ictus (s.m. IV). **stinging**: urens (part. B).

stinking: foetens (adj. B), foetidus (adj. A), foetulentus (adj. A), nauseosus (adj. A) 'sickening', putidus (adj. A) 'rotten', stercoreus (adj. A) 'dungy'; *herba odore alliaceo etiam in sicco valde foetens*, herb with garlic odour even in a dry state strongly smelling.

stipatus (part. A): surrounded, crowded.

Stipe: stipes (s.m. III. ii), *gen. sing.* stipitis, *abl. sing.* stipite, *nom. pl.* stipites, *gen. pl.* stipitum, *abl. pl.* stipitibus, *lit.* 'log, stock, trunk'; *stipes centralis raro excentricus rectus aut incurvus cartilagineus solidus basi leviter attenuatus glaber, in speciminibus siccis fuscescens*, stipe (stalk, stem) central rarely excentric straight or incurved cartilaginous solid at base slightly attenuate glabrous, in dried specimens becoming fuscous; *stipes nigricans basi velo residuo caeterum nudus, siccitate tenuissime striatus, longitudine inter 2 et 5 cm. varians, in procerioribus 0·5 mm. crassus, fragilis intus fistulosus et succo gelatinoso repletus sursum incrassatus*, stipe blackish at base with remains of the velum for the rest naked, in a dried state thinly striate, in length between 2 and 5 cm. varying, in the taller specimens 0·5 mm. thick, fragile inside fistular and with a gelatinous juice filled above thickened; *stipes omnino lateralis verticalis 10 cm. longus valde inaequalis, tuberculis nempe variae magnitudinis exasperatus, caeterum laevigatus et ut pileus crusta laccata obductus, basi saepius dilatata scutatim ligno aut cortici affixus, intus irregulariter lacunosus vel spongiosus*, stipe completely lateral vertical 10 cm. long very unequal in thickness, with tubercles certainly of varied size rough, for the rest

smooth and like the pileus with a varnished crust covered over, by the base
most often swollen in a shield-like
manner to wood or bark attached, inside
irregularly perforated or spongy; *stipite
centrali vel excentrico, sed haud omnino
laterali, recto cartilagineo fistuloso, haud
solido, glabro 10 cm. longo brunneo nudo
laevi, haud viscido, aequali vel apice
dilatato,* with stipe central or excentric,
but never completely lateral, straight
cartilaginous fistular, never solid, glabrous 10 cm. long brown naked smooth,
never viscid, of even thickness or at
the tip expanded; *receptaculum absque
stipite distincto,* receptacle (fruit-body)
without a distinct stipe; *stipite 10-20 cm.
longo stramineo haud purpureo sulcato,
paleis brunneis integris iis rhizomatis
similibus basi vestito, caeterum nudo,*
with the stipe 10-20 cm. long straw-
coloured never purple grooved, with
scales brown entire similar to those of
rhizome at base clothed, otherwise
naked; *clavula in stipitem albidum
attenuata,* club-like receptacles into a
whitish stipe drawn out; *peridium in
stipitem radiciformem 2 mm. longum
crassumque productum,* peridium into a
root-shaped 2 mm. long and thick stipe
lengthened.
Stipella (s.f. I): stipel. **stipellatus** (adj. A)
provided with stipels, i.e. secondary
stipules of compound leaves.
stipitatus (adj. A): stipitate, i.e. provided
with a stipe or little stalk; *ovarium
stipitatum, stipite 2 mm. longo,* ovary
stipitate, with the stipe 2 mm. long. **449**
stipulaceus (adj. A), **stipularis** (adj. B):
stipulaceous, of *or* belonging to stipules.
stipulaneus (adj. A): taking the place of
stipules, formed by the transformation
of stipules; *spina stipulanea,* stipu-
laneous spine (*as in Capparis, Acacia,
etc.*).
Stipule: stipula (s.f. I), *dat. and abl. sing.*
stipula, *nom. pl.* stipulae, *dat. and abl.
pl.* stipulis; *stipulae nullae,* stipules
none; *stipulae semper deficientes,* stipules always lacking; *folia estipulata,*
leaves without stipules; *stipulae cauli
adnatae,* stipules adnate to the stem;
stipulae petiolo adnatae, stipules adnate
to the petiole; *stipulae liberae juxta
basin petioli obviae, parvae, longe persistentes, triangulares,* stipules free next
to base of petiole present, small, long
persistent, triangular; *stipulae inter-
petiolares binae foliis consimiles sed
minores vel ad dentes triangulares redactae vel omnino obsoletae,* stipules between the petioles 2 to the leaves similar

but smaller or to triangular teeth
reduced or entirely obsolete; *folia
stipulis adnatis oblongis apice acutis
1 cm. longis,* leaves with stipules adnate
oblong at the tip acute 1 cm. long.
stipulifer (adj. A): stipule-bearing. **sti-
puliformis** (adj. B): shaped as if a
stipule.
Stipulode: stipulodium (s.n. II), *abl. sing.*
stipulodio, *nom. pl.* stipulodia, *abl. pl.*
stipulodiis.
Stirps (s.f. III): plant, stock, shoot, race;
*rariorum aliquot stirpium per Hispaniam
observatarum historia,* an account of
some rather rare plants observed in
Spain.
Stolon: stolo (s.m. III. vi), *gen. sing.*
stolonis, *abl. sing.* stolone, *nom. pl.*
stolones, *abl. pl.* stolonibus; *caudex
emittens stolones pubescentes rubros vel
virides ad 10 cm. longos et 5 mm. crassos,*
rootstock putting forth stolons (runners)
pubescent red or green to 10 cm. long
and 5 mm. thick; *caudex stolonibus
pubescentibus rubris,* rootstock with
stolons pubescent red; cf. FLAGELLUM,
RHIZOMA, RUNNER, SARMENTUM.
stoloniformis (adj. B): stoloniform, resembling a stolon; *caulis pars basalis
stoloniformis,* of the stem the basal part
stoloniform. **stoloniformiter** (adv.) in a
stoloniform manner, like a stolon.
Stoma: stoma (s.n. III. xi), *abl. sing.*
stomate, *nom. pl.* stomata, *abl. pl.*
stomatibus; *stomata elliptica, cellulis
epidermidis minora vel easdem superficie
fere aequantia vel majora, propatulo
angusto, cellulis accessoriis magnis,*
stomata elliptic, smaller than or almost
the same on the surface as or larger than
the cells of the epidermis, with the
stomatal opening narrow, with the
guard cells large; cf. PROPATULUM.
stomata-bearing: stomatophorus (adj.
A).
Stone (of a fruit): putamen (s.n. III);
*putamen compressum 7 mm. longum
4 mm. latum 2 mm. crassum rugulosum,
a ventre sulco lato profundo in longitudinem exaratum,* stone compressed
7 mm. long 4 mm. wide 2 mm. thick
somewhat rugose, on the ventral side
by a broad deep groove lengthwise furrowed; *see* ENDOCARP.
Stone (rock): saxum (s.n. II), *abl. sing.*
saxo, *abl. pl.* saxis; lapis (s.m. III. ii),
abl. sing. lapide, *abl. pl.* lapidibus.
stone-hard: lapideus (adj. A). **stony**:
lapidosus (adj. A), saxosus (adj. A).
Stony Ground or Place: saxa (s.n. II.
pl.), *abl. pl.* saxis; saxosa (s.n. II. pl.),
abl. pl. saxosis.

Stopper : obturamentum (s.n. II).
Storage Region : regio (s.f. III. vi) penaria.
stored : conditus (part. A).
stout : crassus (adj. A) 'thick', validus (adj. A) 'strong'.
straggling : effusus (part. A).
straight : rectus (adj. A), strictus (part. A).
straight-nerved : rectinervis (adj. B), rectinervius (adj. A). **straightforward** : protinus (adv.). **350, 388, 389**
Strait : fretum (s.n. II), fretus (s.m. IV) ; *frutices ad Fretum Magellanicum crescentes*, shrubs at the Straits of Magellan growing.
stramineus (adj. A) : straw-yellow (H.C.C. *60.4*).
Strand (shore): littus (s.n. III). **Strand** (thread) : filum (s.n. II).
strange : peregrinus (adj. A) 'foreign', mirus (adj. A) 'wonderful', insuetus (adj. A) 'unusual'.
strangulatus (part. A) : throttled, i.e. narrowed and then widened again.
strap-shaped : ligulatus (adj. A), loratus (adj. A), loriformis (adj. B) ; *in Gk. comp.* himanto- ; cf. BAND-SHAPED.
stratosus (adj. A) : in distinct layers. **Stratum** (s.n. II) : layer of tissue.
straw-coloured : stramineus (adj. A).
Stream : rivulus (s.m. II).
Stria (s.f. I) : stria, fine linear marking, line, streak, *or* groove ; *nom. pl.* striae, *abl. pl.* striis ; *striis transversis et longitudinalibus parallelis vel radiantibus subtilibus vel distinctis, 12-14 in 10μ*, with striae transverse and longitudinal parallel or radiating faint or distinct, 12-14 within a length of 10 μ ; *striis raphem non attingentibus*, with striae not reaching the raphe. **striatus** (adj. A) : striate, i.e. marked with striae. **254**
Strictura (s.f. I) : contraction, constriction.
strictus (part. A) : drawn close together, very upright, very straight. **389**
Striga (s.f. I) : striga, a straight rigid closepressed rather short bristle-like hair. **strigosus** (adj. A) : covered with strigae.
Striola (s.f. I) : a very fine linear marking ; *see* STRIA. **striolatus** (adj. A) : striolate, i.e. with fine linear markings.
striped : fasciatus (adj. A), grammatus (adj. A) 'with raised lines', vittatus (adj. A) 'longitudinally striped' ; cf. FASCIATUS.
stripped : denudatus (part. A).
strobilaceus (adj. A), **strobiliformis** (adj. B), **strobilinus** (adj. A) : strobilaceous, i.e. formed of overlapping scales like a pine-cone ; *paniculae femineae e spicis paucis pendulis strobiliformibus bracteis plurifariam laxe imbricatis membranaceis*, panicles female from (made from) spikes few pendulous cone-like with bracts in many rows loosely overlapping membranous. **Strobilus** (s.m. II) : cone ; *strobilus ovoideus vel globosus lignosus, squamis valde incrassatis post anthesin auctis persistentibus*, cone ovoid or globose woody, with scales strongly thickened after anthesis enlarged persistent ; *strobili maturi caerulei vel rubri ½-1 poll. diametro*, mature cones blue or red ½-1 in. in diameter.
Stroma : stroma (s.n. III), *abl. sing.* stromate, *nom. pl.* stromata, *abl. pl.* stromatibus ; *stroma parcum peridermio tectum crustaceum effusum undulatum nigrum*, stroma scanty by the peridermium covered crustaceous stretched out undulate black ; *stromata gregaria erumpentia, peridermio laciniatim rupto cincta, pulvinata*, stromata in groups bursting the surface, by the periderm laciniately broken surrounded, cushion-like.
strombuliformis (adj. B) : twisted in a long spire. **13**
strong : validus (adj. A), fortis (adj. B). **strongly** : valde (adv.).
strong-smelling ; graveolens (adj. B) ; cf. STINKING.
Strophiole : strophiolum (s.n. II), *abl. sing.* strophiolo, *nom. pl.* strophiola, *abl. pl.* strophiolis.
Structura (s.f. I) : structure, organization ; cf. COMPAGES, FABRICA.
Struma (s.f. I) : cushion-like swelling *or* tumour. **strumosus** (adj. A) : provided with a swelling.
Strut : tigillum (s.n. II), q.v.
stuffed : farctus (part. A), farctilis (adj. B). Used when interior is filled with substance of very different texture from the exterior ; cf. FILLED.
stuppeus (adj. A), **stupposus** (adj. A) : covered with matted tow-like hairs.
stylaris (adj. B) : relating to the style. **stylatus** (adj. A) : provided with a style, usually a conspicuous one ; cf. STYLOSUS.
Style : stylus (s.m. II), *gen. sing.* styli, *abl. sing.* stylo, *nom. pl.* styli, *abl. pl.* stylis ; *stylus rectus nunc brevis vel brevissimus nunc filiformis elongatus, in ovario uniloculari saepius excentricus mox lateralis in ovario biloculari centralis, stigmate parvo capitato*, style straight sometimes short or very short sometimes thread-like elongated, on a one-chambered ovary often off the centre and soon lateral, on a two-chambered ovary central, with the stigma small capitate ; *stylus clavatus inferne glaber superne pubescens*, style club-shaped below glabrous above pubescent ; *stylus exsertus curvatus, cum stigmate ad 2 cm. longus, ad 2 mm. latus*, style exserted

curved, including the stigma to 2 cm. long, 2 mm. broad ; *ovarium in stylum glabrum circiter 1 mm. longum transiens*, ovary into a style glabrous about 1 mm. long passing ; *stylus supra ovarium abrupte inflexus inferne glaber superne plus minus longitudinaliter barbatus, intra rostrum carinae incrassatus et cum eo tortus, stigmate obliquo*, style above the ovary abruptly bent inwards below glabrous above more or less longitudinally bearded, within the beak of the keel thickened and together with this twisted, with stigma oblique ; *stylus staminibus duplo brevior*, style than the stamens twice shorter (i.e. half as long) ; *ovarium stylo recto haud curvato albido vel rubro pubescenti 3 cm. longo*, ovary with style straight not curved whitish or red pubescent 3 cm. long ; *styli a basi usque ad medium connati apice liberi divaricati hirsuti ad 4 cm. longi*, styles from base up to the middle united at the tip free extremely divergent hairy up to 4 cm. long ; *styli riguli filiformes albidi, senescentes inferne violacei, ab apice usque ad medium vel etiam usque fere ad basim pubescentes non hispidi*, style somewhat rigid thread-like whitish, with age in the lower part violet, from the tip to the middle or even almost to the base pubescent not hispid ; *discus epigynus crassus styli basin cingens*, disc epigynous thick the base of the style surrounding ; *styli purpurascentes antheras superantes vel staminibus aequilongi, apice stigmatoso unilaterali 3 mm. longo distincte falcato*, styles purplish the anthers overtopping or as long as the stamens, with the one-sided 3 mm. long stigmatic tip distinctly falcate.

Stylidium : stylidium (s.n. II).

Styliductus (s.m. III) : stylar canal.

stylifer (adj. A) : style-bearing.   **styliformis** (adj. B) : like a style.   **stylinus** (adj. A) : belonging to the style.

Stylodium : stylodium (s.n. II).

Stylogonidium : stylogonidium (s.n. II).

Stylopod : stylopodium (s.n. II).

Stylostegium : stylostegium (s.n. II).

stylosus : (adj. A) : having a conspicuous *or* persistent style.

Stylus (s.m. II) : style, q.v.

suaveolens (adj. B) : fragrant, smelling sweetly : cf. ODOUR.

suavis (adj. B) : sweet, pleasant, delightful.

sub (prep.): used *with abl. or acc.* to indicate position (object under which a thing is situated or extends) or time (at which, immediately before or immediately after an action takes place) ; *with abl.* under, below, near (indicating object under,

etc., which thing is situated), during, within, at (indicating time when action takes place) ; *with acc.* under, below, towards (indicating object under which thing extends, the verb being usually one of motion), shortly before, up to, until *or* immediately after, just after (indicating a close approximation in time) ; *sub lente valido*, under a strong lens ; *sub microscopio*, under the microscope ; *sub hoc nomine*, under this name ; *sub anthesi*, at anthesis.

sub- : *in L. comp.*, somewhat, not completely, a little. Before words beginning with *m*, *sub-* becomes *sum-* ; before *r* it becomes *sur-* ; *subacutus*, somewhat acute ; *subalbidus*, somewhat whitish ; *subalpinus*, subalpine, growing below the alpine region marked by the timber line ; *sub-bilocularis*, almost bilocular, the partition not complete ; *subcordatus*, with rounded basal lobes separated by a shallow notch ; *subglobosus*, almost spherical ; *subnudus*, almost naked. The meaning of the numerous analogous compounds, such as *subaculeatus, subaequalis, subalternifolius*, etc., should be self-evident, the original meaning of the adjective being lessened in force by the addition of *sub* meaning 'almost' or 'somewhat'. **111, 167, 227**

subductus (part. A) : drawn from below, pulled up, dredged.

Suber (s.n. III. v) : cork.   **subereus** (adj. A), **suberosus** (adj. A) : corky. **317**

sub-erosus (adj. A) : somewhat erose, slightly gnawed in appearance.

Subfamily : subfamilia (s.f. I), *gen. sing.* subfamiliae ; cf. FAMILY.

Subgenus : subgenus (s.n. III. iv), *gen. sing.* subgeneris ; cf. GENUS.

Subicle : subiculum (s.n. II), *abl. sing.* subiculo ; *subiculum tomentosum extensum e fibrillis ramosissimis flexuosis intertextis constans*, subiculum (mycelium under fruit-body) tomentose outspread composed from fibrils (hyphae) much branched flexuous interwoven.

subiens (part. B) : submitting to, undergoing.

subinde (adv.) : immediately after.

subito (adv.) : suddenly, unexpectedly.

subjectus (part. A) : placed below, lying beneath.

submarinus (adj. A) : under the sea.

submersus (part. A) : submerged, growing under water ; opposite of *emersus* ; *caules plantae submersae 15-20 cm. longi, ei plantae emersae 5-10 cm. longi*, stems of submerged plant 15-20 cm. long, those of emerged plant 5-10 cm. long. **392**

Subsection: subsectio (s.f. III. vi), *gen. sing.* subsectionis ; cf. SECTION.

Subseries: subseries (s.f. V), *gen. sing.* subseriei ; cf. SERIES.

subsidiarius (adj. A) : subsidiary.

Subspecies: subspecies (s.f. V), *gen. sing.* subspeciei ; cf. SPECIES.

Subspecioid: subspecioides (s.m. III), *gen. sing.* subspecioidis, *nom. pl.* subspecioides, *abl. pl.* subspecioidibus.

Substance: substantia (s.f. I), *abl. sing.* substantia ; contextus (s.m. IV), *abl. sing.* contextu ; caro (s.f. III. vi), *abl. sing.* carne, *lit.* 'flesh' ; *substantia pilei tenuis candida, e filamentis ramosis intricatis septatis in tramam similarem descendentibus composita*, substance of the pileus thin pure white, from filaments branched entangled septate into the similar trama descending composed ; *contextus pilei suberosus colore flavo insignis*, context (substance of hyphal mass) of the pileus corky by its yellow colour remarkable ; *species contextu intense colorato distincta*, species by the deeply coloured context distinct.

substituted : succedaneus (adj. A), substitutus (part. A).

Substratum : substratum (s.n. II), *abl. sing.* substrato.

subtended : subtentus (part. A).

subter (adv.) : below, beneath underneath, in a lower place. **subter** (prep. with acc. and abl.) : below, beneath, underneath, under.

subterraneus (adj. A) : underground, in the soil (*opp. of* SUPRATERRANEUS) ; *see* EPIGAEUS, HYPOGAEUS. **470**

subtilis (adj. B) : fine, precise, delicate. **subtiliter** (adv.) : finely, minutely.

subtracted : demptus (part. A).

subtus (adv.) : below, beneath, underneath, in a lower place.

Subula (s.f. I) : a fine sharp point, *lit.* 'an awl'. **subulatus** (adj. A), **subuliformis** (adj. B) : subulate, awl-shaped, i.e. tapering from a narrow or moderately broad base to a very fine point. **subuli-** : *in L. comp.*, subulate- ; *subulifer*, awl-bearing, subulate ; *subulifolius*, subulate-leaved ; *subulisepalus*, with subulate sepals. **114**

subvexus (adj. A) : sloping upwards (*opp. of* DEVEXUS) ; *see* SLOPING.

succedaneus (adj. A) : substituted, taking the place of something else ; cf. STIPULANEUS.

successive : successivus (adj. A). **successively** : deinceps (adv.), invicem (adv.), successive (adv.) ; cf. ALIUS.

succidus (adj. A) : juicy.

succineus (adj. A) : amber-coloured.

succisus (part. A) : abruptly broken off, cut across from below.

succosus (adj. A) : full of juice, sappy.

succubus (adj. A) : succubous, i.e. obliquely inserted on the stem so that the leaf-edge nearest the shoot-tip is overlapped by and covered by the lower edge of the leaf above ; *folia succuba magna valde oblique inserta*, leaves succubous large very obliquely inserted.

succulent : succulentus (adj. A) 'sappy, juicy', carnosus (adj. A) 'abounding in flesh, fleshy'. **327**

Succus (s.m. II) : juice, sap.

Sucker : surculus (s.m. II), q.v.

Sucrose : sucrosum (s.n. II), *gen. sing.* sucrosi.

suddenly : subito (adv.), abrupte (adv.).

sufficiens (part. B) : sufficient, adequate. **sufficienter** (adv.) : sufficiently, enough.

sufflatus (part. A) : blown up, inflated, bloated ; *see* INFLATUS, PHYSO-, VESICARIUS.

suffrutescens (adj. B) : slightly woody. **Suffrutex** (s.m. III. i) : half-shrub, subshrub, perennial plant with only lower part woody. **suffruticosus** (adj. A) : somewhat woody, woody only at base.

suffultus (part. A) : supported, propped, subtended.

suffusus (part. A) : tinged, q.v.

Sugar : saccharum (s.n. II), *gen. sing.* sacchari ; cf. SUCROSE. **sugary** : saccharatus (adj. A), saccharinus (adj. A).

sui (pron.) : of itself.

suitable : aptus (part. A), idoneus (adj. A).

sulcatus (adj. A) : furrowed or grooved. **sulcinervis** (adj. B), **sulcinervius** (adj. A) : with grooved (i.e. sunken) nerves. **Sulcus** (s.m. II) : furrow *or* groove.

Sulphate : sulphas (s.m. III), *gen. sing.* sulphatis. **Sulphide** : sulphidum (s.n. II), *gen. sing.* sulphidi. **Sulphur** : sulphur (s.n. III), *gen. sing.* sulphuris ; *less often* sulfur (s.n. III). **sulphur yellow** : sulphureus (adj. A) ; *less often* sulfureus (adj. A), H.C.C.1. **sulphurated** : sulphuratus (adj. A) ; *in fonte sulphurata*, in a sulphur spring. **sulphuric** : sulphuricus (adj. A) ; *acidum sulphuricum*, sulphuric acid.

Summary : summarium (s.n. II), *nom. pl.* summaria.

Summer : aestas (s.f. III. ii) ; *aestate ineunte, inita aestate*, at the beginning of summer. **pertaining to summer** ; aestivalis (adj. B), aestivus (adj. A) ; cf. SOLSTITIALIS.

summopere (adv.) : very much, exceedingly.

Summum (s.n. II) : the top, highest place. **summus** (adj. A) : uppermost, highest ; *folia summa*, the uppermost leaves.

Sumptus (s.m. IV) : cost, charge, expense ; *sumptu auctoris*, at the author's expense ; cf. IMPENSA. **sumptus** (part. A) : taken.

sunken : depressus (part. A) 'pressed down', impressus (part. A), 'pressed into', immersus (part. A) 'immersed'.

sunny : apricus (adj. A).

super : (adv. *and* prep. with acc. or abl.) : above, over, on top, during ; *in L. comp.*, over, extra, above.

superans (part. B) : overtopping, longer than, rising above ; *inflorescentia folium caulinum superans*, inflorescence overtopping the cauline leaf. **superatus** (part. A) : overtopped ; *capsula foliis superata*, capsule overtopped by the leaves.

superaxillaris (adj. B), **supra-axillaris** (adj. B) : growing above an axil.

superficialis (adj. B) : occurring on the upper surface. **superficiaris** (adj. B) : on the surface of an organ. **Superficies** (s.f. V) : the upper surface, face.

superfluus (adj. A) : superfluous, unnecessary.

superimpositus (part. A) : placed upon, overlapping.

Superintendent : praefectus (s.m. II), curator (s.m. III. v).

superior (adj. compar.) : higher, upper, former, preceding.

superior : superus (adj. A); *ovarium inferum vel semisuperum vel superum*, ovary inferior or half-superior or superior (*in relation to insertion of sepals, petals and stamens*).

superjectus (part. A) : lying above.

superne (adv.) : upwards, above.

superpendens (part. B) : overhanging.

superpositus (part. A) : placed over *or* upon, vertically above another part.

superus (adj. A) : upper, higher, placed above, superior in position.

supervolutivus (adj. A) : (*in vernation*) when one edge is rolled inwards and is covered by the opposite edge rolled inwards around it. **369**

supinus (adj. A) : bent backwards, prostrate ; cf. PROCUMBENS.

suppetens (part. B) : at hand, available.

suppeto (verb 3rd Conj.) : be at hand, be present ; *flores masculi non suppetebant*, male flowers were not available.

supported : suffultus (part. A), fulcratus (part. A), fultus (part. A). **supporting** : sustinens (part. B), fulcrans (part. B), fulciens (part. B).

supra (adv. and prep. with acc.) : on the upper side, above beyond, over.

supradecompositus (adj. A) : supradecompound, i.e. so many times divided that the degree of division is not readily evident. **205**

subterraneus (adj. A) : above-ground (*opp. of* SUBTERRANEUS) ; cf. EPIGAEUS, HYPOGAEUS.)

supremus (adj. A) : highest, topmost.

sur- : *in L. comp.*, somewhat. Variant of sub- (q.v.), used before words beginning with *r*, e.g. *surrancidus*, somewhat rank ; *surrectus*, almost straight.

Surculus (s.m. II) : sucker, shoot, young branch.

Surface : pagina (s.f. I), *gen. sing.* paginae, *abl. sing.* pagina, *nom. pl.* paginae, *abl. pl.* paginis ; cf. SUPERFICIES.

surgens (part. B) : arising, rising up.

surrounded : circumcinctus (part. A), circumnexus (part. A). **surrounding** : cingens (part. B), ambiens (part. B) ; *nectarium crassum styli basin cingens*, nectary thick the style base encircling.

sursum (adv.) : upwards, from below ; *sursum deorsum*, up and down.

suspended : dependens (part. B), suspensus (part. A).

sustinens (part. B) : upholding, supporting.

sutural : suturalis (adj. B). **Suture** : sutura (s.f. I), *acc. sing.* suturam, *abl. sing.* sutura, *nom. pl.* suturae, *acc. pl.* suturas, *abl. pl.* suturis ; *fructus legumen dictus in valvas 2 secus suturam superiorem vel interiorem et costam seu suturam dorsalem vel inferiorem vel rarius more folliculi ad suturam superiorem tantum dehiscens*, fruit called a legume in valves 2 along the upper or inner suture and the midrib or dorsal or lower suture or very rarely in the manner of a follicle at the upper suture alone dehiscing ; *semina suturae superiori ad margines valvarum alternatim affixa*, seeds to the upper suture at the margins of the valves alternately attached ; *ovula juxta suturam vexillarem* (*i.e. suturam vexillo obversam*) *plura biseriata*, ovules by the side of the vexillary suture (i.e. the suture turned towards the vexillum) many in two series.

Swamp : palus (s.f. III. ii), *gen. sing.* paludis, *abl. sing.* palude, *nom. pl.* paludes, *gen. pl.* paludum, *abl. pl.* paludibus. **swampy, pertaining to swamps** : palustris (adj. B).

Swarm : grex (s.m. III. i).

Swelling : tumor (s.m. III. v) ; *spinae geminae interdum basi in tumorem magnum vel maximum confluentes*, spines paired sometimes at base in a large or very large swelling grown together. **swelling up** : tumescens (part B), tumens (part. B) ; cf. GIBBA, GIBBOSUS.

swimming : natans (part. B) ; *cellula cito natans*, cell rapidly swimming ; *trichomata libere natantia*, trichomes freely swimming. **390**

swinging : oscillans (part. B).

swollen : tumidus (adj. A). *Also in special senses*, gibbus (adj. A), strumosus (adj. A), ventricosus (adj. A), inflatus (part. A), sufflatus (part. A), praegnans (adj. B). swollen- : *in Gk. comp.*, onco-, oedo-.

sword-shaped : ensatus (adj. A), ensiformis (adj. B), gladiatus (adj. A). **116**

Syllabus (s.m. II) : list, register.

Sylloge (s.f. I) : gathering, summary, collection of examples, assembly (*used only in book-titles*).

Sylva (s.f. I), Silva (s.f. I) : wood, forest, woodland ; *silva* is usual in class L., *sylva* in bot. L.

Sylvarius (s.m. II) : forester, forest-officer ; cf. FORESTER, SALTUARIUS.

sylvaticus (adj. A), silvaticus (adj. A), sylvestris (adj. B), silvestris (adj. B) : pertaining to woods, growing wild (*opp. to* CULTUS, SATIVUS). Sylvicola (s.f. I) : inhabitant of woods.

Symbola (s.f. I) : contribution ; *nom. pl.* symbolae ; *symbolae Antillanae*, West Indian contributions.

Symbolus (s.m. II) : sign, mark, token, symbol ; *nom. pl.* symboli.

sympetalus (adj. A) : gamopetalous, i.e. having united petals.

sympodial : sympodialis (adj. B). Sympodium : sympodium (s.n. II).

Sympodule : sympodula (s.f. I).

Symposium : symposium (s.n. II).

syn- : *in Gk. comp.*, with, together. It becomes *sym-* before the letters *b, m* and *p*, as in *symbiosis, symmetricus, sympetalus, symphyostemonus*.

Synandrium : synandrium (s.n. II), *abl. sing.* synandrio.

synantherus (adj. A), synanthericus (adj. A) : with anthers cohering together into a tube or ring ; cf. SYNGENESUS.

synanthus (adj. A), synanthius (adj. A) : with the flowers (*used of leaves produced at the same time as the flowers*); cf. COAETANUS, HYSTERANTHUS, TIME.

Syncarp : syncarpium (s.n. II), *abl. sing.* syncarpio. syncarpous : syncarpus (adj. A).

synclistus (adj. A) : indehiscent.

syngenesus (adj. A) : with anthers united together into a tube or ring ; cf. SYNANTHERUS.

Synnema : synnema (s.n. III. xi).

synoecius (adj. A), synoicus (adj. A) : synoecious, i.e. having male and female flowers or organs mixed together in the same inflorescence.

Synonym : synonymum (s.n. II), *nom. pl.* synonyma, *abl. pl.* synonymis. Synonymy : synonymia (s.f. I) ; *nomenclator botanicus, seu synonymia plantarum universalis, enumerans ordine alphabetico nomina atque synonyma*, botanical nomenclator or whole synonymy of plants, listing in alphabetical order names and synonyms.

Synopsis (s.f. III) : general view, synopsis.

syntheticus (adj. A) : built of separate elements put together, as an allopolyploid species.

Syntype : syntypus (s.m. II) ; cf. TYPUS.

Systema (s.n. III. xi) : a whole consisting of several parts, system, orderly arrangement ; *ambitus totius systematis ramificationis*, outline of the whole system of branching.

systylus (adj. A) : with several styles united into one body.

T

tabacarius (adj. A) : relating to tobacco, e.g. used for making tobacco pipes, as in *Bambusa tabacaria*. tabacinus (adj. A) : tobacco-coloured, pale brown.

tabescens (part. B), tabidus (adj. A) : wasting away, becoming stunted, *hence* aborted.

Tabula (s.f. I) : a print from a plate, *hence* full-page illustration in a book; pileus of certain fungi.

tabularis (adj. B) : flattened horizontally, plate-like, (*in geographical epithets*) growing on Table Mountain, South Africa.

tabulatus (adj. A) : provided with floors, consisting of layer upon layer, i.e. with transverse septa at intervals in a fruit.

tactilis (adj. B) : sensitive to touch.

Tactus (s.m. IV) : touch.

taeni-, taenio- : *in Gk. and L. comp.*, band-like, strap-shaped; *taenifrons*, with band-like fronds ; *taeniophyllus*, with band-like leaves. Taenia (s.f. I) : ribbon, band. taenianus (adj. A) : long, somewhat flattened and contracted in various places, like a tapeworm (Taenia). taeniatus (adj. A), taeniformis (adj. B) : band- or ribbon-like. **87**

Tail : cauda (s.f. I), *abl. sing.* cauda. tailed : caudatus (adj. A); cf. URO-. **152**

taken away from : ademptus (part. A), demptus (part. A). taken out of : excerptus (part. A).

Talea (s.f. I) : a cutting used for propagation.

talis (adj. B) : such, of such a kind. taliter (adv.) : in such wise.

tall : elatus (part. A), celsus (adj. A), procerus (adj. A), excelsus (adj. A), praelongus (adj. A), altus (adj. A). **340**

tam (adv.) : so far, equally, as.

tamdiu (adv.) : so long (*of time*).
tamen (conj.) : notwithstanding, never-theless.
tandem (adv.) : at length, finally.
tangerinus (adj. A) : tangerine-orange (H.C.C. 9).
tangled : implexus (part. A), implicatus (part. A), implicitus (part. A).
tantopere (adv.) : so greatly, so very, to such a large extent.
tantum (adv.) : to such a degree, only, merely, barely.
tantummodo (adv.) : merely.
taper-pointed : acuminatus (adj. A).
tapering : contractus (part. A) 'drawn together', angustatus (part. A) 'nar-rowed', decrescens (part. A) 'growing less', deminutus (part. A) 'lessened', protractus (part. A) 'lengthened out', usually qualified by adv. such as *grada-tim*, gradually, *longe*, long, *cuneatim*, cuneately, *sensim*, gently ; *lamina basi in petiolum alatum gradatim decrescens*, blade at base into the winged petiole gradually diminishing.
tapeworm-shaped : taenianus (adj. A), q.v.
Tap-root : radix (s.f. III) palaris (adj. B) ; *radice palari*, with a tap-root.
tarde (adv.) : slowly.
tardiflorus (adj. A) : late-flowering ; cf. SEROTINUS. tardus (adj. A) : late, slow.
tartareus (adj. A) : tartareous, having a rough crumbling surface like tartar. 332
Taste : sapor (s.m. III. v), *abl. sing.* sapore ; gustus (s.m. IV), *abl. sing.* gustu ; *pileus odore et sapore vix manifestis*, pileus with smell and taste scarcely evident ; *caro sapore vix sensibili, haud amaro vel amariusculo*, flesh with taste scarcely perceptible, never bitter or somewhat bitter ; *sapore nullo vel dulci*, with taste none or sweet. tasteless : insipidus (adj. A); *opposite of* SAPIDUS ; *caro inodora et insipida*, flesh odourless and tasteless.
tawny : fulvus (adj. A), ravus (adj. A).
Taxon : taxon (s.n. II), *gen. sing.* taxi, *abl. sing.* taxo, *nom. pl.* taxa, *gen. pl.* taxorum, *abl. pl.* taxis. Taxonomy : taxonomia (s.f. I).
tear-shaped : lacrimiformis (adj. B), (*some-times but incorrectly*) lachrymaeformis. 12
tearing : findens (part. B).
Tectum (s.n. II) : roof ; *plantae tectorum*, plants of roofs.
tectus (part. A) : covered, hidden, con-cealed.
Teeth : *see* TOOTH.
tegens (part. B) : covering, concealing.
Tegmen (s.n. III. vi), Tegmentum (s.n. II) : covering, *hence* used by older authors

for the glume of grasses, inner coat of a seed.
Tegula (s.f. I) : tile, tiled roof, involucral scale, phyllary.
Tegumentum (s.n. II) : indusium.
Tela (s.f. I) : web, tissue, mycelium.
teleianthus (adj. A) : perfect-flowered, i.e. hermaphrodite.
Teliospore : teliospora (s.f. I), teleutospora (s.f. I).
telmat- : *in Gk. comp.*, referring to wet meadows or pools.
temere (adv.), temeriter (adv.) : at random, fortuitously.
temperate : temperatus (part. A) ; *regio temperata*, temperate region ; *regiones temperatae*, temperate regions ; *species in siccis regionum temperatarum hemi-sphaerae borealis indigenae*, species (pl.) in dry places of the temperate regions of the northern hemisphere indigenous ; *in hemisphaerae borealis regionibus temperatis et frigidis*, in temperate and cold regions of the northern hemisphere ; *species per zonas temperatas et calidas dispersae*, species (pl.) through tem-perate and warm zones dispersed ; *hepaticae in terris temperatis frequentes, in calidis et frigidis rariores*, liverworts in temperate lands frequent, in hot and cold ones rarer.
Temperature : temperatura (s.f. I).
temporarily : temporaliter (adv.), in tem-pus, ad interim. temporary : tempo-rarius (adj. A), temporalis (adj. B).
Tempus (s.n. III. iv) : time, q.v. ; *tempore florendi*, at the time of flowering ; cf. ANTHESIS.
temulentus (adj. A) : drunken, intoxicated.
ten : decem (num. adj. indecl.) 'ten', decimus (adj. A) 'tenth', decies (adv.), deciens (adv.) 'ten times'. ten- : *in L. comp.*, decem-, *in Gk. comp.*, deca-; *decapetalus*, 10-petalled ; *decemdentatus*, 10-toothed ; *decangularis*, abbr. of *decemangularis*, 10-angled.
Tenaculum (s.n. II) : tenacle, i.e. circle of cilia, holdfast.
tenax (adj. B) : holding fast, tough (*opp. to* FRAGILIS).
Tendril : cirrhus (s.m. II) (*usu. applied to leaf-tendrils*), capreolus (s.m. II) (*usu. applied to shoot-tendrils*).
tenellus (adj. A) : delicate.
tenens (part. B) : holding.
Tentaculum (s.n. II) : sensitive glandular hair, as in Drosera.
Tentamen (s.n. III. iv) : attempt.
tenth : decimus (adj. A).
tenui- : *in L. comp.*, slender, thin ; *tenui-caulis*, with slender stem ; *tenuisectus*, finely cut. tenuis (adj. B) : thin, fine,

slender. **Tenuitas** (s.f. III. ii) : thinness.
tenuiter (adv.) : finely, lightly.
tenus (prep. with abl.) : as far as.
Tepal : tepalum (s.n. II), *gen. sing.* tepali, *abl. sing.* tepalo, *nom. pl.* tepala, *gen. pl.* tepalorum, *abl. pl.* tepalis.
tephro- : *in Gk. comp.*, grey-, ash-grey ; *tephropeplus*, with a grey covering.
Tepidarium (s.n. II) : moderately heated greenhouse.
tepidus (adj. A) : moderately warm, luke-warm.
ter (adv.) : three times, thrice.
terebrans (part. B) : boring, perforating, *hence* moving in a spirally twisting manner ; *motus trichomatum regulariter et lente terebrans, haud irregularis et celer*, motion of filaments regularly and slowly turning spirally, not irregular and rapid.
teres (adj. B) : terete, i.e. circular in transverse sections, tapering or nar-rowly cylindric ; *caulis teres*, stem terete ; *folia teretia*, leaves terete ; *caulibus foliisque teretibus*, with stems and leaves terete. **tereti-** : *in L. comp.*, terete-. *tereticaulis*, with terete stem ; *teretifolius*, with terete leaves. **tereti-usculus** (adj. A) : somewhat terete. **28**
tergeminatus (adj. A), **tergeminus** (adj. A) : tergeminate, as when a common petiole bears at its tip two leaflets, between which arise two secondary petioles each bearing at its tip two leaflets. **218**
Term : terminus (s.m. II), q.v.
terminal : terminalis (adj. B), terminatricus (adj. A), apicalis (adj. B). **terminated** : terminatus (part. A). **terminating** : terminans (part. B). **466**
Terminology : glossologia (s.f. I), termi-nologia (s.f. I).
Terminus (s.m. II) : technical word, term ; *termini botanici*, botanical terms.
ternarius (adj. A) : consisting of threes.
ternato-pinnatus (adj. A) : ternately pinnate, i.e. with three secondary petioles arising from the tip of a common petiole. **ternatus** (adj. A) : ternate, in threes, consisting of threes. **terni** (num. distr. adj. pl.) : three each, three together. **terni-** : *in L. comp.*, three- ; *ternifolius*, with three leaves or with the leaf consisting of three leaflets. **ternus** (adj. A) : three. **219, 479**
Terra (s.f. I) : earth, ground, soil, land.
terracotta : testaceus (adj. A).
terrestris (adj. B) : growing on the ground *or* soil, as opposed to rocks or trees.
terreus (adj. A) : earth-coloured, brown-ish. **terricola** (s.c. I used as adj. A) : dwelling on the ground.
tertiarius (adj. A) : tertiary. **tertius** (adj. A) : third.

Tesca (s.n. II. pl.) wastes, deserts, wild regions.
tessellated : tessellatus (adj. A).
tessularis (adj. B) : more or less cubical, all sides equal.
Testa (s.f. I) : outer coat of seed, *lit.* 'a piece of burned clay' ; *cf.* SEED-COAT.
testaceus (adj. A) : brick-red (H.C.C. 0. 16), 'brownish-yellow like that of un-glazed earthenware' (Lindley), terracotta.
teste (abl. sing. of *testis*) : according to, *lit.* by the witness (of) ; *teste Smith et Jones*, according to Smith and Jones ; *testibus Smith et Jones*, according to Smith and to Jones ; *cf.* FIDE.
testiculatus (adj. A) : testiculate, i.e. with two globose bodies, e.g. tubers, side by side. **66**
tetra- : *in Gk. comp.*, four-, 4- ; *tetra-gonolobus*, with 4-angled pods ; *tetra-gonus*, 4-angled ; *tetragynus*, with 4 styles or carpels ; *tetramerus*, with parts in fours ; *tetrandrus*, 4-stamened ; *tetra-petalus*, 4-petalled ; *tetrapterus*, 4-winged ; *tetrasepalus*, 4-sepalled ; *tetra-spermus*, 4-seeded ; *see* FOUR-, QUADR-.
tetradidymus (adj. A) : eight-fold or with four pairs. **tetradynamus** (adj. A) : tetradynamous, i.e. with four long stamens and two short stamens. **tetra-dymus** (adj. A) : having four cells.
tetrahedral : tetraedricus (adj. A), te-traedrus (adj. A), tetrahedralis (adj. B). **tetrahedrally** : tetraedrice (adv.).
Tetrad : tetras (s.f. III), *gen. sing.* tetradis ; tetradum (s.n. II), *gen. sing.* tetradi.
Tetraspore : tetraspora (s.f. I) ; *cf.* SPORE.
textilis (adj. B) : woven.
Textura (s.f. I) : tissue ; *textura angularis*, tissue of short polyhedral cells without intercellular spaces; *textura epidermoidea*, tissue of closely interwoven irregularly disposed hyphae without interhyphal spaces, the walls united, usually forming a membranous or epidermis-like tissue ; *textura globularis*, tissue of short rounded cells with intercellular spaces ; *textura intricata*, tissue of interwoven irregularly disposed hyphae with distinct interhyphal spaces, the walls not united ; *textura oblita*, tissue of more or less parallel hyphae all in one direction, with narrow lumina and strongly thickened walls, cohering ; *textura porrecta*, tissue of more or less parallel hyphae all in one direction, with wide lumina and non-thickened walls, not cohering ; *cf.* Dissing in *Bot. Tidsskr.* 60 : 109 (1964).
thalamiflorus (adj. A) : thalamifloral, i.e. having the petals and stamens arising directly and separately from the re-ceptacle.

Thalamium: thalamium (s.n. II).
Thalamus (s.m. II): the receptacle *or* torus.
thalassicus (adj. A): sea-green, bluish-green.
thalliformis (adj. B): like a thallus; cf. THALLODES. **thallinus** (adj. A), **thallodialis** (adj. B), **thallodicus** (adj. A): thalline, pertaining *or* belonging to a thallus; *margo thallinus cum thallo concolor, integer*, thalline margin the same colour as the thallus, entire. **thallodes** (adj. B), **thalloides** (adj. B): like a thallus; cf. THALLIFORMIS. **Thallus**: thallus (s.m. II); *thallus epiphloeodes crustaceus uniformis tenuis (60-80μ crassus) late expansus, substratum arcte obducens, griseus opacus, sorediis et insidiis destitutus, in margine linea obscuriore non cinctus*, thallus growing on the surface of bark crustaceus uniform thin (60-80μ thick) broadly outspread, the substratum tightly covering, grey opaque, by soredia and insidia forsaken (i.e. lacking soredia and insidia), at the margin by a darker line not encircled; *thallus pro maxima parte endolithicus*, thallus for the most part growing within stone; *thalli superficies trichomatibus instructa*, of the thallus the upper side with trichomes arrayed; cf. PHYCOMA.
than: quam (adv.), q.v.
that: ut (conj.), used with subjunctive of verbs; *folia ita disposita ut verticillata videantur*, leaves so arranged that they appear verticillate.
the: no equivalent: 'the' can usually be omitted but, when needed for emphasis or to make a distinction, can sometimes be expressed by *ille* indicating celebrity or *qui* or by a repetition of the word concerned; *pinnae variabiles, pinna longissima 3 cm. longa*, pinnae variable, with the longest one 3 cm. long; *pinnae quarum longissima 3 cm. longa*, pinnae of which the longest one 3 cm. long. cf. ILLE.
Theca (s.f. I): theca, *lit.* 'a case', hence applied to the sporangium of a fern, the lateral half of an anther, the capsule of a moss, the ascus of a lichen, etc.; *theca horizontalis vel nutans pyriformis, pallide cuprea, operculo brevi conico acuto*, theca horizontal or nodding pear-shaped, pale copper, with the operculum short conical acute; *operculo thecae dimidium metiente*, with the operculum measuring half of the theca (i.e. half the length of the theca); *laevitate thecae a congeneribus recedit*, by the smoothness of the theca it departs from others of the same genus; *thecae immaturae solum visae*, only immature thecae

seen; *antherae obovatae, connectivo apice dilatato, thecis apice distantibus basi contiguis per totam longitudinem rima dehiscentibus*, anthers obovate, with the connective broadened at the apex, the thecae separated at the apex touching at the base for the whole length by a fissure dehiscing; *antherae thecis duabus bilocularibus loculis longitudinaliter dehiscentibus*, anthers with two bilocular thecae with loculi longitudinally dehiscing.
-theca (s.f. I): *in Gk. comp.*, -cover, -case, -container.
Thecium: thecium (s.n. II).
thele-: *in Gk. comp.*, nipple-; *thelecarpus*, with a nipple-like fruit; *thelephorus*, bearing nipple-like projections; *thelespermus*, with seeds having nipple-like projections.
thely-: *in Gk. comp.*, female.
then: tum (adv.).
thence: inde (adv.), illinc (adv.).
therefore: ergo (adv.), ideo (adv.), igitur (adv.), itaque (adv.).
Thermae (s.f. I. pl.): warm springs; *habitat thermas aponinas*, it inhabits the warm springs of Abano. **thermalis** (adj. B): relating to warm springs or water; *in aqua thermali stagnanti*, in stagnant warm water.
Thesaurus (s.m. II): hoard, storehouse, treasury.
thick: crassus (adj. A), latus (adj. A) 'broad', densus (adj. A) 'closely packed', crassiusculus (adj. A) 'somewhat thick'. **thick-**: *in L. comp.*, crassi-, *in Gk. comp.*, pachy-; *crassifolius, pachyphyllus*, thick-leaved; *crassilabius, pachychilus*, thick-lipped; *crassinervius, pachyneurus*, thick-nerved; *crassipes, pachypodus*, with a thick support (petiole, peduncle or pedicel). **thickened**: incrassatus (part. A), inspissatus (adj. A). **thickening**: spissescens (part. B). 326
Thicket: dumetum (s.n. II), *abl. pl.* dumetis.
Thickness: crassities (s.f. V), crassitudo (s.f. III. vi); *crassities setae porcinae*, the thickness of a pig's bristle; *caulis crassitie straminis triticei vel pennae corvinae vel gallinaceae*, stem with the thickness of straw of wheat or of the feather of a raven or domestic fowl.
thick-skinned: pachydermus (adj. A), pachydermicus (adj. A).
thin: tenuis (adj. B), gracilis (adj. B) 'slender', exilis (adj. B) 'meagre', dilutus (part. A) 'pale, diluted'.
Thinium (s.n. II): dune.
thinly: tenuiter (adv.), rare (adv.) 'not densely'.

Thinness: tenuitas (s.f. III. ii).

third : tertius (adj. A) ; triens (s.m. III).

thirty : triginta (num. adj. indecl.) 'thirty', tricensimus (adj. A) 'thirtieth', tricies (adv.), triciens (adv.) 'thirty times'.

this : hic, haec, hoc (demonst. pron.), *gen. sing.* hujus ; *hic . . . ille, hic . . . alter*, this . . . that.

tholiformis (adj. B) : dome-shaped. **Tholus** (s.m. II) ; dome, cupola.

Thorn : spina (s.f. I), *abl. sing.* spina, *nom. pl.* spinae, *abl. pl.* spinis. **thorny** : spinosus (adj. A), senticosus (adj. A) ; cf. PRICKLY.

though : quamquam (conj.) 'albeit', velut (conj.) 'just as', etsi (conj.) 'notwithstanding, but'.

Thread : filum (s.n. II). **thread-like** : filiformis (adj. B) ; *in Gk. comp.*, nemato-.

three : tres (num. adj.) 'three', tertius (adj. A) 'third', ter (adv.) 'three times, thrice', terni (num. distr. adj. pl.) 'three each, three together' ; *folia tria foliolis tribus*, leaves 3 with leaflets 3 ; *laciniae sex, quarum tres exteriores reflexae, tres interiores erectae*, segments 6, of which the 3 outer reflexed, 3 inner erect ; *ovarium triloculare trigonum, stylis tribus*, ovary 3-chambered 3-angled, with styles 3 ; *styli tres*, styles 3 ; *folia verticillata terna vel quaterna*, leaves whorled three or four together. **three-** : *in L. and Gk. comp.*, tri-; *trigonus, triangularis, triangulus, triquetrus*, 3-angled ; *trichromus, trichrous, tricolor*, 3-coloured ; *trianthus, triflorus*, 3-flowered ; *triphyllus, trifolius*, with 3 leaves *or* leaflets ; *tripleurus, tricostatus*, 3-ribbed ; *tripterus, trialatus*, 3-winged ; *trimorphus, triformis*, existing in 3 forms, e.g. with short, intermediate and long stamens or with 3 types of florets or fruits; *see* TRI-. **41, 42, 345**

thrice : ter (adv.).

thriving : vigens (part. B) ; *species ad saxa vel ad terram vigens*, a species on rock or on the ground thriving ; *species ad corticem arboris vigentes*, species (pl.) on the bark of a tree thriving.

-thrix (s.f. III) : *in Gk. comp.*, hair ; *gen. sing.* -trichis ; *callithrix*, beautiful hair ; *chrysothrix*, golden hair ; cf. TRICH-.

Throat : faux (s.f. III. i), *abl. sing.* fauce, *nom. pl.* fauces, *abl. pl.* faucibus ; *corolla fauce hirsuto flavo*, corolla with throat hairy yellow ; *stamina fauci vel sub fauce inserta*, stamens on the throat or below the throat inserted ; cf. MOUTH.

through : per (prep. with acc.) ; *planta per frutices humiles scandens*, plant through

dwarf shrubs climbing ; *species per varias regiones dispersae*, species (pl.) through various regions dispersed.

throughout : penitus (adv.), omnino (adv.), ubique (adv.).

thus : ita (adv.), sic (adv.) ; cf. THEREFORE.

Thylacoid : thylacoides (s.f. III).

Thyriothecium : thyriothecium (s.n. II).

Thyrse : thyrsus (s.m. II), *acc. sing.* thyrsum, *abl. sing.* thyrso.

thyrsiformis (adj. B), **thyrsoideus** (adj. A) : thyrsoid, like a thyrse.

Thyrsus (s.m. II) : thyrse, i.e. a more or less ovoid or ellipsoid panicle, with cymose branches.

thysano- : *in Gk. comp.*, fringe-; *thysanochilus*, with a fringed lip ; *thysanostegius*, with a fringed covering.

Tide : aestus (s.m. IV), *acc. sing.* aestum, *gen. sing.* aestus, *abl. sing.* aestu, *nom. and acc. pl.* aestus, *gen. pl.* aestuum, *abl. pl.* aestibus ; *alga in saxis inter marinorum aestuum accessum et recessum emersis crescens*, seaweed growing on rocks between flow and ebb of the sea tides exposed ; *in lacubus minuente aestu relictis*, in pools left at the ebbing of the tide ; *flexuus atque refluxus maris*, flow and ebb of the sea.

tight : arctus (adj. A) 'drawn together'. **tightly** : arcte (adv.)

Tigillum : tigillum (s.n. II), *abl. sing.* tigillo, *nom. pl.* tigilla, *abl. pl.* tigillis ; cf. *Bull. Brit. Mus. (N.H.) Bot.* 3 : 50 (1963).

tigrinus (adj. A) : tiger-like, i.e. spotted like a jaguar (*Felis onca*), the American 'tiger' or, less often, barred like the Asiatic tiger (*Felis tigris*).

Time : tempus (s.n. III), *abl. sing.* tempore ; *planta ab antiquissimis temporibus cognita sed ultimis temporibus neglecta*, plant known from most ancient times but in the latest times neglected. Adverbial expressions relating to time include : *tempore florendi*, at the time of flowering, *tempore liberationis*, at the time of release, *aliquamdiu, aliquantisper*, for a while, *interim*, meanwhile, *mox*, soon, *parumper*, for a little while, *semel*, a single time, *semper*, all the time, *simul*, at the same time. Adjectives include : *coaetaneus*, of the same age, produced at the same time, *hysteranthius, hysteranthius*, following the flowers, produced after flowering, *longaevus*, of great age, ancient, *primaevus*, youthful, *synanthus, synanthius*, produced at the same time as the flowers ; cf. AGE, ANNOTINUS, ANTHESIS, FLOWERING, HORNOTINUS, HACTENUS, PAULISPER.

times : usually expressed by adv. ending -plo or -ies, e.g. *2-vel 3-plo, duplo vel* *triplo*, two or three times, *sexies*, six times, *pluries*, several times, *multoties*, many times, *interdum*, at times.

Tinctor (s.m. III) : dyer ; *tinctorum*, of the dyers. **tinctorius** (adj. A) : used in dyeing.

Tinea (s.f. I) : clothes moth, ringworm ; *tinea barbae capitis corporis cruris pedis unguium*, ringworm of the beard, head, body, groin, foot, nail.

tinged : suffusus (part. A), tinctus (part. A). **tingeing** : tingens (part. B). *See* p. 253.

tiny : minutus (adj. A) ; cf. LILLIPUTANUS.

Tip : apex (s.m. III. i), *acc. sing.* apicem, *gen. sing.* apicis, *abl. sing.* apice, *nom. pl.* apices, *gen. pl.* apicum, *abl. pl.* apicibus ; *apicem versus*, towards the tip ; *ab apice usque ad imum*, from the top down to the bottom ; *apice, ad apicem*, at tip.

Tissue : contextus (s.m. IV), textura (s.f. I), tela (s.f. I).

to : ad (prep. with acc.), versus (prep. with acc.) ; *plantae usque ad 2 m. altae*, plants up to 2 m. high.

tobacco-brown : tabacinus (adj. A).

Tofus (s.m. II) : tufa.

together : simul (adv.), una (adv.) 'at the same time or place', cum (prep. with abl.) 'together with'.

tomentellus (adj. A) : minutely tomentose.

tomentosus (adj. A) : tomentose, i.e. thickly and evenly covered with short more or less appressed curled or curved matted hairs. **tomentulosus** (adj. A) : minutely tomentose. **Tomentum** (s.n. II) : tomentum, i.e. dense interwoven hair covering. **274**

Tomus (s.m. II) : volume, book.

tongue-shaped : linguiformis (adj. B), lingulatus (adj. A). **-tongued** : *in L. comp.*, -linguis (adj. B), *in Gk. comp.*, -glossus (adj. A) ; *latilinguis, platyglossus*, broad-tongued (*usu. applied to the lip or labellum*) ; cf. LIP. **39**

tonsus (part. A) : shaven, i.e. having become glabrous.

Tooth : dens (s.m. III. ix), *abl. sing.* dente, *nom. pl.* dentes, *abl. pl.* dentibus ; *filamentorum interiorum dentes laterales breves obtusi vel acuti*, of the inner filaments the teeth lateral short obtuse or acute ; *filamenta interiora basi dentata, dentibus lateralibus acuminatis*, inner filaments toothed at base, with the teeth lateral acuminate. **toothed** : dentatus (adj. A) (*when the teeth are sharp and point outwards*) ; denticulatus (adj. A) (*when these teeth are minute*) ; serratus (adj. A) (*when the teeth are sharp and point forwards or towards the apex*) ; serrulatus (adj. A) (*when these teeth are minute*). **-toothed** : *in L. comp.*,

-dens, dentatus, *in Gk. comp.*, -odon, -odontus ; *paucidens, paucidentatus*, oligodon, oligodontus, few-toothed. **toothless** : edentatus (adj. A), edentulus (adj. A). **182, 183**

Top : *see* APEX, TIP, VERTEX.

top-shaped : turbinatus (adj. A), *lit.* 'cone-shaped'. **10**

tophaceus (adj. A) : tufa-like, with a papillose *or* gritty surface.

Tophulus : tophulus (s.m. II).

topmost : summus (adj. A).

Topotypus (s.m. II) : topotype, i.e. specimen from the type-locality agreeing with the type-specimen.

torn : laceratus (part. A), lacerus (adj. A). **189**

tornatus (part. A) : rounded off.

torosus (adj. A), **torulosus** (adj. A) : cylindrical with bulges *or* contractions at intervals ; cf. MONILIFORMIS. **53**

torquatus (adj. A) : adorned with a collar *or* zone, twisted.

Torrent : torrens (s.m. III. ix), *acc. sing.* torrentem, *gen. sing.* torrentis (*a contraction of* fluvius (s.m. II) torrens) ; *in Gk. comp.*, rhyac- ; *see* CATARACT, RIVER.

torridus (adj. A) : dry, dried up, parched.

Torsio (s.f. III) : torsion, twisting.

torsivus (adj. A) : twisted spirally.

torti- : *in L. comp.*, twisted ; *tortifolius*, with twisted leaves ; *tortispinus*, with twisted spines. **tortilis** (adj. B) : liable to twist, twisted. **tortuosus** (adj. A) : bent *or* twisted in different directions, involved, complicated. **tortus** (part. A) : twisted. **414**

torulosus (adj. A) : *see* TOROSUS.

Torus (s.m. II) : torus, receptacle.

tot (adj. indecl.) : so many ; *tot quot*, as many as ; *see* STAMEN. **totidem** (adj. indecl.) : just so many, just as many. **toties** (adv.) : so many times.

totus (adj. A) : all, all the, entire, total.

Touch : tactus (s.m. IV) ; *folia ad tactum mollia*, leaves soft to the touch.

touching : contiguus (adj. A), contingens (part. B).

tough : tenax (adj. B).

towards : versus (prep. with acc.).

tower-shaped : turriformis (adj. B).

Town : oppidum (s.n. II), *gen. sing.* oppidi ; cf. CITY.

toxicarius (adj. A) : poisonous, q.v.

Trabecula : trabecula (s.f. I), *nom. pl.* trabeculae, *lit.* 'a little beam'. **trabeculate** : trabeculatus (adj. A). **trabeculose** : trabeculosus (adj. A).

Tracheid : tracheida (s.f. I), *nom. pl.* tracheidae.

trachy- : *in Gk. comp.*, rough.

Tractatus (s.m. IV) : treatise, tract.
traditus (part. A) : handed over, delivered, communicated.
trahens (part. B) : dragging, trailing.
trailing (creeping) : serpens (part. B).
trailing (dragging) : trahens (part. B).
Trama : trama (s.f. I), *abl. sing.* trama, *lit.* 'weft or filling of a web', *hence* applied to layer of hyphae in gill of agarics.
tranquillus (adj. A) : calm, still ; *see* QUIET.
trans (prep. with acc.) : across, over beyond, on the farther side (*opp. of* CIS- *in comp.*) ; *transalpinus*, beyond the Alps, i.e. on the north side of the Alps.
Transactions : acta (s.n. II. pl.).
Transection : transectio (s.f. IV).
transeptatus (adj. A) : with all cross walls transverse.
transferred : translatus (part. A).
transformatus (part. A) : changed in shape.
transiens (part. B) : passing over into, being changed into.
Transition : transitus (s.m. IV), transitio (s.f. III) ; *zona transitionis*, zone of transition.
transitivus (adj. A) : passing over. **transitorius** (adj. A) : intermediate, passing from one to the other. **Transitus** (s.m. IV) : transition.
translatus (part. A) : transferred.
translucens (part. B), **translucidus** (adj. A) : clear, allowing light to shine through.
transmitted : transmissus (part. A) : *stratum aurantiacum luce reflexa flavum luce transmissa*, layer orange by reflected light, yellow by transmitted light.
transmutatus (part. A) : changed.
transparent : diaphanus (adj. A), hyalinus (adj. A), pellucidus (adj. A), translucens (part. B), translucidus (adj. A), limpidus (adj. A).
Transsectio (s.f. III) : transection.
Transtrum (s.n. II) : cross-beam, bar.
transverse : transversalis (adj. B), transversarius (adj. A), transversus (adj. A).
transversely : transverse (adv.), transversim (adv.), transversaliter (adv.).
trapezialis (adj. B), **trapeziformis** (adj. B), **trapezoideus** (adj. A) : trapeziform, i.e. asymmetrically four-sided or like a triangle with the top cut off. **121**
trapping : illaqueans (part. B) : *hyphae vermiculos nematoideos illaqueantes*, hyphae trapping (ensnaring) eelworms (nematodes, little worms).
Travel : iter (s.n. III), *nom. pl.* itinera. **relating to travel** : itinerarius (adj. A).
traversed : perductus (part. A), 'led through', peragratus (part. A) 'travelled through' ; cf. PERCURSUS.
treble : triplus (adj. A). **trebly** : ter (adv.), tripliciter (adv.).

Tree : arbor (s.f. III. v), *nom. pl.* arbores ; *arbor Americae tropicae parva et humilis vel mediocris vel etiam procera, trunco usque ad 1 m. diametro, 3 m. peripheria, ligno albido fragili, cortice cinereo fissili, ramis patentibus*, tree of tropical America small and low or medium-sized or even tall, with the trunk up to 1 m. in diameter, 3 m. in circumference, the wood whitish fragile, the bark grey splitting, the branches spreading.
tree-like : dendroideus (adj. A); dendriticus (adj. A) (*used of hairs*) ; arboreus (adj. A) (*used of whole plant*). **238**
trellis-like : cancellatus (adj. A), clathratus (adj. A). **243**
trembling : tremulus (adj. A).
tremelloideus (adj. A) : gelatinous, jellylike, resembling in this the genus Tremella or 'trembling fungi'.
tremulus (adj. A) : trembling.
tres (num. adj.) : three, q.v.
tri- : *in L. and Gk. comp.*, three- ; *triandrus*, 3-stamened ; *tribracteatus*, 3-bracted ; *tricephalus*, 3-headed ; *tricoccus*, with 3 cocci, i.e. breaking into 3 one-seeded parts ; *tricornis*, 3-horned ; *tricuspis, tricuspidatus*, with 3 cusps ; *tridentatus*, 3-toothed ; *trifidus*, 3-cleft ; *trifurcus, trifurcatus*, with 3 forks or branches ; *triglans*, with 3 nuts in an involucre ; *trigynus*, with 3 carpels *or* styles ; *trijugus*, with 3 pairs of pinnae ; *trilobatus, trilobus*, 3-lobed ; *trilocularis*, 3-chambered ; *trimerus*, with parts in threes ; *trinervis, trinervius*, 3-nerved ; *triovulatus*, with 3 ovules ; *tripartitus*, 3-parted ; *tripetalus*, 3-petalled ; *tripinnatus*, 3 times pinnate ; *trisectus*, 3-cleft to the base ; *trisepalus*, 3-sepalled ; *trispermus*, 3-seeded ; *tristylus*, 3-styled ; *trisulcatus*, 3-furrowed ; *triternatus*, 3 times ternate ; *trivittatus*, 3-banded ; *triuncialis*, 3 inches long ; see THREE-. **161, 223, 224, 345**
Triangle : triangulum (s.n. II). **triangular** : triangularis (adj. B), triangulatus (adj. A), triangulus (adj. A), deltatus (adj. A), deltoideus (adj. A). These may be qualified by *perdepresse*, 'very shallowly', and adverbs listed under TRULLATUS, q.v. **triangular in transverse section** : triqueter (adj. A). **triangularly** : triangulariter (adv.), triangule (adv.). **120**
Tribe : tribus (s.f. IV), *gen. sing.* tribus, *abl. sing.* tribu, *nom. pl.* tribus, *gen. pl.* tribuum, *abl. pl.* tribubus.
tribuliformis (adj. B) : tribuliform, i.e. with four projecting and diverging spines somewhat like the Roman *tribulus*, a four-pronged iron implement used to impede cavalry ; cf. TRINACRIFORMIS.

tricensimus, tricesimus (adj. A) : thirtieth.

trich-, tricho- : *in Gk. comp.*, hairy or hair-like ; *trichantherus*, with hairy anthers ; *trichanthus*, with hairy flower ; *trichocalyx*, with hairy calyx ; *trichodon*, with hairy teeth ; *trichocoleus*, with hairy sheath ; *trichophyllus*, with hairy leaves *or* fine hair-like leaves.

Trichoblast : trichoblastus (s.m. II).

Trichogyne : trichogyne (s.f. III) *or* trichogyna (s.f. I), *gen. sing.* trichogynes *or* trichogynae, *abl. sing.* trichogyne *or* trichogyna, *nom. pl.* trichogynes *or* trichogynae, *gen. pl.* trichogynum *or* trichogynarum, *abl. pl.* trichogynibus *or* trichogynis.

trichoideus (adj. A) : hair-like, as fine as a hair.

Trichome : trichoma (s.n. III. xi), *gen sing.* trichomatis, *abl. sing.* trichomate, *nom. and acc. pl.* trichomata, *gen. pl.* trichomatum, *abl. pl.* trichomatibus ; *trichomata simplicia libera mobilia cochleatim tortilia apicem versus attenuata*, trichomes simple free mobile spirally twisted towards apex, narrowed ; *trichomatibus ad genicula manifeste constrictis, in parte basali 8 μ medio 7 μ crassis, apicem versus gradatim attenuatis et in pilum longum hyalinum 3 μ crassum egredientibus*, with trichomes at junctions (genicula) distinctly constricted, in basal part 8 μ, at middle 7 μ thick, towards the apex gradually narrowed and into a hair long hyaline 3 μ thick going forth ; *trichomata elongata inferne recta superne uncinata vel per totam longitudinem in spiram laxam plus minusve irregularem contorta, apice attenuata*, trichomes elongated, below straight, above hooked or for the whole length in a loose spiral more or less irregularly twisted, at the tip attenuate.

Trichophore : trichophorum (s.n. II).

trichotomus (adj. A) : trichotomous, i.e. having the divisions always in threes.

triciens (adv.), **tricies** (adv.) : thirty times.

Triens (s.f. III) : a third part.

trifariam (adv.), **trifarius** (adj. A) : arranged in three ranks.

triginta (num. adj. indecl.) : thirty.

Trigone : trigona (s.f. I), *nom. pl.* trigonae, *abl. pl.* trigonis ; *cellulae minutae trigonis magnis ad angulos auctae*, cells minute with trigones (thickenings of angles) large at the angles enlarged.

trigonus (adj. A) : having three angles and three plane faces between them. **41**

trihilatus (adj. A) : with three apertures or pores.

trilete : triletus (adj. A) ; *sporis triletis*, having trilete spores, i.e.

radially symmetric with three-rayed marking.

trimus (adj. A) : three years old.

trinacriformis (adj. B) : three-pronged.

triple : triplex (adj. B), triplus (adj. A).

triplex (adj. B) : three-fold, triple.

triplicato- : *in L. comp.*, threefold ; *triplicato-ternatus*, triternate.

tripliciter (adv.) : in a three-fold manner.

triplinervis (adj. B), **triplinervius** (adj. A) : triple-nerved, the midrib sending off a strong nerve on each side above the base of the blade. **346**

triplostichus (adj. A) : in *or* having three rows ; cf. TRISTICHUS.

triqueter (adj. A), **triquetrus** (adj. A) : three-edged, three-angled, the angles usu. sharp. **42**

tristichus (adj. A) : in *or* having three rows ; cf. TRIFARIUS, TRIPLOSTICHUS.

tristis (adj. B) : sad, dull-coloured.

tritus (part. A) : rubbed, bruised.

trivialis (adj. B) : commonplace, ordinary ; *nomen triviale*, specific epithet ; *nomina trivialia forte admitti possunt modo, quo in Pane suecico usus sum* ; *constarent haec vocabulo unico, vocabulo libere undequaque desumpto* ; *ratione haec praecipue evicti, quod differentia saepe longa evadit, ut non ubique commode usurpetur, et dein mutationi obnoxia, novis detectis speciebus, e.g. Pyrola irregularis, Pyrola Halleriana, Pyrola secunda, Pyrola umbellata, Pyrola uniflora* (Linnaeus, *Phil. bot.* 202 ; 1751), trivial names may be admitted after a fashion, as I have used them in Pan suecicus ; they consist of a single word, a word freely taken from anywhere ; the chief reason, which cannot be gainsaid, is that the differential character is often so long, that it cannot everywhere be conveniently used and is subject to change through new species being discovered, e.g. Pyrola irregularis, Pyrola Halleriana, Pyrola secunda, Pyrola umbellata, Pyrola uniflora.

trochlearis (adj. B), **trochleiformis** (adj. B) : shaped like a pulley-wheel. **77**

trocho- : *in Gk. comp.*, wheel-like.

trombiformis (adj. B) : narrowly funnel-shaped.

tropaeolinus (adj. A) : nasturtium red (H.C.C. 14) ; cf. CAPUCINUS.

tropical : tropicus (adj. A).

trough-shaped : alveiformis (adj. B).

true : genuinus (adj. A), verus (adj. A).

trullatus (adj. A), **trulliformis** (adj. B) : angular-ovate, trullate, i.e. shaped rather like a bricklayer's trowel, broadest below the middle with two equal straight sides meeting at the apex and two shorter straight sides meeting at base. It may be qualified by the adverbs *anguste*, narrowly, *late*, broadly, *latissime*, very broadly, and *depresse*, depressed. *See* Fig. 19 F (p. 318).

truly : vere (adv.).

trumpet-shaped : buccinatus (adj. A), buccinatorius (adj. A) (when somewhat curved) ; tubaeformis (adj. B), tubatus (adj. A) (when almost straight). The Roman *tuba* was a straight-sided instrument, the *bucina* a strongly curved one ; cf. FUNNEL-SHAPED, TROMBIFORMIS. **54**

truncatus (part. A): truncate, i.e. ending very abruptly as if cut straight across. **158, 171**

Trunk : truncus (s.m. II).

Tuba (s.f. I) : trumpet ; cf. TRUMPET-SHAPED.

tubaeformis (adj. B), **tubatus** (adj. A): trumpet-shaped, q.v. **54**

Tube : tubus (s.m. II), *abl. sing.* tubo, *nom. pl.* tubi, *abl. pl.* tubis ; sipho (s.m. III. vi), *abl. sing.* siphone, *nom. pl.* siphones, *abl. pl.* siphonibus ; *corollae tubus cylindricus inferne albus supra medium rubescens vel ruber, extus glaber, intus pubescens vel etiam annulo pilorum sub apice ornatus, c. 1 cm. longus 4 mm. latus*, of the corolla the tube cylindric below white above the middle reddish or red, outside glabrous, inside pubescent or even with a ring of hairs below the top ornamented, about 1 cm. long 4 mm. wide ; *corolla e tubo angusto 1 cm. longo sensim ampliata, fauce nuda, tubo ima basi saepius annulo piloso vel carnuloso instructo, staminibus tubo medio insertis*, corolla from a narrow tube 1 cm. long gradually expanded, with the throat naked, with the tube at the very base most often with a pilose or rather fleshy ring furnished, with the stamens to the tube at the middle attached.

Tuber : tuber (s.n. III. v), *gen. sing.* tuberis, *abl. sing.* tubere, *nom. pl.* tubera, *abl. pl.* tuberibus ; *tuber magnum globosum vel irregulare 10 cm. latum, carne albida amara*, tuber large globose or irregular, with flesh whitish bitter ; *tubera geminata ellipsoidea vel dauciformia 2-4 cm. longa*, tubers paired ellipsoid or carrot-shaped 2-4 cm. long ; *herba tubere parvo cavo*, herb with tuber small hollow.

tuberans (adj. B), **tuberascens** (adj. B): becoming swollen or tuberous.

Tuberculum (s.n. II): tubercle. **tubercularis** (adj. B) : having tubercles or like a tubercle. **tuberculatus** (adj. A):

tuberculate, i.e. covered with wart-like projections. **tuberculiformis** (adj. B): like a tubercle. **268**

tuberifer (adj. A) : tuber-bearing. **tuberosus** (adj. A): producing tubers *or* swollen into a tuber.

tubiformis (adj. B) : tube-like ; cf. TUBAE-FORMIS. **tubiflorus** (adj. A), **tubuliflorus** (adj. A): with symmetrical tubular (*as distinct from rayed*) florets, with tubular flowers.

tubular : tubularis (adj. B), tubulosus (adj. A), siphonaceus (adj. A) ; cf. FISTULOSUS. **6**

tubulatus : trumpet-shaped, q.v.

Tubule : tubulus (s.m. II) : *tubuli ad stipitem decurrentes flavi*, tubules on to the stipe decurrent yellow ; *caro ad tubulos purpurea*, flesh at the tubules purple. **tubuliformis** (adj. B): like a tubule.

Tubus (s.m. II) : tube, q.v.

Tufa : tofus (s.m. II).

Tuft : caespes (s.m. III. iii). **tufted** : caespitosus (adj. A), cespitosus (adj. A).

tum (adv.) : then, at that time, thereupon, and also, but also, if so, furthermore. Used in enumerations of characters indicating sequence, as with *primum*, *deinde*, *prostremo*, or contrast, as with *quum* ; *descriptio e speciminibus plurimis quum siccis tum vivis*, description from very many specimens not only dried but also living.

tumens (part. B): swelling, being swollen.

tumescens (part. B): swelling up.

tumidus (adj. A): tumid, swollen, thickened, protuberant ; cf. PRAEGNANS.

Tumor (s.m. III. v): tumour, swelling.

Tumulus (s.m. II) : mound, hillock.

tunc (adv.): then, immediately.

Tundra : tundra (s.f. I).

Tunic : tunica (s.f. I), *abl. sing.* tunica, *nom. pl.* tunicae, *abl. pl.* tunicis, *lit.* 'an under-garment' ; *tunica praecipua tenuissime membranacea demum in fibras parallelas soluta*, chief tunic (covering) very thinly membranous at length into fibres parallel broken up ; *tunica cribraria fibris reticulatis colore stramineo pallido*, tunic sieve-like with fibres reticulate with the colour strawy pale ; *bulbus tunicis pergamenis punctatis, interioribus candidis exterioribus nigricantibus*, bulb with tunics parchment-like dotted, with the inner ones white the outer ones becoming black ; *herba bulbi tunicis reticulato-fibrosis castaneis*, herb with tunics of the bulb reticulate-fibrousc hestnut-coloured ; cf. BULB.

tunicatus (adj. A): tunicate, having coats

or envelopes *or* a thin separable covering.

Turbarium: (s.n. II) : peat bog.

turbatus (adj. A) : disturbed, disordered.

turbinatus (adj. A) : turbinate, i.e. top-shaped or obconical. **10**

Turfosum (s.n. II) : peat moor. **turfosus** (adj. A) : peaty.

turgidus (adj. A) : inflated, swollen with air *or* water, slightly swelling; cf. DISTENTUS. **95**

Turion : turio (s.m. III. vi); *turio juvenilis erectus*, young turion erect; *turiones flagellares arcuati pilosi, aculeis parvi armati, superne glandulis stipitatis adspersi*, turions whip-like arching pilose, with prickles small armed, above with glands stalked sprinkled; *see* PRIMOCANE.

Turma (s.f. I) : troop, squadron, throng, group of species; *species e turma Selaginellae bisulcatae*, species from (i.e. belonging to) the group of (i.e. typified by) Selaginella bisulcata.

Turn : anfractus (s.m. IV); *chlorophoro singulo anfractibus 2-5*, with a single chloroplast having 2-5 turns.

turn, in : invicem (adv.); cf. VICISSIM.

turned towards : versus (adv.) (*usu. preceded by adv. or name of object in acc.*); obversus (part. A); *apicem versus*, towards the tip; *sursum versus*, upwards; *sutura vexillo obversa*, suture turned towards the vexillum, i.e. on the side nearest the vexillum. Cf. DIRECTION.

turning : change of state or process of becoming is usually expressed by part. ending *-escens* or *-ascens*; *thallus lutescens*, thallus turning yellow.

turnip-shaped : napiformis (adj. B), rapiformis (adj. B).

turriformis (adj. B) : tower-shaped.

twelve : duodecim (num. adj. indecl.) 'twelve', duodecimus (adj. A) 'twelfth', duodecies (adv.), duodeciens (adv.) 'twelve times'. **twelve-** : *in Gk. comp.*, dodeca-; *dodecandrus*, 12-stamened.

twenty : viginti (num. adj. indecl.) 'twenty', vicensimus (adj. A) 'twentieth', vicies (adv.) *or* viciens (adv.) 'twenty times'.

twice : bis (adv.).

Twig : ramunculus (s.m. II), *abl. sing.* ramunculo, *nom. pl.* ramunculi, *abl. pl.* ramunculis; *see* VIRGA.

twining : volubilis (adj. B). Direction of twining is indicated by the adverb *sinistrorsum*, 'towards the left side', or *dextrorsum*, 'towards the right side', the phrase *extus vis.* or *externe vis.*, 'seen from outside' or *e latere vis.*, 'seen from the side' distinguishing the

viewpoint of an observer with the stem in front of him from that of a person who imagines himself entwined within its coil (*e centro vis.*, 'seen from the centre') or climbing a spiral stairway; cf. A. Gray in *Amer. J. Sc.* III, 3 : 162 (1880), Schmucker in *Beih. Bot. Centralbl.* 41, i : 51 (1924); *caulis sinistrorsum (externe visus) volubilis*, stem to the left (seen from the outside) twining; *frutices saepius volubiles*, shrubs most often twining; *herbae caulibus volubilibus*, herbs with twining stems; cf. ANTIHELICTE, CLOCKWISE, HELICTE. **418**

twinned : gemellus (adj. A), geminus (adj. A), geminatus (adj. A), binatus (adj. A), didymus (adj. A). **232, 503**

Twist : convoluta (s.f. I), spira (s.f. I); *cellulae spirales 8-9 convolutas ostendentes*, spiral cells showing 8-9 twists; cf. TURN. **twisted** : tortus (part. A), tortilis (adj. B), torsivus (adj. A); *in Gk. comp.* strepto-. **382**

two : duo (adj. num.) 'two', secundus (adj. A) *or* alter (adj. B) 'second', bini (adj. num. distr. pl.) 'two each', bis (adv.) 'twice'; *folia quaterna, in quo verticillo duo longiora, duo breviora*, leaves four together, in each whorl two longer, two shorter; *angulis binis*, with two angles. **two-** : *in L. comp.*, bi-, *in Gk. comp.*, di-; *bicolor, bicoloratus, dichrous, dichromus*, two-coloured; *biflorus, dianthus*, two-flowered (but the generic name *Dianthus* is a contraction of *Diosanthos*, flower of Zeus); *bifarius, distichus*, distichous; *bicornis, bicornutus, diceras*, with two horns; *bifolius, diphyllus*, with two leaves *or* leaflets; *bistratus, distromaticus*, two-layered; *bicontortus, dicyclus*, with two circular twists; *biformis, dimorphus*, of two shapes; *bispicatus, distachyus*, with two spikes; *bialatus, dipterus*, two winged; *see* BI-, DI-, TWINNED.

tylacanthus (adj. A) : having spines on ridges, the primary rows bearing the spine-cells being more prominent than the secondary; cf. AULACANTHUS.

tylo- : *in Gk. comp.*, with knobs, lumps or projections.

tympaniformis (adj. B) : drum-shaped.

Tympanum (s.n. II) : epiphragm.

Type : typus (s.m. II), *abl. sing.* typo; *generitypus, typus generis*, type-species of a genus; *holotypus*, the one specimen or element used by the author of a name or designated by him as nomenclatural type; *isotypus*, duplicate of the holotype; *lectotypus*, specimen selected from original material to serve as nomenclatural type when the holotype is missing or not designated; *neotypus*, specimen selected for working purposes as representative when all of original material is missing; *paratypus*, specimen cited with the original description other than the holotype; *syntypus*, one of the specimens used by the author when no holotype was designated or when two or more were simultaneously designated as type; cf. TOPOTYPUS.

typical: typicus (adj. A); *terra typica restricta* : restricted type locality. typically : typice (adv.).

tyrius (adj. A): tyrian purple (H.C.C. 7. 27).

U

ubi (adv.) : in which place, where, when.

ubicumque (adv.) : where, anywhere.

ubique (adv.) : everywhere, in any place whatever, throughout.

udus (adj. A) : wet, moist, damp, soaked ; *see* MADIDUS.

uliginosus (adj. A) : marshy, growing in marshes ; *see* PALUSTRIS.

ullus (adj. A) : any, anyone.

Ulna (s.f. I) : an ell, 2 feet, approx. 65 cm. ulnaris (adj. B) : 2 feet long.

ulterior (adj. compar.) : farther, on the farther side. ulterius (adv.): beyond, farther on. ultime (adv.) : extremely. ultimus (adj. A) : farthest, most distant, ultimate, last. ultimately : ad extremum, ad finem, extremum (adv.), postremo (adv.).

ultra (adv.) : on the other side, beyond, farther. ultra (prep. with acc.) : on the farther side of, past, beyond, above, more than.

ultro citroque, ultro et citro (adv.) : to and fro, backwards and forwards.

Umbel : umbella (s.f. I), *gen. sing.* umbellae, *abl. sing.* umbella, *nom. pl.* umbellae, *abl. pl.* umbellis, *lit.* 'sunshade, parasol'; *umbella bulbillis carens, capsulifera, multiflora, irregularis*, umbel lacking bulbils, capsule-bearing, many-flowered, irregular ; *spatha umbellam aequans vel paulo longior vel raro brevior*, spathe equalling the umbel or a little longer or rarely shorter ; *umbella simplex*, simple umbel. umbellate : umbellatus (adj. A).

umbelliformis (adj. B) : shaped like an umbel ; cf. CORYMBOSE.

Umbellula (s.f. I) : partial umbel, ultimate umbel in a compound umbel. umbellulatus (adj. A) : furnished with partial umbels.

umber : umbrinus (adj. A).

umbilicatus (adj. A), umbiliciformis (adj. B) : navel-like, having a small central depression or hollow; also used by some authors in the sense of PELTATUS.

Umbilicus : umbilicus (s.m. II), *abl. sing.* umbilico.

Umbo : umbo (s.m. III. vi), *abl. sing.* umbone. umbonatus (adj. A) : having a rounded projection *or* umbo in the middle. 20

Umbra (s.f. I) : shade, shadow.

umbraculiformis (adj. B) : umbrella-shaped. 89

Umbraculum : umbraculum (s.n. II).

umbrinus (adj. A) : umber, brown.

umbrosus (adj. A) : shady, growing in shade.

un- : the negative or contrary expressed in English by the prefix 'un-' is often rendered in Latin by the prefix *in-* or *im-* (before *b, m* or *p*) or *e-* or *ex-* (before vowels) or the adverb *haud* or *non*.

una (adv.) : at the same time, together.

unarmed : inermis (adj. B), nudus (adj. A). 260

uncatus (adj. A) : hooked, bent inwards. 147

uncertain : incertus (adj. A), dubius (adj. A), ambiguus (adj. A).

unchangeable, unchanging : immutabilis (adj. B). unchanged : immutatus (adj. A).

Uncia (s.f. I) : twelfth part, $\frac{1}{12}$ foot, 1 inch, approx. 2·5 cm. ; same as POLLEX, q.v. uncialis (adj. B) : 1 inch long.

unciformis (adj. B) : hook-shaped. uncinatus (adj. A) : barbed, hooked.

uncommon : rarus (adj. A). uncommonly : raro (adv.).

unctulus (adj. A), unctuosus (adj. A): having an oily *or* greasy appearance. unctus (part. A) : greasy, oiled. 302

Uncus (s.m. II) : hook, barb.

undatim (adv.) : in a wavy manner. undatus (adj. A) : wavy.

unde (adv.) : from which place, whence.

undecided : incertus (adj. A).

undeciens (adv.), undecies (adv.) : eleven times, elevenfold. undecim (num. adj. indecl.) : eleven. undecimus (adj. A) : eleventh.

under (prep.) : sub (prep. with abl., when no motion is implied, and acc.), subter (prep. with abl. and acc.). under (adj.) : inferus (adj. A), inferior (adj. compar. B) ; *folia inferiora*, underleaves.

undergoing : subiens (part. B) ; *cellulae divisiones subeuntes*, cells undergoing divisions.

underground : subterraneus (adj. A), hypogaeus (adj. A).

underneath : infra (adv. and prep. with acc.), subter (adv. and prep. with abl. and acc.), subtus (adv.).

Undershrub : suffrutex (s.m. III. i).

undeveloped : immaturus (adj. A).
undique (adv.) : on all sides.
undivided : indivisus (adj. A), simplex (adj. B).
undulate : undulatus (adj. A), undatus (adj. A). **132**
undulato-striatus (adj. A) : having wavy elevated lines.
unequal : inaequalis (adj. B), impar (adj. B), dispar (adj. B) ; *foliis disparibus, inferiore grandiusculo reliquis multo minoribus*, with leaves unequal, the lower one rather large, the rest much smaller. **unequally** : inaequaliter (adv.), impariter (adv.) ; *imparipinnatus*, unequally pinnate. **unequal-sided** : inaequilaterus (adj. A), irregularis (adj. B) ; *foliola valde inaequilatera, latere altero quam alterum multo breviore*, leaflets very unequal-sided, with one side than the other much shorter. **134, 136**
uneven : inaequalis (adj. B), asper (adj. A) 'rough' used of uneven places.
unexpected : inopinatus (adj. A), inexpectatus (adj. A).
unexplored : inexploratus (adj. A).
unfavourable : iniquus (adj. A), adversus (adj. A).
unfinished : inchoatus (part. A), imperfectus (adj. A).
unfruitful : infecundus (adj. A), sterilis (adj. B).
unguicularis (adj. B) : ½ inch (1·3 cm.) long, clawed. **unguiculatus** (adj. A) : clawed. **Unguis** (s.m. III. xii) : claw, narrowed basal part of a petal, length of a fingernail, ½ inch, 1·3 cm.
ungulatus (adj. A), **unguliformis** (adj. B) : hoof-shaped, clawed.
uni- : *in L. comp.*, one- ; *uniaristatus*, with one awn ; *unibracteatus*, with one bract ; *unicapsularis*, with all the carpels united into one capsule ; *unicaulis*, with a single stalk *or* stem ; *unicellularis*, one-celled ; *unifarius*, in one row ; *uniglumis*, with one glume ; *unijugus*, with one pair of leaflets ; *unilabiatus*, one-lipped ; *unilateralis*, one-sided ; *unilocularis*, one-chambered ; *uninervis*, one-nerved ; *uniovulatus*, with the ovule solitary ; *uniseptatus*, with one septum ; *uniserialis, uniseriatus*, in one row ; *unisexualis*, of one sex, i.e. having only an androecium or a gynoecium, not both together in one flower ; *univalvis*, one-valved ; *univittatus*, one-banded ; *see* MON-, ONE-. **225, 344, 490**
unicus (adj. A) : one and no more, single, solitary, growing singly ; cf. SINGULARIS.
unifariam (adv.), **unifarius** (adj. A) : in one row.

uniform : aequabilis (adj. B), uniformis (adj. B). **uniformly** : uniformiter (adv.), aeque (adv.), aequabiliter (adv.).
unilateral : unilateralis (adj. B) ; cf. SECUNDUS. **490**
uninterrupted : continuus (adj. A). **501**
Union : junctio (s.f. III), conjunctio (s.f. III), copulatio (s.f. III) ; cf. CONJUGATION, JOIN.
unisexual : unisexualis (adj. B), diclinis (adj. B) ; *flores unisexuales*, flowers unisexual, i.e. having male organs in one flower, female in another.
unistratose : unistratosus (adj. A).
Unit : monas (s.f. III), *gen. sing.* monadis.
united : conjunctus (part. A), unitus (part. A), connatus (part. A).
uniuscujusque : *see* UNUSQUISQUE.
universalis (adj. B) : general, of *or* belonging to the whole ; *involucrum universale*, general involucre ; *volva universalis*, universal veil.
Universe (adv.) : in general, generally. **in universum** (adv. phrase) : as a whole.
University : universitas (s.f. III. ii), academia (s.f. I) (*used only of the older European universities*) ; *delectus seminum ex Horto Cantabrigiensis Academiae*, a selection of seeds from the Cambridge University Garden ; *Hortus publicus Academiae Lugduno-Batavae*, Botanic Garden of Leiden University.
unknown : ignotus (adj. A), incognitus (adj. A).
unlawful : illegitimus (adj. A).
unless : nisi (conj.).
unlike : dissimilis (adj. B, with gen. or dat. of noun compared), diversus (part. A) ; *species H. excelsae habitu dissimilis*, species unlike H. excelsa in habit.
unpleasant : ingratus (adj. A) ; cf. STINKING.
unpolished : impolitus (adj. A).
unquam (adv.) : at any one time.
unripe : immaturus (adj. A), crudus (adj. A).
unspotted : astictus (adj. A), immaculatus (adj. A).
until : dum (conj.), ad (prep.).
untouched : intactus (adj. A).
untrue : falsus (adj. A), mendosus (adj. A).
unus (adj. A) : one.
unusquisque (comp. pron. m.), **unaquaeque** (f.), **unumquidque** (n.) : each single one, each one singly, each (*of a number of objects, in contrast to* uterque *which refers to each one of a pair*) ; *dentes triangulares, nervo ex uniuscujusque apice decurrente*, teeth triangular, with the nerve from the apex of each single one decurrent ; *in unoquoque loculo*, in each loculus.
unusual : infrequens (adj. B), insolitus (adj. A), singularis (adj. B), egregius (adj. A),

insuetus (adj. A). **unusually**: insolenter (adv.), egregie (adv.), raro (adv.).
unwearied: indefessus (adj. A).
up to: usque ad (prep. with acc.).
upholding: sustinens (part. B).
upon: super (prep. with acc.) 'on top', de (prep. with abl.) 'concerning'.
upper: superus (adj. A), supernus (adj. A); *compar.* superior (adj. A), 'yet higher, higher than'; *superl.* supremus (adj. A), summus (adj. A) 'highest'. **upper side, on the**: supra (adv.). **uppermost**: summus (adj. A), supremus (adj. A).
upright: erectus (part. A), verticalis (adj. A).
upwards: sursum (adv.).
urbanus (adj. A): pertaining to towns and cities as distinct from the country. **Urbs** (s.f. III): city.
urceolatus (adj. A): pitcher-, vase- or urn-shaped, i.e. hollow, more or less rounded and distinctly contracted at the mouth, with the limb small. **Urceolus** (s.m. II): urceole. 73
Uredinium: uredinium (s.n. II).
uredinoid: uredinoideus (adj. A).
Urediospore: urediospora (s.f. I).
Uredium: uredium (s.n. II).
Uredosorus: uredosorus (s.m. II).
Uredospore: urediospora (s.f. I), uredospora (s.f. I), urediniospora (s.f. I).
urens (part. B): stinging.
urniformis (adj. B): urn-shaped.
uro-, -urus: *in Gk. comp.*, tail-, -tailed, i.e. with an elongated or tail-like appendage; *urophyllus*, tail-leaved, i.e. with leaves having an elongated tip; *urosepalus*, with tailed *or* appendaged sepals; *macrurus*, with a large tail.
Use: usus (s.m. IV), *gen. sing.* usus, *abl. sing.* usu. **useful**: utilis (adj. B). **usefully**: utiliter (adv.). **Usefulness**: utilitas (s.f. III. ii), *gen. sing.* utilitatis, *abl. sing.* utilitate. **useless**: inutilis (adj. B).
usitatus (part. A): usual, customary, habitual, ordinary.
usneic: usneicus (adj. A): *acidum usneicum*, usnic acid.
usque (adv.): all the way to, continuously, as far as (*usu. followed by* ad *with object in* acc.); *capitulis usque 4 cm. longis*, with heads up to 4 cm. long; *usque adhuc*, up to now, until now; *usque ad apicem*, up to the tip; *usque ad Floridam*, as far as Florida.
usual: usitatus (part. A), solitus (part. A), usualis (adj. B). **usually**: plerumque (adv.), vulgo (adv.).
usurpativus (adj. A): wrongly used; *sub nomine usurpativo*, under the misapplied name.
Usus (s.m. IV): use, q.v.

ut, uti (adv.): how, in what manner. **ut** (conj.): as, like, as for example, so that; *stipulae ut videtur nullae*, stipules as it seems none; *foliis et bracteis ut in typo*, with leaves and bracts as in the type; *ut e statu sicco apparet*, as from the dried state it appears; *ut auctores generi attribuunt*, as authors attribute to the genus; *ut in diagnosi descripta*, as described in the diagnosis.
utcunque (adv.): however.
uterque (pron.): each (of two), either, both.
utilis (adj. B): useful, beneficial. **Utilitas** (s.f. III. ii): usefulness. **utiliter** (adv.): usefully.
utique (adv.): in any case, certainly.
Utricle: utriculus (s.m. II), *abl. sing.* utriculo, *nom. pl.* utriculi, *abl. pl.* utriculis; *utriculi anguste ovati compressi c. 3·5 mm. longi, inferiores squamis breviores, superiores squamis longiores, omnes squamis multo latiores, membranei glabri papillosi apicem versus pluricostati in rostrum breve sensim desinentes*, utricles narrowly ovate compressed about 3·5 mm. long, the lower ones shorter than the scales, the upper ones longer than the scales, all much broader than the scales, membranous glabrous papillose towards the tip many-ribbed in a short beak gradually ending.
utricularis (adj. B), **utriculatus** (adj. A), **utriculosus** (adj. A): bladder-like, bladdery, possessing bladders, inflated; cf. VESICARIUS.
utrinque (adv.), **utrimque** (adv.), **utrinsecus** (adv.): on both sides, on the one side and on the other.
utroque (adv.): to both sides, in both directions.
uvarius (adj. A), **uviformis** (adj. B): like a bunch of grapes, i.e. with clustered rounded parts; cf. BOTRY-.
uvidus (adj. A): moist, wet, humid.

V

vaccinus (adj. A): dun in colour.
vacillans (part. B): swinging to and fro; cf. OSCILLANS, VERSATILIS.
Vacuole: vacuola (s.f. I), *abl. sing.* vacuola, *nom. pl.* vacuolae, *abl. pl.* vacuolis; *protoplasma roseum in centro vacuolam gaseosam praebens*, protoplasm rose in the centre a gas vacuole displaying; *sine vacuola gaseosa centrali*, without a central gas vacuole; *sine vacuolis gaseosis*, without gas vacuoles; *cytoplasma hyalinum, interdum vacuolis digestivis instructum*, cyto-

plasm hyaline, sometimes with digestive vacuoles provided; *vacuolis contractilibus numerosis per totam cellulae peripheriam sparsis*, with contractile vacuoles numerous over the whole circumference of the cell dispersed.

Vacuum (s.n. II): an empty space; *seriebus cellularum vacuum internum cingentibus*, with rows of cells surrounding the inner empty space.

vacuus (adj. A): empty; cf. CASSUS.

vadosus (adj. A): shallow, full of shallows (*used only of water*). **Vadum** (s.n. II): shallow place in water.

vagans (part. B): wandering.

vage (adv.): here and there, far and wide, dispersedly.

Vagina (s.f. I): sheath, q.v.; *vagina gelatinosa*, gelatinous sheath. **vaginalis** (adj. B): relating to a sheath. **vaginans** (adj. B): sheathing. **vaginatus** (adj. A): sheathed. **445**

vaginervis (adj. B), **vaginervius** (adj. A): having the veins arranged without any apparent order. **359**

Vaginule: vaginula (s.f. I).

vagus (adj. A): uncertain, having no particular direction, in several directions. **431**

valde (adv.): strongly, intensely, exceedingly, decidedly.

validly: rite (adv.): *nomen non rite publicatum*, name not validly published.

validus (adj. A): strong, robust-growing.

Vallecula (s.f. I): furrow between ridges (*juga*) on fruits of Umbelliferae; *valleculae in quoque carpello 4*, furrows on each carpel 4; *vittae ad valleculas angustas solitariae*, vittae solitary in the narrow furrows; *valleculis univittatis*, with furrows having one vitta. **valleculatus** (adj. A): provided with furrows.

Valley: vallis (s.f. III. viii), convallis (s.f. III. viii) 'valley enclosed on all sides', fauces (s.f. pl. III. i) 'gorge'.

valvaceus (adj. A): valvate, provided with valves. **valvaris** (adj. B), **valvatus** (adj. A): valvate; *dehiscentia valvaris*, dehiscence by valves; *aestivatio valvata*, aestivation with parts touching at edges but not overlapping. **380**

Valve: valva (s.f. I), *gen. sing.* valvae, *dat. sing.* valvae, *abl. sing.* valva, *nom. pl.* valvae, *gen. pl.* valvarum, *dat. and abl. pl.* valvis, *lit.* 'leaf of a folding door'; *valva integra reflexa*, valve entire reflexed; *perigonii valvae fructiferae omnes calliferae reticulato-nervosae, callis prominentibus lanceolatis levibus haud rugosis*, of the perigon the fruiting valves all callus-bearing reticulately nerved, with callosities (tubercles) prominent lanceolate smooth not rugose;

capsula bilocularis bivalvis loculicide vel septicide dehiscens, valvis integris membranaceis valvarum marginibus inflexis, capsule 2-chambered 2-valved loculicidally or septicidally dehiscing, with valves entire membranous with margins of valves inflexed; *valvae dissimiles, una tantum rhaphem nodulumque centralem praebens*, valves unlike, one only a raphe and central nodule furnishing; *valvae rotundatae vel ellipticae*, valves rounded or elliptic; *valvis ellipticis, non tumidis, regulariter usque ad apices obtusos attenuatis*, with valves elliptic, not swollen, regularly up to the blunt tips drawn out.

-valved : -valvis (adj. B).

Valve-view: facies (s.f. V) valvaris, facies frontalis; cf. VIEW.

Valvule: valvula (s.f. I), declined as *valva*; *valvula inferior trinervis acuta mutica*, lower valvule (lemma) 3-nerved acute but without an appendage; *valvula superiora aut nulla aut minima aut ovario major*, upper valvule (palea) lacking or very small or than the ovary larger; *antherae a basi ad apicem valvula revoluta decidua dehiscentes*, anthers from base to tip by a revolute deciduous valvule dehiscing; *antherae valvulis sursum dehiscentes*, anthers by valvules from below upwards dehiscing.

vanishing: evanescens (part. B), evanidus (adj. A); *costa sub apice evanida*, midrib vanishing before reaching the tip.

variable: variabilis (adj. B), varius (adj. A), mutabilis (adj. B) (*used of colour*); cf. VERSIFORMIS. **varians** (part. B): varying. **Variation**: variatio (s.f. III. vi).

varicosus (adj. A): abnormally enlarged in places.

varie (adv.): variously, diversely.

variegated: variegatus (part. A).

Variety: varietas (s.f. III. ii), *gen. sing.* varietatis, *abl. sing.* varietate, *nom. pl.* varietates, *gen. pl.* varietatum, *abl. pl.* varietatibus.

vario (verb, conj. I): diversify, change, vary; *maxime variat structura statura magnitudine latitudine et forma*, most greatly it varies in structure stature size width and form.

Variole: variola (s.f. I), *abl. sing.* variola.

various: varius (adj. A); *semina forma situ et directione varia*, seeds as to form position and direction varied. **variously**: varie (adv.), diverse (adv.).

varnished: laccatus (adj. A), vernicosus (adj. A).

varying: varians (part. B); *fructus magnitudine variantes*, fruits varying in size, fruits of variable size.

Vas (s.n. III. iv): vessel, duct; *vasa laticis*, lactiferous ducts; *vasa scalariformia*, scalariform vessels; *fasciculo vasorum unico in sectione litteram V simulante*, with a single bundle of vessels in section resembling the letter V.

vascular: vascularis (adj. B); *plantae vasculares*, vascular plants, i.e. phanerogams and pteridophytes.

Vasculum (s.n. II): vasculum, field collecting case for botanical specimens; cf. *Proc. Bot. Soc. Brit. Isles*, 3 : 135-150 (1959).

vase-shaped: urceolatus (adj. A).

vast: immensus (adj. A).

vectus (part. A): carried.

vegetabilis (adj. B): belonging *or* relating to plants; *regnum vegetabile*, the plant kingdom.

Vegetatio (s.f. III. vi): vegetation.

vegetativus (adj. A): vegetative.

vegetus (adj. A): fresh, vigorous (*opp. of* MARCIDUS).

Veil: velum (s.n. II), *abl. sing.* velo.

Veining: nervatura (s.f. I), venatio (s.f. III. vi) *not to be confused with class. L.* venatio 'hunting'; the following are the chief terms used to describe veining. **Anastomosis** (cross-connexion of veins forming network): anastomosis (s.f. III). **Angle of Divergence**: angulus (s.m. II). Following Lindley, when the angle formed by the midrib and the diverging vein or nerve is between 10° and 20° the vein may be said to be *nearly parallel* (vena subparallela, *abl. pl.* venis subparallelis); when between 20° and 40°, *diverging* (vena divergens, *abl. pl.* venis divergentibus); when between 40° and 60°, *spreading* (vena patens, *abl. pl.* venis patentibus); between 60° and 80°, *divaricating* (vena divaricata, *abl. pl.* venis divaricatis); between 80° and 90°, *right-angled* (vena rectangularis, *abl. pl.* venis rectangularibus); between 90° and 120°, *oblique* (vena obliqua, *abl. pl.* venis obliquis); beyond 120°, *reflexed* (vena retroflexa, *abl. pl.* venis retroflexis). It is usually better to state the angle direct, e.g. *sub angulo circa 40°-50°*. **Area between Veins**: intervenium (s.n. II). **Area enclosed by Veins or Veinlets, Vein-islet**: areola (s.f. I). **Midrib** (central or main vein): costa (s.f. I), nervus medius, nervus centralis. **Midrib of Fern-pinna**: costula (s.f. I). **Nerve** (used for principal or more conspicuous unbranched veins starting from the midrib or base of the blade, as distinguished from those which divide or branch and are termed veins or veinlets):

nervus (s.m. II), nervus secundarius (the midrib being *nervus medius*), nervus lateralis. **nerved** (ribbed): nervatus (adj. A), nervosus (adj. A). **netted**: reticulatus (adj. A). **Network of Veinlets**: rete (s.n. III. x). **Vein**: vena (s.f. I), *acc. sing.* venam, *gen. sing.* venae, *abl. sing.* vena, *nom. pl.* venae, *acc. pl.* venas, *gen. pl.* venarum, *abl. pl.* venis. **Veining, Types of**: when the veins (nerves) enter the blade at the base and run more or less parallel to the margin without branching from base to tip, the venation is termed *parallel*, with the veins (nerves) straight (venis rectis) or *acrodrome*, with veins curved (venis curvatis). In *penni-parallel* venation (venatio pinnatiparallela) the veins (nerves) are parallel with each other but run outwards from the midrib. When the veins form a network, the venation is *reticulate* (venatio reticulata). When three or more principal veins of a network diverge outwards from the base of the blade, the venation is *radiate, palmate, digitate* or *pedate* (venatio radiata, v. palmata, v. digitata, v. pedata) or in a peltate leaf *actinodrome* (venatio actinodroma). When the veins (nerves) diverge outwards from a midrib, the venation is *pinnate* (venatio pinnata) and is further distinguished as *undivided* or *craspedodrome* (venatio craspedodroma) when the principal veins run straight to the margin without dividing, as *looped* or *brochidodrome* (venatio brochidodroma) when they run outwards but curve markedly before reaching the margin and unite with the vein above, thereby forming a loop, as *arched* or *camptodrome* (venatio camptodroma) when they run outwards but do not reach the margin, arch upwards and break up or terminate without forming loops. Most of these terms were introduced by C. von Ettingshausen, *Die Blatt-Skelette der Dikotyledonen* (Vienna, 1861); *folia nervis lateralibus utroque latere 14-17 subhorizontalibus parallelis i.e. sub angulo fere recto e nervo mediano abeuntibus*, leaves with lateral nerves at each side 14-17 almost horizontal parallel i.e. at almost a right angle from the central nerve (midrib) departing; *sub angulo circa 40°-50° prodeuntibus*, at angle of about 40°-50° going forth; *folia nervis utroque costae latere 10-15 marginem versus valde arcuatis*, leaves with nerves 10-15 each side of midrib towards margin strongly arched; *folia valde reticulata nervis*

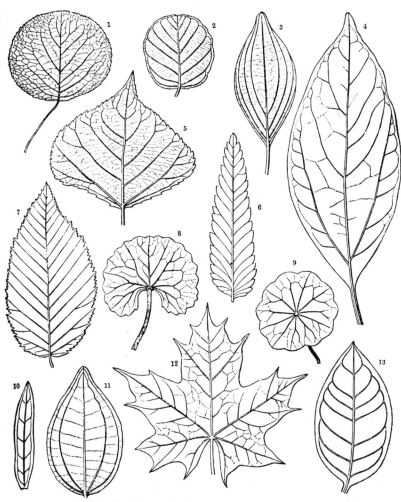

Fig. 40   Types of Veining, with one main Nerve
1, reticulatus;   2, brochidodromus;   3, 4, camptodromus;   5, reti-
culato-pinnatus;   6, 7, craspedromus;   8, 9, reticulatus;   10, brochidodromus;   11, camptodromus;   12, radiatus;   13, brochidodromus
(from A. Kerner von Marilaun, *Pflanzenleben*; 1887)

atque rete venularum utrinque subaequaliter manifestis, leaves strongly reticulate with nerves and network of veinlets on both surfaces almost equally evident; *nervis supra obsoletis vel nullis subtus pro-minulis reticulato-anastomosantibus, areo-lis minutis,* with nerves on the upper side inconspicuous or lacking on the lower side standing out slightly and reticu-lately joining together, the enclosed

areas minute; *folia triplinervia, nervo medio supra per totam longitudinem impresso subtus crassissimo elevato, pari laterali 3-5 mm. supra basin abeunte supra plus minus impresso 1-2 mm. a margine remoto usque ad apicem pro-ducto, venulis transversalibus numerosis 2-3 mm. inter se distantibus,* leaves triple-nerved, with middle nerve (midrib) on the upper side for the whole length

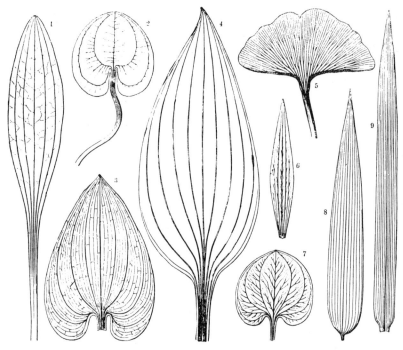

Fig. 41 Types of Veining, with several Nerves
1, acrodromus (solidinervis), 2-4, campylodromus; 5, flabellato-
furcatus; 6, acrodromus; 7, pedato-acrodromus; 8, 9, parallelus
(from A. Kerner von Marilaun, *Pflanzenleben*; 1887)

impressed, on the lower side very thick raised, with the lateral pair 3-5 mm. above the base going forth on the upper side more or less impressed 1-2 mm. from the margin distant up to the apex produced, with transverse veinlets numerous 2-3 mm. between themselves apart; *folia (nervulo submarginali tenui neglecto) e basi trinervia*, leaves (with the almost marginal thin veinlet ignored) from base three-nerved; *nervo medio supra inferne impresso sed ad apicem versus evanido subtus elevato*, with middle nerve (midrib) on the upper side in lower part impressed but towards apex vanishing on lower side raised; *nervi secundarii sub angulo 60° excurrentes recti indivisi vel furcati*, secondary nerves at angle of 60° issuing forth straight undivided or forked; *folia subtus praesertim ad nervos nervulosque hirsuta*, leaves below especially at nerves and nervules hairy; *folia secus venas elevatas pubescentia*, leaves along

the raised veins pubescent; *folia subtus praeter venas virides satis rubra*, leaves below except for the green veins quite red; *venae pinnatae tenuissimae aut creberrimae flabellato-multifurcatae aut distantes furcatae venulis divergentibus*, veins pinnate very slender either very crowded many times forked in a fan-like way or remote forked with veinlets diverging; *venae tenues ramosissimae venulisque in maculas (areolas) hexagonoideas inaequales anastomosantes et reticulum densum efformantes*, veins slender much branched and with the veinlets into spots (areoles) hexagonal unequal joining together and a dense network forming; *venae simplices in apicem dentium frondis excurrentes*, veins simple into apex of teeth of frond running out; *species quoad foliorum nervaturam distincta*, species as to the nervation of the leaves distinct; *venae marginem non attingentes sed ante marginem arcuatim confluentes*, veins not reaching the margin but before the margin by arching joined together; *venae liberae, parte tertia superiore soros gerentes, marginem vix attingentes*, veins free, in the upper third bearing sori, the margin hardly reaching. **veinless**: avenius (adj. A). **Veinlet**: venula (s.f. I). **343-364**

vel (conj.): or, q.v.

Velamen (s.n. III. vi): cover, covering; *stratum tenue saxa limumque velamine continuo obducens*, layer thin spreading over rocks and mud as a continuous cover; *velamen radicum*, velamen, i.e. the moisture-absorptive covering of aerial roots of tropical orchids and aroids.

velatus (part. A): covered, partially concealed from view.

Vellus (s.n. III): fleece, wool, down; *herba vellere longorum pilorum obtecta*, herb with a wool of long hairs covered.

Velum (s.n. II): veil; *velum partiale, velum hymeniale*, partial veil of agarics; *velum universale*, universal veil or volva.

velut (adv.), **veluti** (adv.): just as, like, as, for example.

velutinus (adj. A): velvety, densely covered with fine short soft erect hairs. **275**

Velvetum (s.n. II): velvet.

Vena (s.f. I): vein: *see* VEINING.

venenatus (part. A): poisonous, q.v.

venenosus (adj. A): very poisonous.

venetus (adj. A): venice-blue.

venosus (adj. A): having many branched veins *or* conspicuously veined. **364**

Venter (s.m. III. v): expanded basal part of an archegonium, ventral surface.

ventralis (adj. B): ventral, i.e. on the inner face or the one towards the axis.

ventraliter (adv.): ventrally.

ventricosus (adj. A): swollen, especially on one side. **97**

Venula (s.f. I): veinlet; *see* VEINING.

venustus (adj. A): beautiful, graceful.

Ver (s.n. III. v): spring; *ineunte vere*, at the beginning of spring.

verdigris: aerugineus (adj. A), aeruginosus (adj. A).

vere (adv.): truly, in fact, rightly, exactly; *see* REVERA, VERO.

vergens (part. B): trending towards.

veris (gen. sing. of *Ver*): of the season of spring; *see* VERNALIS, VERNUS.

verisimiliter (adv.): very likely, probably.

vermicularis (adj. B): worm-shaped, almost cylindrical and bent in places, marked with irregular waves *or* bent lines. **52**

Vermiculus (s.m. II): little worm; *vermiculi nematoidei*, eelworms.

vermiformis (adj. B): worm-shaped.

vermilion: cinnabarinus (adj. A).

vernacular: vernaculus (adj. A); *nomen vernaculum*, vernacular name.

vernalis (adj. B): vernal, pertaining to spring.

Vernatio (s.f. III. vi): vernation, the manner in which leaves are arranged within the leaf-bud. When of a folded kind this may be *conduplicate* (vernatio conduplicata), with the leaf folded lengthwise along the midrib so that the two halves of the upper side face one another; *pleated* or *plicate* (vernatio plicata), with the leaf folded several times lengthwise along the primary veins like the pleats of a closed fan; *reclinate* (vernatio reclinata), with the leaf bent downwards; *wrinkled, crumpled* or *corrugated* (vernatio corrugata); *equitant* (vernatio equitans), with the leaves overlapping entirely and in parallel; *obvolute* (vernatio obvoluta), when the margin of one leaf overlaps that of the leaf opposite. When of a rolled kind the vernation may be *revolute* (vernatio revoluta), with both margins of the leaf rolled back towards the midrib on the lower side; *involute* (vernatio involuta), with both margins rolled forward towards the midrib on the upper side; *convolute* (vernatio convoluta, v. convolutiva, v. supervolutiva), when the leaf is wholly rolled lengthwise from one margin, so that one margin is at the centre of the coil and the other outside; *circinate* (vernatio circinata), when the leaf is rolled spirally from the apex downwards; *folia juniora convolutiva nec conduplicata*, young leaves convolute not conduplicate; *folia vernatione plicata*, leaves with plicate vernation. **365-386**

vernicosus (adj. A): varnished.

vernus (adj. A): vernal, pertaining to spring.

vero (adv.): in truth, in fact, certainly, exactly ; *see* REVERA, VERO.

veronicinus (adj. A): veronica-violet (H.C.C. 6.39).

verosimiliter (adv.): very likely, probably.

Verruca (s.f. I): wart, wart-like outgrowth *or* swelling. **verrucatus** (adj. A), **verrucosus** (adj. A): warty. **verruciformis** (adj. B): shaped like a wart. **Verrucula** (s.f. I): small wart. **verruculosus** (adj. A): covered with small wart-like outgrowths; cf. TUBERCULATUS. **268**

versatilis (adj. B): versatile, turning freely on its support, attached on the back so as to be capable of movement. **448**

versicolor (adj. B), **versicolorus** (adj. A):
variously coloured *or* changing colour;
cf. MUTABILIS.

versiformis (adj. B): of different shapes,
altering in shape with age.

versum (adv.): turned in the direction of.

versus (adv. and prep. with acc.): towards,
q.v.

Vertex (s.m. III. i): the top, highest
point; *vertice*, at the top; *a vertice*,
from above, down from above.

verticalis (adj. B): vertical, placed in a
direction from the base to the tip,
perpendicular. **396**

Verticillaster: verticillaster (s.m. II), *nom.
pl.* verticillastri, *abl. pl.* verticillastris;
*verticillastri nunc multiflori axillares vel
ad apices ramorum racemosi nunc in
capitula terminalia conferti nunc omnes
pauciflori*, verticillasters (false-whorls)
sometimes many-flowered axillary or at
tips of branches racemose sometimes in
terminal heads crowded sometimes all
few-flowered.

verticillate (adv.), **verticillatim** (adv.):
verticillately, in a whorled manner.
verticillatus (adj. A): verticillate,
whorled. **Verticillus** (s.m. II): whorl,
ring of organs on the same plane. **478**

verus (adj. A): true, genuine (*not to be
confused with* veris).

very: usu. expressed by use of the adj.
superlative ending *-issimus* or *-illimus*,
sometimes by the adv. *maxime* 'in the
highest degree', *valde* 'strongly', *minime*
'least of all', *magnopere* 'greatly', *bene*
'well', or the adj. prefix *per-*, e.g.
perpusillus, very small.

vesicarius (adj. A): bladder-like, inflated.

Vesicula (s.f. I): vesicle, small bladder,
air-cavity. **vesicularis** (adj. B), **vesicu-
latus** (adj. A): bladder-like. **vesiculosus**
(adj. A): covered with little bladders *or*
blisters.

vespertinus (adj. A): belonging to the
evening, q.v.; cf. DIURNUS, NOCTURNUS.

Vessel: vas (s.n. III. iv), q.v.

vestiens (part. B): clothing.

vestigialis (adj. B): vestigial. **Vestigium**
(s.n. II): vestige, remnant, trace.

Vestimentum (s.n. II): clothing, covering.

vestitus (part. A): clothed.

veternus (adj. A), **vetus** (adj. A), **vetustus**
(adj. A): aged.

vexillaris (adj. B): vexillary, i.e., in
aestivation of Leguminosae, with the
standard petal much larger than the
others and folded around them. **385**

Vexillum: vexillum (s.n. II), *abl. sing.*
vexillo; *see* STANDARD PETAL, WING.

Via (s.f. I): road, path. **viaticus** (adj. A):
growing along roads *or* paths.

Vibex (s.f. III): the mark of a blow, scar.

vibratile: vibratorius (adj. A).

vicarious: vicarius (adj. A).

vice (adv.): instead of, for, on account of.

viceni (adv.): growing in twenties. **vicensimus** (adj. A): twentieth. **viciens**
(adv.), **vicies** (adv.): twenty times.

Vicinia (s.f. I), **Vicinitas** (s.f. III. ii):
neighbourhood, nearness. **vicinus** (adj.
A): near, neighbouring.

vicissim (adv.): on the other hand, in turn.

videtur (3rd pers. sing. pres. pass. of
video): 'it seems'; *ut videtur*, as you
will, apparently; *frons ex icone pedalis
videtur*, frond according to the illustration appears to be one foot long.

viduus (adj. A): deprived of, without.

View: aspectus (s.m. IV); *aspectu
frontali*, in frontal view. Often expressed
by *visus* (part. A), indicating position
from which seen; cf. SEEN.

vigens (part. B): thriving, flourishing.

viginti (num. adj. indecl.): twenty.

vigorous: fortis (adj. B), vegetus (adj. A).

Villi (s.m. II. pl.): long weak hairs.
villosus (adj. A): villous, i.e. shaggy
with fairly long soft straight not interwoven ascending hairs. **273**

Vimen (s.n. III): a long flexible shoot, an
osier. **viminalis** (adj. B): bearing shoots
for plaiting and wicker-work.

vimineus (adj. A): having long flexible
shoots, used for wicker-work.

vinaceus (adj. A), **vinicolor** (adj. B),
vinosus (adj. A): wine-coloured,
purplish-red.

violaceus (adj. A): violet (H.C.C. 36);
violaceus refers to the blue-red colours
nearer blue, *purpureus* nearer red.

violet: violaceus (adj. A), ianthinus (adj.
A). **violet-**: *in L. comp.*, violaceo-, *in
Gk. comp.*, ion-, iono-; *ionandrus*, with
violet stamens; *ionanthus*, with violet
flowers; *violaceopictus*, painted with
violet; *violiflorus*, with flowers like a
Viola.

virellus (adj. A): greenish, somewhat
green. **virens** (part. B): green. **virescens**
(part. B): becoming green.

Virga (s.f. I): slender green branch, twig,
scion, rod, stripe; cf. VIRGULA.

virgatus (adj. A): twiggy, long and slender,
or streaked, rod-like.

virgineus (adj. A): pure white.

Virgula (s.f. I): a little twig or wand.

Viridarium (s.n. II): pleasure garden,
flora.

viridi-: *in L. comp.*, green-; *viridiflorus*,
green-flowered. **viridescens** (part. B):
becoming green. **viridianus** (adj. A):
viridian-green (H.C.C. 55). **viridis** (adj.
B): green. **viridulus** (adj. A): greenish.

virinus (adj. A): relating to a virus.

virosus (adj. A): stinking, poisonous.

Virus: virus (s.n. II), *gen. sing.* viri, *nom. pl.* vira, *gen. pl.* virorum (to be distinguished from *virorum*, of men).

viscid: viscidus (adj. A), viscosus (adj. A); cf. GLUTINOSUS. **300**

visible: visibilis (part. B), manifestus (adj. A) 'apparent, evident', aspectabilis (adj. B) 'worthy of being seen'.

visus (part. A): seen; *specimina ab auctore visa*, specimens seen by the author; *species a nobis non visa*, species by us not seen; *see* SEEN, VIEW.

Vita (s.f. I): life.

Vitamin: vitaminum (s.n. II), *gen. sing.* vitamini, *abl. sing.* vitamino, *nom. pl.* vitamina, *gen. pl.* vitaminorum, *abl. pl.* vitaminis.

vitellinus (adj. A): egg-yolk yellow, 'dull yellow just turning to red' (Lindley).

viti-: *in L. comp.*, pertaining to the vine (*Vitis vinifera*); *viticola*, dweller on the vine; *vitifolius*, vine-leaved (but *viticifolius*, with leaves like Vitex).

vitreus (adj. A): of glass, glassy, i.e. transparent and green-tinged; cf. TRANSPARENT. **Vitrum** (s.n. II): glass.

Vitta (s.f. I): aromatic oil-tube in fruit of Umbelliferae, longitudinal rib of diatom, stripe, band; *vittae tenues vel tenuissimae ad valleculas solitariae inconspicuae*, vittae slender or very slender solitary in the furrows inconspicuous; *vitta marginali cellulis scleroticis formata*, with marginal band formed by sclerotic cells.

vittatus (adj. A): longitudinally striped, bearing vittae.

vittiformis (adj. B): band-shaped.

vivens (part. B): living.

vividus (adj. A): vivid, bright, pure in colour.

viviparus (adj. A): viviparous, i.e. germinating *or* sprouting while still attached to parent; cf. PROLIFERUS.

vivus (adj. A): living, fresh; *bracteolae in vivo albae, in sicco brunneae*, bracteoles in a living state white, in a dried state brown.

vix (adv.): with difficulty, scarcely, barely.

volcanic: volcanicus (adj. A), vulcanicus (adj. A), vulcanius (adj. A); *in terra volcanico exusta*, on burnt-out volcanic soil; *in montibus vulcanicis*, on volcanic mountains; *in portu Nagasaki post explosiones vulcanicas submarinas cum Fucis variis appulsa*, in the port of Nagasaki after submarine volcanic explosions with various Fuci brought to land. **Volcano**: mons (s.m. III. ix) ignivomus; *in monte olim ignivomo*, on the mountain formerly vomiting fire.

volubilis (adj. B): twining, q.v. **418**

Volume (book): volumen (s.n. III. vi), tomus (s.m. II).

volutus (part. A): rolled up.

Volva: volva (s.f. I), *abl. sing.* volva, *nom. pl.* volvae, *abl. pl.* volvis; *volva arcte vaginata irregulariter 4-5-lobata extus grisea*, volva closely sheathed irregularly 4-5-lobed outside grey. **volvatus** (adj. A): provided with a volva.

-vorus (adj. A): *in L. comp.*, devouring, consuming, feeding upon; *pigmentivorus*, consuming pigments, destroying paint.

vulcanicus (adj. A), **vulcanius** (adj. A): volcanic, q.v.

vulgaris (adj. B), **vulgatus** (part. A): common, general, ordinary.

vulgo (adv.): commonly, generally.

vulneratus (part. A): wounded, damaged.

-vulnerus (adj. A): *in L. comp.*, -wounded. **Vulnus** (s.n. III): wound.

vulviformis (adj. B): like a cleft with projecting edges.

W

Wall: paries (s.m. III. ii), *gen. sing.* parietis, *dat. sing.* parieti, *abl. sing.* pariete; *ovula parieti ovarii affixa subhorizontalis*, ovules to the wall of the ovary attached almost horizontal.

wanting: carens (part. B, transitive) 'being without'; intransitive 'wanting' expressed by *deficiens, nullus, deest, desunt*; *caulis foliis carens*, stem wanting leaves; *folia deficientia*, leaves lacking; cf. DEEST, LACKING, WITHOUT.

warm: calidus (adj. A) 'hot', tepidus (adj. A) 'just warm'; cf. THERMALIS.

Wart: verruca (s.f. I). **wart-like**: verruciformis (adj. B). **warty**: verrucatus (adj. A), verrucosus (adj. A), phymatodeus (adj. A): cf. TUBERCULATUS.

Wasteland: incultum (s.n. II), locus (s.m. II) incultus.

wasting away: tabescens (part. B), tabidus (adj. A).

Water: aqua (s.f. I), *gen. sing.* aquae, *abl. sing.* aqua, *nom. pl.* aquae, *gen. pl.* aquarum, *abl. pl.* aquis; *plantae in aquis tranquillis haud rapide fluentibus crescentes*, plants in still never rapidly flowing waters growing; *aqua pluvialis*, rain water; *aqua dulcis*, fresh water; *aqua marina*, sea water; *aqua subsalsa*, brackish water; *summa aqua*, the surface of the water; *aquae marinae et dulcis hospites*, of water sea and fresh the guests, i.e. inhabitants of sea water and fresh water. **water-inhabiting**: aquaticus (adj. A), aquatilis (adj. B).

watery; aquaticus (adjA), aquosus (adjA)

Waterfall : cataracta (s.f. I).

waved : sinuatus (part. A) (*applied to flat edges curving strongly in and out*), undulatus (adj. A) (*applied also to edges waved upwards and downwards*). **132**

Wax : cera (s.f. I), *abl. sing.* cera. **waxgold** : cerinus (adj. A). **waxy** : ceraceus (adj. A), cereus (adj. A). **324**

weak : infirmus (adj. A), debilis (adj. B), invalidus (adj. A) ; *of colours*, pallidus (adj. A), dilutus (part. A). **weakly** : infirme (adv.), leniter (adv.) 'mildly, gently' ; *of colours*, pallide (adv.), dilute (adv.).

wedge-shaped : cuneatus (part. A), cuneiformis (adj. B). **113, 175**

Week : hebdomas (s.f. III), *gen. sing.* hebdomadis ; *coloniae aetate duarum vel trium hebdomadum*, colonies at the age of two or three weeks, 2- or 3-week-old colonies. **weekly** : hebdomadalis (adj. B).

well : bene (adv.).

West : occidens (s.m. III. ix), *gen. sing.* occidentis ; *ad occidentem*, to the west. **west, western** : occidentalis (adj. B), (*as an epithet only*) hesperius (adj. A).

wet : humidus (adj. A), udus (adj. A), uvidus (adj. A), irriguus (adj. A) ; cf. MOIST. **wetted** : madefactus (part. A), madidus (adj. A).

when : quum (conj.), ubi (adv.) ; *petala longitudine varia, erecta ubi brevia, patentissima ubi elongata*, petals in length varying, erect when short, most outspread when elongated.

whence : unde (adv.).

where : ubi (adv.). **wherever** : ubicumque (adv.).

wherefore : quamobrem.

whether : *see* OR.

which : qui (rel. pron.), q.v.

while : dum (conj.).

whip-like : flagelliformis (adj. B). **47**

white : albus (adj. A) 'dull white', candidus (adj. A) 'glossy white', albidus (adj. A) 'whitish', niveus (adj. A) 'snow-white', eburneus (adj. A) 'ivory-white' (i.e. with yellow tinge), lacteus (adj. A) 'milk-white' (i.e. with bluish tinge), albicans (part. B) 'becoming white', virgineus (adj. A) 'pure white'. **white-** : *in L. comp.*, albi-, albo-, *in Gk. comp.*, leuc-, leuco-, *also* chion-, chiono- 'snowy', galact-, galacto- 'milky'.

whitened : dealbatus (part. A). **whitish** : albidus (adj. A), exalbidus (adj. A). **309**

Whole : totum (s.n. II). **whole** : totus (adj. A), omnis (adj. B), integer (adj. A) 'undivided'. **as a whole** : in universum.

Whorl : verticillus (s.m. II), *acc. sing.* verticillum, *abl. sing.* verticillo, *nom. pl.*

verticilli, *abl. pl.* verticillis ; *folia in verticillum disposita*, leaves in a whorl arranged ; *caulis verticillis usque 8-foliatis*, stem with whorls up to 8-leaved ; *ramuli verticillorum inter se dissimiles, primarii plerumque 8, secundarii minores circa 16, duobus ordinibus*, branchlets of the whorls between themselves dissimilar, the primary ones commonly 8, the secondary ones smaller about 16, in two series. **whorled** : verticillatus (adj. A), verticillaris (adj. B). **in a whorled manner** : verticillatim (adv.), verticillate (adv.). **478**

wide : latus (adj. A). **widely** : late (adv.). **widened** : dilatatus (part. A). **Width** : latitudo (s.f. III vi).

wild : ferus (adj. A), sylvestris (adj. B), incultus (adj. A).

willowy : salignus (adj. A).

wilting : languescens (part. B).

Wind : ventus (s.m. II). **wind-** : *in Gk. comp.*, anemo-.

winding : maeandriformis (adj. B), sinuosus (adj. A), tortuosus (adj. A) ; cf. TWINING.

Window : fenestra (s.f. I), *abl. sing.* fenestra ; *fenestra magna pellucida viridis*, window large transparent green ; *fenestra apicalis*, apical window ; *fenestra basalis*, basal window.

windowed : fenestralis (adj. B), fenestratus (adj. A).

wine-coloured : vinaceus (adj. A), vinicolor (adj. B), vinosus (adj. A).

Wing : ala (s.f. I), *acc. sing.* alam, *gen. sing.* alae, *abl. sing.* ala, *nom. pl.* alae, *gen. pl.* alarum, *abl. pl.* alis ; *seminum testa in alam expansa*, the testa of seeds into a wing expanded ; *alae oblongae purpureae, carina longiores vel carinam aequantes vexillo vix breviores*, wings oblong purple, longer than the keel or equalling the keel scarcely shorter than the standard ; *corolla alis oblongis carina longioribus et vexillo brevioribus*, corolla with oblong wings longer than the keel and shorter than the standard petal. **wing-** : *in L. comp.*, alato-, *in Gk. comp.*, ptero- ; *alatocaulis, pterocaulis*, with winged stem ; *pterocarpus*, with winged fruits. **winged** : alatus (adj. A) ; *in Gk. comp.*, -pterus. **wing-shaped** : aliformis (adj. B). **60**

Winter : hiems (s.f. III. vi), *gen. sing.* hiemis, *abl. sing.* hieme ; *hieme florens*, flowering in winter. **pertaining to winter** : hiemalis (adj. B), hibernus (adj. A), brumalis (adj. B) ; cf. PER HIEMANS.

Winterbud : hibernaculum (s.n. II).

wiped clean : detersus (part. A).

wire-like : filo metallico similis (adj. B).

with : cum (prep. with abl.) 'together with'. Usually expressed by the abl. case alone without a prep., sometimes expressed by acc. using *praebens* (part. B), 'offering' or *habens* (part. B) 'having'.

withered : marcidus (adj. A), emarcidus (adj. A). **Withered but persistent parts** : induviae (s.f. I. pl.), *abl. pl.* induviis. withering : marcescens (part. B).

within : intra (adv. and prep. with acc.), intus (adv.), interius (adv.).

without (lacking) : sine (prep. with abl.), absque (prep. with abl.) ; exclusus (part. A. with abl.) 'excluded' is sometimes appropriate ; *sine numero*, without a number ; *absque descriptione latina*, without a Latin description ; *cum vel sine spinis*, with or without spines ; cf. DEEST, EXPERS, LACKING, WANTING.

without (outside) : extra (adv. and prep. with acc.), extus (adv.) : cf. OUTSIDE.

wonderful : mirus (adj. A). **wonderfully** : mire (adv.), mirimodis (adv.).

Wood (timber) : lignum (s.n. II), *abl. sing.* ligno.

Wood (woodland) : silva (s.f. I) *less used than medieval* sylva (s.f. I), *gen. sing.* sylvae, *abl. sing.* sylva, *nom. pl.* sylvae, *acc. pl.* sylvas, *gen. pl.* sylvarum, *abl. pl.* sylvis ; nemus (s.n. III. iv), *nom. pl.* nemora, *gen. pl.* nemorum, *abl. pl.* nemoribus.

Woodcut : xylographia (s.f. I), *nom. pl.* xylographiae ; cf. ILLUSTRATION.

wooden, woody : ligneus (adj. A), lignosus (adj. A) ; cf. XYL-. **325**

Wool : lana (s.f. I), *abl. sing.* lana ; vellus (s.n. III), *abl. sing.* vellere. **wool-** : *in L. comp.*, lani-, lanos-, *in Gk. comp.*, erio-, lasio- ; *lanosantherus, lasiantherus*, with woolly anthers. **woolly** : lanatus (adj. A), laneus (adj. A), lanuginosus (adj. A). **276**

World : orbis (s.m. III. vii), *gen. sing.* orbis, *also* orbis terrae, orbis terrarum; *herbae in alpestribus totius orbis crescentes*, herbs in high places of the whole world growing ; *species inter tropicos in utroque orbe vigentes*, species between the tropics on both sides of the world thriving ; *in regionibus intertropicis utriusque hemisphaerii*, in intertropical regions of both hemispheres. **Old World** (s.) : orbis vetus, orbis antiquus ; *per totum orbis antiqui hemisphaerium boreale*, through the whole northern hemisphere of the Old World. **Old World** (adj.) : gerontogaeus (adj. A.) ; *species gerontogaeae*, Old World species. **New World** (s.) : orbis novus, America. **New World** (adj.) : neogaeus (adj. A), americanus (adj. A).

world-wide : cosmopolitanus (adj. A), per orbem terrarum late dispersus (part. A) ; *herbae cosmopolitanae, inter tropicos rarae*, herbs world-wide, between the tropics rare.

worm-shaped : lumbricalis (adj. B), lumbriciformis (adj. B), vermiformis (adj. B) ; cf. ANGUILLIFORMIS. **52**

Wound : vulnus (s.n. III) ; *see* INJURY. wounded : vulneratus (part. A). **-wounded** : *in L. comp.*, -vulnerus.

woven : textus (part. A).

Wrinkle : ruga (s.f. I). **wrinkled** : rugosus (adj. A), rugatus (part. A), caperatus (part. A), corrugatus (part. A) ; *in Gk. comp.*, rhyti-, rhytido-. **375**

written : scriptus (part. A).

wrong : falsus (adj. A). **wrongly** : false (adv.), male (adv.).

X

xanth-, xantho- : *in Gk. comp.*, yellow; *xanthochymus*, with yellow sap *or* latex ; *xanthorrhizus*, with yellow roots.

xerampelinus (adj. A) : 'dull red with a strong mixture of brown' (Lindley).

xero- : *in Gk. comp.*, dry ; *xerophilus*, loving dry places ; *xerophyllus*, with dry leaves.

xiph-, xipho- : *in Gk. comp.*, sword-like ; *xiphodon*, with sword-like teeth.

xiphoideus (adj. A) : sword-like ; *see* ENSIFORMIS, GLADIATUS.

xyl-, xylo-, -xylon : *in Gk. comp.*, woody, relating to wood ; *xylophilus*, woodloving, living on (and usually destroying) wood ; *xylorrhizus*, with woody roots *or* rootstock ; *melanoxylon*, with black wood.

Xylem : xylema (s.n. III), *gen. sing.* xylematis.

Xylographia (s.f. I) : woodcut.

Xylopodium : xylopodium (s.n. II).

Y

Year : annus (s.m. II) ; cf. AGE. **yearly** : annuus (adj. A).

Yeast : fermentum (s.n. II).

yellow : luteus (adj. A), flavus (adj. A), aureus (adj. A), vitellinus (adj. A). Pure yellows include *mimosinus*, mimosa-yellow (H.C.C. 60.2), *canarinus*, canary-yellow (H.C.C. 2), *aureolinus*, aureolin (H.C.C. 3), *stramineus*, straw-yellow (H.C.C. 60.4), *citrinus*, lemon-yellow (H.C.C. 4). Pale greenish-yellows

include *primulinus*, primrose-yellow
(H.C.C. *60*.1), *sulphureus*, sulphur-
yellow (H.C.C. 1), *flavus dresdanus*,
dresden-yellow (H.C.C. 64), passing into
luteo-viridis, uranium-green (H.C.C. 63),
and *citrino-viridis*, *viridis citrinus*,
citron-green (H.C.C. 64). The addition
of red gives *ranunculinus*, buttercup-
yellow (H.C.C. 5), *indico-flavus*, indian-
yellow (H.C.C. 6), *croceus*, saffron-
yellow (H.C.C. 7), passing into *aurantiacus*, orange (H.C.C. 12). Very pale
yellow or yellowish colours are indicated
by *luteolus, flavidus, ochroleucus, eburneus*. Greyed-yellows include *bubalinus*,
buff, chamois, *succineus*, amber, *isabellinus, ochraceus*, ochre-yellow. **yellow-** :
in L. comp., flav-, flavi-, flavo-, luteo-,
in Gk. comp., chrys-, chryso-, xanth-,
xantho- ; *flavinervius, xanthoneurus*,
yellow-nerved. **yellowish** : flavidus (adj.
A), luteolus (adj. A).
yet : tamen (conj.) 'notwithstanding',
attamen (adv.) 'but yet', quanquam
(conj.) 'although, and yet', saltem
(adv.) 'at least', etiam (conj.) 'and also,
even yet'. **as yet** : ad huc (adv.). **not
yet** : nondum (adv.).
yoked : jugatus (adj. A) ; *in L. comp.*,
-jugus, *in Gk. comp.*, -zygus, zygo-.
young : juvenis (adj. B) ; cf. AGE. **younger** :
junior (comp. adj. B) ; *rami juniores
angulati, vetustiores teretes*, younger
branches angled, older ones terete.

Youth : juventus (s.f. III. ii) ; *juventute*,
in youth. **youthful** : juvenilis (adj. B),
primaevus (adj. A) ; cf. AGE.

Z

zantho- : *in Gk. comp.*, variant of XANTHO-.
zebrinus (adj. A) : striped fairly regularly
with white *or* yellow.
zigzag : valde flexuosus (adj. A), fractiflexus (adj. A), anfractuoso-flexuosus
(adj. A) ; *modo dicto gallice et anglice
'zigzag'*, in the manner called 'zigzag'
in French and English.
Zinc : zincum (s.n. II), *gen. sing.* zinci.
zonatim (adv.) : in a zoned *or* banded
manner. **zonatus** (adj. A) : zoned,
banded, marked circularly. **Zone** : zona (s.f. I), *gen. sing.* zonae. **zone-
less** : azonus (adj. A).
zoo- : *in Gk. comp.*, relating to animals.
zygo- : *in Gk. comp.*, joined, yoked ;
zygomeris, with parts joined in pairs.
Zygodesma (s.n. III) : clamp ; cf. FIBULA.
zygomorphic : zygomorphus (adj. A).
Zygospore : zygospora (s.f. I), *abl. pl.*
zygosporis.
Zygote : zygota (s.f. I), *nom. pl.* zygotae,
abl. pl. zygotis ; *zygotis ellipsoideis
circa 50 μ longis*, with zygotes ellipsoid
about 50 μ long.
zymogenus (adj. A) : ferment-producing.

CHAPTER XXVI

General Bibliography

AINSWORTH, G. C. & BISBY, G. R. 1971. *Dictionary of the Fungi*. 6th ed. Kew, Surrey.

BACCI, A. 1955. *Lexicon eorum Vocabulorum quae difficilius Latine redduntur.* 3rd ed. Rome.

BAILEY, L. H. 1946. Terms employed in palm-literature. *Gentes Herb.*, 7 : 178-189.

BARANOV, A. 1971. *Basic Latin for Plant Taxonomists.* Lehre.

BENTHAM, G. 1861. *Flora Hongkongensis.* London.

BISCHOFF, G. W. 1833-44. *Handbuch der botanischen Terminologie und Systemkunde.* 3 vols. Nürnberg.

—— 1857. *Wörterbuch der beschreibenden Botanik.* 2nd ed. Stuttgart.

BROWN, R. W. 1956. *Composition of scientific Words.* 2nd ed. Washington, D.C.

CABRERA, A. L. 1946. Nociones sobre redacción de diagnosis y terminología botánica empleada en la misma. *Bol. Soc. Argent. Bot.*, 1 : 253-279.

CANDOLLE, ALPHONSE DE. 1880. *La Phytographie, ou l'Art de décrire les Végétaux.* Paris.

CANDOLLE, AUGUSTIN PYRAMUS DE. 1813. *Théorie élémentaire de la Botanique.* Paris (2nd ed., 1819 ; 3rd ed., 1844).

CASH, E. K. 1965. *A Mycological English-Latin Glossary (Mycologia Memoir No. 1).* New York and London.

COBBETT, W. 1819. *A Grammar of the English Language . . . for the use of Soldiers, Sailors, Apprentices and Plough-boys.* London. [Later issued as Cobbet's *Easy Grammar.*]

DAHLGREN, K. V. O. 1951. Philosophia botanica, ett 200-arsminne. *Svenska Linné-Sällskap. Årsskr.*, 33-34 : 1-30.

ETTINGSHAUSEN, C. VON. 1861. *Die Blattskelete der Dikotyledonen.* Vienna.

FEATHERLY, H. I. 1954. *Taxonomic Terminology of the Higher Plants.* Ames, Iowa.

FORBES, F. B. 1884. On the botanical terms for pubescence. *J. Bot. (London)*, 22 : 232-235.

GERMAIN DE SAINT-PIERRE, E. 1852. *Guide du Botaniste.* Paris.

—— 1870. *Nouveau Dictionnaire de Botanique.* Paris.

GRAY, A. 1879. *The botanical Textbook*, 6th ed. Part 1. *Structural Botany.* New York and Chicago.

ILLIGER, J. K. W. 1800. *Versuch einer systematischen völlstandigen Terminologie für das Thierreich und Pflanzenreich.* Helmstädt.

JACKSON, B. D. 1900. *A Glossary of botanic Terms.* London (4th ed., 1928, reprinted 1960).

JIRÁSEK, V. 1963. Lateinische Formen der taxonomischen Rangstufen der Kultur- und Wildpflanzen. *Novit. Bot. Univ. Carol. Prag.*, 1963 : 12-19.

JOSSERAND, M. 1952. *La Description des Champignons supérieurs (Encyclopédie mycologique* 21). Paris.

KENNEDY, B. H. 1962. *The Revised Latin Primer.* New ed., edited by J. F. Mountford. London.

KERNER VON MARILAUN, A. 1894-95. *The Natural History of Plants,* Translated by F. W. Oliver and others. 2 vols. London, etc. [Terminology of venation, 1 : 629-635].

KREMP, G. O. W. 1965. *Morphologic Encyclopedia of Palynology.* Tuczon.

KRETSCHMER, P. 1899. *Sprachregeln für die Bildung und Betonung zoologischer und botanischer Namen.* Berlin.

LAWRENCE, G. H. M. 1955. *Introduction to Plant Taxonomy.* New York.

LINDLEY, J. 1832. *An Introduction to Botany.* London (2nd ed., 1835 ; 3rd ed., 1839 ; 4th ed. in 2 vols., 1848).

—— 1847. *The Elements of Botany . . . and a Glossary of technical Terms.* London.

—— 1951. *Glosologia de los Terminos usados en Botánica.* Traducida de la segund edición inglesa [*Introduction to Botany*, 2nd ed., pp. 370-429 ; 1835] por T. Enrique Rothe. Tucumán.

—— 1964. *Excerpt from illustrated Dictionary of botanical Terms.* Introduction by Alice Eastwood. Foreword by J. J. Graham. Stanford, California [reprinted from *Introduction to Botany*, 4th ed., 1848].

LINK, H. F. 1798. *Philosophiae botanicae novae seu Institutionum phytographicarum Prodromus.* Göttingen.

LINNAEUS, C. 1751. *Philosophia botanica.* Stockholm.

—— 1762. *Termini botanici . . . sistit J. Elmgren.* Uppsala [Reprinted in Linnaeus, *Amoen. Acad.*, 6 : 217-246 ; 1763].

MOLL, J. W. 1934. *Phytography as a Fine Art.* Leiden.

MURLEY, M. R. 1951. Seeds of the Cruciferae of Northeastern North America. *Amer. Midland Nat.*, 46 : 1-81.

MURRILL, W. A. 1905. Terms applied to the surface and surface appendages of Fungi. *Torreya*, 5 : 60-66.

NYBAKKEN, O. 1959. *Greek and Latin in scientific Terminology.* Ames, Iowa.

PRISZTER, SZ. 1963. *A Növényszervtan Terminológiája (A Keszth Mezögazd. Akad. Kiadv.* 1961 no. 7). Budapest.

RAUSCHERT, S. 1963. Beitrag zur Verheitlichung der soziologischen Nomenklatur. *Mitteil. Floristisch-soziol. Arbeitsgem.* N.F. 10 : 232-249.

RICKETT, H. W. 1954. Materials for a dictionary of botanical terms. *Bull. Torrey Bot. Club*, 81 : 1-15 [a], 188-198 [b].

—— 1956. —— *Bull. Torrey Bot. Club*, 81 : 419-445 [a] ; 83 : 342-354 [b].

RIZZINI, C. T. 1964. Sistematizaçao terminologia da folha. *Rodriguesia,* 23-24 (1960–61) : 193-208.

ROE, K. E. 1971. Terminology of hairs in the genus Solanum. *Taxon* 20 : 501-508.

SCHULZE, G. M. 1953. Beiträge zur deskriptiven Terminologie. Engler, *Bot. Jahrb.*, 76 : 109-133.

SNELL, W. H. & DICK, E. A. 1971. *A Glossary of Mycology.* 2nd ed. Cambridge, Mass.

STEARN, W. T. 1955. Linnaeus's 'Species Plantarum' and the language of botany. *Proc. Linnean Soc. London*, 165 : 158-164.

—— 1956. Shapes of leaves. R. Hort. Soc., London, *Suppl. to Dict. of Gardening*, 318-322.

—— 1957. *An Introduction to the 'Species Plantarum' and cognate botanical works of Carl Linnaeus* (Prefixed to Ray Society facsimile of Linnaeus, *Species Plantarum*, vol. 1). London.

—— 1959. The background of Linnaeus's contributions to the methods and nomenclature of systematic biology. *Systematic Zoology*,7 : 4-22.

—— 1961. Botanical gardens and botanical literature in the eighteenth century. *Cat. Bot. Books R. M. M. Hunt*, 2 : xli-cxl.

SYSTEMATICS ASSOCIATION COMMITTEE FOR DESCRIPTIVE TERMINOLOGY. 1960. Preliminary list of works relevant to descriptive biological terminology. *Taxon*, 9 : 245-257.

—— 1962. Terminology of simple symmetrical plane shapes (Chart 1). *Taxon*, 11 : 145-156, 245-247.

THEODOROV, A., KIRPICZNIKOV, M. & ARTJUSCHENKO, Z. 1956–62. *Organographia illustrata Plantarum vascularium* [vol. 1] *Folium.* [vol. 2] *Caulis et Radix.* 2 vols. Moscow & Leningrad.

TRYON, R. 1960. A glossary of some terms relating to the fern leaf. *Taxon*, 9 : 104-109.

WERNER, C. F. 1961. *Wortelemente lateinische-griechischer Fachausdrücke in den biologischen Wissenschaften.* 2nd ed. Leipzig.

WIKÉN, E. 1951. *Latin för Botanister och Zoologer.* Malmö.

WILMOTT, A. J. 1931. The necessity for precision in descriptive terminology. *Fifth Internat. Bot. Congr., Cambridge, Report of Proc.*, 540-543.

WOODCOCK, E. C. 1959. *A New Latin Syntax.* London.

WOODS, R. S. 1966. *An English-Classical Dictionary for the Use of Taxonomists.* Pomona College.

ZABINKOVA, N. & KIRPICZNIKOV, M. 1957. *Lexicon latino-rossicum pro Botanicis.* Moscow & Leningrad.

ZANDER, R. 1948. *Kleines botanisches Fremdwörterbuch.* 2nd ed. Ludwigsburg.

SYNOPSIS POLYGLOTTA

id est, gallica (*f*), hispanica (*e*), lusitanica (*p*), germanica (*d*), suecica (*s*) et rossica (*r*).

Index

This index does not include words incidentally mentioned as examples; entries in the Vocabulary, being alphabetically arranged and provided with cross-references, are also excluded unless illustrated.

557

AUCTOR ET UXOR